EIGHTH EDITION

ACCOUNTANTS' HANDBOOK

VOLUME TWO:
SPECIAL INDUSTRIES AND SPECIAL TOPICS

EIGHTH EDITION

ACCOUNTANTS' HANDBOOK

VOLUME TWO:
SPECIAL INDUSTRIES
AND SPECIAL TOPICS

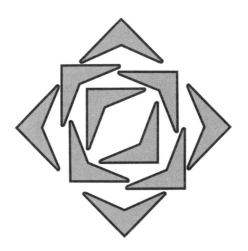

D.R. CARMICHAEL
STEVEN B. LILIEN
MARTIN MELLMAN

JOHN WILEY & SONS, INC.
New York • Chichester • Weinheim • Brisbane • Singapore • Toronto

"Accounting for Income Taxes" by J. T. Ball and E. Raymond Simpon. Copyright © 1996 by Financial Accounting Standards Board.
Copyright 1923, 1932, 1934, 1943, 1956 and © 1970 by The Ronald Press Company
Copyright © 1981, 1991, and 1996 by John Wiley & Sons, Inc.

Library of Congress Cataloging-in-Publication Data:

Accountant's handbook / edited by D.R. Carmichael, Steven B. Lilien,
    Martin Mellman. ---8th ed.
         p.   cm.
    Includes bibliographical references and index.
    ISBN 0-471-13031-1 (set). --- ISBN 0-471-14705-2 (vol. 1). --- ISBN
 0-471-14707-9 (vol. 2)---ISBN 0-471-25478-9 (vol. 1 paper)---
ISBN 0-471-25475-4 (vol. 2 paper)
    1. Accounting---Encyclopedias.   2. Accounting---Handbooks, manuals,
etc.   I. Carmichael, D. R. (Douglas R.), 1941--   II. Lilien,
Stevens B.   III. Mellman, Martin.
HF5621.A22   1996
657---dc20   95-26400

CONTENTS

VOLUME TWO: SPECIALIZED INDUSTRIES AND SPECIAL TOPICS

CHAPTER **23**

OIL, GAS, AND OTHER NATURAL RESOURCES

Richard P. Graff, CPA
Coopers & Lybrand L.L.P.
Joseph B. Feiten, CPA
Coopers & Lybrand L.L.P.

CONTENTS

23.1 INTRODUCTION

Accounting for oil and gas activities can be extremely complex because it encompasses a wide variety of business strategies and vehicles. The industry's diversity developed in response to the risk involved in the exploration process, the volatility of prices, and the fluctuations in supply and demand for oil and gas. In addition to having a working knowledge of accounting procedures, the oil and gas accountant should be familiar with the operating characteristics of companies involved in oil and gas activities and understand the impact of individual transactions.

Oil and gas activities cover a wide spectrum—ranging from exploration activities to the refining, transportation, and marketing of products to consumers. Since SEC accounting rules regulate exploration and production activities more stringently, this chapter deals primarily with the SEC aspect of oil and gas accounting. Accounting for refining activities is similar in many ways to other process manufacturing businesses. Likewise, transportation and marketing do not differ significantly from one end product to another.

23.2 OIL AND GAS EXPLORATION AND PRODUCING OPERATIONS

Oil- and gas-producing activities begin with the search for prospects—parcels of acreage that management thinks may contain economically viable oil or gas formations. For the most likely prospects, the enterprise may contract with a geological and geophysical (G&G) company to test and assess the subsurface formations and their depths. Based on the G&G studies, the enterprise evaluates the various prospects, rejecting some and accepting others as suitable for acquisition of lease rights (prospecting may be done before or after obtaining lease rights).

Specialists called **landmen** may be used to obtain lease rights. A landman is in effect a lease broker who searches titles and negotiates with property owners. Although the landman may be part of the company's staff, oil and gas companies often acquire lease rights to properties through independent landmen. Consideration for leasing the mineral rights usually includes a bonus (an immediate cash payment to the lessor) and a royalty interest retained by the lessor (a specified percentage of subsequent production minus applicable production taxes).

Once the leases have been obtained and the rights and obligations of all parties have been determined, exploratory drilling begins. Because drilling costs run to hundreds of thousands or millions of dollars, many companies reduce their capital commitment and related risks by seeking others to participate in **joint venture arrangements.** Participants in a joint venture are called **joint interest owners;** one owner, usually the enterprise that obtained the leases, acts as operator. The operator manages the venture and reports to the other, nonoperator participants. The operator initially pays the drilling costs and then bills those costs to the nonoperators. In some cases, the operator may collect these costs from nonoperators in advance.

The operator acquires the necessary supplies and subcontracts with a drilling company for drilling the well. The drilling time may be a few days, several months, or even a year or longer depending on many factors, particularly well depth and location. When the hole reaches the desired depth, various instruments are lowered that **"log the well"** to detect the presence of oil or gas. The joint interest owners evaluate the drilling and logging results to determine whether sufficient oil or gas can be extracted to justify the cost of completing the well. If the evaluation is negative, the well is plugged and abandoned as a **dry hole.** If sufficient quantities of crude oil or natural gas (hydrocarbons) appear to be present, the well is completed and equipment is installed to extract and separate the hydrocarbons from the water coming from the underground reservoir. Completion costs often equal or exceed the initial drilling costs.

Before production begins (sometimes even before the well is drilled), the enterprise selects oil and gas purchasers and negotiates sales contracts. To transport the oil or gas from the well, a trunk line may be built to the nearest major pipeline; crude oil also may be stored in tanks at the production site and removed later by truck. Generally, the various parties prepare and sign division orders, which are revenue distribution contracts specifying each party's share of revenues. If the division order specifies that the purchaser is to pay all revenues to the operator, the operator must distribute the appropriate amounts to the other joint interest owners and the lessor(s).

(a) FACTORS DETERMINING SUCCESS OR FAILURE OF EXPLORATION ACTIVITIES.

The various factors that determine the success or failure of oil and gas exploration activities include many uncertainties, some of which are discussed below. These factors set the oil and gas industry apart from many other capital-intensive industries.

- *Anticipated Success of Drilling.* According to figures compiled by the American Petroleum Institute and the American Association of Petroleum Geologists, only 15% to 20% of exploratory wells have traditionally been successful, whereas the success rate for development wells (wells in areas known to contain oil or gas) approximates 80%. In addition to the risks associated with finding commercial quantities of oil and gas, exploration activities are affected by drilling risks such as stuck drill pipes, blowouts, and improper completions.

- *Taxation.* A substantial portion of the revenues from the sale of crude oil and natural gas goes directly or indirectly to the federal and state governments in the form of severance taxes, ad valorem taxes, and income taxes. In the late 1970s, Congress enacted the **Windfall Profit Tax** on domestic crude oil. On August 25, 1988, the Windfall Profit Tax was repealed for all crude oil removed after that date. After the various taxes, royalties to the landowner, and production costs have been deducted, the producer's income from the sale of crude oil and natural gas may be only a small percentage of gross revenues. Except for certain tax credits relating to "Tight Sands" and coalbed methane gas production, most tax-related incentives have been eliminated through tax legislation since 1986.

- *Product Price and Marketability.* Although U.S. oil prices are no longer controlled by the U.S. government, they are dependent, in part, on production levels set by the Organization of Petroleum Exporting Countries (OPEC). The OPEC countries and the Former Soviet Union control 80% of the world's oil and gas reserves. The increase of oil prices in the late 1970s and early 1980s had a twofold impact—conservation was encouraged and exploration for oil reserves outside the OPEC countries increased. As a result, OPEC's market share of world oil sales dropped significantly from 1973 to 1986. With the new reserves in the North Sea, Mexico, and the North Slope displacing OPEC sales, the OPEC countries were forced to curtail production in order to support the price of oil on the world market.

  The price of high quality crude oil peaked at $42 per barrel in late 1979. In the late 1980s, the price fluctuated around $15 to $20 per barrel. Following Iraq's invasion of Kuwait in 1990, the price of crude briefly rose to around $40 per barrel only to fall back to the $20 range after the liberation of Kuwait in early 1991. By the Fall of 1991, concern over oil prices focused on the interruption of Iraq and Kuwait oil exports and on the break up of the USSR as the world's largest oil producer. Its republics' severe economic problems and substantial decline in oil production over the past several years coupled with booming demand in East Asia for petroleum products raise concerns that increased oil production outside the Former Soviet Union may not be adequate to meet world demand after the year 2000 unless oil prices rise in real terms. Because the United States must import half of the crude oil it needs, U.S. oil producers typically do not encounter problems selling their produced oil.

The U.S. government no longer regulates the price of natural gas. The U.S. prices of natural gas vary by region and are generally lower in the summer than winter in response to lower demand for gas in the summer. In many areas of the United States, gas production is curtailed, particularly in the summer. In recent years, gas purchasing has shifted from local pipelines to end users whereby the local pipelines serve as common carriers, rather than purchasers, of gas.

Because of the recent volatility in oil and gas prices, a number of price hedging mechanisms have been developed, including futures contracts, long-term hedging arrangements, and product swaps.

- *Timing of Production.* How quickly oil and gas are produced directly affects the payback period of an investment and its financial success or failure. The timing of production varies with the geologic characteristics of the reservoir and the marketability of the product. Reservoirs may contain the same gross producible reserves, yet the timing of production causes significant differences in the present value of the future revenue stream.

- *Acreage and Drilling Costs.* Many U.S. companies are focusing on exploration outside the United States. The U.S. is a mature exploration area producing 10% of the world's oil production from 63% of the world's oil wells. The global availability of quality exploration acreage, drilling personnel, and supplies has increased, whereas the related costs have dropped significantly since the boom period of the late 1970s and early 1980s.

23.3 ACCOUNTING FOR JOINT OPERATIONS

Oil- and gas-producing activities are recorded in the same general manner as most other activities that use manual or automated revenue, accounts payable, and general ledger systems. There are significant differences in the data gathering and reporting requirements, however, depending on whether the entity is an operator or a nonoperator. The two major accounting systems unique to oil- and gas-producing activities are the **joint interest billing system** and the **revenue distribution system.** The operator's joint interest billing system must properly calculate and record the operator's net cost as well as the costs to be billed to the nonoperators. Likewise, the revenue distribution system should properly allocate cash receipts among venture participants; this entails first recording the amounts payable to the participants and later making the appropriate payments.

As discussed previously, joint interest operations evolved because of the need to share the financial burden and risks of oil- and gas-producing activities. Joint operations typically take the form of a simple joint venture evidenced by two formal agreements, generally referred to as an exploration agreement and an operating agreement. These agreements define the geographic area involved, designate which party will act as operator of the venture, define how revenue and expenses will be divided, and set forth the rights and responsibilities of all parties to the agreement. The operating agreement also establishes how the operator is to bill the nonoperators for joint venture expenditures and provides nonoperators with the right to conduct "joint interest audits" of the operator's accounting records.

Accounting for joint operations is basically the same as accounting for operations when a property is completely owned by one party, except that in joint operations, revenues and expenses are divided among all of the joint venture partners. The following section discusses accounting for joint operations, first from the operator's standpoint and then from the non-operators' perspective.

(a) OPERATOR ACCOUNTING.   The operator typically records revenue and expenses for a well on a 100%, or "gross," basis and then allocates the revenue and expenses to the nonoperators based on ownership percentages maintained in the division order and joint interest master files. One approach is to record the full invoice or remittance advice amount and use contra or clearing accounts that set up the amounts due from or to the nonoperators. Recording transactions by means of contra accounts facilitates generation of information that management uses to review operations on a gross basis.

Before drilling and completing a well, the operator prepares an **authorization for expenditure (AFE)** itemizing the estimated costs to drill and complete the well. Although AFEs are normally required by the operating agreement, they are so useful as a capital budgeting tool that they are routinely used for all major expenditures by oil and gas companies, even if no joint venture exists. In addition to AFEs, the operator's field supervisor or engineer at the well site prepares a daily drilling report, which is an abbreviated report of the current status and the drilling or completion activity of the past 24 hours. That report may be compared with a drilling report prepared by the drilling company (also called a "tour" report). Some daily drilling reports indicate estimated cumulative costs incurred to date.

For shallow wells that are quickly and easily drilled, the AFE subsidiary ledger, combined with the daily drilling report, may provide the basis for the operator's estimate of costs incurred but not invoiced. For other wells, however, the engineering department prepares an estimate of cumulative costs incurred through year-end as a basis for recording the accrual and, if material, the commitments for future expenditures. Since an oil and gas company's accruable liabilities are primarily costs related to wells in progress, the engineering estimates may in some instances replace the auditor's usual tests for unrecorded liabilities in this area.

The operator normally furnishes the nonoperators with a monthly summary billing that shows the amount owed the operator on a property-by-property basis. The summary billing is accompanied by a separate joint operating statement for each property. The joint operating statement contains a description of each expenditure and shows the total expenditures for the property. The statement also shows the allocation of expenditures among the joint interest participants. The operator usually does not furnish copies of third-party invoices supporting items appearing on the joint interest billing, but the third-party invoices can be examined and copied during the nonoperators' audit of the joint account. The operator may also furnish the nonoperators a production report and at a later date remit checks to the nonoperators for their share of production.

(b) NONOPERATOR ACCOUNTING.   From the nonoperators' standpoint, the accounting for joint operations is basically the same as that followed by the operator. It is not unusual for a company to act as an operator on some properties and a nonoperator on others. To be able to make comparisons and evaluations that include both types of properties, nonoperators should also record items on a gross basis. A nonoperator should develop a control procedure for reviewing the joint operating statement to determine whether the operator is complying with the joint operating agreement, is billing the nonoperator only valid charges at the appropriate percentages, and is distributing the appropriate share of revenue.

(c) OTHER ACCOUNTING PROCEDURES.   The operating agreement may permit the operator to charge the joint venture a monthly fixed fee to cover its internal costs incurred in operating the joint venture. Alternatively, the agreement may provide for reimbursement of the operator's actual costs.

The parties in a joint operation may agree either to share costs in a proportion that is different from that used for sharing revenue or to change the sharing percentages after a specific event takes place. Typically, that event is **"payout,"** the point at which certain venturers have recovered their initial investment or an agreed-upon multiple of the investment. All parties involved in joint operations encounter payout situations at some time. Controls must be designed to monitor payout status to ensure that all parties are satisfied that items have been properly allocated in accordance with the joint operating agreement.

(d) OVERVIEW OF ACCOUNTING STANDARDS.   The following pronouncements set forth generally accepted accounting principles unique to oil and gas producing activities:

- Statement of Financial Accounting Standards (SFAS) No. 19, which describes a "successful efforts" method of accounting.
- SFAS No. 25, which recognizes that other methods may be appropriate.
- SEC Regulation S-X, Article 4, Section 10 (also referred to as S-X Rule 4-10), which prescribes two acceptable methods for public entities—either the successful efforts method described in SFAS No. 19 or a "full cost" method, as described in S-X Rule 4-10.
- SFAS No. 69, which requires supplementary disclosures of oil and gas producing activities.

Additional guidance and interpretations are found in FASB Interpretations, SEC Staff Accounting Bulletins, surveys in industry accounting practices, and petroleum accounting journals, and petroleum accounting textbooks.

The primary differences between the successful efforts and full cost methods center around costs to be capitalized and those to be expensed. As the name implies, under the successful efforts method, only those costs that lead to the successful discovery of reserves are capitalized, while the costs of unsuccessful exploratory activities are charged directly to expense. Under the full cost method, all exploration efforts are treated as capital costs under the theory that the reserves found are the result of all costs incurred. Both methods are widely used; however, larger companies tend to follow the successful efforts method.

Under income tax law and regulations, all exploration and development costs, except leasehold and equipment costs, are generally expensed as incurred. Petroleum producing companies with significant refining or marketing activities (called "Integrateds" as opposed to "Independents") must capitalize 30% of intangible well costs to be amortized over sixty months. Leasehold costs are expensed by complex depletion deductions which, for independents, can exceed actual costs. Equipment costs are depreciated using accelerated methods. Many independent U.S. oil and gas-producing companies pay the alternative minimum tax.

23.4 ACCEPTABLE ACCOUNTING METHODS

(a) The Successful Efforts Method

(i) Basic Rules.   The following points summarize the major aspects of the **successful efforts method** of accounting for oil and gas property costs:

- The costs of all G&G studies to find reserves are charged to expense as incurred.
- Lease acquisition costs for **unproved** properties are initially capitalized. Unproved properties are those on which no economically recoverable oil or gas has been demonstrated to exist. Unproved properties are to be assessed for impairment at least annually.
- If an unproved property becomes **impaired** because of such events as pending lease expiration or an unsuccessful exploratory well (dry hole), the loss is recognized and a valuation allowance is established to reflect the property's impairment. Two approaches to impairment are used (1) Property-by-property (typically used by small companies or

situations involving significant acreage costs), or (2) A formula approach based on factors such as historical success ratios and average lease terms (typically used by larger companies with a significant number of smaller properties).

- Once proved reserves are found on a property, the property is considered **proved** and the acquisition costs are amortized on a **unit-of-production** basis over the property's producing life based on total proved reserves (both developed and undeveloped reserves). The SFAS No. 25 definition of proved reserves may be summarized as the estimated volumes of oil and gas that geological and engineering data demonstrate with reasonable certainty to be recoverable in future years from known reservoirs under existing economic and operating conditions.

- If both oil and gas are produced from the property, the unit is normally equivalent barrels or mcfs, whereby gas is converted to equivalent barrels (or barrels are converted to equivalent mcfs) based on relative energy content. A common conversion factor is 5.6 mcfs to 1 equivalent barrel.

- For a property containing both oil and gas, the unit may reflect either oil or gas if:

  —The relative property of oil and gas extracted in the current period is expected to continue in the future, or

  —The reflected mineral clearly dominates the other for both current production and reserves.

- Carrying costs required to retain rights to unproved properties (delay rentals, ad valorem taxes, etc.) are charged to expense.

- Exploratory wells are capitalized initially as wells-in-progress and expensed if proved reserves are not found. Successful exploratory wells are capitalized, as are their completion costs (setting casing and other costs necessary to begin producing the well).

- Costs of drilling development wells (even the rare dry ones) are capitalized.

- Costs of successful exploratory wells, along with the costs of drilling development wells on the lease, are amortized on a unit-of-production basis over the property's proved developed reserves on:

  —A property-by-property basis, or

  —The basis of some reasonable aggregation of properties with a common geologic or structural feature or stratigraphic condition, such as a reservoir or field

- Once production has begun, all regular production costs are charged to expense.

- Capitalized interest, under the requirements of SFAS 34, would also be capitalized as part of the cost of unevaluated properties during the evaluation phase.

(ii) Exploratory versus Development Well Definition. Because Reg. S-X requires that the costs of dry exploratory wells be charged to expense, whereas the costs of dry development wells are capitalized, it is important to properly classify wells. Reg. S-X, Rule 4-10, defines the two categories of wells as follows:

- Development Well. A well drilled within the proved area of an oil or gas reservoir to the depth of a stratigraphic horizon known to be productive.

- Exploratory Well. A well drilled to find and produce oil or gas in an unproved area, to find a new reservoir in a field previously found to be productive of oil or gas in another reservoir, or to extend a known reservoir. Generally, an exploratory well is any well that is not a development well, a service well, or a stratigraphic test well.

These definitions may not coincide with those that have been commonly used in the industry (typically, the industry definition of a development well is more liberal than Reg. S-X, Rule 4-10). This results in two problems:

- Improper classification of certain exploratory dry holes as development wells (the problem occurs primarily with stepout or delineation wells drilled at the edge of a producing reservoir).
- Inconsistencies between the drilling statistics found in the forepart of Form 10-K (usually prepared by operational personnel) and the supplementary financial statement information required by SFAS No. 69 (usually prepared by accounting personnel).

(iii) Treatment of Costs of Exploratory Wells Whose Outcome Is Undetermined.   As set out below, Reg. S-X, Rule 4-10, effectively curtails extended deferral of the costs of an exploratory well whose outcome has not yet been determined:

(g) *Accounting for the costs of exploratory wells and exploratory-type stratigraphic test wells if the successful efforts method of accounting is followed.* The costs of drilling exploratory wells and the costs of drilling exploratory-type stratigraphic test wells shall be capitalized as part of the reporting entity's uncompleted wells, equipment, and facilities pending determination of whether the well has found proved reserves. If the well has found proved reserves, the capitalized costs of drilling the well shall become part of the entity's wells and related equipment and facilities (even though the well may not be completed as a producing well); if, however, the well has not found proved reserves, the capitalized costs of drilling the well, net of any salvage value, shall be charged to expense. The determination of whether proved reserves are found is usually made on or shortly after completion of drilling the well and the capitalized costs shall either be charged to expense or be reclassified as part of the costs of wells and related equipment facilities at that time. Information that becomes available after the end of the period covered by the financial statements but before those financial statements are issued shall be taken into account in evaluating conditions that existed at the balance sheet date. Occasionally, an exploratory well or an exploratory-type stratigraphic test well may be determined to have found oil and gas reserves, but classification of those reserves as proved cannot be made when drilling is completed. In those cases, one of three subparagraphs set forth below shall apply. Paragraphs (g)(1) and (2) are intended to prohibit, in all cases, the deferral of the costs of exploratory wells that find some oil and gas reserves merely on the chance that some event totally beyond the entity's control will occur, e.g., on the chance that the selling prices of oil and gas will increase sufficiently to result in classification of reserves as proved that are not commercially recoverable at current prices.

(1) *Exploratory wells that find oil and gas reserves in an area requiring a major capital expenditure, such as a trunk-pipeline, before production could begin.* On completion of drilling, an exploratory well may be determined to have found oil and gas reserves, but classification of those reserves as proved depends on whether a major capital expenditure can be justified which, in turn, depends on whether additional exploratory wells find a sufficient quantity of additional reserves. In that case, the cost of drilling the exploratory well shall continue to be carried as an asset pending determination of whether proved reserves have been found only as long as both of the following conditions are met: (i) the well has found a sufficient quantity of reserves to justify its completion as a producing well if the required capital expenditure is made, and (ii) drilling of additional wells is underway or firmly planned for the near future. Otherwise, the exploratory well shall be assumed to be impaired, and its costs shall be charged to expense.

(2) *All other exploratory wells that find oil and gas reserves.* In the absence of a determination as to whether the reserves that have been found can be classified as proved, the costs of drilling such an exploratory well shall not be carried as an asset for more than one year following completion of drilling. If, after that year has passed, a determination that proved reserves have been found cannot be made, the well shall be assumed to be impaired, and its costs shall be charged to expense.

(3) *Exploratory-type stratigraphic test wells that find oil and gas reserves.* On completion of drilling, such a well may be determined to have found oil and gas reserves, but classification of those reserves as proved depends on whether a major capital expenditure (usually a production platform) can be justified which, in turn depends on whether additional

exploratory-type stratigraphic test wells find a sufficient quantity of additional reserves. In that case, the cost of drilling the exploratory-type stratigraphic test well shall continue to be carried as an asset pending determination of whether proved reserves have been found only as long as both of the following conditions are met: (i) The well has found a quantity of reserves that would justify its completion for production had it not been simply a stratigraphic test well, and (ii) drilling of the additional exploratory-type stratigraphic test well is underway or firmly planned for the near future. Otherwise, the exploratory-type stratigraphic test well shall be assumed to impaired, and its costs shall be charged to expense.

(iv) Successful Efforts Impairment Test.   SFAS No. 121 on impairment of long-lived assets amends SFAS No. 19 and requires application of SFAS No. 121 impairment rules to capitalized costs of proved oil and gas properties for companies following the successful efforts method of accounting.

(v) Conveyances.   SFAS No. 19 and Reg. S-X, Rule 4-10(m) provides rules to account for mineral property conveyances and related transactions. Conveyances of "production payments" repayable in fixed monetary terms, i.e., loans in substance, are accounted for as loans. Conveyances of production payments repayable in fixed production volumes from specified production are deemed to be property sales whereby proved reserves are reduced but the proceeds from sale of a production payment are credited to deferred revenue to be recognized as revenue as the seller delivers future petroleum volumes to the holder of the production payment. Gain or loss is not recognized for conveyances of (1) a pooling of assets in a joint venture to find, develop, or produce oil and gas or (2) such assets in exchange for other assets used in oil and gas producing activities. Gain is not recognized (but loss is) for conveyance of a partial property interest when substantial uncertainty exists as to the recovery of costs for the retained interest portion or when the seller has substantial obligation for future performance such as drilling a well. For other conveyances, gain or loss is recognized unless prohibited under accounting principles applicable to enterprises in general.

(b) THE FULL COST METHOD

(i) Basic Rules.   Under Reg. S-X, Rule 4-10, oil and gas property costs are accounted for as follows:

- All costs associated with property acquisition, exploration and development activities shall be capitalized by *country-wide* cost center. Any internal costs that are capitalized shall be limited to those costs that can be *directly* identified with the acquisition, exploration and development activities undertaken by the reporting entity for its own account, and shall not include any costs related to production, general corporate overhead or similar activities.
- Capitalized costs within a cost center shall be amortized on the unit-of-production basis using proved oil and gas reserves, as follows:
  —Costs to be amortized shall include (A) all capitalized costs, less accumulated amortization, excluding the cost of certain unevaluated properties not being amortized; (B) the estimated future expenditures (based on current costs) to be incurred in developing proved reserves; and (C) estimated dismantlement and abandonment costs, net of estimated salvage values. [The current rule is referring to undiscounted future dismantlement and abandonment costs, net of estimated salvage values ("net abandonment costs"). In early 1996, the FASB issued an exposure draft for a proposed SFAS on accounting for certain liabilities related to closure or removal of long-lived assets. If adopted as drafted, the new SFAS would amortize capitalized costs that include a charge corresponding to the accrued liability for net abandonment costs. The liability reflects a present value discounted at a safe rate of interest.]
  —Amortization shall be computed on the basis of physical units, with oil and gas converted to a common unit of measure on the basis of their approximate relative energy

content, unless economic circumstances (related to the effects of regulated prices) indicated that use of revenue is a more appropriate basis of computing amortization. In the latter case, amortization shall be computed on the basis of current gross revenues from production in relation to future gross revenues (excluding royalty payments and net profits disbursements) based on current prices from estimated future production of proved oil and gas reserves (including consideration of changes in existing prices provided for only by contractual arrangements). The effect on estimated future gross revenues of a significant price increase during the year shall be reflected in the amortization provision only for the period after the price increase occurs.

In some cases it may be more appropriate to depreciate natural gas cycling and processing plants by a method other than the unit-of-production method.

Amortization computations shall be made on a consolidated basis, including investees accounted for on a proportionate consolidation basis. Investees accounted for on the equity method shall be treated separately.

(ii) Exclusion of Costs From Amortization.   SEC Financial Report Reg. S-X, Rule 4–10, allows two alternatives:

- Immediate inclusion of all costs incurred in the amortization base.
- Temporary exclusion of **all** acquisition and exploration costs incurred that directly relate to unevaluated properties and certain costs of major development projects.

Unevaluated properties are defined as those for which no determination has been made of the existence or nonexistence of proved reserves. Costs that may be excluded are all those costs **directly** related to the unevaluated properties (i.e., leasehold acquisitions costs, delay rentals, G&G, exploratory drilling, and capitalized interest). The cost of exploratory dry holes should be included in the amortization base as soon as the well is deemed dry.

These excluded costs must be assessed for impairment annually, either:

- individually for each significant property (i.e., capitalized cost exceeds 10% of the net full cost pool), or
- in the aggregate for insignificant properties using the successful efforts approach discussed in Rule 4-10(c)(1) (i.e., by transferring the excluded property costs into the amortization base ratably on the basis of such factors as the primary lease terms of the properties, the average holding period, and the relative proportion of properties on which proved reserves have been found previously).

(iii) The Full Cost Ceiling Test.   SFAS No. 121 impairment rules are effectively superseded by the following full cost "ceiling test" specified in Reg. S-X, Rule 4–10(i):

(i) For each cost center capitalized costs, less accumulated amortization and related deferred income taxes, shall not exceed an amount (the cost center ceiling) equal to the sum of: (A) The present value of estimated future net revenues computed by applying current prices of oil and gas reserves (with consideration of price changes only to the extent provided by contractual arrangements) to estimated future production of proved oil and gas reserves as of the date of the latest balance sheet presented, less estimated future expenditures (based on current costs) to be incurred in developing and producing the proved reserves computed using a discount factor of ten percent and assuming continuation of existing economic conditions; plus (B) the cost of properties not being amortized pursuant to paragraph (i)(3)(ii) of this section; plus (C) the lower of cost or estimated fair value of unproven properties included in the costs being amortized; less (D) income tax effects related to differences between the book and tax basis of the properties referred to in paragraphs (i)(4)(i)(B) and (C) of this section.

(ii) If unamortized costs capitalized within a cost center, less related deferred income taxes, exceed the cost center ceiling, the excess shall be charged to expense and separately disclosed during the period in which the excess occurs. Amounts thus required to be written off shall not be reinstated for any subsequent increase in the cost center ceiling.

Part D, income tax effects, is poorly worded and refers to the income tax effects related to the ceiling components in parts A, B, and C allowing for consideration of the oil and gas properties' tax bases and related depletion carryforwards and related net operating loss carryforwards.

Two other unique aspects of the full cost ceiling test are:

- *Ceiling Test Exemption for Purchases of Proved Properties.* A petroleum producing company might purchase proved properties for more than the present value of estimated future net revenues, causing net capitalized costs to exceed the cost center ceiling on the date of purchase. To avoid the writedown, the company may request from the SEC staff a temporary (usually one year) waiver of applying the ceiling test. The company must be prepared to demonstrate that the purchased properties' additional value exists beyond reasonable doubt. For more details see SAB No. 47, Topic 12, D-3a.

- *Effect of Subsequent Event.* If, after year-end but prior to the audit report date, either (1) additional reserves are proved up on properties owned at year-end, or (2) price increases become known, then such subsequent events may be considered in the year-end ceiling test to mitigate a writedown of capitalized costs.

  The avoidance of a writedown must be adequately disclosed, but the subsequent events should not be considered in the required disclosures of the company's proved reserves and standardized measure of discounted future net cash flows relating to such reserves (as further described in this Chapter's section on Financial Statement Disclosures). For more details, see SAB No. 47, Topic 12, D-3b.

(iv) Conveyances.   Reg. S-X, Rule 4-10(i)(6) provides that accounting for conveyances will be the same as for successful efforts accounting except that sales of oil and gas properties are to be accounted for as adjustments of capitalized costs with no recognition of gain or loss ("unless such adjustments would significantly alter the relationship between capitalized costs and proved reserves"). Exceptions are also made in some circumstances for property sales to partnerships and joint ventures in that (1) proceeds that are reimbursements of identifiable, current transaction expenses may be credited to income and (2) a petroleum company may recognize in income "management fees" from certain types of managed limited partnerships. When a company acquires an oil and gas property interest in exchange for services (such as drilling wells), income may be recognized in limited circumstances.

23.5 ACCOUNTING FOR NATURAL GAS IMBALANCES

Accounting techniques are basically the same whether revenue is generated by selling crude oil or natural gas. However, joint venture participants usually sell their crude oil collectively but may individually market and sell their shares of natural gas production. When a joint venture owner physically takes and sells more or less gas than its entitled share, a "gas imbalance" is created that is later reversed by an equal, but opposite, imbalance or by settlement in cash.

For example, if two joint venture participants each own 50% working interests in a well, and one company decides to sell gas on the spot market but the other company declines to sell due to a low spot price (or other factors), the company selling gas will receive 100% of revenue after paying the royalty interests. The selling company is in an overproduced capacity with respect to the well (the company is entitled to 50% of the gas after royalties but will receive 100%). A gas imbalance can also occur between a gas producer and the gas transmission company that receives the producer's gas but delivers a different volume to the producer's customer.

Gas-producing companies account for gas imbalances under either the Sales method, or the Entitlements method.

(a) SALES METHOD.   Under the sales method, the company recognizes revenue and a receivable for the volume of gas sold, regardless of ownership of the property. For example, if Company A owns a 50% net revenue interest in a gas property but sells 100% of the production in a given month, the company would recognize 100% of the revenue generated. In a subsequent month, if Company A sells no gas (and the other owners "make up" the imbalance), Company A would recognize zero revenue. Company A would reduce its estimate of proved reserves for any future production that it must give up to meet a gas imbalance obligation and increase proved reserves for any additional future production it has a right to receive from other joint venture participants to eliminate an existing gas imbalance.

Although this method is rather simple from a revenue accounting standpoint, it presents other problems. Regardless of the revenue method chosen, the operator will issue joint interest billing statements for expenses based on the ownership of the property. Depending on the gas-balancing situation, the sales method may present a problem with the matching of revenues and expenses in a period. If a significant imbalance exists at the end of an accounting period, the accountant may be required to analyze the situation and record additional expenses (or reduce expenses depending on whether the property is overproduced or underproduced).

(b) ENTITLEMENTS METHOD.   Under the entitlements method, the company recognizes revenue based on the volume of sales to which it is entitled by its ownership interest. For example, if Company A owns a 50% net revenue interest but sells 100% of the production in a given month, the company would recognize 50% of the revenue generated. Company A would recognize a receivable for 100% of the revenue with the difference being recorded in a payable (or deferred revenue) account. When the imbalance is corrected, the payable account will become zero, thus indicating that the property is "in balance."

This method correctly matches revenues and expenses but presents another accounting issue. If a property is significantly imbalanced, Company A may find itself in a position that reserves are insufficient to bring the well back to a balanced condition. If Company A is underproduced in this situation, a receivable (or deferred charge) may be recorded in the asset category that has a questionable realization. In addition, the company is really under- or overproduced in terms of volumes (measured in cubic feet) of gas. A value per cubic foot is assigned based on the sale price at the period of imbalance. If the price is significantly different when the correction occurs, the receivable may not show a zero balance in the accounting records.

(c) GAS BALANCING EXAMPLE

Facts: Company A owns a 50% net revenue.
Gas sales for January are 5,000 mcf @ $2.00 per MCF.
Gas sales for February are 5,000 mcf @ $2.00 per MCF.
In January, Company A sells 100% of gas production to its purchaser.
In February, Company sells zero gas to its purchaser.

JANUARY ACCOUNTING ENTRIES

Under the Sales Method	Debit	Credit
Accounts receivable, gas sales	$10,000	
Gas revenue		$10,000
Under the Entitlements Method		
Accounts receivable, gas sales	$10,000	
Gas revenue		$ 5,000
Payable		$ 5,000

FEBRUARY ACCOUNTING ENTRIES

Under the Sales Method   No entries are recorded

Under the Entitlements Method

Payable $ 5,000
    Gas revenue $ 5,000

23.6 HARD-ROCK MINING

(a) MINING OPERATIONS.   The principal difference between hard-rock mining companies and companies involved in oil and gas producing activities, previously discussed in this chapter, relates to the nature, timing, and extent of expenditures incurred for exploration, development, production, and processing of minerals.

Generally in the mining industry, a period of as long as several years elapses between the time exploration costs are incurred to discover a commercially viable body of ore and the expenditure of development costs, which are usually substantial, to complete the project. Therefore, the economic benefits derived from a project are long-term and subject to the uncertainties inherent in the passage of time. In contrast, the costs related to exploring for deposits of oil and gas are expended generally over a relatively short time. Major exceptions would be offshore and foreign petroleum exploration and development.

Like petroleum exploration and production, the mining industry is capital intensive. Substantial investments in property, plant, and equipment are required; usually they represent more than 50% of a mining company's total assets. The significant capital investments of mining companies and the related risks inherent in any long-term major project may affect the recoverability of capitalized costs.

The operational stages in mining companies vary somewhat depending on the type of mineral, because of differences in geological, chemical, and economic factors. The basic operations common to mining companies are exploration, development, mining, milling, smelting, and refining.

Exploration is the search for natural accumulations of minerals with economic value. Exploration for minerals is a specialized activity involving the use of complex geophysical and geochemical equipment and procedures. There is an element of financial risk in every decision to pursue exploration, and explorers generally seek to minimize the costs and increase the probability of success. As a result, before any fieldwork begins, extensive studies are made concerning which types of minerals are to be sought and where they are most likely to occur. Market studies and forecasts, studies of geological maps and reports, and logistical evaluations are performed to provide information for use in determining the economic feasibility of a potential project.

Exploration can be divided into two phases, prospecting and geophysical analysis. *Prospecting* is the search for geological information over a broad area. It embraces such activities as geological mapping, analysis of rock types and structures, searches for direct manifestations of mineralization, taking samples of minerals found, and aeromagnetic surveys. *Geophysical analysis* is conducted in specific areas of interest localized during the prospecting phase. Rock and soil samples are examined, and the earth's crust is monitored directly for magnetic, gravitational, sonic, radioactive, and electrical data. Based on the analysis, targets for trenching, test pits, and exploratory drilling are identified. Drilling is particularly useful in evaluating the shape and character of a deposit. Analysis of samples is necessary to determine the grade of the deposit.

Once the grade and quantity of the deposit have been estimated, the mining company must decide whether developing the deposit is technically feasible and commercially viable. The value of a mineral deposit is determined by the intrinsic value of the minerals present and by the nature and location of their occurrence. In addition to the grade and quality of the ore, such factors as the physical accessibility of the deposit, the estimated costs of production, and the value of joint products and by-products are key elements in the decision to develop a deposit for commercial exploitation.

The *development* stage of production involves planning and preparing for commercial operation. Development of surface mines is relatively straightforward. For open-pit mines, which are surface mines, the principal procedure is to remove sufficient overburden to expose the ore. For strip mines, an initial cut is made to expose the mineral to be mined. For underground mines, data resulting from exploratory drilling is evaluated as a basis for planning the shafts and tunnels that will provide access to the mineral deposit.

Substantial capital investment in mineral rights, machinery and equipment, and related facilities generally is required in the development stage.

Mining breaks up the rock and ore to the extent necessary for loading and removal to the processing location. A variety of mining techniques exists to accomplish this. The drilling and blasting technique is utilized frequently; an alternative is the continuous mining method, in which a boring or tearing machine is mounted on a forward crawler to break the material away from the rock face.

After removal from the mine site, the ore is ready for *milling*. The first phase of the milling stage involves crushing and grinding the chunks of ore to reduce them to particle size. The second milling procedure is concentration, which involves the separation of the mineral constituents from the rock.

Smelting is the process of separating the metal from impurities with which it may be chemically bound or physically mixed too closely to be removed by concentration. Most smelting is accomplished through fusion, which is the liquefaction of a metal under heat. In some cases, chemical processes are used instead of, or in combination with, heating techniques.

Refining is the last step in isolating the metal. The primary methods utilized are fire refining and electrolytic refining. Fire refining is similar to smelting. The metal is kept in a molten state and treated with pine logs, hydrocarbon gas, or other substances to enable impurities to be removed. Fire refining generally does not allow the recovery of by-products. Electrolytic refining uses an electrical current to separate metals from a solution in such a way that by-products can be recovered.

(b) SOURCES OF GENERALLY ACCEPTED ACCOUNTING PRINCIPLES.   Accounting and reporting issues in the mining industry are discussed in AICPA Accounting Research Study No. 11, *Financial Reporting in the Extractive Industries* (1969). In 1976, the Financial Accounting Standards Board (FASB) issued a discussion memorandum, *Financial Accounting and Reporting in the Extractive Industries,* which analyzed issues relevant to the extractive industries. Neither of these attempts, however, culminated in the issuance of an authoritative pronouncement for mining companies. At present, therefore, the accounting practices prevalent among mining companies are the principal source of generally accepted accounting practices for the industry.

23.7 ACCOUNTING FOR MINING COSTS

(a) EXPLORATION AND DEVELOPMENT COSTS.   Exploration and development costs are major expenditures of mining companies. The characterization of expenditures as either exploration, development, or production usually determines whether such costs are capitalized or expensed. For accounting purposes, it is useful to identify five basic phases of exploration and development: prospecting, property acquisition, geophysical analysis, development before production, and development during production.

Prospecting usually begins with obtaining (or preparing) and studying topographical and geological maps. Prospecting costs, which are generally expensed as incurred, include (1) options to lease or buy property; (2) rights of access to lands for geophysical work; and (3) salaries, equipment, and supplies for scouts, geologists, and geophysical crews.

Property acquisition includes both the purchase of property and the purchase or lease of mineral rights. Costs incurred to purchase land (including mineral rights and surface rights) or to lease mineral rights are capitalized. Acquisition costs may include lease bonus and lease extension costs, lease brokers commissions, abstract and recording fees, filing and patent fees and other related expenses.

Geophysical analysis is performed to discover specific deposits of minerals. The related costs (commonly referred to as exploration costs) are accounted for in a number of different ways. Most companies expense all those costs as incurred; others capitalize them until such time as the existence or absence of an economically recoverable mineral reserve is established. If no reserve is established, the costs are written off. "Full cost" accounting is discussed at length earlier in this chapter, but has not gained general acceptance in the mining industry.

A body of ore reaches the development stage when the existence of an economically recoverable mineral reserve is established and the decision has been made to develop the body of ore for mining. Development costs include expenditures associated with drilling, removing overburden (waste rock), sinking shafts, driving tunnels, building roads and dikes, purchasing processing equipment and equipment used in developing the mine, and constructing supporting facilities to house and care for the work force. In many respects, the expenditures in the development stage are similar to those incurred during exploration. As a result, it is sometimes difficult to distinguish the point at which exploration ends and development begins. For example, the sinking of shafts and driving of tunnels may begin in the exploration stage and continue into the development stage. In most instances, the transition from the exploration to the development stage is the same for both accounting and tax purposes.

Generally, all costs incurred during the development stage before production starts are capitalized; usually they are reduced by the proceeds from the sale of any production during the development period. Development ore (ore extracted in the process of gaining access to the body of ore) is normally incidental to the development process.

Development also takes place during the production stage. The accounting treatment of development costs incurred during the ongoing operation of a mine depends on the nature and purpose of the expenditures. Costs associated with expansion of capacity are generally capitalized; costs incurred to maintain production are normally included in production costs in the period in which they are incurred. In certain instances, the benefits of development activity will be realized in future periods, such as when the "block caving" and open-pit mining methods are used. In the block caving method, entire sections of a body of ore are intentionally collapsed to permit the mass removal of minerals; extraction may take place two to three years after access to the ore is gained and the block prepared. In an open-pit mine, there is typically an expected ratio of overburden to mineral-bearing ore over the life of the mine. The cost of stripping the overburden to gain access to the ore is expensed in those periods in which the actual ratio of overburden to ore approximates the expected ratio. In certain instances, however, extensive stripping is performed to remove the overburden in advance of the period in which the ore will be extracted. When the benefits of either development activity are to be realized in a future accounting period, the costs associated with the development activity should be deferred and amortized during the period in which the ore is extracted or the product produced.

Statement of Financial Accounting Standards (SFAS) No. 7, "Accounting and Reporting by Development Stage Enterprises" (Accounting Standards Section De4), states that "an enterprise shall be considered to be in the development stage if it is devoting substantially all of its efforts to establishing a new business" and "the planned principal operations have not commenced" or they "have commenced, but there has been no significant revenue therefrom." Although SFAS No. 7 specifically excludes mining companies from its application, the definition of a development stage enterprise is helpful in defining the point in time at which a mine's development phase ends and its production phase begins. Mining companies usually use one of two points in time:

1. When both the mine and the mill produce on a regularly scheduled basis at the planned activity levels, or
2. When ore is extracted on a regular basis without regard to the milling capability.

Determining when the production phase begins is important for accounting purposes because, in general, at that time, certain development costs are no longer capitalized, and revenue from the sale of ore is included in sales revenue rather than as a reduction of capitalized development costs. The point at which production is considered to begin is sometimes stipulated in loan agreements and may initiate debt payments. Determining the commencement of production is also significant for federal income tax purposes. The point at which a mine is considered to begin production is generally the same for both accounting and tax purposes.

(b) PRODUCTION COSTS.   When the mine begins production, production costs are expensed. The capitalized property acquisition, exploration, and development costs are recognized as costs of production through their depreciation or depletion, generally on the unit-of-production method over the expected productive life of the mine.

The principal difference between computing depreciation in the mining industry and in other industries is that useful lives of assets that are not readily movable from a mine site must not exceed the estimated life of the mine, which in turn is based on the remaining economically recoverable ore reserves. In some instances, this may require depreciating certain mining equipment over a period that is shorter than its physical life.

Depreciation charges are significant because of the highly capital-intensive nature of the industry. Moreover, those charges are affected by numerous factors, such as the physical environment, revisions of recoverable ore estimates, environmental regulations, and improved technology. In many instances, depreciation charges on similar equipment with different intended uses may begin at different times. For example, depreciation of equipment used for exploration purposes may begin when it is purchased and use has begun, while depreciation of milling equipment may not begin until a certain level of commercial production has been attained.

Depletion (or depletion and amortization) of property acquisition, exploration, and development costs related to a body of ore is calculated in a manner similar to the unit-of-production method of depreciation. The cost of the body of ore is divided by the estimated quantity of ore reserves or units of metal or mineral to arrive at the depletion charge per unit. The unit charge is multiplied by the number of units extracted to arrive at the depletion charge for the period. This computation requires a current estimate of economically recoverable mineral reserves at the end of the period.

It is often appropriate for different depletion calculations to be made for different types of capitalized exploration and development expenditures. For instance, one factor to be considered is whether capitalized costs relate to gaining access to the total economically recoverable ore reserves of the mine or only to specific portions.

Usually, estimated quantities of economically recoverable mineral reserves are the basis for computing depletion and amortization under the unit-of-production method. The choice of the reserve unit is not a problem if there is only one product; if, however, as in many extractive operations, several products are recovered, a decision must be made whether to measure production on the basis of the major product or on the basis of an aggregation of all products. Generally, the reserve base is the company's total proved and probable ore reserve quantities; it is determined by specialists, such as geologists or mining engineers. Proved and probable reserves typically are used as the reserve base because of the degree of uncertainty surrounding estimates of possible reserves. The imprecise nature of reserve estimates makes it inevitable that the reserve base will be revised over time as additional data becomes available. Changes in the reserve base should be treated as changes in accounting estimates in accordance with APB

Opinion No. 20, "Accounting Changes" (Accounting Standards Section A06), and accounted for prospectively.

(c) INVENTORY.   A mining company's inventory generally has two major components—(1) metals and minerals and (2) materials and supplies that are used in mining operations.

(i) Metals and Minerals.   Metal and mineral inventories usually comprise broken ore; crushed ore; concentrate; materials in process at concentrators, smelters, and refineries; metal; and joint and by-products. The usual practice of mining companies is not to recognize metal inventories for financial reporting purposes before the concentrate stage, that is, until the majority of the nonmineralized material has been removed from the ore. Thus, ore is not included in inventory until it has been processed through the concentrator and is ready for delivery to the smelter. This practice evolved because the amounts of broken ore before the concentrating process ordinarily are relatively small, and consequently the cost of that ore and of concentrate in process generally is not significant. Furthermore, the amount of broken ore and concentrate in process is relatively constant at the end of each month, and the concentrating process is quite rapid—usually a matter of hours. In the case of leach operations, generally the mineral content of the ore is estimated and costs are inventoried. However, practice varies and some companies do not inventory costs until the leached product is introduced into the electrochemical refinery cells.

Determining inventory quantities during the production process is often difficult. Broken ore, crushed ore, concentrate, and materials in process may be stored in various ways or enclosed in vessels or pipes.

With few exceptions, mining companies carry metal inventory at the lower of cost or market value, with cost determined on a LIFO, FIFO, or average basis. Occasionally, mining companies value inventories of precious metals in finished and salable form at net realizable value, which approximates market but exceeds cost. Although this policy is acceptable, it is rarely applied, and then only if there is an assured market at quoted prices.

Valuation of product inventory is also affected by worldwide imbalances between supply and demand for certain metals. Companies sometimes produce larger quantities of a metal than can be absorbed by the market. In that situation, management may have to write the inventory down to its net realizable value; determining that value, however, may be difficult if there is no established market or only a thin market for the particular metal.

Product costs for mining companies usually reflect all normal and necessary expenditures associated with cost centers such as mines, concentrators, smelters, and refineries. Inventory costs comprise not only direct costs of production, but also an allocation of overhead, including mine and other plant administrative expenses. Depreciation, depletion, and amortization of capitalized exploration, acquisition, and development costs also should be included in inventory.

If a company engages in tolling (described in subsection 23.7(d)), it may have significant production inventories on hand that belong to other mining companies. Usually it is not possible to physically segregate inventories owned by others from similar inventories owned by the company. Memorandum records of tolling inventories should be maintained and reconciled periodically to physical counts.

(ii) Materials and Supplies.   Materials and supplies usually constitute a substantial portion of the inventory of most mining companies, sometimes exceeding the value of metal inventories. This is because a lack of supplies or spare parts could cause the curtailment of operations. In addition to normal operating supplies, materials and supplies inventories often include such items as fuel and spare parts for trucks, locomotives, and other machinery. Occasionally, because of the significance of the cost of certain spare parts and the need to have them on hand to ensure the uninterrupted operation of production equipment, mining companies capitalize spare parts and treat them as equipment (accounting for them as "emergency spare parts" or "insurance spares") rather than inventory. These emergency spare parts are depreciated over the same period as the equipment with which they are associated. Most mining companies use perpetual inventory systems to account for materials and supplies because of their high unit value.

Materials and supplies inventories normally are valued at cost minus a reserve for surplus items and obsolescence.

(d) COMMODITIES, FUTURES TRANSACTIONS.   Mining companies usually have significant inventories of commodities that are traded in worldwide markets, and frequently enter into long-term forward sales contracts specifying sales prices based on market prices at time of delivery. To protect themselves from the risk of loss that could result from price declines, mining companies often "hedge" against price changes by entering into futures contracts. Companies sell contracts when they expect selling prices to decline or are satisfied with the current price and want to "lock in" the profit (or loss) on the sale of their inventory. To establish a hedge when it has or expects to have a commodity (e.g., copper) in inventory, a company sells a contract that commits it to deliver that commodity in the future at a fixed price. The company usually closes out the futures position at or near the delivery date of the hedge inventory by buying the contract back at the current market price.

The accounting for commodity futures contracts depends on whether the contract qualifies as a hedge under Statement of Financial Accounting Standards No. 80, *Accounting for Futures Contracts* (SFAS 80) (Accounting Standards Section F80). In order for the contract to qualify as a hedge two conditions must be met: 1) the item to be hedged must expose the company to price or interest rate risk; and 2) the contract must reduce that exposure and must be designated as a hedge. In determining its exposure to price or interest rate risk, a company must take into account other assets, liabilities, firm commitments and anticipated transactions that may already offset or reduce the exposure. Moreover, SFAS 80 prescribes a correlation test between the hedged item and the hedging instrument that requires a company to examine historical relationships and to monitor the correlation after the hedging transaction was executed, thus permitting cross hedging provided there is high correlation between changes in the values of the hedged item and the hedging instrument.

For contracts which qualify as hedges, unrealized gains and losses on the futures contracts are generally deferred and are recognized in the same period in which gains or losses from the items being hedged are recognized. Speculative contracts, in contrast, are accounted for at market value.

In 1992, the FASB initiated a project on hedge accounting and accounting for derivatives and synthetic instruments. As this publication goes to print, the FASB has tentatively concluded that commodity based derivatives should be included within the scope of its project and that

- All free-standing derivatives would be marked to market.
- An entity would have to specify (i.e., designate) whether a derivative was trading or risk management.
- Gains or losses on trading derivatives would be recorded in earnings.
- Gains or losses on risk management derivatives would be reported as a separate component of equity and recognized in earnings when realized.
- Any exposure and any type of derivative would qualify for risk management.

Deliberations continue on the subject. Their discussions are important to the mining industry since their tentative conclusions represent major changes that could impact mining companies.

As an intermediate measure, prior to the finalization of rules related to accounting for hedges, derivatives and synthetic instruments, the FASB decided in December 1993 to undertake a short-term project aimed at improving financial statement disclosures about derivatives.

This short-term project led to the issuance of FASB Statement 119 in October 1994, entitled "Disclosure about Derivative Financial Instruments and Fair Value of Financial Instruments" (SFAS 119).

SFAS 119 requires companies to disclose the following:

- The face amount of the contract by class of financial instrument;
- The nature and terms of the contract, including a discussion of the credit and market risks and cash requirements of those instruments; and
- Their related accounting policy.

With respect to hedging transactions, new disclosures include: a discussion of the company's objectives and strategies for holding or issuing these instruments; and descriptions of how those instruments are reported in the financial statements.

Additionally, disclosures for hedges of anticipated transactions have been expanded to require: a description of the hedge, the period of time the transaction is expected to occur, and deferred gains or losses. Contracts that either require the exchange of a financial instrument for a nonfinancial commodity or permit settlement of an obligation by delivery of a nonfinancial commodity are exempt from disclosure requirements of this statement. However, depending upon the significance of use of derivatives by particular companies, additional disclosure may be prudent to accurately portray the manner in which the entity protects itself against price fluctuations.

(e) ENVIRONMENTAL CONCERNS.   Mining operations and exploration activities are subject to governmental regulation for the protection of the environment. These laws are continually changing and are becoming more restrictive. The primary basis for regulation of environmental contamination, hazardous waste disposal and cleanup are:

- The Resource Conservation and Recovery Act of 1976 (RCRA), which regulates the generation, treatment, storage and disposal of both solid and hazardous wastes;
- The Comprehensive Environmental Response, Compensation and Liability Act of 1980 (CERCLA or Superfund), which addresses the nationwide risk to human health and the environment created by inactive hazardous waste landfills and contaminated sites, focusing on the cleanup of existing hazardous waste and dump sites.

In addition to the aforementioned federal regulations, virtually all states have enacted similar regulations.

Each of the these regulations could have a significant impact on any mining company. However, Superfund activities remain in the limelight largely because of the significant costs associated with the related remediation. To date, the EPA has identified 27,000 to 30,000 potential Superfund sites. Some have estimated the cleanup costs at $25 million per site. Experts predict that this could produce a total liability for past contamination of $500 billion.

Recording a liability for potential environmental cleanup costs is no different than accounting for any other contingency in accordance with SFAS 5, *Accounting for Contingencies.* SFAS 5 requires an accrual of a loss when it is probable the liability has been incurred and the amount of loss can be reasonably estimated. When an environmental liability is to be accrued will depend on the unique facts and circumstances. From a practical standpoint, as the remediation process progresses toward finalization, there is increasing likelihood that an estimate or at least a range of loss can be determined and, therefore, a liability should be recorded. However, estimating the amount of the contingent liability may be difficult in the early stages of cleanup without final decisions being made as to cleanup methodologies, cost allocations among Potentially Responsible Parties ("PRP"s), or final design and implementation of remedial plans.

FASB Interpretation No. 14, *Reasonable Estimation of the Amount of a Loss* (an interpretation of SFAS 5), states that when it is probable that an asset has been impaired or a liability has been incurred, and the reasonable estimate of the loss is a range, an amount should be accrued for the loss. When some amount within the range appears to be a better estimate than any other amount within the range, that amount should be accrued. When no amount within the range is a better estimate than any other amount, the minimum amount in the range should be accrued.

Management should assess potential environmental cleanup costs by collecting all available pertinent information and developing a sensible range of estimates considering best and worst case scenarios. From this range, the most probable amount should be accrued.

In addition to SFAS 5 and FIN 14, Staff Accounting Bulletin No. 92, *Accounting and Disclosures Relating to Loss Contingencies,* contains additional guidance for SEC registrants. SAB 92 reaffirms the requirements of FIN 14 and requires that recognition of a loss equal to the lower limit of the range is necessary even if the upper limit of the range is uncertain, and states that it is inappropriate to delay accrual of a loss until sufficient information is available to determine the best estimate of an ultimate liability.

An environmental liability should be evaluated independently from any potential claim for recovery (a two-event approach) and the loss arising from the recognition of a liability should be reduced only when a claim for recovery is "probable" of realization. This position, set forth in ETIF Issue No. 93-5, "Accounting for Environmental Liabilities," is an interpretation of the provisions of SFAS 5 regarding contingent assets which are usually not recognized prior to realization. Further, ETIF 93-5 reached a consensus that discounting environmental liabilities to reflect the time value of money is permissible, but not required, only if the aggregate amount of the obligation and the amount and timing of the cash payments are fixed or reliably determinable for a specific cleanup site.

(f) SHUT-DOWN OF MINES.   As a result of environmental considerations, mining companies may incur significant costs for restoration, reclamation, and rehabilitation of mining facilities after the mining process has been completed. Those costs should be accrued during the revenue-producing period.

Volatile metal prices may make active operations uneconomical from time to time, and, as a result, mining companies will shut down operations, either temporarily or permanently. When operations are temporarily shut down, a question arises as to the carrying value of the related assets. If a long-term diminution in the value of the assets has occurred, a write-down of the carrying value to net realizable value should be recorded. This decision is extremely judgmental and depends on projections of whether viable mining operations can ever be resumed. Those projections are based on significant assumptions as to prices, production, quantities, and costs; because most minerals are worldwide commodities, the projections must take into account global supply and demand factors.

When operations are temporarily shut down, the related facilities usually are placed in a "standby mode" that provides for care and maintenance so that the assets will be retained in a reasonable condition that will facilitate resumption of operations. Care and maintenance costs are usually recorded as expenses in the period in which they are incurred. Examples of typical care and maintenance costs are security, preventive and protective maintenance, and depreciation.

A temporary shutdown of a mining company's facility can raise questions as to whether the company can continue as a going concern.

(g) ACCOUNTING FOR THE IMPAIRMENT OF LONG LIVED ASSETS.   The Financial Accounting Standards Board ("FASB") issued a standard in March 1995 on Accounting for the Impairment of Long-Lived Assets and Long-Lived Assets To Be Disposed Of. The Standard is effective for financial statements for fiscal years beginning after December 15, 1995. This statement provides definitive guidance on when the carrying amount of long-lived assets should be reviewed for impairment. It also establishes a common methodology for assessing and measuring the impairment of long-lived assets. Additionally, assets to be disposed of which do not qualify as a segment will now be accounted for under the provisions of this statement.

The Standard requires long-lived assets held and used by an entity (e.g. plant and equipment and capitalized exploration and development costs) to be reviewed for impairment whenever events or changes indicate that the carrying value of the assets may not be recoverable. In the case of mining companies, events such as falling commodity prices, increasing environmental liabilities and operating costs and reductions in reserves are circumstances indicating that long-lived assets may be impaired.

The proposed test for recoverability involves a two-step approach. First, a comparison of carrying values of long-lived assets to the undiscounted estimated future cash flows expected to result from their use or eventual disposition, is to be performed. If asset carrying values are greater than such cash flows, an impairment loss would be recognized immediately. The second step involves measuring the amount of the impairment loss which is the amount by which the carrying amount of the asset exceeds the fair value of the asset. Fair value of assets shall either be measured by their market value or selling prices of similar assets. If no market price is available, then fair value is based on discounted future cash flows. The use of discounted cash flows in the measurement criteria would therefore result in larger asset writedowns than the initial test for impairment would indicate.

It is important for mining companies to perform a realistic analysis of estimated future cash flows when reviewing assets for impairment, especially in view of the fact that restoration of previously recognized impairment losses is prohibited and that impairment measurement will result in a larger writedown under the standard. In this regard, the estimate of cash flows is to be management's best estimate based on reasonable supportable assumptions and projections. The use of commodity prices (e.g. futures prices) other than spot would be permissible providing they are reasonable and supportable.

23.8 ACCOUNTING FOR MINING REVENUES

(a) SALES OF MINERALS.   Generally, minerals are not sold in the raw-ore stage because of the insignificant quantity of minerals relative to the total volume of waste rock. (There are, however, some exceptions, such as iron ore and coal.) The ore is usually milled at or near the mine site to produce a concentrate containing a significantly higher percentage of mineral content. For example, the metal content of copper concentrate typically is 25 to 30%, as opposed to between $\frac{1}{2}$ and 1% for the raw ore. The concentrate is frequently sold to other processors; occasionally, mining companies exchange concentrate to reduce transportation costs. After the refining process, metallic minerals may be sold as finished metals, either in the form of products for remelting by final users (e.g., pig iron or cathode copper) or as finished products (e.g., copper rod or aluminum foil).

Sales of raw ore and concentrate entail determining metal content based initially on estimated weights, moisture content, and ore grade. Those estimates are subsequently revised, based on the actual metal content recovered from the raw ore or concentrate, or settlement is based on actual recoveries. Estimates generally are made by both the seller and the buyer; the difference is usually split.

Sales prices are often based on the market price on a commodity exchange such as the COMEX (New York Commodity Exchange) or LME (London Metal Exchange) at the time of delivery. Sometimes a time other than delivery is used to set the price; for example, the average of daily COMEX prices for the two-week period subsequent to delivery of the minerals could be used. In those circumstances, it might be necessary to record revenue based on an estimate of the total sales value of the shipment at the point of sale and adjust the amount when the sales price has been determined.

Generally, revenue should be recognized only when all of the following conditions have been met:

- The product has been shipped and is no longer under physical control of the seller (or title to the product has already passed to the buyer);
- The quantity and quality of the product can be determined with reasonable accuracy; and
- The selling price can be determined with reasonable accuracy.

Mining companies often encounter problems with the last two conditions because final quantities and prices may not be established at the time of delivery. Provisional invoices commonly are recorded using estimated quantities and prices that are adjusted when details of the deliveries are finalized.

(b) TOLLING AND ROYALTY REVENUES.   Companies with smelters and refineries may also realize revenue from tolling, which is the processing of metal-bearing materials of other mining companies for a fee. The fee is based on numerous factors, including the weight and metal content of the materials processed. Normally, the processed minerals are returned to the original producer for subsequent sale. To supplement the recovery of fixed costs, companies with smelters and refineries frequently enter into tolling agreements when they have excess capacity.

For a variety of reasons, companies may not wish to mine certain properties that they own. Mineral royalty agreements may be entered into that provide for royalties based on a percentage of the total value of the mineral or of gross revenue, to be paid when the minerals extracted from the property are sold.

23.9 SUPPLEMENTARY FINANCIAL STATEMENT INFORMATION—ORE RESERVES

SFAS No. 89, "Financial Reporting and Changing Prices" (Accounting Standards Section C28), eliminated the requirement that certain publicly traded companies meeting specified size criteria must disclose the effects of changing prices and supplemental disclosures of ore reserves. However, Item 102 of Securities and Exchange Commission Regulation S-K requires that publicly traded mining companies present information related to production, reserves, locations, developments, and the nature of the registrant's interest in properties.

23.10 ACCOUNTING FOR INCOME TAXES

Chapter 18 addresses general accounting for income taxes. Tax accounting for oil and gas production as well as hard rock mining is particularly complex and cannot be fully covered in this chapter. However, two special deductions need to be mentioned—percentage depletion and immediate deduction of certain development costs.

Many petroleum and mining production companies are allowed to calculate depletion as the greater of cost depletion or percentage depletion. Cost depletion is based on amortization of property acquisition costs over estimated recoverable reserves. Percentage depletion is a statutory depletion deduction that is a specified percentage of gross revenue at the well-head or mine (15% for oil and gas) for the particular mineral produced and is limited to a portion of the property's taxable income before deducting such depletion. Percentage depletion may exceed the depletable cost basis.

The determination of gross income from mining is based on the value of the mineral at the cutoff point (i.e., before application of nonmining processes). To the extent that minerals are sold to independent third parties at the cutoff point, the sales price generally determines gross income from mining. For an integrated mining company, gross income should be determined by using a representative field or market price for an ore or mineral of similar kind of grade. Absent such price, gross income can be determined under the proportionate profits method, which attributes an equal amount of profit to each dollar of mining and nonmining cost incurred.

For both petroleum and mining companies, exploration and development costs other than for equipment are largely deductible when incurred. However, all mining companies and the major, integrated petroleum companies must capitalize 30% of such exploration and development costs and amortize that portion over 60 months. Mining companies must also recapture the previously deducted exploration costs when and if the related mine attains commercial production.

23.11 FINANCIAL STATEMENT DISCLOSURES

SFAS No. 69 details supplementary disclosure requirements for the oil and gas industry, most of which are required only by public companies. Both public and nonpublic companies, however, must provide a description of the accounting method followed and the manner of disposing of capitalized costs. Audited financial statements filed with the SEC must include supplementary disclosures, which fall into four categories:

- Historical cost data relating to acquisition, exploration, development, and production activity,
- Results of operations for oil and gas producing activities,
- Proved reserve quantities, and
- Standardized measure of discounted future net cash flows relating to proved oil and gas reserve quantities (also known as SMOG [standardized measure of oil and gas]). For foreign operations, SMOG also relates to produced quantities subject to certain long-term purchase contracts held by a party involved in producing the quantities.

The supplementary disclosures are required of companies with significant oil- and gas-producing activities; significant is defined as 10% or more of revenue, operating results, or identifiable assets. The statement provides that the disclosures are to be provided as supplemental data; thus they need not be audited. The disclosure requirements are described in detail in the statement, and examples are provided in an appendix to SFAS No. 69. If the supplemental information is not audited, it must be clearly labeled as unaudited. However, auditing interpretations (Au Section 9558) required the financial statement auditor to perform certain limited procedures to these required, unaudited supplementary disclosures.

Proved reserves are inherently imprecise because of the uncertainties and limitations of the data available.

Most large companies and many medium-sized companies have qualified engineers on their staffs to prepare oil and gas reserve studies. Many also use outside consultants to make independent reviews. Other companies, who do not have sufficient operations to justify a full-time engineer, engage outside engineering consultants to evaluate and estimate their oil and gas reserves. Usually, reserve studies are reviewed and updated at least annually to take into account new discoveries and adjustments of previous estimates.

The standardized measure is disclosed as of the end of the fiscal year. SMOG reflects future revenues computed by applying unescalated, year-end oil and gas prices to year-end proved reserves. Future price changes may only be considered if fixed and determinable under year-end sales contracts. The calculated future revenues are reduced for estimated future development costs, production costs and related income taxes (using unescalated, year-end cost rates) to compute future net cash flows. Such cash flows, by future year, are discounted at a standard 10% per annum to compute the standardized measure.

Significant sources of the annual changes in the year-end standardized measure and year-end proved oil and gas reserves should be disclosed.

23.12 SOURCES AND SUGGESTED REFERENCES

Brock, Horace R., Jennings, Dennis R., and Feiten, Joseph B., *Petroleum Accounting—Principles, Procedures, and Issues,* 4th ed., Professional Development Institute, Denton, TX, 1996.

Council of Petroleum Accountants Societies, *Bulletin No. 24, Producer Gas Imbalances* as revised, Kraftbilt Products, Tulsa, 1991.

Ellis, Richard W., McCarthy, Dennis J., and Skidmore, Constance E., *Financial Reporting and Tax Practices In Nonferrous Mining,* 18th ed., Coopers & Lybrand L.L.P., New York, 1995.

Financial Accounting Standards Board, "Financial Accounting and Reporting by Oil and Gas Producing Companies," Statement of Financial Accounting Standards No. 19, FASB, Stamford, CT, 1977.

———, "Suspension of Certain Accounting Requirements for Oil and Gas Producing Companies," Statement of Financial Accounting Standards No. 25, FASB, Stamford, CT, 1979.

———, "Disclosures about Oil and Gas Producing Activities," Statement of Financial Accounting Standards No. 69, FASB, Stamford, CT, 1982.

O'Reilly, V. M., *Montgomery's Auditing,* 12th ed., Wiley, New York, 1996.

Securities and Exchange Commission, "Financial Accounting and Reporting for Oil and Gas Producing Activities Pursuant to the Federal Securities Laws and the Energy Policy and Conservation Act of 1975," Regulation S-X, Rule 4-10, as currently amended, SEC, Washington, DC, 1995.

———, "Interpretations Relating to Oil and Gas Accounting," SEC Staff Accounting Bulletins, Topic 12, SEC, Washington, DC, 1995.

CHAPTER 24

REAL ESTATE AND CONSTRUCTION

Nicholas Cammarano, Jr., CPA
Price Waterhouse LLP

CONTENTS

24.1 THE REAL ESTATE INDUSTRY

(a) OVERVIEW.   The real estate industry does not easily lend itself to definition. It encompasses a variety of interests (developers, investors, lenders, tenants, homeowners, corporations, etc.) with a divergence of objectives (tax benefits, security, long-term appreciation, etc.). The industry is also a tool of the federal government's income tax policies (evidenced by the rules on mortgage interest deductions and restrictions on "passive" investment deductions).

Although the industry consists primarily of many private developers and builders, the economic dynamics of the 1980s have brought new forces to the real estate industry. The most important of these forces are:

1. *The U.S. Government.* The savings and loan and bank crises have left the federal government the single largest property owner in the United States.

2. *Foreign Investment.* Long-term growth, stability, and favorable exchange rates have led many foreign investors to U.S. real estate. Notwithstanding the recent publicity given the influx of Japanese investment, European investors, who have been in the United States for a longer time, outpace the amount of Japanese investment and will probably continue to do so for the foreseeable future.

3. *U.S. Pension Funds and Insurance Companies.* Driven by similar forces as the foreign investors, these companies have been increasing the amount of their funds invested in real estate. The amount to be invested in real estate in the next 10 years has been estimated to be in excess of $100 billion.

4. *Corporations.* In response to the pressures on corporate management to increase shareholder value, many corporations have been forced to focus more attention on their real estate assets. This is easy to understand because occupancy (real estate) costs are generally the second largest expense for a company after personnel costs. In fact, many of the takeovers of the 1980s were based upon the underutilization of the target corporations' assets.

As we move through the 1990s, many uncertainties face the real estate industry. Overbuilding and the extent of repossessed assets held by the U.S. government will continue to plague the recovery of many real estate markets. The sources and extent of available capital for financings and construction will continue to be a concern. This concern will be centered on the ability and willingness of the financing institutions in various markets to reenter the real estate lending arena and the willingness of foreign investors to fill a void left by the financial institutions.

24.2 SALES OF REAL ESTATE

(a) ANALYSIS OF TRANSACTIONS.   Real estate sales transactions are generally material to the entity's financial statements. "Is the earnings process complete?" is the primary question that must be answered regarding such sales. In other words, assuming a legal sale, have the risks and rewards of ownership been transferred to the buyer?

(b) ACCOUNTING BACKGROUND.   Prior to 1982, guidance related to real estate sales transactions was contained in two AICPA Accounting Guides: "Accounting for Retail Land Sales" and "Accounting for Profit Recognition on Sales of Real Estate." These guides had been supplemented by several AICPA Statements of Position that provided interpretations.

In October 1982, SFAS No. 66, "Accounting for Sales of Real Estate," was issued as part of the FASB project to incorporate, where appropriate, AICPA Accounting Guides into FASB Statements. This Statement adopted the specialized profit recognition principles of the above guides.

The FASB formed the Emerging Issues Task Force (EITF) in 1984 for the early identification of emerging issues. The EITF has dealt with many issues affecting the real estate industry, including issues that clarify or address SFAS No. 66.

Regardless of the seller's business, SFAS No. 66 covers all sales of real estate, determines the timing of the sale and resultant profit recognition, and deals with seller accounting only. This Statement does not discuss nonmonetary exchanges, cost accounting and most lease transactions or disclosures.

The two primary concerns under SFAS No. 66 are:

- Has a sale occurred?
- Under what method and when should profit be recognized?

The concerns are answered by determining the buyer's initial and continuing investment and the nature and extent of the seller's continuing involvement. The guidelines used in determining these criteria are complex and, within certain provisions, arbitrary. Companies dealing with these types of transactions are often faced with the difficult task of analyzing the exact nature of a transaction in order to determine the appropriate accounting approach. Only with a thorough understanding of the details of a transaction can the accountant perform the analysis required to decide on the appropriate accounting method.

(c) CRITERIA FOR RECORDING A SALE.   SFAS No. 66 (pars. 44–50) discussed separate rules for Retail Land Sales (see subsection 24.2(h)). The following information is for all real estate sales other than retail land sales. To determine whether profit recognition is appropriate, a test must first be made to determine whether a sale may be recorded. Then there are additional tests related to the buyer's investment and the seller's continued involvement.

Generally, real estate sales should not be recorded prior to **closing.** Since an exchange is generally required to recognize profit, a sale must be consummated. A sale is consummated when all the following conditions have been met:

- The parties are bound by the terms of a contract.
- All consideration has been exchanged.
- Any permanent financing for which the seller is responsible has been arranged.
- All conditions precedent to closing have been performed.

Usually all those conditions are met at the time of closing. On the other hand, they are not usually met at the time of a **contract to sell** or a preclosing.

Exceptions to the "conditions precedent to closing" have been specifically provided for in SFAS No. 66. They are applicable where a sale of property includes a requirement for the seller to perform future construction or development. Under certain conditions, partial sale recognition is permitted during the construction process because the construction period is extended. This exception usually is not applicable to single-family detached housing because of the shorter construction period.

Transactions that should not be treated as sales for accounting purposes because of **continuing seller's involvement** include the following:

- The seller has an option or obligation to repurchase the property.
- The seller guarantees return of the buyer's investment.
- The seller retains an interest as a general partner in a limited partnership and has a significant receivable.
- The seller is required to initiate or support operations or continue to operate the property at its own risk for a specified period or until a specified level of operations has been obtained.

If the criteria for recording a sale are not met, either the deposit, financing, lease, or profit sharing (co-venture) methods should be used, depending on the substance of the transaction.

(d) ADEQUACY OF DOWN PAYMENT. Once it has been determined that a sale can be recorded, the next test relates to the **buyer's investment.** For the seller to record full profit recognition, the buyer's down payment must be adequate in size and in composition.

(i) Size of Down Payment. The minimum down payment requirement is one of the most important provisions in SFAS No. 66. Appendix A of this pronouncement, reproduced here as Exhibit 24.1, lists minimum down payments ranging from 5% to 25% of sales value based on

	Minimum Initial Investment Payment Expressed as a Percentage of Sales Value
Land:	
Held for commercial, industrial, or residential development to commence within two years after sale	20%
Held for commercial, industrial, or residential development after two years	25%
Commercial and industrial property:	
Office and industrial buildings, shopping centers, and so forth:	
Properties subject to lease on a long-term lease basis to parties having satisfactory credit rating; cash flow currently sufficient to service all indebtedness	10%
Single-tenancy properties sold to a user having a satisfactory credit rating	15%
All other	20%
Other income-producing properties (hotels, motels, marinas, mobile home parks, and so forth):	
Cash flow currently sufficient to service all indebtedness	15%
Start-up situations or current deficiencies in cash flow	25%
Multifamily residential property:	
Primary residence:	
Cash flow currently sufficient to service all indebtedness	10%
Start-up situations or current deficiencies in cash flow	15%
Secondary or recreational residence:	
Cash flow currently sufficient to service all indebtedness	10%
Start-up situations or current deficiencies in cash flow	25%
Single-family residential property (including condominium or cooperative housing)	
Primary residence of buyer	5%[a]
Secondary or recreational residence	10%[a]

[a] As set forth in Appendix A, "if collectibility of the remaining portion of the sales price cannot be supported by reliable evidence of collection experience, the minimum initial investment shall be at least 60% of the difference between the sales value and the financing available from loans guaranteed by regulatory bodies, such as the FHA or the VA, or from independent financial institutions.

This 60% test applies when independent first mortgage financing is not utilized and the seller takes a receivable from the buyer for the difference between the sales value and the initial investment. If independent first mortgage financing is utilized, the adequacy of the initial investment on sales of single-family residential property should be determined in accordance with SFAS No. 66 (par. 53).

Exhibit 24.1.   Minimum initial investment requirements. *Soure:* SFAS No. 66, "Accounting for Sales of Real Estate" (Appendix A), FASB, 1982.

Situation	Cash Received by Seller at Closing	Components of Cash Received by Seller at Closing		Assumption of Seller's Nonrecourse Mortgage
		Buyer's Initial Investment	Buyer's Independent 1st Mortgage	
1.	100	20	80	
2.	100	0	100	
3.	20	20		80
4.	0	0		100
5.	20	20		
6.	20	20		
7.	80	20	60	
8.	20	20		60
9.	20	20		
10.	0	0		
11.	0	0		
12.	0	0		
13.	80	0	80	
14.	10	10		
15.	10	10		
16.	90	10	80	
17.	10	10		80
18.	10	10		

Assumptions:
Sales price: $100.
Seller's basis in property sold: $70.
Initial investment requirement: 20%.
All mortgage obligations meet the continuing investment requirements of Statement 66.

Exhibit 24.2.   Examples of the application of the EITF consensus on Issue No. 88-24. *Source:* EITF Issue No. 88-24, "Effect of Various Forms of Financing under FASB Statement No. 66," (Exhibit 88-24A), FASB, 1988.

usual loan limits for various types of properties. These percentages should be considered as specific requirements because it was not intended that exceptions be made. Additionally, EITF consensus No. 88-24 "Effect of Various Forms of Financing under FASB Statement No. 66," discusses the impact of the source and nature of the buyer's down payment on profit recognition. Exhibit A to EITF 88-24 has been reproduced here as Exhibit 24.2.

If a newly placed permanent loan or firm permanent loan commitment for maximum financing exists, the minimum down payment must be the higher of (1) the amount derived from Appendix A or (2) the excess of sales value over 115% of the new financing. However, regardless of this test, a down payment of 25% of the sales value of the property is usually considered sufficient to justify the recognition of profit at the time of sale.

An example of the down payment test—Appendix A compared to the newly placed permanent loan test—is given below:

Seller Financing[1]	Assumption of Seller's Recourse Mortgage[2]	Recognition under Consensus Paragraph	Profit Recognized at Date of Sale[3]		
			Full Accrual	Installment	Cost Recovery
		#1	30		
		#1	30		
		#1	30		
		#1	30		
80(1)		#2	30		
	80	#2	30		
20(2)		#2	30		
20(2)		#2	30		
20(2)	60	#2	30		
	100	#3		0	0
100(1)		#3		0	0
20(2)	80	#3		0	0
20(2)		#3		10	10
90(1)		#3		3	0
	90	#3		3	0
10(2)		#3		20	20
10(2)		#3		20	20
10(2)	80	#3		3	0

[1] First or second mortgage indicated in parentheses.

[2] Seller remains contingently liable.

[3] The profit recognized under the reduced profit method is dependent on various interest rates and payment terms. An example is not presented due to the complexity of those factors and the belief that this method is not frequently used in practice. Under this method, the profit recognized at the consummation of the sale would be less than under the full accrual method, but normally more than the amount under the installment method.

ASSUMPTIONS

Initial payment made by the buyer to the seller on sale of an apartment building	$ 200,000
First mortgage recently issued and assumed by the buyer	1,000,000
Second mortgage given by the buyer to the seller at prevailing interest rate	200,000
Stated sales price and sales value	$1,400,000
115% of first mortgage (1.15 × $1,000,000)	1,150,000
Down payment necessary	$ 250,000

RESULT

Although the down payment required under Appendix A is only $140,000 (10% of $1,400,000), the $200,000 actual down payment is inadequate because the test relating to the newly placed first mortgage requires $250,000.

The down payment requirements must be related to **sales value,** as described in SFAS No. 66 (par. 7). Sales value is the stated sales price increased or decreased for other consideration that clearly constitutes additional proceeds on the sale, services without compensation, imputed interest, and so forth.

Consideration payable for development work or improvements that are the responsibility of the seller should be included in the computation of sales value.

(ii) Composition of Down Payment. The primary acceptable down payment is cash, but additional acceptable forms of down payment are:

- Notes from the buyer (only when supported by irrevocable letters of credit from an independent established lending institution).
- Cash payments by the buyer to reduce previously existing indebtedness.
- Cash payments that are in substance additional sales proceeds, such as prepaid interest that by the terms of the contract is applied to amounts due the seller.

Other forms of down payment that are not acceptable are:

- Other noncash consideration received by the seller, such as notes from the buyer without letters of credit or marketable securities. Noncash consideration constitutes down payment only at the time it is converted into cash.
- Funds that have been or will be loaned to the buyer builder/developer for acquisition, construction, or development purposes or otherwise provided directly or indirectly by the seller. Such amounts must first be deducted from the down payment in determining whether the down payment test has been met. An exemption from this requirement was provided in paragraph 115 of SFAS No. 66, which states that if a future loan on normal terms from a seller who is also an established lending institution bears a fair market interest rate and the proceeds of the loan are conditional on use for specific development of or construction on the property, the loan need not be subtracted in determining the buyer's investment.
- Funds received from the buyer from proceeds of priority loans on the property. Such funds have not come from the buyer and therefore do not provide assurance of collectibility of the remaining receivable; such amounts should be excluded in determining the adequacy of the down payment. In addition, EITF consensus No. 88-24 provides guidelines on the impact that the source and nature of the buyer's initial investment can have on profit recognition.
- Marketable securities or other assets received as down payment will constitute down payment only at the time they are converted to cash.
- Cash payments for prepaid interest that are not in substance additional sales proceeds.
- Cash payments by the buyer to others for development or construction of improvements to the property.

(iii) Inadequate Down Payment. If the buyer's down payment is inadequate, the accrual method of accounting is not appropriate, and either the deposit, installment, or cost recovery method of accounting should be used.

When the sole consideration (in addition to cash) received by the seller is the buyer's assumption of existing nonrecourse indebtedness, a sale could be recorded and profit recognized if all other conditions for recognizing a sale were met. If, however, the buyer assumes recourse debt and the seller remains liable on the debt, he has a risk of loss comparable to the risk involved in holding a receivable from the buyer, and the accrual method would not be appropriate.

EITF consensus No. 88-24 states that the initial and continuing investment requirements for the full accrual method of profit recognition of SFAS No. 66 are applicable unless the seller receives one of the following as the full sales value of the property:

- Cash, without any seller contingent liability on any debt on the property incurred or assumed by the buyer.
- The buyer's assumption of the seller's existing nonrecourse debt on the property.
- The buyer's assumption of all recourse debt on the property with the complete release of the seller from those obligations.
- Any combination of such cash and debt assumption.

(e) RECEIVABLE FROM THE BUYER.   Even if the required down payment is made, a number of factors must be considered by the seller in connection with a receivable from the buyer. They include:

- Collectibility of the receivable.
- Buyer's continuing investment—amortization of receivable.
- Future subordination.
- Release provisions.
- Imputation of interest.

(i) Assessment of Collectibility of Receivable.   Collectibility of the receivable must be reasonably assured and should be assessed in light of factors such as the credit standing of the buyer (if recourse), cash flow from the property, and the property's size and geographical location. This requirement may be particularly important when the receivable is relatively short term and collectibility is questionable because the buyer will be required to obtain financing. Furthermore, a basic principle of real estate sales on credit is that the receivable must be adequately secured by the property sold.

(ii) Amortization of Receivable.   Continuing investment requirements for full profit recognition require that the buyer's payments on its total debt for the purchase price must be at least equal to level annual payments (including principal and interest) based on amortization of the full amount over a maximum term of 20 years for land and over the **customary term of a first mortgage** by an independent established lending institution for other property. The annual payments must begin within 1 year of recording the sale and, to be acceptable, must meet the same composition test as used in determining adequacy of down payments. The customary term of a first mortgage loan is usually considered to be the term of a new loan (or the term of an existing loan placed in recent years) from an independent financial lending institution.

All indebtedness on the property need not be reduced proportionately. However, if the seller's receivable is not being amortized, realization may be in question and the collectibility must be more carefully assessed. Lump-sum (balloon) payments do not affect the amortization requirement as long as the scheduled amortization is within the maximum period and the minimum annual amortization tests are met.

For example, if the customary term of the mortgage by an independent lender required amortizing payments over a period of 25 years, then the continuing investment requirement would be based on such an amortization schedule. If the terms of the receivable required principal and interest payments on such a schedule only for the first 5 years with a balloon at the end of year 5, the continuing investment requirements are met. In such cases, however, the collectibility of the balloon payment should be carefully assessed.

If the amortization requirements for full profit recognition as set forth above are not met, a reduced profit may be recognized by the seller if the annual payments are at least equal to the total of:

- Annual level payments of principal and interest on a maximum available first mortgage.
- Interest at an appropriate rate on the remaining amount payable by the buyer.

The reduced profit is determined by discounting the receivable from the buyer to the present value of the lowest level of annual payments required by the sales contract excluding requirements to pay lump sums. The present value is calculated using an appropriate interest rate, but not less than the rate stated in the sales contract.

The amount calculated would be used as the value of the receivable for the purpose of determining the reduced profit. The calculation of reduced profit is illustrated in Exhibit 24.3.

The requirements for amortization of the receivable are applied cumulatively at the closing date (date of recording the sale for accounting purposes) and annually thereafter. Any excess of down payment received over the minimum required is applied toward the amortization requirements.

(iii) Receivable Subject to Future Subordination.   If the receivable is subject to future subordination to a future loan available to the buyer, profit recognition cannot exceed the amount determined under the cost recovery method unless proceeds of the loan are first used to reduce the seller's receivable. Although this accounting treatment is controversial, the cost recovery method is required because collectibility of the sales price is not reasonably assured. The future subordination would permit the primary lender to obtain a prior lien on the property, leaving only a secondary residual value for the seller, and future loans could indirectly finance the buyer's initial cash investment. Future loans would include funds received by the buyer arising from a permanent loan commitment existing at the time of the transaction unless such funds were first applied to reduce the seller's receivable as provided for in the terms of the sale.

The cost recovery method is not required if the receivable is subordinate to a previous mortgage on the property existing at the time of sale.

(iv) Release Provisions.   Some sales transactions have provisions releasing portions of the property from the liens securing the debt as partial payments are made. In this situation, full profit recognition is acceptable only if the buyer must make, at the time of each release, cumulative payments that are adequate in relation to the sales value of property not released.

Assumptions:

Down payment (meets applicable tests)		$ 150,000
First mortgage note from independent lender at market rate of interest (new, 20 years—meets required amortization)		750,000
Second mortgage notes payable to seller, interest at a market rate is due annually, with principal due at the end of the 25th year (the term exceeds the maximum permitted)		100,000
Stated selling price		$1,000,000
Adjustment required in valuation of receivable from buyer:		
Second mortgage payable to seller	$100,000	
Less: present value of 20 years annual interest payments on second mortgage (lowest level of annual payments over customary term of first mortgage—thus 20 years not 25)	70,000	30,000
Adjusted sales value for profit recognition		$ 970,000

The sales value as well as profit is reduced by $30,000.
In some situations profit will be entirely eliminated by this calculation.

Exhibit 24.3.   Calculation of reduced profit.

(v) Imputation of Interest. Careful attention should be given to the necessity for imputation of interest under APB Opinion No. 21, "Interest on Receivables and Payables," since it could have a significant effect on the amount of profit or loss recognition. As stated in the first paragraph of APB Opinion No. 21: "The use of an interest rate that varies from prevailing interest rates warrants evaluation of whether the face amount and the stated interest rate of a note or obligation provide reliable evidence for properly recording the exchange and subsequent related interest."

If imputation of interest is necessary, the mortgage note receivable should be adjusted to its present value by discounting all future payments on the notes using an imputed rate of interest at the prevailing rates available for similar financing with independent financial institutions. A distinction must be made between first and second mortgage loans because the appropriate imputed rate for a second mortgage would normally be significantly higher than the rate for a first mortgage loan. It may be necessary to obtain independent valuations to assist in the determination of the proper rate.

(vi) Inadequate Continuing Investment. If the criteria for recording a sale has been met but the tests related to the collectibility of the receivable as set forth herein are not met, the accrual method of accounting is not appropriate and the installment or cost recovery method of accounting should be used. These methods are discussed in subsection 24.2(j) of this chapter.

(f) SELLER'S CONTINUED INVOLVEMENT. A seller sometimes continues to be involved over long periods of time with property legally sold. This involvement may take many forms such as participation in future profits, financing, management services, development, construction, guarantees, and options to repurchase. With respect to profit recognition when a seller has continued involvement, the two key principles are as follows:

- A sales contract should not be accounted for as a sale if the seller's continued involvement with the property includes the same kinds of risk as does ownership of property.
- Profit recognition should follow performance and in some cases should be postponed completely until a later date.

(i) Participation Solely in Future Profits. A sale of real estate may include or be accompanied by an agreement that provides for the seller to participate in future operating profits or residual values. As long as the seller has no further obligations or risk of loss, profit recognition on the sale need not be deferred. A receivable from the buyer is permitted if the other tests for profit recognition are met, but no costs can be deferred.

(ii) Option or Obligation to Repurchase the Property. If the seller has an **option or obligation to repurchase** property (including a buyer's option to compel the seller to repurchase), a sale cannot be recognized (SFAS No. 66, par. 26). However, neither a commitment by the seller to assist or use his best efforts (with appropriate compensation) on a resale nor a right of first refusal based on a bona fide offer by a third party would preclude sale recognition. The accounting to be followed depends on the repurchase terms. EITF consensus No. 86-6 discusses accounting for a sale transaction when antispeculation clauses exist. A consensus was reached that the contingent option would not preclude sale recognition if the probability of buyer noncompliance is remote.

When the seller has an obligation or an option that is reasonably expected to be exercised to repurchase the property at a price higher than the total amount of the payments received and to be received, the transaction is a **financing arrangement** and should be accounted for under the financing method. If the option is not reasonably expected to be exercised, the deposit method is appropriate.

In the case of a repurchase obligation or option at a lower price, the transaction usually is, in substance, a lease or is part lease, part financing and should be accounted for under the lease method. Where an option to repurchase is at a market price to be determined in the future, the transaction should be accounted for under the deposit method or the profit-sharing method.

(iii) General Partner in a Limited Partnership with a Significant Receivable.   When the seller is a general partner in a limited partnership and has a significant receivable related to the property, the transaction would not qualify as a sale. It should usually be accounted for as a profit-sharing arrangement. A significant receivable is one that is in excess of 15% of the maximum first lien financing that could be obtained from an established lending institution for the property sold.

(iv) Lack of Permanent Financing.   The buyer's investment in the property cannot be evaluated until adequate permanent financing at an acceptable cost is available to the buyer. If the seller must obtain or provide this financing, obtaining the financing is a prerequisite to a sale for accounting purposes. Even if not required to do so, the seller may be presumed to have such an obligation if the buyer does not have financing and the collectibility of the receivable is questionable. The deposit method is appropriate if lack of financing is the only impediment to recording a sale.

(v) Guaranteed Return of Buyer's Investment.   SFAS No. 66 (par. 28) states: "If the seller guarantees return of the buyer's investment, . . . the transaction shall be accounted for as a financing, leasing or profit-sharing arrangement."

Accordingly, if the terms of a transaction are such that the buyer may expect to recover the initial investment through assured cash returns, subsidies, and net tax benefits, even if the buyer were to default on debt to the seller, the transaction is probably not in substance a sale.

(vi) Other Guaranteed Returns on Investment—Other than Sale-Leaseback.   When the seller guarantees cash returns on the buyer's investment, the accounting method to be followed depends on whether the guarantee is for an extended or limited period and whether the seller's expected cost of the guarantee is determinable.

Extended Period.   SFAS No. 66 states that when the seller contractually guarantees cash returns on investments to the buyer for an extended period, the transaction should be accounted for as a financing, leasing, or profit-sharing arrangement. An "extended period" was not defined but should at least include periods that are not limited in time or specified lengthy periods, such as more than 5 years.

Limited Period.   If the guarantee of a return on the buyer's investment is for a limited period, SFAS No. 66 indicates that the deposit method of accounting should be used until such time as operation of the property covers all operating expenses, debt service, and contractual payments. At that time, profit should be recognized based on performance (see subsection 24.2(j)). A "limited period" was not defined but is believed to relate to specified shorter periods, such as 5 years or less.

Irrespective of the above, if the guarantee is determinable or limited, sale and profit recognition may be appropriate if reduced by the maximum exposure to loss as described below.

Guarantee Amount Determinable.   If the amount can be reasonably estimated, the seller should record the guarantee as a cost at the time of sale, thus either reducing the profit or increasing the loss on the transaction.

Guarantee Amount Not Determinable.   If the amount cannot be reasonably estimated, the transaction is probably in substance a profit-sharing or co-venture arrangement.

Guarantee Amount Not Determinable But Limited.   If the amount cannot be reasonably esti-mated but a maximum cost of the guarantee is determinable, the seller may record the maxi-mum cost of the guarantee as a cost at the time of sale, thus either reducing the profit or increasing the loss on the transaction. Alternatively, the seller may account for the transaction as if the guarantee amount is not determinable. Implications of a seller's guarantee of cash flow on an operating property that is not considered a sale-leaseback arrangement are dis-cussed in subsection 24.2(f)(x).

(vii) Guaranteed Return on Investment—Sale-Leaseback.   A guarantee of cash flow to the buyer sometimes takes the form of a leaseback arrangement. Since the earnings process in this situation has not usually been completed, profits on the sale should generally be deferred and amortized.

Accounting for a sale-leaseback of real estate is governed by SFAS No. 13, "Accounting for Leases," as amended by SFAS No. 28, "Accounting for Sales with Leasebacks," SFAS No. 98, "Accounting for Leases: Sale-Leaseback Transactions Involving Real Estate," and SFAS No. 66. SFAS No. 98 specifies the accounting by a seller-lessee for a sale-leaseback transaction involv-ing real estate, including real estate with equipment. SFAS No. 98 provides that:

- A sale-leaseback transaction involving real estate, including real estate with equipment, must qualify as a sale under the provisions of SFAS No. 66 as amended by SFAS No. 98, before it is appropriate for the seller-lessee to account for the transaction as a sale. If the transaction does not qualify as a sale under SFAS No. 66, it should be accounted for by the deposit method or as a financing transaction.

- A sale-leaseback transaction involving real estate, including real estate with equipment, that includes any continuing involvement other than a normal leaseback in which the seller-lessee intends to actively use the property during the lease should be accounted for by the deposit method or as a financing transaction.

- A lease involving real estate may not be classified as a sales-type lease unless the lease agreement provides for the transfer of title to the lessee at or shortly after the end of the lease term. Sales-type leases involving real estate should be accounted for under the pro-visions of SFAS No. 66.

Profit Recognition.   Profits should be deferred and amortized in a manner consistent with the classification of the leaseback:

- If the leaseback is an operating lease, deferred profit should be amortized in proportion to the related gross rental charges to expense over the lease term.

- If the leaseback is a capital lease, deferred profit should be amortized in proportion to the amortization of the leased asset. Effectively, the sale is treated as a financing transac-tion. The deferred profit can be presented gross; the author's preference is to offset the deferred profit in the balance sheet against the capitalized asset.

In situations where the leaseback covers only a minor portion of the property sold or the period is relatively minor compared to the remaining useful life of the property, it may be appropriate to recognize all or a portion of the gain as income. Sales with minor leasebacks should be ac-counted for based on the separate terms of the sale and the leaseback unless the rentals called for by the leaseback are unreasonable in relation to current market conditions. If rentals are considered to be unreasonable, they must be adjusted to a reasonable amount in computing the profit on the sale.

The leaseback is considered to be minor when the present value of the leaseback based on reasonable rentals is 10% or less of the fair value of the asset sold. If the leaseback is not considered to be minor (but less than substantially all of the use of the asset is retained through a leaseback) profit may be recognized to the extent it exceeds the present value of the minimum lease payments (net of executory costs) in the case of an operating lease or the recorded amount of the leased asset in the case of a capital lease.

Loss Recognition.   Losses should be recognized immediately to the extent that the undepreciated cost (net carrying value) exceeds the fair value of the property. Fair value is frequently determined by the selling price from which the loss on the sale is measured. Many sale-leasebacks are entered into as a means of financing, or for tax reasons, or both. The terms of the leaseback are negotiated as a package. Because of the interdependence of the sale and concurrent leaseback, the selling price in some cases is not representative of fair value. It would not be appropriate to recognize a loss on the sale that would be offset by future cost reductions as a result of either reduced rental costs under an operating lease or depreciation and interest charges under a capital lease. Therefore, to the extent that the fair value is greater than the sale price, losses should be deferred and amortized in the same manner as profits.

(viii) Services without Adequate Compensation.   A sales contract may be accompanied by an agreement for the seller to provide management or other services without adequate compensation. Compensation for the value of the services should be imputed, deducted from the sales price, and recognized over the term of the contract. See discussion of implied support of operations in subsection 24.2(f)(x) below if the contract is noncancelable and the compensation is unusual for the services to be rendered.

(ix) Development and Construction.   A sale of undeveloped or partially developed land may include or be accompanied by an agreement requiring future seller performance of development or construction. In such cases, all or a portion of the profit should be deferred. If there is a lapse of time between the sale agreement and the future performance agreement, deferral provisions usually apply if definitive development plans existed at the time of sale and a development contract was anticipated by the parties at the time of entering into the sales contract.

In addition, SFAS No. 66 (par. 41) provides that "The seller is involved with future development or construction work if the buyer is unable to pay amounts due for that work or has the right under the terms of the arrangement to defer payment until the work is done."

If the property sold and being developed is an operating property (such as an apartment complex, shopping center, or office building) as opposed to a nonoperating property (such as a land lot, condominium unit, or single-family detached home), subsection 24.2(f)(x) below may also apply.

Completed Contract Method.   If a seller is obligated to develop the property or construct facilities and total costs and profit cannot be reliably estimated (e.g., because of lack of seller experience or nondefinitive plans), all profit, including profit on the sale of land, should be deferred until the contract is completed or until the total costs and profit can be reliably estimated. Under the completed contract method, all profit, including profit on the sale of land, is deferred until the seller's obligations are fulfilled.

Percentage of Completion Method (Cost-Incurred Method).   If the costs and profit can be reliably estimated, profit recognition over the improvement period on the basis of costs incurred (including land) as a percentage of total costs to be incurred is required. Thus, if the land was a principal part of the sale and its market value greatly exceeded cost, part of the profit that can be said to be related to the land sale is deferred and recognized during the development or construction period.

The same rate of profit is used for all seller costs connected with the transaction. For this purpose, the cost of development work, improvements, and all fees and expenses that are the

Assumptions:

1. Sale of land for commercial development—$475,000.
2. Development contract—$525,000.
3. Down payment and other buyer investment requirements met.
4. Land costs—$200,000.
5. Development costs $500,000 (reliably estimated)—$325,000 incurred in initial year.

Calculation of profit to be recognized in initial year:

Sale of land	$ 475,000
Development contract price	525,000
Total sales price	1,000,000
Costs:	
Land	200,000
Development	500,000
Total costs	700,000
Total profit anticipated	$ 300,000
Cost incurred through end of initial year:	
Land	$ 200,000
Development	325,000
Total	$ 525,000
Profit to be recognized in initial year − 525,000 ÷ 700,000 × 300,000 =	$ 225,000

Exhibit 24.4.   Percentage of completion, or cost-incurred, method.

responsibility of the seller should be included. The buyer's initial and continuing investment tests, of course, must be met with respect to the total sales value. Exhibit 24.4 illustrates the cost incurred method.

(x) Initiation and Support of Operations.   If the property sold is an operating property, as opposed to a nonoperating property, deferral of all or a portion of the profit may be required under SFAS No. 66 (pars. 28–30). These paragraphs establish guidelines not only for **stated support** but also for **implied support.**

Although the implied support provisions do not usually apply to undeveloped or partially developed land, they do apply if the buyer has commitments to construct operating properties and there is stated or implied support.

Assuming that the criteria for recording a sale and the test of buyer's investment are met, the following sets forth guidelines for profit recognition where there is stated or implied support.

Stated Support.   A seller may be required to support operations by means of a guaranteed return to the buyer. Alternatively, a guarantee may be made to the buyer that there will be no negative cash flow from the project, buy may not guarantee a positive return on the buyer's investment. For example, EITF consensus No. 85-27 "Recognition of Receipts from Made-Up Rental Shortfalls," considers the impact of a master lease guarantee. The broad exposure that such a guarantee creates has a negative impact on profit recognition.

Implied Support.   The seller may be presumed to be obligated to initiate and support operations of the property sold, even in the absence of specified requirements in the sale contract or related document. The following conditions under which support is implied are described in footnote 10 of SFAS No. 66:

- A seller obtains an interest as general partner in a limited partnership that acquires an interest in the property sold.
- A seller retains an equity interest in the property, such as an undivided interest or an equity interest in a joint venture that holds an interest in the property.
- A seller holds a receivable from a buyer for a significant part of the sales price and collection of the receivable is dependent on the operation of the property.
- A seller agrees to manage the property for the buyer on terms not usual for the services to be rendered and which is not terminable by either seller or buyer.

Stated or Implied Support.   When profit recognition is appropriate in the case of either stated or implied support, the following general rules apply:

- Profit is recognized on the ratio of costs incurred to total costs to be incurred. Revenues for gross profit purposes include rent from operations during the rent-up period; costs include land and operating expenses during the rent-up period as well as other costs.
- As set forth in SFAS No. 66 (par. 30):

[S]upport shall be presumed for at least two years from the time of initial rental unless actual rental operations cover operating expenses, debt service, and other contractual commitments before that time. If the seller is contractually obligated for a longer time, profit recognition shall continue on the basis of performance until the obligation expires.

- Estimated rental income should be adjusted by reducing estimated future rent receipts by a safety factor of $33\frac{1}{3}\%$ unless signed lease agreements have been obtained to support a projection higher than the rental level thus computed. As set forth in SFAS No. 66 (par. 29), when signed leases amount to more than $66\frac{2}{3}\%$ of estimated rents, no additional safety factor is required but only amounts under signed lease agreements can be included.

(xi) Partial Sales.   A partial sale includes the following:

- A sale of an interest in real estate.
- A sale of real estate where the seller has an equity interest in the buyer (e.g., a joint venture or partnership).
- A sale of a condominium unit.

Sale of an Interest in Real Estate.   Except for operating properties, profit recognition is appropriate in a sale of a partial interest if all the following conditions exist:

- Sale is to an independent buyer.
- Collection of sales price is reasonably assured.
- The seller will not be required to support the property, its operations, or related obligations to an extent greater than its proportionate interest.
- Buyer does not have preferences as to profits or cash flow. (If the buyer has such preferences, the cost recovery method is required.)

In the case of a sale of a partial interest in operating properties, if the conditions set forth in the preceding paragraph are met, profit recognition must reflect an adjustment for the implied presumption that the seller is obligated to support the operations.

Seller Has Equity Interest in Buyer.   No profit may be recognized if the seller controls the buyer. If seller does not control the buyer, profit recognition (to the extent of the other investors' proportionate interests) is appropriate if all other necessary requirements for profit recognition are satisfied. The portion of the profit applicable to the equity interest of the seller/investor should be deferred until such costs are charged to operations by the venture. Again, with respect to a sale of operating properties, a portion of the profit relating to other investors' interests may have to be spread as described in subsection 24.2(f)(x) because there is an implied presumption that the seller is obligated to support the operations.

(g) SALES OF CONDOMINIUMS.   Although the definition of "condominium" varies by state, the term generally is defined as a multiunit structure in which there is fee simple title to individual units combined with an undivided interest in the common elements associated with the structure. The common elements are all areas exclusive of the individual units, such as hallways, lobbies, and elevators.

A **cooperative** is contrasted to a condominium in that ownership of the building is generally vested in the entity, with the respective stockholders of the entity having a right to occupy specific units. Operation, maintenance, and control of the building are exercised by a governing board elected by the owners. This section covers only sales of condominium units.

(i) Criteria for Profit Recognition.   The general principles of accounting for profit on sales of condominiums are essentially those previously discussed for sales of real estate in general. The following criteria must be met prior to recognition of any profit on the sale of a dwelling unit in a condominium project:

- All parties must be bound by the terms of the contract. For the buyer to be bound, the buyer must be unable to require a refund. Certain state and federal laws require appropriate filings by the developer before the sales contract is binding; otherwise, the sale may be voidable at the option of the buyer.
- All conditions precedent to closing, except completion of the project, must be performed.
- An adequate cash down payment must be received by the seller. The minimum down payment requirements are 5% for a primary residence and 10% for a secondary or recreational residence.
- The buyer must be required to adequately increase the investment in the property annually; the buyer's commitment must be adequately secured. Typically, a condominium buyer pays the remaining balance from the proceeds of a permanent loan at the time of closing. If, however, the seller provides financing, the same considerations as other sales of real estate apply concerning amortization of the buyer's receivable.
- The developer must not have an option or obligation to repurchase the property.

(ii) Methods of Accounting.   Sales of condominium units are accounted for by using the closing (completed contract) method or the percentage of completion method. Most developers use the **closing method.**

Additional criteria must be met for the use of the **percentage of completion** method:

- The developer must have the ability to estimate costs not yet incurred.
- Construction must be beyond a preliminary stage of completion. This generally means at least beyond the foundation stage.
- Sufficient units must be sold to assure that the property will not revert to rental property.
- The developer must be able to reasonably estimate aggregate sales proceeds.

Closing Method.   This method involves recording the sale and related profit at the time a unit closes. Since the unit is completed, actual costs are used in determining profit to be recognized.

All payments or deposits received prior to closing are accounted for as a liability. Direct selling costs may be deferred until the sale is recorded. Where the seller is obligated to complete construction of common areas or has made guarantees to the condominium association, profit should be recognized based on the relationship of costs already incurred to total estimated costs, with a portion deferred until the future performance is completed.

Percentage of Completion Method.   This method generally involves recording sales at the date a unit is sold and recognizing profit on units sold as construction proceeds. As a result, this method allows some profit recognition during the construction period. Although dependent on estimates, this method may be considered preferable for some long-term projects. A lack of reliable estimates, however, would preclude the use of this method.

Profit recognition is based on the percentage of completion of the project multiplied by the gross profit arising from the units sold. Percentage of completion may be determined by using either of the following alternatives:

- The ratio of costs incurred to date to total estimated costs to be incurred. These costs could include land and common costs or could be limited to construction costs. The costs selected for inclusion should be those that most clearly reflect the earnings process.
- The percentage of completed construction based on architectural plans or engineering studies.

Under either method of accounting, if the total estimated costs exceed the estimated proceeds, the total **anticipated loss** should be charged against income in the period in which the loss becomes evident so that no anticipated losses are deferred to future periods. See further discussion of this method in the section entitled "Construction Contracts."

(iii) Estimated Future Costs.   As previously mentioned, future costs to complete must be estimated under either the closing method or the percentage of completion method. Estimates of future costs to complete are necessary to determine net realizable value of unsold units. Estimated future costs should be based on adequate architectural and engineering studies and should include reasonable provisions for:

- Unforeseen costs in accordance with sound cost estimation practices.
- Anticipated cost inflation in the construction industry.
- Costs of offsite improvements, utility facilities, and amenities (to the extent that they will not be recovered from outside third parties).
- Operating losses of utility operations and recreational facilities. (Such losses would be expected to be incurred for a relatively limited period of time—usually prior to sale of facilities or transfer to some public authority.)
- Other guaranteed support arrangements or activities to the extent that they will not be recovered from outside parties or be the responsibility of a future purchaser.

Estimates of amounts to be recovered from any sources should be discounted to present value as of the date the related costs are expected to be incurred.

Estimated costs to complete and the allocation of such costs should be reviewed at the end of each financial reporting period, with costs revised and reallocated as necessary on the basis of current estimates, as recommended in SFAS No. 67, "Accounting for Costs and Initial Rental Operations of Real Estate Projects." How to record the effects of changes in estimates depends on whether full revenues have been recorded or whether reporting of the revenue has been deferred due to an obligation for future performance or otherwise.

When sales of condominiums are recorded in full, it may be necessary to accrue certain estimated costs not yet incurred and also related profit thereon. Adjustments of accruals for costs applicable to such previously recognized sales, where deferral for future performance was not required, must be recognized and charged to costs of sales in the period in which they become known. See subsection 24.2(g)(ii) for further discussion.

In many cases, sales are not recorded in full (such as when the seller has deferred revenue because of an obligation for future performance to complete improvements and amenities of a project). In these situations, the adjustments should not affect previously recorded deferred revenues applicable to future improvements but should be recorded prospectively in the current and future periods. An increase in the estimate of costs applicable to deferred revenues will thus result in profit margins lower than those recorded on previous revenues from the project.

An exception exists, however, when the revised total estimated costs exceed the applicable deferred revenue. If that occurs, the total anticipated loss should be charged against income in the period in which the need for adjustment becomes evident.

In addition, an increase in estimated costs to complete without comparable increases in market value could raise questions as to whether the estimated total costs of the remaining property exceed the project's net realizable value.

APB Opinion No. 20, "Accounting Changes," has been interpreted to permit both the cumulative catch-up method and the prospective method of accounting for changes in accounting estimates. It should be noted that SFAS No. 67 (pars. 42–43) requires the prospective method.

(h) RETAIL LAND SALES. Retail land sales, a unique segment of the real estate industry, is the retail marketing of numerous lots subdivided from a larger parcel of land. The relevant accounting guidance originally covered by the AICPA Industry Accounting Guide, "Accounting for Retail Land Sales," and now included in SFAS No. 66, applies to retail lot sales on a volume basis with down payments that are less than those required to evaluate the collectibility of casual sales of real estate. Wholesale or bulk sales of land and retail sales from projects comprising a small number of lots, however, are subject to the general principles for profit recognition on real estate sales.

(i) Criteria for Recording a Sale. Sales should not be recorded until:

- The customer has made all required payments and the period of cancellation with refund has expired.
- Aggregate payments (including interest) equal or exceed 10% of contract sales price.
- The selling company is clearly capable of providing land improvements and offsite facilities promised as well as meeting all other representations it has made.

If these conditions are met, either the accrual or the installment method must be used. If the conditions are not met, the deposit method of accounting should be used.

(ii) Criteria for Accrual Method. The following tests for the use of accrual method should be applied on a project-by-project basis:

- The seller has fulfilled the obligation to complete improvements and to construct amenities or other facilities applicable to the lots sold.
- The receivable is not subject to subordination to new loans on the property, except subordination for home construction purposes under certain conditions.
- The **collection experience** for the project indicates that collectibility of receivable balances is reasonably predictable and that 90% of the contracts in force 6 months after sales are recorded will be collected in full. A down payment of at least 20% shall be an acceptable indication of collectibility.

To predict collection results of current sales, there must be satisfactory **experience on prior sales** of the type of land being currently sold in the project. In addition, the collection period must be sufficiently long to allow reasonable estimates of the percentage of sales that will be fully collected. In a new project, the developers' experience on prior projects may be used if they have demonstrated an ability to successfully develop other projects with the same characteristics (environment, clientele, contract terms, sales methods) as the new project.

Collection and **cancellation experience** within a project may differ with varying sales methods (such as telephone, broker, and site visitation sales). Accordingly, historical data should be maintained with respect to each type of sales method used.

Unless all conditions for use of the accrual method are met for the entire project, the installment method of accounting should be applied to all recorded sales of the project.

(iii) Accrual Method.   Revenues and costs should be accounted for under the accrual method as follows:

- The **contract price** should be recorded as gross sales.
- Receivables should be discounted to reflect an appropriate interest rate using the criteria established in APB Opinion No. 21.
- An **allowance for contract cancellation** should be recorded and deducted from gross sales to derive net sales.
- Cost of sales should be calculated based on net sales after reductions for sales reasonably expected to cancel.

(iv) Percentage of Completion Method.   Frequently, the conditions for use of the accrual method are met, except the seller has not yet completed the improvements, amenities, or other facilities required by the sales contract. In this situation the percentage of completion method should be applied provided both of the following conditions are met:

- There is a reasonable expectation that the land can be developed for the purposes represented.
- The project's improvements have progressed beyond preliminary stages, and there are indications that the work will be completed according to plan. Indications that the project has progressed beyond the preliminary stage include the following:

   Funds for the proposed improvements have been expended.

   Work on the improvements has been initiated.

   Engineering plans and work commitments exist relating to the lots sold.

   Access roads and amenities such as golf courses, clubhouses, and swimming pools have been completed.

In addition, there shall be no indication of significant delaying factors such as the inability to obtain permits, contractors, personnel, or equipment, and estimates of costs to complete and extent of progress toward completion shall be reasonably dependable.

The following general procedures should be used to account for revenues and costs under the percentage of completion method of accounting:

- The amount of revenue recognized (discounted where appropriate pursuant to APB Opinion No. 21) is based on the relationship of costs already incurred to the total estimated costs to be incurred.
- Costs incurred and to be incurred should include land, interest and project carrying costs incurred prior to sale, selling costs, and an estimate for future improvement costs.

Estimates of future improvement costs should be reviewed at least annually. Changes in those estimates do not lead to adjustment of deferred revenue applicable to future improvements that has been previously recorded unless the adjusted total estimated costs exceeds the applicable revenue. When cost estimates are revised, the relationship of the two elements included in the revenue not yet recognized—cost and profit—should be recalculated on a cumulative basis to determine future income recognition as performance takes place. If the adjusted total estimated cost exceeds the applicable deferred revenue, the total anticipated loss should be charged to income. When anticipated losses on lots sold are recognized, the enterprise should also consider recognizing a loss on land and improvements not yet sold.

Future performance costs such as roads, utilities, and amenities may represent a significant obligation for a retail land developer. Estimates of such costs should be based on adequate engineering studies, appropriately adjusted for anticipated inflation in the local construction industry, and should include reasonable estimates for unforeseen costs.

(v) Installment and Deposit Methods. If the criteria for the accrual or percentage of completion methods are not satisfied, the installment or deposit method may be used. See subsection 24.2(j) below for a general discussion of these methods.

When the conditions required for use of the percentage of completion method are met on a project originally recorded under the installment method, the percentage of completion method of accounting should be adopted for the entire project (current and prior sales). The effect should be accounted for as a change in accounting estimate due to different circumstances. See subsection 24.2(g)(iii) for further discussion of methodology.

(i) ACCOUNTING FOR SYNDICATION FEES. On February 6, 1992, the AICPA issued a Statement of Position (SOP) that provides guidance on accounting for real estate syndication income. The SOP states that it should be applied to transactions for which the initial closing with investors occurs after March 15, 1992.

Syndicators expect to earn fees and commissions from a variety of sources (both up-front fees such as lease-up fees, construction supervision fees, financing fees, and fees for as an incentive), property management or participation in future profit or appreciation. At the time of the syndication, partnerships usually pay cash to the syndicator for portions of their up-front fees. These fees are usually paid from investor contributions or the proceeds of borrowings. Subsequent fees are expected to be paid from operations, refinancings, sale of property or remaining investor payments. Current practice in accounting for these fees is diverse, thus necessitating the issuance of the guidance.

The SOP states that SFAS 66 would apply to the recognition of profit on the sales of real estate by syndicators to partnerships. It concludes that profit on real estate syndication transactions be accounted for in accordance with SFAS 66, even if the syndicator never had ownership interests in the properties acquired by the real estate partnerships.

The SOP states that fees charged by syndicators (except for syndication fees and fees for future services) should be included in the determination of "sales value" in conformity with SFAS 66. It further states that SFAS 66 does not apply to the fees excluded from "sales value." Fees for future services should be recognized when the earning process is complete and collection of the fee is reasonably assured.

This SOP would require that income recognition on syndication fees and fees for future services be deferred if the syndicator is exposed to future losses or costs from either material involvement with the properties, partnerships or partners or uncertainties regarding the collectibility of partnership notes. The income should be deferred until the losses or costs can be reasonably estimated.

The SOP requires that for the purpose of determining whether buyers' initial and continuing investments satisfy the requirements for recognizing full profit in accordance with SFAS 66, cash received by syndicators should be allocated to unpaid syndication fees before being allocated to the initial and continuing investment. After the syndication fee is fully paid, additional cash received should first be allocated to unpaid fees for future services, to the extent those services have been performed by the time the cash is received, before being allocated to the initial and continuing investment.

(j) ALTERNATE METHODS OF ACCOUNTING FOR SALES.   As previously discussed, in some circumstances the accrual method is not appropriate and other methods must be used. It is not always clear which method should be used or how it should be applied. Consequently, it is often difficult to determine the appropriate method and whether alternative ones are acceptable.

The methods prescribed where the buyer's initial or continuing **investment is inadequate** are the deposit, installment, cost recovery, and reduced profit methods.

The methods prescribed for a transaction that cannot be considered a sale because of the **seller's continuing involvement** are the financing, lease, and profit sharing (or co-venture) methods.

(i) Deposit Method.   When the substance of a real estate transaction indicates that a sale has not occurred, for accounting purposes, as a result of the buyer's inadequate investment, recognition of the sale should be deferred and the deposit method used. This method should be continued until the conditions requiring its use no longer exist. For example, when the down payment is so small that the substance of the transaction is an **option arrangement,** the sale should not be recorded.

All cash received under the deposit method (including down payment and principal and interest payments by the buyer to the seller) should be reported as a deposit (liability). An exception is interest received that is not subject to refund may appropriately offset carrying charges (property taxes and interest on existing debt) on the property. Note also the following related matters:

- Notes receivable arising from the transaction should not be recorded.
- The property and any related mortgage debt assumed by the buyer should continue to be reflected on the seller's balance sheet, with appropriate disclosure that such properties and debt are subject to a sales contract. Even nonrecourse debt assumed by the buyer should not be offset against the related property.
- Subsequent payments on the debt assumed by the buyer become additional deposits and thereby reduce the seller's mortgage debt payable and increase the deposit liability account until a sale is recorded for accounting purposes.
- Depreciation should be continued.

Under the deposit method, a sale is not recorded for accounting purposes until the conditions in SFAS No. 66 are met. Therefore, for purposes of the **down payment tests,** interest received and credited to the deposit account can be included in the down payment and sales value at the time a sale is recorded.

If a buyer defaults and forfeits his nonrefundable deposit, the deposit liability is no longer required and may be credited to income. The circumstances underlying the **default** should be carefully reviewed since such circumstances may indicate **deteriorating value** of the property. In such a case it may be appropriate to treat the credit as a valuation reserve. These circumstances may require a provision for additional loss. See subsections 24.3(l) and 24.5(b) for further discussion.

(ii) Installment Method.   When the substance of a real estate transaction indicates that a sale has occurred for accounting purposes, but that **collectibility** of the total sales price cannot be reasonably estimated (i.e. inadequate buyer's investment), the installment method may be appropriate. However, circumstances may indicate that the cost recovery method is required or is otherwise more appropriate. For example, when the deferred gross profit exceeds the net carrying value of the related receivable, profit may have been earned to the extent of such excess.

Profit should be recognized on cash payments, including principal payments by the buyer on any debt assumed (either recourse or nonrecourse), and should be based on the ratio of total profit to total sales value (including a first mortgage debt assumed by the buyer, if applicable). Interest received on the related receivable is properly recorded as income when received.

The total sales value (from which the deferred gross profit should be deducted) and the cost of sales should be presented in the income statement. Deferred gross profit should be shown as a deduction from the related receivable, with subsequent income recognition presented separately in the income statement.

(iii) Cost Recovery Method.   The cost recovery method must be used when the substance of a real estate transaction indicates that a sale has occurred for accounting purposes but no profit should be recognized until costs are recovered. This may occur when (1) the receivable is subject to future subordination, (2) the seller retains an interest in the property sold and the buyer has preferences, (3) uncertainty exists as to whether all or a portion of the cost will be recovered, or (4) there is uncertainty as to the amount of proceeds. As a practical matter, the cost recovery method can always be used as an alternative to the installment method.

Under the cost recovery method, no profit is recognized until cash collections (including principal and interest payments) and existing debt assumed by the buyer exceed the cost of the property sold. Cash collections in excess of cost should be recorded as revenue in the period of collection.

Financial statement presentation under the cost recovery method is similar to that for the installment method.

(iv) Reduced Profit Method.   When the substance of a real estate transaction indicates that a sale has occurred for accounting purposes, but the continuing investment criteria for full profit recognition is not met by the buyer, the seller may sometimes recognize a reduced profit at the time of sale (see additional discussion in subsection 24.2(e)(ii)). This alternative is rarely used since a full accrual of anticapted costs of continuing investment will permit full accrual of the remaining profit.

(v) Financing Method.   A real estate transaction may be, in substance, a financing arrangement rather than a sale. This is frequently the case when the seller has an **obligation to repurchase** the property (or can be compelled by the buyer to repurchase the property) at a price higher than the total amount of the payments received and to be received. In such a case the financing method must be used.

Accounting procedures under the financing method should be similar to the accounting procedures under the deposit method, with one exception. Under the financing method, the difference between (1) the total amount of all payments received and to be received and (2) the repurchase price is presumed to be interest expense. As such, it should be accrued on the interest method over the period from the receipt of cash to the date of repurchase. As in the deposit method, cash received is reflected as a liability in the balance sheet. Thus, at the date of repurchase, the full amount of the repurchase obligation should be recorded as a liability.

In the case of a **repurchase option,** if the facts and circumstances at the time of the sale indicate a presumption or a likelihood that the seller will exercise the option, interest should be accrued as if there were an obligation to repurchase. This presumption could result from the value of the property, the property being an integral part of development, or from management's intention. If such a presumption does not exist at the time of the sale transaction, interest should not be accrued and the deposit method is appropriate.

(vi) Lease Method.   A real estate transaction may be, in substance, a lease rather than a sale. Accounting procedures under the lease method should be similar to the deposit method, except as follows:

- Payments received and to be received that are in substance deferred rental income received in advance should be deferred and amortized to income over the presumed lease period. Such amortization to income should not exceed cash paid to the seller.

- Cash paid out by the seller as a guarantee of support of operations should be expensed as paid.

The seller may agree to make **loans** to the **buyer** in support of operations, for example, when cash flow does not equal a predetermined amount or is negative. In such a situation, deferred rental income to be amortized to income should be reduced by all the loans made or reasonably anticipated to be made to the buyer, thus reducing the periodic income to be recognized. Where the loans made or anticipated exceed deferred rental income, a loss provision may be required if the collectibility of the loan is questionable.

(vii) Profit-Sharing or Co-Venture Method.   A real estate transaction may be, in substance, a profit-sharing arrangement rather than a sale. For example, a **sale** of **real estate** to a **limited partnership** in which the seller is a general partner or has similar characteristics is often a profit-sharing arrangement. If such a transaction does not meet the tests for recording a sale, it usually would be accounted for under the profit-sharing method. This accounting method should also be followed when it is clear that the buyer is acting merely as an agent for the seller.

Under the profit-sharing method, giving consideration to the seller's continued involvement, the seller would be required to account for the operations of the property through its income statement as if it continued to own the properties.

24.3 COST OF REAL ESTATE

(a) CAPITALIZATION OF COSTS.   In October 1982, the FASB issued SFAS No. 67. This Statement incorporates the specialized accounting principles and practices from the AICPA SOPs No. 80-3, "Accounting for Real Estate Acquisition, Development and Construction Costs," and No. 78-3, "Accounting for Costs to Sell and Rent, and Initial Rental Operations of Real Estate Projects," and those in the AICPA Industry Accounting Guide, "Accounting for Retail Land Sales," that address costs of real estate projects. SFAS No. 67 establishes whether costs associated with acquiring, developing, constructing, selling, and renting real estate projects should be capitalized. Guidance is also provided on the appropriate methods of allocating capitalized costs to individual components of the project.

SFAS No. 67 also established that a rental project changes from nonoperating to operating when it is substantially completed and held available for occupancy, but not later than one year from cessation of major construction activities.

What are the general precepts? Costs incurred in real estate operations range from "brick and mortar" costs that clearly should be capitalized to general administrative costs that clearly should not be capitalized. Between these two extremes lies a broad range of costs that are difficult to classify. Therefore, judgmental decisions must be made as to whether such costs should be capitalized.

(b) PREACQUISITION COSTS.   These costs include payments to obtain options to acquire real property and other costs incurred prior to acquisition such as legal, architectural, and other professional fees, salaries, environmental studies, appraisals, marketing and feasibility studies, and soil tests. Capitalization of costs related to a property that are incurred before the enterprise acquires the property, or before the enterprise obtains an option to acquire it, is appropriate provided all of the following conditions are met:

- The costs are directly identifiable with the specific property.
- The costs would be capitalized if the property had already been acquired.
- Acquisition of the property or of an option to acquire the property is probable (that is, likely to occur). This condition requires that the prospective purchaser is actively seeking

acquisition of the property and has the ability to finance or obtain financing for the acquisition. In addition, there should be no indication that the property is not available for sale.

Capitalized preacquisition costs should be included as project costs on acquisition of the property or should be charged to expense when it is probable that the property will not be acquired. The charge to expense should be reduced by the amount recoverable by the sale of the options, plans, and so on.

(c) LAND ACQUISITION COSTS.   Costs directly related to the acquisition of land should be capitalized. These costs include option fees, purchase cost, transfer costs, title insurance, legal and other professional fees, surveys, appraisals, and real estate commissions. The purchase cost may have to be increased or decreased for **imputation of interest** on mortgage notes payable assumed or issued in connection with the purchase, as required under APB Opinion No. 21.

(d) LAND IMPROVEMENT, DEVELOPMENT, AND CONSTRUCTION COSTS.   Costs directly related to improvements of the land should be capitalized by the developer. They may include:

- Land planning costs, including marketing and feasibility studies, direct salaries, legal and other professional fees, zoning costs, soil tests, architectural and engineering studies, appraisals, environmental studies, and other costs directly related to site preparation and the overall design and development of the project.
- Onsite and offsite improvements, including demolition costs, streets, traffic controls, sidewalks, street lighting, sewer and water facilities, utilities, parking lots, landscaping, and related costs such as permits and inspection fees.
- Construction costs, including onsite material and labor, direct supervision, engineering and architectural fees, permits, and inspection fees.
- Project overhead and supervision, such as field office costs.
- Recreation facilities, such as golf courses, clubhouse, swimming pools, and tennis courts.
- Sales center and models, including furnishings.

General and administrative costs not directly identified with the project should be accounted for as period costs and expensed as incurred.

Construction activity on a project may be suspended before a project is completed for reasons such as insufficient sales or rental demand. These conditions may indicate an impairment of the value of a project that is other than temporary, which suggests valuation problems. See section entitled "Valuation Problems" below.

(e) ENVIRONMENTAL ISSUES.   In Emerging Issues Task Force Issue No. 90-8, "Capitalization of Costs to Treat Environmental Contamination," the EITF reached a consensus that, in general, costs incurred as a result of environmental contamination should be charged to expense. Such costs include costs to remove contamination, such as that caused by leakage from underground tanks; costs to acquire tangible property, such as air pollution control equipment; costs of environmental studies; and costs of fines levied under environmental laws. Nevertheless, those costs may be capitalized if recoverable but only if any one of the following criteria is met:

- The costs extend the life, increase the capacity, or improve the safety or efficiency of property owned by the company, provided that the condition of the property after the costs are incurred must be improved as compared with the condition of the property when originally constructed or acquired, if later.

- The costs mitigate or prevent environmental contamination that has yet to occur and that otherwise may result from future operations or activities. In addition, the costs improve the property compared with its condition when constructed or acquired, if later.

- The costs are incurred in preparing for sale that property currently held for sale.

In EITF Issue No. 93-5, "Accounting for Environmental Liabilities," the EITF reached a consensus that an environmental liability should be evaluated independently from any potential claim for recovery (a two-event approach) and that the loss arising from the recognition of an environmental liability should be reduced only when it is probable that a claim for recovery will be realized.

The EITF also reached a consensus that discounting environmental liabilities for a specific clean-up site to reflect the time value of money is allowed, but not required, only if the aggregate amount of the obligation and the amount and timing of the cash payments for that site are fixed or reliably determinable.

The EITF discussed alternative rates to be used in discounting environmental liabilities but did not reach a consensus on the rate to be used. However, the SEC Observer stated that SEC registrants should use a discount rate that will produce an amount at which the environmental liability theoretically could be settled in an arm's-length transaction with a third party. That discount rate should not exceed the interest rate on monetary assets that are essentially risk-free and have maturities comparable to that of the environmental liability. In addition, SEC Staff Accounting Bulletin 92 requires registrants to separately present the gross liability and related claim recovery in the balance sheet. SAB 92 also requires other accounting and disclosure requirements relating to product or environmental liabilities.

(f) INTEREST COSTS.   Prior to 1979, many developers capitalized interest costs as a necessary cost of the asset in the same way as "bricks and mortar" costs. Others followed an accounting policy of charging off interest cost as a period cost on the basis that it was solely a financing cost that varied directly with the capability of a company to finance development and construction through equity funds. This long-standing debate on capitalization of interest cost was resolved in October 1979 when the FASB published SFAS No. 34, "Capitalization of Interest Cost," which provided specific guidelines for accounting for interest costs. The guidelines set forth herein are based to a large extent on the provisions of SFAS No. 34.

SFAS No. 34 requires capitalization of interest cost as part of the historical cost of acquiring assets that need a period of time in which to bring them to that condition and location necessary for their intended use. The objectives of capitalizing interest are to obtain a measure of acquisition cost that more closely reflects the enterprise's total investment in the asset and to charge a cost that relates to the acquisition of a resource that will benefit future periods against the revenues of the periods benefited. Interest capitalization is not required if its effect is not material.

(i) Assets Qualifying for Interest Capitalization.   Qualifying assets include real estate constructed for an enterprise's own use or real estate intended for sale or lease. Qualifying assets also include investments (equity, loans, and advances) accounted for by the equity method while the investee has activities in progress necessary to commence its planned principal operations, but only if the investee's activities include the use of such to acquire qualifying assets for its operations.

Capitalization is not permitted for assets in use or ready for their intended use, assets not undergoing the activities necessary to prepare them for use, assets that are not included in the consolidated balance sheet, or investments accounted for by the equity method after the planned principal operations of the investee begin. Thus land that is not undergoing activities necessary for development is not a qualifying asset for purposes of interest capitalization. If activities are undertaken for developing the land, the expenditures to acquire the land qualify for interest capitalization while those activities are in progress.

(ii) Capitalization Period.   The capitalization period commences when:

- Expenditures for the asset have been made.
- Activities that are necessary to get the asset ready for its intended use are in progress.
- Interest cost is being incurred.

Activities are to be construed in a broad sense and encompass more than just physical construction. All steps necessary to prepare an asset for its intended use are included. This broad interpretation includes administrative and technical activities during the preconstruction stage (such as developing plans or obtaining required permits).

Interest capitalization must end when the asset is substantially complete and ready for its intended use. A real estate project should be considered substantially complete and held available for occupancy upon completion of major construction activity, as distinguished from activities such as routine maintenance and cleanup. In some cases, such as in an office building, tenant improvements are a major construction activity and are frequently not completed until a lease contract is arranged. If such improvements are the responsibility of the developer, SFAS No. 67 indicates that the project is not considered substantially complete until the earlier of (1) completion of improvements or (2) one year from cessation of major construction activity without regard to tenant improvements. In other words, a one-year grace period has been provided to complete tenant improvements.

If substantially all activities related to acquisition of the asset are suspended, interest capitalization should stop until such activities are resumed. However, brief interruptions in activities, interruptions caused by external factors, and inherent delays in the development process do not necessarily require suspension of interest capitalization.

Under SFAS No. 34, interest capitalization must end when the asset is **substantially complete** and **ready for its intended use.** For projects completed in parts, where each part is capable of being used independently while work continues on other parts, interest capitalization should stop on each part that is substantially complete and ready for use. Examples include individual buildings in a multiphase or condominium project. For projects that must be completed before any part can be used, interest capitalization should continue until the entire project is substantially complete and ready for use. Where an asset cannot be used effectively until a particular portion has been completed, interest capitalization continues until that portion is substantially complete and ready for use. An example would be an island resort complex with sole access being a permanent bridge to the project. Completion of the bridge is necessary for the asset to be used effectively.

Interest capitalization should not stop when the capitalized costs exceed net realizable value. In such instances, a valuation reserve should be recorded or appropriately increased to reduce the carrying value to net realizable value (see subsection 24.3(l)).

(iii) Methods of Interest Capitalization.   The basic principle is that the amount of interest cost to be capitalized should be the amount that theoretically could have been avoided during the development and construction period if expenditures for the qualifying asset had not been made. These interest costs might have been avoided either by foregoing additional borrowing or by using the funds expended for the asset to repay existing borrowings in the case where no new borrowings were obtained.

The amount capitalized is determined by applying a **capitalization rate** to the average amount of accumulated capitalized expenditures for the asset during the period. Such expenditures include cash payments, transfer of other assets, or incurrence of liabilities on which interest has been recognized, and they should be net of progress payments received against such capitalized costs. Liabilities such as trade payables, accruals, and retainages, on which interest is not recognized, are not expenditures. Reasonable approximations of net capitalized expenditures may be used.

The author's preference is for the capitalization rate to be based on the weighted average of the rates applicable to borrowings outstanding during the period. Alternatively, if a specific new borrowing is associated with an asset, the rate on that borrowing may be used. If the average amount of accumulated expenditures for the asset exceeds the amounts of specific new borrowings associated with the asset, a weighted average interest rate of all other borrowings must be applied to the excess. Under this alternative, judgment will be required to select the borrowings to be included in the weighted average rate so that a reasonable measure will be obtained of the interest cost incurred that could otherwise have been avoided. It should be remembered that the principle is not one of capitalizing interest costs incurred for a specific asset, but one of capitalizing interest costs that could have been avoided if it were not for the acquisition, development, and construction of the asset.

The amount of interest cost capitalized in an accounting period is limited to the total amount of interest cost incurred in the period. However, interest cost should include amortization of premium or discount resulting from imputation of interest on certain types of payables in accordance with APB Opinion No. 21 and that portion of minimum lease payments under a capital lease treated as interest in accordance with SFAS No. 13.

(iv) Accounting for Amount Capitalized. Interest cost capitalized is an integral part of the cost of acquiring a qualifying asset, and therefore its disposition should be the same as any other cost of that asset. For example, if a building is subsequently depreciated, capitalized interest should be included in the depreciable base the same as bricks and mortar.

In the case of interest capitalized on an investment accounted for by the equity method, its disposition should be made as if the investee were consolidated. In other words, if the assets of the investee were being depreciated, the capitalized interest cost should be depreciated in the same manner and over the same lives. If the assets of the investee were developed lots being sold, the capitalized interest cost should be written off as the lots are sold.

(g) TAXES AND INSURANCE. Costs incurred on real estate for property taxes and insurance should be treated similarly to interest costs. They should be capitalized only during periods in which activities necessary to get the property ready for its intended use are in progress. Costs incurred for such items after the property is substantially complete and ready for its intended use should be charged to expense as incurred.

(h) INDIRECT PROJECT COSTS. Indirect project costs that relate to a specific project, such as costs associated with a project field office, should be capitalized as a cost of that project. Other indirect project costs that relate to several projects, such as the costs associated with a construction administration department, should be capitalized and allocated to the projects to which the cost related. Indirect costs that do not clearly relate to projects under development or construction should be charged to expense as incurred.

The principal problem is defining and identifying the cost to be capitalized. It is necessary to consider all of the following points:

- Specific information should be available (such as timecards) to support the basis of allocation to specific projects.
- The costs incurred should be incremental costs; that is, in the absence of the project or projects under development or construction, these costs would not be incurred.
- The impact of capitalization of such costs on the results of operations should be consistent with the pervasive principle of matching costs with related revenue.
- The principle of conservatism should be considered.

Indirect costs related to a specific project that should be considered for capitalization include direct and indirect salaries of a field office and insurance costs. Costs that are not directly related to the project should be charged to expense as incurred.

(i) GENERAL AND ADMINISTRATIVE EXPENSES.   Real estate developers incur various types of general and administrative expenses, including officers' salaries, accounting and legal fees, and various office supplies and expenses. Some of these expenses may be closely associated with individual projects, whereas others are of a more general nature. For example, a developer may open a field office on a project site and staff it with administrative personnel, such as a field accountant. The expenses associated with the field office are directly associated with the project and are therefore considered to be overhead. On the other hand, the developer may have a number of expenses associated with general office operations that benefit numerous projects and for which specifically identifiable allocations are not reasonable or practicable. Those administrative costs that cannot be clearly related to projects under development or construction should be charged to current operations.

(j) AMENITIES.   Real estate developments often include **amenities** such as golf courses, utilities, clubhouses, swimming pools, and tennis courts. The accounting for the costs of these amenities should be based on management's intended disposition as follows:

- *Amenity to Be Sold or Transferred with Sales Units.* All costs in excess of anticipated proceeds should be allocated as common costs because the amenity is clearly associated with the development and sale of the project. Common costs should include estimated net operating costs to be borne by the developer until they are assumed by buyers of units in the project.
- *Amenity to Be Sold Separately or Retained by Developer.* Capitalizable costs of the amenity in excess of its estimated fair value on the expected date of its substantial physical completion should be allocated as common costs. The costs capitalized and allocated to the amenity should not be revised after the amenity is substantially completed and available for use. A later sale of the amenity at more or less than the determined fair value as of the date of substantial physical completion, less any accumulated depreciation, should result in a gain or loss in the period in which the sale occurs.

(k) ABANDONMENTS AND CHANGES IN USE.   Real estate, including rights to real estate, may be abandoned, for example, by allowing a mortgage to be foreclosed or by allowing a purchase option to lapse. Capitalized costs, including allocated common costs, of real estate abandoned should be written off as current expenses or, if appropriate, to allowances previously established for that purpose. They should not be allocated to other components of the project or to other projects, even if other components or other projects are capable of absorbing the losses.

Donation of real estate to municipalities or other governmental agencies for uses that will benefit the project are not abandonment. The cost of real estate donated should be allocated as a common cost of the project.

Changes in the intended use of a real estate project may arise after significant development and construction costs have been incurred. If the change in use is made pursuant to a formal plan that is expected to produce a higher economic yield (as compared to its yield based on use before change), the project costs should be charged to expense to the extent the capitalized costs incurred and to be incurred exceed the estimated value of the revised project when it is substantially completed and ready for its intended use.

If no formal plans exist, the project costs should be charged to expense to the extent they exceed the estimated net realizable value of the property based on the assumption it will be sold in its present state.

(I) SELLING COSTS.   Costs incurred to sell real estate projects should be accounted for in the same manner as, and classified with, construction costs of the project when they meet both of the following criteria:

- The costs incurred are for tangible assets that are used throughout the selling period or for services performed to obtain regulatory approval for sales.
- The costs are reasonably expected to be recovered from sales of the project or incidental operations.

Examples of costs incurred to sell real estate projects that ordinarily meet the criteria for capitalization are costs of model units and their furnishings, sales facilities, legal fees for the preparation of prospectuses, and semipermanent signs.

SFAS No. 67 states that other costs incurred to sell real estate projects should be capitalized as prepaid costs if they are directly associated with and their recovery is reasonably expected from sales that are being accounted for under a method of accounting other than full accrual. Costs that do not meet the criteria for capitalization should be expensed as incurred.

Capitalized selling costs should be charged to expense in the period in which the related revenue is recognized as earned. When a sales contract is canceled (with or without refund) or the related receivable is written off as uncollectible, the related unrecoverable capitalized selling costs are charged to expense or to an allowance previously established for that purpose.

24.4 ALLOCATION OF COSTS

After it has been determined what costs are capitalized, it becomes important to determine how the costs should be allocated, because these costs will enter into the calculation of cost of sales of individual units. Although a number of methods of allocation can be used in different circumstances, judgment often must be used to make sure that appropriate results are obtained.

(a) METHODS OF ALLOCATION.   Capitalized costs of real estate projects should first be assigned to individual components of the project based on specific identification. If specific identification on an overall basis is not practicable, capitalized costs should be allocated as follows:

- Land costs and all other common costs should be allocated to each land parcel benefitted. Allocation should be based on the relative fair value before construction.
- Construction costs should be assigned to buildings on a specific identification basis and allocated to individual units on the basis of relative value of each unit.

In the usual situation, sales prices or rentals are available to compute relative values. In rare situations, however, where relative value is impracticable, capitalized costs may be allocated based on the area method/or the relative cost method as appropriate under the circumstances.

The following sections describe the specific identification, value, and area methods of cost allocation.

(i) Specific Identification Method.   This method of cost allocation is based on determining actual costs applicable to each parcel of land. It rarely is used for land costs because such costs usually encompass more than one parcel. However, it frequently is used for direct construction costs because these costs are directly related to the property being sold. This method should be used wherever practicable.

(ii) Value Method.   The relative value method is the method usually used after costs have been assigned on a specific identification basis. Under this method, the allocation of common costs should be based on relative fair value (before value added by onsite development and construction activities) of each land parcel benefitted. In multiproject developments common costs are normally allocated based on estimated sales prices net of direct improvements and selling costs. This approach is usually the most appropriate because it is less likely to result in deferral of losses.

With respect to condominium sales, certain units will usually have a higher price because of location. With respect to time-sharing sales, holiday periods such as Easter, Fourth of July, and Christmas traditionally sell at a premium. Depending on the resort location, the summer or winter season will also sell at a premium as compared with the rest of the year. Caution should be exercised to ensure that the sales values utilized in cost allocation are reasonable.

(iii) Area Method.   This method of cost allocation is based on square footage, acreage, or frontage. The use of this method will not always result in a logical allocation of costs. When negotiating the purchase price for a large tract of land, the purchaser considers the overall utility of the tract, recognizing that various parcels in the tract are more valuable than others. For example, parcels on a lake front are usually more valuable than those back from the lake. In this situation, if a simple average based on square footage or acreage was used to allocate costs to individual parcels, certain parcels could be assigned costs in excess of their net realizable value.

Generally, the area method should be limited to situations where each individual parcel is estimated to have approximately the same relative value. Under such circumstances, the cost allocations as determined by either the area or value methods would be approximately the same.

24.5 VALUATION PROBLEMS

(a) IMPAIRMENT.   FASB Statement No. 121, "Accounting for the Impairment of Long-Lived Assets and for Long-Lived Assets to Be Disposed Of," was issued in March 1995 and is effective for fiscal years beginning after December 15, 1995. The Statement establishes accounting standards for the impairment of long-lived assets, certain identifiable intangibles, and goodwill related to those assets to be held and used. It also establishes accounting standards for long-lived assets and certain identifiable intangibles to be disposed of.

(i) Assets to Be Held and Used.   The Statement establishes the following process for recognizing and measuring impairment on long-lived assets and certain identifiable intangibles to be held and used:

1. **Indicators.** First, the Statement provides a list of indicators that serve as a warning light when the value of an asset to be held and used may have been impaired. The presence of any of the following indicators evidence a need for additional investigation:
   — a significant decrease in the market value of an asset.
   — a significant change in the extent or manner in which an asset is used or a significant change in an asset.
   — a significant adverse change in legal factors or in business climate that could affect the value of an asset or an adverse action or assessment by a regulator.
   — an accumulation of costs significantly in excess of the amount originally expected to acquire or construct an asset.

— a current period operating or cash flow loss combined with a history of operating or cash flow losses or a projection or forecast that demonstrates continuing losses associated with an asset used for the purpose of producing revenue.

The list of indicators is not intended to be all-inclusive. Other events or changes in circumstances may indicate that the carrying amount of an asset that an entity expects to hold and use may not be recoverable.

2. **Gross Cash Flow Analysis.** Second, an entity that detects one or more of the indicators discussed above should evaluate whether the sum of the expected future net cash flows (undiscounted and without interest charges) associated with an asset to be held and used are at least equal to the asset's carrying amount. The FASB imposed a high threshold for triggering the impairment analysis. The selection of a cash flow test based on undiscounted amounts will trigger the recognition of an impairment loss less frequently than would a test based on fair value.

3. **Measurement.** Finally, for assets to be held and used, the Statement requires an impairment loss to be measured as the amount by which the carrying amount of the impaired asset exceeds its fair value. The distinction between the recognition process, which uses undiscounted cash flows, and the measurement process, which uses fair value or discounted cash flows, is significant. As a result of a relatively minor change in undiscounted cash flows, the impairment measurement process might kick in, thus causing the balance sheet amount to drop off suddenly in any period in which undiscounted cash flows fall below a long-lived asset's carrying amount. Once assets to be held and used are written down, the Statement does not permit them to be written back up. Thus, a new depreciable cost basis is established after a write-down and subsequent increases in the value or recoverable cost of the asset may not be recognized until its sale or disposal.

(ii) Assets to Be Disposed Of. FASB Statement No. 121 requires long-lived assets for which authorized management has committed to a disposal plan, whether by sale or abandonment, to be reported at the lower of carrying amount or fair value less cost to sell. The cost to sell generally includes the incremental direct costs to transact the sale, such as broker commissions, legal and title transfer fees, and closing costs. Costs generally excluded from cost to sell include insurance, security services, utility expenses, and other costs of protecting or maintaining the asset. Subsequent upward adjustments to the carrying amount of an asset to be disposed of may not exceed the carrying amount of the asset before an adjustment was made to reflect the decision to dispose of it.

(iii) Real Estate Development. For homebuilders and other real estate developers, FASB Statement No. 121 classifies land to be developed and projects under development as assets to be held and used until development is complete. As a result, unlike assets to be disposed of, such assets are analyzed in light of the impairment indicator list and gross cash flows generated before any consideration is given to measuring an impairment loss. In the absence of such a provision, nearly all long-term projects, regardless of their overall profitability would be subject to write-downs in their early stages of development, only to be reversed later in the life of the project. Upon completion of development, the project is reclassified as an asset to be disposed of.

(iv) Goodwill. Goodwill identified with a potentially impaired asset should be combined with the carrying amount of that asset in determining whether the sum of the expected future cash flows is less than the carrying amount. Goodwill resulting from a purchase method business combination should be allocated to the assets being tested for recoverability on a pro rata basis using the relative fair values of the assets acquired at that date unless there is evidence to suggest that some other allocation method is more appropriate.

(b) NET REALIZABLE VALUE. Until the effective date of SFAS No. 121, the guidance in SFAS No. 67, which was published in October 1982, remains in effect. The glossary of SFAS No. 67 defines net realizable value as the "estimated selling price in the ordinary course of business less estimated costs of completion (to the stage of completion assumed in determining the selling price), holding, and disposal." SFAS No. 67 (par. 24) also states the general principle that the carrying amount of a real estate project should not exceed NRV on an individual project basis.

The following discussion of NRV incorporates the principal matters contained in SFAS No. 67; however, it should be noted that the FASB has placed an impairment of assets project on its agenda (November 1988). The current schedule calls for a discussion memorandum to be issued in 1990. Accordingly, new guidance on this subject may be issued.

As a general principle, real estate held for sale, or development and sale, should be included in the balance sheet at the lower of cost or net realizable value. The major questions that arise in applying this principle are:

- What types of real estate should be subject to NRV guidelines?
- How should the principle of lower of cost or NRV be applied to real estate projects?
- How should estimated selling prices be determined?
- Should cost of completion include the cost (especially interest cost) to carry the inventory to date of sale?

If the cost of the project exceeds NRV an allowance should be provided. However, the capitalization of costs should not cease, but an additional allowance should be provided.

(c) INVENTORY VERSUS LONG-TERM INVESTMENT. Real estate held for sale, or for development and sale, generally falls into the category of inventory. This includes such properties as land (including raw land and land under development), condominiums, and single-family housing, as well as income properties held for sale. Inventories do not include:

- Income properties held for long-term investment.
- Real property used in the business.
- Land held for future development or construction of property as a long-term investment or as property used in the business.

It is not appropriate for income properties to be declared to be held for investment solely to avoid losses that otherwise would have to be recorded under rules for inventories.

Factors that should be considered in the evaluation of real estate held for sale or for development and sale are:

- The company's financial ability to hold or to develop the properties in question.
- The company's plans for the properties, including information about its past practices and experience.
- The company's plans for the timing of development and sale.
- Appraisals of the property prepared either by independent appraisers or by the company staff.

(d) INDIVIDUAL OR GROUP BASIS. As a general rule, due to the low volume and high dollar value of the individual sales transactions in the real estate industry—and as required by SFAS No. 67—the lower of cost or net realizable value test should be determined on the basis of an evaluation of the individual unit.

(e) DETERMINATION OF NET REALIZABLE VALUE

(i) Selling Price. The estimated selling price should usually be determined on the basis of a sale in the ordinary course of business, which would allow a reasonable time to find a willing purchaser under normal market conditions, exclusive of any adjustment for anticipated inflation. If, however, the intention is to dispose of the property on an immediate sale basis or if the owner does not have the financial ability to hold the property, the estimated selling price should be determined on an immediate liquidation basis.

The nature of the property will affect the method used to determine its selling price. Selling prices for bulk undeveloped land should ordinarily be based on comparable sales prices, allowing a reasonable time to find a purchaser.

Certain future events, such as prospective developments or possible future legislation, should not be factored into the determination of the estimated selling prices except to the extent that such events are being recognized currently in the marketplace. Possible future zoning should not be considered unless it is reasonably certain that it can be obtained.

In determining selling prices for property under development (such as retail lots, single-family homes, and condominiums) current sales prices should be used. Where experience is lacking or where there has been relatively low sales volume, selling prices of comparable transactions in the local area should be used.

Income properties usually are valued on the basis of their estimated future net cash flow and a capitalization (or discount) rate, which varies with the type of project and the financial markets. Estimated future cash flow should be based on full or stabilized operations with appropriate reductions for the estimated cash flow shortfalls prior to stabilization. When using this approach to determine estimated selling prices, pro forma operating costs should be based on costs that are comparable to the estimated future revenues rather than on historical averages. For example, future net cash flow should be adjusted to reflect recent increases in utility costs.

(ii) Cost of Completion, Including Interest and Property Taxes. The total cost of completion of properties being evaluated should include all additional costs to be incurred to complete the properties to be sold. These costs should include the effects of inflation and should be determined on a basis consistent with the determination of costs that are capitalizable or included in inventory.

There has been considerable controversy as to whether future interest costs should be considered in determining NRV. It has long been the author's view that the future interest costs should be included in the calculation if such interest costs were capitalized as a part of the cost of the project. The FASB issued, in October 1979, SFAS No. 34, which requires the capitalization of interest cost as part of the historical cost of development and construction of real estate projects. (See subsection 24.3(d) for further discussion of SFAS No. 34.) The thrust of the Statement is that interest costs during the improvement period should not be treated differently from bricks and mortar. In addition, SFAS No. 67 states that capitalization should not stop when accounting principles require recognition of a lower carrying value for the asset. The allowance required to reduce the acquisition cost to a lower carrying value should be established or increased appropriately.

Although SFAS No. 34 does not directly address the question of what, if any, interest costs should be included in the computation of net realizable value, the only logical conclusion from the statement is that the estimated future capitalizable interest costs should be included in this computation. The controversy, however, has not been resolved over whether to include other future interest costs in determining net realizable value. Other future interest costs would include such costs until the estimated time of sale with respect to undeveloped land or, for developed real estate, after substantial completion. The author's view is that such additional interest costs should not be included.

There have been two approaches generally used to include future interest costs in the calculation of net realizable value. One method, which is consistent with SFAS No. 34, is to include the interest cost in the estimated aggregate cost of the property. To the extent that it exceeds the estimated future sale proceeds, interest cost is recognized currently in the loss provision. Another method indirectly reflects future interest costs by discounting estimated future sales proceeds (net of estimated cash disbursements exclusive of interest) to present value. The resulting amount is compared to costs accumulated to date to determine any loss provision required. Effectively, the former method measures the loss as the difference between total estimated costs to be incurred and estimated proceeds at the future date, while the latter measures the loss as the difference in cost and value at a current date. The latter method is illustrated in the Appendices to AICPA SOP No. 75-2, "Accounting Practices of Real Estate Investment Trusts" and is therefore used by these entities as well as savings and loan associations, as specified in the AICPA *Accounting Guide*. Although that statement requires an interest rate based on an average cost of capital (i.e., total interest cost divided by the aggregate of debt and equity), it should be noted that the FASB rejected that approach for purposes of interest capitalization in SFAS No. 34.

How should future property taxes, insurance and indirect project costs be accounted for in the determination of NRV? Similar to interest, to the extent that these future costs are expected to be capitalized, such costs should be included in the estimated cost of completion.

(iii) Costs of Disposal.   Such costs include marketing, selling, advertising, points, fees, and commissions.

(f) REVERSAL OF RESERVES.   Because of the many factors that can affect recoverability of investments in real estate, the estimated loss on an individual unit or project may not be the same as the ultimate loss sustained on the disposition of the property. Where the valuation is based on estimates, the reduction in value is treated as a valuation reserve that could be adjusted periodically based on a relatively complete reevaluation.

If the valuation has been determined based on known losses caused by specific sales contracts or commitments, the property should be written down to net realizable value. In both instances, once a reserve has been established, the project may not be "written up" to original cost, as the reserve establishes a new cost basis.

24.6 CONSTRUCTION CONTRACTS

Although most real estate developers acquire land in order to develop and construct improvements for their own use or for sale to others, some develop and construct improvements solely for others. There are also many general contractors whose principal business is developing and constructing improvements for others and rarely, if ever, do they own the land.

This section covers guidelines for accounting for development and construction contracts where the contractor does not own the land but is providing such services for others. The principal issue in accounting for construction contracts is when to record income. Construction contracts are generally of two types: fixed price and cost-plus. Under fixed price contracts, a contractor agrees to perform services for a fixed amount. Although the contract price is fixed, it may frequently be revised as a result of change orders as construction proceeds. If the contract is longer than a few months, the contractor usually receives advances from the customer as construction progresses.

Cost-plus contracts are employed in a variety of forms, such as cost plus a percentage of cost or cost plus a fixed fee. Sometimes defined costs may be limited and penalties provided in situations where stated maximum costs are exceeded. Under cost-plus agreements, the contractor is usually reimbursed for its costs as costs are incurred and, in addition, is paid a specified fee. In most cases, a portion of the fee is retained until the construction is completed and accepted. The method of recording income under cost-plus contracts generally is the same as for fixed price contracts and is described below.

(a) AUTHORITATIVE LITERATURE.   In 1955 the AICPA Committee on Accounting Procedures issued ARB No. 45 "Long-Term Construction-Type Contracts." This document described the generally accepted methods of accounting for long-term construction-type contracts for financial reporting purposes and described the circumstances in which each method is preferable.

In 1981 the AICPA issued SOP No. 81-1, "Accounting for Performance of Construction-Type and Certain Production-Type Contracts." This Statement culminated extensive reconsideration by the AICPA of construction-type contracts. The recommendations set forth therein provide guidance on the application of ARB No. 45 but do not amend that bulletin. In 1982, the FASB issued SFAS No. 56, "Contractor Accounting" which states that the specialized accounting and reporting principles and practices contained in SOP No. 81-1 are preferable accounting principles for purposes of justifying a change in accounting principles.

Prior to the issuance of SOP 81-1, authoritative accounting literature used the terms "long-term" and "short-term" in identifying types of contracts. SOP No. 81-1 chose not to use those terms as identifying characteristics because other characteristics were considered more relevant for identifying the types of contracts covered. The guidelines set forth below are based largely on SOP No. 81-1.

(b) METHODS OF ACCOUNTING.   The determination of the point or points at which revenue should be recognized as earned and costs should be recognized as expenses is a major accounting issue common to all business enterprises engaged in the performance of construction contracting. Accounting for such contracts is essentially a process of measuring the results of relatively long-term events and allocating those results to relatively short-term accounting periods. This involves considerable use of estimates in determining revenues, costs, and profits and in assigning the amounts to accounting periods. The process is complicated by the need to continually evaluate the uncertainties that are inherent in the performance of contracts and by the need to rely on estimates of revenues, costs, and the extent of progress toward completion.

There are two generally accepted methods of accounting for construction contracts: the percentage of completion method and the completed contract method. The determination of the preferable method should be based on an evaluation of the particular circumstances as the two methods are not acceptable alternatives for the same set of circumstances. The method used and circumstances describing when it is used should be disclosed in the accounting policy footnote to the financial statements.

(i) Percentage of Completion Method.   The use of this approach depends on the ability of the contractor to make reasonably dependable estimates. The percentage of completion method is the author's preference as an accounting policy in circumstances in which reasonably dependable estimates can be made and in which all the following conditions exist:

- The contract is clear about goods or services to be provided, the consideration to be exchanged, and the manner and terms of settlement.
- The buyer can be expected to pay for the services performed.
- The contractor can be expected to be able to perform his contractual obligations.

The percentage of completion method is the author's preference because this method presents the economic substance of activity more clearly and timely than the completed contract method. It should be noted that estimates of revenues, costs and percentage of completion are the primary criteria for income recognition. Billings may have no real relationship to performance and generally are not a suitable basis for income recognition.

(ii) Completed Contract Method. This method may be used in circumstances in which an entity's financial position and results of operations would not vary materially from those resulting from the percentage of completion method. The completed contract method is the author's preference in circumstances in which estimates cannot meet the criteria for reasonable dependability or in which there are inherent hazards that caused forecasts to be doubtful.

(iii) Consistency of Application. It is possible that a contractor may use one method for some contracts and the other for additional contracts. There is no inconsistency, since consistency in application lies in using the same accounting treatment for the same set of conditions from one accounting period to another. The method used, and circumstances when it is used, should be disclosed in the accounting policy footnote to the financial statements.

(c) PERCENTAGE OF COMPLETION METHOD. This method is the author's preference because it recognizes the legal and economic results of contract performance on a timely basis. Financial statements based on the percentage of completion method present the economic substance of a company's transactions and events more clearly and more timely than financial statements based on the completed contract method, and they present more accurately the relationships between gross profit from contracts and related period costs. The percentage of completion method informs the users of the general purpose financial statements concerning the volume of a company's economic activity.

In practice, several methods are used to measure the extent of progress toward completion. These methods include the cost-to-cost method, the efforts-expended method, the units-of-delivery method and the units-of-work-performed method. These methods are intended to conform to the recommendations of ARB 45 (par. 4), which states:

> . . . that the recognized income be that percentage of estimated total income, either:
>
> **a.** that incurred costs to date bear to estimated total costs after giving effect to estimates of costs to complete based upon most recent information, or
> **b.** that may be indicated by such other measure of progress toward completion as may be appropriate having due regard to work performed.

One generally accepted method of measuring such progress is the stage of construction, as determined through engineering or architectural studies.

When using the "cost incurred" approach, there may be certain costs that should be excluded from the calculation. For example, substantial quantities of standard materials not unique to the project may have been delivered to the job site but not yet utilized. Or engineering and architectural fees incurred may represent 20% of total estimated costs whereas only 10% of the construction has been performed.

The principal disadvantage of the percentage of completion method is that it is necessarily dependent on estimates of ultimate costs that are subject to the uncertainties frequently inherent in long-term contracts.

The estimation of total revenues and costs is necessary to determine estimated total income. Frequently a contractor can estimate total contract revenue and total contract cost in single amounts. However, on some contracts a contractor may be able to estimate only total contract revenue and total contract cost in ranges of amounts. In such situations, the most likely amounts within the range should be used, if determinable. If not, the least favorable amounts should be used until the results can be estimated more precisely.

(i) Revenue Determination.   Estimating revenue on a contract is an involved process. The major factors that must be considered in determining total estimated revenue include the basic contract price, contract options, change orders, claims, and contract provisions for incentive payments and penalties. All these factors and other special contract provisions must be evaluated throughout the life of a contract in estimating total contract revenue.

(ii) Cost Determination.   At any time during the life of a contract, total estimated contract cost consists of two components: costs incurred to date and estimated cost to complete the contract. A company should be able to determine costs incurred on a contract with a relatively high degree of precision. The other component, estimated cost to complete, is a significant variable in the process of determining income earned and is thus a significant factor in accounting for contracts. SOP No. 81-1 states that the following practices should be followed in estimating costs to complete:

a. Systematic and consistent procedures that are correlated with the cost accounting system should be used to provide a basis for periodically comparing actual and estimated costs.

b. In estimating total contract costs the quantities and prices of all significant elements of cost should be identified.

c. The estimating procedures should provide that estimated cost to complete includes the same elements of cost that are included in actual accumulated costs; also, those elements should reflect expected price increases.

d. The effects of future wage and price escalations should be taken into account in cost estimates, especially when the contract performance will be carried out over a significant period of time. Escalation provisions should not be blanket overall provisions but should cover labor, materials, and indirect costs based on percentages or amounts that take into consideration experience and other pertinent data.

e. Estimates of cost to complete should be reviewed periodically and revised as appropriate to reflect new information.

(iii) Revision of Estimates.   Adjustments to the original estimates of the total contract revenue, cost, or extent of progress toward completion are often required as work progresses under the contract, even though the scope of the work required under the contract has not changed. Such adjustments are changes in accounting estimates as defined in APB Opinion No. 20. Under this Opinion, the cumulative catch-up method is the only acceptable method. This method requires the difference between cumulative income and income previously recorded to be recorded in the current year's income.

The following example illustrates the percentage of completion method.

A contracting company has a lump-sum contract for $9 million to build a bridge at a total estimated cost of $8 million. The construction period covers 3 years. Financial data during the construction period is as follows:

	Year 1	Year 2	Year 3
		(thousands of dollars)	
Total estimated revenue	$9,000	$9,100	$9,200
Cost incurred to date	$2,050	$6,100	$8,200
Estimated cost to complete	6,000	2,000	—
Total estimated cost	$8,050	$8,100	$8,200
Estimated gross profit	$ 950	$1,000	$1,000
Billings to date	$1,800	$5,500	$9,200
Collections to date	$1,500	$5,000	$9,200
Measure of progress	25%	75%	100%

The amount of revenue, costs, and income recognized in the three periods would be as follows:

	To Date	Recognized Prior Year *(thousands of dollars)*	Current Year
Year 1 (25% completed)			
Earned revenue ($9,000,000 × 0.25)	$2,250.0		$2,250.0
Cost of earned revenue			
($8,050,000 × 0.25)	2,012.5		2,012.5
Gross profit	$ 237.5		$ 237.5
Gross profit rate	10.5%		10.5%
Year 2 (75% completed)			
Earned revenue ($9,100,000 × 0.75)	$6,825.0	$2,250.0	$4,575.0
Cost of earned revenue			
($8,100,000 × 0.75)	6,075.0	2,012.5	4,062.5
Gross profit	$ 750.0	$ 237.5	$ 512.5
Gross profit rate	11.0%	10.5%	11.2%
Year 3 (100% completed)			
Earned revenue	$9,200.0	$6,825.0	$2,375.0
Cost of earned revenue	8,200.0	6,075.0	2,125.0
Gross profit	$1,000.0	$ 750.0	$ 250.0
Gross profit rate	10.9%	11.0%	10.5%

Source: AICPA.

(d) COMPLETED CONTRACT METHOD.   This method recognizes income only when a contract is completed or substantially completed, such as when the remaining costs to be incurred are not significant. Under this method, costs and billings are reflected in the balance sheet but there are no charges or credits to the income statement.

As a general rule, a contract may be regarded as substantially completed if remaining costs and potential risks are insignificant in amount. The overriding objectives are to maintain consistency in determining when contracts are substantially completed and to avoid arbitrary acceleration or deferral of income. The specific criteria used to determine when a contract is substantially completed should be followed consistently. Circumstances to be considered in determining when a project is substantially completed include acceptance by the customer, departure from the site, and compliance with performance specifications.

The completed contract method may be used in circumstances in which financial position and results of operations would not vary materially from those resulting from use of the percentage of completion method (for example, in circumstances in which an entity has primarily short-term contracts). In accounting for such contracts, income ordinarily is recognized when performance is substantially completed and accepted. For example, the completed contract method, as opposed to the percentage of completion method, would not usually produce a material difference in net income or financial position for a small contractor that primarily performs relatively short-term contracts during an accounting period.

The completed contract method is the author's preference in circumstances in which estimates cannot meet the criteria for reasonable dependability under the percentage of completion method or where there are inherent hazards of the nature of those discussed in SOP No. 81-1. However, for circumstances in which there is an assurance that no loss will be incurred on a contract (for example, when the scope of the contract is ill-defined but the contractor is protected by a cost-plus contract or other contractual terms), the percentage of completion method based on a zero profit margin, rather than the completed contract method, should be used until more precise estimates can be made.

The significant difference between the percentage of completion method applied on the basis of a zero profit margin and the completed contract method relates to the effects on the income statement. Under the zero profit margin approach to applying the percentage of completion method, equal amounts of revenue and cost, measured on the basis of performance during the period, are presented in the income statement and no gross profit amount is presented in the income statement until the contract is completed. The zero profit margin approach to applying the percentage of completion method gives the users of general purpose financial statements an indication of the volume of a company's business and of the application of its economic resources.

The principal advantage of the completed contract method is that it is based on results as finally determined, rather than on estimates for unperformed work that may involve unforeseen costs and possible losses. The principal disadvantage is that it does not reflect current performance when the period of the contract extends into more than one accounting period. Under these circumstances, it may result in irregular recognition of income.

(e) PROVISION FOR LOSSES.   Under either of the methods above, provision should be made for the entire loss on the contract in the period when current estimates of total contract costs indicate a loss. The provision for loss should represent the best judgment that can be made in the circumstances.

Other factors that should be considered in arriving at the projected loss on a contract include target penalties for late completion and rewards for early completion, nonreimbursable costs on cost-plus contracts, and the effect of change orders. When using the completed contract method and allocating general and administrative expenses to contract costs, total general and administrative expenses that are expected to be allocated to the contract are to be considered together with other estimated contract costs.

(f) CONTRACT CLAIMS.   Claims are amounts in excess of the agreed contract price that a contractor seeks to collect from customers or others for customer-caused delays, errors in specifications and designs, unapproved change orders, or other causes of unanticipated additional costs. Recognition of amounts of additional contract revenue relating to claims is appropriate only if it is probable that the claim will result in additional contract revenue and if the amount can be reliably estimated.

These requirements are satisfied by the existence of all the following conditions:

- The contract or other evidence provides a legal basis for the claim.
- Additional costs are caused by circumstances that were unforeseen at the contract date and are not the result of deficiencies in the contractor's performance.
- Costs associated with the claim are identifiable and are reasonable in view of the work performed.
- The evidence supporting the claim is objective and verifiable.

If the foregoing requirements are met, revenue from a claim should be recorded only to the extent that contract costs relating to the claim have been incurred. The amounts recorded, if material, should be disclosed in the notes to the financial statements.

Change orders are modifications of an original contract that effectively change the provisions of the contract without adding new provisions. They may be initiated by either the contractor or the customer. Many change orders are unpriced; that is, the work to be performed is defined, but the adjustment to the contract price is to be negotiated later. For some change orders, both scope and price may be unapproved or in dispute. Accounting for change orders depends on the underlying circumstances, which may differ for each change order depending on the customer, the contract, and the nature of the change. Priced change orders represent an adjustment to the contract price and contract revenue, and costs should be adjusted to reflect these change orders.

Accounting for unpriced change orders depends on their characteristics and the circumstances in which they occur. Under the completed contract method, costs attributable to unpriced change orders should be deferred as contract costs if it is probable that aggregate contract costs, including costs attributable to change orders, will be recovered from contract revenues. For all unpriced change orders, recovery should be deemed probable if the future event or events necessary for recovery are likely to occur. Some factors to consider in evaluating whether recovery is probable are the customer's written approval of the scope of the change order, separate documentation for change order costs that are identifiable and reasonable, and the entity's favorable experience in negotiating change orders (especially as it relates to the specific type of contract and change order being evaluated). The following guidelines should be used in accounting for unpriced change orders under the percentage of completion method:

- Costs attributable to unpriced change orders should be treated as costs of contract performance in the period in which the costs are incurred if it is not probable that the costs will be recovered through a change in the contract price.
- If it is probable that the costs will be recovered through a change in the contract price, the costs should be deferred (excluded from the cost of contract performance) until the parties have agreed on the change in contract price or, alternatively, they should be treated as costs of contract performance in the period in which they are incurred, and contract revenue should be recognized to the extent of the costs incurred.
- If it is probable that the contract price will be adjusted by an amount that exceeds the costs attributable to the change order and the amount of the excess can be reliably estimated, the original contract price should also be adjusted for that amount when the costs are recognized as costs of contract performance if its realization is probable. However, since the substantiation of the amount of future revenue is difficult, revenue in excess of the costs attributable to unpriced change orders should only be recorded in circumstances in which realization is assured beyond a reasonable doubt, such as circumstances in which an entity's historical experience provides assurance or in which an entity has received a bona fide pricing offer from the customer and records only the amount of the offer as revenue.

If change orders are in dispute or are unapproved in regard to both scope and price, they should be evaluated as claims.

24.7 OPERATIONS OF INCOME-PRODUCING PROPERTIES

(a) RENTAL OPERATIONS.   Operations of income-producing properties represent a distinct segment of the real estate industry. Owners are often referred to as "real estate operators." Income-producing properties include office buildings, shopping centers, apartments, industrial buildings, and similar properties rented to others. A lease agreement is entered into between the owner/operator and the tenant for periods ranging from one month to many years, depending on the type of property. Sometimes an investor will acquire an existing income-producing property or alternatively will have the builder or developer construct the property. Some developers, frequently referred to as "investment builders," develop and construct income properties for their own use as investment properties.

SFAS No. 13 is the principal source of standards of financial accounting and reporting for leases. Under SFAS No. 13, a distinction is made between a **capital lease** and an **operating lease.** The lessor is required to account for a **capital lease** as a sale or a financing transaction. The lessee accounts for a capital lease as a purchase. An **operating lease,** on the other hand, requires the lessor to reflect rent income, operating expenses, and depreciation of the property over the lease term; the lessee must record rent expense.

Accounting for leases is discussed in Chapter 17 and therefore is not covered in depth here. Certain unique aspects of accounting for leases of real estate classified as operating leases, however, are covered below.

(b) RENTAL INCOME.   Rental income from an operating lease should usually be recorded by a lessor as it becomes receivable in accordance with the provisions of the lease agreement.

FTB No. 85-3 provides that the effects of scheduled rent increases, which are included in minimum lease payments under SFAS No. 13, should be recognized by lessors and lessees on a straight-line basis over the lease term unless another systematic and rational allocation basis is more representative of the time pattern in which the leased property is physically employed. Using factors such as the time value of money, anticipated inflation, or expected future revenues to allocate scheduled rent increases is inappropriate because these factors do not relate to the time pattern of the physical usage of the leased property. However, such factors may affect the periodic reported rental income or expense if the lease agreement involves contingent rentals, which are excluded from minimum lease payments and accounted for separately under SFAS No. 13, as amended by SFAS No. 29.

A lease agreement may provide for scheduled rent increases designed to accommodate the lessee's projected physical use of the property. In these circumstances, FTB No. 88-1 provides for the lessee and the lessor to recognize the lease payments as follows:

   a. If rents escalate in contemplation of the lessee's physical use of the leased property, including equipment, but the lessee takes possession of or controls the physical use of the property at the beginning of the lease term, all rental payments including the escalated rents, should be recognized as rental expenses or rental revenue on a straight-line basis in accordance with paragraph 15 of Statement No. 13 and Technical Bulletin 85-3 starting with the beginning of the lease term.
   b. If rents escalate under a master lease agreement because the lessee gains access to and control over additional leased property at the time of the escalation, the escalated rents should be considered rental expense or rental revenue attributable to the leased property and recognized in proportion to the additional leased property in the years that the lessee has control over the use of the additional leased property. The amount of rental expense or rental revenue attributed to the additional leased property should be proportionate to the relative fair value of the additional property, as determined at the inception of the lease, in the applicable time periods during which the lessee controls its use.

(i) Cost Escalation.   Because of increased inflation, more lessors require that the lessee pay operating costs of the leased property such as utilities, real estate taxes, and common area maintenance. Some lessors require the lessee to pay for such costs when they escalate and exceed a specified rate or amount. In some cases, the lessee pays these costs directly. More commonly, however, the lessor pays the costs and is reimbursed by the lessee. In this situation, the lessor should generally record these reimbursement costs as a receivable at the time the costs are accrued, even though they may not be billed until a later date. Since these costs are sometimes billed at a later date, collectibility from the lessee should, of course, be considered.

(ii) Percentage Rents.   Many retail leases, such as those on shopping centers, enable the lessor to collect additional rents, based on the excess of a stated percentage of the tenant's gross sales over the specified minimum rent. While the minimum rent is usually payable in periodic level amounts, percentage rents (sometimes called "overrides") are usually based on annual sales, often with a requirement for periodic payments toward the annual amount.

SFAS No. 29 (par. 13), "Determining Contingent Rentals," states: "Contingent rentals shall be includable in the determination of net income as accruable."

(c) RENTAL COSTS.   The following considerations help determine the appropriate accounting for project rental costs.

(i) Chargeable to Future Periods.   Costs incurred to rent real estate should be deferred and charged to future periods when they are related to and their recovery is reasonably expected from future operations. Examples include initial direct costs such as commissions, legal fees, costs of credit investigations, and costs of preparing and processing documents for new leases acquired, and that portion of compensation applicable to the time spent on consummated leases. Other examples include costs of model units and related furnishings, rental facilities, semipermanent signs, grand openings, and unused rental brochures, but not rental overhead, such as rental salaries (see "Period Costs" below).

For leases accounted for as operating leases, deferred rental costs that can be directly related to revenue from a specific operating lease should be amortized over the term of the related lease in proportion to the recognition of rental income. Deferred rental costs that cannot be directly related to revenue from a specific operating lease should be amortized to expense over the period of expected benefit. The amortization period begins when the project is substantially completed and held available for occupancy. Estimated unrecoverable deferred rental costs associated with a lease or group of leases should be charged to expense when it becomes probable that the lease(s) will be terminated.

For leases accounted for as sales-type leases, deferred rental costs must be charged against income at the time the sale is recognized.

(ii) Period Costs.   Costs that are incurred to rent real estate projects that do not meet the above criteria should be charged to expense as incurred. SFAS No. 67 specifically indicates that rental overhead, which is defined in its glossary to include rental salaries, is an example of such period costs. Other examples of expenditures that are period costs are initial indirect costs, such as that portion of salaries and other compensation and fees applicable to time spent in negotiating leases that are not consummated, supervisory and administrative expenses, and other indirect costs.

(d) DEPRECIATION.   Under GAAP, the costs of income-producing properties must be depreciated. Depreciation, as defined by GAAP, is the systematic and rational allocation of the historical cost of depreciable assets (tangible assets, other than inventory, with limited lives of more than 1 year) over their useful lives.

In accounting for real estate operations, the most frequently used methods of depreciation are straight-line and decreasing charge methods. The most common **decreasing charge methods** are the declining balance and sum-of-the-years-digits methods. **Increasing charge methods,** such as the sinking fund method, are not generally accepted in the real estate industry in the United States. There is much merit to the sinking fund method (which is accepted in Canada) particularly for long-term leases, but it needs further study and authoritative literature before it should be considered acceptable in the real estate industry here.

The major components of a building, such as the plumbing and heating systems, may be identified and depreciated separately over their respective lives. This method, which is frequently used for tax purposes, usually results in a more rapid write-off.

(e) INITIAL RENTAL OPERATIONS.   When a real estate project is substantially complete and held available for occupancy, the procedures listed here should be followed:

- Rental revenue should be recorded in income as earned.
- Operating costs should be charged to expense currently.
- Amortization of deferred rental costs should begin.
- Full depreciation of rental property should begin.

- Carrying costs, such as interest and property taxes, should be charged to expense as accrued.

If portions of a rental project are substantially completed and occupied by tenants or held available for occupancy and other portions have not yet reached that stage, the substantially completed portions should be accounted for as a separate project. Costs incurred should be allocated between the portions under construction and the portions substantially completed and held available for occupancy.

(f) RENTAL EXPENSE.   Rental expense under an operating lease normally should be charged to operations by a lessee over the lease term on a basis consistent with the lessor's recording of income, with the exception of periodic accounting for percentage rent expense, which should be based on the estimated annual percentage rent.

24.8 ACCOUNTING FOR INVESTMENTS IN REAL ESTATE VENTURES

(a) ORGANIZATION OF VENTURES.   The joint venture vehicle—the sharing of risk—has been widely utilized for many years in the construction, mining, and oil and gas industries as well as for real estate developments. Real estate joint ventures are typically entered into in recognition of the need for external assistance, for example, financing or market expertise. The most common of these needs is capital formation.

Real estate ventures are organized either as corporate entities or, more frequently, as partnerships. Limited partnerships are often used because of the advantages of limited liability. The venture is typically formed by a small group, with each investor actively contributing to the success of the venture and participating in overall management, and with no one individual or corporation controlling its operations. The venture is usually operated separately from other activities of the investors. Regardless of the legal form of the real estate venture, the accounting principles for recognition of profits and losses should be the same.

(b) ACCOUNTING BACKGROUND.   Accounting practices in the real estate industry in general and, more specifically, accounting for investments in real estate ventures, have varied. The result was lack of comparability and, in some cases, a lack of comprehension. Therefore the following relevant pronouncements were issued:

- *APB Opinion No. 18.* In response to the wide variation in accounting for investments, the APB, in March 1971, issued Opinion No. 18, "The Equity Method of Accounting for Investments in Common Stock." This opinion became applicable to investments in unincorporated ventures, including partnerships, because of an interpretation promulgated in November 1971.
- *AICPA Statement of Position No. 78-9.* The AICPA recognized the continuing diversity of practice and in December 1978 issued SOP No. 78-9, "Accounting for Investments in Real Estate Ventures." This statement was issued to narrow the range of alternative practices used in accounting for investments in real estate ventures and to establish industry uniformity. A task force of the AICPA's Real Estate Committee is considering proposed amendments to SOP 78-9. It is anticipated that the task force will focus primarily on the criteria for allocating venture losses among investors.
- *SFAS No. 94.* In response to the perceived problem of off-balance sheet financing, of which unconsolidated majority-owned subsidiaries were deemed to be the most significant aspect, the FASB issued SFAS No. 94, "Consolidation of All Majority-Owned Subsidiaries," in October 1987. SFAS No. 94 eliminated the concept of not consolidating nonhomogeneous operations and replaced it with the concept that the predominant factor

in determining whether an investment requires consolidation should primarily be control rather than ownership of a majority voting interest. This Statement is also applicable to investments in unincorporated ventures, including partnerships.

- *AICPA Notice to Practitioners, ADC Loans, February 1986.* Recognizing that financial institutions needed guidance on accounting for real estate acquisition, development, and construction (ADC) arrangements, the AICPA issued the above notice (also known as the Third Notice). The notice provides accounting guidance on ADC arrangements that have virtually the same risks and potential rewards as those of joint ventures. It determined that accounting for such arrangements as loans would not be appropriate and provides guidance on the appropriate accounting.

  The SEC incorporated the notice into SAB No. 71 "Views Regarding Financial Statements of Properties Securing Mortgage Loans." SAB No. 71, and its amendment SAB No. 71A, provide guidance to registrants on the required reporting under this notice. Also, EITF Issue Nos. 84-4 and 86-21, as well as SAB No. 71, extend the provisions of this notice to all entities, not just financial institutions. It should be noted that a Task Force of the AICPA, formed in early 1990, is considering several aspects of accounting by lenders for ADC loans.

The task force is in the final stages of developing a statement of position after analyzing the comments received on the October 27, 1993 exposure draft, "Identifying and Accounting for Real Estate Loans That Qualify as Real Estate Investments." It is anticipated that the final SOP will elevate the authority of significant portions of the third Notice, modify others, and provide new guidance on how to account for a loan after it has been classified as an investment.

(c) INVESTOR ACCOUNTING PROBLEMS. The accounting literature mentioned above covers many of the special problems investors encounter in practice. The major areas are:

- Investor accounting for results of operations of ventures.
- Special accounting problems related to venture losses.
- Investor accounting for transactions with a real estate venture, including capital contributions.
- Financial statement presentation and disclosures.

A **controlling investor** should account for its income and losses from real estate ventures under the principles that apply to investments in subsidiaries, which usually require **consolidation** of the venture's operations. A **noncontrolling investor** should account for its share of income and losses in real estate ventures by using the equity method. Under the equity method, the initial investment is recorded by the investor at cost; thereafter, the carrying amount is increased by the investor's share of current earnings and decreased by the investor's share of current losses or distributions.

In accounting for transactions with a real estate venture, a controlling investor must **eliminate all intercompany profit.** When the investor does not control the venture, some situations require that all intercompany profit be eliminated, whereas in others, intercompany profit is eliminated by the investor only to the extent of its ownership interest in the venture. For example, as set forth in AICPA SOP No. 78-9, even a noncontrolling investor is precluded from recognizing any profit on a **contribution of real estate or services** to the venture. Accounting for other transactions covered by SOP 78-9 includes sales of real estate and services to the venture, interest income on loans and advances to the venture, and venture sales of real estate or services to an investor.

With regard to **financial statement presentation,** a controlling investor is usually required to consolidate venture operations. A noncontrolling investor should use the equity method, with the carrying value of the investment presented as a single amount in the balance sheet and the investor's share of venture earnings or losses as a single amount in the income statement. The proportionate share approach, which records the investor's share of each item of income, expense, asset, and liability, is not considered acceptable except for legal undivided interests.

The material above is only a very brief summary of comprehensive publications, and there are exceptions to some of those guidelines. In accounting for real estate venture operations and transactions, judgment must be exercised in applying the principles to assure that economic substance is fairly reflected no matter how complex the venture arrangements.

(d) ACCOUNTING FOR TAX BENEFITS RESULTING FROM INVESTMENTS IN AFFORD-ABLE HOUSING PROJECTS.   The Revenue Reconciliation Act of 1993 provides tax benefits to investors in entities operating qualified affordable housing projects. The benefits take the form of tax deductions from operating loses and tax credits. In EITF Issue No. 94-1, "Accounting for Tax Benefits Resulting from Investments in Affordable Housing Projects," the EITF reached a consensus that a limited partner in a qualified low income housing project may elect to use the effective yield method (described below) if the following conditions are met:

1. The availability of the limited partner's share of the tax credits is guaranteed by a creditworthy entity through a letter of credit, tax indemnity agreement or other arrangement.
2. The limited partner's projected yield based solely on the cash flows from the guaranteed tax credits is positive.
3. The limited partner's liability for both legal and tax purposes is limited to its capital investment.

Under the effective yield method, the investor recognizes tax credits as they are allocated and amortizes the initial cost of the investment to provide a constant effective yield over the period that tax credits are allocated to the investor. The effective yield is the internal rate of return on the investment, based on the cost of the investment and the guaranteed tax credits allocated to the investor. Any expected residual value of the investment should be excluded from the effective yield calculation. Cash received from operations of the limited partnership or sale of the property, if any, should be included when realized or realizable.

Under the effective yield method, the tax credit allocated, net of the amortization of the investment in the limited partnership, is recognized in the income statement as a component of income taxes attributable to continuing operations. Any other tax benefits received should be accounted for pursuant to FASB Statement No. 109, "Accounting for Income Taxes."

An investment that does not qualify for accounting under the effective yield method should be accounted for under SOP 78-9, which requires use of the equity method unless the limited partner's interest is so minor as to have virtually no influence over partnership operating and financial policies. The EITF did not establish a "bright line" as to what percentage ownership threshold is required under SOP 78-9 for selecting between the cost and equity methods. The AICPA is currently reconsidering the guidance in SOP 78-9 in its project titled, Accounting for Investors' Interests in Unconsolidated Real Estate Joint Ventures.

If the cost method is used, the excess of the carrying amount of the investment over its residual value should be amortized over the period in which the tax credits are allocated to the investor. Annual amortization should be based on the proportion of tax credits received in the current year to total estimated tax credits to be allocated to the investor. The residual value should not reflect anticipated inflation.

During the deliberations of EITF Issue No. 94-1, the staff of the Securities and Exchange Commission announced that they had revised their position on accounting for investments in limited partnerships. Previously, the SEC had not objected to the use of the cost method for limited partnership investments of up to 20%, provided the investor did not have significant influence as defined in APB Opinion No. 18, "The Equity Method of Accounting for Investments in Commons Stock." However, the revised position is that the equity method should be used to account for limited partnership investments, unless the investment is "so minor that the limited partner may have virtually no influence over partnership operating and financial policies." In practice, investments of more than 3–5% would be considered more than minor. For public companies, this guidance is to be applied to any limited partnership investment made after May 18, 1995. This would include not only the investments in low income housing projects, but all real estate partnerships and any other types of limited partnership investments (like oil and gas, etc.).

24.9 FINANCIAL REPORTING

(a) FINANCIAL STATEMENT PRESENTATION.   There are matters of financial statement presentation—as opposed to footnote disclosures—that are unique to the real estate industry. The financial reporting guidelines in this section are based on the principles set forth in authoritative literature and reporting practice.

(i) Balance Sheet.   Real estate companies frequently present nonclassified balance sheets; that is, they do not distinguish between current and noncurrent assets or liabilities. This is because the operating cycle of most real estate companies exceeds one year.

Real estate companies normally list their assets on the balance sheet in the order liquidity, in the same manner as other companies. A second popular method, however, is to list the real estate assets first, to demonstrate their importance to the companies. In either case, **real estate assets** should be disclosed in the manner that is most demonstrative of the company's operations. These assets are often grouped according to the type of investment or operation as follows:

- Unimproved land.
- Land under development.
- Residential lots.
- Condominium and single-family dwellings.
- Rental properties.

(ii) Statement of Income.   Revenues and costs of sales are generally classified in a manner consistent with that described for real estate investments. In 1976 the Financial Accounting Standards Board issued SFAS No. 14, "Financial Reporting for Segments of a Business Enterprise," which states that the financial statements of an enterprise should include certain information about the industry segments of the enterprise. An industry segment is defined in paragraph 10(a) as "a component of an enterprise engaged in providing a product or service or a group of related products and services primarily to unaffiliated customers (i.e. customers outside the enterprise) for profit." Some developers, however, have traditionally considered themselves to be in only one line of business.

(b) ACCOUNTING POLICIES.   Because of the alternatives currently available in accounting for real estate developments, it is especially important to follow the guidelines of APB Opinion No. 22, "Disclosure of Accounting Policies." The Opinion states (par. 12) that disclosures should include the accounting principles and methods that involve any of the following:

A selection from existing acceptable alternatives.

Principles and methods peculiar to the industry in which the reporting entity operates, even if such principles and methods are predominantly followed in that industry.

Unusual or innovative applications of generally accepted accounting principles (and, as applicable, of principles and methods peculiar to the industry in which the reporting entity operates).

The following lists certain accounting policy disclosures that are appropriate in the financial statements of a real estate company, as opposed to a manufacturing or service enterprise.

1. *Profit Recognition.* The accounting method used to determine income should be disclosed. Where different methods are used, the circumstances surrounding the application of each should also be disclosed. Similarly, a comment should be included indicating the timing of sales and related profit recognition.

2. *Cost Accounting.* The method of allocating cost to unit sales should be disclosed (e.g., relative market values, area, unit, specific identification). Financial statement disclosure should include, where applicable, capitalization policies for property taxes and other carrying costs, and policies with respect to capitalization or deferral of start-up or preoperating costs (selling costs, rental costs, initial operations).

3. *Net Realizable Value.* Inventory is required to be carried at the lower of cost or NRV. The method of determining NRV should preferably be disclosed.

4. *Investment in Real Estate Ventures.* Disclosures of the following accounting policies should be made:

    a. Method of inclusion in investor's accounts (e.g., equity or consolidation).

    b. Method of income recognition (e.g., equity or cost).

    c. Accounting principles of significant ventures.

    d. Profit recognition practices on transactions between the investor and the venture.

(c) **NOTE DISCLOSURES.**   The following list describes other financial statement disclosures that are appropriate in the notes to the financial statements of a real estate developer.

Real Estate Assets. If a breakdown is not reflected on the balance sheet, it should be included in the footnotes. Disclosure should also be made of inventory subject to sales contracts that have not been recorded as sales and the portion of inventory serving as collateral for debts.

Inventory Write-Downs. Summarized information or explanations with respect to significant inventory write-downs should be disclosed in the footnotes because write-downs are generally important and unusual items.

Nonrecourse Debt. Although it is not appropriate to offset nonrecourse debt against the related asset, a note to the financial statements should disclose the amount and interrelationship of the nonrecourse debt with the cost of the related property.

Capitalization of Interest. SFAS No. 34 requires the disclosure of the amount of interest expensed and the amount capitalized.

Deferral of Profit Recognition. When transactions qualify as sales for accounting purposes but do not meet the tests for full profit recognition and, as a result, the installment or cost recovery methods are used, disclosure should be made of significant amounts of profit deferred, the nature of the transaction, and any other information deemed necessary for complete disclosure.

Investments in Real Estate Ventures. Typical disclosures with respect to significant real estate ventures include names of ventures, percentage of ownership interest, accounting and tax policies of the venture, the difference, if any, between the carrying amount of the investment and the investor's share of equity in net assets and the accounting policy regarding amortization of the difference, summarized information as to assets, liabilities, and results of operations or separate financial statements, and investor commitments with respect to joint ventures.

Construction Contractors. The principal reporting considerations for construction contractors relate to the two methods of income recognition: the percentage of completion method and the completed contract method.

When the completed contract method is used, an excess of accumulated costs over related billings should be shown in a classified balance sheet as a current asset, and an excess of accumulated billings over related costs should be shown as a current liability. If costs exceed billings on some contracts, and billings exceed costs on others, the contracts should ordinarily be segregated so that the asset side includes only those contracts on which costs exceed billings, and the liability side includes only those on which billings exceed costs.

Under the percentage of completion method, assets may include costs and related income not yet billed, with respect to certain contracts. Liabilities may include billings in excess of costs and related income with respect to other contracts.

The following disclosures, which are required for SEC reporting companies should generally be made by a nonpublic company whose principal activity is long-term contracting:

- Amounts billed but not paid by customers under retainage provisions in contracts, and indication of amounts expected to be collected in various years.

- Amounts included in receivables representing the recognized sales value of performance under long-term contracts where such amounts had not been billed and were not billable at the balance sheet date, along with a general description of the prerequisites for billing and an estimate of the amount expected to be collected in one year.

- Amounts included in receivables or inventories representing claims or other similar items subject to uncertainty concerning their determination or ultimate realization, together with a description of the nature and status of principal items, and amounts expected to be collected in one year.

- Amount of progress payments (billings) netted against inventory at the balance sheet date.

(d) CURRENT VALUE. On October 10, 1994, the AICPA Accounting Standards Executive Committee issued an exposure draft of a proposed statement of position (SOP), Reporting by Real Estate Companies of Supplemental Current-Value Information. As described in the exposure draft, the measurement of current value would consider the entity's intent and ability to realize asset values and settle liabilities. In addition, the reported amounts would represent the values of specific balance sheet elements—not the value of the entity as a whole. The AICPA has attempted to ensure that the final SOP, when and if issued, will serve solely as the basis for optional supplemental disclosure and not as the framework for an "other comprehensive basis of accounting" (OCBOA).

The exposure draft was developed from the AICPA Real Estate Committee's 1984 Guidance for an Experiment on Reporting Current Value Information for Real Estate, which provided for a comprehensive approach and a piecemeal approach to the presentation of current value information. Although the piecemeal approach is not discouraged, the current project focuses primarily on the comprehensive approach, in which all assets and liabilities are reported at their current amounts in balance sheet form.

Both the Experiment and the exposure draft recommend presentation of current value information side-by-side with the corresponding GAAP information in comparative form. Although the Experiment discussed the idea of including current value statements of operating performance and changes in equity, those statements are not addressed in the exposure draft. Instead, the exposure draft focuses on the disclosure of interperiod changes in revaluation equity—the difference between (1) the net current value of assets and liabilities and (2) the corresponding net carrying amount determined in conformity with GAAP.

(i) Deferred Taxes. The reporting of the deferred income tax liability in the current value balance sheet has been controversial. The exposure draft would permit either of the following two methods to be used in determining the deferred income tax liability to be reported in the current value balance sheet:

- Method 1—The reported deferred income tax liability is equal to the discounted amount of the estimated future tax payments, adjusted for the use of existing net operating loss carryforwards or other carryforwards. The determination of the deferred income tax liability is based on the enacted income tax rates and regulations at the balance sheet date (even if not in effect at that date). The exposure draft contains a deemed sale provision at the end of the fifteenth year, with the discounted amount of the tax that would be paid on such a sale included in the reported liability.
- Method 2—The reported deferred income tax liability is based on enacted rates and regulations at the balance sheet date (even if not in effect at that date). The enacted rate is multiplied by the difference between the current value of total net assets and liabilities and their tax bases, adjusted for the use of existing net operating loss carryforwards or other carryforwards. Although this method of determining the anticipated tax liability is conceptually inconsistent with the principle of determining current value based on the discounted amount of estimated future cash flows, the method was included in the exposure draft because it is easy to apply as a result of the fact that it reflects the effect of an immediate and complete liquidation of the reporting entity's portfolio.

(e) ACCOUNTING BY PARTICIPATING MORTGAGE LOAN BORROWERS. On July 5, 1995, the AICPA issued an exposure draft of a proposed statement of position (SOP), Accounting by Participating Mortgage Loan Borrowers. The proposed SOP would establish the borrower's accounting for a participating mortgage loan if the lender participates in increases in the market value of the mortgaged real estate project, the results of operations of that mortgaged real estate project or both. This proposed SOP requires the following:

- At origination, the borrower should record the participating mortgage loan without allocating any of the proceeds to a liability related to the participating feature.
- At the end of each reporting period, a participation liability should be reported equal to the amount that would be required to extinguish the participation liability if (a) the participating mortgage loan matured or was refinanced at that date, or (b) the mortgaged property was sold at that date. When establishing or adjusting the participation liability, the corresponding charge or credit should be to debt discount.
- As estimates of the participation liability change because of changes in estimates of the market value of the property, the borrower should recalculate the effective interest rate to reflect the changes in expected future payments. The borrower should recalculate that rate assuming that (a) the amount of the expected future payment will be paid on the due date of the loan and (b) the recalculated expected future payment amount was known at the inception of the loan. The debt discount related to the participation liability should be adjusted, with a corresponding charge or credit to interest expense, to the amount that would have existed had the new effective interest rate been applied since the origination of the participating mortgage loan.
- Certain disclosures, such as aggregate loan amounts, loan terms and the effect of cumulative adjustments, must be included in the financial statements.

This proposed SOP would be effective for fiscal years beginning after June 15, 1996.

24.10 SOURCES AND SUGGESTED REFERENCES

Accounting Principles Board, "The Equity Method of Accounting for Investments in Common Stock," APB Opinion No. 18, Interpretation No. 18-2, AICPA, New York, November 1971.

————, "The Equity Method of Accounting for Investments in Common Stock," APB Opinion No. 18, AICPA, New York, March 1971.

————, "Accounting Changes," APB Opinion No. 20, AICPA, New York, 1971.

————, "Interest on Receivables and Payables," APB Opinion No. 21, AICPA, New York, August 1971.

————, "Disclosure of Accounting Policies," APB Opinion No. 22, AICPA, New York, April 1972.

American Institute of Certified Public Accountants, "Inventory Pricing," "Restatement and Revision of Accounting Research Bulletins," Accounting Research Bulletin No. 43, AICPA, New York, June 1953.

————, "Long-Term Construction-Type Contracts," Accounting Research Bulletin No. 45, AICPA, New York, October 1955.

————, "Audit and Accounting Guide for Construction Contractors," Accounting Guide, AICPA, New York, 1981.

————, "Guide for the Use of Real Estate Appraisal Information," Accounting Guide, AICPA, New York, 1987.

————, Issues Paper on "Accounting for Allowances for Losses on Certain Real Estate and Loans and Receivables Collaterialized by Real Estate," AICPA, New York, June 1979.

————, "Accounting Practices of Real Estate Investment Trusts," Statement of Position No. 75-2, AICPA, New York, June 27, 1975.

————, "Accounting for Costs to Sell and Rent, and Initial Real Estate Operations of, Real Estate Projects," Statement of Position No. 78-3, AICPA, New York, 1978.

————, "Accounting for Investments in Real Estate Ventures," Statement of Position No. 78-9, AICPA, New York, December 29, 1978.

————, "Accounting for Real Estate Acquisition, Development and Construction Costs," Statement of Position No. 80-3, AICPA, New York, 1980.

————, "Accounting for Performance of Construction-Type and Certain Production-Type Contracts," Statement of Position 81-1, AICPA, New York, July 15, 1981.

————, Third Notice to Practitioners, "Accounting for Real Estate Acquisition, Development, and Construction Arrangements," AICPA, New York, February 10, 1986.

Financial Accounting Standards Board, "Acquisition, Development, and Construction Loans," EITF Issue No. 84-4, FASB, Stamford, CT, 1984.

————, "Recognition of Receipts from Made-Up Rental Shortfalls," EITF Issue No. 85-27, FASB, Stamford, CT, 1985.

————, "Antispeculation Clauses in Real Estate Sales Contracts," EITF Issue No. 86-6, FASB, Stamford, CT, 1986.

————, "Application of the AICPA Notice to Practitioners Regarding Acquisition, Development, and Construction Arrangements to the Acquisition of an Operating Property," EITF Issue No. 86-21, FASB, Stamford, CT, 1986.

————, EITF Abstracts: A Summary of Proceedings of the FASB Emerging Issues Task Force, "Profit Recognition on Sale of Real Estate with Insurance Mortgages on Surety Bonds," EITF Issue No. 87-9, FASB, Norwalk, CT, 1988.

————, "Effect of Various Forms of Financing under FASB Statement No. 66," EITF Issue No. 88-24, FASB, Norwalk, CT, 1988.

————, "Accounting for Leases," Statement of Financial Accounting Standards No. 13, FASB, Stamford, CT, November 1976.

————, "Financial Reporting for Segments of a Business Enterprise," Statement of Financial Accounting Standards No. 14, FASB, Stamford, CT, 1976.

————, "Accounting for Sales with Leasebacks (an amendment of FASB Statement No. 13)," Statement of Financial Accounting Standards No. 28, FASB, Stamford, CT, 1979.

————, "Determining Contingent Rentals (an amendment of FASB Statement No. 13)," Statement of Financial Accounting Standards No. 29, FASB, Stamford, CT, 1979.

————, "Capitalization of Interest Cost," Statement of Financial Accounting Standards No. 34, FASB, Stamford, CT, October 1979.

————, "Designation of AICPA Guide and Statement of Position (SOP) 81-1 on Contractor Accounting and SOP 81-2 Concerning Hospital-Related Organizations as Preferable for Purposes of Applying APB Opinion 20," Statement of Financial Accounting Standards No. 56, FASB, Stamford, CT, February 1982.

————, "Accounting for Sales of Real Estate," Statement of Financial Accounting Standards No. 66, FASB, Stamford, CT, October 1982.

————, "Accounting for Costs and Initial Rental Operations of Real Estate Projects," Statement of Financial Accounting Standards No. 67, FASB, Stamford, CT, October 1982.

————, "Consolidation of all Majority-Owned Subsidiaries," Statement of Financial Accounting Standards No. 94, FASB, Stamford, CT, October 1987.

————, "Statement of Cash Flows," Statement of Financial Accounting Standards No. 95, FASB, Stamford, CT, November 1987.

————, "Accounting for the Impairment of Long-Lived Assets and for Long-Lived Assets to Be Disposed Of," Statement of Financial Accounting Standards No. 121, FASB, Norwalk, CT, March 1995.

————, "Accounting for Leases," Statement of Financial Accounting Standards No. 98, FASB, Norwalk, CT, May 1988.

————, "Accounting for Operating Leases with Scheduled Rent Increases," FASB Technical Bulletin No. 85-3, FASB, Stamford, CT, November 1985.

————, "Issues Relating to Accounting for Leases," FASB Technical Bulletin No. 88-1, FASB, Norwalk, CT, December 1988.

Klink, James J., *Real Estate Accounting and Reporting: A Guide for Developers, Investors, and Lenders,* 2nd ed., Wiley, New York, 1985.

Price Waterhouse, "Accounting for Condominium Sales," New York, 1984.

————, "Accounting for Sales of Real Estate," New York, 1983.

————, "Cost Accounting for Real Estate," New York, 1983.

————, "Investor Accounting for Real Estate Ventures," New York, 1979.

Securities and Exchange Commission, "Reporting Cash Flow and Other Related Data," Financial Reporting Policy 202, SEC, Washington, DC.

————, "Requirement for Financial Statements of Special Purpose Limited Partnerships," Financial Reporting Policy 405, SEC, Washington, DC.

————, "Preparation of Registration Statements Relating to Interests in Real Estate Limited Partnerships," Guide 5, SEC, Washington, DC.

————, "Special Instructions for Real Estate Operations to Be Acquired," Regulation S-X, Article 3, Rule 3-14, SEC, Washington, DC.

————, "Consolidation of Financial Statements of the Registrant and its Subsidiaries," Regulation S-X, Article 3A, Rule 3A-02, SEC, Washington, DC.

————, "Views on Financial Statements of Properties Securing Mortgage Loans," Staff Accounting Bulletin 71-71A (Topic No. 1I), SEC, Washington, DC.

————, "Offsetting Assets and Liabilities," Staff Accounting Bulletin Topic No. 11D, SEC, Washington, DC.

CHAPTER **25**

FINANCIAL INSTITUTIONS

William J. Lewis, CPA and Linda K. Seitz, CPA

Price Waterhouse LLP, Banks and Savings Institutions

Maryann E. Murphy, CPA and Keith E. Olson, CPA

Price Waterhouse LLP, Mortgage Banking Activities

Thomas J. Romeo, CPA and Gary C. Meltzer, CPA

Price Waterhouse LLP, Investment Companies

Mary B. Heath, CPA and Mary Ann Masucci, CPA

Price Waterhouse LLP, Taxation

CONTENTS

25.1 OVERVIEW

(a) CHANGING ENVIRONMENT.   The financial institutions industry has changed significantly in the last decade. Regulatory changes and increased competition have further blurred the lines between depository institutions, mortgage banking activities, investment companies, credit unions, investment banks, insurance companies, finance companies, and securities brokers and dealers. Anticipated future regulatory changes such as merging depository institution charters, further regulating derivatives, repealing Glass-Steagall (which effectively prohibits commercial banks from underwriting securities or otherwise engaging in investment banking activities), and the possibility of granting insurance powers to banks may, in the future, make today's blurred lines appear virtually transparent.

Competition has increased, as all types of financial entities conduct business directly with potential depositors and borrowers. Transactions traditionally executed through depository institutions are now handled by all types of financial institutions. Increased competition has heightened the depository institutions' desire for innovative approaches to attracting depositors and borrowers, higher levels of noninterest income and continued consolidation and restructuring of banking operations.

New interstate banking laws passed in 1994, combined with increased competition may result in further consolidation within the financial institutions industry. Acquisitions and mergers between and among the types of financial institutions could magnify the consolidation process.

(b) ROLE IN THE ECONOMY.   Financial institutions in their basic role provide a medium of exchange; however, they may also serve as a tool to regulate the economy. In a complex financial and economic environment, the regulation of financial institutions—directly and indirectly—is used to impact economic activity.

(c) TYPES OF FINANCIAL INSTITUTIONS.   Many types of financial institutions exist. The more common types are described. In view of the range and diversity within financial institutions, this chapter will focus on three major types of entities/activities—banks and savings institutions, mortgage banking activities, and investment companies.

(i) Banks and Savings Institutions.   Banks and savings institutions (including thrifts) continue in their traditional role as financial intermediaries. They provide a link between entities that have capital and entities that need capital; and also provide an efficient means for payment and transfer of funds between entities. Banks also provide a wide range of services to their customers, such as cash management and fiduciary services.

More recently, global and larger domestic bank holding companies have begun forming subsidiaries to engage in securities activities. Many bankers and politicians believe Glass-Steagall and the Bank Holding Company Act will be repealed and that the results will be new definitions for banks and savings institutions, as well as for other financial institutions.

(ii) Mortgage Banking Activities.   Mortgage banking activities include the origination, sale, and servicing of mortgage loans. Mortgage loan origination activities are performed by entities such as mortgage banks, mortgage brokers, credit unions, and commercial banks and savings institutions. Mortgages are purchased by government-sponsored entities, sponsors of mortgage-backed security programs, and private companies such as insurance companies, other mortgage banking entities, and pension funds.

(iii) Investment Companies.   Investment companies pool shareholders' funds to provide the shareholders with professional investment management. Typically, an investment company sells its capital shares to the public, invests the proceeds to achieve its investment objectives, and distributes to its shareholders the net income and net gains realized on the sale of its investments. The types of investment companies include management investment companies, unit investment trusts, collective trust funds, investment partnerships, certain separate accounts of insurance companies, and offshore funds.

Investment companies grew significantly in the early 1990s, primarily due to growth in mutual funds. More recently, many investment companies are adopting complex capital structures to increase flexibility in pricing and access to alternative distribution channels.

(iv) Credit Unions.   Credit unions are member-owned, not-for-profit cooperative financial institutions, organized around a defined membership. The members pool their savings, borrow funds, and obtain other related financial services. A credit union relies on volunteers who represent the members. Its primary objective is to provide services to its members, rather than to generate earnings for its owners.

More recently, many credit unions have made arrangements to share branch offices with other credit unions and depository institutions to reduce operating costs.

(v) Investment Banks.   Investment banks or merchant banks deal with the financing requirements of corporations and institutions. They may be organized as corporations or partnerships.

(vi) Insurance Companies.   The primary purpose of insurance is the spreading of risks. The two major types of insurance are life, and property and liability. The primary purpose of life insurance is to provide financial assistance at the time of death. It typically has a long period of coverage. Property and liability insurance companies provide policies to individuals (personal lines) and to business enterprises (commercial lines). Examples of personal lines include homeowner's and individual automobile policies. Examples of commercial lines include general liability and workers' compensation.

Banks, mutual funds, and health maintenance organizations are aggressively trying to expand into products traditionally sold by insurance companies. Also, the potential impact on insurance companies from health care reform remains uncertain.

(vii) Finance Companies.   Finance companies provide lending and financing services to consumers (consumer financing) and to business enterprises (commercial financing). Some finance companies engage solely in consumer or commercial financing; others provide both types. Subgroups within the finance company sector include diversified finance, mortgage finance, credit card, and leasing companies. Captive finance entities represent manufacturers, retailers, wholesalers, and other business enterprises who provide financing to encourage customers to buy their products and services. Captive financing may be provided directly by the company or through affiliated companies. Many captive finance companies have expanded their financing activities to include a wide range of products and services sold by unaffiliated businesses.

More recently, mortgage finance companies and diversified finance companies have increased their presence by increasing the number of loans made to higher risk niches at higher yields.

(viii) Securities Brokers and Dealers. Securities brokers and dealers perform various functions within the securities industry. Brokers, acting in an agency capacity, buy and sell securities and commodities for their customers and charge a commission. Dealers or traders, acting in a principal capacity, buy and sell for their own account and trade with customers and other dealers. In addition to buying and selling securities and commodities, securities brokers and dealers may underwrite or participate in the underwriting of securities, assist in the private placement of securities, offer investment advisory services, extend credit to customers who have purchased securities on margin, and act as depositories in holding securities owned by their customers. Securities brokers and dealers may market highly specialized investments, such as oil and gas and real estate participations, livestock programs, and equipment leasing ventures.

More recently, globalization of the securities and commodities industry continues and many broker-dealers are placing additional emphasis on accessing new markets.

(ix) Real Estate Investment Trusts. The new class of real estate investment trusts (REITs) (those formed since 1991) basically are self-contained real estate companies. They are designed to align the interests of active management and passive investors, to generate cash flow growth and create long-term value. These newer REITs are very different from the leveraged construction lenders caught in the last REIT crash of the mid-1970s.

25.2 BANKS AND SAVINGS INSTITUTIONS

(a) PRIMARY RISKS OF BANKS AND SAVINGS INSTITUTIONS. General business and economic risk factors exist for many industries; however, increased competition among banks and savings institutions and within the financial institution industry has resulted in the industry's aggressive pursuit of profitable activities. Techniques for managing assets and liabilities and financial risks have been enhanced in order to maximize income levels. Technological advances have accommodated increasingly complex transactions such as the sale of securities backed by cash flows from other financial assets. Regulatory policy has radically changed the business environment for banks, savings, and other financial institutions. Additionally, there are other risk factors common to most banks and savings institutions, based on their business activities. The other primary risk factors are described next.

(i) Interest-Rate Risk. This is the risk that adverse movements in interest rates may result in loss of profits since banks and savings institutions routinely earn on assets at one rate and pay on liabilities at another rate. Techniques used to minimize interest-rate risk are a part of asset/liability management.

(ii) Liquidity Risk. This is the risk that an institution may be unable to meet its obligations as they become due. An institution may acquire funds short-term and lend funds long-term to obtain favorable interest rate spreads thus creating liquidity risk if depositors or creditors demand repayment.

(iii) Asset-Quality Risk. This is the risk that the loss of expected cash flows due to, for example, loan defaults and inadequate collateral, will result in significant losses. Examples include credit losses from loans and declines in the economic value of mortgage servicing rights, resulting from prepayments of principal during periods of falling interest rates.

(iv) Fiduciary Risk. This is the risk of loss arising from failure to properly process transactions or handle the custody, management, or both, of financial related assets on behalf of third parties. Examples include administering trusts, managing mutual funds, and servicing the collateral behind asset-backed securities.

(v) Processing Risk.   This is the risk that transactions will not be processed accurately or timely, due to large volumes, short periods of time, unauthorized access of computerized records, or the demands placed on both computerized and manual systems. Examples include electronic funds transfers, loan servicing, and check processing.

(vi) Disclosures of Certain Significant Risks and Uncertainties.   AICPA Statement of Position (SOP) 94-6, "Disclosure of Certain Significant Risks and Uncertainties," requires institutions to include in their financial statements disclosures about (1) the nature of their operations and (2) the use of estimates in the preparation of their financial statements.

SOP 94-6 also requires disclosure regarding:

> *Certain Significant Estimates.* Estimates used in the determination of the carrying amounts of assets or liabilities or in gain or loss contingencies is required to be disclosed when information available prior to issuance of the financial statements indicates that (a) it is at least reasonably possible that the estimate of the effect on the financial statements of a condition, situation, or set of circumstances that existed at the date of the financial statements will change in the near term due to one or more future confirming events, and (b) the effect of the change would be material to the financial statements.
>
> SOP 94-6 further states that (a) the disclosure should indicate the nature of the uncertainty and include an indication that it is at least reasonably possible that a change in the estimate will occur in the near term and (b) if the estimate involves a loss contingency covered by Statement of Financial Accounting Standards (SFAS) No. 5, "Accounting for Contingencies," the disclosure should also include an estimate of the possible loss or range of loss, or state that such an estimate cannot be made.
>
> *Current Vulnerability Due to Certain Concentrations.* Institutions are required to disclose concentrations, as defined in the Statement, if based on information known to management prior to issuance of the financial statements, (a) the concentration exists at the date of the financial statements, (b) the concentration makes the institution vulnerable to the risk of a near-term severe impact, and (c) it is at least reasonably possible that the events that could cause the severe impact will occur in the near term.

(b) REGULATION AND SUPERVISION OF BANKS AND SAVINGS INSTITUTIONS.
The permissible activities of banks are governed by federal and state regulations, which in some cases prohibit the conduct of interstate banking. These restrictions gave rise to the development of the bank holding companies during the early part of the century. The Bank Holding Company Act of 1956 (Act of 1956) was enacted to regulate the types of services these companies could offer that are broader in scope than those permissible under banking regulations. Under the Act of 1956, bank holding companies may engage in various activities, in addition to the more traditional banking functions, including:

- Mortgage banking.
- Finance companies for general, consumer, and commercial activities.
- Leasing.
- Debt and equity investments in qualifying community development projects.
- Investment, financial, and economic advisory services.
- Securities brokerage and futures commissions merchant activities.
- Underwriting certain credit-related insurances.
- Real estate and personal property appraising.

In addition, on a case-by-case basis, the Federal Reserve Board may allow even greater powers to bank holding companies. For example, since 1987, the Federal Reserve Board has allowed separately capitalized bank holding company subsidiaries to engage in limited securities underwriting and dealing—"Section 20" powers.

(c) REGULATORY BACKGROUND.   Banks and savings institutions have special privileges and protections granted by government. These incentives, such as credit through the Federal Reserve System and federal insurance of deposits, have not been similarly extended to commercial enterprises. Accordingly, the benefits and responsibilities associated with their public role as financial intermediaries have brought banks and savings institutions under significant governmental oversight.

As a result of the financial repercussions of the Great Depression, the government took certain measures to maintain the stability of the country's financial system. Several new regulatory and supervisory agencies were created to promote economic stability, particularly in the banking industry, and strengthen the regulatory and supervisory agencies that were in existence at the time. Among the agencies created were the Federal Deposit Insurance Corporation (FDIC), the Securities and Exchange Commission (SEC), the Federal Home Loan Bank Board (FHLBB), and the Federal Savings and Loan Insurance Corporation (FSLIC). The agencies that were strengthened included the Office of the Comptroller of the Currency (OCC) and the Federal Reserve System (FRS). These entities were responsible for designing and establishing policies and procedures for the regulation and supervision of national and state banks, foreign banks doing business in the United States, and other depository institutions. This regulatory and supervisory structure, created during the 1930s, was in place for almost 60 years. During 1989, congress enacted the Financial Institutions Reform, Recovery and Enforcement Act (FIRREA), which changed the regulatory and supervisory structure of thrift institutions. FIRREA eliminated the FHLBB and the FSLIC. In their place, it created the Office of Thrift Supervision (OTS) as the primary regulator of the thrift industry and the Savings Association Insurance Fund (SAIF) as the thrift institutions' insurer to be administered by the FDIC.

Even though several of the aforementioned federal agencies have overlapping regulatory and supervisory responsibilities over depository institutions, in general terms, the OCC has primary responsibility for national banks; the FRS has primary responsibility over state banks that are members of the FRS, all bank holding companies and their non-bank subsidiaries and most U.S. branches of foreign banks; the FDIC has primary responsibility for all state-insured banks that are not members of the FRS (nonmember banks); and the OTS has primary responsibility for thrift institutions. Exhibit 25.1 lists these regulatory responsibilities.

Bank Classifications*	OCC	State Banking Department	Federal Reserve	FDIC
National banks	X			
State banks and trust companies				
Federal Reserve members		X	X	
Nonmembers				
FDIC insured		X		X
Mutual Savings Banks		X		X
Noninsured		X		
Bank holding companies			X	

*All national banks are members of the Federal Reserve System. All national banks and state chartered member banks are insured by the FDIC.

Exhibit 25.1.   Regulatory supervision.

(i) Office of the Comptroller of the Currency (OCC).   The OCC was created in 1863 by the National Currency Act, later renamed the National Bank Act. The OCC is under the general direction of the Secretary of the Treasury. The Comptroller is appointed by the President, subject to Senate confirmation. The OCC shares the responsibility for regulating and supervising the banking industry with the FRS and the FDIC. Its primary objective is to promote safety and stability within the national banking system by regulating, supervising, and assessing the condition of national banks.

A national bank must obtain the approval of the OCC before it can be organized to do business. Once created, national banks must report continuously to the OCC and submit to its extensive regulating activities. The regulatory and supervisory functions of the OCC include:

- Examining national banks and federal branches of foreign banks as often as it deems necessary.
- Overseeing the organization, conversion, merger, establishment of branches, relocation, and dissolution of national banks.
- Determining insolvency and referring insolvent banks to the FDIC.
- Administering the registration and reporting requirements of the 1934 Act as applied to national banks.

(ii) Federal Reserve System (FRS).   The FRS was created by Congress in 1913 by the Federal Reserve Act. The primary role of the FRS is to establish and conduct monetary policy, as well as to regulate and supervise a wide range of financial activities. The structure of the FRS includes a board of governors, the Federal Reserve banks, and the member banks. The board of governors consists of seven members appointed by the President, subject to Senate confirmation. National banks must be members of the FRS. State banks are not required to, but may elect to become members. The member banks and other financial institutions are required to keep reserves with the FRS and member banks must subscribe to the capital stock of the reserve bank in the district to which they belong.

Since all national banks are supervised by the OCC, the FRS primarily regulates and supervises member state banks, including administering the registration and reporting requirements of the 1934 Act.

The regulatory and supervisory functions and other services provided by the FRS include:

- Examining the Federal Reserve banks, state member banks, bank holding companies, their nonbank subsidiaries, and state licensed U.S. branches of foreign banks.
- Requiring reports of member and other banks.
- Setting discount rate.
- Issuing loans to members and other depository institutions.
- Approving or denying FRS membership applications and applications for branches, mergers, or creation of bank holding companies.
- Supplying currency when needed.
- Regulating foreign transactions of its member banks and the transactions of foreign banks doing business in the United States.
- Enforcing legislation and issuing rules and regulations dealing with "truth in lending."
- Issuing regulations to prevent deceptive and unfair bank practices.
- Providing procedures for transfer of funds throughout the country.

(iii) Federal Deposit Insurance Corporation (FDIC).   The FDIC was created under the Banking Act of 1933. The main purpose for its creation was to insure bank deposits in order to maintain economic stability in the event of bank failures. FIRREA restructured the FDIC during

1989 to carry out broadened functions by insuring thrift institutions as well as banks. Therefore, the FDIC now insures all depository institutions except credit unions.

The FDIC is an independent agency of the U.S. government, managed by a five-member board of directors, consisting of the Comptroller of the Currency, the Director of the Office of Thrift Supervision, and three other members appointed by the President, subject to Senate confirmation.

The FDIC insures deposits under two separate funds—the Bank Insurance Fund and the Savings Association Insurance Fund (SAIF). From its Bank Insurance Fund, the FDIC insures national and state banks that are members of the FRS. These institutions are required to be insured. Also insured from this fund are state nonmember banks and branches of foreign banks, which are not required to be insured by the FDIC, but may elect to do so.

From its SAIF, the FDIC insures all federal savings and loan associations and federal savings banks. These institutions are required to be insured. The state thrift institutions are also insured from this fund.

Currently, each account, subject to certain FDIC rules, in a depository institution is insured to a maximum of $100,000. Other responsibilities of the FDIC include:

- Administering the registration and reporting requirements of the 1934 Act as applied to state nonmember banks.
- Supervising the liquidation of insolvent insured depository institutions.
- Providing financial support and additional measures to prevent insured depository institution failures.
- Supervising state nonmember insured banks by conducting bank examinations, regulating bank mergers, consolidations, and establishment of branches and establishing other regulatory controls.

(iv) Office of Thrift Supervision (OTS). During 1989, FIRREA created the OTS under the Department of the Treasury. The OTS regulates federal and state thrift institutions and thrift holding companies. As a principal rule maker, examiner, and enforcement agency, OTS exercises primary regulatory authority to grant federal thrift institution charters, approve branching applications, and allow mutual-to-thrift charter conversions. OTS is headed by a presidentially appointed director. The 12 district Federal Home Loan Banks continue to be the primary source of credit for thrift institutions.

(d) REGULATORY ENVIRONMENT. The early 1980s were marked by the removal of interest-rate ceilings, changes in reserve requirements, powers, and related deregulatory actions. However, significant losses incurred in the late 1980s are early 1990s by the federal government as a result of insured deposit taking institution failures, drove legislators in 1989 and 1991 to increase regulatory oversight. Both FIRREA and the Federal Deposit Insurance Corporation Improvement Act of 1991 (FDICIA) were directed toward protection of federal deposit insurance funds through early detection of and intervention in problem institutions, with an emphasis on capital adequacy.

In addition to safety and soundness considerations, current banking regulations recognize economic issues, such as the desire for banks and savings institutions to successfully compete with other, less regulated, financial services providers, as well as to address social issues, such as community reinvestment, nondiscrimination and fair treatment in consumer credit, including residential lending. Costs and benefits of regulations are weighed as the approach to regulation of the industry is redefined.

(e) FDICIA SECTION 112. Regulations implementing Section 36 of the Federal Deposit Insurance Act ("FDI Act"), as added by Section 112 of FDICIA became effective July 2, 1993. These regulations imposed additional audit, reporting, and attestation responsibilities on management, directors (especially the audit committee), internal auditors, and independent accountants of banks and savings institutions with $500 million or more in total assets. The reporting requirements were effective for fiscal years ending on or after December 31, 1993.

(i) The Regulation and Guidelines.   The regulation itself is skeletal—only about 800 words; however, it is accompanied by Appendix A to Part 363—Guidelines and Interpretations that contain 37 guidelines, providing an explanation to its meaning and operation. The guidelines often leave discretion with an institution or its board, while simultaneously providing guidance that, if followed, would provide a safe harbor from examiner criticism.

(ii) Basic Requirements.   Each FDIC-insured depository institution with assets in excess of $500 million at the beginning of its fiscal year ("covered institutions") is subject to the following requirements:

Annual Report. Covered institutions must file an annual report, within 90 days of its fiscal year end, with the FDIC and its other appropriate state or federal bank regulator. The annual report must include:

(a) Audited financial statements prepared in accordance with GAAP and audited by an Independent Public Accountant (IPA) meeting the qualifications.

(b) A management report signed by its chief executive and chief financial officer or chief accounting officer containing:

  • A statement of management's responsibilities for:

    —Preparing the annual financial statements.

    —Establishing and maintaining an adequate internal control structure and procedures for financial reporting.

    —Complying with particular laws designated by the FDIC as affecting the safety and soundness of insured depositories.

  • Assessment by management of:

    —The effectiveness of the institution's internal control structure and procedures for financial reporting as of the end of the fiscal year.

    —The institution's compliance, during the fiscal year, with the designated safety and soundness laws. The FDIC designated only two kinds of safety and soundness laws to be addressed in the compliance report: (1) federal statutes and regulations concerning transactions with insiders, and (2) federal and state statutes and regulations restricting the payment of dividends.

(c) An attestation report, by an IPA, on internal control structure and procedures for financial reporting. The institution's IPA must examine, attest to, and report separately on, management's assertions about internal controls and about compliance. The attestations are to be made in accordance with generally accepted standards for attestation engagements. FDIC has established procedures for IPAs to follow in testing compliance. A covered institution may elect to have its internal auditors perform these procedures. If it does so, the IPA then must review the work of internal auditors and test a limited sample of transactions.

On February 6, 1996, the Board of the FDIC amended the procedures that IPAs follow in testing compliance to streamline the procedures and to reduce regulatory burden.

Audit Committee. Covered institutions must establish an independent audit committee comprised of directors who are independent of management. An audit of a "large" (total assets in excess of $3 billion, measured as of the beginning of each fiscal year) bank or thrift must meet additional qualifications. The entire board of directors annually is required to adopt a resolution documenting its determination that the audit committee has met all FDIC-imposed requirements.

The audit committee is required to review with management and the IPA the basis for the reports required by the FDIC's regulation. FDIC suggests, but does not mandate, additional audit committee duties, including overseeing internal audit, selecting the IPA, and reviewing significant accounting policies.

Each subject institution must provide its independent accountant with copies of the institution's most recent reports of condition and examination; any supervisory memorandum of understanding or written agreement with any federal or state regulatory agency; and a report of any action initiated or taken by federal or state banking regulators.

(iii) Holding Company Exception.   The requirements of the FDIC's regulation, in some instances, may be satisfied by a bank's or savings association's parent holding company. The requirement for audited financial statements always may be satisfied by providing audited financial statements of the consolidated holding company. The requirements for other reports, as well as for an independent audit committee, may be satisfied by the holding company if:

(a) The holding company's services and functions are comparable to those required of the depository institution.
(b) The depository institution has total assets as of the beginning of the fiscal year either of:
  (i) Less than $5 billion, or
  (ii) Equal to or greater than $5 billion and a CAMEL composite rating of 1 or 2. Section 314(a) of the Riegle Community Development and Regulatory Improvement Act of 1994 amended Section 36(i) of the FDI Act to expand the holding company exception to equal to or greater than $5 billion. The requirement that the institution must have a CAMEL composite rating of 1 or 2 remained unchanged.

The appropriate federal banking agency may revoke the exception for any institution with total assets in excess of $9 billion for any period of time during which the appropriate federal banking agency determines that the institution's exception would create a significant risk to the affected deposit insurance fund.

(iv) Availability of Reports.   All of management's reports are made publicly available. The independent accountant's report on the financial statements and attestation report on financial reporting controls is also made publicly available. The independent accountant's agreed-upon procedures report and any management letter, while filed with the FDIC, and the appropriate federal banking agency (and any appropriate state bank supervisor) are not included in the annual report and, therefore, are not publicly available.

(f) CAPITAL ADEQUACY GUIDELINES.   Capital is one of the primary tools used by regulators to monitor the financial health of insured banks and savings institutions. Statutorily mandated supervisory intervention is focused primarily on an institution's capital levels relative to regulatory standards. The federal banking agencies detail these requirements in their respective regulations under capital adequacy guidelines. The capital adequacy requirements are implemented through quarterly regulatory financial reporting ("Call Reports" and "Thrift Financial Reports").

(i) Risk-Based and Leverage Ratios.   Capital adequacy is measured mainly through two risk-based capital ratios and a leverage ratio, with thrifts subject to an additional tangible capital ratio.

(ii) Tier I and Tier II Components.   Regulatory capital is composed of two components: core capital or Tier I, and supplementary capital or Tier II. Tier I capital includes elements such as: common stock, surplus, retained earnings, minority interest in consolidated subsidiaries and qualifying preferred stock. Tier II capital includes, with certain limitations, elements such as: general loan loss reserves, certain forms of preferred stock, qualifying term subordinated debt, perpetual debt and other hybrid debt/equity instruments. Tier II capital elements individually and together are variously restricted in proportion to Tier I capital, which is intended to be the dominant capital component. Certain deductions are made to determine regulatory capital, including: goodwill and other disallowed intangibles, excess portions of qualifying intangibles and deferred tax assets, investments in unconsolidated subsidiaries, and reciprocal holdings of other bank's capital instruments. Adjustments made to equity under generally accepted accounting principles for unrealized gains and losses on debt and equity securities available for sale under FASB Statement No. 115 are excluded from Tier I and Total Capital, except for unrealized losses on equity securities available for sale with readily determinable market values. Any regulatory capital deduction is also made to average total assets for ratio computation purposes. A thrift's tangible capital is generally defined as Tier I capital less intangibles.

(iii) Risk-Weighted Assets.   The capital ratios are calculated using the applicable regulatory capital component in the numerator and either risk-weighted assets or total adjusted on-balance sheet assets as the denominator, as appropriate. Risk-weighted assets are ascertained pursuant to the regulatory guidelines which allocate gross average assets among four categories of risk weights (0%, 20%, 50%, and 100%). The allocations are based mainly on type of asset, type of obligor, and nature of collateral, if any. Gross assets include on-balance sheet assets, credit equivalents of certain off-balance exposures, and certain assets sold with recourse that are treated as financings for regulatory reporting purposes.

Credit equivalents of off-balance sheet exposures are determined by the nature of the exposure. For example, direct credit substitutes (e.g., standby letters of credit) are credit converted at 100% of the face amount. Other off-balance sheet activities are subject to the current exposure method, which is composed of the positive mark-to-market value (if any) and an estimate of the potential increase in credit exposure over the remaining life of the contract. These "add-ons" are estimated by applying defined credit conversion factors, differentiated by type instrument and remaining maturity, to the contact's notional value.

(iv) Capital Calculations and Minimum Requirements.   The capital ratios, calculations, and minimum requirements are presented in Exhibit 25.2.

Federal regulators are currently considering further modifications to the risk-based capital rules to include interest rate risk and market risk elements in the regulatory capital adequacy calculations.

(g) PROMPT CORRECTIVE ACTION.   The federal banking agencies are statutorily mandated to assign each FDIC insured depository institution to one of five capital categories, quantitatively defined by the risk-based and leverage capital ratios.

Capital Ratio	Calculation	Minimum Requirement
Total risk-based ratio	Tier I + Tier II/Risk-weighted assets	≥ 8.0%
Tier I risk-based ratio	Tier I/Risk-weighted assets	≥ 4.0%
Tier I leverage capital ratio	Tier I/Average on-balance sheet assets	≥ 4.0%*
Tangible ratio (Thrifts)	Tangible capital/On-balance sheet assets	≥ 1.5%
* 3.0% for institutions CAMEL/MACRO rated "1" (overall).		

Exhibit 25.2.   Capital Ratio Calculations and Minimum Requirements.

1. *Well Capitalized.* If capital level significantly *exceeds* the required minimum level for each relevant capital category.

2. *Adequately Capitalized.* If capital level *meets* the minimum level.

3. *Undercapitalized.* If capital level *fails to meet one or more* of the minimum levels.

4. *Significantly Undercapitalized.* If capital level is *significantly below one or more* of the minimum levels.

5. *Critically Undercapitalized.* If the ratio of *tangible equity* (as statutorily defined) *to total assets is 2% or less.*

Institutions falling in the last three of these categories are subject to a variety of "prompt corrective actions," such as limitations on dividends, prohibitions on acquisitions and branching, restrictions on asset growth, and removal of officers and directors. Irrespective of the ratios reported, the agencies may downgrade an institution's capital category based on adverse examination findings.

The regulatory capital ratio ranges defining the "prompt corrective action" capital categories are summarized in Exhibit 25.3.

(h) REGULATORY EXAMINATIONS.   Federally insured banks and savings institutions are required to have periodic full-scope, on-site examinations by the appropriate agency. In certain cases, an examination by a state regulatory agency is accepted. Full-scope and other examinations are intended primarily to provide early identification of problems at insured institutions rather than as a basis for expressing an opinion in fair presentation of the institution's financial statements.

(i) Scope.   The scope of an examination is generally unique to each institution based on risk factors assessed by the examiner and some examinations are targeted to a specific area of operations, such as real estate lending or trust operations. Separate compliance examination programs also exist to address institutions' compliance with laws and regulations in areas such as consumer protection, insider transactions and reporting under the Bank Secrecy Act.

(ii) Regulatory Rating Systems.   Regulators use regulatory rating systems and assign ratings to banks, thrifts, holding companies, parents of foreign banks and U.S. branches and agencies of foreign banking organizations. The rating scales vary, although each is based on a 5-point system, with "1" (or "A") being the highest rating. The rating systems are presented in

Capital Category	Total Risk-Based Ratio		Tier 1 Risk-Based Ratio		Tier 1 Leverage Capital Ratio
Well capitalized	≥ 10%	and	≥ 6%	and	≥ 5%
Adequately capitalized	≥ 8%	and	≥ 4%	and	≥ 4%*
Undercapitalized	< 8%	or	< 4%	or	< 4%*
Significantly undercapitalized	< 6%	or	< 3%	or	< 3%
Critically undercapitalized	If the ratio of tangible equity (as statutorily defined) to total assets is 2% or less.				
* 3% for institutions that have a rating of "1" under the regulatory CAMEL, MACRO, or related rating system; that are not anticipating or experiencing significant growth; and that have well-diversified risk.					

Exhibit 25.3.   Regulatory Capital Categories.

Entity	Assigns Rating	Rating Scale	Rating Components
Banks and Thrifts	OCC, FDIC, OTS, and FRB	**CAMEL** Ratings 1–5	Capital adequacy Asset quality Management's performance Earnings Liquidity
Bank holding companies	FRB	**BOPEC** Ratings 1–5	Bank's CAMEL rating Operation of nonbanking subs. Parent's strength Earnings Capital adequacy
Parents of foreign banks with U.S. branches or agencies	FRB	**SOSA*** (Strength of Support Assessment) Ratings A–E.	General country factors. Institution specific issues. Ability of parent to maintain adequate internal controls and compliance with procedures in United States
U.S. branches and agencies of foreign banking organizations	FRB, OCC, and FDIC	**ROCA** Ratings 1–5	Risk management Operational controls Compliance Asset quality

* SOSA ratings will not be disclosed to the bank, branch, or home supervisor. Ratings are for U.S. internal supervisory use only.

Exhibit 25.4.   Regulatory Rating Systems.

Exhibit 25.4. Additionally, in November 1995, the FRB issued SR-95-51, "Rating the Adequacy of Risk Management Processes and Internal Controls at State Member Banks and Bank Holding Companies" stating that Federal Reserve System examiners, beginning in 1996, are instructed to assign a formal supervisory rating to the adequacy of an institution's risk management processes, including its internal controls.

(i) ENFORCEMENT ACTIONS.   Regulatory enforcement is carried out through a variety of informal and formal mechanisms. Informal enforcement measures are consensual between the bank and its regulator but not legally enforceable. Formal measures carry the force of law and are issued subject to certain legal procedures, requirements, and penalties. Examples of formal enforcement measures include ordering an institution to cease and desist from certain practices of violations, removing an officer, prohibiting an officer from participating in the affairs of the institution or the industry, assessing civil money penalties, and terminating insurance of an institution's deposits. As previously discussed, other mandatory and discretionary actions may be taken by regulators under "prompt corrective action" provisions of the Federal Deposit Insurance Act.

(j) DISCLOSURE OF CAPITAL MATTERS.   Beginning in 1996, the AICPAs *Audit Guide for Banks and Savings Institutions* will require that the GAAP financial statements of banks and savings associations include footnote disclosures of regulatory capital adequacy/prompt corrective action categories. The following describes the minimum disclosures:

1. A description of the regulatory capital requirements, including those established by the prompt corrective action provisions.
2. The actual or possible material effects of noncompliance with such requirements.

3. Whether the institution is in compliance with the regulatory capital requirements, including (1) the institution's required and actual ratios and amounts of Tier I leverage, Tier I risk-based, total risk-based capital, and for savings institutions, tangible capital and, (2) factors that may significantly affect capital adequacy such as potentially volatile components of capital, qualitative factors, and regulatory mandates.

4. The prompt corrective action category in which the institution was classified as of its most recent notification, as of each balance sheet date presented.

5. Whether management believes any conditions or events since notification have changed the institution's category, as of the most recent balance sheet date.

If, as of the most recent balance sheet date presented, the institution is either (1) not in compliance with capital adequacy requirements, (2) considered less than adequately capitalized under the prompt corrective action provisions, or (3) both, the possible material effects of such conditions and events on amounts and disclosures in the financial statements should be disclosed. Additional disclosures may be required where there is substantial doubt about the institution's ability to continue as a going concern.

As with all footnotes to the financial statements, any management representations included in the footnotes, such as with respect to capital matters, would be subject to review by the independent accountant.

(k) SECURITIES AND EXCHANGE COMMISSION (SEC)

(i) Background.   The SEC was created by Congress in 1934 to administer the Securities Act of 1933 (1933 Act) and the Securities Exchange Act of 1934 (1934 Act). The SEC is an independent agency of the U.S. government, consisting of five commissioners appointed by the President, subject to Senate confirmation.

The 1933 Act requires companies to register securities with the SEC before they may be sold, unless the security or the transaction is exempt. Banks are exempt from the registration requirements of the 1933 Act; however, bank holding companies and their nonbank subsidiaries are not. The 1934 Act, among other things, requires extensive and continuous reporting by companies that issue securities listed on the national exchanges or by companies with more than 500 security holders and more than $5 million in assets. Banks are not exempt from the requirements of the 1934 Act. However, the registration and reporting provisions related to banks are administered by the federal bank regulatory agencies instead of the SEC.

(ii) Reporting Requirements.   SEC registrants are required to comply with certain industry-specific financial statement requirements, set forth in Article 9 for Bank Holding Companies of SEC Regulation S-X. In addition, they must comply with other nonfinancial disclosures required by Guide 3 for Bank Holding Companies, of Regulation S-K.

In December 1995, the SEC released for comment proposed amendments to Regulation S-X, Regulation S-K, and various forms (collectively, the "proposal"). The proposal clarifies and expands existing requirements for financial statement footnote disclosures (for both dealers and corporate end-users) about accounting policies for derivatives and requires disclosures outside the financial statements of qualitative and quantitative information about the market risk inherent in derivatives and other financial instruments.

Additionally, the SEC is undertaking a review of Guide 3 to evaluate potential changes to improve the usefulness of financial institution disclosures.

(l) FINANCIAL STATEMENT PRESENTATION

(i) Income Statements.   Banks and savings institutions place heavy emphasis on the interest margin, that is, the difference between interest earned and the cost of funds. Accordingly, a specialized income statement format has evolved that focuses on net interest income. Supplemental income statement information may be provided separately to show the impact of investing in certain tax-exempt securities. Such "taxable equivalent" data purports to illustrate income statement data as if such tax-exempt securities were fully taxable.

(ii) Balance Sheets.   The balance sheets of banks and savings institutions are not classified into short-term and long-term categories for assets and liabilities but are generally presented in descending order of maturity. Supplemental information is also presented by many banking institutions showing average balances of assets and liabilities and the associated income or expense and average rates paid or earned.

(iii) Statements of Cash Flow.   The statements of cash flow are presented in accordance with SFAS No. 95, "Statement of Cash Flows," amended by SFAS No. 102, "Statement of Cash Flows-Exemption of Certain Enterprises and Classification of Cash Flows from Certain Securities Acquired for Resale (an amendment of FASB Statement No. 95)" and SFAS No. 104, "Statement of Cash Flows-Net Reporting of Certain Cash Receipts and Cash Payments and Classification of Cash Flows for Hedging Transactions (an amendment of FASB Statement No. 95)." The amendments permit certain financial institutions, such as banks and savings institutions to net the cash flows for selected activities such as trading, deposit taking, and loan activities.

(iv) Commitments and Off-Balance Sheet Risk.   Banks and savings institutions offer a variety of financial services and, accordingly, they enter into a wide range of financial transactions and issue a variety of financial instruments. Depending on the nature of these transactions, they may not appear on the balance sheet and are only disclosed in the footnotes to the financial statements. For further discussion regarding off-balance sheet risk refer to subsections 25.2(o) and 25.2(t).

(m) ACCOUNTING GUIDANCE.   In addition to the main body of professional accounting literature that comprises generally accepted accounting principles (GAAP), more specific industry guidance is provided in the industry-specific Audit and Accounting Guides published by the American Institute of Certified Public Accountants (AICPA), specifically "Banks and Savings Institutions" which is expected to be issued in 1996. Currently, the "Audit of Banks" and the "Audits of Savings Institutions" guides provide the authoritative guidance for banks and savings institutions. Additionally, the Emerging Issues Task Force (EITF) of the FASB addresses current issues.

(n) GAAP AND REGULATORY ACCOUNTING PRACTICES (RAP).   General purpose financial statements are prepared in accordance with GAAP; however, financial information provided to the regulatory agencies may be prepared on a RAP basis to satisfy specific regulatory objectives. Regulations require banks and savings institutions to file quarterly "Call Reports" and "Thrift Financial Reports (TFRs)," respectively. These quarterly reports are used by regulators as a basis for supervisory action, a source of statistical information, and for other purposes. The TFR is prepared on a basis consistent with GAAP; however, the Call Report requires certain accounting and reporting conventions which differ from GAAP.

The Federal Deposit Insurance (FDI) Act requires that other regulatory filings follow accounting principles consistent with GAAP. Regulators are permitted for regulatory reporting purposes to require an accounting principle that is no less stringent than GAAP if they believe the more stringent principle will (1) more accurately reflect the capital of insured banks and savings institutions, (2) provide for more effective supervision, and (3) better facilitate prompt corrective action and least-cost resolution of troubled institutions.

Examples of areas where accounting practices for regulatory Call Reporting purposes differ from GAAP include hedge accounting, excess servicing fee receivables, in-substance defeasance of debt, sales of assets with recourse, valuation of certain intangibles, and offsetting assets and liabilities.

In November 1995, the federal bank regulating agencies announced intent to eliminate RAP/GAAP differences in the Call Report by moving to GAAP beginning with the March 1997 reporting period.

(o) LOANS AND COMMITMENTS.   Loans are the most significant product of most banks and savings institutions and generate the largest proportion of their revenues. Institutions originate, purchase and sell (in whole or in part), and securitize loans. The parameters used to create the loan portfolio include many of the institution's key strategies, such as credit risk strategy, diversification strategy, liquidity, and interest rate margin strategy. Accordingly, the composition of the loan portfolio varies by institution. The loan portfolio is critical to the institutions' overall asset/liability management strategy.

(i) Types of Loans.   Loans are offered on a variety of terms to meet the needs of the borrower and of the institution. The following are the types of loan arrangements normally issued:

> *Commercial Loans.* Institutions have developed different types of credit facilities to address the needs of commercial customers. Some of the characteristics which distinguish these facilities are: security (whether the loan is collateralized or unsecured); term (whether the loan matures in the short term, long term, on demand or on a revolving credit arrangement); variable or fixed interest rates; and, currency (whether the loan is repayable in the local currency of in a foreign currency).
>
> Loan facilities can be tailored to match the needs of commercial borrowers and may include many combinations of specific loan terms. Some of the common general types are described next.
>
> *Secured Loans.* Collateral (security) to a loan is usually viewed as a characteristic of any type of loan, rather than as a loan category itself. Nevertheless, it is not uncommon for institutions to analyze their loan portfolios, in part, by looking at the proportion of secured credits and the entire balance.
>
> Much bank lending is not supported by specific security. The less creditworthy a potential borrower, however, the more likely it becomes that an institution will require some form of collateral in order to minimize its risk of loss.
>
> Loan security is normally not taken with the intention of liquidating it in order to obtain repayment. Maintenance and liquidation of collateral is, in fact, often time consuming and unprofitable for the foreclosing bank. Most loan security takes the form of some kind of fixed or floating claim over specified assets or a mortgage interest in property.
>
> *Lines of Credit.* Lines of credit, including facilities which are referred to as "revolving lines of credit," originate with an institution extending credit to a borrower with a specified maximum amount and a stated maturity. The borrower then draws and repays funds through the facility in accordance with its requirements. Lines of credit are useful for short-term financing of working capital or seasonal borrowings. A commitment fee is usually charged on the unused portion of the facility.
>
> *Demand Loans.* Demand loans are short-term loans which may be "called" by the institution at any time, hence the term "demand." Demand loans are often unsecured and are normally made to cover short-term funding requirements. There is usually no principal reduction during the loan term, the entire balance coming due on maturity.
>
> *Term Loans.* Term loans are often used to finance the acquisition of capital assets such as plant and equipment. Due to their longer term, they involve greater credit risk than short-term advances (all other things being equal). To reduce that credit risk, these loans typically are secured and require amortization of principal over the loan term. Loan agreements often contain restrictive covenants which require the borrower to maintain specified financial ratios and to refrain from defined types of transactions for as long as the loan is outstanding.

Asset-Based Lending. Asset-based lending is a form of revolving line of credit that is related directly to the value of specific underlying assets (typically accounts receivable or inventory). The primary difference between asset-based lending and a simple line of credit is the direct correlation, upon which the institution insists, between the funds advanced and the underlying security. While funds may be advanced on a line of credit up to the approved maximum amount, they may be drawn under an asset-based lending arrangement only to the extent allowed by predetermined formulas related to collateral value. Requests for funds are normally monitored closely and repayments may be demanded where collateral values fall.

Syndications. A syndicated loan is one where a number of institutions, in a form of joint venture, provide funds which they would individually be unwilling or unable to provide. Syndications are used for customers whole scale of financing is too great for any single institution to accommodate without distorting its loan portfolio. In addition, consortium banks group together banks from different countries to specialize in and centralize large scale finance for specific projects.

The members of a syndicate appoint one or more of themselves as the managing bank for the syndicate. In certain cases, the borrower might appoint the managing bank, in which case the other members would commonly appoint an agent bank to act on their behalf. The managing bank is responsible for negotiating with the borrower, preparing the appropriate documentation, collecting the loan funds from the syndicate and disbursing them to the borrower and collecting amounts due from the borrower and distributing them to the syndicate members.

Apart from the managing bank, the syndicate members will not necessarily have any direct dealings with the borrower, although the borrower is aware of the existence of the syndicate. Credit risk rests with each syndicate member to the extent of its participation.

Participations. Bank sell loans, or part shares in loans, to other financial institutions for a number of reasons: to serve large customers whose financing needs exceed their lending ability; to diversify their loan portfolios; to alter the maturity structure of their loan portfolios; or to increase their liquidity. Participation agreements usually specify such matters as the method of payment of proceeds from the borrower, responsibilities in the event of default and interest in collateral. Loans may be sold with or without recourse and on terms which may or may not agree with those of the underlying loan.

Loans which are "participated out" (i.e., sold) are normally reported on the seller's balance sheet net of the sold portion (which is reported with other loan assets by the buyer). The fact that another institution has researched and agreed to extend the loan does not reduce the risk of the purchasing bank.

Loans Held for Resale. Loans may be originated by an institution which intends to resell them to other parties. They may be purchased with the intention to resell. The reasons for such transactions vary. Some institutions wish to provide a type of loan service to their customers which they do not wish to retain in their portfolio. Some institutions use loan origination as a source of fee income. Some purchase debt to use as securitization for other instruments which they package and sell to specialized markets.

Real Estate Loans. Real estate loans may be made for commercial or personal purposes and most banks differentiate their portfolios between the two uses. The rationale for this segregation lies in the fact that while both are classified as real estate lending, the portfolios are subject to different types of risk and/or different degrees of risk. Also, the type and level of expertise required to successfully manage residential and commercial real estate loan portfolios differs as the type of financing provided to the homeowner is typically not the same as to an owner or developer of commercial real estate.

Incremental knowledge with respect to the particular financing provided, especially concerning construction loans, appraisal methods, comparable properties in the area, the status of the economy surrounding the property, use of the property, other future property developments in the area, occupancy rates, projected operating cash flows and so on, must be obtained and constantly updated to manage successfully commercial real estate property lending.

Mortgage Loans. Real estate mortgage loans are term loans collateralized by real estate. The loans are generally fairly long term, though some are short term with a large principal ("balloon") payment due at maturity. The loan commitments usually involve a fee to be paid by the borrower upon approval or upon closing.

Some institutions originate residential mortgage loans for sale to investors. Under these arrangements, the bank usually continues to service the loans on a fee basis. The sale allows the bank to provide mortgage financing services for its customers without funding a large volume of loans.

Construction Loans. Construction loans are used to finance the construction of particular projects and normally mature at the scheduled completion date. They are generally secured by a first mortgage on the property and are backed by a purchase (or "takeout") agreement from a financially responsible permanent lender. They may include the financing of loan interest through the construction period.

Construction loans are vulnerable to a number of risks related to the uncertainties which are characteristic of building projects. Examples of risks associated with construction loans include construction delays, nonpayment of material bills or subcontractors, and the financial collapse of the project contractor prior to project completion.

Construction loan funds are generally disbursed on a standard payment plan (for relatively small, predictable projects) or a progress payment plan (for more complex projects). Extent of completion may be verified by an architect's certification or by evidence of labor and material costs.

Direct Lease Financing. Leasing is a form of debt financing for fixed assets which, although differing in legal form, is similar to substance to term lending. Like a more conventional loan, the institution's credit concerns in extending lease financing are ones of cash flow, credit history, management and projections of future operations. The type of property to be leased and its marketability in the event of default or termination of the lease are concerns quite parallel to the bank's evaluation of collateral. In a leasing arrangement, the bank formally owns the property rather than having a lien upon it.

Lease financing arrangements may be accounted for either as financings (i.e., as loans) or as operating leases depending upon the precise terms of the transaction and upon the applicable accounting principles.

Consumer Loans. Consumer loans—personal loans to individual borrowers—can originate through a bank's own customers (direct loans) or through merchants with whom the borrowers deal (indirect loans). They may relate specifically to the purchase of items which can serve as collateral for the borrowing (e.g., vehicles, mobile homes, boats, furniture) or to other needs which provide no basis for a security interest (e.g., vacations, income tax payments, medical expenses, educational costs). Consumer loans may be made on an installment, single payment or demand basis. They are often broken down into classifications which describe the purpose of the financing (student loans or home equity loans) or the terms of disbursement and repayment (installment loans, credit card loans, check credit).

Installment Loans. Installment loans are the most common type of consumer credit. Their terms normally include repayment over a specified period of time with fixed minimum periodic (usually monthly) payments. Interest rates are generally fixed upon origination but may be variable over the term of the loan. The term is generally determined by the type of purchase being financed and is usually relatively short—10 years or less.

Standby Letters of Credit. A standby letter of credit is a promise made by an institution to provide compensation to a third party on behalf of its customer in the event that the customer fails to perform in accordance with the terms specified by an underlying contract.

Standby letters of credit may be available under a credit facility or may be issued for a specified amount with an expiration date. Normally, payment under such agreements depends on performance or lack of performance of some act required by the underlying contract.

Standby letters of credit are typically recorded as contingent liabilities in memorandum records and are offset by customer liability memorandum accounts. In the event that funds are disbursed under a standby letter of credit agreement, the drawing would be recorded as a loan.

Sovereign Risk. Sovereign risk lending involves the granting of credit facilities to foreign governments or to companies based in foreign countries. The facilities are normally denominated in a currency other than the domestic currency of the borrower and are typically used to finance imports or to refinance existing foreign currency debt.

In addition to all of the customary considerations surrounding credit risk, sovereign risk lending involves economic, social and political considerations which bear on the ability of the borrower to repay foreign currency obligations.

Trade Finance.

(a) Letters of credit. Letters of credit are instruments used to facilitate trade (most commonly international trade) by substituting an institution's credit for that of a commercial importing company. A letter of credit provides assurance to a seller that he will be paid for goods shipped. At the same time, it provides assurance to the buyer that payment will not be made until conditions specified in the sales contract have been met.

Letter of credit transactions can vary in any number of ways. The issuing and advising institutions may deal with each other through their own local correspondent banks. Some of the documents may flow in different patterns. The requirements for payment and security will certainly vary from transaction to transaction. One of the attractive features of letter of credit financing from the customer's point of view is its flexibility. Facilities can be tailored to individual transactions or groups of transactions.

(b) Bankers' Acceptances. A bankers' acceptance is like a letter of credit in that it provides a seller of goods with a guarantee of payment, thus facilitating trade. The institution's customer is the buyer who, having established an acceptance facility with the bank, notifies the seller to draw up a bill of exchange. The bank "accepts" that bill (by physically stamping "accepted" on its face and having an authorized bank officer sign it) and, in so doing, commits itself to disburse funds on the bill's due date.

A banker's acceptance represents both an asset and a liability to the accepting bank. The asset is a receivable from the bank's customer, the buyer in the transaction. The liability is a payable to the holder of the acceptance. The bank's accounting for open acceptances varies from country to country. In some countries, the asset and liability are both reflected on the bank's balance sheet. In others, they are netted against each other and thus become, in effect, off-balance sheet items. In EU Countries, they appear as memorandum items on the face of the balance sheet.

By substituting its own credit for that to the buying company, the accepting bank creates a financial instrument which is readily marketable. Bankers' acceptances trade as bearer paper on active secondary markets.

(ii) Accounting for Loans

Principal. Loans expected to be held until maturity should be reported at outstanding principal, net of chargeoffs, specific valuation accounts, and any deferred fees or costs, or unamortized premiums or discounts on purchased loans. Total loans should be reduced by the allowance for credit losses.

Loans held for sale should be reported at the lower of cost or market value. Mortgage loans held for sale should be reported at the lower of cost or market value in conformity with SFAS No. 65, "Accounting for Certain Mortgage Banking Activities," as amended by SFAS

No. 122, "Accounting for Mortgage Servicing Rights." Mortgage-backed securities held for sale in conjunction with mortgage banking activities shall be classified as trading securities and reported at fair value in conformity with SFAS No. 115, "Accounting for Certain Investments in Debt and Equity Securities."

Interest. Interest income on all loans should be accrued and credited to interest income as it is earned, using the interest method. Interest income on certain impaired loans should be recognized in accordance with SFAS No. 114, "Accounting by Creditors for Impairment of a Loan," as amended by SFAS No. 118, "Accounting by Creditors for Impairment of a Loan-Income Recognition and Disclosures."

The accrual of interest is usually suspended on loans that are in excess of 90 days past due, unless the loan is both well secured and in the process of collection. When a loan is placed on such nonaccrual status, interest that has been accrued but not collected is reversed, and interest subsequently received is recorded on a cash basis or applied to reduce the principal balance depending on the bank's assessment of ultimate collectibility of the loan. An exception to this rule is that many banks do not place certain types of consumer loans on nonaccrual since they automatically charge off such loans within a relatively short period of becoming delinquent—generally within 120 days.

Loan Fees. Various types of fees are collected by banks in connection with lending activities. SFAS No. 91, "Accounting for Nonrefundable Fees and Costs Associated with Originating or Acquiring Loans and Initial Direct Costs of Leases (an amendment of FASB Statements No. 13, 60, and 65 and a recission of FASB Statement No. 17)," requires that the majority of such fees and associated direct origination costs be offset. The net amount must be deferred as part of the loan (and reported as a component of loans in the balance sheet) and recognized in interest income over the life of the loan and/or loan commitment period as an adjustment of the yield on the loan. The requirements for cost deferral under this standard are quite restrictive and require direct linkage to the loan origination process. Activities for which costs may be deferred include (1) evaluating the borrower, guarantees, collateral, and other security; (2) preparation and processing of loan documentation for loan origination; and (3) negotiating and closing the loan. Certain costs are specifically precluded from deferral, for example, advertising and solicitation, credit supervision and administration, costs of unsuccessful loan originations and other activities not directly related to the extension of a loan.

Loan fees and costs for loans originated or purchased for resale are deferred and are recognized when the related loan is sold.

Commitment fees to purchase or originate loans, net of direct origination costs, are generally deferred and amortized over the life of the loan when it is extended. If the commitment expires, then the fees are recognized in other income on expiration of the commitment. There are two main exceptions to this general treatment:

- If past experience indicates that the extension of a loan is unlikely, then the fee is recognized over the commitment period.
- Nominal fees, which are determined retroactively, on a commitment to extend funds at a market rate, may be recognized in income at the determination date.

Certain fees may be recognized when received, primarily loan syndication fees. Generally, the yield on the portion of the loan retained by the syndicating bank must at least equal the yield received by the other members of the syndicate. If this is not the case, a portion of the fees designated as a syndication fee must be deferred and amortized to income to achieve a yield equal to the average yield of the other banks in the syndicate. The distinctions between syndications and participation are becoming less distinct; as a result, Emerging Issues Task Force (EITF) Issue No. 88-17, "Allocation of Recorded Investment When a Loan or Part of a Loan is Sold," provides guidance with respect to criteria for in substance syndications. According to the EITF consensus, generally if at least 50% of the loan balance is sold within 60 days of origination and the risks and rewards of the seller and purchaser are shared proportionately from the date of sale, then the transaction can be considered to be a syndication, with appropriate fee recognition principles applied.

Purchased loans are recorded at cost net of fees paid/received. The difference between this recorded amount and the principal amount of the loan is amortized to income over the life of the loan to produce a level yield. Acquisition costs are not deferred, but are expensed as incurred.

Acquisition, Development, and Construction Arrangements. Certain transactions that appear to be loans are considered effectively to be investments in the real estate property financed. These transactions are required to be presented separately from loans and accounted for as real estate investments using the guidance set forth in the AICPA Notice to Practitioners dated February 1986. Factors indicating such treatment include arrangements whereby the financial institution:

1. Provides substantially all financing to acquire, develop and, construct the property, that is, borrower has little or no equity in the property.
2. Funds the origination or commitment fees through the loan.
3. Funds substantially all interest and fees through the loan.
4. Has security only in the project with no recourse to other assets or guarantee of the borrower.
5. Can recover its investment only through sale to third parties, refinancing, or cash flow of the project.
6. Is unlikely to foreclose on the project during development since no payments are due during this period and therefore the loan cannot normally become delinquent.

Troubled Debt Restructurings and Impaired Loans. Banks may routinely restructure loans to meet a borrower's changing circumstances. The new loan terms are reflected in the financial statements essentially as if a new loan has been made. However, if "a creditor for economic or legal reasons related to the debtor's financial difficulties grants a concession . . . that it would not otherwise consider," then SFAS No. 15, "Accounting by Debtors and Creditors for Troubled Debt Restructurings" applies. SFAS No. 15 was substantially amended by SFAS No. 114.

(a) Troubled Debt Restructurings. Troubled debt restructurings may include one or more of the following:

- Transfers of assets of the debtor or an equity interest in the debtor to partially or fully satisfy a debt.
- Modification of debt terms, including reduction of one or more of the following (1) interest rates with or without extensions of maturity date(s), (2) face or maturity amounts, and (3) accrued interest.

Prior to the release of SFAS No. 114, under a SFAS No. 15 restructuring involving a modification of terms, the creditor accumulated the undiscounted total future cash receipts and compared them to the recorded investment in the loan. If these cash receipts exceeded the recorded investment in the loan, no loss or impairment was deemed to exist; however, if the total cash receipts did not exceed the recorded investment, the recorded investment was adjusted to reflect the total undiscounted future cash receipts. For restructurings involving a modification of terms that occurred before the effective date of SFAS No. 114, this accounting still applies as long as the loan does not become impaired relative to the restructured terms. Restructurings involving a modification of terms after the effective date of SFAS No. 114 must be accounted for in accordance with SFAS No. 114.

(b) Impaired Loans. In May 1993, SFAS No. 114, "Accounting by Creditors for Impairment of a Loan (an amendment of FASB Statements No. 5 and 15)," was released. This Statement was issued primarily to provide more consistent guidance on the application of SFAS No. 5 loss criteria and to provide additional direction on the recognition and measurement of loan impairment in determining credit reserve levels. The statement was required beginning in 1995.

SFAS No. 114 applies to all impaired loans, uncollateralized as well as collateralized, except: large groups of smaller balance homogeneous loans that are collectively evaluated for impairment such as credit card, residential mortgage, and consumer installment loans; loans that are measured at fair value or at the lower of cost or fair value; leases; and debt securities, as defined in SFAS No. 115, "Accounting for Certain Investments in Debt and Equity Securities."

A loan is impaired when, based on current information and events, it is probable (consistent with its use in SFAS No. 5—an area within a range of the likelihood that a future event or events will occur confirming the fact of the loss) that a creditor will be unable to collect all amounts due according to the contractual terms of the loan agreement. As used in SFAS No. 114 and in SFAS No. 5, as amended, all amounts due according to the contractual terms means that both the contractual interest payments and the contractual principal payments of a loan will be collected as scheduled in the loan agreement.

It is important to note that an insignificant delay or insignificant shortfall in the amount of payments does not require application of SFAS No. 114. A loan is not impaired during a period of delay in payment if the creditor expects to collect all amounts due including interest accrued at the contractual interest rate for the period of delay.

SFAS No. 114 provides that the measurement of impaired value should be based on one of the following methods:

(a) Present value of expected cash flows discounted at the loan's effective interest rate;

(b) The observable value of the loan's market price; or

(c) The fair value of the collateral if the loan is collateral dependent.

The effective rate of a loan is the contractual interest rate adjusted for any net deferred loan fees or costs, premium or discount existing at the origination or acquisition of the loan. For variable rate loans, the loan's effective interest rate may be calculated based on the factor as it changes over the life of the loan or it may be fixed at the rate in effect at the date the loan meets the SFAS No. 114 impairment criterion. However, that choice should be applied consistently for all variable rate loans.

All impaired loans do not have to be measured using the same method; the method selected may vary based on the availability of information and other factors. However, the ultimate valuation should be critically evaluated in determining whether it represents a reasonable estimate of impairment.

If the measure of the impaired loan is less than the recorded investment in the loan (including accrued interest, net deferred loan fees or costs, and unamortized premium or discount), a creditor should recognize an impairment by creating a valuation allowance with a corresponding charge or credit to bad-debt expense.

Subsequent to the initial measurement of impairment, if there is a significant change (increase or decrease) in the amount or timing of an impaired loan's expected future cash flows, observable market price, or fair value of the collateral, a creditor should recalculate the impairment by applying the procedures described above and by adjusting the valuation allowance. However, the net carrying amount of the loan should at no time exceed the recorded investment in the loan.

Any restructurings performed under the provisions of SFAS No. 15 need not be reevaluated unless the borrower is not performing in accordance with the contractual terms of the restructuring.

In-substance Foreclosures. SFAS No. 114 clarified the definition of in-substance foreclosures as used in SFAS No. 15, "Accounting by Debtors and Creditors for Troubled Debt

Restructurings," by stating that the phrase "foreclosure by the creditor" in paragraph 34 should be read to mean "*physical* possession of debtor's assets regardless of whether formal foreclosure proceedings take place." Further, until foreclosure occurs, these assets should remain as loans in the financial statements.

(p) CREDIT LOSSES.   Credit loss estimates are subjective, and, accordingly, require careful judgments in assessing loan collectibility and in estimating losses.

(i) Accounting Guidance.   SFAS No. 114, "Accounting by Creditors for Impairment of a Loan (an amendment of FASB Statements No. 5 and 15)" and SFAS No. 5, "Accounting for Contingencies (as amended by SFAS No. 118, Accounting by Creditors for Impairment of Loan-Income Recognition and Disclosures)" are the primary sources of guidance on accounting for the allowance for loan losses. SFAS No. 5 requires that an estimated loss from a contingency should be accrued by a charge to income if both of the following conditions are met:

- Information available prior to issuance of the financial statements indicates that it is **probable** that an asset had been impaired or a liability had been incurred at the date of the financial statements. It is implicit in this condition that it must be probable that one or more future events will occur confirming the fact of the loss.
- The amount of loss can be reasonably estimated.

SFAS No. 5 states that when a loss contingency exists, the likelihood that the future event or events will confirm the loss or impairment of an asset (whether related to contractual principal or interest) can range from remote to probable. **Probable** means the future event or events are likely to occur; however, the conditions for accrual are not intended to be so rigid that they require virtual certainty before a loss is accrued.

The allowance for loan losses should be adequate to cover probable credit losses related to specifically identified loans as well as probable credit losses inherent in the remainder of the loan portfolio that have been incurred as of the balance sheet date. Credit losses related to off-balance sheet instruments should also be accrued if the conditions of SFAS No. 5 are met.

Actual credit losses should be deducted from the allowance and the related balance should be charged off in the period in which they are deemed uncollectible. Recoveries of loans previously charged off should be added to the allowance when received.

SFAS No. 114, addresses the accounting by creditors for impairment of certain loans, as discussed in subsection 25.2(o)(ii).

(ii) Regulatory Guidance.   The regulatory agencies issued the "Interagency Policy on the Allowance for Loan and Lease Losses" in December 1993. The policy statement provides guidance with respect to the nature and purpose of the allowance; the related responsibilities of the board of directors, management, and the bank examiners; adequacy of loan review systems; and issues related to international transfer risk.

The policy statement also includes an analytical tool to be used by bank examiners for assessing the reasonableness of the allowance; however, the policy statement cautions the bank examiners against placing too much emphasis on the analytical tool, rather than performing a full and thorough analysis.

The Office of the Comptroller of the Currency (OCC) also provides guidance in its Banking Circular 201, Allowance for Loan and Lease Losses, for regulatory financial reporting purposes.

In January 1995, the Federal Reserve Board (FRB) announced elimination of its requirement that uninsured U.S. branches and agencies of foreign banks establish and maintain loan loss allowances separate from those of the foreign banks. The FRB emphasized its continuing policy requiring uninsured U.S. branches and agencies of foreign banks to establish and maintain procedures for identifying loan losses. The OCC clarified that the FRB's decision does not alter the OCC's requirement that each branch or agency maintain loan loss allowances as required by the OCC's February 1992 Banking Circular 201 and July 1993 Agency Circular No. 1 (OCC Bulletin 95-15).

(iii) Allowance Methodologies. An institution's method of estimating credit losses is influenced by many factors, including the institution's size, organization structure, business environment and strategy, management style, loan portfolio characteristics, loan administration procedures, and management information systems.

Common Factors to Consider. Although allowance methodologies may vary between institutions, the factors to consider in estimating credit losses are often similar. Examples of common factors included in most allowance methodologies are as follows:

a. National and Local economic and business conditions.
b. Types of loans and growth in the portfolio.
c. Experience, ability, and depth of lending management and staff.
d. Lending policies and procedures.
e. Level and trends of problem loans such as past due, nonaccrual and classified loans.
f. Quality of the institution's loan review system and the degree of oversight by the institution's board of directors.
g. Existence and effect of any concentrations of credit.
h. Effect of external factors such as competition and legal and regulatory requirements.

Supplemental data such as historical loss rates or peer group analyses can be helpful; however, they are not, by themselves, sufficient basis for an allowance methodology.

Portfolio Segments. Another common practice is dividing the loan portfolio into different segments. Each segment typically includes similar characteristics such as risk classification and type of loan. Segments typically include large problem loans by industry or collateral type, and homogeneous pools of smaller loans, such as credit cards, automobile loans, and residential mortgages.

Credit Classification Process. A credit classification process involves categorizing loans into risk categories and is often applied to large loans which are evaluated individually. The categorization is based on conditions that may affect the ability of borrowers to service their debt, such as current financial information, historical payment experience, credit documentation, public information, and current trends. Many institutions classify loans using a rating system that incorporates the regulatory classification system. These definitions are as follows:

(a) *Special Mention.* Some loans are considered criticized, but not classified. Such loans have potential weaknesses that deserve management's close attention. If left uncorrected, these potential weaknesses may result in deterioration of the repayment prospects for the assets or of the institution's credit position at some future date. Special-mention loans are not adversely classified and do not expose an institution to sufficient risk to warrant adverse classification.

(b) *Substandard.* Loans classified as substandard are inadequately protected by the current sound worth and paying capacity of the obligor or of the collateral pledged, if any. Loans so classified must have a well-defined weakness or weaknesses that jeopardize the liquidation of the debt. They are characterized by the distinct possibility that the institution will sustain some loss if the deficiencies are not corrected.

(c) *Doubtful.* Loans classified as doubtful have all the weaknesses inherent in those classified as substandard, with the added characteristic that the weaknesses make collection or liquidation in full, on the basis of currently existing facts, conditions, and values, highly questionable and improbable.

(d) *Loss.* Loans classified as loss are considered uncollectible and of such little value that their continuance as bankable assets is not warranted. This classification does not mean that the loan has absolutely no recovery or salvage value, but rather that it is not practical or desirable to defer writing off this basically worthless asset even though partial recovery may be effected in the future.

Pools of Smaller-Balance Homogeneous Loans. Loans not evaluated individually are included in pools and loss rates are derived for each pool. The loss rates are adjusted for changes in trends and conditions.

Foreign Loans. The Interagency Country Exposure Risk Committee (ICERC) requires certain loans to have allocated transfer risk reserves (ATRRs). ATRRs are minimum specific reserves related to loans in particular countries and, therefore, must be reviewed by each institution. The ICERC's supervisory role is pursuant to the International Supervision Act of 1983. The collectibility of foreign loans that do not have ATRRs should be assessed in the same way as domestic loans.

Documentation, Completeness and Frequency. The institution's allowance methodology should be based on a comprehensive, adequately documented and consistently applied analysis. The analysis should consider all significant factors that affect collectibility of the portfolio and should be based on an effective loan review and credit grading (classification) system. Additionally, the evaluation of the adequacy of the allowance should be performed as of the end of each quarter and appropriate provisions should be made to maintain the allowance at an adequate level.

(q) LOAN SALES AND MORTGAGE BANKING ACTIVITIES. Banks may originate and sell loans for a variety of reasons, such as generating income streams from servicing and other fees, increasing liquidity, minimizing interest rate exposure, enhancing asset/liability management, and maximizing their use of capital.

(i) Underwriting Standards. When loans are originated for resale, the origination process includes not only finding an investor, but also preparing the loan documents to fit the investor's requirements. Loans originated for resale must normally comply with specific underwriting standards regarding items such as borrower qualifications, loan documentation, appraisals, mortgage insurance and loan terms. Individual loans that do not meet the underwriting standards are typically eliminated from the pool of loans eligible for sale. Generally, the originating institutions may be subject to recourse by the investor for underwriting exceptions identified subsequent to the sale of the loans and any related defaults by borrowers.

(ii) Securitizations. A common method of transforming real estate assets into liquid marketable securities is through securitization. Securitization is where loans are sold to a separate entity which finances the purchase through the issuance of debt securities or undivided interest in the loans. The real estate securities are backed by the cash flows of the loans.

"Already, approximately 60 percent of residential mortgages ultimately are financed through securitization." Securitization of residential real estate loans has expanded to include commercial and multifamily mortgages; auto and home equity loans; credit cards; and leases.

The accounting guidance for sales of loans through securitizations is discussed in section 25.3, "Mortgage Banking Activities."

(iii) Loan Servicing. When loans are sold, the selling institution sometimes retains the right to service the loans for a servicing fee which is collected over the life of the loans as payments are received. The servicing fee is often based on a percentage of the principal balance of the outstanding loans. A typical servicing agreement requires the servicer to perform the billing, collection and remittance functions, as well as maintaining custodial bank accounts. The servicer may also be responsible for certain credit losses.

The accounting guidance for purchasing, acquiring and selling mortgage servicing rights is discussed in section 25.3.

(iv) Valuation. The accounting guidance addressing the valuation of loans held for sale is discussed in section 25.3.

(r) REAL ESTATE INVESTMENTS, REAL ESTATE OWNED, AND OTHER FORECLOSED ASSETS. The type and nature of assets included in real estate investments, former bank premises and other foreclosed assets can vary significantly. Such assets are described next.

(i) Real Estate Investments. Certain institutions make direct equity investments in real estate projects and other institutions may grant real estate loans which have virtually the same risks and rewards as those of joint venture participants. Both types of transactions are considered to be real estate investments and such arrangements are treated as if the institution has an ownership interest in the property.

Specifically, GAAP for real estate investments is established in the following authoritative literature:

- AICPA Statement of Position 78-9, "Accounting for Investments in Real Estate Ventures";
- SFAS No. 34, "Capitalization of Interest Cost";
- SFAS No. 58, "Capitalization of Interest Cost in Financial Statements That Include Investments Accounted for by the Equity Method";
- SFAS No. 66, "Accounting for Sales of Real Estate"; and,
- SFAS No. 67, "Accounting for Costs and Initial Rental Operations of Real Estate Projects."

(ii) Former Bank Premises. Many institutions have former premises that are no longer used in operations. Such former bank premises may be included in real estate owned.

(iii) Foreclosed Assets. Foreclosed assets include all assets received in full or partial satisfaction of a receivable and include real and personal property; equity interests in corporations, partnerships, and joint ventures; and beneficial interests in trusts. However, the largest component of real estate owned by banks and savings institutions is comprised of foreclosed real estate assets.

Guidance on accounting for and reporting of foreclosed assets is established in the following authoritative literature:

- SFAS No. 15, "Accounting by Debtors and Creditors for Troubled Debt Restructurings";
- SFAS No. 121, "Accounting for the Impairment of Long-Lived Assets and for Long-Lived Assets to Be Disposed Of"; and,
- Statement of Position (SOP) 92-3, "Accounting For Foreclosed Assets."

SFAS No. 121, which is effective for financial statements for fiscal years beginning after December 15, 1995 with earlier application encouraged, requires that long-lived assets to be disposed of be reported at the lower of carrying amount or fair value less cost to sell, except for assets that are covered by APB Opinion 30, "Reporting the Results of Operations-Reporting the Effects of Disposal of a Segment of a Business and Extraordinary, Unusual and Infrequently Occurring Events and Transactions." Assets that are covered by APB Opinion 30, are reported at the lower of carrying amount or net realized value. SFAS No. 121, when adopted, takes precedence over SOP 92-3.

SFAS No. 121 also states that long-lived assets to be held and used by an institution should be reviewed for impairment whenever events or changes in circumstances indicate that the carrying amount of an asset may not be recoverable. In performing the review for recoverability, the institution should estimate the future cash flows expected to result from the use of the asset and its eventual disposition. If the sum of the expected future cash flows is less than the carrying amount of the asset, including related goodwill, an impairment loss is recognized. Otherwise, an impairment loss is not recognized. The Statement requires that measurement of an impairment loss for long-lived assets that an institution expects to hold and use should be based on the fair value of the asset. At foreclosure, or physical possession, the asset should be reported at its fair value, if it will be held and used, or at its fair value less cost to sell, if it will be disposed of.

(s) INVESTMENTS IN DEBT AND EQUITY SECURITIES.   Banks use a variety of financial instruments for various purposes, primarily to provide a source of income through investment or resale and to manage interest-rate and liquidity risk as part of an overall asset/liability management strategy. Investment securities are classified in three categories: held-to-maturity, available-for-sale, and trading.

Banks are generally restricted in the types of financial instruments that they may deal in, underwrite, purchase or sell. Essentially banks may only deal in U.S. government and U.S. government agency securities; municipal bonds; and certain other bonds, notes, and debentures. These restrictions are also limited based on capitalization.

(i) Accounting for Investments in Debt and Equity Securities.   SFAS No. 115 "Accounting for Certain Investments in Debt and Equity Securities," addresses the accounting and reporting for investments in equity securities that have readily determinable fair values and for all investments in debt securities. Such securities are classified in three categories and accounted for as follows:

Held-to-Maturity. Securities for which an institution has both the ability and positive intent to hold to maturity are classified as held-to-maturity and are carried at amortized cost (any difference between cost and fair value is recorded as a premium or discount which is amortized to income using the level yield method over the life of the security).

Trading. Securities which are purchased and held principally for the purpose of selling them in the near term are carried at fair value, with unrealized gains and losses included in earnings.

Available for Sale. All other securities are classified as available-for-sale and carried at fair value, with unrealized gains and losses included as a separate component of equity.

SFAS No. 115, addresses changes in circumstances that may cause an enterprise to change its intent to hold a certain security to maturity without calling into question its intent to hold other debt securities to maturity in the future.

Entities are required to determine whether a decline in fair value below the amortized cost basis is other than temporary. If such a decline is judged to be other than temporary, the cost basis of the individual security should be written down to fair value as the new cost basis. The amount of the write down should be treated as a realized loss and recorded in earnings. The new cost basis shall not be changed for subsequent recoveries.

Investment securities are required to be recorded on a trade date basis. Interest income on investment securities is recorded separately as a component of interest income. Realized gains and losses on available-for-sale securities and realized and unrealized gains and losses on trading securities are recorded as a separate component of noninterest income or loss. Upon the sale of an available-for-sale security, any unrealized gain or loss previously recorded in the separate component of equity is reversed and recorded as a separate component of noninterest income or loss.

Transfers between the three categories are performed at fair value. Transfers out of held-to-maturity should be rare.

(ii) Wash Sales. Gains and losses represent the results of actual sales of securities. Wash sales may not be considered to be completed sales transactions if securities are sold and substantially similar securities are repurchased within a short period of time. In these cases, no gain or loss is recorded. In order for a sale to have occurred, there must be a reasonable period between the sale and purchase of substantially similar securities and during which the bank must have been at risk.

(iii) Short Sales. An institution may sell a security it does not own with the intention of buying or borrowing securities at an agreed-upon future date to cover the sale. Given the nature of these transactions, such sales should be within the trading portfolio. Obligations incurred in these short sales should be reported as liabilities and recorded at fair value at each reporting date with change in fair value recorded through income.

(iv) Securities Borrowing and Lending. An institution may borrow securities from a counterparty to fulfill its obligations and may advance cash, pledge other securities, or issue letters of credit as collateral for borrowed securities. The institution that borrows the securities records cash advanced as collateral as a receivable from the lender of securities counterparty. Any rebate (interest received by the borrower on the cash it advances) is reported as interest income. When the borrowed securities are returned, the cash is returned, typically in an amount equal to the market value of the securities borrowed. Disclosure of securities pledged as collateral is required to be made in the financial statements.

When securities are loaned, a liability is established for the cash advanced. The amount of cash or other collateral required may change depending on the value of the securities. Any rebate is reported as interest expense.

Balances from borrowed and loaned securities should be presented gross on the balance sheet unless netting is permitted under FASB Interpretation No. 39, "Offsetting of Amounts Related to Certain Contracts (an interpretation of APB Opinion No. 10 and FASB Statement No. 105."

Additional guidance on accounting for and reporting of investments in debt and equity securities is established in the following:

- FASB Technical Bulletin (TB) No. 94-1, "Application of SFAS No. 115 to Debt Securities Restructured in a Troubled Debt Restructuring" which clarifies that any loan that was restructured in a troubled debt restructuring involving a modification of terms would be subject to SFAS No. 115 if the debt instrument meets the definition of a security;

- SFAS No. 91, "Accounting for Nonrefundable Fees and Costs Associated with Originating or Acquiring Loans and Initial Direct Costs of Leases" which specifies that discounts or premiums associated with the purchase of debt securities should be accreted or amortized using the interest method; and

- SFAS No. 15, "Accounting by Debtors and Creditors for troubled Debt Restructurings" which applies to troubled debt restructurings involving debt securities.

Additional guidance on the implementation of SFAS No. 115 has been provided in a FASB Special Report, "A Guide to Implementation of Statement 115 on Accounting for Certain Investments in Debt and Equity Securities."

(t) FUTURES, FORWARDS, OPTIONS, SWAPS, AND SIMILAR FINANCIAL INSTRUMENTS. Futures, forwards, swaps, and options and other financial instruments with similar characteristics (collectively, derivatives) have become important financial management tools for banks. Many derivatives' values are more volatile than those of other financial instruments—potentially alternating between favorable and adverse values in a short period of time.

The notional principal amounts of these transactions are not recorded on the balance sheet of the bank but are recorded in memorandum accounts in view of the nature of these transactions.

Derivatives can generally be described as either forward-based or option-based, or combinations of the two. A forward-based contract (futures, forwards, and swap contracts) obligates one party to buy and a counterparty to sell an underlying financial instrument, foreign currency, or commodity at a future date at an agreed-upon price. An option-based derivative (options, interest rate caps and interest rate floors) are one-sided in that if the right is exercised, only the holder can have a favorable outcome and the writer can have only an unfavorable outcome. Most derivatives are generally combinations of these two types of contracts.

Authoritative guidance is limited and continues to evolve. Guidance does not exist for certain customized instruments. Institutions may use derivatives for speculation or risk management and this use currently influences the accounting for derivatives. In general, derivatives used for speculation are accounted for at market value while derivatives used for risk management or hedging purposes (subject to certain restrictions and conditions as detailed below) are accounted for on an accrual basis. At times the distinction between speculation and risk management can be blurred and as a result, FASB has a long-term project concerning how derivatives should be accounted for.

The most common types of derivatives are discussed next.

(i) Futures.   A futures contract is an agreement to make or take delivery of a financial instrument (interest rate instrument, currency, and certain stock indices) at a future date. Most futures contracts are closed out prior to the delivery date by entering into an offsetting contract. The accounting for exchange traded futures contracts is set forth in SFAS No. 80, "Accounting for Futures Contracts," which requires that all contracts that do not meet certain very stringent criteria for hedge accounting should be marked-to-market with realized and unrealized gains and losses recorded in income. Although the criteria for hedge accounting are more stringent than those under SFAS No. 52, "Foreign Currency Translation," SFAS No. 80 is more flexible in that it allows hedging of anticipated transactions. SFAS No. 80 requires both of the following conditions be met for a futures contract to qualify as hedge:

(a)   The item to be hedged exposes the bank to price or interest rate risk.
(b)   The hedge reduces the exposure and is designated as a hedge. There must be a high correlation between changes in the value of the hedged item and the type of futures contract used for hedging.

The effect of changes in the value of the futures contract is recognized as an adjustment of the value of the hedged item or is deferred and recognized in its measurement in the case of a futures transaction.

(ii) Forwards.   A forward contract is a contract between two parties to purchase and sell a specified quantity of a financial instrument, foreign currency, or commodity at a specified price, with delivery and settlement at a specified future date. Such contracts are not traded on exchanges.

(iii) Options.   Option contracts provide the purchaser of the option with the right, but not the obligations, to buy (or sell) a specified instrument, such as currencies, interest rate products, or futures. They also put the seller under the obligation to deliver (or take delivery of) the instrument to the buyer of the option but only at the buyer's option.

There is no authoritative comprehensive accounting guidance for options and practice is somewhat diverse. The AICPA 1986 Options Issues Paper, "Accounting for Options," provided recommendations but was not intended to establish standards and contained viewpoints that differed from the conclusions of SFAS No. 52 and No. 80. FASB advised that SFAS No. 115, "Accounting for Certain Investments in Debt and Equity Securities," should be followed with respect to options that meet the definition of an equity security and have a readily deter-minable fair value.

In practice, options are typically accounted for at market value with resultant gains and losses included in trading income unless hedging criteria is met. Premiums paid or received are recorded in the balance sheet as trading assets and other liabilities. When options are exer-cised, liquidated, or expire, the value of the premium paid or received remaining on the balance sheet is included in the calculation of the gain or loss on the option position. Option writing is usually considered speculative and is accounted for as detailed above. If the follow-ing criteria are met, then hedge accounting may be used for purchased options:

(a) The option must reduce exposure by the transaction being hedged. (This differs from the more stringent SFAS No. 80 requirement to assess enterprise risk.)

(b) High correlation between changes in the market value of the hedged item and the option must be probable.

(c) The price of the hedged item and the option must have a clear relationship.

(d) The option must be designated as a hedge.

(iv) Interest-Rate Swaps.   These are contracts between parties to exchange sets of cash flows based on a predetermined notional principal. Only the cash flows are exchanged (usually on a net basis) with no principal exchanged; it is merely a reference point to determine the amounts of cash flows. Swaps are used to change the nature or cost of existing transactions, for example, exchanging fixed rate debt cash flows for floating rate cash flows. The principal types of swaps are interest rate swaps and currency swaps.

There is no authoritative guidance for the accounting for swap transactions and there is some diversity in practice between institutions. However, predominant practice appears to be that speculative swaps are marked-to-market, whereas swaps meeting hedging criteria are ac-counted for on an accrual basis over the life of the swap; that is, the net cash inflow or outflow is recorded as a component of net interest income on a normal accrual basis.

(v) Foreign Exchange Contracts.   These contracts are used both to provide a service to cus-tomers and as a part of the institution's trading or hedging activities. The bank profits by maintaining a margin between the purchase price and sale price. Contracts may be for current trades (spot contract), future dates (forward contract), or swap contracts. The bank may also enter into these contracts to hedge a foreign currency exposure.

The accounting for foreign exchange contracts is set forth in SFAS No. 52, which requires mark-to-market accounting for trading contracts (the difference between the contracted rate for the contract and the currently available rate for the same maturity date). The realized and unrealized gains and losses on these contracts are recorded as a component of other income. No separate accounting recognition is given to the premium or discount for these contracts.

Certain contracts are accounted for differently provided they meet the required criteria under SFAS No. 52 for hedge accounting, including such factors as the contract being desig-nated and effective as a hedge of the hedged item or commitment. For these transactions a dis-count or premium is calculated at inception which comprises the difference between the spot and forward rates at that date. Typically, this premium or discount is then amortized to income over the life of the hedged item irrespective of the recognition of a gain or loss on the hedge contract. Gains and losses on hedge contracts (the difference between the spot rate at the bal-ance sheet date and the spot rate at inception) generally follow the gains and losses on the hedged item and therefore are recorded in income, when incurred, over the life of the hedged item.

(vi) Interest Rate Caps.   These are contracts in which a cap writer, in return for a premium, agrees to make cash payments to the cap holder equal to the excess of the market rate over the strike price multiplied by the notional principal amount if rates go above specified interest rate (strike price). The cap holder has the right, not the obligation to exercise the option and if rates move down, the cap holder will lose only the premium paid. The cap writer has virtually unlimited risk resulting from increases in interest rates above the cap rate.

(vii) Interest Rate Floors.   These are contracts in which a floor writer, in return for a premium, agrees to limit the risk of declining interest rates based on a notional amount such that if rates go below a specified interest rate (strike price), the floor holder will receive cash payments equal to the difference between the market rate and the strike price multiplied by the notional principal amount. As with interest rate caps, the floor holder has the right, not the obligation, to exercise the option and if rates move up, the floor holder will lose only the premium paid. The floor writer has risk resulting from decreases in interest rates below the floor rate.

(viii) Interest Rate Collars.   These are combinations of interest rate caps and interest rate floors, that is, one held and one written.

(ix) Swaptions.   These are option contracts to enter into an interest-rate swap contract at some future date or to cancel an existing swap in the future.

Authoritative Guidance on accounting for and reporting of derivatives is provided in the following:

- SFAS No. 52, "Foreign Currency Translation," which provides guidance on accounting for forwards, futures and swaps involving foreign currencies;
- SFAS No. 80, "Accounting for Futures Contracts," which establishes standards of accounting for exchange-traded futures other than foreign currencies;
- SFAS No. 105, "Disclosure of Information about Financial Instruments with Off-Balance-Sheet Risk and Financial Instruments with Concentrations of Credit Risk";
- SFAS No. 107, "Disclosure about Fair Value of Financial Instruments";
- SFAS No. 119, "Disclosures about Derivative Financial Instruments and Fair Value of Financial Instruments."

Other sources include:

- FASB Staff Paper, "Might Synthetic Instrument Accounting Be Substituted for Hedge Accounting for Some 'Hedging' Relationships?," which addresses the concepts of synthetic instrument accounting;
- A report prepared by the Financial Instruments Task Force of the Accounting Standards Executive Committee, "Derivatives—Current Accounting and Auditing Literature" which is a compilation of accounting and auditing guidance; and
- A special report prepared by FASB, "Major Issues Related to Hedge Accounting," which reports on a consensus of a working group of representatives of various standard-setting bodies throughout the world on the recognition and measurement of derivative financial instruments.
- SEC has proposed an amendment to Regulation S-X, S-K and various forms including Form 20F for disclosures of derivatives and other financial instruments.

In addition, the EITF has addressed a number of specific issues concerning derivatives and the SEC staff has provided additional guidance with respect to interest rate swaps designated to equity securities.

(u) DEPOSITS.   Generally, the most significant source of a bank's funding is customer deposits. Institutions now offer a wide range of deposit products having a variety of interest rates, terms and conditions. The more common types of deposits are described below.

(i) Demand Deposits. Customer deposit accounts from which funds may be withdrawn on demand. Checking and negotiable order of withdrawal (NOW) accounts are the most common form of demand deposits. Deposits and withdrawals are typically made through a combination of deposits, check writing, automatic teller machines (ATMs), point of sale terminals, electronic funds transfers, and preauthorized deposits and payment transactions, such as a payroll deposits and loan payments.

(ii) Savings Deposits. Interest-bearing deposit accounts which normally carry with them certain access restrictions or minimum balance requirements. Passbook and statement savings accounts and money market accounts are the most common form of savings accounts. Deposits and withdrawals are typically made at teller windows, ATMs, by electronic funds transfers, or by preauthorized payment. Money market accounts often permit the customer to write checks, although the number of checks that may be written is limited.

(iii) Time Deposits. Interest-bearing deposit accounts which are subject to withdrawal only after a fixed term. Certificates of deposit (CDs), individual retirement accounts (IRAs), and open accounts are the most common form of time deposits.

CDs may be issued in bearer form or registered form and may be negotiable and non-negotiable. Negotiable CDs, for which there is an active secondary market, are generally short-term and are most commonly sold to corporations, pension funds, and government bodies in large denominations, such as $100 thousand to $1 million. Nonnegotiable CDs are generally in smaller denominations and depositors are subject to a penalty fee if they elect to withdraw their funds prior to the stated maturity.

IRAs, Keogh accounts and self-employed-person accounts (SEPs) are generally maintained as CDs; however, because of the tax benefits to depositors, they typically have longer terms than most CDs.

Brokered deposits are time deposits that are third-party deposits placed by or through the assistance of a deposit broker. Deposit brokers sometimes sell interests in placed deposits to third parties. Federal law restricts the acceptance and renewal of brokered deposits by an institution based on its capitalization.

(v) FEDERAL FUNDS AND REPURCHASE AGREEMENTS. Federal Funds and repurchase agreements are often used as a source of liquidity and as a cost-effective source of funds.

(i) Federal Funds Purchased. Generally, short-term funds maturing overnight bought between banks which are members of the Federal Reserve System in the United States Federal funds transactions can be secured or unsecured. If the funds are secured, U.S. government securities are placed in a custody account for the seller.

(ii) Repurchase Agreements. The sale of a security for cash with an agreement to repurchase the same or similar security at a later date.

(w) DEBT. Banks and savings institutions use long- and short-term borrowings as a source of funds.

(i) Long-Term Debt. Debentures and notes are the most common form of long-term debt; however, institutions also use long-term mortgages, obligations and commitments under capital leases, and mandatorily redeemable preferred stock to provide long-term funding. Funds are also borrowed through Eurodollar certificates; collateralized mortgage obligations (CMOs) and real estate mortgage investment conduits (REMICS); mortgage-backed bonds; mortgage-revenue bonds; and Federal Home Loan Bank (FHLB) advances. The terms of long-term debt vary; they may be secured or unsecured and they may be convertible.

(ii) Short-Term Debt. Repurchase agreements and federal funds purchased are the most common form of short-term debt, and are discussed in subsection 25.2(v).

Commercial paper is another common source of short-term funding. Commercial paper is an unsecured short-term promissory note issued by bank or savings institution holding companies.

Member institutions may borrow from their regional Federal Reserve Bank in the form of discounts and advances, which are primarily used to cover shortages in the required reserve account and also in times of liquidity problems.

Mortgage back bonds are any borrowings (other than those from an FHLB) collateralized in whole or in part by one or more real estate loans.

(x) TAXATION. Taxation of financial institutions is extremely complex; specific discussion is therefore beyond the scope of this book. However, certain significant factors affecting bank and thrift taxation are discussed below.

(i) Loan Loss Reserves

Banks. Prior to the Tax Reform Act of 1986 (1986 Act), banks were permitted to deduct loan loss provisions based on either the experience method or on a percentage of eligible loans method. The 1986 Act modified IRC Section 585 which now allows only a "small" bank with $500 million or less in average assets (calculated by taking into account the average assets of all other members of an institution's controlled group, if applicable) to calculate an addition to the bad debt reserve using the experience method.

A "large" bank with over $500 million in assets may not use the reserve method. It is limited to the specific charge-off method under IRC Section 166. If a bank becomes a large bank, it is required to recapture its reserve, usually over a four-year period. A deduction under Section 166 is generally allowed for wholly or partially worthless debt for the year in which the worthlessness occurs. The total or partial worthlessness of a debt is a facts-and-circumstances, loan-by-loan determination. A bank may make a conformity election, however, which provides a presumptive conclusion of worthlessness for charge-offs made for regulatory purposes.

In comparison to GAAP, the specific charge-off method generally results in an unfavorable temporary difference (i.e., the book expense is recognized prior to the tax deduction being allowed), because the actual charge-off of a loan usually occurs later than the time the reserve is established for it.

Thrifts. Section 593 provides for a special loan loss reserve for an institution which meets the thrift asset test—60% of assets must be "qualifying assets" (generally cash, government obligations, and loans secured by residential real property) as described in Section 7701(a)(19)(C). Under Section 593, a thrift is allowed an addition to its reserve based upon either the percentage of taxable income or an experience method reserve. The percentage of taxable income method allows a thrift to claim a bad debt deduction equal to 8% of modified taxable income after net operating loss. The experience method deduction is the amount needed to bring the reserve up to the greater of (1) an amount based upon a six-year average of net charge-offs to loan ratio; or (2) the base-year reserve. A thrift may also use the specific charge-off method to compute its bad debt deduction for the year.

(ii) Mark-to-Market. Contrary to normal realization-based tax accounting principles, IRC Section 475 requires "dealers in securities" to recognize gain or loss through "marking-to-market" their securities holdings, unless such securities are validly identified by the taxpayer as excepted from the provisions.

As used in this context, the terms "dealer" and "securities" have very broad application. Virtually all financial institutions are considered dealers in securities for mark-to-market purposes though regulations provide exceptions for certain institutions not engaging in more than de minimis dealer activities. Securities required to be marked (unless validly identified as excepted) include notes, bonds, and other evidences of indebtedness; stock; notional principal contracts; and options, forwards, and other derivative financial instruments.

Securities that may be identified as excepted from the mark-to-market provisions are:

Securities "held for investment."

Notes and other evidences of indebtedness (and obligations to acquire such) that are acquired or originated by the taxpayer in the ordinary course of a trade or business which are "not held for sale."

Hedges of positions or liabilities that are not securities in the hands of the taxpayer, and hedges of positions or liabilities that are exempt from mark-to-market under the two foregoing provisions. This does not apply for hedges held as a dealer.

To be excepted from mark-to-market, the security must be identified by the taxpayer on a contemporaneous basis (generally, day of acquisition) as meeting one of the exceptions.

Whether or not a security is required to be marked-to-market for financial accounting purposes is *not* dispositive for purpose of determining whether such security is treated as "held for investment" or "not held for sale."

Some financial institutions identify all or a significant portion of their loans to customers as excepted from the mark-to-market provisions because they intend to hold those loans to maturity. A possible exception are mortgages that are originated for sale (pipeline or warehoused loans), which do not meet the exception criteria and must be marked-to-market.

(iii) Tax-Exempt Securities.   For tax purposes, gross income does not include interest on any obligation of a state or political subdivision thereof (e.g., county, city). Interest on certain nonqualified private activity bonds, unregistered bonds and arbitrage bonds does not qualify for this exemption.

A deduction is not allowed for interest expense on indebtedness incurred to purchase or carry tax-exempt obligations. Deposit-taking financial institutions (banks and thrifts) are subject to a special two-part formula to determine how much of the total interest expense of an institution is disallowed interest expense.

Interest expense related to tax-exempt obligations acquired after August 1986 is wholly disallowed, and is calculated by multiplying total interest expense by the ratio of the tax basis of such obligations to the tax basis of all assets.

Interest expense related to tax-exempt obligations acquired between January 1983 and August 1986 is 20% disallowed, and is calculated in a manner similar to that just described.

Certain qualified tax-exempt obligations (generally, obligations issued by an entity that will not issue more than $10 million of tax-exempt obligations during the year, and that are not private activity bonds) issued after August 1986 are treated as if issued prior to that date (i.e., subject to the 20% disallowance rule rather than the 100% disallowance rule).

(iv) Nonaccrual Loans.   Generally, interest on a loan must be accrued as income unless the taxpayer can demonstrate that the interest is uncollectible at the time of accrual. The tax rule is dependent on the facts and circumstances for the non-accrual loans at issue. FAS No. 114 uses a "probable" test in determining when a loan is impaired. When it is probable that a creditor will be unable to collect all amounts due according to the contractual terms of the loan agreement, the loan is considered impaired. Use of this analysis may now provide substantiation of the tax treatment for impairment of loans.

(v) Hedging.   Financial institutions that are involved in hedging transactions treat the gain or loss from these transactions as ordinary for tax purposes. A hedging transaction must be entered into primarily to reduce a taxpayer's risk of interest rate changes, price changes, or currency fluctuations. A taxpayer must also have risk on an overall (or macro) basis. A hedge of a single ordinary asset or liability will be respected if it is reasonably expected to reduce the taxpayer's overall risk. Hedges entered into as part of an overall risk reduction program also will qualify.

"Fixed to floating" hedges (e.g., hedges that convert a fixed rate liability into a floating rate liability) may satisfy the risk reduction requirement if, for example, a taxpayer's income varies with interest rates. In addition, hedges entered into to reverse or counteract another hedging transaction may qualify for ordinary gain or loss treatment.

Hedges of ordinary liabilities qualify as "hedging transactions" regardless of the use of the proceeds from the borrowing. Consequently, gain or loss from a hedge of a liability used to fund the purchase of a capital asset will be ordinary.

The timing of the gain or loss from a hedging transaction must reasonably be "matched" with the gain or loss of the item being hedged. This applies to global hedges and other hedges of aggregate risk.

If a taxpayer disposes of a hedged item but retains the hedge, the taxpayer generally must mark-to-market the hedge on the date that the taxpayer disposes of the hedged item.

There are detailed identification and recordkeeping requirements with which an institution must comply to support its treatment of hedging transactions. Failure to comply could lead to characterization of losses from these transactions as capital losses (which may only be used to offset capital gains).

(vi) Loan Origination Fees and Costs.   For financial accounting purposes, SFAS No. 91 requires that all loan origination fees (including loan commitment fees and points) be deferred and generally recognized over the life of the related loan or commitment period as an adjustment of yield. For tax accounting purposes, loan fees received as cash payments incident to a lending transaction (e.g., points) that are not for services (e.g., most commitment fees) are deferred. Points received in connection with a lending transaction are applied as a reduction to the issue price of the loan, and generally create original issue discount (OID) to be recognized over the life of the loan on a constant yield method. In instances where the OID on a loan is de minimis (as defined in regulations), the OID is recognized in proportion to principal payments.

For book purposes, the costs associated with origination of a loan are deferred and recognized over the life of the loan together with the origination fees. For tax purposes, institutions generally deduct these costs currently because there is no published guidance requiring capitalization.

(vii) Foreclosed Property

Banks.   Generally, a bank recognizes gain or loss on foreclosure of property securing a loan, but is not permitted to deduct any further decrease in or impairment of value. Any decrease in value occurring after foreclosure is recognized when the property is disposed of by the institution. If real property acquired through foreclosure is operated in a trade or business after foreclosure (e.g., as rental property), the institution may deduct depreciation (and other operating expenses) computed in accordance with general tax depreciation provisions.

Thrifts.   A special rule applies in the case of a thrift that forecloses on a property. Under Section 595, the acquisition of property is treated as a non-taxable event with no gain or loss recognized at time of foreclosure and no depreciation allowed on the property. A subsequent write-down charged to the reserve for bad debts is allowed if the fair market value of the property is less than the tax basis of the loan. Upon final disposition, the gain or loss is credited or charged to the reserve for bad debts.

(viii) Leasing Activities.   Direct financing activities may qualify as financings for tax purposes. As a result, a bank will be considered the owner of the leased property for tax purposes. Accordingly, rental income and depreciation deductions on the leased asset will be recognized for tax purposes but not for financial reporting purposes. This will result in a difference between book and tax accounting under SFAS No. 109.

(y) FIDUCIARY SERVICES AND OTHER FEE INCOME

(i) Fiduciary Services.   In their fiduciary capacity, banks must serve their clients' interests and must act in good faith at a level absent in most other banking activities. In view of this high degree of fiduciary responsibility, banks usually segregate the responsibilities of the trust department from that of the rest of the bank. This segregation is designed to maintain a highly objective viewpoint in the fiduciary area. Fiduciary services range from the simple safekeeping of valuables to the investment management of large pension funds.

Custodial, safekeeping, and safe deposit activities involve the receipt, storage, and issuance of receipts for a range of valuable assets. This may involve the holding of bonds, stocks, and currency in escrow pending the performance under a contract, or merely the maintenance of a secure depository for valuables or title deeds. As custodian, the bank may receive interest and dividends on securities for the account of customers.

Investment management may be discretionary, whereby the bank has certain defined powers to make investments, or nondiscretionary, whereby the bank may only execute investment transactions based on customers' instructions. The former obviously involves a higher degree of risk to the institution and creates an obligation to make prudent investment decisions.

Other fiduciary services include trust administration, stock registrar, and bank trustee. Trust administration involves holding or management of property, such as pension funds and estates, for the benefit of others. Stock registrar and bank trustee functions include the maintenance of records and execution of securities transactions, including changes in ownership and payment of dividends and interest.

Since the assets and liabilities of the trust department of the bank are held in an agency capacity, they are not recorded on the balance sheet of the bank. These activities can, however, generate significant fee income, which is recorded when earned in the statement of income.

(ii) Other Fee Income.   Emphasis on fee income-generating activities has increased in response to both the risk-based capital guidelines, which created more pressure to reduce the size of the balance sheet, and also a general increase in competition in the financial services industry.

Some of the principal forms of fee-generating activity include:

Annuities. Banks sell fixed and variable annuities.

Brokerage. Banks may arrange for the purchase and sale of securities on behalf of customers in return for a commission.

Corporate and Advisory-Services. These activities involve advice on mergers and acquisitions, capital raising, and treasury management in return for a fee.

Private Banking. This activity involves investment planning, tax assistance, and credit extensions to wealthy individuals.

Private Placements. This activity normally involves the placement of securities on a *best efforts* basis as opposed to an underwriting commitment.

Underwriting. Banks may guarantee to purchase certain allowable securities if they are not fully subscribed to in an offering.

401(k) Plans and Mutual Funds. Banks may distribute mutual funds in a 401(k) plan.

Many of the activities, particularly underwriting, are subject to restriction by regulation as to the type of securities that may be transacted, and separately capitalized subsidiaries may be required. These restrictions are subject to change at the current time and may be significantly relaxed in the near future.

These activities generate fee income that is recorded when earned. Certain activities are conducted in conjunction with credit extension activities, and therefore particular attention is required to ensure that fees generated are appropriately recorded. It is essential to distinguish between fees that may be recorded immediately and fees that are essentially loan origination fees to be accounted for over the life of the loan (SFAS No. 91).

25.3 MORTGAGE BANKING ACTIVITIES

(a) ACCOUNTING.   The concentration of mortgage-related activities in banks and savings institutions heightens the importance of the specific accounting rules relating to these activities. SFAS No. 65, "Accounting for Certain Mortgage Banking Activities, as amended by SFAS 122, Accounting for Mortgage Saving Rights," provides specific guidance on accounting issues relevant to mortgage banking activity. Some of the most relevant accounting issues covered by SFAS No. 65 and other pronouncements are described below.

(b) MORTGAGE LOANS AND MORTGAGE-BACKED SECURITIES.   Mortgage loans are loans granted to debtors for real estate purchases, refinancing, and improvements; the loans are secured by the underlying property. Mortgage-backed securities are securities issued by a governmental agency or corporation (e.g., GNMA or FHLMC) or by private issuer (e.g., FNMA, banks and mortgage banking enterprises). Mortgage-backed securities generally are referred to as mortgage participation certificates or pass-through certificates (PC's). A PC represents an undivided interest in a pool of specific mortgage loans. Periodic payments of FHLMC and FNMA PCS are guaranteed by those corporations but are not backed by the U.S. government. It should be noted that, in accordance with FIRREA, the FHLMC was restructured and privatized.

(i) Valuation.   The valuation of mortgage loans for financial reporting purposes depends on whether they are held to maturity or for sale. Mortgage loans held to maturity should be reported at cost. Mortgage loans held for sale must be reported at the lower of cost or market value, determined as of the balance sheet date. The amount by which cost exceeds market value must be accounted for as a valuation allowance. Changes in the valuation allowances must be included in the determination of net income of the period in which the change occurs. Mortgage-backed securities held for sale in conjunction with mortgage banking activities must be classified as trading securities and reported at fair value in accordance with SFAS No. 115 "Accounting for Certain Investments in Debt and Equity Securities."

(ii) Transferred to a Long-Term Investment or Securitized.   A mortgage loan transferred to a long-term investment classification must be transferred at the lower of cost or market value on the transfer date. The securitization of a mortgage loan held for sale must be accounted for as the sale of the mortgage loan and the purchase of a mortgage-backed security classified as a trading security at fair value. Any difference between the carrying amount of the loan and its outstanding principal balance must be recognized as an adjustment to yield by the interest method. A mortgage loan must not be classified as a long-term investment unless the mortgage banking enterprise has both the ability and the intent to hold the loan for the foreseeable future or until maturity.

(iii) Market Value.   The market value of mortgage loans and mortgage-backed securities held for sale must be determined by type of loan. At a minimum, separate determinations of market value for residential (one- to four-family dwellings) and commercial mortgage loans must be made. Either the aggregate or individual loan basis may be used in determining the lower of cost or market value for each type of loan. Market value for loans subject to investor purchase commitments (committed loans) and loans held on a speculative basis must be determined separately as follows:

Committed Loans and Mortgage-Backed Securities. Market value for mortgage loans covered by investor commitments must be based on commitment prices. If the fair value of a mortgage-backed security subject to an investor purchase commitment exceeds the commitment price, the implicit loss on the commitment must be recognized.

Uncommitted Loans. Market value for uncommitted loans must be based on the market in which the mortgage banking enterprise normally operates.

Uncommitted Mortgage-Backed Securities. Fair value for uncommitted mortgage-backed securities that are collateralized by a mortgage banking enterprise's own loans ordinarily must be based on the market value of the securities.

Capitalized costs of acquiring rights to service mortgage loans, associated with the purchase or origination of mortgage loans must be excluded from the cost of mortgage loans for the purpose of determining the lower of cost or market value if the investment has a definitive plan to sell the loans.

(c) LOAN ORIGINATION FEES AND COSTS.   Mortgage loan origination and commitment fees are a significant income component of mortgage banking activity. Based on diversity in practice among financial institutions regarding accounting for nonrefundable fees and costs associated with lending activities, the FASB undertook the loan origination fees and costs project and issued SFAS No. 91, "Accounting for Nonrefundable Fees and Costs Associated with Originating or Acquiring Loans and Initial Direct Costs of Leases," making accounting practices uniform for such fees and costs. Accounting for loan origination and commitment fees and associated costs has been previously discussed in subsection 25.2(o)(ii).

(d) SERVICING FEES.   A mortgage banking institution generally retains the right to service mortgage loans it sells to investors. The process of performing loan administration functions (collecting, maintaining mortgage loan records, etc.) is referred to as "servicing." In compensation for this service, a servicing fee is charged based on a percentage of the unpaid principal balance of the loans.

If mortgage loans are sold with servicing retained and the stated servicing fee rate differs materially from a current (normal) servicing fee rate, the sales price must be adjusted, for purposes of determining gain or loss on the sale, to provide for the recognition of a normal servicing fee in each subsequent year. The amount of the adjustment must be the difference between the actual sales price and the estimated sales price that would have been obtained if a normal servicing fee rate had been specified. The adjustment ordinarily will approximate the present value, based on an appropriate interest rate, of the difference between normal and stated servicing fees over the estimated life of the mortgage loans. The adjustment and any gain or loss to be recognized must be determined as of the date the mortgage loans are sold. In addition, if normal servicing fees are expected to be less than estimated servicing costs over the estimated life of the mortgage loans, the expected loss on servicing the loans must be accrued at the date.

The FASB's EITF reached a consensus in Issue No. 88-11, "Allocation of Recorded Investment When a Loan or Part of a Loan Is Sold," that the difference between the normal and stated servicing fees, if any, over the estimated life of the loan should be calculated using prepayment, default, and interest-rate assumptions that market participants would use for similar financial instruments and should be discounted using an interest rate that a purchaser unrelated to the seller of such a financial instrument would demand. Prepayment estimates should be based on the prepayment experience for similar instruments.

(e) SERVICING RIGHTS

(i) Purchasing, Acquiring, and Selling Mortgage Servicing Rights.   A mortgage banking enterprise may purchase mortgage servicing rights separately or it may acquire mortgage servicing rights by purchasing or originating mortgage loans and selling or securitizing those loans with servicing rights retained. When a mortgage banking enterprise purchases or originates mortgage loans, the cost of acquiring those loans includes the cost of the related mortgage servicing rights. If the mortgage banking enterprise sells or securitizes the loans and retains the mortgage servicing rights, the enterprise must allocate the total cost of the mortgage loans (the recorded investment in the mortgage loans including net deferred loan fees or costs and any purchase premium or discount) to the mortgage servicing rights and the loans (without the mortgage servicing rights) based on their relative fair values if it is practicable to estimate those fair values as follows:

Definitive Plan to Sell or Securitize. A mortgage banking enterprise that purchases or originates mortgage loans with a definitive plan to sell or securitize those loans and retain the mortgage servicing rights must allocate the cost of the mortgage loans based on the relative fair values at the date of purchase or origination. The allocation must be based on the assumption that a normal servicing fee will be received and that the rights to the remaining cash flows from the underlying mortgage loans will be sold or securitized. A definitive plan exists if (1) the mortgage banking enterprise has obtained, before the purchase or origination date, commitments from permanent investors to purchase the mortgage loans or related mortgage-backed securities, makes a commitment within a reasonable period (usually not more than 30 days after the purchase or origination date) to sell the mortgage loans or related mortgage-backed securities to a permanent investor or underwriter, or has made, before the purchase or origination date, commitments to deliver the mortgage loans for securitization and (2) estimates of the selling price have been made.

No Definitive Plan. A mortgage banking enterprise that does not have a definitive plan at the purchase or origination date and later sells or securitizes the mortgage loans and retains the mortgage servicing rights must allocate the amortized cost of the mortgage loans based on the relative fair values at the date of sale or securitization.

If Not Practicable to Estimate. If it is not practicable to estimate the fair values of the mortgage servicing rights and the mortgage loans (without the mortgage servicing rights), the entire cost of purchasing or originating the mortgage loans must be allocated to the mortgage loans (without servicing rights) and no cost must be allocated to the mortgage servicing rights.

(ii) Impairment of Mortgage Servicing Rights

Stratification. For the purpose of evaluating and measuring impairment of capitalized mortgage servicing rights, a mortgage banking enterprise must stratify those rights based on one or more of the predominant risk characteristics of the underlying loans. Those characteristics may include loan type, size, note rate, date of origination, term, and geographic location. However, a mortgage banking enterprise may continue to apply its previous accounting policies for stratifying mortgage servicing rights to those mortgage servicing rights that were capitalized prior to fiscal years beginning after December 15, 1995.

Valuation Allowance. Impairment must be recognized through a valuation allowance for an individual stratum. The amount of impairment recognized must be the amount by which the capitalized mortgage servicing rights for a stratum exceed their fair value. The fair value of mortgage servicing rights that have not been capitalized must not be used in the evaluation of impairment.

Subsequent Measurement. Subsequent to the initial measurement of impairment, the mortgage banking enterprise must adjust the valuation allowance to reflect changes in the measurement of impairment. Fair value in excess of amount capitalized as mortgage servicing rights (net of amortization), however, must not be recognized.

Fair Value. The fair value of an asset is the amount at which the asset could be bought or sold in a current transaction between willing parties, that is, other than in a forced or liquidation sale. Quoted market prices in active markets are the best evidence of fair value and must be used as the basis for the measurement, if available. If quoted market prices are not available, the estimate of fair value must consider prices for similar assets and the results of valuation techniques to the extent available in the circumstances. Examples of valuation techniques include the present value of estimated expected future cash flows using a discount rate commensurate with the risks involved, option-pricing models, matrix pricing, option-adjusted spread models, and fundamental analysis. Valuation techniques for measuring mortgage servicing rights should be consistent with the objective of measuring fair value and should incorporate assumptions that market participants would use in their estimates of future servicing income and expense, including assumptions about prepayment, default, and interest rates.

(iii) Amortization of Capitalized Mortgage Servicing Rights. The amount capitalized as the right to service mortgage loans (net of any valuation allowances) must be amortized in proportion to, and over the period of, estimated net servicing income (servicing revenue in excess of servicing costs). For this purpose, estimates of future servicing revenue must include expected late charges and other ancillary revenue and should be adjusted for loan prepayment estimates. Estimates of expected future servicing costs must include direct costs associated with performing the servicing function and appropriate allocations of other costs. Estimated future servicing costs may be determined on an incremental cost basis.

(f) LOAN PLACEMENT FEES. Fees for arranging a commitment directly between a permanent investor and a borrower (loan placement fees) should be recognized as revenue when all significant services have been performed. In addition, if a mortgage banking enterprise obtains a commitment from a permanent investor before or at the time a related commitment is made to a borrower and if the commitment to the borrower will require (1) simultaneous assignment of the commitment to the investor and (2) simultaneous transfer to the borrower of the amount received from the investor, the related fees should also be accounted for as loan placement fees.

25.4 INVESTMENT COMPANIES

(a) BACKGROUND. An investment company (referred to as a "fund" or a "mutual fund") generally pools investors' funds to provide them with professional investment management and diversification of ownership in the securities markets. Typically, an investment company sells its capital shares to the public and invests the net proceeds in stock, bonds, government obligations, or other securities, intended to meet the fund's stated investment objectives. A brief history of investment companies is included at item 1.07 of "Audits of Investment Companies," the *AICPA Audit and Accounting Guide.* One of the more notable distinctions between investment companies and companies in other industries is the extremely high degree of compliance to which registered investment companies must adhere.

(i) SEC Statutes. The SEC is responsible for the administration and enforcement of the following statutes governing investment companies:

> **The Investment Company Act of 1940.** Regulates registered investment companies (having more than 100 shareholders) and provides extensive rules and regulations that govern recordkeeping, reporting, fiduciary duties, and other responsibilities of an investment company's management.
> **The Investment Advisers Act of 1940.** Requires persons who are paid to render investment advice to individuals or institutions, including investment companies, to register with the SEC, and regulates their conduct and contracts.
> **The Securities Act of 1933.** Relates primarily to the initial public offering and distribution of securities (including the capital shares of investment companies).

The Securities Exchange Act of 1934. Regulates the trading of securities in secondary markets after the initial public offering and distribution of the securities under the 1933 Act. Periodic SEC financial reporting requirements pursuant to § 13 or § 15(d) of the 1934 Act are satisfied by the semiannual filing of Form N-SAR pursuant to § 30 of the 1940 Act.

(ii) Types of Investment Companies. Three common methods of classification are (1) by securities law definition, (2) by investment objectives, and (3) by form of organization.

Classification by Securities Law Definition. Securities law divides investment companies into three types: management companies, face amount certificate companies, and unit investment trusts. The most common classification is the management company. The term "mutual fund" refers to an open-end management company as described under § 5 of the 1940 Act. Such a fund stands ready to redeem its shares at net asset value whenever requested to do so and usually continuously offers its shares for sale, although it is not required to do so. A closed-end management company does not stand ready to redeem its shares when requested (although it may occasionally make tender offers for its shares) and generally does not issue additional shares, except perhaps in connection with a dividend reinvestment program. Its outstanding shares are usually traded on an exchange, often at a premium or discount from the fund's underlying net asset value. In addition to open-end and closed-end management companies, there are also management companies which offer the ability for shareholders to periodically redeem their shares on specified dates or intervals.

Other management investment companies include Small Business Investment Companies and Business Development Companies (SBICs and BDCs). Management companies, at their own election, are further divided into diversified companies and non-diversified companies. A fund that elects to be a diversified company must meet the 75% test required under § 5(b)(1) of the 1940 Act. Nondiversified companies are management companies that have elected to be nondiversified and do not have to meet the requirements of § 5(b)(1).

The 1940 Act also provides for face amount certificate companies, which are rather rare, and unit investment trusts. Unit investment trusts are established under a trust indenture by a sponsoring organization that acquires a portfolio (often tax-exempt or taxable bonds that are generally held to maturity) and then sells undivided interests in the trust. Units of the trust generally are not offered continuously, nor do the trusts generally make any additional portfolio acquisitions. Units remain outstanding until they are tendered for redemption or the trust is terminated.

Separate accounts of an insurance company that underlie variable annuity and variable life insurance products are also subject to the requirements of the 1940 Act. They may be established as management companies or as unit investment trusts. Variable annuities and variable life products are considered to be both securities subject to the 1933 Act and insurance products subject to regulation by state insurance departments.

Classification by Investment Objectives. Investment companies can also be classified by their investment objectives or types of investments, for example, growth funds, income funds, tax-exempt funds, global funds, money market funds, and equity funds. At the end of 1994, the Investment Company Institute, an industry trade association, reported the existence of 5,630 funds, divided among 22 types of funds.

Classification by Form of Organization. Investment companies can also be classified by their form of organization. Funds may be organized as corporations or trusts (and, to a lesser extend, as partnerships).

Incorporation offers the advantages of detailed state statutory and interpretative judicial decisions governing operations, limited liability of shareholders, and in normal cases, requires no exemptions to comply with the 1940 Act.

The business trust, or Massachusetts Trust, is an unincorporated business association established by a declaration or deed of trust and governed largely by the law of trusts. In general, a business trust has the advantages of unlimited authorized shares, no annual meeting requirement, and long duration. However, Massachusetts Trusts have a potential disadvantage, in that there is unlimited liability to the business trust shareholders in the event of litigation or other negative factors. Generally, however, the Trust undertakes to indemnify the shareholders against loss.

(b) FUND OPERATIONS.   When a new fund is established, it enters into a contract with an investment adviser (often the sponsoring organization) to manage the fund and, within the terms of the fund's stated investment objectives, to determine what securities should be purchased, sold, or exchanged. The investment adviser places orders for the purchase or sale of portfolio securities for the fund with brokers or dealers selected by it. The officers of the fund, who generally are also officers of the investment adviser or fund administrator, give instructions to the custodian of the fund holdings as to delivery of securities and payments of cash for the account of the fund. The investment adviser normally furnishes, at its own expense, all necessary services, facilities, and personnel in connection with these responsibilities. The investment adviser may also act as administrator; administrative duties include preparation of regulatory filings and managing relationships with other service providers. The investment adviser and administrator are usually paid for these services through a fee based on the value of net assets.

The distributor or underwriter for an investment company markets the shares of the fund—either directly to the public ("no-load" funds) or through a sales force. The sales force may be compensated for their services through a direct sales commission included in (deducted from) the price at which the fund's shares are offered (redeemed), through a distribution fee (also referred to as a "12b-1 plan fee") paid by the fund as part of its recurring expenses, or in both ways. Rule 12b-1 under the 1940 Act permits an investment company to pay for distribution expenses, which otherwise are paid for by the distributor and not the fund.

A fund has officers and directors (and in some cases, trustees) but generally has no employees, the services it requires being provided under contract by others. Primary servicing organizations are summarized below.

(i) Fund Accounting Agent.   The fund accounting agent maintains the fund's general ledger and portfolio accounting records and computes the net asset value per share, usually on a daily basis. In some instances, this service is provided by the investment adviser or an affiliate of the adviser, or a nonaffiliated entity may perform this service. The fund accounting agent, or in some cases a separate administrative agent, may also be responsible for preparation of the fund's financial statements, tax returns, semiannual and annual filings with the SEC on Form N-SAR, and the annual registration statement filing.

(ii) Custodian.   The custodian maintains custody of the fund's assets, collects income, pays expenses, and settles investment transactions. The 1940 Act provides for three alternatives in selecting a custodian. The most commonly used is a commercial bank or trust company that meets the requirements of §§ 17 and 26 of the 1940 Act. The second alternative is a member firm of a national securities exchange; the third alternative is for the fund to act as its own custodian and utilize the safekeeping facilities of a bank or trust company. Section 17(f) and Rule 17f-2 of the 1940 Act provide for specific audit procedures to be performed by the fund's independent accountant when either alternative two or three is used.

(iii) Transfer Agent.   The fund's transfer agent maintains the shareholder records and processes the sales and redemptions of the fund's capital shares. The transfer agent processes the capital share transactions at a price per share equal to the net asset value per share of the fund next determined by the fund accounting agent (forward pricing). In certain instances, shareholder servicing—the direct contact with shareholders, usually by telephone—is combined with the transfer agent processing.

(c) ACCOUNTING.   The AICPA Audit and Accounting Guide, "Audits of Investment Companies" (1994) provides specific guidance on accounting issues relevant to investment companies. The SEC has set forth in Accounting Series Release (ASR) No. 118, "Accounting for Investment Securities by Registered Investment Companies" (Financial Reporting Policies, Section 404.03, "Accounting, Valuation, and Disclosure of Investment Securities"), its views on accounting for securities by registered investment companies.

Because for federal income tax purposes the fund is a conduit for the shareholders, the operations of an investment company are normally influenced by federal income tax to the shareholder. Accordingly, conformity between book and tax accounting is usually maintained whenever practicable under GAAP. In general, investment companies carry securities, which is their most significant asset, at current value, not at historical cost. In such a "mark-to-market" environment, conforming book and tax accounting usually has no effect on net asset value and only has a reclassification effect on income. On this basis, the Audit and Accounting Guide permits federal income tax accounting as an acceptable accounting policy in many areas.

Uniquely, most mutual funds close their books daily and calculate a net asset value per share, which forms the pricing basis for shareholders who are purchasing or redeeming fund shares. SEC Rules 2a-4 and 22c-1 set forth certain accounting requirements, including a one cent per share materiality criterion used by funds when pricing shares. Because of this daily closing of the books, mutual funds and their agents must maintain well-controlled and current accounting systems to provide proper records for their highly compliance-oriented industry.

The SEC has promulgated extensive rules under each of the statutes that it administers, including the following:

> **Article 6 of Regulation S-X** (and Rule 3-18 of Article 3 and Rule 12-12 of Article 12). Sets forth requirements as to the form and content of, and requirements for, financial statements filed with the SEC, including what financial statements must be presented and for hat periods.
>
> **Regulation S-K Item 302—Supplementary Financial Information.** Requires disclosure of selected quarterly financial data of closed-end funds meeting specified size and trading requirements.
>
> **Financial Reporting Policies.** Section 404 relates specifically to registered investment companies.

(d) FINANCIAL REPORTING

(i) New Registrants.   Any company registered under the 1940 Act that has not previously had an effective registration statement under the 1933 Act, must include in its initial registration statement, financial statements and financial highlights of a date within 90 days prior to the date of filing. For a company that did not have any prior operations, this would be limited to a seed capital statement of assets and liabilities and related notes.

Section 14 of the 1940 Act requires that an investment company have a net worth of at least $100,000. Accordingly, a new investment company is usually incorporated by its sponsor with seed capital of that amount.

(ii) General Reporting Requirements.   SEC reporting requirements are outlined in § 30 of the 1940 Act and the related rules and regulations thereunder, which supersede any requirements under § 13 or § 15(d) of the 1934 Act to which an investment company would otherwise be subject. A registered investment company is deemed by the SEC to have satisfied its requirement under the 1934 Act to file an annual report by the filing of semiannual reports on Form N-SAR.

The SEC requires that every registered management company send to its shareholders, at least semiannually, a report containing financial statements and financial highlights. Only the financial statements and financial highlights in the annual report are required to be audited.

Some funds prepare quarterly reports to shareholders, although they are not required to do so. They generally include a portfolio listing and in relatively few cases, they include full financial statements. Closed-end funds listed on an exchange have certain quarterly reporting requirements under their listing agreements with the exchange.

(iii) Financial Statements. Article 6 of Regulation S-X deals specifically with investment companies and requires the following statements:

- A statement of assets and liabilities (supported by a separate listing of portfolio securities) or a statement of net assets, which includes a detailed list of portfolio securities at the reporting date.
- A statement of operations for the year.
- A statement of changes in net assets for the latest two years.

SFAS No. 95 provides that a statement of cash flows should be included with financial statements prepared in accordance with GAAP. SFAS No. 102 exempts investment companies from providing a statement of cash flows, provided certain conditions are met. A statement of changes in net assets should be presented even if the statement of cash flows is presented because it presents the changes in shareholders' equity required by GAAP.

(e) TAXATION. Investment companies are subject to federal income taxes and certain state and local taxes. However, investment companies registered under the 1940 Act may qualify for special federal income tax treatment as regulated investment companies (RICs) under the IRC and may deduct dividends paid to shareholders. If a fund fails to qualify as a RIC, it will be taxed as a regular corporation, and the deduction for dividends paid by the fund is disallowed. Subchapter M (§§ 851 to 855) of the IRC applies to RICs. Chapter 4 of the Audit Guide discusses the tax considerations related to RICs.

To qualify as a RIC, the fund must:

- Be registered under the 1940 Act.
- Derive less than 30% of its gross income from sales of securities held less than 3 months (the so-called short-short test).
- Derive 90% of its total income from dividends, interest, and gross gains on sales of securities.
- Have 50% of its assets composed of cash, U.S. government securities, securities of other funds, and "other issues," as defined.
- Have not more than 25% of the value of its total assets invested in the securities (other than U.S. government securities or the securities of other regulated investment companies) of any one issuer or of two or more issuers controlled by the fund that are determined to be engaged in the same or similar trades or businesses.
- Distribute at least 90% of its net investment company taxable income and net tax-exempt interest income to its shareholders.

Also, to avoid a 4% nondeductible excise tax, a fund must distribute, by December 31 of each year, 98% of its ordinary income measured on a calendar year basis and 98% of its net capital gains measured on a fiscal year basis ending October 31. Actual payment of the distribution must be before February 1 of the following year.

(f) FILINGS. SEC registration forms applicable to investment companies include the following:

Form N-8A. The notification of registration under the 1940 Act.

Form N-1A. The registration statement of open-end management investment companies under the 1940 and the 1933 Acts. (It is not to be used by SBICs, BDCs, or insurance company separate accounts.) The Form describes in detail the company's objectives, policies, management, investment restrictions, and similar matters. The Form consists of the prospectus, the statement of additional information (SAI), and a third section of other information, including detailed information on the SEC-required yield calculations. Posteffective amendments on Form N-1A, including updated audited financial statements, must be filed and become effective under the 1933 and 1940 Acts within 16 months after the end of the period covered by the previous audited financial statements if the fund is to continue offering its shares.

Form N-SAR. A reporting form used for semiannual and annual reports by all registered investment companies that have filed a registration statement that has become effective pursuant to the 1933 Act, with the exception of face amount certificate companies and BDCs. Face amount certificate companies file periodic reports pursuant to § 13 or § 15(d) of the 1934 Act.

Management investment companies file the form semiannually; unit investment trusts are only required to file annually. There is no requirement that the form or any of the items be audited. The annual report filed by a management investment company must be accompanied by a report on the company's system of internal accounting controls from its independent accountant. The requirement for an accountant's report on internal accounting controls does not apply to SBICs or to management investment companies not required by either the 1940 Act of any other federal or state law or rule or regulation thereunder to have an audit of their financial statements.

Form N-2. A registration statement for closed-end funds comparable to the N-1A for open-end funds. Under Rule 8b-16 of the 1940 Act, if certain criteria are met in the Annual Report of a closed-end fund, the fund may not need to annually update its Form N-2 filing with the SEC.

Forms N-1, N-3, N-4, N-8B-2, and S-6. The registration statements for various types of insurance-related products including variable annuities and variable life insurance.

Form N-14. The statement for registration of securities issued by investment companies in business combination transactions under the 1933 Act. It contains information about the companies involved in the transaction, including historical and pro forma financial statements.

(g) INVESTMENT PARTNERSHIPS—SPECIAL CONSIDERATIONS. Investment partnerships may be described generally as limited partnerships organized under state law to trade and/or invest in securities. They are sometimes also referred to as "hedge funds," which has become a generic industry term for an investment partnership (or another nonpublic investment company), although this may be a misnomer depending on the partnership's investment strategy. Investment partnerships, if certain conditions are met, are generally not required to register under the Investment Company Act of 1940 (1940 Act) and are also generally not subject to the Internal Revenue Code rules and regulations that apply to regulated investment companies (RICs).

An investment partnership is governed by its partnership agreement. This is the basis for legal, structural, operational and accounting guidelines. The majority of the capital in an investment partnership is owned by its limited partners. The general partner usually has a minimal investment in the partnership, if any at all. Limited partners may be a variety of entities, including private and public pension plans, foreign investors, insurance companies, bank holding companies and individuals. There are legal, regulatory and accounting and tax considerations associated with each of the above types of investors. For example, investment in an investment partnership by pension plans may subject the investment partnership to the rules and regulations of the Employee Retirement Income Security Act of 1974 ("ERISA") (generally, investment partnerships will not be subject to ERISA if less than 25% of the partnership's capital is derived from pension or other employee benefit plan assets); foreign investors may be subject to foreign withholding taxes; and the number of partners in an investment partnership may subject the investment partnership to registration under the 1940 Act (generally, an investment partnership must have fewer than 100 partners to avoid registration under the 1940 Act).

The limited partners are generally liable for the repayment and discharge of all debts and obligations of the investment partnership, but only to the extent of their respective interest in the partnership. They usually have no part in the management of the partnership and have no authority to act on behalf of the partnership in connection with any matter. The general partner can be an individual, a corporation or other entity. The general partner usually has little or no investment in the investment partnership (often 1% of total contributed capital) and is responsible for the day-to-day administration of the investment partnership. The general partner, however, usually has unlimited liability for the repayment and discharge of all debts and obligations of the partnership irrespective of its interest in the partnership. The general partner may also be the investment adviser or an affiliate of the adviser.

Although investment partnerships are generally not "investment companies" as defined in federal securities laws, they do meet the definition of investment companies as contained in the AICPA "Audit and Accounting Guide on Audits of Investment Companies" (1994 edition). Accordingly, the Guide is generally applicable to investment partnerships. There are, however, certain disclosure requirements in the Guide to which most partnerships have historically taken exception and have not followed. The AICPA has clarified the appropriate disclosure for partnerships in its issuance of SOP 95-2 "Financial Reporting for NonPublic Investment Partnerships" which is applicable for fiscal years beginning after December 15, 1994. The new disclosure requirements include the requirement for a summary portfolio of investments and have clarified the accounting treatment for incentive fees and the presentation of the statement of operations.

A partnership is classified as a pass-through entity for tax purposes, meaning that the partners, not the partnership, are taxed on the income, expenses, gains, and losses incurred by the partnership. The partners recognize the tax effects of the partnership's operations regardless of whether any distribution is made to such partners. This differs from a corporation which incurs an entity level tax on its earnings and whose owners (stockholders) incur a second level of tax when the corporation's profits are distributed to them.

(h) OFFSHORE FUNDS—SPECIAL CONSIDERATIONS.   Offshore funds may be described generally as investment funds set up to permit international investments with minimum tax burden on the fund shareholders. This is achieved by setting up the funds in countries with favorable tax laws, as well as countries with non-burdensome administrative regulations. Popular offshore locations include Bermuda, the Cayman Islands, and the Netherlands Antilles.

An offshore fund's shares are offered to investors (generally non-U.S.) residing outside the country in which the fund is domiciled. Assuming the offshore fund is not publicly sold in the U.S. and does not have more than 100 U.S. shareholders, the offshore fund will not be subject to SEC registration or reporting requirements. Because of the lack of regulatory restrictions, offshore funds often have higher risk investment strategies than U.S. regulated funds.

A major U.S. tax advantage to non-U.S. shareholders of investing in U.S. securities through an offshore fund as opposed to a U.S. domiciled fund is the avoidance of certain U.S. withholding taxes. By investing through the offshore fund, the shareholder avoids withholding taxes on most U.S.-sourced interest income and short-term capital gains which would be subject to withholding taxes if the amounts were paid to the non-U.S. shareholder through a U.S.

domiciled fund. Offshore funds also avoid the U.S. IRC distribution requirements imposed on U.S. funds. This allows for the potential "roll-up" of income in the fund (i.e., the deferral of income recognition for the shareholder for tax purposes, depending on the tax residence of the shareholder).

Even though the fund is a non-U.S. entity, it could be subject to U.S. taxes applicable to U.S. entities, if the fund carries on most or all of its investment activities in the U.S. and is considered as having its principal office in the U.S. Pursuant to U.S. IRC Reg. Sec. 1.864-2(c)2, offshore funds with U.S. investment activities will not be considered to have their principal office in the U.S. (and therefore not subject to U.S. taxes at the fund level) if all or a substantial portion of ten specific functions are carried on at or from an office or offices located outside the U.S. These ten functions are commonly referred to as the "ten commandments."

25.5 SOURCES AND SUGGESTED REFERENCES

Accounting Principles Board Opinion 30, "Reporting the Results of Operations-Reporting the Effects of Disposal of a Segment of a Business and Extraordinary, Unusual and Infrequently Occurring Events and Transactions," AICPA, New York, 1973.

American Institute of Certified Public Accountants Audit and Accounting Guide "Audits of Banks and Savings Institutions" (expected to be issued in 1996). Currently guidance is provided in American Institute of Certified Public Accountants Audit and Accounting Guide "Audits of Savings Institutions," AICPA, 1995, and the American Institute of Certified Public Accountants Industry Audit Guide, "Audits of Banks," AICPA, New York, 1995.

———, "Audits of Investment Companies," AICPA, New York, 1994.

Cammarano, Nicholas and Jr. James J. Klink. *Real Estate Accounting and Reporting: A Guide for Developers, Investors, and Lenders. 3rd ed.* (New York: John Wiley & Sons, 1995).

Financial Accounting Standards Board, Statement of Financial Accounting Standards No. 5, "Accounting for Contingencies," FASB, Stamford, CT, 1975.

———, Statement of Financial Accounting Standards No. 15, "Accounting by Debtors and Creditors for Troubled Debt Restructurings," FASB, Stamford, CT, 1977.

———, Statement of Financial Accounting Standards No. 34, "Capitalization of Interest Cost," FASB, Stamford, CT, 1979.

———, Statement of Financial Accounting Standards No. 52, "Foreign Currency Translation," FASB, Stamford, CT, 1981.

———, Statement of Financial Accounting Standards No. 58, "Capitalization of Interest Cost in Financial Statements That Include Investments Accounted for by the Equity Method," FASB, Stamford, CT, 1982.

———, Statement of Financial Accounting Standards No. 65, "Accounting for Certain Mortgage Banking Activities," FASB, Stamford, CT, 1982.

———, Statement of Financial Accounting Standards No. 66, "Accounting for Sales of Real Estate," FASB, Stamford, CT, 1982.

———, Statement of Financial Accounting Standards No. 67, "Accounting for Costs and Initial Rental Operations of Real Estate Projects," FASB, Stamford, CT, 1982.

———, Statement of Financial Accounting Standards No. 77, "Reporting by Transferors for Transfers of Receivables with Recourse," FASB, Stamford, CT, 1983.

———, Statement of Financial Accounting Standards No. 80, "Accounting for Futures," FASB, Stamford, CT, 1984.

———, Statement of Financial Accounting Standards No. 91, "Accounting for Nonrefundable Fees and Costs Associated with Originating or Acquiring Loans and Initial Direct Costs of Leases (an amendment of FASB Statements No. 13, 60, and 65 and a rescission of FASB Statement No. 17)," FASB, Stamford, CT, 1986.

———, Statement of Financial Accounting Standards No. 95, "Statement of Cash Flow," FASB, Norwalk, CT, 1987.

————, Statement of Financial Accounting Standards No. 102, "Statement of Cash Flows-Exception of Certain Enterprises and Classification of Cash Flows from Certain Securities Acquired for Resale (an amendment of FASB Statement No. 95.)," FASB, Norwalk, CT, 1989.

————, Statement of Financial Accounting Standards No. 104, "Statement of Cash Flows-Net Reporting of Certain Cash Receipts and Cash Payments and Classification of Cash Flows from Hedging Transactions (an amendment of FASB Statement No. 95)," FASB, Norwalk, CT, 1989.

————, Statement of Financial Accounting Standards No. 105, "Disclosure of Information about Financial Instruments Off-Balance Sheet Risk and Financial Instruments with Concentrations of Credit Risk," FASB, Norwalk, CT, 1990.

————, Statement of Financial Accounting Standards No. 107, "Disclosures About Fair Value of Financial Instruments," FASB, Norwalk, CT, 1991.

————, Statement of Financial Accounting Standards No. 114, "Accounting by Creditors for Impairment of a Loan (an amendment of FASB Statements 5 and 15)," FASB, Norwalk, CT, 1993.

————, Statement of Financial Accounting Standards No. 115, "Accounting for Certain Investments in Debt and Equity Securities," FASB, Norwalk, CT, 1993.

————, Statement of Financial Accounting Standards No. 118, "Accounting by Creditors for Impairment of a Loan-Income Recognition and Disclosures (an amendment of FASB Statement 114)," FASB, Norwalk, CT, 1994.

————, Statement of Financial Accounting Standards No. 119, "Disclosures about Derivative Financial Instruments and Fair Value of Financial Instruments," FASB, Norwalk, CT, 1994.

————, Statement of Financial Accounting Standards No. 121, "Accounting for the Impairment of Long-Lived Assets and for Long-Lived Assets to Be Disposed Of," FASB, Norwalk, CT, 1995.

————, Statement of Financial Accounting Standards No. 122, "Accounting for Mortgage Servicing Rights," FASB, Norwalk, CT, 1995.

————, Interpretation No. 39, "Offsetting of Amounts Related to Certain Contracts (an interpretation of APB Opinion No. 10 and FASB Statement No. 105)," FASB, Norwalk, CT, 1992.

Accounting Standards Division, Statement of Position, 78-9, "Accounting for Investments in Real Estate Ventures," AICPA, New York, 1978.

————, Statement of Position, 92-3, "Accounting For Foreclosed Assets," AICPA, New York, 1992.

————, Statement of Position, 94-6, "Disclosure of Certain Significant Risks and Uncertainties," AICPA, New York, 1994.

————, Statement of Position, 95-2, "Financial Reporting for Nonpublic Investment Partnerships," AICPA, New York, 1995.

Financial Accounting Standards Board, EITF Abstracts: A Summary of Proceedings of the FASB Emerging Issues Task Force, EITF Issue No. 88-11, "Allocation of Recorded Investment When a Loan or Part of a Loan Is Sold," FASB, Norwalk, CT, 1995.

————, EITF Abstracts: A Summary of Proceedings of the FASB Emerging Issues Task Force, EITF Issue No. 88-17, "Accounting for Fees and Costs Associated with Loan Syndications and Loan Participations," FASB, Norwalk, CT, 1989.

Securities and Exchange Commission, "Codification of Financial Reporting Policies", Financial Reporting Release No. 1, Section 404.03, "Accounting, Valuation, and Disclosure of Investment Securities," (Accounting Series Release No. 118, "Accounting for Investment Securities by Registered Investment Companies"), Warren, Gorham & Lamont, Boston, MA, 1995.

CHAPTER 26

RETAIL ACCOUNTING

Robert M. Zimmerman, CPA
Coopers & Lybrand L.L.P.

CONTENTS

This chapter has not been updated since its submission in 1992. It will be updated with the forthcoming supplement and will contain the following pronouncements that have a bearing for the revised chapter: SFAS No. 121, Accounting for the Impairment of Long-Lived Assets and for Long-Lived Assets to be Disposed of; EITF 94-3, Liability Recognition for Certain Employee Termination Benefits and Other Costs to Exit an Activity (including Certain Cost Incurred in a Restructuring); and SOP 93-7, Reporting on Advertising Costs. The reader should also consider SEC staff positions on pre-opening costs (see Chapter 16). Robert M. Zimmerman is a retired partner at Coopers & Lybrand L.L.P.

Based on chapters of RETAIL ACCOUNTING AND FINANCIAL CONTROL fifth edition by Robert M. Zimmerman, Robert M. Kaufman, Gregory Finerty and James O. Egan of Coopers & Lybrand.

26.1 INTRODUCTION

There are no special regulatory or licensing requirements in this industry, nor is the activity performed by retailers complicated or arcane, each segment of retailing is unique (e.g., high fashion boutiques versus fast food restaurants). In addition, each company within a retail segment must establish a unique identity with its customers. This identity is generally based on some combination of location, assortment, service, and price. This customization usually has a direct bearing on business operations and, therefore, on accounting and financial controls.

Retailing, as an industry, has many characteristics that differentiate it from other forms of commercial activity. Three of these characteristics are of overriding importance:

1. High volume of low-value transactions.
2. Broad exposure of merchandise to theft or damage by employees, customers, and suppliers.
3. Constantly changing product offerings.

These conditions, in turn, impact other aspects of the business such as personnel, space utilization, pricing, organization structure, and technology.

26.2 TYPES OF RETAIL FORMATS

Retailing is an intensely competitive industry that constantly changes the products being offered to its customers and the ways in which these products are offered. One-stop shopping competes with niche specialization; full service competes with low price. Traditional forms of organization are consolidating while new concepts keep bubbling up and succeeding.

Retail formats can be generally defined according to three primary dimensions: structure, merchandise, and size. Structure and merchandise may be used concurrently or separately. For example, retail formats can be broadly differentiated as Food and General Merchandise; however, in-store retailing is different from shop-at-home businesses, regardless of merchandise.

The third dimension, size, is important according to degree. That is, once a retailer grows beyond a certain size, in one location or many, business operations and controls will change. This cannot be calculated by formula, but should be recognized in practice.

The following categorization establishes an order; however, as just discussed, reality may not be as straightforward. Retailers are constantly evolving in response to the needs of customers. New combinations of products and display are critical to survival.

    I. Food
        A. Grocery
            1. Supermarket
            2. Convenience Stores
        B. Dining
            1. Fast Food
            2. Fine Dining
            3. Food Service
    II. General Merchandise
        A. Department, Discount, and Chain Stores
        B. Specialty Stores
            1. Apparel
            2. Hard Goods

The classification of any specific retailer into one of these categories may be difficult, and more importantly, of little value, for example:

- Very few department stores carry the full line of merchandise that was originally carried while many specialty stores are truly multidepartmental.
- Everyday low pricing or heavy promotional activity exists across all retail formats.
- Area registers can be found in discounters and front-end checkout lanes can be found in nondiscounters.
- Chain store distribution techniques are being used by most multilocation retailers.

What is important is the implementation of systems and controls that provide accurate, timely information at the lowest possible cost. Historically, it was not economically feasible for retailers to manage or control at the item level. Because of their high volume of low-value transactions it was sufficient to develop groupings of merchandise (departments, class, subclass) and manage them through average gross margin and open-to-buy calculations. Item level activity is important since it is at this level that stores and their customers actually buy, but it was not usually the level of control. Advances in automation are changing this scenario.

Technological changes in retailing have been pursued in order to improve merchandising and operations (the right reasons). The development of SKU-level (Stock Keeping Unit) databases that can accurately reflect order, receipt, sales, and on-hand information, in units and dollars, is changing merchandising and operating techniques. These developments are just beginning to be felt in the accounting areas, but it is reasonable to expect that the Retail Inventory Method may be replaced or augmented with more specific, cost accounting-like techniques such as Direct Product Profitability (DPP). Electronic Data Interchange (EDI) is resulting in imaginative new linkages between businesses up and down the distribution and financial chain. Accounting and control systems must keep pace with these changes. It is unlikely that new developments will render existing accounting concepts obsolete, but it is certain that accounting techniques must evolve in order to take advantage of new opportunities and to satisfy new requirements.

26.3 INVENTORY CONTROL

(a) METHODS OF INVENTORY MEASUREMENT.   There are three principal methods of measuring merchandise on hand:

1. Physical inventories, whether taken on a cycle basis or at the end of the fiscal period.
2. Book inventory controls maintained on a cost basis.
3. Book inventory controls maintained on a retail basis.

The method of measurement by physical inventories represents the opposite extreme from methods whereby inventory is valued by means of book records or stock ledgers maintained on the basis of cost or retail.

The physical inventory approach minimizes use of accounting records as transactions occur and relies principally upon summaries, such as totals of sales or purchases. Operations are checked periodically by inventories of physical stock.

Under the book control methods, every transaction is accounted for and the book records reflect the inventories that should be currently on hand. Physical inventories are still necessary at intervals in order to compare the results of the inventories with the corresponding book figures. Differences may reflect actual loss of merchandise, errors in the processing of transactions, errors in the counting or summarization of the physical inventory, or combinations of any of these factors.

(i) Measurement by Physical Inventories.   In retail operations where inventory is comparatively small and can be readily counted and summarized, inventory can be taken with great frequency—monthly, weekly, or even daily. For such operations this procedure affords a satisfactory method for determining profits and monitoring the movement of merchandise stock. The stock on hand, when compared to purchases and sales, determines whether there has been a gain or a loss, and reveals any merchandise shortage.

The physical inventory method is a practical method for many small retail stores but in some cases may indicate a need for greater control. As with all physical inventories, the valuation of inventories must give appropriate consideration to any unrecognized impairment in the value of merchandise if profits are to be properly measured.

Cost Method.   Certain retailers value inventory utilizing the cost method, tracking sales at retail and by specific stock-keeping unit (SKU). Traditionally this method has been practical for retail operations that carry a limited number of SKUs, such as jewelry stores, furniture dealers, and automobile dealers. Some departments within a department store may be kept on the cost method, such as jewelry and fur departments. As computers and computer users have become more sophisticated, it has become increasingly practical for even retailers with many SKUs to use this method.

The Book Record.   The cost method requires recordkeeping for each SKU carried at cost. Traditionally cost has included purchase cost, including the cost of transportation. Merchandise available for sale includes inventory as of the beginning of the period plus cost of purchases. Cost of sales, determined on an item-by-item basis, plus markdowns (at cost) are deducted from goods available for sale to arrive at inventory on hand. If the retail operation normally experiences shrinkage, an estimate of this shrinkage should also be deducted from cost to arrive at inventory on hand. This inventory on hand would then be checked by periodic physical inventories.

While most retailers using the cost method include only invoice cost plus cost of transportation, others have included certain distribution and buying costs in the cost ledger. These retailers argue that such costs fall under the Accounting Research Bulletin (ARB)

No. 43 definition of inventory costs as "the sum of the applicable expenditures and charges directly or indirectly incurred in bringing an article to its existing condition and location." The ARB No. 43 definition of "cost" requires the application of judgment. Only those costs incurred which actually add value to the merchandise may be capitalized.

It is impossible to provide an all-encompassing list of "approved" costs; however, several examples will demonstrate the general principles. Such costs would include the salaries of buyers (or a proportionate share of these salaries if buyers also perform other functions) and the costs incurred on buying trips. Another cost might be a distribution center's rent, utilities, and labor. In the case of retail chains using distribution centers, most of the costs incurred at the centers relate to physically moving the merchandise through to its ultimate saleable location. The distribution process also adds value by moving the goods from the point-of-sale to the consumer.

One requirement of the cost method is that physical inventories must be taken by SKU. While the retailer may want to know the retail value of its inventory, such information is not necessary in the initial valuation of ending inventory. However, if the value of certain inventory items are decreasing, due to over-stocks, obsolescence, or any other reason, the retail value of an item is important in insuring that ending inventory is valued at the lower of cost or market.

Cost of the physical inventory should be determined on the same basis as the book inventories. For example, if book cost includes only invoice cost plus transportation, reduced by applicable markdowns, physical inventory cost should include only these same costs.

The decision may be made to write down the inventory to reflect current market decisions (i.e., lower of cost or market). Such writedowns may be reflected as a direct writedown of a specific SKU or as a general inventory reserve.

Cost of Sales.   Under the cost method, sales must be tracked by SKU and then the cost of the item sold must be determined. Here lies one of the major drawbacks of the cost method. Whatever costs are included in inventory costs (i.e., invoice cost, transportation, distribution) must be allocated, recorded, and controlled by SKU. This can be a very cumbersome process unless there are either very few SKUs or elaborate computer systems. Under the retail method sales need to be tracked only by selling price by department (although many retailers do track sales by SKU).

Price Changes.   Price changes resulting from a diminution in value of the inventory should normally be reflected in the cost files. The book cost of a particular item is compared to the expected selling price (or "Market") less estimated costs to be incurred to sell that item (including carrying costs, labor, and so on). If the net market price is less than cost, failure to adjust the cost files will result in an overstatement of gross profit in the current period as the deterioration in value has not been reflected in the period in which it has occurred. Timely recognition of the reduction in market price preserves the normal gross margin percentage of the period in which the affected merchandise is sold.

For this reason, retailers often include an estimate of cost markdowns for interim reporting periods, adjusting these estimates to actual upon taking a physical inventory. These reserves are normally carried as general reserves since it would be impractical to allocate them to specific SKUs. The reserves are reversed at the beginning of the period and new reserves provided during the period, as applicable. This treatment more properly reflects income during interim periods as opposed to providing inventory adjustments at year-end only.

It should be noted that the above method properly reflects two types of markdowns in cost of sales during any period. The first is the markdown taken on individual items sold during the period as a result of lower of cost or market adjustments. The second is the general markdown reserve provided net of the reversal of previous general reserves or the specific writedowns taken against closing inventory, if a physical count has been taken.

(ii) Costing by Price Lines. The cost records may be subdivided into the price lines of each merchandise classification, with statistics as to the number of units handled in each price line. Given this data, average costs per unit within price lines are readily available. Cost of sales for a period may then be obtained by multiplying the number of units sold by the average cost per unit. This avoids the onerous chore of separately costing each individual sale.

Under this plan markdowns arise through transfer of units to a lower price line. Upon such transfer the cost of markdowns is readily computed since it represents the difference between cost values of units in the respective price lines multiplied by the number of units. Units of shrinkage are also costed by application of the average rates.

The taking and pricing of physical inventories is similarly facilitated since inventory counts are made by price lines and costed out using the respective average unit costs.

As noted, the biggest deterrent to the use of the cost method has been the need to keep detail cost files on an item-by-item basis. With only a few items, this can be done fairly easily. However, for retailers with thousands of SKUs, in the past such detail records have been cumbersome, and sometimes prohibitively expensive, to keep. Sales must be individually costed and certain costs such as transportation must be allocated.

However, today the record keeping burden has been eased by the availability of more sophisticated computer hardware and software. Yet item level costing may still be impractical for many retailers.

(b) RETAIL METHOD. The retail method was developed in response to the difficulty of costing individual items. The retail method records purchases and sales at retail, recognizes price changes and then computes an estimated value for ending inventory at cost.

It is easier to control and summarize the values of physical inventories at marked retail prices than at cost. To do the latter requires either the use of cost figures in code on price tickets or a search in files for cost figures. There is always the possibility that a cost code may be decipherable by persons who are not entitled to have this information. For most retailers, it is impossible or impractical to obtain the actual cost of all goods on hand from the purchase files.

(i) Advantages of the Retail Method. The retail method has the following advantages:

1. It permits periodic determination of inventories and profits without resorting to physical inventories.
2. It provides for a level of managerial control over gross margin by recording initial markon and changes in pricing through to maintained markon. Such changes include markdowns and stock shortages.
3. It renders feasible the taking of departmental inventories at various dates, other than the general fiscal closing, with appropriate adjustment of the related departmental book record.
4. It makes it possible to take physical inventories more easily since they require merely the summarization of marked retail prices which are readily available to counting personnel.
5. It obtains reductions in inventory values, evidenced by decreases in selling prices, as an automatic by-product of the method as soon as retail prices are remarked and processed by the retail accounting system.
6. It discloses the amount of stock shortages.
7. It facilitates the knowledgeable preparation of merchandise budgets.
8. It provides a basis for insurance coverage and settlements.
9. It tends to disclose, through apparently erroneous results, deficiencies in internal control systems and operating procedures.

(ii) The Retail Method as an Averaging Method. There is one major disadvantage: the retail method is basically an averaging technique. As such it is subject to distortion by the inclusion of extremes in the mix and can produce possible inaccuracies in the derivation of inventory values.

Under the retail method, the cost of merchandise on hand at any time is arrived at by deducting from retail the cumulative markon, generally representing the combined result of the markon of the opening inventory and the markon of purchases for the period to date. The cumulative markon is an average relation between the total cost of all merchandise (generally including opening inventory at cost) handled for the period and the total retail of the same merchandise. The cumulative markon is removed from ending inventory at retail by multiplying the cost multiplier percentage by the ending inventory at retail. The resulting amount is inventory at estimated cost. Since the cost multiplier excludes the impact of markdowns and as a result, the retail method provides an inherently conservative estimate of the cost of inventory.

A simple example will illustrate this point. If a coat is marked down from $150 to $100 and the normal gross margin is 50%, the markdown period will reflect a markdown cost of $25 as the inventory is reduced from an original cost of $75 (.5 × $150) to $50 (.5 × $100). If the coat is subsequently sold for $100, the normal margin of 50% is preserved as the retailer realizes a gross profit of 50% ($100 − $50). The retail method allows markdowns to affect inventory costs in the period in which they occur rather than the period in which they are sold; obviously the more conservative and logical choice.

Cost multipliers are generally maintained by department and therefore represent an average of all goods in the department. Given the employment of this averaging principle, the merchandise cost of sales determined for a department under the retail method is not exact cost. Operation of the retail method and its underlying theory are discussed later in this chapter.

The retail method, like any other inventory method, must be tested periodically by comparison with physical inventories, and book figures should be adjusted to the physical count unless there is reason to doubt the accuracy of the physical count. Also like any other method of inventory control, its successful use is dependent upon the care with which all pertinent factors are recognized and reflected in the accounts. No method of control will give satisfactory results if accounting detail is compiled carelessly, inaccurately, or with the omission of material factors. Furthermore, as noted earlier, it is fundamentally a method of averages. Accordingly, its successful use depends upon its application to departments where average results, especially the use of an average cost multiplier percentage, do not distort the general picture. Any group of transactions where the extremes are frequently so great as to make average figures meaningless is not suited to the retail method. Usually, though, by subdivision a reasonably homogeneous inventory grouping can be achieved, making feasible the use of this method.

(c) CHOICE OF METHOD. Over the years the retail method has been widely adopted. For department stores and for many other forms of retail operation, this method probably combines, more satisfactorily than any other, information and control at the lowest cost. It is, however, a serious mistake to disregard or ignore the advantages of the other methods for use under certain circumstances. In some large retail stores there will be departments where the cost control method serves the requirements of the business more adequately than the retail method, and other departments where the taking of frequent physical inventories without use of detailed control records may be preferable.

(d) OPERATION OF THE RETAIL METHOD. Operation of the retail method requires merchandise statistics at retail as well as at cost, and summarization of transactions by each department or other appropriate merchandise classification rather than aggregate totals. With respect to inventories, "cost" figures are calculated using the retail method; some retailers use an alternative term, "mercantile," to refer to this estimated cost.

The merchandise statistics for each department or classification start with opening inventory at cost and at retail. Purchases are added at cost (plus other capitalizable costs) and at retail (equal to the marked selling price). There are also added markups at retail. Totals of these items represent merchandise handled during the period at cost and at retail. Utilizing these totals the cumulative markon is obtained. This is the difference between retail and cost of merchandise handled.

For purposes of valuing the year-end inventory, most retailers include the markon inherent in the opening inventory in computing the cumulative markon and the cost-multiplier. However, this is not a universal practice. Recognizing that they are increasingly subject to periods of changes in the mix of merchandise and changing markon percentage, some retailers have either exclusively used the markon on the current year's purchases or more heavily weighted this markon percentage in the year-end inventory valuation process. Such an approach, of course, is predicated on the assumption that the closing inventory is comprised primarily of merchandise purchased during the current year. The method selected to compute the cumulative markon percentage should be that which most appropriately reflects the retailer's circumstances and should be applied on a consistent basis.

To obtain closing inventory at retail, the total of retail deductions is subtracted from the total of merchandise handled at retail. Total retail deductions comprise the sum of net sales, markdowns, allowances, sales discounts, and shrinkage (estimated or actual). Closing inventory at retail is reduced to cost by deducting the cumulative markon inherent in the ending inventory at retail. The cost of ending inventory is calculated by multiplying the ending inventory at retail by the complement of the cumulative markon percentage, more commonly known as the "cost multiplier."

The ending inventory at cost, $6,775, represents 64.04% (complement of the cumulative markon percentage) of $10,580, the closing inventory at retail. (See Exhibit 26.1.)

	Cost	Retail	Cumulative Markon Percentage
Opening inventory	$5,683	$ 8,795	
Purchases and transportation and other capitalizable costs, net	3,482	5,372	
Markups (less cancellations)		145	
Total merchandise handled	$9,165	$14,312	35.96
Net sales		$ 3,369	
Markdowns (less cancellations)		280	
Sales discounts		15	
Shrinkage (estimated or actual)		68	
Total retail deductions		$ 3,732	
Ending inventory	$6,775	$10,580	35.96

(A) Cumulative markon = $\dfrac{\text{Total retail of}}{\text{merchandise handled}} - \dfrac{\text{Total cost of}}{\text{merchandise handled}}$ = $14,312 − $9,165

= $5,147

(B) Cumulative markon percentage = $\dfrac{\text{Cumulative markon}}{\text{Total retail of merchandise handled}} = \dfrac{\$\,5,147}{\$14,312}$

= .3596 or 35.96%

(C) Cost-multiplier = $\dfrac{\text{Total cost of merchandise handled}}{\text{Total retail of merchandise handled}} = \dfrac{\$9,165}{\$14,312}$ = .6404 or 64.04%

(D) Cost-multiplier percentage = 100 − Cumulative markon percentage = 64.04 = 100 − 35.96

(E) Ending inventory at cost = Cost-multiplier $\times \dfrac{\text{Ending inventory}}{\text{at retail}}$ = (.6404) ($10,580) = $6,775

Exhibit 26.1.   Illustration.

(e) THE STOCK LEDGER.   The principal record used in the retail method is a stock ledger which includes information for each department or departmental sub-division. Single-line specialty stores, as well as some other operations, may maintain stock ledgers by merchandise classifications (or price lines, styles, etc.) rather than by departments.

In other cases the stock ledger may be maintained by store or by departments within branch stores. It may be most useful, and least expensive, to maintain the ledger by store in cases where the merchandise classifications are limited and the product mix consistent from period to period.

Most retail chains find store ledgers impractical and although they track results of operations by store, the stock ledger is maintained by department. In many cases it is not sufficient to divide the stock ledger into broad department categories such as men's clothing or electronics. The diverse nature of the merchandise within such groupings may combine goods with an inappropriately extreme range of cost multipliers which could distort the calculation of inventory cost. Exhibit 26.6 provides a clear illustration of the danger in averaging unrelated items.

Retail operations are sometimes divided into two seasons with cumulative merchandise statistics kept on a seasonal rather than an annual or other periodic basis. For example, department stores on a January 31 fiscal year basis may record merchandise statistics for the spring season, from February 1 to July 31, and then start the records anew for the fall season, August 1 to January 31. However, this is not a universal practice; in the interests of simplicity and reduced recordkeeping requirements, the records are often kept on an annual basis and statistics are accumulated without regard to seasonal breakdowns. There is no loss of accuracy if merchandise purchases and the mix of ending inventory do not vary significantly on a seasonal basis.

The stock ledgers may be either abbreviated or detailed. With an abbreviated ledger a supplementary record is kept to accumulate purchase totals; where the ledger is detailed, the various purchase elements are entered directly. Exhibit 26.2 and 26.3 illustrate the abbreviated form of departmental stock ledger (a form used by most retail chains). Exhibit 26.2 illustrates the total page of such a stock ledger maintained on a year-to-date basis. Exhibit 26.3 is typical of the seasonal type of stock ledger and this case illustrates summary information by department. Exhibit 26.4 is prepared on the same seasonal basis as Exhibit 26.3; however, this ledger analyzes the same information on a store by store basis.

As illustrated in Exhibit 26.5 a detailed form of stock ledger consists of three principal parts: an upper section for accumulating cost of merchandise handled; a middle section for accumulating the corresponding retail, and a lower section for determining closing inventory at retail and cost, and gross margin.

Regardless of the form, the purpose of these stock ledgers is to record, on a summary basis for each department, all the transactions of the season or the year.

A variation on this theme is a method which uses a separate sheet for monthly records for each department and showing cumulative results for the season or year. This latter method has the advantage of summarizing on one page the key merchandise data of each month and of the period to date in addition to serving as the main record of transactions. Copies of the report can be supplied to buyers and executives as a monthly report of merchandising results, thereby avoiding the duplicate work of transcribing figures from the stock ledger of the monthly report of operations.

This type of form, as illustrated in Exhibit 26.5 reflects the accumulations of statistics on an annual rather than a seasonal basis, with the data for the departments of all stores combined in a single stock ledger and operating report. The theory underlying the pooled or common department concept is the universal applicability of a common departmental markon, with all retail deductions (markdowns, allowances, discounts, and shrinkage) shared in proportion to sales. Consequently, the same gross margin on the sales is "earned" by the department regardless of store location.

An abbreviated form of stock ledger is most likely to be used when the records are kept on a weekly basis and where the departmental figures are subdivided by such factors as merchandise

	Current Month November	Year to Date November
Markon %		
Cost %		
Initial markon %		
Cost Additions:		
Opening inventory		
Opening freight		
Purchases		
Freight		
(Discounts)		
Total		
Retail Additions:		
Opening inventory		
Purchases		
Markups		
Total		
Retail Reductions:		
Sales		
Markdowns		
Shortage %		
Shortage		
Total		
Closing Inventory:		
Retail		
Cost		
Cost of Sales		
Gross profit dollars		
Gross profit % sales		

Exhibit 26.2.   Stock ledger—departmental recap.

classifications, price lines, or store locations. When the stock records are kept on a monthly basis, the abbreviated form is much more likely to be used as the more detailed version becomes cumbersome; too much information may obscure important merchandising trends.

The following discussion will use the stock ledger illustrated in Exhibit 26.6 to demonstrate how the stock ledger actually performs its recordkeeping function. Remember that the primary duties of the stock ledger are to measure merchandise, to estimate the cost of inventory at the end of the period (and therefore profit for the period) and to monitor the elements of gross margin.

(i) Merchandise Handled.   This term includes opening inventory and all elements of purchases that enter into the determination of cumulative markon. Purchases included consist of the following items:

1. Invoiced cost of domestic purchases, less merchandise returns, rebates, allowances and discounts.
2. Landed cost of imported merchandise; that is invoiced cost plus duty, freight, insurance, commissions, etc., less returns and allowances.
3. Inward transportation charges (at cost only).

DEPARTMENT SUMMARY
Month of April 19XX

Dept.	#	Beginning Balance	Purchases	Markups	Goods Available	Physical Inv. Adj.	Markdowns	Reserve for Shrink	Sales	Ending Balance	Gross Profit Season to Date	Gross Profit Current Month
01	R											
	C											
22	R											
	C											
28	R											
	C											
34	R											
	C											
45	R											
	C											
66	R											
	C											
All Depts.	R											
	C											

Exhibit 26.3. Seasonal stock ledger.

SUMMARY BY STORE
Month of April 19XX

Dept.	#	Beginning Balance	Purchases	Markups	Goods Available	Physical Inv. Adj.	Markdowns	Reserve for Shrink	Sales	Ending Balance	Gross Profit	
											Season to Date	Current Month
2	R											
	C											
3	R											
	C											
5	R											
	C											
6	R											
	C											
7	R											
	C											
8	R											
	C											
9	R											
	C											
10	R											
	C											
12	R											
	C											
14	R											
	C											
16	R											
	C											
17	R											
	C											
18	R											
	C											
19	R											
	C											
20	R											
	C											
21	R											
	C											
All Stores	R											
	C											

Exhibit 26.4. Seasonal stock ledger.

MERCHANDISE STATEMENT

Month of			Year to Date	
Amount	%		%	Amount
	1	Cost: Inventory—Beginning of period		
	2	Domestic purchases (Net)		
	3	Freight—in		
	4	Foreign purchases (Net)		
	5	Transfers (Net)		
	6			
	7	Cumulative cost (% = 7/14 for year)		
	8	Retail: Inventory—Beginning of period		
	9	Domestic purchases (Net)		
	10	Foreign purchases (Net)		
	11	Markups		
	12	Transfers (Net)		
	13			
	14	Cumulative retail (Markon % = 7/14 FR. 100)		
	15	Net sales: Store 1		
	16	Store 2		
	17	Store 3		
	18	Store 4		
	19	Store 5		
	20	Store 6		
	21			
	22			
	23	Total net sales		
	24	Markdowns (% = 24/23)		
	25	Allowances to customers (% = 25/23)		
	26	Discounts to employees (% = 26/23)		
	27	Shrink (% = 27/23)		
	28	Total retail stock ded. (23 to 27 incl.)		
	29	Inventory: Retail—End of period (14 − 28) (Ratio = 29/23)		
	30	Inventory cost—End of period (29 × %7 Yr. to date)		
	31	Workroom and other costs (% = 31/23)		
	32	Gross margin before discounts (23 + 30 − 7 − 31) (% = 32/23)		
	33	Cash discounts (____% of 28 for month) (% = 33/23)		
	34	Gross margin (32+33)		

_____Dept no.
_____ 19____ Period

Dept no._____
Period _____ 19____

Exhibit 26.5. Inventory dollar control.

Month of July 19XX

Department _____ Dept. _____

Period	Merchandise Handled		Retail Deductions				Closing Inventory at Retail	Alteration and Workroom Costs	Mark-on %	Mark-down %	Sales Discount %	Shrinkage Provision %	Alteration Costs %	Gross Margin
	Cost	Retail	Net Sales	Mark-Downs	Sales Discounts	Shrinkage Provisions	Totals							
Inventory Feb. 1														
Month of February														
Season to Date														
Month of March														
Season to Date														
Month of April														
Season to Date														
Month of May														
Season to Date														
Month of June														
Season to Date														
Month of July														
Season to Date														

Exhibit 26.6. Departmental stock ledger.

4. Department transfers in, less transfers out.

5. Markups, less cancellations and other corrections of retail (at retail only).

6. Invoices in transit.

The retail and cost amounts of purchases (excluding invoices in transit) are detailed and accumulated by department in a subsidiary purchases ledger. In some retail companies, the cost of freight may be combined with the cost of the merchandise rather than identified separately.

Markups and corrections of retail must also be accumulated in a subsidiary price change ledger. The totals from these systems feed (after review for errors) into the stock ledger.

Smaller retailers may track those components manually and may even use a manually prepared stock ledger. Again, all components of purchases are accumulated departmentally in the equivalent of a purchase journal. Totals may be carried directly to the stock ledger or in some cases, the totals of the various components of purchases may be summarized in a supplemental report. The separate accumulation of purchase elements permits a review of the factors that enter into the computation of the cost multiplier. An example of such a summary is shown in Exhibit 26.7.

(ii) Invoices in Transit.   In the determination of purchases for the stock ledger, a question arises as to whether merchandise handled should include all merchandise received or only merchandise which has cleared through the receiving and marking rooms and has been recorded on the equivalent of a purchase journal. In practice, certain merchandise is always "in transit"; that is, the invoices have not been recorded on the purchase journal although the merchandise has been received. The preferred method is to adjust the totals for these unrecorded purchases using the actual amount if known or an estimate if that is all that is available. The result is a more accurate description of operating results and more precise open-to-buy statistics.

As a practical matter, many retailers do not adjust purchases at month-end for invoices in transit because they are not a significant factor. For many retailers, the dollar amount of invoices relating to merchandise received but not yet recorded is only a small portion of the total dollar amount of invoices in transit; the majority normally represent those dated prior to month-end for which the related merchandise has not yet been received.

When invoices in transit are not a significant factor the easiest procedure is to omit a purchase adjustment. An adjustment for invoices in transit would require the retailer to summarize

		Month of April 19XX			
Department_____					
		Period_____		Period_____	
		Cost	Retail	Cost	Retail
1.	Domestic invoices (net)	$2,466	$3,722		
2.	Foreign invoices (net) at landed cost	850	1,500		
3.	Freight-in charges	76	—		
4.	Transfers-in	60	100		
5.	Markups, etc.	—	145		
6.	Invoices in transit, close of period (if any)	102	157		
		$3,554	$5,624		
7.	Invoices in transit, beginning of period (if any)	85	135		
8.	Transfers-out	30	50		
		$ 115	$ 185		
9.	Total purchases	$3,439	$5,439		

Exhibit 26.7.   Purchase record summary.

the invoice cost of the related merchandise and then determine the retail amount for the same goods. The retail amount can generally be estimated, by department, using the known relationship between cost and retail for purchases recorded in the purchase journal or stock ledger. The retailer can then adjust purchases recorded for the month in the stock ledger using the summarized cost and estimated retail; this adjustment is reversed in the subsequent month and a new amount is accrued for that month-end.

Whether or not the adjustment is made most retailers do examine invoices in transit very carefully at year-end in order to verify that purchases include all invoices for which merchandise has been received or to determine that the amount of unrecorded goods is not significant. Retailers also scrutinize invoices in transit more carefully at the time of physical inventories in order to eliminate any record keeping errors and identify the "real" amount of merchandise shortage (shrink).

(iii) Cost-Multiplier.   As defined earlier, the cumulative markon of a department is the difference between retail and cost of the total merchandise handled. The cumulative markon percentage is the cumulative markon as a percentage of total merchandise handled at retail. This percentage can be applied to ending inventory at retail to calculate the amount to be subtracted from this to reduce such inventory to an estimated cost.

It is mathematically simpler to use the complement of the markon percentage in computing inventory at cost, so generally it is the complement percentage (otherwise known as the "cost-multiplier") which is reflected in the stock ledger. The cost-multiplier is calculated by dividing the total cost of merchandise handled by the corresponding retail amount.

The cumulative markon and cost-multipliers should be reviewed carefully and compared with those prior accounting periods. This review serves two purposes: first to insure that the calculation of the cost-multiplier (and therefore ending inventory at cost) is correct and consistent with prior periods; and second, to note important trends in merchandising results which may influence future merchandising decisions.

(iv) Net Sales.   Net sales represent sales net of all returns, allowances and discounts. Sales returns are deducted from gross sales because the merchandise has been restored to stock. When allowances are granted, no merchandise is returned to stock. To the extent that allowances are offset against sales they must be added to markdowns, so that there is a complete accounting for merchandise at retail.

(v) Markdowns.   Markdowns are entered as credits to inventory on the stock ledger in recognition of the reduction of the selling price from the retail originally recorded. Sales of marked down merchandise are credited to stock only at reduced prices.

Markdowns are frequently classified by causative factor, with a view to providing some insight into the effectiveness of buying and merchandising policies. The following classification of such factors is commonly used:

1. Promotional purchase remainders.
2. Slow-moving or inactive stocks.
3. Planned "event" or promotional markdowns.
4. Special sales from stock.
5. Price adjustments.
6. Broken assortments, remnants, discontinued lines, and damaged merchandise.
7. Allowances to customers.

Some retailers use the same price change form to record all types of price changes, including markdowns. Summarization of these price change forms will supply the necessary information

Department:	#49			Store:	# 22
Type of change:	Markdown—clearance			Price change form:	#001
Effective date:	01/15/XX			Authorization:	#245

SKU #	Merchandise Description	Old Retail Price	New Retail Price	Quantity Changed	Extended Value
5194	Boy's Coat	15.99	10.88	25	127.75

Buyer's Signature: M. Smith
Taken by: J. Doe
Date of price change: 01/17/XX

Exhibit 26.8.   Price change form.

regarding the amounts of markups and markup cancellations, markdowns and markdown cancellations, and corrections of retail. Exhibit 26.8 illustrates a typical form for recording price changes. More and more retailers are today recording markdowns at the point of sale, thus eliminating the need for these price change forms.

(vi) Sales Discounts.   Sales discounts, primarily to employees, are deducted from the gross sales prices at the time of the sale. Charge account discounts are not deducted from sales prices at the time of sale, and inventory (at retail) is reduced for the full amount of the sale. Subsequently the sales price is reduced to reflect the discount at the time of payment of the charge account and the amount of these charge accounts discounts is allocated departmentally and deducted from departmental sales, with a corresponding addition to sales discounts.

(vii) Shrinkage.   The provision for shrinkage as entered in the stock ledger is accumulated throughout the year as an estimate of probable shrinkage based upon past experience. Book inventories have, therefore, already been reduced by an estimated amount of shrinkage before they are compared with physical inventories. If a difference exists between a physical inventory and a book inventory already reduced by an estimated shrinkage, the difference is equivalent to a correction of the estimated shrinkage. It indicates that the estimate of shrinkage was either too large or too small and an adjustment is in order, so that the stock ledger will reflect the actual inventory at the date of the physical inventory.

If the indicated adjustment is large enough to reduce shrinkage below a minimum deemed "normal" for the specific department, or, on the other hand, to increase it to an abnormally large figure, a study should be conducted to determine the cause. Usually no significant adjustments (especially reductions) to the provision for shrinkage are made until the book records and the summarization of the physical inventory have been reviewed for possible errors.

(viii) Ending Inventory.   Ending inventory at retail is obtained by subtracting total retail deductions from the total of merchandise handled at retail and is subject to check by a physical inventory. Physical inventories are taken by some retailers on a cycle basis and by others seasonally (typically July and January), but all retailers should perform physical inventories at least once a year. The inventory amount shown by the stock ledger is adjusted to the amount of physical inventory through the shrinkage provision.

The cost of ending inventory, whether the unadjusted book balance or the amount of the physical inventory, results from the multiplication of the retail amount by the cost-multiplier.

(ix) Gross Margin.   Gross margin equals the excess of net sales for the period over the total costs of merchandise sold. Total merchandise costs are the sum of opening inventory at cost, purchases at cost (net of discounts earned), less closing inventory at cost.

The examples of stock ledgers illustrated in this book do not include columns for the cost of sales (total merchandise costs). Although such columns could be included in stock ledgers the examples exclude them in recognition of industry practice and in order to focus attention on the more important statistic—gross margin. Gross margin is the foremost ratio in judging the results of departmental operations because it indicates how far the realized (or "maintained") markon percentage has fallen short of the cumulative markon percentage.

The stock ledger illustrated in Exhibit 26.6 provides a method of determining the percentage of gross margin through the use of certain other percentages. It is a short-cut method which avoids computation of inventory amounts at cost and total merchandise costs, and eliminates several mathematical steps. The various percentages used in this form generally are computed as desirable statistical information, and thus do not involve additional work. The procedure for utilizing this form in deriving the percentage of gross margin may be illustrated by assuming that the following data have been obtained from a stock ledger:

	Amounts	Percentages of Net Sales
Opening inventory at cost	$ 20,880*	
Purchase at cost	51,794*	
Merchandise handled at retail	126,518*	
Net sales	92,743	
Markdowns	5,653	6.10%
Sales discounts	1,079	1.16
Shrinkage provisions	368	0.40
Ending inventory at retail	26,675	

*From these totals the cumulative markon percentage of 42.56% is calculated:

$$\frac{126,518 - 20,880 - 51,794}{126,518}$$

From the foregoing percentages the percentage of gross margin is determined, as follows:

Percentage of cumulative markon		42.56%
Retail reduction percentages to be reduced to cost:		
Markdowns	6.10%	
Sales discounts	1.16	
Shrinkage provisions	0.40	
Total	7.66%	
Percentage of retail deductions reduced to cost,		
7.66 × 57.44 (which is 100 − 42.56)		4.40
Percentage of gross margin		38.16%

(f) PREPARING A GROSS MARGIN STATEMENT.   As a proof of the percentage of gross margin derived under the above formula, a method of preparing a departmental statement of gross margin from data in the stock ledger is illustrated below. As will be noted from the data used in the preceding example, the elements of a complete gross margin statement that are lacking are ending inventory at cost and the amount of gross margin. Ending inventory and gross margin are derived while setting up the statement.

	Amounts		Percentages of Net Sales	
Net sales	$92,743	$92,743	100.00%	100.00%
Markdowns	5,653		6.10	
Sales discounts	1,079		1.16	
Provision for shrinkage	368		.40	
Retail sales and reductions	$99,843		107.66%	
Merchandise costs:				
Inventory, beginning of period	$20,880			
Purchases	51,794			
Cost of merchandise handled	72,674			
Inventory, end of period	15,322			
Cost of merchandise sold	57,352	57,352		61.84
Gross margin		$35,391		38.16%

Net sales, opening inventory at cost, and purchases at cost, are available and can be entered directly on the statement. Since the percentage of gross margin is available, the corresponding amount is readily computed and entered. Net sales less gross margin gives total merchandise costs which may also be entered. The missing item, closing inventory at cost, is then calculated by deducting the cost of merchandise sold from the cost of merchandise handled. The amount of ending inventory at cost can be verified by multiplying the ending inventory at retail, $26,675, by the cost-multiplier, 57.44 (complement of the markon percentage of 42.56).

(g) CONTROLS OVER THE STOCK LEDGER.   One of the most basic controls found in accounting is the reconciliation of subsidiary ledger amounts to the corresponding general ledger or control totals. The utilization of control totals plays an important role in the arena of retail accounting. The figures reflected in the stock ledgers determine both the end of period inventory balance and the results of operations for the period. These subsidiary ledger amounts must be compared to the corresponding control totals to insure that operating results are being calculated properly.

As was stated earlier in this chapter, the cost method is more practicable than the retail method for certain departments. Some retailers employ both methods at the same time, with the cost method used for only a comparatively small number of departments.

The stock ledgers used for the retail method may also be used for recording, in the appropriate columns only, the results of the operations of the departments controlled by the cost method. Where figures under both methods are included in a single stock record, the latter is controlled by accounts in the general ledger representing totals for all departments. Sometimes the figures for departments controlled by the retail method are controlled in the general ledger separately from cost department figures, with two distinct stock records being maintained.

The stock ledger (or ledgers) will include totals summarizing activity for all departments and/or all stores. These totals must be periodically reconciled (typically on a monthly basis) with amounts reflected in the general ledger. If there is a single stock ledger it will contain separate control totals for retail departments and cost departments, and a total of all departments. The control totals in the stock ledgers represent totals of the respective dollar columns of the individual departments. It should be noted that since the total inventory at cost for the retail departments is the sum of the amounts computed for each department, total inventory at cost cannot be computed from the control totals. Total ending inventory at cost can only be obtained by adding up the amounts calculated for each department.

Usually, the general ledger contains control accounts for net sales and cost of purchases, the latter including all the elements of purchases.

Two different procedures are followed with respect to the inventory account in the general ledger. Under one method the amount is not changed during a season or even during a fiscal year, whereas under the other the amount is changed each month to bring it into agreement with the stock ledger. Under the first method the general ledger is not in agreement, as to inventories or net profits, with the interim monthly balance sheets and income accounts. Under the other approach the books are always in agreement with financial statements. For this reason the latter method is most commonly employed.

It is not necessary to close out sales, purchases, expenses, discounts, and so on, to a monthly profit and loss account if an account is opened to reflect the change in inventory during the period. This makes it possible to obtain all the required elements of the income account directly from the general ledger, except closing inventory, which equals the opening inventory as adjusted by the account which reflects interim changes.

(h) STOCK LEDGER ELEMENTS NOT SUBJECT TO CONTROL.   There are two important component elements of the stock ledger without equivalent control totals on the general ledger. These are the retail amounts of purchases and price changes (most significantly markdowns). The retail of purchases as recorded in the stock ledger should represent the sum of the originally marked retail prices of merchandise placed in stock. Ordinarily, there is no mathematical proof of the accuracy of the retail of purchases. This means there may be errors in extensions or in tabulations, but they cannot be discovered by cross checking against a control account. This possible source of error in the operation of the retail method is important and merits particular attention.

Markdown calculations and tabulations represent another source of possible errors under the retail method. They cannot be controlled to the same degree as sales. In this respect also, it is important that sufficient attention be directed to obtaining accuracy in the figures. There should be an accountability for the numerical sequence of all price change reports, and calculations and summarizations should be verified. In addition, each price change form should be examined for authorized signatures which evidence that the price changes have actually been made on the merchandise. Many retailers employ an audit process (similar to sales audit) to check and verify that these retail amounts have been properly recorded.

The inability to reconcile purchases at retail and retail price changes with control totals on the general ledger also encourages retailers to use exception reports to detect errors. In the case of purchases, computerized systems can be programmed to detect unusual markons for specific purchases. For example, if the retail amount for a purchase is recorded below the item's cost or with an unusually low markon, the purchase can be detected and listed on an exception report. In the case of manual systems, the equivalent review would obviously be tedious. Similar exception reports can be generated for retail price changes.

When all transactions are properly recorded under the retail method, the shrinkage disclosed by the retailer's records should properly represent the results of thefts, price tampering, and damage to or loss of merchandise. However, in practice, paperwork errors inevitably occur and a portion of shrink reflects their impact.

(i) RETAIL METHOD FORMULAS.   Under the retail method there is an interrelation among cumulative markon, retail reductions and gross margin. The interrelation may be expressed by formulas applicable both to dollar amounts and to percentages. The percentages are expressed in terms of the common denominator, retail. Cumulative markon percentage is based upon the retail of merchandise handled during a period, but percentages of retail reductions, and gross margin are based upon the retail of merchandise sold during the period.

Illustrations of certain of these formulas follow.

	Amounts	Percentages on Net Sales	Percentages on Merchandise Handled
Net sales	$92,743	100.00%	
Markdowns	5,653	6.10	
Sales discounts	1,079	1.16	
Shrinkage provisions	368	0.40	
Total retail reductions	7,100	7.66	
Cost of merchandise sold	57,352	61.84	
Gross margin	35,391	38.16	
Cumulative markon			42.56%
Cost multiplier percentage			57.44

(i) Cost of Merchandise Sold.   Cost of merchandise sold equals the sum of net sales and total retail reductions, reduced to cost by application of the cost-multiplier percentage. The same formula is used to derive percentage of cost of merchandise sold. For example:

	Dollars At Retail	Dollars Retail × 57.44%	Percentages At Retail	Percentages Retail × 57.44%
Net sales	$92,743	$53,272	100.00%	57.44%
Total retail reductions	7,100	4,078	7.66	4.40
Cost of merchandise sold	$99,843	$57,350	107.66%	61.84%

(ii) Gross Margin.   Formulas for gross margin and percentage of gross margin may be stated as follows:

1. Gross margin equals net sales less the cost of merchandise sold. The cost of merchandise sold equals: (a) sales at retail × cost-multiplier *plus* (b) retail reductions (i.e., markdowns, provision for shrinkage, sales discounts) × cost-multiplier. Since the complement of the cost-multiplier is the cumulative markon, we can rearrange the terms above to achieve an alternate formula for gross margin:

2. Gross margin *also* equals: (a) net sales × the cumulative markon (b) less other retail reductions at cost.

3. Percentage of gross margin equals gross margin as a percentage of net sales. However, in light of the formula for gross margin expressed above this can alternatively be calculated as the percentage of cumulative markon minus the percentage of retail reductions at cost.

Illustration of these formulas, based upon the figures already used, is as follows:

	At Retail	At Cost
A. Net Sales $92,743		
Cost of merchandise sold	$53,272	(1)
Retail reductions	7,100	4,078(2)

Gross margin = Net sales − Cost of merchandise sold − Retail reductions at cost;
in this case: 92,743 − 53,272 − 4,078 = 35,393.
(1) 92,743 × .5744
(2) 7,100 × .5744

Note: Cost-multiplier equal to 57.44%.

B. Alternate Calculation

Since in this case the cumulative markon = $100 - 57.44 = 42.56$, gross margin also equals: $(92,743)(42.56) - (7,100)(.5744) = 39,471 - 4,078 = 35,393$. Note that each calculation produces the same result, a gross margin of 35,393.

C. Gross Margin Percentage equals:

$35,393 + 92,743 = 38.16\%$ or as alternatively calculated, $.4256 - 4,078/92,743 = .4256 - .044 = 38.16\%$.

The above example illustrates how gross margin is reduced from the margin that would have been earned on the basis of cumulative markon, by the adverse effect of markdowns, sales discounts, and shrinkage.

(iii) Cumulative Markon Percentage. Manipulation of the above equations produces an alternate formula for cumulative markon percentage. Since gross margin equals the cumulative markon *less* reductions at cost, we can realign the variables to prove that cumulative markon equals gross margin *plus* retail reductions at cost. Cumulative markon percentage can then be redefined as:

$$\frac{\text{Gross margin} + \text{Retail reductions}}{\text{Net sales} + \text{Retail reductions}}$$

Or using the data from the previous example:

$$\frac{35,393 + 7,100}{92,743 + 7,100} = \frac{42,493}{99,843} = 42.56\%$$

Note that retail reductions are restored at retail because cumulative markon excludes such reductions. Cumulative markon percentage can also be defined in terms of the applicable percentages of the other factors:

Cumulative markon percentage = Gross margin percentage + Retail reductions as a percentage of sales

In this example: $38.16 + 4.4 = 42.56\%$.

Cost of Sales

Cost of sales is based upon the following factors:

Inventory, beginning of period	—
Purchases	—
Total = Gross cost of merchandise handled	—
Deduct: Inventory, end of period	—
Difference = Gross cost of merchandise sold	—
Deduct: Discounts earned	—
Difference = Total net merchandise costs	—

The factors stated are those which appear in a formal statement of cost of sales. However, other factors of cost-sales discounts, markdowns, and shrinkages—are not separately presented in a formal statement of cost of sales and gross margin.

Sales discounts are reflected in net sales, because the net sales are less than they would have been if the sales prices had not been reduced in the form of discounts to customers.

Markdowns are reflected partly in net sales and partly in inventories; that is, in sales for items which have been marked down and sold, and in inventory for markdowns taken on items which are unsold at the end of the period.

In the absence of errors in connection with recordkeeping or physical inventories, shrinkage represents losses caused by disappearance, destruction, or other unrecorded disposition (e.g., samples) of merchandise which might otherwise have been sold to produce gross margin. The effect of shrinkage on gross margin is reflected through inventories, since there is less merchandise to be carried forward to the new accounting period. Shrinkage increases the cost of sales although it has no direct relationship to sales.

Sales discounts, markdowns, and shrinkage are recorded in retail amounts, and percentages of these amounts are expressed in relationship to net sales. Net sales constitute a common denominator for expressing relationships, and the effect of these various elements upon gross margin can be determined from ratios based upon this common denominator. The amount of loss from sales discounts, markdowns, and shrinkages is not the retail at which they are recorded, but is the difference between retail and the cumulative markon contained in such retail. In other words, the amount lost is the amount required to purchase enough merchandise for sale on the basis of the cumulative markon, to realize the retail total of sales discounts, markdowns, and shrinkages. For this reason, the cost of these elements is determined by multiplying their retail amount by the cost-multiplier (100 minus percentage of cumulative markon).

(j) DISPOSITION OF MARKON.   The gross income of a retail operation arises principally from markons. As stated in preceding discussions, some part of initial markon is lost through shrink and markdowns. The remainder of markon is used to meet operating expenses and provide profit. It is critical to profitability that a sufficient initial markon is provided when setting prices and that subsequently this markon is safeguarded so that as little as possible is lost in reductions. It is informative to have a record of the portion of remaining markon used to meet operating expenses and the balance that is realized as operating profit. Exhibits 26.9,

RECONCILIATION BETWEEN MARKON PROVIDED AND TOTAL OPERATING INCOME

	Markon	Markon Percentages	Dollar Amounts of Items	
			Cost	Retail
Provided:				
Markon in inventory, beginning of period	$175,000	35.00	$ 325,000	$ 500,000
Markon in current purchases	562,500	37.50	937,500	1,500,000
Markups less cancelations	10,000			10,000
Total provided	$747,500	37.19	$1,262,500	$2,010,000
Available for future:				
Markon in inventory, close of period	223,140	37.19	376,860	600,000
			$ 885,640	$1,410,000
		Percentage Used to Total Markon		
Total used	$524,360	70.15		

Exhibit 26.9.   Report of markon and its disposition.

RECONCILIATION BETWEEN MARKON PROVIDED AND TOTAL OPERATING INCOME

		Percentages of Total Markon Used	Percentages on Sales
Total markon used	$524,360	100.00%	40.34
Lost:			
Markdowns, less cancellations	$70,000	13.25	5.39
Sales discounts	15,000	2.86	1.15
Shortages	30,000	5.72	2.31
Total reductions	$115,000	21.93	8.85
Earned:			
Gross margin before discounts	409,360	78.07	31.49
Discounts earned	40,000		3.08
Gross margin after discounts	$449,360		34.57
Expended: Operating expenses	400,000	76.28	30.77
Realized:			
Operating income:			
From markon	9,360	1.79%	.72
From discounts earned	40,000		3.08
	$ 49,360		3.80

Note: Deductions at retail amount to $1,415,000, of which retail deductions are $115,000, leaving $1,300,000 for sales.

Exhibit 26.10. Report of markon and its disposition.

RECONCILIATION BETWEEN MARKON PROVIDED AND TOTAL OPERATING INCOME

	Markon		Markon Percentages
Provided:			
Markon in inventory, beginning of period	$175,000		35.00
Markon in current purchases	562,500		37.50
Markups, less cancelations	10,000		
Total provided		$747,500	37.19
Available for future:			
Markon in inventory, end of period		223,140	37.19
			Percentages Used to Total Markon
Total used		$524,360	70.15
			Percentages Used to Total Markon
Total markon used		$524,360	100.00
Lost:			
Markdowns, less cancelations	70,000		13.35
Sales discounts	15,000		1.86
Shortages	30,000		5.72
Total reductions	$115,000		
		115,000	21.93
Earned: Gross margin before discounts		$409,360	78.07
Expended: Operating expenses		400,000	76.28
Realized: Operating income before discounts earned		9,360	1.79
Discounts earned		40,000	
Operating income		$ 49,360	

Exhibit 26.11.   Report of markon and its disposition.

26.10, and 26.11 illustrate various forms of analyzing initial markon and its subsequent reductions.

In effect, these reports show how departmental statements for a designated period may be prepared to show markon originally provided, the portion carried forward to a future period in the closing inventory, and the disposition of the amount available, with the uses made of markons realized. By indicating the percentages of markon used for various purposes, as related to total markon provided, a clear picture of the disposition of markon is supplied. This serves to emphasize the importance of conserving for expenses and profit as large a portion of markon as possible, rather than losing it in reductions and unknown costs.

Different types of forms can be utilized to present these data for separate departments, for groups of departments, or for retail departments in total. The first form provides more detail than the second in order to make clearer the manner in which the figures are compiled. While the second form omits some figures, it does supply the pertinent data. Reports may be made monthly, for other intermediate periods, or for seasons or fiscal years.

The Tax Reform Act of 1986 (TRA '86) significantly affected the way retailers must account for their inventory costs. The Internal Revenue Code now requires retailers to capitalize a portion of the costs of buying and warehousing merchandise. The primary impact of the TRA '86 is to decrease a retailer's allowable expenses for tax purposes and, therefore, under most conditions, increase the retailer's expense and liability. Prior to the TRA '86, the costs of buying (defined broadly in include buyer's salaries and fringe benefits, the costs of buying trips and an allocated portion of the MIS, Human Resources, and Accounting department costs) were considered period costs for federal income tax purposes and eligible for deduction in the period in which they were incurred. Similarly, the costs of warehousing merchandise, including warehouse rent, depreciation, utilities, labor, and an allocated portion of general and administrative support, were also period costs.

A secondary impact of the TRA '86 was the administrative and accounting burden caused by the requirement to assemble or create the information necessary to comply with the TRA '86. As an example, many retailers found that the Act required them to conduct a survey to determine what percentage of buyers' time was actually spent buying merchandise and by extension, what portion of their salaries would be capitalizable.

Many retailers had expensed such costs for both book and tax purposes prior to the TRA '86. As a result, these retailers were faced with a dilemma; should they continue with their previous financial reporting practices and maintain separate inventory records for tax purposes or capitalize the required costs for both book and tax purposes? One benefit of capitalizing additional costs for book purposes is that earnings (already higher for tax purposes with the consequent tax implications noted above) would be increased. It should be noted, however, that not all costs capitalizable for tax purpose would be capitalizable for book purposes. Generally accepted accounting principles (GAAP) would preclude capitalization of general and administrative costs as well as the excess of accelerated (tax) depreciation over the straight-line calculations generally used for book purposes.

Another important factor influencing retailers' choices is industry practice. As more retailers choose to capitalize additional costs for book purposes, it becomes more likely that others will also change. Subsequent to the introduction of the TRA '86, a number of retailers have chosen to change their method of inventory accounting for book purposes as well. This change is appropriate if it is judged to be a preferable accounting method, that is, a better matching of revenues and related expenses.

If the impact of the change in accounting for inventory is material, then the retailer's financial statements must comply with the disclosure requirements of Accounting Principles Board (APB) Opinion No. 20, Accounting Changes. These disclosure requirements include a description of the change in accounting principle, reflection of a cumulative effect of the change in the current period's income statement and pro forma disclosure of earnings (for all income statements presented) as if the change was applied retroactively.

(k) RIGHT OF RETURN.   Most retailers accept merchandise returns from customers in the ordinary course of business. In some instances the right of return is a matter of written contract. In many other instances it is a matter of practice rather than formal policy, to enhance customer relations, promote business, and so on.

SFAS No. 48, Paragraph 6, details the conditions that must be met in order for a sale to be recognized:

1. The price must be fixed or determinable.
2. Payment has either been made or obligated without further contingency.
3. The buyer's obligation remains even if the product is stolen or destroyed (risk passes to the buyer).
4. Buyer and seller are unrelated.
5. Seller does not have significant future performance obligations.
6. The amount, if any, of future returns can be estimated within reason.

Thus, to record a sale, an estimate needs to be made at the end of each accounting period of the amount of future returns. This requires an understanding of the customer return policies which vary widely from company to company. Some do not accept any returns other than for damages or exchanges, some accept returns within a certain amount of time, and still others accept returns at almost any time and for any reason. Normally past history is a good method of estimating. However, changes in circumstances, business, products, or other factors could make the calculation more complex. For example, a retailer could find it difficult to estimate returns due to:

1. Changes in technology.
2. Changes in demand.
3. Absence of many homogeneous transactions or the existence of a few very large transactions whereby one or a few returns could be significant.

Despite the existence of any of the above factors, in order to recognize a sale, some estimate of returns needs to be made. The nature of the estimate depends on the type of reason for the returns. For example:

1. If the return is due to damage, an accrual should be made for the costs to fix the products.
2. If the return will be for a cash refund or credit on future merchandise, the accrual should be for the gross profit realized on the sale. When the product is physically returned, the difference between the cash actually refunded and the accrual established is debited to inventory.
3. If returns are accepted only for an exchange for a similar item (i.e., a return due to color, size, etc.), retailers commonly do not establish a reserve. The belief is that the selling process is completed and there is no incremental costs due to the exchange and no accrual is necessary. This is acceptable if it can be clearly demonstrated, by past history and policy, that this is the case. If the merchandise being sold is unique and if cash is refunded if a like item is not available, this argument may not be valid.

The estimate of the reserve for merchandise returns must be continually reviewed for changes in policy or circumstances and in consideration of changes in the historical pattern of returns.

As a result of returned merchandise for which credit to buy other merchandise is issued, the retailer carries a liability on the books. It is normal that some of these credits are never redeemed. It is important for retailers to understand state and local escheat laws which usually provide guidance as to what should be done with these credits, as well as with abandoned gift certificates. In most cases, after a period of time (one to two years), if the customer cannot be located, the credited funds should be turned over to the state. Retailers that have adopted the policy of taking these credits into income are often in violation of these laws and face the possibility of fines and/or penalties.

26.4 STORE ISSUES

Thus far, this chapter has dealt with issues specific to the retail industry and especially those in the area of retail merchandise accounting. Retailers are faced with numerous other accounting issues, some of which are relevant primarily to their industry, some of which are more general in nature. The more important of these issues are discussed in this section, along with its relevance to, and impact on, the retail business.

(a) PREOPENING COSTS. Planning for store openings involves personnel from all of a company's operational areas, including store operations, merchandising, financial, data processing, and so on. This planning often begins many months before the store actually opens for business. Most of the costs involved with such openings are considered to be period costs and are expenses as incurred, either because they are not incremental costs, cannot be specifically identified, or because of doubt as to whether or not the store will actually open. However, certain other costs are truly incremental, can be specifically identified as being applicable to a store that either has or is guaranteed to open and are incurred prior to the opening of the store. These costs may be deferred and amortized over a relatively short period of time after the store opens. Examples of the more common of these costs are:

1. Rent incurred in leasing a store for a period prior to its actual opening. For stores built by the retailer, the accounting rules relative to capitalization of interest cost should be followed.
2. Advertising the opening of a store.
3. Direct, incremental payroll costs related to a specific store, including costs to train store personnel, set up the store, and so on.
4. Travel costs incurred by company personnel to visit the location, plan the opening, and so on.
5. Data processing costs related specifically to a new store.
6. Security costs.
7. Utility costs.

There are additional costs that may also qualify for deferral depending on the specific circumstances of each company. Except in very rare situations, no corporate costs or allocations would be included as preopening costs. Additionally, any deferral of costs would end as soon as the store opens for business. Deferred costs must be both directly related to a specific store and incremental.

Each retailer needs to establish a corporate policy for the amortization of any deferred costs. This policy should be followed for all similar types of stores opened by the company. The policy should be established based on the justification for the deferral.

Several different amortization policies have been adopted by retailers and remain acceptable, depending on the specific facts and circumstances. The most widely followed policies are:

1. *Expense as Incurred.* Despite the common practice of deferring preopening costs, many retailers elect to expense all costs as incurred. This policy reflects both conservative accounting and the tenuous nature of success for any store.
2. *Amortize over the Remainder of the Fiscal Year.* This policy is most often applicable to retailers with accounting years ending in December or January. For most retail operations, the Christmas season represents the major selling season. Certain retailers believe that preopening costs should be spread over at least one prime selling season to best match revenues and costs. Other retailers justify this policy as the best to spread costs over a short period of time after a store opens rather than burdening an interim period with unusually high costs. This is also a conservative accounting policy as all costs are fully expensed prior to the end of the fiscal year. The exception to this would be for costs related to a store not yet opened by the end of the year, thus applicable preopening costs would be deferred from one year to the next.
3. *Amortize over the 12 Months after a Store Opens.* This policy was more prevalent in the past than currently. The theory is that one entire 12-month selling season should bear the burden of these deferred costs. It is less conservative than the above policies as it results in deferred costs on the balance sheet at the end of any fiscal year in which stores were opened. For this reason, many retailers have switched to the policies noted in (1) and (2) above. However, it does remain an acceptable policy in most cases.

4. *Amortize over a Two- or Three-Year Period.* This policy has been adopted by relatively few retailers and is far less conservative than those described above. Certain retailers have argued that the life cycle for developing their business is more than one year. One example might be membership clubs where membership builds up slowly over a period of time. A second example might be a mail order business that needs to build up its customer lists. Those that feel this is an unacceptable policy argue that all new retail operations take a period of time to build up to "normal" volume.

In order to justify this policy, the retailer must provide strong proof of the longer life based on existing facts and circumstances, that is, a demonstrated pattern of slowly growing volume resulting, in part, from those costs incurred prior to the store opening. Additionally, there must be virtual certainty that the store will remain in operation for the period of amortization.

This policy brings with it a high degree of risk and is not widely accepted within the industry. Careful consideration is necessary before adopting an amortization period greater than one year.

Any amortization policy for preopening costs other than those noted above is considered unacceptable. For example, it would not be proper to amortize these costs over the term of the lease or over a period of time greater than two or three years. This is due to both the risk involved with any retail location and the difficulty in absolutely associating specific preopening costs with future benefits. For tax return purposes, preopening costs are generally expensed as incurred, thus giving rise to deferred taxes.

(b) LEASE ACCOUNTING. One of the larger expenses for most retailers is the lease expense for store and warehouse facilities, as well as furniture, fixtures, and vehicles. While some retailers do own some or all of their locations, most have viewed leasing as a means of financing their operations. Leasing, as opposed to buying, ties up less capital and passes certain risks to the lessor. While leasing results in less control over the property itself, many retailers are willing to pass up this control to free additional funds for inventory, further expansion, and so on, or because they have weak credit ratings and could not finance a property. While leasing may free additional debt capacity, the major debt rating agencies, as well as most banks, do calculate a debt factor based on the existing operating leases. This factor may either be a present value calculation of future rental payments or a multiple of rent expense.

For many retailers, leases are one of their more valuable assets. A fair market value lease today may become a bargain lease in the future for a variety of reasons, including inflation, the maturing of a shopping center, a long fixed rent term and/or bargain renewal options, and so on. Some retailers, as a result of the size of their stores and/or their reputation, are able to obtain substantially below market lease terms from day one. Such stores are generally referred to as "anchor" stores because of their positioning in shopping centers.

Any lease must be classified as either operating or capital. This classification determines the method of accounting for that particular lease. Operating leases are those that do not create equity for the lessee, whether true or economic equity. Capital leases do create equity, whether legally or economically, as a result of the terms of the transaction. SFAS No. 13, issued in November 1976, established four criteria for capital leases. A least that meets any one or more of these criteria is classified as capital:

1. The lease transfers ownership of the property to the lessor by the end of the lease term.
2. The lease contains a bargain purchase option.
3. The lease term . . . is equal to 75% or more of the estimated economic life of the leased property . . . .
4. The present value at the beginning of the lease term of the minimum lease payments . . . , excluding executory costs such as insurance, maintenance and taxes to be paid by the lessor, including any profit thereon, equals or exceeds 90% of the excess of

the fair value of the leased property . . . to the lessor, at inception of the lease over any related investment tax credit retained by the lessor and expected to be realized by him.

In some circumstances, criteria 4 may be difficult to analyze because the fair market value of the leased property may not be objectively determinable. For example, many specialty retail operations lease a relatively small space in a large shopping mall. SFAS No. 13, Paragraph 28 notes that, "if the fair value of the leased property is not objectively determinable, the lessee shall classify the lease . . ." using criteria 3 above only. This does not mean that all leases involving small stores in a larger center would qualify under these circumstances since the fair value is often determinable based on construction cost estimates, and so on. Rather, the specific circumstances surrounding any lease must be closely reviewed.

In order to determine the proper classification of capital versus operating lease, the lessee must know the basic terms of the lease plus:

1. The economic life of the leased property.
2. The executory costs, if any, included in the lease payments.
3. Their incremental borrowing rate or the lessor's implicit rate built into the lease if that rate is known and is less than the lessee's rate.
4. Any option periods included in the lease and any purchase options.

(i) Disclosure.   Operating leases, unlike capital leases, require income statement and footnote disclosure only, rather than balance sheet classification. Disclosure requirements are for all such leases with initial or remaining noncancellable lease terms greater than one year. These disclosures include:

1. The amount of net expense for each period for which an income statement is presented. Minimum rentals, contingent rentals, and sublease income should be disclosed.
2. Total future minimum rental payments and the minimum payments for each of the next five years.
3. Total minimum sublease income to be received in the future.

As noted previously, a capital lease is one that either legally or economically implies ownership. Therefore, the balance sheet must include an asset and obligation related to those leases. SFAS No. 13, Paragraph 10, defines the amount of the asset and obligation as "an amount equal to the present value at the beginning of the lease term of the minimum lease payments during the lease term, excluding that portion of the payment representing executory costs such as insurance, maintenance and taxes to be paid by the lessor, together with any profit thereon." This amount cannot exceed the fair value of the property at lease inception.

During the lease period the asset is amortized as follows:

1. If classified as a capital lease since the lease transfers ownership to the lessee or the lease contains a bargain purchase option the amortization should match the lessee's normal depreciation policy for assets owned.
2. If classified as a capital lease for other than the reasons noted in (1) above, the amortization period should be the lease term.

The lease payment should be allocated to the lease obligation and interest to result in a constant rate of interest on the remaining obligation, that is, using the "interest" method.

The financial statement should separately identify the lease assets and obligations and related amortization. The footnotes should disclose:

1. The future minimum lease payments in total and for each of the succeeding five years.
2. For noncancellable leases, the minimum sublease rentals to be received.
3. Contingent rentals incurred for each period for which an income statement is presented.

For all leases there should be disclosure of the general nature of the leasing arrangements including the basis for determining contingent rentals, renewal or purchase options and restrictions imposed by the leases.

(ii) Step Function Leases.   As a result of confusion concerning the accounting for operating leases with scheduled rent increases during the lease term, the FASB issued FTB 85-3 (FASB Technical Bulletin 85-3) in November 1985 and FTB 88-1 in December 1988. These bulletins cover all scheduled rent increases, whether as a result of normal increases over time, rent, holidays, to recognize the impact of inflation, and so on. The bulletins do not cover contingent rents, such as percentage rents. Contingent rents are accounted for as an expense as paid or incurred. The bulletins also do not cover capital leases, as scheduled rent increases for capital leases are an integral element of the calculation of the asset and related liability.

The bulletins state that rent expense must be recognized on a straight-line basis over the life of the lease, regardless of the timing of the actual payments. The following illustrations demonstrate application of this:

Case 1. A standard lease with a 20-year term and schedule lease payments of $50,000 per year plus 1% of gross revenue in excess of a stated amount.

In this example, the expense recognized each year would be the $50,000 scheduled rent plus any percentage rent based on the gross revenues.

Case 2. A 20-year lease with no rent in year 1 as an inducement to sign the lease, rent of $45,000 in years 2 through 5, $50,000 in years 6 through 15 and $64,000 in years 16 through 20.

In this example, total scheduled lease payments over the 20-year term are $1,000,000, the same as the scheduled rent in Case 1. The expense recognized would be $50,000 each year ($1,000,000 divided by 20 years) even though no rent is paid in year one and only $45,000 per year in years 2 through 5.

It should be remembered that contingent rentals, such as the percentage rent in Case 1, are not included in this calculation. If you assume that the contingent rent in Case 1 is $10,000 in year 20, rent expense that year would be $60,000, versus $50,000 in year 20 for Case 2. Thus, the expense is lower that year for Case 2 although the actual cash paid is higher ($64,000 vs. $60,000).

The only exception to recognizing expense on a straight line basis would be in the relatively rare situation whereby this method does not truly represent the time pattern in which the leased property is physically utilized. Factors such as the time value of money, inflation, or future revenues do not relate to the time pattern of usage considered by the technical bulletin. Thus they do not provide exceptions to the straight-line method.

As noted, percentage rents are not included in the step function lease calculations. However, the period for determining the percentage rent often crosses over the company's fiscal year end. In such situations, an accrual should be set up, both at year-end and on an interim basis, for the estimated percentage rent. This estimate should be based on past history, budgeted sales and any other relevant factors.

(iii) Landlord Concessions.   Often a landlord will offer rent concessions to a prospective tenant to encourage them to move from one location to another. These concessions may include paying a tenant's moving costs, reimbursement for leasehold improvements in the current location, or assuming any remaining lease obligations.

Generally, payments by the landlord for moving costs or leasehold improvements should be recognized by the tenant as a reduction of rent expense in the new location on a straight-line basis over the term of the new lease. Additionally, if the tenant is not able to terminate the old lease or sublease their existing space, or must sublease the space at a loss, the expected loss should be recognized currently. In most instances, any nonreimbursed costs related to a move should be recognized currently rather than deferred. In fact, it is unlikely that the SEC would accept deferral of any such costs.

(iv) Tax Treatment.   Both capital and operating leases can result in different expense recognition for books and tax returns, giving rise to deferred taxes. For tax returns, the expense is normally based on the terms of the lease, that is, the actual timing of payments contemplated. For a capital lease the combination of amortization expense and interest on the lease obligation generally exceeds the actual rent paid in the early years of the lease and is less in the later years as the obligation decreases. This gives rise to deferred tax debits in the early years of the lease, absent other factors affecting taxes outside the lease area. The debit eventually decreases to zero as the lease expires.

For operating leases with scheduled lease payments on a straight-line basis, generally the book and tax expense would be the same. However, for step function leases, the tax expense is based on actual rents paid or accrued under the lease term. In the previous example, the tax expense would be zero in year 1, $45,000 in year 2, and so on. The book expense would be $50,000 in both years. As with the capital lease example, above, book expense exceeds tax expense in the early years of this lease, resulting in deferred tax debits that again reduce to zero as the lease expires. In the unusual case of schedule rent decreases, deferred tax credits could result.

(v) Sale-Leasebacks.   Some retailers have tried to combine the best benefits of both owning and leasing by utilizing sale-leaseback arrangements. They actually provide the funds to build their locations and then sell the real estate to an investor. The selling price is based on market conditions and the terms the retailer sets for its leasing back of the property. Such an arrangement provides the retailer with control over the actual physical structure as well as lease terms that they determine. Normally the sale results in a gain recognized by the retailer, if a true sale occurs.

SFAS No. 98 provides further guidance on when sale-leaseback accounting is applicable. Basically, the transaction must include a normal leaseback, must have payment terms that demonstrate the buyer-lessor's initial and continuing involvement in the property and must transfer all risks and rewards of ownership (demonstrated by the absence of any other continuing involvement, other than normal lease, by the seller-lessee).

With recent changes in the tax laws, the investors in such arrangements are generally more interested in the true economic value of the real estate, as measured by cash flow and/or potential appreciation, rather than in tax benefits. Institutional investors have become much more active in this market since a scarcity of quality real estate in which to invest has developed. Quality, in this case, is determined as much by the quality of the tenant itself as by the location of the property.

(c) STORE CLOSING RESERVE.   Frequently retailers make the decision to close one or a group of stores or operations within a store. Closings can be the result of:

1. Ongoing evaluation of the profitability of all stores.
2. Closing of all stores in a specific geographic location.

3. Closing of a group of stores or a specific, separate type of operation within a store.
4. Closing of a store to move to a new location in the same area.

The accounting treatment for and related disclosure of store closings depends on which of the above categories is applicable. Most closings are part of the normal operations of a retailer, thus the related changes are included with income from operations. If material, these changes might be included as a separate line item with footnote disclosure. Other closings may qualify as a discontinued segment. A more detailed explanation of the proper disclosures will be presented later in this chapter.

(i) Costs to Be Accrued.   Once the decision is made to close a store or stores or an operation within stores, the costs of these closings should be accrued. These should be costs directly related to the decision to close. The more frequent types of costs include:

Inventory Markdowns.   Generally closings result in greater than normal markdowns in inventory when it is determined that the cost of these markdowns, whether in pure dollars, time and effort of people, and so on, is less than the cost of moving the merchandise to another store, remarking, and other related activities. If this is the case, then an estimate of the markdowns in excess of normal markdowns should be accrued when the decision is made, assuming that the markdowns will result in a loss from operations.

If a loss is also expected as a result of normal markdowns that amount should also be accrued. This could well be the situation as the store could be closing since it is in a poor location losing money. If the merchandise is to be moved to another location, the costs of moving, reticketing, and so on must be accrued since moving merchandise from store to store does not add value to the inventory.

Occupancy Costs.   If the location is owned, the book value of the location plus an estimate of the costs to sell the space, including costs to maintain the location until it is sold, must be compared to an estimate of the selling price. If a loss is estimated, then that loss should be accrued. If a gain is estimated, the gain should not be recognized until realized. If the space is to be leased rather than sold, and if it is reasonably expected that the lease income will cover operating costs, the only accrual required is for operating *losses* estimated to be incurred until the property is leased.

If the property is leased, a calculation must be made of the present value of all future minimum rental costs, including base rent, common area costs, security, utilities, and so on throughout the base rental period. The amount calculated should be reduced by expected sublease income, if any. Again, if a loss results, it should be accrued. If a gain results, it would be recognized as earned over the life of the lease and sublease.

For an example of the above, assume a lease with 10 years remaining and a base rent of $50,000 per year. Additional costs include a 5% common area charge, or $2500 per year, plus insurance, maintenance, etc. costs of $5000 per year. Total payments over the remaining base lease term would be $57,500 per year. Using a 10% discount rate, the present value of these payments would be $363,000. Assume that the property can be sub-let for $45,000 per year, including all costs, and that it is estimated that it will take one year to sublease. The present value, again at a 10% rate, of $45,000 per year in years two through 10 is $247,000. The difference of $116,000 ($363,000–$247,000) should be accrued when the decision to close is made.

In most cases, sublease calculations require estimates, as no formal commitment exists. There may be situations whereby a formal sublease arrangement has been entered into, but for a period shorter than the base rental period. In the previous example assume the sublease was signed already, but only covering years one through five, with an option period for five more years. Judgment would need to be exercised to decide whether or not the base sublease period was enough of a commitment to establish value for the location. It may be argued that five years is a significant commitment and, therefore, it is very likely that either the lease will be extended or the property subleased again for the final five years at a rent of at least $45,000 per year. Thus, the sublease calculation would be for years two through ten at $45,000 per year, not just the five years committed.

As mentioned, this is a judgment area. A one-year lease is probably not a good measure of fair value for a sublease. However, an eight-year sublease on a ten-year base lease may create a different problem since it is likely to be difficult to sublease for only two years. It is important to ensure that sound business assumptions are used for the above calculations.

Payroll Costs.   Payroll and payroll related costs should be accrued once the decision to close has been made. This includes direct payroll of those involved in actually closing the operations, preparing it for sublease, severance pay, vacation pay, additional pension costs, and so on. It may also include moving costs of a personnel to be kept by the company.

Fixtures and Leaseholds.   The net book value of all fixtures and leaseholds in the store, reduced by the cash to be received upon selling these items (net of costs to dispose) should be accrued.

Depending upon the specific circumstances, there could be other costs that should be accrued. The above are the more prevalent ones, associated with most closings.

(ii) Disclosure.   Most closings represent ongoing evaluations of various locations by management and normal business decisions to discontinue one or several stores. Any loss on such closings would be included with continuing operations. Depending on the materiality of the amount involved, it might be included as a separate line within the income statement or, more often, disclosed in the footnotes to the financial statements. Some retailers have adopted the policy of footnote disclosure of any such closing losses every year, regardless of the amount. They believe that these are recurring events that are important to the reader of the financial statements, thus warranting disclosure.

Occasionally a retailer will close an entire segment of the business. If material, the disclosure rules are different than noted above. APB No. 30 discusses discontinued operations and the accounting treatment for disposals of a segment as "A component of an enterprise whose activities represent a separate major line of business or class of customer." For a retail operation with several divisions, each in a different retail operation, that is, a department store division, a specialty clothing division, a supermarket division, and so on, identifying a segment might be fairly easy. However, for others this may not be the case. It is important to note that the following criteria must be met for the operation to qualify as a segment.

26.5 RETAILER'S FINANCIAL STATEMENT ANALYSIS

Financial statements are the most widely used media for disseminating information about a company. While complying with accounting standards and governmental reporting requirements, they can function as an excellent public relations tool.

Financial statements are one resource for analyzing a company. Financial statements provide historical information and should be used to supplement the financial statement user's understanding of the business. The numbers need to be correlated with what is going on in the business.

There are no operating problems that do not have financial reporting overtones. For example, poor merchandising leads to slow moving inventory and the possible need for a reserve for future markdowns. Conversely, there are no financial reporting problems that do not have operating implications. For example, customer accounts receivable collection problems (with proprietary or "house" accounts), which must be evaluated to determine the adequacy of the allowance for doubtful accounts, do not arise in a vacuum. They could arise from the faulty assignment of customer credit limits, or from sporadic and/or ineffective collection policies.

Certain operating and accounting issues are unique or of more significance to retailers. This section discusses financial reporting disclosures and issues of importance to retailers.

(a) THE RETAILER'S INCOME STATEMENT

(i) Net Sales. Net sales of a store are defined as "gross sales less returns and allowances (except policy adjustments) and less discounts to employees and others."

In some stores the service departments such as restaurants and salons represent an important part of store operations. For this reason, their sales and results of operations may be reported separately from the conventional retail departments that sell merchandise at normal markons. Under these circumstances, frequent consolidation of the retail and service departments results in distorted relationships which are not comparable with figures of other retailers.

Gross sales do not include receipts from customers for *alterations* which are applied as reductions of workroom and alteration costs. For the sake of simplicity, workroom and alteration costs would be included in other costs of sales in the condensed income statement.

Sales taxes collected on merchandise sold and installment carrying charges should be excluded from sales. *Installment carrying charges* are an element of other income, net, and are shown as finance charge income in the accompanying statement.

In the event *contract and wholesale* operations are a significant factor, the related sales, costs and expenses should be segregated from the more conventional retail operations. Contract or wholesale volume is typically obtained at lower profit margins than realized by the regular retail business. Consequently, consolidation of such diverse elements results in abnormal relationships in the total all-store combined figures. If the combination of wholesale and retail operations produces operating results deemed distortive, the store's income account should be broken down into two or more separate sections.

(ii) Cost of Goods Sold. Income statements for retailers are frequently more condensed than those seen in other businesses. Retailers have adopted a format for the income statement that reflects the cost of acquiring merchandise and preparing it for sale, such as special packaging, as part of cost of goods sold. Retailers believe that this format more realistically presents the real costs incurred in making merchandise available to consumers at retail. This format also indirectly responds to criticisms directed toward the large spread between retail prices and merchandise costs as reflected in published statements.

Traditionally, the special format of income statement published by publicly owned companies, and responsive to financial reporting rules of the Securities and Exchange Commission, classifies "occupancy and buying costs" as part of cost of goods sold. Since there is not precise uniformity in the identification of these elements of expenses, there can be differences in interpretation and grouping among retailers, thereby reducing the degree of comparability.

For example, one discount department store lists "cost of goods sold, transportation, and buying expenses" as the captioned amount of cost of sales. Grocery stores are not as descriptive and merely state the captioned cost of sales as "cost of goods sold." It is not clear whether they are including buying and occupancy costs in this captioned amount.

Given the lack of uniformity in grouping costs and expenses, as well as a certain unwillingness to disclose data deemed competitively disadvantageous, some major retail companies have adopted a different format for external reporting purposes. This format groups all costs and expenses together, exclusive of certain designated items (normally, maintenance and repairs, depreciation, taxes other than income taxes, rentals, retirement expense, and interest expense).

Some companies, while grouping all costs and expenses together, have chosen to show cost of goods sold as a separately captioned amount. In effect, there are three general schools of thought in presenting costs and expenses for a company engaged in retailing:

1. *Traditional Method*

   Cost of goods sold, including occupancy and buying costs:

   Selling, general and administrative expenses.

   Depreciation.

   Interest expense.

2. *"Exclusive of" Method*

   Cost of goods sold and expenses, exclusive of the following items:

   Maintenance and repairs.

   Depreciation.

   Taxes other than those based on income.

   Rentals.

   Retirement expense.

   Interest expense.

3. *Combination Method*

   Cost and expenses of retail operations:

   Cost of goods sold.

   Selling, general and administrative expenses.

   Maintenance and repairs.

   Depreciation.

   Taxes, other than those based on income.

   Rentals.

   Retirement expenses.

   Interest expense.

   Total costs and expenses.

There can be many variations to meet specific situations. From an accounting standpoint it may be preferable to see occupancy and buying costs classified as part of cost of goods sold, however the other forms of presentation also have merit. Whatever format is chosen, it should be used consistently, period to period, to enable the readers to make appropriate comparisons.

It is apparent that the special formats of the income statement were designed largely as vehicles for the public presentation of operating statistics. Practically speaking, these formats do not provide the detailed insights necessary to effectively monitor and control the ongoing operations of a retail enterprise. In effect, the special formats would be used only when preparing formal statements for public dissemination.

(iii) Leased Department Operations.   Retailers often have leased department operations. Financial statement presentations of these operations vary from company to company. Since the retailer receives only a commission from the leased department operator, based generally on gross sales, the cost of the merchandise handled and operating expenses of the lessee are not known. Some retailers report the amount of commissions from leased departments as an element of other income, not to be included in gross margin. However, the National Retail Federation (NRF) Retail Accounting Manual considers such commissions as an element of gross margin. When using this format, the company should indicate that sales do include leased department sales. In these instances, the difference between the leased department sales and the commissions from leased departments is reflected as a charge to cost of goods sold.

In offering merchandise for sale to the general public, the retailer is not distinguishing between owned department and leased department merchandise. Including leased department sales in the retailer's net sales reflects the total sales of the retail company. Proponents of this alternative agree that the use of the leased department, rather than a company-operated department, is a merchandising decision, often made because of the special nature and/or highly specialized merchandising requirements of leased operations. The company can operate these departments if it so chooses; therefore, a true reflection of its selling capacity is *all sales.*

Although this argument may have some merit, it is preferable to show total net sales, including leased department sales, from which leased department sales are deducted to arrive at owned department sales. Commissions from leased departments are then shown separately. This alternative handles the problem of reflecting total selling capacity, while not distorting owned-sales/cost-of-sales relationships.

The sample income statement in Exhibit 26.12 reflects separate disclosure to leased department sales and leased department income and combines leased department expenses with store operating, administrative, and general expenses.

(iv) Operating Expenses.   Operating expenses should be planned by functional groups and actual performance should be measured against plan on a periodic basis. Separate statistical statements showing the details of operating expenses are normally prepared in conjunction with the income statement. The amount of detail any one company may wish to report will vary depending upon the size of the operation, the organizational structure, and the level to which responsibility can be reasonably assigned.

A considerable portion of Book 1 of the NRMA Retail Accounting Manual is devoted to the area of expense accounting and reporting. It should be consulted for specific details. This chapter will consider only the basic concepts of expense reporting.

In preparing their Retail Accounting Manual, the NRMA was confronted with certain practical problems. A chart of accounts had to be provided for expense accumulation, summarization, and reporting that could be used by most retailers regardless of size or type of operation. At the same time, some degree of uniformity in reporting practices had to be maintained in order to make figure exchange feasible.

	Fiscal Year Ended January 26, 19X1
Total Sales	$XXX XXX
Less: Leased department sales	X XXX
Net sales	$XXX XXX
Leased department income	XXX
Interest and other income	XXX
Total income	$XXX XXX
Costs and expenses:	
Cost of goods sold, transportation, and buying expenses	XXX XXX
Store operating, administrative, and general expenses, including leased department expenses	XX XXX
Depreciation and amortization	XXX
Interest and debt expense	XXX
Total costs and expenses	$XXX XXX
Income before state and federal taxes on income	X XXX
Taxes on income	XXX
Net income	$XXX XXX
Earnings per common share	$X.XX

Exhibit 26.12.   Sample income statement format.

As a solution, the NRMA breaks down the various functions or centers of activity into 10 expense summaries, with 44 expense centers within these summaries, which can be used by even the smallest of retail operations:

010	Property and equipment
100	Company management
200	Accounting and management information
300	Credit and accounts receivable
400	Sales promotion
500	Services and operations
600	Personnel
700	Merchandise receiving, storage, and distribution
800	Selling and supporting services
900	Merchandising

Companies that wish to show more detail can utilize the 44 expense centers provided within these expense summaries. For example, expense summary 400, sales promotion, has the following expense centers:

400	Sales promotion	
	410	Sales promotion management
	420	Advertising
	430	Shows, special events, and exhibits
	440	Display

A company may use any or all of these expense centers, depending on its needs. However, if all the expense centers within a specific summary are not used, the expense elements pertaining to the unused centers should be included in the management expense center of each summary. In the 400 summary example cited above, if a company did not wish to use the expense center 430—shows, special events, and exhibits—any expenses incurred for these types of activities would be included in 410, sales promotion management.

For companies desiring an even finer breakdown of expenses, the NRMA provides 22 subexpense centers. Each company can decide which, if any, of these subexpense centers to use. Sales promotion would cover the following if all of the expense areas of activity were used:

400	Sales promotion	
	410	Sales promotion management
	420	Advertising
	421	Newspaper
	425	Radio
	426	TV
	427	Direct mail
	428	Other
	430	Shows, special events, and exhibits
	431	Public relations
	432	Merchandise shows
	434	Special events and exhibits
	440	Display
	441	Display production
	444	Sign shop

In addition to capturing expense by areas of activity, the NRMA Retail Accounting Manual also classifies expenses by natural division, describing the type of expense. There are 17 basic natural divisions of expense as follows:

01	Payroll
03	Media costs
04	Taxes
06	Supplies
07	Services purchased
08	Unclassified
09	Travel
10	Communications
11	Pensions
12	Insurance
13	Depreciation
14	Professional services
16	Bad debts
17	Equipment rentals
18	Outside maintenance
20	Real property rentals
92	Credits and outside revenues

Provision is also made for three transfer accounts. Although not comprising basic natural divisions, they are used in addition to the natural divisions:

02	Allocated fringe benefits
90	Expense transfers-in
91	Expense transfers-out

A great deal of attention and emphasis has been brought to bear in planning and controlling expense by area of responsibility. As an integral segment of the monthly or period financial reporting package, management should receive a statement similar to the one shown in Exhibit 26.13. This statement displays expense by expense summary compared to budget, and to last year, and additionally shows variances from budget. These amounts are shown both for the current month or period (or four- or five-week) and season or year-to-date. The statement as presented shows only the 10 expense summaries, companies that use expense centers and/or subcenters may wish to display those as well.

Management should also be provided with a monthly (or four- or five-week period) statement of operating expenses by natural division. (Exhibit 26·14 on pp. 26·42–26·43). Each supervisor assigned responsibility for a work center should be provided periodically with a natural expense breakdown of their work center. This is done by displaying the natural divisions of expense applicable to each center for the current month versus budget, and season or year-to-date actual versus budget.

(b) THE RETAILER'S BALANCE SHEET.   Components of the typical retailer's balance sheet have fairly standard captions and format; however, the content of the particular accounts can have some unique qualities. This section addresses the contents of balance sheet captions.

(i) Cash.   Cash may include cash on hand and cash in the bank; payroll, disbursements, concentration accounts, as well as individual store deposit accounts. Concentration accounts are used by retailers to move funds from all the individual store bank accounts. The retailer's cash account would also include the deposit amounts for bankcards such as MasterCard and Visa,

Classification and Name of Expense	Month				Period / Season to Date			
	This Year Amount %	Budget Amount %	Budget Ver. Amount %	Last Year Amount %	This Year Amount %	Budget Amount %	Budget Ver. Amount %	Last Year Amount %
010 Property and Equipment								
100 Company Management								
200 Accounting and Management Info.								
300 Credit and Accounts Receivable								
400 Sales Promotion								
500 Services and Operations								
600 Personnel								
700 Merchandise Receiving, Storage, and Distribution								
800 Selling and Supporting Services								
900 Merchandising								
Total Expenses								

Exhibit 26.13. Comparative statement of operating expenses by expense summary. *Source:* Retail Accounting Manual, NRF.

where the retailer's account is credited with the funds the same day the credit card documentation is provided to the bank. Cash accounts may also be established for foreign purchases under letters of credit.

(ii) Accounts Receivable. Accounts receivable would normally include regular customer accounts, revolving charge, installment, layaway and deferred billing accounts, and amounts due from third party charge companies such as American Express. Accounts receivable may in some instances also include the other bank card receivables, net of service fee charges, if they are not reflected in cash. The inclusion of bank card receivables in accounts receivable or cash generally depends on the processing time for the bank card deposits and availability of the funds to the retailer.

(iii) Other Receivables. Other receivables may include leased department receivables, loans and advances to officers and employees, amounts due from cosmetics and other demonstrators, debit balances in accounts payable including amounts due from vendors for merchandise returns, advertising rebates, volume allowances and freight claims. Offsetting amounts due from a vendor against the liability to that vendor is permissible in accordance with FASB Technical Bulletin No. 88-2.

(iv) Bad Debt Reserves or Allowances. Reserves or allowances for bad debts are recorded by retailers for both customer receivables and other receivables. In addition to the bad debt losses relating to customer accounts, a retailer frequently incurs losses for uncollectible freight claims and vendor debit balances. As with customer accounts, other receivables require ongoing, constant collection efforts if writeoffs are to be avoided.

Given the large number of individual customer accounts, it is impossible to determine the adequacy of bad debt reserves by reference to each customer account. Retailers must rely on historical aging and bad debt writeoff statistics and trends. In addition, retailers must consider changes in the economies in which stores are located, as well as policy changes instituted. For example, a liberalization of the retailer's credit policy will affect the retailer's aging and will have to be taken into account when analyzing and estimating the bad debt reserve requirements. For interim reporting purposes, retailers frequently record an estimated or budgeted amount, often a percentage of net sales based on prior year actual.

At year-end, the appropriate bad debt reserves must be determined using various formula approaches. One approach is based on the accounts receivable aging. The aggregate reserve is developed by applying specific percentages to the various aging categories, with increasingly higher percentages utilized for older age categories. The percentages utilized should be based on a historical analysis which correlates bad debt experience with aging; tempered for current business developments and policies.

An alternative, but less desirable, approach is to relate historical bad debt losses to net sales over several years and record the reserve based on that percentage relationship. This approach should recognize that, to a certain extent, bad debts recognized in the current year will relate to sales recorded in the prior year. Accordingly, a knowledgeable correlation will have to be made between the timing of sales and the corollary bad debt reserve requirement.

(v) Inventory. Merchandise inventories are normally the most significant asset on the retailer's balance sheet. The inventory category normally includes inventory that has been received as well as inventory that is in transit. Inventory costs include inward freight, express, and cartage. Foreign purchased inventory costs include all shipping cost, insurance costs, and duties paid—commonly called "landed costs." Landed cost may include outside buying office expenses or commission fees. All inventory costs should be recorded net of trade discounts.

Inventory reserves may be required because, at any point in time, a diminution in the value and saleability of inventory may have occurred but has not yet been reflected in currently

		01	02	03	04	06	07	08	09	10
		Payroll	Allocated Fringe Benefits (Dr) / (Cr)	Media Costs	Taxes	Supplies	Services Purchased	Unclassified	Travel	Communications
010	Property and equipment									
020	Real estate, buildings, and building equipment				X					
030	Furniture, fixtures, and non-building equipment				X					
100	Company management									
110	Executive office	X	X		X	X	X	X	X	
130	Branch management	X	X			X	X	X	X	
140	Internal audit	X	X			X		X	X	
150	Legal and consumer activities	X	X			X		X	X	
200	Accounting and management information									
210	Control management, general accounting, and statistical	X	X			X	X	X	X	X
220	Sales audit	X	X			X	X	X		
230	Accounts payable	X	X			X	X	X		
240	Payroll and timekeeping department	X	X			X	X	X	X	X
280	Data processing	X	X		X	X	X	X	X	X
300	Credit and accounts receivable									
310	Credit management	X	X			X	X	X	X	
330	Collection	X	X			X	X	X	X	
340	Accounts receivable and bill adjustment	X	X			X	X	X		X
350	Cash office	X	X			X	X	X		
360	Branch/store selling location offices	X	X			X	X	X		
400	Sales promotion									
410	Sales promotion management	X	X			X	X	X	X	
420	Advertising	X	X	X		X	X	X	X	X
430	Shows, special events, and exhibits	X	X			X	X	X	X	
440	Display	X	X			X	X	X	X	
500	Services and operations									
510	Service and operations management	X	X			X	X	X	X	
530	Security	X	X			X	X	X	X	
550	Telephones and communications	X	X			X		X		X
560	Utilities	X	X			X		X		
570	Housekeeping	X	X			X	X	X		
580	Maintenance and repairs	X	X			X	X	X		
600	Personnel									
610	Personnel management	X	X			X	X	X	X	
620	Employment	X	X			X	X	X	X	
640	Training	X	X			X	X	X	X	
660	Medical and other employee services	X	X (Cr)			X	X	X	X	
670	Supplementary benefits	X	X (Cr)		X	X	X	X		
700	Merchandise receiving, storage, and distribution									
710	Management of merchandise receiving, storage & distribution	X	X			X	X	X	X	
720	Receiving and marking	X	X			X	X	X	X	
730	Reserve stock storage	X	X			X		X	X	
750	Shuttle services	X	X			X	X	X		
800	Selling and supporting services									
810	Selling supervision	X	X			X	X	X	X	
820	Direct selling	X	X			X		X	X	
830	Customer services	X	X			X		X	X	X
840	Selling support services	X	X			X		X	X	
860	Central wrapping and packing	X	X			X		X		
880	Delivery	X	X		X	X	X	X	X	
900	Merchandising									
910	Merchandising management	X	X			X	X	X	X	
920	Buying	X	X			X	X	X	X	
930	Merchandise control	X	X			X		X		

Exhibit 26.14.   Summary of natural divisions by expense center.

| 11 | 12 | 13 | 14 | 16 | 17 | 18 | 20 | 90 | 91 | 92 | |
Pensions	Insurance	Depreciation	Professional Services	Bad Debts	Equipment Rentals	Outside Maintenance and Equipment Service Contracts	Real Property Rentals	Expense Transfers In (Dr)	Expense Transfers Out (Cr)	Credits and Outside Revenues (Cr)	
											010
	X	X			X		X			X	020
	X	X			X					X	030
											100
	X		X								110
											130
											140
			X								150
											200
			X					X			210
								X			220
								X			230
								X			240
	X	X	X		X	X		X	X	X	280
											300
								X			310
				X				X			330
											340
								X		X	350
										X	360
											400
			X								410
			X					X		X	420
								X		X	430
										X	440
											500
			X								510
			X								530
		X			X	X			X		550
											560
										X	570
						X			X	X	580
											600
			X								610
											620
											640
											660
	X		X							X	670
X	X		X							X	670
											700
											710
		X		X	X		X				720
											730
		X		X	X		X				750
											800
											810
								X		X	820
										X	830
										X	840
										X	860
	X	X		X	X				X	X	880
											900
			X								910
											920
								X			930

marked retail prices. Inventory reserves are an offset to retail merchandise inventory, and may include reserves for future markdowns, as well as for shortages, discounts and allowances.

Markdowns taken subsequent to the end of the period should be reviewed to determine whether unrecorded markdowns were inherent in such inventory.

At least three opinions exist as to when a reserve for subsequent markdowns should be established. Only two approaches have been accepted in practice. The most conservative could be termed the balance sheet approach. Under this approach, the reserve would include any markdowns taken in the month subsequent to year end on the theory that such markdowns were inherent in the year-end inventory.

A second method, the income statement approach, states that February, normally the month after year-end, should have a normal level of markdowns to reflect the customary presidents' birthdays sales and other sales. Therefore, the reserve only includes markdowns which are deemed abnormal. For example, a decline in turnover or significant deterioration in merchandise aging may necessitate significant markdowns which should be rolled back and for which a reserve should be established at year-end. Either of these two methods is appropriate as long as the method is used consistently. The last method which is not recommended is that the reserve should only contain markdowns authorized prior to year end.

The establishment of the reserve is highly judgmental and requires discussions with merchandise managers and buyers in addition to the chief financial officer in order to identify and quantify required future markdowns. The reserves should be calculated based on actual experience for the period immediately following balance sheet dates. The reserves may be estimated on an overall basis, but should be corroborated by reference to merchandise categories within the various departments.

Various methods can be used to estimate a reserve. One approach would be to establish a reserve by applying designated percentages, by aging category of inventory, reserving higher percentages for out-of-season stock than for current season stock. Alternatively, differing percentages can be applied to the excess inventory within each aging category, with such excess estimated by reference to planned sales. It is important to remember that no formula replaces judgment and knowledge about the specific problem areas in each department.

(vi) Prepaid Expenses. Prepaid expenses may include prepaid rent, supplies (including bags, boxes and other wrapping supplies), and prepaid advertising, and catalog expenses. Also included in this caption are prepaid maintenance contracts and store preopening expenses (for new stores expected to be opened in the following year). Business licenses may be another component of prepaid expenses for a retailer. Only advance payments should be included in prepaid expenses.

(vii) Property and Equipment. In addition to owned land and buildings, categories of assets included as property and equipment that are significant to retailing include leasehold improvements, point-of-sale and computer equipment, and store fixtures.

(viii) Beneficial Leaseholds. The asset beneficial leaseholds normally will be recorded in connection with the acquisition of a retail enterprise. Beneficial leaseholds are the values assigned to the benefits derived from acquiring unexpired leases containing more favorable rates than would be obtained if the leases were negotiated currently. Generally determined by an outside appraisal firm, these intangible assets are recorded at fair market values, net of related income taxes. Beneficial leaseholds are generally amortized on a straight-line basis over the related remaining lease terms. Since stores are leased over different periods and at varying rents, beneficial leaseholds should be recorded and amortized on a store-by-store basis. Separate records, by store, are also necessary in the event of a store closing since the related intangible asset will have to be written off. If the total amount is insignificant, however, it may be more efficient to amortize the entire amount over the average remaining lease term for all leases.

(ix) Accounts Payable. Accounts payable are frequently segregated into accounts payable for retail merchandise which would include the liability for merchandise in transit and freight, and accounts payable for store operating and home office expenses.

(x) Accrued Expenses. Probably the most significant accrued expense for retailers is accrued rent, common area maintenance due landlords, and accrued minimum rent liability. The latter is the most controversial, arising from the promulgation of FASB Technical Bulletin No. 85-3, Accounting for Operating Leases with Scheduled Rent Increases which requires scheduled rent increases covered under escalation clauses to be recognized on a straight-line basis over the lease term. For example, assume a five-year lease with the following rent schedule:

Year(s)	Annual Rent	Total Payments
1 and 2	$15,000	$ 30,000
3 and 4	20,000	40,000
5	30,000	$ 30,000
Total rent payable over five years.		$100,000

Under generally accepted accounting principles, the rent expense charged against income would be $20,000 each year ($100,0005-year term). The FASB has taken the position that a lease is similar to owning a building in that it is being used for the same time and purpose each year. Therefore, each year should be charged with a pro-rata share of the rent. Others argue that in circumstances where the rent was negotiated at a lower rate in the early years of the lease, in anticipation of sales increases in the future, a proper matching of revenues and expenses occurs when the rent is expensed as incurred (i.e., based on the rent schedule). For all practical purposes, this latter argument is not acceptable under generally accepted accounting principles.

Other accrued expense items which are normally significant for retailers include:

- Accrued advertising.
- Accrued payroll and incentive bonuses, particularly selling commissions.
- Accrued vacation pay.
- Accrued personal property and real estate taxes.
- Accrued sales and use taxes.

There may also be a liability for future returns of merchandise sold included in accrued expenses. Typically, retailers do not establish a reserve for future returns since it is normally deemed immaterial to the balance sheet as well as to the income statement.

(xi) Customer Liabilities. Customer liabilities include customer-related items such as gift certificates outstanding, customers' advance deposit payments and mail order deposits.

(xii) Reserve for Store Closings. A reserve for store closings should be established when a decision to close a store is made by management. Major factors to be considered in determining the reserve amount include:

- Severance pay and related employee benefits and employer's share of taxes.
- Beneficial leasehold unamortized balance.
- Net book value of furniture and fixturings, less any salvage value.
- Lease buyout payment or present value of minimum lease payments net of any sublease rental income which can be realistically anticipated.

- Losses on disposal of inventory.
- Handling and shipping costs to transfer the merchandise to other stores.
- Settlements with leased department operators.
- Impact on collectibility of customer accounts.
- Operating losses from the decision date to the actual store closing.

The impact of each of these items should be quantified for inclusion in the reserve for store closings.

(xiii) Deferred Taxes.   Deferred taxes which are typical for retailers arise from the use of accelerated depreciation methods solely for tax reporting purposes:

- Differences in the timing of the recognition of pension and deferred compensation expense,
- Differences between book and tax inventory costing,
- Deferred taxes applicable to the allowance for doubtful accounts, and
- Book and tax differences in accounting for leases.

(xiv) Other Liabilities.   Income taxes payable and other liabilities, both current and noncurrent, are similar in their content to those found in nonretailers' balance sheets. For a sample retail income statement and balance sheet, see Exhibit 26.15. Other statements such as the statement of cash flow and the statement of shareholders' equity are similar in presentation and format to those of nonretail companies.

(c) NOTES TO THE RETAILER'S FINANCIAL STATEMENTS.   Certain footnote disclosures are unique to retailers. Key information regarding a retailer's financial reporting can be obtained by reviewing the accounting policies and other notes to the financial statements.

(i) Accounting Policy Footnote Disclosures

Fiscal Year.   In general merchandise retailing, the fiscal year is typically the last Saturday of a month, often January. For grocery stores, it is frequently the last Saturday in December. The natural yearly cycle of business activity, particularly focusing on seasonality of the business, should be persuasive when selecting a year-end. It is preferable to select a fiscal year-end at the time business activities are at their lowest level, rather than during a peak season. Considerations include:

- When inventories are at, or near, a minimum level to facilitate the taking, summarization, and valuation of physical inventories.
- When the working capital ratio is highest (typically after peak selling season when inventories have been converted into cash and/or receivables, and payables should be at low levels).
- Availability of employees to complete year-end closing within required reporting deadlines (90 days as mandated by SEC and loan covenant requirements) and without conflicting with peak season selling activities or normal employee vacation practices.

In addition, the tax consequences of selecting a particular year-end date should be considered (federal, state and property) with a view to minimizing the overall corporate tax burden.
Other internal considerations include the impact on:

- Budgeting requirements and comparability of data.
- Internal reporting and comparability of data.
- Contractual, incentive and bonus plan arrangements.

Assets	January 26, 19X1
Current Assets:	
Cash	$ XXX
Marketable securities, at cost which approximates market	XXX
Receivables:	X XXX
Trade	XX
Other	XX
Total Receivables	X XXX
Merchandise inventories	XX XXX
Prepaid expenses and other current assets	XXX
Total Current Assets	XX XXX
Property and Equipment:	
Land and buildings	X XXX
Property under capital leases	XXX
Fixtures and equipment	X XXX
Leasehold improvements	XXX
Beneficial leasehold interests	XXX
	XX XXX
Less: Accumulated depreciation and amortization	X XXX
Net Fixed Assets	XX XXX
Other Assets and Deferred Charges	XXX
Excess of Purchase Price over Acquired Net Assets ("Goodwill"), Net	XXX
	$XXX XXX
Current Liabilities:	
Accounts payable:	
Trade	$ X XXX
Leased department concessionaires and other	XXX
Total Accounts Payable	X XXX
Current maturities of long-term debt and capital lease obligations	XXX
Accrued payroll	XXX
Accrued expenses	X XXX
Other liabilities	XXX
Dividends payableXXX	
Taxes on income	
Total Current Liabilities	XX XXX
Deferred income taxes, noncurrent portion	XXX
Deferred compensation	XXX
Capital lease obligations	XXX
Long-term debt	X XXX
Other long-term liabilities	XXX
Stockholders' Equity:	
Common stock $.XX par value per share:	
Authorized XX XXX shares	
Issued and outstanding XX,XXX shares	X XXX
Additional paid-in capital	X XXX
Retained earnings	XX XXX
Less: Common stock in treasury, XX shares at cost	XX
Total Stockholders' Equity	XX XXX
	$XXX XXX

Exhibit 26.15.   Sample balance sheet format.

Basis of Presentation.   Of particular significance is the treatment of leased department sales, for example, whether such sales are included or excluded from net sales.

Merchandise Inventories.   Inventories should be indicated as being stated at the lower of cost or market, with the specific cost method indicated, normally the retail method, LIFO method or specific identification.

Property and Equipment.   There should be an indication that these assets are reflected at cost with information regarding the depreciation methodology used and the average lives used for depreciation purposes by category of asset.

Store Preopening Costs.   This policy note should address whether store preopening costs are charged to operations in the year a new store is opened, or capitalized and amortized over a period of time generally not longer than 12 to 18 months. Preopening costs include those related to employee training, preopening rent and advertising, and new credit card promotions. Indirect general and administrative costs should be expensed as incurred.

Deferred Revenues.   Appliance, electronics or furniture stores may sell service contracts beyond the period covered by the manufacturer's warranty. The policy regarding recognition of revenue arising from the sale of these contracts should be stated. For example, a statement may be included that revenue from the sales of these contracts is recognized over the life of the contract, in a manner that matches revenues to direct expenses and projected product service costs.

Revenue Recognition.   Layaways and other customer deposit/sales can be recognized when the deposit is received, with appropriate consideration for sales cancellation experience, or when final payment is made and the customer takes the merchandise. The policy for revenue recognition on these transactions should be stated.

Finance charge income must be recognized when earned, assuming it is deemed to be fully collectible. Otherwise, an appropriate allowance for uncollectible amounts should be established. The method utilized for recognizing finance charge income should be included in the policy statement. Retailers are required by the SEC to disclose the amount of their finance charge income and where it is included in the income statement. Some retailers have chosen to show finance charge income as "other income," others have chosen to reflect it as "revenue before cost of goods sold." The most prevalent treatment, however, is to treat finance charge income as a reduction of selling, general and administrative expense. The rationale is that this income represents a recovery of a portion of the costs incurred to realize credit sales and to process and maintain customer accounts receivable.

(ii) Inventories.   For inventory valuation purposes, retailers need to comply with the general rule that inventory must be stated at the lower of cost or market.

In complying with this requirement, retailers will use the retail method, the LIFO method which effectively is superimposed on the retail method, or one of the cost methods (normally specific identification on average cost).

The market value of inventory is the estimated sales price of merchandise less the normal departmental markon. Application of the retail method will automatically provide an inventory value which is the lower of cost or market assuming the sales price affixed to the merchandise is realistic. This occurs because the cost multiplier used (normally on a departmental basis) to convert the retail of merchandise to cost results in an inventory value which "ensures" the realization of a normal gross margin upon sale of the merchandise. This result is achieved notwithstanding the dollar amount of markdowns taken on merchandise.

The cost method is utilized by retailers with a limited number of SKU items and price lines such as furniture chains, and by specialty retailers with high ticket items such as furs and jewelry. Detailed inventory records must be maintained, normally on a SKU basis or by merchandise classifications. Historically, the cost method is burdensome because the individual sales must be costed out which requires the maintenance of detailed item or classification cost records, making it practical only for retailers with a limited number of items or styles of merchandise. This is changing with the increased capabilities of computers to maintain cost on an item basis, and some retailers have begun to question the need to use the retail method.

The gross profit method, which is an estimating method, is used primarily by drugstore and convenience store chains. In this method, beginning inventory and purchases are reported at cost, and cost of goods sold is calculated using a gross profit percentage. The gross profit percentage is estimated. Physical inventories, costed at actual, are then required in order to adjust the records to actual cost. The estimated gross profit resulting from the use of this method may be suspect because there is never any assurance that the gross profit for any period has not been affected by the mix of merchandise sold. Moreover, gross profits can be manipulated to distort the results of operations by changing the estimated gross profit percentage, a distortion that will not surface pending the taking of a physical inventory. Other problems with the gross profit method are as follows:

- The company does not know, with reasonable accuracy, the amount of inventory on hand at any date in time, particularly in connection with the taking of a physical inventory. Consequently, they are unable to ascertain or quantify the shortage experienced for a period.
- Management has no assurance that its monthly gross profit reporting is accurate. Bearing in mind the absence of any departmental data regarding purchases at cost and retail, and the related impact on gross profit of any significant changes in the mix of merchandise sold. Additionally, the absence of data on departmental markdowns can further distort inventories, particularly when taken in conjunction with the discretion exercised by store managers in establishing and/or revising retail prices.

The retail method is used most often in modern retailing. Under this methodology, which is a form of perpetual inventory maintained at retail prices, effectively, merchandise is controlled by the retail price instead of the cost. Accountability for all changes in the marked selling prices of merchandise is an absolute requirement. In this averaging method, cost multipliers are used to convert inventory from retail to cost at the end of any period. This method provides an excellent control over the retailer's major asset, as well as critical merchandising data (e.g., data regarding initial markon, markdowns, and shortages). Certain definite advantages that are inherent in its use are as follows:

- It permits periodic determination of inventories and profits without resorting to physical inventories.
- It allows the taking of departmental inventories at various dates, other than the general fiscal closing, with appropriate adjustment of the related departmental book record.
- Physical inventories can be taken more expeditiously since they represent compilations of marked retail prices which are readily available to counting personnel.
- Depreciation of inventory values, evidenced by a reduction in selling prices, is obtained as an automatic by-product of the method as soon as retail prices are reduced.
- It discloses the initial markon of purchases, the effect of markdowns on profits, and the amount of stock shortages.
- It facilitates the knowledgeable preparation of merchandise budgets.
- It provides a basis for insurance coverage and settlements.
- And lastly, it tends to disclose, through apparently erroneous results, deficiencies in operational and internal control systems and procedures or in their implementation.

(iii) Debt.   The footnote disclosure relating to debt includes, in addition to the amounts outstanding, the interest rates, maturity dates, and the most restrictive covenants of the underlying loan agreements, available lines of credit, and collateral for the indebtedness. For retailers, the collateral frequently includes receivables, inventory and tangible fixed assets.

(iv) Lease Commitments.   Retailers are heavy users of leased physical facilities and to a lesser extent, of leased fixtures and leased equipment. These leases must be classified as operating or capital leases in accordance with SFAS No. 13, "Accounting for Leases." This pronouncement, and its subsequent interpretations and amendments, presents numerous problems. Store leases are typically required to be capitalized, but each lease must be evaluated to determine whether it meets the criteria for a capital lease.

With capital leases, an asset and an offsetting liability are recorded. Under operating leases, all costs are reflected as rent expense and no asset or liability recorded. In determining the applicability of SFAS No. 13 capitalization criteria, certain factors are unique to retailing, and require the use of judgment as there are few clear-cut answers. For example, in evaluating the economic life of the property being leased, the economic life of the mall or strip center must be considered as well. In addition, leases frequently include options which must be evaluated to determine whether there are bargain renewal options within the definition of SFAS No. 13. Given the required level of judgment in applying the criteria of SFAS No. 13, two retailers with identical leases in the same mall may reach differing conclusions on the appropriate accounting treatment. The issue of whether a lease is a capital versus an operating lease should be addressed on a store-by-store basis.

The disclosures required by SFAS No. 13 for leases include the future minimum lease payments, as of the date of the latest balance sheet, in the aggregate and for each of the five succeeding years. These amounts should be present valued. It is important to note that minimum rents do not include percentage rents, which are very common in retailing.

The total rental expense for each period for which an income statement is presented must also be disclosed, with separate amounts for minimum rents, percentage or contingent rents, and sublease rentals. A brief description of the basis on which percentage rents are computed should be included, as should the fact that options to renew and escalation clauses exist.

In situations where a retail company has closed stores with remaining lease obligations, these obligations must be included in full in the above disclosures.

(v) Other Off-Balance Sheet Financing.   SFAS No. 105 requires most off-balance sheet financing arrangements, in addition to operating lease arrangements, must be disclosed in the notes to the financial statements. These may include disclosures related to guarantees of indebtedness of other companies or individuals.

Exhibit 26.16 reflects an example of the disclosures for notes unique to a retailer's financial statements. Other notes such as disclosures for income taxes, pension and employee benefits, accrued expenses, postretirement benefits, capital stock and option plans are all similar to the disclosures seen in the footnotes to the financial statements of nonretailers.

(vi) Interim Reporting.   Many companies defer certain costs when incurred and spread them over the course of their fiscal year to better match revenues and related expenses. This is probably more relevant for the retail industry than any other due to the seasonality of most retail operations. Certain costs are incurred early in the fiscal year to benefit the peak selling seasons later in the year. By deferring costs, interim reporting is often more meaningful and comparable from year to year. The more seasonal the business, the more relevant the deferral. The costs that are the most likely to be deferred are those that fluctuate with the level of sales and can be separately identified. Still other costs need to be accrued during interim periods based on estimated results for the year.

A. Summary of Accounting Policies:
   1. *Fiscal Year.*   The Company's fiscal year ends on the last Saturday in January.
   2. *Inventory Valuation.*   Merchandise inventories are stated at lower than cost, using the retail last-in, first-out (LIFO) costing method, or market.
   3. *Preopening Costs.*   In 19X1 the Company began charging preopening costs to operations in the month a new store opens. Previously, costs associated with opening stores were amortized on a straight-line basis following the opening of each new store over a two year period.
   4. *Finance Charge Revenues.*   Finance charges on customer credit accounts are recognized in the period in which they are earned. Unearned finance charges on installment sales contracts are recognized over the contract life.
   5. *Closed Facilities under Lease.*   Estimated net future costs related to facilities closed prior to the termination of the related lease agreement are expensed at the time the final decision is made to close the facility. Such costs are recorded at their present value and include future anticipated expenditures required by the lease agreement and other related occupancy costs. Additional costs expensed are those associated with the reduction of fixed assets to realizable values and other costs related to the closings.
   6. *Deferred Revenues.*   The Company sells service contracts beyond the manufacturer's warranty period. Revenue from the sale of these contracts is recognized over the life of the contract in a manner which matches revenues to direct selling expenses and projected product service costs. Selling expenses and product service costs relating to the service contracts are charged to operations as incurred.
   7. *Property and Equipment.*   Land, buildings, fixtures, and equipment and leasehold improvements are recorded at cost. Property under capital leases is recorded at the lower of the net present value of lease payments or fair market value. Major replacements and betterments are capitalized. Maintenance and repairs are charged to earnings as incurred. Cost of assets sold or retired and the related amounts of accumulated depreciation are eliminated from the accounts in the year of disposal, with the resulting gain or loss included in earnings.
   8. *Depreciation and Amortization.*   For financial statement purposes, depreciation and amortization of fixtures and equipment and leasehold improvements are provided on the straight-line method principally over a 10-year period. Depreciation of buildings is provided on a straight-line method principally over a 25-year period. Property under capital leases is amortized on a straight-line basis over the lease terms.
   9. *Beneficial Leasehold Interests.*   Beneficial leaseholds are recorded at fair market value net of related tax effect and relate to the unexpired leases of the ABC stores acquired in the ABC merger. Amortization is provided on a straight-line basis over the remaining life of the store leases. Amortization of beneficial leaseholds was approximately $XXX in 19X1 and accumulated amortization at January 26, 19X1 was $XXX.

B. Inventories:
   The Company values substantially all of its inventories utilizing the retail last-in, first-out (LIFO) method for stores and the LIFO method for wholesale and warehouse operations. If the first-in, first-out (FIFO) cost method had been used, inventories would have been increased by $XX,XXX at January 26, 19X1.

C. Lease Commitments:
   The Company's retail operations are conducted primarily in leased properties. Initial lease terms normally range from 15 to 25 years with renewal options generally available. In most cases, management expects that, in the normal course of business, leases will be renewed or replaced by other leases. The leases are either gross leases, which provide for annual rentals that include executory expenses such as real estate taxes, insurance, common areas and other operating costs paid by the lessor; ornet leases which provide that the Company pay the above-mentioned expenses. In addition, the Company subleases portions of certain stores and nearby facilities to subtenants whose operations are intended to complement the Company's marketing strategy.
   Contingent rent expense, which is based on sales, includes $XXX incurred on capital leases for 19X1.
   Certain leases have provisions which could require restoration of leased premises at the termination of the lease. The accounting for capital leases includes estimates for significant restoration

(continued)

Exhibit 26.16.   Sample notes to financial statements.

obligations, while restoration costs related to operating leases are accrued at the time they are reasonably determinable and it is considered probable that the Company will incur such costs.

Future minimum lease activity as of January 26, 19X1 is as follows (000s omitted):

	Lease Payments		Sublease Income	
Fiscal Year Ending	**Capital Leases**	**Operating Leases**	**Capital Leases**	**Operating Leases**
19X2	$	$	$	$
19X3				
19X4				
19X5				
19X6				
Thereafter				
Total minimum lease payments	XX XXX		X XXX	(XXX)
				(XXX)
Less amount representing estimated executory costs	XXX			
Net minimum lease payments	XX XXX			
Less amount representing interest	X XXX			
Present value of net minimum lease payments	XX XXX			
Less currently payable	XXX			
Long-term capital lease obligation	$XX XXX			

Amortization of capital leases was approximately $X in 19X1. Accumulated amortization of capital leases at January 26, 19X1 was $X. Rent expense was as follows (000s omitted):

	Fiscal Year Ended January 26, 19X1
Minimum rent on operating leases	$XX XXX
Contingent rentals	XXX
Sublease rentals	(XXX)

Exhibit 26.16.   *Continued.*

The more common costs that are deferred or accrued during the year include:

1. *Occupancy Costs.* Normally rent and related costs are fairly constant during year. Therefore, such cost would be a much higher percentage of sales during slow periods of the year versus the peak selling seasons, unless deferred. While some companies do defer such costs, this is not the common practice.
2. *Advertising.* Retailers often incur advertising expenses weeks or even months before realizing the benefits of the advertising. Thus, some of these costs may be deferred, during an interim period of a year, and expensed during the related selling season or as a percentage of sales.
3. *Warehousing and Freight.* Merchandise must be purchased well in advance of sales. Depending on buying decisions of the particular retailer, merchandise often is stored in warehouse or stores for a period of time. Warehousing costs tend to be higher during the slower seasons as the merchandise is delivered, sorted, labeled, and so forth in anticipation of peak seasons. The significance of the warehouse deferral is also dependent on whether or not the retailer capitalized some or all of the warehouse costs in inventory.

4. *Payroll.* Some payroll costs are variable as additional personnel are usually hired for peak seasons. For this reason store payroll costs are not usually deferred. However, certain payroll costs are fixed and specifically relate to inventory, such as merchandise buyer costs, warehouse personnel, etc. and may be deferred.

5. *Inventory Shortage.* An estimate of inventory shortage as a percentage of sales should be accrued during the course of the year, absent a complete physical inventory during the year.

6. *Insurance and Supplies.* These are generally less significant than the above costs, but often are absorbed based on a budgeted percentage of sales during the year.

7. *Bonuses.* Often bonuses are paid based on earnings for the company's fiscal year. If it is likely that such bonuses will be paid, the expense should be spread over the course of the year, either rateably or, more often, as a percentage of sales.

During the course of the year, these costs can be absorbed using several methods including:

- Based on budgeted sales, absorbed evenly each month.
- Based on the budgeted expenses for the year.
- Based on a percentage of actual sales, and so on.

The important point is that the method used should be the most applicable under the circumstances, and should be applied consistently.

It should be noted that such deferrals and accruals relate only to costs during the course of the year. These costs must be absorbed by year-end, as they are separate from normal prepaid expenses that may be deferred between years.

In addition to deferring expense, some retailers also defer gross profit during the year. Gross profit for many retailers is lower during the peak selling seasons than during the rest of the year. During the peak seasons competition is the greatest and promotional advertising increases. In an effort to maximize sales and gross profit dollars, the decision is often made to accept a lower gross profit percentage. For these reasons some retailers have justified the accrual of a constant gross profit percentage during the year, normally based on budgeted gross profit for the entire year. For retailers with fiscal year-ends shortly after peak selling seasons, such a policy would result in the deferral of income in the early periods of the year. To support the deferral, it is important that the reasonableness of the budgeted gross profit for the year be continually reviewed.

Depending on the type of retail operation and the cyclical nature of the business, certain deferrals are more applicable to some retailers than others. Due to the importance of proper reporting of income on an interim basis, deferrals should be reviewed annually to ensure that they remain proper and reasonable. Additionally, interim reports of most retailers should note that their business is seasonal and that the interim results may not be indicative of the full year. Certain retailers include a trailing 12-month statement with interim reports for just such reasons.

(d) SUMMARY. The Financial Executives' Division of the National Retail Federation has developed and promoted the adoption of standard content and format for retailers' financial statements. The key reference for the preparation of a retailer's financial statements is their Retail Accounting Manual, Books I & II. These manuals place emphasis on merchandise accounting and management reporting, and contain a detailed explanation of expense center accounting.

Book I also discusses merchandise accounting, with particular emphasis on the determination of gross margin. It details the accounting for nonretail operations such as cost departments, workrooms and other costs associated with sales. Another area discussed in Book I is management reporting for retailers. This section details various types of reports which may be helpful in management's analysis of the company and its performance.

Book II includes a chart of accounts for the balance sheet with detailed explanations of what is typically included in each. It discusses cash management, with particular emphasis on forecasting, and items to be considered in maximizing cash flow. There is also a section dealing with the issues facing a retailer considering a change to the LIFO inventory costing method, including a detailed explanation of the various LIFO calculations required.

Other sections cover warehousing and distribution, fixed asset accounting, budgeting, and financial reporting as it relates to the impact of changing prices and current cost. The final section of Book II provides guidelines for records retention.

26.6 SOURCES AND SUGGESTED REFERENCES

American Institute Certified Public Accountants, "Restatement and Revision of Accounting Research Bulletins," Accounting Research Bulletin No. 43, AICPA, New York, 1953.

Accounting Principles Board, "Accounting Changes," APB Opinion 20, AICPA, New York, 1971.

Financial Accounting Standards Board, "Revenue Recognition When Right of Return Exists, Statement of Financial Standards No. 48, FASB, Norwalk, CT, 1981.

————, Accounting for Leases, Statement of Financial Standards No. 13, FASB, Norwalk, CT, 1976.

————, Accounting for Leases: Sale-Leaseback Transactions Involving Real-Estate Sales-Type Leases of Real Estate Definition of Lease Term Initial Direct Costs of Direct Financing Leases, Statement of Financial Accounting Standards Board No. 98, FASB, Norwalk, CT, 1989.

————, Accounting for Operating Leases with Scheduled Rent Increases, Technical Bulletin No. 85-3, FASB, Norwalk, CT, 1985.

————, "Disclosure of Information about Financial Instruments with Off-Balance-Sheet Risk and Financial Instruments with Concentrations of Credit Risk," Statement of Financial Accounting Standards No. 105, FASB, Stamford, CT, 1987.

————, Issues Relating to Accounting for Leases Time Pattern of the Physical Use of the Property in an Operating Lease. Lease Incentives in an Operating Lease. Applicability of Leveraged Lease Accounting to Existing Assets of the Lessor. Money-Over-Money Lease Transactions. Wrap Lease Transactions, Technical Bulletin 88-1, FASB, Norwalk, CT, 1988.

Retail Accounting Manual, National Retail Federation, New York, 4th Printing, 1985.

Zimmerman, R. M., Kaufman, R. M., Finerty, Gregory S., and Egan, J. O., *Retail Accounting and Financial Control,* 5th ed. Wiley, New York, 1990.

CHAPTER 27

REGULATED UTILITIES

Benjamin A. McKnight III, CPA
Arthur Andersen & Co., LLP

CONTENTS

Mr. McKnight wishes to acknowledge the assistance provided by Alan D. Felsenthal and Robert W. Hriszko, both of Arthur Andersen & Co., LLP.

27.1 THE NATURE AND CHARACTERISTICS OF REGULATED UTILITIES

(a) INTRODUCTION TO REGULATED UTILITIES.   Many types of business have their rates for providing services set by the government or other regulatory bodies, for example, utilities, insurance companies, transportation companies, hospitals, and shippers. The enterprises addressed in this chapter are limited to electric, gas, telephone, and water (and sewer) utilities that are regulated on an **individual cost-of-service** basis. Effective business and financial involvement with the utility industry requires an understanding of what a utility is, the regulatory compact under which utilities operate, and the interrelationship between the rate decisions of regulators and the resultant accounting effects.

(b) DESCRIPTIVE CHARACTERISTICS OF UTILITIES.   Regulated utilities are similar to other businesses in that there is a need for capital and, for private sector utilities, a demand for investor profit. Utilities are different in that they are dedicated to public use—they are obligated to furnish customers service on demand—and the services are considered to be necessities. Many utilities operate under monopolistic conditions. A regulator sets their prices and grants an exclusive service area, which probably serves a relatively large number of customers. Consequently, a high level of public interest typically exists regarding the utility's rates and quality of service.

Only a utility that has a monopoly of supply of service can operate at maximum economy and, therefore, provide service at the lowest cost. Duplicate plant facilities would result in higher costs. This is particularly true because of the capital-intensive nature of utility operations, that is, a large capital investment is required for each dollar of revenue.

Because there is an absence of free market competitive forces such as those found in most business enterprises, regulation is a substitute for these missing competitive forces. The goal of regulation is to provide a balance between investor and consumer interests by substituting regulatory principles for competition. This means regulation is to:

1. Provide consumers with adequate service at the lowest price.
2. Provide the utility the opportunity, **not a guarantee,** to earn an adequate return so that it can attract new capital for development and expansion of plant to meet customer demand.
3. Prevent unreasonable prices and excessive earnings.
4. Prevent unjust discrimination among customers, commodities and locations.
5. Insure public safety.

To meet the goals of regulation, regulated activities of utilities typically include:

1. Service area.
2. Rates.
3. Accounting and reporting.
4. Issuance of debt and equity securities.
5. Construction, sale, lease, purchase, and exchange of operating facilities.
6. Standards of service and operation.

27.2 HISTORY OF REGULATION

Some knowledge of the history of regulation is essential to understanding utilities. Companies that are now regulated utilities find themselves in that position because of a long sequence of political events, legislative acts, and judicial interpretations.

Rate regulation of privately owned business was not an accepted practice during the early history of the United States. This concept has evolved because important legal precedents have established not only the right of government to regulate but also the process that government bodies must follow to set fair rates for services. The background and the facts of *Munn v.*

Illinois (94 U.S. 113 (1877)) are significant and basic to the development of ratemaking since the case established a U.S. legal precedent for the right of government to regulate and set rates in cases of public interest and necessity.

(a) *MUNN V. ILLINOIS.* In 1871, the Illinois State Legislature passed a law that prescribed the maximum rates for grain storage and that required licensing and bonding to ensure performance of the duties of a public warehouse. The law reflected the popular sentiment of midwestern farmers at that time against what they felt was a pricing monopoly by railroads and elevators. Munn and his partner, Scott, owned a grain warehouse in Chicago. They filed a suit maintaining that they operated a private business and that the law deprived them of their property without due process.

The case ultimately reached the U.S. Supreme Court. The Court decided that, when private property becomes "clothed with a public interest," the owner of the property has, in effect, granted the public an interest in that use and "must submit to be controlled by the public for the common good." The Court was impressed by Munn and Scott's monopolistic position while furnishing a service practically indispensable to the public.

From the precedent of *Munn,* railroads, a water company, a grist mill, stockyards, and finally gas, electric, and phone companies were brought under public regulation. Thus, when utilities finally came into existence in the 20th century, the framework for regulation already was in place and did not have to be decided by the courts. When state legislatures began to set up utility commissions, it was the *Munn* decision that established beyond question their right to do so.

(b) *CHICAGO, MILWAUKEE & ST. PAUL RY. CO. V. MINNESOTA.* A second important case which began to establish the principle of "due process" in ratemaking is *Chicago, Milwaukee & St. Paul Railroad Co. v. Minnesota ex rel. Railroad & Warehouse Comm.* (134 U.S. 418 (1890)). In this important case the courts first began to address the issue of standards of reasonableness in regulation. The U.S. Supreme Court decided that a Minnesota law was unconstitutional because it established rate regulation but did not permit a judicial review to test the reasonableness of the rates. The Court found that the state law violated the due process provisions of the 14th Amendment because the utility was deprived of the power to charge reasonable rates for the use of its property, and if the utility was denied judicial review, then the company would be deprived of the lawful use of its property, and ultimately, the property itself.

(c) *SMYTH V. AMES.* A third important case, *Smyth v. Ames* (169 U.S. 466 (1898)), established the precedent for the concept of "fair return upon the fair value of property." During the 1880s the state of Nebraska passed a law that reduced the maximum freight rates that railroads could charge. The railroads' stockholders brought a successful suit that prevented the application of the lowered rates. The state appealed the case to the U.S. Supreme Court, which unanimously ruled that the rates were unconstitutionally low by any standard of reasonableness.

In its case, the state maintained that the adequacy of the rates should be tested by reference to the present value, or reproduction cost, of the assets. This position was attractive to the state because the current price level had been declining. The railroad was built during the Civil War, a period that was marked by a high price level and substantial inflation, and the railroad believed that its past costs merited recognition in a "test of reasonableness."

In reaching its decision, the Court began the formulation of the "fair value" doctrine, which prescribed a test of the reasonableness and constitutionality of regulated rates. The Supreme Court's opinion held that a privately owned business was entitled to rates that would cover reasonable operating expenses plus a fair return on the fair value of the property used for the convenience of the public.

The *Smyth v. Ames* decision also established several rate-making terms still in use today. This was the first attempt by the courts to define rate-making principles. These terms include:

1. *Original Cost of Construction.* The cost to acquire utility property.
2. *Fair Return.* The amount that should be earned on the investment in utility property.
3. *Fair Value.* The amount on which the return should be based.
4. *Operating Expenses.* The cost to deliver utility services to the public.

Each of these three landmark cases, especially *Smyth v. Ames,* established the inability of the legislative branch to effectively establish equitable rates. They also demonstrated that the use of the judicial branch is an inefficient means of accomplishing the same goal. In *Smyth v. Ames,* the U.S. Supreme Court, in essence, declared that the process could be more easily accomplished by a **commission** composed of persons with special skills and experience and the qualifications to resolve questions concerning utility regulation.

27.3 REGULATORY COMMISSION JURISDICTIONS

A view of the overlays of regulatory commissions will be helpful in understanding their unique position and responsibilities.

(a) FEDERAL REGULATORY COMMISSIONS.   The interstate activities of public utilities are under the jurisdiction of several federal regulatory commissions. The members of all federal regulatory commissions are appointed by the executive branch and are confirmed by the legislative branch. The judicial branch can review and rule on decisions of each commission. This form of organization represents a blending of the functions of the three separate branches of government.

- The **Federal Communications Commission (FCC),** established in 1934 with the passage of the Communications Act, succeeded the Federal Radio Commission of 1927. At that time the FCC assumed regulation of interstate and foreign telephone and telegraph service from the Interstate Commerce Commission, which was the first federal regulatory commission (created in 1887). The FCC prescribes for communications companies a uniform system of accounts (USOA) and depreciation rates. It also states the principles and standard procedures used to separate property costs, revenues, expenses, taxes, and reserves between those applicable to interstate services under the jurisdiction of the FCC and those applicable to services under the jurisdiction of various state regulatory authorities. In addition, the FCC regulates the rate of return carriers may earn on their interstate business.
- The **Federal Energy Regulatory Commission (FERC)** was created as an agency of the cabinet-level Department of Energy in 1977. The FERC assumed many of the functions of the former Federal Power Commission (FPC), which was established in 1920. The FERC has jurisdiction over the transmission and sale at wholesale of electric energy in interstate commerce. The FERC also regulates the transmission and sale for resale of natural gas in interstate commerce and establishes rates and prescribes conditions of service for all utilities subject to its jurisdiction. The entities must follow the FERC's USOA and file a Form 1 (electric) or Form 2 (gas) annual report.
- The SEC was established in 1934 to administer the Securities Act of 1933 and the Securities Exchange Act of 1934. The powers of the SEC are restricted to security transactions and financial disclosures—not operating standards. The SEC also administers the Public Utility Holding Company Act of 1935 (the 1935 Act), which was passed because of financial and services abuses in the 1920s and the stock market crash and subsequent depression of 1929–1935. Under the 1935 Act, the SEC was given powers to regulate the accounting, financing, reporting, acquisitions, allocation of consolidated income taxes, and parent–subsidiary relationships of electric and gas utility holding companies.

(b) STATE REGULATORY COMMISSIONS.   All 50 states have established agencies to regulate rates. State commissioners are either appointed or elected, usually for a specified term. Although the degree of authority differs, they have authority over utility operations in intrastate commerce. Each state commission sets rate-making policies in accordance with its own state statutes and precedents. In addition, each state establishes its prescribed forms of reporting and systems of accounts for utilities. However, most systems are modifications of the federal USOA.

27.4 THE RATE-MAKING PROCESS

(a) HOW COMMISSIONS SET RATES.   The process for establishing rates probably constitutes the most significant difference between utilities and enterprises in general. Unlike an enterprise in general, where market forces and competition establish the price a company can charge for its products or services, rates for utilities are generally determined by a regulatory commission. The process of establishing rates is described as **rate making.** The administrative proceeding to establish utility rates is typically referred to as a **rate case** or **rate proceeding.** Utility rates, once established, generally will not change without another rate case.

The establishment of a rate for a utility on an individual cost-of-service basis typically involves two steps. The first step is to determine a utility's general level of rates that will cover operating costs and provide an opportunity to earn a reasonable rate of return on the property dedicated to providing utility services. This process establishes the utility's required revenue (often referred to as the **revenue requirement** or **cost-of-service**). The second step is to design specific rates in order to eliminate discrimination and unfairness from affected classes of customers. The aggregate of the prices paid by all customers for all services provided should produce revenues equivalent to the revenue requirement.

(b) THE RATE-MAKING FORMULA.   This first step of rate regulation, on an individual cost-of-service basis, is the determination of a utility's total revenue requirement, which can be expressed as a rate-making formula:

$$\text{Rate Base} \times \text{Rate of Return} = \text{Return (Operating Income)}$$
$$\text{Return} + \text{Allowable Operating Expenses} = \text{Required Revenue (Cost of Service)}$$

1. *Rate Base.* The amount of investment in utility plant devoted to the rendering of utility service upon which a fair rate of return may be earned.
2. *Rate of Return.* The rate determined by the regulatory agency to be applied to the rate base to provide a fair return to investors. It is usually a composite rate that reflects the carrying costs of debt, dividends on preferred stock, and a return provision on common equity.
3. *Return.* The rate base multiplied by rate of return.
4. *Allowable Operating Expenses.* Merely the costs of operations and maintenance associated with rendering utility service. Operating expenses include:
   a. Depreciation and amortization expenses.
   b. Production fuel and gas for resale.
   c. Operations expenses.
   d. Maintenance expenses.
   e. Income taxes.
   f. Taxes other than income taxes.
5. *Required Revenue.* The total amount that must be collected from customers in rates. The new rate structure should be designed to generate this amount of revenue on the basis of current or forecasted levels of usage.

(c) RATE BASE. A utility **earns** a return on its rate base. Each investor-supplied dollar is entitled to such a return until the dollar is remitted to the investor. Some of the items generally included in the rate base computation are utility property and plant in service, a working capital allowance, and in certain jurisdictions or circumstances, plant under construction. Generally, nonutility property, abandoned plant, plant acquisition adjustments, and plant held for future use are excluded. Deductions from rate base typically include the reserve for depreciation, accumulated deferred income taxes, which represent cost-free capital, certain unamortized deferred investment tax credits, and customer contributions in aid of construction. Exhibit 27.1 provides an example of the computations used to determine a rate base.

(d) RATE BASE VALUATION. Various methods are used in valuing rate base. These methods apply to the valuation of property and plant and include:

1. Original cost.
2. Fair value.
3. Weighted cost.

(i) Original Cost. The original cost method, the most widely used method, corresponds to GAAP, which require historical cost data for primary financial statement presentation. In addition, all regulatory commissions have adopted the USOA, requiring original cost for reporting purposes. Original cost is defined in the FERC's USOA as "the cost of such property to the person first devoting it to public service." This method was originally adopted by various commissions during the 1930s, at which time inflation was not a major concern.

(ii) Fair Value. The fair value method is defined as **not** the cost of assets but rather what they are really worth at the time rates are established. The following three methods of computing fair value are most often used:

1. *Trended Cost.* Utilizes either general or specific cost indices to adjust original cost.
2. *Reproduction Cost New.* A calculation of the cost to reproduce existing plant facilities at current costs.
3. *Market Value.* Involves the appraisal of specific types of plant.

(iii) Weighted Cost. The weighted cost method for valuation of property and plant is used in some jurisdictions as a compromise between the original cost and the fair value methods. Under this method, some weight is given to both original cost and fair value. Regulatory

AVERAGE NET INVESTMENT RATE BASE	
	In Millions
Plant in service	$350
Less reserve for depreciation	(100)
Net plant in service	250
Add:	
Working capital allowance	3
Construction work-in-progress	20
Deduct:	
Accumulated deferred income taxes	(14)
Advances in aid of construction	(2)
Average net investment rate base	$257

Exhibit 27.1. Example of a utility rate base computation.

agencies in some weighted cost jurisdictions use a 50/50 weighting of original cost and fair value, whereas others use 60/40 or other combinations.

(iv) Judicial Precedents—Rate Base.   In a significant rate base case, *Federal Power Commission v. Hope Natural Gas Co.* (320 U.S. 591 (1944)), the original cost versus fair value controversy finally came to a head. A number of important points came out of this case, including the **Doctrine of the End Result.** The U.S. Supreme Court's decision did not approve original cost or fair value. Instead, it said a rate-making body can use any method, including no formula at all, so long as the end result is reasonable. It is not the theory but the impact of the theory that counts.

(e) RATE OF RETURN AND JUDICIAL PRECEDENTS.   The rate of return is the rate determined by a regulator to be applied to the rate base to provide a fair return to investors. In the capital market, utilities must compete against nonregulated companies for investors' funds. Therefore, a fair rate of return to common equity investors is critical.

Different sources of capital with different costs are involved in establishing the allowed rate of return. Exhibits 27.2 and 27.3 show the computations used to determine the rate of return.

The cost of long-term debt and preferred stock is usually the "embedded" cost, that is, long-term debt issues have a specified interest rate, whereas preferred stock has a specified dividend rate. Computing the cost of equity is more complicated because there is no stated interest or dividend rate. Several methods have been used as a guide in setting a return on common equity. These methods reflect different approaches, such as earnings/price ratios, discounted cash flows, comparable earnings, and perceived investor risk.

The **cost** of each class of capital is weighed by the percentage that the class represents of the utility's total capitalization.

Two important cases provide the foundation for dealing with rate of return issues: *Bluefield Water Works & Improvement Co. v. West Virginia Public Service Comm.* (262 U.S. 679 (1923)) and the *Hope Gas* case. The important rate of return concepts that arise from these cases are as follows:

1. A company is entitled to, but not guaranteed, a return on the value of its property.
2. Return should be equal to that earned by other companies with comparable risks.
3. A utility is not entitled to a return such as that earned by a speculative venture.

COST OF CAPITAL AND RATE OF RETURN

	In Millions
Capitalization	
Stockholder's equity:	
Common stock ($8 par value, 5,000,000 shares outstanding	$ 40
Other paid-in capital	45
Retained earnings	28
Common stock equity	113
Preferred stock (9% dividend rate)	16
Total stockholders' equity	129
Long-term debt (7.50% average interest rate)	128
	$257

Exhibit 27.2.   Example of a utility capitalization structure.

	Dollars In Millions	Capitalization Ratios	Annual Cost Rate	Weighted Cost
Long-term debt	$128	50	7.5%	3.75%
Preferred stock	16	6	9.0	.54
Common stock equity	113	44	13.0	5.71
Cost of capital	$257	100		10.00%

Exhibit 27.3.   Computation of the overall rate of return.

    4. The return should be reasonably sufficient to:
        a. Assure confidence and financial soundness of the utility.
        b. Maintain and support its credit.
        c. Enable the utility to raise additional capital.
    5. Efficient and economical management is a prerequisite for profitable operations.

(f) OPERATING INCOME.   Operating income for purposes of establishing rates is computed based on **test-year** information, which is normally a recent or projected 12-month period. In either case, historic or projected test-year revenues are calculated based on the current rate structure in order to determine if there is a revenue requirement deficiency. The operating expense information generally includes most expired costs incurred by a utility. As illustrated in Exhibit 27.4, the operating expense information, after reflecting all necessary pro forma adjustments, determines operating income for rate-making purposes.

    Above-the-line and **below-the-line** are frequently used expressions in public utility, financial, and regulatory circles. The above-the-line expenses on which operating income appears are those that ordinarily are directly included in the rate-making formula; below this line are the excluded expenses (and income). The principal cost that is charged **below-the-line** is interest on debt since it is included in the rate-making formula as a part of the rate-of-return computation and not as an operating expense. The inclusion or exclusion of a cost above-the-line is important to the utility since this determines whether it is directly includable in the rate-making formula as an operating expense.

COST OF SERVICE INCOME STATEMENT—TEST YEAR
(Twelve Months Ended 12/31/XX)

Operating revenue	$300,000
Operating expenses	
Commercial	45,000
Maintenance	45,000
Traffic	49,000
General and administrative	61,000
Depreciation	60,000
General taxes	6,000
Income taxes	
Federal current and deferred	10,000
State current and deferred	2,000
ITC, net	1,300
Total operating expenses	279,300
Operating income	$ 20,700

Exhibit 27.4.   Example of a utility operating income computation.

RATEMAKING FORMULA

(Rate of Return × Rate Base) + Cost of Service = Revenue Requirement	
Test-year operating revenue	$300,000,000
Test-year operating expense	279,300,000
Test-year operating income	20,700,000
Rate base	257,000,000
Desired rate of return	10%
Assumed federal tax rate	46%
Rate base	$257,000,000
× Rate of return	× .10
Operating income requirement	25,700,000
+ Operating Expenses	+ 283,559,259 (A)
Revenue requirement	$309,259,259

(A) $279,300,000 Operating expenses
          4,259,259 Pro forma tax adjustment based on
              $5,000,000 operating income deficiency
              ($25,700,000 − $20,700,000) and 46% tax rate

                                                                $283,559,259

Exhibit 27.5.   Example of the revenue requirement computation based on Exhibits 1 through 4.

A significant consideration in determining the revenue requirement is that the rate of return computed is the rate **after income taxes** (which are a part of operating expenses). In calculating the revenue required, the operating income (rate of return times rate base) deficiency must be **grossed up** for income taxes. This is most easily accomplished by dividing the operating income deficiency by the complement of the applicable income tax rate. For example, if the operating income deficiency is $5,000,000 and the income tax rate is 46%, the required revenue is $5,000,000/.54, or $9,259,259. By increasing revenues $9,259,259, income tax expense will increase by $4,259,259 ($9,259,259 × 46%), with the remainder increasing operating income by the deficiency amount of $5,000,000. This concept is illustrated as part of an example revenue requirement calculation based on the information presented in Exhibit 27.5.

Exhibit 27.6 shows a shortcut method of computing the revenue requirement, which calculates the operating income deficiency and then grosses that up for income taxes. The answer under either method is the same.

When the rate-making process is complete, the utility will set rate tariffs to recover $309,259,259. At this level, future revenues will recover $283,559,259 of operating expenses

REVENUE REQUIREMENT

Desired operating income	$ 25,700,000
Actual operating income	20,700,000
Operating income deficiency	$ 5,000,000
Gross up factor for income taxes (1 − 46%)	÷ .54
Revenue deficiency	$ 9,259,259
Test-year operating revenue	300,000,000
Revenue requirement	$309,259,259

Exhibit 27.6.   Shortcut computation of the utility revenue requirement.

and provide a return of $25,700,000. This return equates to a 10% earnings level on rate base. The $25,700,000 operating income will go toward paying $9,600,000 of interest on long-term debt ($128,000,000 × 7.5%) and preferred dividends of $1,440,000 ($16,000,000 × 9%), leaving net income for the common equity holders of $14,660,000—which approximates the desired 13% return on common equity of $113,000,000. However, the rate-making process only provides the **opportunity** to earn at that level. If future sales volumes, operating costs, or other factors change, the utility will earn more or less than the allowed amount.

27.5 INTERRELATIONSHIP OF REGULATORY REPORTING AND FINANCIAL REPORTING

(a) ACCOUNTING AUTHORITY OF REGULATORY AGENCIES. Regulatory agencies with statutory authority to establish rates for utilities also prescribe the accounting that their jurisdictional regulated entities must follow. Accounting may be prescribed by a USOA, by periodic reporting requirements, or by accounting orders.

Because of the statutory authority of regulatory agencies over both accounting and rate setting of regulated utilities, some regulators, accountants, and others believe that the agencies have the final authority over the form and content of financial statements published by those utilities for their investors and creditors. This is the case even when the stockholders' report, based on regulatory accounting requirements, would not be in accordance with GAAP.

Actually, this issue has not arisen frequently because regulators have usually reflected changes in GAAP in the USOA that they prescribe. For example, the new USOA of the FCC, effective in 1988, has GAAP as its foundation, with departures being permitted as necessary, because of departures from GAAP in ratemaking. But the general willingness of regulators to conform to GAAP does not answer the question of whether a regulatory body has the final authority to prescribe the accounting to be followed for the financial statements included in the annual and other reports to stockholders or outsiders, even when such statements are not prepared in accordance with GAAP.

The landmark case in this area is the *Appalachian Power Co. v. Federal Power Commission* (328 F.2d 237 (4th Cir.), *cert. denied,* 379 U.S. 829 (1964)). The FPC (now the FERC) found that the financial statements in the annual report of the company were not in accordance with the accounting prescribed by the FPC's USOA. The FPC was upheld at the Circuit Court level in 1964 and the Supreme Court denied a writ of certiorari. The general interpretation of this case has been that the FPC had the authority to order that the financial statements in the annual report to stockholders of its jurisdictional utilities be prepared in accordance with the USOA, even if not in accordance with GAAP.

During subsequent years, the few differences that have arisen have been resolved without court action, and so it is not clear just what authority the FERC or other federal agencies may now have in this area. The FERC has not chosen to contest minor differences, and one particular utility, Montana Power Company, met the issue of FPC authority versus GAAP, by presenting, for several years, two balance sheets in its annual report to shareholders. One balance sheet was in accordance with GAAP, which reflected the ratemaking prescribed by the state commission, and one balance sheet was in accordance with the USOA of the FPC, which had ordered that certain assets be written off even though the state commission continued to allow them in the rate base. The company's auditors stated that the first balance sheet was in accordance with GAAP and that the second balance sheet was in accordance with the FPC USOA.

In a more recent instance, the FERC has allowed a company to follow accounting that the FERC believes reflects the ratemaking even though the accounting does not comply with a standard of the FASB. The SEC has ruled that the company must follow GAAP. As a result, the regulatory treatment was reformulated to meet the FASB standard, and so the conflict was resolved without going to the courts.

(b) SEC AND FASB.   The FASB has no financial reporting enforcement or disciplinary responsibility. Enforcement with regard to entities whose shares are traded in interstate commerce arises from SEC policy articulated in ASR No. 150, which specifies that FASB standards (and those of its predecessors) are required to be followed by registrants in their filings with the SEC. Thus, the interrelationship between the FASB and the SEC operates to achieve, virtually without exception for an entity whose securities trade in interstate commerce, the presentation of financial statements that reflect GAAP. Although this jurisdictional issue is neither resolved nor disappearing, it appears that the SEC currently exercises significant, if not controlling, influence over the general-purpose financial statements of all public companies, including regulated utilities.

(c) RELATIONSHIP BETWEEN RATE REGULATION AND GAAP

(i) Historical Perspective.   Ratemaking on an individual cost-of-service basis is designed to permit a utility to recover its costs that are incurred in providing regulated services. Individual cost-of-service does not guarantee cost recovery. However, there is a much greater assurance of cost recovery under individual cost-of-service ratemaking than for enterprises in general. This likelihood of cost recoverability provides a basis for a different application of GAAP, which recognizes that ratemaking can affect accounting.

As such, a rate regulator's ability to recognize, not recognize, or defer recognition of revenues and costs in established rates of regulated utilities adds a unique consideration to the accounting and financial reporting of those enterprises. This unique economic dimension was first recognized by the accounting profession in paragraph 8 of ARB No. 44 (Revised), "Declining-Balance Depreciation:"

> Many regulatory authorities permit recognition of deferred income taxes for accounting and/or rate-making purposes, whereas some do not. The committee believes that they should permit the recognition of deferred income taxes for both purposes. However, where charges for deferred income taxes are not allowed for rate-making purposes, accounting recognition need not be given to the deferment of taxes if it may reasonably be expected that increased future income taxes, resulting from the earlier deduction of declining-balance depreciation for income-tax purposes only, will be allowed in the future rate determinations.

A year later, in connection with the general requirement to eliminate intercompany profits, paragraph 6 of ARB No. 51, "Consolidated Financial Statements," concluded:

> However, in a regulated industry where a parent or subsidiary manufactures or constructs facilities for other companies in the consolidated group, the foregoing is not intended to require the elimination of intercompany profit to the extent that such profit is substantially equivalent to a reasonable return on investment ordinarily capitalized in accordance with the established practice of the industry.

(ii) The Addendum to APB Opinion No. 2.   In 1962, the APB decided to express its position on applicability of GAAP to regulated industries. The resulting statement initially reported in the *The Journal of Accountancy* in December, 1962, later became the Addendum to APB Opinion No. 2, "Accounting for the Investment Credit" (the Addendum), and provided that:

1. GAAP applies to all companies—regulated and nonregulated.
2. Differences in the application of GAAP are permitted as a result of the rate-making process because the rate regulator creates economic value.
3. Cost deferral on the balance sheet to reflect the rate-making process is appropriately reflected on the balance sheet only when recovery is clear.

4. A regulatory accounting difference without ratemaking impact does not constitute GAAP. The accounting must be reflected in rates.

5. The financial statements of regulated entities other than those prepared for regulatory filings should be based on GAAP with appropriate recognition of ratemaking consideration.

The Addendum provided the basis for utility accounting for almost 20 years. During this period, utilities accounted for certain items differently than enterprises in general. For example, regulators often treat capital leases as operating leases for rate purposes, thus excluding them from rate base and allowing only the lease payments as expense. In that event, regulated utilities usually treated such leases as operating leases for financial statement purposes. This resulted in lower operating expenses during the first few years of the lease.

Also, utilities capitalize both debt and equity components of funds used during construction, which is generally described as an allowance for funds used during construction (AFUDC). The FASB, under SFAS No. 34, "Capitalization of Interest Cost," allows nonregulated companies to capitalize only the debt cost. Because property is by far the largest item in most utility companies' balance sheets and because they do much of their own construction, the effect of capitalizing AFUDC is frequently very material to both the balance sheet and the statement of income.

Such differences, usually concerning the timing of recognition of a cost, were cited as evidence that the Addendum allowed almost any accounting treatment if directed by rate regulation. There was also some concern that the Addendum applied to certain industries that were regulated, but not on an individual cost-of-service basis. These as well as other issues ultimately led to the FASB issuing SFAS No. 71, "Accounting for the Effects of Certain Types of Regulation," which attempted to:

1. Provide a clear conceptual basis to account for the economic impact of regulation.

2. Emphasize the concept of one set of accounting principles for all enterprises.

3. Enhance the quality of financial reporting for regulated enterprises.

27.6 SFAS NO. 71: "ACCOUNTING FOR THE EFFECTS OF CERTAIN TYPES OF REGULATION"

(a) SCOPE OF SFAS NO. 71.   SFAS No. 71 specifies criteria for the applicability of the Statement by focusing on the nature of regulation rather than on specific industries. As stated in paragraph 5 of SFAS No. 71:

[T]his statement applies to general-purpose external financial statements of an enterprise that has regulated operations that meet all of the following criteria:

1. The enterprise's rates for regulated services or products provided to its customers are established by or are subject to approval by an independent, third-party regulator or by its own governing board empowered by statute or contract to establish rates that bind customers.

2. The regulated rates are designed to recover the specific enterprise's costs of providing the regulated services or products.

3. In view of the demand for the regulated services or products and the level of competition, direct and indirect, it is reasonable to assume that rates set at levels that will recover the enterprise's costs can be charged to and collected from customers. This criterion requires consideration of anticipated changes in levels of demand or competition during the recovery period for any capitalized costs.

Based on these criteria, SFAS No. 71 provides guidance in preparing general-purpose financial statements for most investor-owned, cooperative, and governmental utilities.

The FASB's sister entity, the GASB, has been empowered to set pervasive standards for government utilities to the extent applicable and, accordingly, financial statements issued in accordance with GAAP must follow GASB standards. However, in the absence of an applicable pronouncement issued by the GASB, differences between accounting followed under GASB or other FASB pronouncements and accounting followed for ratemaking purposes should be handled in accordance with SFAS No. 71.

(b) AMENDMENTS TO SFAS NO. 71.   After the issuance of SFAS No. 71, the FASB became concerned about the accounting being followed by utilities (primarily electric companies) for certain transactions. Significant economic events were occurring, such as:

1. Disallowances of major portions of recently completed plants.
2. Very large plant abandonments.
3. Phase-in plans.

All of these events in one way or another prevented utilities from recovering costs currently and, in some instances, did not allow recovery at all. As a result, the FASB amended SFAS No. 71 in December 1986 with SFAS No. 90, "Regulated Enterprises—Accounting for Abandonments and Disallowances of Plant Costs," and in August 1987 with SFAS No. 92, "Regulated Enterprises—Accounting for Phase-in Plans."

(c) OVERVIEW OF SFAS NO. 71.   The major issues addressed in SFAS No. 71 relate to the following:

1. Effect of ratemaking on GAAP.
2. Evidence criteria for recording regulatory assets and liabilities.
3. Application of GAAP to utilities.
4. Proper financial statement disclosures.

SFAS No. 71 sets forth (pars. 9–12) general standards of accounting for the effects of regulation. In addition, there are specific standards that are derived from the general standards and various examples (Appendix B) of the application of the general standards.

(d) GENERAL STANDARDS.   In SFAS No. 71, the FASB recognized that a principal consideration introduced by rate regulation is the cause-and-effect relationship of costs and revenues—an economic dimension that, in some circumstances, should affect accounting for regulated enterprises. Thus, a regulated utility should capitalize a cost (as a regulatory asset) or recognize an obligation (as a regulatory liability) if it is probable that, through the rate-making process, there will be a corresponding increase or decrease in future revenues.

(i) Regulatory Assets.   Paragraph 9 of SFAS No. 71 states that the "rate action of a regulator can provide reasonable assurance of the existence of an asset." All or part of an **incurred** cost that would otherwise be charged to expense should be capitalized if:

1. It is **probable** that future revenues in an amount approximately equal to the capitalized cost will result from inclusion of that cost in **allowable** costs for ratemaking purposes.
2. The regulator intends to provide for the recovery of that specific incurred cost rather than to provide for expected levels of similar future costs.

Thus, a regulated utility should capitalize a cost that would otherwise be charged to expense if future recovery in rates is probable. This general standard is not totally applicable to regulatory treatment of costs of **abandoned plants** and **phase-in plans.** The accounting accorded abandoned plant costs and phase-in plans is specified in SFAS Nos. 90 and 92.

To illustrate this provision in paragraph 9, assume a regulated utility has an incurred cost of $9 million for terminating a long-term fuel supply contract. The contract buyout was based on the utility's analysis that available alternative sources of fuel made such action economically beneficial to its customers. Further, the affected regulator's historical policy has been to allow similar costs to be recovered through customer rates over a 3-year period, so the utility concludes that future recovery is probable. In this situation, paragraph 9 of SFAS No. 71 should be applied, and a $9 million regulatory asset should be recorded on the utility's balance sheet. The utility will typically request recovery of the $9 million in connection with its next rate case. Once the regulator specifically provides for the amount of and period for recovery, the regulatory asset should be amortized in a consistent manner, above-the-line.

The term **probable** was defined in SFAS No. 71 differently from the way it had been defined in SFAS No. 5, "Accounting for Contingencies." One of the most significant amendments to SFAS No. 71, in SFAS No. 90, is the change in the definition of "probable" from the dictionary definition (better than a 50% certainty) to the SFAS No. 5 definition (likely to occur). The change has a considerable effect on the degree of assurance required, and therefore the timing, for recognizing in financial statements the economic impact of regulation.

The terms **allowable costs** and **incurred costs,** as defined in SFAS No. 71, also required further attention, which was provided by the FASB in SFAS No. 92. The two terms were often applied interchangeably so that, in practice, the provisions of SFAS No. 71, paragraph 9, were interpreted to permit the cost of equity return to be deferred and capitalized for future recovery as a regulatory asset. The FASB, in SFAS No. 92, stated that equity return (or an allowance for earnings on shareholders' investment) is not "an incurred cost that would otherwise be charged to expense. Accordingly, such an allowance shall not be capitalized pursuant to paragraph 9 of SFAS No. 71."

At various 1993 meetings, the FASB's Emerging Issues Task Force (EITF) reached a final consensus for certain issues involving the application of SFAS No. 71 with respect to regulatory assets.

During the discussion of Issue No. 92-12, "Accounting for OPEB Costs by Rate-Regulated Enterprises," the EITF reached a tentative conclusion that if a rate-regulated enterprise initially fails to meet the regulatory asset recognition requirements described in the consensus reached on Issue No. 92-12 for OPEB costs (see subsection 27.11(e)), but meets those requirements in a subsequent period, then a regulatory asset related to SFAS No. 106, "Employers' Accounting for Postretirement Benefits Other Than Pension," costs should be recognized in the period in which those requirements are met. At a later 1993 meeting, the EITF considered Issue No. 93-4, "Accounting for Regulatory Assets," and finalized the tentative conclusion reached in Issue No. 92-12 for OPEB costs.

With respect to the broader issue, the EITF also reached a consensus for Issue No. 93-4 that a cost that does not meet the asset recognition criteria in paragraph 9 of SFAS No. 71 at the date the cost is incurred should be recognized as a regulatory asset when it does meet those criteria at a later date.

Additionally, the EITF reached a second consensus under Issue No. 93-4 that the carrying amount of a regulatory asset recognized pursuant to the criteria in paragraph 9 of SFAS No. 71 should be reduced to the extent that the asset has been impaired. Impairment of a regulatory asset should be judged in the same manner as for assets of enterprises in general.

However, several members of the FASB and its staff took exception to the EITF's latter consensus for Issue No. 93-4. Subsequently, the FASB included in SFAS No. 121, "Accounting for the Impairment of Long-Lived Assets and for Long-Lived Assets to Be Disposed Of," amendments to paragraphs 9 and 10 of SFAS No. 71.

Effectively, the amendment to paragraph 9 requires a *probable* of future recovery test to be met each balance sheet date in order for a regulatory asset to remain recorded. And, the amendment to paragraph 10 extends the dollar-for-dollar write-off requirement in paragraph 7 of SFAS No. 90 for disallowed newly completed plant to all regulatory assets, except those associated with abandoned plants.

(ii) Asset Impairment.   SFAS No. 121 and the provisions of SFAS Nos. 71 and 90 result in different impairment approaches for four categories of assets. Impairments of regulatory assets that have been recorded based on the criteria of paragraph 9 of SFAS No. 71 are to be recognized whenever the criteria of that paragraph are no longer met. Disallowances of costs of recently completed plants continue to be covered by paragraph 7 of SFAS No. 90. The accounting for plant abandonments and related regulatory assets continue to be based on paragraphs 3–6 to SFAS No. 90. Other assets that are not regulatory assets covered by SFAS No. 71 or SFAS No. 90 (abandoned plant costs) or recently completed plant costs covered by SFAS No. 90 are addressed by the general provisions of SFAS No. 121.

(iii) Regulatory Liabilities.   The general standards also recognize that the rate action of a regulator can impose a liability on a regulated enterprise, usually to the utility's customers.
The following are typical ways in which regulatory liabilities can be imposed:

1. A regulator may require refunds to customers (revenue collected subject to refund).
2. A regulator can provide current rates intended to recover costs that are expected to be incurred in the future. If those costs are not incurred, the regulator will reduce future rates by corresponding amounts.
3. A regulator can require that a gain or other reduction of net allowable costs be given to customers by amortizing such amounts to reduce future rates.

Paragraph 12 of the general standards states that "actions of a regulator can eliminate a liability only if the liability was imposed by actions of the regulator." The practical effect of this provision is that a utility's balance sheet should include all liabilities and obligations that an enterprise in general would record under GAAP, such as for capital leases, pension plans, compensated absences, and (once SFAS No. 109, "Accounting for Income Taxes," is adopted) income taxes.

(e) SPECIFIC STANDARDS.   SFAS No. 71 also sets forth specific standards for several accounting and disclosure issues.

(i) AFUDC.   Paragraph 15 allows the capitalization of AFUDC, including a designated cost of equity funds, if a regulator requires such a method, rather than using SFAS No. 34 for purposes of capitalizing the carrying cost of construction.
Rate regulation has historically provided utilities with two methods of capturing and recovering the carrying cost of construction:

1. Capitalizing AFUDC for future recovery in rates.
2. Recovering the carrying cost of construction in current rates by including construction work-in-progress in the utility's rate base.

The computation of AFUDC is generally prescribed by the appropriate regulatory body. The predominant guidance has been provided by the FERC and FCC. The FERC has defined AFUDC as "the net cost for the period of construction of borrowed funds used for construction purposes and a reasonable rate on other funds when so used." The term "other funds," as used in this definition, refers to equity capital.
The FERC formula for computing AFUDC is comprehensive and takes into consideration:

1. Debt and equity funds.
2. The levels of construction.

3. Short-term debt.
4. The costs of long-term debt and preferred stock are based on the traditional embedded cost approach, using the preceding year-end costs.
5. The cost rate for common equity is usually the rate granted in the most recent rate proceeding.

The FCC instructions also provide for equity and debt components. In allowing AFUDC, the FERC and FCC recognize that the capital-carrying costs of the investments in construction work-in-progress are as much a cost of construction as other construction costs such as labor, materials, and contractors.

In contrast to regulated utilities, nonregulated companies are governed by a different standard, SFAS No. 34. Under the FASB guidelines:

> [T]he amount of interest to be capitalized for qualifying assets is intended to be that portion of interest cost incurred during the assets acquisition periods that theoretically could have been avoided (for example, by avoiding additional borrowings or by using the funds expended for the assets to repay existing borrowings) if expenditures for the assets had not been made.

Furthermore, the FASB statement allows only debt interest capitalization and does not recognize an equity component.

The specific standard in SFAS No. 71 states that capitalization of such financing costs can occur only if both of the following criteria are met.

1. It is **probable** that future revenue in an amount at least equal to the capitalized cost will result from the inclusion of that cost in allowable costs for rate-making purposes.
2. The future revenue will be provided to permit recovery of the previously incurred cost rather than to provide for expected levels of similar future costs.

In practice, many have interpreted the standard under SFAS No. 71 to mean that AFUDC should be capitalized if it is reasonably possible (not necessarily probable under SFAS No. 5) that the costs will be recovered. This same reasoning was also applied to the capitalization of other incurred costs such as labor and materials. Thus, capitalization occurred so long as recovery was reasonably possible and a loss was not probable.

As previously indicated, SFAS No. 90 amends the definition of probable included in SFAS No. 71 such that probable is now defined under the stringent technical definition in SFAS No. 5. In addition, paragraph 8 of SFAS No. 90 clarified that AFUDC capitalized under paragraph 15 can occur only if "subsequent inclusion in allowable costs for rate-making purposes is probable." Accordingly, the standard for capitalizing AFUDC is different from the standard applied to other costs, such as labor and materials.

The FASB also concluded in SFAS No. 92, paragraph 66, that:

> [I]f the specific criteria in paragraph 15 of SFAS No. 71 are met but AFUDC is not capitalized because its inclusion in the cost that will become the basis for future rates is not probable, the regulated utility may not alternatively capitalize interest cost in accordance with SFAS No. 34.

(ii) Intercompany Profit.   Paragraph 16 of SFAS No. 71 generally reaffirms the provision in ARB No. 51 that intercompany profits on sales to regulated affiliates should not be eliminated in general-purpose financial statements if the sales price is reasonable and it is probable that future revenues allowed through the rate-making process will approximately equal the sales price.

(iii) Accounting for Income Taxes.   In paragraph 18 of SFAS No. 71, the FASB recognized that, in some cases, a regulator flows through the tax effects of certain timing differences as a reduction in future rates. In such cases, if it is **probable** that future rates will be based on income taxes payable at that time, SFAS No. 71 did not permit deferred taxes to be recorded in accordance with APB Opinion No. 11, "Accounting for Income Taxes."

In February, 1992, SFAS No. 71 was amended by SFAS No. 109 and paragraph 18 was replaced by the following:

> A deferred tax liability or asset shall be recognized for the deferred tax consequences of temporary differences in accordance with FASB Statement No. 109, "Accounting for Income Taxes."

(iv) Refunds.   Paragraph 19 of SFAS No. 71 addresses the accounting for significant refunds. Examples include refunds granted gas distribution utilities from pipelines and telephone refunds occurring where revenues are estimated in one period and "trued-up" at a later date or where revenues are billed under bond pending settlement of a rate proceeding.

For refunds recognized in a period other than the period in which the related revenue was recognized, disclosure of the effect on net income and the years in which the related revenue was recognized is required if material. SFAS No. 71 provides presentation guidance that the effect of such refunds may be disclosed by displaying the amount, **net** of income tax, as a line item in the income statement, but not as an extraordinary item.

Adjustments to prior **quarters** of the **current** fiscal year are appropriate for such refunds, provided all of the following criteria are met:

1. The effect is material (either to operations or income trends).
2. All or part of the adjustment or settlement can be specifically identified with and is directly related to business activities of specific prior interim periods.
3. The amount could not be reasonably estimated prior to the current interim period but becomes reasonably estimable in the current period.

This treatment of prior interim periods for utility refunds is one of the restatement exceptions contained in paragraph 13 of SFAS No. 16, "Prior Period Adjustments."

(v) Deferred Costs Not Earning a Return.   Paragraph 20 of SFAS No. 71 requires disclosure of costs being amortized in accordance with the actions of a regulator but not being allowed to earn a return during the recovery period. Disclosure should include the remaining amounts being amortized (the amount of the nonearning asset) as well as the remaining recovery period.

(vi) Examples of Application.   Appendix B in SFAS No. 71 contains examples of the application of the general standards to specific situations. These examples, along with the basis for conclusions (Appendix C) are an important aid in understanding the provisions of SFAS No. 71 and the financial statements of utilities.

Items discussed include:

1. Intangible assets.
2. Accounting changes.
3. Early extinguishment of debt.
4. Accounting for contingencies.
5. Accounting for leases.
6. Revenue collected subject to refund.
7. Refunds to customers.
8. Accounting for compensated absences.

27.7 SFAS NO. 90: "REGULATED ENTERPRISES—ACCOUNTING FOR ABANDONMENTS AND DISALLOWANCE OF PLANT COSTS"

(a) CONCERN WITH SFAS NO. 71—DISALLOWANCES AND ABANDONMENTS.

After SFAS No. 71 was issued, various regulatory agencies began to question the cost of certain new plants and to discuss major disallowances. Also, several electric generating units in advanced stages of construction were abandoned. In several states, courts ruled that the affected utilities could not recover the costs of those abandoned plants through rates.

The related accounting for these significant economic events was unsettled in practice and viewed by many as being potentially troublesome. For example, large cost disallowances were ordered by regulators, but no losses were being currently reported by affected utilities under the theory that, on an overall basis, the total cost would be recovered. By including the return earned on the **allowed** portion of the new plant, the plant cost would be recovered even though it might earn less than a full return.

To illustrate, say a plant costing $2 billion is placed in service and the regulator disallows $200 million from rate base and depreciation recovery. As long as the future cash flows from the $1.8 billion allowed portion exceed $2 billion, then no write-off would be recorded because the asset was not "impaired" in an accounting sense. This accounting treatment was considered to be consistent with the provisions of SFAS No. 71 (par. 10), which states:

> [T]he carrying amount of any related asset shall be reduced to the extent that the asset has been impaired. Whether the asset has been impaired shall be judged the same as for enterprises in general.

Similarly, as long as cost recovery for abandonments was probable (no matter over how long a time period), no immediate loss was required under GAAP. Thus, if a $3 billion project were abandoned and a regulator allowed recovery of $100 million for 30 years, no write-off would result.

The FASB recognized, in its basis for conclusions included in SFAS No. 90, that the accounting provisions of SFAS No. 71 require regulated utilities "to recognize probable increases in future revenues due to a regulator's actions as assets by capitalizing incurred costs that would otherwise be charged to expense." Accordingly, regulated utilities "should also recognize probable decreases in revenues due to a regulator's actions as reductions in assets." The accounting for disallowances and abandonments discussed above is inconsistent with this conclusion, so SFAS No. 71 was amended by SFAS No. 90.

(b) SIGNIFICANT PROVISIONS OF SFAS NO. 90.

The provisions of SFAS No. 90 are limited to the narrow area of accounting for abandonments and disallowances of plant costs and not to other assets, regulatory or otherwise.

(i) Accounting for Regulatory Disallowances of Newly Completed Plant.

When a *direct disallowance* of a newly completed plant is **probable** and **estimable,** a loss should be recorded, dollar for dollar, for the disallowed amount. After the write-down is achieved, the reduced asset forms the basis for future depreciation charges. Application of this requirement to the regulatory disallowance situation cited above would result in an immediate write-off for $200 million of the $2 billion plant cost.

An **indirect disallowance** occurs when, in certain circumstances, no return or a reduced return is permitted on all or a portion of the new plant for an extended period of time. To determine the loss resulting from an indirect disallowance, the present value of the future revenue stream allowed by the regulator should be determined by discounting at the most recent allowed rate of return. This amount should be compared with the recorded plant amount and the difference recorded as a loss. Under this discounting approach, the remaining asset should be depreciated consistent with the ratemaking and in a manner that would produce a constant return on the undepreciated asset equal to the discount rate.

(ii) Accounting for Plant Abandonments.   In the case of abandonments, when no return or only a partial return is permitted, at the time the abandonment is both **probable** and **estimable** the asset should be written off and a separate new asset should be established based on the present value of the future revenue stream. The entities' incremental borrowing rate should be used to measure the new asset. During the recovery period, the new asset should be amortized to produce zero net income based on the theoretical debt, and interest should be assumed to finance the abandonment.

FTB No. 87-2, "Computation of a Loss on an Abandonment," supports discounting the abandonment revenue stream using an after-tax incremental borrowing rate. Until SFAS No. 96 is adopted, the tax effects of the abandonment loss should be based on the statutory rate for the year of abandonment. This is the rate supported under APB Opinion No. 11 and APB Opinion No. 20, "Accounting Changes."

(iii) Income Statement Presentation.   SAB No. 72 (currently cited as SAB Topic 10E) concludes that the effects of adoption of SFAS No. 90 should not be reported as an extraordinary item. SAB No. 72 states that such charges should be reported **gross** as a component of other income and deductions and **not shown net-of-tax.** The following presentation complies with the requirements of SAB No. 72.

Operating income	$XX
Other income (expense)	
Allowance for equity funds used during construction	XX
Disallowed plant cost	(XX)
Income tax reduction for disallowed plant cost	XX
Interest income	XX
Income taxes applicable to other income	XX
Income before interest charges	$XX

27.8 SFAS NO. 92: "REGULATED ENTERPRISES—ACCOUNTING FOR PHASE-IN PLANS"

(a) CONCERN WITH SFAS NO. 71—PHASE-IN PLANS.   Subsequent to the issuance of SFAS No. 71, a combination of circumstances has caused traditional rate-making procedures to result in a phenomenon called "rate spike." Rate spike is a major, one-time increase in rates that can occur from the inclusion of the cost of new plants in rates under traditional rate-making procedures. Rate spikes have in part been caused by the high cost of nuclear power plants, which escalated far beyond initial expectations. Also, demand for many utilities' services has not grown in recent years to the extent that was expected when the decision was made to construct many of the recently completed plants. As a result, plants that were expected to be necessary to meet demand have created excess capacity. In addition, the increased efficiency of the new plants has not been sufficient to offset the high construction and capitalized capital costs of those plants and the return on investment that would have been included in rates under traditional rate-making procedures.

Phase-in plans were developed to alleviate the problem of rate spike by:

1. Moderating the initial increase in rates that would otherwise result from placing newly completed plants in service by deferring some of that rate increase to future years and providing the utility with return on investment for those deferred amounts.

2. Creating a pattern of gradually increasing allowable costs for the initial years of the plant's service life instead of the traditional pattern of an increase in allowable costs

followed by decreasing allowable costs for utility plants after the plants are placed in service.

The major aspects of phase-in plans that the FASB found troublesome related to the conceptual problems these plans create and these various factors seemed to undermine the credibility of financial reporting under SFAS No. 71. These conceptual concerns include:

1. The mere fact that phase-in plans defer cost recovery to future periods seems to contradict the requirement in SFAS No. 71 that rates set at levels designed to recover a utility's costs are collectible from customers.
2. SFAS No. 71 requires that rates be designed to recover a utility's cost of service. Under a phase-in plan, cost recovery can be deferred to future periods, and consequently, current rates can be based upon criteria other than cost of service.
3. Some phase-in plans provide for capitalization of equity costs **after** a plant begins operations.

The FASB reached two major conclusions about phase-in plans in SFAS No. 92.

1. If such plans result in costs deferred and capitalized for financial reporting purposes, a stringent set of criteria must be met so as to not undermine the credibility of SFAS No. 71.
2. Capitalization of phase-in plan costs should only be permitted if substantial construction of the affected plant occurred before January 1, 1988. If not, no phase-in plan accounting under SFAS No. 92 is permitted for the newly completed plant. This provision affects the newly completed plants of all regulated utilities subject to SFAS No. 71.

(b) SIGNIFICANT PROVISIONS OF SFAS NO. 92. A phase-in plan, as defined in SFAS No. 92, is a method of ratemaking that meets all of the following criteria:

1. Adopted **in connection with a major, newly** completed plant of the utility or one of its suppliers or a major plant scheduled for completion in the near future.
2. Defers the rates intended to recover allowable costs beyond the period in which those allowable costs would be charged to expense under GAAP applicable to enterprises in general.
3. Defers the rates intended to recover allowable costs beyond the period in which those rates would have been ordered under ratemaking methods **routinely** used prior to 1982 by that regulator for **similar** allowable costs of that utility.

This definition is **not** limited to **electric** utility plants and encompasses, for example, methods of depreciation slower than straight-line (sinking fund depreciation) and the treatment of a capital lease under SFAS No. 13 as an operating lease for ratemaking purposes. Deferral of costs associated with newly completed plants before a rate order is issued, which is often referred to as a short-term or rate synchronization deferral, is specifically excluded from being defined as a phase-in plan.

(i) Accounting for Phase-In Plans. SFAS No. 92 requires allowable costs deferred for future recovery under a phase-in plan related to plants completed before January 1, 1988, and plants on which substantial physical construction has been performed before January 1, 1988, to be capitalized if each of four criteria is met. Consequently, for a major, newly completed plant that does not meet the January 1, 1988, cutoff date, post in-service deferrals for financial reporting purposes are limited to a time frame that ends when rates are adjusted to reflect the cost of operating the plant. The criteria to determine whether capitalization continues to be appropriate are as follows:

1. The plan has been agreed to by the regulator.
2. The plan specifies when recovery will occur.
3. All allowable costs deferred under the plan are scheduled for recovery within 10 years of the date when deferrals begin.
4. The percentage increase in rates scheduled for each future year under the plan is not greater than the percentage increase in rates scheduled for each immediately preceding year.

If any of these criteria are not met, allowable costs deferred under the plan would not be capitalized for financial reporting purposes. Instead, those costs would be recognized in the same manner as if there were no phase-in plan.

(ii) Financial Statement Classification.   From a financial statement viewpoint, costs deferred should be classified and reported as a separate item in the income statement in the section relating to those costs. For instance, if capital costs are being deferred, they should be classified below-the-line. If depreciation or other operating costs are being deferred, the "credit" should be classified above-the-line with the operating costs. Allowable costs capitalized should not be reported net as a reduction of other expenses. Amortization of phase-in plan deferrals typically should be above-the-line (similar to recovering AFUDC via depreciation). This income statement presentation is consistent with guidance provided by the SEC's staff in the "Official Minutes of the Emerging Issues Task Force Meeting" (February 23, 1989, Open Meeting).

(iii) AFUDC.   SFAS No. 92 clarifies that AFUDC-equity can be capitalized in general purpose financial statements only during construction (based on par. 15 of SFAS No. 71) or as part of a qualifying phase-in plan. Thus, it is clear that, after January 1, 1988, AFUDC-equity can no longer be capitalized in connection with short-term, rate synchronization deferrals. It should also be noted that, in connection with the adoption of SFAS No. 92, such deferrals can be recorded only when it is probable—based on SFAS No. 5—that such costs will be recovered in future rates. This is consistent with the discussion on SFAS No. 90 relating to capitalizing AFUDC.

(iv) Interrelationship of Phase-In Plans and Disallowances.   Amounts deferred pursuant to SFAS No. 92 should also include an allowance for earnings on stockholders' investment. If the phase-in plan meets the criteria in SFAS No. 92 and the regulator prevents the enterprise from recovering either some amount of its investment or some amount of return on its investment, a disallowance occurs that should be accounted for in accordance with SFAS No. 90.

(v) Financial Statement Disclosure.   A utility should disclose in its financial statements the terms of any phase-in plans in effect during the year. If a phase-in plan exists but does not meet the criteria in SFAS No. 92, the financial statements should include disclosure of the net amount deferred for ratemaking purposes at the balance sheet date and the net change in deferrals for ratemaking purposes during the year for those plans. In addition, the nature and amounts of any allowance for earnings on stockholders' investment capitalized for ratemaking purposes but not capitalized for financial reporting are to be disclosed.

27.9 SFAS NO. 101: "REGULATED ENTERPRISES— ACCOUNTING FOR THE DISCONTINUATION OF APPLICATION OF FASB STATEMENT NO. 71"

All major telephone companies have discontinued application of SFAS No. 71. Deregulation and competition, as well as political pressures, have brought the broader issue of the necessity of SFAS No. 71 into question.

1. Are rates really cost based?
2. If a portion of the business becomes deregulated, is the remainder of the enterprise really individual cost-of-service rate regulated and still subject to SFAS No. 71?

(a) **SIGNIFICANT PROVISIONS OF SFAS NO. 101.** SFAS No. 101 deals with the required accounting **once** a utility concludes that it should discontinue application of SFAS No. 71. Although it does not specify **when** a utility should discontinue application, SFAS No. 101 does provide the following examples of potential cause for a utility not meeting the scope criteria in SFAS No. 71, paragraph 5.

1. Deregulation.
2. Regulation that is no longer cost based.
3. Competition that precludes selling utility services at cost-recoverable rates.

(b) **REGULATORY ASSETS AND LIABILITIES.** Once a utility concludes that all or a part of a company's operations no longer comes under SFAS No. 71, it should discontinue application of that Statement and report discontinuation by eliminating from its balance sheet the effects of any actions of regulators that had been recognized as assets and liabilities pursuant to SFAS No. 71 but would not have been recognized as assets and liabilities by enterprises in general. The guidance in SFAS No. 101 indicates that all regulatory-created assets and liabilities should be written off unless the right to receive payment or the obligation to pay exists as a result of past events and regardless of expected future transactions.

Examples of such regulatory-created assets and liabilities include:

1. Deferred storm damage.
2. Deferred plant abandonment loss.
3. Receivables or payables to future customers under purchased gas or fuel adjustment clauses (unless amounts are receivable or payable regardless of future sales).
4. Deferred gains or losses or reacquisition of debt.
5. Revenues subject to refund as future sales price adjustments.

(c) **FIXED ASSETS AND INVENTORY.** SFAS No. 101 also states:

> However, the carrying amounts of plant, equipment and inventory measured and reported pursuant to SFAS No. 71 should not be adjusted unless those assets are impaired (as measured by enterprises in general), in which case the carrying amounts of those assets should be reduced to reflect that impairment.

The carrying amount of inventories measured and reported pursuant to SFAS No. 71 would not be adjusted—to eliminate, for example, intercompany profit—absent loss recognition by applying the "cost or market, whichever is lower" rule set forth in Chapter 4, "Inventory Pricing," of ARB No. 43, "Restatement and Revision of Accounting Research Bulletins."

Reaccounting is required for **true** regulatory assets that have been **misclassified** as part of plant, such as postconstruction cost deferrals recorded as part of plant, and for systematic underdepreciation of plant in accordance with ratemaking practices.

(d) **INCOME TAXES.** An apparent requirement of SFAS No. 101 when SFAS No. 71 is discontinued is that net-of-tax AFUDC should be displayed gross along with the associated deferred income taxes. This requirement is based on the notion that the net-of-tax AFUDC presentation is pursuant to industry practice and not SFAS No. 71. The interaction of this requirement along with the SFAS No. 101 treatment of excess deferred income taxes and the transition provision in SFAS No. 109 must be considered in connection with discontinuing the application of SFAS No. 71.

(e) INCOME STATEMENT PRESENTATION.   The net effect of the above adjustments should be included in income of the period of the change and classified as an extraordinary item in the income statement.

27.10 OTHER SPECIALIZED UTILITY ACCOUNTING PRACTICES

(a) UTILITY INCOME TAXES AND INCOME TAX CREDITS.   Income tax expense is important to utilities because it generally is one of the largest items in the income statement and usually is a key factor in the determination of cost of service for ratemaking purposes. Deferred income taxes represent a significant element of internally generated funds and a major financing source for the extensive construction programs that utilities have historically experienced. In addition, the complexity of the IRC and of the various regulations to which utilities are subject causes a significant amount of controversy. As a result, the method of accounting for income taxes—"normalization" versus "flow-through" ratemaking—is often a specific issue in rate proceedings. The ratemaking method is an important area of concern to analysts and can be a factor in establishing the cost of equity and new debt offerings.

(i) Interperiod Income Tax Allocation.   The accounting for differences between income before income taxes and taxable income has been and continues to be a subject of much discussion. GAAP, whether under APB Opinion No. 11 or SFAS No. 109, require that a "provision for deferred taxes" be made for the tax effect of most of such differences. This practice of interperiod tax allocation is referred to in the utility industry as **normalization.**

The term "normalization" evolved because income taxes computed for accounting purposes on the normalization basis would cause reported net income to be a "normal" amount had the utility not adopted, for example, a particular tax return method for a deduction that created the tax-book difference. Under the deferred tax, or normalization concept, the taxes that would be payable, except for the use of the tax return deduction that created the tax-book difference, are merely deferred, not saved. For example, when tax depreciation exceeds book depreciation in the early years of property life, deferred taxes are charged to expense with a contra credit to a reserve. In later years, when the tax write-offs are lower than they otherwise would be, the higher taxes when payable are charged against this reserve. To illustrate the concept, assume the following facts:

	Year 1	Year 2	Year 3
Revenues	$1,000	$1,000	$1,000
Other expenses	600	600	600
Book depreciation	200	200	200
Tax depreciation	300	200	100
Tax rate	34%	34%	34%

Exhibit 27.7 sets forth how normalized (deferred) tax accounting would be recorded in Year 1 for the tax and book depreciation difference of $100.

(ii) Flow-Through.   "Flow-through" is a cash basis concept wherein the reductions in current tax payments from tax deductions, such as received by using accelerated depreciation, are flowed through to customers via lower cost-of-service and revenue requirements. Under this approach, income tax expense is equal to the currently payable amount only. No recognition (deferred taxes) is given to the tax effect of differences between book income before income taxes and taxable income. Under a "partial" allocation approach, deferred taxes are provided on certain differences but are ignored on others.

The principal argument used by those who support flow-through accounting is that a provision for deferred taxes does not constitute a current cost, and therefore such a deferment should

DEFERRED TAX ACCOUNTING

	Income Statement	Tax Return	Timing Difference
Revenue	$1,000	$1,000	$ —
Depreciation	(200)	(300)	100
Other expenses	(600)	(600)	—
Income before taxes	$ 200	$ 100	$100
Federal income taxes:			
Payable currently (34% × $100)	$ 34	$ 34	
Deferred (34% × $100)	34		$ 34
Total	$ 68		
Operating income	$ 132		

Exhibit 27.7.   Illustration of "normalized" tax accounting.

not be made. Income tax expense for the year should only include those taxes legally payable with respect to the tax return applicable to that year, and any provision in excess of taxes payable represents "phantom" taxes or "customer contributed capital." Further, when property additions are growing, as they are for certain utilities, and if no change were made to the tax law, deferred tax provisions **in the aggregate** would continue to grow and would never turn around (or reverse); thereby the tax timing differences are, in fact, "permanent differences."

Exhibit 27.8 sets forth how flow-through tax accounting would be recorded in Year 1 for the tax and book depreciation difference of $100.

Although Exhibit 27.8 shows a "bottom line" impact from the elimination of deferred tax expense, such accounting is not acceptable. GAAP requires deferred tax accounting with SFAS No. 71, permitting departures only when regulators affect revenues. To be acceptable, therefore, the regulator would lower revenue requirements due to the omission of deferred tax expense as an element of the utility's cost-of-service for ratemaking purposes. The action of the regulator in this case is to defer a cost that will be recoverable through increased rates in the future.

As previously discussed, utility regulators determine operating income first and then add allowable expenses to derive operating revenue. In Exhibit 27.7, $132 is presumed to be the

"FLOW-THROUGH" ACCOUNTING ASSUMING NO DECREASE IN CUSTOMER RATES

	Income Statement	Tax Return	Timing Difference
Revenue	$1,000	$1,000	$ —
Depreciation	(200)	(300)	100
Other expenses	(600)	(600)	—
Income before taxes	$ 200	$ 100	$100
Federal income taxes:			
Payable currently (34% × $100)	$ 34	$ 34	
Deferred (34% × $0)	—		$ —
Total	$ 34		
Net Income	$ 166		

Exhibit 27.8.   Illustration of "flow-through" accounting with no impact on customer rates.

result of multiplying rate base × rate of return. The same operating income of $132 in the normalization example would be developed first under the flow-through concept and, with the elimination of deferred tax expense of $34, only $948 of revenue would be required to produce the $132 of operating income under flow-through. The proper application of flow-through is shown in Exhibit 27.9.

This $52 reduction in revenues (by eliminating only $34 of deferred tax expense) is caused by the tax-on-tax effect, which is discussed under the ratemaking formula. In short, the elimination of the deferred tax expense results in a direct reduction of revenues, causing current tax expense also to be reduced. This effect is the primary reason so much attention is focused on normalization versus flow-through ratemaking for income taxes.

The comparison of the normalization and flow-through concepts in Exhibit 27.10 illustrates that operating income continues to be $132 under both methods and that the $52 of savings in revenue requirement in Year 1 due to flow-through is offset by $52 of higher rates in Year 3. For simplicity, this example ignores the rate base reducing effects of deferred taxes.

The comparison illustrates the principal argument for normalization—that revenues are at a level, or normal, amount, whereas revenue varies greatly under flow-through. Advocates of normalization note that normalization distributes income tax expense to time periods, and therefore to customers' revenue requirements, consistently with the costs (depreciation) that are affecting income tax expense. As the rate-making process necessarily involves the deferral of costs such as plant investment and distribution of these costs over time, normalization is used to produce a consistent determination of income tax expense.

Normalization also recognizes that the "using up" of tax basis of depreciable property (or using up an asset's ability to reduce taxes) creates a cost. This cost should be recognized as the tax payments are reduced. Basing tax expense solely on taxes payable without recognizing the cost of achieving reductions in tax payments is not consistent with accrual accounting. Although flow-through ratemaking ignores this current cost, this cost does not disappear any more than the nonrecognition of depreciation for ratemaking would make that cost disappear.

(iii) Provisions of the Internal Revenue Code.   Complicating the regulatory treatment and financial reporting of income taxes for utilities are significant amounts of deferred income taxes that are "protected" under provisions of the IRC. That is, normalization is required with respect to certain tax and book depreciation differences if the utility is to remain eligible for accelerated depreciation. A historical perspective of tax incentives and tax legislation, as they relate to the utility industry, is helpful in understanding why the regulatory treatment of income tax is of such importance.

"FLOW-THROUGH" ACCOUNTING ASSUMING DECREASE IN CUSTOMER RATES			
	Income Statement	Tax Return	Timing Difference
Revenue	$948	$948	—
Depreciation	(200)	(300)	$100
Other expenses	(600)	(600)	—
Income before taxes	$148	$ 48	$100
Federal income taxes:			
Payable currently (34% × $48)	16	16	
Deferred	—		—
Total	$ 16		
Net income	$132		

Exhibit 27.9.   Illustration of "flow-through" accounting with a decrease in rates.

COMPARISON OF NORMALIZATION AND FLOW-THROUGH

	Normalization				Flow-Through			
	Year 1	Year 2	Year 3	Total	Year 1	Year 2	Year 3	Total
Revenues	$1,000	$1,000	$1,000	$ 3,000	$ 948	$1,000	$1,052	$ 3,000
Depreciation	(200)	(200)	(200)	(600)	(200)	(200)	(200)	(600)
Other expenses	(600)	(600)	(600)	(1,800)	(600)	(600)	(600)	(1,800)
Income before income taxes	200	200	200	600	148	200	252	600
Income taxes								
Payable currently	34	68	102	204	16	68	120	204
Deferred taxes	34	—	(34)	—	—	—	—	—
	68	68	68	204	16	68	120	204
Operating income	$ 132	$ 132	$ 132	$ 396	$ 132	$ 132	$ 132	$ 396

Exhibit 27.10.   Illustration of normalization versus flow-through differences.

(iv) The Concept of Tax Incentives.   The first significant tax incentive that was generally available to all taxpayers was a provision of the 1954 Code that permitted accelerated methods of depreciation. Prior to enactment of this legislation, tax depreciation allowances were generally limited to those computed with the straight-line method, which is traditionally used for financial reporting and ratemaking purposes. The straight-line method spread the cost of the property evenly over its estimated useful life. The accelerated depreciation provisions of the 1954 Code permitted taxpayers to take greater amounts of depreciation in the early years of property life and lesser amounts in later years. Although accelerated methods permit taxpayers to recover capital investments more rapidly for tax purposes, deductions are limited to the depreciable cost of property. Thus, only the timing, not the ultimate amount of depreciation, is affected.

Because utilities are capital intensive in nature, accelerated depreciation provisions generate significant amounts of tax deferrals. Additionally, other sources of deferred taxes can be relatively small in some industries but are magnified in the utility industry because of its large construction programs. Among the major differences, generally referred to as **basis differences,** are interest, pensions, and taxes capitalized as costs of construction for book purposes but deducted currently (as incurred) as expenses for tax purposes. Once again, it is the timing, not the ultimate cost, that is affected.

Accelerated methods and lives were intended by the U.S. Congress to generate capital for investment, stimulate expansion, and contribute to high levels of output and employment. The economic benefit to the taxpayer arising from the use of accelerated depreciation and capitalized costs is the time value of the money because of the postponement of tax payments. The availability of what are effectively interest-free loans, obtained from the U.S. Treasury, reduces the requirements for other sources of capital, thereby reducing capital costs. Prior to the Tax Reform Act of 1986, these capitalized overheads represented significant deductions for tax purposes. However, subsequent to that Act, such amounts are now capitalized into the tax basis of the asset and depreciated for tax purposes as well. Thus, the benefits that once resulted from basis differences have, to a large extent, been eliminated.

(v) Tax Legislation.   A brief history of the origin of accelerated tax depreciation and the intent of the U.S. Congress in permitting liberalized depreciation methods is helpful in understanding the regulatory and accounting issues related to income taxes.

Tax Reform Act of 1969.   The accelerated tax depreciation methods initially made available to taxpayers in 1954 were without limitations in the tax law as to the accounting and ratemaking methods used for public utility property. However, in the late 1960s, the U.S. Treasury Department and Congress became concerned about larger-than-anticipated tax revenue losses as a result of rate regulatory developments. Although both Congress and the Treasury realized that accelerated tax deductions would initially reduce Treasury revenues by the tax effect, they had not anticipated that flow-through would about double (at the then 48% tax rate) the Treasury's tax loss because of the tax-on-tax effect. Depending on the exact tax rate, about one-half the reduction in payments to the Treasury came from the deduction of accelerated depreciation and the other one-half from the immediate reduction in customer rates from the use of flow-through. It was this second one-half reduction of Treasury revenues that was considered unacceptable. Furthermore, immediate flow-through of these incentives to utility customers negated the intended Congressional purpose of the incentives themselves. It was the utility customers who immediately received all of the benefit of accelerated depreciation. Accordingly, the utility did not have all the Treasury "capital" that was provided by Congress for investment and expansion.

Faced with larger-than-anticipated Treasury revenue losses, Congress enacted TRA '69. By adding § 167(1), it limited the Treasury's exposure to revenue losses by making the accelerated depreciation methods available to public utility properties only if specific qualifying standards as to accounting and ratemaking were met. Although § 167(1) did not dictate to state regulatory commissions a ratemaking treatment they should follow with respect to the tax effects of accelerated depreciation, the Act provided that:

1. If a utility had not used accelerated depreciation prior to 1970, it would not be allowed to use accelerated tax depreciation in the future unless it normalized for ratemaking and accounting purposes.

2. Utilities that had been using accelerated tax depreciation and were normalizing for accounting and ratemaking purposes would not be allowed to use accelerated depreciation in the future unless they continued to normalize for accounting and ratemaking purposes.

3. Companies that were currently on a flow-through basis were allowed to continue on a flow-through basis in the future. However, an election was offered to such companies by which they could elect to be in a position where they would lose accelerated depreciation on future expansion additions unless they were normalizing for ratemaking and accounting purposes with respect to such future expansion property additions.

Revenue Act of 1971.   The Revenue Act of 1971, signed into law on December 10, 1971, codified the Asset Depreciation Range (ADR) system for determining depreciation for tax purposes. Under ADR, lives were shortened, thereby accelerating tax depreciation even further. The ADR regulations prescribed the same standards regarding normalization versus flow-through ratemaking as were set forth in TRA '69.

Economic Recovery Act of 1981.   The Economic Recovery Act of 1981, signed into law on August 31, 1981, continued to allow acceleration of depreciation tax deductions and included normalization rules for public utility property with respect to depreciation under the Accelerated Cost Recovery System. Normalization is mandatory under the Act for accelerated depreciation taken on all public utility property placed in service after December 31, 1980.

Tax Reform Act of 1986.   TRA '86 reduced the acceleration of depreciation tax deductions and continued normalization requirements for public utility property. In addition, the maximum federal tax rate for corporations was reduced from 46% to 34%. This reduction in the federal tax rate not only reduces tax payments currently being made, but will also reduce future tax payments (assuming continuation of the present tax rate) that result from the reversal of previously recorded deferred tax amounts—effectively forgiving a portion of the loan from the U.S. Treasury.

TRA '86 (§ 203(e)) provided that deferred taxes related to certain depreciation method and life differences on public utility property in excess of the new 34% statutory rate be used to reduce customer rates using the average rate assumption method. This method generally requires the development of an average rate determined by dividing the aggregate normalized timing differences into the accumulated deferred taxes that have been provided on those timing differences. As the timing differences begin to reverse, the turnaround occurs at this average rate. Under this method, the so-called excess in the reserve for deferred taxes is reduced over the remaining life of the property.

If a regulatory commission requires reduction in the deferred tax balance more rapidly than under this method, book depreciation must be used for tax purposes. There is no provision in TRA '86 for any protection of other deferred taxes, such as book/tax basis differences, life differences on pre-ADR assets, salvage value on ADR assets, repair allowance, and so on. In addition, the deferred taxes on depreciation method and life differences provided at rates in excess of 46% are not protected under the average-rate assumption method.

(vi) "Accounting for Income Taxes"—APB Opinion No. 11.   In December 1967 the APB issued Opinion No. 11, which requires that, in general, deferred taxes be provided for all tax-timing differences. Under the deferred method, deferred taxes provided are not meant to be a provision for the taxes that will be payable in the future but, rather, a deferral of the benefit received. Thus, under APB Opinion No. 11, deferred tax assets and liabilities are not adjusted when tax rates or other provisions of the income tax law change. Instead, they turn around during the reversal period at the tax rates used when the deferred taxes were originally provided. The deferred method is the professional standard today for all industries, with one major exception. That exception is for those utilities that are regulated on a flow-through basis if certain requirements are met with respect to increased rates being provided to recover higher future taxes. Income tax accounting for regulated enterprises is also addressed in SFAS No. 71 and, under this existing literature, deferred taxes for timing differences flowed through to reduce customer rates typically are not recorded for financial reporting purposes. However, the cumulative net amount of any income tax timing differences for which deferred taxes have not been provided must be disclosed in the footnotes to a utility's financial statements.

(vii) "Accounting for Income Taxes"—SFAS No. 109.   In February 1992 the FASB issued SFAS No. 109, which shifts the focus of income tax accounting from the income statement to an asset and liability approach. SFAS No. 109 retains the current requirement to record deferred taxes whenever income or expenses are reported in different years for financial reporting and tax purposes. However, it changes the way companies compute deferred taxes by requiring deferred tax assets and liabilities to be adjusted whenever tax rates or other provisions of the income tax law change. This is referred to as the "liability method" of providing deferred income taxes. SFAS No. 109 also requires utility companies to record tax liabilities for all temporary differences (defined as differences between the book and tax bases of assets and liabilities recorded on their respective balance sheets), even those that have previously been flowed through. For many utilities, these amounts are significant.

The liability method represents a change from the existing "deferred method" embodied in APB Opinion No. 11. However, in most situations, the amounts of the deferred tax provision under each of these concepts would be the same. In addition, ratemaking calculations of income tax expense may continue under an APB Opinion No. 11 type approach long after SFAS No. 109 is implemented.

As a result of adopting SFAS No. 109, utilities will adjust their accumulated deferred income tax balances to the level obtained by multiplying the statutory tax rate by existing temporary differences. Because this amount may be more or less than what has been permitted to be recovered through the rate-making process, regulatory assets or liabilities will also be recorded for financial reporting purposes. These regulatory assets and liabilities represent the future recovery or reduction in revenues as a result of previous income tax policies of regulatory commissions.

To illustrate the unique effects of utilities adopting SFAS No. 109, two significant transactions will be described—recording of amounts previously flowed through as a reduction in customer rates and the effects of a change in tax rates.

1. *Recording of Amounts Previously Flowed Through.* SFAS No. 109 requires utilities to record accumulated deferred taxes using the liability approach for all temporary differences whether normalized or flowed through. Accordingly, paragraph 18 of SFAS No. 71 is superseded by SFAS No. 109. Furthermore, the FASB has concluded that the asset (liability) created by a regulatory promise to allow recovery (or require a settlement) of flow-through amounts is best measured by the expected cash flow to be provided as the temporary difference turns around and is recovered (settled) in rates. Thus, a regulatory asset or liability is established at the revenue requirement level, taking into account the tax-on-tax impact. In the Statement, these regulatory assets/liabilities are characterized as "probable future revenue/probable reduction in future revenue."

The corresponding accumulated deferred income tax (ADIT) liability represents the income taxes that would result in connection with recovering both the temporary difference itself and the newly recorded regulatory asset. Accordingly, the computation of the amount to be recorded for prior flow-through is:

> Temporary differences flowed through
> × Gross-up (tax-on-tax) factor
> × Tax rate
> _____
> Dr. Regulatory asset/Cr. ADIT liability

SFAS No. 109 requires the regulatory asset and ADIT liability to be displayed separately for general-purpose financial reporting.

2. *Effects of a Change in Tax Rates.* Under the liability method in SFAS No.109, the ADIT liability is reported at the enacted settlement tax rate. Thus, deferred tax liabilities or assets established at rates in excess of the current statutory rate (35%) should be reduced to that level. Utilities are required to record the reduction in the ADIT liability but presumably will not immediately recognize the reduction in the results of operations because:

a. The average rate assumption method provision contained in TRA '86 prohibits excess deferred taxes related to protected depreciation differences from being used to reduce customer rates more rapidly than over the life of the asset giving rise to the difference. Under this method, the excess in the deferred tax reserve is not reduced until the temporary differences giving rise to deferred taxes begin to turn around.

b. Regulators may adopt a similar methodology for nonprotected excess deferred taxes.

For these reasons, the credit to offset the reduction in the ADIT liability required by the liability method should be reclassified by regulated utilities as a separate liability. Consistent with the asset recovery scenario discussed previously, the FASB measures this separate liability as the cash flow impact of settling the specific liability (i.e., the future reduction in the revenue requirement). Accordingly, a gross-up factor must be applied to the excess deferred tax liability. The concept is illustrated with the following skeleton entry:

> Temporary difference
> × Enacted tax rate
> _____
> Required ADIT liability
> − Existing deferred taxes on temporary difference
> _____
> Excess deferred taxes
> × Gross-up factor
> _____
> Dr. ADIT liability/Cr. Other liabilities

Other temporary differences that will result in the recording of ADIT and regulatory assets/liabilities are unamortized ITC balances (see next section), amounts recorded on a net-of-tax basis (SFAS No. 109 prohibits such presentations), and AFUDC-equity (previously recorded on an after-tax basis). Considering the large amounts of construction activity, the AFUDC-equity ADIT and regulatory assets may be significant.

At the time of adoption, paragraph 58 of SFAS No. 109 sets forth transitional guidance whereby a single temporary difference between the book and tax bases of **plant in service** could be computed and the net effect recorded on the balance sheet.

The important concept to consider is that SFAS No. 109, in and of itself, did not alter ratemaking/revenue requirements and therefore SFAS No. 71 requires regulatory assets/

liabilities for differences in the recognition of the timing of income tax expense via that process. Thus, flow-through of tax expense may continue for regulatory purposes, but SFAS No. 109 will require financial statements to report the deferred income tax liability with an offsetting regulatory asset to recognize that such cost will be recovered at a future date.

(viii) Investment Tax Credit.   The accounting and ratemaking aspects of the ITC are discussed separately because the economics and the effect are different from those of the acceleration in the write-off of costs for tax purposes. The ITC represents a permanent savings in taxes rather than a deferral. Although the tax credit should be used to reduce expense, the accounting and ratemaking question is not one of flow-through but rather is a question as to which year's tax expense should be reduced and the benefit passed on to utility customers.

Accounting for ITC.   Based on APB Opinion Nos. 2 and 4, the two accounting methods in use are to:

1. Flow the tax reduction through to income over the life of the property giving rise to the investment tax credit (service-life method), or
2. Reduce tax expense in the current year by the full amount of the credit (initial year flow-through method).

Tax Legislation and Regulatory Treatment.   The service-life method is required by the IRC in order for many utilities to claim ITC. In 1964, in connection with the investment credit, the U.S. Congress specifically established certain ratemaking requirements, stating that federal regulatory agencies could not use the investment credit to reduce cost of service except over the service life of the related property. Congress also extended the practice of including ratemaking requirements in the tax law when it enacted the job development tax credit in 1971 and provided that, except where a special election was made by a limited number of eligible companies, the benefits of the job development credit were to be shared between consumers and investors and that the consumers' share was to be passed on to them over the life of the property.

If the ratemaking and the accounting are not in accordance with the irrevocable election made by the company pursuant to the 1971 Act, the utility taxpayer can be denied ITC. The four available options were:

1. No portion of the investment credit would be used to reduce cost-of-service for rate purposes, but the unamortized credit could be used to reduce rate base (general rule).
2. The ratemaking authority could reduce the cost-of-service for no more than the annual amortization of the investment credit over the book life of the property giving rise to the credit, and the unamortized balance of the credit could not be used to reduce rate base (ratable flow-through).
3. Utilities that were flow-through for accelerated depreciation under the standards of the Tax Reform Act of 1969 were permitted to elect to continue to follow the flow-through method for the investment credit. This election does not preclude the use of a service-life method of amortization of the credit if the regulatory commission agreed.
4. If the appropriate regulatory agency declared there was a shortage of supply, companies in the natural gas or steam heat business would lose the credit if the ratemaking body either reduced the cost of service or reduced the rate base.

With few exceptions, electric utilities, gas distribution companies, and telephone companies are now on the service-life amortization method for all or most of the investment credit, in most cases using the ratemaking method covered by Option 2 above. Natural gas pipeline companies elected the "shortage of supply" option. As a result, no element of the credit could be passed on to customers. They were in the same position as nonregulated companies and could use either the initial year flow-through or service-life method for accounting purposes. However, in 1986, the FERC determined that there was no longer a shortage of gas supply and these companies would follow Option 1 for any credits subsequently realized.

The 1986 Act repealed the ITC, generally effective for property placed in service after December 31, 1985. The Act requires that a utility continue to follow its present method of accounting for amortizing the ITC. For failure to continue its present method, a utility will be forced to recapture the greater of (1) ITC for all open years or (2) unamortized ITC of the taxpayer or ITC not previously restored to rate base.

(b) REVENUE RECOGNITION.   Under GAAP as applied in practice, there are three acceptable methods of accounting for utility (principally gas and electric) revenues or related costs of gas and electricity, as follows:

1. To include in revenues the amounts **billed** for service for which meters were read during the period, and to include in expenses the cost of gas or electricity for the period (**billed revenue** method).

2. To include in revenues the estimated amount applicable to gas or electricity **delivered** to customers during the period, whether or not the meters have been read and bills rendered, and to include in expenses the cost of gas or electricity for the period (**unbilled revenue** method).

3. To include in revenues the amounts billed for service for which meters were read during the period, and to include in expenses the cost of gas or electricity applicable to such revenues, that is, to defer the cost of electricity or gas for the period that relates to service rendered during the period for which no revenues have been recognized (**deferred cost** method).

Acceptance of the **billed revenue** method is based on long-standing industry practice. From an accounting and reporting point of view, the **unbilled revenue** method is regarded as preferable and the **deferred cost** method as acceptable.

(c) REVENUE RECOGNITION—ALTERNATIVE REVENUE PROGRAMS.   There are various financial reporting issues related to the accounting by rate regulated utilities for the effects of certain alternative revenue programs adopted in a number of regulatory jurisdictions. Although the specific objectives of various recent programs are intended to address relatively new regulatory policies, the basic form and economic substances of the related regulatory treatment has been widespread and around for many years. The major alternative revenue programs currently in use include the following.

1. *Weather Normalization Clauses.* These clauses operate in a manner similar to fuel adjustment clauses and are designed to protect both rate payers and shareholders from the effects of significant changes in unit sales due to weather. Amounts billed or refunded are generally computed by multiplying the difference between actual units sold and units included in the rate-making process times base rates (excluding variable fuel costs). The intent of such a clause is to recover nonfuel cost of service (incurred costs) and return (including equity).

2. *Operating/Plant Performance Measurements.* These programs are designed to hold a utility's management accountable and to effectively reward or penalize shareholders for meeting or not meeting established performance measurements. The reward or penalty can be a specific amount or an amount based on an increase or decrease in the return

allowed by the regulator. The amount is usually based on performance for a specific measurement and period (typically an annual period) and billed or refunded to customers prospectively after regulatory review.

3. *Demand Side Management (DSM).* Many utility companies have implemented various load management and conservation programs that have been designed to address capacity shortages, potential peak demand reductions, money-saving opportunities for customers, and environmental concerns. Such programs include payments made to customers to assist in installation of cost-effective electric load reduction measures, incentives paid to customers for proven conservation and load management measures, retrofit programs directed at large customers to remodel or update operating equipment, numerous projects to reduce individual customer energy use (such as bill credits for more efficient lighting and water heaters, energy efficient appliances, residential weatherization and insulation), developing standby generation and interruptible service rates.

DSM programs reduce sales so regulators are taking various actions to remove this disincentive by:

1. Permitting recovery of and return on program costs,
2. Permitting compensation for lost revenues, or
3. Granting bonuses or incentives for meeting goals and objectives.

These programs typically enable the regulated utility to adjust rates in the future (usually as a surcharge applied to future billings) in response to past activities, transactions, or completed events.

In practice, accounting for amounts due to customers has not been an issue. These amounts represent refunds of revenues collected during the measurement period and are accounted for as contingent liabilities or regulatory liabilities that meet the conditions for accrual under SFAS No. 5 or paragraph 11 of SFAS No. 71, respectively.

The primary accounting question for these programs is whether the economic substance of regulatory actions should be accrued and recorded as assets for financial reporting purposes when it is probable that amounts for program costs and revenue shortfalls will be recovered from customers and no other event is required in the future other than billing. Financial reporting issues related to this question include (1) the limitations on accruing equity return or profit under SFAS No. 71; (2) distinguishing between an incurred and allowable (equity) cost under SFAS No. 71, and situations in which the deferral/capitalization of such costs create regulatory assets for financial reporting purposes; and (3) distinguishing regulatory assets from GAAP assets.

At its May 21, 1992 meeting, the EITF addressed Issue No. 92-7, "Accounting by Rate-Regulated Utilities for the Effects of Certain Alternative Revenue Programs," and reached a consensus that once the specific events permitting billing of the additional revenues under a program have been completed, the regulated utility should recognize the additional revenues if all of the following conditions are met.

1. The program is established by an order from the utility's regulatory commission that allows for automatic adjustment of future rates. Verification of the adjustment to future rates by the regulator would not preclude the adjustment from being considered automatic.
2. The amount of additional revenues for the period is objectively determinable and is probable of recovery.
3. The additional revenues will be collected within 24 months following the end of the annual period in which they are recognized.

For purposes of applying the consensus, the conditions or accruing revenue effectively determine what accounting model is being followed for asset recognition—a GAAP-based model as followed by enterprises in general or an SFAS No. 71 model. Accordingly, if the conditions of Issue No. 92-7 are met, an asset with many of the characteristics of a GAAP receivable is recorded. The ability to accrue revenue for a program measurement period is an all or nothing determination with respect to the 24-month collection period condition. In other words, if there is a 36-month collection period, no amount is accruable for the program. Thus, revenue collected within the first 24 months of a 36-month collection period is not accruable.

In situations where revenue is not accruable as a GAAP asset, paragraph 9 of SFAS No. 71 should be followed to the extent that probable future revenue is being provided to recover *incurred costs* and a regulatory asset exists.

Prior to 1987, the majority of public utilities did not record unbilled revenues in their financial statements for several reasons, one of which related to income taxes. TRA '86 has prospectively eliminated the favorable tax treatment that was previously accorded unbilled revenues and, consequently, numerous utilities have changed to the unbilled revenue method of accounting for financial statement purposes. Beginning in 1987, all utilities must accrue unbilled revenues for income tax purposes regardless of whether such revenues are accrued for financial statement purposes.

(d) ACCOUNTING FOR PENSION PLANS.   The application of SFAS No. 87, "Employers' Accounting for Pensions," can result in different pension accounting principles for ratemaking and financial reporting purposes. Paragraph 210 of SFAS No. 87 addresses the issue of rate-regulated enterprises and the applicability of SFAS No. 71 and states that:

> [SFAS No. 71] may require that the difference between net periodic pension cost as defined in this Statement and amounts of pension cost considered for ratemaking purposes be recognized as an asset or a liability created by the actions of the regulator. Those actions of the regulator charge the timing of recognition of net periodic cost as an expense; they do not otherwise affect the requirements of this Statement.

For example, if a regulator continues to allow a higher level of pension expense based on funding determined under APB Opinion No. 8 or some other acceptable actuarial method, a prepaid pension expense and corresponding regulatory liability to ratepayers—displayed broad—should be recorded on the balance sheet for the difference between the amount funded and recovered from customers and the amount to be recognized as pension expense under SFAS No. 87. In this situation, the balance sheet liability must be included in the reconciliation of the funded status of the plan to the reported balance sheet amount. This reconciliation is illustrated in "A Guide to Implementation of Statement No. 87 on Employers' Accounting for Pensions" (Amble and Cassel, 1986, Table 1, p. 8).

The Guide also illustrates how these balance sheet entries and net periodic pension cost should be recorded and classified in the financial statements. The Guide encompasses an unearned revenue notion. The resulting presentation is somewhat foreign to the typical utility income statement display for the effects of regulation because revenues are reduced and operating expenses will not reflect the amount of pension expense that has been included in cost-of-service by the regulator. Because of the potential for confusion and the questionable usefulness of the Guide's income statement treatment for a utility, in practice pension expense in the income statement is typically equal to the amount recovered in rates. In such situations, the disclosures required by SFAS No. 87, as illustrated in the Guide (Table 2, p. 8), should be modified.

Portions of a pension plan footnote might look as follows (required comparative information is not illustrated):

The reconciliation of the funded status of the retirement plans to the pension liability recorded by a utility is as follows as of December 31, 19XX:

Fair value of plan assets	$XXX
Projected benefit obligation	(XXX)
Excess of plan assets over projected benefit obligation	XXX
Unrecognized net loss from past experience Different than that assumed	XXX
Unrecognized net asset	XXX
Regulatory effect recorded	(734)
Pension liability	$XXX

Components of annual net pension expense:

Service cost (benefits earned during the period)	$XXX
Interest cost on projected benefit obligation	XXX
Actual return on plan assets	XXX
Net amortization and deferral	XXX
Regulatory effect based on funding	734
Net pension expense	$XXX

(e) ACCOUNTING FOR POSTRETIREMENT BENEFITS OTHER THAN PENSIONS.   In December 1990, the FASB issued SFAS No. 106 which concludes that such benefits, commonly referred to as OPEB costs, represents deferred compensation which should be accounted for on an accrual basis. SFAS No. 106 is required to be adopted in 1993.

Regulators have historically provided regulated utilities rate recovery of OPEB costs on a pay-as-you-go basis. Since SFAS No. 106 was issued, various regulators have allowed SFAS No. 106 expense, or some level of funding above pay-as-you-go, for rate-making purposes. Others, such as the FERC, have specifically issued a policy statement adopting SFAS No. 106-based regulatory treatment for OPEB costs. However, a few regulatory jurisdictions have indicated that they will continue to limit cost recovery through rates to pay-as-you-go or to some other regulatory treatment that will result in significant deferrals of OPEB costs for future recovery in rates. In situations where SFAS No. 106 is not adopted for regulatory purposes, regulatory asset recognition, for the annual difference between SFAS No. 106 costs and costs allowable in rates, would only be appropriate if future rate recovery of the regulatory asset is *probable,* as defined in SFAS No. 5.

The SEC staff was particularly concerned with the evidence that would be available to support the *probable* determination of future recovery, as required by paragraph 9 of SFAS No. 71 for establishing a regulatory asset. When unusual costs have been or will be incurred that have not been previously addressed by a regulator, this *sufficient evidence* hurdle becomes even harder to meet, particularly with today's changing regulatory environment, increasing competition and the costs in question, which have some unique characteristics when deferred.

In order to provide authoritative guidance as to the appropriate accounting and what constitutes sufficient evidence that a regulatory asset exists, the EITF created Issue No. 92-12, "Accounting for OPEB Costs by Rate-Regulated Enterprises."

On January 21, 1993, the EITF reached a final consensus for Issue No. 92-12 that a regulatory asset related to SFAS No. 106 costs should not be recorded in a regulated utility's financial statements if the regulator continues to *limit inclusion* of OPEB costs in rates *to a pay-as-you-go basis.* Several EITF members noted that the application of SFAS No. 71 for financial reporting purposes requires that a rate-regulated enterprise's rates be designed to recover the specific enterprise's costs of providing the regulated service or product and that enterprise's cost of providing a regulated service or product includes SFAS No. 106 costs.

Further, the EITF reached a final consensus in Issue 92-12 that a rate-regulated enterprise *should not* recognize a regulatory asset for financial reporting purposes for the difference between SFAS No. 106 costs and OPEB costs included in the regulated utility's rates unless the company (a) determines that it is *probable* that future revenue in an amount at least equal to the deferred cost (regulatory asset) will be recovered in rates and (b) meets *all* of the following criteria:

1. The regulated company's regulator has issued a rate order, including a policy statement or a generic order applicable to enterprises within the regulator's jurisdiction, that allows the deferral of SFAS No. 106 costs and subsequent inclusion of those deferred costs in rates;

2. Annual SFAS No. 106 costs, including *normal* amortization of the transition obligation, should be included in rates within approximately five years of SFAS No. 106 adoption. The change to full SFAS No. 106 in rates may take place in multiple steps, but the deferral period should not exceed approximately five years.

3. The combined deferral and recovery period approved by the regulator should not exceed approximately 20 years. If a regulatory approves a total deferral and recovery period of more than twenty years, a regulatory asset should not be recognized for any costs not recovered by the end of the approximate 20-year period.

4. The percentage increase in rates scheduled under the regulatory recovery plan for each future year should be no greater than the percentage increase in rates scheduled under the plan for each immediately preceding year. This criterion is similar to that required for phase-in plans in paragraph 5(d) of SFAS No. 92. The EITF observed that recovery of the regulatory asset in rates on a straight-line basis would meet this criterion.

(f) OTHER FINANCIAL STATEMENT DISCLOSURES

(i) Purchase Power Contracts.   Many utilities enter into long-term contracts for the purchase of electric power in order to meet customer demand. The SEC's SAB No. 28 (currently cited as SAB Topic 10D) sets forth the disclosure requirements related to long-term contracts for the purchase of electric power. This release states:

> The cost of power obtained under long-term purchase contracts, including payments required to be made when a production plant is not operating, should be included in the operating expenses section of the income statement. A note to the financial statements should present information concerning the terms and significance of such contracts to the utility company including date of contract expiration, share of land output being purchased, estimated annual cost, annual minimum debt service payment required and amount of related long-term debt or lease obligations outstanding.

Purchasers of power under contracts that specify a level of power to be made available for a specific time period usually account for such contracts as purchase commitments with no recognition of an asset for the right to receive power and no recognition of a liability for the obligation to make payments (that is, the contracts are accounted for as executory agreements). However, some power purchase contracts may have characteristics similar to a lease in that the contract confers to the purchaser the right to use specific property, plant and equipment. Factors indicating that a power purchase contract is, in substance, a lease include the following:

1. The contract specifies the generating facility or group of generating facilities that will make power available and the amount of power to be purchased varies with the level of power made available from the specified facilities. For example, the contracted power is 100 percent of the power available from Power Plant X.

2. The purchaser of the power bears significant risk related to the construction of the specified facilities. For example, the power purchase contract is entered into prior to the construction of the generating facility and the price of the power is dependent in part on the ultimate cost of constructing the plant.

3. The purchaser of the power bears significant risk related to the specified facility's operating and fuel costs. For example, a fixed amount is payable whether the generating facility is available for use 30% or 80% of the billing period and a variable amount is payable based on actual operating and maintenance and fuel costs.

4. The purchaser of the power is involved in the dispatching and operation of the facility.

The determination of whether a power purchase contract is an executory agreement or a lease is a judgmental decision based on the substance of the contract. The fact that an agreement is labeled a "power purchase agreement" is not conclusive. If a contract "conveys the right to use property, plant and equipment," the contract should be accounted for as a lease. Other power purchase contracts should be accounted for as executory agreements with disclosure as required by SFAS No. 47, "Disclosure of Long-Term Obligations."

(ii) Financing through Construction Intermediaries.   Utilities using a construction intermediary should include the intermediary's work-in-progress in the appropriate caption of utility plant on the balance sheet. SAB No. 28 (currently cited as SAB Topic 10A) requires the related debt to be disclosed and included in long-term liabilities. Capitalized interest included as part of an intermediary's construction work-in-progress should be recognized as interest expense (with an offset to AFUDC-debt) in the income statement.

A note to the financial statements should describe the organization and purpose of the intermediary and the nature of its authorization to incur debt to finance construction. The note should also disclose the interest rate and amount of interest capitalized for each period in which an income statement is presented.

(iii) Jointly Owned Plants.   SAB No. 28 (currently cited as SAB Topic 10C) also requires a utility participating in a jointly owned power station to disclose the extent of its interests in such plant(s). Disclosure should include a table showing separately for each interest the amount of utility plant in service, accumulated depreciation, the amount of plant under construction, and the proportionate share. Amounts presented for plant in service may be further subdivided into subcategories such as production, transmission, and distribution. Information concerning two or more generating plants on the same site may be combined if appropriate.

Disclosure should address the participant's share of direct expenses included in operating expenses on the income statement (e.g., fuel, maintenance, other operating). If the entire share of direct expenses is charged to purchased power, then disclosure of this amount, as well as the proportionate amounts related to specific operating expenses on the joint plant records, should be indicated.

A typical footnote is as follows:

(x) Jointly Owned Electric Utility Plant

Under joint ownership agreements with other state utilities, the company has undivided ownership interests in two electric generating stations and related transmission facilities. Each of the respective owners was responsible for the issuance of its own securities to finance its portion of the construction costs. Kilowatthour generation and operating expenses are divided on the same basis as ownership with each owner reflecting its respective costs in its statements of income. Information relative to the company's ownership interest in these facilities at December 31, 19XX, is as follows:

	Unit 1	Unit 2
Utility plant in service	$XXX,XXX	$XX,XXX
Accumulated depreciation	$XXX,XXX	$XX,XXX
Construction work-in-progress	$ XX,XXX	$ XX
Plant capacity—Mw	XXX	XXX
Company's share	XX%	XX%
In-service date	1974	1981

(iv) Decommissioning Costs and Nuclear Fuel.   In January 1978, the SEC published SAB No. 19 (currently cited as Topic 10B), which addressed estimated future costs of storing spent nuclear fuel as well as decommissioning costs of nuclear generating plants. SAB No. 19 requires footnote disclosure of the estimated decommissioning or dismantling costs and whether a provision for these costs is being recorded/recognized in rates. If decommissioning or dismantling costs are not being provided for, disclosure of the reasons for not doing so and the potential financial statement impact should be made.

The term "decommissioning" means to safely remove nuclear facilities from service and reduce residual radioactivity to a level that permits termination of the Nuclear Regulatory Commission (NRC) license and release of the property for unrestricted use. The NRC has issued regulations requiring affected utilities with nuclear generation to prepare formal financial plans providing assurance that decommissioning funds in an amount at least equal to prescribed minimums will be accumulated prospectively over the remaining life of the related nuclear power plant. The NRC minimum is based on decontamination of the reactor facility but not demolition and site restoration. The amounts are based on generic studies and represent the NRC's estimate of the minimum funds needed to protect the public safety and are not intended to reflect the actual cost of decommissioning. Companies making annual sinking fund contributions are required by the NRC to maintain external trust funds. SFAS No. 107, "Disclosure About Fair Value of Financial Instruments," and SFAS No. 115, "Accounting for Certain Investments in Debt and Equity Securities," should be addressed with respect to decommissioning trusts.

Significant financial reporting considerations related to nuclear decommissioning costs have not been fully resolved. On June 15, 1994, the FASB added a project to its agenda on accounting for obligations to decommission nuclear power plants. Generally, the estimated decommissioning obligation for nuclear power plants has been recognized over the life of the plant as a component of depreciation. The objective of the FASB's project is to determine if and when a liability for nuclear decommissioning should be recognized. The project addressed how to measure the resulting liability and whether a corresponding asset is created, once it was determined if a liability should be recognized. Deliberations took place throughout 1995.

In September 1995, the FASB expanded the scope of the project to include costs similar to decommissioning. The project is now entitled: Accounting for Liabilities Related to Closure and Removal of Long-Lived Assets. The FASB issued an Exposure Draft entitled "Accounting for Certain Liabilities Related to Closure on Removal of Long-Lived Assets," dated February 7, 1996, with the following tentative conclusions:

- Legal and constructive obligations for closure and removal of long-lived assets should be accounted for as a liability and accrued as the obligation is incurred, with corresponding recognition of an increase in the depreciable cost of the related asset/plant.
- The liability should be measured based on discounted future cash flows (as opposed to current cost).
- The discounted future cash flows should be based on current prices adjusted for inflation, efficiencies that are expected from experience with similar activities, and consideration of reasonable future advances in technology.

- The method of determination of future cash flows considers nearly all of the factors that create uncertainty in these future cash flows. Consequently, a risk-free (U.S. Treasury securities) rate is the appropriate discount rate to use because otherwise, measurement of the obligation would compensate for certain risks in both the cash flows and the discount rate. The same *type* of rate should be used for *increases* in the obligation for an entity's new actions, such as additional contamination. Effectively, over time, a weighted-average risk-free discount rate would evolve.

- For purposes of measuring a change in estimate of an *existing* obligation, the discount rate should be fixed. In other words, at each balance sheet date the existing estimated obligation should be updated/remeasured using the best current information available with respect to the measurement assumptions discussed above, which includes inflation. However, the risk-free discount rate initially used should not be changed for that obligation.

- Trust funds should not be offset against the liability nor does funding of those trusts extinguish the liability.

- Changes at each balance sheet date in the estimated liability should be recognized as an increase or decrease in the plant asset and depreciation should be revised prospectively.

- Depreciation of long-lived assets should not exceed the historical cost of those assets. Therefore cost of removal recognized through depreciation should not exceed the salvage value of those assets.

- The proposed effective date is for financial statements issued for fiscal years beginning after December 15, 1996.

Although the Edison Electric Institute asked the FASB to add this project to its agenda, the primary reason that it exists is because the SEC staff has questioned current accounting practices related to decommissioning costs for nuclear generating stations. The SEC staff will continue to accept current practice until the FASB completes its project. In the interim, however, the SEC staff has been requesting that certain additional decommissioning cost related disclosures (well beyond the requirements of the SEC's SAB 19) be included in the footnotes to financial statements.

SAB No. 19 also suggests disclosure of the estimated future storage or disposal costs for spent fuel recorded as nuclear fuel amortization. The note should also disclose whether estimated future storage or disposal costs and residual salvage value recognized in prior years are being recovered through a fuel clause or through a general rate increase.

(v) Environmental Accounting Matters.   Environmental matters are viewed by some as the "business" issues of the 1990s. Accordingly, this area is one of major focus for most enterprises including regulated utilities, as significant environmental liabilities and obligations grow.

Environmental laws fall in two general categories; first, those that govern the activities of businesses in protecting the environment and, second, those that cover the clean-up (or remediation) of land and property contaminated by past activities. The contamination results from Polychlorinated Biphenyl (PCBs), asbestos, and residual associated with manufactured gas plant sites.

In addition to being held responsible for clean-up costs or incurring fines and newly imposed taxes for noncompliance, a company may be sued for personal injury or property damage under common law. For example, lawsuits may be filed by nearby residents of a contaminated site, or employees may sue for disease allegedly contracted due to exposure to dangerous toxins. These suites are commonly known as "toxic torts." Frequently, toxic tort lawsuits will follow notification by the Environmental Protection Agency (EPA) or a state regulatory authority ordering the company to take certain remedial actions.

There are many problems with developing, for accounting and financial reporting purposes, a reasonable estimate of an environmental obligation. In general terms, the estimation process is difficult because of the long period involved from notification to clean up, including the lack of reliable data, evolving technologies and allocating the total estimated cost. Early investigations and initial estimates of total remediation costs may be unreliable because not enough work has been performed to assess the complexity of the site (the location and number of toxic materials), agreeing how much area needs to be remediated, how clean the site must be after remediation, and the appropriate remediation process. Furthermore, changing regulatory standards and the use of different standards by different EPA regions also add complexity to a cost estimate. In addition, evolving technology may make a remediation process that is available today obsolete in the future when the actual remediation takes place.

Further complicating the estimation process is determining each potentially responsible party's (PRP) share of the total cost. While a participant's share is frequently determined by factors such as weight, volume or toxicity of the substances contributed by each PRP, that is not always the case. Also, a particular PRP's actual share of the ultimate cost may not be known until final settlement is reached. Finally, a PRP may assert that its ultimate liability should be reduced for expected recoveries from other PRP's as well as from owners under contractual indemnification provisions.

The initial event that typically triggers a possible environmental clean-up liability is the action that contributed to the contamination. As noted above, this included a broad range of activities, from having created the waste material to acquiring, years later, a company that is itself, a PRP. An internal review by company personnel or an environmental audit by an outside consultant is one means of identifying a potential clean-up liability, which until notification by the EPA or state authority, constitutes an unasserted claim.

The applicable accounting literature includes SFAS No. 5, "Accounting for Contingencies," and FASB Interpretation No. 14, "Reasonable Estimation of the Amount of a Loss." In addition, guidance is included in the following:

- EITF Issue No. 93-5, "Accounting for Environmental Liabilities."
- FASB Interpretation No. 39, "Offsetting of Amounts Related to Certain Contracts," and the SEC Staff's SAB No. 92.
- FASB's Emerging Issues Task Force (EITF) Issue No. 89-13, "Accounting for the Cost of Asbestos Removal" and Issue No. 90-8, "Capitalization of Costs to Treat Environmental Contamination."

SFAS No. 5 states then an estimated loss from a lost contingency should be accrued by a charge to income if it is probable that a liability has been incurred and the amount of the loss can be reasonably estimated. FIN No. 14, an interpretation of SFAS No. 5, states that if the estimated amount of probable loss is within a range of amounts, and some amount within the range appears to be a better estimate than any other, then the amount should be accrued. If no amount with the probable range is a better estimate, the minimum amount in the range should be accrued.

Under the consensus reached on EITF Issue No. 93-5, an environmental liability should be evaluated independently from any potential claim for recovery. Any loss arising from the recognition of an environmental liability should be reduced by a potential claim for recovery only when that claim is probable of recovery. SAB No. 92 indicates, however, that accounting guidance generally precludes the offsetting of assets and liabilities, except when a right of setoff exists. The general prohibition was recently strengthened by the issuance of FIN No. 39, which is effective for financial statements issued for periods beginning after December 15, 1993. The SEC staff, in SAB No. 92, takes the position that presentation of liabilities net of any claims for recovery will not be appropriate after FIN No. 39 is required to be applied.

The EITF also reached a consensus under Issue No. 93-5 that discounting an environmental liability for a specific clean-up site to reflect the time value of money is appropriate only if the aggregate amount of the obligation and the amount and timing of the cash payments are fixed or reliably determinable for that site. Further, any asset that is recognized relating to a claim for recovery of a liability that is accrued on a discounted basis should be also discounted to reflect the time value of money.

The SEC staff in SAB No. 92 concludes that the discount rate used should be the rate that will produce an amount at which the environmental liability could be settled with a third party. If that rate is not determinable, the discount rate should not exceed the interest rate on monetary assets that are essentially risk-free and have maturities comparable to that on the environmental liability.

SAB No. 92 also sets forth the SEC staff's position that environmental costs meeting the criteria of paragraph 9 of SFAS No. 71 should be presented on the balance sheet as regulatory asset and should not be offset against the liability. Also, a rate-regulated enterprise should not delay recognition of a probable and estimate liability for environmental costs until a regulator determines whether the cost is an allowable cost for ratemaking purposes.

SEC registrants should consider the disclosure requirements of Item 101 (Description of Business), 103 (Legal Proceedings), and 303 (Management's Discussion and Analysis) of Regulations S-K and S-B. The SEC has issued two interpretive releases, Securities Act Release No. 6130 (September 27, 1979) and Financial Reporting Release No. 36 (May 18, 1989) that provide additional disclosure guidance with respect to environmental matters.

(vi) SFAS Nos. 71 and 101—Expanded Footnote Disclosure.   The current relevance of SFAS No. 71 is a much discussed financial reporting topic for rate-regulated enterprises. In SEC staff comment letters, rate-regulated registrants are typically requested to discuss and quantify the effect on the company's financial statements of the application of SFAS No. 71, and what the impact would be of discontinuing SFAS No. 71. Factors that make such discussions meaningful include: (1) deregulation and resulting competition for a variety of services; (2) discounting of approved tariffs; (3) rate designs or new forms of regulation that are not based on the cost of providing utility service; (4) criticism of continual cost deferrals under the provisions of SFAS No. 71 and the financial difficulties experienced by certain entities with significant deferrals; and (5) actual and expected discontinuations of application of SFAS No. 71 by a growing number of entities, particularly telecommunication companies. An example of the footnote disclosure being represented by the SEC staff follows.

Note 1: Summary of Significant Accounting Policies

Regulatory Assets and Liabilities:

The Company is subject to the provisions of Statement of Financial Accounting Standards 71, "Accounting for the Effects of Certain Types of Regulation." Regulatory assets represent probable future revenue to the Company associated with certain costs which will be recovered from customers through the ratemaking process. Regulatory liabilities represent probable future reductions in revenues associated with amounts that are to be credited to customers through the ratemaking process. Regulatory assets and liabilities reflected in the Consolidated Balance Sheets as of December 31 (in thousands) relate to the following:

	19XX	19XX
Deferred Income Taxes	$ XX,XXX	$ XX,XXX
Deferred Income Tax Credits	(X,XXX)	(X,XXX)
Energy Efficiency Costs	XX,XXX	XX,XXX
Order 636 Transition Costs	XX,XXX	X,XXX
Debt Financing Costs	XX,XXX	X,XXX
Plant Costs	XX,XXX	XX,XXX
Postretirement Benefit Costs	XX,XXX	XX,XXX
Nuclear Plant Outage Costs	X,XXX	—
Rate Case Costs	XXX	X,XXX
Environmental Costs	X,XXX	X,XXX
Overrecovered Fuel Adjustment Clause	(X,XXX)	(X,XXX)
	$XXX,XXX	$XXX,XXX

As of December 31, 19XX, $XXX,XXX of the Company's regulatory assets and all of its regulatory liabilities are being reflected in rates charged to customers over periods ranging from 5 to 28 years. The Company intends to request recovery of its remaining regulatory assets in a general rate case filing expected in 19XX. For additional information regarding deferred income taxes, Order 636 transition costs, environmental costs and postretirement benefit costs, see footnotes 3, 4(e), 4(f) and 12, respectively.

If a portion of the Company's operations becomes no longer subject to the provisions of SFAS No. 71, a write off of related regulatory assets and liabilities would be required, unless some form of transition cost recovery (refund) continues through rates established and collected for the Company's remaining regulated operations. In addition, the Company would be required to determine any impairment to the carrying costs of deregulated plant and inventory assets.

27.11 SOURCES AND SUGGESTED REFERENCES

Accounting Principles Board, "Accounting for the "Investment Credit,"' APB Opinion No. 4, AICPA, New York, 1964.

———, "Accounting for Income Taxes," APB Opinion No. 11, AICPA, New York, 1967.

———, "Accounting Changes," APB Opinion No. 20, AICPA, New York, 1971.

Amble, Joan L., and Cassel, Jules M., "A Guide to Implementation of Statement 87 on Employers' Accounting for Pensions," FASB, Stamford, CT, 1986.

American Institute of Certified Public Accountants, "Restatement and Revision of Accounting Research Bulletins," Accounting Research Bulletin No. 43, AICPA, New York, 1953.

———, "Declining-Balance Depreciation," Accounting Research Bulletin No. 44, AICPA, New York, July 1958.

———, "Consolidated Financial Statements," Accounting Research Bulletin No. 51, AICPA, New York, August 1959.

Financial Accounting Standards Board, "Official Minutes of the Emerging Issues Task Force Meeting," FASB, Norwalk, CT, February 23, 1989.

———, "Accounting for Contingencies," Statement of Financial Accounting Standards No. 5, FASB, Stamford, CT, 1975.

———, "Prior Period Adjustments," Statement of Financial Accounting Standards No. 16, FASB, Stamford, CT, 1977.

———, "Capitalization of Interest Cost," Statement of Financial Accounting Standards No. 34, FASB, Stamford, CT, 1979.

———, "Accounting for the Effects of Certain Types of Regulation," Statement of Financial Accounting Standards No. 71, FASB, Stamford, CT, 1982.

———, "Accounting for OPEB Costs by Rate-Regulated Enterprises," Issue No. 92-12, Financial Accounting Standards Board, Emerging Issues Task Force, Norwalk, CT, January 1993.

———, "Employers' Accounting for Postretirement Benefits Other Than Pension," Statement of Financial Accounting Standards No. 106, FASB, Stamford, CT, December 1990.

———, "Accounting for Regulatory Assets," Issue No. 93-4, Financial Accounting Standards Board, Emerging Issues Task Force, Norwalk, CT, March 1993.

———, "Accounting for Income Taxes," Statement of Financial Accounting Standards No. 109, FASB, Norwalk, CT, February 1992.

———, "Accounting by Rate-Regulated Utilities for the Effects of Certain Alternative Revenue Programs," Issue No. 92-7, Financial Accounting Standards Board, Emerging Issues Task Force, Norwalk, CT, July 1992.

———, "Accounting for Environmental Liabilities," Issue No. 93-5, Financial Accounting Standards Board, Emerging Issues Task Force, Norwalk, CT, March 1993.

———, "Offsetting of Amounts Related to Certain Contracts," Interpretation No. 39, Financial Accounting Standards Board, Norwalk, CT, March 1992.

———, Staff Accounting Bulletin No. 92, SEC, Washington, DC, June 1993.

————, "Accounting for the Cost of Asbestos Removal," Issue No. 89-13, Financial Accounting Standards Board, Emerging Issues Task Force, Norwalk, CT, October 1989.

————, "Capitalization of Costs to Treat Environmental Contamination," Issue No. 90-8, Financial Accounting Standards Board, Emerging Issues Task Force, Norwalk, CT, July 1990.

————, "Regulated Enterprises—Accounting for Abandonments and Disallowances of Plant Costs," Statement of Financial Accounting Standards No. 90, FASB, Stamford, CT, 1986.

————, "Regulated Enterprises—Accounting for Phase-in Plans," Statement of Financial Accounting Standards No. 92, FASB, Stamford, CT, 1987.

————, "Regulated Enterprises—Accounting for the Discontinuation of Application of FASB Statement No. 71," Statement of Financial Accounting Standards No. 101, FASB, Norwalk, CT, 1988.

————, "Computation of a Loss on an Abandonment," FASB Technical Bulletin No. 87-2, FASB, Stamford, CT, December 1987.

————, "Accounting for the Impairment of Long-Lived Assets and for Long-Lived Assets to Be Disposed Of," Statement of Financial Accounting Standards No. 121, FASB, Norwalk, CT, March 1995.

————, "Accounting for Certain Liabilities Related to Closure or Removal of Long-Lived Assets," Proposed Statement of Financial Accounting Standards, FASB, Norwalk, CT, February 1996.

Securities and Exchange Commission, "Interpretation Describing Disclosure Concerning Expected Future Costs of Storing Spent Nuclear Fuel and of Decommissioning Nuclear Electric Generating Plants," Staff Accounting Bulletin No. 19, SEC, Washington, DC, January 1978.

————, "Financing by Electric Utilities Through Use of Construction Intermediaries," Staff Accounting Bulletin No. 28, SEC, Washington, DC, December 1978.

————, "Utilities—Classification of Disallowed Costs or Costs of Abandoned Plants," Staff Accounting Bulletin No. 72, SEC, Washington, DC, November 1987.

CHAPTER 28

STATE AND LOCAL GOVERNMENT ACCOUNTING

Andrew J. Blossom, CPA
KPMG Peat Marwick LLP
Andrew Gottschalk, CPA
KPMG Peat Marwick LLP
John R. Miller, CPA
KPMG Peat Marwick LLP

CONTENTS

28.1 INTRODUCTION

The rapid changes that have occurred in the environment of state and local governments during the past few years have prompted sweeping changes to governmental accounting practice and theory. The evolution of governmental accounting and reporting standards has made great strides since the formation of the GASB and the Single Audit Act of 1984. Related to the changes is greater scrutiny by federal and state agencies as they begin to realize the importance of audit quality in the governmental environment. Governmental enterprises are no longer the "shoebox" operations imagined by many people. Rather, government is a large business—a very large business. Officials in government need to be and are much more sophisticated now than similar personnel were only a few years ago. In other words, the increasing complexity of the governmental environment, the increasing demands for public accountability, and the challenges and opportunities that face today's governments require accounting systems that provide fast, accurate, and timely information to the government's decision makers.

Going forward and dealing with the challenges of issues like deteriorating infrastructure, an aging work force, and public health care, including the AIDS epidemic, are likely to be key concerns of the individuals who operate the state and local governments. However, the nature and organization of a government's daily activities form an important foundation that must be understood in order to deal with the greater challenges of the future.

28.2 THE NATURE AND ORGANIZATION OF STATE AND LOCAL GOVERNMENT ACTIVITIES

(a) STRUCTURE OF GOVERNMENT.   For the most part, government is structured on three levels: federal, state, and local. This chapter deals only with state and local governments.

States are specific identifiable entities in their own right, but accounting at the state level is associated more often than not with the individual state functions, such as departments of revenue, retirement systems, turnpike authorities, and housing finance agencies.

Local governments exist as political subdivisions of states, and the rules governing their types and operation are different in each of the 50 states. There are, however, three basic types of local governmental units: **general purpose local governments** (counties, cities, towns, villages, and townships), **special purpose local governments,** and **authorities.**

The distinguishing characteristics of general purpose local governments are that they:

- Have broad powers in providing a variety of government services, for example, public safety, fire prevention, public works.
- Have general taxing and bonding authority.
- Are headed by elected officials.

Special purpose local governments are established to provide specific services or construction. They may or may not be contiguous with one or more general purpose local governments.

Authorities and agencies are similar to special purpose governments except that they have no taxing power and are expected to operate with their own revenues. They typically can issue only revenue bonds, not general obligations bonds.

(b) OBJECTIVES OF GOVERNMENT.   The purpose of government is to provide the citizenry with the highest level of services possible given the available financial resources and the legal requirements under which it operates. The services are provided as a result of decisions made during a budgeting process that considers the desired level and quality of services. Resources are then made available through property taxes, sales taxes, income taxes, general and categorical grants from the federal and state governments, charges for services, fines, licenses, and other sources. However, there is generally no direct relationship between the cost of the services rendered to an individual, and the amount that the individual pays in taxes, fines, fees, and so on.

Governmental units also conduct operations that are financed and operated in a manner similar to private business enterprises, where the intent is that the costs of providing the goods or services be financed or recovered primarily through charges to the users. In such situations, governments have many of the features of ordinary business operations.

(c) ORGANIZATION OF GOVERNMENT.   A government's organization depends on its constitution (state level) or charter (local level) and on general and special statutes of state and local legislatures. When governments were simpler and did not provide as many services as they do today, there was less tendency for centralization. The **commission** and **weak mayor** forms of governments were common. The financial function was typically divided among several individuals.

As government has become more complex, however, the need for strong professional management and for centralization of authority and responsibility has grown. There has been a trend toward the **strong mayor** and **council-manager** forms of government. In these forms, a chief financial officer, usually called the **director of finance** or **controller,** is responsible for maintaining the financial records and preparing financial reports; assisting the CEO in the preparation of the budget; performing treasury functions such as collecting revenues, managing cash, managing investments, and managing debt; and overseeing the tax assessment function. Other functions that may report to the director of finance are purchasing, data processing, and personnel administration.

Local governments are also making greater use of the **internal audit** process. In the past, the emphasis by governmental internal auditors was on **preaudit,** that is, reviewing invoices and other documents during processing for propriety and accuracy. The internal auditors reported to the director of finance. Today, however, governmental internal auditors have been removing themselves from the preaudit function by transferring this responsibility to the department responsible for processing the transactions. They have started to provide the typical internal audit function, that is, conducting reviews to ensure the reliability of data and the safeguarding of assets, and to become involved in **performance auditing** (i.e., reviewing the efficiency and effectiveness of the government's operations). They have also started to report, for professional (as opposed to administrative) purposes, to the CEO or directly to the governing board. Finally, internal auditors are becoming more actively involved in the financial statement audit and single audit of their government.

(d) SPECIAL CHARACTERISTICS OF GOVERNMENT.   Several characteristics associated with governments have influenced the development of governmental accounting principles and practices:

- Governments do not have any owners or proprietors in the commercial sense. Accordingly, measurement of earnings attributable or accruing to the direct benefit of an owner is not a relevant accounting concept for governments.
- Governments frequently receive substantial **financial inflows** for both operating and capital purposes from sources other than revenues and investment earnings, such as taxes and grants.
- Governments frequently obtain **financial inflows** subject to legally binding **restrictions** that prohibit or seriously limit the use of these resources for other than the intended purpose.
- A government's authority to raise and expend money results from the adoption of a **budget** that, by law, usually must balance (e.g., the estimated revenues plus any prior years' surpluses need to be sufficient to cover the projected expenditures).
- The power to raise revenues through taxes, licenses, fees, and fines is generally defined by law.
- There are usually restrictions related to the tax base that govern the purpose, amount, and type of indebtedness that can be issued.
- Expenditures are usually regulated less than revenues and debt, but they can be made only within approved budget categories and must comply with specified purchasing procedures when applicable.

- State laws may dictate the local government accounting policies and systems.
- State laws commonly specify the type and frequency of financial statements to be submitted to the state and to the government's constituency.
- Federal law, the Single Audit Act of 1984, defines the audit requirements for state and local governments receiving more than $100,000 in federal financial assistance.

In short, the environment in which governments operate is complex and legal requirements have a significant influence on their accounting and financial reporting practices.

28.3 SOURCE OF ACCOUNTING PRINCIPLES FOR STATE AND LOCAL GOVERNMENT ACCOUNTING

Governmental accounting principles are not a complete and separate body of accounting principles, but rather are part of the whole body of GAAP. Since the accounting profession's standard-setting bodies have been concerned primarily with the accounting needs of profit-seeking organizations, these principles have been defined primarily by groups formed by the state and local governments. In 1934, the **National Committee on Municipal Accounting** published "A Tentative Outline—Principles of Municipal Accounting." In 1968, the **National Committee on Governmental Accounting** (the successor organization) published *Governmental Accounting, Auditing, and Financial Reporting* (GAAFR), which was widely used as a source of government accounting principles. The AICPA Industry Audit Guide, "Audits of State and Local Governmental Units," published in 1974, stated that the accounting principles outlined in the 1968 GAAFR constituted GAAP for government entities.

The financial difficulties experienced by many governments in the mid-1970s led to a call for a review and modification of the accounting and financial reporting practices used by governments. Laws were introduced in Congress, but never enacted, that would have given the federal government the authority to establish governmental accounting principles. The FASB, responding to pressures, commissioned a research study to define and explain the issues associated with accounting for all nonbusiness enterprises, including governments. This study was completed in 1978 and the Board developed SFAC No. 4 for nonbusiness organizations. The statement defined nonbusiness organizations, the users of the statements, the financial information needs of these users, and the information that is necessary to meet these needs.

(a) NATIONAL COUNCIL ON GOVERNMENTAL ACCOUNTING (NCGA). The NCGA was the successor of the National Committee reconstituted as a permanent organization. One of its first projects was to "restate," that is, update, clarify, amplify, and reorder the GAAFR to incorporate pertinent aspects of "Audits of State and Local Governmental Units." The restatement was published in March 1979, as NCGA Statement 1, "Governmental Accounting and Financial Reporting Principles." Shortly thereafter, the AICPA Committee on State and Local Government Accounting recognized NCGA Statement 1 as authoritative and agreed to amend the Industry Audit Guide accordingly. This restatement was completed, and a new guide was published in 1986. Thus NCGA Statement 1 became the primary reference source for the accounting principles unique to governmental accounting. However, in areas not unique to governmental accounting, the complete body of GAAP still needed to be considered.

(b) GOVERNMENTAL ACCOUNTING STANDARDS BOARD (GASB). In 1984, the Financial Accounting Foundation (FAF) established the GASB as the primary standard setter for GAAP for governmental entities. Under the jurisdictional agreement GASB has the primary responsibility for establishing accounting and reporting principles for government entities. GASB's first action was to issue Statement No. 1, "Authoritative Status of NCGA Pronouncements and AICPA Industry Audit Guide," which recognized the NCGA's statements and interpretations and the AICPA's audit guide as authoritative. The Statement also recognized the pronouncements of the FASB issued prior to the date of the agreement as applicable to governments. FASB pronouncements issued after the organization of GASB do not become effective unless GASB specifically adopts them.

The GASB has operated under this jurisdictional arrangement since 1984. However, the arrangement came under scrutiny during the GASB's mandatory 5-year review conducted in 1988. The Committee to Review Structure of Governmental Accounting Standards released its widely read report in January 1989 on the results of its review and proposed to the FAF, among other recommendations, a new jurisdictional arrangement and GAAP hierarchy for governments. These two recommendations prompted a great deal of controversy within the industry. The issue revolved around the Committee's recommended jurisdictional arrangement for the separately issued financial statements of certain "special-entities." (Special entities are organizations that can either be privately or governmentally owned and include colleges and universities, hospitals, and utilities.) The Committee recommended that FASB be the primary accounting standard-setter for these special entities when they issue separate, stand-alone financial statements and that GASB be allowed to require the presentation of "additional data" in these stand-alone statements. This arrangement would allow for greater comparability between entities in the same industry (e.g., utilities) regardless of whether the entities were privately or governmentally owned and still allow government-owned entities to meet their "public accountability" reporting objective.

This recommendation and a subsequent compromise recommendation were unacceptable to many and especially to the various public interest groups such as the Government Finance Officers Association (GFOA) who, 10 months after the Committee's report, began discussions to establish a new body to set standards for state and local government. These actions prompted the FAF to consider whether a standard-setting schism was in the interest of the public and the users of financial statements. Based on this consideration, the FAF decided that the jurisdictional arrangement established in 1984 should remain intact.

In response to the jurisdictional arrangement described above, the AICPA issued Statement on Auditing Standards No. 69, *The Meaning of Present Fairly in Conformity with Generally Accepted Accounting Principles in the Independent Auditor's Report,* which creates a hierarchy of GAAP specifically for state and local governments. SAS No. 69 raises AICPA SOPs and audit and accounting guides to a level of authority above that of industry practice. As a result, FASB pronouncements will not apply to state and local governments unless the GASB issues a standard incorporating them into GAAP for state and local government. In September 1993, the GASB issued Statement No. 20, "Accounting and Financial Reporting for Proprietary Funds and Other Governmental Entities That Use Proprietary Fund Accounting." The Statement provides interim guidance on business-type accounting and financial reporting for proprietary activities, pending further research by the GASB that is expected to result in the issuance of one or more pronouncements on the accounting and financial reporting model for proprietary activities.

Statement No. 20 requires proprietary activities to apply all applicable GASB Statements as well as FASB pronouncements, Accounting Principles Board Opinions, and Accounting Research Bulletins issued on or before November 30, 1989, unless those pronouncements conflict or contradict with a GASB pronouncement. A proprietary activity may also apply, at its option, all FASB pronouncements issued after November 30, 1989, except those that conflict or contradict with a GASB pronouncement.

The GASB subsequently issued Statement No. 29, "The Use of Not-for-Profit Accounting and Financial Reporting Principles by Governmental Entities," which amended Statement No. 20 to indicate that proprietary activities could apply only those FASB statements that were developed for business enterprises. FASB statements and interpretations whose provisions are limited to not-for-profit organizations or address issues primarily of concern to those organizations may not be applied. These actions, along with the increased activity of the FASB in setting standards for not-for-profit organizations, have resulted in increasing differences in GAAP between nongovernmental entities and state and local governments.

These differences also highlight the importance of determining whether a particular entity is a state or local government. While it is obvious that states, cities, and counties are governments, other units of government are less clear. Is a university considered a government if it is supported 70% by taxes allocated by the state? What if the percentage is only 15%? If a hospital is created by a county but the county has no continuing involvement with the hospital, is the hospital a government? The GASB acknowledged these concerns in the Basis for Conclusions of Statement No. 29 in stating:

> Some respondents believe that the fundamental issue underlying this Statement—identifying those entities that should apply the GAAP hierarchy applicable to state and local governmental entities—will continue to be troublesome until there is an authoritative definition of such "governmental entities." The Board agrees—but does not have the authority to unilaterally establish a definition—and intends to continue to explore alternatives for resolving the issue.

As indicated, this determination is not currently addressed in professional literature. The decision as to whether a particular entity should follow the hierarchy for state and local governments or nongovernmental entities is a matter of professional judgment based on the individual facts and circumstances for the entity in question.

28.4 GOVERNMENTAL ACCOUNTING PRINCIPLES AND PRACTICES

(a) SIMILARITIES TO PRIVATE SECTOR ACCOUNTING.   Since the accounting principles and practices of governments are part of the whole body of GAAP, certain accounting concepts and conventions are as applicable to governmental entities as they are to accounting in other industries:

- *Consistency.* Identical transactions should be recorded in the same manner both during a period and from period to period.
- *Conservatism.* The uncertainties that surround the preparation of financial statements are reflected in a general tendency toward early recognition of unfavorable events and minimization of the amount of net assets and net income.
- *Historical Cost.* Amounts should be recognized in the financial statements at the historical cost to the reporting entity. Changes in the general purchasing power should not be recognized in the basic financial statements.
- *Matching.* The financial statements should provide for a matching, but in government it is a matching of revenues and expenditures with a time period to ensure that revenues and the expenditures they finance are reported in the same period.
- *Reporting Entity.* The focus of the financial report is the economic activities of a discrete individual entity for which there is a reporting responsibility.
- *Materiality.* Financial reporting is concerned only with significant information.
- *Full Disclosure.* Financial statements must contain all information necessary to understand the presentation of financial position and results of operations and to prevent them from being misleading.

(b) USERS AND USES OF FINANCIAL REPORTS.   Users of the financial statements of a governmental unit are not identical to users of a business entity's financial statements. The GASB Concepts Statement No. 1 identifies three groups of primary users of external governmental financial reports:

- *Those to Whom Government Is Primarily Accountable—The Citizenry.* The citizenry group includes citizens (whether they are classified as taxpayers, voters, or service recipients), the media, advocate groups, and public finance researchers. This user group is concerned with obtaining the maximum amount of service with a minimum amount of taxes and wants to know where the government obtains its resources and how those resources are used.

- *Those Who Directly Represent the Citizens—Legislative and Oversight Bodies.* The legislative and oversight officials group includes members of state legislatures, county commissions, city councils, boards of trustees, and school boards, and those executive branch officials with oversight responsibility over other levels of government. These groups need timely warning of the development of situations that require corrective action, financial information that can serve as a basis for judging management performance, and financial information on which to base future plans and policies.

- *Those Who Lend or Participate in the Lending Process—Investors and Creditors.* Investors and creditors include individual and institutional investors and creditors, municipal security underwriters, bond-rating agencies (Moody's Investors Service, and Standard & Poor's, etc.), bond insurers, and financial institutions.

The uses of a government's financial reports are also different. GASB Concepts Statement No. 1 also indicates that governmental financial reporting should provide information to assist users in (1) assessing accountability and (2) making economic, social, and political decisions by:

- *Comparing Actual Financial Results with the Legally Adopted Budget.* All three user groups are interested in comparing original or modified budgets with actual results to get some assurance that spending mandates have been compiled with and that resources have been used for the intended purposes.

- *Assisting in Determining Compliance with Finance-Related Laws, Rules, and Regulations.* In addition to the legally mandated budgetary and fund controls other legal restrictions may control governmental actions. Some examples are bond covenants, grant restrictions, and taxing and debt limits. Financial reports help demonstrate compliance with these laws, rules, and regulations.

  Citizens are concerned that governments adhere to these regulations because noncompliance may indicate fiscal irresponsibility and could have severe financial consequences such as acceleration of debt payments, disallowance of questioned costs, or loss of grants.

  Legislative and oversight officials are also concerned with compliance as a follow-up to the budget formulation process.

  Investors and creditors are interested in the government's compliance with debt covenants and restrictions designed to protect their investment.

- *Assisting in Evaluating Efficiency and Effectiveness.* Citizen groups and legislators, in particular, want information about service efforts, costs, and accomplishments of a governmental entity. This information, when combined with information from other sources, helps users assess the economy, efficiency, and effectiveness of government and may help form a basis for voting or funding decisions.

- *Assessing Financial Condition and Results of Operations.* Financial reports are commonly used to assess a state or local government's financial condition, that is, its financial position and its ability to continue to provide services and meet its obligations as they come due.

  Investors and creditors need information about available and likely future financial resources, actual and contingent liabilities, and the overall debt position of a government to evaluate the government's ability to continue to provide resources for long-term debt service.

  Citizens' groups are concerned with financial condition when evaluating the likelihood of tax or service fee increased.

Legislative and oversight officials need to assess the overall financial condition, including debt structure and funds available for appropriation, when developing both capital and operating budget and program recommendations.

With the users and the uses of financial reports clearly defined, the GASB developed the following overall objectives of governmental financial reporting:

1. Financial reporting should assist in fulfilling a government's duty to be publicly accountable and should enable users to assess that accountability by:
   a. Providing information to determine whether current-year revenues were sufficient to pay for current-year services.
   b. Demonstrating whether resources were obtained and used in accordance with the entity's legally adopted budget and compliance with other finance-related legal or contractual requirements.
   c. Providing information to assist users in assessing the service efforts, costs, and accomplishments of the governmental entity.
2. Financial reporting should assist users in evaluating the operating results of the governmental entity for the year by providing information:
   a. About sources and uses of financial resources.
   b. About how the governmental entity financed its activities and met its cash requirements.
   c. Necessary to determine whether the entity's financial position improved or deteriorated as a result of the year's operations.
3. Financial reporting should assist users in assessing the level of services that can be provided by the governmental entity and its ability to meet its obligations as they become due by:
   a. Providing information about the financial position and condition of a governmental entity. Financial reporting should provide information about resources and obligations, both actual and contingent, current and noncurrent, and about tax sources, tax limitations, tax burdens, and debt limitations.
   b. Providing information about a governmental entity's physical and other nonfinancial resources having useful lives that extend beyond the current year, including information that can be used to assess the service potential of those resources.
   c. Disclosing legal or contractual restrictions on resources and risks of potential loss of resources.

In April 1994, the GASB issued Concepts Statement No. 2, "Service Efforts and Accomplishments Reporting," which expands on the consideration of service efforts and accomplishments (SEA) reporting included in Concepts Statement No. 1. The GASB believes that the government's duty to be publicly accountable requires the presentation of SEA information. Concepts Statement No. 2 identifies the objective of SEA reporting as providing "more complete information about a governmental entity's performance that can be provided by the operating statement, balance sheet, and budgetary comparison statements and schedules to assist users in assessing the economy, efficiency, and effectiveness of services provided." The Concepts Statement also indicates SEA information should meet the characteristics of relevance, understandability, comparability, timeliness, consistency, and reliability. The GASB acknowledges the need for continued experimentation and development of SEA measures prior to the issuance of SEA reporting standards.

(c) SUMMARY STATEMENT OF PRINCIPLES. Because governments operate under different conditions and have different reporting objectives than commercial entities, 12 basic principles applicable to government accounting and reporting have been developed. These principles are generally recognized as being essential to effective management control and financial reporting. In other words, understanding these principles and how they operate is extremely important to the understanding of governments. The 12 principles defined for state and local government in GASB Codification § 1100 are as follows:

(i) Accounting and Reporting Capabilities.   A governmental accounting system must make it possible both (1) to present fairly the financial position and results of financial operations of the funds and account groups of the governmental unit in conformity with GAAP, which include full disclosure; and (2) to determine and demonstrate compliance with finance-related legal and contractual provisions.

(ii) Fund Accounting Systems.   Governmental accounting systems should be organized and operated on a fund basis. A "fund" is defined as a fiscal and accounting entity with a self-balancing set of accounts recording cash and other financial resources, together with all related liabilities and residual equities or balances, and changes therein, which are segregated for the purpose of carrying on specific activities or attaining certain objectives in accordance with special regulations, restrictions, or limitations.

(iii) Types of Funds.   The following types of funds should be used by state and local governments.

Governmental Funds

1. *The General Fund.* To account for all financial resources except those required to be accounted for in another fund.
2. *Special Revenue Funds.* To account for the proceeds for specific revenue sources (other than expendable trusts, or major capital projects) that are legally restricted to expenditures for specified purposes.
3. *Capital Projects Funds.* To account for financial resources to be used for the acquisition or construction of major capital facilities (other than those financed by proprietary funds and trust funds).
4. *Debt Service Funds.* To account for the accumulation of resources for, and the payment of, general long-term debt principal and interest.

The GASB Codification also discusses special assessment funds. However, the issuance of GASB Statement No. 6, "Accounting and Financial Reporting for Special Assessments," in January 1987, eliminated the special assessment fund type for financial reporting purposes. The Statement does, however, allow special assessment funds to exist for budget purposes.

Proprietary Funds

1. *Enterprise Funds.* To account for operations (1) that are financed and operated in a manner similar to private business enterprises, where the intent of the governing body is that the cost (expenses, including depreciation) of providing goods or services to the general public, on a continuing basis be financed or recovered primarily through user charges; or (2) where the governing body has decided that periodic determination of revenues earned, expenses incurred, and/or net income is appropriate for capital maintenance, public policy, management control, accountability, or other purposes.
2. *Internal Service Funds.* To account for the financing of goods or services provided by one department or agency to other departments or agencies of the governmental unit, or to other governmental units, on a cost-reimbursement basis.

Fiduciary Funds. Trust and agency funds account for assets held by a governmental unit in a trustee capacity or as an agent for individuals, private organizations, other governmental units, and other funds. These include (1) expendable trust funds, (2) nonexpendable trust funds, (3) pension trust funds, and (4) agency funds.

(iv) Number of Funds. Governmental units should establish and maintain those funds required by law and sound financial administration. Only the minimum number of funds consistent with legal and operating requirements should be established, however, since unnecessary funds result in inflexibility, undue complexity, and inefficient financial administration.

(v) Accounting for Fixed Assets and Long-Term Liabilities. A clear distinction should be made between (1) proprietory and similar trust fund fixed assets and general fixed assets and (2) proprietory and similar trust fund long-term liabilities and general long-term debt.

1. Fixed assets related to specific proprietary funds or similar trust funds should be accounted for through those funds. All other fixed assets of a governmental unit should be accounted for through the general fixed assets account group.
2. Long-term liabilities of proprietary funds and trust funds should be accounted for through those funds. All other unmatured, general long-term liabilities of the governmental unit should be accounted for through the general long-term debt account group.

(vi) Valuation of Fixed Assets. Fixed assets should be accounted for at cost or, if the cost is not practicably determinable, at estimated cost. Donated fixed assets should be recorded at their estimated fair value at the time received.

(vii) Depreciation of Fixed Assets. Depreciation of general fixed assets should not be recorded in the accounts of governmental funds. Depreciation of general fixed assets may be recorded in cost accounting systems or calculated for cost funding analyses, and accumulated depreciation may be recorded in the general fixed assets account group.
   Depreciation of fixed assets accounted for in a proprietary fund should be recorded in the accounts of that fund. Depreciation is also recognized in trust funds where expenses, net income, and/or capital maintenance are measured.

(viii) Accrual Basis in Governmental Accounting. The modified accrual or accrual basis of accounting, as appropriate, should be used in measuring financial position and operating results.

1. Governmental fund revenues and expenditures should be recognized on the modified accrual basis. Revenues should be recognized in the accounting period in which they become available and measurable. Expenditures should be recognized in the accounting period in which the fund liability is incurred, if measurable, except for unmatured interest on general long-term debt, which should be recognized when due.
2. Proprietary fund revenues and expenses should be recognized on the accrual basis. Revenues should be recognized in the accounting period in which they are earned and become measurable; expenses should be recognized in the period incurred, if measurable.
3. Fiduciary fund revenues and expenses or expenditures (as appropriate) should be recognized on the basis consistent with the fund's accounting measurement objective. Nonexpendable trust and pension trust funds should be accounted for on the accrual basis; expendable trust funds, on the modified accrual basis. Agency fund assets and liabilities should be accounted for on the modified accrual basis.
4. Transfers should be recognized in the accounting period in which the interfund receivable and payable arise.

(ix) Budgeting, Budgetary Control, and Budgetary Reporting.   An annual budget should be adopted by every governmental unit. The accounting system should provide the basis for appropriate budgetary control. Budgetary comparisons should be included in the appropriate financial statements and schedules for governmental funds for which an annual budget has been adopted.

(x) Transfer, Revenue, Expenditure, and Expense Account Classification.   Interfund transfers and proceeds of general long-term debt issues should be classified separately from fund revenues and expenditures or expenses.

Governmental fund revenues should be classified by fund and source. Expenditures should be classified by fund, function (or program), organization unit, activity, character, and principal classes of objects.

Proprietary fund revenues and expenses should be classified in essentially the same manner as those of similar business organizations, functions, or activities.

(xi) Common Terminology and Classification.   A common terminology and classification should be used consistently throughout the budget, the accounts, and the financial reports of each fund.

(xii) Interim and Annual Financial Reports.   Appropriate interim financial statements and reports of financial position, operating results, and other pertinent information should be prepared to facilitate management control of financial operations, legislative oversight, and, where necessary or desired, external reporting.

A comprehensive annual financial report covering all funds and account groups of the governmental unit should be prepared and published, including appropriate combined, combining, and individual fund statements; notes to the financial statements; required supplementary information; schedules; narrative explanations; and statistical tables.

General purpose financial statements may be issued separately from the comprehensive annual financial report. Such statements should include the basic financial statements, notes to the financial statements, and any required supplementary information essential to a fair presentation of financial position and operating results and cash flows of proprietary funds and nonexpendable trust funds.

(d) DISCUSSION OF THE PRINCIPLES.   To enable readers to more fully understand the 12 principles, a discussion of each of the principles appears below.

(e) LEGAL COMPLIANCE.   **Principle 1** of governmental accounting (GASB Codification § 1100.101) states:

> A governmental accounting system must make it possible both: (a) to present fairly and with full disclosure the financial position and results of financial operations of the funds and account groups of the governmental unit in conformity with generally accepted accounting principles; and (b) to determine and demonstrate compliance with finance-related legal and contractual provision.

Several state and local governments have accounting requirements that differ from GAAP; for example, cash basis accounting is required, and capital projects must be accounted for in the general fund. Because of this situation, the **legal compliance** principle used to be interpreted as meaning that, when the legal requirements for a particular entity differed from GAAP, the legal requirements became GAAP for the entity. This interpretation is no longer viewed as sound. When GAAP and legal requirements conflict, governments should present their basic financial report in accordance with GAAP and, if the legal requirements differ materially from GAAP, the legally required reports can be published as supplemental data to the basic financial report or, if these differences are extreme, it may be preferable to publish a separate legal basis report.

However, conflicts that arise between GAAP and legal provisions do not require maintaining two sets of accounting records. Rather, the accounting records typically would be maintained in accordance with the legal requirements but would include sufficient additional information to permit preparation of reports in accordance with GAAP.

(f) FUND ACCOUNTING. **Principle 2,** fund accounting, is used by governments because of (1) legally binding restrictions that prohibit or seriously limit the use of much of a government's resources for other than the purposes for which the resources were obtained, and (2) the importance of reporting the accomplishment of various objectives for which the resources were entrusted to the government.

GASB Codification § 1100.102, defines a fund for accounting purposes as:

> A fiscal and accounting entity with a self-balancing set of accounts recording cash and other financial resources, together with all related liabilities and residual equities or balances, and changes therein, which are segregated for the purposes of carrying on specific activities or obtaining certain objectives in accordance with special regulations, restrictions, or limitations.

Thus a fund may include accounts for assets, liabilities, fund balance or retained earnings, revenues, expenditures, or expenses. Accounts may also exist for appropriations and encumbrances, depending on the budgeting system used.

(g) TYPES AND NUMBER OF FUNDS. Because of the various nature of activities carried on by government, it is often important to be able to account for certain activities separately from others (i.e., when required by law). **Principles 3 and 4** define seven basic fund types in which to account for various governmental activities. The purpose and operation of each fund type differs, and it is important to understand these differences and why they exist. Every fund maintained by a government should be classified into one of these seven fund types:

- General fund.
- Special revenue funds.
- Debt service funds.
- Capital projects funds.
- Enterprise funds.
- Internal service funds.
- Trust and agency funds.

The general fund, special revenue funds, debt service funds, and capital projects funds are considered **governmental funds** since they record the transactions associated with the general services of a local governmental unit (i.e., police, public works, fire prevention) that are provided to all citizens and are supported primarily by general revenues. For these funds, the primary concerns, from the financial statement reader's point of view, are the types and amounts of resources that have been made available to the governmental unit and the uses to which they have been put.

The enterprise funds and internal services funds are considered **proprietary funds** because they account for activities for which the determination of net income is important.

The trust and agency funds are considered **fiduciary funds.** There are basically three types of trust funds: expendable trust funds that operate in a manner similar to governmental funds, nonexpendable trust funds and pension trust funds that operate in a manner similar to proprietary funds, and agency funds that account for funds held by a government entity in an agent capacity. Agency funds consist of assets and liabilities only and do not involve the measurement of operations.

Although a government should establish and maintain those funds required by law and sound financial administration, it should set up only the minimum number of funds consistent with legal and operating requirements. The maintenance of unnecessary funds results in inflexibility, undue complexity, and inefficient financial administration. For instance, in the past, the proceeds of specific revenue sources or resources that financed specific activities as required by law or administrative regulation had to be accounted for in a special revenue fund. However, governmental resources restricted to purposes usually financed through the general fund should be accounted for in the general fund, provided that all legal requirements can be satisfied. Examples include state grants received by an entity for special education. If a separate fund is not legally required, the grant revenues and the grant-related expenditures should be accounted for in the fund for which they are to be used.

Another way to minimize funds is by accounting for debt service payments in the general fund and not establishing a separate debt service fund unless it is legally mandated or resources are actually being accumulated for future debt service payments (i.e., for term bonds or in sinking funds).

Furthermore, one or more identical accounts for separate funds should be combined in the accounting system, particularly for funds that are similar in nature or are in the same fund group. For example, the cash accounts for all special revenue funds may be combined, provided that the integrity of each fund is preserved through a distinct equity account for each fund.

(i) General Fund.   The **general fund** accounts for the revenues and expenditures not accounted for in other funds and finances most of the current normal functions of governmental units—general government, public safety, highways, sanitation and waste removal, health and welfare, culture, and recreation. It is usually the largest and most important accounting activity for state and local governments. Property taxes are often the principal source of general fund revenues, but substantial revenues may also be received from other financing sources.

The general fund balance sheet is typically limited to current assets and current liabilities. The GASB Codification emphasizes this practice by using the terms **expendable assets** and **current liabilities** when describing governmental funds, of which the general fund is one. Thus the fund balance in the general fund is considered available to finance current operations.

A governmental unit, however, often makes long-term **advances** to independent governmental agencies, such as redevelopment authorities or housing agencies, or provides the capital necessary to establish an internal service fund. The advances are recorded in the general fund as an advance receivable. Although in most cases collectibility is assured, repayment may extend over a number of years. The inclusion of a noncurrent asset in the general fund results in a portion of the general fund's fund balance not being readily available to finance current operations.

To reflect the unavailability of an advance to finance current activities, a fund balance reserve is established to segregate a portion of the fund balance from the general fund in an amount equal to the advance that is not considered currently available. Establishing this reserve does not require a charge to operations; rather, it is a segregation of the fund balance in the available general fund and is established by debiting unreserved fund balance and crediting reserved fund balance. The reserve is reported in the fund balance section of the balance sheet.

(ii) Special Revenue Funds.   **Special revenue funds** should be established to account for the proceeds of specific revenue sources (other than expendable trusts, or major capital projects) that are legally restricted to expenditure for specified purposes and for which a separate fund is legally required. Examples are parks, schools, and museums, as well as particular functions or activities, such as highway construction or street maintenance.

A special revenue fund may have a definite limited life, or it may remain in effect until discontinued or revoked by appropriate legislative action. It may be used for a very limited purpose, such as the maintenance of a historic landmark, or it may finance an entire function of government, such as public education or highways.

A special revenue fund may be administered by the regularly constituted administrative and financial organization of the government; by an independent body or special purpose local district, such as a park board or the board of directors of a water district; or by a quasi-independent body. In some cases, the fund may be administered by an independent board, but the government maintains the accounting records because the independent board does not have the necessary personnel or other facilities.

Some of the activities mentioned above could also be accounted for in an enterprise fund. Deciding which type of fund to use is often difficult. Basically, unless the government determines that the activity should be financed and operated in a manner similar to that for private business enterprises, the activity should be accounted for as a special revenue fund. A special revenue fund is not appropriate, however, when the costs, including depreciation, of providing goods or services to the general public on a continuing basis are to be financed or recovered primarily through user charges. Also, a special revenue fund is not appropriate when the government has decided that periodic determination of revenues earned, expenses incurred, or net income is appropriate for capital maintenance, public policy, management control, accountability, or other purposes.

(iii) Debt Service Funds.   **Debt service funds** exist to account for the accumulation of resources for, and the payment of, long-term debt principal and interest other than that which is issued for and serviced primarily by an enterprise or similar trust fund. A debt service fund is necessary only if it is legally required or if resources are being accumulated for future payment. Although governments may incur a wide variety of debt, the more common types are described below.

Term (or sinking fund) bonds are being replaced by **serial bonds** as the predominant form of state and local government debt. For term bonds, debt service consists of annual additions of resources being made to a cumulative "investment fund" for repayment of the issue at maturity. The additions, also called "sinking fund installments," are computed on an actuarial basis, which includes assumptions that certain rates of interest will be earned from investing the resources accumulating in the investment fund. If the actual earnings are less than the planned earnings, subsequent additions are increased; if the earnings are greater than planned, the excess is carried forward until the time of the final addition of the fund. Because term bond principal is due at the end of the bond's term, the expenditure for repayment of principal is recognized at that time.

Debt service on serial bonds, however, generally consists of preestablished principal payments that are due on an annual basis and interest payments based on either fixed or variable rates that are due on a semiannual basis. No sinking fund is involved in the repayment of serial bonds.

The revenues for a debt service fund come from one or more sources, with property taxes being the predominant source. Taxes that are specified for debt service appear as a **revenue** of the debt service fund. Taxes for general purposes (i.e., not specified but nevertheless used for debt service) are considered to be an operating transfer to the debt service fund from the fund in which the revenue is recorded, oftentimes the general fund.

Enterprise activity earnings may be another resource for servicing general obligation debt. In these instances, the general obligation debt should be classified as enterprise debt (a liability of the enterprise fund), and the debt service payments should be recorded in the enterprise fund as a reduction of the liability, not in the debt service fund. The debt service transactions would be recorded in the debt service fund only if the enterprise fund was not expected to be responsible for repaying the debt on an ongoing basis. Essentially, if the enterprise fund became unable to service the principal and interest and the general governmental unit assumed responsibility for servicing the debt, then the debt service fund would be used.

More recently, governmental units have been exploring alternative financing activities including lease-purchase arrangements and issuance of zero-coupon or deep discount debt. The issues surrounding lease-purchase arrangements involve legal questions about whether such arrangements constitute debt of a government since they often do not require voter approval prior to incurring the debt. Zero-coupon and deep discount debt issues center on the manner of presenting and amortizing the bond discount amount in the government's financial statements.

Quite often, a **refunding bond** is issued to replace or consolidate prior debt issues. Determining the appropriate accounting principles to apply to refunding bonds depends primarily on whether the bonds are included in an enterprise fund or in the general long-term debt account group. GASB Statement No. 7, "Advance Refundings Resulting in Defeasance of Debt," outlines the appropriate accounting and reporting principles. For the refunding of debt recorded in the GLTDAG, the proceeds of the refunding issue become an "other financing source" of the fund receiving the proceeds of the refunding bond (oftentimes a debt service fund created to service the original issue or a capital projects fund). Since the proceeds are used to liquidate the original debt, an "other financing use" is also recorded in the debt service or capital projects fund in an amount equal to the remaining principal, interest, and other amounts due on the original debt. The outstanding principal of the issue being refunded is removed from the GLTDAG, and the principal amount of the new debt is then recorded in the GLTDAG.

EXAMPLE

Assuming the proceeds of the refunding bond issue (new debt) are $10,000,000 and the unpaid principal of the existing debt (old debt) recorded in the GLTDAG is $7,000,000, the following journal entries are needed to record the advance refunding in a debt service fund.

Debt Service Fund

Cash	$10,000,000	
Other financing services—bond proceeds		$10,000,000
To record proceeds of new debt		
Other financing uses—payment to bondholders	7,000,000	
Cash		7,000,000
To record defeasance of old debt		

GLTDAG

Bonds payable	7,000,000	
Amounts to be provided		7,000,000
To record extinguishment of old debt		
Amounts to be provided	10,000,000	
Bonds payable		10,000,000
To record new debt outstanding		

If, as a result of the refunding, the liability to the bondholders is satisfied, the refunding is referred to as a legal defeasance of debt or **current refunding.** However, refundings often do not result in the immediate repayment of the debt but rather assets are placed in a trust to be used to repay the debt as it matures. These refundings are called **advance refundings** or an "in-substance defeasance." To qualify for an in-substance defeasance, the proceeds of the refunding bonds are placed in an irrevocable trust and invested in essentially risk-free securities, usually obligations of the U.S. Treasury or other government agencies, so that the risk-free securities, together with any premiums on the defeased debt, and expenses of the refunding operation will be sufficient for the trust to pay off the debt to the bondholders when it becomes due. The accounting for an in-substance defeasance is identical to legal defeasances except that payment is made to a trustee rather than to bondholders. The trustee then pays principal and interest to the bondholders based on the maturity schedule of the bond. In addition, the recording of payments of proceeds to the trustee as another financing use is limited to the amount of proceeds.

Advance refundings of debt recorded in a proprietary fund follow the accounting principles outlined in GASB Statement No. 23, "Accounting and Financial Reporting for Refundings of Debt Reported by Proprietary Activities." Statement No. 23 requires that the difference between the reacquisition price and the net carrying amount of the old debt be deferred and amortized as a component of interest expense over the remaining life of the old or the life of the new debt, whichever is shorter.

Regardless of whether the defeased debt was recorded in the GLTDAG or a proprietary fund, GASB Statement No. 7 requires the disclosure of a description of the refunding transaction; the cash flow gain or loss, which is the difference between the total cash outflow of the new debt (i.e., principal, interest, etc.) and the remaining cash outflow of the old debt; and the economic gain or loss, which is the difference between the present values of the cash flows of the new and old debt.

For advance refundings, each year after the defeasance, the footnotes to the financial statements should disclose the remaining amount of debt principal that the trustee has to pay to bondholders.

(iv) Capital Projects Funds. The purpose of a **capital projects fund** is to account for the receipt and disbursement of resources used for the acquisition of major capital facilities other than those financed by enterprise funds. Capital projects are defined as outlays for major, permanent fixed assets having a relatively long life (e.g., buildings), as compared with those of limited life (e.g., office equipment). Capital projects are usually financed by bond proceeds, but they can also be financed from other resources, such as current revenues or grants from other governments.

Capital outlays financed entirely from the direct revenues of the general fund or a special revenue fund and not requiring long-term borrowing may be accounted for in the fund providing such resources rather than in a separate capital projects fund. Assets with a relatively short life—hence not capital projects—are usually financed from current revenues or by short-term obligations and are accounted for in the general or special revenue fund.

Accounting for Capital Projects Fund Transactions. Bonds are issued and capital projects are started under a multiyear capital program. In some instances, it is necessary to secure referendum approval to issue general obligation bonds. Obligations are then incurred and expenditures made according to an annual capital projects budget.

When a project is financed entirely from general obligation bond proceeds, the initial entry to be made in the capital projects fund when the bonds are sold is:

Cash	$XXX	
Other financing source—		
Proceeds of general obligation bonds		$XXX

Whereas the proceeds of the bonds are accounted for in the capital projects funds, the liability for the face amount of the bonds is recorded in the general long-term debt account group.

If bonds are sold at a **premium** (i.e., above par value) the premium increases the other financing sources. Oftentimes, the premium is transferred—by a debit to "other financing sources" and a credit to "cash"—to the debt service fund established to service the debt for the project. If the bonds are sold at a **discount** (i.e., below par value), the discount reduces the amount recorded as other financing sources in the capital projects fund. Bond issuance costs either paid out of available funds or withheld from the bond proceeds usually are accounted as debt service expenditures in the capital projects or debt service funds operating statement.

Bond Anticipation Notes.   Governments sometimes issue **bond anticipation notes** (BANs) prior to the sale of bonds, planning to retire the notes with the proceeds of the bond issue to which the notes are related. The reasons would be:

- The governmental unit wants to accelerate initiation of a project, and issuance of the long-term bonds will require more time than is required to issue BANs.
- The governmental unit does not want to undertake long-term financing until the project is complete and ready for use. Hence bond anticipation notes are used to provide construction financing.
- The current and projected interest rates make it prudent to issue short-term notes first and to defer issuance of long-term bonds.
- The individual capital projects to be financed from the proceeds of the bond sale are so small as to make the sale of bonds to finance each project impracticable.

The cash proceeds and the liabilities resulting from the sale of BANs should be recorded in the capital projects fund as follows:

Cash	$XXX	
Bond anticipation notes payable		$XXX

When the long-term bonds are sold, an "other financing source" should be recorded and the BANs payable debited in an amount equal to the portion of the BANs redeemed as follows:

Bond participation notes payable	$XXX	
Other financing sources		$XXX

If the BANs are not redeemed with long-term bond proceeds or other funds by the end of the year, and the governmental unit has both the intent and the ability (as those terms are defined in SFAS No. 6, "Classification of Short-Term Obligations Expected to Be Refinanced," pars. 10 and 11) to redeem the BANs with long-term debt, the bond anticipation notes payable account should be debited and an "other financing source" should be credited. The BANs payable and the offsetting amount to be provided should be established in the general long-term debt group account. If the governmental unit does not have the intent or ability to redeem the BANs with long-term debt, it is appropriate to leave the liability in the capital projects fund. The ability to redeem the BANs could be demonstrated by a post balance sheet issuance of long-term debt or the entering into of a long-term financing arrangement for the BANs.

Project Budgets.   When debt is issued to finance an entire capital project, it is usually done so at the beginning of the project in an amount equal to the total estimated project cost. Accordingly, a portion of the proceeds may remain unexpended over a considerable period of time. To the maximum extent possible, these excess proceeds should be invested in interest-bearing investments. However, consideration should be given to the federal arbitrage regulations that limit the amount of interest that can be earned from investing the proceeds of a tax-exempt bond issue. If certain limits are exceeded, the bond's tax-exempt status may be lost or severe penalties could be imposed on the issuer.

Project budgets are typically established for capital projects to control costs and to guard against cost overruns. All expenditures needed to place the project in readiness, that is, indirect as well as direct costs, should be recorded against this budget. The actual expenditures, however, will probably be either less or greater than the amounts authorized. Therefore, in the absence of any legal restrictions, any unspent balance should be transferred to the appropriate sources. If the project was financed only from bond proceeds, the transfer should be to the debt service fund from which the bond issue is to be repaid. If the resources were drawn from more than one source, such as bond proceeds and current revenues, the transfer should be split among the sources in proportion to their contributions. If the expenditures were greater than authorized and a deficit exists, sufficient funds must be transferred to liquidate any commitments.

As construction of the project is completed, the costs should be recorded in the general fixed assets account group with the following entry:

| Construction in progress | $XXX | |
| Investment in general fixed assets | | $XXX |

When the project is finally completed, the entry in the general fixed assets account group would then be:

| Buildings | $XXX | |
| Construction in progres | | $XXX |

The amount of construction in progress would be transferred to the buildings account in the general fixed assets account group when the project is completed.

(v) Enterprise Funds. Enterprise funds are the funds that governments use to account for services to the public when most of the costs involved are paid for in the form of charges by the users of such services. Examples are electric utilities, water, sanitary sewer, gas, local transportation systems, airports, public housing, parking lots, golf courses, and swimming pools. The substantial federal and state grants to certain types of enterprise activities, however, as well as the rising costs of these services and the public's unwillingness to pay the full amounts, have meant that many of these activities are no longer financed predominantly by user charges. Hence, the activities theoretically would have to be accounted for in the general fund or as special revenue funds, and not enterprise funds.

Nonetheless, in many instances it is still highly desirable to account for many of these activities as enterprise funds, because it is often important to know the full costs of the activities, to monitor the amount of outside support required for them, and to know the extent of costs paid for by **user charges.** Accordingly, the definition of enterprise funds (GASB Codification § 1300.104) addresses these issues. Enterprise funds are used:

To account for operations (a) that are financed and operated in a manner similar to private business enterprises—where the intent of the governing body is that the costs (expenses, including depreciation) of providing goods and services to the general public on a continuing basis be financed or recovered primarily through user charges; or (b) where the governing body has decided that periodic determination of revenues earned, expenses incurred and/or net income is appropriate for capital maintenance, public policy, management control, accountability, or other purposes.

Enterprise activities are frequently administered by departments of the general purpose government, for example, a municipal water department or a state parks department. They can also be the exclusive function of a local special district, such as a water district, power authority, or bridge and tunnel authority.

User charges are one significant source of enterprise fund resources; revenue bond proceeds are another. Revenue bonds are long-term obligations, the principal and interest of which are paid from the earnings of the enterprise for which the bond proceeds were spent. The enterprise revenues may be pledged to the payment of the debt, and the physical properties may carry a mortgage that is to be liquidated in the event of default.

Revenue bond **indentures** usually also contain several requirements concerning the use of the bond proceeds, the computation and reporting of revenue bond **coverage,** and the establishment and use of restricted asset accounts for handling revenue bond debt service requirements.

For instance, a revenue bond indenture may require the establishment of various bond accounts including a construction account, operations and maintenance account, current debt service account, future debt service account, and revenue and replacement account. This does not necessarily mean establishing individual accounting funds for each bond issue. Instead, the accounting and reporting requirements can be met through the use of various accounts within an accounting fund.

The revenue bond construction account normally represents cash and investments (including interest receivable) segregated by the bond indenture for construction. Construction liabilities payable from restricted assets should be reported as "contracts payable from restricted assets." As with all restricted accounts, construction assets and the liabilities to be paid from them generally should not be classified as current assets and liabilities. The difference between the restricted construction asset and liability accounts is not required to be reported as a reserve in retained earnings.

A revenue bond operations and maintenance account often is established pursuant to a bond indenture. Resources for this account are provided through bond proceeds and/or operating income or net income. This account generally accumulates assets equal to operating costs for one month. Once this account has been established, additional proceeds from future bond issues generally are necessary only to the extent the costs associated with these expanded operations are expected to increase. This account is normally balanced by a reserve for revenue bond operations and maintenance account in retained earnings.

Bond indentures may also include a covenant requiring the establishment of a restricted account for the repayment of bond principal and interest. Resources for this account also are provided through bond proceeds and/or operating income or net income. Normally, assets accumulated for debt service payments (i.e., principal and interest) due within one year are classified in the revenue bond current debt service account. This account is at least partially associated with the bonds payable—current account and the accrued interest payable account. Any difference between the revenue bond current debt service account and related current bonds payable and accrued interest payable should be reported as reserved retained earnings. When accounts are restricted for debt service payments beyond the next 12 months, a revenue bond future debt service account should be established.

The final restricted account typically established pursuant to a covenant within a bond indenture is the revenue bond renewal and replacement account. Bond proceeds and/or net income are often restricted for payments of unforeseen repairs and replacements of assets originally acquired with bond proceeds. Provided that liabilities have not been incurred for this purpose, the revenue bond renewal and replacement account is balanced by the reserve for revenue bond renewal and replacement account in retained earnings.

The following general rule should be considered when determining the amount of retained earnings to reserve in restricted asset accounts: Unless otherwise required by the bond indenture, retained earnings should only be reserved for amounts of restricted assets in excess of related liabilities.

Another restricted asset often found in enterprise funds is the amount resulting from the deposits customers are required to make to ensure payment of their final charges and to protect the utility against damage to equipment located on the customer's property. These funds are not available for the financing of current operations and, generally, the amount, less the charges outstanding against the account, must be returned to the customer upon withdrawing from the system. Also, these deposits may, depending on legal and policy requirements, draw interest at some stipulated rate.

In some instances, revenue bonds are also secured by the full faith and credit of the governmental unit. This additional security enables the bonds to obtain better acceptance in the securities market. If the bonds are to be serviced by the enterprise activity, the cash, liability, principal, and interest payments should be accounted for in the enterprise fund. Even if the bonds are secured only by full faith and credit and not by a revenue pledge, but the intention is to use enterprise revenues to service the bonds, they should be accounted for as if they were revenue bonds. If, however, general obligation bond proceeds are used to finance the enterprise activity and there is no intention to service the bonds with enterprise fund resources, the amounts provided to the enterprise fund should be recorded as a contribution from the fund recording the proceeds of the bond, typically, the general fund.

Other sources of contributions also provide significant resources for enterprise activities. Such resources include contributions of permanent capital by other funds or other governmental bodies; contributions in aid of construction by customers or other members of the general public; the aforementioned proceeds of a bond issue to be repaid from general fund revenues, federal grants, or state grants; connection charges to users of utility services; payments by real estate developers for installing utility lines; and similar receipts.

If such resources are externally restricted for capital acquisitions or construction, they should be reported as **contributed capital.** Fixed assets acquired with these contributions should be capitalized at full cost and depreciated over the estimated useful life of the fixed assets. The depreciation on fixed assets acquired by grants, entitlements, and shared revenues received from other governments may be closed to the appropriate contributed capital account rather than retained earnings. If this option is followed, such depreciation is "added back" to the enterprise fund's net income or loss, thereby increasing the net income or reducing the net loss that is closed to retained earnings.

Another resource is the support provided by or to other funds of the government. For instance, an enterprise fund will frequently use the services or commodities of a central facility operated as an internal service fund. Conversely, the general fund departments will use the services of an electric utility fund.

It is important to handle these relationships on a businesslike basis. All services rendered by an enterprise fund for other funds of the government should be billed at predetermined rates, and the enterprise should pay for all services received from other funds on the same basis that is utilized to determine charges for other users. The latter will often include **payments in lieu of taxes** to the general fund in amounts comparable to the taxes that would have been paid by the enterprise were it privately owned and operated, or an "administrative charge" if the enterprise does not have its own management capacity and instead uses management services provided by the general government. Unless this is done, the financial operations of a government-owned enterprise will be distorted, and valid comparisons of operating results with those for similar privately owned enterprise cannot be made. However, other considerations, such as the amount of planned idle capacity, have an impact on the comparability of public and private enterprise funds.

Interfund operating transfers may also occur between an enterprise fund and governmental funds. Operating subsidy transfers from the general fund or special revenue fund are possible. There may also be transfers from an enterprise to finance general fund expenditures.

Finally, there are the nonoperating income and expenses, which are incidental to, or by-products of, the enterprise's primary service function. Nonoperating income consists of such items as interest earnings, rent from nonoperating properties, intergovernmental revenues, and sale of excess supplies. Nonoperating expenses include items such as interest expense and fiscal agents' fees.

(vi) Internal Service Funds.   **Internal service funds** finance and account for special activities that are performed and commodities that are furnished by one department or agency of a governmental unit to other departments or agencies of that unit or to other governmental units on a cost-reimbursement basis. The services differ from those rendered to the public at large, which are accounted for in general, special revenue or enterprise funds. Examples of activities in which internal service funds are established include central motor pools, duplication services, central purchasing and stores departments, and insurance and risk-management activities.

When an internal service fund is established, resources are typically obtained from capital contributions from other operating funds, such as the general fund or an enterprise fund, or from long-term advances from other funds that are to be repaid from earnings. The entry to be made when the fund is created varies depending on the source of the capital.

The cost of services rendered and commodities furnished, including labor, depreciation on all fixed assets used by the funds other than buildings financed from capital projects, and overhead, are charged to the departments served. These departments reimburse the internal service fund by recording expenditures against their budgeted appropriations. The operating objective of the fund is to recover costs incurred to provide the service, including depreciation. Accordingly, the operations of the fund should not result in any significant profit or loss. Whenever it uses the services of another fund, such as an enterprise fund, the fund pays for and records the costs just as if it had dealt with an outside organization.

Since exact overhead charges are usually not known when bills are prepared, the departments being served are usually billed for direct costs plus a uniform rate for their portion of estimated overhead. Any difference in actual overhead expenses may be charged or credited to the departments at fiscal year-end or adjusted for in a subsequent year. At the end of each fiscal year, net income or loss must be determined. The excess of net billings to the department over costs is closed to the retained earnings account.

(vii) Trust and Agency Funds.   The purpose of **trust and agency funds** is to account for assets held by a governmental unit in a trustee capacity or as an agent for individuals, private organizations, other governmental units, or other funds.

Trust Funds.   Usually in existence for an extended period of time, **trust funds** deal with substantial vested interests and involve complex administrative problems. The government's records must provide adequate information to permit compliance with the terms of the trust as defined in the trust document, statutes, ordinances, or governing regulations. For instance, if depreciable property were included in a nonexpendable trust fund, depreciation would have to be recorded as an expense and not included in the distributable income, to keep the principal intact. Similarly, gains and losses on the sale of investments may, unless otherwise specified in the trust agreement, be credited or charged to trust principal.

Expendable and Nonexpendable Trust Funds.   Within the trust fund category there are **expendable trust funds,** where the principal as well as the income may be expended, and **nonexpendable trust funds,** where the principal must be preserved intact. These funds require a precise determination of revenues and expenditures (expenses) in accordance with the trust document so that only the correct net income will be expended.

Pension Trust Funds.   Another type of trust fund is the **pension trust fund,** in which governments account for the money held for the future retirement benefit of their employees, that is, their retirement systems. The resources of this fund are the members' contributions, contributions from the government employer, and earnings on investments in authorized securities. The expenses are the authorized retirement allowances and other benefits, refunds of contributions to members who resign prior to retirement, and administrative expenses. Professional actuaries make periodic actuarial studies of the retirement systems and compute the amounts that should be provided so that the benefits can be paid as required.

The proper accounting for pension trust funds has been on the GASB's agenda since its creation. GASB initially allowed governments to choose from three different methods of accounting and financial reporting but required certain disclosures from all governments. The GASB has finally completed its consideration of pensions and issued three statements: Statement No. 25, "Financial Reporting for Defined Benefit Pension Plans and Note Disclosures for Defined Contribution Plans," Statement No. 26, "Financial Reporting for Postemployment Healthcare Plans Administered by Defined Benefit Pension Plans," and Statement No. 27, "Accounting for Pensions by State and Local Government Employers." Statements No. 25 and 26 address issues related to accounting by pension plans and pension trust funds. Statement No. 27

addresses accounting and financial reporting for those employers who participate in a pension plan.

Statement No. 25 establishes two basic financial statements for pension plans: the statement of plan net assets and the statement of changes in plan net assets. These two financial statements are designed to provide current information about plan assets and financial activities. These statements are supplemented by two schedules that provide actuarial information from a long-term perspective: the schedule of funding progress and the schedule of employer contributions. These schedules are reported as required supplemental information. Statement No. 25 sets requirements for note disclosure that include a brief plan description, a summary of significant accounting principles, and information about contributions, legally required reserves, and investment concentrations. Statement No. 25 is effective for fiscal years beginning after June 15, 1996. Statement No. 26 establishes reporting standards for postemployment healthcare plans that are administered as part of a defined benefit plan and must be implemented concurrently with Statement No. 25.

Statement No. 27 is directed at employers which participate in a pension plan and reflects two underlying principles. First, the pension cost recognized should be related to the annual required contribution (ARC) as determined by an actuary for funding purposes. Second, the actuarial methods and assumptions used by employers should be consistent with those used by the plan in its separate reporting.

In implementing these basic principles Statement No. 27 requires the ARC to be recognized as pension expense in proprietary funds and nonexpendable trust funds. Governmental and expendable trust funds will recognize pension expenditure to the extent that the ARC is expected to be liquidated with expendable available resources. The remainder is recorded as a liability in the GLTDAG. If an employer does not contribute the ARC (or has contributed in excess of the ARC), pension expense/expenditure no longer equals the ARC. In these cases the ARC is adjusted to remove the effects of the actuarial adjustments included in the ARC and to reflect interest on previous under or over funding.

Although Statement No. 27 tries to minimize the differences between accounting for pensions and funding pensions, it does place certain limits or "parameters" on the actuary's calculation of the ARC. These parameters are consistent with parameters established for accounting for the plan itself in Statement No. 25. These parameters relate to the pension obligation, actuarial assumptions, economic assumptions, actuarial cost method, actuarial valuation of assets and amortization of unfunded actuarial accrued liability.

Statement No. 27 establishes disclosure requirements which vary depending on whether the government merely participates in pension plan administered by another entity or includes a pension trust fund. Disclosure requirements also vary for governments with a pension trust fund based on whether the pension plan issues separate publicly available financial statements. These disclosure requirements generally include a plan description, funding policy, pension cost components, actuarial valuation information and trend data.

Agency Funds. Used by governments to handle cash resources held in an agent capacity, **agency funds** require relatively simple administration. The typical agency funds used by state and local governments include (1) tax collection funds, under which one local government collects a tax for an overlapping governmental unit and remits the amount collected less administrative charges to the recipient; (2) payroll withholdings, under which the government collects the deductions and periodically remits them in a lump sum to the appropriate recipient; (3) clearance funds, used to accumulate a variety of revenues from different sources and to apportion them to various operating funds; and (4) deferred compensation plans organized under IRC § 457.

(viii) Special Assessment Activities. **Special assessment activities** pertain to (1) the financing and construction of certain public improvements, such as storm sewers, which are to be paid for wholly or partly from special assessments levied against the properties benefited by such improvements, or (2) the providing of services that are normally provided to the public as general governmental functions and that would otherwise be financed by the general fund or a special revenue fund. Those services may include street lighting, street cleaning, and snow plowing. The payment by the property owners or taxpayers receiving the benefit distinguishes these activities from activities that benefit the entire community and are paid for from general revenues or general obligation bond proceeds. Sometimes, however, a special assessment bond, which is often used to finance the special assessment improvement, also carries the additional pledge of the full faith and credit of the governmental unit.

It should be emphasized that whereas GASB Statement No. 6 eliminated the requirement to report special assessment funds in an entity's general purpose financial statement, accounting for special assessment activities is still an important part of governmental accounting.

Capital improvement special assessment projects have two distinct and functionally different phases. The initial phase consists of financing and constructing the project. In most cases, this period is relatively short in duration, sometimes lasting only a few months, and rarely more than a year or two. The second phase, which may start at the same time as, during, or after the initial phase, consists of collecting the assessment principal and interest levied against the benefited properties and repaying the cost of financing the construction. The second phase is usually substantially longer than the first.

There are many ways of financing a capital improvement special assessment project. Assessments may be levied and collected immediately. Funds will then be available to pay construction costs, and it will not be necessary to issue special assessment bonds. Alternatively, a project may be constructed using the proceeds from short-term borrowing. When the project is complete and the exact cost is known, special assessment bonds are issued to provide the exact amount of money and the short-term borrowings are repaid. A third—and perhaps the most common—financing alternative is for the government to levy a special assessment for the estimated cost of the improvement, issue bonds to provide the funds, construct the improvement using the bond proceeds, and then collect the assessments over a period of years, using the collections to service the bonds.

Five basic types of transactions are associated with a capital project type special assessment:

1. Levying the special assessment.
2. Issuing special assessment bonds.
3. Constructing the capital project.
4. Collecting the special assessment.
5. Paying the bond principal and interest.

Because the special assessment fund has been eliminated for financial reporting purpose, the transactions related to special assessment activities are typically reported in the same manner, and on the same basis of accounting, as any other capital improvement and financing transaction. Transactions of the construction phase of the project should generally be reported in a capital projects fund, and transactions of the debt service phase should be reported in a debt service fund, if one is required.

At the time of the levy, special assessments receivable should be recognized and offset by deferred revenue; deferred revenue should be reduced as the assessments become measurable and available. The fixed assets constructed or acquired (other than those related to an enterprise fund) should be reported in the general fixed assets account group, and the outstanding long-term debt should be reported in the general long-term debt account group.

The entry to record the special assessment levy is shown below.

Special assessments receivable	$XXX	
Special assessment revenue		$XXX
Deferred special assessment revenue		$XXX

When the current special assessments and the governmental unit's share are collected, the following entry is made:

Cash	$XXX	
Special assessments receivable		$XXX

The issuance of special assessment bonds at par is recorded by the following entries:

Capital Projects Fund

Cash	$XXX	
Other financing sources—bond proceeds		$XXX

GLTDAG

Amounts to be provided	$XXX	
Bonds payable		$XXX

If the bonds are issued at a premium or discount, the debit to "cash" for the proceeds received, and the credit to "other financing sources" would be adjusted accordingly.

The entry for the retirement of special assessment bonds and for the construction of the special assessment project would follow the accounting principles outlined in the discussion on capital projects. The usual entries are made for expenditures and for encumbrances if such a system exits. At the end of the year, the revenues and expenditures should be closed to the fund balance to reflect the balance that may be expended in future periods.

Although the accounting for special assessment construction activities is quite similar to other financing and construction activities, the major issue relating to special assessment activities involves the definition of special assessment debt. Special assessment debt is often defined as those long-term obligations, secured by a lien on the assessed properties, for which the primary source of repayment is the assessments levied against the benefiting properties.

However, the nature and composition of debt associated with special assessment-related capital improvements is not always consistent with this definition. Rather, it can vary significantly from one jurisdiction to another. Capital improvements involving special assessments may be financed by debt that is:

1. General obligation debt that is not secured by liens on assessed properties but nevertheless will be repaid in part by special assessment collections.
2. Special assessment debt that is secured by liens on assessed properties and is also backed by the full faith and credit of the government as additional security.
3. Special assessment debt that is secured by liens on assessed properties and is not backed by the full faith and credit of the government but is, however, fully or partially backed by some other type of general governmental commitment.
4. Special assessment debt that is secured by liens on assessed properties, is not backed by the full faith and credit of the government, and is not backed by any other type of general governmental commitment; the government is not liable under any circumstance for the repayment of this category of debt, should the property owner default.

In some cases special assessment debt is payable entirely by special assessment collections from the assessed property owners; in other cases the debt may be repaid partly from special assessment collections and partly from the general resources of the government, either because the government is a property owner benefiting from the improvements or because the government has agreed to finance part of the cost of the improvement as a public benefit. The portion of special assessment debt that will be repaid directly with governmental resources is, in essence, a general obligation of the government. If the government owns property that benefits from the improvements financed by special assessment debt as in item 4 above, or if a public benefit assessment is made against the government, the government is obligated for the public benefit portion and the amount assessed against its property, even though it has no liability for the remainder of the debt issue.

Because the special assessment debt can have various characteristics, the extent of a government's liability for debt related to a special assessment capital improvement can also vary significantly. For example, the government may be primarily liable for the debt, as in the case of a general obligation issue; it may have no liability whatsoever for special assessment debt; or it may be obligated in some manner to provide a secondary source of funds for repayment of special assessment debt in the event of default by the assessed property owners. A government is obligated in some manner for special assessment debt if (1) it is legally obligated to assume all or part of the debt in the event of default or (2) the government may take certain actions to assume secondary liability for all or part of the debt—and the government takes, or has given indications that it will take, those actions.

Stated differently, the phrase "obligated in some manner" is intended to include all situations other than those in which (1) the government is prohibited (by constitution, charter, statute, ordinance, or contract) from assuming the debt in the event of default by the property owner or (2) the government is not legally liable for assuming the debt and makes no statement, or gives no indication, that it will, or may, honor the debt in the event of default.

Debt issued to finance capital projects that will be paid wholly or partly from special assessments against benefited property owners should be reported as follows:

1. General obligation debt that will be repaid, in part, from special assessments should be reported like any other general obligation debt.

2. Special assessment debt for which the government is obligated in some manner should be reported in the GLTDAG, except for the portion, if any, that is a direct obligation of an enterprise fund, or that is expected to be repaid from operating revenues of an enterprise fund.

    a. The portion of the special assessment debt that will be repaid from property owner assessments should be reported as "special assessment debt with governmental commitment."

    b. The portion of special assessment debt that will be repaid from general resources of the government (the public benefit portion, or the amount assessed against government-owned property) should be reported and classified in the GLTDAG like other general obligation debt.

3. Special assessment debt for which the government is not obligated in any manner should not be displayed in the government's financial statements. However, if the government is liable for a portion of that debt (the public benefit portion, or as a property owner), that portion should be reported as in subparagraph 2b above.

(h) FIXED ASSETS: VALUATION AND DEPRECIATION.   Principles 5, 6, and 7 discuss accounting for fixed assets. Governments account for their general fixed assets, that is, the fixed assets not belonging to an enterprise fund, an internal service fund, or a similar trust fund in the **general fixed assets account group.** This account group is established to maintain accountability for the fixed assets even though they do not belong to any individual fund, but rather to the governmental unit as an instrumentality. Furthermore, they do not represent net financial resources available for expenditure, but items for which financial resources have been used. Thus their inclusion in a specific fund would distort the fund balance.

Fixed assets in enterprise funds, internal service funds, and similar trust funds should be accounted for in the respective fund.

To be classified as a fixed asset, a specific piece of property should have three attributes: It should be tangible, have a life at least longer than the current fiscal year, and have a significant value. Reporting of **public domain** or **"infrastructure" fixed assets,** that is, roads, bridges, curbs and gutters, streets, sidewalks, drainage systems, lighting systems, and similar assets that are immovable and have value only to the governmental unit, is optional. General fixed assets acquired through noncancelable leases, as the term is defined by SFAS No. 13, "Accounting for Leases," should be capitalized and a liability for the present value of the future lease payments should be recorded in the general long-term debt account group.

The amount recorded for fixed assets should be historical cost, or estimated historical cost if the original cost is not available. Cost should include not only the purchase price or construction cost, but also all ancillary charges necessary to place the asset in its intended location ready to use: freight and transportation charges, site preparation expenditures, professional fees, and legal claims directly attributable to the asset's acquisition. If the asset is constructed by the governmental unit's own personnel, the amount recorded should result from a complete accounting of the costs of labor, materials, equipment usage, and overhead. Donated fixed assets should be recorded at their estimated fair value on the date donated.

Capitalization of interest is required for assets constructed in enterprise and similar trust funds if the amount is material. The interest capitalization policy should be disclosed for all assets constructed and capitalized, including assets in the general fixed assets account group.

(i) Accounting for Acquisition and Disposal of Fixed Assets. The expenditures for general fixed assets are recorded in the general fund, special revenue fund, or capital projects fund. The entry that records the asset is made in the general fixed assets account group as follows:

Buildings	$XXX	
Investment in general fixed assets		$XXX

The debit entry should reflect the asset classification: land, buildings, improvements other than buildings, equipment, construction in progress. The credit is normally made to "investment in general fixed assets."

(ii) Subsidiary Property Records. The maintenance of **subsidiary property records** aids in the control of fixed assets. The subsidiary records should contain such information as classification code, date of acquisition, name and address of vendor, unit charged with custody, location, cost, fund and account from which purchased, method of acquisition, estimated life, and repair and maintenance data.

(iii) Disposal or Retirement of Fixed Assets. In the **disposal or retirement** of a general fixed asset the amount for which the asset is recorded must be removed from the asset side of the general fixed assets account group, and an equal amount must be deducted from the investment in fixed assets. If the asset is sold, the amount obtained in cash or by evidence of indebtedness should be recorded in the appropriate governmental fund. The same amount should be credited to a revenue account, such as sale of fixed assets or miscellaneous revenues or other financing sources.

(iv) Depreciation. Depreciation of general fixed assets is not recorded in the operating statements of governmental funds because governmental funds report expenditures and depreciation is an **expense.** Depreciation can be recorded, however, in the cost accounting systems or calculated for purposes of cost analysis. Accumulated depreciation may also be recorded in the general fixed assets account group by increasing the accumulated depreciation account and decreasing the investment in the general fixed asset account.

Depreciation of fixed assets accounted for in a proprietary fund should be recorded in that fund. Depreciation is also recognized in trust funds where expenses, net income, or capital maintenance is measured.

(i) LONG-TERM LIABILITIES. Principle 5 indicates that all unmatured long-term indebtedness of the government not directly related to or expected to be repaid from proprietary funds, or similar trust funds, is **general long-term debt** and should be accounted for in the **general**

long-term debt account group. General long-term debt is not limited to liabilities arising from debt issuances, but may also include lease purchase agreements, long-term portion of compensated absences, judgments and claims, and other commitments that are not current liabilities properly recorded in the governmental funds. Matured long-term indebtedness should be recorded in the debt service fund, if maintained, or another governmental fund. Long-term indebtedness directly related to and expected to be repaid from proprietary or trust fund resources should be included in those funds.

Typically, the general long-term debt of a state and local government is secured by the general credit and revenue-raising powers of the government rather than by the assets acquired for specific fund resources. Furthermore, just as general fixed assets do not represent financial resources available for appropriation and expenditure, the unmatured principal of general long-term debt does not require current appropriation and expenditure of a governmental fund's financial resources. Thus, to include it as a governmental fund liability would be misleading for management control and accountability functions for the current period. However, this issue is being examined by the GASB in its financial reporting model project as discussed in subsection 28.7(a) of this chapter.

General long-term debt should be classified appropriately as term bonds, serial bonds, and other general long-term liabilities (i.e., unpaid sick leave and vacation, unpaid pensions, etc.). Balancing accounts would show the amount available in the debt service funds for payment of debt principal and the amount that must be provided in future years for such payments.

(i) Accounting for Long-Term Debt. The entry to establish the long-term debt payable in the general long-term debt account group is made when the bonds are issued and the proceeds are recorded in a governmental fund. It is as follows:

Amount to be provided for repayment of bonds	$XXX	
Bonds payable		$XXX

When funds are accumulated in the debt service funds for payment of the bonds, the following entry is made in the general long-term debt account group:

Amount available in debt service funds	$XXX	
Amount to be provided for repayment of bonds		$XXX

When the bonds mature, one of the following entries is recorded, depending on whether the matured bonds are paid from current revenues or from accumulated resources in a debt service fund:

Bonds payable	$XXX	
Amount to be provided for repayment of bonds		$XXX
Bonds payable	$XXX	
Amount available in debt service funds		$XXX

The amount to be recorded in the general long-term debt account group for noncurrent liabilities on lease-purchase agreement is generally the lower of the present value at the beginning of the lease term of the minimum lease payments due during the noncancelable lease term excluding executory costs, and the fair value of the leased property at the inception of the lease. This amount should be adjusted at the end of each year to reflect the payments on the lease liability.

(ii) Deficit Bonds. **Deficit bonds** result from governments' ending a fiscal year with a deficit and issuing bonds, payable in future years, to finance the deficit. The bonds are classified as "deficit bonds payable" in the general long-term debt account group. The offsetting debit would be the "amount to be provided for repayment of deficit bonds." The credit attributable to the proceeds of the deficit bonds should be to a general fund account entitled "fund balance provided by deficit bonds."

In subsequent years, as these bonds are liquidated from the excesses of revenues over expenditures (prior to consideration of debt service of the deficit bonds), the deficit bonds payable and the amount to be provided for redemption of deficit bonds are reduced. The fund balance provided by deficit bonds should also be reduced by closing the principal portion of debt service payments of the deficit bonds to the account. Thus, at any point, the total amount to be provided for repayment of the deficit bonds in the general long-term debt account group will be equal to "fund balance provided by deficit bonds" in the general fund.

(j) MEASUREMENT FOCUS AND BASIS OF ACCOUNTING. The accounting and financial reporting treatment applied to a fund is determined by its measurement focus. The measurement focus refers to what is being expressed in reporting an entity's financial performance and position. A particular measurement focus is accomplished by considering not only which resources are measured, but also when the effects of transactions or events involving those resources are recognized (the basis of accounting). **Principle 8** describes the basis of accounting used by governments.

(i) Measurement Focus. All governmental funds and expendable trust funds are accounted for by using a current financial resources measurement focus. With this measurement focus, only current assets and current liabilities are included on the balance sheet. Operating statements of these funds present increases (i.e., revenues and other financing sources) and decreases (i.e., expenditures and other financing uses) in net current assets.

All proprietary funds, nonexpendable trust funds and pension trust funds are accounted for on a flow of economic resources measurement focus. With this measurement focus, all assets and liabilities associated with the operation of these funds are included on the balance sheet. Fund equity (i.e., net total assets) is segregated into contributed capital and retained earnings components. Proprietary fund-type operating statements present increases (e.g., revenues) and decreases (e.g., expenses) in net total assets.

(ii) Basis of Accounting. The **basis of accounting** determines when revenues, expenditures, expenses, and transfers—and the related assets and liabilities—are recognized in the accounts and reported in the financial statements. Specifically, it relates to the timing of the measurements made, regardless of the measurement focus. For example, whether depreciation is recognized depends on whether expenses or expenditures are being measured rather than on whether the cash or accrual basis is used.

Cash Basis.   Under the **cash basis** of accounting, revenues and transfers in are not recorded in the accounts until cash is received, and expenditures or expenses and transfers out are recorded only when cash is disbursed.

The cash basis is frequently encountered, but its use is not generally accepted for any governmental unit. With the cash basis, it is difficult to compare expenditures with services rendered, because the disbursements relating to those services may be made in the fiscal period following that in which the services occurred. Also, statements prepared on a cash basis do not show financial position and results of operations on a basis that is generally accepted.

Accrual Basis.   Under the **accrual basis** of accounting, most transactions are recorded when they occur, regardless of when cash is received or disbursed. Items not measurable until cash is received or disbursed are accounted for at that time.

The accrual basis is considered a superior method of accounting for the economic resources of any organization because it results in accounting measurements that are based on the substance of transactions and events, rather than merely on the receipt or disbursement of cash.

Modified Accrual Basis.   As indicated previously, the financial flows of governments, such as taxes and grants, typically do not result from a direct exchange for goods or services and thus cannot be accrued based on the completion of the earnings process and an exchange taking place. Governments have thus devised the **"susceptible to accrual"** concept as the criterion for determining when inflows are accruable as revenue. A revenue is susceptible to accrual when it is both **measurable** and **available** to finance current operations. An amount is measurable when the precise amount is known because the transaction is completed, or when it can be accurately estimated using past experience or other available information. An amount is available to finance operations when it is (1) **physically available,** that is, collectible within the current period or soon enough thereafter to be used to pay liabilities of the current period; and (2) **legally available,** that is, authorized for expenditure in the current fiscal period and not applicable to some future period.

On the expenditure side, a government's main concern, for governmental funds at least, is to match the financial resources used with the financial resources obtained. This measure of whether current-year revenues were sufficient to pay for current-year services is referred to as interperiod equity. A measure of interperiod equity shows whether current-year citizens received services but shifted part of the payment burden to future-year citizens or used up previously accumulated resources. Conversely, such a measure would show whether current-year revenues were not only sufficient to pay for current-year services, but also increased accumulated net resources.

This adaptation of the accrual basis to the conditions surrounding government activities and financing has been given the term **modified accrual.** Modified accrual is currently used in all governmental fund types (i.e., the general fund, special revenue funds, etc.) where the intent is to determine the extent to which provided services have been financed by current resources.

In proprietary funds the objective is to determine net income, and the accounting should be essentially the same as commercial accounting. Hence, proprietary funds use the economic resources measurement focus and the accrual basis without the need for modification described above.

(iii) Revenue Transactions.   The modified accrual basis of accounting is applied in practice for revenue transactions as follows:

1. **Property taxes** are recorded as revenue when the taxes are levied, provided that they apply to and are collected in the current period or soon enough thereafter to finance the current period's expenditures. The period after year-end generally should not exceed 60 days. The amount recorded as revenue should be net of estimated uncollectible taxes, abatements, discounts, and refunds. (Property taxes that are measurable but not available—and hence not susceptible to accrual—should be deferred and recognized as revenue in the fiscal year they become available.)

2. **Taxpayer-assessed income, gross receipts, and sales taxes** should be recorded as revenues when susceptible to accrual.

3. **Miscellaneous revenues** such as **fines and forfeits,** athletic fees, and inspection charges are generally recognized when cash is received because they are usually not measurable and available until they are received.

4. **Grants** should be recorded when the government has an irrevocable right to the grant. If expenditure of funds is the prime factor for determining eligibility for the grant funds, revenue should be recognized when the expenditure is made. A more detailed discussion of grant accounting is provided in subsection 28.5(a).

5. **Interest earned on special assessment levies** may be accrued when due rather than when earned if it approximately offsets interest expenditures on special assessment indebtedness that is also recorded when due.

(iv) Expenditure Transactions.   Expenditure transactions under the modified accrual basis are treated as follows:

1. **Interest** on long-term debt should be recorded as an expenditure when due.

2. **Inventory items** may be considered expenditures either when purchased (the purchases method) or when used (the consumption method). Under either method significant amounts of inventory at the end of a fiscal year should be reported as an asset on the balance sheet.

3. **Expenditures for insurance** and similar services extending over more than one accounting period need not be allocated between or among accounting periods, but they may be accounted for as expenditures of the period of acquisition.

4. **Interest expenditures** on special assessment indebtedness may be recorded when due if they are approximately offset by interest earnings on special assessment levies that are also recorded when due.

5. **Vacation and sick leave benefits** should be recorded when a liability has been incurred that is payable from expendable available resources.

(k) BUDGETARY ACCOUNTING.   **Principle 9** describes the requirements related to budgeting. **Budgeting,** or the allocation of scarce resources to enable established objectives to be accomplished, is the central element in a government's planning, financial management, control, and public accountability processes. The **budget** is the financial plan embodied into law, introduced and enacted in the same manner as any other ordinance or statute. Thus it enables governments to demonstrate that they are meeting a major objective of governmental accounting, namely, compliance with the law.

Budgets are the goals of governments in the same way that net income and return on investment are the goals to corporate organizations. A financial report that compares the actual results with the budgeted results is the means by which a governmental unit demonstrates accountability and managerial performance. Accordingly, an annual operating budget is usually developed for and adopted by every governmental fund.

(i) Types of Operating Budgets.   Several types of annual operating budgets are used in contemporary public finance. Among the more common are the following:

- Line item budget.
- Program budget.
- Performance budget.
- Zero-base budget.

Line Item Budgeting.   Listing the inputs for resources that each organizational unit requests for each **line** (or **object**) of expenditure is referred to as **line item budgeting.** This simple approach produces a budget that governing bodies and administrators can understand, based on their own experience. It provides for tight control over spending and is the most common local government budgeting approach, although this popularity is due primarily to tradition.

Line item budgeting is criticized because it emphasizes inputs rather than outputs, analyzes expenditures inadequately, and fragments activities among accounts that bear little relation to purposes of the government. However, all budgeting systems use objects for the buildup of costs and for execution of the budget.

Overcoming criticisms of a line item budgeting system can be accomplished by:

- Improving the budget structure to encompass all funds and organizational units in a manner that enables the total resources available to a particular organizational unit or responsibility center to be readily perceived.

- Developing a level of detail for the object categories that permits adequate analysis of proposed expenditures and effective control over the actual expenditures.
- Improving the presentation of historical data to stimulate the analysis of trends.
- Providing a partial linking of outputs to the objects of expenditures.

Program Budgeting.   Formulating expenditure requests on the basis of the services to be performed for the various programs the government provides is known as **program budgeting**. A program budget categorizes the major areas of citizen needs and the services for meeting such needs into programs. Goals and objectives are stated for each program, normally in relatively specific, quantified terms. The costs are estimated for the resources required (e.g., personnel and equipment) to accomplish the objective for each program. The governing body can then conduct a meaningful review of budget requests by adding or deleting programs or placing different emphasis on the various programs.

Program budgeting has existed for many years, but relatively few governments have adopted it, partly because line budgeting is so familiar and comprehensible. Lack of acceptance also results from the difficulty of developing operationally useful program budgets that meet the governmental notion of accountability, that is, control of the number of employees and other expense items, rather than achievement of results in applying such resources.

The operational usefulness of program budgeting has also been questioned as a result of the complexity of the **program structure,** the vagueness of goals and objectives, the lack of organizational or individual responsibility for program funds that span several departments or agencies, and the inadequacy of accounting support to record direct and indirect program costs.

Nevertheless, program budgeting can be an extremely effective approach for a government willing to devote the effort. The steps that departments should take to implement the system are:

- Identify programs and the reasons for their existence.
- Define the goals of programs.
- Define kinds and levels of services to be provided in light of **budgetary guidelines** (council- or CEO-furnished guidelines, e.g., budget priorities, budget assumptions, and budget constraints).
- Develop budget requests in terms of resources needed, based on the programs' purposes, the budgetary guidelines, the projected levels of services, and the previous years' expenditure levels for the programs.
- Submit budget requests for compilation, review, and approval.

Performance Budgeting.   Formulating expenditure requests based on the work to be performed is the primary function of **performance budgeting.** It emphasizes the work or service performed, described in quantitative terms, by an organizational unit performing a given activity; for example, number of tons of waste collected by the Sanitation Department and case work load in the Department of Welfare. These performance data are used in the preparation of the annual budget as the basis for increasing or decreasing the number of personnel and the related operating expenses of the individual departments.

The development of a full-scale performance budget requires a strong budget staff, constructive participation at all levels, special accounting and reporting methods, and a substantial volume of processed statistical data. Primarily for these reasons, performance budgeting has been less widely used than line item budgeting.

The approach to developing a performance budgeting system is as follows:

- Decide on the extent to which functions and activities will be segmented into work units and services for formulation and execution of the budget.

- Define the functions in services performed by the government, and assemble them into a structure.
- Identify and assemble or develop work load and efficiency measures that relate to service categories.
- Estimate the total costs of the functions and services.
- Analyze resource needs for each service in terms of personnel, equipment, and so on.
- Formulate the first-year performance budget. For the first year, set the budget appropriations and controls at a higher level than the data indicate.
- Perform cost accounting for the functional budget category; initiate statistical reporting of the work load measures; match resources utilized to actual results.

Zero-Base Budgeting.   In the preparation of a budget, **zero-base budgeting** projects funding for services at several alternative levels, both lower and higher than the present level, and allocates funds to services based on rankings of these alternatives. It is an appropriate budgeting system for jurisdictions whose revenues are not sufficient for citizen demands and inflation-driven expenditure increases, where considerable doubt exists as to the necessity and effectiveness of existing programs and services, and where incremental budgeting processes have resulted in existing programs and their funding being taken as a given, with attention devoted to requests for new programs.

Zero-base budgeting can be used with any existing budgeting system, including line item, program, or performance budgeting. The budget format can remain unchanged.

The steps to implement zero-base budgeting are as follows:

- Define **decision units,** that is activities that can be logically grouped for planning and providing each service.
- Analyze decision units to determine alternative service levels, determine the resources required to operate at alternative levels, and present this information in **decision packages.**
- Rank the decision packages in a priority order that reflects the perceived importance of a particular package to the community in relation to other packages.
- Present the budget to the governing body for a review of the ranking of the decision packages.

(ii) Budget Preparation.   The specific procedures involved in the preparation of a budget for a governmental unit are usually prescribed by state statute, local charter, or ordinance. There are, however, certain basic steps:

- Preparation of the budget calendar.
- Development of preliminary forecasts of available revenues, recurring expenditures, and new programs.
- Formulation and promulgation of a statement of executive budget policy to the operating departments.
- Preparation and distribution of budget instructions, budget forms, and related information.
- Review of departmental budget requests and supporting work sheets.
- Interview with department heads for the purpose of adjusting or approving their requests in a tentative budget.
- Final assembly of the tentative budget, including fixing of revenue estimates and the required tax levy.
- Presentation of the tentative budget to the legislative body and the public.
- Conduction of a public hearing, with advance legal notice.
- Adoption of final budget by the legislative body.

Revenue and Expenditure Estimates.   The property tax has been the traditional basic source of revenue for local government. The amount to be budgeted and raised is determined by subtracting the estimated nonproperty taxes and other revenues, plus the reappropriated fund balance, from budgeted expenditures. This amount, divided by the assessed valuation of taxable property within the boundaries of the governmental unit, produces the required tax rate.

Many jurisdictions have legal ceilings on the property tax rates available for general operating purposes. Additionally, taxpayer initiatives have forced governments to seek new revenue sources. Accordingly, governmental units have turned increasingly to other types of revenue, such as sales taxes, business and nonbusiness license fees, charges for services, state-collected, locally shared taxes, and grants-in-aid from the federal and state governments. Department heads, however, ordinarily have little knowledge of revenue figures. As a result, the primary responsibility for estimating these revenues usually lies with the budget officer and the chief finance officer.

Most governmental units, as a safeguard against excessive accumulation of resources, require that any **unappropriated fund balance** in the general fund be included as a source of financing in the budget of that fund for the succeeding fiscal year. Most controlling laws or ordinances provide for inclusion of the estimated surplus (fund balance) at the end of the current year, although many require that the includable surplus be the balance at the close of the last completed fiscal year.

Departmental estimates of expenditures and supporting work programs or performance data generally are prepared by the individual departments, using forms provided by the central budget agency. Expenditures are customarily classified to conform to the standard account classification of the governmental unit and thus permit comparison with actual performance in the current and prior periods.

Personal Services.   Generally, **personal services** are supported by detailed schedules of proposed salaries for individual full-time employees. Nonsalaried and temporary employees are usually paid on an hourly basis, and the budget requests are normally based on the estimated number of hours of work.

Estimates of materials and supplies and other services, ordinarily quite repetitive in nature, are most often based on current experience, plus an allowance, if justified, for rising costs. Capital outlay requests are based on demonstrated need for specific items of furniture or equipment by individual departments.

In recent years, governmental units, particularly at the county, state, and federal levels, have disbursed substantial sums annually that are unlike the usual current operating expenditures. These sums include welfare or **public assistance payments,** contributions to other governmental units, benefit payments, and special grants. They are properly classified as "other charges." Estimates of these charges are generally based on unit costs for assistance, legislative allotments, requests from outside agencies or governmental units, and specified calculations.

In addition to departmental expenditures, the budget officer must estimate certain nondepartmental or general governmental costs not allocated to any department or organizational unit. Examples include pension costs and retirement contributions, which are not normally allocated, election costs, insurance and surety bonds, and interest on tax notes.

Although most governments still operate under laws that require the budget to be balanced precisely, an increasing number permit a surplus or contingency provision in the expenditure section of the budget. This is usually included to provide a reserve to cover unforeseen expenditures during the budget year.

The expenditure budget may be approved by a board, a commission, or other governing body before presentation to the central budget-making authority.

Presentation of the Budget.   To present a comprehensive picture of the proposed fund operations for a budget year, a budget document is prepared that is likely to include a budget message, summary schedules and comparative statements, detailed revenue estimates, detailed expenditure estimates, and drafts of ordinances to be enacted by the legislative body.

The contents of a budget message should set forth concisely the salient features of the proposed budget of each fund and will generally include the following: (1) a total amount showing amounts of overall increase and decrease, (2) detailed amounts and explanations of the increases and decreases, and (3) a detailed statement of the current financial status of each fund for which a budget is submitted, together with recommendations for raising the funds needed to balance the budget of each fund. It should identify the relationship of the operating budget to the capital program and capital budget, which are submitted separately.

Adoption of the Budget.   Most states adopt the budget by the enactment of one or more statutes. Many cities require the formality of an ordinance for the adoption of the budget. In other cases, the budget is adopted by resolution of the governing body.

Appropriations.   Because **appropriations** constitute maximum expenditure authorizations during the fiscal year, they cannot be exceeded legally unless subsequently amended by the legislative body (although some governments permit modifications up to a prescribed limit to be made by the executive branch). Unexpended or unencumbered appropriations may lapse at the end of a fiscal year or may continue as authority for subsequent period expenditures, depending on the applicable legal provisions.

It may be necessary for the legislative agency to adopt a separate appropriation resolution or ordinance, or the adoption of the budget may include the making of appropriations for the items of expenditure included therein. Provision for the required general property tax levy is usually made at this time, either by certifying the required tax rates to the governmental unit that will bill and collect the general property tax or by enacting a tax levy ordinance or resolution.

(iii) Budget Execution.   The budget execution phase entails obtaining the revenues, operating the program, and expending the money as authorized. The accounts are usually structured on the same basis on which the budget was prepared. Many governments maintain budgetary control by integration of the budgetary accounts into the general and subsidiary ledger. The entry is as follows:

Estimated revenues	$XXX	
Appropriations		$XXX

If estimated revenues exceed appropriations, a credit for the excess is made to "budgetary fund balance"; if they are less the appropriations, the difference is debited to "budgetary fund balance."

Individual sources of revenues are recognized in subsidiary revenue accounts. A typical revenue ledger report is illustrated in Exhibit 28.1. This format provides for the comparison, at any date, of actual and estimated revenues from each source.

To control expenditures effectively, the individual amounts making up the total appropriations are recorded in subsidiary expenditures accounts, generally called "appropriation ledgers." Exhibit 28.2 presents an example of an appropriation ledger. It should be noted that this format provides for recording the budget appropriation and for applying expenditures and **encumbrances** (see below) relating to the particular classification against the amount appropriated at any date.

When the managerial control purposes of integrating the budgetary accounts into the general ledger have been served, the budgetary account balances are reversed in the process of closing the books at year-end. Budgetary accounting procedures thus have no effect on the financial position or results of operations of a governmental entity.

NAME OF GOVERNMENTAL UNIT
Budget versus Actual Revenue
by Revenue Source
for Accounting Period June 30, 19X2

Fund Type: The General Fund

Revenues	Budgeted	Actual	Variance
015 Real & per. revenue recognized			
0110 Real & p. prop rev. recognized	$459,449,213	$460,004,317	$ (555,104)
Revenue class total	459,449,213	460,004,317	(555,104)
020 Motor vehicle & other excise			
0121 M/V taxes—current year	16,000,000	22,727,905	(6,727,905)
0122 M/V taxes—prior 1987	0	2,886,605	(2,886,605)
0123 M/V taxes—1986	0	32,051	(32,051)
0124 M/V taxes—1985	0	45,378	(45,378)
0125 M/V taxes—1984 & prior	0	85,393	(85,393)
0126 M/V taxes—1972—prior	0	2	(2)
0127 Boat excise—cur yr 1988	15,000	40,414	(25,414)
0128 Boat excise—1987	0	155	(155)
0131 M.V. lessor surcharge	200	60	139
Revenue class total	16,015,200	25,817,963	(9,802,764)
025 Local excise taxes			
0129 Hotel/motel room excise	13,500,000	13,580,142	(80,142)
0130 Aircraft fuel excise	12,400,000	12,960,966	(560,966)
Revenue class total	25,900,000	26,541,108	(641,108)
030 Departmental & other revenue			
0133 Penalties & int-prop. taxes	1,000,000	1,746,007	(746,007)
0134 Penalties & int.-M/V taxes	525,000	620,124	(95,124)
0135 Penalties & int.-sidewalk	0	115	(115)
0136 Penalties & interest/tax title	5,000,000	3,835,517	1,164,483
0138 Penalties & int./boat excise	0	3	(3)
3101 Data processing services	100	6,849	(6,749)
3103 Purchasing services	50,000	69,038	(19,038)
3104 Recording of legal instruments	150	291	(141)
3105 Registry division—fees	750,000	761,238	(11,238)
3107 City record/sale of publicatn	10,000	25,353	(15,353)
3108 Assessing fees	1,600	914	686
3109 Liens	400,000	373,410	26,590
3120 City clerk—fees	250,000	231,970	18,030
3130 Election—fees	12,000	10,633	1,367
3140 City council/sale of pubicatn	200	310	(110)
3199 Other general services	35,000	18,691	16,309
3202 Police services	350,000	365,102	(15,102)
3211 Fire services	1,150,000	1,582,355	(432,355)
3221 Civil defense	40,000	161,835	(121,835)
3301 Parking facilities	3,350,000	3,775,810	(425,810)
Revenue class total	$ 12,924,050	$ 13,585,565	$ (661,515)

Exhibit 28.1.   A typical revenue ledger report.

NAME OF GOVERNMENTAL UNIT
Budget Versus Actual Expenditures
and Encumbrances by Activity
for Accounting Period June 30, 19X2

Fund Type: The General Fund

Expenditures		Budgeted	Actual	Variance
1100 Human services				
011-384-0384	Rent equity board	$ 1,330,977	$ 1,274,531	$ 56,446
011-387-0387	Elderly commission	2,534,005	2,289,549	244,456
011-398-0398	Physically handicapped comm	180,283	159,768	20,515
011-503-0503	Arts & humanities office	211,916	207,219	4,697
011-740-0741	Vet serv-veterans serv div	2,871,616	2,506,363	365,253
011-740-0742	Vet serv-veterans graves reg	158,270	146,392	11,878
011-150-1505	Jobs & community services	370,053	369,208	845
Activity total		7,657,120	6,953,030	704,090
1200 Public safety				
011-211-0211	Police department	116,850,000	117,145,704	(295,704)
011-221-0221	Fire department	80,594,068	79,587,423	1,006,645
011-222-0222	Arson commission	189,244	175,670	13,574
011-251-0251	Transportation-traffic div	13,755,915	13,707,890	48,025
011-252-0252	Licensing board	542,007	449,825	92,182
011-251-0253	Transportation-parking clerk	7,520,539	7,474,462	46,077
011-261-0260	Inspectional services dept	10,004,470	10,003,569	901
Activity total		229,456,243	228,544,543	911,700
1300 Public works				
011-311-0311	Public works department	64,900,000	60,281,837	4,618,163
011-331-0331	Snow removal	2,250,000	2,360,326	(110,326)
Activity total		67,150,000	62,642,163	4,507,837
1400 Property & development				
011-180-0180	RPD-general administration div	432,740	416,569	16,171
014-180-0183	Real property dept county	1,027,660	354,328	673,332
011-180-0184	RPD-buildings division	6,010,155	6,038,464	(28,309)
011-180-0185	RPD-property division	1,847,650	1,806,427	41,223
011-188-0186	PFD-code enforcement division	504,013	458,984	45,029
011-188-0187	PFD-administration division	4,677,365	4,697,167	(19,802)
011-188-0188	PFD-construction & repair div	3,063,637	2,808,266	255,371
Activity total		$ 17,563,220	$ 16,580,205	$ 983,015

Exhibit 28.2. A typical appropriation ledger report.

Encumbrances. An **encumbrance,** which is unique to governmental accounting, is the reservation of a portion of an applicable appropriation that is made because a contract has been signed or a purchase order issued. The encumbrance is usually recorded in the accounting system to prevent overspending the appropriation. When the goods or services are received, the expenditure is recorded and the encumbrance is reversed. The entry to record an encumbrance is as follows:

Encumbrances	$XXX	
Reserve for encumbrances		$XXX

The entries that are made when the goods or services are received are:

Reserve for encumbrances	$XXX	
Encumbrances		$XXX
Expenditures	$XXX	
Vouchers payable		$XXX

Many governments report encumbrances that are not liquidated at year-end in the same way as expenditures because the encumbrances are another use of budgetary appropriations. The total amount of encumbrances not liquidated by year-end may be considered as a reservation of the fund balance for the subsequent year's expenditures, based on the encumbered appropriation authority carried over.

Allotments.   Another way to maintain budgetary control is to use an allotment system. With an allotment system, the annual budget appropriation is divided and allotted among the months or quarters in the fiscal year. A department is not permitted to spend more than its allotment during the period.

The International City Managers' Association lists the following purposes of an allotment system:

1. To make sure that departments plan their spending so as to have sufficient funds to carry on their programs throughout the year, avoiding year-end deficiencies and special appropriations.
2. To eliminate or reduce short-term tax anticipation borrowing by making possible more accurate forecast control of cash position throughout the fiscal year.
3. To keep expenditures within the limits of revenues that are actually realized, avoiding an unbalanced budget in the operation of any fund as a whole.
4. To give the chief administrator control over departmental expenditures commensurate with the administrative responsibility, allowing the administrator to effect economies in particular activities as changes in work load and improvements in methods occur.

Interim Reports.   The last element in the budget execution process is interim financial reports. These are prepared to provide department heads, senior management, and the governing body with the information needed to monitor and control operations, demonstrate compliance with legal and budgetary limitations, anticipate changes in financial resources and requirements due to events or developments that are unknown or could not be foreseen at the time the budget was initially developed, or take appropriate corrective action. Interim reports should be prepared frequently enough to permit early detection of variances between actual and planned operations, but not so frequently as to adversely affect practicality and economy. For most governmental units, interim reports on a monthly basis are necessary for optimum results. With smaller units, a bimonthly or quarterly basis may be sufficient. With sophisticated data-processing equipment, it may be possible to automatically generate the appropriate information daily.

Governmental units should prepare interim financial reports covering the following:

Revenues.
Expenditures.
Cash projections.
Proprietary funds.

Capital projects.

Grant programs.

The form and content of these reports should reflect the government's particular circumstances and conditions.

(iv) Proprietary Fund Budgeting.   The nature of most operations financed and accounted for through proprietary funds is such that the demand for the goods or services largely determines the appropriate level of revenues and expenses. Increased demand causes a higher level of expenses to be incurred but also results in a higher level of revenues. Thus, as in commercial accounting, **flexible budgets** prepared for several levels of possible activity typically are better for planning, control, and evaluation purposes than are fixed budgets.

Accordingly, budgets are not typically adopted for proprietary funds. Furthermore, even when flexible budgets are adopted, they are viewed not as appropriations but as approved plans. The budgetary accounts are generally not integrated into the ledger accounts because it is considered unnecessary. Budgetary control and evaluation are achieved by comparing interim actual revenues and expenses with planned revenues and expenses at the actual level of activity for the period.

In some instances, fixed dollar budgets are adopted for proprietary funds either to meet local legal requirements or to control certain expenditures (e.g., capital outlay). In such cases, it may be appropriate to integrate budgetary accounts into the proprietary fund accounting system in a manner similar to that discussed for governmental funds.

(v) Capital Budget.   Many governments also prepare a **capital budget.** A capital budget is a plan for capital expenditures to be incurred during a single budget year from funds subject to appropriation for projects scheduled under the **capital program.** The annual capital budget is adopted concurrently with the operating budgets of the governmental unit, being subject to a public hearing and the other usual legal procedures.

The capital budget should not be confused with a **capital program** or **capital project budget.** A capital program is a plan for capital expenditures to be incurred over a period of years, usually 5 or 6 years. The capital project budget represents the estimated amount to be expended on a specific project over the entire period of its construction. The capital budget authorizes the amounts to be expended on all projects during a single year. Controlling this amount is important for the proper use of available funds.

(l) CLASSIFICATION AND TERMINOLOGY.   **Principles 10** and **11** establish the requirements surrounding classification and terminology. Governmental fund revenues should be classified by fund and source. The major revenue source classifications are taxes, licenses and permits, intergovernmental revenues, charges for services, fines and forfeits, and miscellaneous. Governmental units often classify revenues by organizational units. This classification may be desirable for purposes of management control and accountability, as well as for auditing purposes, but it should supplement rather than supplant the classifications by fund and source.

(i) Classification of Expenditures.   There are many ways to classify governmental fund expenditures in addition to the basic fund classification. Function, program, organizational unit, activity, character, and principal class of object are examples. Typically, expenditures are classified by character (current, intergovernmental, capital outlay, and/or debt service). Current expenditures are further classified by function and/or program.

- *Character Classification.* Reporting expenditures according to the physical period they are presumed to benefit. The major character classifications are (1) current expenditures, which benefit the current fiscal period; (2) capital outlays, which are presumed to benefit both the present and future fiscal periods; and (3) debt service, which benefits prior fiscal periods as well as current and future periods. Intergovernmental expenditures is a fourth character classification that is used when one governmental unit makes expenditures to another governmental unit.

- *Function Classification.* Establishing groups of related activities that are aimed at accomplishing a major service or regulatory responsibility. Standard function classifications are as follows:

    General government.

    Public safety.

    Health and welfare.

    Culture and recreation.

    Conservation of natural resources.

    Urban redevelopment and housing.

    Economic development and assistance.

    Education.

    Debt service.

    Miscellaneous.

- *Program Classification.* Establishing groups of activities, operations, or organizational units that are directed at the attainment of specific purposes or objectives, for example, protection of property, or improvement of transportation. Program classification is used by governmental units employing program budgeting.

- *Organizational Unit Classification.* Grouping expenditures according to the governmental unit's organization structure. Organizational unit classification is essential to responsibility reporting.

- *Activity Classification.* Grouping expenditures according to the performance of specific activities. Activity classification is necessary for the determination of cost per unit of activity, which in turn is necessary for evaluation of economy and efficiency.

- *Object Classification.* Grouping expenditures according to the types of items purchased or services obtained, for example, personal services, supplies, other services and charges. Object classifications are subdivisions of the character classification.

Excessively detailed object classifications should be avoided since they complicate the accounting procedure and are of limited use in financial management. The use of a few object classification is sufficient in budget preparation; control emphasis should be on organization units, functions, programs, and activities rather than on the object of expenditures.

(ii) Classifications of Other Transactions.   Certain transactions, although not revenues or expenditures of an individual fund or the governmental entity as a whole, are increases or decreases in the equity of an individual fund. These transactions are classified as **other financing sources and uses** and are reported in the operating statement separately from fund revenues and expenditures. The most common other financing sources and uses are:

- *Proceeds of Long-term Debt Issues.* Such proceeds (including leases) are not recorded as fund liabilities; for example, proceeds of bonds and notes expended through the capital project or debt service funds.

- *Operating Transfers.* These include legally authorized transfers from a fund receiving revenues to the fund through which the resources are to be expended; examples are transfers of tax revenues from a special revenue fund to a debt service fund and transfers from an enterprise fund other than payments in lieu of taxes to finance general fund expenditures.

Other interfund transactions are:

- *Interfund Loans and Advances.* These funds are disbursed by one fund for the benefit of another. If the funds will be repaid shortly, the amount should be reclassified as **due from** other funds by the lending fund and **due to** other funds by the receiving fund. When two funds owe each other, the amounts receivable and payable should not be offset in the accounts. However, for purposes of reporting, current amounts due from and due to the same funds may be offset and the net amounts shown in the respective fund balance sheets.

  If the advance is long-term in nature and the asset will not be available to finance current operations, a fund balance reserve equal to the amount of the advance should be established.

- *Quasi-External Transactions.* These transactions would be treated as revenues, expenditures, or expenses if they involved organizations external to the governmental unit. Examples are payments in lieu of taxes from an enterprise fund to the general fund; internal service fund billings to departments; routine employer contributions from the general fund to a pension trust fund; and a routine service charge for inspection, engineering, utilities, or similar services provided by a department financed from one fund to a department financed from another fund.

  Amounts should be accounted for as revenues in the recipient fund and as expenditures in the disbursing fund.

- *Reimbursements.* These transactions constitute reimbursements of a fund for expenditures or expenses initially made from it that are properly applicable to another fund. An example is an expenditure properly chargeable to a special revenue fund but initially made from the general fund, which is subsequently reimbursed. The transaction should be recorded as an expenditure or expense in the reimbursing fund and as a reduction of an expenditure or expense in the reimbursed fund.

(iii) Residual Equity Transfers.   Another type of interfund transaction, **residual equity transfers,** is not classified as an other financing source or use because it is a change in fund balance that is not considered in the determination of the results of operations. A **residual equity transfer** is a nonrecurring or nonroutine transfer of equity between funds. Examples are a general fund's contribution of capital to an enterprise fund or an internal service fund; the subsequent return of all or part of such contribution to the general fund; and transfers of residual balances of discontinued funds to the general fund or a debt service fund.

(iv) Classification of Fund Equity.   Fund equity is the difference between a fund's assets and its liabilities. In the governmental funds, it is called the "fund balance"; in the proprietary funds, it consists of retained earnings and contributed capital.

The important amount in the fund equity account for governmental funds is the amount available for future appropriation and expenditure (i.e., unreserved and undesignated fund balance); therefore governments should clearly delineate amounts that are not available for such purposes. Fund balance can be segregated into reserved and unreserved amounts. Unreserved fund balance can be segregated further into designated and undesignated amounts.

Reservations of fund balance identify (1) third-party claims against resources of the entity that have not materialized as liabilities at the balance sheet date, or (2) the existence of assets that, because of their nonmonetary nature or lack of liquidity, represent financial resources not available for current appropriation or expenditure; for example, inventories, prepaid expenses, and noncurrent assets (usually receivables). Such reserves are not intended as valuation allowances, but merely demonstrate the current unavailability of the subject assets to pay current expenditures.

Designations of fund balance identify tentative plans for or restrictions on the future use of financial resources. Such designations should be supported by definitive plans and approved by either the government's CEO or the legislature. Examples of such designations include the earmarking of financial resources for capital projects and contingent liabilities.

Reserves and designations are established by debiting unreserved, undesignated fund balance and crediting the reserve or designation. The reserve is not established by a charge to operations. Since reserves relate to certain assets not being available for future appropriation, establishing a reserve may create or increase a negative unreserved fund balance. Designations, on the other hand, may not create or increase a negative unreserved fund balance because the designation represents an internal plan.

Another type of fund equity, existing only in the proprietary funds, is **contributed capital.** It represents the amount of fund equity or permanent capital contributed to a proprietary fund by another fund or by customers, developers, other members of the general public, or other government bodies toward the cost of capital facilities.

(v) Investment in General Fixed Assets.   Although presented in the fund equity section of a governmental unit's balance sheet, **investment in general fixed assets** is not considered fund equity.

(vi) Accounting Coding.   Charts of accounts in governments range from simple three-digit codes designed for manual accounting systems to multidigit codes that use the logical arrangement of numbers within the codes to signify such things as fund, organizational unit, program, fiscal year, activity, and source of revenue.

(m) EXTERNAL FINANCIAL REPORTING.   Prior to 1979, governments traditionally prepared external financial reports by preparing financial statements for every fund maintained by the government. This often resulted in lengthy financial reports. External financial reporting has evolved to require the presentation of financial statements on a more aggregated basis and the inclusion of legally separate entities that have special relationships. Principle 12 relates to financial reporting and is discussed below.

(i) The Financial Reporting Entity.   GASB Statement No. 14, "The Financial Reporting Entity" establishes standards for defining and reporting on the financial reporting entity.

The statement indicates that the financial reporting entity consists of (a) the primary government (PG), (b) organizations for which the PG is financially accountable, and (c) other organizations that, if omitted from the reporting entity, would cause the financial statements to be misleading.

The statement also outlines the basic criteria for including organizations in or excluding organizations from the reporting entity. All organizations for which the PG is *financially* accountable should be included in the reporting entity. Such organizations include:

1. The organizations that make up the PG's legal entity, and
2. Component units. That is, organizations that are legally separate from the PG but:
   - The PG's officials appoint a voting majority of the organization's governing board *and*
   - Either the PG is able to impose its will on that organization *or* there is a potential for the organization to provide specific financial benefits to, or to impose specific financial burdens on the PG.

Organizations not meeting the above criteria are excluded from the reporting entity.

Reporting the inclusion of the various entities comprising the reporting entity can be done using two methods: blending or discrete presentation. Most component units should be included in the financial reporting entity by discrete presentation. Some component units, despite being legally separate entities, are so intertwined with the PG that, in substance, they are the same as the primary government and should be "blended" with the transactions of the PG.

Certain other entities are not considered component units because the PG, while responsible for appointing the organization's board members, is not financially accountable. Such entities are considered related organizations. These related organizations as well as joint ventures and jointly governed organizations should be disclosed in the reporting entity's footnotes.

(ii) Pyramid Concept and General Purpose Financial Statements. GASB Codification § 1900 recommends that governments use the **pyramid concept** for external financial reporting. Specifically, they should prepare **general purpose financial statements** (GPFS) composed of the following:

- Combined balance sheet—all fund types, account groups, and discretely presented component units (Exhibit 28.3).
- Combined statement of revenues, expenditures, and changes in fund balances—all governmental fund types, expendable trust funds, and discretely presented component units (Exhibit 28.4).
- Combined statement of revenues, expenditures, and changes in fund balances—budget and actual—general and special revenue fund types (Exhibit 28.5).
- Combined statement of revenues, expenses, and changes in retained earnings—all proprietary fund types, similar trust funds, and discretely presented component units (Exhibit 28.6).
- Combined statement of cash flows—all proprietary fund types, nonexpendable trust fund types, and discretely presented component units (Exhibit 28.7).
- Notes to financial statements.
- Required supplementary information.

Even though the GASB encourages each governmental entity to prepare a **comprehensive annual financial report** (CAFR) the GPFS constitutes fair presentation of financial position and results of operations in accordance with GAAP and could be opined upon as such by an independent auditor. The statements would be suitable for inclusion in an official statement for a securities offering and for widespread distribution to users requiring less detailed information about the governmental unit's finances than is contained in the CAFR described below.

The following should be noted for each recommended GPFS:

- *Combined balance sheet—all fund types, account groups, and discretely presented component units.*

  The term "equities" is used for contributed capital, investment in general fixed assets, retained earnings, and fund balances, with the four separated on the balance sheet.

  The fund types and account groups are classified into the following categories: governmental fund types, proprietary fund types, fiduciary fund types, and account groups. (Classifying the fiduciary funds with the governmental and proprietary fund, as appropriate, is an acceptable alternative.)

  The totals of the amounts of all types and account groups may be reported for each caption. Totals may be reported for the reporting entity as a whole or the reporting entity as a whole and the primary government. Totals for only the primary government are not permitted. If totals are reported, the total column should be headed "memorandum only."

  Interfund and similar eliminations may or may not be made in arriving at the total. If eliminations are made, this fact should be disclosed by headings on the statement, and the

NAME OF GOVERNMENTAL UNIT
Combined Balance Sheet—All Fund Types, Account Groups, and Discretely Presented Component Units
December 31, 19X2

ASSETS	Governmental Fund Types				Proprietary Fund Types		Fiduciary Fund Types	Account Groups		Totals (Memorandum Only)		Totals (Memorandum Only)
	General	Special Revenue	Debt Service	Capital Projects	Enterprise	Internal Service	Trust and Agency	General Fixed Assets	General Long-Term Debt	Primary Government	Component Units	Reporting Entity
Cash	$258,500	$101,385	$185,624	$659,100	$257,036	$29,700	$216,701	—	—	$1,708,046	$1,656,960	$3,365,006
Cash with fiscal agent	—	—	102,000	—	—	—	—	—	—	102,000	—	102,000
Investments, at cost or amortized cost	65,000	37,200	160,990	—	1,239,260	—	—	—	—	1,502,450	893,227	2,395,677
Receivables (net of allowances for uncollectibles):												
Taxes	58,300	2,500	3,829	—	—	—	580,000	—	—	644,629	49,003	693,632
Accounts	8,300	3,300	—	100	29,130	—	—	—	—	40,830	38,326	79,156
Special assessments	—	—	458,930	—	—	—	—	—	—	458,930	—	458,930
Notes	—	—	—	—	2,350	—	—	—	—	2,350	—	2,350
Loans	—	—	—	—	—	—	35,000	—	—	35,000	—	35,000
Accrued interest	50	25	1,907	—	650	—	2,666	—	—	5,298	—	5,298
Lease receivable from primary government	—	—	—	—	—	—	—	—	—	—	810,000	810,000
Due from other funds	2,000	—	—	—	2,000	12,000	11,189	—	—	27,189	—	27,189
Due from component units	65,000	—	—	—	—	—	—	—	—	65,000	—	65,000
Due from other governments	30,000	75,260	—	640,000	—	—	—	—	—	745,260	—	745,260
Advances to internal service funds	65,000	—	—	—	—	—	—	—	—	65,000	—	65,000

Inventory of supplies, at cost	7,200	5,190	—	—	23,030	40,000	—	—	—	75,420	—	75,420
Prepaid expenses	—	—	—	—	1,200	—	—	—	—	1,200	—	1,200
Restricted assets:												
Cash	—	—	—	—	113,559	—	—	—	—	113,559	—	113,559
Investments, at cost or amortized cost	—	—	—	—	176,800	—	—	—	—	176,800	—	176,800
Investment in joint venture	—	—	—	—	2,300,000	—	—	—	—	2,300,000	—	2,300,000
Land	—	—	—	—	211,100	20,000	—	$1,259,500	—	1,490,600	3,841,936	5,332,536
Buildings	—	—	—	—	447,700	60,000	—	2,855,500	—	3,363,200	9,517,000	12,880,200
Accumulated depreciation	—	—	—	—	(90,718)	(4,500)	—	—	—	(95,218)	(2,175,193)	(2,270,411)
Improvements other than buildings	—	—	—	—	3,887,901	15,000	—	1,036,750	—	4,939,651	2,844,213	7,783,864
Accumulated depreciation	—	—	—	—	(348,944)	(3,000)	—	—	—	(351,944)	(1,406,015)	(1,757,959)
Machinery and equipment	—	—	—	—	1,841,145	25,000	—	452,500	—	2,318,645	8,991,402	11,310,047
Accumulated depreciation	—	—	—	—	(201,138)	(9,400)	—	—	—	(210,538)	(2,421,766)	(2,632,304)
Construction in progress	—	—	—	—	22,713	—	—	1,722,250	—	1,744,963	—	1,744,963
Amount available in debt service funds	—	—	—	—	—	—	—	—	$ 256,280	256,280	—	256,280
Amount to be provided for retirement of general long-term debt	—	—	—	—	—	—	—	—	2,749,790	2,749,790	193,000	2,942,790
Amount to be provided from special assessments	—	—	—	—	—	—	—	—	458,930	458,930	—	458,930
Total Assets	$559,350	$224,860	$913,280	$1,299,200	$8,675,514	$184,800	$2,084,816	$7,326,500	$3,465,000	$24,733,320	$22,832,093	$47,565,413

(continued)

Exhibit 28.3. Sample combined balance sheet.

28 · 45

		Governmental Fund Types			Proprietary Fund Types		Fiduciary Fund Types	Account Groups		Totals (Memorandum Only)		Totals (Memorandum Only)
LIABILITIES AND FUND EQUITY	General	Special Revenue	Debt Service	Capital Projects	Enterprise	Internal Service	Trust and Agency	General Fixed Assets	General Long-Term Debt	Primary Government	Component Units	Reporting Entity
Liabilities:												
Vouchers payable	$118,261	$ 33,850	—	$ 49,600	$ 131,071	$ 15,000	$ 3,350	—	—	$ 351,132	$ 635,298	$ 986,430
Contracts payable	57,600	18,300	—	119,000	8,347	—	—	—	—	203,247	98,412	301,659
Judgments payable	—	2,000	—	33,800	—	—	—	—	—	35,800	—	35,800
Accrued liabilities	—	—	—	10,700	16,870	—	4,700	—	—	32,270	—	32,270
Payable from restricted assets:												
Construction contracts	—	—	—	—	17,760	—	—	—	—	17,760	—	17,760
Fiscal agent	—	—	—	—	139	—	—	—	—	139	—	139
Accrued interest	—	—	—	—	32,305	—	—	—	—	32,305	—	32,305
Revenue bonds	—	—	—	—	48,000	—	—	—	—	48,000	—	48,000
Deposits	—	—	—	—	63,000	—	—	—	—	63,000	—	63,000
Due to other taxing units	—	—	—	—	—	—	680,800	—	—	680,800	—	680,800
Due to other funds	24,189	2,000	—	1,000	—	—	—	—	—	27,189	—	27,189
Due to primary government	—	—	—	—	—	—	—	—	—	—	65,000	65,000
Due to student groups	—	—	—	—	—	—	1,850	—	—	1,850	—	1,850
Deferred revenue	15,000	—	$555,000	—	—	—	—	—	—	570,000	—	570,000
Advance from general fund	—	—	—	—	—	65,000	—	—	—	65,000	—	65,000
Matured bonds payable	—	—	100,000	—	—	—	—	—	—	100,000	—	100,000
Matured interest payable	—	—	2,000	—	—	—	—	—	—	2,000	—	2,000
Lease payable to component unit	—	—	—	—	—	—	—	—	$ 810,000	810,000	—	810,000
General obligation bonds payable	—	—	—	—	700,000	—	—	—	2,100,000	2,800,000	193,000	2,993,000
Special assessment debt with governmental commitment	—	—	—	—	—	—	—	—	555,000	555,000	—	555,000
Revenue bonds payable	—	—	—	—	1,798,000	—	—	—	—	1,798,000	2,776,000	4,574,000
Total Liabilities	215,050	56,150	657,000	214,100	2,815,492	80,000	690,700	—	3,465,000	8,193,492	3,767,710	11,961,202

Fund Equity:												
Investment in general fixed assets	—	—	—	—	—	—	—	7,326,500	—	7,326,500	7,836,545	15,163,045
Contributed capital	—	—	—	—	3,692,666	95,000	—	—	—	3,787,666	8,841,640	12,629,306
Retained earnings:												
Reserved for revenue bond retirement	—	—	—	—	129,155	—	—	—	—	129,155	—	129,155
Unreserved	—	—	—	—	2,038,201	9,800	—	—	—	2,048,001	1,359,581	3,407,582
Fund Balances:												
Reserved for encumbrances	38,000	46,500	—	1,076,500	—	—	—	—	—	1,161,000	475,100	1,636,100
Reserved for inventory of supplies	7,200	5,190	—	—	—	—	—	—	—	12,390	—	12,390
Reserved for advance to internal service funds	65,000	—	—	—	—	—	—	—	—	65,000	—	65,000
Reserved for loans	—	—	—	—	—	—	50,050	—	—	50,050	—	50,050
Reserved for endowments	—	—	—	—	—	—	134,000	—	—	134,000	—	134,000
Reserved for employees' retirement system	—	—	—	—	—	—	1,426,201	—	—	1,426,201	—	1,426,201
Unreserved:												
Designated for debt service	—	—	256,280	—	—	—	—	—	—	256,280	—	256,280
Designated for subsequent years' expenditures	50,000	—	—	—	—	—	—	—	—	50,000	—	50,000
Undesignated	184,100	117,020	—	8,600	—	—	(216,135)	—	—	93,585	551,517	645,102
Total Fund Equity	344,300	168,710	256,280	1,085,100	5,860,022	104,800	1,394,116	7,326,500	—	16,539,828	19,064,383	35,604,211
Total Liabilities and Fund Equity	$559,350	$224,860	$913,280	$1,299,200	$8,675,514	$184,800	$2,084,816	$7,326,500	$3,465,000	$24,733,320	$22,832,093	$47,565,413

The notes to the financial statements are an integral part of this statement.

Exhibit 28.3. *Continued.*

NAME OF GOVERNMENTAL UNIT
Combined Statement of Revenues, Expenditures, and Changes in Fund Equity—
All Governmental Fund Types, Expendable Trust Funds, and Discretely Presented Component Units
for the Fiscal Year Ended December 31, 19X2

| | Governmental Fund Types | | | | Fiduciary Fund Type | Totals (Memorandum Only) | | Totals (Memorandum Only) |
	General	Special Revenue	Debt Service	Capital Projects	Expendable Trust	Primary Government	Component Units	Reporting Entity
Revenues:								
Taxes	$ 881,300	$ 189,300	$ 79,177	—	—	$1,149,777	$ 675,327	$1,825,104
Special assessments	—	—	55,500	—	—	55,500	—	55,500
Licenses and permits	103,000	—	—	—	—	103,000	13,942	116,942
Intergovernmental revenues	186,500	831,100	41,500	$1,250,000	—	2,309,100	233,474	2,542,574
Charges for services	91,000	79,100	—	—	—	170,100	—	170,100
Fines and forfeits	33,200	—	—	—	—	33,200	—	33,200
Miscellaneous revenues	19,500	71,625	36,235	3,750	$ 200	131,310	—	131,310
Total revenues	1,314,500	1,171,125	212,412	1,253,750	200	3,951,987	922,743	4,874,730
Expenditures:								
Current:								
General government	121,805					121,805	233,587	355,392
Public safety	258,395	480,000				738,395		738,395
Highways and streets	85,400	417,000				502,400		502,400
Sanitation	56,250					56,250		56,250
Health	44,500					44,500		44,500
Welfare	46,800					46,800		46,800
Culture and recreation	40,900	256,450				297,350		297,350
Education	509,150				2,420	511,570	658,923	1,170,493
Capital outlay				1,939,100		1,939,100	102,500	2,041,600
Debt service:								
Principal retirement			115,500			115,500	33,400	148,900
Interest and fiscal charges			68,420			68,420	14,800	83,220
Total Expenditures	1,163,200	1,153,450	183,920	1,939,100	2,420	4,442,090	1,043,210	5,485,300
Excess of Revenues over (under) Expenditures	151,300	17,675	28,492	(685,350)	(2,220)	(490,103)	(120,467)	(610,570)

Other Financing Sources (Uses):								
Proceeds of general obligation bonds	—	—	—	1,175,000	—	1,175,000	—	1,175,000
Proceeds of special assessment debt	—	—	—	190,500	—	190,500	—	190,500
Operating transfers in	—	—	—	74,500	2,530	77,030	—	77,030
Operating transfers out	(74,500)	—	—	—	—	(74,500)	—	(74,500)
Operating transfers from primary government	—	—	—	—	—	—	100,000	100,000
Operating transfers to component units	—	—	—	(275,000)	—	(275,000)	—	(275,000)
Total Other Financing Sources (Uses)	(74,500)	—	—	1,165,000	2,530	1,093,030	100,000	1,193,030
Excess of Revenues and Other Sources over (under) Expenditures and Other Uses	76,800	17,675	28,492	479,650	310	602,927	(20,467)	582,460
Net Income from Golf Course Operations	—	—	—	—	—	—	2,350	2,350
Fund Equity—January 1	267,500	151,035	227,788	605,450	26,555	1,278,328	1,352,056	2,630,384
Fund Equity—December 31	$ 344,300	$ 168,710	$227,788	$1,085,100	$26,865	$1,881,255	$1,352,056	$3,215,194

The notes to the financial statements are an integral part of this statement.

Exhibit 28.4. **Combined statement of revenues, expenditures, and changes in fund equity—all governmental fund types, expendable trust funds, and discretely presented component units.**

NAME OF GOVERNMENTAL UNIT
**Combined Statement of Revenues, Expenditures, and
Changes in Fund Balances—Budget and Actual—
General and Special Revenue Fund Types
for the Fiscal Year Ended December 31, 19X2**

	General Fund			Special Revenue Funds			Totals (Memorandum Only)		
	Budget	Actual	Variance— Favorable (Unfavorable)	Budget	Actual	Variance— Favorable (Unfavorable)	Budget	Actual	Variance— Favorable (Unfavorable)
Revenues									
Taxes	$ 882,500	$ 881,300	$ (1,200)	$ 189,500	$ 189,300	$ (200)	$1,072,000	$1,070,600	$ (1,400)
Licenses and Permits	125,500	103,000	(22,500)	—	—	—	125,500	103,000	(22,500)
Intergovernmental Revenues	200,000	186,500	(13,500)	837,600	831,100	(6,500)	1,037,600	1,017,600	(20,000)
Charges for Services	90,000	91,000	1,000	78,000	79,100	1,100	168,000	170,100	2,100
Fines and Forfeits	32,500	33,200	700	—	—	—	32,500	33,200	700
Miscellaneous Revenues	19,500	19,500	—	81,475	71,625	(9,850)	100,975	91,125	(9,850)
Total Revenues	1,350,000	1,314,500	(35,500)	1,186,575	1,171,125	(15,450)	2,536,575	2,485,625	(50,950)
Expenditures									
Current:									
General government	129,000	121,805	7,195	—	—	—	129,000	121,805	7,195
Public safety	277,300	258,395	18,905	494,500	480,000	14,500	771,800	738,395	33,405
Highways and streets	84,500	85,400	(900)	436,000	417,000	19,000	520,500	502,400	18,100
Sanitation	50,000	56,250	(6,250)	—	—	—	50,000	56,250	(6,250)

	General Fund			Special Revenue			Total (Memorandum Only)		
	Budget	Actual	Variance	Budget	Actual	Variance	Budget	Actual	Variance
Health	47,750	44,500	3,250	—	—	—	47,750	44,500	3,250
Welfare	51,000	46,800	4,200	—	—	—	51,000	46,800	4,200
Culture and Recreation	44,500	40,900	3,600	272,000	256,450	15,550	316,500	297,350	19,150
Education	541,450	509,150	32,300	—	—	—	541,450	509,150	32,300
Total Expenditures	1,225,500	1,163,200	62,300	1,202,500	1,153,450	49,050	2,428,000	2,316,650	111,350
Excess of Revenues over (under) Expenditures	124,500	151,300	26,800	(15,925)	17,675	33,600	108,575	168,975	60,400
Other Financing Sources (Uses)									
Operating Transfers Out	(74,500)	(74,500)	—	—	—	—	(74,500)	(74,500)	—
Excess of Revenues over (under) Expenditures and Other Uses	50,000	76,800	26,800	(15,925)	17,675	33,600	34,075	94,475	60,400
Fund Balances—January 1	202,500	202,500	—	151,035	151,035	—	353,535	353,535	—
Fund Balances—December 31	$252,500	$279,300	$26,800	$135,110	$168,710	$33,600	$387,610	$448,010	$60,400

The notes to the financial statements are an integral part of this statement.

Exhibit 28.5. Combined statement of revenues, expenditures, and changes in fund balances—budget and actual—general and special revenue fund types.

NAME OF GOVERNMENTAL UNIT
Combined Statement of Revenues, Expenses, and Changes in Fund Equity—
All Proprietary Fund Types, Similar Trust Funds, and Discretely Presented Component Units
for the Fiscal Year Ended December 31, 19X2

	Proprietary Fund Types		Fiduciary Fund Types		Totals (Memorandum Only)		Totals (Memorandum Only)
	Enterprise	Internal Service	Nonexpendable Trust	Pension Trust	Primary Government	Component Units	Reporting Entity
Operating Revenues:							
Charges for services	$ 672,150	$ 88,000			$ 760,150	$1,189,631	$ 1,949,781
Interest			$ 2,480	$ 28,460	30,940	—	30,940
Contributions				160,686	160,686	—	160,686
Gifts			45,000		45,000		45,000
Total Operating Revenues	672,150	88,000	47,480	189,146	996,776	1,189,631	2,186,407
Operating Expenses:							
Personal services	247,450	32,500			279,950	587,258	867,208
Contractual services	75,330	400			75,730	252,701	328,431
Supplies	20,310	1,900			22,210	174,356	196,566
Materials	50,940	44,000			94,940	101,800	196,740
Heat, light, and power	26,050	1,500			27,550	83,749	111,299
Depreciation	144,100	4,450			148,550	460,102	608,652
Benefit payments				21,000	21,000		21,000
Refunds				25,745	25,745		25,745
Total Operating Expenses	564,180	84,750		46,745	695,675	1,659,966	2,355,641
Operating Income (Loss)	107,970	3,250	47,480	142,401	301,101	(470,335)	(169,234)

Nonoperating Revenues (Expenses):

Operating grants	55,000	—	—	—	55,000	410,000	465,000
Net income from joint venture	145,000	—	—	—	145,000	—	145,000
Interest revenue	3,830	—	—	—	3,830	82,522	86,352
Rent	5,000	—	—	—	5,000	—	5,000
Interest expense and fiscal charges	(92,988)	—	—	—	(92,988)	(248,320)	(341,308)
Tax revenues	—	—	—	—	—	100,000	100,000
Total Nonoperating Revenues	115,842	—	—	—	115,842	344,202	460,044
Income (Loss) before operating transfers	223,812	3,250	47,480	142,401	416,943	(126,133)	290,810
Operating Transfers In (Out)	—	—	(2,530)	—	(2,530)	—	(2,530)
Operating Transfers from Primary Government	—	—	—	—	—	175,000	175,000
Net Income	223,812	3,250	44,950	142,401	414,413	48,867	463,280
Fund Equity—January 1	4,963,544	101,550	139,100	1,040,800	6,244,994	9,445,032	15,690,026
Contributions—Capital Grants	672,666	—	—	—	672,666	400,000	1,072,666
Fund Equity—December 31	$5,860,022	$104,800	$184,050	$1,183,201	$7,332,073	$9,893,899	$17,225,972

The notes to the financial statements are an integral part of this statement.

Exhibit 28.6. Combined statement of revenues, expenses, and changes in fund equity—all proprietary fund types, similar trust funds, and discretely presented component units.

CITY OF EXAMPLE, ANY STATE
Statement of Cash Flows—All Proprietary Fund Types, Similar Trust Funds, and Discretely Presented Component Units
for the Fiscal Year Ended December 31, 19X2

	Enterprise	Internal Service	Nonexpendable Trust	Totals (Memorandum Only) Primary Government	Component Units	Reporting Entity
Cash Flows from Operating Activities						
Operating Income	$ 107,970	$ 3,250	$ 47,480	$ 158,700	$(470,335)	$ (311,635)
Adjustments to Reconcile Operating Income to Net Cash Provided by Operating Activities:						
Depreciation	144,100	4,450	—	148,550	460,102	608,652
Change in Assests and Liabilities:						
Decrease in other current liabilities payable from restricted assets	(8,946)	—	—	(8,946)	—	(8,946)
Increase in other restricted assets	(1,624)	—	—	(1,624)	—	(1,624)
Decrease in accounts receivable	5,570	—	5,000	10,570	17,435	28,005
Increase (decrease) in inventory of supplies	(11,250)	(14,000)	—	(25,250)	2,385	(22,865)
Increase in prepaid expenses	(460)	—	—	(460)	—	(460)
Decrease in due from other funds	6,000	8,000	—	14,000	—	14,000
Increase (decrease) in vouchers payable	72,471	(5,000)	—	67,471	—	67,471
Increase (decrease) in other liabilities	12,160	—	—	12,160	(72,749)	(60,589)
Decrease in contracts payable	(551,653)	—	—	(551,653)	(69,288)	(620,941)
Total Adjustments	(333,632)	(6,550)	5,000	(335,182)	337,885	2,703
Net Cash Provided (Used) by Operating Activities	(225,662)	(3,300)	52,480	(176,482)	(132,450)	(308,932)

Cash Flows from Noncapital Financing Activities

Retirement of General Obligation Bonds	(50,000)	—	(50,000)	—	(50,000)
Interest Expense and Fiscal Charges	(92,988)	—	(92,988)	(75,342)	(168,330)
Operating Grants Received	55,000	—	55,000	785,000	840,000
Operating Transfers (to) from Other Funds	—	(2,530)	(2,530)	—	(2,530)
Repayment of Advance from General Fund	—	—	(10,000)	—	(10,000)
Net Cash Provided (Used) by Noncapital Financing Activities	(87,988)	(2,530)	(100,518)	709,658	609,140

Cash Flows from Capital and Related Financing Activities:

Acquisition and Construction of Capital Assets	(324,453)	(7,000)	(331,453)	(632,246)	(963,699)
Proceeds from Sale of Revenue Bonds	127,883	—	127,883	—	127,883
Retirement on Revenue Bonds Payable	(52,000)	—	(52,000)	(325,000)	(377,000)
Capital Contributed by Subdividers	672,666	—	672,666	400,000	1,072,666
Rent	5,000	—	5,000	—	5,000
Net Cash Provided (Used) by Capital and Related Financing Activities	429,096	(7,000)	422,096	(557,246)	(135,150)

Cash Flows from Investing Activities:

Purchase of Investment Securities	—	(46,640)	(46,640)	(94,273)	(276,063)
Proceeds from Sale and Maturities of Investment Securities	—	1,000	1,000	30,519	31,519
Interest and Dividends on Investments	3,830	—	3,830	83,716	87,646
Net Cash Provided (Used) by Investing Activities	3,830	(45,640)	(41,810)	(50,844)	(92,654)
Net Increase (Decrease) in Cash and Cash Equivalents	119,276	4,310	103,286	(30,882)	72,404
Cash and Cash Equivalents at Beginning of Year	137,760	12,391	200,151	552,318	752,469
Cash and Cash Equivalents at End of Year	$ 257,036	$ 16,701	$ 303,437	$ 521,436	$ 824,873

Exhibit 28.7. Statement of cash flows—all proprietary fund types and nonexpendable trust funds.

nature of the elimination should be explained in the accompanying notes (if not obvious from the financial statements).

The presentation of comparative totals for the prior year for each caption is encouraged because this information is useful to the statement.

Comparative data for fund types is not typically presented because such a presentation will unduly complicate the statement.

- *Combined statement of revenues, expenditures, and changes in fund balances—all governmental fund types, expendable trust funds, and discretely presented component units.*

The statement should be classified as follows:

	Revenues
−	Expenditures
	Excess of revenues over (under) expenditures
±	Other financing sources (uses)
	Excess of revenues and other sources over (under) expenditures and other uses
+	Fund balance—beginning of period
	Fund balance—end of period

Alternatively, such statements may be presented as follows:

	Revenues
+	Other financing sources
	Total revenue and other sources
	Expenditures
+	Other uses (e.g., operating transfers to other funds)
	Total expenditures and other uses
	Excess of revenues and other sources over (under) expenditures and other uses
+	Fund balance—beginning of period
	Fund balance—end of period

It is also acceptable to open the statement of revenues, expenditures, and changes in fund balance with "fund balance—beginning of period." For example:

	Fund balance—beginning of period
	Revenues
+	Other financing sources
	Total revenues and other sources
	Expenditures
+	Other uses (e.g., operating transfers to other funds)
	Total expenditures and other uses
	Excess of revenues and other sources over (under) expenditures and other uses
	Fund balance—end of period

Excessive detail should be avoided in choosing the captions for reporting revenues and expenditures. Appropriate revenue and expenditure captions were discussed in section 28.4(1) of this chapter.

- *Combined statement of revenues, expenditures, and changes in fund balances—budget and actual—general and special revenue fund types.*

This statement provides the comparison of the budgeted amounts and the actual results for those governmental fund types for which a legally adopted budget was prepared. The budget data should be obtained from the legally adopted budget. If the budget is not a legal document, the amounts may be those that the governing body or management considers its annual budget.

If the budget has been revised, the budget amounts should reflect the latest revised budget and the column should be headed "revised budget." If the revised budget differs substantially from the original budget, the original budget should also be reported.

The budget amounts and actual results should be on the same basis of accounting. Often, that basis is in conformity with GAAP. However, if the budget is prepared on a basis not consistent with GAAP, the actual results should be reported in conformity with the basis used to prepare the budget. In addition a reconciliation between the results on a budgeting basis and the results on a GAAP basis should be reported in the statement of revenues, expenditures, and changes in fund balance or in a note to the financial statements.

A note to the financial statements should disclose any material amounts of expenditures over appropriations at the legal level of control in an individual fund that is not disclosed in the combined statement of revenues, expenditures, and changes in fund balances—budget and actual—general and special revenue fund types.

- *Combined statement of revenues, expenses, and changes in retained earnings—all proprietary fund types, similar trust funds, and discretely presented component units.*

The format for this statement should be as follows:

	Operating revenues
−	Operating expenses
	Operating income (loss)
±	Nonoperating revenues (expenses)
	Income before operating transfers
±	Operating transfers from (to) other funds
	Net income (loss) before extraordinary items
±	Extraordinary items
	Net income (loss)
+	Retained earnings—beginning of period
	Retained earnings—end of period

Bond proceeds are not reported in the statement of revenues, expenses, and changes in retained earnings.

Contributed capital represents a contribution of permanent equity capital, not revenue. Hence it is not reported in the statement of revenues, expenses, and changes in retained earnings. Instead, an analysis of activity in the contributed capital account is presented in a note to the financial statements.

If the governmental unit has several enterprise funds involved in diverse activities, the information concerning the individual activities should be segmented in a note to the financial statements. Enterprise fund segment disclosures are required if (1) material long-term liabilities are outstanding, (2) the disclosures provide essential assurance that the

GPFS are not misleading, or (3) the disclosures are necessary to assure interperiod comparability.

- *Combined statement of cash flows—all proprietary fund types, nonexpendable trust fund types, and discretely presented component units.*

  This statement can be presented on either the direct or indirect method of reporting cash flows. The statement should report net cash provided or used in each of the four categories (operating, investing, capital and related financing, and noncapital financing), as well as the net effect of those flows on cash and cash equivalents during the period in a manner that reconciles beginning and ending cash and cash equivalents.

A comprehensive listing of required footnote disclosures can be found in GASB Codification § 2300. However, typical notes for a government's financial report may provide such disclosures as:

- Summary of significant accounting policies.
- Cash and investments (including derivatives).
- Property taxes.
- Long-term debt and debt refundings.
- Leases.
- Fixed assets.
- Encumbrances.
- Pensions.
- Budget basis of accounting and budget/GAAP reconciliation.
- Deficits in funds and individual fund interfund payables and receivables.
- Segment information.
- Legal violations.
- Commitments and contingencies.
- Litigations.
- Subsequent events.
- Related party transactions.
- Joint ventures and jointly governed organizations.
- Individual component unit disclosures.

The summary of significant accounting policies note should contain, among other things, the following items:

- A brief description of the governmental unit and its form of government.
- Identification of any associated governmental units included in the reporting entity.
- Basis of presentation.
- Identification and description of the funds maintained by the governmental unit.
- Basis of accounting, including the manner in which the susceptible to accrual concept is applied to the major revenue classification.
- Policies for establishing the budgets.
- Description of encumbrance accounting if used and identification of the funds using encumbrance accounting.
- Investment valuation policy.
- Definition of cash and cash equivalents.

- Inventory valuation policy.
- Fixed assets valuation policy.
- Depreciation policy.
- Lease capitalization policy.
- Interest capitalization policy.
- Infrastructure capitalization policy.
- Basis for the establishment of reserves.
- Vacation and sick leave policy.
- Meaning and nature of any unusual accounts.

Required supplementary information (RSI) should be disclosed as part of the GPFS for governmental employers participating in defined benefit single-employer or agent multiple-employer pension plans and for the financial statements of PERS. Also, certain RSI should be disclosed for risk financing and certain insurance-related activities of state and local government entities. RSI differs from other types of information outside the basic financial statements because the GASB considers the information an essential part of the financial reporting of certain entities and because authoritative guidelines for the measurement and presentation of the information have been established.

(iii) Comprehensive Annual Financial Report.   The **comprehensive annual financial report** (CAFR) differs from the GPFS in the level of detail and the quantity of data presented. The additional data are *not* necessary for fair presentation of financial position or results of operation in accordance with GAAP, but they are useful and informative for certain readers of a government's financial report. Furthermore, the CAFR may be the vehicle for providing the necessary information for fulfilling the legal and other disclosure requirements of higher levels of government, bondholders, and similar groups. It is also useful in demonstrating management's stewardship responsibilities since alongside the comparative budgets, it presents in more detail the use of the available resources.

The recommended contents of the CAFR includes:

- Introductory section.

    Title page. Contains the title "Comprehensive Annual Financial Report," the name of the governmental unit, the period of time covered, and the names of the principal government officials. Component units that issue separate statements should indicate the primary government of which it is a component. A title such as, "City Hospital, a component unit of City, Any State" is recommended.

    Table of contents. Identifies the presence and location of each item included in the report.

    Transmittal letter. From the government's chief finance officer (or CEO), providing significant aspects of financial operations during the period. The letter may include, for example, changes in financial policies; discussion of internal controls; changes in operating results or expected revenues, expenditures, and debt; significant elements of financial management including cash and risk management; financial problems encountered; budget procedures and current budget; and a preview of the significant developments or changes contemplated in the coming year including economic conditions, outlook, and major initiatives.

- Financial section.

    Independent auditor's report.

    General purpose financial statements. Includes all required financial statements and related notes as previously described.

Combining financial statements. Used when a governmental unit has more than one fund of a given type.

Individual fund financial statements. Used when this information is not provided in a separate column in a combining statement or it is desirable to present a level of detail that would be excessive for the GPFS or the combining statements. Examples are detail comparisons to budgets that cannot be reflected on the combining statements, comparative data for prior years, or a demonstration of an individual fund's compliance with legal provisions.

Required supplementary information. Included when disclosure is required by the GASB.

Schedules necessary to demonstrate compliance. Included when such are required by state law or by a bond covenant.

Other schedules desired by the government. Used for reporting particular kinds of information that are spread throughout the numerous financial statements and that can be brought together and presented in greater detail than in the individual statements, or that show the details of a specific amount or amounts presented in the GPFS, the combining statements, or the individual fund financial statements.

- Statistical section.

Statistical tables cover a period of several years and contain data drawn from more than just the accounting records. Their purpose is to present social, economic, and financial trends, and the fiscal capacity of the governmental unit. The following titles indicate recommended statistical tables for a local government's comprehensive annual financial report:

General Governmental Expenditures by Function—Last Ten Fiscal Years.

General Revenues by Source—Last Ten Fiscal Years.

Property Tax Levies and Collections—Last Ten Fiscal Years.

Assessed and Estimated Actual Value of Taxable Property—Last Ten Fiscal Years.

Property Tax Rates-All Overlapping Governments—Last Ten Fiscal Years.

Special Assessment Billings and Collections—Last Ten Fiscal Years.

Ratio of Net General Bonded Debt to Assessed Value and Net Bonded Debt Per Capita—Last Ten Fiscal Years.

Computation of Legal Debt Margin (if not in GPFS).

Computation of Overlapping Debt (if not in GPFS).

Ratio of Annual Debt Service Expenditures for General Bonded Debt to Total General Government Expenditures—Last Ten Fiscal Years.

Revenue Bond Coverage—Last Ten Fiscal Years.

Demographic Statistics.

Property Values, Construction, and Bank Deposits—Last Ten Fiscal Years.

Principal Taxpayers.

Miscellaneous Statistics.

- Single Audit Section.

Although not a required part of a CAFR, some governments include in a separate section the information, including auditor's reports, required by the Single Audit Act of 1984.

(iv) Certificate of Achievement Program. Governmental units may submit their CAFRs to the GFOA (180 North Michigan Avenue, Chicago, IL 60601) for evaluation in accordance with the standards of financial reporting established by the GASB and the GFOA. If the report substantially adheres to these standards, the government is awarded a **Certificate of**

Achievement for Excellence in Financial Reporting. The certificate is only valid for one year. It may be reproduced in the government's annual report and should be included in the subsequent year's CAFR. Annually, the GFOA publishes a list of the governments that hold valid certificates.

Many governments endeavor to obtain the certificate. They realize that credit rating agencies and others familiar with governmental accounting and financial reporting recognize that governments holding a certificate typically maintain complete financial records and effectively report their financial information to permit detail analyses to be performed. This characteristic can improve the government's bond rating.

(v) Popular Reports.   Governments also prepare **popular reports** to communicate with persons who are neither interested in a complete set of financial statements or able to review them. Popular reports, also called **condensed summary data,** are at the top of the financial reporting "pyramid."

There are three types of popular reports. The first is an aggregation of the data from the financial statements that disregards the distinction among fund types and account groups and the different bases of accounting and presents the data as if all the assets, liabilities, equities, revenues, and expenditures (expenses) pertain, not to the fund types, but to the government as a whole. This results in a presentation similar to that made by corporations and their subsidiaries. In such cases, the government usually eliminates significant interfund transactions before arriving at totals.

The second approach is to visually present the entity's financial information, for instance, by using pie charts or bar graphs. A common presentation is to present one pie to show the composition of revenue by cutting the pie into slices with each slice representing a major revenue source. The size of the slice would reflect the magnitude of the respective revenue source. Similar pie charts can be used to show the major categories of expenditures, the major categories of assets, and the major categories of liabilities.

The third approach, taken by a few governments, is to issue consolidated financial statements, similar to those proposed by the AICPA in a project on experimental financial reporting. Such a consolidated approach replaces the funds and account groups by a single "fund" that is used to report the financial position and results of operations of the entire oversight unit or reporting entity. Intragovernmental transactions are eliminated in the consolidation process and a single basis of accounting (normally accrual) is used for all transactions.

Consolidated financial statements typically include a balance sheet, operating statement, and statement of cash flows. Because the accrual basis of accounting is normally used, fixed assets are reported in the single fund and depreciated. Also, long-term obligations are reported in the single fund, with the result that debt service principal payments are treated as balance sheet rather than operating statement transactions.

28.5 GRANT ACCOUNTING

(a) DEFINITIONS.   A **grant** is a contribution or gift of cash, or other assets from another government to be used or expended for a specified purpose, activity, or facility. Some grants are restricted by the grantor for the acquisition or construction of fixed assets. These are **capital grants.** All other grants are **operating grants.**

An **entitlement** is the amount of payment to which a government is entitled pursuant to an allocation formula contained in applicable statutes. A **shared revenue** is a revenue levied by one government but shared on a predetermined basis with another government. Grants, entitlements, and shared revenues have become major sources of revenues for governments. Frequently, however, special accounting and reporting requirements are associated with these grants.

(b) FUND IDENTIFICATION.   All grants, entitlements, and shared revenues should be accounted for in one of the seven fund types. The identity of the fund should be based on the purpose or requirements of the grant. For instance, grants, entitlements, or shared revenues received for purposes normally financed through the general fund may be accounted for within that fund, provided that applicable legal requirements can be appropriately satisfied. Resources received for the payment of principal or interest on general long-term debt may be accounted for in a debt service fund. Capital grants or shared revenues received for capital acquisitions or construction, other than those associated with enterprise and internal service funds, may be accounted for in a capital projects fund. However, it is not always necessary to establish a separate fund for an individual grant, entitlement, or shared revenue. Existing funds should be used to the extent possible in order to comply with the minimal number of funds principle.

If a grant, entitlement, or shared revenue may be used for more than one purpose and the recipient has not determined the purposes for which it intends to use the funds, the resources may be accounted for in an agency fund pending determination of their use. When the determination is made, the assets and revenues should be recognized in the appropriate fund and removed from the agency fund. Since most grants, entitlements, or shared revenues are either unrestricted as to purpose or restricted to a specific purpose, there is seldom a need to use an agency fund.

(c) REVENUE AND EXPENDITURE (EXPENSE) RECOGNITION.   Grants, entitlements, and shared revenues recorded in governmental funds should be recognized as revenue when they become susceptible to accrual, that is, measurable and available. Legal and contractual requirements should be carefully reviewed. If the restriction is more form than substance, revenue should be recognized at the time of receipt or earlier. If the grant is earned by the recipient government as funds are expended for a specific restricted purpose, revenue should be recognized when the expenditures are made for that purpose. The latter are called **"expenditure-driven" grants.**

Grants, entitlements, and shared revenues received before the revenue recognition criteria are met should be reported as deferred revenue and reported as a liability account in the government's financial statements. Resources not received should be reported as a receivable if the revenue recognition criteria have been met. If the resources have not been received and the revenue recognition criteria have not been met, the grants should not be reported on the balance sheet at all. They may, however, be disclosed in the notes to the financial statements.

Grants, entitlements, and shared revenues that are received by a proprietary fund for operating purposes, or that may be used for operations or capital purposes at the discretion of the recipient government, should be recognized as nonoperating revenue when earned. Resources restricted to the acquisition or construction of capital assets should be recorded as contributed capital.

Operating expenses should include depreciation on all depreciable fixed assets, including assets acquired with contributed capital. Depreciation recognized on assets acquired or constructed with contributed capital may be charged to the contributed capital account by "adding back" the depreciation on such assets to net income before closing it to retained earnings.

To promote greater consistency with respect to the accounting and financial reporting for grants and similar financial assistance by state and local governments, the GASB issued Statement No. 24, "Accounting and Financial Reporting for Certain Grants and Other Financial Assistance." Statement No. 24 addresses issues relating to the recognition, measurement and reporting of grants and other financial assistance received and given by state and local governments including:

- "Pass-through" grants.
- Food stamps and similar voucher programs.
- "On-behalf" payments of fringe benefits and salaries.

28.6 AUDITS OF GOVERNMENTAL UNITS

Audits of governmental units with financial statements can be performed in accordance with:

- Generally accepted auditing standards (GAAS).
- *Government Auditing Standards* (the "Yellow Book").
- The Single Audit Act of 1984 and OMB Circular A-128.

When performing an audit in accordance with GAAS, the guidance contained in the *AICPA Professional Standards* is followed. This is the same guidance followed by auditors when auditing the financial statement of commercial entities and typically results in the issuance of an opinion of the financial statements and perhaps a management letter. *Government Auditing Standards,* also known as the "Yellow Book" (U.S. Comptroller General, rev. 1994), establishes the concept of an expanded scope audit that includes both financial and compliance features. According to the Yellow Book, a financial audit can help determine whether:

1. The financial statements of an audited entity present fairly the financial position and the results of financial operations in accordance with GAAP.
2. The entity has complied with laws and regulations that may have a material effect on the financial statements.

The Yellow Book incorporates the AICPA Professional Standards mentioned above and sets forth additional standards and requirements, including the following:

1. A review is to be made of compliance with applicable laws and regulations, as set forth in federal audit guides and other applicable reference sources.
2. The auditor reports on the entity's compliance with laws, regulations, contracts and shall also include material instances of noncompliance and instances or indications of illegal acts found during or in connection with the audit.
3. The auditors shall report on their consideration of the entity's internal control structure made as part of the financial audit.

    They shall identify as a minimum:

    a. Scope of auditor's work in obtaining an understanding of the internal control structure and assessing risk.

    b. The reportable conditions including separate identification of material weaknesses identified as a result of the auditor's work.
4. Auditors performing government audits are required to obtain 80 hours of continuing education every 2 years, of which 24 hours should be directly related to government. At least 20 of the 80 hours should be completed in each year of the 2-year period.
5. Audit organizations performing government audits are required to establish an internal quality control system and participate in an external quality control review program.
6. The auditor communicates certain information related to the conduct of the audit to the audit committee or to the individuals with whom they have contracted for the audit.

(a) THE SINGLE AUDIT ACT OF 1984. As a result of the Single Audit Act of 1984, many state and local governments are required to obtain a periodic audit of the federal funds they receive—usually once a year. The audits are normally performed by an independent CPA or public accountant, or, in some states, by the government's internal audit personnel. A few jurisdictions have an independently elected or appointed auditor who conducts the audit. Single audits are conducted in accordance with GAAS, *Government Auditing Standards,* and the Single Audit Act and its implementing regulation OMB Circular A-128.

The objectives of the Act are:

- To improve the financial management of state and local governments with respect to federal financial assistance programs through improved auditing.
- To establish uniform requirements for audits of federal financial assistance provided to state and local governments.
- To promote the efficient and effective use of audit resources.
- To ensure that federal departments and agencies, to the maximum extent practicable, rely on and use audit work performed pursuant to the requirements of the Single Audit Act.

Though the single audit builds on the annual financial statement audit currently required by most state and larger local governments, it places substantial additional emphasis on the consideration and testing of internal controls and the testing of compliance with laws and regulations.

The Single Audit Act and OMB Circular A-128 require the auditor to determine whether:

- The financial statements of the government, department, agency, or establishment present fairly its financial position and the results of operations in conformity with GAAP.
- The organization has internal and other control structures to provide reasonable assurance that it is managing federal financial assistance programs in compliance with applicable laws and regulations.
- The organization has complied with laws and regulations that may have a material effect on its financial statements and on each major federal financial assistance program.

The governmental units that are subject to single audits include those that *receive* $100,000 or more of federal financial assistance in any fiscal year. If a government receives between $25,000 and $100,000 of federal assistance, the entity has the option of having a single audit or separate grant audits performed. For those governments receiving less than $25,000 in assistance, there is an exemption from the Single Audit Act requirements.

The Single Audit Act provides auditors with guidance on the focus of the audit by defining a level of audit work based on the concept of "major" and "nonmajor" federal assistance programs. Major programs (not grants) are typically the larger programs in which an entity participates and are determined on a sliding scale by the relationship between the expenditures of the program and the total federal expenditures of the entity. For most small and medium-sized governments a major program is defined as the larger of $300,000 or 3% of the total federal *expenditures* for all federal programs.

For larger governments whose total federal expenditures exceed $100 million, the Single Audit Act defines a major federal financial assistance program based on a sliding scale.

The Single Audit Act and OMB Circular A-128 require the auditor to issue several reports:

For the entity:

- A report on the audit of the general purpose or basic financial statements of the entity as a whole, or the department, agency, or establishment covered by the audit.
- A report on internal control based on an understanding and assessment of the internal control structure obtained as a part of the audit of the general purpose or basic financial statements.
- A report on compliance with laws and regulations that may have a material effect on the financial statements.

For its federal financial assistance programs:

- A report on a supplementary schedule of the entity's federal financial assistance programs, showing total expenditures for each federal assistance program.

- A report on compliance with laws and regulations identifying all findings of noncompliance and questioned costs.
- A report on internal control structure used in administering federal financial assistance programs.

In March 1990, the Office of Management and Budget (OMB) issued OMB Circular A-133, "Audits of Institutions of Higher Education and Other Nonprofit Organizations." The audit objectives contained in OMB Circular A-133 are patterned after the Single Audit Act of 1984 (described in the preceding section) and brings under the single audit umbrella nonprofit organizations receiving federal funds. Although the Circular was issued primarily for nonprofit organizations receiving federal funds, institutions of higher education which are operated by a state or local government may elect to conduct a single audit under the provisions of OMB Circular A-133 versus the audit requirements associated with the Single Audit Act of 1984.

In 1995, OMB began a process intended to combine the regulations governing single audits into a single document. As a part of this process, OMB proposed changes to Circular A-133. OMB indicated that these changes would serve as a model for requested changes to the Single Audit Act of 1984 and that if those changes were made, Circular A-128 would be abolished and that state and local governments would follow Circular A-133. The major proposals in this revision include:

- Use of the concept of risk in determining which programs to audit.
- Raising the threshold for an audit to $300,000.
- Reduce the time period for submission of the single audit results from 13 to 9 months.
- Expansion of the scope to include hospitals.

(b) OTHER CONSIDERATIONS.   Most government officials and auditors of governmental units realize that a good audit should furnish more than an opinion on the financial statements. Other services a governmental auditor can provide are pinpointing the key information upon which decisions should be based and contributing to the presentation of this information in a manner that facilitates decision making; uncovering deficiencies in the accounting system and providing suggestions for improving the efficiency and effectiveness of the system; and obtaining and presenting information useful for marketing securities.

Obtaining a qualified auditor, particularly one who can provide the additional services described above, requires that the selection be based on qualifications and experience, and not solely cost. The National Intergovernmental Audit Forum in its handbook "How to Avoid a Substandard Audit: Suggestions for Procuring an Audit," indicates:

Public entities should never select auditors without considering five basic elements of an effective audit procurement process:

- planning (determining what needs to be done and when),
- fostering competition by soliciting proposals (writing a clear and direct solicitation document and disseminating it widely),
- technically evaluating proposals and qualifications (authorizing a committee of knowledgeable persons to evaluate the ability of prospective auditors to effectively carry out the audit),
- preparing a written agreement (documenting the expectations of both the entity and the auditor), and
- monitoring the auditor's performance (periodically reviewing the progress of that performance).

This handbook provides detailed information about the five elements of procurement listed above as well as the use of audit committees in a government environment and other useful information about the auditor procurement process.

(i) Governmental Rotation of Auditors.   The **automatic rotation of auditors** after a given number of years is a common practice in many governments; however, it is not always beneficial. Many governments have followed this policy, believing that they will (1) receive a fresh outlook from the audit, (2) spread the work among several firms, and (3) encourage lower fees. In actuality, automatic rotation may be harmful in that it could deprive the government of the extensive knowledge of the entity developed by the current auditor. It may also impair auditing effectiveness since a new auditor may need to spend considerable time learning the government's system—the government may actually incur more cost since its personnel will need to spend time explaining the organization, systems, and data to the new auditors, and the new auditors will need to spend valuable time reviewing information that is already part of the previous auditor's workpapers. Although a government should continuously monitor its auditor's performance to assure that the service obtained is commensurate with the cost, the entity should normally change auditors only because of dissatisfaction with services and not for the sake of receiving a lower fee.

(ii) Audit Committees.   In recent years, governments have started establishing **audit committees** similar to those in the private sector. Some appropriate tasks for a local government's audit committee are:

- Reviewing significant financial information for reliability, timeliness, clarity, appropriateness of disclosure, and compliance with GAAP and legal requirements.
- Ascertaining that the internal control structure is appropriately designed and functioning effectively.
- Evaluating independent audit firms and selecting one for approval by the appropriate body.
- Overseeing the scope and performance of the independent audit function.
- Ensuring that the auditors' recommendations for improvements in internal controls and operating methods receive management's attention and are implemented on a timely basis.
- Providing an effective communications link between the auditors and the full governing board.

The primary benefit of an audit committee is in assisting the full governing board to fulfill its responsibilities for the presentation of financial information about the governmental unit. There are also secondary benefits: The other parties involved in the issuance of financial information—management and independent and internal auditors—can perform their roles more effectively if an audit committee is involved in the process. Finally, there are advantages for the government's constituencies—in particular, the taxpayers and bondholders.

28.7 PROPOSED CHANGES AND OTHER MATTERS

(a) FINANCIAL REPORTING MODEL.   GASB Statement No. 11 required the introduction of accrual-basis operating statements for governmental activities. The effective date of Statement No. 11 was delayed indefinitely by Statement No. 17. This delay was to allow the GASB to complete additional research on the financial reporting model, capital reporting, pension accounting, risk financing and insurance projects. Recent actions by the GASB have made it apparent that the GASB intends to develop a new statement which would completely replace Statement No. 11.

In June 1995, the GASB issued a Preliminary Views (PV) document entitled "Governmental Financial Reporting Model: Core Financial Statements." The approach outlined in the PV document would replace the financial reporting pyramid as discussed in subsection 28.4(m)(ii) with a "dual perspective" approach. The dual perspective is based on the belief that different sets of financial statements should provide different information to meet different users needs. The PV document outlines plans for governmental financial statements that would include two basic sets of financial statements. One set, called the "fund perspective," would be very much the same as governments currently present their financial statements as discussed in the remainder of this chapter. Another set of financial statements, called the "entity-wide perspective," would present the financial statements of the entire government in a single column. However, the amounts included in the entity-wide perspective would be based on an economic resources measurement focus and the accrual basis of accounting. This would result in the same transactions being reported in different ways at the two perspectives.

(b) OTHER ISSUES AT THE GASB.   The GASB is also dealing with other current issues facing state and local governments. As a part of the financial reporting model project, the GASB also intends to address conceptual issues such as the definition of an asset and related presentation issues such as what footnotes should be required. Meanwhile, the GASB is also addressing other topics of interest. The GASB has been researching postemployment benefits other than pensions in anticipation of developing a statement regarding recording these liabilities. The GASB has also added a project to its agenda to address the appropriate valuation of investments.

(c) ACCOUNTING FOR MUNICIPAL SOLID WASTE LANDFILL CLOSURE AND POST-CLOSURE CARE COSTS.   GASB Statement No. 18, "Accounting for Municipal Solid Waste Landfill Closure and Post-closure Care Costs," provides guidance in response to the issuance of U.S. Environmental Protections Agency rule, "Solid Waste Disposal Facility Criteria," which requires owners and operators of municipal solid waste landfills (MSWLFs) to perform various closure functions and post-closure monitoring and maintenance functions as a condition for the right to operate a MSWLF.

The guidance applies to MSWLFs that accept municipal solid waste and are required to incur closure and post-closure care costs. Specifically, the guidance would require recognition of MSWLF closure and post-closure care costs as an expenditure/expense and as a liability in each period in which the landfill accepts waste. Recognition would be based on a systematic and rational method that assigns estimated total current costs to periods based upon landfill use rather than the passage of time.

The estimated total current cost of MSWLFs closure and post-closure consist of the following costs:

- Equipment and facilities used in post-closure monitoring and care.
- Final cover.
- Maintenance and monitoring the landfill during the post-closure period.

State and local governments with MSWLFs will be required to disclose in the financial statements the nature and source of landfill closure and post-closure care costs and the fact that the costs are being recognized based on estimated total current costs while the landfill is operating regardless of when related disbursements are made. In addition, disclosure of financing arrangements for closure and post-closure care costs would be required along with an indication of whether or not such financing arrangements were in compliance with applicable laws and regulations.

(d) AUDIT QUALITY.   Perhaps one of the hottest topics in the government industry today is audit quality. The results of recent GAO studies of the quality of audits of government units have indicated that audit fieldwork and reporting were deficient in a significant number of audit engagements. Because the auditor is one defense mechanism against improper spending of federal funds, the GAO looks unfavorably on auditors who are performing substandard work and has taken steps to alleviate the problem. *Government Auditing Standards* includes a requirement for auditors performing government audits to meet minimum continuing professional education requirements and for auditing firms to have independent quality control reviews at least once every 3 years.

(e) SUMMARY.   Governmental accounting and reporting is changing and expanding at an increasing rapid rate. Coupling this with public accountability issues, the federal government's pressure for increased audit quality, and the penalties for substandard audit performance results in increasing levels of audit risk. Government audits, often considered low-risk engagements by many, are quickly becoming areas of extremely high risk. Auditing professionals need to recognize the risk associated with government engagements now and in the future before incurring severe penalties or embarrassment. The technical issues involved in government auditing are on a par with those in the commercial environment but auditors have much less experience and less technical guidance to fall back on.

Dealing with these technical issues requires well-trained, highly motivated individuals and can no longer be left to less experienced members of the audit team. Dealing with the *real* issues governments are facing (e.g., infrastructure, AIDS, prison overcrowding, drugs, etc.) requires even more from the individuals in the profession. Like it or not, government accounting and reporting is being thrust into the spotlight and will be scrutinized by a multitude of individuals and groups. It is imperative that individuals in the industry realize this fact and begin now to prepare for the future.

APPENDIX 28.1: PRONOUNCEMENTS ON STATE AND LOCAL GOVERNMENT ACCOUNTING

Government Accounting Standard Board		*Effective Date*
Statement No. 1	Authoritative Status of NCGA Pronouncements and AICPA Industry Audit Guide	On issuance (7/84)
Statement No. 2	Financial Reporting of Deferred Compensation Plans Adopted under the Provisions of Internal Revenue Code Section 457	Financial statements for periods ending after 2/15/86
Statement No. 3	Deposits with Financial Institutions, Investments (including Repurchase Agreements), and Reverse Repurchase Agreements	Financial statements for periods ending after 2/15/86
Statement No. 4	Applicability of FASB Statement No. 87, "Employers' Accounting for Pensions," to State and Local Governmental Employers	On issuance (9/86)
Statement No. 5	Disclosure of Pension Information by Public Employee Retirement Systems and State and Local Governmental Employers	Financial reports issued for fiscal years beginning after 12/15/86
Statement No. 6	Accounting and Financial Reporting for Special Assessments	Financial statements for periods beginning after 6/15/87

Government Accounting Standard Board—Continued		Effective Date
Statement No. 7	Advance Refundings Resulting in Defeasance of Debt	Fiscal periods beginning after 12/15/86
Statement No. 8	Applicability of FASB Statement No. 93, Recognition of Depreciation by Not-for-Profit Organizations, to Certain State and Local Governmental Entities	Fiscal periods beginning after 5/15/87
Statement No. 9	Reporting Cash Flows of Proprietary and Nonexpendable Trust Funds and Governmental Entries, that use Proprietary Fund Accounting	Fiscal periods beginning after 12/15/89
Statement No. 10	Accounting and Financial Reporting for Risk Financing and Related Insurance Issues	Pools—Fiscal periods beginning after 6/15/90 Other—Fiscal periods beginning after 6/15/93
Statement No. 11	Measurement Focus and Basis of Accounting—Governmental Fund Operating Statements	Fiscal periods beginning after 6/15/94
Statement No. 12	Disclosure of Information on Postemployment Benefits Other than Pension Benefits by State and Local Governmental Employers	Fiscal periods beginning after 6/15/90
Statement No. 13	Accounting for Operating Leases with Scheduled Rent Increases	Leases with terms beginning after 6/30/90
Statement No. 14	The Financial Reporting Entity	Fiscal periods beginning after 12/15/92
Statement No. 15	Governmental College and University Accounting and Financial Reporting Models	Fiscal periods beginning after 6/15/92
Statement No. 16	Accounting for Compensated Absences	Fiscal periods beginning after June 15, 1993
Statement No. 17	Measurement Focus and Basis of Accounting—Governmental Fund Operating Statements: Amendment of Effective Dates of GASB Statement No. 11 and Related Statements	Immediately
Statement No. 18	Accounting for Municipal Solid Waste Landfill Closure and Post-closure Care Costs	Fiscal periods beginning after June 15, 1993
Statement No. 19	Governmental College and University Omnibus Statement	Fiscal periods beginning after June 15, 1993
Statement No. 20	Accounting and Financial Reporting for Proprietary Funds and Other Governmental Entities That Use Proprietary Fund Accounting	Fiscal periods beginning after December 15, 1993
Statement No. 21	Accounting for Escheat Property	Fiscal periods beginning after June 15, 1994
Statement No. 22	Accounting for Taxpayer-Assessed Tax Revenues in Governmental Funds	Fiscal periods beginning after June 15, 1994
Statement No. 23	Accounting and Financial Reporting for Refundings of Debt Reported by Proprietary Activities	Fiscal periods beginning after June 15, 1994
Statement No. 24	Accounting and Financial Reporting for Certain Grants and Other Financial Assistance	Fiscal periods beginning after June 15, 1995

(continued)

	Government Accounting Standard Board—Continued	*Effective Date*
Statement No. 25	Financial Reporting for Defined Benefit Pension Plans and Note Disclosures for Defined Contribution Plans	Fiscal periods beginning after June 15, 1996, Statement No. 26 must be implemented simultaneously
Statement No. 26	Financial Reporting for Postemployment Healthcare Plans Administered by Defined Benefit Pension Plans	Fiscal periods beginning after June 15, 1996, Statement No. 25 must be implemented simultaneously
Statement No. 27	Accounting for Pensions by State and Local Governmental Employers	Fiscal periods beginning after June 15, 1997
Statement No. 28	Accounting and Financial Reporting for Securities Lending Transactions	Fiscal periods beginning after December 15, 1995
Statement No. 29	The Use of Not-for-Profit Accounting and Financial Reporting Principles by Governmental Entities	Fiscal periods beginning after December 15, 1995
Interpretation No. 1	Demand Bonds Issued by State and Local Governmental Entities	Fiscal periods ending after 6/15/85
Technical Bulletin No. 84-1	Purpose and Scope of GASB Technical Bulletins and Procedures for Issuance	None
Technical Bulletin No. 87-1	Applying Paragraph 66 of GASB Statement 3	On issuance (1/87)
Technical Bulletin No. 94-1	Disclosures about Derivatives and Similar Debt and Investment Transactions	Fiscal periods ending after December 15, 1994
Concepts Statement No. 1	Objectives of Financial Reporting	None
Concepts Statement No. 2	Reporting Service Efforts and Accomplishments	None

	National Council on Governmental Accounting	*Effective Date*
Statement 1	Governmental Accounting and Financial Reporting Principles	Fiscal years ending after 6/30/80
Statement 2	Grant, Entitlement, and Shared Revenue Accounting by State and Local Governments	Fiscal years ending after 6/30/80
Statement 3	Defining the Governmental Reporting Entity (Superceded)	Prospectively for fiscal years ending after 12/31/82
Statement 4	Accounting and Financial Reporting Principles for Claims and Judgments and Compensated Absences	Fiscal years beginning after 12/31/82; ¶20 extended indefinitely by NCGAI 11
Statement 5	Accounting and Financial Reporting Principles for Lease Agreements of State and Local Governments	Fiscal years beginning after 6/30/83
Statement 6	Pension Accounting and Financial Reporting: Public Employee Retirement Systems and State and Local Government Employers	Extended indefinitely by NCGAI 8
Statement 7	Financial Reporting for Component Units Within the Governmental Reporting Entity	Prospectively for fiscal years ending after 6/30/84
Interpretation 1	GAAFR and the AICPA Audit Guide (Superseded)	Issued 4/86; superseded by NCGAS 1

National Council on Governmental Accounting—Continued		*Effective Date*
Interpretation 2	Segment Information for Enterprise Funds	Prospectively for fiscal years ending after 9/30/80
Interpretation 3	Revenue Recognition—Property Taxes	Fiscal years beginning after 9/30/81
Interpretation 4	Accounting and Financial Reporting for Public Employee Retirement Systems and Pension Trust Funds (Superseded)	Fiscal years beginning after 6/15/82; superseded by NCGAS 6 and repealed by NCGAI 8
Interpretation 5	Authoritative Status of Governmental Accounting, Auditing, and Financial Reporting (1968)	On issuance (3/82)
Interpretation 6	Notes to the Financial Statements Disclosure	Prospectively for fiscal years beginning after 12/31/82
Interpretation 7	Clarification as to the Application of the Criteria in NCGA Statement 3. "Defining the Governmental Reporting Entity"	On Issuance (9/83)
Interpretation 8	Certain Pension Matters	Fiscal years ending after 12/31/83
Interpretation 9	Certain Fund Classifications and Balance Sheet Accounts	Fiscal years ending after 6/30/84
Interpretation 10	State and Local Government Budgetary Reporting	Fiscal years ending after 6/30/84
Interpretation 11	Claim and Judgment Transactions for Governmental Funds	On issuance (4/84)

GASB Exposure Drafts Outstanding 9/30/95

Financial Reporting for Reverse Repurchase Agreements (an interpretation of GASB Statement No. 3)

Account and Financial Reporting for Capitalization Contributions to Public Entity Risk Pools (an interpretation of GASB Statements No. 10 and 14)

Risk Financing Omnibus Statement (an amendment of GASB Statement No. 10)

The Financial Reporting Entity: Affiliated Organizations

28.8 SOURCES AND SUGGESTED REFERENCES

American Institute of Certified Public Accountants, "Audits of State and Local Government Units," Industry Audit and Accounting Guide, AICPA, New York, 1994.

———, "AICPA Professional Standards," AICPA, New York, 1995.

Financial Accounting Standards Board, "Classification of Short-Term Obligations Expected to Be Refinanced," Statement of Financial Accounting Standards No. 6, FASB, Stamford, CT, 1975.

———, "Accounting for Leases," Statement of Financial Accounting Standards Board No. 13, FASB, Stamford, CT, 1975.

———, "Objectives of Financial Reporting by Nonbusiness Organizations," Statement of Financial Accounting Concepts No. 4, FASB, Stamford, CT, 1980.

General Accounting Office, "Government Auditing Standards," GAO, Washington, DC, 1994.

Governmental Accounting Standards Board, "Codification of Governmental Accounting and Financial Reporting Standards," GASB, Stamford, CT, 1995.

Government Finance Officers Association, "Governmental Accounting, Auditing and Financial Reporting," GFOA, Chicago, IL, 1994. (Study guide available)

CHAPTER 29

NOT-FOR-PROFIT ORGANIZATIONS

Roger S. Bruttomesso, CPA

Price Waterhouse LLP

Richard F. Larkin, CPA

Price Waterhouse LLP

CONTENTS

The authors wish to acknowledge that the exhibits and inspiration for this work were derived from the work *Financial and Accounting Guide for Not-for-Profit Organizations,* by Price Waterhouse LLP, authors Malvern J. Gross Jr., Richard F. Larkin, Roger S. Bruttomesso, and John J. McNally (John Wiley & Sons, Inc., 5th Edition, 1995).

29.1 THE NOT-FOR-PROFIT ACCOUNTING ENVIRONMENT

Not-for-profit organizations range from the large and complex to the small and simple. They include hospitals, colleges and universities, voluntary social service organizations, religious organizations, associations, foundations, and cultural institutions. All are confronted with accounting and reporting challenges. All are presently covered by authoritative accounting literature. This chapter discusses not-for-profit accounting and reporting conventions and examines accounting pronouncements, auditing concerns, and the regulatory environment applicable to different types of not-for-profit organizations. Health care organizations are covered in Chapter 30.

(a) RECENT CHANGES IN ACCOUNTING PRINCIPLES. Not-for-profit accounting is undergoing a period of profound change. In the recent past, authoritative accounting principles and reporting practices were established for many not-for-profit organizations that previously had neither.

In 1972, the AICPA issued an Industry Audit Guide for hospitals. In 1973, an Industry Audit Guide for colleges and universities was issued. And in 1974, a third not-for-profit Industry Audit Guide, for voluntary health and welfare organizations, was issued. In 1990, the AICPA issued a new audit and accounting guide, "Audits of Providers of Health Care Service," to replace the 1972 hospital audit guide.

In late 1978, the AICPA issued SOP No. 78-10, "Accounting Principles and Reporting Practices for Certain Nonprofit Organizations." SOP No. 78-10 defines accounting principles and reporting practices for all not-for-profit organizations **not** covered by earlier guides.

For several years, as the most current broad-scope pronouncement of the accounting profession on not-for-profit accounting, the SOP was the authoritative reference for not-for-profit accounting and reporting questions for the organizations covered, and it was consulted for guidance by other organizations on questions not addressed in their respective audit guides.

In 1979, the FASB issued SFAS No. 32, which recognized principles prescribed by AICPA Industry Audit Guides and Statements of Position as preferable when considering a change in accounting principles.

These guides and the SOP had a dramatic effect on not-for-profit accounting, as they represented the first authoritative attempt to codify accounting principles and reporting practices for the not-for-profit industry. However, inconsistencies exist among the four guides, and they frequently contradict one another on key accounting concepts. Also, the accounting principles presented in the guides have limited authority as they constituted GAAP only until formal standards were set on this subject by the FASB. Steps to relieve this confusion have been in process.

By the early 1980s, persons interested in not-for-profit accounting issues had identified the following key areas of accounting that would have to be considered in unifying the diverse not-for-profit accounting practices.

- Reporting entity (when controlled and affiliated organizations should be included in an entity's financial statements).
- Depreciation.
- Joint costs of multipurpose activities, particularly those involving a fund-raising appeal (on what basis such costs should be divided among the various purposes served).
- Revenue recognition for expendable/restricted receipts (when, in which fund, and how such items should be reported as revenue).
- Display (what format should be used to present financial data).
- Valuation of investments.
- Contributions (how these should be valued, when and how they should be reported).
- Grants awarded to others (when these should be accrued and expensed by the grantor).

Before accounting principles could be written, concepts had to be developed. The FASB had originally excluded not-for-profits from concepts development, but later started a separate project for not-for-profits. The first concepts statement under this project was issued in 1980. SFAC No. 4, "Objectives of Financial Reporting by Nonbusiness Organizations," proved to be so similar to the corresponding statement for businesses (SFAC No. 1) that the FASB started thinking in terms of only one set of concepts. Indeed, SFAC No. 2 was amended to include not-for-profits; SFAC No. 6 (Elements of Financial Statements) covers both types of entities, although some parts of this statement deal separately with the two sectors. The FASB has now developed accounting principles in several areas for the not-for-profit sector.

(b) CURRENT STATUS OF ACCOUNTING PRINCIPLES.   The FASB identified five areas in which it planned to develop accounting principles for not-for-profits: depreciation, contributions, the reporting entity, financial statement display, and investments:

(i) Recently-Issued Standards

- Depreciation is the subject of SFAS No. 93. Effective in 1990, this requires all not-for-profits to depreciate long-lived tangible assets, except that museum collections and similar assets often considered to be inexhaustible need not be depreciated if verifiable evidence of their inexhaustibility is available.

- Accounting for contributions received and made, and for museum collections is the subject of FASB Statement No. 116, effective beginning in 1995. Upon adoption it requires a number of significant changes to accounting practices previously followed by many not-for-profit organizations. It requires immediate revenue recognition for all unconditional gifts and pledges, regardless of the presence of donor restrictions, and regardless of the intended period of payment (pledges payable in future periods will be discounted to present value). Donors will follow a similar policy for recording expenses and liabilities. Donated services of volunteers will be recorded by charities if certain criteria are met. Museum collection items will be capitalized unless certain criteria are met.

  The requirement for immediate recognition of revenue for purpose and time restricted gifts results from FASB's conclusion in SFAC No. 6 that unspent expendable restricted gifts do not normally meet the definition of a liability (deferred revenue).

- Financial statement format was initially the subject of initial work by an AICPA task force. FASB issued a statement of financial accounting standards No. 117 on financial statement format in June 1993. It becomes effective in 1995, at the same time as the new standard on contributions (previous bullet).

- In 1995 the FASB issued SFAS 124, "Accounting for Certain Investments Held by Not-for-Profit Organizations." Briefly, its requirements are that all marketable securities be reported at current value in the balance sheet, and that unrealized losses be reported in the unrestricted class of net assets (absent donor restrictions or law which would require reporting losses in a restricted class.) A more detailed summary of this standard follows.

ACCOUNTING FOR CERTAIN INVESTMENTS HELD BY NOT-FOR-PROFIT ORGANIZATIONS
SUMMARY OF FASB STATEMENT 124—NOVEMBER 1995

Effective date: Fiscal years beginning after December 15, 1995

Accounting for securities:
   Coverage: Equity securities (including options, warrants, rights) which have readily determinable fair values—except those accounted for on the equity method or investments in consolidated subsidiaries; Debt securities (not included derivatives).

   Accounting principle: All covered securities shall be reported at fair value in a balance sheet.

Reporting investment gains/losses and income:
   Investment gains/losses and income shall be reported in the statement of activities as changes in unrestricted net assets, unless their use is restricted by explicit donor-imposed

stipulations or by law, in which case they are reported in the appropriate restricted class. If a donor has explicitly restricted investment income from a fund, but is silent about gains, gains are considered to have the same restriction as income.

Reporting losses on investments of donor-restricted endowment funds:
    In the absence of donor stipulations or law to the contrary:

> Losses shall reduce temporarily restricted net assets to the extent that donor-imposed restrictions on net appreciation of the fund have not been met before the loss occurs.

> Any remaining loss shall reduce unrestricted net assets.

> If losses reduce the assets of a donor-restricted endowment fund below the level required by donor stipulations or by law, gains that restore the fair value of the assets of the fund to the required level shall be classified as unrestricted.

Definitions:
Debt security:	Any security representing a creditor relationship, including: redeemable preferred stock, convertible debt.
Equity security:	Any security representing an ownership interest in an enterprise, or the right to acquire or dispose of such interest at fixed or determinable prices. (Does not include convertible debt or redeemable preferred stock.)
Fair value:	The amount at which an asset could be bought or sold in a current transaction between willing parties. Quoted market price, if available.

Summary of SFAS Nos. 116 and 117

IMPLEMENTATION SCHEDULE.   Both statements were issued in June 1993. They are effective for fiscal years beginning after December 15, 1994 (e.g., for a June 30 year-end entity, for the fiscal year ending June 30, 1996). There is an optional one-year delayed effective date for small (total assets less than $5,000,000, and annual expenses less than $1,000,000) entities. Early adoption is encouraged. Adoption of No. 117 must be made retroactively; adoption of No. 116 can be made either retroactively or prospectively. Copies are available from the FASB Order Department: P.O. Box 5116, Norwalk, CT 06856.

SFAS NO. 117 (DISPLAY).   Statement No. 117 requires organizations to present aggregated financial data: total assets, liabilities, net assets (fund balances), and change in net assets. Some not-for-profits already do, but many have not done this in the past. Organizations are free to present data disaggregated by classes of net assets (corresponding to funds), but, except for donor-restricted revenue, net assets, and change in net assets, no detail by class is explicitly required.

Three classes of net assets are defined: Unrestricted, Temporarily restricted, and Permanently restricted. Net assets of the two restricted classes are created *only* by donor-imposed restrictions on their use. All other net assets, including board-designated or appropriated amounts, are legally unrestricted, and must be reported as part of the unrestricted class, although they may be separately identified within that class as designated if the organization wishes.

Permanently restricted net assets will consist mainly of amounts restricted by donors as permanent endowment. Some organizations may also have certain capital assets on which donors have placed perpetual restrictions. Temporarily restricted net assets will often contain a number of different types of donor-restricted amounts: unspent purpose-restricted expendable gifts for operating purposes, pledges payable in future periods, unspent explicitly time-restricted gifts, unspent amounts restricted for the acquisition of capital assets, certain capital assets, unmatured annuity and life income funds, and term endowments.

One requirement that will be a significant change for many organizations is the reporting of all expenses in the unrestricted class, regardless of the source of the financing of the expenses. As expendable restricted revenue will be reported in the temporarily restricted class, when these amounts are spent, a reclassification (transfer) will be made to match the restricted revenue with the unrestricted expenses. This practice is presently followed by hospitals, but not by other types of organizations.

A second new requirement is that all capital gains or losses on investments and other assets or liabilities will be reported in the unrestricted class, no matter which class holds the underlying assets/liabilities, unless there are explicit donor restrictions, or applicable law, which require the reporting of some or all of the capital gains/losses in a restricted class. This practice will often have the effect of increasing the reported unrestricted net asset balance (and decreasing the other net asset balances), compared with present reporting principles.

All organizations must report expenses by functional categories (program, management, fund-raising). Voluntary health and welfare organizations must also report expenses by natural categories (salaries, rent, travel, etc.) in a matrix format; other organizations are encouraged to do so. Reporting in functional categories will be new for some organizations, mainly those which do not raise significant amounts of contributions from the general public, such as trade associations, country clubs, and many local churches.

A new financial statement for many organizations will be a statement of cash flows, showing where the organization received and spent its cash. Cash flows will be reported in three categories: operating flows, financing flows (including receipt of nonexpendable contributions), and investing flows. This statement has been required for businesses for several years by Statement of Financial Accounting Standards No. 95, which should be consulted for further information.

Statement No. 95 permits either of two basic methods for preparing the statement of cash flows: the "direct" or the "indirect" method. Briefly, the indirect method starts with the excess of revenues over expenses and reconciles this number to operating cash flows. The direct method reports operating cash receipts and cash disbursements, directly adding these to arrive at operating cash flows. We believe the direct method is much more easily understood by readers of financial statements, and thus recommend its use.

Much of the information used to prepare a statement of cash flows is derived from data in the other two primary financial statements, some of it from the preceding year's statements. Thus, when planning to prepare this statement for the first time, it will be helpful to start a year in advance so that the necessary prior-year data will be available when needed.

Sample financial statements, illustrating formats which contain the disclosures required by Statement No. 117, are shown in Appendix C to the Statement.

SFAS No. 116 (CONTRIBUTIONS).   This document establishes one set of standards for all recipients of contributions, replacing the four different standards in the four AICPA audit guides. It also sets standards for donors of gifts; no explicit standards have heretofore existed, except for private foundations. For-profit organizations are also covered by this part of the document.

Certain types of transactions are not considered contributions: transactions that are in substance purchases of goods or services (even though they may be called grants), and transactions in which a recipient of a "gift" is merely acting as an agent or intermediary for, and passes the gift on to, another organization. Unfortunately, there is not much specific guidance for how to distinguish these two situations from real contributions; organizations will have to use judgment on a case-by-case basis.

SFAS No. 116 explicitly introduces a new concept into accounting for contributions: the conditional promise to give (pledge). This concept has implicitly existed for a long time, but has never before been articulated so clearly. A conditional pledge is one that depends on the occurrence of some specified *uncertain* future event to become binding on the pledgor.

Examples of such events are the meeting of a matching requirement by the pledgee, or natural or man-made disasters such as a flood or fire. The mere passage of time is not a condition. Note that the concept of a condition is completely separate from that of a restriction. Conditions relate to events that must occur prior to a pledge becoming binding on the pledgor; restrictions relate to limits on the use of a gift after receipt.

Unconditional pledges are recorded at the time verifiable evidence of the pledge is received. Conditional pledges are not recorded until the condition is met, at which time they become unconditional. Pledges payable in future periods are considered implicitly time-restricted, and are reported in the temporarily restricted class of net assets until they are due. Long-term pledges are also discounted to their present value to reflect the time value of money (in accordance with Accounting Principles Board Opinion No. 21); this will be a new practice for most organizations. Accretion of the discount to par value will be reported as contribution income.

All contributions are reported as revenue, in the class of net assets (unrestricted, temporarily restricted, or permanently restricted) appropriate to any donor restrictions on the gift, at the time of receipt of the gift. This applies to unconditional pledges as well as cash gifts. The presence or absence of explicit or implicit donor-imposed time or purpose restrictions on the use of a gift do not affect the timing of revenue recognition, only the class in which they are reported. This principle will be a significant change in practice for many organizations which have heretofore deferred donor-restricted gifts and all pledges until a later period when the restriction was met or the pledge collected. The effect will be to report higher net asset amounts, mainly in the temporarily restricted class, than under existing principles. This principle has generated a lot of controversy between those who favor retaining the present deferral method and advocates of the new standard.

Accounting by donors for pledges and other contributions will follow the same principles with respect to recognition and timing as the donees, though of course all the accounting entries are reversed: expense instead of revenue, pledges payable instead of pledges receivable. Also, for-profit donors do not categorize their financial reports into classes because this concept only applies to not-for-profits.

The reporting of the value of donated services of volunteers will also change for many organizations under SFAS No. 116. The new standard requires reporting such a value if either of two criteria is met: (1) the services create or enhance non-financial assets, or (2) the services require specialized skills, are provided by persons possessing those skills, and would typically otherwise have to be purchased by the recipient if volunteers were not available. If neither criterion is met, the services may not be recorded. Organizations should start to reconsider which of their volunteer services meet either of the two criteria.

Another matter that was controversial during the process of developing SFAS No. 116 was the question of accounting for museum collections. An early FASB proposal was to require capitalization of such assets. After much discussion of the subject, FASB agreed to allow noncapitalization of these items, if certain conditions relating to the items were met, and certain footnote disclosures made.

Decisions.   Organizations have a number of decisions available to them under SFAS Nos. 116 and 117. These are:

Restricted Contributions:

- Do we wish to report restricted contributions whose restrictions are met in the same accounting period as that in which they are received as restricted or as unrestricted support? (Contributions ¶ 14, third sentence)
- Do we wish to adopt a policy which implies that on gifts of long-lived assets, there exists a time restriction which expires over the useful life of the donated assets? (Contributions ¶ 16)

Basic financial statement format:

- What titles do we wish to use for the balance sheet and for the statement of activity? (No particular titles are required or precluded by SFAS No. 117)
- Do we wish to present additional detail in the statement of financial position of assets and liabilities by class? (Display ¶ 156, next-to-last sentence)
- Which of the sample formats for the Statement of Activities do we wish to follow? (Display ¶ 157 and its examples that follow)
- Do we wish to present a measure of "operations"? (Display ¶¶ 23, 163–167) (See Appendix 29-F for further guidance)
- Do we wish to prepare the statement of cash flows using the direct or the indirect method? (Statement of Financial Accounting Standards No. 95, "Statement of Cash Flows," ¶¶ 27–28)
- Do we wish to present comparative financial data for prior year(s)? (Display ¶ 70)

Classification of expenses:

- On the face of the statement of activities, do we wish to categorize expenses by functional or by natural classifications? (Display ¶ 26, second and third lines)
- If we are not required to disclose expenses in natural categories, do we wish to make such disclosure voluntarily? (Display ¶ 26, last sentence)
- If expenses have not previously been categorized by function, what categories (beyond the basic categories of program, management, fundraising, membership-development) do we wish to present? (Display ¶¶ 26–28)

Do we wish to disclose the fair value of contributed services received but not recognized as revenues? (Contributions ¶ 10, last sentence).

Collection items:

- If our organization has assets that meet the definition of collection items at Contributions ¶ 11, do we wish to capitalize these assets or not?
- If we have not previously capitalized but now wish to capitalize these items, do we wish to do so retroactively, or only prospectively? (Contributions ¶ 12)
- If we choose to capitalize these items retroactively, how do we wish to determine their value for this purpose? (Contributions, footnote 4)

Do we wish to present nonmonetary information, as discussed in Display footnote 6?

Adoption date: (Contributions ¶ 28; Display ¶ 31).

- Do we wish to adopt the standards earlier than the required adoption date?
- If we qualify as a "small" organization (total assets less than $5 million and annual expenses less than $1 million), do we wish to delay adoption until the later permitted date?
- Do we wish to adopt the contributions standard retroactively or prospectively?
- If we choose to adopt the contributions standard retroactively, do we wish to adopt ¶ 17 (relating to recognition of expiration of restrictions) prospectively? (¶ 30)

Do we wish to retain our present fund *accounting* system and convert our financial data to the new class structure by worksheets prior to preparing the financial statements, or do we wish to convert our entire accounting system to reflect the three-class structure discussed at Display ¶ 3 and Appendix D?

The division of net assets (formerly called fund balance) into three classes—unrestricted, temporarily restricted, and permanently restricted—as set forth in SFAC No. 6, and other matters discussed in that document, will likely have a significant effect on the format of the financial statements of many not-for-profit organizations.

(ii) Projects in Process.   As of early 1996, the FASB and the AICPA have completed or are working on the following additional projects.

- Combination of related organizations: In 1995 the FASB issued an exposure draft of a proposed statement on consolidated financial statements, which will apply to not-for-profit, as well as for-profit, organizations. Briefly, its requirements are that an organization shall consolidate all organizations over whose assets it has legal or effective control. A more detailed summary of its proposals follows.

FASB EXPOSURE DRAFT ON CONSOLIDATIONS—OCTOBER 1995
SUMMARY OF PRINCIPAL PROVISIONS RELEVANT TO NOT-FOR-PROFITS

Effective Date: Fiscal years beginning after 15 December 1996

Scope: Applies to all entities that control other entities, regardless of the form of organizations involved.

Policy: A controlling entity shall consolidate all entities that it controls; unless control is temporary at the time that the entity becomes a subsidiary.

Control:

Control of an entity is power over its assets—power to use or direct the use of the individual assets of another entity in essentially the same ways as the controlling entity can use its own assets.

Ways to control another entity's assets are having the power to:
- establish the policies of the controlled entity, as well as its operating and capital budgets;
- select, compensate, and terminate personnel responsible for implementing its policies and decisions.

The presence of legal restrictions which limit the freedom of discretion in the exercise of control does not overcome the existence of control itself. Such restrictions include those imposed by law, regulation, and contract. An example of the latter is a donor-imposed restriction on net assets of a not-for-profit entity. A controlling entity can cause the assets of the controlled entity to be used to remove certain restrictions, such as by paying off debt or paying penalties resulting from breach of contract, and fulfilling donor-imposed stipulations (if possible to be fulfilled).

Control can be achieved in two ways: legal control; effective control.
- Legal control is normally achieved by having power to select a majority of a governing body (governing board, or partnership interest); voting stock ownership is most common example.
- Effective control is control other than legal control.

Assessing the Existence of Control:

If by legal means, existence is usually apparent.

If by other means, careful consideration of relevant facts and circumstances is required. Absent evidence to the contrary, effect control shall be presumed if any of the following exist:

- Large minority voting interest (approx. 40%) and no other party or organized group has a significant interest;
- Ability, demonstrated by a recent election, to dominate the process of governing board selection;
- Unilateral ability to obtain majority voting interest by converting securities into voting securities;
- A relationship with an entity that: it (the reporting entity) has established, that has no voting rights, and that has provisions in its governing documents that (1) cannot be changed by entities other than the creator, and (2) limit the entity to activities that the creating entity can schedule to provide substantially all future net cash inflows or other future economic benefits to its creator;
- Unilateral ability to dissolve the entity and assume control of its assets;
- Being the sole general partner in a limited partnership.

Other indicators, while not determinative, should be considered in each case:
- Ability to cast a majority of votes in elections of directors;
- Ability to control the nomination and voting process for directors;
- Ability to appoint directors to fill temporary vacancies;
- Right to a majority of the net assets in the event of liquidation or other distribution;
- Being the sole creator of the other entity;
- A relationship that requires the two entities to work together for their purposes, for example, an organization is formed for the primary purpose of:
  - holding and investing assets to generate income for another entity;
  - holding assets to pay the debts of another entity;
  - raising contributions for a specific charitable organization.

Examples of relationships which generally are *not* indicative of control:
- Manager and managed entity;
- Trustees, trust, and beneficiaries; (Note that a beneficiary's irrevocable interest in a trust is an asset of the beneficiary, but it does not give the beneficiary control of the assets of the trust itself.) (Gives examples of third-party charitable trust)
- Grant-making foundations and their sponsors (e.g., corporate foundation);
- Federations, membership organizations, other associations, and their members, including associations of religious organizations (dioceses, synods, etc.);

- Impairment of long-lived assets: The Board has issued a standard, No. 121 (applicable to both for-profit and not-for-profit entities) which would require a reduction in the reported value of such assets if it appeared that future cash flows related to the assets were less than the existing book value of the assets. In general, not-for-profits will be able to consider contributions in assessing whether assets are considered impaired.

- New audit guides: Work is continuing on the new guides (one for health care organizations (see Chapter 30), and one for all other not-for-profit organizations) which will replace the existing guides and SOP No. 78-10. The guides will, of course, be consistent with the requirements of SFAS Nos. 116 and 117; they will provide additional explanations and guidance on matters covered in the FASB standards, as well as clarify certain matters which FASB did not cover in detail. Exposure drafts of the new guides were issued in 1995, and final documents are expected in 1996.

- Combination of related organizations: A statement of position on this topic, No. 94-3, was issued in 1994. Its requirements for combination are based on the extent of control of and economic interest in the related organization. (See subsection 29.2(k).)

- Joint costs of multipurpose activities: Comments have been received on the exposure draft issued but final work remains to be done.

(c) **GOVERNMENT AUDIT REQUIREMENTS.**   Not-for-profit entities are increasingly subject to audit requirements imposed by government agencies. These requirements are discussed in subsection 29.6(f) of this chapter.

29.2 NOT-FOR-PROFIT ACCOUNTING PRINCIPLES AND REPORTING PRACTICES

(a) **PRINCIPAL ACCOUNTING AND REPORTING CHANGES RESULTING FROM MATTERS COVERED IN NEW LITERATURE.**   The various new accounting standards discussed in this chapter will have a profound impact on accounting and financial reporting for all types of not-for-profit organizations. A list of the most significant changes follows. Some are already issued; some are expected to be issued in the near future. Many of these are discussed in more detail elsewhere in this chapter.

Accounting for contributions (see SFAS No. 116 and the AICPA Audit Guide exposure draft)

- Pledges are recorded when an unconditional promise to give is communicated to the donee.
- A conditional promise to give is not reported until the condition is met.
  - (The distinction between conditional and restricted gifts is not always clear.)
- Pledges are discounted to their present value (PV), and are reported net of an allowance for the estimated uncollectible amount.
  - (There is a question about how to report the allowance.)
- All gifts, including pledges and restricted gifts, are reported as revenue when received.
- Donors (including for-profit donors) must follow the same rules as donees (in reverse—an unconditional pledge must be recorded as an expense and a liability when made). **(Fund-raisers should take note of this, as it will affect some donors' willingness to make unconditional pledges.)**
- Split interest gifts are essentially treated as pledges; these include:
  - Gift annuities, remainder annuity trusts, unitrusts, pooled income funds, lead trusts.
  - Irrevocable trusts held by others are reported in the beneficiary's financial statements.
- Gifts-in-kind are recorded at fair value—including property, use of property, equipment, inventory for sale or use, services by other organizations (including bargain purchases).
- Donated services of individual volunteers are recorded only when specified criteria are met:
  - —The services create or enhance nonfinancial assets (building something), or
  - —The services require specialized skills, the volunteer possesses those skills, and the donee would typically have to purchase the services if the volunteer were not available (the services involve a significant and central activity of the entity).
- A pass-through entity may not be able to record gifts as revenue, depending on the circumstances of the gift.
- A museum does not have to capitalize its collection if certain criteria are met.

Financial statement format (see SFAS No. 117 and the AICPA Audit Guide exposure draft)

- Required disclosures are: totals of assets, liabilities, net assets, change in net assets.
- Net assets (formerly, fund balance) and revenue are categorized into three classes:

—Unrestricted; temporarily restricted; permanently restricted (per donor restrictions only).

—Restrictions imposed by nondonors do not change category (e.g., contracts).

• Required disclosures for each class are: net assets, change in net assets.

• A statement of cash flows is required (the "direct" method is preferred).

• All expenses are reported in the unrestricted class.

—Temporarily restricted net assets are reclassified to match related expenses.

• Expenses are reported on a functional basis (program, management, fund-raising).

• Revenues and expenses are reported gross, not net (exception: investment management fees).

—Related items (e.g., sales/cost of sales) may be shown as: gross, deduction, net.

• (See below for treatment of capital gains/losses.)

• Affiliated entities are combined if specified criteria are met (SOP 94-3):

—For-profit affiliate: criteria based on ownership.

—Not-for-profit affiliate: criteria based on control and economic interest.

Accounting for investments (see SFAS No. 117 and 124)

• Marketable securities are reported at current market value.

• There is a question about which accounting rule is to be followed by associations and clubs (see SFAS No. 115).

• Capital gains and losses on endowment are reported mostly in the unrestricted class, unless state law or a donor stipulation specifies otherwise.

Other matters

• Depreciable assets must be depreciated (see SFAS No. 93).

• Not-for-profits must follow requirements of Generally Accepted Accounting Principles (GAAP) (see SOP No. 94-2).

• Joint costs of multipurpose activities can be allocated to program functions only if certain criteria are met:

• Purpose; audience; content, including a call to action other than giving (see SOP No. 87-2; its replacement).

• (Contribution rules in SFAS No. 116 do not affect the timing of revenue recognition for advance payments of earned income: dues, fees, sales, season tickets, etc.—these are still deferred until earned).

(b) BASIS OF ACCOUNTING: CASH OR ACCRUAL.   Not-for-profit organizations frequently maintain their records on a **cash basis,** a bookkeeping process that reflects only transactions involving cash. On the other hand, most commercial organizations, as well as many medium and large not-for-profit organizations, keep accounts on an **accrual basis.** In accrual basis accounting, income is recognized when earned and expenses are recognized when incurred. For bookkeeping purposes either basis is acceptable.

Each accounting basis has certain advantages. The principal advantage of cash basis accounting is **simplicity**—its procedures are easy to learn and easy to execute. Because of this simplicity, a cash basis accounting system is **less complicated and expensive** to maintain than an accrual basis system. A less complicated system will be easier for a volunteer bookkeeper who does not feel comfortable with the more complicated accrual methods. Because there is often no material difference in financial results between cash and accrual basis accounting for small organizations, the incremental cost of an accrual basis system may be unwarranted. In addition, many not-for-profit organizations think it more **prudent** to keep their books on a cash basis. They often do not want to recognize income prior to the actual receipt of cash.

The principal advantage of accrual basis accounting is that it portrays financial position and results of operations on a more **realistic** basis—a complex organization with accounts receivable and bills outstanding can present realistic financial results only on the accrual basis. In addition, accrual basis accounting usually achieves a better **matching** of revenue and related expenses. Also, many individuals who use the financial statements of not-for-profit organizations, such as bankers, local businesspeople, and board members, are often more familiar with accrual basis accounting.

Organizations wanting the accuracy of accrual basis accounting, but not wishing to sacrifice the simplicity of cash basis bookkeeping, have alternatives. They may maintain their books on a cash basis and at year-end record all payables, receivables, and accruals. These adjustments would permit presentation of accrual basis financial statements.

An organization can also keep its books on a cash basis, except for certain transactions that are recorded on an accrual basis. A popular type of "modified cash basis" accounting is to record accounts payable as liabilities are incurred, but to record income on a cash basis as received.

(c) FUND ACCOUNTING.   Fund accounting is the process of segregating resources into sets of self-balancing accounts on the basis of either restrictions imposed by donors or designations imposed by governing boards.

In the past, most not-for-profit organizations have followed fund accounting procedures in accounting for resources. This was done because many organizations regard fund accounting as the most appropriate means of exercising stewardship over funds. Reporting all the details of funds, however, is not required of all not-for-profit organizations, and in many cases is not recommended. Fund accounting, if carried to its logical extreme, requires a separate set of accounts for each restricted gift or contribution; this leads to confusing financial statements that often present an organization as a collection of individual funds rather than as a single entity. Today, many not-for-profit organizations are combining funds and eliminating fund distinctions for reporting purposes to facilitate financial statement users' understanding of the organization as a whole.

The new FASB Standard on financial reporting CSFAS No. 117 specifically requires the reporting of certain financial information by what it calls "classes" rather than funds.

An infinite variety of funds is possible. To limit the number of funds reported, broad fund classifications may be used. One scheme commonly used today is classification of resources by type of donor restriction. Another criterion for classifying funds is the degree of control an organization possesses over its resources. Under this approach, funds are combined for reporting purposes into two groupings—**unrestricted** and **restricted.** A third approach classifies resources on the basis of their availability for current expenditure on an organization's programs. Under this approach, funds are combined into two categories, **expendable** and **nonexpendable.**

When resources are classified by type of donor restriction, four fund groupings are commonly used—current unrestricted, current restricted, endowment, and fixed asset funds.

The **current unrestricted fund** contains assets over which the board has total managerial discretion. This fund includes unrestricted contributions, revenue, and other income and can be used in any manner at any time to further the goals of the organization. For all not-for-profit organizations, "board-designated" funds should be included with current unrestricted funds. Board-designated funds are voluntary segregations of unrestricted fund balances approved by the board for specific future projects or purposes.

Current restricted funds are resources given to an organization to be expended for specific operating purposes.

Endowment funds are amounts donated to an organization with the legal restriction that the principal be maintained inviolate and in perpetuity. Investment income on such funds is generally unrestricted and should be reported in the current unrestricted fund. Occasionally, endowment gifts stipulate restricted uses for the investment income, and such restricted income should be reported in the appropriate fund.

The **fixed asset fund** represents the land, buildings, and equipment owned by an organization. Since these assets are usually unrestricted in the sense that the board can employ (or dispose of) them in any manner it wishes to further the goals of the organization, fixed assets need not be reported in a separate fund, and may be reported as part of the current unrestricted fund.

(i) Reclassification of Funds into Classes.   Under SFAS No. 117, organizations must access each component of each fund on an individual basis to determine into which class that fund balance (net assets) should be classified. This assessment, as to the temporarily and permanently restricted classes, is based only on the presence or absence of donor-imposed restrictions. All funds without donor-imposed restrictions must be classified as unrestricted, regardless of the existence of any board designations or appropriations.

Following is a chart showing typical classes into which various types of fund balances will normally be classified:

Funds	Unrestricted	Temporarily Restricted	Permanently Restricted
Endowment	Quasi	Term	Permanent
Specific purpose, or current restricted	Board-designated	Donor-restricted	N/A
Loan	Board-designated	Donor-restricted[1]	Revolving[1]
Split-interest (annuity, life income, etc.)	Voluntary excess reserves	Unmatured	Permanent[2]
Fixed asset	Expended[3]; Board-designated	Donor-restricted unexpended; Expended donated[4]	
General/Operating	Unrestricted	Donor-time restricted	N/A
Custodian	All (on balance sheet only)[5]	N/A	N/A

[1] A permanently restricted loan fund would be one where only the income can be loaned, or, if the principal can be loaned, repayments of principal by borrowers are restricted to be used for future loans. A loan fund in which principal repayments are available for any use would be temporarily restricted until the loans are repaid, at which time such amounts would become unrestricted.

[2] For example, an annuity fund which, upon maturity, becomes a permanent endowment.

[3] Expended donor-restricted plant funds will be either unrestricted or temporarily restricted, depending on the organization's choice of accounting principle under ¶ 16 of SFAS No. 116.

[4] Fixed assets could be permanently restricted if a donor has explicitly restricted the proceeds from any future disposition of the assets to reinvestment in fixed assets. Museum collection items received subject to a donor's stipulation that they be preserved and not sold might also be considered permanently restricted.

[5] Note that because no transactions related to custodian funds are reported in the income statement of the holder of the assets, and because there is never a fund balance amount (assets are always exactly offset by liabilities), reporting of such funds as separate items becomes an issue only when a balance sheet is disaggregated into classes. The logic for reporting the assets and liabilities of custodian funds in the unrestricted class is that such assets are not the result of *donor*-restricted *gifts,* which is a requirement for recording items in one of the restricted classes.

(d) RECLASSIFICATIONS.   The use of fund accounting necessitates transfers in some situations to allocate resources between funds or classes. Financial statement readers often find it difficult to comprehend such reclassifications. In addition, if not properly presented, reclassifications may give the impression that an organization is willfully manipulating amounts reported as income.

To minimize confusion and the appearance of deception, transfers must not be shown as either **income** or **expenses** of the transferring fund. Reclassifications of the total organization are merely an internal reallocation of resources and in no way result in income or expense recognition.

Columnar statements, which present the activity of each class in separate, side-by-side columns, facilitate clear, comprehensive presentation of reclassifications.

(e) APPROPRIATIONS.   Appropriations (or designations) are internal authorizations to expend resources in the future for specific purposes. They are neither expenditures nor legal obligations. When appropriation accounting is followed, appropriated amounts should be set aside in a separate account as part of the net assets of an organization.

Appropriation accounting is both confusing and subject to abuse. It is confusing because "appropriation" is an ambiguous term, and many readers do not understand that it is neither a current expenditure nor a binding obligation for a future expenditure. It is subject to abuse because, when treated incorrectly, appropriations can appear to reduce the current year's excess of revenue over expenses to whatever level the board wants. The board can then, at a later date, restore "appropriated" funds to the general use of the organization.

The use of appropriation accounting is not recommended. If an organization wishes to follow appropriation accounting techniques and wants to conform with GAAP, it must be certain that appropriations are not presented as expenses, and that they appear only as part of the net assets of the organization. Expenses incurred out of appropriated funds should be charged as expenses in the year incurred, and the related appropriations should be reversed once an expense has been incurred.

Disclosure in notes is an alternative to appropriation accounting. Under this approach, an organization does not refer to appropriations in the body of its financial statements but instead discloses such amounts only in notes to the financial statements.

(f) FIXED ASSETS.   Treatment of fixed assets is sometimes a perplexing accounting issue confronting not-for-profit organizations. There are three reasons some not-for-profit organizations have historically not recorded a value for fixed assets on their balance sheets. First, many not-for-profit organizations have not been as interested in matching income and expenses as are businesses. This being the case, management of these organizations has felt no compelling need to record assets and then charge depreciation expense against current income. Second, the principal asset of some not-for-profit organizations is real estate that was often acquired many years previously. In these inflationary times, many organizations do not wish to carry at cost and depreciate assets now worth several times their original purchase price. Third, many not-for-profit organizations plead poverty as a means of raising funds. By not recording fixed assets, they appear less substantial than they in fact are.

Confusion concerning fixed assets has been heightened by lack of a universally accepted treatment for fixed assets. Historically, there have been three common alternatives for handling fixed assets: immediate write-off, capitalization (with or without depreciation), and write-off, followed by capitalization.

Immediate write-off is the simplest method of treating fixed assets and is used most frequently for small organizations and those on a cash basis. Under this method, an organization expenses fixed asset purchases immediately on the statement of income and expenses.

The principal advantage of approach is simplicity—the bookkeeping complexities of capitalization are avoided, and the amount of excess revenue over expenses reported on the statement of income and expenses more closely reflects the amount of money at the board's disposal.

The major disadvantage of immediate write-off is that the historical costs of an organization's fixed assets are not recorded, and its balance sheet does not present the true net worth of the organization. Another disadvantage is that expensing fixed assets may produce fluctuations in net income that are largely unrelated to operations. Finally, this approach does not conform with GAAP.

A second alternative available to an organization is to **capitalize** all major fixed asset purchases. Under this approach, all major fixed assets are reflected on the organization's balance sheet.

The principal advantage of this approach is that it conforms with GAAP and permits an auditor to express an unqualified opinion on an organization's financial statements. It also documents the amount of assets the organization controls, permitting evaluation of management performance, and allows the organization to follow depreciation accounting.

The major disadvantage of capitalization is that it renders financial statements more complex. An unsophisticated statement reader may conclude that an organization has more funds available for current spending than it actually has.

A third alternative is to immediately **write off** fixed asset purchases on the statement of income and expenses and **then capitalize** these assets on the balance sheet. This method permits an organization to report expenditures for fixed asset purchases on the statement of income and expenses, thus offsetting any excess of income over expenses that may have been caused by contributions received for fixed assets on its balance sheet.

However, this approach is very confusing, is inconsistent with other accounting conventions, does not permit depreciation accounting in a traditional sense, and does not constitute GAAP. Accordingly, the use of this approach is strongly discouraged.

(g) DEPRECIATION.   Depreciation has been as thorny a problem for not-for-profit organizations as the problem of fixed assets. If an organization capitalizes fixed assets, it is immediately confronted with the question of whether it should depreciate them: that is, allocate the cost over the estimated useful life of the assets.

Depreciation accounting is now a generally accepted practice for most not-for-profit organizations and since 1990 it constitutes GAAP for all not-for-profit organizations. (Prior to that year it was optional for colleges.) SFAS No. 93, "Recognition of Depreciation by Not-for-Profit Organizations," requires not-for-profit organizations to record depreciation on fixed assets. Many arguments in favor of recording depreciation, such as the following, are valid for not-for-profit organizations:

1. Depreciation is a cost of operations. Organizations cannot accurately measure the cost of providing a product or service or determine a fair price without including this cost component.
2. Most organizations replace at least some fixed assets out of recurring income. If depreciation is not recorded, an organization may think that its income is sufficient to cover costs when, in reality, it is not.
3. If depreciation is not recorded, income may fluctuate widely from year to year, depending on the timing of asset replacement and the replacement cost of assets.
4. Organizations that are "reimbursed" by a government agency for the sale of goods or services must depreciate fixed assets if they wish to recapture all costs incurred.
5. Some not-for-profit organizations pay federal income tax on "unrelated business income." Depreciation should be reported as an expense to reduce income subject to tax.

Depreciation is computed in the same manner as that used by commercial enterprises. Depreciation is reported as an item of expense on the statement of income and expenses, and accumulated depreciation is reported under the "fixed assets" caption on the balance sheet.

If fixed asset purchases are capitalized but not written down through regular depreciation charges in the statement of income and expenses, it may be necessary to periodically write down their carrying value so that the balance sheet is not overstated. The preferred method of achieving this is to report the write-down as an expense on the statement of income and expenses and to reduce the asset value on the balance sheet.

(h) INVESTMENT INCOME. Dividends and interest earned on unrestricted investment funds, including board-designated funds, should be reported as income in the unrestricted class.

Unrestricted investment income earned on endowment funds should also be reported as income directly in the unrestricted class.

Restricted investment income should be reported directly in the appropriate restricted fund. For example, if the donor of an endowment fund gift specifies that the investment income be used for a particular purpose, investment income should be reported directly in the temporarily restricted class rather than the unrestricted or the permanently restricted class.

(i) GAINS AND LOSSES ON INVESTMENTS. The new FASB reporting standard in Statement 117 will require many organizations to change their method of reporting gains and losses on endowment funds from the method previously used and described in the seventh edition of this book. Briefly, the new method will involve determining which portion of the gains are legally restricted, either by explicit donor restrictions or by applicable laws to which the organization is subject. All gains not so restricted will be reported directly in the unrestricted class, rather than in the endowment fund as at present.

Realized gains or losses on unrestricted investment funds should be reported directly in the unrestricted class. Unrestricted capital gains or losses may be reported in the statement of income and expenses as an income item along with dividends and interest, or they may be reported separately from other investment income, above the caption "Change in net assets."

Realized gains or losses on endowment investments were traditionally treated as adjustments to principal of the endowment fund. They have not been considered as income and were thought to possess the same restrictions as those that are attached to the principal. The legal status of gains or losses on endowment funds—as unrestricted income or as a component of restricted principal—is, however, currently discussed in SFAS No. 117. Where permitted by state law, such gains or losses should be treated as income and reported with dividends and interest in the unrestricted class above the caption "change in net assets." Restricted gains or losses may be treated in a similar manner except that they are reported in the appropriate restricted class.

Unrealized gains or losses did not pose accounting questions for not-for-profit organizations prior to 1973 because, before that year, investments could be carried only at cost and gains or losses were realized only at the time investments were sold or otherwise disposed of.

After 1973 the tenor of accounting pronouncements on the carrying value of investments and the treatment of unrealized gains or losses changed dramatically. In 1973 and 1974 the AICPA Industry Audit Guides for colleges and universities and voluntary health and welfare organizations permitted those organizations to carry their investments at either cost or market. Hospitals were required in 1978 to carry equity investments at market if the fair value dipped below cost. SOP No. 78-10 permits covered organizations to carry investments at market or the lower of cost or market.

When investments are carried at market, gains and losses are recognized on a continuing basis. Realized and unrealized gains or losses should be reported together in a single caption: "net increase (decrease) in carrying value of investments." It is appropriate to report this increase or decrease in the same section in which investment dividends and interest are reported.

In 1995 SFAS 124 was issued. Its requirement includes:

- Equity securities that have readily determinable fair market values and all debt securities shall be reported at current fair value;
- In the absence of donor stipulations or law to the contrary:
  - Capital losses shall reduce temporarily restricted net assets to the extent that donor-imposed restrictions on net appreciation of the fund have not yet been met;
  - Any remaining loss shall reduce unrestricted net assets;
  - Gains that restore previous losses shall be reported in the unrestricted class.

Even when investments are carried at cost, if market value declines "permanently" below cost, the carrying value of this investment should be written down to the market value. This is accomplished by setting up a "provision for decline in market value of investments" in the statement of income and expenses in the same section where realized gains or losses are presented.

(j) CONTRIBUTIONS. Support for a not-for-profit organization can be received in many different forms. Each of the types of contributions will be discussed in a separate section of this chapter.

In 1993, the controversy about proper accounting for contributions was settled by the issuance of FASB Statement of Financial Accounting Standards No. 116, *Accounting for Contributions Received and Contributions Made.* In brief, it says that all contributions, whether unrestricted or restricted, and in whatever form: cash, gifts-in-kind, securities, pledges, or other forms, are revenue in full immediately upon receipt of the gift or an unconditional pledge. (Restricted contributions are not deferred until the restriction is met, as is now the practice by many organizations.) The revenue is reported in the class of net assets appropriate to any donor-imposed restriction on the gift (unrestricted, if there is no donor-imposed restriction). It also contains guidance on accounting for donated services of volunteers, and an exception to the normal rule when dealing with museum collection objects.

(i) Expendable Current Support

Unrestricted Contributions. This section of the chapter will discuss simple unrestricted cash gifts. Unrestricted gifts in other forms, such as pledges, gifts of securities, and gifts of equipment and supplies, are discussed in later sections. The general principles discussed here apply to all unrestricted gifts, in whatever form received.

HISTORICAL PRACTICES.   All unrestricted contributions should be recorded in the current unrestricted fund. This principle is fairly well accepted and followed by most not-for-profit organizations. What has not been uniformly followed is a single method of reporting such unrestricted contributions. Some organizations followed the practice of adding unrestricted contributions directly to the fund balance either in a separate Statement of Changes in Fund Balances, or in the fund balance section where a combined Statement of Income, Expenses, and Changes in Fund Balances was used. Others reported some or all of their contributions directly in an unrestricted investment fund, and worse still, some reported unrestricted contributions directly in the endowment fund as though such amounts were restricted. The result of all these practices has been to make it difficult for the readers of the financial statements to recognize the amount and nature of contributions received. Sometimes this was done deliberately in an attempt to convince the readers that the organization badly needed more contributions.

ACCOUNTING FOR UNRESTRICTED CONTRIBUTIONS.   All unrestricted contributions should be reported in the unrestricted class of net assets in a Statement of Income and Expenses or, if a combined Statement of Income, Expenses, and Changes in Net Assets is used, such unrestricted contributions should be shown before arriving at the "Excess of income over expenses" caption. It is *not acceptable* to report unrestricted contributions in a separate Statement of Changes in Net Assets or to report such gifts in a restricted class of net assets.

BARGAIN PURCHASES.   Organizations are sometimes permitted to purchase goods or services at a reduced price that is granted by the seller in recognition of the organization's charitable or educational status. In such cases, the seller has effectively made a gift to the buyer. This gift should be recorded as such if the amount is significant. For example, if a charity buys a widget for $50 that normally sells for $80, the purchase should be recorded at $80, with the $30 difference being reported as a contribution.

It is important to record only true gifts in this way. If a lower price is really a normal discount available to any buyer who requests it, then there is no contribution. Such discounts include quantity discounts, normal trade discounts, promotional discounts, special offers, or lower rates (say, for professional services) to reflect the seller's desire to utilize underused staff, or sale prices to move slow-moving items off the shelves.

Current Restricted Contributions.   Current restricted contributions are contributions that can be used to meet the current expenses of the organization, although restricted to use for some specific purpose, or during or after some specified time. An example of the former would be a gift "for cancer research" (a "purpose restriction"), and of the latter, a gift "for your 19X6 activities" (a "time restriction"). In practice, the distinction between restricted gifts and unrestricted gifts is not always clear. In many cases, the language used by the donor leaves doubt as to whether there really is a restriction on the gift.

Current restricted contributions cause reporting problems, in part because the accounting profession took a long time to resolve the appropriate accounting and reporting treatment for these types of gifts. The resolution arrived at is controversial because many believe it is not the most desirable method of accounting for such gifts.

The principal accounting problem relates to the question of what constitutes "income" or "support" to the organization. Is a gift that can only be used for a specific project or after a specified time "income" to the organization at the time the gift is received, or does this restricted gift represent an amount which should be looked on as being held in a form of escrow until it is expended for the restricted purpose (cancer research in the above example), or the specified time has arrived (19X6 in the above example)? If it is looked on as something other than income, what is it—deferred income or part of a restricted net asset balance?

If a current restricted gift is considered income or support in the period received—whether expended or not—the accounting is fairly straightforward. It would be essentially the same as for unrestricted gifts, described earlier, except that the gift is reported in the temporarily restricted class rather than in the unrestricted class of net assets. But if the other view is taken, the accounting can become complex.

The approach required by SFAS No. 116 is to report a current restricted gift as income or support in full in the year received, in the temporarily restricted class of net assets. In this approach, gifts are recognized as income as received and expenditures are recognized as incurred. The unexpended income is reflected as part of temporarily restricted net assets.

Observe, however, that in this approach a current restricted gift received on the last day of the reporting period will also be reflected as income, and this would increase the excess of support over expenses reported for the entire period. Many boards are reluctant to report such an excess in the belief this may discourage contributions or suggest that the board has not used all of its available resources. Those who are concerned about reporting an excess of income over expenses are therefore particularly concerned with the implications of this approach: a large unexpected current restricted gift may be received at the last minute, resulting in a large excess of income over expenses.

Others, in rejecting this argument, point out that the organization is merely reporting what has happened and to report the gift otherwise is to obscure its receipt. They point out that in reality all gifts, whether restricted or unrestricted, are really at least somewhat restricted and only the degree of restriction varies; even "unrestricted" gifts must be spent realizing the stated goals of the organization, and therefore such gifts are effectively restricted to this purpose even though a particular use has not been specified by the contributor.

There are valid arguments on both sides. This approach is the one recommended in the AICPA Audit Guide for Voluntary Health and Welfare Organizations and therefore has been very widely followed. It will now become the method used by all not-for-profit organizations if they want their independent auditor to be able to say that their financial statements are prepared in conformity with generally accepted accounting principles.

GRANTS FOR SPECIFIC PROJECTS.   Many organizations receive grants from third parties to accomplish specific projects or activities. These grants differ from other current restricted gifts principally in the degree of accountability the recipient organization has in reporting back to the granting organization on the use of such monies. In some instances, the organization receives a grant to conduct a specific research project, the results of which are turned over to the grantor. The arrangement is similar to a private contractor's performance on a commercial for-profit basis. In that case, the "grant" is essentially a purchase of services. It would be accounted for in accordance with normal commercial accounting principles, which call for the revenue to be recognized as the work under the contract is performed. In other instances, the organization receives a grant for a specific project, and while the grantee must specifically account for the expenditure of the grant in detail and may have to return any unexpended amounts, the grant is to further the programs of the grantee rather than for the benefit of the grantor. This kind of grant is really a gift, not a purchase.

The line between ordinary current restricted gifts and true "grants" for specific projects is not important for accounting purposes because the method of reporting revenue is now the same for both. What can get fuzzy is the distinction between grants and purchase of services contracts. Most donors of current restricted gifts are explicit as to how their gifts are to be used, and often the organization will initiate a report back to the donors on the use of their gifts. However, restricted gifts and grants usually do not have the degree of specificity that is attached to purchase contracts. Appendix 29–A contains a checklist to help readers distinguish between gifts and purchase contracts in practice.

Prepayment versus cost-reimbursement. Grants and contracts can be structured in either of two forms: in one the payor remits the amount up front and the payee then spends that money. In the other, the payee must spend its own money from other sources and is reimbursed by the payor.

In the case of a purchase contract, amounts remitted to the organization in advance of their expenditure should be treated as deferred income until such time as expenditures are made which can be charged against the contract. At that time, income should be recognized to the extent earned. Where expenditures have been made but the grantor has not yet made payment, a receivable should be set up to reflect the grantor's obligation.

In the case of a true grant (gift), advance payments must be recognized as revenue immediately upon receipt, as is the case with all contributions under SFAS No. 116. Reimbursement grants are recognized as revenue as reimbursements become due, that is, as money is spent which the grantor will reimburse. This is the same method as is used under cost-reimbursement purchase contracts.

Some organizations have recorded the entire amount of the grant as a receivable at the time awarded, offset by deferred grant income on the liability side of the Balance Sheet. This is no longer appropriate under SFAS No. 116. If the entire grant amount qualifies as an unconditional pledge (see below), then that amount must be recorded as revenue, not deferred revenue.

Investment Securities.   Frequently an organization will receive contributions that are in the form of investment securities: stocks and bonds. These contributions should be recorded in the same manner as cash gifts. The only problem usually encountered is difficulty in determining a reasonable basis for valuation in the case of closely-held stock with no objective market value.

The value recorded should be the fair market value at the date received. Marketable stocks and bonds present no serious valuation problem. They should be recorded at their market value on the date of receipt or, if sold shortly thereafter, at the amount of proceeds actually received. However, the "shortly thereafter" refers to a sale within a few days or perhaps a week after receipt. Where the organization deliberately holds the securities for a period of time before sale, the securities should be recorded at their fair market value on the date of receipt. This will result in a gain or loss being recorded when the securities are subsequently sold (unless the market price remains unchanged).

For securities without a published market value, the services of an appraiser may be required to determine the fair value of the gift. See subsection 29.2(b) for further discussion of investments.

(ii) Gifts-in-Kind

Fixed Assets (Land, Buildings, and Equipment), and Supplies.   Contributions of fixed assets can be accounted for in one of two ways. SFAS No. 116 permits such gifts to be reported as either unrestricted or temporarily restricted income at the time received. If the gift is initially reported as temporarily restricted, the restriction is deemed to expire ratably over the useful life of the asset: that is, in proportion to depreciation for depreciable assets. The expiration is reported as a reclassification from the temporarily restricted to the unrestricted class of net assets. Nondepreciable assets such as land would remain in the temporarily restricted class indefinitely—until disposed of. (Recognizing the gift as income in proportion to depreciation recognized on the asset is not in conformity with generally accepted accounting principles.)

Supplies and equipment should be recorded at the amount which the organization would normally have to pay for similar items. A value for used office equipment and the like can usually be obtained from a dealer in such items. The valuation of donated real estate is more difficult, and it is usually necessary to get an outside appraisal to determine the value.

Museum Collections.   SFAS No. 116 makes an exception for recording a value for donated (and purchased) museum collection objects, if certain criteria are met and certain disclosures are made. Owners of such objects do not have to record them, although they may if they wish.

Contributed Services of Volunteers.   Many organizations depend almost entirely on volunteers to carry out their programs, and sometimes supporting functions. Should such organizations place a value on these contributed services and record them as "contributions" in their financial statements?

CRITERIA FOR RECORDING.   The answer is yes, under certain circumstances. These circumstances exist only when *either* of the following conditions is satisfied:

1. The services create or enhance nonfinancial assets; or
2. The services:
   a. Require specialized skills,
   b. Are provided by persons possessing those skills, and
   c. Would typically have to be purchased if not provided by donation.

If neither criterion is met, SFAS No. 116 precludes recording a value for the services, although disclosure in a footnote is encouraged. These criteria differ considerably from criteria in the earlier audit guides/statement of position.

Creating or enhancing fixed assets.   The first criterion is fairly straightforward. It covers volunteers constructing or making major improvements to buildings or equipment. It would also cover things like building sets or making costumes for a theater or opera company, and writing computer programs, since the resulting assets could be capitalized on the balance sheet. The criterion says "nonfinancial" assets so as *not* to cover volunteer fundraisers who, it could be argued, are "creating" assets by soliciting gifts.

Specialized skills. The second criterion has three parts, all of which must be met for recording to be appropriate. The first part deals with the nature of the services themselves. The intent is deliberately to limit the types of services that must be recorded, thus reducing the burden of tracking and valuing large numbers of volunteers doing purely routine work, the aggregate financial value of which would usually be fairly small. SFAS No. 116 gives very little guidance about how to identify, in practice, those skills which would be considered "specialized," as opposed to nonspecialized. There is a list of skills that are considered specialized, but it merely recites a list of obvious professions such as doctors, lawyers, teachers, carpenters. What is lacking is an operational definition of specialized that can be applied to all types of services. Appendix 29–B contains a checklist to help readers make this distinction in practice.

The second part of the criterion will usually cause no problems in practice, as persons practicing the types of skills contemplated should normally possess the skills (if not, why are they performing the services?)

Would otherwise purchase. The third part of the criterion will be the most difficult of all to consider, as it calls for a pure judgment by management. Would the organization or would it not purchase the services? This is similar to one in SOP No. 78-10, which reads as follows:

> The services performed are significant and form an integral part of the efforts of the organization as it is presently constituted; the services would be performed by salaried personnel if donated services were not available . . . ; and the organization would continue the activity.

Probably the most important requirement is that the services being performed are an essential part of the organization's program. The key test is whether the organization would hire someone to perform these services if volunteers were not available.

This is a difficult criterion to meet. Many organizations have volunteers involved in peripheral areas which, while important to the organization, are not of such significance that paid staff would be hired in the absence of volunteers. But this is the acid test: If the volunteers suddenly quit, would the organization hire replacements? Appendix 29–C contains a checklist to help readers assess this criterion.

BASIS ON WHICH TO VALUE SERVICES.   An additional criterion that is not explicitly stated in SFAS No. 116 in connection with donated services is that there must be an objective basis on which to value these services. It is usually not difficult to determine a reasonable value for volunteer services where the volunteers are performing professional or clerical services. By definition, the services to be recorded are only those for which the organization would in fact hire paid staff if volunteers were not available. This suggests that the organization should be able to establish a reasonable estimate of what costs would be involved if employees had to be hired.

In establishing such rates, it is not necessary to establish individual rates for each volunteer. Instead, the volunteers can be grouped into general categories and a rate established for each category.

Some organizations are successful in getting local businesses to donate one of their executives on a full- or part-time basis for an extended period of time. In many instances, the amount paid by the local business to the loaned executive is far greater than the organization would have to pay for hired staff performing the same function. The rate to be used in establishing a value should be the lower rate. This also helps to get around the awkwardness of trying to discern actual compensation.

An organization may wish not to record a value unless the services are significant in amount. There is a cost to keep the records necessary to meet the reporting requirements and unless the resulting amounts are significant it is wasteful for the organization to record them.

ACCOUNTING TREATMENT.   The dollar value assigned to contributed services should be reflected as income in the section of the financial statements where other unrestricted contributions are shown. In most instances, it is appropriate to disclose the amount of such services as a separate line.

On the expense side, the value of contributed services should be allocated to program and supporting service categories based on the nature of the work performed. The amounts allocated to each category are not normally disclosed separately. If volunteers were used for constructing fixed assets, the amounts would be capitalized rather than being charged to an expense category. Unless some of the amounts are capitalized, the recording of contributed services will not affect the excess of income over expenses, since the income and expense exactly offset each other.

The footnotes to the financial statements should disclose the nature of contributed services and the valuation techniques followed.

Use of Facilities. Occasionally a not-for-profit organization will be given use of a building or other facilities either at no cost or at a substantially reduced cost. A value should be reflected for such a facility in the financial statements, both as income and as expense. The value to be used should be the fair market value of facilities which the organization would otherwise rent if the contributed facilities were not available. This means that if very expensive facilities are donated the valuation to be used should be the lower value of the facilities which the organization would otherwise have rented. Implicit in this rule is the ability to determine an objective basis for valuing the facilities. If an organization is given the use of facilities that are unique in design and have no alternative purpose, it may be impossible to determine what they would have to pay to rent comparable facilities. This often occurs with museums that occupy elaborate government-owned buildings.

Where a donor indicates that the organization can unconditionally use such rent-free facilities for more than a one-year period, the organization should reflect the arrangement as a pledge, and record the present value of the contribution in the same way as other pledges.

(iii) Support Not Currently Expendable

Endowment Gifts. Donor-restricted endowment fund contributions should be reported as revenue upon receipt in a restricted class of net assets: temporary in the case of a term endowment gift, otherwise permanent.

Gifts of term endowment are later reclassified to the unrestricted class when the term of the endowment expires. (If upon expiration of the endowment restriction, the gift is still restricted—likely for some operating purpose—it would not be reclassified until money was spent for that purpose. If upon expiration of the term endowment restriction, the gift becomes permanently restricted, it should be recorded in that class initially.)

Pledges (Promises to Give). A pledge[1] is a promise to contribute a specified amount to an organization. Typically, fund-raising organizations solicit pledges because a donor either does not want to or is not able to make a contribution in cash in the amount desired by the organization at the time solicited. In giving, as with consumer purchases, the "installment plan" is a way of life. Organizations find donors are more generous when the payments being contributed are smaller and spread out over a period of time.

A pledge may or may not be legally enforceable. The point is largely moot because few organizations would think of trying to legally enforce a pledge. The unfavorable publicity that would result would only hurt future fund raising. The only relevant criteria are: Will the pledge be collected and are pledges material in amount?

If these criteria are satisfied, then there are two accounting questions: Should a pledge be recorded as an asset at the time the pledge is received? If the answer is "yes," the next question is: When should the pledge be recognized as income?

---

[1] SFAS No. 116 uses the term "promise to give" to refer to what is more commonly called a pledge.

RECORDING AS AN ASSET.   For many organizations, a significant portion of their income is received by pledge. The timing of the collection of pledges is only partially under the control of the organization. Yet over the years most organizations find they can predict with reasonable accuracy the collectible portion of pledges, even when a sizable percentage will not be collected. Accounting literature requires that unconditional pledges the organization expects to collect be recorded as assets and an allowance established for the portion that is estimated to be uncollectible.

Historically, there was considerable difference of opinion on this subject, with the AICPA Audit Guides and the Statement of Position taking different positions. The college audit guide said recording of pledges was optional, and most colleges did not record them until collected. The other three guides required recording pledges, although their criteria and method of recording differed slightly. Now, SFAS No. 116 requires *all* organizations to record unconditional pledges.

CONDITIONS VERSUS RESTRICTIONS.   The requirement in SFAS No. 116 is to record *unconditional* pledges as assets. Unconditional means, without conditions. What is meant by conditions? FASB defines a condition as "a future and uncertain event" that must occur for a pledge to become binding on the pledgor. There are two elements to this definition: future and uncertain. Future means it hasn't happened yet; this is fairly clear. Uncertain is, however, more subject to interpretation. How uncertain? This will be a matter of judgment in many cases.

If a donor pledges to give to a charity "if the sun rises tomorrow," that is not an uncertain event; the sun will rise tomorrow, at a known time. If a donor pledges to give $10,000 to the Red Cross, "if there's an earthquake in California," that is very uncertain (a geologist will say the eventual probability of an earthquake happening is 100%, but the timing is completely uncertain). This latter pledge would be conditional upon an earthquake occurring. Once an earthquake occurs, then the donor's pledge is unconditional (the condition has been removed), and the pledge would be recorded by the Red Cross.

Another example of a condition is a matching pledge (also known as a challenge grant). A donor pledges to give an amount to a charity if the charity raises a matching amount from other sources. (The "match" need not be one for one; it can be in any ratio the donor specifies.) In this case, the charity is not entitled to receive the donor's gift until it has met the required match. Once it does, it will notify the donor that the pledge is now due.

A third type of donor stipulation sounds like a condition, but it may or may not actually be one. A donor pledges to contribute to a symphony orchestra "if they will perform my favorite piece of music [specified by name]." (A cynical person would call this a bribe.) Yes, this is an uncertain future event, since the piece of music has not yet been performed, but how uncertain is it? If the orchestra might very well have played the piece anyway, then the "condition" is really trivial, and the event would not be considered uncertain. However, if the piece were one that the orchestra would be very unlikely to perform without the incentive represented by the pledge in question, then the event would be considered uncertain, and the pledge conditional. In this case, the condition is fulfilled when the orchestra formally places the music on its schedule and so informs the donor.

Note that the concept of a condition is quite different from that of a restriction. Conditions deal with events which must occur before a charity is entitled to receive a gift. Restrictions limit how the charity can use the gift after receipt. Unconditional pledges can be either unrestricted or restricted; so can conditional pledges. Donor stipulations attached to a gift or pledge must be read carefully to discern which type of situation is being dealt with. For example, "I pledge $20,000 *if* you play my favorite music" is conditional but unrestricted (the donor has not said the gift must be used to pay for the performance). Whereas "I pledge $20,000 *for* [the cost of] playing my favorite piece of music" is restricted, but unconditional. In the latter case, the donor has said the pledge will be paid, but can only be used for that performance. The difference in wording is small, but the accounting implications are great. The conditional pledge is not recorded at all until the condition is met; the unconditional restricted pledge is recorded as revenue (in the temporarily restricted class) upon receipt of notification of the pledge. Appendix 29–D contains a checklist to help readers determine whether an unconditional pledge actually exists. Appendix 29–E contains a checklist to help distinguish conditions from restrictions.

DISCOUNTED TO PRESENT VALUE.   Prior to SFAS No. 116, pledges were recorded at the full amount which would ultimately be collected. None of the accounting literature for not-for-profit organizations talked about discounting pledges to reflect the time value of money. There had been for many years an accounting standard applicable to business transactions which does require such discounting (APB No. 21), but not-for-profit organizations universally chose to treat this as not applicable to them, and accountants did not object.

SFAS No. 116 does require recipients (and donors) of pledges payable beyond the current accounting period to discount the pledges to their present value, using an appropriate rate of interest. Thus, the ability to receive $1,000 two years later is really only equivalent to receiving about $900 (assuming about a 5% rate of interest) now, because the $900 could be invested and earn $100 of interest over the two years. The higher the interest rate used, the lower will be the present value of the pledge, since the lower amount would earn more interest at the higher rate and still be worth the full $1,000 two years hence.

The appropriate rate of interest to use in discounting pledges will be a matter of some judgment. In many cases, it will be the average rate the organization is currently earning on its investments or its idle cash. If the organization is being forced to borrow money to keep going, then the borrowing rate should be used. Additional guidance is in SFAS No. 116 and APB No. 21.

As the time passes between the initial recording of a discounted pledge and its eventual collection, the present value increases since the time left before payment is shorter. Therefore, the discount element must be gradually "accreted" up to par (collection) value. This accretion should be recorded each year until the due date for the pledge arrives. The accretion is recorded as contribution income. (This treatment differs from that specified in APB No. 21 for business debts for which the accretion is recorded as interest income.)

PLEDGES FOR EXTENDED PERIODS.   There is one limitation to the general rule that pledges be recorded as assets. Occasionally, donors will indicate that they will make an open-ended pledge of support for an extended period of time. For example, if a donor promises to pay $5,000 a year for 20 years, would it be appropriate to record as an asset the full 20 years' pledge? In most cases, no; this would distort the financial statements. Most organizations follow the practice of not recording pledges for future years' support beyond a fairly short period. They feel that long-term open-ended pledges are inherently conditional upon the donor's continued willingness to continue making payments, and thus are harder to collect. These arguments have validity, and organizations should consider very carefully the likelihood of collection before recording pledges for support in future periods beyond five years.

ALLOWANCE FOR UNCOLLECTIBLE PLEDGES.   Not all pledges will be collected. People lose interest in an organization; their personal financial circumstances may change; they may move out of town. This is as true for charities as for businesses, but businesses will usually sue to collect unpaid debts; charities usually won't. Thus another important question is how large the allowance for uncollectible pledges should be. Most organizations have past experience to help answer this question. If over the years, 10% of pledges are not collected, then unless the economic climate changes, 10% is probably the right figure to use.

RECOGNITION AS INCOME.   The second, related question is: When should a pledge be recognized as income? This used to be a complicated question, requiring many pages of discussion in earlier editions of this book. Now, the answer is easy: immediately upon receipt of an unconditional pledge. This is the same rule that applies to all kinds of gifts under SFAS No. 116.

Conditional pledges are not recorded until the condition is met, at which time they are effectively unconditional pledges. Footnote disclosure of unrecorded conditional pledges should be made.

Under the earlier audit guides/statement of position, pledges without purpose restrictions were recorded in the unrestricted fund. Only if the pledge has a purpose restriction would it be recorded in a restricted fund. Even pledges with explicit time restrictions were still recorded in the unrestricted fund, to reflect the flexibility of use that would exist when the pledge was collected. Under SFAS No. 116, all pledges are considered implicitly time-restricted, by virtue of their being unavailable for use until collected. Additionally, time-restricted gifts, including all pledges, are now reported in the temporarily restricted class of net assets. They are then reclassified to the unrestricted class when the specified time arrives.

This means that even a pledge not payable for 10 years, or a pledge payable in many installments is recorded as revenue in full (less the discount to present value) in the temporarily restricted class in the year the pledge is first received. This is a major change from earlier practice, which generally deferred the pledge until the anticipated period of collection.

Sometimes a charity may not want to have to record a large pledge as immediate revenue; it may feel that its balance sheet is already healthy and recording more income would turn away other donors. If a pledge is unconditional, there is no choice: The pledge must be recorded. One way to mitigate this problem is to ask the donor to make the pledge conditional; then it is not recorded until some later time when the condition is met. Of course, there is a risk that the donor may not be as likely ever to pay a conditional pledge as one that is understood to be absolutely binding, so nonprofit organizations should consider carefully before requesting that a pledge be made conditional.

SFAS No. 116 requires that donors follow the same rules for recognition of the expense of making a gift as recipients do for the income: that is, immediately upon payment or of making an unconditional pledge. Sometimes a charity will find a donor reluctant to make a large unconditional pledge, but willing to make a conditional pledge. Fund raisers should be aware of the effect of the new accounting principles in SFAS No. 116 on donors' giving habits, as well as on recipients' balance sheets.

Bequests.   A bequest is a special kind of pledge. Bequests should never be recorded before the donor dies—not because death is uncertain, but because a person can always change a will, and the charity may get nothing. (There is a special case: the pledge payable upon death. This is not really a bequest, it is just an ordinary pledge, and should be recorded as such if it is unconditional.)

After a person dies, the beneficiary organization is informed that it is named in the will, but this notification may occur long before the estate is probated and distribution made. Should such a bequest be recorded at the time the organization first learns of the bequest or at the time of receipt? The question is one of sufficiency of assets in the estate to fulfill the bequest. Since there is often uncertainty about what other amounts may have to be paid to settle debts, taxes, other bequests, claims of disinherited relatives, and so on, a conservative, and recommended, approach is not to record anything until the probate court has accounted for the estate and the amount available for distribution can be accurately estimated. At that time, the amount should be recorded in the same manner as other gifts.

Thus, if an organization is informed that it will receive a bequest of a specific amount, say $10,000, it should record this $10,000 as an asset. If instead the organization is informed that it will receive 10% of the estate, the total of which is not known, nothing would be recorded yet although footnote disclosure would likely be necessary if the amount could be sizeable. Still a third possibility exists if the organization is told that while the final amount of the 10% bequest is not known, it will be at least some stated amount. In that instance, the minimum amount would be recorded with footnote disclosure of the contingent interest.

SPLIT-INTEREST GIFTS.   The term "split-interest" gifts is used to refer to irrevocable trusts and similar arrangements (also referred to as deferred gifts) where the interest in the gift is split between the donor (or another person specified by the donor) and the charity. These arrangements can be divided into two fundamentally different types of arrangements: lead interests and remainder interests. Lead interests are those in which the benefit to the charity "leads" or precedes the benefit to the donor (or other person designated by the donor). To put this into the terminology commonly used by trust lawyers, the charity is the "life tenant," and someone else is the "remainderman." The reverse situation is that of the "remainder" interest, where the donor (or the donor's designee) is the life tenant and the charity is the remainderman, that is the entity to which the assets become available upon termination (often called the maturity) of the trust or other arrangement. There may or may not be further restrictions on the charity's use of the assets and/or the income therefrom after this maturity.

Under both types of arrangement the donor makes an initial lump-sum payment into a fund. The amount is invested, and the income during the term of the arrangement is paid to the life tenant. In some cases, the arrangement is established as a trust under the trust laws of the applicable state. In other cases, no separate trust is involved, rather the assets are held by the charity as part of its general assets. In some cases involving trusts, the charity is the trustee; in other cases, a third party is the trustee. Typical third-party trustees include banks and trust companies or other charities such as community foundations. Some arrangements are perpetual, that is, the charity never gains access to the corpus of the gift; others have a defined term of existence that will end either upon the occurrence of a specified event such as the death of the donor (or other specified person) or after the passage of a specified amount of time.

To summarize to this point, the various defining criteria applicable to these arrangements are:

- The charity's interest may be a lead interest or a remainder interest.
- The arrangement may be in the form of a trust or it may not.
- The assets may be held by the charity or held by a third party.
- The arrangement may be perpetual or it may have a defined term.
- Upon termination of the interest of the life tenant, the corpus may be unrestricted or restricted.

LEAD INTERESTS.   There are two kinds of such arrangements as normally conceived.[2] These are:

1. Charitable lead trust.
2. Perpetual trust held by a third party.

In both of these cases, the charity receives periodic payments representing distributions of income, but never gains unrestricted use of the assets which produce the income. In the first case, the payment stream is for a limited time; in case two, the payment stream is perpetual.

A *charitable lead trust* is always for a defined term, and usually held by the charity. At the termination of the trust, the corpus (principal of the gift) reverts to the donor or to another person specified by the donor (may be the donor's estate). Income during the term of the trust is paid to the charity; the income may be unrestricted or restricted. In effect, this arrangement amounts to an unconditional pledge, for a specified period, of the income from a specified amount of assets. The current value of the pledge is the discounted present value of the estimated stream of income over the term of the trust. Although the charity manages the assets during the term of the trust, it has no remainder interest in the assets.

---

[2] It is also possible to consider both a simple pledge and a permanent endowment fund as forms of lead interests. In both cases, the charity receives periodic payments, but never gains unrestricted use of the assets which generate the income to make the payments. A pledge is for a limited time; an endowment fund pays forever.

A *perpetual trust held by a third party* is the same as the lead trust, except that the charity does not manage the assets, and the term of the trust is perpetual. Again the charity receives the income earned by the assets, but never gains the use of the corpus. In effect there is no remainderman. This arrangement is also a pledge of income, but in this case the current value of the pledge is the discounted present value of a perpetual stream of income from the assets. Assuming a perfect market for investment securities, that amount will equal the current quoted market value of the assets of the trust or, if there is no quoted market value, then the "fair value," which is normally determined based on discounted future cash flows from the assets.

Some may argue that since the charity does not and never will have day-to-day control over the corpus of this type of trust, it should only record assets and income as the periodic distributions are received from the trustee. In fact, that is the way the income from this type of gift has historically been recorded. In the authors' view, this is overcome by the requirement in SFAS No. 116 that long-term unconditional pledges be recorded in full (discounted) when the pledge is initially received by the pledgee. Since SFAS No. 116 requires that the charity immediately record the full (discounted) amount of a traditional pledge, when all the charity has is a promise of future gifts, with the pledgor retaining control over the means to generate the gifts, then the charity surely must record immediately the entire amount (discounted) of a "pledge" where the assets that will generate the periodic payments are held in trust by a third party, and receipt of the payments by the charity is virtually assured.

A variation of this type of arrangement is a trust held by a third party in which the third party has discretion as to when and/or to whom to pay the periodic income. Since in this case the charity is not assured in advance of receiving any determinable amount, no amounts should be recorded by the charity until distributions are received from the trustee; these amounts are then recorded as contributions.

REMAINDER INTERESTS.   There are four types of these arrangements. These are:

1. Charitable remainder annuity trust.
2. Charitable remainder unitrust.
3. Charitable gift annuity.
4. Pooled income fund (also referred to as a life income fund).

These arrangements are always for a limited term, usually the life of the donor and/or another person or persons specified by the donor—often the donor's spouse. The donor or the donor's designee is the life tenant; the charity is the remainderman. Again, in the case of a trust, the charity may or may not be the trustee; in the case of a charitable gift annuity, the charity usually is the holder of the assets. Upon termination of the arrangement, the corpus usually becomes available to the charity; the donor may or may not have placed further temporary or permanent restrictions on the corpus and/or the future income earned by the corpus.

In many states, the acceptance of these types of gifts is regulated by the state government—often the department of insurance—since, from the perspective of the donor, these arrangements are partly insurance contracts, essentially similar to a commercial annuity.

A *charitable remainder annuity trust* (CRAT) and *charitable remainder unitrust* (CRUT) differ only in the stipulated method of calculating the payments to the life tenant. An annuity trust pays a stated dollar amount that remains fixed over the life of the trust; a unitrust pays a stated percentage of the then current value of the trust assets. Thus, the dollar amount of the payments will vary with changes in the market value of the corpus. Accounting for the two types is the same except for the method of calculation of the amount of the present value of the life interest payable to the life tenant(s). In both cases, if current investment income is insufficient to cover the stipulated payments, corpus may have to be invaded to do so; however, the liability to the life tenant is limited to the assets of the trust.

A *charitable gift annuity* (CGA) differs from a CRAT only in that there is no trust; the assets are usually held among the general assets of the charity (some charities choose to set aside a pool of assets in a separate fund to cover annuity liabilities), and the annuity liability is a general liability of the charity—limited only by the charity's total assets.

A *pooled income fund* (PIF, also sometimes called a life income fund) is actually a creation of the Internal Revenue Code Section 642(c)(5), which, together with Sec. 170, allows an income tax deduction to donors to such funds. (The amount of the deduction depends on the age(s) of the life tenant(s), and the value of the life interest and is less than that allowed for a simple charitable deduction directly to a charity, to reflect the value which the life tenant will be receiving in return for the gift.) The fund is usually managed by the charity. Many donors contribute to such a fund, which pools the gifts and invests the assets. During the period of each life tenant's interest in the fund, the life tenant is paid the actual income earned by that person's share of the corpus. (To this extent, these funds function essentially as mutual funds.) Upon termination of a life interest, the share of the corpus attributable to that life tenant becomes available to the charity.

ACCOUNTING FOR SPLIT-INTEREST GIFTS.   The essence of these arrangements is that they are pledges. In some cases, the pledge is of a stream of payments to the charity during the life of the arrangement (lead interests). In other cases, the pledge is of the value of the remainder interest. Calculation of the value of a lead interest is usually straightforward, as the term and the payments are well-defined. Calculation of remainder interests is more complicated, since life expectancies are usually involved and the services of an actuary will likely be needed.

SFAS No. 116 gives very little guidance specific to split-interests. The AICPA not-for-profit organizations committee will be including more definitive guidance in the new audit guide to be issued in 1996.

(k) RELATED ORGANIZATIONS.   Practice has varied regarding when not-for-profit entities combine the financial statements of affiliated organizations with those of the central organization. Part of the reason for this is the widely diverse nature of relationships among such organizations, which often creates difficulty in determining when criteria for combination have been met.

(i) Definition of the Reporting Entity.   There are two issues here but they involve the same concepts. First is the question of gifts to affiliated fund-raising entities and whether the affiliate should record the gift as its own revenue, followed by gift or grant expense when their money is passed on to the parent organization, or should record the initial receipt as an amount held on behalf of the parent. Such gifts are often called *pass-through gifts* since they pass through one entity to another entity. Second is the broader question of when the financial data of affiliated entities should be combined with that of a central organization for purposes of presenting the central organization's financial statements. If the data are combined, the question of pass-through gifts need not be addressed since the end result is the same regardless of which entity records gifts initially.

The concept underlying the combining of financial data of affiliates is to present to the financial statement reader information that portrays the complete financial picture of a group of entities that effectively function as one entity. In the business setting, the determination of when a group of entities is really just a single entity is normally made by assessing the extent to which the "parent" entity has a controlling financial interest in the other entities in the group. In other words, can the parent use for its own benefit the financial resources of the others without obtaining permission from any party outside the parent? When one company owns another company, such permission would be automatic; if the management of the affiliate refused, the parent would exercise its authority to replace management.

In the not-for-profit world, such "ownership" of one entity by another rarely exists. Affiliated organizations are more often related by agreements of various sorts, but the level of control embodied in such agreements is usually far short of ownership. The "Friends of the Museum" may exist primarily to support the Museum, but it is likely a legally independent organization with only informal ties to its "parent." The Museum may ask, but the Friends may choose its own time and method to respond. Further, the Museum may have no way to legally compel the Friends to do its bidding if the Friends resist.

The issue for donors is, if I give to the Friends, am I really supporting the Museum? Or if I am assessing the financial condition of the Museum, is it reasonable to include the resources of the Friends in the calculation? Even though the Friends is legally separate, and even though the Friends does not have to turn its assets over to the Museum, isn't it reasonable to assume that if the Museum got into financial trouble, the Friends would help?

Examples of other types of relationships often found among not-for-profits include: a national organization and local affiliates; an educational institution and student and alumni groups, research organizations and hospitals; a religious institution and local churches, schools, seminaries, cemeteries, broadcasting stations, pension funds, and charities. Since each individual relationship may be different, it requires much judgment to decide which entities should be combined and which should not.

Existing accounting literature includes some guidance, but more is needed. The basic rules for businesses are:

- ARB Opinion No. 51, "Consolidated Financial Statements."
- APB Opinion No. 18, "The Equity Method of Accounting for Investments in Common Stock."
- SFAS No. 94, "Consolidation of All Majority-Owned Subsidiaries."

While, strictly speaking, these rules apply to not-for-profits only in the context of a for-profit subsidiary, the concepts embodied therein and the related background discussions are helpful to someone considering the issue. Rules for not-for-profits are in the AICPA SOP No. 94-3, which replaces the rules in the audit guides/SOP (par. 7.07-7.11 of Audits of Voluntary Health and Welfare Organizations; par. 11.09 of Audits of Colleges and Universities; par. 42–48 of SOP No. 78-10). These rules focus largely on the question of whether one not-for-profit controls another. Exhibit 29.1 is designed to help not-for-profits and their accountants decide whether sufficient control exists to require combination.

In 1994, the AICPA issued a new statement of position (SOP No. 94-3) on combining related entities when one is a not-for-profit organization. This SOP will require:

- When a not-for-profit organization owns a majority of the voting equity interest in a for-profit entity, the not-for-profit must consolidate the for-profit into its financial statements, regardless of how closely related the activities of the for-profit are to those of the not-for-profit.

- If the not-for-profit organization owns less than a majority interest in a for-profit but still has significant influence over the for-profit, it must report the for-profit under the equity method of accounting, except that the not-for-profit may report its investment in the for-profit at market value if it wishes. If the not-for-profit does not have significant influence over the for-profit, it should value its investment in accordance with the applicable audit guide.

- When a not-for-profit organization has a relationship with another not-for-profit in which the "parent" both exercises control over the board appointments of and has an economic interest in the affiliate, it must consolidate the affiliate.

- If the not-for-profit organization has either control *or* an economic beneficial interest but not both, disclosure of the relationship and significant financial information is required.

- If the parent controls the affiliate by means other than board appointments, and has an economic interest, consolidation is permitted but not required. If the affiliate is not consolidated, extensive footnote disclosures about the affiliate are required.

Following is a list of factors which may be helpful to not-for-profit organizations in deciding whether to combine financial statements of affiliated organizations and to auditors in assessing the appropriateness of the client's combination decision. Many of these factors are not absolutely determinative by themselves, but must be considered in conjunction with other factors.

Factors Whose Presence Indicate Control	**Factors Whose Presence Indicate Lack of Control**
Organization Relationship	
1. A is clearly described as controlled by, for the benefit of, or an affiliate of R in some of the following: 　Articles/charter/by-laws 　Operating/affiliation agreement 　Fund-raising material/membership brochure 　Annual report 　Grant proposals 　Application for tax-exempt status.	A is described as independent of R or no formal relationship is indicated.
Governance	
2. A's board has considerable overlap in membership with R; common officers.	There is little or no overlap.
3. A's board members and/or officers are appointed by R, or are subject to approval of R's board, officers, or members.	A's board is self-perpetuating with no input from R.
4. Major decisions of A's board, officers or staff are subject to review, approval, or ratification by R.	A's decisions are made autonomously; or even if in theory subject to such control, R has in fact never or rarely exercised control and does not intend to do so.
Financial	
5. A's budget is subject to review or approval by R.	Budget not subject to R's approval.
6. Some or all of A's disbursements are subject to approval or countersignature by R.	Checks may be issued without R's approval.
7. A's excess of revenue over expenses or fund balances or portions thereof are subject to being transferred to R at R's request, or are automatically transferred.	Although some of A's financial resources may be transferred to R, this is done only at the discretion of A's board.
8. A's activities are largely financed by grants, loans or transfers from R, or from other sources determined by R's board.	A's activities are financed from sources determined by A's board.
9. A's by-laws indicate that its resources are intended to be used for activities similar to those of R.	A's by-laws limit uses of resources to purposes which do not include R's activities.
10. A's fund-raising appeals give donors the impression that gifts will be used to further R's programs.	Appeals give the impression that funds will be used by A.

(continued)

Exhibit 29.1.   Factors related to control which may indicate that an affiliated organization (A) should be combined with the reporting organization (R), if other criteria for combination are met.

Factors Whose Presence Indicate Control	Factors Whose Presence Indicate Lack of Control
Operating	
11. A shares with R many of the following operating functions: Personnel/payroll Purchasing Professional services Fund-raising Accounting, treasury Office space	Few operating functions are shared; or reimbursement of costs is on a strictly arm's-length basis with formal contracts.
12. Decisions about A's program or other activities are made by R or are subject to R's review or approval.	A's decisions are made autonomously.
13. A's activities are almost exclusively for the benefit of R's members.	Activities benefit persons unaffiliated with R.
Other	
14. A is exempt under IRC Section 501(c) (3) and R is exempt under some other subsection of 501(c), and A's main purpose for existence appears to be to solicit tax-deductible contributions to further R's interest.	A's purposes appear to include significant activities apart from those of R.

Exhibit 29.1. *Continued.*

When one organization (C, in the following exhibit) raises funds for another organization (R, in the exhibit), and either C is not required to be consolidated into R under the above rules, or C is consolidated into R, but C also issues separate financial statements, the question of whether C should record amounts raised by it on behalf of R should be reported by C as its revenue (contribution income) or as amounts held for the benefit of R (a liability). If such amounts are reported by C as a liability, C's statement of revenue and expenses will not ever include the funds raised for R. This issue is of considerable concern to organizations such as federated fund-raisers (such as United Ways), community foundations, and other organizations such as foundations affiliated with universities, which raise (and sometimes hold) funds for the benefit of other organizations. Paragraphs 4 and 53 of SFAS No. 116 indicate that when the pass-through entity has little or no discretion over the use of the amounts raised (i.e. the original donor—D in the exhibit—has specified that C must pass the gift on to R) that C should not report the amount as a contribution to it. As this is written, FASB has issued an exposure draft discussing this issue further, but has not yet reached a definitive conclusion. Exhibit 29.2 is a list of factors to be considered in assessing whether a pass-through entity should record amounts raised for others as revenue or as a liability.

By "economic interest" is meant generally four kinds of relationship: an affiliate which raises gifts for the parent, an affiliate which holds assets for the parent, an affiliate that performs significant functions assigned to it by the parent, or the parent has guaranteed the debt of or is otherwise committed to provide funds to the affiliate.

(I) CASH FLOWS.   SFAS No. 95, which requires businesses to present a statement of cash flows (in lieu of the former statement of changes in financial position), did not apply to not-for-profits. The new FASB standard on financial statements (No. 117) requires the presentation of a statement of cash flows. A sample statement of cash flows, following the example in the statement, is illustrated in Exhibit 29.3.

Following is a list of factors which may be helpful to:

- Not-for-profit organizations in deciding whether assets received by them are contributions within the meaning of SFAS No. 116, or are transfers in which the entity is acting as an agent, trustee, or intermediary;
- Auditors, in assessing the appropriateness of the client's decision.

No one factor is usually determinative by itself; all relevant factors should be considered together.

D = Original Noncharitable Donor (Individual or Business)

C = Initial Charitable Recipient/Donor (Sometimes there is more than one charity in the chain.)

R = Ultimate Charitable or Individual Recipient

Factors Whose Presence Indicate Recording by C as Revenue and Expense May Not Be Appropriate	Factors Whose Presence Indicate Recording by C as Revenue and Expense May Be Appropriate
General factors—relevant to all gifts:	
1. D has restricted the gift by specifying that it must be passed on to R.*	D has not restricted the gift in this manner.
2. C is controlled by D or by R.	D or R do not control C.
3. Two or more of D, C, and R are under common control, have overlapping boards or management, share facilities or professional advisors.*	Factor not present.
4. Even without the intermediation of C, D would still easily be able to make the gift to R.	Without such intermediation, D would not easily be able to make a gift to R (D is unaware of existence of R or of R's needs, geographic separation, etc.).*
5. The stated program activities of C and R are similar.	The program activities are not particularly similar.
6. C has solicited the gift from D under the specific pretense of passing it on to R.*	C has solicited the gift ostensibly for C's own activities.
7. C does not ever obtain legal title to the assets composing the gift.*	C does at some time obtain legal title to the assets.
8. D and/or other entities under common control are major sources of support for C.	Factor not present.
9. R and/or other entities under common control are major destinations for C's charitable resources.	Factor not present.
9a. Both factors 8 and 9 are present.*	One but not both present.
10. The "chain" from D to R consists of several C's.	The chain consists of only one or very few C's.
11. Gifts passed from D to C are frequently in exactly the same dollar amount (or very close) as gifts subsequently passed from C to R.*	Factor not present.
12. Times elapsed between receipt and disbursement of particular amounts by C are short (less than a month).	Times elapsed are relatively long or variable.

Exhibit 29.2. Factors to be considered in deciding whether a "Pass-Through" gift is truly revenue and expense to charity (C).

Factors Whose Presence Indicate Recording by C as Revenue and Expense May Not Be Appropriate	**Factors Whose Presence Indicate Recording by C as Revenue and Expense May Be Appropriate**
13. C makes pledges to R, payment of which is contingent on receipt of gifts from D.	Factor not present.
14. C was created only shortly prior to receiving the gift, and/or C appears to have been created specifically for the sole purpose of passing gifts from D on to R.*	Factor not present.
Factors especially relevant to gifts-in-kind:	
15. C never takes physical possession of the gift at an owned or rented facility.	C does have physical possession of the items at some time, at a facility normally owned or rented by it.
16. The nature of the items is not consistent with the program service activities of C as stated in its Form 1023, 990, organizing documents, fund-raising appeals, annual report.*	The nature is consistent with C's stated program activities.
17. The gift was not solicited by C.	C specifically solicited the particular items from D.
18. The quantity of items is large in relation to the foreseeable needs of C or its donees.	Factor not present.
19. Factor not present.	Members of the board or staff of C have specific technical or professional expertise about the items, and actively participate in deliberations about where to obtain the items and how best to use them.*
20. D appears to be the only source from which C considers acquiring the item. Same for C/R.	C has several potential or actual sources for the item. Same for R.
21. C receives numerous types of items dissimilar in their purpose or use.	Factor not present.
22. C receives items from D and passes them on to R in essentially the same form.	C "adds value" to the items by sorting, repackaging, cleaning, repairing or testing them.*
23. C *and* either or both of D and R have little in the way of program services other than distribution of gifts in kind to other charities.	Either C or *both* D and R have significant program services other than distribution of gifts in kind.
24. The value assigned to the items by D or C appears to be inflated.	Factor not present.
25. There is a consistent pattern of transfers of items along the same "chain" (D to C to R, etc.).	Factor not present.
26. Factor not present.	C incurs significant expenses (freight, insurance, storage, etc.) in handling the items.

*Factors considered to be generally more significant.

Exhibit 29.2. *Continued.*

NATIONAL ASSOCIATION OF ENVIRONMENTALISTS
STATEMENT OF CASH FLOWS
For the Year Ended December 31, 19X2

Operating cash flows:	
Cash received from:	
Sales of goods and services	$ 198,835
Investment income	14,607
Gifts and grants:	
Unrestricted	230, 860
Restricted	37,400
Cash paid to employees and suppliers	(265,854)
Cash paid to charitable beneficiaries	(83,285)
Interest paid	(350)
Net operating cash flows	132,213
Financing cash flows:	
Nonexpendable gifts	31,500
Proceeds from borrowing	5,000
Repayment of debt	(5,000)
Net financing cash flows	31,500
Investing cash flows:	
Purchase of building and equipment	(38,617)
Purchase of investments	(60,000)
Proceeds from sale of investments	50,000
Net investing cash flows	(48,617)
Net increase in cash	115,096
Cash: Beginning of year	11,013
End of year	$ 126,109

Reconciliation of Excess of Revenues over Expenses to Operating Cash Flows:

Excess of Revenues over Expenses	$ 161,316
Add: Depreciation expense	13,596
Less: Appreciation of investments	(33,025)
Changes in: Receivables	(6,939)
Payables and deferred income	28,765
Nonexpendable contributions	(31,500)
Operating cash flows	$ 132,213

Exhibit 29.3.   Statement of Cash Flows, derived from data included in Exhibits 29.4 and 29.5.

(m) GOVERNMENTAL VERSUS NONGOVERNMENTAL ACCOUNTING. In 1989, the Financial Accounting Foundation, overseer of the FASB and its counterpart in the governmental sector, the GASB (see discussion in Chapter 28, "State and Local Government Accounting") resolved the question of the jurisdiction of each body. A question related to several types of organizations, mainly not-for-profits, which exist in both governmental and nongovernmental forms. These types include institutions of higher education, museums, libraries, hospitals, and others. The issue is whether it is more important to have, for example, all hospitals follow a single set of accounting principles, or to have all types of governmental entities do so. This matter was resolved by conferring on GASB jurisdiction over all governmental entities.

29.3 VOLUNTARY HEALTH AND WELFARE ORGANIZATIONS

The term, "Voluntary Health and Welfare Organization" first entered the accounting world with the publication in 1964 of the first edition of the so-called "Black Book," *Standards of Accounting and Financial Reporting for Voluntary Health and Welfare Organizations,* by the National Health Council and the National Social Welfare Assembly. The term has been retained through two successor editions of that book, and was used by the American Institute of Certified Public Accountants (AICPA) in the title of its "audit guide," *Audits of Voluntary Health and Welfare Organizations,* first published in 1967.

In 1974, the AICPA issued a revised audit guide, prepared by its Committee on Voluntary Health and Welfare Organizations. This Audit Guide was prepared to assist the independent auditor in examinations of voluntary health and welfare organizations. Included in the revised Audit Guide is a discussion of accounting and reporting principles that were considered appropriate for this type of organization. Since 1974, the audit guide has been slightly revised to reflect certain technical changes in the wording of auditors' reports.

In 1993, the Financial Accounting Standards Board (FASB) issued two new accounting pronouncements, SFAS No. 116, *Accounting for Contributions Received and Contributions Made,* and No. 117, *Financial Statements of Not-for-Profit Organizations,* which supersede many provisions of the AICPA audit guide. Also, as this book is being written, the AICPA Not-for-Profit Organizations Committee is preparing a new audit and accounting guide that will replace the existing guides for voluntary health and welfare organizations, colleges, and universities, and other not-for-profit organizations (discussed later in this chapter).

This chapter summarizes the accounting and reporting principles discussed in the new FASB standards, and, to the extent that they have not been superseded by the new FASB standards, the provisions of the AICPA voluntary health and welfare audit guide. For the most part, the FASB standards prescribe the same accounting treatment for a given transaction by all types of not-for-profit organizations. One exception to that rule is a requirement that voluntary health and welfare organizations continue to present a statement of functional expenses. Other types of organizations are not required to present this statement, although they may if they wish. More detailed discussions of certain accounting and reporting standards in the new FASB documents will also be found elsewhere in this chapter. For example, a full discussion of accounting for contributions is in subsection 29.2(j)(iii).

"Voluntary health and welfare organizations" are those not-for-profit organizations that "derive their revenue primarily from voluntary contributions from the general public to be used for general or specific purposes connected with health, welfare, or community services."[3] Note that there are two separate parts to this definition: first, the organization must derive its revenue from voluntary contributions from the general public, and second, the organization must be involved with health, welfare, or community services.

Many organizations fit the second part of this definition, but receive a substantial portion of their revenues from sources other than public contributions. For example, an opera company would not be a voluntary health and welfare organization because its primary source of income is box office receipts, although it exists for the common good. A YMCA would be excluded because normally it receives most of its revenues from dues and program fees. On the other hand, a museum would be excluded, even if it were to receive most of its revenue from contributions, since its activities are educational, not in the areas of health and welfare.

(a) FUND ACCOUNTING

(i) Classification of Funds.   This topic was discussed earlier in this chapter. There it was noted that, after the issuance of SFAS No. 117, this concept relates only to internal bookkeeping

---

[3] Page v. *Audits of Voluntary Health and Welfare Organizations.* Copyright (c) 1974 by the American Institute of Certified Public Accountants, Inc. Hereinafter in this chapter the word "Guide" refers to this publication.

and reporting, not to external financial reporting. The Guide lists the funds commonly used, and the types of transactions normally associated with each fund. The fund groupings listed by the Guide and the type of transactions recorded in each are discussed below. When this and subsequent sections refer to funds, the reference is to how a transaction is *recorded.* When discussing how information is *reported* in financial statements issued to the public, references will be to the three classes of net assets in SFAS No. 117.

Current Unrestricted Fund.   This fund "accounts for all resources over which the governing Board has discretionary control to use in carrying on the operations of the organization . . . except for unrestricted amounts invested in land, buildings, and equipment that may be accounted for in a separate fund."[4] These are all of the completely unrestricted resources of the organization, including board-designated endowment funds or other resources allocated by the board for some specific purpose.

Prior to the issuance of this Guide, many voluntary health and welfare organizations set up separate board-designated funds which were reported on separately from the other unrestricted activities of the organization. This Guide, and SFAS No. 117, specifically provide that all such unrestricted income, and net assets must be reported in a single category so that the reader can quickly see the total amount the organization's board has at its disposal. At the time, this was a major and significant change. It means that for these organizations, board-designated amounts must be included in the unrestricted class for financial statement purposes. The prior practice followed by many organizations of "designating" certain gifts as endowments (and then reporting these gifts directly in a restricted endowment category) is not permissible.

This does not prevent the board from "designating" certain portions of the current unrestricted net assets *balance* for specific purposes, but such designations must be reported only in the net assets section of the Balance Sheet.

Current Restricted Fund.   These are the amounts that have been given to the organization for a specific "operating" or "current" purpose. Excluded from this classification would be amounts given for endowment purposes or for acquisition of fixed assets.

Current restricted funds would include only amounts given to the organization by outside persons or organizations. They would not include amounts which the board had "designated" for some future purposes.

Land, Building, and Equipment Fund.   If this fund is maintained, it is used to record the organization's net investment in its fixed assets. Also included in this fund are donor-restricted contributions that have been given for the purpose of purchasing fixed assets.

While the Guide provides for this separate land, building, and equipment fund, it does not prohibit the organization from combining this fund (excluding unexpended donor-restricted building fund gifts) with the current unrestricted fund. Many organizations in the past have preferred to use a separate fixed asset fund, principally so that the current unrestricted fund would exclude long-term assets such as fixed assets or other funds. This meant that the current unrestricted fund was then a form of "current working capital" fund. Under this Guide, however, the presentation outside of the unrestricted fund of separate board-designated endowment or other funds is no longer permitted. As a result, many organizations have concluded that there is no practical reason for segregating fixed assets in a separate fund and have combined their fixed asset fund and their current unrestricted fund. When this is done the title of the current unrestricted fund would become "unrestricted fund."

The major reason why this Guide still permits the use of a separate fixed asset fund is historical usage. That is, most not-for-profit organizations have traditionally carried their fixed assets in a separate fund and the authors of the Guide concluded that the continued use of this

---

[4] Page 2, *ibid.*

separate fund would not distort the financial picture, provided the plant fund is reported with all other funds in a single columnar-format statement (see Exhibit 29.4).

Endowment Fund.   This fund is to be used for all assets donated to the organization with the stipulation by the donor that only the income earned can be used. Generally, the income itself is not restricted and can be used to carry out the organization's principal activities, although occasionally gifts are received that have restrictions on the uses to be made of the income. It is also possible to receive gifts that are restricted for a period of years, after which time the principal can be used as desired by the board (called "term endowment"). Another possibility is an endowment gift under which the income earned on the principal of the gift is paid to the donor during his or her life but becomes completely unrestricted at his or her death (called by various terms including: "deferred gifts," "charitable remainder trusts," "split-interest gifts").

It is important to note that this endowment fund is to be used only for gifts that have been restricted by the donor. Occasionally a donor, while not formally placing restrictions on a gift, will orally express the "desire" that the gift be put in the endowment fund. However, if the decision is left to the board, such amounts are unrestricted, and should be added to the current unrestricted fund (although they may be designated by the board if it wishes). Legally unrestricted gifts cannot be added to a restricted endowment fund. All amounts in the endowment fund must bear legal restrictions that the board cannot normally alter.

Custodian Fund.   These are funds "established to account for assets received by an organization to be held or disbursed only on instructions of the person or organization from whom they were received."[5] Since these fund are not normally the property of the organization, their activity is not reflected in the Statement of Support, Revenues, and Expenses, and Changes in Net Assets. Their assets and offsetting liabilities are reported in the Balance Sheet.

(b) ACCOUNTING PRINCIPLES.   Summarized in the following paragraphs are the accounting principles (or practices) that are prescribed by the Audit Guide and by SFAS No. 116 and No. 117 for voluntary health and welfare organizations, other than those discussed elsewhere in this chapter.

(i) Accrual Basis.   The Guide concludes that the accrual basis of accounting is normally necessary for financial statements prepared in accordance with generally accepted accounting principles. While cash basis statements are not prohibited, the auditor cannot issue an opinion on cash basis financial statements which states that the statements are prepared in accordance with generally accepted accounting principles, unless these financial statements do not differ materially from the statements prepared on the accrual basis. The same caution is made with respect to modified accrual basis statements (discussed in Chapter 3).

(c) ACCOUNTING FOR ASSETS

(i) Carrying Value of Investments.   The Guide provides that an organization can carry its investments either at market or at cost. Previously, marketable securities could be carried only at cost or, in the case of donated securities, at the fair market value at the date of receipt. In 1995, FASB issued a new standard (SFAS No. 124) on accounting for marketable securities for not-for-profits, as discussed earlier at subsection 29.2(i).

(ii) Fixed Assets Where Title May Revert to Grantors.   As noted in Chapter 6, some organizations purchase or receive fixed assets under research or similar grants which provide that, at the completion of the grant period, the right of possession of these fixed assets technically reverts to the grantor. If the grantor is not expected to ask for their return, a fixed asset,

---

[5] Page 3, *ibid.*

NATIONAL ASSOCIATION OF ENVIRONMENTALISTS
BALANCE SHEET
December 31, 19X2 and 19x1

	December 31, 19X2 Current Funds Unrestricted	Current Funds Restricted	Endowment Funds	Fixed Asset Funds	Total All Funds	December 31, 19X1 Total All Funds
ASSETS						
Current assets:						
Cash	$ 58,392	$17,151	$ 8,416	$ 2,150	$ 86,109	$ 11,013
Savings accounts	40,000				40,000	
Accounts receivable	3,117				3,117	918
Investments, at market	86,195		226,119		312,314	269,289
Pledges receivable	4,509	1,000			5,509	769
Total current assets	192,213	18,151	234,535	2,150	447,049	281,989
Fixed assets, at cost				111,135	111,135	72,518
Less: Accumulated depreciation				(19,615)	(19,615)	(6,019)
Net fixed assets				91,520	91,520	66,499
Total assets	$192,213	$18,151	$234,535	$ 93,670	$538,569	$348,488
LIABILITIES AND NET ASSETS						
Current liabilities:						
Accounts payable	$ 54,181				$ 54,181	$ 25,599
Deferred income	2,516				2,516	2,333
Total current liabilities	56,697				56,697	27,932
Net assets:						
Unrestricted	135,516			$ 93,670	229,186	124,631
Temporarily restricted		$18,151			18,151	5,915
Permanently restricted			$234,535		234,535	190,010
Total	135,516	18,151	234,535	93,670	481,872	320,556
Total liabilities and net assets	$192,213	$18,151	$234,535	$ 93,670	$538,569	$348,488

Exhibit 29.4. A Balance Sheet prepared in columnar format.

whether purchased or donated, should be recorded as an asset and depreciated as with any other asset.

(d) NET ASSETS

(i) Appropriations. The board is permitted to "appropriate" or designate a portion of the unrestricted net assets for some specific purpose. This appropriation or designation, however, would be reported only in the net assets section of the Balance Sheet. The appropriation or designation may *not* be shown as a deduction on the Statement of Support, Revenue and Expenses, and Changes in Net Assets.

Accordingly, it is not appropriate for an organization to charge expenditures directly against "appropriated" balances. The expenditure must be included in the Statement of Support, Revenue and Expenses, and Changes in Net Assets. All an appropriation does is to allow the board to designate *in the net assets section* of the Balance Sheet how it intends to spend the unrestricted net assets in the future.

For example, the unrestricted net assets of the National Association of Environmentalists of $135,516 (Exhibit 29.4) could be split into several amounts, representing the board's present intention of how it plans to use this amount. Perhaps $50,000 of it is intended for Project Seaweed, and the balance is available for undesignated purposes. The net assets section of the Balance Sheet would appear:

Net assets:	
Designated by the board for Project Seaweed	$ 50,000
Undesignated, available for current purposes	85,516
	$135,516

As monies are expended for Project Seaweed in subsequent periods, they would be recorded as an expense in the Statement of Support, Revenue and Expenses, and Changes in Net Assets. At the same time, the amount of the net assets designated by the board for Project Seaweed would be reduced and the amount "undesignated" would be increased by the same amount.

(e) FINANCIAL STATEMENTS. SFAS No. 117 provides for four principal financial statements for voluntary health and welfare organizations, thus superseding the financial statements discussed in the Guide. Examples are shown in this chapter. These four statements are:

1. Balance Sheet (Exhibit 29.4, page 29 · 39)
2. Statement of Support, Revenue and Expenses, and Changes in Net Assets (Exhibit 29.5, page 29 · 41)
3. Statement of Cash Flows (Exhibit 29.3, page 29 · 35)
4. Statement of Functional Expenses (Exhibit 29.6, page 29 · 42)

The sample financial statements presented in SFAS No. 117 are for illustrative purposes only, and some variation from the ones presented may be appropriate, as long as the required disclosure elements are shown.

(i) Balance Sheet. Exhibit 29.4 shows a Balance Sheet for the National Association of Environmentalists. Although SFAS No. 117 only requires (and illustrates) a single-column balance sheet showing the totals of assets, liabilities, and net assets (and net assets by class), many organizations will wish to show more detail of assets and liabilities, but not necessarily by class. This is acceptable.

The statement illustrated in the Audit Guide presents the more conventional Balance Sheet format in which each managed fund group is reported as a separate sub-Balance Sheet.

NATIONAL ASSOCIATION OF ENVIRONMENTALISTS
STATEMENT OF SUPPORT, REVENUE AND EXPENSES, AND CHANGES IN NET ASSETS
For the Year Ended December 31, 19X2

	Unrestricted	Temporarily Restricted	Permanently Restricted	Total
Support:				
Contributions and gifts	$174,600	$38,400	$ 10,000	$223,000
Bequests	60,000		21,500	81,500
Total support	234,600	38,400	31,500	304,500
Revenues:				
Membership dues	20,550			20,550
Research projects	127,900			127,900
Advertising income	33,500			33,500
Subscriptions to nonmembers	18,901			18,901
Dividends and interest income	14,607			14,607
Appreciation of investments	30,000		3,025	33,025
Total revenues	245,458		3,025	248,483
Total support and revenues	480,058	38,400	34,525	552,983
Net assets released from restriction	26,164	(26,164)		
Expenses:				
Program services:				
"National Environment" magazine	110,500			110,500
Clean-up month campaign	126,617			126,167
Lake Erie project	115,065			115,065
Total program services	352,182			352,182
Supporting services:				
Management and general	33,516			33,516
Fund raising	5,969			5,969
Total supporting services	39,485			39,485
Total expenses	391,667			391,667
Excess (deficit) of revenues over expenses	114,555	12,236	34,525	161,316
Other changes in net assets:				
Transfer of unrestricted resources to				
meet challenge grant	(10,000)		10,000	—
Change in net assets	104,555	12,236	44,525	161,316
Net assets, beginning of year	124,631	5,915	190,010	320,556
Net assets, end of year	$229,186	$18,151	$234,535	$481,872

Exhibit 29.5. Income statement in the columnar format recommended in the AICPA Audit Guide for Voluntary Health and Welfare Organizations, which meets the requirements of SFAS 117.

Exhibit 29.4 has been presented in a columnar format because this presentation is more meaningful to most readers. The Guide does not prohibit a columnar presentation but indicates that care must be taken to ensure that the restricted nature of certain resources is clearly shown.

Funds versus Classes. Note that the columns on the balance sheet reflect the funds used for bookkeeping purposes. This is permissible, as long as the net asset amounts for each of the three classes defined in SFAS No. 117 are shown in the net assets section of the balance sheet.

Comparison Column. In Exhibit 29.4 we have shown the totals for the previous year to provide a comparison for the reader. SFAS No. 117 does not require presentation of a comparison column, but it is recommended.

Designation of Unrestricted Net Assets. While it is a little more awkward to show when the Balance Sheet is presented in a columnar fashion as in Exhibit 29.4, it is still possible to

NATIONAL ASSOCIATION OF ENVIRONMENTALISTS
STATEMENT OF FUNCTIONAL EXPENSES
For the Year Ended December 31, 19X2

	Total All Expenses	Program Services				Supporting Services		
		"National Environment" Magazine	Clean-up Month Campaign	Lake Erie Project	Total Program	Management and General	Fund Raising	Total Supporting
Salaries	$170,773	$ 24,000	$ 68,140	$ 60,633	$152,773	$15,000	$3,000	$18,000
Payroll taxes and employee benefits	22,199	3,120	8,857	7,882	19,859	1,950	390	2,340
Total compensation	192,972	27,120	76,997	68,515	172,632	16,950	3,390	20,340
Printing	84,071	63,191	18,954	515	82,660	1,161	250	1,411
Mailing, postage, and shipping	14,225	10,754	1,188	817	12,759	411	1,055	1,466
Rent	19,000	3,000	6,800	5,600	15,400	3,000	600	3,600
Telephone	5,615	895	400	1,953	3,248	2,151	216	2,367
Outside art	14,865	3,165	11,700	—	14,865	—	—	—
Local travel	1,741	—	165	915	1,080	661	—	661
Conferences and conventions	6,328	—	1,895	2,618	4,513	1,815	—	1,815
Depreciation	13,596	2,260	2,309	5,616	10,185	3,161	250	3,411
Legal and audit	2,000	—	—	—	—	2,000	—	2,000
Supplies	31,227	—	1,831	28,516	30,347	761	119	880
Miscellaneous	6,027	115	4,378	—	4,493	1,445	89	1,534
Total	$391,667	$110,500	$126,617	$115,065	$352,182	$33,516	$5,969	$39,485

Exhibit 29.6. An analysis of the various program expenses showing the natural expense categories making up each of the functional or program categories.

29 · 42

disclose the composition of the unrestricted net assets of $135,516. This is shown earlier in this chapter, on page 29 · 40.

Investments Carried at Market. As previously noted, the National Association of Environmentalists carries its investments at market rather than at cost. The Guide indicates that where this is done the statement should disclose the unrealized appreciation (or depreciation). This particular organization has disclosed this information in footnotes to the financial statements rather than on the face of the statement itself.

(ii) Statement of Support, Revenue and Expenses, and Changes in Net Assets. Exhibit 29.5 shows a Statement of Support, Revenue and Expenses, and Changes in Net Assets for the National Association of Environmentalists. This is the format shown in SFAS No. 117, with some modifications (discussed below).

Reporting of Expenses

FUNCTIONAL CLASSIFICATION OF EXPENSES. Traditionally, not-for-profit organizations used to report in terms of amounts spent for salaries, rent, supplies, etc. (called a "natural" expense classification). The Guide took a major step forward when it stated that not-for-profit organizations exist to perform services and programs and therefore should be reporting principally in terms of individual program activities or functions. SFAS No. 117 also reaches the same conclusion. Exhibit 29.5 shows the expenses of the National Association of Environmentalists reported on a functional basis. This type of presentation requires management to tell the reader how much of its funds were expended for each program category and the amounts spent on supporting services, including fund raising.

Further, SFAS No. 117 and the Guide state that this functional reporting is not optional. Although SFAS No. 117 requires that disclosure of expenses by function must be made either in the primary financial statements or in the footnotes, the Guide requires that the Statement of Support, Revenue and Expenses, and Changes in Net Assets must be prepared on this functional or program basis.

In many instances, the allocation of salaries between functional or program categories should be based on time reports and similar analyses. Other expenses such as rent, utilities, and maintenance will be allocated based on floor space. Each organization will have to develop time and expense accumulation procedures that will provide the necessary basis for allocation. Organizations have to have reasonably sophisticated procedures to be able to allocate expenses between various categories. An excellent reference source is the third edition (1988) of the "Black Book," *Standards of Accounting and Financial Reporting for Voluntary Health and Welfare Organizations.*

PROGRAM SERVICES. Not-for-profit organizations exist to perform services either for the public or for the members of the organization. They do not exist to provide employment for their employees or to perpetuate themselves. They exist to serve a particular purpose. The Audit Guide re-emphasizes this by requiring the organization to identify major program services and their related costs. Some organizations may have only one specific program category, but most will have several. Each organization should decide for itself into how many categories it wishes to divide its program activities.

SUPPORTING SERVICES. Supporting services are those expenses which do not directly relate to performing the functions for which the organization was established, but which nevertheless are essential to the continued existence of the organization.

The Statement of Support, Revenue and Expenses, and Changes in Net Assets must clearly disclose the amount of supporting services. These are broken down between fund raising and administrative (management and general) expenses. This distinction between supporting and program services is required, as is the separate reporting of fund raising.

Management and general expenses. This is probably the most difficult of the supporting categories to define because a major portion of the time of top management usually will relate more directly to program activities than to management and general. Yet many think, incorrectly, that top management should be considered entirely "management and general." The Statement of Position (#78-10) defines management and general expenses as follows:

> Management and general costs are those that are not identifiable with a single program or fund-raising activity but are indispensable to the conduct of those activities and to an organization's existence, including expenses for the overall direction of the organization's general board activities, business management, general recordkeeping, budgeting, and related purposes. Costs of overall direction usually include the salary and expenses of the chief officer of the organization and his staff. However, if such staff spend a portion of their time directly supervising program services or categories of supporting services, their salaries and expenses should be prorated among those functions. The cost of disseminating information to inform the public of the organization's "stewardship" of contributed funds, the publication of announcements concerning appointments, the annual report, and so forth, should likewise be classified as management and general expenses.

Some suggested methods of computing the allocation of certain types of expenses to the various functions are described in the Statement of Position. Other methods may also be appropriate and could be used.

Fund-raising expenses. Fund-raising expenses are a very sensitive category of expense because a great deal of publicity has been associated with certain organizations that appear to have very high fund-raising costs. The cost of fund raising includes not only the direct costs associated with a particular effort, but a fair allocation of the overhead of the organization, including the time of top management.

Fund-raising expenses are normally recorded as an expense in the Statement of Activity at the time they are incurred. It is not appropriate to defer such amounts. Thus the cost of acquiring or developing a mailing list that has value over more than one year would nevertheless be expensed in its entirety at the time the list was purchased or the costs incurred. The reason for this conservative approach is the difficulty accountants have in satisfying themselves that costs that might logically be deferred will in fact be recovered by future support related thereto. Further, if substantial amounts of deferred fund-raising costs were permitted, the credibility of the financial statements would be in jeopardy, particularly in view of the increased publicity surrounding fund-raising expenses.

If fund-raising is combined with a program function, such as educational literature that also solicits funds, the total cost should be allocated between the program and fund-raising functions on the basis of the use made of the literature, as determined from its content, reason for distribution, and audience, if the criteria of Statement of Position No. 87-2 are met. These criteria are discussed in the next section.

Cost of obtaining grants. Organizations soliciting grants from governments or foundations have a cost that is somewhat different from fund-raising costs. Where such amounts are identifiable and material in amount, they should be separately identified and reported as a supporting service.

ALLOCATION OF JOINT COSTS OF MULTIPURPOSE ACTIVITIES.   In 1987, the AICPA issued a Statement of Position (No. 87-2), amending the Voluntary Health and Welfare Audit Guide and SOP No. 78-10, thus covering the great majority of not-for-profit organizations. It provides that if it can be demonstrated that a bona fide program or management function has been conducted in conjunction with an appeal for funds, joint costs should be allocated between fund raising and the appropriate other function. Otherwise, such joint costs are to be reported as fund-raising expense. Allocation, when made, should be on the basis of content of the activity; the audience to whom the activity is targeted; the action, if any, requested of the audience; and other evidence as to the intent of the activity.

Typically such costs are for a mailing which contains both educational information and an appeal for contributions. The direct cost of printing the educational information is reported as a program service expense, and that of printing the appeal is reported as fund-raising expense. The difficult questions are whether and, if so, how to allocate the joint costs: the envelope and (mainly, as it is usually the largest cost component) the postage to send the piece. The accountant must also consider what costs are properly allocable; for example should part of the salary of the person who organizes the mailing be included as a joint cost?

Charities, understandably, want to allocate as much as possible to program expense, as they believe this will make a better impression on donors and prospective donors, thus motivating them to greater giving to the charity. Those who regulate charities and who assess the performance of charities are concerned that some charities may be over-allocating to program, to make their reported expenses more appealing than is actually the case.

The requirements of SOP No. 87-2 are that joint costs are presumed to be fund-raising unless it can be demonstrated that a bona fide program or management function has also been conducted. Demonstrating this requires verifiable indications such as the nature of the content of the activity, the characteristics of the audience targeted by the activity, and the nature of any action requested of the recipients. This is the "whether to allocate" part of the question. If this is answered no, the other two parts are moot. Being the passive recipient of information is, in and of itself, of no value to someone, no matter how useful the information might potentially be. The potential usefulness of the information is realized only if the recipient is urged to take some beneficial action based on the information. The action need not be taken immediately, as long as the recipient is urged to take it at some later appropriate time, for example, when the symptoms of a disease appear. Nor need the action directly benefit the recipient; it might be something that benefits others: specific groups, humanity, or the environment generally.

As to what and how to allocate, the not-for-profit accounting literature has heretofore offered very little guidance. Standard books on cost accounting may be helpful in discussing general principles useful for answering these questions.

ALL EXPENSES REPORTED AS UNRESTRICTED.   This is a new requirement in SFAS No. 117, and a significant change for almost all not-for-profit organizations (except hospitals). In the past, expenses were reported in the same fund as the revenue which was used to pay for the expenses. Thus unrestricted revenue, and expenses paid for out of that revenue, were shown together in the unrestricted fund. Current restricted revenue, and the expenses paid for out of that revenue, were in the current restricted fund. (No expenses could ever be paid out of the permanent endowment fund, due to the nature of the restriction of those amounts.)

With the adoption of SFAS No. 117, all expenses, regardless of the origin of the resources used to finance the expenses, will be shown in the unrestricted class of net assets; no expenses will be in the temporarily restricted class. This is shown in Exhibit 29.5. The method of relating the restricted revenue to the expenses financed out of that revenue is to reclassify an amount of temporarily restricted net assets equal to the expenses to the unrestricted net assets class ($26,164 in Exhibit 29.5).

COLUMNAR PRESENTATION.   The statement presentation is in a columnar format and, as can be observed in Exhibit 29.5, includes all three classes on one statement. It is also possible to present the information in a single column. In this format, information for the three classes is shown sequentially, including the change in net assets for the class, followed by the total change in net assets for the year. An advantage of such a format is the ease of showing comparative prior year information for each class; a disadvantage is the inability to present a total column.

It should be noted that this statement provides a complete picture of all activity of this organization for the year—not just the activity of a single class or fund. Further, by including a "total" column on the statement, the reader is quickly able to see the overall activity and does not have to add together several amounts to get the complete picture. This represents a major advance in not-for-profit accounting.

The illustrated financial statements in the Guide show figures in the "total" column for both the revenues and expenses categories. The illustrated statements do not, however, show figures in this total column for the caption "Excess of revenues over expenses," or for the captions that follow. SFAS No. 117 requires the statements to show total net assets, and the total change in net assets; thus most organizations will choose to present a complete total column if a columnar format is used.

UNRESTRICTED ACTIVITY IN A SINGLE COLUMN.   One of the most significant features of this presentation is that all legally unrestricted revenues and all expenses are reported in the single column representing the unrestricted class of net assets. The use of a single column in which all unrestricted activity is reported greatly simplifies the presentation and makes it more likely that a nonaccountant will be able to comprehend the total picture of the organization.

Many organizations, of course, will want to continue to keep board-designated accounts within their bookkeeping system. This is fine. But, for reporting to the public, all unrestricted amounts must be combined and reported as indicated in this illustration.

While not recommended, there would appear to be no prohibition to an organization's including additional columns to the *left* of this total "unrestricted" column to show the various unrestricted board-designated categories of funds which make up the total unrestricted class. However, where an organization does so it must clearly indicate that the total unrestricted column represents the total unrestricted activity for the year and that the detailed columns to the left are only the arbitrarily subdivided amounts making up this total. Probably an organization is better advised to show such detail in a separate supplementary schedule, if at all.

Where an organization chooses to show its unrestricted class broken into two columns and has only one class with restricted resources, it may be acceptable to eliminate the total unrestricted column in the interest of simplicity. An example of the column headings might be:

Unrestricted			
General Fund	Investment Fund	Temporarily Restricted	Total All Classes

The key to whether this would be acceptable is the extent of activity in the various columns. For example, if the temporarily restricted class in the above illustration were relatively minor in amount, then the total column would largely reflect the unrestricted class (i.e., the general fund and the investment fund). This is a judgmental question.

TEMPORARILY RESTRICTED COLUMN.   The "temporarily restricted" column represents those amounts which have been given to the organization for a specified purpose other than for permanent endowment. It should be observed that the amounts reported as revenues in this fund represent the total amount the organization received during the year, and not the amount that was actually expended.

USE OF SEPARATE FIXED ASSET (PLANT) FUND.   The Guide provides for the use of a separate plant fund, although, as noted earlier, it does not require its use. SFAS No. 117 does not mention a separate fixed asset category; rather it includes amounts related to fixed assets in the three classes of net assets discussed earlier. Even though a fixed asset fund is maintained in the organization's bookkeeping system, for external financial reporting purposes, the organization would include most of the amounts of the fixed asset fund in the unrestricted class. This has the additional advantage of reducing the number of columns and eliminating the need for certain reclassifications.

Appreciation of Investments.   This organization has elected to carry its investments at market. This means that the organization must reflect appreciation (or depreciation) on its Statement of Support, Revenue and Expenses, and Changes in Net Assets. In this instance, the net appreciation of investments was $33,025. Assuming there were no sales or purchases of investments during the year, this amount would have been determined by comparing the market value of the investments at the end of the year with the market value at the beginning of the year. Normally, however, there will be some realized gain or loss during the year. While there is no technical objection to reporting the realized gain or loss separately from the unrealized appreciation (or depreciation), there seems little significance to this distinction.

ACTIVITY OF RESTRICTED FUNDS RECORDED AS REVENUES AND EXPENSES.   It is significant to note that the Guide called for recording changes in the restricted funds in an income statement format, including their excess of revenues over expenses. (In the past, many argued that such restricted activity should not be reported in an income statement format but rather as individual "changes" in net assets without any indication of the overall net change for the year.)

 This approach is significant because it permits the reader to see the total activity of the organization—both restricted and unrestricted. Thus the Guide appears to be saying that we have a single entity on which we are reporting as distinct from several subentities for which there is no total. SFAS No. 117 also has adopted this philosophy. In this example, the total excess of revenues over expenses was $161,316, whereas the activity of the unrestricted class resulted in an excess of only $114,555. Certainly the reader has a right to know of these other amounts in a manner that will permit seeing a total picture.

OTHER CHANGES IN NET ASSETS.   This section represents certain reclassifications. Since all unrestricted amounts are reported as a single column there are very few of these. In this illustration, $10,000 was reclassified from the unrestricted class to the permanently restricted class to match a challenge grant received that year.

OPERATING STATEMENT.   A variation on this statement which some may wish to use is to present a subtotal of "operating" revenue in excess of "operating" expenses. This would focus the reader's attention on what the organization considers its core "operations," as distinguished from matters which it considers peripheral or incidental to its operations. SFAS No. 117 permits, but does not require, this presentation. If an organization chooses this presentation, it will decide for itself what it considers to be its operations, versus other activities. Appendix 29–F contains a checklist to help organizations decide what they wish to consider as operating versus nonoperating transactions.

(iii) Statement of Cash Flows (Formerly Changes in Financial Position).   A Statement of Cash Flows is a summary of the resources made available to an organization during the year and the uses made of such resources. Until 1978, no similar statement was required for not-for-profit organizations, but commercial organizations have had to prepare a Statement of Changes in Financial Position for many years.[6] In 1978, Statement of Position No. 78-10 added a requirement for organizations covered by it to prepare a Statement of Changes in Financial Position.

 Beginning in 1988, businesses were required to prepare a Statement of Cash Flows in place of a Statement of Changes in Financial Position. However, the accounting standard[7] which

---

[6] Required by Accounting Principles Board Opinion No. 19.

[7] FASB Statement of Financial Accounting Standards No. 95.

mandated this change excluded not-for-profit organizations from its coverage. This effectively left them under the earlier rule requiring only organizations following the Statement of Position to prepare a Statement of Changes in Financial Position. Other not-for-profits could prepare such a statement but were not required to. Now SFAS No. 117 requires presentation of a Statement of Cash Flows by all not-for-profit organizations. Full discussion of preparation of this statement is in SFAS No. 95.

Exhibit 29.3 shows a Statement of Cash Flows. In some ways it is similar to a Statement of Cash Receipts and Disbursements, in that it presents cash received and spent. It differs by grouping transactions into three groups: Operating, Investing, and Financing cash flows. Also, there is less detail of specific types of operating cash flows, since such detail is already shown for revenue and expenses in Exhibit 29.5.

(iv) Statement of Functional Expenses.   Exhibit 29.6 is a statement that analyzes functional or program expenses and shows the natural expense categories which go into each functional category. It is primarily an analysis to give the reader insight as to the major types of expenses involved. In order to arrive at the functional expense totals shown in the Statement of Support, Revenue and Expenses, and Changes in Net Assets, an analysis must be prepared that shows all of the expenses going into each program category. The Statement of Functional Expenses merely summarizes this detail for the reader.

DEPRECIATION.   In the illustrative financial statement in the Guide, depreciation expense is shown as the very last item on the statement, and all other expenses are subtotaled before depreciation is added. This presentation was illustrated in the Guide because of the concern of many not-for-profit organizations in showing depreciation as an expense. By subtotaling all expenses before adding depreciation, the Guide emphasizes the somewhat different nature of depreciation expense. Exhibit 29.6 includes depreciation among the other expense categories. Either presentation is acceptable.

29.4 COLLEGES AND UNIVERSITIES

With the issuance of FASB Statement Nos. 116 and 117, some of the accounting and reporting rules for colleges and universities discussed in this section have changed. Section 29.4 presents a summary of the changes.

The AICPA Industry Audit Guide, "Audits of Colleges and Universities," issued in 1973, has been the most authoritative pronouncement on accounting principles and reporting practices for colleges and universities. The guide was revised in 1974 by an AICPA SOP, "Financial Accounting and Reporting by Colleges and Universities," which modified certain descriptions and classifications of current funds revenue, expenditures, and transfers.

(a) ACCOUNTING PRINCIPLES.   Fund accounting is a prominent element of college and university accounting. Depreciation and current restricted gifts, in addition, pose special accounting problems.

(i) Accrual Basis of Accounting.   Colleges and universities should follow accrual basis accounting. All accounts should be maintained on an accrual basis unless unrecorded amounts are immaterial, including such often overlooked accruals and deferrals as investment income and interest on student loans. Revenue from and expenditures for summer sessions should be reported in the fiscal year in which most of the session occurs.

(ii) Fund Accounting.   Colleges and universities have historically followed fund accounting procedures. Fund accounting continues to find favor at colleges and universities because many gifts and grants that colleges receive possess external restrictions that must be carefully monitored, and also because many colleges voluntarily set aside some current unrestricted funds as "endowment" to produce future income.

The following six fund groupings are generally used by colleges and universities.

Current funds are resources available for carrying out the general activities of an institution. In public reporting, current unrestricted funds are usually reported separately from current restricted funds, that is, funds restricted by donors or grantors for specific current purposes.

Loan funds are resources available for loans to students, faculty, and staff. If only the investment income from restricted endowment funds can be used for loans, only the income should be reported in the loan fund.

Endowment and similar funds consist of three types of endowment resources:

1. **True endowment,** where the donor stipulates that the principal must be maintained inviolate and in perpetuity, and only the income earned thereon may be expended.
2. **Term endowment,** where the donor stipulates that, upon the passage of time or the incidence of an event, the principal may be used for current operations or specific purposes.
3. **Quasi endowment,** where the board of trustees voluntarily retains as principal a portion of current funds to produce current and future income.

Annuity and life income funds are endowment resources of which the college owns only the principal and not the income earned thereon. In accepting an annuity or life income gift, the college agrees to pay the contributor all income earned or a specific amount for a stated period of time. (See the discussion of split-interest gifts at subsection 29.2(j)(iii).)

Plant funds consist of four fund groupings, and separate financial data for each are often reported:

1. **Unexpended plant funds** are used for plant additions or improvements.
2. **Renewal and replacement funds** are transferred from current funds for **future** renewal or replacement of the existing plant. These funds provide for the future integrity of the physical plant.
3. **Retirement of indebtedness funds** are set aside to service debt interest and principal. It is often appropriate to designate which funds are set aside under mandatory contractual agreements with lenders and which funds are voluntarily designated.
4. **Investment in plant** records the actual cost of all land, buildings, and equipment owned by the college. Donated plant is recorded at market value at the date of the gift.

Agency funds are funds over which an institution exercises **custodial** but not **proprietary** authority. An example is funds that are owned by a student organization but are deposited with the college.

(iii) Encumbrance Accounting.   Encumbrance accounting is not acceptable for financial statements of colleges and universities. It is inappropriate to report, as expenditures or liabilities, commitments for materials or services not received by the reporting date. A portion of the current unrestricted fund may be designated to satisfy purchase orders, provided that the designation is made only in the fund balances (net assets) section of the balance sheet.

(iv) Fixed Assets.   Material fixed assets should be capitalized and recorded on the balance sheet. A college cannot write off or "expense" fixed assets as acquired.

(v) Depreciation.   The requirements of the AICPA audit guide on this subject have been superseded by SFAS Nos. 93 and 117. See discussion at subsection 29.2(g).

(vi) Investments.   See subsections 29.2(h) and 29.2(i) for discussion of this topic. Unrestricted investment income, including unrestricted endowment fund income, should be reported as revenue in the current unrestricted fund in the period earned. Restricted investment income should be reported as revenue directly in the fund to which the restrictions pertain.

(vii) Contributions.   See subsection 29.2(j) for discussion of this topic.

(b) REPORTING PRACTICES.   Colleges and universities have generally prepared three financial statements:

1. A statement of changes in fund balances.
2. A balance sheet.
3. A statement of current funds revenues, expenditures, and other changes.

(i) Statement of Changes in Fund Balances.   The statement of changes in fund balances is the most comprehensive and important statement prepared by colleges and universities. It summarizes the financial activity of all funds of an institution.

The format of this statement is similar to that of an income statement. Expenditures are ostensibly subtracted from revenue, yielding the net change for the period. However, the statement of changes in fund balances is **not** a statement of income and expenses. "Revenue and other additions" and "expenditures and other deductions" include many items that do not constitute revenue or expense in a strict accounting sense. "Other additions" and "other deductions" include such nonrevenue and nonexpense items as "expended for plant facilities" and "retirement of indebtedness," which would normally be treated as adjustments to the fund balance of particular fund groups or included in a statement of changes in financial position.

All restricted gifts, bequests, and grants received during the period are reported as revenue in the current restricted fund. This treatment differs from that followed in the statement of current funds revenues, expenditures, and other changes, where restricted gifts, bequests, and grants are reported as revenue only to the extent expended.

The "net increase (decrease) before transfers" caption did not, given the mixed nature of the revenue and expenditure items, represent excess of revenue over expenditures for the period. It does, however, present the activity of each fund prior to transfers. A "total" column facilitates evaluation of a college as a single entity, rather than as a collection of individual funds. In recent years, more accountants prefer, and more institutions are presenting, these items.

Transfers between funds are segregated from the revenues and expenditures sections of the statement. Transfers mandated by contractual agreements were reported separately from voluntary transfers. This statement, as well as the statement of current fund revenues, expenditures, and other changes will now be replaced with a statement of revenue, expenses, and changes in net assets, in accordance with SFAS No. 117.

A statement of changes in fund balances should contain a "net increase (decrease) for the year" caption. This caption, recommended by the audit guide, communicates the net change in fund balances for the period for each fund and for the institution as a whole.

(ii) Balance Sheet.   The audit guide permits balance sheet presentation in either a "columnar" or "layered" format. Exhibit 29.7 illustrates a columnar balance sheet, which presents an overview of an entire organization.

(iii) Statement of Revenues, Expenses, and Changes in Net Assets.   Exhibit 29.8 presents this statement, which replaces the old statement of current funds revenues, expenditures, and other changes and statement of changes in fund balances. This statement reports all activity—unrestricted and restricted—of an institution.

MARY AND ISLA COLLEGE
BALANCE SHEET
June 30, 19X1

	Current Funds	Loan Funds	Endowment and Similar Funds	Plant Funds	Total All Funds
ASSETS					
Current assets:					
Cash	$1,195,000	$16,000	$ 310,000	$ 80,000	$ 1,601,000
Short-term investments	930,000			550,000	1,480,000
Accounts receivable	18,000	80,000			98,000
Inventories	20,000				20,000
Prepaid expenses	25,000				25,000
Total	2,188,000	96,000	310,000	630,000	3,224,000
Long-term investments			4,215,000		4,215,000
Invested in plant, net of depreciation				23,450,000	23,450,000
Interfund receivable (payable)	(560,000)		510,000	50,000	—
Total assets	$1,628,000	$96,000	$5,035,000	$24,130,000	$30,889,000
LIABILITIES AND NET ASSETS					
Current liabilities:					
Accounts payable	$ 573,000			$ 35,000	$ 608,000
Current portion of debt				170,000	170,000
Tuition deposits	110,000				110,000
Total	683,000			205,000	888,000
Long-term debt				580,000	580,000
Refundable advances		$30,000			30,000
Net assets:					
Unrestricted	810,000	16,000	$3,010,000	23,025,000	26,861,000
Temporarily restricted	135,000		510,000	320,000	965,000
Permanently restricted		50,000	1,515,000		1,565,000
Total	945,000	66,000	5,035,000	23,345,000	29,391,000
Total liabilities and net assets	$1,628,000	$96,000	$5,035,000	$24,130,000	$30,889,000

Exhibit 29.7.   An example of a columnar presentation of a Balance Sheet for a small college using fund accounting recommended in the AICPA Audit Guide.

29.5 OTHER NOT-FOR-PROFIT ORGANIZATIONS

(a) ACCOUNTING PRINCIPLES.   Not-for-profit organizations not covered by a specific AICPA Industry Audit Guide are covered by SOP No. 78-10. Issued in 1978, the SOP does not contain an effective date because of the expectation that differences with forthcoming FASB pronouncements on not-for-profit accounting would eventually be resolved. Organizations covered by the SOP include professional and trade associations, private and community foundations, religious organizations, libraries, museums, private schools, and performing arts organizations.

(i) Accrual Basis Accounting.   The SOP requires that not-for-profit organizations **report** on the accrual basis if they wish to describe their financial statements as being prepared in accordance with GAAP. If the difference between cash basis and accrual basis statements is immaterial, an organization may remain on a cash basis and still effectively report on a GAAP basis.

MARY AND ISLA COLLEGE
STATEMENT OF REVENUES, EXPENSES, AND CHANGES
IN NET ASSETS
For the Year Ended June 30, 19X1

	Unrestricted	Temporarily Restricted	Permanently Restricted	Total
Operating revenues:				
Tuition and fees	$ 1,610,000			$ 1,610,000
Governmental appropriations	400,000			400,000
Research grants		$ 190,000		190,000
Auxiliary activities	125,000			125,000
Net assets released from restrictions	550,000	(550,000)		
Total operating revenues	2,685,000	(360,000)		2,325,000
Operating expenses:				
Educational:				
Engineering	930,000			930,000
Arts	410,000			410,000
Business	625,000			625,000
Research	850,000			850,000
Supporting:				
Administrative	495,000			495,000
Fund raising	90,000			90,000
Auxiliary activities	95,000			95,000
Total operating expenses	3,495,000			3,495,000
Excess of operating expenses over revenues	(810,000)	(360,000)		(1,170,000)
Other revenues:				
Gifts and bequests	900,000	240,000	$ 395,000	1,535,000
Investment income	350,000	47,000		397,000
Realized and unrealized appreciation	130,000		20,000	150,000
Total other revenues	1,380,000	287,000	415,000	2,082,000
Excess of revenues over expenses	570,000	(73,000)	415,000	912,000
Net assets, beginning of year	26,291,000	1,038,000	1,150,000	28,479,000
Net assets, end of year	$26,861,000	$ 965,000	$1,565,000	$29,391,000

Exhibit 29.8.   An example of an all-inclusive Statement of Revenues, Expenses, and Changes in Net Assets.

(ii) Fund Accounting.   The SOP does not require the use of fund reporting by organizations wishing to prepare financial statements in accordance with GAAP. Instead, organizations should properly segregate unrestricted resources from resources possessing externally imposed restrictions. Fund reporting may be used if helpful in achieving this segregation.

(iii) Fixed Assets.   Fixed assets should be capitalized. Capitalization should be based on cost for purchased assets and fair market value at date of gift for donated fixed assets. If historical cost is unobtainable, another reasonable basis, such as cost-based appraisal value, may be used.

(iv) Museum Collections.   Museums and similar organizations may capitalize their collections but are not required to do so. Other fixed assets (e.g., buildings) owned by such organizations should be capitalized.

(v) Depreciation.   Once capitalized, fixed assets that are exhaustible should be depreciated. Inexhaustible fixed assets, such as landmarks, monuments, and historical treasures, need not be depreciated if the criteria in SFAS No. 93 are met. Houses of worship must be depreciated after the effective date of SFAS No. 93. See subsection 29.2(g) for further discussion.

(vi) Investments.   See subsections 29.2(h) and 29.2(i) for a discussion of this topic.

(vii) Contributions.   See subsection 29.2(j) for a discussion of this topic.

(viii) Subscription and Membership Income.   Subscription and membership income should be recognized in the periods in which the organization provides goods or services to subscribers or members. This usually requires deferring such amounts when received and recognizing them ratably over the membership or subscription period. Special calculations, based on life expectancy, are required when so-called life memberships are involved.

(ix) Functional Reporting of Program Services.   SOP No. 78-10 required that organizations that receive a significant level of support in the form of contributions from the general public should report expenses on a functional or program basis. Other organizations could classify expenses on a natural (or object) basis or on a functional basis, as they see fit. SFAS No. 117 requires all organizations to report functionally, except that if it is not yet clear whether associations and clubs must do this. This question will be resolved by the new AICPA audit guide (see subsection 29.1(b)(ii)).

(x) Management and General Expenses.   Management and general expenses are defined in SOP No. 78-10 as those costs that cannot be exclusively identified with a single program or activity, but are nonetheless vital to the conduct of the programs and activities of an organization. An appropriate portion of management and general expenses should be allocated to programs or activities receiving benefits.

(xi) Fund-Raising Expenses.   Fund-raising expenses are defined by the SOP as costs incurred to induce others to contribute resources (e.g., money, time, or materials) without receipt of direct economic benefits in return. Fund-raising costs include a fair allocation of overhead, as well as direct costs. Fund-raising costs should be expensed when incurred. If fund-raising activities are combined with program functions, such as mailing educational literature to prospective contributors, the total cost should be allocated between functions on the basis of how the literature is used, as determined by content, reason for distribution, and expected audience, in accordance with SOP No. 87-2.

(xii) Grants to Others.   Organizations that award grants should record a grant as a liability and an expense in the period in which the recipient is entitled to the grant. This is usually the period in which the grant is authorized, even though some of the payments may not be made until later periods.

Under SFAS No. 116, grantors will account for grants in the same way as grantees—except backwards–expense and liability instead of revenue and receivable. See subsection 29.2(j) for a discussion of accounting for restricted gifts and pledges.

(b) REPORTING PRACTICES.   Three primary financial statements are required by SOP No. 78-10:

1. A balance sheet.
2. A statement of activity.
3. A statement of changes in financial position or a statement of cash flows.

A comprehensive statement of changes in financial position was not previously required of any category of not-for-profit organization.

A statement of functional expenses may be presented if desired. See subsections 29.2(c) and 29.3(e) for a discussion of SFAS No. 117.

29.6 AUDIT CONSIDERATIONS FOR A NOT-FOR-PROFIT ORGANIZATION

(a) GENERAL CONSIDERATIONS. An audit of the financial statements of a not-for-profit organization is similar to an audit of a for-profit enterprise, and generally accepted auditing standards should be followed. A not-for-profit organization, however, seeks to provide an optimal level of services, rather than to maximize profits, and its financial statements, accordingly, focus on the activity and balances of different classes and funds. This in turn, influences the conduct of the audit.

(b) INTERNAL CONTROL STRUCTURE. Some not-for-profit organizations do not have effective internal control structures. The size of staff may be inadequate to achieve a proper segregation of duties, and the nature of some transactions often precludes sufficient checks and balances. Internal control structure deficiencies are often mitigated by adoption of procedures including the following: (1) involvement of senior management and directors in the operation of the organization; (2) restricting check signing to senior management and directors; (3) implementing effective bank reconciliation procedures; (4) preparing annual budgets and promptly investigating variances from budget estimates; and (5) depositing investment securities with independent custodians.

(c) MATERIALITY. The issue of what is material is equally important for not-for-profit and for-profit organizations. In for-profit enterprises, evaluating materiality involves considering the effect of alternate accounting treatments and disclosures on decisions by investors, and it relates to net income and earnings per share. These measures are generally not applicable to not-for-profit organizations. Instead, evaluating materiality involves considering the effects of accounting treatments and disclosures on decisions by contributors, and it relates to revenue, expenditures, and the cost of individual programs.

(d) TAXES. Not-for-profit organizations are generally exempt from income taxes and are often exempt from property and sales taxes. Tax liabilities, however, may arise from tax on unrelated business income, tax on net income resulting from a loss of tax-exempt status, or certain excise taxes applicable to private foundations.

(e) CONSOLIDATION. Not-for-profit organizations do not "own" other organizations in the sense that businesses own other businesses. Not-for-profit organizations, however, may exercise effective control over affiliates or related organizations; in such instances, preparation of combined financial statements may be appropriate.

(f) COMPLIANCE AUDITING. In recent years, federal and state governments have become more active in requiring recipients of government money to submit auditor reports on various aspects of financial operations. These usually include opinions on financial data for the organization as a whole and, for government grants, reports on internal controls and compliance with laws and regulations. The exact requirements may differ depending on the type of recipient (college, hospital, etc.), the agency that made the grant, whether the money was received directly or through another level of government, and the amount of money received. It is important for the auditor to ascertain any compliance auditing requirements prior to beginning fieldwork, so that the auditor can perform the work necessary to issue the required reports. Specific requirements are contained in a number of different documents including SAS No. 74.

"Compliance Auditing Considerations in Audits of Governmental Entities and Recipients of Governmental Financial Assistance"; the Department of Health and Human Services audit guide, "Guidelines for Audits of Federal Awards to Nonprofit Organizations"; various circulars issued by the Office of Management and Budget (principally A-21, A-110, A-122, A-128, A-133); and "Government Auditing Standards," issued by the GAO (generally referred to as the "Yellow Book"). Compliance auditing requirements are also found in the OMB "Compliance Supplement for Single Audits of State and Local Governments" (Revised 1990) and "Compliance Supplement for Single Audits of Educational Institutions and Other Nonprofit Organizations."

Additional guidance for compliance auditing is in AICPA SOP No. 92-9, "Audits of Not-for-Profit Organizations Receiving Federal Awards," and PCIE (President's Council on Integrity and Efficiency) Position Statement No. 6, "Questions and Answers on OMB Circular A-133." Compliance auditing is discussed further in Chapter 28, "State and Local Government Accounting."

(g) UNIQUE AUDITING AREAS.   Auditing areas unique to not-for-profit organizations include the following:

- **Collections of museums, libraries, zoological parks, and similar organizations.** Auditing considerations include valuation of assets, capitalization, accessions and deaccessions, security, insurance coverage, and observation of inventory. Certain procedures are appropriate even though the collection is not capitalized.

- **Contributions.** Auditing considerations include ascertaining that amounts reported as contributions are properly stated. Audit tests for noncash contributions include testing their assigned value. Auditors are particularly concerned about the possibility that contributions that were intended for the organization may never have been received and recorded.

- **Fees for performance of services, including tuition, membership dues, ticket revenue, and patient fees.** Auditing considerations include confirming that revenue is computed at proper rates, collected, and properly recorded for all services provided.

- **Functional allocation of expenses.** Auditing considerations include appropriateness of allocations among functions, reasonableness of allocation methods, accuracy of computations, and consistency of allocation bases with bases of prior periods. These considerations are especially important when joint costs of multipurpose activities (discussed above) are involved.

- **Restricted resources.** Auditing considerations include ascertaining that transactions are for the restricted purpose and are recorded in the proper restricted fund.

- **Grant awards to others.** Auditing considerations include confirming grant awards with recipients and ascertaining that grants are recorded in the proper accounting period.

- **Tax compliance.** Not-for-profits are subject to IRC sections that differ from those regularly applicable to businesses. Auditors must review compliance with these sections. Areas of particular concern are conformity with exempt purpose, unrelated business income, lobbying, status as a public charity (if applicable), and special rules applicable to private foundations.

APPENDIX 29–A: FACTORS TO BE CONSIDERED IN DISTINGUISHING CONTRACTS FOR THE PURCHASE OF GOODS OR SERVICES FROM RESTRICTED GRANTS

Following is a list of factors that may be helpful to not-for-profit organizations in deciding how to account for the receipt of payments that might be considered as being either for the purchase of goods or services from the organization, or as restricted-purpose gifts or grants to the organization (as contemplated in par. 3 of SFAS No. 116). These factors can also be used by auditors in

Factors Whose Presence Would Indicate Payment Is for the Purchase of Goods or Services	*Factors Whose Presence Would Indicate the Payment Is a Restricted Grant for a Specific Purpose*

Factors related to the agreement between the payor and the payee:

1. The expressed intent is for the payee to provide goods/services to the payor, or to other specifically identified recipients, as determined by the payor.	The expressed intent is to make a gift to the payee to advance the programs of the payee.
2. There is a specified time and/or place for delivery of goods/services to the payor or other recipient.	Time and/or place of delivery of any goods/services is largely at the discretion of the payee.
3. There are provisions for economic penalties, beyond the amount of the payment, against the payee for failure to meet the terms of the agreement.	Any penalties are expressed in terms of required delivery of goods/services, or are limited to return of unspent amounts.
4. The amount of the payment per unit is computed in a way that explicitly provides for a "profit" margin for the payee.	The payment is stated as a flat amount, or a fixed amount per unit based only on the cost (including overhead) of providing the goods/service.
5. The total amount of the payment is based only on the quantity of items delivered.	The payment is based on a line item budget request, including an allowance for actual administrative costs.
6. The tenor of the agreement is that the payor receives approximately equivalent value in return for the payment.	The payor does not receive approximately equivalent value.

Factors related to the goods/services (items) covered by the payment:

7. The items are closely related to commercial activity regularly engaged in by the payor.	The items are related to the payee's program services.
8. There is substantial benefit to the payor itself from the items.	The items are normally used to provide goods/services considered of social benefit to society as a whole, or to some defined segment thereof (e.g., children, persons having a disease, students), which might not otherwise have ready access to the items.
9. If the payor is a governmental unit, the items are things the government itself has explicitly undertaken to provide to its citizens; the government has arranged for another organization to be the actual service provider.	The government is in the role of subsidizing provision of services to the public by a non-governmental organization.
10. The benefits resulting from the items are to be made available only to the payor or to persons or entities designated by the payor.	The items, or the results of the activities funded by the payment, are to be made available to the general public, or to any person who requests and is qualified to receive them. Determination of specific recipients is made by the payee.
11. The items are to be delivered to the payor or to other persons or entities closely connected with the payor.	Delivery is to be made to persons or entities not closely connected with the payor.
12. Revenue from sale of the items is considered unrelated business income (IRC Section 512) to the payee.	Revenue is "related" income to the payee.
13. In the case of sponsored research, the payor determines the plan of research and the desired outcome, and retains proprietary rights to the results.	The research plan is determined by the payee; desired outcomes are expressed only in general terms (e.g., to find a cure for a disease), and the rights to the results remain with the payee or are considered in the public domain.
14. The payment supports applied research.	The payment supports basic research.

assessing the reasonableness of the client's decision. Additional discussion of this distinction can be found in the instructions to IRS Form 990, lines 1a–c, and in IRS Regulation 1.509(a)-3(g). No one of these factors is normally determinative by itself; all relevant factors should be considered together.

APPENDIX 29–B: FACTORS TO BE CONSIDERED IN ASSESSING WHETHER CONTRIBUTED SERVICES ARE CONSIDERED TO REQUIRE SPECIALIZED SKILLS. (PER PARAGRAPH 9 OF SFAS NO. 116, "ACCOUNTING FOR CONTRIBUTIONS RECEIVED")

Following is a list of factors that may be helpful to recipients of contributed services of volunteers in assessing whether the skills utilized by the volunteers in the performance of their services are considered to be "specialized" within the meaning of Paragraph 9 of SFAS No. 116. These factors may also aid auditors in assessing the appropriateness of the client's judgment. This list of factors is not intended to be used in determining how to value or account for such services. In some cases, no one of these factors is necessarily determinative by itself; all relevant factors should be considered together.

Factors whose presence is often indicative that skills are "specialized":

1. Persons who regularly hold themselves out to the public as qualified practitioners of such skills are required by law or by professional ethical standards to possess a license or other professional certification, or specified academic credentials. Alternatively, if possession of such license/certification/credentials is optional, the person performing the services does possess such formal certification.

2. Practitioners of such skills are required, by law or professional ethics, to have obtained a specified amount of technical pre-job or on-the-job training, to obtain specified amounts of continuing professional education, a specified amount of practical work experience, or to complete a defined period of apprenticeship in the particular type of work.

3. Proper practice of the skills requires the individual to possess specific artistic or creative talent and/or a body of technical knowledge not generally possessed by members of the public at large.

4. Practice of the skills requires the use of technical tools or equipment. The ability to properly use such tools or equipment requires training or experience not generally possessed by members of the public at large.

5. There is a union or professional association whose membership consists specifically of practitioners of the skills, as opposed to such groups whose members consist of persons who work in a broad industry, a type of company, or a department of a company. Admission to membership in such organization requires demonstrating one or more of the factors 1, 2, or 3. (Whether the person whose skills are being considered actually belongs to such organization is not a factor in assessing whether the skills are considered to be specialized, though it may be relevant in assessing whether the person possesses the skills.)

6. Practitioners of such skills are generally regarded by the public as being members of a particular "profession."

7. There is a formal disciplinary procedure administered by a government or by a professional association, to which practitioners of such skills are subject, as a condition of offering their skills to the public for pay.

8. Practice of the skills by persons who do so in their regular work is ordinarily done in an environment in which there is regular formal review or approval of work done by supervisory personnel or by professional peers.

APPENDIX 29-C CHECKLIST: FACTORS TO BE CONSIDERED IN DETERMINING WHETHER AN ORGANIZATION WOULD TYPICALLY NEED TO PURCHASE SERVICES IF NOT PROVIDED BY DONATION

The following is a list of factors which may be helpful to:

- Not-for-profit organizations, in deciding whether or not contributed services meet the third part of the criterion in par. 9b of SFAS No. 116;
- Auditors, in assessing the reasonableness of the client's decision.

No one of these factors is normally determinative by itself; all relevant factors and the strength of their presence should be considered together.

Factors Whose Presence Would Indicate the Services Would Typically Need to Be Purchased	*Factors Whose Presence Would Indicate the Services Would Typically Not Need to Be Purchased*
1. The activities in which the volunteers are involved are an integral part of the reporting organization's ongoing program services (as stated in its IRS Form 1023/4, fundraising material, and annual report), or of management or fundraising activities that are essential to the functioning of the organization's programs.	The activities are not part of the reporting organization's program, or of important management or fundraising activities, or are relatively incidental to those activities; the services primarily benefit the program activities of another organization.
2. Volunteer work makes up a significant portion of the total effort expended in the program activity in which the volunteers are used.	Volunteer work is a relatively small part of the total effort of the program.
3. The program activity in which the volunteers function is a significant part of the overall program activities of the organization.	The program activity is relatively insignificant in relation to the organization's overall program activities.
4. The reporting organization has an objective basis for assigning a value to the services.	No objective basis is readily available.
5. The organization has formal agreements with third parties to provide the program services which are conducted by the volunteers.	Factor not present.
6. The reporting organization assigns volunteers to specific duties.	Assignment of specific duties to volunteers is done by persons or entities other than the reporting organization, or the volunteers largely determine for themselves what is to be done within broad guidelines.
7. The volunteers are subject to ongoing supervision and review of their work by the reporting organization.	The activities of the volunteers are conducted at geographic locations distant from the organization, or factor otherwise not present.
8. The organization actively recruits volunteers for specific tasks.	Volunteers are accepted but not actively recruited, or, if recruited, specific tasks are not mentioned in the recruiting materials.

Factors Whose Presence Would Indicate the Services Would Typically Need to Be Purchased	*Factors Whose Presence Would Indicate the Services Would Typically Not Need to Be Purchased*
9. If the work of the volunteers consists of creating or enhancing non-financial assets, the assets will be owned and/or used primarily by or under the control of the reporting organization after the volunteer work is completed. If the assets are subsequently given away by the organization to charitable beneficiaries, the organization decides who is to receive the assets.	The assets will immediately be owned or used primarily by other persons or organizations.
10. If there were to be a net increase in net assets resulting from the recording of a value for the services (even though in practice, there usually is not), the increase would better meet the criteria for presentation as revenue, rather than a gain, as set forth in SFAC No. 6, par. 78–79, 82–88, and 111–113.	The net increase would better meet the criteria of a gain, rather than revenue.
11. Management represents to the auditor that it would hire paid staff to perform the services if volunteers were not available.	Management represents that it would not hire paid staff; or it is obvious from the financial condition of the organization that it is unlikely that financial resources would be available to pay for the services.

Auditors are reminded that management representations, alone, do not normally constitute sufficient competent evidential matter to support audit assertions; however they may be considered in conjunction with other evidence.

Factors particularly relevant in situations where the volunteer services are provided directly to charitable or other beneficiaries of the reporting organization's program services (e.g., Legal Aid society), rather than to the organization itself:

12. The reporting organization assumes responsibility for the volunteers with regard to workers compensation and liability insurance, errors or omissions in the work, satisfactory completion of the work.	The organization has explicitly disclaimed such responsibility.
13. The reporting organization maintains ongoing involvement with the activities of the volunteers.	The organization functions mainly as a clearinghouse for putting volunteers in touch with persons or other organizations needing help, but has little ongoing involvement.

APPENDIX 29–D: FACTORS TO BE CONSIDERED IN ASSESSING WHETHER A DONOR HAS MADE A BONA FIDE PLEDGE TO A DONEE

Following is a list of factors that may be helpful to donees, in assessing whether a pledge (unconditional promise to give, as contemplated in pars. 5–7, 22, 23 of SFAS No. 116) has, in fact, been made. These factors may also help auditors in assessing the appropriateness of the client's judgment. This list of factors is not intended to be used in deciding on proper accounting (for either the pledge asset or the related revenue/net assets), or to assess collectibility, although some of the factors may be relevant to those decisions as well. In many cases no one of these factors is necessarily determinative by itself; all relevant factors should be considered together.

Factors Whose Presence May Indicate a Bona Fide Pledge Was Made	*Factors Whose Presence May Indicate a Bona Fide Pledge Was Not Made*
1. Factors related to the solicitation process:	
____ a. There is evidence that the recipient explicitly solicited formal pledges.	The pledge was unsolicited, or the solicitation did not refer to pledges.
____ b. Public announcement[1] of the pledge has been made (by donor or donee)	No public announcement has been made.
____ c. Partial payment on the pledge has been made (or full payment after balance sheet date).	No payments have yet been made, or payments have been irregular, late, or less than scheduled amounts.
2. Factors related to the "pledge" itself:	
____ a. Written evidence created by the donor clearly supports the existence of an unconditional promise to give. (D)	There is no written evidence[2]; the only written evidence was prepared by the donee, or written evidence is unclear.
(D) This factor, if present, would normally be considered determinative.	

____ b. The evidence includes words such as:
 	
    promise
    agree
    will
    binding, legal
	There is written evidence, but it includes words such as:
	    intend, plan
	    hope
	    may, if
	    expected

____ c. The pledge appears to be legally enforceable. (Consult an attorney if necessary.) (Note also factor 4a.)	Legal enforceability is questionable or explicitly denied.
____ d. There is a clearly-defined payment schedule stated in terms of either calendar dates or the occurrence of specified events whose occurrence is reasonably probable.	A payment schedule is not clearly defined, or events are relatively unlikely to occur.
____ e. The calendar dates or events comprising the payment schedule will (are expected to) occur within a relatively short time[3] after the balance sheet date (or in the case of events, have already occurred).	The time (period) of payment contemplated by the donor is relatively far in the future.
____ f. The amount of the pledge is clearly specified or readily computable.	The amount is not clear or readily computable.
____ g. The donor has clearly specified a particular purpose for the gift, e.g., endowment, fixed assets, loan fund, retire long-term debt, specific program service. The purpose is consistent with ongoing donee activities.	The purpose is vaguely or not specified, or inconsistent with donee activities.
3. Factors relating to the donor:	
____ a. There is no reason to question the donor's ability or intent to fulfill the pledge.	Collectibility of the gift is questionable.
____ b. The donor has a history of making and fulfilling pledges to the donee of similar or larger amounts.	Factor not present.
4. Factors relating to the donee:	
____ a. The donee has indicated that it would take legal action to enforce collection if necessary, or has a history of doing so.	It is unlikely (based on donee's past practices) or uncertain whether the donee would enforce the "pledge."
____ b. The donee has already taken specific action in reliance on the pledge or publicly[1] announced that it intends to do so.[4]	No specific action has been taken or is contemplated.

[1] The announcement would not necessarily have to be made to the general public; announcement in media circulated among the constituency of either the donor or donee would suffice. Examples include newsletters, fund-raising reports, annual reports, a campus newspaper, etc. In the case of announcements by the donee, there should be a reasonable presumption that the donor is aware of the announcement and has not indicated any disagreement with it.

[2] Oral pledges can be considered bona fide under some circumstances. Clearly, in the case of oral pledges, much greater weight will have to be given to other factors if the existence of a bona fide pledge is to be asserted. Also, the auditor will have to carefully consider what audit evidence can be relied on.

[3] What constitutes a relatively short time has to be determined in each case. The longer the time contemplated, the more weight will have to be given to other factors (especially 2b, c, 3a and 4a) in assessing the existence of a pledge. In most circumstances, periods longer than 3 to 5 years would likely be judged relatively long.

[4] Types of specific action contemplated include:

- Commencing acquisition, construction, or lease of capital assets or signing binding contracts to do so
- Making public announcement of the commencement or expansion of operating programs used by the public (e.g., the opening of a new clinic, starting a new concert series, a special museum exhibit)
- Indicating to another funder that the pledge will be used to match part of a challenge grant from that funder
- Soliciting other pledges or loans for the same purpose by explicitly indicating that "x has already pledged";
- Committing proceeds of the pledge in other ways such as awarding scholarships, making pledges to other charities, hiring new staff, etc. (where such uses are consistent with either the donee's stated purposes in soliciting the pledge or the donor's indicated use of the pledge)
- Forbearing from soliciting other available major gifts (e.g., not submitting an application for a foundation grant) because, with the pledge in question, funding for the purpose is considered complete
- Using pledge as collateral for a loan.

APPENDIX 29–E CHECKLIST: FACTORS TO BE CONSIDERED IN DECIDING WHETHER A GIFT OR PLEDGE SUBJECT TO DONOR STIPULATIONS IS CONDITIONAL OR RESTRICTED (AS DISCUSSED IN SFAS NO. 116, PAR. 7, 22–23, 57–71, 75–81)

Donors place many different kinds of stipulations on pledges and other gifts. Some stipulations create legal *restrictions* which limit the way in which the donee may use the gift. Other stipulations create *conditions* which must be fulfilled before a donee is entitled to receive (or keep) a gift.

In SFAS No. 116, FASB defines a condition as an uncertain future event which must occur before a promise based on that event becomes binding on the promisor. In some cases, it is not immediately clear whether a particular stipulation creates a condition or a restriction. (Some gifts are both conditional and restricted.) Accounting for the two forms of gift is quite different, so it is important that the nature of a stipulation be properly identified so that the gift is properly categorized.

Following is a list of factors to be considered by:

- Recipients (and donors) of gifts, in deciding whether a pledge or other gift which includes donor stipulations is conditional or restricted;
- Auditors, in assessing the appropriateness of the client's decision.

In many cases, no one of these factors will be determinative by itself; all applicable factors should be considered together.

Factors Whose Presence in the Communication from the Donor or the Donee-Prepared Pledge Card Would Indicate the Gift May Be Conditional	Factors Whose Presence in the Grant Document, Donor's Transmittal Letter, or Other Gift Instrument, or in the Appeal by the Recipient Would Indicate the Gift May Be Restricted
Factors related to the terms of the gift/pledge:	

1. The document uses words such as:
   If;*
   Subject to;*
   When;
   Revocable.*
	The document uses words such as:
	Must;
	For;
	Purpose;
	Irrevocable.

2. Neither the ultimate amount nor the timing of payment of the gift are clearly determinable in advance of payment.	At least one of the amount and/or timing are clearly specified.
3. The pledge is stated to extend for a very long period of time (over, say, 10 years) or is open-ended. (Often found with pledges to support a needy child overseas, or a missionary in the field.)	The time is short and/or specific as to its end.
4. The donor stipulations in the document refer to *outcomes* expected as a result of the activity (with the implication that if the outcomes are not achieved, the donor will expect the gift to be refunded, or will cancel future installments of a multi-period pledge.[1a])* (Such gifts are likely also restricted.)	The donor stipulations focus on the *activities* to be conducted. Although hoped-for outcomes may be implicit or explicit, there is not an implication that achievement of particular outcomes is a requirement.[1b]*
5. There is an explicit requirement that amounts not expensed by a specified date must be returned to the donor.	There is no such refund provision, or any refund is required only if money is left after completion of the specified activities.
6. The gift is in the form of a pledge.	The gift is a transfer of cash or other non-cash assets.
7. Payment of amounts pledged will be made only on a cost-reimbursement basis.(D)	Payment of the gift will be made up front, or according to a payment schedule, without the necessity for the donee to have yet incurred specific expenses.
8. The gift has an explicit matching requirement (D), or additional funding beyond that already available will be required to complete the activity.	Factor not present.
Factors relating to the circumstances surrounding the gift:	
9. The action or event described in the donor's stipulations is largely outside the control of the management or governing board of the donee.[2a]*	The action or event is largely within the donee's control.[2b]*
10. The activity comtemplated by the gift is one which the donee has not yet decided to do, and it is not yet certain whether the activity will actually be conducted.*	The donee is already conducting the activity, or it is fairly certain that the activity will be conducted.*
11. There is a lower probability that the donor stipulations will eventually be met.	There is a higher probability.
12. As to any tangible or intangible outcomes which are to be produced as a result of the activities, these products will be under the control of the donor. (In such cases, the payment may not be a gift at all; rather it may be a payment for goods or services.)	Any outcomes will be under the control of the donee

D-Presence of this factor would normally be considered determinative. Absence of the factor is not necessarily determinative.

*Factors which would generally be considered more important.

[1a] Examples of outcomes contemplated by this factor include:
- Successful creation of a new vaccine;
- Production of a new television program;
- Commissioning a new musical composition;
- Establishing a named professorship;
- Reduction in the teenage pregnancy rate in a community;
- Construction of a new building;
- Mounting a new museum exhibit.

[1b] Examples of activities contemplated by this factor include (but see Factor 10**):
- Conduct of scientific or medical research;
- Broadcasting a specified television program;
- Performing a particular piece of music;
- Paying the salary of a named professor;
- Counseling teenagers judged at risk of becoming pregnant;
- Operating a certain facility;
- Providing disaster relief.

[2a] Examples of events contemplated by this factor include:
- Actions of uncontrolled third parties, e.g.:
  - other donors making contributions to enable the donee to meet a matching requirement of this gift;
  - a government granting approval to conduct an activity (e.g., awarding a building or land use permit, or a permit to operate a medical facility);
  - an owner of other property required for the activity making the property available to the organization (by sale or lease);
- Natural and manmade disasters;
- Future action of this donor (such as agreeing to renew a multi-period pledge in subsequent periods);
- The future willingness and ability of a donor of personal services to continue to provide those services (see SFAS No. 116, par. 70, third sentence).

(Events outside of the donee's control, but which are virtually assured of happening anyway at a known time and place (e.g., astronomical or normal meteorological events), and the mere passage of time, are not conditions.)

[2b] Examples of events contemplated by this factor include (but see Factor 10**):
- Eventual use of the gift for the specified purpose (e.g., those listed in Note 1b above), or retention of the gift as restricted endowment;
- Naming a building for a specified person;
- Filing with the donor routine performance reports on the activities being conducted.

** There is a presumption here that the right column of Factor 10 applies.

APPENDIX 29–F: CONSIDERATION OF WHETHER ITEMS MAY BE REPORTED AS OPERATING OR NON-OPERATING (WITHIN THE CONTEXT OF ¶ 23 OF SFAS NO. 117)

Paragraph 23 of SFAS No. 117 leaves it to each organization (if it wishes to present a subtotal of "operating" results) to determine what it considers to be operating versus non-operating items in a statement of activity. If it is not obvious from the face of the statement what items are included or excluded in the operating subtotal, footnote disclosure of that distinction shall be made. Following are some items that might be considered as non-operating. This is not intended to express any preferences, nor to limit the types of items that a particular organization might report as non-operating, but merely to provide a list for consideration of various types of items.

Items that would usually be considered non-operating as to the current period:

- Extraordinary items
- Cumulative effects of accounting changes
- Correction of errors of prior periods
- Prior period adjustments, generally
- Results of discontinued operations.

Items that many persons might consider non-operating in some situations:

- Unrealized capital gains on investments carried at market value
- Unrelated business income (as defined in the Internal Revenue Code Section 512), and related expenses
- Contributions that qualify as "unusual grants," as defined in IRS Regulation § 1.509(a)-3(c)(3)
- Items that meet some, but not all, of the criteria in APB No. 30/SFAS No. 4 for extraordinary items, or APB No. 30/SFAS No. 16 for prior period adjustments.

Items that some persons might consider non-operating in some situations:

- Bequests and other "deferred gifts" (annuity, life income funds, etc.) received
- Gains and losses, generally (as defined in SFAC No. 6, pars. 82–89)
- Sales of goods/services which, although they are not considered unrelated under the Internal Revenue Code, are nevertheless peripheral to the organization's major activities
- Some "auxiliary activities" of colleges
- Revenue and expenses related to program activities not explicitly listed on the organization's IRS Form 1023
- Revenue and expenses directly related to transactions which are reported as financing or investing cash flows in the statement of cash flows; e.g., investment income not available for operating purposes, interest expense, write-offs of loans receivable, nonexpendable gifts (as contemplated by ¶ 30d of SFAS No. 117), adjustment of annuity liability
- Contributions having the characteristics of an "initial capital" contribution to an organization, even though they do not meet the requirements of an extraordinary item or an unusual grant.

Notes: The characterization of an item of expense as operating versus non-operating is not driven by its classification as program, management, or fund-raising expense.

In general, expenses should follow related revenue: e.g., if contributions are considered operating, then fundraising expenses normally would be also, and vice versa.

29.7 SOURCES AND SUGGESTED REFERENCES

American Institute of Certified Public Accountants, New York:

Accounting Standards Division, "Accounting for Joint Costs of Informational Materials and Activities of Not-for-Profit Organizations that Include a Fund-Raising Appeal," Statement of Position No. 87-2, 1987. (In process of revision)

Accounting Standards Division, "The Application of the Requirements of Accounting Research Bulletins, Opinions of the Accounting Principles Board, and Statements and Interpretations of the Financial Accounting Standards Board to Not-for-Profit Organizations," Statement of Position No. 94-2, 1994.

Accounting Standards Division, "Reporting of Related Entities by Not-for-Profit Organizations," Statement of Position No. 94-3, 1994.

Auditing Standards Division, "Compliance Auditing Considerations in Audits of Governmental Entities and Recipients of Governmental Financial Assistance," Statement on Auditing Standards No. 74, 1995.

Committee on College and University Accounting and Auditing, "Audits of Colleges and Universities, Including Statement of Position Issued by the Accounting Standards Division," Industry Audit Guide, 2nd ed., 1975. (In process of revision)

Committee on Not-for-Profit Organizations, "Audits of Not-for-Profit Organizations Receiving Federal Awards," Statement of Position No. 92-9, 1992.

Committee on Not-for-Profit Organizations, "Audit Guide for Not-for-Profit Organizations," to be published in 1996.

Committee on Voluntary Health and Welfare Organizations, "Audits of Voluntary Health and Welfare Organizations," Industry Audit Guide, 2nd ed., 1988. (In process of revision)

Health Care Committee, "Audits of Providers of Health Care Services, Including Statement of Position Issued by the Accounting Standards Division," Industry Audit Guide, 1990. (In process of revision)

Subcommittee on Nonprofit Organizations, "Audits of Certain Nonprofit Organizations," including "Accounting Principles and Reporting Practices for Certain Nonprofit Organizations," Statement of Position No. 78-10, 2nd ed., 1988. (In process of revision)

Anthony, R. N., *Financial Accounting in Nonbusiness Organizations: An Exploratory Study of Conceptual Issues,* Financial Accounting Standards Board, Norwalk, CT, 1978.

Anthony, R. N., and Young, D. W., *Management Control in Nonprofit Organizations,* Richard D. Irwin, Homewood, IL, 3rd ed., 1984.

Blazek, J., *Tax Planning and Compliance for Tax-Exempt Organizations: Forms, Checklists, Procedures,* John Wiley & Sons, New York, 2nd ed., 1993.

Cary, W. L., and Bright, C. B., *The Law and the Lore of Endowment Funds—Report to the Ford Foundation,* New York, 1969.

Daughtrey, W. H., Jr., and Gross, M. J., Jr., *Museum Accounting Handbook,* American Association of Museums, Washington, DC, 1978.

Financial Accounting Standards Board, Norwalk, CT:

Statements of Financial Accounting Concepts:

No. 4, "Objectives of Financial reporting By Nonbusiness Organizations," 1980;

No. 6, "Elements of Financial Statements," 1985.

Statements of Financial Accounting Standards:

No. 93, "Recognition of Depreciation by Not-for-Profit Organizations," Norwalk, CT, 1987.

No. 95, "Statement of Cash Flows," 1987.

No. 116, "Accounting for Contributions Received and Contributions Made," 1993.

No. 117, "Financial Statements of Not-for-Profit Organizations," 1993.

No. 124, "Accounting for Certain Investments Held by Not-for-Profit Organizations," 1995.

Evangelical Joint Accounting Committee, "Accounting and Financial Reporting Guide for Christian Ministries," Christian Management Association, Diamond Bar, CA, Revised edition, 1995.

Gross, Larkin, Bruttomesso, and McNally, *Financial and Accounting Guide for Not-for-Profit Organizations,* New York, John Wiley & Sons, 5th ed., 1995.

Holder, W. W., *The Not-for-Profit Organization Reporting Entity,* Philanthropy Monthly Press, New Milford, CT, 1986.

Hopkins, B. R., *A Legal Guide to Starting and Managing A Nonprofit Organization,* New York, John Wiley & Sons, 2nd ed., 1993.

Hopkins, B. R., *The Law of Tax-Exempt Organizations,* New York, John Wiley & Sons, 6th ed., 1992.

Hopkins, B. R., *The Law of Fund-Raising,* New York, John Wiley & Sons, 1991.

Hummel, J., *Starting and Running a Nonprofit Organization,* Minneapolis: University of Minnesota Press, 1980.

Larkin, R. F., "Accounting," Chapter 31 of *The Nonprofit Management Handbook—Operating Policies and Procedures,* New York, John Wiley & Sons, 1993; and 1994 Supplement.

Larkin, R. F., "Accounting Issues Relating to Fundraising," Chapter 2 of *Financial Practices for Effective Fundraising,* San Francisco, Jossey-Bass, Inc., 1994.

National Association of College and University Business Officers, *Financial Accounting and Reporting Manual for Higher Education,* Washington, DC, 1990. (In process of revision)

National Association of Independent Schools, *Business Management for Independent Schools,* 3rd ed., Boston: Author, 1987. (In process of revision)

National Health Council, National Assembly for Social Policy and Development, Inc., and United Way of America, *Standards of Accounting and Financial Reporting for Voluntary Health and Welfare Organizations,* 3rd ed., NHC, NASPD, and UWA, New York, 1988. (In process of revision)

Price Waterhouse LLP, New York:

> *The Audit Committee, the Board of Trustees of Not-for-Profit Organizations and the Independent Accountant,* 1992.

> *Effective Internal Accounting Control for Nonprofit Organizations,* 1988.

> *Not-for-Profit Organizations' Implementation Guide for SFAS Statements 116 and 117,* 1993.

United States Department of Health and Human Services, "Guidelines for Audits of Federal Awards to Nonprofit Organizations," DHHS, Washington, 1989.

United States General Accounting Office, "Government Auditing Standards," GAO, Washington, DC, 1994 Revision.

United States Office of Management and Budget Circulars, OMB, Washington:

> No. A-21, "Cost Principles for Educational Institutions," 1979. (In process of revision)

> No. A-110, "Uniform Administrative Requirements for Grants and Agreements with Institutions of Higher Education, Hospitals, and Other Nonprofit Organizations," 1993.

> No. A-122, "Cost Principles for Nonprofit Organizations," 1980. (In process of revision)

> No. A-128, "Audits of State and Local Governments," 1985. (In process of revision)

> No. A-133, "Audits of Institutions of Higher Education and Other Nonprofit Institutions," 1990. (In process of revision)

United States President's Council on Integrity & Efficiency, "Questions and Answers on OMB Circular A-133," Position Statement No. 6, PCIE, Washington, 1992.

United Way of America, Alexandria, VA:

> *Accounting and Financial Reporting: A Guide for United Ways and Not-For Profit Human Service Organizations,* 2nd ed., 1989.

> *Budgeting: A Guide for United Ways and Not-for-Profit Human Service Organizations,* 1975.

CHAPTER 30

PROVIDERS OF HEALTH CARE SERVICES

Martha Garner, CPA
Price Waterhouse LLP
Woodrin Grossman, CPA
Price Waterhouse LLP

CONTENTS

30.1 THE HEALTH CARE INDUSTRY

(a) OVERVIEW. Health care in the United States is provided by entities operating in all sectors of the economy. In the private sector, health care entities may be operated by religious organizations, owned by investors seeking a return on their investment or sponsored by local communities. Public sector health care entities are operated at the federal, state, and local government levels. Consequently, health care providers may be subject to different accounting and reporting standards depending upon their "ownership" and form of organization.

Traditionally, the primary providers of health care services have been physicians, hospitals, and nursing homes. In the 1980s, cost containment pressures in the industry forced the development of less costly means of delivering certain services. Health maintenance organizations and other prepaid health care plans, home health agencies, ambulatory surgery centers, and specialty hospitals are among the alternative delivery systems and diversifications that have flourished in this climate. The rapidly growing elderly population has also focused attention on retirement communities, particularly those that offer residents health care services ranging from emergency nursing services to long-term inpatient-type care. In short, today's health care providers cover a broad spectrum of activities.

(b) TAX-EXEMPT PROVIDERS. This sector consists mainly of health care entities that are organized, sponsored or operated by communities, religious groups, or private universities and medical schools. The fees charged by these not-for-profit business-oriented health care providers are intended to help the organization maintain its self-sustaining status rather than to maximize profit for an owner's benefit.

Tax-exempt health care entities are usually exempt from federal and state income taxes if they are operated exclusively for religious, charitable, scientific, or educational purposes and if no part of their net earnings inures to the benefit of any private shareholder or individual. However, they may be subject to taxes on income that is derived from activities not related to their tax-exempt purpose. Tax-exempt providers are allowed to generate profits in order to be able to meet financial obligations, improve patient care, expand facilities, and participate in research, training, education, and other activities that advance the entity's charitable purpose.

Although many tax-exempt health care entities may receive support from religious and fraternal organizations, individuals, corporations, and other donors or grantors, most are essentially self-sustaining; that is, they finance their capital needs primarily from the proceeds of debt issues and their operating needs largely from fees they charge for health care services rendered. As a result, accountability to creditors is more of a driving force in matters pertaining to financial statement presentation and disclosure of tax-exempt health care providers than it is for nonprofit organizations that rely primarily on outside support. Comparability with financial statements of providers in the governmental and investor-owned sectors is also important. Consequently, tax-exempt health care providers must keep up with accounting standards of the business sector as well as the not-for-profit sector.

(c) GOVERNMENTAL PROVIDERS.   Governmental health care entities are owned and operated by federal, state, city, or county governments or other political subdivisions. The sponsoring government may participate directly in the operation of the facility, or there may be little interaction between the facility and the governmental unit. Such entities generally receive varying levels of subsidies from their sponsoring governments. This may range from heavy subsidization to no financial support, depending on the entity's circumstances.

Federally sponsored hospitals include hospitals operated by the Veterans' Administration, military hospitals, federal prison hospitals, and certain long-term specialty hospitals. Federal hospitals follow federal accounting guidelines, and are excluded from the scope of this chapter.

For accounting and financial reporting purposes, state and local governmental health care providers are grouped into two categories. One group uses accounting and reporting rules designed for governmental entities whose operations are basically self-sustaining—the governmental equivalents of commercial businesses—and by other types of governmental entities for whom information on net income and capital maintenance is important. These entities generally follow what is termed "enterprise" fund accounting, and are referred to as "governmental business-type activities" by the Governmental Accounting Standards Board (GASB), which is the primary standard-setting body for governmental organizations. Other types of governmental operations generally follow "governmental-type" fund accounting. These operations often are set up as departments underneath the umbrella of a city, county or state government.

Thus far the GASB has not defined the term *governmental organization*. A November 1993 GASB/FASB paper, "Applicability of GASB Standards," provides a nonbinding definition of *governmental* that primarily is based on an entity's legal structure. A summary of the circumstances that would result in an entity being considered governmental, based on the GASB/FASB paper, follows:

- A municipal corporation (including cities, towns, counties, townships, villages, parishes, boroughs, school districts, special districts, public authorities, and so forth).
- Any organization declared by statute to be a "public corporation" or a "body corporate and politic."
- Any entity created that possesses one or more of the following characteristics: officers are popularly elected, the entity has power to tax, the entity has power to directly issue tax-exempt debt, or the entity can be dissolved by the government that created it and its assets assumed without compensation.

- Other factors that could indicate an entity is governmental include the right to governmental privileges, classification as governmental by the U.S. Bureau of Census, evidence of managerial control by a governmental entity, possession of other sovereign powers, exemption of income from federal taxation and, if an entity is acquired by the government rather than created by government, the purpose of the acquisition and its expected permanence.

The clarification of the requirements that result in an entity being classified as governmental is still uncertain until FASB or GASB issues a pronouncement that goes through due process.

(d) INVESTOR-OWNED PROVIDERS.   Investor-owned health care organizations are also known as "proprietary" providers. They may be organized as stock corporations (publicly traded or privately held), partnerships, or sole proprietorships. The majority of for-profit health care organizations are publicly traded, and therefore are also subject to Securities and Exchange Commission (SEC) reporting requirements.

30.2 AUTHORITATIVE PRONOUNCEMENTS

(a) GENERALLY ACCEPTED ACCOUNTING PRINCIPLES (GAAP)—PRIVATE SECTOR.
Tax-exempt business-oriented providers (as distinguished from voluntary health and welfare organizations, which are outside the scope of this chapter) generally follow the same accounting rules as do investor-owned health care providers, adjusting only for the special not-for-profit reporting requirements that have been established for those entities by the FASB. An example of an area in which the FASB has issued differing requirements is presentation of the income statement.

(b) GENERALLY ACCEPTED ACCOUNTING PRINCIPLES (GAAP)—PUBLIC SECTOR.
Since its inception in 1984, the Governmental Accounting Standards Board (GASB) has issued 29 statements and a number of interpretations of financial accounting and reporting standards that set forth accounting principles that must be followed by state and local government entities. Many GASB standards modify the requirements of FASB standards.

For purposes of applying the GASB standards, state and local governmental health care providers are grouped into two categories. One group uses accounting and reporting rules designed for governmental entities whose operations are basically self-sustaining—the governmental equivalents of commercial businesses—and by other types of governmental entities for whom information on net income and capital maintenance is important. These entities generally follow enterprise fund accounting, and are referred to by the GASB as governmental business-type activities or governmental enterprises. Other types of governmental operations generally follow true governmental fund accounting principles, identified by funds with names such as special revenue, debt service, and capital projects. These operations often are set up as departments under the umbrella of a city, county, or state government.

Most governmental health care organizations operate as enterprise-fund organizations because they are financed and operated in a manner similar to private-business enterprises. The principal feature of an enterprise fund is that its costs of providing goods and services are recovered through the use of charges for these goods and services rather than through tax revenues.

SAS No. 69, "The Meaning of 'Present Fairly in Conformity with Generally Accepted Accounting Principles' in the Independent Auditor's Report," significantly changed the hierarchy of GAAP for governmental health care enterprises. GAS No. 20, "Accounting and Financial Reporting for Proprietary Funds and Other Government Entities that Use Proprietary Fund Accounting, and GAS No. 29, "The Use of Not-for-Profit Accounting and Financial

Reporting Principles for Governmental Entities," provide interim guidance with respect to applying the provisions of SAS No. 69 to governmental enterprises that use business-type accounting and reporting principles (pending completion of a current GASB project in process on the accounting and reporting model for proprietary activities.). Relevant provisions are summarized as follows:

- Such health care enterprises should apply all GASB pronouncements (other than those that are clearly inapplicable, such as the GASB statements directed at nonbusiness type activities).

- In addition, they should apply all FASB Statements and Interpretations, APB Opinions, and ARBs issued on or before November 30, 1989, that do not conflict with or contradict GASB pronouncements.

- Furthermore, such enterprises *may* elect to apply all FASB Statements and Interpretations issued after November 30, 1989, that do not conflict with or contradict GASB pronouncements (GAS No. 20, par. 7). Entities that choose to apply these "new" FASB pronouncements must apply them on an all-or-none basis (this is, they may not pick and choose among the pronouncements they wish to apply). The GASB's intent in allowing this option was to permit those governmental providers that traditionally have been accounted for in the same manner as investor-owned and tax-exempt health care enterprises to continue to do so, pending the GASB's issuance of accounting and financial reporting standards for proprietary activities. Therefore, governmental providers that elect this option may apply only those "new" FASB pronouncements that are developed for *business enterprises*. They may not apply FASB Statements and Interpretations whose provisions are limited to not-for-profit organizations (for example, FAS No. 117), or those that address issues concerning primarily such organizations (such as FAS No. 116).

- The AICPA audit and accounting guide, *Health Care Organizations,* is specifically applicable to governmental providers that elect to follow GAS No. 20, par. 7. and it was cleared by the GASB prior to issuance. Therefore, under the governmental GAAP hierarchy it constitutes category (b) guidance for those entities. However, the guide incorporates the guidance set forth in FAS No. 116 (for contributions) and FAS No. 117 (for financial statement display); these FASB pronouncements are not applicable to governmental health care enterprises (GAS No. 29). As a result, governmental providers are required to disregard the provisions of *Health Care Organizations* with regard to contributions and financial statement display. For those areas, governmental providers should instead continue to follow the guidance set forth in the predecessor guide, *Audits of Providers of Health Care Services.*

(c) SEC REPORTING REQUIREMENTS. Although a great many investor-owned health care organizations are publicly-traded, at this time there are no unique SEC rules pertaining specifically to health care providers.

(d) HFMA PRINCIPLES AND PRACTICES BOARD. In 1975, the Healthcare Financial Management Association (HFMA), a major trade organization in the health care industry, founded a Principles and Practices Board (P&P Board). This committee consists of distinguished individuals in the field of health care accounting and finance who set forth advisory recommendations on health care accounting and reporting issues which are not addressed in FASB statements or the Guide. Although these statements have no authoritative status, they are valuable to the health care community because they disseminate well thought out opinions, along with views on the issues and relevant background information, regarding issues on which information would not otherwise be available. Information on statements issued by the P&P Board can be obtained from HFMA; Two Westbrook Corporate Center, Suite 700; Westchester, IL 60154; (800) 252-HFMA.

(e) AICPA AUDIT GUIDE. The AICPA is the primary source of guidance relating to industry-specific accounting principles and reporting practices for health care organizations. Throughout this chapter, the principles outlined herein are those contained in the AICPA audit and accounting guide, *Health Care Organizations,** issued in 1996.

Generally speaking, the Guide applies to all entities whose principal operations involve providing (or agreeing to provide, in the case of prepaid health care arrangements) health care services to individuals. This includes (but is not limited to) hospitals, including specialty facilities such as psychiatric or rehabilitation hospitals; nursing homes; subacute care facilities; HMOs and other providers of prepaid health care services; CCRCs; home health companies; ambulatory care companies such as clinics, medical group practices, individual practice associations, and individual practitioners; emergency care facilities; surgery centers; outpatient rehabilitation and cancer treatment centers; and integrated health care delivery systems (also called health networks) that include one or more of these types of organizations. It also applies to organizations whose primary activities are the planning, organization, and oversight of entities providing health care services, such as parent or holding companies of health care providers.

There are some exceptions to this general rule, based on the health care organization's ownership characteristics.

- The audit guide applies to all such entities described above that are operated in the investor-owned sector.
- With regard to entities described above that operate in the not-for-profit sector, the guide adds another parameter to the definition: in addition to the provision of health care services the organization must also derive all or almost all of its revenues from provision of goods and services. This is directed at certain health care organizations which provide health care services, but whose primary source of income is contribution income rather than revenues earned in exchange for providing (or agreeing to provide) health care services. Those types of organizations (defined in FAS No. 117, par. 168 as "voluntary health and welfare organizations") thereafter would fall within the scope of the AICPA Audit and Accounting Guide *Audits of Not-for-Profit Organizations,* rather than the health care guide.
- The guide is specifically applicable to governmental providers that elect to follow GAS No. 20, par. 7, and it was cleared by the GASB prior to issuance. Therefore, it meets the GASB's criteria for classification as category (b) guidance under the governmental GAAP hierarchy. However, governmental health care enterprises are instructed in GAS No. 29 to disregard the provisions of the guide that deal with contributions and financial statement display based on FAS No. 116 and FAS No. 117 (see subsection 30.2(b)). For those areas, governmental providers should instead continue to follow the guidance set forth in the predecessor guide *Audits of Providers of Health Care Services.*

30.3 ACCOUNTING PRINCIPLES

(a) FUND ACCOUNTING. Not-for-profit and governmental hospitals traditionally have used fund accounting for recordkeeping and financial reporting purposes. This accounting technique helps those providers to carry out their fiduciary responsibilities in ensuring that donor-restricted resources are used only for the purposes specified by the donor or grantor. For health care organizations, only two major fund groupings are permitted: *general funds* and *donor-restricted funds.* For purposes of external financial reporting, these internal fund

---

*Previous editions were the *Hospital Audit Guide* (1972) and *Audits of Providers of Health Care Services* (1990).

groupings must be classified into one or more of three broad classes of net assets: unrestricted, temporarily restricted or permanently restricted.

(i) Unrestricted (General) Funds.   Assets and liabilities which are free of any donor-imposed restrictions are included in this fund grouping. They represent the net assets available for any purpose, at the discretion of the provider's board of directors or trustees. This fund grouping generally includes the provider's working capital, long-term debt, and investment in property plant and equipment. It also includes assets whose use is limited to a particular purpose (see subsection 30.3(b)).

(ii) Donor-Restricted Funds.   Assets that are specifically restricted to use for a particular purpose by an external donor or grantor, along with any related obligations, are included in this fund grouping. Although donor-imposed restrictions may require individual gifts or grants to be kept separate for record-keeping purposes, as a general rule they may be grouped for financial reporting purposes. Groupings are determined based on whether the restrictions are temporary or permanent, and on the uses for which the resources are intended. The nature of restrictions on donor-restricted resources, if such amounts are material, should be disclosed in the financial statements.

(b) ASSETS WHOSE USE IS LIMITED.   The balance sheet caption "assets whose use is limited" includes:

- Assets whose use is limited by external parties (other than donors or grantors) under terms of debt indentures, trust agreements such as self-insurance arrangements, and assets required to be set aside to meet statutory reserve requirements (such as those required under state law for many HMOs).
- Assets set aside by the governing board for identified purposes (i.e., board-designated assets). The board retains control over them and may, at its discretion, subsequently use them for other purposes.

Providers who wish to report board-designated assets under this caption on the balance sheet must distinguish them from externally designated assets whose use is limited. This distinction is considered important because of the degree of control an organization is able to maintain over the uses of internally designated funds.

(c) AGENCY FUNDS.   Health care entities may act as agents for other parties; as such, they receive and hold assets that are owned by others. An example of this would be patients' or residents' funds. These are funds held by the facility for the patient's or resident's own personal use, such as for purchasing periodicals, making trips outside the facility, or for other incidentals. Usually, these funds are kept in an account separate from the facility's own cash accounts. In accepting responsibility for these assets, the entity incurs a liability to the owner either to return them in the future or to disburse them to another party on behalf of the owner. Transactions involving agency funds (for example, disbursements, interest earned) should not have any economic impact on the provider's operations. Consequently, they should not be included in the provider's income statement.

(d) PATIENT AND RESIDENT SERVICE REVENUE.   In hospitals and nursing homes, the primary source of income is patient service revenue, which arises from routine nursing services to patients and from other professional (ancillary) services. In a home health agency, revenue primarily arises from home visits and other services to patients. These types of revenue also are referred to as patient service revenue (or sometimes as client service revenue). The primary revenues in a CCRC arise from monthly service fees paid by residents (if called for by the contract), amortization of deferred entrance fees, and services provided to nonresidents in the community's nursing home (if applicable). This is known as *resident service revenue.*

In hospitals, nursing homes, and home health agencies, a significant portion of health care services are paid for by third parties such as Medicare, Medicaid, Blue Cross, commercial insurance companies, and prepaid health care plans such as HMOs. The domination of any particular type of payor varies by industry, based on the payor's primary orientation. For example, the Medicare program is geared toward short-term acute care services or rehabilitative care. The Medicaid program, on the other hand, is designed to provide health care services to low-income individuals for an unlimited period of time, which often may include long-term health care services. Like Medicare, commercial insurance companies also are major payors for acute care and rehabilitative services.

- For hospitals, the primary payors are Medicare, Medicaid, commercial insurance, Blue Cross, and prepaid health care plans.
- Nearly half of the patients cared for in nursing homes are considered "private pay" (that is, the patient or their family pays for the care). For the remainder, Medicaid is the dominant third-party payor. Little commercial insurance coverage presently exists for nursing home care, and Medicare provides very limited nursing home benefits.
- The Medicare program often is the primary source of revenue for short-term rehabilitation services in the home health industry. Home health agency services may also be paid for by grants from local governments and charitable organizations (such as United Way). Because of the unilateral nature of these payments, amounts received from these types of organizations should be accounted for as contributions or grants, rather than as amounts received from third-party payors. Other sources of revenue for home health agencies include commercial insurance and Medicaid.
- Entrance fees and monthly service fees in CCRCs are paid by the residents themselves; therefore, third-party payors have little involvement (except for payment of some services provided in the health care section of the facility).

Under many of these payment arrangements, providers receive payment amounts that are less than their full established rates. For internal recordkeeping purposes, providers should record revenue (and the related receivables) from providing services to patients or residents at their established rates, regardless of how much payment the provider actually expects to collect. The revenue should be recorded on an accrual basis; in other words, it should be recognized as services are rendered. Any differences between the established rates for covered services and the amounts paid by third parties should be accounted for as a contractual adjustment (also called a contractual allowance). These adjustments also should be recorded on an accrual basis.

Because providers often less in payment than their full established rates, and the amounts received bear little relationship to established charges, reporting gross charges in the financial statements has little meaning for many financial statement users. Consequently, the Guide instructs providers to report only the amount of their net service revenue (that is, gross charges less contractual adjustments and other deductions from revenue) in the Statement of Operations. This is more of an issue for hospitals, nursing homes and home health agencies than it is for CCRCs, which usually have little in the way of contractual allowances.

(e) PREMIUM REVENUE.   Premium revenue constitutes the primary income source of prepaid health care plans such as HMOs and PPOs, and of integrated delivery systems. Premium revenue arises when a prepaid health care plan accepts a fixed, predetermined amount in exchange for *agreeing to provide* services to a specified group of individuals (regardless of the level of services actually provided).

(f) SETTLEMENTS WITH THIRD-PARTY PAYORS.   Payments under contracts with third-party payors such as Medicare, Medicaid and HMOs often are based on estimates. In most cases, these payments are subject to adjustment either during the contract term or afterward, when the actual level of services provided under the contract is known. Often, final settlements are determined after the close of the fiscal period to which they apply. In the interim, additional information may be available which will necessitate revision of the estimate. Such settlements have the potential to materially affect the health care entity's financial position and results of operations. The health care entity must make its best estimate of these adjustments on a current basis, and reflect these amounts in the Statement of Operations. To the extent that the subsequent actual adjustments are more or less than the estimate, such amounts should be reflected in the Statement of Operations for the period in which the final adjustment becomes known. It is not appropriate to reflect such amounts as prior period adjustments. The Guide requires disclosure of material differences between third-party settlement estimates and subsequent revisions, consistent with the trend toward providing more information regarding estimates.

(g) BAD DEBTS. The Guide defines bad debt expense as "the provision for actual or expected uncollectibles resulting from the extension of credit." The provision for bad debts should be determined on an accrual basis and reported as an expense.

(h) CHARITY CARE. Providers often render services free of charge (or at discounted rates) to individuals who have no means to pay for them. The accounting for the writeoff of charges pertaining to charity services is similar to that for bad debts; an allowance for charity services should be established, which is a valuation account related to patient accounts receivable. The provision for charity services should be determined on an accrual basis and accounted for as a deduction from gross revenue.

Special rules apply to the reporting of charity care in the provider's financial statements. According to the Guide, charity care results from an entity's policy to provide health care services free of charge to individuals who meet certain financial criteria. Because no cash flows are expected from these services, charges pertaining to charity services do not qualify for recognition as revenue in the provider's financial statements. The provider is considered to have given away the services, rather than having "sold" them. Receivables reported in the balance sheet for health care services and the related valuation allowance similarly should not include amounts related to charity care. These prohibitions hold true on the face of the financial statements and in any note disclosures or supplemental schedules that accompany the financial statements.

However, the Guide does not intend for all mention of charity care to disappear from the financial statements. Charity care represents an important element of the services provided by many facilities. Accordingly, the Guide requires specific disclosures regarding charity care to be made in the notes to the financial statements. A statement of management's policy with regard to providing charity care, and the fact that charity services do not result in the production of revenue, should be included in the entity's "summary of significant accounting policies." The level of charity care provided for each of the years covered by the financial statements also must be disclosed in the notes to the financial statements. The level of care provided may be measured in a variety of ways, such as at established rates, costs, patient days, occasions of service, or other statistics. The method used to measure the charity care should also be disclosed. These disclosures are applicable to for-profit providers as well as not-for-profit providers.

The Guide recognizes that distinguishing charity care writeoffs from bad debt writeoffs is not easy in the health care environment. Because charity care results from an entity's policy to provide health care services free of charge to individuals who meet certain financial criteria, the establishment of a formal management policy clearly defining charity care should result in a reasonable determination, according to the Guide.

Some facilities may choose to provide information concerning gross service revenue and deductions from revenue in either the notes to the financial statements or in a supplemental schedule. If this type of financial statement disclosure is made, the amount shown as gross service revenue may not include charges attributable to services provided to charity patients, and deductions from revenue may not include the provision for charity care.

Contributions, bequests, and grants received that are restricted to be used for care of charity patients are considered to be directly related to the provision of health care services, and are normally classified as "other revenue" when they are expended for their intended purpose, regardless of the provider's accounting policy with regard to other types of contributions and grants. It is not appropriate to account for and report such funds as a reduction of the provision for charity care.

(i) REPORTING REVENUES, EXPENSES, GAINS, AND LOSSES. By definition, income arising from the direct provision of health care services to patients, clients, or residents is classified as revenue, and the cost of providing those services similarly is classified as expense. Similarly, premium income in HMOs is directly related to the provision of, arranging for, or agreeing to provide health care services and therefore should be classified as revenue. Costs related to the provision of, arranging for, or agreeing to provide health care services in a prepaid health care plan should be classified as expense.

Aside from the provision of health care services, a number of other activities are normal in the day-to-day operation of a health care facility. Such income should be accounted for separately from health care service revenue. Examples include:

- Sales of medical and pharmacy supplies to employees, physicians, and others.
- Proceeds from sales of cafeteria meals and guest trays to employees, medical staff, and visitors.
- Proceeds from sales of scrap, used x-ray film, etc.
- Proceeds from sales at gift shops, snack bars, newsstands, parking lots, vending machines, and other service facilities operated by the entity.
- Income from education programs.
- Rental of facility space.
- Income from transportation services provided to residents.
- Investment income.

(j) CONCENTRATIONS OF CREDIT RISK. FASB Statement No. 105, *Disclosure of Information About Financial Instruments With Off-Balance Sheet Risk and Financial Instruments With Concentrations of Credit Risk,* requires disclosure of information about significant concentrations of credit risk from third parties for all financial instruments. The term "financial instruments" as used in FAS No. 105 includes trade accounts receivable. Concentration of credit risk is usually an issue for hospitals and physician groups because of the emergency nature of many of the services provided and because they generally tend to treat patients from their local or surrounding communities. An economic event, such as the closing of a large industrial plant, may leave many of the community's residents without insurance. Since an accident or illness requiring an individual to incur hospitalization expense usually is not a matter of choice, many who partake of a provider's services are unable to pay for those services. Hospitals that participate in federal programs cannot deny services to patients who are perceived to be bad credit risks. Therefore, hospitals frequently extend a great deal of unsecured credit. It should be noted that the concentration of credit risk for an individual hospital is different that it would be for a national multihospital system that includes the individual hospital. When the individual facilities' financial statements are consolidated into statements prepared for the entire system, the credit risk is spread over a much larger geographic area, and is therefore not as concentrated. These concepts are illustrated by the following disclosure examples:

- *Disclosure in stand-alone financial statements of a local hospital.* The Hospital is located in (City, State). The Hospital grants credit without collateral to its patients, most of whom are local residents and are insured under third-party payor agreements. Net receivables from patients and third-party payors were as follows:

	19X1	19X0
Medicare and Medicaid	45%	43%
Blue Cross	10	13
Other private third-party payors	33	34
Self-pay	12	10
	100%	100%

- *Disclosure in consolidated financial statements of a national hospital chain.* The Company receives payment for services rendered to patients from (i) the federal and state governments under the Medicare and Medicaid programs, (ii) privately sponsored managed care programs for which payment is made based on terms defined under formal contracts, and (iii) other payors. The following table summarizes the percent of gross accounts receivable from all payors as of (Month/Day), 19X2 and 19X1, respectively:

	19X1	19X0
Government	39%	36%
Contracted	23	20
Other	38	44
	100%	100%

Receivables from government agencies represent the only concentrated group of credit risk for the Company and management does not believe that there are any credit risks associated with these governmental agencies. Contracted and other receivables consist of receivables from various payors, including individuals involved in diverse activities, subject to differing economic conditions, and do not represent any concentrated credit risks to the Company. Furthermore, management continually monitors and adjusts its reserves and allowances associated with these receivables.

(k) CONTRIBUTIONS. *Health Care Organizations* "scopes out" (i.e., excludes) health care providers that derive their revenues primarily from contributions from the general public, rather than from fees received in exchange for goods and services. Those organizations instead are required to follow the financial reporting requirements applicable to voluntary health and welfare organizations and other eleemosynary organizations (discussed in Chapter 29).

(i) Tax-Exempt Providers. For tax exempt providers, the accounting and reporting of contributions received and contributions made is generally governed by FAS No. 116, adjusted in certain areas by more restrictive implementing guidance issued by the AICPA Health Care Committee. The guidance contained in *Health Care Organizations* reflects that implementing guidance on how FAS No. 116 should be applied to tax-exempt health care organizations.

A comprehensive treatment of FAS No. 116 is contained in Chapter 29. The major areas in which *Health Care Organizations* differs from FAS No. 116 are as follows:

- The most significant difference pertains to "capital" contributions—that is, donations received or pledged toward upgrading or replacing a facility's land, buildings and equipment. Gifts or grants that are restricted for construction or renovation projects, property or equipment purchases, or capital debt retirement are added to unrestricted net assets when the assets are received. The guide requires tax-exempt health care providers to exclude such contributions from net income (i.e., report them below the operating indicator in the Statement of Operations).

- The guide requires providers to recognize the expiration of donor restrictions at the time the asset is placed in service. This is a narrowing of the options available to other types of not-for-profit organizations under FAS No. 116.

(ii) Governmental Providers. GAS No. 29 prohibits governmental health care providers from adopting FAS No. 116's accounting and reporting requirements. Instead, governmental health care entities should follow the guidance set forth in the predecessor guide, *Audits of Providers of Health Care Services.* That guidance is summarized in the following paragraphs.

Unrestricted Contributions, Bequests, and Grants. These items are recorded in the Statement of Revenues and Expenses. As a general rule, they will be classified as either "nonoperating gains" or "other revenue" depending on whether they are "ongoing, major or central" or "peripheral or incidental" to the health care entity's operations.

Restricted Contributions, Bequests, and Grants. Contributions, grants, and bequests that are restricted by the donor or grantor to be used in a particular manner must be shown as an addition to the appropriate restricted fund balance on the Statement of Changes in Fund Balances in the year received. The accounting for the disposition of the restricted contribution depends on the nature of the fund, as shown next.

Specific Purpose Funds. Resources received from donors or grantors that are restricted for specific operating purposes are recorded as additions to the appropriate restricted fund balance when received. When expended for their intended purpose, they are transferred out of the specific purpose fund and reported in the Statement of Revenue and Expenses.

Plant Replacement and Expansion Funds. Resources received from donors or grantors that are restricted for additions to property and equipment or for capital debt retirement are recorded as additions to the appropriate restricted fund balance when received. When expended for their intended purpose, they are reclassified to the general fund balance; they are not reported as revenue. Similarly, property and equipment donated for hospital operations should be recorded as an addition to the restricted fund balance in an amount equal to the fair value at the date of receipt; a transfer to the general fund balance should be made when the assets are placed in service.

Term Endowment Funds. Term endowments are reported as additions to the appropriate restricted fund balance when received. When donor-imposed time or conditional restrictions are satisfied on term endowments, they are reported in the Statement of Revenue and Expenses if there is no further restriction on their use.

Permanent Endowments. Permanent endowments are reported as additions to the appropriate restricted fund balance when received. Permanent endowments can never be expended, so they will always remain in a restricted endowment fund balance.

Pledges. Pledges, less an allowance for uncollectible amounts, should be recorded as a receivable in the year the pledge is made. Income from unrestricted pledges should be recorded on the entity's books in the same manner as any other unrestricted gift. Restricted pledges should be reported as additions to the appropriate restricted fund balances.

Donated Services. The nature and extent of donated services in health care entities varies, ranging from limited participation in fund-raising activities to significant participation in operating the facility. The value of donated services generally is not recorded in the financial statements of health care entities.

Donated Assets.   Donations of assets other than cash should be recorded at the fair market value of the assets on the date of the contribution. Donations of property and equipment are discussed in the section, Plant, Replacement and Expansion Funds. Donations of other types of assets (such as investments or supplies), if unrestricted, are recorded in the Statement of Revenues and Expenses. If restricted, such donations are recorded as an addition to the appropriate restricted fund balance; a transfer to the general fund is reported when the donated asset is used for the specific purpose for which it was intended.

(iii) Donated Funds Held in Trust by Others.   Occasionally a donor will set up with an outside trustee an endowment fund, the income from which is to be given to the health care entity. If the health care entity is the remainderman in the trust, the donated funds may be reported in the entity's balance sheet (depending on the terms of the trust document).

If the health care entity does not control the principal and is not the remainderman in the trust, these funds should not be included in the entity's balance sheet, although their existence should be disclosed. If the trustee is obligated to make distributions to the hospital, these distributions should be reported on an accrual basis as investment income. The right to future income and the amount of principal held in the trust may be disclosed if appropriate. If the trustee has discretion over distributions, the entity reports the distribution as instructed under the trust instrument or by the trustee.

(iv) Fund-Raising Foundations.   Frequently, not-for-profit health care entities will create separate "foundations" to raise and hold funds for their benefit. The primary motivation of setting up these separate organizations has been to insure that third-party payors could not insist that unrestricted gifts be used to offset hospital costs for in determining third-party settlement amounts. The Guide contains guidance on determining whether the health care entity must combine its financial statements with those of related fund-raising foundations, or make disclosures of those relationships.

When separate statements are prepared for related fund-raising foundations, the reporting should follow the guidance contained in the AICPA guide, *Not-for-Profit Organizations.*

The GASB is studying issues related to fund-raising and other organizations affiliated with governmental entities to determine what, if any, characteristics of these organizations should warrant their inclusion in the financial statements of the primary entity. This creates the potential for different treatment of these organizations by public sector and private sector health care organizations.

(l) INVESTMENTS

(i) Investments in Debt Securities and Certain Equity Securities

- *Investor-Owned Providers.* For-profit health care enterprises are required to follow the accounting and reporting requirements set forth in FASB Statement No. 115, "Accounting for Certain Investments in Debt and Equity Securities."
- *Tax-exempt providers.* Tax-exempt providers are subject to the requirements of FAS No. 124, *Accounting for Certain Investments of Not-for-Profit Organizations,* as interpreted by the AICPA Health Care Committee and cleared by the FASB. That guidance is provided in *Health Care Organizations.* Generally speaking, for classification purposes within the statement of operations, guidance similar to FAS No. 115 with respect to classification and reporting of unrealized gains/losses by class of investments (i.e., trading securities) should be followed. Unrealized gains/losses on trading portfolios are reported as a component of net income (i.e., above the operating indicator); other unrealized gains/losses will be reported outside of (below) net income in the statement of operations.
- *Governmental providers.* Governmental providers that follow the provisions of GAS No. 20, par. 7 follow the requirements of FAS No. 115. All others are required to follow

the guidance set forth in the predecessor guide, *Audits of Providers of Health Care Services.* GASB Statement No. 3, *Deposits with Financial Institutions, Investments (including Repurchase Agreements), and Reverse Repurchase Agreements* requires all governmental providers to make certain note disclosures about the credit and market risks of their investments, and provides guidance on accounting for repurchase and reverse repurchase agreements.

(ii)   Unconsolidated Affiliates.   Investments in unconsolidated affiliates (such as joint ventures) are accounted for in accordance with APB Opinion No. 18.

(iii)   Other Securities.   Other types of investments not addressed above (such as real estate or oil and gas interests) should be reported at the lower of amortized cost or a reduced amount if an impairment in their value is deemed to be other than temporary.

(m) DEFERRED START-UP COSTS FOR NEW FACILITIES.   Certain sectors of the health care industry have experienced rapid growth through opening new facilities. In certain circles, there are indications that the SEC will accept deferral of development costs for these facilities (such as certificate of need costs, legal costs, and costs to obtain permits) and also will accept certain costs incurred during the period prior to opening the new facility. Deferred development costs normally are written off over ten years. Deferred pre-opening costs normally are written off over three years; however, in some cases entities have been able to make an argument for amortizing costs that will be reimbursed by Medicare for five years. The rationale to do so is to provide better matching of operating expenses with the periods in which they are expected to be paid by the Medicare program.

(n) DISCLOSURE OF OFF-BALANCE SHEET RISK.   FASB Statement No. 105, *Disclosure of Information About Financial Instruments With Off-Balance Sheet Risk and Financial Instruments With Concentrations of Credit Risk,* requires certain disclosures when there are material financial instruments with off-balance-sheet risk of accounting losses, such as guarantees on loans to physicians or related parties. An example of such a disclosure for a health care entity is as follows:

> The Company has other investments, notes receivable and investments in and advances to companies and affiliates in the long-term care industry totalling $100 million. These companies have high debt-to-equity ratios as a result of leveraged buyout transactions. These amounts are expected to be repaid from cash flows of the individual companies. Collateral consists of first or second mortgages, personal guarantees, and pledges of certain other assets.

(o) PROPERTY AND EQUIPMENT.   The property and equipment accounts represent the provider's actual investment in plant assets, land, building, leasehold improvements, and equipment. Property that is not used for general operations (such as property held for future expansion or investment purposes) should be presented separately from property used in general operations.

Property and equipment should be recorded at cost, or at fair market value if donated. Where historical cost records are not available, an appraisal at historical cost should be made and the amounts recorded in the provider's books.

The amount of depreciation expense should be shown separately (or combined with amortization of leased assets) in the Statement of Operations. The Guide states that the American Hospital Association's "Estimated Useful Lives of Depreciable Hospital Assets" publication may be helpful in determining the estimated useful lives of fixed assets of health care providers.

(p) INTANGIBLE ASSETS.   The increased level of mergers and acquisitions among health care organizations has heightened the SEC's interest in filings by public health care companies, particularly with regard to purchase price allocation, goodwill amortization periods, contingent consideration, and goodwill impairment.

(i) Allocation of Purchase Price.   APB No. 16 requires that all identifiable assets purchased in an acquisition transaction be assigned a portion of the cost of the acquired company. The SEC is concerned that in sectors of the industry where tangible assets often are not significant, such as in the health care management sector, such identifiable intangible assets are not being valued separately and amortized. As a result, the SEC has increased its scrutiny of allocation of purchase price issues in filings by health care companies. In evaluating the propriety of accounting and reporting of intangibles, the SEC is focusing on allocations to purchased intangibles such as management contracts, workforce in place, covenants not to compete, etc.

(ii) Goodwill Amortization Period.   A related area of heightened SEC scrutiny concerns the length of the amortization period assigned to both identifiable intangible assets and goodwill. In particular, the SEC has announced that it will challenge assignments of lives of more than 20 years to goodwill, alleging that significantly increased competition, industry consolidation, changing third-party reimbursement requirements, technological innovation and an uncertain regulatory future make it difficult to assert that an acquired business will survive and provide a competitive advantage for longer than that time. However, longer lives of up to 40 years sometimes are sustained if the facts and circumstances of a health care company's particular situation warrant it.

(iii) Contingent Consideration.   Contingent consideration, also referred to as "earn-out" arrangements, provide for additional amounts to be paid to the selling shareholders contingent on the occurrence of specified events or transactions in the future. One accounting question associated with contingent consideration is whether it should be accounted for as additional purchase price or as compensation expense. This issue may be particularly relevant in the acquisition of a healthcare provider if the owners of the selling company are physicians or other health care professionals who continue to be employed by and provide health care services on behalf of the combined entity after the acquisition.

This issue recently was addressed in EITF No. 95-8, *Accounting for Contingent Consideration Paid to the Shareholders of an Acquired Company in a Purchase Business Combination.* The EITF reached a consensus that the determination of whether contingent consideration should be recorded as part of the purchase price or as compensation expense is a matter of judgment that will depend on the relevant facts and circumstances.

(iv) Goodwill Impairment.   The current industry climate of restructuring, mergers and realignments has increased the risk that previously recorded goodwill and other intangibles may be impaired. For example, a merger may result in the reduction of services provided by a particular entity within the combined organization and significantly reduce its ability to generate future cash flows. Even more significant may be the health care provider that is left out of all integrated delivery systems in a particular geographic area and loses its ability to compete. In these instances, the carrying amounts of recorded intangible assets may not be recoverable and provisions of FAS No. 121 will need to be applied.

(q) LEASES.   Governmental health care entities with certain types of operating leases must follow the additional accounting and disclosure requirements of GASB Statement No. 13, *Accounting for Operating Leases with Scheduled Rent Increases.*

(r) LONG-TERM DEBT REFUNDINGS.   Health care entities generally follow the same accounting and reporting rules for extinguishments of debt as do other business enterprises.

GASB Statement No. 7, *Advance Refundings Resulting in Defeasance of Debt,* requires governmental providers to made additional disclosures regarding the economic gain or loss resulting from an advance refunding resulting in defeasance of debt. The accounting and financial reporting requirements for advance refundings (and current refundings) entered into by governmental health care entities are set forth in GASB Statement No. 23, *Accounting and Financial Reporting for Refundings of Debt Reported by Proprietary Activities.*

(s) MALPRACTICE CONTINGENCIES.   The Guide states that the ultimate costs of malpractice claims should be accrued when the incidents occur that give rise to the claims, if certain criteria are met. These criteria include a determination that a liability has been incurred and an ability to make a reasonable estimate of the amount of the loss. In particular, the Guide indicates clearly that health care providers that have not transferred to a third-party all risk for medical malpractice claims arising out of occurrences prior to the financial statement date will probably be required to make an accrual. The Guide provides guidance in accounting for uninsured asserted and unasserted medical malpractice claims, claims insured by captive insurance companies, claims insured under retrospectively-rated or claims-made insurance policies, and claims paid from self-insurance trust funds. Governmental health care entities should also consider the accounting and disclosure requirements of GASB Statement No. 10, *Accounting and Financial Reporting for Risk Financing and Related Insurance Issues,* with regard to contingencies such as malpractice.

(t) PENSIONS AND OTHER POST-EMPLOYMENT BENEFITS (OPEB).   Private-sector health care entities follow the same accounting and reporting rules for pensions and other post-employment benefits as do other business enterprises. Governmental health care entities have different pension accounting and disclosure requirements; these are set forth in GASB Statement No. 4, *Applicability of FASB Statement No. 87, "Employers' Accounting for Pensions," to State and Local Government Employers,* GASB Statement No. 5, *Disclosure of Pension Information by Public Employee Retirement Systems and State and Local Governmental Employers,* and GASB Statement No. 27, *Accounting for Pensions by State and Local Governmental Employees.* With regard to OPEB, GASB Statement No. 12, *Disclosure of Information on Postemployment Benefits Other Than Pension Benefits by State and Local Governmental Employers* provides that state and local government employers are not required to adopt FASB's guidance on accounting and financial reporting of OPEB because the GASB is working on a project dealing with those issues; however, it does not prohibit governmental providers operated as enterprise funds from adopting the FASB's rules, if they desire to do so.

(u) RELATED ORGANIZATIONS.   Most for-profit health care entities are part of multientity corporate structures. The accounting and reporting rules applicable to those entities are the same as those for investments made by any other for-profit business.

   In response to the massive changes that have taken place in the health care industry during the last two decades, there has been a widespread movement to diversify the activities of not-for-profit and governmental health care providers. This diversification has been reflected in the proliferation of complex multientity corporate structures, as well as in more numerous mergers and acquisitions. Such changes in organizational structure are often undertaken to recognize results of diverse activities, enhance access to capital, respond to regulatory pressures, help the entity to compete more effectively, or to protect assets. The Guide provides guidance for determining whether or not the health care entity must combine or consolidate its financial statements with those of related organizations.

   GASB Statement No. 14, *The Financial Reporting Entity,* sets forth standards for defining and reporting on the governmental financial reporting entity; it also established standards for reporting participation in joint ventures. It is applicable to the separately issued financial statements of governmental component units, which specifically includes governmental health care providers; it should also be applied to such component units when they are included in a governmental reporting entity. The statement also requires certain disclosures about the entity's relationships with organizations other than component units, including related organizations, joint ventures, and jointly owned operations, among others.

(v) TIMING DIFFERENCES. For Medicare cost reporting purposes, certain items are accounted for in different periods than they are reported in for financial reporting purposes. The "timing differences" that arise from these items are recognized in the periods in which the differences arise and the periods in which they reverse. Common examples involve deferred compensation arrangements, uses of different depreciation methods for financial reporting and cost reporting purposes, malpractice expense, and reporting of gains or losses on debt extinguishments.

Changes in Medicare regulations may cause some of these timing differences to become permanent. In such cases, the Guide states that the effect should be recorded in the period when it is determined that they will not be recovered or realized. However, the Guide does not state whether the effect should be included in operations or classified as an extraordinary item in the financial statements. Neither does it address how to handle timing differences in times of regulatory uncertainty. This pertains to situations in which Congress passes legislation requiring Medicare to change certain rules by a certain date; however, such laws generally provide no specific information on how to measure the impact of the change. That information is usually not available until implementing regulations are issued. In the interim, providers are not able to reasonably estimate the financial impact of the change on their deferred Medicare assets and liabilities, even though they know that impairment may exist. Finally, the Guide does not comment on whether new timing differences should continue to be set up in periods of regulatory uncertainty.

Advisory Statement No. 13 of HFMA's P&P Board, *Timing Differences Pertaining to Third-Party Payment,* addresses these issues. That advisory statement recommends that no adjustment should be made to the carrying value of existing deferred assets or liabilities in periods of regulatory uncertainty until reasonably certain provisions of enabling legislation or final implementing regulations with regard to the new payment system are available. In the interim, any material contingencies should be disclosed when reasonably certain provisions of enabling legislation or final implementing regulations become available, the effect of the adjustment should be reported in the Statement of Operations in the same manner as was the transaction that originally gave rise to the timing difference. If the transaction was an extraordinary item (such as a gain or loss on a bond defeasance), the adjustment should be reported as extraordinary; if the transaction was included in results of operations, the adjustment should also be included in results of operations. Timing differences that originate in periods of regulatory uncertainty represent gain or loss contingencies that should be disclosed in the financial statements, if material. When reasonably certain provisions of enabling legislation or final implementing regulations become available, regulations are issued, the availability of any future benefits or diminishments can be measured and should be recorded at that time.

Timing differences may exist for other types of third-party payors as well. The provisions discussed above would be applicable to those types of timing differences as well as Medicare timing differences.

30.4 SPECIAL ACCOUNTING PROBLEMS OF SPECIFIC TYPES OF PROVIDERS

(a) CONTINUING CARE RETIREMENT COMMUNITIES. Continuing-care retirement facilities (CCRCs) are organizations that provide or guarantee residential and health care services for persons who may reside in apartments, other living units, or a nursing center. They are usually characterized by an obligation to provide future services, and some sort of up-front payment on the part of the resident, part of which may be refundable. Unique accounting issues pertaining to CCRCs include: refundable fees, fees repayable to residents from reoccupancy proceeds, nonrefundable fees, the obligation to provide future services, and the use of facilities to current residents, and costs of acquiring continuing-care contracts.

(i) Refundable Advance Fees.   Frequently, continuing care contracts provide for some or all of a resident's advance fee (also called an entrance fee) to be refunded if the resident dies or withdraws from the CCRC. In many cases, the refundable portion decreases with time or other contractual provisions.

If provisions of the contract allow a refund to be made, an estimate should be made each year of the amount of refundable advance fees that are expected to be refunded to current residents upon death or withdrawal. The estimate would be based on the individual facility's own experience or, if not available, on the experience of comparable facilities. The estimated amount refundable would be reported as a liability. The remainder of the advance fee would be accounted for as deferred revenue. As time passes or other contract provisions cause the amount refundable to decrease, the portion that becomes nonrefundable should be reclassified to deferred revenue and amortized into income. The amortization of this deferred revenue is discussed in section (iv) below.

The gross amount of contractual refund obligations under existing contracts at the balance sheet date should be disclosed for each year the balance sheet is presented. The CCRC's refund policy should also be disclosed in the notes to the financial statements. Amounts refunded should be classified in the statement of cash flows as a financing transaction.

These conclusions do not apply to refunds that are contingent upon the resale of the unit. Those situations are discussed in section (iii).

(ii) Nonrefundable Advance Fees.   Most contracts provide that at least some portion of the entrance fee will not be refundable upon the resident's death or withdrawal. Some contracts do not allow any of the entrance fee to be refunded. According to the Guide, nonrefundable fees represent payment for future services to be provided over the life of the resident (unless the contract terms state otherwise). Therefore, nonrefundable amounts should be reported as deferred revenue when received and amortized into income as described in section (iv) below.

Upon the death or withdrawal of a resident, any unamortized deferred revenue from nonrefundable advance fees pertaining to his or her contract should immediately be reclassified to revenue.

(iii) Fees Refundable to Residents from Reoccupancy Proceeds of a Contract Holder's Unit.   Some contracts provide that entrance fees will be refunded only when and if the contract holder's unit is resold to a new resident. Presumably, each subsequent contract would similarly allow a refund only in the event the unit is again sold. The Guide states that in such situations, the portion of advance fees that is refundable upon reoccupancy should be reported as deferred revenue (provided that law and management policy and practice support the withholding of refunds under this condition).

CCRCs generally structure contracts in this manner to recover the cost of the facilities over their economic lives; therefore, the amount reported as deferred revenue should be amortized to income over the remaining useful life of the facility. The basis and method of amortization should be consistent with the method for calculating depreciation, and should be disclosed in the notes to the financial statements.

No liability for the refund amount exists until the unit is in fact resold. At that time, the liability will be paid from the proceeds of the unit's resale. If the amount received from the new resident is greater than the amount to be refunded to the former resident, the excess also should be considered deferred revenue (provided that the resale contract also contains a provision that refundability is contingent on subsequent resale of the unit).

(iv) Amortization of Nonrefundable Advance Fees.   Deferred revenue from nonrefundable advance fees should be amortized into income on a straight-line basis over each individual resident's remaining life expectancy (or the contract term, if it is shorter). The period of amortization would be adjusted annually based on the actuarially-determined estimated remaining life expectancy of each individual, or joint and last survivor life expectancy of each pair of residents occupying the same unit. The amortization of each resident's nonrefundable fees should not exceed the amount available to the CCRC under state regulations, contract provision, or management policy.

Although the individual life method may appear to be a time-consuming process that requires substantial recordkeeping, once the data is developed, calculated and accumulated, it should not require a significant amount of time to calculate deferred nonrefundable fees for each individual. The individual life method is preferable because it smooths out fluctuations and results in a more accurate accrual of earned revenue than does the group method. (Under the group method, residents are grouped by average age, entry year, type or size of unit, or some other method, and a life expectancy is determined for the group using life expectancy tables.)

CCRCs should assess whether they have sufficient historical information about life expectancies, or whether they will have to use regional or national actuarially-determined data instead. CCRC-specific data may be the most appropriate, especially for CCRCs that cater to affluent populations. Such groups often are in better health, and live longer than average. Whatever statistical information is selected for amortizing deferred revenue must also be used for determining the obligation for future services.

As indicated, the straight-line method should be used to amortize the deferred revenue, except in certain circumstances where costs are expected to be significantly higher in the later years of residence. In those cases, a method that reflects the timing of the costs of the expected services may be used. The amortization method used should be disclosed in a note to the financial statements.

In the income statement, the amortization of deferred revenue from advance fees should be reported in resident fees earned.

(v) Obligation to Provide Future Services. CCRCs generally commit to provide services and the use of facilities to residents for the rest of their lives. Annually, the CCRC needs to assess its contractual arrangements with existing residents to determine whether the expected future revenues from those contracts will be sufficient to cover the costs of providing services and use of facilities over the rest of the residents' lives.

Many CCRCs require residents to pay periodic fees that may be increased, if necessary. CCRCs that have no restrictions upon their ability to cover future costs, and those which have a history of profitable operations, may not encounter problems in this area. More likely to be affected are CCRCs that have contracts which restrict the amount of periodic fee increases, and CCRCs having contracts which only require residents to pay an advance fee. In this situation, no additional funds can be required to be paid, regardless of how long a resident lives or if the resident requires more services than anticipated.

If the estimated costs of future services are determined to exceed anticipated revenues, the CCRC has entered into a loss contract. Losses resulting from such contracts—the obligation to provide future services—should be recorded in the period in which they are determined to exist. In determining the loss, contracts should be grouped by type, such as "contracts with a limit on annual increases in fees"/"contracts with unlimited fee increases."

According to the Guide, "anticipated revenues" include third-party payments (e.g., those from Blue Cross/Blue Shield), contractually or statutorily committed investment income from sources related to CCRC activities, contributions pledged by donors to support CCRC activities, periodic fees expected to be collected, and the balance of deferred nonrefundable advance fees. Examples of "estimated costs of future services" include costs of resident care, dietary costs, health care facility costs, general, and administrative costs, interest expense, depreciation, and amortization costs.

At the time of initial determination that a loss exists, the CCRC would record a liability (the "obligation to provide future services and the use of facilities is excess of amounts received or to be received for such services") and make a corresponding charge to income (the "provision for obligation to provide future services and use of facilities"). The Guide provides a formula for calculating the liability, as follows:

- Present value of future net cash flows;
- minus the balance of unamortized deferred revenue;
- plus depreciation of facilities to be charged related to the contracts;
- plus unamortized costs of acquiring the related initial continuing-care contracts, if applicable.

For purposes of determining the present value of future net cash flows, the Guide defines cash inflows as revenue contractually committed to support the residents, and inflows resulting from monthly fees, including anticipated increases in accordance with contract terms. Cash outflows are defined as operating expenses, including interest expense but excluding selling and general and administrative expenses. Cost increases resulting from inflation should be factored into the amount of operating expenses included in the computation. The difference between cash inflows and cash outflows should be discounted to present value. The Guide states that the expected inflation rate and other factors should be taken into account in determining the discount rate to be used.

A formula for determining the depreciation of facilities to be charged to current residents is provided in the Guide. Basically, the purpose of this formula is to exclude from the loss computation any depreciation allocable to revenue-producing service areas.

For both the net present value of cash flows and the depreciation of facilities, the computation should be made on a resident-by-resident basis within each contract group, using the resident's remaining life expectancy. The life spans used should be the same as those used in calculating the amortization of deferred revenue.

Each year, the liability should be recalculated. Increases or decreases in the liability would be reported in the income statement as a separate line item, "change in obligation to provide future services and use of facilities," with appropriate note disclosure. In the balance sheet, the obligation to provide future services should be presented separately as a long-term liability, if it is material.

The notes to the financial statements should include a description of the obligation to provide future services. The Guide shows this note in the summary of significant accounting policies. Because the appropriateness of discounting is under consideration by the FASB, CCRCs should also disclose the carrying amount of the liability that is presented at present value—if it is not separately disclosed in the balance sheet—and the interest rate used to discount the liability.

(vi) Costs of Acquiring Initial Continuing Care Contracts.   Most CCRCs capitalize the costs of obtaining contracts to initially fill the facility. These costs represent an investment that will result in future revenues from amortization of nonrefundable advance fees (and future periodic fees, in some cases).

The Guide requires costs associated with acquiring initial contracts that occur within a certain time period to be capitalized. These include:

- Certain costs of processing contracts, such as evaluating the financial condition of a prospect, evaluating and recording guarantees and other security arrangements, negotiating contract terms, processing documents, and closing the transactions.
- Costs in connection with soliciting potential residents (such as model units, signs, sales brochures, tours, grand openings, and sales salaries); however, this does not include advertising or administrative costs, interest, rent, depreciation, or any other occupancy or equipment costs.

• The portion of an employee's compensation and benefits that relates to the initial contract acquisition.

Once capitalized, such costs should be amortized to operations using the straight-line method over the average expected remaining life of the CCRC's residents (or the contract term, if shorter).

The time period during which capitalization is allowed is limited to those costs that are incurred through the date of substantial occupancy, but no later than one year from the date of completion of construction. Costs of acquiring contracts after a CCRC is substantially occupied or one year following completion should be expensed when incurred.

(b) PREPAID HEALTH CARE PLANS.   Prepaid health care plans provide or arrange for the delivery of health care services to a specified group of individuals in exchange for a fixed, predetermined fee. The most common form of prepaid health care organization is the HMO.

Some have questioned the need for developing specific guidance for the HMO industry when GAAP for insurance companies might be applied to certain similar transactions entered into by HMOs. The fundamental difference noted in the accounting guidance for the two industries is that HMOs undertake to provide (or arrange for the provision of) health care services in addition to their role as a third-party payor. Because FASB Statement No. 60 and other relevant insurance industry principles are applicable only to contracts that involve payment for health care services (not to contracts that extend to the provision of health care services), specialized guidance was needed.

(i) Expense Recognition Issues.   The event that triggers an HMO to recognize claim expense is the provision of health care services to an enrolled member, not the occurrence of an accident or illness. In order to achieve a proper matching of the HMO's revenues and expenses, as a general rule the costs of providing health care services to HMO members should be reported in the periods in which those services are actually rendered. This is true even if the subscriber is being treated for an illness that requires long term treatment. It is not appropriate to estimate and accrue the expense of the entire spell of illness in the period in which the diagnosis is made. However, in certain situations it is appropriate for HMOs to accrue the costs of health care services. These are set forth in the following items.

Contractual or Regulatory Obligation.   If an HMO member is hospitalized at the end of the premium period, in situations where the contract or prevailing regulations obligate the HMO to continue to provide care to members after the end of the premium period, the HMO will have to accrue the total costs of these hospitalization services. An example would be if the HMO is contractually obligated to continue to provide coverage for hospital stays that are "in progress" at the end of the premium period.

IBNR Accruals.   "Incurred but not reported" (IBNR) accruals must be estimated and reserves recorded for services that have been rendered by providers but not reported to the HMO as of the financial statement date. This will include recurring claims from the HMO's contracted providers, claims from specialists, and claims arising from situations in which a subscriber requires medical care outside of the HMO's service area (such as while traveling). In such cases, the HMO should accrue the costs of any services rendered during the fiscal period for which payment has not been made as of the close of the fiscal period, even if the subcontracting provider has not yet billed the HMO for those services.

The IBNR reserve is one of the key risk areas for an HMO, not only because it has a major effect on an HMO's financial statements but also because it serves as one of the early warning signals of utilization problems. Finance personnel must work closely with utilization management and contacting personnel to analyze cost and utilization data, which is essential to conducting lag schedule analyses and formulating the reserves.

Termination of Contract.   Another situation in which an accrual of health care costs might be required is when a contract between an HMO and an employer is terminated. For instance, a staff model HMO might contract with a major industrial corporation to establish a medical clinic on or near the premises of a plant. In a staff model HMO, the costs of providing health care services to the plant's employees are relatively fixed, because the clinic's physicians and support personnel are generally salaried employees. If the contract with the corporation is terminated, expenses associated with the clinic that the HMO will be unable to avoid, such as guaranteed salaries, rent, or depreciation, should be accrued net of any related anticipated revenues.

(ii) Loss Contracts.   If premiums are set too low or if utilization by the members is unusually high, the HMO will sustain an economic loss in fulfilling that particular contract. Losses should be accrued when an HMO's projected health care costs and maintenance costs pertaining to a particular group of contracts exceed the anticipated premium revenues and stop-loss insurance recoveries under those contracts. The costs considered should include fixed costs as well as variable costs; in other words, the computation should include costs that would be incurred regardless of whether or not a particular contract is in force, such as staff physician's salaries and costs attributable to facilities owned by the HMO. The costs considered should also include all direct costs of the contracts along with indirect costs identifiable with or allocable to the contracts, as is customary in any type of contract accounting. Generally this requires inclusion of all HMO costs other than general and administrative, selling, marketing and interest.

To determine whether a loss accrual is necessary, an HMO will need to analyze the unexpired contracts in force at the end of each reporting period. Contracts should be grouped in the manner discussed below and the aggregate health care costs, maintenance expenses, premium revenue, and stop-loss recoveries projected for the contracts in each group. If the aggregate expenses for the contract period are expected to exceed the aggregate revenues for the contract period, the amount of the excess should be accrued as a loss on that group of contracts. Furthermore, if any of the contracts in a "loss group" have guaranteed renewal provisions and the HMO is constrained by statutory requirements or community rating practices from increasing the premiums charged on those contracts, the HMO should also accrue any losses it expects to incur attributable to the guaranteed renewal periods.

The groupings used for loss determination correspond with the groupings used by the HMO in establishing its premium rates. For HMOs that use community rating (i.e., one premium rate is established for all members in a given enrollment population; for instance, a particular geographic area or actuarial class), the contracts grouped together for loss determination would be those considered to be part of the same enrollment "pool" for premium determination. HMOs that are experience-rated would group their contracts along the same lines as are used for rate-setting purposes, such as by type of employer. (In an experience-rated HMO, members covered by each contract constitute a separate population base for rate-setting purposes; therefore, premiums are based on the actual or anticipated health care costs of each contract.)

(iii) Risk Pools.   Risk pools provide a vehicle for sharing favorable and unfavorable experiences among providers (and sometimes the payor) by creating incentives for physicians and hospitals to control utilization of services. The type of incentive offered may be positive (gain-sharing pool) or negative (loss-sharing pool), or may combine both positive and negative incentives (combined risk-sharing pool). Risk pool settlements retroactively determine the amount of fees a provider will receive under a given risk contract; therefore, the settlements affect the amount of health care expense that should be recognized by the HMO. The HMO should accrue risk pool settlements payable to physicians, hospitals, and other providers based on relevant factors such as experience to date.

In situations where settlements are due from providers under risk-sharing arrangements, a receivable will exist. Whether or not this receivable can be collected may be a significant item for HMOs, because the amounts can be large relative to net income. It is not uncommon for HMOs ultimately to write such receivables off. Alternatively, some HMOs "recover" the receivable over a period of years by withholding payments from compensation to providers calculated at greater than market rates. Receivables of this nature should be presented net of an allowance for uncollectibles; that allowance may be difficult to estimate due to the factors discussed above. Such receivables may be separately disclosed, if they are material.

(iv) Stop-Loss Insurance. HMOs often purchase stop-loss insurance (also called excess-of-loss reinsurance) to protect themselves against the risk of loss incurred in the process of satisfying the claims of HMO subscribers. HMOs should report stop-loss insurance premiums as a health care cost. Stop-loss insurance recoveries should be reported as a reduction of the related premium expense; they should not be reported as revenue. Amounts recoverable (i.e., receivable) from insurers under stop-loss policies should be reported as assets, reduced by appropriate valuation allowances; it is not appropriate to offset such amounts against amounts payable for health care costs.

(v) Acquisition Costs. HMOs incur certain costs in connection with writing contracts and obtaining new members. These costs may be general in nature, such as marketing staff salaries, general promotional literature, and other advertising; or they may be directly related to the acquisition of specific contracts, such as the costs of specialized brochures and advertising and commissions paid to agents or brokers. Acquisition costs should be expensed as incurred.

(vi) Billing and Reconciliation. It is imperative that an HMO monitor the status of outstanding bills and accounts receivable, that monthly bills be reconciled to amounts received on a timely basis, and that discrepancies be followed up promptly. This facilitates the identification of employers to be terminated for nonpayment but, more importantly, facilitates the identification of retroactive member additions and terminations. This assists in maintaining the integrity of the eligibility database, so that health care services are provided to, and claims and capitation paid only for, enrolled members. Failure to perform his function on a timely basis can seriously threaten the financial stability of an HMO.

30.5 FINANCIAL REPORTING PRACTICES

(a) USERS OF FINANCIAL STATEMENTS. The primary users of health care companies' general purpose financial statements are providers of capital who make rating and investment decisions in competitive capital markets; suppliers of goods and services to the industry with whom health care companies maintain credit relationships; stockholders and other owners; the Securities and Exchange Commission (SEC), and regulators such as state Departments of Insurance and other oversight groups.

(b) BASIC FINANCIAL STATEMENTS. Investor-owned and tax-exempt health care providers generally prepare four financial statements:

1. Balance sheet.
2. Income statement/Statement of Operations.
3. Statement of changes in stockholders' equity/statement of changes in net assets.
4. Statement of cash flows.

Financial statement display requirements for tax-exempt health care providers are set forth in FASB Statement No. 117, as adjusted by implementing guidance set forth by the AICPA

Health Care Committee and cleared by the FASB. The guidance contained in *Health Care Organizations* reflects that implementing guidance on how FASB Statement No. 117 should be applied to the financial statements of tax-exempt health care organizations.

GASB Statement No. 29 prohibits governmental health care providers from adopting FASB Statement No. 117's financial statement display requirements. Instead, governmental health care entities continue to follow the financial statement display guidance set forth in the predecessor guide, *Audits of Providers of Health Care Services*. Under that guide, the four basic statements prepared by governmental health care entities are:

1. Balance sheet.
2. Statement of revenue and expenses.
3. Statement of changes in fund balances.
4. Statement of cash flows.

Health Care Organizations provides illustrative financial statements for investor-owned, tax-exempt, and governmental health care organizations. Those statements illustrate the application of the reporting practices contained in the guide. Specific types of health care organizations are presented, but only to illustrate a wide diversity of reporting practices. It is not intended that these illustrations represent either the only types of disclosure nor the only statement formats that would be appropriate. For example, the reporting of revenue, gains, expenses and losses varies depending on the relationship of the underlying transaction to the entity's operations. More or less detail should appear in the financial statements or notes, depending on the circumstances.

(c) BALANCE SHEET.   The primary difference between a balance sheet prepared for a for-profit provider and one prepared for a not-for-profit provider is the presentation of the facility's net assets (net worth). In for-profit balance sheets, net assets are referred to as "stockholders' equity"; in not-for-profit statements, they are referred to as unrestricted, temporarily restricted, or permanently restricted net assets.

In balance sheets prepared for governmental providers, it is essential that a clear separation be made between general funds and donor-restricted funds. How this is accomplished depends on whether the provider uses **single-fund** or multifund (**layered** or **pancake**) reporting. In "single fund" (also called "aggregated") reporting, all assets, liabilities, and fund balance amounts are displayed in a single aggregated balance sheet, with fund differentiation indicated by notation in the fund balance section and disclosure in the notes to the financial statements. When a single-fund balance sheet is prepared, assets of the restricted fund (excluding amounts due to or from other funds) are included under the caption, "Assets Whose Use Is Limited Or Restricted." Amounts required to satisfy restricted fund current liabilities are classified as current assets.

Due-to/due-from accounts generally are not reported on a single-fund balance sheet. In general, due-to/due-from accounts are eliminated and the corresponding amounts of cash balances adjusted as if the cash were actually exchanged. Notes to the financial statements should include disclosure of the amount of restricted assets included in the balance sheet, including details of their composition and the nature of restrictions imposed by donors for specific purposes and permanent endowment funds; and details of interfund borrowing agreements, if applicable.

(d) INCOME STATEMENT.   The guide states that health care organizations should report the results of their operations in a "statement of operations" (e.g., an income statement) which clearly sets forth the organizations's results of operations for the period (e.g., net income). It also stipulates that the following transactions should be presented *outside of* net income (also referred to as the "operating indicator") in the statement of operations:

- Equity transfers involving other entities that control the reporting entity, are controlled by the reporting entity, or are under common control with the reporting entity.
- Contributions of long-lived assets.
- Other items required by GAAP to be reported separately, such as extraordinary items, the effects of discontinued operations, and the cumulative effect of accounting changes.
- Receipt of restricted contributions, including temporary or permanent restrictions (which instead are reported in the statement of changes in temporarily/permanently restricted net assets).

The guide further states that if an organization's use of the term *operations* is not apparent from the details provided on the face of the statement, there should be appropriate note disclosure of the nature of the reported measure of operations or the items excluded from operations.

These requirements are primarily directed at not-for-profit health care providers, in an attempt to preserve consistency in financial reporting of results of operations among health care organizations of all ownership types. Absent these specific instructions, not-for-profit providers would be required to follow the financial reporting requirements of FAS No. 117 which eliminate the requirement to present an income statement, instead requiring a "statement of activity." The statement of activity combines the information traditionally presented in the income statement with the information traditionally reported in the statement of changes in equity/fund balance/net assets to arrive at the organization's "net increase/decrease in net assets" for the year. There is no requirement to define any results of operations for the year.

The audit guide imposes additional restrictions on the FAS No. 117 requirements for healthcare providers as follows: Not-for-profit health care organizations are to report their total income or loss from operations in a statement that, at a minimum, also presents the total changes in unrestricted net assets. The statement of operations must include the "operating indicator" discussed above.

Therefore, FAS No. 117's requirement to show the changes in net assets for the year is met and the results of operations also are apparent. Although the Statement of Operations prepared under these parameters will not parallel exactly the statement of revenue and expenses traditionally presented, it will produce a statements that more closely resemble the traditional income statement presentation now used by providers.

FAS No. 117 also imposes two requirements affecting the reporting of expenses. First, it requires that all expenses of the organization be shown in the unrestricted class of net assets; no expenses may be reported in the temporarily or permanently restricted classes. This is not a significant issue for most not-for-profit health care providers, who traditionally have run most expenses through the income statement. The second requirement mandates the reporting of expenses by functional categories such as "program," "management" and "fundraising." Traditionally, providers have reported expenses classified along "revenue/cost center" lines (e.g., nursing services, other professional services, general services) or "natural" lines (e.g., salaries and wages, employee benefits, supplies, purchased services). The guide emphasizes the option provided in FAS No. 117 which allows not-for-profit healthcare organizations to continue their traditional presentation on the face of the financial statement, as long as the functional reporting requirements are presented in the notes to the financial statements.

The functional reporting requirements may not be as onerous to implement as may first appear. A great deal of flexibility is allowed in the degree to which the functional information is reported. Some providers may choose to present only two categories: "health services" and "general and administrative." Others may desire to more detail. Whatever degree of detail is selected, the functional allocations should be based on full cost allocations.

As stated previously, GASB Statement No. 29 prohibits governmental health care providers from applying the display requirements of FAS No. 117. Instead, they are instructed to continue to follow the financial statement display requirements of FAS No. 117. Instead, they are instructed to continue to follow the financial statement display requirements of the predecessor guide, *Audits of Providers of Health Care Services.* Consequently, the statement of revenue and expenses is the governmental provider's equivalent of the income statement/statement of operations. It is limited to activity reported in the facility's general fund.

Some providers are required to disclose information pertaining to major customers. SEC-registered companies are required to disclose segment information. Governmental health care enterprises must comply with the segment reporting requirements of NCGA Interpretation 2, "Segment Information for Enterprise Funds."

Based upon all the foregoing discussion, it is obvious that the statement of operations has the potential to become an extremely detailed document. Some providers will choose to present a great deal of detail; others will present income statements that are highly condensed, providing only summary totals of major classifications of revenue and expense. Details, if desired, may also be presented in the accompanying notes or in supplemental schedules or statements. Each provider must determine the level of detail that is most meaningful for full disclosure.

Some SEC registrants have received comment letters from the SEC requesting that their income statements display operating expenses at a level of detail "consistent with the AICPA audit guide for health care providers." As stated previously, the sample financial statements are illustrative and are not intended to establish a practice that would require this level of disclosure.

(i) EBITDA vs. Income from Operations.   For the owners and lenders involved in an LBO of an investor-owned health care company, an important number is earnings before interest, taxes, depreciation, and amortization (EBITDA). This is an important amount because it shows the cash flow available to service debt and is often used in calculations in debt covenants. In reporting their results of operations, some companies have attempted to reflect EBITDA as "income from operations." The SEC has taken exception to this practice, as it believes it is not appropriate to reflect depreciation as a nonoperating item.

(e) STATEMENT OF CHANGES IN NET ASSETS/EQUITY.   A Statement of Changes in Net Assets/Equity should report all changes that have occurred during the reporting period in all equity, net asset, and fund balance accounts maintained by the provider.

(f) STATEMENT OF CASH FLOWS OF GENERAL FUNDS.   A statement of cash flows must be prepared by all health care providers. For-profit providers follow the guidance in FASB Statement No. 95, *Statement of Cash Flows,* in preparing the statements of cash flows. Tax-exempt providers follow the reporting guidance contained in FASB Statement No. 117, which is similar to FAS No. 95.

Governmental providers follow the guidance in GASB Statement No. 9, *Reporting Cash Flows of Proprietary and Nonexpendable Trust Funds and Governmental Entities That Use Proprietary Fund Accounting,* in preparing their statement of cash flows. That statement's requirements differ from those of FASB Statement Nos. 95 and 117 in the following ways:

- The GASB cash flow statement has four categories: operating, investing, capital financing, and noncapital financing. The capital financing category is used for acquiring and disposing of capital assets, borrowing money for acquiring capital assets, and repaying the amounts borrowed. All other financing is classified as noncapital.

- Some items are classified differently by the GASB than they are by the FASB. For example, fixed assets are classified as capital financing activities under GASB Statement No. 9, but are considered to be investing activities under FASB Statement No. 95. Certain types of contributions and interest income also are classified in different categories by the GASB than by the FASB.

- The GASB cash flow statement excludes nonoperating gains and losses (that is, it reconciles cash flows to income from operations).

30.6 SOURCES AND SUGGESTED REFERENCES

American Hospital Association, *Estimated Useful Lives of Depreciable Hospital Assets,* AHA, Chicago, IL, 1993.

American Institute of Certified Public Accountants, Health Care Committee, "Audits of Providers of Health Care Services," Industry Audit and Accounting Guide, AICPA, New York, 1990.

————, "HealthCare Organizations," Industry Audit and Accounting Guide, AICPA, New York, 1996.

Governmental Accounting Standards Board, "Codification of Governmental Accounting and Financial Reporting Standards," GASB, Norwalk, CT, 1996.

Healthcare Financial Management Association. "Timing Differences Pertaining to Third-Party Payment," Principles and Practices Board Statement No. 13, HFMA, Westchester, IL, 1992.

CHAPTER 31

ACCOUNTING FOR GOVERNMENT CONTRACTS

Margaret M. Worthington, CPA

Price Waterhouse LLP

CONTENTS

31.1 UNIQUE ACCOUNTING REQUIREMENTS FOR FEDERAL CONTRACTORS

Doing business with the federal government is significantly different from doing business with commercial organizations, because the federal government operates within a very formalized statutory and regulatory framework when it procures products and services. These differences are often reflected in special cost estimating, cost accounting, billing and project management requirements that are imposed on federal contractors. Consequently, systems used by federal contractors must not only provide the information that is necessary to effectively price contracts and control contract incurred costs but must comply with those special requirements.

This chapter is designed to provide a practical discussion of those unique federal contracting requirements. Several of those requirements are discussed below:

- *Cost Principles.* When government agencies buy custom-made goods and services, the forces of supply and demand cannot necessarily be relied upon to establish fair and reasonable prices. Consequently, in negotiated contracts, the estimated and/or actual cost of performance, becomes a dominant factor in setting prices. The government established cost accounting requirements that apply to such contracts. Cost principles contained in Part 31 of the Federal Acquisition Regulation (FAR) and the various agency FAR supplements provide specific criteria as to the costs that may be included in contract proposals, claims and billings submitted to the government. The cost principles change as a result of efforts by Congress and the executive departments to eliminate perceived abuses and/or streamline the procurement process. These changes generally tend to reduce the cost of products and services purchased by the federal government.

- *Cost Accounting Standards (CAS).* Congress created the Cost Accounting Standards Board to enhance the uniformity and consistency of cost accounting practices by 1) narrowing the range of alternative practices and 2) holding contractors accountable for cost accounting practice changes. Nineteen cost accounting standards and disclosure statement filing requirements have been promulgated.

- *Defective Pricing.* The Truth in Negotiation Act, as amended, is designed to ensure that the government has the opportunity to review all significant and relevant cost or pricing data available to the contractor in arriving at proposed prices of negotiated contracts. If, after the negotiation, it is determined that not all such data were submitted to the government, the contract price is subject to downward adjustment for any price increase resulting from the contractor's or subcontractor's failure to comply.

31.2 MANAGEMENT INFORMATION SYSTEM REQUIREMENTS

A well-designed management information system provides more than a summary of contract costs. To compete effectively in any market, management must receive the information necessary to plan and control its business. For a government contractor, the planning phase begins when a contract proposal is prepared. During that process, contract performance is broken down into meaningful work packages with cost estimates, performance schedules, and performance responsibility assigned to appropriate cost centers. When the contract is awarded, such data should be used to establish the performance and cost baseline for monitoring actual performance. If comparisons of actuals with the baseline reveal unfavorable variances during performance, corrective action may then be taken promptly.

In the current complex federal acquisition environment, companies must, at a minimum, have systems and controls that provide adequate accounting, estimating, and project management information.

(a) COST ACCOUNTING SYSTEMS.   A government contractor's cost accounting system must identify and accumulate contract costs incurred to support billings under flexibly priced contracts or progress payments under fixed-price contracts. Cost ledgers can be designed in a variety of ways to permit efficient accumulation of costs for billing purposes. In practice, these records vary considerably, based on the individual company's need for information and the complexity of the contract requirements.

Contractors performing contracts for which cost or pricing data must be submitted before contract definitization must have cost accounting systems that comply with FAR and CAS requirements.

For flexibly priced contracts (cost-reimbursement, fixed-price-incentive, or fixed-price-redeterminable), allowable costs incurred form the basis for contract remuneration. Thus, accurate charging by contract is imperative. To ensure the reliability of recorded labor charges, a contractor must have an adequate internal control system for collecting and distributing labor costs. Accurate labor charging also encompasses accounting for all hours worked. If salaried employees work a significant number of hours in excess of the standard work week, a risk of labor mischarging to the government may be asserted if all hours worked are not accounted for. Although no specific regulatory provisions mandate the use of total time accounting, government auditors have long asserted that accounting for all hours worked is a basic requirement of FAR 31.201-4 and CAS 418, which provide that costs should be charged to contracts on the basis of relative benefits received. The Defense FAR Supplement (DFARS), which applies to the defense contracts and subcontracts, explicitly requires contracts of $100,000 or more for services to be acquired on the basis of the number of hours to be received to identify both direct and indirect hours included in the proposal to which uncompensated overtime rates apply.[1] The DFARS provision also mandates consistency between the accounting practices used to estimate uncompensated overtime and the cost accounting practices used to accumulate and report uncompensated overtime hours.

Most negotiated government contracts contain a clause similar to the one contained in FAR 52.215-2, which provides that "the Contractor shall maintain . . . records and other evidence sufficient to reflect properly all costs claimed to have been incurred or anticipated to be incurred directly or indirectly in performing this contract." The regulations do not require contractors to maintain any specific type of accounting system. Rather, FAR 31.201-1 states that "any generally accepted method of determining or estimating costs that is equitable and is consistently applied may be used, including standard costs properly adjusted for applicable variances."

In a job-order costing system, costs are collected using a work-order process. Such a process normally involves assigning a job or project number to final cost objectives (e.g., contracts) and certain indirect activities (e.g., IR&D/B&P projects and plant rearrangement projects). Contractors, particularly in a production environment, are not required by the regulations to account for costs by contract (e.g., maintain a job-order cost accounting system). A cost accounting system in a production environment is generally driven by the contractor's products and/or production processes. The cost accounting system should be deemed adequate if production costs are appropriately, equitably, and consistently allocated to all final cost objectives. This point was emphasized in *Texas Instruments, Inc.,* [2] in which the Armed Services Board of Contract Appeals (ASBCA) concluded that the contractor's process cost system, which was used to accumulate the costs of units to be delivered under both government and commercial orders, complied with CAS and applicable procurement regulations.

For firm-fixed-price contracts that require submission of cost or pricing data prior to agreement on contract price, an adequate cost accounting system is required even though costs incurred on the contract do not affect the monies ultimately paid to the contractor upon contract completion. The cost accounting system provides data for follow-on contract cost pricing, tracking contract performance, and supporting cost-based progress payment requests. To price follow-on contracts, information on the rate of improvement in performing repetitive tasks on subsequent production (i.e., learning curves) is important. Well-designed cost accounting systems can enable estimators to identify the costs or hours incurred on prior contracts or production lots. The ability to segregate nonrecurring costs from recurring costs is also critical for follow-on pricing. The design of the accounting system is all-important in providing valuable input for the estimating or planning process for contract costs.

With regard to using standard costs to project future performance, the DCAA *Contract Audit Manual,* Section 9-314, provides that "the basic principle underlying the use of standard costs in estimating is that the standard cost plus the estimated variance must reasonably approximate the expected actual costs."[3]

---

[1] DFARS 252.237-7019.
[2] *Texas Instruments, Inc.,* ASBCA No. 18621, March 10, 1979, 79-1 BCA 13,800.
[3] Superintendent of Documents Government Printing Office, Defense Contracts Audit Manual 7640-1, Washington, DC 20402, Catalog No. D-1, 4612:7640.1/1283.

The obvious necessity is to capture and accumulate costs in a manner that reflects the cost of performance in individual government contracts. To do this, certain costs that can be identified specifically with contracts and/or products are treated as direct costs and are charged in that manner. Typically, direct costs include material, subcontracts, and labor, but they are by no means limited to these. As stated earlier, FAR 31.201-4 requires that costs charged directly to contracts be allocated "on the basis of the relative benefits received or other equitable relationship."

Indirect costs, or other costs that benefit more than one contract, must be pooled and allocated to contracts on some equitable basis. According to FAR 31.203(b), the general criteria for establishing indirect cost pools are:

> Indirect costs shall be accumulated by logical cost groupings with due consideration of the reasons for incurring such costs. Each grouping should be determined so as to permit the distribution of the grouping on the basis of the benefits accruing to the several cost objectives. Commonly, manufacturing overhead, selling expenses, and general and administrative (G&A) expenses are separately grouped. Similarly, the particular case may require subdivision of these groupings. . . . When substantially the same results can be achieved through less precise methods, the number and composition of cost groupings should be governed by practical considerations and should not unduly complicate the allocation.

FAR 31.203(b) and (c) similarly provide flexibility in determining what allocation base to use in distributing costs from the indirect cost pools to contracts:

> This necessitates selecting a distribution base common to all cost objectives to which the grouping is to be allocated. The base should be selected so as to permit allocation of the grouping on the basis of the benefits accruing to the several cost objectives . . .

> Once an appropriate base for the distribution of indirect costs has been accepted, it shall not be fragmented by the removal of individual elements. All items properly includable in an indirect cost base should bear a pro-rata share of indirect costs irrespective of their acceptance as Government contract costs. For example, when a cost input base is used for the distribution of G&A costs, all items that would properly be part of the cost input base, whether allowable or unallowable, shall be included in the base and bear their pro-rata share of G&A costs.

The FAR requirement to allocate allowable G&A costs to both allowable and unallowable costs comprising the total cost input base was upheld by the Federal Circuit in 1993.[4]

Accounting for indirect costs presents a challenge to those uninitiated in government contracting. Through the acquisition regulations and cost accounting standards, the government has promulgated specific rules on the allocability of indirect costs. However, these rules still permit considerable flexibility in the number and types of pools that can be selected and the methods used for allocating indirect costs.

Whichever methods are selected for classifying and allocating direct or indirect costs, a key requirement is the existence of adequate audit trails. An accounting system provides satisfactory audit trails if: (1) every transaction is traceable from its origin to its final posting in the books of account, including the ledger summarizing costs by contract; (2) every posting to accounts, including the ledger summarizing contract costs, is susceptible to breakdown into identifiable transactions; and (3) adequate documentation (e.g., time cards or vendors' invoices) is available and accessible to support the accuracy and validity of individual transactions.

The allocation of indirect costs in a highly automated environment presents an even greater challenge, since typical overhead allocation bases, such as direct labor, may represent only a minor component of total factory costs. Automated production environments generally necessitate multiple cost pools allocated over nonlabor bases, such as machine usage. This requirement

---

[4] *Rice v. Marietta Corp.*, CAFC No. 93-1025, December 28, 1993, 13 F.3d 1563.

is currently evident in activity based costing or advanced cost management systems that have been implemented by a number of government contractors. In an automated environment, requirements for audit trails still exist; however, additional controls over input to the system and program logic are essential to validate the accuracy of such systems.

(b) COST ESTIMATING SYSTEMS. Cost or pricing data must be submitted prior to award of a contract of $500,000 or more unless

- The price is based on adequate price competition;
- The price is based on an established catalog or market price of a commercial item sold in substantial quantities to the general public;
- The price is set by law or regulations; or
- The item to be acquired is a commercial item for which the price is determined to be reasonable through price analysis.

In estimating the costs to be incurred on government contracts, contractors' cost estimating systems must incorporate large amounts of data generated from a myriad of sources and departments. These data often include historical data, vendor quotations, projections based on changes in production methods, changes in technology, volume changes, management decisions, and estimates of future costs. As such, the data obtained from the cost accounting system must suit the needs of the cost estimating system.

The accuracy of the contractor's cost estimating system is critical, since estimating mistakes can only harm the contractor. If estimates are understated, a loss may be sustained on the contract. If proposed costs are overstated, the company may be vulnerable to a downward price adjustment as a result of defective pricing.

When certified cost or pricing data are required, the offeror has little latitude in the detail and format of the cost proposal submitted to the government. Standard Form 1411 Contract Pricing Proposal Cover Sheet specifies how the data should be submitted. Instructions for preparing the form (see Exhibit 31.1), which are contained in FAR 15.804-6(b)(2), outline the documentation needed to support the proposed price and require, as a minimum, separate supporting schedules, detailing various cost elements, for each proposed contract line item. The schedules should also reflect any specific requirements established by the contracting office. In addition to submitting detailed cost data, the company's cost proposal should include any information reasonably required to explain the estimating process used, including judgmental factors applied, the methods used in the estimates (including projections), and the nature and amounts of any contingencies included in the proposed price.

Today's increasingly sophisticated manufacturing cost collection and reporting systems provide substantial information for estimating the costs of future efforts. To the extent that shop-floor report systems, formal Material Requirements Planning Systems, and other systems are used, the information they contain should be considered in developing cost estimates.

Cost proposals must be compatible with the cost-accounting system that the contractor anticipates using to measure and accumulate costs during contract performance. To comply with government requirements for CAS covered contracts, the cost-accounting system must be able to produce information on the specific cost elements and in the same detail as proposed.

Relevant information that becomes available before final contract negotiation must be provided to the contracting officer. The contractor should maintain a record of all data provided, the date and to whom provided, and, if feasible, copies of all data provided to the contracting officer and/or the auditor.

FAR 15.811 identifies only broad factors to be considered in determining the acceptability of a contractor's estimating system.

- The source of data used for estimates and procedures for ensuring that the data are accurate, complete and current.

Materials	Provide a consolidated priced summary of individual material quantities included in the various tasks, orders, or contract line items being proposed and the basis for pricing (vendor quotes, invoice prices, etc.) Include raw materials, parts, components, assemblies, and services to be produced or performed by others. For all items proposed, identify the items and show the source, quantity, and price.
	For those acquisitions (e.g., subcontracts, purchase orders, material orders) exceeding the pertinent threshold set forth at 15.804-2(a)(1) priced on a competitive basis, also provide data showing degree of competition, and the basis for establishing the source and reasonableness of price. For interorganization transfers priced at other than cost of the comparable competitive commercial work of the division, subsidiary, or affiliate of the contractor, explain the pricing method (see 31.205-26(e)).
	When an exception from the requirement to submit cost or pricing data is claimed, whether the item was produced by others or by the offeror, provide justification for the exception as required by 15.804-3(e).
	For those acquisitions (e.g., subcontracts, purchase orders, material orders) exceeding the pertinent threshold set forth at 15.804-2(a)(1) priced on a noncompetitive basis, also provide data showing the basis for establishing source and reasonableness of price. For standard commercial items fabricated by the offeror that are generally stocked in inventory, provide a separate cost breakdown if priced based on cost. For interorganizational transfers priced at cost, provide a separate breakdown of cost by elements. As required by FAR 15-806-2(a) provide a copy of cost or pricing data submitted by the prospective source in support of each subcontract, or purchase order that is either: (i) $1,000,000 or more, or (ii) both more than the pertinent threshold set forth at 15.804-2(a)(1)(iii) and (iv) and more than 10 percent of the prime contractor's proposed price. The contracting officer may require submission of cost or pricing data in support of proposals in lower amounts. Submit the results of the analysis of the prospective source's proposal as required by FAR 15.806. When the submission of a prospective source's cost or pricing data is required as described above, it shall be included as part of the offeror's initial pricing proposal.
Direct labor	Provide a time-phased (e.g., monthly, quarterly) breakdown of labor hours, rates, and cost by appropriate category, and furnish bases for estimates.
Indirect Costs	Indicate how offeror has computed and applied offeror's indirect costs, including cost breakdowns, and showing trends and budgetary data, to provide a basis for evaluating the reasonableness of proposed rates. Indicate the rates used and provide an appropriate explanation.
Other Costs	List all other costs not otherwise included in the categories described above (e.g., special tooling, travel, computer and consultant services, preservation, packaging and packing, spoilage and rework, and Federal excise tax on finished articles) and provide bases for pricing.
Facilities Capital Cost of Money	When the offeror elects to claim facilities capital cost of money as an allowable cost, the offeror must submit Form CASB-CMF and show the calculation of the proposed amounts (see FAR 31.205-10).

Exhibit 31.1.   (Excerpts from Table 15–2 Instructions for submission of a Contract Pricing Proposal, FAR 15.804-6(b).)

- The documentation in support of the estimate.
- The assignment of responsibilities for originating reviewing and approving estimates.
- The coordination and communication between organizational elements responsible for cost estimates.
- Management support, controls and training.

The DOD FAR Supplement, provides much more specific criteria. As stated in DFARS 215.811-70(b)(ii), all defense contractors must have estimating systems that consistently produce well-supported proposals that are acceptable as a basis for negotiation of fair and reasonable prices. The characteristics of an adequate estimating system and the indicators of potentially significant estimating deficiencies, as set forth in DFARS 215.811, are contained in Exhibits 31.2 and 31.3.

(c) MATERIAL MANAGEMENT AND ACCOUNTING SYSTEMS (MMAS).   While no specific requirements relating to material cost accounting are contained in FAR, DFARS 252.242-7004, addresses "systems for planning, controlling, and accounting for the acquisition, use and disposition of material." As stated in DFARS 242.7202, all defense contractors must reasonably forecast material requirements, assure that costs of purchased and fabricated material are charged or allocated to a contract on the basis of valid time-phased requirements and maintain

---

(1) General. An adequate system should provide for the use of appropriate source data, utilize sound estimating techniques and good judgment, maintain a consistent approach, and adhere to established policies and procedures.

(2) Evaluation. In evaluating the adequacy of a contractor's estimating system, the ACO should consider whether the contractor's estimating system, for example—

   (i) Establishes clear responsibility for preparation, review and approval of cost estimates;

   (ii) Provides a written description of the organization and duties of the personnel responsible for preparing, reviewing, and approving cost estimates;

  (iii) Assures that relevant personnel have sufficient training, experience and guidance to perform estimating tasks in accordance with the contractor's established procedures;

  (iv) Identifies the sources of data and the estimating methods and rationale used in developing cost estimates;

   (v) Provides for appropriate supervision throughout the estimating process;

  (vi) Provides for consistent application of estimating techniques;

 (vii) Provides for detection and timely correction of errors;

(viii) Protects against cost duplication and omissions;

  (ix) Provides for the use of historical experience, including historical vendor pricing information, where appropriate;

   (x) Requires use of appropriate analytical methods;

  (xi) Integrates information available from other management systems, where appropriate;

 (xii) Requires management review including verification that the company's estimating policies, procedures and practices comply with this regulation;

(xiii) Provides for internal review of and accountability for the adequacy of the estimating system, including the comparison of projected results to actual results and an analysis of any differences;

(xiv) Provides procedures to update cost estimates in a timely manner throughout the negotiation process; and

 (xv) Addresses responsibility for review and analysis of the reasonableness of subcontract prices.

Exhibit 31.2.   Characteristics of an Adequate Estimating System, DFARS 215.811-70(d).

The following examples indicate conditions that may produce or lead to significant estimating deficiencies—

(i) Failure to ensure that relevant historical experience is available to and utilized by cost estimators as appropriate;

(ii) Continuing failure to analyze material costs or failure to perform subcontractor cost reviews as required;

(iii) Consistent absence of analytical support for significant proposed cost amounts;

(iv) Excessive reliance on individual personal judgment where historical experience or commonly utilized standards are available;

(v) Recurring significant defective pricing findings within the same cost element(s);

(vi) Failure to integrate relevant parts of other management systems (e.g., production control or cost accounting) with the estimating system so that the ability to generate reliable cost estimates is impaired;

(vii) Failure to provide established policies, procedures and practices to persons responsible for preparing and supporting estimates.

Exhibit 31.3. Indicators of Potentially Significant Estimating Deficiencies, DFARS 215.811-70(d)(3).

a consistent, equitable and unbiased logic for costing material transactions. Ten standards (see Exhibit 31.4), are used in determining whether systems comply with the DOD policy. The standards, developed jointly by DOD and industry representatives, are vigorous and difficult to meet.

One of the key requirements is that inventories be based on "valid time phased requirements." The accuracy requirements, 98% for the bill of materials and 95% for the master production schedule, are designed to ensure that the right materials are assigned to contracts based on the time-phased requirements. Difficulties arise when the bill of materials and/or production schedule are not updated, thus raising doubt as to whether the materials being procured are actually required and are only procured when they are needed for current production. Selecting the time period to measure the master production schedule is difficult, yet critical to achieving the accuracy requirements. Initially, the schedule should follow the production cycle, but problems often occur when the government (1) concurrently contracts for spares which have a much shorter cycle or (2) changes delivery requirements. Selecting a time period that is too short or too long can result in an accuracy level that falls below the 95% required to meet the standard. Many defense contractors have found it difficult to demonstrate that DOD has not been harmed materially by not meeting the bill of materials or production schedule accuracy standards. Because of the problems in quantifying the impact of not meeting the standards, it is also difficult to demonstrate a cost benefit of not correcting such deficiencies.

The 95% accuracy standard for physical inventory is designed to ensure that parts reported in the system for government contracts actually are in inventory and inventories allocated to defense contracts and included in requests for progress payments have actually been used on those contracts. However, accuracy levels for physical inventories may be difficult to achieve when a contractor uses the gross numbers of items in the inventory. To establish the accuracy levels of inventories, defense contractors are periodically required to take complete physical inventories or cycle counts. During these counts, contractors can stratify inventories based on the value of the items and establish differing accuracy levels for various strata. For example, a specialized electronic component with a unit value of several thousand dollars may be put in a stratum that requires 100% accuracy; whereas a bolt with a value of less than one cent may be in a stratum that requires 60% accuracy. A potential result of using multiple strata is that

MMAS systems shall have adequate internal accounting and administrative controls to assure system and data integrity; and comply with the following:

(1)   Have an adequate system description including policies, procedures and operating instructions compliant with the FAR and DFARS;

(2)   Ensure that costs of purchased and fabricated material charged or allocated to a contract are based on valid time phased requirements as impacted by minimum/economic order quantity restrictions. A 98% bill of material accuracy and a 95% master production schedule accuracy are desirable as a goal in order to assure that requirements are both valid and appropriately time phased. If systems have accuracy levels below these, the Contractor shall demonstrate that there is no material harm to the government due to lower accuracy levels, and the cost to meet the accuracy goals is excessive in relation to the impact on the Government;

(3)   Provide a mechanism to identify, report and resolve system control weaknesses and manual override. Systems should identify operational exceptions such as excess/residual inventory as soon as known;

(4)   Provide audit trails and maintain records . . . necessary to evaluate system logic and to verify through transaction testing that the system is operating as desired;

(5)   Establish and maintain adequate levels of record accuracy, and include reconciliation of recorded inventory quantities to physical inventory by part number on a periodic basis. A 95% accuracy level is desirable. If systems have an accuracy level below 95%, the Contractor shall demonstrate that there is no material harm to the government due to lower accuracy level, and the cost to meet the accuracy goal is excessive in relation to the impact on the Government;

(6)   Provide detailed descriptions of circumstances which will result in manual or system generated transfers of parts;

(7)   Maintain a consistent, equitable, and unbiased logic for costing of material transactions. The Contractor shall maintain and disclose a written policy describing the transfer methodologies. The costing methodology may be standard or actual cost, or any of the inventory costing methods in 48 CFR 9904.411-50(b). Consistency must be maintained across all contract and customer types, and from accounting period to accounting period for initial charging and transfer charging. The system should transfer parts and associated costs within the same billing period. In the few circumstances where this may not be appropriate, the Contractor may use a "loan/payback" technique only if approved by the ACO. When the technique is used, the Contractor shall have controls to ensure (A) Parts are paid back expeditiously; (B) Procedures and controls are in place to correct any overbilling that might occur; (C) Monthly, at a minimum, identification of the borrowing contract and the date the part was borrowed, and (D) The cost of the replacement part is charged to the borrowing contract;

(8)   Where allocations from common inventory accounts are used, have controls in addition to the requirements of standards in paragraphs (b)(2) and (7) of this clause to ensure that: (i) reallocations and any credit due are processed no less frequently than the routine billing cycle; (ii) inventories retained for requirements which are not under contract are not allocated to contracts; and (iii) algorithms are maintained based on valid and current data;

(9)   Notwithstanding FAR 45.505-3(f)(1)(ii), have adequate controls to ensure that physically commingled inventories that may include material for which costs are charged or allocated to fixed-price, cost-reimbursement, and commercial contracts do not compromise requirements of any of the standards in paragraphs (f)(1) through (8) of this clause. Government furnished materials shall not be—(i) Physically commingled with other material; or (ii) Used in commercial work; and

(10)   Be subjected to periodic internal audits to ensure compliance with established policies and procedures.

Exhibit 31.4.   Material Management and Accounting System Standards, DFARS 252.242-7004.

inaccuracy in one strata may cause the accuracy of the entire inventory to fall below the 95% level; however, using multiple strata may make it easier to demonstrate that DOD has not been harmed due to the lower accuracy in low-value parts.

Another key requirement addresses the transfer of parts between contracts, since transfers can affect billings based on cost. Transfers must be well documented, consistently applied and use appropriate and equitable pricing methodologies. Loan/payback systems use the principle that contracts that receive transfers of parts due to changed requirements should bear the cost of the parts purchased to replace the items transferred; such systems are permitted only when the loan and the payback are accomplished in the same billing period or, with governments approval, when billings are adjusted to mitigate any overbilling.

System programming and records must be maintained in machine-readable form for the record retention period outlined in 31.2(e). This requirement also points out the government's changing view of what constitutes an adequate audit trail.

(d) PROJECT MANAGEMENT SYSTEMS.   The ability to monitor and project costs on government contracts is of increasing importance. The government is particularly concerned about overpaying cost-based progress payments and not being forewarned about potential cost overruns.

The preparation of a comprehensive estimate of contract costs at completion is key to assessing progress and determining if problems exist. These estimates should be prepared at least quarterly to ensure the reliability of interim financial statements and to avoid surprises that come too late for effective corrective action. Management must be informed promptly and periodically of the key facts concerning contract performance. Inherent in such systems is a configuration management function that tracks changes to the technical "baseline" of a product. Project management systems need to timely provide such information as:

- Actual cost to date.
- Budgeted cost for work scheduled.
- Budgeted cost for work performed.
- Estimated cost to complete.
- Estimated cost at completion.
- Contract amount (including changes).
- Projected overrun or underrun.
- Contract scheduled completion date.
- Expected completion date.
- Projected slippage.

To ensure that it can monitor the contractor's progress on major procurements, DOD inserts a clause into certain large contracts requiring a cost/schedule control system. The criteria necessary to comply with this clause are described in *Cost/Schedule Control Systems Criteria Joint Implementation Guide.*[5] Basically, a cost/schedule control system breaks down the contract into work packages, identifies organizations and managers who are responsible, develops a schedule, and budgets the costs by those work packages.

The "Limitation of Cost" clause (FAR 52.232-20) used in fully funded cost-reimbursement contracts and the "Limitation of Funds" clause (FAR 52.232-22) inserted in incrementally funded cost-reimbursement contracts, obligate the contractor to notify the government of anticipated overruns or underruns when, within the next 60 days, the cumulative cost incurred to

---

[5] Departments of the Air Force, Army, Navy, and the Defense Supply Agency. Cost/Schedule Control Systems Criteria Joint Implementation Guide (Washington, DC, AFMCP 173-5, AMC-P 715-5, NAV 50 P3627, DLAH 8400.2, DCAA P7641.47).

date in performing the contract are expected to exceed 75% of the estimated cost of, or funds allotted to, the contract. The contractor must also notify the government of anticipated overruns or underruns anytime the total contract cost is expected to be substantially more or less than the estimated cost or allotted funds. The government is not obligated to reimburse the contractor for any cost in excess of the contract estimated cost or funds allotted to the contract. Nor is the contractor obligated to continue performance or incur any costs in excess of the contract estimated costs or funds allotted. The "Limitation of Cost or Funds" clauses are designed to give the government an opportunity to decide whether it can and will provide additional funds necessary to complete the work. The reporting requirements of these clauses, require government contractors to maintain project management systems that allow for timely notification of potential cost overruns. Boards of contract appeals and the courts have ruled in numerous instances that inadequate accounting or project management systems are not valid excuses for not providing the notice required by the clauses.[6]

(e) BILLING SYSTEMS

(i) Cost-Reimbursement Contracts. The "Allowable Cost and Payment" clause (FAR 52.216-7) provides for reimbursement of costs incurred in contract performance that are deemed "allowable" by the contracting officer, in accordance with applicable cost principles and contract terms.

Notwithstanding the specific provisions of the cost principles (discussed in subsection 31.3(a)) the clause limits cost reimbursement contract billings to:

- Recorded costs for items or services purchased directly for the contract that, at the time of request for reimbursement, have been paid (not applicable to small business).
- Costs incurred, but not necessarily paid, for materials issued from the contractor's stored inventory, direct labor, direct travel, other direct in-house costs, and properly allocable and allowable indirect costs.
- Pension, deferred profit-sharing, and employee stock-ownership plan contributions that are, as a minimum, funded on a quarterly basis.
- Progress payments that have been paid to subcontractors.

The contractor's cost accounting system is used to determine properly allocable costs. As discussed in subsection 31.3(b) the allocation of costs to a government contract may be subject to some or all of the provisions of the CASB's rules, regulations, and standards.

In establishing the allowable indirect costs under a contract, indirect cost rates are applied to allowable contract base costs. Since indirect cost rates can be definitively determined only at the completion of a contractor's fiscal year, estimated rates are required to reimburse contractors on an interim basis. These rates, referred to as billing rates, are based on the anticipated final annual rates. To prevent substantial overpayment or underpayment, the billing rates should be adjusted as needed during the year. The contractor must determine the continued appropriateness of previously established billing rates given the passage of time and experience. The administrative contracting officer or auditor responsible for determining the final indirect cost rates is usually responsible for establishing the billing rates to be used.

Final indirect cost rates, which are generally determined after the contractor's fiscal period ends, are used to determine indirect expenses applicable to cost-reimbursement-type contracts, as well as fixed price redeterminable and incentive-type contracts. The contractor is required to submit the final indirect cost rate proposal to the Administrative Contracting Officer (ACO) and auditor within 90 days after expiration of the fiscal year. The proposal must include cost

---

[6] *Defense Systems Concepts, Inc.,* ASBCA No. 44540, November 13, 1992, 93-2 BCA 25,568.

data supporting the indirect cost rate computations (i.e., indirect costs and base costs incurred for the year, as well as an identification of the flexibly priced contracts to which the rates apply).

Contractors also must certify that expressly unallowable costs have been excluded and that indirect costs are properly allocable to contracts. The certification requirements should not be taken lightly. Contractors should ensure that effective internal controls exist to properly screen unallowable costs from indirect expense proposals. FAR 42.703-2 requires execution of the certificate whenever provisional billing rates or final indirect cost rate proposals are submitted. The certificate must be signed by a senior management official at a level no lower than vice president or chief financial officer. A contract clause entitled "Certificate of Indirect Costs" (see Exhibit 31.5) is included in contracts that provide for interim reimbursement of indirect costs, establishment of final indirect cost rates, or cost-based progress payments.

Including unallowable costs in proposals for settlement of indirect costs also subjects contractors to certain monetary penalties prescribed in FAR 31.110 and 42.709.

(ii) Fixed-Price Contracts. Under the provisions of the "Progress Payments" clause (FAR 52.232-16), fixed-price contracts requiring the use of significant contractor working capital for extended periods generally provide for progress payments if the contractor is reliable, is in satisfactory financial condition, and has an adequate accounting and control system. Payments are made as work progresses, as measured by eligible costs incurred, percentage of completion, or other measure of the specific stages of physical completion. Progress payments based on percentages or stages of physical completion are normally restricted to construction-type contracts or shipbuilding, conversion, alteration, or repair contracts. Consequently, most progress payments are based on incurred costs.

Customary progress payments are generally considered reasonably necessary when a contract or a grouping of contracts exceeds $1 million ($100,000 for small business concerns) and when lead time between the initial incurrence of cost and the first delivery or completion of service extends six months (four months for small business concerns). Progress payments are not permissible if the items are quick-turnover types for which progress payments are not a customary commercial practice.

Payments are based on specified percentages applied to the eligible cost incurred by the contractor in performing the contract.

Eligible costs include all expenses of contract performance that are allowable, reasonable, allocable to the contract, consistent with sound and generally accepted accounting principles and practices, and not otherwise excluded by the contract. However, costs eligible for reimbursement under monthly progress payments are limited to:

- Recorded allowable costs that, at the time of request for reimbursement, have been paid for items or services purchased directly for the contract. (For small businesses, these costs need not be paid.)

- Allowable costs incurred, but not necessarily paid, for materials issued from the contractor's stored inventory, direct labor, direct travel, other direct in-house costs, and properly allocable and allowable indirect costs.

- Allowable pension, deferred profit-sharing, and employee stock-ownership plan contributions that are funded on a quarterly basis.

- Unliquidated progress payments to subcontractors. (However, these costs are fully allowed and not subject to reduction by applying progress payment rates.)

(f) RECORD-RETENTION REQUIREMENTS. The audit-negotiation clause (FAR 52.215-2) required in negotiated contracts or modifications and the audit-sealed bidding clause (FAR 52.214-26) required in contract modifications awarded under sealed bidding form the

(a) The Contractor shall—(1) Certify any proposal to establish or modify billing rates or to establish final indirect cost rates; (2) Use the format in paragraph (c) of this clause to certify; and (3) Have the certificate signed by an individual of the Contractor's organization at a level no lower than a vice president or chief financial officer of the business segment of the Contractor that submits the proposal.

(b) Failure by the Contractor to submit a certificate, as described in this clause, shall result in payments of indirect costs at rates unilaterally established by the Government.

(c) The certificate of indirect costs shall read as follows:

CERTIFICATE OF INDIRECT COSTS

This is to certify that to the best of my knowledge and belief:

1. I have reviewed this indirect cost proposal submitted herewith;

2. All costs included in this proposal (identify proposal and date) to establish billing or final indirect cost rates for (identify period covered by rate) are allowable in accordance with the requirements of contracts to which they apply and with the cost principles of the Federal Acquisition Regulation (FAR) applicable to those contracts;

3. This proposal does not include any costs which are unallowable under applicable cost principles of the FAR or its supplements, including but not limited to: advertising and public relations costs, contributions and donations, entertainment costs, fines and penalties, lobbying costs, defense of fraud proceedings, and good will; and

4. All costs included in this proposal are properly allocable to Government contracts on the basis of a beneficial or causal relationship between the expense incurred and the contracts to which they are allocated in accordance with applicable acquisition regulations.

I declare under penalty of perjury that the foregoing is true and correct.

Firm: _____

Signature: _____

Name of Corporate Official: _____

Title: _____

Date of Execution: _____

(End of clause)

Exhibit 31.5.   Certificate of Indirect Costs Clause, FAR 52.242-4.

basis of the government's access to contractor records, and require that contractors provide the contracting officer, or a representative of the contracting officer who is a government employee, with access to certain records whenever:

• Cost or pricing data is required;
• A cost reimbursement or flexibly priced contract is used; or
• Cost, funding, or performance reports are required by the contract.

The audit clauses must be flowed-down to all the subcontracts over $10,000.

In these situations, contractors must make available relevant books, records, documents and other data or evidence, and accounting procedures and practices. The data must be maintained for three years after final payment, except where shorter retention periods are prescribed in FAR 4.705 for certain specified types of data. Exhibit 31.6 summarizes these exceptions.

Retention Requirements	
2 Year Data	**4 Year Data**
Labor cost distribution cards	Accounts receivable invoice and supporting data
Petty cash records	Material, work order or service order files
Time cards	Cash advance recapitulations
Payroll checks	Paid, canceled and voided checks
Material and supply requisitions	Accounting payment records and supporting data
	Payroll registers
	Maintenance work orders
	Equipment property records
	Expendable usage records
	Material inspection & receiving reports
	Purchase orders and supporting data
	Production and quality records

Exhibit 31.6.   Summary of record retention requirements in FAR 4.705.

31.3 SPECIFIC ACCOUNTING REQUIREMENTS

(a) **COST PRINCIPLES.**   The FAR and departmental FAR supplement cost principles apply to contracts and subcontracts awarded on or after April 1, 1984. While a concerted effort has been underway in recent years to enhance the uniformity in determining what costs are acceptable, agency differences still exist. Contractors should be aware of such differences so that any proposals, claims, and billings submitted to a particular agency conforms to that organization's unique cost principles. Major agencies which have issued cost principle supplements are listed in Exhibit 31.7.

(i) **Advance Agreements on Particular Cost Items (FAR 31.109).**   Because the cost principles apply broadly to many accounting systems in varying contract situations, the reasonableness and allocability of certain cost items to a given contract may be difficult to determine, particularly when firms or organizational divisions within firms are not subject to effective competitive restraints.

   To avoid possible disallowance or dispute based on unreasonableness or nonallocability, contractors are encouraged to seek advance agreement with the government on the treatment of

Organization	Procurement Acquisition Regulation	FAR System Chapter No.
Federal agencies	FAR	1
DOD	DFARS	2
GSA	GSAR	5
AID	AID FAR Supplement	7
VA	VA FAR Supplement	8
DOE	DEAR	9
EPA	EPA FAR Supplement	15
NASA	NASA FAR Supplement	18
ICA	ICA FAR Supplement	19

Exhibit 31.7.   Cost principles contained in the Federal Acquisition Regulations System.

special or unusual costs. Advance agreements should be negotiated before the cost covered by the agreement is incurred. Agreements must be in writing, executed by both contracting parties, and incorporated in the applicable contracts. Contracting officers are not authorized to enter into advance agreements for the treatment of cost inconsistent with the other provisions of the cost principles.

In the present era of reduced military spending, many companies are facing critical issues of downsizing their operations. Fundamental to optimizing the financial impact of these strategies is the use of advance agreements. Advance agreements can be effectively used to mitigate the adverse impact of these strategies on the recovery of costs on government contracts. Restructuring that results from downsizing and/or business combinations often causes the incurrence of significant nonrecurring costs (e.g., severance payments, early retirement incentives, idle facilities and idle capacity) and accounting practice changes. These increased overhead costs generally are not recoverable under existing firm-fixed-price contracts since the prices for these contracts have already been established.[7] Since restructuring decisions benefit future operations, contractors may wish to negotiate advance agreements to recover such costs over future periods. By amortizing the costs over future years, contractors may recover a portion of such costs in pricing new firm-fixed-price contracts. Advance agreements are required for recovery of restructuring costs on defense contracts.

Other costs for which advance agreements may be particularly important include:

- Compensation for personal services.
- Precontract costs.
- Travel and relocation costs as related to special or mass personnel movements and maximum per diem rates.
- Travel via contractor-owned, -leased, or -chartered aircraft.
- Costs of idle facilities and idle capacity.
- Mass severance pay to employees.
- Plant reconversion.

Given the potentially controversial nature of many of the costs listed in FAR 31.109, it is readily understandable why they are suggested as items for which advance agreements may be appropriate.

(ii) Composition of Total Allowable Costs.   The cost principles of commercial organizations define the "total cost of a contract" as the sum of the allowable direct and indirect costs allocable to the contract, less allocable credits, plus any allocable cost of money. Credits are defined as the applicable portion of income, rebates, allowances, and other credits that relate to allowable costs. Credits can be given to the government as either cost reductions or cash refunds.

The distinction between direct and indirect costs is a significant concept in the cost principles. A direct cost is identifiable with a specific final cost objective (e.g., the contract), whereas indirect costs are incurred for more than one cost objective. However, direct costs of insignificant amounts may be treated as indirect costs for administrative convenience. Consistent application of criteria for identifying costs as either direct or indirect is emphasized. Once a cost is identified as a direct cost to a particular contract, the same type of cost, incurred in similar circumstances, may not be included in any indirect expense pool allocated to that contract or any other contract.

---

[7] Increased costs are only recoverable on FFP CAS-covered contracts if the increased costs result from a cost accounting practice change that the Administrative Contracting Offer deems to be desirable.

The cost principles do not prescribe which costs should be charged as direct as opposed to indirect. The criteria for charging direct versus indirect should be based on an analysis of the nature of the particular contractor's business and contracts. The criteria should be codified into a written statement of accounting principles and practices for classifying costs and for allocating indirect costs to contracts.

(iii) Factors Affecting Allowability (FAR 31.201).   Costs are not allowable merely because they were determined by application of the company's established accounting system. Factors considered in determining the allowability of individual cost items include: (1) reasonableness; (2) allocability; (3) cost accounting standards, if applicable, or generally accepted accounting principles and practices appropriate in the particular circumstances; (4) terms of the contract; and (5) limitations specified in the cost; principles. A company should succeed in obtaining reimbursement for incurred costs if the contracting officer believes that all these criteria have been met.

Reasonableness.   Reasonableness has been one of the more difficult concepts in the regulations because of the substantially subjective nature of the concept. The cost principles consider a cost to be reasonable if, in its nature and amount, it does not exceed that which would be incurred by a prudent person in the conduct of competitive business. The cost principles recognize that reasonableness must often be determined on a case-by-case basis, considering the specific circumstances, nature, and amount of the cost in question. Reasonableness determinations depend upon a variety of considerations and circumstances including:

- Is the cost generally recognized as ordinary and necessary for conducting business or performing the contract?
- Does the cost reflect sound business practices, arm's length bargaining, and the requirements of federal and state laws and regulations?
- Would a prudent business person take similar action, considering his or her responsibilities to the business owners, employees, customers, the government, and the public?
- Are significant deviations from established contractor practices inordinately increasing contract costs?

Allocability.   Although the concept of cost allocability is not complicated, its application can become extremely difficult and frequently controversial. The cost principles consider a cost to be allocable if it is assignable or chargeable to one or more cost objectives in accordance with the relative benefits received or other equitable relationship. Subject to the foregoing, a cost is allocable to a government contract if it:

- Is incurred specifically for the contract;
- Benefits both the contract and other work, or both government work and other work, and can be distributed to them in reasonable proportion to the benefits received; or
- Is necessary to the overall operation of the business, although a direct relationship to any particular cost objective cannot be shown.

If it is direct, the entire cost is recoverable against a specific contract; if indirect, only an appropriate portion of the expense can be recovered on a given contract. Frequently, disagreements focus on the extent of "benefit" to the government. There is no requirement that benefit to the government be capable of precise measurement.

Cost-Accounting Standards or Generally Accepted Accounting Principles.   Certain cost accounting standards have been specifically incorporated into the cost principles. A practice inconsistent with those standards is subject to disallowance under the cost principles as well as a finding of noncompliance with the standards.

If cost accounting standards are not applicable, generally accepted accounting principles (GAAP) may be an authoritative reference for determining appropriate accounting treatment.

While no single reference source exists for all established accounting principles, the American Institute of Certified Public Accountants, *Codification of Statements on Auditing Standards,* contains a fairly complete summary of the body of knowledge that might be classified as GAAP. Rule 203 of the AICPA *Code of Professional Ethics* identifies statements and interpretations issued by the Financial Accounting Standards Board, Accounting Principles Board opinions, and AICPA accounting research bulletins as authoritative pronouncements that require compliance. In the absence of these authoritative sources, AICPA notes that:

> . . . the auditor should consider other possible sources of established accounting principles, such as AICPA accounting interpretations, AICPA industry audit guides and accounting guides and industry accounting practices. Depending on their relevance in the circumstances, the auditor may also wish to refer to APB statements, AICPA statements of position, pronouncements of other professional associations and regulatory agencies, such as the Securities and Exchange Commission, and accounting textbooks and articles. . . . [8]

Although GAAP have been defined for a variety of financial reporting practices, cost accounting standards address the allocability of costs to specific final cost objectives (e.g., contracts). Consequently, the courts and boards of contract appeals have generally given considerable weight to GAAP only when more definitive accounting treatment is not prescribed in the acquisition regulations or the contract itself. The boards and courts have cautioned against relying on GAAP to determine the allocability of costs to government contracts by noting that "such principles have been developed for asset valuation and income measurement and 'are not cost accounting principles' as such, although 'cost accounting concepts . . . may evolve out of them.' "[9] When the cost accounting treatment permitted by GAAP is contrary to the criteria provided in the cost accounting standards, cost principles, or the contract, these latter criteria generally prevail.

Selected Costs.   The cost principles have changed over the years with disturbing regularity in response to unique aspects of government contracting, such as public policy considerations, administrative convenience, and congressional interest. The acquisition regulations require that expressly unallowable costs, plus all directly associated costs, be identified and excluded from proposals, billings, and claims submitted to the government. "Directly associated costs" are defined as those that would not have been incurred if the other cost (e.g., the unallowable cost), had not been incurred. Salary costs of employees who engage in activities that result in unallowable costs, such as acquisitions and mergers, are generally subject to question only if the employees expend a substantial portion of their time on the unallowable activity; however, for certain proscribed activities (e.g., legislative lobbying and certain legal proceedings), the salary costs are themselves unallowable, regardless of amount.

The cost principles do not address each cost that may be incurred, and the absence of a cost principle for a particular cost item does not imply that it is either allowable or unallowable. FAR 31.204 (c) states:

> When more than one subsection in 31.205 is relevant to a contractor cost, the cost shall be apportioned among the applicable subsections, and the determination of allowability of each portion shall be based on the guidance contained in the applicable subsection. When a cost, to which more than one subsection in 31.205 is relevant, cannot be apportioned, the determination of allowability shall be based on the guidance contained in the subsection that most specifically deals with, or best captures the essential nature of, the cost at issue.

---

[8] American Institute of Certified Public Accountants, Codification of Statements on Auditing Standards No. 1-39, 1982, A U sec. 411, para. 02.
[9] *Celesco Industries,* ASBCA No. 22401, January 31, 1980, 80-1 BCA 14,271.

Cost items described in the cost principles are listed in Exhibit 31.8, with a brief summary as to whether or not the cost is allowable.

(b) COST ACCOUNTING STANDARDS. The cost accounting standards affect most companies doing business with the federal government and have significantly affected many accounting systems. In addition to the records needed for financial reporting and tax return preparation, contractors must often maintain a third set of records to comply with the standards. These problems are a particular concern to contractors whose government business is immaterial in relation to their total business.

The impact of CAS on accounting systems varies with the amount of government business performed by the contractor, the contractor's size, and the sophistication of its record-keeping function. Contractors may desire to change their cost accounting practices used for financial reporting purposes to conform with cost accounting standards, if such costing techniques are responsive to operational requirements. Other contractors may choose to maintain separate memorandum records to establish the cost accounting practices used for government contract costing purposes.

Preamble A to CAS 401 addresses the use of memorandum records as follows:

> Commentators stated that the purpose of the standards would require each contractor to revise his formal system of accounts in order to maintain them on a basis used for estimating Government contracts. The Board did not intend that requirement. The standard does not contain any requirement that a contractor must revise his formal system of accounts. Cost accounting records are supplemental to, and generally subsidiary to a contractor's financial records. However, it is necessary that the cost accounting records be reconcilable to the contractor's general financial records.

The impact of cost accounting standards goes beyond the need to develop and maintain new accounting systems. Standards can affect companies' profits and resulting capital accumulation and, if such effect is adverse, can discourage companies from pursuing government work and thus weaken the base of suppliers available to satisfy the government's needs. Significant issues raised by industry are that CASB standards are too detailed and rigid, favor the government, give little attention to alternatives, and do not sufficiently weigh costs against benefits to be derived.

However, there have been some positive effects from cost accounting standards. By requiring more objective allocation techniques and by limiting alternative accounting procedures through more specified criteria, contract costing has become more comparable and consistent. CAS regulations have also provided a structured framework for effecting changes in cost accounting practices. Finally, the disclosure statement has proven to be a useful document for gaining a mutual understanding of the practices to be used in costing government contracts. Compliance with cost accounting standards should not be taken lightly. Failure to comply can result in adverse adjustments of costs and profits.

The original Cost Accounting Standards Board (CASB) established in 1970 by Public Law 91-379, ceased to exist after Congress declined to further fund the board. During its turbulent life, CASB promulgated accounting practice disclosure requirements and 19 cost accounting standards. In 1988, Public Law 100-379 reestablished a five-member CASB within the Office of Federal Procurement Policy, and chaired by the OFPP Administrator. The other four members consist of a DOD member (appointed by the Secretary of Defense), a GSA member (appointed by the Administrator of General Services), an industry member, and a private-sector member knowledgeable in cost accounting matters. The latter two are appointed by the OFPP Administrator. The DOD and GSA members are currently the Director of the DCAA and the GSA Assistant Inspector General for Auditing, respectively.

The CASB is directed by statute to promulgate standards to achieve uniformity and consistency in the cost accounting principles followed by prime contractors and subcontractors in

Public relations & advertising costs	−1	Substantially unallowable
Automatic data processing equipment leasing costs	−2	Allowable with restrictions
Bad debts	−3	Unallowable
Bonding costs	−4	Allowable
Civil defense costs	−5	Mixed allowable/unallowable
Compensation for personal services	−6	Allowable with restrictions
Contingencies	−7	Unallowable
Contribution and donations	−8	Unallowable
Cost of money	−10	Allowable
Depreciation	−11	Allowable (but see 31.205-52)
Economic planning costs	−12	Allowable
Employee morale, health, welfare, food service, and dormitory costs and credits	−13	Allowable with restrictions
Entertainment costs	−14	Unallowable
Fines and penalties and mischarging costs	−15	Unallowable
Gains and losses on disposition of depreciable property or other capital assets	−16	Allowable (Gains limited to depreciation taken)
Idle facilities and idle capacity costs	−17	Allowable with restrictions
Independent research and development and bid and proposal costs	−18	Allowable
Insurance	−19	Substantially allowable
Interest and other financial costs	−20	Unallowable
Labor relations costs	−21	Allowable
Legislative lobbying costs	−22	Unallowable
Losses on other contracts	−23	Unallowable
Maintenance and repair costs	−24	Allowable
Manufacturing and production engineering costs	−25	Allowable
Material costs	−26	Allowable
Organization costs	−27	Unallowable
Other business expenses	−28	Allowable
Plant protection costs	−29	Allowable
Patent costs	−30	Allowable with restrictions
Plant reconversion costs	−31	Substantially unallowable
Precontract costs	−32	Allowable with restrictions
Professional and consultant service costs	−33	Allowable with restrictions
Recruitment costs	−34	Allowable with restrictions
Relocation costs	−35	Allowable with restrictions
Rental costs	−36	Allowable with restrictions
Royalties and other costs for use of patents	−37	Allowable with restrictions
Selling costs	−38	Allowable with restrictions
Service and warranty costs	−39	Allowable
Special tooling and special test equipment costs	−40	Allowable
Taxes	−41	Allowable with restrictions
Termination costs	−42	Generally allowable
Trade, business, technical, and professional activity costs	−43	Allowable
Training and educational costs	−44	Allowable with restrictions
Transportation costs	−45	Allowable
Travel costs	−46	Allowable with restrictions
Costs related to legal and other proceedings	−47	Substantially unallowable
Deferred research and development costs	−48	Generally unallowable
Goodwill	−49	Unallowable
Executive lobbying costs	−50	Unallowable
Cost of alcoholic beverages	−51	Unallowable
Asset valuations resulting from business combinations	−52	Unallowable

Exhibit 31.8.   FAR 31.205 selected costs.

estimating, accumulating, and reporting costs for pricing, administering, and settling negotiated prime contracts and subcontracts in excess of $500,000. The board is authorized to issue and amend regulations and to exempt from its standards certain classes or categories of contractors. The CAS regulations also require contractors to:

- Disclose in writing their cost accounting principles, including methods of distinguishing direct costs from indirect costs and the basis used for allocating indirect costs; and
- Agree to contract price adjustments in favor of the government, with interest, for any net increased costs resulting from failure either to comply with duly promulgated cost accounting standards or to consistently follow their cost accounting principles in pricing contract proposals and in accumulating and reporting contract performance cost.

The CASB's Rules, Regulations and Standards are codified in Title 48 of the Code of Federal Regulations, Chapter 99.

(i) Contract Coverage.   CAS coverage is determined at the segment or business unit level of a company. A "segment" is defined as a subdivision of an organization, such as a division, product department, or plant, which usually has profit responsibility and/or produces a product or service. A "business unit" can be either an individual segment or an entire business organization that is not divided into segments.

CAS coverage criteria is as follows:

- Business units that have not received a negotiated prime contract or subcontract in excess of $500,000, which required submission of a cost data, are exempt from CAS.
- Negotiated contracts/subcontracts which require submission of cost data and are not subject to one of the CAS exemptions, are subject to either the "full" CAS clause or the "modified" CAS clause.
  - Negotiated contracts/subcontracts over $500,000 but less than $25 million are eligible for "modified" coverage if the business unit's total CAS-covered awards in the preceding cost accounting period were either less than $25 million or greater than $25 million but no CAS covered award exceeded $1 million. A contractor who is eligible to use "modified" coverage has to elect such coverage; otherwise, "full" coverage will apply.
  - Negotiated contracts/subcontracts over $500,000 but less than $25 million are subject to "full" coverage if the business unit's total CAS-covered awards in the preceding cost accounting period were $25 million or more, provided at least one CAS covered award exceeded $1 million.
  - A single CAS-covered award of $25 million or more is subject to "full" coverage.

Exemptions and Waivers.   Contracts awarded on the basis of sealed bidding are statutorily exempt from CAS. Contracts for which the negotiated prices are $500,000 or less or are based on established catalog or market prices of commercial items sold in substantial quantities to the general public or on prices set by law or regulation are also statutorily exempt from CAS coverage. In 1976, the Comptroller General ruled that statutory exemptions are mandatory and "do not allow for agency discretion as to whether to grant the exemption."[10] Adequate price competition is not a statutory exemption from CAS.

In addition to the statutory exemptions, the CASB has exempted from its rules, regulations, and standards the following:

---

[10] *Gulf Oil Trading Co.,* Comp. Gen. No. B-184333, March 11, 1976, 22 CCF 80,153.

- Any contract or subcontract awarded to a small business concern, as defined by Small Business Administration regulations.
- Any contract or subcontract awarded to a foreign government or its agencies or instrumentalities.
- Any contract or subcontract awarded to a foreign concern, except for CAS 401 and 402.
- Any contract or subcontract made with a United Kingdom contractor for performance substantially in the United Kingdom, provided that the contractor has filed with the U.K. Ministry of Defence a completed CASB disclosure statement. If the contractor is already required to follow U.K. government accounting conventions, the disclosed practices must be in accordance with the requirements of those conventions.
- Any firm-fixed-price contract or subcontract awarded without submission of cost data.
- Contracts executed and performed entirely outside the United States or its territories and possessions.

CASB is also authorized to waive, at the request of designated executive agency officials, all or part of its standards or rules for particular contracts or subcontracts. Such waivers are granted on the basis of whether the procurement agency establishes, to CASB's satisfaction, that the contract involved is essentially a sole-source procurement with such urgency that finding an alternative supplier is not feasible.

Contract Clauses.   An agency implements CAS by including a notice in the solicitation to offerors and inserting a CAS clause in the negotiated contract. Contracts subject to CASB regulations include either the full-coverage clause or the modified-coverage clause, a distinction which, in fact, determines the number of standards to be applied. Both clauses also contain provisions for handling disputes, examining contractor's records, and flowing down an applicable CAS clause to all covered subcontracts.

Full CAS Coverage—Organizations Other Than Educational Institutions.   The clause applicable to full coverage ("Cost Accounting Standards," FAR 52.230-2) requires a contractor to:

- Describe in writing its cost accounting practices when a business unit is part of a company that is required to submit a disclosure statement.
- Follow its cost accounting practices consistently.
- Comply with all cost accounting standards in effect either on the contract award date or on the date of the signed certificate of current cost or pricing.
- Comply prospectively with all cost accounting standards that become applicable during contract performance.
- Agree to an adjustment of contract price, or cost allowance (as described below) when it fails to comply with existing standards or to follow its cost accounting practices and when making changes to its existing practices.

Modified Coverage—Organizations Other Than Educational Institutions.   The clause applicable to modified coverage ("Disclosure and Consistency of Cost Accounting Practices," FAR 52.230-3) requires a contractor not otherwise exempt to:

- Comply with 99404.401, 99404.402, 99404.405, and 99404.406.
- Describe in writing its cost accounting practices when a business unit is part of a company that is required to submit a disclosure statement.
- Consistently follow its cost accounting practices.

- Agree to an adjustment of contract price, or cost allowance (as described below) when it fails to comply with applicable standards or to follow established cost accounting practices.

CAS Coverage—Educational Institutions.   Educational institution not otherwise exempt must:

- Comply with 99505.501, 99505.502, 99505.503, and 99505.506 (comparable to 99404.401, 99404.402, 99404.405, and 99404.406).
- Describe in writing their cost accounting practices when required.
- Consistently follow their cost accounting practices.
- Agree to an adjustment of contract price or cost allowance when they fail to comply with applicable standards or to follow established cost accounting practices.

CAS Administration Clause.   The clauses for CAS coverage are accompanied by an "Administration of Cost Accounting Standards" (FAR 52.230-5) clause, which outlines the procedures and time requirements for the contractor to notify the contracting officer about anticipated changes in any cost accounting practice. The notification must include a written description of any change to be made, together with a general dollar cost impact showing the shift of costs between CAS-covered contracts by contract type and other work. For changes required to implement a new standard, the description must be provided within 60 days of the date of award of the contract requiring the change. For any other change, it is required not less than 60 days before the effective date of the proposed change. For noncompliance, the written description must be provided within 60 days after the date of agreement of such noncompliance. Other dates for providing the written descriptions may be mutually agreed to by the contracting parties.

The "administration" clause also requires a contractor to submit a cost-impact proposal, in the form and manner specified by the contracting officer, within 60 days after the contracting officer's determination of adequacy and compliance of the descriptions submitted above. The proposal is generally required to be submitted on a contract-by-contract basis. The clause permits the ACO to withhold up to 10% of subsequent payments due under the contract until a required cost-impact proposal is submitted.

In addition, the "administration" clause requires a contractor to agree to appropriate contract or subcontract amendments to reflect price adjustments or cost allowances resulting from changes in cost accounting practices or noncompliance. It also provides for the flow of CAS requirements down to lower-tier subcontractors that are not otherwise exempt from CAS. Further, the contractor must advise the contracting officer within 30 days, or any other mutually agreed-upon date, of an award of a CAS-covered subcontract.

Proper administration of this clause requires a system for identifying contracts and subcontracts containing the CAS clauses.

Price Adjustments for Changes in Cost Accounting Practices or for Correction of Noncompliant Practices.   Three types of CAS contract price adjustments can arise, as outlined below:

1. A contract is eligible for equitable adjustment when the contractor (1) is initially required to apply a standard or (2) implements an accounting change that the contracting officer has found to be desirable and not detrimental to the government's interests. The price adjustment is the net increase or decrease in costs resulting from the application of the new standard(s) or desirable changes to all covered contracts. Equitable adjustments may cause the government to pay increased costs to the contractor or may reduce the contract prices.

   Equitable adjustments resulting from a contractor's requirement to apply a new standard are limited to the prospective effect of the new standard on costs and prices of covered price contracts and subcontracts awarded before the standard's effective date. Thus, all uncompleted contracts subject to CAS must be recosted and repriced in accordance with the new requirements to determine the amount of the equitable adjustment.

Equitable adjustments resulting from desirable changes occur when an accounting practice changes during the performance of CAS-covered contracts. These adjustments are applied prospectively from the change date to covered prime contracts and subcontracts awarded before the accounting change occurred. Criteria to be used in determining whether an accounting change is desirable encompass the tests of being appropriate, warranted, equitable, fair, or reasonable.

2. CAS-covered contracts and subcontracts are adjusted prospectively for the effect of voluntary changes in practice that the contracting officer has not found to be in the government's interest. The price adjustment is the net increased cost to the government resulting from the application of the revised practice to all covered contracts. Adjustments are made only in favor of the government.

3. CAS-covered contracts and subcontracts are adjusted retroactively to reflect a contractor's failure to comply with applicable standards and disclosed practices. Adjustments arising from noncompliance are made only in favor of the government. The net adjustment is the resulting increased cost plus interest at the annual rate established by the Internal Revenue Service. Cost increases and decreases may be offset on affected covered contracts.

"Increased cost" is defined as: (1) cost paid by the government that, as a result of a changed practice or a CAS noncompliance, is higher than the cost that would have been paid had the change or noncompliance not occurred; and (2) the excess of the negotiated price on a fixed-price contract over the price that would have been negotiated if the proposal had been priced in accordance with the practices actually used during contract performance.

The primary purpose of the contract adjustment procedures is to hold contractors accountable for the practices used to cost government contracts. To accomplish this important objective, CASB defined a cost accounting practice and a cost accounting practice change.

The term "cost accounting practice" is defined in 48 CFR 9903.302-1 as any accounting method or technique used to measure cost, assign cost to cost accounting periods, or allocate cost to cost objectives. Cost measurement encompasses accounting methods and techniques to define cost components, determine bases for cost measurement, and establish criteria for alternative cost measurement techniques. Cost assignment encompasses the criteria used to determine the timing of the cost occurrence (e.g., the cost accounting period(s) to which the cost should be charged). Examples of assignment methods or techniques include the accrual versus cash basis of accounting. Cost allocations encompass methods or techniques to accumulate cost, to determine whether a cost is to be directly or indirectly allocated, to determine the composition of cost pools, and to determine the appropriate allocation base.

In a significant decision involving Martin Marietta,[11] ASBCA and the Court of Appeals for the Federal Circuit ruled that realignments of cost pools that do not change the composition of the pools or the allocation base are not cost accounting practice changes.

A "cost accounting practice change" is defined in 48 CFR 9903.302-2 as an alteration in a cost accounting practice except that:

• The initial adoption of a cost accounting practice for the first time a cost is incurred, or a function is created, is not a change in cost accounting practice. Also, the partial or total elimination of a cost or the cost of a function is not a change in cost accounting practice.

---

[11] *Martin Marietta Corp.,* ASBCA Nos. 38920, 41565, Sept. 4, 1992, BCA 25, 175, CAFC No. 93-1164, February 10, 1995, 47 F.2d1134.

In accordance with that definition, ASBCA ruled in NI Industries, Inc.[12] that neither the termination of a defined benefit pension plan nor the adoption of a replacement defined contribution plan constituted a change in cost accounting practice.

- The revision of a cost accounting practice for a cost that previously had been immaterial is not a change in cost accounting practice.

To clarify the definition, the CASB regulation also provides practical examples of such changes.

On March 8, 1995, the CASB issued Interpretation 95-01, "Allocation of Contractor Restructuring Costs Under Defense Contracts." The interpretation applies to standards 403, 404, 406, 409, and 418 as they relate to restructuring costs associated with CAS-covered awards. Although CASB did not follow the promulgation process established in Part 990, government and industry generally agree with the guidance contained in Interpretation 95-01. The interpretation recognizes that restructuring costs may be either expensed or deferred and amortized over a period not to exceed five years. Restructuring costs incurred for the first time may be treated as the initial adoption of a cost accounting practice if the contractor does not have an established or disclosed practice covering such costs. If a contractor previously expensed restructuring costs and wishes to defer and amortize future costs, the resultant change in cost accounting practice may be presumed to be desirable and not detrimental to the interests of the government, thus enabling the contractor to obtain equitable adjustment for the impact of such costs on CAS-covered awards.

(ii) Disclosure Statements

Purposes and Uses.   The disclosure statement requirement reflects CASB's legislative mandate to require contractors and subcontractors, as a condition of contracting, to disclose in writing their cost accounting principles, including methods of distinguishing direct costs from indirect costs and the basis used for allocating indirect costs. The disclosure statement provides a written, measurable baseline from which to measure compliance and the consistent application of accounting practices. Contractors must adhere to their own certified practices.

To describe and document a contractor's accounting practices, CASB developed a detailed statement, (CASB-DS-1), for commercial and nonprofit organizations and CASB-DS-2 for educational institutions. The administrative contracting officer is designated to review the adequacy of the statements and to notify the contractor of any reporting deficiencies. The ACO delegates this review to DCAA.

Disclosure statements will not be made public when, as a condition of filing the statement, a contractor requests confidentiality. Contractors should designate those parts of the statement they wish to have kept confidential.

Exemption Provisions.   Disclosure statements must only be filed by those organizations (1) whose negotiated CAS covered prime contracts and subcontracts, at all divisions and subsidiaries during the company's prior fiscal year, exceeded $25 million and at least one award exceeded $1 million, or (2) that received a single award of a $25 million CAS-covered contract or subcontracts. Once the organization has met the filing threshold based on prior year CAS covered awards, only segments whose CAS covered awards in the prior year exceeded $30 million and 10% of sales must actually submit disclosure statements. The statements must be filed within 90 days after the close of the fiscal year in which the threshold was exceeded. When the cost accounting practices are identical for more than one business unit, only one statement need be submitted, but each unit must be identified. Any business unit that is

---

[12] *NI Industries, Inc.*, ASBCA No. 34943, November 29, 1991, 92-1 BCA 24,631; affirmed April 6, 1992, 92-2 BCA 24,980.

selected for award of a single CAS-covered defense award of $25 million must submit the disclosure statement before award. Amendments to disclosure statements are processed by submitting the changed pages, together with a new cover sheet, to the cognizant ACO and auditor.

To avoid the requirement for universities to file disclosure statements at the same time, CASB devised a method for phasing in disclosure statement filings applicable to contracts awarded on or before December 31, 1995. A business unit of an educational institution that is listed on Exhibit A of OMB Circular A-21:

- Must submit the statement within six months after award of a covered contract if the institution is numbered 1 to 20 on the Exhibit.
- Must submit the statement between 6 and 12 months after award of a covered contract if the institution is numbered 21 to 50 on the Exhibit.
- Must submit the statement between 1 year and 18 months after award of a covered contract if the institution is numbered 51 to 99 on the Exhibit.

For a business unit of an educational institution that is not listed in Exhibit A of OMB Circular A-21, a disclosure statement must be submitted within six months after award of a covered contract. Awarding agencies are authorized to waive preaward Disclosure Statement submission for awards between January 1, 1996 through June 30, 1997, if a due date for submission has previously been established.

Determination of Adequacy.   Submission of an adequate disclosure statement, when required, is necessary before a contract may be legally awarded. An adequate disclosure statement must be current, accurate, and complete. Furthermore, the ACO must specifically determine whether a statement is adequate and must notify the contractor of that determination in writing. Although contract should not be awarded until the ACO has determined that the disclosure statement is adequate, contracting officers have waived the requirement for an adequacy determination before award when necessary to protect the government's interest.

The flow-down provisions of the CAS clause require subcontractors to submit disclosure statements if they have met the filing requirements. While the CAS regulations provide for submission of subcontractor disclosure statements to the prime contractors, FAR 30.203 permits subcontractors to submit disclosure statements to the government instead of to the prime contractor. This may be necessary if the subcontractor does not want to divulge competitive information to the prime contractor, or if the subcontractor is already performing as a government prime contractor. Even if the disclosure statement is submitted to the government, this action does not relieve the prime contractor of its responsibility for ascertaining subcontractor compliance with the requirements of the CAS clause. CASB noted in its regulations that a prime contractor might wish to include an indemnification clause in its subcontracts.

Determination of Compliance.   Neither the CAS regulations nor the acquisition regulations require the ACO to determine, before contract award, that the disclosure statement complies with applicable standards. However, the acquisition regulations require that, after the adequacy determination, the auditor review the disclosed practices for compliance with applicable standards and report the audit findings to the ACO. The ACO is required to obtain a revised disclosure statement and negotiate any required price adjustments if the disclosed practices are determined to be in noncompliance with applicable standards. Some of the items in the disclosure statement pertain to cost accounting practices addressed in specific standards. Prudent contractors should consider the requirements of applicable standards in their disclosure statement responses.

Contents and Problem Areas.   The key to avoiding a deficient disclosure statement is complete disclosure. Auditors are admonished to be alert for vague, incomplete, or ambiguous answers which could lead to alternative accounting interpretations. Materiality is a major factor in determining the level of detail required to be disclosed; consideration should be given to whether a change in accounting procedures would materially affect the flow of costs. Contractors should use the statement's continuation sheets to expand on specific responses and to clearly convey the accounting practices followed. A description of the DS-1 follows.

- *Cover Sheet and Certification.* Identifies the reporting unit, its address, and the official to be contacted regarding the statement. A certification of the statement's completeness and accuracy must be executed by an authorized signatory of the reporting unit.
- *General Information (Part I).* Includes industry classification, sales volume, proportion of government business to total, type of cost system, and extent of integration of the cost system with the general accounts.
- *Direct Costs (Part II).* Contractors are asked to define direct material, direct labor, and other direct costs and to disclose the bases for making direct charges. Accounting for variances under standard costs is explored in depth. In describing classes of labor, sufficient information is required to distinguish the principal labor rate categories.
- *Direct vs. Indirect Costs (Part III).* Contractors must designate how various functions, cost elements, and transactions are treated and, if indirect, what aggregate pools are used. Disagreements have involved the extent of detail required to describe the criteria for determining whether costs are charged directly or indirectly.
- *Indirect Costs (Part IV).* Allocation bases must be identified and described for all overhead, service center, and general and administrative pools used by the contractor.
- *Depreciation and Capitalization (Part V).* The criteria for capitalization, the methods of depreciation used, the bases for determining useful lives, and the treatment of gains and losses from disposition are to be specified.
- *Other Costs and Credits (Part VI).* This part covers the methods used for charging or crediting vacation, holiday, sick pay, and other compensation for personal absence.
- *Deferred Compensation and Insurance Costs (Part VII).* Descriptions are required of pension plans and the determination of pension costs, as well as certain types of deferred compensation and insurance costs. Each reporting unit must complete this section even if the information must be obtained from the home office.
- *Corporate or Group Expenses (Part VIII).* Pooling patterns and allocation bases for distributing corporate group expenses (home-office expenses) to organizational segments must be specified and described.

The DS-2 for educational institutions is similar to the DS-1. It contains a cover sheet and certification and seven parts.

- General Information (Part I).
- Direct Costs (Part II).
- Indirect Costs (Part III).
- Depreciation and Use Allowances (Part IV).
- Other Costs and Credits (Part V).
- Deferred Compensation and Insurance Costs (Part VI).
- Central System or Group Expenses (Part VII).

For organizations other than educational institutions, a separate disclosure statement (Parts I–VII) must be submitted for each covered segment (e.g., profit center, division, or other organizational unit). Also, a separate Part VIII must be submitted for each group or home office with costs allocated to one or more CAS-covered segment. The section should not be completed by divisions to which home-office expenses are allocated.

Amendments to disclosure statements must be submitted to the same agencies to which original filings were made. Revised data on sales for items 1.4.0–1.7.0 of Part I and 8.2.0 of Part VIII must be submitted annually at the beginning of the contractor's fiscal year. Only those pages affected by a change are to be resubmitted with a new cover sheet when the disclosure statement is revised or amended.

(iii) The Cost Accounting Standards.   The 19 standards and four interpretations promulgated for commercial and nonprofit organizations and the four standards promulgated for educational institutions to date have run the gamut from generalized statements providing for little more than consistency in certain circumstances to highly detailed dissertations on the treatment of specific costs. Which category a specific standard falls into should be readily evident from a review of the standard.

Each standard has an effective date and an applicability date. In some standards, these dates are the same. The effective date designates the point in time when pricing of future covered contracts must reflect the requirements of the standard. Additionally, only those contracts existing when a standard became effective are eligible for equitable adjustment. The applicability date marks the time by which the contractor's accounting and reporting systems must actually conform to the standard.

Provided below are brief summaries of the 19 CASB standards. To fully understand each standard, the entire standard, including prefatory comments (preambles), should be read. (The complete standards appear in 48 CFR, Part 9904 and 9905.) The Standards are discussed in the following order:

	Standards Applicable to	
	Commercial and Nonprofit Organizations	*Educational Institutions*
Consistency Standards	9904.401, 9904.402	9905.501, 9905.502
Allocation Standards	9904.403, 9904.410, 9904.418, 9904.420	
Fixed Asset Accounting Standards	9904.404, 9904.409, 9904.414, 9904.417	
Compensation Standards	9904.408, 9904.412, 9904.413, 9904.415	
Miscellaneous Standards	9904.405, 9904.406, 9904.411, 9904.416	9905.505, 9905.506

Consistency in Estimating, Accumulating, and Reporting Costs (9904.401 and 9905.501).
The purpose is to ensure consistency in each of the contractor's cost accounting practices used to estimate, accumulate, and report costs on government contracts. The objective is to enhance the likelihood that a contractor will treat comparable transactions alike.

- The practices used in estimating costs for a proposal must be consistent with the cost accounting practices followed by the contractor in accumulating and reporting actual contract costs. The standards permit grouping of like costs when it is not practicable to estimate contract costs by individual cost element or function. However, costs estimated for proposal purposes must be presented in such a manner and in sufficient detail so that any significant cost can be compared with the actual cost accumulated and reported.
- The standards specifically require consistency in: (1) classification of elements or functions of cost as direct or indirect; (2) indirect cost pools to which each element or function of cost is charged or proposed to be charged; and (3) methods used in allocating indirect costs to the contract.

The standards do not require that costs, as presented in proposals, reflect exactly the same detail as the actual costs that are accumulated and reported; it requires only that the practices be consistent and in sufficient detail to permit a valid comparison. The important consideration is to produce reasonable "trails" from the cost included in the proposal to those accumulated in the accounting records and subsequently reported to the government.

Interpretation No. 1 responded to questions concerning consistency in estimating and recording scrap or other losses of direct materials. The interpretation does not prescribe the level of detail required to be maintained. However, it requires, when a significant part of material cost is estimated by means of percentage factors, that the practice be supported by appropriate accounting, statistical, or other relevant records that document the actual scrap or other losses.

Consistency in Allocating Costs Incurred for the Same Purpose (9904.402 and 9905.502). The standards require that each type of cost be allocated only once and on only one basis. The standards prohibit a contract from being charged more than once for the same type of cost by requiring that a cost incurred for the same purpose, in like circumstances, be classified as either direct cost only or indirect cost only. However, the standards also relate to the system's design as a whole and not necessarily to the treatment on individual contracts. Thus, the standards also prohibit a specific contract from being charged direct for a cost if the same cost incurred in like circumstances is also included in an overhead pool, but not allocated to that contract.

The key element is whether the cost is incurred for the same purpose and in like circumstances. If either the purpose or the circumstances differ, then the accounting practices related to the two separate transactions need not be consistent and would not be covered by this standard. If a contractor has submitted a disclosure statement, it should provide sufficient criteria for determining whether a particular cost in a given circumstance is treated as a direct or indirect cost.

Interpretation No. 1 concludes that B&P costs are not always incurred for the same purpose and in like circumstances. B&P costs specifically required by contractual terms and conditions can, on a consistent basis, be properly treated as direct costs, while other contractor B&P costs may be recorded as indirect costs.

Allocation of Home Office Expenses to Segments (9904.403).   This standard governs the allocation of the home office expenses to the segments (business units) under its control and divides home office expenses into three categories:

- Expenses incurred for specific segments. Such costs should be allocated directly to those segments to the maximum extent practical.
- Expenses incurred for various segments, such as centralized services, certain line and staff management, and centralized payments and accruals, whose relationship to those segments can be measured on some objective basis. Such expenses should be grouped in logical and homogeneous expense pools and allocated on the most objective basis available.
- Expenses incurred to manage the organization as a whole that have no identifiable relationship to any specific segment or segments. The aggregate of such residual expenses must be allocated to segments either: (1) on the basis of a three-factor formula (payroll dollars, operating revenue, and net book value of tangible capital assets plus inventories); or (2) on any basis representative of the segments' total activity. The three-factor formula is required when total residual expenses exceed stated proportions of the aggregate operating revenues of all segments for the previous fiscal year.

A special allocation of home office expenses to particular segments is permitted when it can be shown that the benefits from the expense pool to the segment(s) are significantly different from the benefits accruing to the segments.

Interpretation No. 1, permits use of segment book income as a factor in allocating income tax expense to segments only when the segment book income is expressly used by the taxing jurisdiction in computing the income tax.

Allocation of Business Unit General and Administrative Expenses to Final Cost Objectives (9904.410).   The standard narrowly defines "G&A expenses" to include only expenses that are incurred for the general management and administration of the business unit as a whole and that do not have a directly measurable relationship to particular cost objectives. Home office expenses that meet the definition of segment G&A expense are includable in the receiving segment's G&A expense pool. Insignificant expenses that do not qualify by definition as G&A expenses may be included in G&A expense pools. Other significant requirements of the standard are:

- The G&A expense pool must be allocated to final cost objectives (i.e., contracts) by means of one of three cost input bases: (1) total cost input (total production costs), (2) value-added cost input (total production costs excluding material and subcontract costs), or (3) single-element cost input (direct labor dollars or hours), whichever is most appropriate in the circumstances.
- A special allocation is permitted when the benefits from G&A expense to a particular final cost objective significantly differ from the benefits accruing to other final cost objectives. When a special allocation is used, the expense allocated must be excluded from the residual G&A pool, and the cost input of the cost objective must be removed from the cost input base used.

Allocation of Direct and Indirect Cost (9904.418).   The standard requires that a contractor have a written policy for distinguishing between direct and indirect costs and that such costs be consistently classified. A "direct cost" is defined as a cost that is identified specifically with a particular final cost objective. An "indirect cost" is defined as a cost that is identified with two or more final cost objectives or with at least one intermediate cost objective. Pertinent provisions of the standard are:

- Indirect costs must be accumulated in homogeneous cost pools. A cost pool is considered homogeneous if: (1) the major activities in the pool have similar beneficial/causal relationships to cost objectives, or (2) separate allocations of costs of dissimilar activities would not result in substantially different amounts. ASBCA ruled in Litton Systems, Inc.[13] that the standard does not necessarily prohibit the use of multi-facility average direct labor or overhead rates.
- Materiality is a key consideration in whether heterogeneous cost pools must be separately allocated. No changes in the existing indirect cost pool structure are required if the allocations resulting from the existing base(s) are not materially different from the allocations that would result from using discrete homogeneous cost pools.
- A cost pool that includes a significant amount of direct labor or direct material management activities should be allocated on a base representative of the activity being managed. A cost pool that does not include a significant amount of labor or material management activities e.g., service center, should be allocated in accordance with the following hierarchy of preferred bases: (1) a resource consumption measure, (2) an output measure, and (3) a surrogate representative of resources consumed.
- A special allocation of indirect costs is permitted where a particular cost objective receives significantly more or less benefit from an indirect cost pool than would result from a normal allocation of such costs.

---

[13] *Litton Systems, Inc.,* ASBCA No. 37131, February 3, 1994, 94-2 BCA 26,731.

Accounting for Independent Research and Development Costs and Bid and Proposal Costs (9904.420).   CAS provides criteria for accumulating IR&D and B&P costs and for allocating those costs to final cost objectives. IR&D expenses are identified as technical effort that is neither sponsored by a grant nor required for performance of a contract, and that falls into the area of basic and applied research, development, or systems and other concept formulation studies. B&P costs are those incurred in preparing, submitting, or supporting any bid or proposal that is neither sponsored by a grant, nor required for contractor performance. The standard covers such costs incurred at both the home office and the business unit levels. The major provisions are:

- IR&D and B&P costs must be identified and accumulated by project, except when the costs of individual projects are not material.

- IR&D and B&P project costs include all allocable costs except business unit G&A. In essence, IR&D and B&P projects are treated like final cost objectives except for the allocation of G&A expenses.

- IR&D and B&P projects performed by one segment for another segment are considered final cost objectives of the performing segment, rather than IR&D and B&P projects, unless the work is part of an IR&D or B&P project of the performing segment. In that case, the IR&D or B&P project will be transferred to the home office for reallocation to the benefiting segments.

- IR&D and B&P costs accumulated at the home office level are allocated to specific segments where projects are identified with such segments; otherwise, the costs are allocated to all segments using the CAS 403 residual expense allocation base. Segment IR&D and B&P costs are allocated to contracts using the G&A base.

- A special allocation of IR&D and B&P costs is appropriate at either the home office or the segment level if a particular segment (for home office costs) or a particular final cost objective (for segment costs) receives significantly more or less benefit from IR&D and B&P costs than would result from the normal allocation of such costs.

Capitalization of Tangible Assets (9904.404).   Contractors must establish and adhere to a written policy on tangible asset capitalization. The policy must designate the economic and physical characteristics on which the policy is based and identify, to the maximum extent practicable, the components of plant and equipment that are capitalized when asset units are initially acquired or replaced. Additionally, the contractor's policy must designate minimum service life and minimum acquisition cost criteria for capitalization, which may not exceed two years and $1,500, respectively. Other provisions are:

- Tangible capital assets constructed for a contractor's own use must be capitalized at amounts that include general and administrative expenses when such expenses are identifiable with the constructed assets and are material in amount. When the constructed assets are identical or similar to the contractor's regular product, such assets must be capitalized at amounts that include a full share of indirect costs.

- Donated assets that meet the contractor's criteria for capitalization must be capitalized at their fair value.

- Individual low-cost items acquired for the initial outfitting of a tangible capital asset, such as furnishings for an office, which in the aggregate represent a material investment, must be capitalized consistent with the contractor's written policy. Minimum acquisition cost criterion higher in the aggregate than the criterion for such original complements may be designated, provided it is reasonable in the contractor's circumstances.

- Costs incurred that extend the life or increase the productivity of an asset (betterments and improvements) must be capitalized when they exceed the contractor's specified minimum acquisition cost criterion for betterments and when the asset has a remaining life in excess of two years.

- The standard presently subjects capital assets acquired in a business combination under the purchase method to a step-up in basis. The CASB's Notice of Proposed Rulemaking dated March 8, 1995, would prescribe different government contract cost accounting treatments of assets acquired in business combinations, dependent on whether or not the seller's asset costs had been chargeable to CAS covered contracts prior to the business combination.

Depreciation of Tangible Capital Assets (9904.409).   This standard sets forth criteria for assigning costs of tangible capital assets to cost accounting periods and for allocating such costs to cost objectives within such periods. The more important provisions are:

- Estimated service lives for contracting purposes must be reasonable approximations of expected actual periods of usefulness, supported by records of past retirements, disposals, or withdrawals from service. A two-year period, measured from the beginning of the fiscal year in which a contractor must first comply with the standard, is available to develop and maintain such records. Lives based on past experience may be modified to reflect expected changes in physical or economic usefulness, but the contractor bears the burden of justifying estimated service lives that are shorter than those experienced. Estimated service lives used for financial accounting purposes also must be used for government contract costing purposes until adequate records supporting the periods of usefulness are available, if the estimated lives are not unreasonable under the standard's criteria. Assets acquired for which the contractor has no available data or prior experience must be assigned service lives based on a projection of expected usefulness.
- The depreciation method used for financial accounting purposes must be used for contract costing unless it: (1) does not reasonably reflect the expected consumption of services as measured by the expected activity or physical output of the assets; or (2) is unacceptable for federal income tax purposes. If the method used for financial accounting purposes does not meet these tests, the contractor must adopt a method that best measures the expected consumption of services. When a contractor selects a depreciation method for new assets that is different from the method used for like assets in similar circumstances, that new method must be supported by a projection of the expected consumption of services. If the method selected is also used for external financial reporting and is acceptable for income tax purposes, it will be generally accepted.
- Gains or losses on the disposition of assets recognized for contract costing purposes are limited to the difference between the original acquisition cost and the undepreciated balance. The gain or loss, if material in amount, must be allocated in the same manner as depreciation cost; however, if such amounts are immaterial, they may be included in an appropriate indirect cost pool.

Contractors must apply the standard to assets acquired after the beginning of the next fiscal year, following receipt of a covered contract, and are required to support asset lives used in computing depreciation within two years of becoming subject to the standard. This standard does not apply when compensation for the use of tangible capital assets is based on use allowances in lieu of depreciation.

Cost of Money as an Element of the Cost of Facilities Capital (9904.414).   The standard recognizes facilities capital cost of money as an allocable contract cost. The standard provides criteria for measuring and allocating the cost of capital committed to facilities. The more important provisions of the standard are:

- FCCOM is an imputed cost which is identified with the facilities capital associated with each indirect expense pool. Cost of money is allocated to contracts over the same base used to allocate the other expenses in the cost pool in which it is included. For example, manufacturing cost of money is allocated to contracts using the same manufacturing direct labor base that is used to allocate manufacturing overhead.
- The cost of money rate is based on rates published semiannually by the Secretary of the Treasury.
- Form CASB-CMF is used for calculating cost of money factors.
- Procedures for calculating cost of money are:
  — The average net book value of facilities for each indirect expense pool is identified from accounting data used for contract costing. Unless there is a major fluctuation, the beginning and ending asset balances for the year may be averaged to arrive at the average net book value. The facilities capital values should be the same values used to generate depreciation or amortization that is allowed for federal contract costing purposes plus the value of land that is integral to the regular operation of the business unit.
  — The cost of money devoted to facilities capital for each indirect pool is the product of these net book values and the cost of money rates published by the Secretary of the Treasury.
  — FCCOM factors are computed by dividing the cost of money for each pool by the appropriate allocation base.
  — FCCOM is separately estimated, accumulated, and reported for each contract.

Worksheet memorandum records may be used to allocate FCCOM to the incurred base costs of flexibly priced contracts.

Cost of Money as an Element of the Cost of Capital Assets under Construction (9904.417). The standard provides for including an imputed cost of money in the capitalized cost of assets constructed for a contractor's own use. The concept is the same as that in 9904.414, which provides criteria for measuring and allocating cost of money as part of the cost of facilities capital. Pertinent provisions are:

- The cost of money to be capitalized must reflect the application of the commercial borrowing rates published semiannually by the Secretary of the Treasury to a representative investment amount for the period that considers the rate at which construction costs are incurred.
- Other methods for calculating cost of money, such as the method used for financial reporting, may be used, provided the result is not substantially different from the amount calculated as described above.

Accounting for Costs of Compensated Personal Absence (9904.408). The standard provides criteria for measuring, for a cost accounting period, costs of vacation, sick leave, holiday, and other compensated personal absences, such as jury duty, military training, mourning, and personal time off. The standard requires that the costs of compensated personal absences be assigned to the cost accounting period or periods in which the entitlement was earned (accrual basis) and that such costs for an entire cost accounting period be allocated pro rata on an annual basis among that period's final cost objectives. The more significant principles that govern the allocation of these costs are:

- Entitlement is determined when the employer becomes liable to compensate the employee for such absence if the employee were terminated. Probationary periods may be included as a part of the service time creating entitlement.

- An adjustment occasioned by the initial adoption of the standard, the adoption of a new plan, or a change of an existing plan must be carried in a "suspense account" and recognized as a contract cost only to the extent that the suspense account balance at the beginning of the cost accounting period exceeds the ending liability for such compensated absence in a future fiscal year.

Composition and Measurement of Pension Cost (9904.412). The standard establishes the components of pension cost, the bases for measuring such cost, and the criteria for assigning pension cost to cost accounting periods. Two types of pension plans are recognized: a defined-contribution plan in which benefits are determined by the amount of the contributions established in advance, and a defined-benefit plan in which the benefits are stated in advance and the amount to be paid is actuarially calculated to provide for the future stated benefits. Multi-employer collective-bargaining plans and state university plans are considered to be defined-contribution plans. The more important provisions of the standard are:

- For defined-contribution plans, the components of pension cost for a cost accounting period are the payments made, less dividends and other credits. For defined-benefit plans, the components are the normal cost, a part of the unfunded liability, plus interest equivalent and adjustment of actuarial gains and losses.

- Unfunded actuarial liabilities must be consistently amortized in equal annual installments, and such liabilities must be determined by using the same actuarial assumptions as are used for the other pension cost components. Unfunded liabilities for new plans and improvements in existing plans must be amortized within 10 to 30 years.

- Actuarial assumptions must be separately identified. Assumptions used should reflect long-term rather than short-term trends.

- Pension liability costs may be assigned to a cost accounting period only to the extent that the liability is funded.

- For qualified plans, computed pension costs are assigned to a cost accounting period and allocable to cost objectives only to the extent funded. However, if the computed cost exceeds the maximum tax deductible amount, the excess (referred to as an assignable cost deficit) is assigned to future periods and amortized over 10 years. Any unfunded actuarial liability that occurs in the first cost accounting after the assignable pension cost has been so limited will be treated like an actuarial gain or loss and amortized over 15 years. If the computed cost is less than zero (e.g., the plan is fully funded and net actuarial gains exceed normal cost), the computed negative pension cost (referred to as an assignable cost credit) is also assigned to future periods and amortized over 10 years.

- For nonqualified plans which provide nonforfeitable benefits (and the right to the nonforfeitable benefit is communicated to the participant):
  — The computed cost is assignable and allocable to the extent that it is funded through a funding agency at a level at least equal to the percentage of the complement of the highest corporate tax rate in effect on the first day of the accounting period. Because this contribution is not deductible for federal income tax purposes, the required funding level is equal to the after-tax effect of the amount funded for qualified plans.
  — Funding at a lower level than the complement of the highest tax rate will result in a proportional reduction in assigned costs. For example, if the computed pension cost is $100 and the highest tax rate is 35%, pension cost funding of $65 would be required; if only $50 is funded, 77% ($50/$65) of the $100 computed cost or $77 will be assignable and allocable to the current period.

- For nonqualified defined benefit plans which do not meet the communication, nonforfeiture, or funding criteria or are accounted for under the pay-as-you-go cost method, the amount assignable and allocable is the net benefit paid for the period, plus a level 15-year annual installment required to amortize any amount paid to irrevocably settle an obligation for current of future benefits.

SFAS 87 and CAS 412 are not compatible. Consequently, two sets of pension cost calculations must be made by federal contractors that are subject to application of the cost principles for commercial organizations (FAR Subpart §31.2) or full CAS coverage.

Adjustment and Allocation of Pension Cost (9904.413).   The standard provides guidelines for (1) measuring actuarial gains and losses and assigning them to cost accounting periods, (2) valuing pension fund assets, and (3) allocating pension costs to segments. The more important provisions of the standard are:

- Actuarial gains and losses must be calculated annually and amortized over a 15-year period. The amount included in the current year must include the amortized amount of the gain or loss for the year plus interest for the unamortized balance as of the beginning of the period.
- Any recognized pension fund valuation method may be used. However, if the method results in a value that is outside a corridor of 80 to 120% of the assets' market value, the value must be adjusted to the nearest boundary of the corridor.
- Pension costs for segments generally may be calculated either on a composite basis or by separate computation. However, pension costs must be separately calculated for a segment when the costs at the segment are materially affected by certain conditions. Contractors that separately calculate pension costs for one or more segments have the option of establishing a separate segment for inactive participants, such as retirees.
- When a segment is closed or a plan is terminated, the difference between the actuarial liability for the segment and the market value of the assets allocated to the segment as of the closure date must be determined. The difference represents an adjustment of previously determined pension costs. The government's share of any pension plan reversion is determined by the following fraction computed over a period representative of the government's participation on the pension plan:

$$\frac{\text{Pension costs allocated to CAS covered awards}}{\text{Total pension costs}}$$

The government's share of the plan reversion may be obtained through modifications to contracts or by some other techniques.

Accounting for the Cost of Deferred Compensation (9904.415).   The standard provides criteria for measuring deferred compensation costs and assigning such costs to cost accounting periods. The standard covers deferred compensation awards made in cash, stock, stock options, or other assets.

- Deferred compensation costs must be assigned to current cost accounting periods whenever a valid obligation has been incurred (accrual basis) and future funding is assured. If no obligation is incurred before payment, the cost should be assigned to the period(s) of payment. The following criteria are provided for determining whether a valid obligation for deferred compensation costs has been incurred.
  — A future payment is required.
  — The payment is to be made in money, other assets, or shares of stock of the contractor.
  — The amount due can be measured with reasonable accuracy.
  — The recipient is known.

—There is a reasonable probability that any conditions required for the payment will occur.

—There is a reasonable probability that any stock options will be exercised.

• The cost of deferred compensation (i.e., amounts to be paid in the future) must be measured by the present value of the future benefits to be paid. A commercial borrowing rate published semiannually by the Secretary of the Treasury is prescribed for discounting the future payments.

• For awards that require future service, costs should be assigned to cost accounting periods as the future services are performed.

• The cost of deferred compensation must be reduced by forfeitures in the cost accounting periods in which the forfeitures occur. A recipient's voluntary failure to exercise stock options is not considered a forfeiture.

• The cost assignable for stock awards is the market value of the stock on the date the shares are awarded.

• The cost assignable for stock options is the excess of the market value of the stock over the option price on the date the options for the specific number of shares are awarded. Consequently, no cost is assigned to options awarded at market value.

Accounting for Unallowable Costs (9904.405 and 9905.505). The standards do not provide criteria for determining the allowability of costs which is a function of the appropriate procurement or reviewing authority. Rather they establish the accounting treatment and reporting requirements after the costs are determined to be unallowable. The fundamental requirements of the standard are:

• Contractors must identify in their accounting records, and exclude from any proposal, billing, or claim, costs specifically described as unallowable either by the express wording of laws or regulations or by mutual agreement of the contracting parties.

• Contractors must identify: (1) costs designated as unallowable as a result of a written decision by a contracting officer pursuant to contract disputes procedures; (2) any costs incurred for the same purpose and in like circumstances as those specifically identified as unallowable; and (3) the costs of any work project not contractually authorized.

• Costs that are mutually agreed to be directly associated with unallowable costs must be identified and excluded from proposals, billings, or claims. Costs that are designated as directly associated with unallowable costs pursuant to contract disputes procedures must be identified in the accounting records. A directly associated cost is any cost that is generated solely as a result of the incurrence of another cost, and would not have been incurred had the other cost not been incurred.

• Costs specifically described as unallowable, as well as directly associated costs, must be included in any indirect allocation base or bases in which they would normally be included.

Cost Accounting Period (9904.406 and 9905.506). Except in the following specific circumstances, the standards require a contractor to use its normal fiscal year as its cost accounting period.

• When costs of an indirect function exist for only part of a cost accounting period, they may be allocated to cost objectives of that same part of the period.

• Another fixed annual period other than a fiscal year may be used upon mutual agreement with the government if it is an established practice and is consistently used.

• Transitional periods may be used in connection with a change in fiscal year. If the transition period between the end of the previous fiscal year and the beginning of the next fiscal year is three months or less, it may be (1) treated as a stand-alone cost accounting period, (2) combined with the previous fiscal year, or (3) combined with the next regular fiscal year. If the transition period is more than three months, it must be treated as a stand-alone period.

- Where an expense, such as pension cost, is identified with a fixed, recurring annual period that is different from the contractor's cost accounting period, and is consistently employed, its use may be continued.

The cost accounting period used for accumulating costs in an indirect cost pool must be the same as the period used for establishing related allocation bases. Indirect expense rates used for estimating, accumulating, and reporting costs—including progress payments and public vouchers—should be based on the established annual cost accounting period.

Use of Standard Costs for Direct Material and Direct Labor (9904.407).   The standard provides criteria for establishing and revising standard costs, as well as disposing of variances from standard costs, for those contractors who elect to use such costs in estimating, accumulating, and reporting costs of direct material and direct labor. The standard was promulgated because practices concerning the use of standard costs had not been well defined in government procurement regulations. This standard requires that:

- Standard costs must be entered into the books of account.
- Standard costs and related variances must be accounted for at the production unit level. The standard defines a "production unit" as a group of activities that either uses homogeneous input (e.g., direct labor and material) or yields homogeneous outputs.
- Practices relating to setting and revising standards, using standard costs, and disposing of variances must be stated in writing and consistently followed.
- Variances must be allocated to cost objectives at least annually on the basis of material or labor cost at standard, labor hours at standard, or units of output, whichever is most appropriate in the circumstances. If variances are immaterial, they may be included in appropriate indirect cost pools for allocation to applicable cost objectives.

Accounting for Acquisition Costs of Material (9904.411).   The standard sets forth criteria for accumulating and allocating material costs and contains provisions on the use of certain inventory-costing methods. The more important requirements of this standard are:

- First-in, first-out; last-in, first-out; weighted or moving average; and standard cost are all acceptable methods of inventory costing. The method(s) selected must be used consistently for similar categories of material within the same business unit and must be applied "in a manner which results in systematic and rational costing of issues of materials to cost objectives." Although this standard permits the use of the last-in, first-out method, the provision that the method used should result in systematic and rational costing has been interpreted to require costing on a reasonably current basis.
- The cost of units of a category of material can be directly allocated, as long as the cost objective is identified at the time of purchase or production.
- The cost of material used for indirect functions may be allocated to cost objectives through an indirect cost pool when it is not a significant element of production cost. When the cost of such inventories remaining at the end of any cost accounting period significantly exceeds the cost at the beginning of the period, the difference must be capitalized as inventory and the indirect cost pool reduced correspondingly.
- Contractors are required to maintain in writing, and consistently apply, their accounting policies and practices for accumulating and allocating costs of materials.

Accounting for Insurance Costs (9904.416).   The standard provides criteria for measuring, assigning, and allocating insurance costs. The principle requirement of the standard is that the insurance cost assigned to a cost accounting period is the projected average loss for that period plus insurance administration expenses. Other important provisions are:

- Insurance premiums or payments to a trusteed fund, properly prorated and adjusted for applicable refunds, dividends, or additional assessments, should represent the projected average loss.

- For exposure to risk of loss not covered by insurance premiums or payments to a trusteed fund, a program of self-insurance accounting must be developed. If insurance can be purchased against the self-insured risk, the cost of such insurance may be used to estimate the projected average loss. If purchased insurance is not available, the projected average loss should be based on the contractor's experience, relevant industry experience, and anticipated conditions using appropriate actuarial principles. Actual losses can only be charged to insurance expense when they are expected to approximate the projected average loss or are paid to retirees under a self-insurance program.

- Actual loss experience must be evaluated regularly for comparison with the self-insurance cost used to estimate the projected average loss. Actual losses should be measured by the actual cash value of property destroyed, amounts paid or accrued to repair damages, amounts paid or accrued to estates and beneficiaries, and amounts paid or accrued to compensate claimants.

- Insurance costs should generally be allocated on the basis of the factors used to determine the premium or assessment.

- Necessary records must be maintained to substantiate amounts of premiums, refunds, dividends, losses, and self-insurance charges and the measurements and allocation of insurance costs.

(c) CONTRACT CHANGES AND TERMINATIONS.   One of the unique aspects of federal contracting is that the government has the right to change the terms and conditions of an existing contract or cancel the contract through a contract termination.

(i) Contract Changes.   The "Changes" clause permits an equitable adjustment to the contract for any changes made within the general scope of the contract. The purpose of the equitable adjustment is to reimburse either the contractor of the government for the reasonable cost or savings resulting from the difference in cost of performance with and without the change, while not disturbing the profit or loss that will be experienced on the unchanged portion of the contract.

Delays in contract performance that are caused by the government also entitle a contractor to recovery of such increased costs as unabsorbed overhead, idle labor and equipment costs, loss of efficiency, and incremental costs due to performance in a later, higher-cost period.

The government prefers to negotiate the equitable adjustment before the changed work is performed. However, if the contractor cannot estimate the cost of anticipated performance with a sufficient degree of confidence, it may be necessary to wait until after the costs have been incurred to negotiate the equitable adjustment. The use of retroactive pricing places some additional burdens on the contractor to "prove" the incurred cost. Even if incurred costs are presumed to be reasonable, they must be shown to have been incurred specifically for performance of the changed effort or allocable to that effort. Records showing incurred costs are generally needed for the contractor to successfully negotiate the adjustment. The government's recognition of the importance of incurred cost data in negotiating contract changes on a retroactive basis is evidenced in FAR 43.203 which states, in part:

> Contractor's accounting systems are seldom designed to segregate the costs of performing changed work. Therefore, before prospective contractors submit offers, the contracting office should advise them of the possible need to revise their accounting procedures to comply with the cost segregation requirements of the Change Order Accounting clause. (FAR 52.243-6)

Under this clause, contractors may be directed to segregate change-order costs in their accounting records. FAR 43.203 indicates that the following costs are normally segregable and accountable under the terms of the clause:

- Nonrecurring costs (e.g., engineering costs and costs of obsolete work or reperformed work).
- Costs of added distinct work caused by the change order (e.g., new subcontract work, new prototypes, or new retrofit or backfit kits).
- Costs of recurring work (e.g., labor and material costs).

While specific accounting records should assist in measuring the impact of changes, preparation of the request for equitable adjustment will also likely require the use of various estimating techniques.

(ii) Contract Terminations.   When a federal contract is terminated for convenience the contractor is generally entitled to recoup its full cost of performance prior to a termination. However, preparing termination settlement proposals can be both challenging and complex because most cost accounting systems are designed to handle normal operations—contracts performed to completion—not contracts that are prematurely terminated. Thus when a contract is terminated, established procedures for allocating direct and indirect costs may not be appropriate for determining cost of performance. For example, if a contractor incurs significant costs in setting up a new contract production line and charges such costs to overhead, the contractor's established method of allocating overhead to that contract will not provide equitable recovery of the startup cost if the contract is terminated at an early stage of performance. However, once a contractor departs from its usual accounting practices, there is an implication of "double counting" (i.e., charging the same type of cost indirectly in one instance and directly in another). FAR and CAS, fortunately, recognize that double counting exists only when "costs incurred for the same purpose, in like circumstances are charged inconsistently" and that terminations constitute different circumstances.

The cost principle on termination costs (FAR 31.205-42) recognizes that: "Contract terminations generally give rise to the incurrence of costs or the need for special treatment of costs that would not have arisen had the contract not been terminated." The cost principle specifically addresses the allowability of:

- Costs, such as depreciation, that cannot be discontinued as of the date of the termination but that the contractor has taken all reasonable steps to mitigate, e.g., sales or lease of the assets.
- Initial costs such as initial plant rearrangement, production planning, and training, and
- Loss of useful value of special tooling and special machinery and equipment, which cannot reasonably be used on other work and for which the government's interest can be protected, e.g., title passage.
- Termination settlement costs that are incurred solely because of the termination.

In calculating the costs to be included in termination settlement proposals, the FAR Part 49 termination provisions further discuss a fairness concept in addition to the specific allowability criteria tests found in FAR 31.205-42. The FAR provides criteria for equitable recovery of costs by permitting such costs to be deleted from the indirect costs to which they were originally charged and to be recovered as a direct cost on the terminated contract.

The total amount of the termination settlement is limited to the contract price of the items terminated, plus settlement expenses. If a contractor would have sustained a loss on a fixed price contract if it were completed, the termination settlement must be reduced by a loss adjustment factor developed by dividing the total contract price by the estimated cost at completion (i.e., total cost incurred before the termination, plus the estimated costs to complete the contract if the termination had not occurred.) If the costs incurred on a completely or partially terminated contract have been increased because of government action or inaction, a request for equitable adjustment should be prepared, concurrent with the termination settlement proposal, to demonstrate that the contract price should be increased prior to any calculation of a loss factor.

When contractor personnel are engaged in termination settlement activities, allowable settlement labor should be burdened with applicable indirect costs, such as payroll taxes, fringe benefits, occupancy costs, and immediate supervision. Significant settlement expenses should be accumulated under separate account or work order legal and accounting fees, that is charged to the terminated order.

CHAPTER 32

PENSION PLANS AND OTHER POSTRETIREMENT AND POSTEMPLOYMENT BENEFITS

Vincent Amoroso, FSA
KPMG Peat Marwick LLP
Paul C. Wirth, CPA
KPMG Peat Marwick LLP

CONTENTS

32.1 BACKGROUND, ENVIRONMENT, AND OVERVIEW

(a) INTRODUCTION.   The accounting for pensions and other forms of retirement and postemployment benefits underwent dramatic transformation in the 1980s and early 1990s. These changes placed a significant burden on companies and their accountants to understand the intricate concepts of accounting for pension and other types of benefits, assets, obligations, and periodic costs. This chapter has been written to explain those accounting concepts and to assist the reader in understanding and implementing them. The focus will be on the two distinct set of accounting standards that apply to pension and retirement plans—**SFAS No. 35,** "Accounting and Reporting by Defined Benefit Pension Plans," and **SFAS Nos. 87 and 88,** "Employers' Accounting for Pensions" and "Employers' Accounting for Settlements and Curtailments of Defined Benefit Pension Plans and for Termination Benefits." SFAS No. 35 applies to the preparation of financial statements for the pension plan, as an entity. SFAS Nos. 87 and 88, on the other hand, specify the accounting to be followed in the financial statements of the plan sponsor. They also established new standards for measuring a company's annual pension cost and balance sheet pension obligations. Additionally, the intricacies of SFAS No. 106, "Employers' Accounting for Postretirement Benefits Other Than Pensions," and SFAS No. 112, "Employers' Accounting for Postemployment Benefits" will be explored.

(b) DEVELOPMENT OF THE PRIVATE PENSION SYSTEM.   Before consideration of the accounting requirements specified by SFAS Nos. 35, 87, and 88, some background information regarding the pension system may be useful. It will outline why companies sponsor retirement programs and how plans are changing in response to a changing environment.

(i) The Past.   The U.S. private pension system traces its origins to 1875 when the first formal plan was established by a company in the railroad industry. In addition to fostering humanitarian objectives, the early plans were established to achieve a well-defined **management goal**—to affect the age composition of the work force. By using such plans, manufacturing firms could ease out older workers who were less productive and service industries were able to provide promotion opportunities for younger employees. Pension plans were typically established in conjunction with mandatory retirement policies. Tax-driven motives were noticeably absent because there were no meaningful tax incentives until 1942 when corporate tax rates were increased dramatically to finance World War II.

The private U.S. pension system started during the **industrial revolution.** Emerging national companies could not continue their past practice of accommodating aged workers with informal ad hoc policies. One by one, big companies with the financial ability to do so adopted formal retirement arrangements to solve this problem. The list includes the Standard Oil Companies, DuPont, U.S. Steel, and Bell Companies. By 1930 nearly 400 major corporations with more than 4 million workers, representing approximately one-sixth of the private work force, had adopted formal pension plans.

The seeds of federal regulation were sown before the Depression. Many plans were implemented and operated by companies to achieve their goals without regard to **employee rights.** Courts viewed these contracts as one-sided and issued decisions that construed plans as gratuities.

(ii) The Period of Growth.   Plan sponsors' motives for providing pensions have become less homogeneous since World War II. During this period of unprecedented economic prosperity, companies have responded in droves to **increased taxes** and **union demands** (or threats of organization) by establishing plans. Exhibit 32.1 shows the growth in pension coverage between 1940 and 1980.

Higher tax rates coupled with federal wage controls that had been imposed to stifle war-related inflation triggered a spurt of growth in plan formation during the 1940s. Exhibit 32.1 shows that pension coverage doubled in this decade.

The wide-reaching economic prosperity of the 1950s and 1960s had a profound effect on the pension system; coverage almost tripled during this period (see Exhibit 32.1). Through collective bargaining, unions succeeded in establishing plans in many booming industries. Companies with unfilled orders willingly paid the price of starting a program. In addition, plans

NUMBER OF WORKERS COVERED BY PRIVATE PENSION PLANS	
Year	**Number**
1940	4,100,000
1950	9,800,000
1960	18,700,000
1970	26,300,000
1980	35,800,000

Exhibit 32.1.   Growth in pension coverage. *Source:* Alicia H. Munnell, *Economics of Private Pensions,* The Brookings Institution, 1982, p. 11.

were established for nonunion employees to assure parity with unionized co-workers. In companies without unions, plans were developed to ward off organization drives. As the economic pie grew, the one-company worker came to expect that he would be rewarded with a secure retirement for his loyal and long service. He was not disappointed. By the dawn of the congressional debates that culminated in the passage of pension reform legislation in 1974, pension plans had been adopted by virtually all established large and medium-sized companies. Pension coverage is still spotty, however, in smaller companies that operate on thin margins.

Small professional corporations have maintained a proliferation of pension plans as tax shelters during the 1980s. Accumulation of assets and tax savings for the proprietor(s) are the usual goals of these plans. In many ways federal pension regulation has been driven by tax authorities' desire to correct perceived abuses in this segment of the pension system.

(iii) The Present.   The private system is currently under significant **pressure from external forces.** Through repeated changes in the 1980s the federal government is reducing available tax incentives and increasing administrative complexity and, therefore, compliance costs. Foreign competition, corporate restructuring and downsizing, and growing merger activity have caused many companies to rethink their pension policies. Changes in the make-up of the labor force also are having an effect on the makeup of pension programs.

For now, change in plan design and types of plans used for providing retirement income are the only discernible trends in the responses of plan sponsors. Companies are increasingly turning to so-called **nonqualified plans** (see Sponsor Accounting for Nonqualified Plans). Plans such as 401(k) and thrift or matching programs are becoming an increasingly important part of plan sponsors' deferred compensation policies. Younger employees prefer these savings plans because of their visibility, and the predictability of their annual costs appeals to many employers.

(c) PLAN ADMINISTRATION.   Employers still establish plans to affect the age composition of its work force by providing income security during employees' retirement years. A plan's level of benefit and other important features—such as early retirement provisions—balance the sponsor's management goals and cost tolerance. Once a program is established, its administration is dictated by specific plan language, which in turn is affected significantly by federal law.

The **Employee Retirement Income Security Act of 1974** (ERISA) established minimum standards applicable to virtually all employee plans. Certain unfunded nonqualified plans are exempted. Through a succession of amendments since 1974, the original legal standards have been modified and are now considerably more detailed. Employers are not required to start pension plans but, once established, ERISA limits a sponsor's freedom in changing benefits or options. The IRS administers most of the minimum standards, including participation, funding, and vesting and accrual of benefits. The DOL is responsible for the fiduciary and reporting and disclosure requirements. In addition, the DOL assists participants by investigating alleged infractions and by bringing civil action to enforce compliance, if necessary. The **Pension Benefit Guaranty Corporation** (PBGC) administers the termination insurance program established by ERISA.

Plan administration can be viewed as three functions—operation, communication, and compliance. Operating a plan in accordance with its terms requires maintaining sufficient data to determine the proper apportionment of benefits to participants, the calculations needed to apply benefits, and an appropriate level of contributions. Communicating information about benefits to participants assists employees' retirement planning and enhances loyalty. Compliance activities include adopting amendments to conform plans to changing federal requirements and to ERISA's reporting and disclosure requirements. The latter include annual and other reporting to the three pension regulatory agencies and to plan participants.

Most defined benefit pension plans are subject to the **termination insurance program** that was codified by Title IV of ERISA. Covered plans pay annual premiums to the PBGC, which is set as an annual amount per year per participant plus a surcharge applicable to underfunded plans. Within specified time constraints an employer can terminate a fully funded plan at will. A procedure is prescribed for notifying participants and the PBGC. Underfunded plans maintained by employers in financial distress can transfer responsibility to the PBGC for paying benefits guaranteed by the insurance program.

(d) EVOLUTION OF PENSION ACCOUNTING STANDARDS. SFAS Nos. 35, 87, and 88 were the result of approximately 11 years of deliberations by the FASB. However, the controversies concerning the accounting for pension plans well preceded that. As noted in the introduction to SFAS No. 87, since 1956 pension accounting literature has "expressed a preference for accounting in which cost would be systematically accrued during the expected period of actual service of the covered employees."

In 1966, **APB Opinion No. 8,** "Accounting for the Cost of Pension Plans," was issued. Within broad limits, annual pension cost for accounting purposes under APB No. 8 was the same as cash contributions for prefunded plans. Over the years, however, actuarial funding methods have evolved that produce different patterns of accumulating ultimate costs—some are intended to produce level costs, other front-end load costs, and still others tend to back-load costs.

In 1980, the FASB issued SFAS No. 35, which established standards of financial accounting and reporting for the annual financial statements of a defined benefit pension plan. The Statement was considered the FASB's first step in the overall pension project. After SFAS No. 35 was issued, the FASB concluded that the contribution-driven standard prescribed by APB No. 8 was no longer acceptable for employer financial reporting purposes. The proliferation of plans and a total asset pool of nearly $1 trillion (and growing) argued for an accounting approach under which reported costs would be more consistent for a company from one period to the next and more comparable among companies.

SFAS No. 87 and its companion SFAS No. 88 were issued in 1985. These Statements now govern the accounting for virtually all defined benefit pension plans. They prescribe a **single method** for accruing plan liabilities for future benefits that is independent from the way benefits are funded. Standards are prescribed for selecting **actuarial assumptions** used for calculating plan liability and expense components. Most importantly, the discount rate used to calculate the present value of future obligations is market-driven and follows prevailing yields in the bond markets. Taken together, these changes are intended to improve the quality of pension accounting information, but further refinements are possible. SFAS No. 87 states:

> This Statement continues the evolutionary search for more meaningful and useful pension accounting. The FASB believes that the conclusions it has reached are a worthwhile and significant step in that direction, but it also believes that those conclusions are not likely to be the final step in that evolution.

32.2 SPONSOR ACCOUNTING

(a) **SCOPE OF SFAS NO. 87.**   The goal of the FASB in issuing SFAS No. 87 was to establish objective standards of financial accounting and reporting for employers that sponsor pension benefit arrangements for their employees. The Statement applies equally to single-employer plans and multiemployer plans, as well as pension plans or similar benefit arrangements for employees outside the United States. Any arrangement that is similar in substance to a pension plan is covered by the Statement.

The accounting specified in SFAS No. 87 does not supersede any of the **plan** accounting and reporting requirements of SFAS No. 35 (see Plan Accounting). It does, however, affect sponsor accounting by superseding the accounting requirements to calculate pension cost as described in APB No. 8, and the disclosure requirements as stated in SFAS No. 36, "Disclosure of Pension Information."

The Statement does not apply to pension or other types of plans that provide life and/or health insurance benefits to retired employees, although the sponsor of a plan that provides such benefits may elect to account for them in accordance with the provisions of SFAS No. 87. The accounting for the obligations and cost of these other postretirement benefits is the subject of SFAS No. 106 (see Accounting for Postretirement Benefits Other than Pensions).

(b) **APPLICABILITY OF SFAS NO. 87.**   In substance, there are two principal types of single-employer pension plans—**defined benefit plans** and **defined contribution plans.** SFAS No. 87 applies to both kinds of plans; however, most of the provisions of the Statement are directed toward defined benefit plans.

Appendix D of SFAS No. 87 defines these two types of pension plans:

Defined benefit pension plan—A pension plan that defines an amount of pension benefit to be provided, usually as a function of one or more factors such as age, years of service, or compensation. Any pension plan that is not a defined contribution plan is, for purposes of this Statement, a defined benefit plan.

Defined contribution pension plan—A plan that provides pension benefits in return for services rendered, provides an individual account for each participant, and specifies how contributions to the individual's account are to be determined instead of specifying the amount of benefits the individual is to receive. Under a defined contribution pension plan, the benefits a participant will receive depend solely on the amount contributed to the participant's account, the returns earned on investments of those contributions, and forfeitures of other participants' benefits that may be allocated to such participant's account.

The paragraphs that immediately follow address the principal accounting and reporting requirements for a sponsor of a defined benefit pension plan. The provisions of SFAS No. 87 that provide standards for other types of pension plans—defined contribution, multiemployer, and multiple employer plans—are discussed in subsections 32.2(j), 32.2(l), and 32.2(m).

For employers with more than one pension plan, SFAS No. 87 generally applies to each plan separately, although the financial disclosures of the plans in the sponsor's financial statements may be aggregated within certain limitations.

(c) **BASIC ELEMENTS OF PENSION ACCOUNTING.**   The intention of the FASB in adopting SFAS No. 87 was to specify accounting objectives and results rather than the specific computational means of obtaining those results. Accordingly, the Statement permits a certain amount of flexibility in choosing methods and approaches to the required pension calculations.

One of the reasons for the flexibility is that in a defined benefit pension plan an employer promises to provide the employee with retirement income in future years after the employee retires or otherwise terminates employment. The actual amount of pension benefit to be paid usually is contingent on a number of future events, many of which the employer has no control over. These future events are incorporated into the defined benefit plan contract between the employer and employee, and form the basis of the plan's benefit formula.

The benefit formula within a pension plan generally describes the amount of retirement income an employee will receive for services performed during his employment. Since accounting and financial reporting are intended to mirror actual agreements and transactions, it is logical that sponsor accounting for pensions should follow this contract to pay future benefits—that is the plan's benefit formula. However, two problems arise from this accounting premise: How will the amount and timing of benefit payments be determined, and over what years of service will the cost of those pension benefits be attributed?

(i) Attribution.   When drafting SFAS No. 87, the FASB considered whether the determination of net periodic pension cost should be based on a benefit approach or a cost approach. The **benefit approach** determines pension benefits attributed to service to date and calculates the present value of those benefits. The benefit approach recognizes costs equal to the present value of benefits earned for each period. Even when an equal amount of benefit is earned in each period, the cost being recognized will nevertheless increase as an employee approaches retirement. The **cost approach,** on the other hand, projects the present value of the total benefit at retirement and allocates that cost over the remaining years of service. Under the cost approach, the cost charged in the early years of an employee's service is greater than the present value of benefits earned based on the plan's benefit formula. In the later years of an employee's service, the cost is less than the present value of benefits earned so that the cumulative cost by the time the employee retires will be the same as that under the benefits approach.

Exhibit 32.2 depicts the two attribution approaches for determining pension cost based on the aggregate projected benefits to be earned during an employee's career.

As noted previously, accounting is intended to mirror actual agreements. In a defined benefit plan contract, the employer's promise to the employee is specified in terms of how benefits are earned based on service. Accordingly, the benefit approach was selected by the FASB and

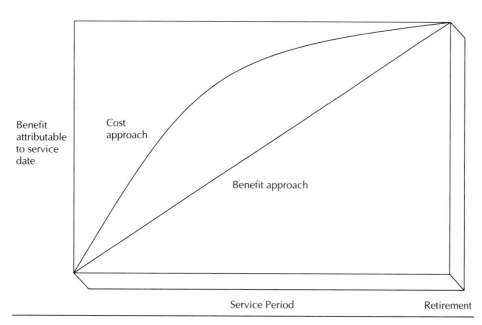

Exhibit 32.2.   Illustration of cost versus benefit approach.

is the single attribution approach permitted by SFAS No. 87. Specifically, the Statement requires:

- For flat benefit plans, the **unit credit actuarial method.**
- For final-pay and career-average-pay plans, the **projected unit credit method.**

Under APB No. 8, any "acceptable actuarial cost method" was permitted for purposes of determining pension cost. Many companies, in an effort to experience more stable costs, among other reasons, chose one of the cost-based methods. A cost-based method tended to front-end load or attribute more cost to the early years of an employee's career, as shown in Exhibit 32.2. Thus, many companies that were funding their pension costs as accrued under the cost attribution approach, accumulated more plan assets than they would have under the benefit attribution approach.

(ii) Actuarial Assumptions.   The value of plan benefits that form the basis for determining net periodic pension cost are calculated through use of actuarial assumptions. The discount rate reflects the time value of money. Demographic assumptions help determine the probability and timing of benefit payments—for example, assumptions for mortality, termination of employment, and retirement incidence are used to develop expected payout streams. Demographic assumptions are also utilized to establish certain amortization schedules. Prior service costs attributable to plan amendments and experience gains and losses typically are spread over the expected remaining service of active employees. Paragraphs 43–45 of SFAS No. 87 establish standards for selecting assumptions. Each nonfinancial assumption must reflect the **best estimate** of future experience for that assumption.

(iii) Interest Rates.   Under SFAS No. 87, employers are required to utilize two interest rates in measuring plan obligations and computing net periodic pension cost—an assumed **discount rate** and an **expected long-term rate of return on plan assets.**

As implied by its name the expected long-term rate of return on assets should reflect the expected long-term yield on plan assets available for investment during the ensuing year, as well as the reinvestment thereof in subsequent years. The discount rate, however, is a "snapshot" rate determined on the measurement date used for financial reporting. It reflects the underlying rate at which the pension benefits could be effectively settled (by purchasing annuities for example). The Statement refers to two indicators that can be used to estimate the settlement rate—high-quality bond yields and annuity rates published by the PBGC. Commercial annuity quotes (the standard in many cases) are based on fixed-income yields available at the time of the offer and, thus change continuously. The interest rate data presented in Exhibit 32.3 are taken from selected Federal Reserve Bulletins and imply the yield curves for U.S. Treasury securities. The corresponding curves for corporate bonds of noted qualities can be inferred by the long-term yields shown.

Variation in the discount rate used by different plan sponsors is inherent in the process prescribed by the Statement for selecting it. There is, at any time, a range of prices quoted by different insurance companies for the same "block of benefit obligations." Discrepancy in price can reflect differences in the underlying settlement of discount rate. Two other levels of variation exist—insurers tend to prefer obligations dominated by benefits that are already in pay status and they prefer bigger blocks of benefits. The best price (with the highest settlement rate), therefore, would be expected from the most aggressive insurer bidding for a large group of annuities for benefits that are mostly in pay status. Conversely, a lower settlement rate would be expected from a "selective" insurer that is bidding on a small group of annuities for young participants who are not in pay status.

The procedure contemplated by the Statement for selecting a discount rate assumes that there is a reasonable range of rates at any one moment that could be supported. Of course, this range will move as prevailing yields move. Minimizing change in the discount rate used from

	INTEREST RATES (Percent)			
	U.S. Treasury Securities* Years to Maturity	Long-Term Corporate Bonds** Quality		
Date	30	Aaa	A	Baa
1/1/91	7.52	8.22	8.71	9.14
1/1/92	7.39	7.90	8.32	8.75
1/1/93	6.28	6.94	7.33	7.71
1/1/94	7.83	8.43	8.70	9.08
1/1/95	6.58	7.31	7.54	7.91

* Average for the week ending nearest to or coincident with the noted date. *Source:* Federal Reserve Bulletin.

** Averages for the week ending nearest to or coincident with the noted date as determined by Moody's. *Source:* Federal Reserve Bulletin.

Exhibit 32.3.   Interest rate data.

one measurement date to the next is desirable because that will reduce volatility in the recorded expense. Generally, it is not acceptable, however, to keep the discount rate the same in successive years if settlement rates have shifted even if the discount rate remains within the reasonable range of rates for 2 years. For example, assume that prevailing yields are 8.5% to 10.0% at the prior measurement date and 7.0% to 9.0% at the current measurement date, and a plan sponsor used an 8.75% discount rate on both dates. Although 8.75% falls within an otherwise acceptable range, using it for the second year is inconsistent with the significant decline in prevailing rates that was observed for the interim. There may be mitigating circumstances, however—such as a demographic change in the employee group or a change in the plan's sponsor method for approximating the settlement rate—which, in this example, could support leaving the discount rate the same despite the drop in prevailing rates.

A plan may contain provisions affecting the interest rate at which benefit obligations may be settled. Examples include an optional lump sum payment computed using a low interest rate, and retirement annuities that are required to be purchased from an insurance company at specified rates. The assumed discount rate should properly reflect such plan provisions.

(iv) Consistency.   The Statement suggests some consistency among the assumptions used to calculate plan liabilities. In practice this means that identical components of financial assumptions generally should be used. For example, the inflation component of the discount rate, the assumed rate of salary increases, and the rate of increase in Social Security benefits or covered earnings should be the same. This suggestion reflects recent strong swings in inflation, productivity, and prevailing yields, which render rule-of-thumb relationships among such variables speculative.

Notwithstanding the preceding paragraph, the Statement does not require an employer to adopt any specific method of selecting the assumptions. Instead SFAS No. 87 requires the assumptions to be the employer's best estimates. Therefore, it is not deemed a change in accounting principle, as defined in APB Opinion No. 20, "Accounting Changes," if an employer should change its basis of selecting the assumed discount rate, for example, from high-quality bond rates to annuity purchase rates.

One of the best indicators of the reasonableness of assumptions is the amount of **unrecognized net gain or loss** under the plan. If the assumptions are reasonable, the gains and losses should offset each other in the long term. Therefore, when a plan has a pattern of unrecognized gains or losses that does not appear to be self-correcting, the assumptions used to measure benefit obligations and net periodic pension cost may be unrealistic. Assumptions, which do not appear on the surface to be unreasonable, may still be unrealistic if not borne out by actual experience.

(v) Actuarial Present Value of Benefits.   As noted previously, the FASB determined the SFAS No. 87 accounting would be based on the plan's contractual arrangement—that the projection of ultimate benefits to be paid under a pension plan should be based on the plan's benefit formula. Accordingly, SFAS No. 87 utilizes two different measurements in estimating this ultimate pension liability—the **accumulated benefit obligation** (ABO), and the **projected benefit obligation** (PBO). The ABO comprises two components—**vested and nonvested benefits**—both of which are determined based on employee service and compensation amounts to date. Benefits are vested when they no longer depend on remaining in the service of the employer. The PBO is equal to the ABO plus an allowance for future compensation levels, that is, a projection of the actual salary upon which the pension benefit will be calculated and paid (i.e., projection of the final salary in a "final-pay" plan). The relationship of these two obligations is reflected in Exhibit 32.4.

Consider the example of a plan that provides a retirement pension equal to 1% of an employee's average final 5-year compensation for each year of service. The PBO for an employee with 5 years of service is the actuarial present value of 5% of his projected average compensation at his expected retirement date; whereas his ABO is determined similarly but only taking into account his average compensation to date. Further, assume that this employee would be 60% vested in his accrued benefits if his service is terminated today; then his vested benefit obligation is equal to 60% of his ABO.

Unless there is evidence to the contrary, accounting is based on the **going-concern** concept. Accordingly, the PBO is utilized as the basis for computing the service and interest components of the net periodic pension cost since it is more representative of the ultimate pension benefits to be paid than the ABO.

When evaluating a plan's benefit formula to determine how the attribution method should be applied, SFAS No. 87 specifies that the substance of the plan and the sponsor's history of plan amendments should be considered. For example, an employer that regularly increases the benefits payable under a flat-benefit plan may, in substance, be considered to have sponsored a plan with benefits primarily based on employees' compensation. In such cases, the attribution method should reflect the plan's substance, rather than simply conform to its written terms. Similarly, attribution of benefits (and, therefore, recognition of cost) for accounting purposes may differ from that called for in a plan's benefit formula if the formula calls for deferred vesting ("backloading") of benefits. This by far is one of the more subjective areas of SFAS No. 87. Obviously, the determination that there is a commitment by the sponsor to provide benefits beyond the written terms of the pension plan's benefit formula requires careful evaluation and consideration.

If an employer has committed to making certain **plan amendments,** these amendments should be reflected in the PBO even if they may not have been formally written into the plan or

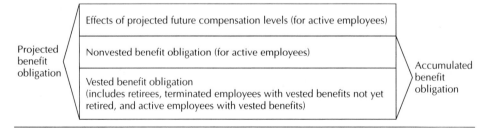

Exhibit 32.4.   Relationship of ABO and PBO.

if some of the changes may not be effective until a later date. Collectively bargained pension plans often provide for benefit increases with staggered effective dates. Such a plan may provide a monthly pension equal to $20 per month for each year of service in the first year of a labor contract, $21 in the second year, and $22 in the third. Once the contract has been negotiated, the PBO should be based on the $22 level.

(vi) Measurement Date.   The date as of which the plan's PBO and assets are measured—for purposes of disclosure in the employer's financial statements and determination of pension cost for the subsequent period—is known as the **measurement date.** Although SFAS No. 87 contemplates that the measurement date coincides with the date of the financial statements, an alternative date not more than 3 months prior may be used. However, a change in the measurement date, for example, from September 30 in one year to December 31 in the next year would constitute a change in accounting principle under APB No. 20. Although most employers have one measurement date each year, some employers remeasure their PBO and select the assumed discount rates on a more frequent basis. The frequency of measurement is part of the employer's accounting methods and may not be changed without proper disclosure of the impact.

Although the projected benefit obligation disclosed in the financial statements is as of the measurement date, it generally is not necessary to determine the PBO using participant data as of that date. Instead the PBO may be estimated from a prior measurement, provided that the result obtained does not differ materially from that if a new measurement is made using current participant data. The fair value of plan assets, on the other hand, should be as of the measurement date.

The period between consecutive measurement dates is known as the measurement period and is used for determining the net periodic pension cost. The cost thus determined is used for the related financial reporting period. Events that occur after the measurement date but still within the financial reporting period generally are excluded from the SFAS No. 87 disclosure requirement. If significant, the cost implications thereof should nevertheless be disclosed in a manner similar to other post year-end events.

(d) NET PERIODIC PENSION COST.   **Net periodic pension cost** represents the accounting recognition of the consequences of events and transactions affecting a pension plan. The amount of pension cost for a specified period is reported as a single net amount in an employer's financial statements. Under SFAS No. 87, net periodic pension cost comprises the following six components:

- Service cost.
- Interest cost.
- Actual return on plan assets.
- Amount of gain or loss being recognized or deferred.
- Amortization of unrecognized prior service cost.
- Amortization of the unrecognized net obligation or net asset existing at the initial application of the Statement.

(i) Service Cost Component.   A defined benefit pension plan contains a benefit formula that generally describes the amount of retirement income that an employee will receive for services performed during their employment. SFAS No. 87 requires the use of this benefit formula in the measurement of annual service cost. The **service cost** component of net periodic pension cost is defined by the Statement as the actuarial present value of pension benefits attributed by the pension benefit formula to employee service during a specified period. Under SFAS No. 87, attribution (the process of assigning pension benefits or cost to periods of employee service) generally is based on the benefit formula (i.e., the benefit attribution approach).

A simplified example will help illustrate this concept. Assume that a pension plan's benefit formula states that an employee shall receive, at the retirement age of 65, retirement income of $15 per month for life, for each year of credited service. Thus a pension of $15 per month can be attributed to each year of employee service. The actuarial present value of the $15 monthly pension represents the service cost component of net periodic pension cost. Although it is customary to determine the service cost at the end of the year, an equally acceptable practice is to compute the service cost at the beginning of the year and to add the interest thereon at the assumed discount rate to the interest cost component.

In certain circumstances the plan's benefit formula does not indicate the manner in which a particular benefit relates to specific services performed by the employee. In this case SFAS No. 87 specifies that the benefit shall be considered to be accumulated as follows:

- If the **benefit is includable in vested benefits,** the benefit shall be accumulated in proportion to the ratio of total completed years of service as of the present to the total completed years of service as of the date the benefit becomes fully vested. A vested benefit is a benefit that an employee has an irrevocable right to receive. For example, receipt of the pension benefit is not contingent on whether the employee continues to work for the employer.

- If the **benefit is not includable in vested benefits,** the benefit shall be accumulated in proportion to the ratio of completed years of service as of the present date to the total projected years of service. An example of a benefit that is not includable in vested benefits is a death or disability benefit that is payable only if death or disability occurs during the employee's active service.

Some pension plans require contributions by employees to cover part of the plan's overall cost. SFAS No. 87 does not specify how the net periodic pension cost should be adjusted for **employee contributions.** An often-used approach is to reduce the service cost component directly by the employee contributions, thus possibly resulting in a negative service cost. Under this approach the plan's PBO encompasses both benefits to be financed by employee contributions and those financed by the employer.

(ii) Interest Cost Component.   In determining the PBO of a plan, SFAS No. 87 gives appropriate consideration to the time value of money, through the use of discounts for interest cost. Therefore, the Statement requires that an employer recognize, as a component of net periodic pension cost, interest on the projected benefit obligation. This **interest cost** component is equal to the increase in the amount of the PBO due to the passage of time. The accretion of interest on the PBO is based on the assumed discount rate.

Since the assumed discount rate is intended to reflect the interest rate at which the PBO currently could be settled, it is imperative that the discount rate assumption be reevaluated each year to determine whether it reflects the best estimate of current settlement rates. As a rule of thumb, if interest rates are in a period of fluctuation, the discount rate generally should change.

(iii) Actual Return on Plan Assets Component.   SFAS No. 87 requires that an employer recognize, as a component of net periodic pension cost, the **actual return or loss on pension plan assets** (see subsection 32.2(e)). The actual return or loss on plan assets equals the difference between the fair value of plan assets at the beginning and end of a period, adjusted for employer contributions and pension benefit payments made during the period. Exhibit 32.5 illustrates the determination of the actual return on plan assets.

A positive return on plan assets decreases the employer's cost of providing pension benefits to its employees, whereas a negative return (loss) increases net periodic pension cost. Note that net periodic pension income is a possibility where very positive earnings are experienced for plan assets held during a period, and those earnings more than offset the other net periodic pension cost components.

Fair value of plan assets, beginning of year	$ 900
Add contributions	100
Subtract benefit payments	(150)
	850
Fair value of plan assets, end of year	931
Actual return on plan assets	$ 81

Exhibit 32.5.   Illustration of the determination of the actual return on plan assets.

Although the Statement purports to offset a plan's cost by the actual return on plan assets, the net periodic pension cost is in fact affected by the **expected return** rather than the actual return since the difference between the actual and expected returns is deferred (see subsection 32.2(d)(iv)—Asset gains and losses). The FASB felt that the actual return is an important piece of information that needs to be disclosed, even though the net periodic pension cost for any period is independent of the actual return earned in that period.

The Statement makes no specific allowance for **administrative or investment expenses** paid directly from the pension fund. These expenses may be reflected in the net periodic pension cost as an offset to the actual investment return on plan assets, and in such case, may also be considered in the selection of the expected long-term rate of return on plan assets. If deemed appropriate, administrative expenses may be treated differently than investment expenses and added to the plan's service cost.

(iv) Amortization of Unrecognized Net Gains and Losses Component. SFAS No. 87 broadly defines gains and losses as changes in the amount of either the PBO or pension plan assets that generally result from differences between the estimates or assumptions used and actual experience. Gains and losses may reflect both the refinement of estimates or assumptions and real changes in economic conditions. Hence, the **gain and loss** component of SFAS No. 87 consists of the net difference between the estimates and actual results of two separate pension items—actuarial assumptions related to pension plan obligations (liability gains and losses) and return on plan assets (asset gains and losses).

Liability gains and losses (increases or decreases in the PBO) stem from two types of events—changes in obligation-related assumptions (i.e., discount rate, assumed future compensation levels) and variances between actual and assumed experience (i.e., turnover, mortality). Liability gains and losses generally would be calculated at the end of each year as the difference between the projected value of the year-end pension obligation based on beginning of the year assumptions and the actual year-end value of the obligation based on the end-of-year assumptions.

Asset gains and losses represent the difference between the actual and expected rate of return on plan assets during a period. These gains and losses are entirely experience-related. As noted in the previous section, the actual return on pension plan assets is equal to the difference between the fair value of pension plan assets at the beginning and end of a period, adjusted for any contributions and pension benefit payments made during that period. The **expected return on pension plan assets** is a computed amount determined by multiplying the market-related value of plan assets (as defined below) by the expected long-term rate of return. The expected long-term rate of return is an actuarial assumption of the average expected long-term interest rate that will be earned on plan assets available for investment during the period.

In order to reduce the potentially volatile impact of gains and losses on net periodic pension cost from year to year, the FASB adopted various **"smoothing" techniques** in SFAS No. 87—**the netting of gains and losses, the market-related value of plan assets, the initial deferral of net gains and losses,** and **the amortization of the net deferred amount.** The impact of the first smoothing technique is obvious; the other techniques are discussed briefly in the following paragraphs.

As noted previously, the **market-related value of plan assets** is utilized in the determination of the expected return on pension plan assets. The market-related value of plan assets can be either the actual fair value of plan assets or a "calculated" value that recognizes the changes in the fair value of plan assets over a period of not more than 5 years. Employers are permitted great flexibility in selecting the method of calculating the market-related value of plan assets. Any method that averages gains and losses over not longer than a 5-year period would be acceptable under the Statement, provided it met two criteria—that the method be both systematic and rational. In fact, changes in the fair value of assets would not have to be averaged at all but could be recognized in full in the subsequent year's net periodic pension cost provided that the method is applied consistently to all gains and losses (on both plan assets and obligations) and is disclosed. An employer also may use different methods for determining the market-related values of plan assets in separate pension plans and in separate asset categories within each plan, provided that the differences can be supported.

SFAS No. 87 specifies that the net gain or loss resulting from the assumptions or estimates used differing from actual experience be deferred and amortized in future periods. **Deferred gains and losses** (excluding any asset gains and losses subsequent to the initial implementation of SFAS No. 87 that have not yet been reflected in the market-related value of assets) are amortized as a component of net periodic pension cost if they exceed the **"corridor."** The corridor is defined as a range equal to plus or minus 10% of the greater of either the PBO or the market-related value of plan assets. If the cumulative gain or loss, as computed, does not lie outside the corridor, no amount of gain or loss needs to be reflected in net periodic cost for the current period. However, if the cumulative gain or loss does exceed the corridor, only the excess is subject to amortization. To visualize the concept of the corridor refer to Exhibit 32.6.

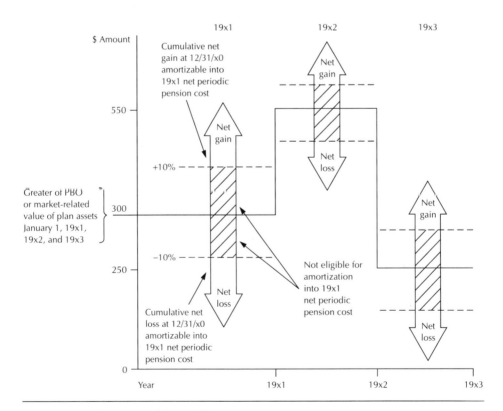

Exhibit 32.6.   Illustration of the corridor.

The **minimum amortization** that is required in net periodic pension cost is the excess amount described above, divided by the average remaining service period of the active employees expected to receive benefits under the plan. Unlike other amortization under SFAS No. 87, the average remaining service period is redetermined each year. The FASB does permit alternative methods of amortization. An employer may decide not to use the corridor method or substitute any alternative amortization method that amortizes an amount at least equal to the minimum. Consequently, an alternative method could recognize the entire amount of the current period's gain or loss in the ensuing period. Any alternative amortization method must be applied consistently from year to year and to both gains and losses, and must be disclosed in the employer's financial statements.

The 10% corridor is designed to avoid amortization of relatively small and temporary gains and losses arising in any one year that can be expected to offset each other in the long run. It is not intended to exclude a portion of gains and losses from ever being recognized in the sponsor's income statement. If a substantial amount of net gain or loss remains unrecognized from year to year, or increases in size, it may imply that the PBO and net periodic pension cost have been overstated or understated.

(v) Amortization of Unrecognized Prior Service Cost Component. Defined benefit pension plans are sometimes amended, usually to provide increased pension benefits to employees. An amendment to a pension plan (or initiation of a pension plan) that grants benefits to employees for services previously rendered generates an increase in the PBO under the plan. This additional PBO is referred to as **prior service cost.** Retroactive pension benefits generally are granted by the employer in the expectation that they will produce future economic benefits, such as increasing employee morale, reducing employee turnover, or improving employee productivity.

Under SFAS No. 87, prior service cost is to be amortized and included as a component of net periodic pension cost. A separate **amortization schedule** is established for each prior service cost based on the expected future service by active employees who are expected to receive employer-provided benefits under the plan. Instead of a declining amortization schedule, a common practice is to amortize the prior service cost on a straight-line basis over the average future service period. Once this amortization schedule has been established, it will generally not be changed unless the period during which the employer expects to realize future economic benefits has shortened or the future economic benefits have become impaired. Decelerating the amortization schedule is prohibited.

If substantially all of the participants of a pension plan are inactive, the prior service cost from a retroactive amendment should be amortized over the remaining life expectancy of those plan participants.

SFAS No. 87 permits the use of alternative amortization methods that more rapidly reduce the amount of unrecognized prior service cost, provided that the alternatives are used consistently. For example, straight-line amortization of unrecognized prior service cost over the average future service period of active employees who are expected to receive benefits under the plan is acceptable. The immediate recognition of prior service cost, however, generally is inappropriate.

As noted previously, a plan amendment typically increases the cost of pension benefits and increases the amount of the PBO. However, there are situations where a plan amendment may decrease the cost of pension benefits, resulting in a decrease in the amount of the PBO. Any decrease resulting from a plan amendment should be applied to reduce the balance of any existing unrecognized prior service cost using a systematic and rational method (i.e., LIFO, FIFO, or pro rata, unless such reduction can be related to any specific prior service cost). Any excess is to be amortized on the same basis as increases in unrecognized prior service cost.

Once the employer has committed to a plan amendment, the net periodic pension cost for the remainder of the year should reflect the additional service cost, interest cost, and amortization related to the amendment. Remeasurement based on the current discount rate may also be called for. Pension cost for any prior periods should not be restated merely on account of the amendment, even if the amendment may be effective retroactively to a prior date.

(vi) Amortization of the Unrecognized Net Obligation or Net Asset Component.   The **unrecognized net obligation or net asset** of a pension plan was determined as of the first day of the fiscal year in which SFAS No. 87 was first applied or if applicable, the measurement date immediately preceding that day. The initial unrecognized net obligation or net asset was equal to the difference between the PBO and fair value of pension plan assets (plus previously recognized unfunded accrued pension cost or less previously recognized prepaid pension cost).

A schedule was set up to amortize the initial unrecognized net obligation or net asset on a straight-line basis over the average remaining service period of employees expected to receive benefits under the plan, except under the following circumstances:

- If the average remaining service period was less than 15 years, an employer could elect to use 15 years.
- If the plan was composed of all or substantially all inactive participants, the employer should use those participants' average remaining life expectancy as the amortization period.

(e) PLAN ASSETS.   **Pension plan assets** generally consist of equity or debt securities, real estate, or other investments, which may be sold or transferred by the plan, that typically have been segregated and restricted in a trust. In contrast to SFAS No. 35, for purposes of SFAS No. 87, plan assets exclude contributions due but unpaid by the plan sponsor. Also excluded are assets that are not restricted to provide plan benefits such as so-called rabbi trusts in which earmarked funds are available to satisfy judgment creditors.

Pension plan assets that are held as an investment to provide pension benefits are to be measured at fair value as of the date of the financial statements or, if used consistently from year to year, as of a date not more than three months prior to that date (this date is defined by the Statement as the measurement date).

In the context of SFAS No. 87, fair value is defined as the amount that a pension plan trustee could reasonably expect to receive from the sale of a plan asset between a willing and informed buyer and a willing and informed seller. The FASB believes that fair value is the appropriate measurement for pension plan assets because it provides the more relevant information in assessing both the plan's ability to pay pension benefits as they become due and the future contributions necessary to provide for unfunded pension benefits already promised.

If an active market exists for a plan investment, fair value is determined by the quoted market price. If an active market does not exist for a particular plan investment, selling prices for similar investments, if available, should be appropriately considered. If no active market exists, an estimate of the fair value of the plan investment may be based on its projected cash flow, provided that appropriate consideration is given to current discount rates and the investment risk involved.

Pension plan assets that are used in the actual everyday operations of a plan—buildings, leasehold improvements, furniture, equipment, and fixtures—should be valued at historical cost less accumulated depreciation or amortization.

(f) RECOGNITION OF LIABILITIES AND ASSETS.   SFAS No. 87 retained the requirement of APB No. 8 to reflect either a liability (accrued pension cost) or an asset (prepaid pension cost) in an employer's statement of financial condition for the difference between the pension cost accrued by the employer and the amount actually contributed to the pension plan. However, the Statement introduced a radically new concept to sponsor accounting—the recognition of **an additional minimum pension liability.**

An additional minimum pension liability must be recorded to the extent that an unfunded ABO (taking into consideration any contribution paid by the employer between the measurement date and the date of the financial statements) exceeds the liability for unfunded accrued pension cost. If a prepaid pension asset exists, the minimum liability that is recorded equals the sum of the prepaid amount and the unfunded ABO. If an additional minimum liability is recognized, an equal amount of **intangible asset** should be recorded provided the asset recognized does not exceed any unrecognized prior service cost plus any unrecognized net liability (but not net asset) at the date of initial application of SFAS No. 87. If the additional liability exceeds the sum of the preceding two items, the remaining debit balance should be recorded as a separate component of stockholders' equity, net of related tax benefits.

The additional liability, intangible asset, and reduction in stockholders' equity are reestablished at each measurement date, and the amounts previously recorded on the balance sheet are reversed. No amortization of the additional liability or intangible asset is required or permitted.

There is no additional asset if plan assets plus (less) accrued (prepaid) pension cost exceed its ABO. Furthermore, the additional liability is determined separately for each plan, and an employer may not reduce the additional liability for one plan by the excess of plan assets in another.

(g) INTERIM MEASUREMENTS. Generally, the determination of interim pension cost should be based on assumptions used as of the previous year-end measurements. Similarly, any additional minimum liability recognized in the year-end financial statements should be carried forward, after adjustment for subsequent accruals and contributions. If, however, more recent measurements of plan assets and pension obligations are available, or if a significant event occurs that ordinarily would call for such measurements (i.e., a plan amendment), that updated information should be used.

(h) FINANCIAL STATEMENT DISCLOSURES. The following **disclosures** should be made in the financial statements of an employer who sponsors a defined benefit pension plan:

- A **description of the pension plan,** including the employee groups covered, type of benefit formula, funding policy, types of assets held and significant nonbenefit liabilities (if any), and the nature and effect of significant matters affecting comparability of information for all periods presented. This general information was required by the FASB to enhance the understanding and comparability of sponsor pension plan accounting.
- The **amount of net periodic pension cost** for each period an income statement is presented, detailing the separate amounts for the (1) service cost component, (2) interest cost component, (3) actual return on plan assets for the period, and (4) net total of other components. The net total of other components comprises the net asset gain or loss from the current period deferred for future recognition, amortization of the net gain or loss from earlier periods, amortization of unrecognized prior service cost, and amortization of the unrecognized net obligation or asset at the initial application of SFAS No. 87.
- A **schedule reconciling the funded status of the plan** with amounts reported in the employer's statement of financial position, showing separately:
  1. The fair value of plan assets.
  2. The PBO, separately identifying the ABO and vested benefit obligation.
  3. The amount of unrecognized prior service cost.
  4. The amount of unrecognized net gain or loss, including asset gains and losses not yet reflected in market-related values.
  5. The **amount of any remaining unrecognized net obligation or net asset** existing at the date of the initial application of SFAS No. 87.
  6. The **amount of additional minimum liability** equal to the unfunded ABO plus (minus) any prepaid (accrued) pension cost.

7. The amount of the **net pension asset or liability that has been recognized in the employer's statement of financial position.** This amount must be equal to the total net result of combining the preceding six items. For purposes of SFAS No. 87, different prepaid and accrued pension cost amounts that may have been created at different times for different reasons may be combined and netted. The portion of accrued pension cost equal to the employer's expected contribution for the next twelve months is classified as a current liability, whereas the remainder should be classified as noncurrent.

Items 1 through 5 are as of the measurement date whereas items 6 and 7 are as of the employer's year-end. When the measurement date precedes the year-end date, plan assets (i.e., item 1) are increased by the amount of contribution paid by the employer during the interim period between the measurement date and the employer's year-end. Except for this modification, the fair value of plan assets should be the actual value as of the measurement date. It is, however, acceptable to estimate the PBO based on a prior measurement such as that done as of the previous measurement date, provided that the result would not be materially different if the PBO had been remeasured using current participant data.

• The **weighted-average assumed discount rate** and, if applicable, the **rate of compensation increase** used in determining the PBO, and the **weighted-average expected long-term rate of return** on pension plan assets. These three assumptions are the most subjective for pension accounting and have the greatest impact on the computations of pension obligations and net periodic pension cost (the assumptions used in measuring the PBO at one fiscal year-end are generally used to determine net periodic pension cost the following fiscal year).

• If applicable, the **amounts and types of securities** of the employer and/or related parties that are included in plan assets, and the approximate **amount of annual benefits of employees and retirees covered by annuity contracts** issued by the employer and related parties. Also, if applicable, the **alternative amortization method used for unrecognized prior service cost** and the **alternative amortization method used to reflect the commitment of an employer to pay more employee benefits than its existing pension benefit formula indicates.**

Though not required, most employers also disclose the measurement date(s) if different from the year-end date.

An employer may combine two or more of its defined benefit pension plans for purposes of financial statement disclosure, including plans with different measurement dates. However, separate reconciliations of funded status are required for plans with assets in excess of ABO and plans with assets less than ABO, and U.S. plans and non-U.S. plans unless they use similar economic assumptions.

(i) ANNUITY CONTRACTS.   All or part of an employer's obligation to provide pension plan benefits to employees may be effectively transferred to an insurance company by the purchase of annuity contracts. An **annuity contract** is an irrevocable agreement in which an insurance company unconditionally agrees to provide specific benefits to designated individuals, in return for a fixed consideration or premium. Hence, by purchasing an annuity contract, an employer transfers to the insurer its legal obligation, and the attendant risks, to provide pension benefits. For purposes of SFAS No. 87, an annuity contract does not qualify unless the risks and rewards associated with the assets and obligations assumed by the insurance company are actually transferred to the insurance company by the sponsor.

An annuity contract may be participating or nonparticipating. In a **participating annuity** contract, the insurance company's investment experience with the funds received for the annuity contract are shared, in the form of dividends, with the purchaser (the employer or the pension fund). The purchase price of a participating annuity is ordinarily higher than that for a nonparticipating annuity, with the excess representing the value of the participation right (i.e., expected future dividends). This excess should be recognized as a plan asset.

Benefits covered by annuity contracts are excluded from the benefit obligations of the plan. The annuity contracts themselves are not counted as plan assets, except for the cost of any participation rights. If any benefits earned in the current period are covered by annuity contracts, the cost of such benefits is equal to the cost to purchase the annuities less any participation right.

Annuity contracts issued by a captive insurance company are not considered annuities for the purpose of SFAS No. 87, since the risk associated with the benefit obligations remains substantially with the employer. Similarly, if there is reasonable doubt that the insurance company will meet its obligations under the contract, it is not considered an annuity contract.

Insurance contracts that are not in substance annuity contracts are accounted for as pension plan assets and are measured at fair value. If a contract has a determinable cash surrender value or conversion value, that is presumed to be its fair value.

A pension fund may have structured a portfolio of fixed-income investments with a cash flow designed to match expected benefit payment. Known as a **dedicated bond portfolio,** its purpose is to protect the pension fund against swings in interest rates. For the purposes of SFAS No. 87, a dedicated bond portfolio is not an annuity contract even if it is managed to remove all or most of the investment risk associated with covered benefit payments.

(j) DEFINED CONTRIBUTION PENSION PLANS. A **defined contribution pension plan** provides for employer contributions that are defined in the plan. A defined contribution plan maintains individual accounts for each plan participant and contains terms that specify how contributions are allocated among participants' individual accounts. Pension benefits are based solely on the amount available in each participant's account at the time of retirement. The amount available in each participant's account at the time of retirement is the total of the amounts contributed by the employer, the returns earned on investments of those contributions, and forfeitures of other participants' accounts that have been allocated to the participant's account.

Under SFAS No. 87, the net periodic pension cost of a defined contribution pension plan is the amount of contributions for the period in which services are rendered by the employees. If a plan calls for contributions after an individual retires or terminates, the estimated cost should be accrued during periods in which the individual performs services.

An employer that sponsors one or more defined contribution pension plans **discloses** the following information separately from its defined benefit pension plan disclosures:

- A **description of the plan(s)** including employee groups covered, the basis for determining contributions, and the nature and effect of significant matters affecting comparability of information for all periods presented.
- The **amount of pension cost** recognized during the period.

For the purposes of SFAS No. 87, any plan that is not a defined contribution pension plan is considered a defined benefit pension plan.

(k) NON-U.S. PENSION PLANS. SFAS No. 87 does not make any special provision for **non-U.S. pension plans.** In some foreign countries it is customary or required for an employer to provide benefits for employees in the event of a voluntary or involuntary severance of employment. In this event, if the substance of the arrangement is a pension plan, it is subject to the provisions of SFAS No. 87 (i.e., benefits are paid for substantially all terminations).

Plans in Puerto Rico or other U.S. territories are considered U.S. plans.

(l) MULTIEMPLOYER PLANS.   A **multiemployer plan** is a plan to which more than one employer contributes, usually pursuant to a labor union agreement. Under these plans, contributions are pooled and separate employer accounts do not exist. As a result, assets contributed by one employer may be used to provide benefits to the employees of other participating employers.

SFAS No. 87 provides no change in the accounting for multiemployer plans. A participating employer should recognize pension cost equal to the contribution required to the plan for the period. The disclosures required by the Statement for multiemployer plans are similar to those for defined contribution pension plans—a description of the plan, including the employee groups covered and type of benefits provided, and the amount of pension cost recognized in the period.

An underfunded multiemployer plan may assess a withdrawing employer a portion of its unfunded benefit obligations. If this **withdrawal liability** becomes either probable or reasonably possible, the provisions of SFAS No. 5, "Accounting for Contingencies," apply.

(m) MULTIPLE EMPLOYER PLANS.   A **multiple employer plan** is similar to a multiemployer plan except that it usually does not include any labor union agreement. It is treated under ERISA as a collection of single-employer plans sponsored by the respective participating employers. If separate asset allocation is maintained among the participating employers (even though pooled for investment purposes), SFAS No. 87 applies individually to each employer with respect to its interest and benefit obligations within the plan. If assets are not allocated among the participating employers (for example, when a number of subsidiaries participate in a plan sponsored by their parent), the organization sponsoring the plan, if one exists, should account for the plan as a single-employer plan, whereas each participating employer should account for this arrangement as a multiemployer plan in its separate financial statements. Disclosure of net periodic pension cost and the reconciliation of the funded status should be for the plan as a whole, with each participating employer further disclosing its own pension cost with respect to this arrangement.

(n) FUNDING AND INCOME TAX ACCOUNTING.   SFAS No. 87 does not address funding considerations, other than to recognize that there may be differences between reported net periodic pension cost and funding. IRS regulations recognize the projected unit credit method as one of several acceptable funding methods. However, when employing the projected unit credit method and the same explicit assumptions used to calculate net periodic pension cost, the range between the permissible maximum and minimum funding amount, may not bracket the net periodic pension cost. This can be caused by the difference in amortization periods for unrecognized pension costs and limitation imposed by the tax law on contributions to relatively well-funded plans. In general, the objective of matching expensing and funding of net periodic pension cost may no longer be appropriate due to tax, legal, and cash flow considerations. In this regard companies must continue to provide deferred taxes, where appropriate, for these differences.

(i) SFAS No. 109.   The method of accounting for income taxes—particularly the way deferred taxes are calculated—was changed by SFAS No. 109, "Accounting for Income Taxes." Its focus is on an asset and liability approach, as opposed to an income statement approach. On a simplified basis, deferred taxes are calculated by applying the tax rates enacted for future years to differences between the financial statement carrying amounts and the tax bases of assets and liabilities. These differences are known as temporary differences.

Temporary differences frequently will arise as a result of differences between the tax basis of pension assets and liabilities and the amounts recognized under SFAS No. 87. For example, assuming that a company funds the pension cost to the extent deductible for tax purposes, a pension asset (prepaid pension cost) will be recognized when the amount funded is in excess of pension cost determined under SFAS No. 87. A pension liability (accrued pension cost) will be recognized when the amount funded is less than the pension cost determined under SFAS No. 87. In addition, settlement gains and losses recognized under SFAS No. 88 will create temporary differences because the transactions generally are not taxable or deductible at the date recognized for financial reporting purposes. Because of the complexities of accounting for pensions, numerous other situations will result in temporary differences.

(ii) Scheduling of Temporary Differences. SFAS No. 109 does not specifically require an entity to schedule the reversal of its temporary differences. However, consideration may be given to the timing and pattern of reversing temporary differences for purposes of assessing the need for a valuation allowance. If the scheduling of future taxable and deductible amounts for temporary differences related to pension assets and liabilities is warranted, either of the following two approaches should be used.

Under the first approach, a temporary difference related to a pension asset would be scheduled to result in a taxable amount in the year(s) that there is expected to be an asset reversion from the pension plan, limited to the amount of the pension asset. A temporary difference attributable to a pension liability recognized for financial reporting purposes would be scheduled to result in deductible amounts based on the pattern of the present values of the estimated tax deductions in future years, limited to the amount of the pension liability.

Under the other approach, a temporary difference related to a pension asset would be scheduled to result in taxable amounts based on estimated pension expense for financial reporting purposes in future years, limited to the amount of the pension asset. Whereas, a temporary difference related to a pension liability would be scheduled to result in deductible amounts based on estimated future tax deductions in excess of future interest calculated on the pension liability that is recognized for financial reporting purposes, limited to the amount of the pension liability.

(o) ILLUSTRATION—APPLICATION OF SFAS NO. 87. Exhibit 32.7 illustrates the application of the major accounting requirements of SFAS No. 87 for a hypothetical defined benefit pension plan having a final-pay benefit formula. To assist the reader, the material has been presented under the following headings: Background Information and Assumptions, Components of Pension Cost, Changes in Projected Benefit Obligation, Valuation of Plan Assets, Amortization of Unrecognized Net Gain or Loss, Unrecognized Gains and Losses, Pension-Related Balance Sheet Accounts, and Financial Statement Disclosures.

32.3 SPONSOR ACCOUNTING FOR NONRECURRING EVENTS

(a) OVERVIEW. An integral concept of pension accounting is that certain pension obligations should be recognized over time rather than immediately. They include gains and losses from experience different from that assumed, the effects of changes in actuarial assumptions on the pension obligations, the cost of retroactive plan amendments, and any unrecognized net obligation or asset at transition established when the plan first complied with SFAS No. 87. The premise of this delayed recognition is that plan amendments are made in anticipation of economic benefits that the employer may derive over the future service periods of its employees, and that gains or losses already incurred may be reversed in the future. When events happen that fundamentally alter or eliminate the premise for delayed recognition, immediate recognition of previously unrecognized amounts may be required.

Examples of such special events include **business combinations,** addressed in paragraph 74 of SFAS No. 87; and **settlements, curtailments,** and **termination benefits,** the subjects of **SFAS No. 88,** which is effective simultaneously with SFAS No. 87. Thus an employer generally may not, for instance, follow the SFAS No. 88 accounting for a settlement unless SFAS No. 87 has been adopted. Relevant paragraphs of **APB Opinion Nos. 8 and 16** are superseded by these new statements, as is **SFAS No. 74** in its entirety.

Although prior accounting opinions and statements, such as APB Opinion No. 8, did require immediate recognition of gains or losses in certain situations, they did not define the

BACKGROUND INFORMATION AND ASSUMPTIONS

Company X, a calendar year entity, adopted SFAS No. 87 on January 1, 1987, as required by the Statement. In prior years, the Company recognized pension cost equal to the maximum annual amount that could be contributed to the plan for federal income tax purposes. The Company funds its contribution to the plan on December 31 of each year.

The Company utilizes the following practices when calculating pension cost for financial statement purposes:

- *Market-Related Value of Plan Assets.* A computed value that recognizes changes in fair value of plan assets (asset gains and losses) over a 5-year period.
- *Amortization of Gains and Losses.* Amortized on a corridor approach (i.e., unrecognized gain or loss is amortized only if it exceeds 10% of the greater of the PBO or the market-related value of plan assets).
- *Amortization of Prior Service Cost.* Amortized on a straight-line basis over the average remaining service period of active employees expected to receive benefits.
- *Measurement Date.* Year-end financial statement date, December 31.

The results of annual actuarial valuations and related actuarial assumptions at the date of initial application of SFAS No. 87 and in subsequent years are:

	December 31			
	19X0*	19X1	19X2	19X3
Accumulated benefit obligation	$ 6,900	$ 8,900	$12,600	$13,100
Projected benefit obligation	10,000	12,100	16,000	16,600
Plan assets (fair value)	7,200	9,000	10,700	12,150
Benefits paid (on December 31)	400	450	500	550
Contribution (on December 31)	1,000	1,100	1,200	1,250
Weighted-average settlement rate	9%	8%	7.5%	8%
Expected long-term rate of return on plan assets	10%	10%	10%	10%
Salary progression rate	6.5%	5.5%	5.5%	5.75%

For all years presented, the average remaining service period of active employees expected to receive benefits is estimated to be 14 years. On December 31, 19X2, a plan amendment was adopted that granted increased benefits to employees based on services previously rendered.

*Reflects adoption date of SFAS 87, January 1, 19X1.

COMPONENTS OF PENSION COST

	Year Ended December 31		
	19X1	19X2	19X3
Service cost[1]	$ 600	$ 650	$ 700
Interest cost[2]	900	968	1,200
Return on plan assets[3]			
Actual return	(1,150)	(1,000)	(750)
Deferred gain (loss)	430	134	(284)
Expected return	(720)	(866)	(1,034)
Amortization of unrecognized prior service cost[4]	0	0	130
Amortization of net loss[5]	0	0	15
Amortization of unrecognized net obligation at transition[6]	200	200	200
Net pension cost	$ 980	$ 952	$1,211

Exhibit 32.7.   Application of SFAS No. 87.

[1] This amount is calculated by the actuary, based on the plan's benefit formula, using assumptions and measurements as of the beginning of the year.

[2] The product of the PBO and the assumed discount (settlement) rate as of the beginning of the year.

[3] See Valuation of Plan Assets.

[4] Represents the cost of the retroactive plan amendment adopted December 31, 19X2 ($1,820), divided by the average remaining service period of active employees (14 years).

[5] See Amortization of Unrecognized Net Gain or Loss.

[6] Represents the unrecognized net loss at transition—the excess of the PBO ($10,000) over the fair value of plan assets ($7,200)—divided by the average remaining service period of active employees (14 years).

CHANGES IN PROJECTED BENEFIT OBLIGATION

	19X1	19X2	19X3
Accumulated benefit obligation, January 1	$ 6,900	$ 8,900	$12,600
Effect of assumed salary progression	3,100	3,200	3,400
Projected benefit obligation, January 1	10,000	12,100	16,000
Anticipated increase (decrease) in PBO during the year:			
Service cost	600	650	700
Interest cost	900	968	1,200
Benefit payments	(450)	(500)	(550)
Projected benefit obligation, December 31	11,050	13,218	17,350
Increase (decrease) in PBO attributable to revised assumptions at end of year:			
Discount rate	1,100	650	(760)
Salary progression rate	(290)	0	80
Other (turnover, etc.)	240	312	(70)
Net loss (gain) deferred	1,050	962	(750)
Effect of retroactive plan amendment adopted December 31, 19X2	0	1,820	0
Actual projected benefit obligation, December 31	$12,100	$16,000	$16,600

VALUATION OF PLAN ASSETS

	Fair Value	Market-Related Value
Fair value of assets, January 1, 19X1	$ 7,200	$ 7,200
Expected return for 19X1[1]	720	720
Difference between actual and expected return:		
Net gain—fair value	430	
Market-related[2]		86
Benefit payments on December 31	(450)	(450)
Sponsor contribution on December 31	1,100	1,100
Value of assets, January 1, 19X2	9,000	8,656
Expected return for 19X2	866	866
Difference between actual and expected return:		
Net gain—fair value	134	
Market-related		113
Benefit payments on December 31	(500)	(500)
Sponsor contribution on December 31	1,200	1,200
Value of assets, January 1, 19X3	10,700	10,335
Expected return for 19X3	1,034	1,034
		(continued)

Exhibit 32.7. *Continued.*

Difference between actual and expected return:		
Net gain—fair value	(284)	
Market-related		56
Benefit payments on December 31	(550)	(550)
Sponsor contribution on December 31	1,250	1,250
Value of assets, January 1, 19X4	$12,150	$12,125

[1] The expected long-term rate of return on plan assets (10%) times the market-related asset value at the beginning of the year.

[2] The market-related value of plan assets is used in calculating the expected return on plan assets. A portion of the cumulative difference between expected and actual return on plan assets (gain or loss) is included each year in the market-related value of plan assets, and the unrecognized gain or loss subject to amortization. Company X's accounting policy states that 20% of the prior year net gain or loss is to be included.

AMORTIZATION OF UNRECOGNIZED NET GAIN OR LOSS

Under SFAS No. 87, the net gain or loss experienced in the current year is subject to amortization in the following year. Since Company X first applied the Statement in 1987, pension cost for 19X1 would not include any amortization. Beginning in 19X2 and for each year thereafter, the Company would be required to calculate whether, under the corridor approach, amortization of net unrecognized gains or losses is to be included in the then current year's pension cost.

The corridor calculation for 19X2 and 19X3 would involve the following:

	19X2	19X3
Unrecognized net gain (loss) at January 1 subject to amortization[1]	$ (964)	$ (1,813)
Corridor = 10% of the greater of the PBO or the market-related value of assets at January 1[2]	1,210	1,600
Unrecognized net gain (loss) in excess of corridor	0	(213)
Divided by average remaining service period (years)	14	14
Amortization of net gain (loss) to be included in pension cost	$ 0	$ (15)

[1] See Unrecognized Gains and Losses.

[2] Applicable amounts are:

	19X2	19X3
PBO—See Changes in Projected Benefit Obligation	$12,100	$16,000
Market-related value of plan assets—See Valuation of Plan Assets	8,656	10,335

UNRECOGNIZED GAINS AND LOSSES

For purposes of the corridor calculation, the unrecognized net gain or loss excludes those asset gains and losses not yet reflected in the calculated market-related value of plan assets. The schedule below displays the elements of the unrecognized net gain or loss and the interaction between it and the unrecognized net gain or loss to be included in the corridor calculation.

	Unrecognized Net Gain (Loss)	Unrecognized Net Gain (Loss) for Purposes of Corridor
January 1, 19X1	$ 0	$ 0
Gains (losses) arising in 19X1:		
Increase in PBO[1]	(1,050)	(1,050)
Difference between actual return and expected return on plan assets[2]	430	86
December 31, 19X1	(620)	(964)

Exhibit 32.7. *Continued.*

Amortization of unrecognized net loss[3]	0	0
Gains (losses) arising in 19X2:		
Increase in PBO	(962)	(962)
Difference between return on plan assets and expected return	134	113
December 31, 19X2	(1,448)	(1,813)
Amortization of unrecognized net loss[3]	15	15
Gains (losses) arising in 19X3:		
Decrease in PBO	750	750
Difference between return on plan assets and expected return	(284)	56
December 31, 19X3	$ (967)	$ (992)

[1] See Changes in Projected Benefit Obligation.
[2] See Valuation of Plan Assets.
[3] See Amortization of Unrecognized Net Gain or Loss.

PENSION-RELATED BALANCE SHEET ACCOUNTS

The interaction between periodic pension cost and funding can best be demonstrated by:

	19X1	19X2	19X3
Prepaid pension cost, January 1	$ 0	$ 120	$ 368
Pension cost	(980)	(952)	(1,211)
Amount contributed (funded)	1,100	1,200	1,250
Prepaid pension cost, December 31	$ 120	$ 368	$ 407

The difference between the accumulated benefit obligation and the fair value of plan assets at the end of each year is:

	December 31		
	19X1	19X2	19X3
Accumulated benefit obligation	$8,900	$12,600	$13,100
Fair value of plan assets	9,000	10,700	12,150
Unfunded (overfunded) accumulated benefit obligation	$ (100)	$ 1,900	$ 950

Company X, as permitted under SFAS No. 87, waited until 19X3 to record an additional minimum liability. On December 31, 19X3, the adjustment necessary to reflect this minimum liability was $1,357 (unfunded ABO of $950 plus prepaid pension cost of $407), with a corresponding intangible asset ($1,357) being recorded. The maximum intangible asset would have been $3,890 (unrecognized prior service cost of $1,690 plus unrecognized net obligation at date of initial application of SFAS No. 87 of $2,200).

FINANCIAL STATEMENT DISCLOSURES

The comparative financial statements of Company X for the year ended December 31, 19X3, would include the following disclosures regarding its pension plan.

Note X

The Company has a defined pension plan covering substantially all of its employees. Benefits are based on years of service and employee's compensation at the time of retirement. The Company's funding policy is to contribute annually the maximum amount that can be deducted for federal income tax purposes.

Pension cost for 19X3, 19X2, and 19X1 consists of the following components:

(continued)

Exhibit 32.7.   *Continued.*

	19X3	19X2	19X1
Service cost	$ 700	$ 650	$ 600
Interest cost	1,200	968	900
Actual return on plan assets	(750)	(1,000)	(1,150)
Deferrals and amortization	61	334	630
Net pension cost	$1,211	$ 952	$ 980

The following assumptions were used:

	As of December 31		
	19X3	19X2	19X1
Weighted-average discount rate for projected benefit obligation (%)	8	7.5	8
Rate of increase in compensation levels for projected benefit obligation (%)	5.75	5.5	5.5
Expected long-term rate of return on plan assets—periodic pension cost (%)	10	10	10

The following table sets forth the plan's funded status and amounts recognized in the Company's statement of financial position at December 31, 19X3 and 19X2:

	December 31	
	19X3	19X2
Actuarial present value of benefit obligations:		
Vested benefit obligation	$(10,400)	$ (9,700)
Accumulated benefit obligation	(13,100)	(12,600)
Projected benefit obligation	(16,600)	(16,000)
Plan assets at fair value	12,150	10,700
Funded status	(4,450)	(5,300)
Unrecognized net loss (gain)	967	1,448
Unrecognized prior service cost	1,690	1,820
Unrecognized net obligation at date of initial application—January 1, 19X1	2,200	2,400
Prepaid (accrued) pension cost prior to recognizing additional liability	407	368
Adjustment necessary to reflect additional minimum liability	(1,357)	—
Prepaid (accrued) pension cost	$ (950)	$ 368

As SFAS No. 87 permits, the Company waited until 19X3 to record an additional minimum liability for unfunded pension benefit obligations. Had the requirement been adopted as of December 31, 19X2, prepaid pension assets would have decreased by $368, other accrued liabilities would have increased by $1,900, and an intangible asset of $2,268 would have been recorded.

Plan assets consist of publicly traded stocks and bonds, and U.S. government securities.

Unrecognized prior service cost is amortized on a straight-line basis over the estimated average service period of employees active at the date of the related plan amendment who are expected to receive plan benefits.

Exhibit 32.7. *Continued.*

methodology by which the special pension recognition should be carried out. As a result, widely divergent practices evolved, with differing effects on the affected employers' subsequent pension costs. In contrast, the new accounting provisions for nonrecurring events are based on standardized measurement methods that are applied within the general framework of SFAS No. 87. As with that Statement, SFAS No. 88 focuses on proper accounting of events in the future and generally allows plans to begin with a clean slate at the initial compliance date regardless of how such events were handled previously. There is also an exception for **immaterial items.**

(b) SETTLEMENT. To constitute a **settlement,** a transaction must (1) be irrevocable, (2) relieve the employer of primary responsibility for a pension benefit obligation, and (3) eliminate significant risks related to the obligations and the assets used to effect the settlement. This is a new accounting concept introduced by SFAS No. 88.

The most common type of settlement is the **purchase of nonparticipating annuities** for or **lump-sum cash payments** to plan participants to discharge all or part of the benefit obligation of the plan, which may or may not be connected with a plan termination. (A participating annuity allows the purchaser to participate in the investment performance and possibly other experience—for example, mortality experience—of the insurance company, through dividends or rate credits. It generally costs more than a nonparticipating annuity, which is based on a fixed price.) Although SFAS No. 88 extends condition (2) in the preceding paragraph to include a transaction that relieves the plan of the responsibility for the benefit obligation, that condition is generally not sufficient, for example, if the benefit obligation is transferred to another plan sponsored by the same or a related employer, or if the annuities are purchased from a subsidiary of the employer.

(i) Timing. The timing of the settlement recognition depends on when all three qualifying conditions for a settlement have been met. For example, a commitment to purchase annuity is not sufficient to constitute a settlement until the benefit obligation risk has been transferred to the insurance company and the premium for the annuities has been paid in cash or in kind, except for minor adjustments. Although a dedicated portfolio designed to match the estimated benefit payments under the plan may eliminate the investment risk on assets backing those payments, it does not constitute a settlement because the plan continues to be exposed to the mortality risk on those payments and also because the portfolio is not irrevocable.

(ii) Gain or Loss. The **maximum gain or loss** subject to settlement recognition is the unrecognized net gain or loss in the plan at the date of settlement, plus any remaining unrecognized net asset (but not a net obligation) at transition. The magnitude of the projected benefit obligation to be settled, as determined by the employer prior to the settlement, is generally not the same as the cost to discharge that obligation, such as the premium for the annuities, and must first be set equal to the latter. This adjustment in the projected benefit obligation generates a gain or loss that is added to unrecognized net gain or loss before the settlement recognition is done. The amount of the **settlement gain or loss** is equal to the maximum gain or loss subject to settlement recognition multiplied by the **settlement percentage,** which is the percentage of the projected benefit obligation of the plan being settled. Computations described in this paragraph are generally performed on a plan-by-plan basis rather than by aggregating all of the employer's plans.

(iii) Use of Participating Annuities. Participating annuities are acceptable instruments to effect a settlement, unless their substance is that the employer remains subject to all or most of the risks and rewards associated with the benefit obligation covered by the annuities or the assets transferred to the insurance company. If the purchase of a participating annuity constitutes a settlement, the maximum gain (but not the maximum loss) must first be reduced by the cost of the participation feature. This means that the participation feature of the annuity contract is excluded from the settlement recognition entirely and its value, which is the present value of the future dividends expected from the insurance company, is carried as a plan asset.

SFAS No. 88 also permits **a de minimis exemption** from settlement recognition if the total cash and annuity settlements in a year do not exceed the sum of the service cost and interest cost components of the net periodic pension cost, provided this accounting practice is followed consistently from year to year.

(c) CURTAILMENT.   A curtailment is an event that significantly reduces the expected years of future service of present employees covered by the plan, or eliminates for a significant number of employees covered by the plan the accrual of defined benefit for some or all of their future services. It is possible for an event, such as a window retirement program, to change significantly the benefit obligation but not the total expected future services and, therefore, not to be a curtailment. Unrelated, individually insignificant reductions in future services do not qualify as a curtailment even if they occur in a single year and are significant in aggregate. Conversely, a series of individually insignificant reductions in future services, which are caused by the same event but take place over more than one fiscal year, should be aggregated to determine if the reduction is sufficiently significant to constitute a curtailment.

Examples of curtailment include reduction in work force, closing of a facility with the employees not employed elsewhere by the employer, disposal of a business segment, window retirement program, termination of a defined benefit plan or freezing of the benefits thereunder. A process known as **termination/reestablishment,** whereby an employer terminates a defined benefit plan, recovers the surplus plan assets, and then establishes a new plan for the same employees that provides the same overall benefits as the terminated plan when benefits from the terminated plan are taken into account, is not a curtailment because the employer's benefit obligation has not been materially altered. Even if the new plan created through the termination/reestablishment process does not reproduce the same overall benefits, the transaction should be treated as a plan amendment and not a curtailment. Similarly, if the employees are covered by multiple plans and the suspension of their benefit accrual under one plan is wholly or partially balanced by increased benefit accrual under another plan of the same or a related employer (e.g., a supplemental retirement plan providing defined benefits, which is offset by the benefits from the suspended plan), the event should be treated not as a curtailment but as simultaneous amendments to the two plans: One reduces benefits and one increases benefits.

The **curtailment gain or loss** to be recognized is the sum of the **prior service cost recognition** and the **projected benefit obligation adjustment,** both determined on a plan-by-plan basis rather than by aggregating all of the employer's plans.

According to statements made by the FASB staff, the **prior service cost recognition** is intended to be the immediate recognition of any unrecognized prior service cost and any remaining unrecognized net obligation (but not a net asset) at transition that relate to those employees whose services have been curtailed. Since these two items are often not available for specific employees or groups of employees, SFAS No. 88 provides a general rule to compute the prior service cost recognition as the product of any unrecognized net obligation at transition, or any prior service cost related to the entire plan, and the applicable **curtailment percentages.** The curtailment percentage is the percentage reduction in the remaining expected future years of service associated with the prior service cost or the net obligation at transition; it is determined separately for each prior service cost and the net obligation at transition. To reduce computational complexity, it is common practice to use an alternative curtailment percentage such as the percentage reduction in future years of service of all employees immediately prior to the curtailment, provided that the results would not be materially distorted.

The **projected benefit obligation adjustment** can be a gain or a loss. If the curtailment reduces the projected benefit obligation, the reduction is applied first against any unrecognized net loss in the plan and the residual amount is recognized as a gain. If the curtailment increases the projected benefit obligation, the increase is applied first against any unrecognized net gain and any remaining unrecognized net asset at transition, and the residual amount is recognized as a loss.

The timing of the curtailment recognition depends on whether the net effect is a gain or a loss. A net gain is recognized when the event has occurred, whereas a net loss is recognized when the event appears probable and its effects are reasonably estimable.

Although Paragraph 31 of **APB Opinion No. 8** had required immediate recognition of any actuarial gains or losses resulting from unusual events, SFAS No. 88 further specifies the conditions necessitating the immediate recognition and the method of determining the amount to be recognized, thus greatly narrowing down the divergence of practice that prevailed prior to SFAS No. 88.

(d) DISPOSAL OF A BUSINESS. When an employer disposes of a business segment, its pension plan may experience a **curtailment,** due to the termination of some employees' services, and a **settlement,** if all or part of the benefit obligation is transferred to the purchaser. Certain **termination benefits** such as severance payments may also be involved. The effects of such curtailment, settlement, and termination benefits should be determined in accordance with SFAS No. 88 and then included in the **gain or loss on the disposal** pursuant to paragraphs 15–17 of APB Opinion No. 30, "Reporting the Results of Operations—Reporting the Effects of Disposal of a Segment of a Business and Extraordinary, Unusual and Infrequently Occurring Events and Transactions," except for the following modifications to the SFAS No. 88 measurements: (1) the curtailment recognition is made regardless of whether the reduction in future services is significant; (2) the de minimis exemption for settlements does not apply; and (3) the difference between any benefit obligation and plan assets transferred to the purchaser is recognized in full as a gain or loss before the settlement percentage is determined. However, if the settlement, by purchasing annuities, for example, could have taken place in the absence of the business disposal, the settlement recognition should not be included in the gain or loss on the disposal.

(e) PLAN MERGER, SPINOFF, AND TERMINATION. The **merger** of two or more pension plans of the same employer does not require any SFAS No. 88 recognition. Prior service costs should be amortized as before. The remaining unrecognized net obligations or assets at transition should be netted and amortized over a reasonably weighted average of the remaining amortization periods previously used by the separate plans. The unrecognized net gains or losses should be aggregated and the minimum amortization thereof should reflect the average remaining service period of the combined employee group.

Spinoff of a portion of a pension plan to an unrelated employer, as may happen after the sale of a business segment, should be handled as a settlement unless there is reasonable doubt that the purchaser will meet the benefit obligation and the seller remains contingently liable for it. A settlement does not occur if an employer divides a pension plan into two or more plans all sponsored by it. In that case any remaining unrecognized net obligation or asset should be allocated among the plans in proportion to their respective projected benefit obligations, as should any unrecognized net gain or loss. Any unrecognized prior service cost should be allocated on the basis of the participants in the surviving plans.

If one of these surviving plans is further **transferred to a subsidiary,** the employer should reduce its prepaid (accrued) pension cost by the amount of prepaid (accrued) pension cost related to the transferred plan and simultaneously record a decrease (increase) in its stockholders' equity by the same amount. The subsidiary, on the other hand, should record the transferred prepaid (accrued) pension cost as an asset liability and an equal amount as an increase (decrease) in its stockholders' equity.

Prior to SFAS No. 88, the accounting effect of the **termination** of a defined benefit plan was largely based on the amount of surplus assets or deficit in the plan. If surplus assets were returned to the employer and there was no successor defined benefit plan, the previously unrecognized amount was typically reflected in the employer's earnings over a period of 10 to 20 years. SFAS No. 88 changed entirely the accounting concept relating to a plan termination. First of all, any remaining unrecognized gain from a **prior asset reversion,** which had been accomplished through a settlement as defined by SFAS No. 88, was recognized immediately upon the initial application date of the Statement as the effect of a change in accounting principle, to the extent that plan assets plus (minus) accrued (prepaid) pension cost exceeded the projected benefit obligation. There would be no further amortization of the remaining amount since it was already reflected in the size of the unrecognized net obligation or asset at transition. The second change introduced by SFAS No. 88 is that a plan termination is accounted for as a combination of a curtailment (i.e., elimination of further benefit accrual, assuming that there is not a successor defined benefit plan) and a settlement. Indeed, the **asset reversion** is no longer the triggering event, and substantially the same accounting effect has been achieved when the benefit accrual is frozen and the benefit obligation settled, even if the plan is not terminated. Any **excise tax** related to the asset reversion should be recognized at the time of the reversion. As noted in subsection 32.3(c), the termination/reestablishment of a defined benefit plan does not constitute a curtailment, but it may nevertheless require a settlement recognition.

Withdrawal from a multiemployer plan may result in additional cost to the employer. The effect of the withdrawal should be recognized when it becomes probable or reasonably possible.

(f) TERMINATION BENEFITS. SFAS No. 74, "Accounting for Special Termination Benefits Paid to Employees," was issued in 1983, ostensibly to address window retirement programs and shutdown benefits. Although it required recognition of the effects of any changes on the previously accrued expenses for those benefits, no recognition method was defined and compliance with the Statement was not widespread.

SFAS No. 88 superseded SFAS No. 74, and as with that Statement, it deals with both pension and nonpension benefits such as severance payments, supplemental unemployment benefits, and life and health insurance benefits, regardless of whether they are paid by a plan or directly by the employer. The amount to be recognized is the amount of any immediate payments plus the present value of any expected future payments. The cost of **special termination benefits** that are offered only for a short period of time should be recognized when the employees accept the offer and the amount can be reasonably estimated. In contrast, **contractual termination benefits,** which are required by the terms of a plan only if a specified event (such as a plant closing) occurs, should be recognized when it is probable that employees will be entitled to benefits and the amount can be reasonably estimated.

Keep in mind that a situation involving termination benefits often also involves a curtailment. The curtailment recognition is first determined using the benefit obligation without the termination benefits. The effect of the termination benefits is then the difference between the benefit obligations determined with and without the termination benefits.

It is not unusual, in the measurement of the projected benefit obligation and the pension cost of a plan, to assume some probability for events that may give rise to termination benefits. In such a situation, the amount of termination benefits to be recognized under SFAS No. 88 is the difference between the projected benefit obligation including the termination benefits and that measured without any termination benefit. For example, a plan may permit early retirement after age 55 with a reduced pension but provide an unreduced pension regardless of age in the event of a change in control of the employer. When a change in control occurs, the amount of termination benefit to be recognized for an employee who is age 40 is the difference in the value of his unreduced pension commencing immediately and his reduced pension commencing when he will reach age 55. Furthermore, if the situation constitutes a curtailment, the projected benefit obligation adjustment is the difference between the value of his reduced pension commencing at age 55 and his projected benefit obligation determined using the regular actuarial assumptions including, if applicable, an allowance for some probability that change-in-control benefits may be invoked. It would not be reasonable to treat the entire change in projected benefit obligation as a gain or loss or to handle the situation solely as a curtailment, merely because the assumptions used to determine the projected benefit obligation prior to the change of control included some allowance for change-in-control benefits.

(g) BUSINESS COMBINATION.   No special accounting treatment is needed if the business combination is accounted for as a pooling of interest. However, if the **purchase method** under APB Opinion No. 16 is used, the purchaser should record a liability (accrued pension cost) equal to the excess of the acquired projected benefit obligation over the acquired plan assets, or an asset (prepaid pension cost) equal to the excess of the acquired plan assets over the acquired projected benefit obligation. Simultaneous with the recording of such purchase accounting liability (asset), **goodwill** is increased (decreased) by an equal amount. Once these adjustments have been made, any previously existing unrecognized prior service cost, net obligation, or asset at transition and net gain or loss are eliminated and no further amortization thereof will be needed. If the acquired company continues to issue its own separate financial statement after the purchase date, its pension cost may be determined without the purchase accounting adjustment and may therefore be different from the pension cost reported by the parent company on its behalf.

The measurement date for the purchase accounting adjustment is the acquisition date, even if the employer customarily uses a measurement date different from its fiscal year-end for all other aspects of SFAS No. 87. In determining the projected benefit obligation at the acquisition date, the effects of certain **postacquisition events** should be reflected. Examples of such events include curtailments (without regard to the significance criterion), termination benefits, and plan amendments that were highly probable at the time of the purchase. To be included in the purchase accounting, these events generally must either occur, or be substantially decided upon, within one year of the acquisition date.

Similar purchase accounting adjustments may also be made for postretirement and post-employment benefits. The restructuring of a company including merger of two or more legal entities generally does not trigger a purchase accounting adjustment for pensions.

(h) SEQUENCE OF MEASUREMENT STEPS.   In a year containing one of the unusual events described above, the employer's pension cost comprises (1) the net periodic pension cost for the period prior to the event, determined without regard to the event; (2) the effect of the event such as the curtailment or settlement recognition; and (3) the net periodic pension cost for the period subsequent to the event, fully reflecting the changes resulting from the event. The **preevent pension cost** in (1) is generally based on the assumptions, such as the discount rate, used for the previous year-end measurement. **Updated projected benefit obligation and plan assets** are then determined as of the event date as if the event had not taken place, using assumptions that are appropriate at that date, including, if applicable, any adjustment to the projected benefit obligation to reflect the actual cost of settling any benefit obligation. The prepaid (accrued) pension cost, as well as any unrecognized prior service cost, net obligation, or asset at transition and net gain or loss, are brought up to date. The effect of the event is next determined on the basis of the updated projected benefit obligation and plan assets. The **postevent pension cost** in item (3) is based on the projected benefit obligation, plan assets, prior service cost, unrecognized net obligation, or asset at transition and net gain or loss that remain after the event.

In determining the postevent pension cost, the remaining amortization period for any unrecognized net obligation or asset at transition will generally not be changed even though the amount to be amortized may have. Similarly the remaining amortization schedule of any prior service cost will generally remain unchanged, unless the period during which the employer expects to realize future economic benefits from the plan amendment is shorter than originally estimated, or if the future economic benefits have been impaired. Amortization of net gain or loss, on the other hand, should reflect the postevent average remaining service period.

In case of **multiple events** occurring within one fiscal year, the process described in the preceding paragraphs may need to be repeated more than once, taking the events one at a time in chronological order. For simultaneous events it is permissible to establish the presumed sequence unless there is compelling reason against the logic of that sequence, provided that the same approach is followed consistently in the future. The sequence selected can materially affect the amount of gain or loss to be recognized. It is also possible for events that originated from the situation to be recognized in different fiscal years, for example, when a plan is terminated in one year but the benefit obligation is not settled until the following year.

Special considerations are needed when the plan's measurement date differs from the employer's fiscal year-end. It is generally not practical to measure the effect of the special event on any date other than the date of the event, since such measurement typically involves the changes in the projected benefit obligation or plan assets on the event date, such as the amounts of benefit obligation and plan assets being transferred to another employer. One approach is to determine the effect of the event using benefit obligation, plan assets, and net gain or loss as of the event date, even though the preevent pension cost was computed using a measurement date different from the fiscal year-end, and then determine the postevent pension cost for the period from the event date to the fiscal year-end. However, the ensuing year-end measurement may again be done at a measurement date that is consistent with that used in the preceding year.

Gain or loss related to events occurring after the measurement date but prior to the employer's fiscal year-end is generally not recognized in the current period, except when it relates to a disposal of business segment that is reflected in the current year or when it results from the termination of a pension plan without a successor defined benefit plan. Even if not recognized, the effect of the event should be disclosed if it is material. The preceding statements apply to quarterly financial statements as well.

(i) DISCLOSURE REQUIREMENTS FOR NONRECURRING EVENTS.   An employer that recognizes a gain or loss for curtailment, settlement, or termination benefits shall disclose the **nature of the event** and the **amount recognized.** Despite the nonrecurring nature of these events, such gain or loss is normally not an extraordinary item as defined in paragraphs 20–22 of APB Opinion No. 30. One exception is when the gain or loss is related to the disposal of a business segment.

(j) ILLUSTRATION—NONRECURRING EVENTS.   Exhibit 32.8 illustrates the application of SFAS No. 88 with respect to settlement, curtailment, and special termination benefits and that of SFAS No. 87 with respect to business combinations accounted for under the purchase method.

32.4 SPONSOR ACCOUNTING FOR NONQUALIFIED PLANS

(a) QUALIFIED VERSUS NONQUALIFIED PLANS.   Qualified pension plans present notable tax advantages to both employer and employee as a form of employee compensation. The immediate advantage to the employer is the ability to deduct currently, within limitations, contributions to the plan. The employee on whose behalf the contribution is made does not, however, have to report the amount as gross income until it is made available to him. This deferral of tax has an added advantage since, in the typical case, benefits are not distributed until retirement, when the employee may be in a lower income tax bracket. The long-term, and perhaps the most important, tax advantage enjoyed by a qualified plan is that the fund or trust that receives and invests the contributions enjoys tax-exempt status. Investments earnings are not taxed until distributed, thus permitting an accelerated rate of growth for the fund.

For a pension plan to be considered qualified for income tax purposes, it must comply with certain IRC requirements, not only in the design of the plan but also in its operations. Some of these requirements are:

- The plan must not discriminate in favor of employees who are officers or shareholders or highly compensated.

BACKGROUND INFORMATION AND ASSUMPTIONS

Company X, which was used to illustrate the application of SFAS No. 87, experienced the following events, all occurring on December 31, 19X3, and in the sequence shown below:

- The projected benefit obligation for pensioners was $6,000 on December 31, 19X3. Company X purchased participating annuities at a cost of $6,200 to discharge this obligation, $600 of which would be expected to be refunded by the insurance company in the form of dividends in future years.
- Company X closed one of its major manufacturing plants and permanently laid off all its workers. These workers would have represented 20% of the future service of all of Company X's employees. The projected benefit obligation with respect to these laid-off workers was $1,500 before the layoff and only $800 after the layoff, ignoring the special benefits described below.
- For those laid-off employees who were eligible for early retirement, Company X offered unreduced early retirement pensions and an additional supplemental pension up to age 62. If not for the plant closing, these employees would have been entitled to a reduced early retirement pension only and no supplement. The value of the supplements and the waiver of the early retirement reduction was $400.
- Also on December 31, 19X3, Company X acquired Company Y, which sponsored a defined-benefit pension plan with a projected benefit obligation of $1,000 and plan assets worth $1,400. Company X has not adopted SFAS No. 96.

EFFECT ON FUNDED STATUS ON DECEMBER 31, 19X3

	Initial Status	Effect of Settlement[1]	Effect of Curtailment[2]	Special Termination Benefit[3]	Acquisition of Company Y[4]	Revised Status
Projected benefit obligation	$(16,600)	$ 6,200	$ 700	$(400)	$(1,000)	$(11,100)
Plan assets (fair value)	12,150	(5,600)	0	0	1,400	7,950
Funded status	$ (4,450)	$ 600	$ 700	$(400)	$ 400	$ (3,150)
Unrecognized net loss (gain)	967	(728)	(239)	0	0	0
Unrecognized prior service cost	1,690	0	(338)	0	0	1,352
Unrecognized net obligation at date of initial application	2,200	0	(440)	0	0	1,760
Prepaid (accrued) pension cost	$ 407	$ (128)	$(317)	$(400)	$ 172	$ (266)

[1] Although the price of the annuity contract was $6,200, the cost for SFAS No. 87 purposes is only $5,600 since $600 of future dividends are anticipated. The $600 will be carried as a plan asset.

In accounting for the settlement the following steps are followed:

First, the $16,600 PBO needs to be reevaluated because the PBO for pensioners was discovered to be $5,600 instead of $6,200. The revised PBO, therefore, is $16,000, of which $5,600 was settled through the annuity purchase. The settlement percentage is 35%.

Second, the unrecognized net loss is reduced from the $967 before the settlement by the $600 "savings" from the annuity contract, leaving a net loss of $367.

(continued)

Exhibit 32.8.   Nonrecurring events.

The settlement loss is $128 (i.e., $367 net loss times settlement percentage of 35%). This loss reduces the prepaid pension cost from $407 to $279.

[2] The 20% reduction in future services expected from the employee is significant enough to constitute a curtailment under SFAS No. 88. The curtailment gain/loss consists of two components—the prior service recognition and the PBO adjustment.

The curtailment loss is calculated as follows:

The remaining unrecognized prior service cost on December 31, 19X3, is $1,690 and the remaining transition obligation is $2,200 for a total of $3,890. The prior service cost recognition is 20% (the curtailment percentage) of the $3,890, or a $778 loss.

The PBO is reduced by $700 on account of the plant closing. However, since the plan still carries an unrecognized net loss of $239 at this point, the $700 saving must first be applied to eliminate the $239 unrecognized loss before the remaining $461 may be recognized as a PBO adjustment gain.

The net curtailment loss is $317 (the $778 prior service cost less the $461 PBO gain). This $317 loss results in an accrued pension cost of $38. The amortization of the prior service cost ($130 in 19X3) will be $160 in 19X4. The respective remaining amortization periods will nevertheless remain unchanged.

[3] The value of the special benefits ($400) is recognized in full immediately and further increases the accrued pension cost from $38 to $438.

[4] Company Y's plan has an excess of $400, the difference between the plan assets of $1,400 and the PBO of $1,000. The $400 excess (less $228 in deferred tax) is recognized in purchase accounting and added to goodwill. Meanwhile the accrued pension cost is reduced by $172, from $438 to $266.

Exhibit 32.8. *Continued.*

- Benefits under the plan must be reasonable in amount when considered with other forms of compensation.
- Plan operations must be conducted in accordance with the plan document and trust agreement.
- The pension fund must be exclusively for the benefit of participants and their beneficiaries.
- The plan must comply with certain minimum funding and reporting requirements.

Over the years these requirements have become increasingly complex and burdensome, thus adding to the costs of administering qualified plans.

It has always been fairly common for an employer to maintain nonqualified retirement plans or to provide individualized deferred compensation arrangements for a selected group of management and highly compensated employees. There is no precise definition of "highly compensated employees" in this context, and it is not linked to the definition of "highly compensated employees" introduced by the Tax Reform Act of 1986. The primary advantages of such nonqualified arrangements are that (1) the coverage can be limited to only a few selected employees; (2) the benefits can be designed to meet the employer's objectives and the employees' needs without having to worry about the myriad of constraints imposed by ERISA and the tax code; and (3) they are exempt from virtually all ERISA reporting and funding requirements except a one-time notice of their existence to the DOL.

During the 1980s, the tax code was repeatedly amended to limit the amount of benefit that can be provided by, and the flexibility in the design of, a qualified plan. As a result nonqualified plans gained increasing importance. Despite these advantages over qualified plans, a nonqualified plan suffers from a serious tax disadvantage. Contributions to the plan, if any, are not currently tax-deductible to the employer as long as the employees' rights to those contributions are subject to a substantial risk of forfeiture. Instead, the employer may deduct the benefits when they are paid. Moreover, there is no tax shelter for any fund that the employer may have set aside to finance the plan. Investment earnings on such fund are taxed directly to the employer, thus retarding the growth of the fund.

An exception to the preceding paragraph is a plan that is funded through a **secular trust** (also known as a vesting trust). In that case the employer's contribution is tax-deductible to the employer and is taxed as income to the employee when the employee's interest has vested. Investment earnings of the trust are generally taxed to the employer unless distributed to the employee. The use of secular trust as the funding vehicle for a nonqualified plan may subject the plan to the reporting, funding, and other requirements of ERISA and the tax code. It is assumed throughout this chapter that the nonqualified plan is not being funded through a secular trust.

(b) NONQUALIFIED PLAN ASSETS.   For accounting and tax purposes, any fund that an employer may have set aside to finance a nonqualified plan is treated as an asset of the employer and not as an asset of the plan in the context of SFAS Nos. 87 and 88. Indeed some plans must be unfunded in order to be exempt from the ERISA funding and reporting requirements. Therefore, such a fund is accounted for like any other general asset of the employer, whereas the cost of the benefits under the plan is determined in accordance with SFAS Nos. 87 and 88 as if there were no plan assets.

In order to improve the security of benefits to the employees, legal devices such as **rabbi trusts** have been used to prohibit or limit access to the plan fund by the employer or its creditors. Nevertheless the assets of a rabbi trust are still considered assets of the employer, and the trust accounting is consolidated with the employer's accounting.

(c) NONQUALIFIED DEFINED CONTRIBUTION PLANS.   Pure nonqualified defined contribution plans are relatively uncommon. To constitute a defined contribution plan, the employer's obligation must be limited to its contributions to the plan, with the employees receiving benefits based on those contributions plus investment earnings thereon. Since most nonqualified plans are either unfunded or funded indirectly through vehicles such as corporate-owned life insurance, the mechanism to operate a defined contribution generally does not exist. A deferred compensation plan that promises a certain rate of interest on compensations deferred by employees is not a defined contribution plan, unless the promised rate is equal to the actual after-tax rate of return on the compensations deferred by the employees. This situation is not changed if the promised rate is based, for example, on the projected rate of return on certain life insurance policies used to finance the plan.

The employer's cost for a defined contribution plan is equal to its contribution to the plan.

(d) NONQUALIFIED DEFINED BENEFIT PLANS.   Both SFAS Nos. 87 and 88 apply to nonqualified plans and to any arrangement that is similar in substance to a pension plan regardless of the form or means of financing. For any other individually designed deferred compensation contract, cost should be accrued in accordance with APB Opinion No. 12 in a systematic and rational manner over the employee's period of active employment, starting from the time the contract is entered into, so that the full cost will have been accrued at the end of the term of active employment.

Examples of nonqualified defined benefit plans are (1) **supplemental retirement plans** for selected employees providing retirement benefits in addition to the employer's qualified pension plans; (2) **benefit restoration plans** to restore to the employees any benefits that may have been restricted by IRC § 401(a) or 415, or by § 401(k) on the maximum amount of compensation that can be deferred; (3) **deferred compensation or termination indemnity plans** promising to credit a rate of interest that is not equal to the after-tax investment return on the assets set aside to finance the plans. **Golden parachutes** are generally accounted for as severance payments. Change-of-control pension provisions in a pension plan, which provides certain special benefits in the event of a change in control of the employer, are handled as termination benefits under SFAS No. 88.

In applying SFAS Nos. 87 and 88 to a nonqualified plan, the following factors should be considered: (1) The discount rate should reflect the effect of any tax liability for annuities that may be purchased to discharge the benefit obligation; (2) there is generally no contribution to the plan since any funds set aside to finance the plan remain assets of the employer, except for benefits paid to the employees or payments made to purchase annuities, for example, to discharge benefit obligations; (3) as a result of (2) above, the expected return on plan assets is zero (whereas the investment return on any assets or funds that may have been appropriated to finance the plan would have already been reported elsewhere as income to the employer); (4) as noted under (2) above, benefit payments are also treated as contributions and, therefore, would reduce the employer's accrued pension cost; and (5) a nonqualified plan linked to a qualified plan, such as a supplemental retirement plan providing benefits that are offset by benefits from a qualified pension plan, should nevertheless be accounted for separately from the qualified plan.

(e) CORPORATE-OWNED LIFE INSURANCE.   No discussion of nonqualified plans can be complete without examining the role played by **corporate-owned life insurance** (COLI). In its simplest form COLI is life insurance taken out by an employer on the lives of its employees, with the employer being the premium payer, owner, and beneficiary of the insurance policies. It is the most widely used financing vehicle for nonqualified plans. COLI can also be owned by a trust established for the plan.

Under current tax laws, even though the insurance premiums paid by the employer are not currently tax-deductible, the insurance proceed payable upon the employee's death is tax-free. More importantly, the growth in the cash value of an insurance policy is not taxed to the employer, except when it is surrendered prior to the employee's death. This creates an indirect tax shelter that can be used to overcome the main tax disadvantage of a nonqualified plan: the lack of tax shelter. However, due to the start-up costs, overheads, and policy cancellation charges typically associated with life insurance policies, the use of COLI as a financing vehicle generally will only succeed if the policies are maintained for an extended period of time, if the employer's own achievable after-tax rate of return stays below that on the COLI policies, and if the preferential treatment of life insurance under the current tax laws will continue.

Another tax advantage offered by COLI has to do with the tax deduction on interest paid on policy loans. Subject to certain conditions, interest paid by the employer on loans taken on COLI policies is tax-deductible (for policies purchased after June 20, 1986, for loans up to $50,000 in total on all policies on any one employee). Suppose the insurance company charges 10% interest on a $1,000 policy loan and the employer's marginal tax rate is 40%. The interest cost to the employer is $100 gross and $60 net of tax. Suppose further that, for the $100 interest paid on the loan, the insurance company would increase the policy's cash value by $90. The net result of these transactions is that the employer has managed to convert $60 after tax into $90 worth of insurance policy cash value, which it will eventually be able to collect as tax-free insurance proceeds.

Because of these tax advantages, COLI can be a more profitable investment than other investments available to the employer. This profit can be used to offset the cost of a nonqualified plan, thus creating the illusion of a no-cost benefit plan. This line of reasoning is often used to promote the sale of COLI policies and the establishment of nonqualified plans. Techniques known as ratable charge method or zero realization method, for example, have been used to demonstrate that premiums paid on COLI policies need not be charged against earnings if the policies are projected to generate a profit over time, or that the cost of a nonqualified plan need not be accrued because it is less than the projected profit from the COLI policies used to finance it. These methods were rejected by FTB No. 85-4, "Accounting for Purchase of Life Insurance," which prescribed the cash surrender value method as the only generally accepted method of accounting for COLI policies. Under the cash surrender value method, premiums are charged against the employer's earnings, any change in cash surrender or contract value is recorded as an adjustment of premiums paid, and the cash surrender value is carried as an asset of the employer. SFAS No. 109, "Accounting for Income Taxes," requires that a deferred tax liability be established for the excess of cash surrender value over premiums paid in situations where the employer's intention to maintain the policies till maturity is in doubt.

Any related nonqualified plan that may have been funded using COLI should be separately accounted for under SFAS Nos. 87 and 88, as described in subsection 32.4(d). The COLI policies, which have already been included in the assets of the employer, are not considered plan assets in this context. Insurance proceeds are recorded as income to the employer. A policy loan is recorded simultaneously as an increase in cash and a reduction in the net cash value of the COLI policy that is carried as an asset on the employer's balance sheet and therefore does not have an impact on the employer's earnings. Interest paid on a policy loan is charged as expense like any other interest payment.

32.5 PLAN ACCOUNTING

(a) BACKGROUND. In March 1980 the FASB issued SFAS No. 35, which established for the first time GAAP for the entity defined as a pension plan. The standard was effective for financial statements for fiscal years beginning after December 15, 1980. SFAS No. 35 was developed only after a great deal of controversy and followed a discussion paper, a public hearing, and two exposure drafts over a period of 5 years. It applies to all plans, including private plans and those of state and local governments. Coming under the standard are defined benefit pension plans that are subject to the financial reporting requirements of ERISA as well as those that are not. It does not apply to plans that are being terminated.

For nongovernmental plans with 100 or more participants as of the beginning of the plan year, a comprehensive annual report (Form 5500) must be filed in accordance with ERISA. The annual report must include:

1. A set of financial statements prepared in accordance with GAAP, with an audit and opinion by an independent qualified public accountant.
2. An actuarial report, including the status of the minimum funding standard account, and opinion by an enrolled actuary.

(b) OBJECTIVE AND CONTENT OF FINANCIAL STATEMENTS. Under SFAS No. 35, the plan itself is the reporting entity, not the trust. The statement is based on a position that the primary objective of a plan's financial statements is to provide information useful in assessing its present and future ability to pay benefits when due. This objective requires the presentation of information about the economic resources of the plan and a measurement of its participants' accumulated benefits. The Statement leaves unresolved, at least for the time being, the issue of whether accumulated plan benefits are accounting liabilities of the plan. Therefore it allows flexibility in presenting the actuarial information by providing that the plan's annual financial statements must include:

1. A **statement** that includes information regarding **net assets available for benefits.**
2. A **statement** that includes information regarding the **changes in net assets** available for benefits.
3. Information regarding the actuarial **present value of accumulated plan benefits** as of the benefit information date (which can either be at the beginning or end of the year).
4. **Information** regarding the effects, if significant, of certain factors effecting the year-to-year change in the actuarial present value of accumulated plan benefits.

SFAS No. 35 provides that the actuarial information required under items 3 and 4 can be presented in separate statements, in the notes to financial statements, or combined with the other required information on the net assets available for benefits and the year-to-year changes therein (provided the information is as of the same date and/or for the same period.)

(c) NET ASSETS AVAILABLE FOR BENEFITS. Plan investments, excluding insurance contracts, must be reported at fair value. Insurance contracts must be reported in accordance with the rules required by certain governmental agencies relating to the plan's annual report filed pursuant to ERISA. Plans not subject to ERISA also would be required to report their insurance contracts as though they had filed that annual report. Exhibit 32.9 is a brief summary of those filing requirements.

Because net assets are the existing means by which a plan can provide benefits, net asset information is necessary to assess a plan's ability to pay benefits when due. Using fair value as the basis to measure a plan's investments provides the most relevant information about resources currently available to pay the participants' benefits. The fair value of an investment is the amount that the plan could reasonably expect to receive for the investment from a current sale between a willing buyer and a willing seller, that is, not in a forced liquidation sale. If there is an active market for the investment, fair value is measured by the **market price** as of the reporting date.

(i) Good Faith Valuations. Investments that do not have a quoted market price, must be valued "in good faith." In determining a good faith value the following factors should be considered:

- Quoted market prices for similar investments.
- Information about transactions or offers regarding the plan's investment.
- Forecast of expected cash flows for that investment.

(ii) Insurance Company Contracts. Contracts with insurance companies take various forms. SFAS No. 110, "Reporting by Defined Benefit Pension Plans of Investment Contracts," requires that insurance contracts be classified as either investment contracts or "true" insurance contracts (i.e., those that incorporate mortality or morbidity risk). Insurance contracts must be valued in accordance with the instructions to either Form 5500 or Form 5500-C/R; that is at fair value or at amounts determined by the insurance enterprise (contract value). The instructions, which are the same for both these forms, provide that contracts under which payments to the insurance companies are allocated to individual participants are **excluded** from plan assets. An **allocated contract** is one under which the insurance company guarantees the benefit payment to the participant, thereby relieving the sponsor, upon payment of the premium, of all risks. **Unallocated insurance contracts,** whereby the plan is responsible for paying benefits to the participants, are included as assets of the plan.

A plan can enter into several types of insurance contract with an insurance company. Classification of these contracts is primarily based on whether (1) the contract assets are allocated to specific participants or (2) the premium payments made by the sponsor are accumulated in an unallocated fund and used to meet benefit payments as they become due or to purchase annuities for participants at some future date, such as at retirement. When reviewing different types of insurance contract for accounting purposes, the major consideration is the determination of the party (i.e., the plan or insurance company) ultimately liable for the benefit payments to participants.

(iii) Deposit Administration Contracts. A deposit administration contract is an unallocated contract under which a specified interest return is typically guaranteed. In addition, experience credits (dividends) may be declared to the plan at the sole discretion of the insurance company. Typically, when a participant retires, an individual annuity is purchased for that participant, the insurance company guarantees payment of the benefits, and the annuity contract is no longer recorded as an asset of the plan.

Under the deposit administration contract, all funds intended for the future payment of benefits to participants are held in an undivided account, generally referred to as the "active

| | Pension Plan with 100 or More Participants | Pension Plans with Fewer than 100 Participants | Welfare Benefit Plans | | One Participant Pension Plan with $100,000 or More of Assets |
			Plans with 100 or More Participants	Plans with Fewer than 100 Participants	
Basic Annual Return/Report Form	Form 5500	Form 5500-C/R	Form 5500	Form 5500-C/R	Form 5500-EZ
Financial Statements to Be Attached to Basic Form					
Statement of assets and liabilities at current value	Yes	No	Yes	No	No
Statement of income, expense, and changes in net assets	Yes	No	Yes	No	No
Notes to financial statements	Yes	No	Yes	No	No
Financial Information in Attached Schedules					
Assets held for investment:					
At the end of year	Yes	No	Yes	No	No
Both acquired and disposed within the plan year	Yes	No	Yes	No	No
Party-in-interest transactions	Yes	Yes	Yes	Yes	No
Obligations in default	Yes	No	Yes	No	No
Leases in default	Yes	No	Yes	No	No
Reportable transactions	Yes	No	Yes	No	No
Report of Independent Public Accountant	Yes	No	Yes	No	No

(continued)

Exhibit 32.9. Employee benefit plans: schedule of DOL filing requirements. *Source:* U.S. Department of Labor.

	Pension Plan with 100 or More Participants	Pension Plans with Fewer than 100 Participants	Welfare Benefit Plans		One Participant Pension Plan with $100,000 or More of Assets
			Plans with 100 or More Participants	Plans with Fewer than 100 Participants	
Schedules for Attachment to Basic Forms					
Schedule A (Insurance Information)[1]	Yes	Yes	Yes	Yes	No
Schedule B (Actuarial Information)[2]	Yes	Yes	No	No	Yes
Schedule SSA (Separated Participants with Deferred Vested Benefits)	Yes	Yes	No	No	No
Annual statement of assets and liabilities of a bank common or collective trust or an insurance company pooled separate account[3]	Yes	No	Yes	No	No
Due Date for Filing					
Number of months after close of plan year	7	7	7	7	7
Additional number of months allowed upon timely filing of a request for extension	2½	2½	2½	2½	2½

[1] Required if benefits are provided by an insurance carrier.

[2] Required if the plan is subject to the minimum funding standards of ERISA (defined benefit pension plan).

[3] If the bank or insurance company files a copy of the annual report directly with the Department of Labor, a plan filing need not contain a separate copy of the annual report.

Exhibit 32.9. *Continued.*

life fund," which is credited with all premium deposits, interest earned on the funds invested, and any dividends or experience credits declared by the insurance company. It is charged with the purchase price of all annuities provided for retired participants and any other benefits paid directly from the account, such as for death or disability, and for all expenses not paid directly by the sponsor. Although the insurance company guarantees an interest return on all funds invested, it does not guarantee that sufficient funds will be available to meet the costs of annuities to be purchased.

(iv) Immediate Participation Guaranteed Contracts.   An immediate participation guaranteed contract is a variation of the deposit administration contract except that an interest return is not guaranteed by the insurance company (a *low* minimum rate may be guaranteed), nor is a dividend credited to the contract. Instead, income is based on the actual interest rates earned by the insurance company. An immediate participation in the insurer's investment performance is a contract right. In accordance with the terms of the contract, the plan makes contributions to the insurance company, which credits the plan's account for the amount of the deposit. For investment purposes, the money (deposits) in the plan's account are commingled with the other assets of the insurance company. The plan's account is credited with interest based on the actual rates (generally referred to as "new money rates") earned by the insurance company according to the individual year in which the funds are deposited. Expenses charged to the plan's account are specified in the insurance contract, and benefit payments are made directly from the fund to retirees and charged to the plan's account. Alternatively, annuities can be purchased at the time the participants retire and the price of the annuity charged directly to the fund. In this case, the fund is adjusted each year based on the insurer's analysis of mortality, benefits paid, and earnings.

When an individual annuity contract is not purchased, the insurance company requires the plan to maintain a minimum balance in the account that is referred to as the "retired life fund." This fund must be sufficient to purchase annuities for all retired participants. Although this fund is effectively transferred to the insurance company in return for the insurance company's agreement to provide benefits, the fund is still included in the contract value as a plan asset.

A problem occurs when the plan year is not the same as the contract year, the latter usually being the insurance company's calendar year. Some insurance companies credit the plan's account with an estimated interest amount during the year and adjust that amount to the actual amount as of the insurance company's year-end. In addition, there could be a significant difference (as much as 11 months) between the insurance company's year-end and the date the actual rate is credited to the plan's account. In these instances the plan administrator, or plan trustees, should make certain that the estimated amount credited to the account as of the plan's year-end is reasonable and appropriate disclosure should be made in the notes to the financial statements.

A **separate-separate account** is an investment arrangement with the insurance company whereby funds deposited (contributions) by the plan are invested by the insurance company. The assets of the separate-separate account are the assets of the insurance company, but they are not commingled with the general assets of the insurance company. The separate-separate account provides the plan sponsor with more flexibility in investing the plan's funds. Investments in a separate-separate account are separately identified, and the account is operated similar to a bank trust fund (see below), although the net assets of the account are included in the insurance company's financial statements.

Because the insurance company legally owns the assets, and also because the plan does not have a beneficial interest in the individual assets held in the account, the plan's investments in these accounts should be presented in the statement of net assets available for benefits on a one-line basis appropriately described as investments in an account with the insurance company.

A **pooled separate account** is an account maintained with an insurance company that consists of assets of two or more participating plans, plans of a controlled group being treated as a single account. Each plan's share in the account is determined on a participation unit or variable unit basis, with the value usually adjusted each business day to reflect the investment performance of the account. The plan account provides a cumulative record of the number of participation units credited to it and the number of units allocated or withdrawn from it. The net balance of participation units credited to the account as of the end of the year, multiplied by the current participation unit value, equals the contract value amount that should be reported as an asset of the plan. Such amounts are reported on a one-line basis in the statement of net assets available for benefits, appropriately described such as, "units of interest in XYZ Insurance Co."

(v) Trusteed Assets.   Typically, a plan administrator or a fiduciary will engage a trustee or an investment adviser to assist with the investment activities of the trust. Generally four different types of trustee arrangements are applicable to a plan's investments.

Under a **nondiscretionary trust arrangement** (also referred to as a **directed trust**), the trustee acts as custodian of the plan's investments and is responsible for collecting investment income and handling trust asset transactions, as directed by the party named as having discretion to make investment decisions. Such an arrangement provides the plan with a good degree of control over the accounting transactions, because investment decisions are made by the plan trustee or fiduciary. The plan ordinarily maintains a record of the instructions given to the trustee concerning the specific investment transactions to be executed.

Under a **discretionary trust arrangement** the plan administrator gives the trustee discretionary authority and control over investments. The trustee has the authority to purchase or sell investment assets within the framework of the trust instruments and usually maintains all the detail records concerning the investment transactions and supporting documentation.

In a **common or commingled trust fund** maintained with a bank, the plan acquires investment units, sometimes referred to as **units of participation,** which are roughly equivalent to shares purchased in a mutual fund. The purchase or redemption price of the units is determined periodically by the bank, on the basis of the current fair market values of the underlying assets of the fund. The trust funds are not included in the bank's financial statements. The units of participation should be reported in the plan's statement of net assets available for benefits on a one-line basis, appropriately described.

A company that sponsors more than one pension plan, or a controlled group of companies in several plans, may place assets relating to some or all of the plans into one combined trust account, commonly referred to as a **master trust.** Each plan may have an undivided interest in the net assets of the trust account, or ownership may be represented by units of participation. A bank ordinarily is the trustee for a combined trust account for which it acts as custodian, and it may have discretionary control over the assets. Although SFAS No. 35 does not deal with accounting for master trusts, the instructions to Form 5500 (and Form 5500-C/R) require that for master trusts, the plan's pro rata share of each category of assets be presented in the financial statements.

(vi) Disclosures for Investments.   Information regarding the plan's investments must be presented in the plan's statement of net assets available for benefits in sufficient detail to identify the general types of investment (e.g., as government securities, short-term securities, corporate bonds, common stocks, mortgages, and real estate). In addition, whether fair values have been measured by quoted price in an active market or determined otherwise must be disclosed.

(vii) Operating Assets.   Assets used in the plan's operations must be presented at cost, less accumulated depreciation or amortization. Such assets would include, for example, buildings, equipment, furniture and fixtures, and leasehold improvements. Although the DOL's instructions to Forms 5500 and 5500-C/R require the presentation of all assets at fair value, it is believed that the DOL will not object to this presentation in the financial statements.

(viii) Contributions Receivable. The plan's financial statements should include as contributions receivable all amounts due the plan, as of the reporting date, from the employer, participants, and other sources of funding (e.g., state subsidies or federal grants). These receivables would include amounts due pursuant to formal commitments as well as legal or contractual requirements.

(d) CHANGES IN NET ASSETS AVAILABLE FOR BENEFITS. The information about a plan's ability to pay benefits when due, provided by its financial statements, is affected whenever transactions or other events affect the net asset or benefit information presented in those statements. Because a plan's ability to pay participants' benefits normally does not remain constant, users of its financial statements are concerned with assessing the plan's ability to pay participants' benefits not only as of a particular point in time, but also on a continuing basis. For this reason, they need to know the **reasons for changes** in the net asset and benefit information reported in successive financial statements.

The FASB concluded, therefore, that plan financial statements should include (1) information regarding the year-to-year change in net assets available for benefits, and (2) disclosure of the effects, if significant, of certain factors affecting the year-to-year change in benefit information.

SFAS No. 35 requires presentation of the statement of changes in net assets available for benefits in sufficient detail to permit identification of the significant changes during the year. The statement should include, at a minimum:

1. The net change in fair value for each significant class of investments, segregated as between investments whose fair values have been measured by quoted prices in an active market and those whose fair values have been determined otherwise.
2. Investment income, excluding the changes of fair value described in item 1.
3. Contributions from employers, segregated as between cash and noncash contributions.
4. Contributions from participants.
5. Contributions from other identified sources such as state subsidies or federal grants.
6. Benefits paid.
7. Payments to insurance companies to purchase contracts that are excluded from plan assets.
8. Administrative expenses.

In presenting this information, gains and losses from investments sold are not segregated from **unrealized gains and losses** relating to investments held at the plan's year-end.

(e) ACTUARIAL PRESENT VALUE OF ACCUMULATED PLAN BENEFITS. Accumulated plan benefits are future benefit payments that are attributable, under the plan's provisions, to employees' service rendered prior to the **benefit information date**—the date as of which the actuarial present value of accumulated plan benefits is presented. Accumulated benefits include benefits for retired or terminated employees, beneficiaries of deceased employees, and present employees or their beneficiaries.

The accumulated benefit information may be presented as of the beginning or end of the plan year. If it is presented as of the beginning of the plan year, the prior year statement of net assets available for benefits and changes therein must also be presented. For example, if the plan year-end is December 31, 1990, and the statement of accumulated plan benefits is based on a benefit information date of December 31, 1989, statements of net assets available for benefits and of changes therein also would be presented for 1989.

Measurement of accumulated plan benefits is based primarily on the employees' history of pay, service, and other appropriate factors as of the information date. **Future salary changes** are not considered, nor is a provision for inflation allowed. However, future increases that are guaranteed under a cost-of-living adjustment should be estimated. **Future years of service** are considered only in determining an employee's expected eligibility for benefits of particular types, such as early retirement, death, and disability benefits. To measure the actuarial present value, assumptions are used to adjust the accumulated plan benefits to reflect the time value of money and the probability of payment between the benefit information date and the expected date of payment. An assumption that the plan is ongoing must underlie those assumptions. Benefit information should relate to the benefits reasonably expected to be paid in exchange for employees' service to the benefit information date.

To the extent possible, plan provisions should apply in measuring accumulated plan benefits. If the benefit for each service year is not determinable from the provisions of the plan, the benefit must be considered to accumulate by years of service rendered in proportion to total years required to earn a particular benefit. Normally, the plan provisions will indicate how to measure accumulated plan benefits. Plan amendments occurring subsequent to the date of the calculation must be excluded from the actuarial computation. In addition, benefits that are guaranteed by a contract with an insurance company (i.e., allocated contracts) are also excluded.

(i) Actuarial Assumptions.   The most important decisions in developing the actuarial present value of accumulated plan benefits are in the selection of actuarial assumptions. The **interest return assumption** (analogous to the discount rate assumption in the section "Sponsor Accounting") is the single most important issue. It is used to discount future benefit payments, as well as to determine the anticipated rates of return on current and prospective assets. The concept of a **best estimate** and the principle of an **explicit approach** are integral to the rationale used in developing actuarial assumptions.

The concept of a "best estimate" is used by the FASB in discussing the actuarial assumptions in SFAS No. 35, possibly because the term is included in the ERISA certification required of an **enrolled actuary.** The reason is not critical, but it is important to realize that the best estimate requirement under ERISA is being interpreted in several ways. Its use for plan accounting purposes may be quite different from the best estimate for a funding basis. The section on sponsor accounting discusses the concept further.

Although there is no specific discussion of what the FASB intended by "best estimate," there is a discussion in the Statement of what is meant by **explicit approach.** It is important to recognize that prior to the Omnibus Budget Reconciliation Act of 1987 the explicit approach, although strongly recommended to actuaries by the American Academy of Actuaries, was not required in developing the ERISA requirements under the **minimum funding standard account.** Because of the importance of this issue, part of SFAS No. 35 is reproduced here:

> **199.** This statement requires that each significant assumption used in determining the benefit information reflect the best estimate of the plan's future experience solely with respect to that assumption. That method of selecting assumptions is referred to as an **explicit approach.** An **implicit approach,** on the other hand, means that two or more assumptions do not individually represent the best estimate of the plan's future experience with respect to those assumptions. Rather, the aggregate effect of their combined use is presumed to be approximately the same as that of an explicit approach. The Board believes that an explicit approach results in more useful information regarding (a) components of the benefit information, (b) changes in the benefit information, and (c) the choice of significant assumptions used to determine the benefit information.

> **200.** The following illustrates the preferability of an explicit approach as it relates to measuring components of the benefit information (that is, vested benefits of participants currently receiving payments, other vested benefits, and nonvested benefits). Under an implicit approach, it might be assumed that the net result of assuming no withdrawal before vesting and increasing assumed rates of return by a specified amount would approximate the same actuarial present value of total accumulated plan benefits as that which would result from using assumed rates of return and withdrawal rates determined by an explicit approach. Even

if that were true, increasing assumed rates of return to compensate for withdrawal before vesting might significantly misstate components of the benefit information. Withdrawal before vesting relates only to nonvested benefits. Therefore, discounting vested benefits at rates of return that have been adjusted to implicitly reflect that withdrawal understates that component of the benefit information and correspondingly overstates the nonvested benefit information.

201. The disadvantage of an implicit approach with respect to information regarding changes in the benefit information can be similarly illustrated. Assume that under an implicit approach, assumed rates of return are decreased to implicitly reflect the effects of a plan's provision for an automatic cost-of-living adjustment (COLA). In that situation, the effect of a plan amendment relating to the automatic COLA, for example, an amendment to increase the "cap" on the COLA from three percent to four percent, might be obscured. If significant, the effect of such an amendment should, pursuant to the requirements of the Statement, be disclosed as the effect of a plan amendment. If an implicit approach is used, however, assumed rates of return would be adjusted to reflect the effects of that amendment and accordingly, some part or all of the effect might be presented as the effect of a change in an actuarial assumption rather than as the effect of a plan amendment (particularly if assumed rates of return are also changed for other reasons).

202. In addition to the foregoing possible disadvantages, an implicit approach might result in less meaningful disclosure of the significant assumptions used to determine the benefit information. For example, disclosure of the assumed rates of return resulting from the implicit approaches described in paragraphs 200 and 201 could mislead users of the financial statements regarding the plan's investment return expectations and could result in noncomparable reporting for two plans with the same investment return expectations. Users might also draw erroneous conclusions about the relationship between the plan's actual and assumed rates of return.

There are economic actuarial assumptions and noneconomic actuarial assumptions. The key issue in developing a plan's economic assumptions is the forecast of **long-term inflation.** The inflation component should be consistently reflected in all the economic assumptions. For example, if the long-term investment return assumption reflects a 5% inflation component, then the estimate of future salary increases should also reflect a 5% inflation component. In plan accounting it is not necessary to develop an assumption for future pay increases or future Social Security benefits. Because very few plans provide for automatic postretirement cost-of-living adjustments, that assumption will seldom be required for plan accounting.

It is clear from SFAS No. 35 that the interest assumption used for accounting purposes will frequently, if not usually, be different from that used for funding. The key requirement in developing an interest assumption, and for that matter any other assumption, is to use a sensible rationale. Judgmental elements in the actuary's development of a recommendation should be highlighted and subject to review and approval by the plan's sponsor. The framework and illustration of such a rationale is discussed in "Sponsor Accounting." Although the result may differ as between sponsor and plan accounting, the same approach can be applied in both instances.

The noneconomic assumptions of **mortality, withdrawal, disability, and early (late) retirement** are referred to in SFAS No. 35, relating to the probability and timing of benefit payments. They are referred to here as noneconomic because they are usually not influenced by the long-term economic forecast, although short-term economic conditions can have a marked impact on withdrawal and early retirement experience. The mortality and disability assumptions are more highly technical. The typical plan sponsor will have to rely more heavily on the actuary's judgment and recommendations when adopting them. The impact of variations in mortality and disability assumptions on the actuarial value of accumulated benefits is not generally very large. The withdrawal and early retirement assumptions can vary considerably from one organization to another, because they are affected by the personnel practices and business circumstances of the plan sponsor. Accordingly, more input from the plan sponsor is appropriate with respect to these assumptions. The discussion of these assumptions under "Sponsor Accounting" applies here as well.

(ii) Disclosures for Actuarial Present Value of Accumulated Plan Benefits. As previously stated, the accumulated benefit information may be presented as a separate financial statement, in a note to the financial statements, or combined with other information in the financial statements. The information must all be located in one place and must be segregated as follows:

- Vested benefits of participants currently receiving benefits.
- Other vested benefits.
- Nonvested benefits.

If employees contribute to the plan, accumulated employee contributions must be disclosed and, if applicable, accumulated interest credited on the contributions, including the interest rate, must also be disclosed.

(iii) Relationship to Disclosures Under SFAS No. 87 and SFAS No. 88. If the plan sponsor also complies with SFAS No. 87, it is required to disclose at its fiscal year-end the accumulated and vested benefit obligations of its plan. These items are the same as the present values of accumulated and vested plan benefits, if the plan's benefit information date is the same as the sponsor's fiscal year-end. **Schedule B to Form 5500** also discloses the present value of vested and nonvested accrued benefits, which are conceptually similar to the disclosures required under SFAS No. 35, except that Schedule B items do not reflect future indexation of the maximum benefit limitations under IRC § 415. Starting with plan years beginning in 1988, additional conditions were placed on the definition of Schedule B present values and the interest rate that may be used to compute them. As a result, they will often (usually) differ from SFAS No. 35 present values.

(f) CHANGES IN THE ACTUARIAL PRESENT VALUE OF ACCUMULATED PLAN BENEFITS. The FASB requires disclosure of the effects, if significant, of certain factors affecting the year-to-year change in the benefit information. If the **benefit information date** is the beginning of the year, the required information regarding the year-to-year change in the benefit information would also relate to the preceding year. Consistent with the requirement for accumulated benefit information, the changes therein also may be presented as a separate financial statement, combined with other information in the financial statements, or in the notes to the financial statements. In addition, the information can be presented either in a reconciliation format or in a narrative format. As a minimum, significant effects of the following factors must be included in the disclosure of the information:

1. Plan amendments.
2. Changes in the nature of the plan, such as a plan spinoff or a merger with another plan.
3. Changes in actuarial assumptions.

Effects that are individually significant should be separately identified.

If only the minimum required disclosure is presented, presentation in a statement format will necessitate an additional unidentified "other" category to reconcile the beginning and ending amounts. Changes in actuarial assumptions are treated as changes in accounting estimates, and therefore previously reported amounts should not be restated.

(g) ILLUSTRATIVE PLAN FINANCIAL STATEMENTS.   Exhibit 32.9 gives the DOL's filing requirements for employee benefit plans of various types. More specifically, Exhibits 32.10 through 32.13 illustrate the financial statements of a defined benefit pension plan. Exhibit 32.10 presents a statement of net assets available for benefits. SFAS No. 35 requires the net asset information to be presented as of the end of the plan year. However, if the information regarding the actuarial present value of accumulated plan benefits is presented as of the beginning of the plan year, the net asset information also must be presented as of that date (i.e., presented as of the end of the current and preceding plan years).

Exhibit 32.11 contains a statement of changes in net assets available for benefits, identifying the significant changes during the plan year. If the information regarding accumulated plan benefits is presented as of the beginning of the plan year, the statement of changes in net assets available for benefits must be presented for two years.

Exhibits 32.12 and 32.13 present a statement of accumulated plan benefits and a statement of changes in accumulated plan benefits. This information can be presented as of a benefit information date that is either the beginning or end of the plan year. In addition, the information can be presented in a combined statement with the related net asset information or included in the notes to the financial statements. The statement presented in Exhibit 32.13 reconciles the year-to-year change in the actuarial present value of accumulated plan benefits. As an alternative to presenting this information in a statement format, disclosure can be made of only the

	December 31, 19X3
Assets	
Investments, at fair value	
United States government securities	$ 350,000
Corporate bonds and debentures	3,500,000
Common stock	
ABC Company	690,000
Other	2,250,000
Mortgages	480,000
Real estate	270,000
	7,540,000
Deposit administration contract, at contract value*	1,000,000
Total investments	8,540,000
Receivables	
Employees' contributions	40,000
Securities sold	310,000
Accrued interest and dividends	77,000
	427,000
Cash	200,000
Total assets	9,167,000
Liabilities	
Accounts payable	70,000
Accrued expenses	85,000
Total liabilities	155,000
Net assets available for benefits	$9,012,000

*Deposit administration contract is reflected at contract value, as opposed to fair value, because such contract was entered into prior to March, 1990 (refer to transition provisions of SFAS No. 110).

Exhibit 32.10.   Statement of net assets available for benefits.

	Year Ended December 31, 19X3
Investment income	
Net appreciation in fair value of investments	$ 207,000
Interest	345,000
Dividends	130,000
Rents	55,000
	737,000
Less investment expenses	39,000
	698,000
Contributions	
Employer	780,000
Employees	450,000
	1,230,000
Total additions	1,928,000
Benefits paid directly to participants	740,000
Purchases of annuity contracts	257,000
	997,000
Administrative expenses	65,000
Total deductions	1,062,000
Net increase	866,000
Net assets available for benefits	
Beginning of year	8,146,000
End of year	$9,012,000

Exhibit 32.11.   Statement of changes in net assets available for benefits.

factors significantly changed in accumulated plan benefits. The information can be disclosed in the notes to the financial statements or presented on the face of the statement of accumulated plan benefits. Factors that usually have a significant effect on accumulated plan benefits include plan amendments, changes in the nature of a plan (e.g., a plan spinoff or merger with another plan), and changes in actuarial assumptions.

(h) ADDITIONAL FINANCIAL STATEMENT DISCLOSURES.   Disclosure of the plan's accounting policies must include a description of the methods and significant assumptions used to determine the fair value of investments and the reported value of contracts with insurance companies. In addition, a description of the method and significant actuarial assumptions used to determine the actuarial present value of accumulated plan benefits must be disclosed in the

	December 31, 19X3
Actuarial present value of accumulated plan benefits	
Vested benefits	
Participants currently receiving payments	$ 3,040,000
Other participants	8,120,000
	11,160,000
Nonvested benefits	2,720,000
Total actuarial present value of accumulated plan benefits	$13,880,000

Exhibit 32.12.   Statement of accumulated plan benefits.

	Year Ended December 31, 19X3
Actuarial present value of accumulated plan benefits at beginning of year	$ 11,880,000
Increase (decrease) during the year attributable to:	
Plan amendment	2,410,000
Change in actuarial assumptions	(1,050,500)
Benefits accumulated	895,000
Increase for interest due to the decrease in the discount period	742,500
Benefits paid	(997,000)
Net increase	2,000,000
Actuarial present value of accumulated plan benefits at end of year	$ 13,880,000

Exhibit 32.13.   Statement of changes in accumulated plan benefits.

notes to the financial statements. Such disclosure would include any significant changes of methods or assumptions between benefit information dates.

In addition to disclosing significant accounting policies, SFAS No. 35 requires the following disclosures:

1. A brief general description of the plan agreement, including vesting and benefit provisions.
2. A description of significant plan amendments made during the year. If significant amendments occur between the latest benefit information date and the plan's year-end and therefore were not reflected in the actuarial present value of accumulated plan benefits, disclosure should be made of this matter.
3. A brief general description of the priority order of participants' claims to the assets of the plan in the event of plan termination and benefits guaranteed by PBGC.
4. Funding policy and any changes in such policy during the plan year.
5. The policy regarding the purchase of contracts with insurance companies that are excluded from plan assets.
6. Tax status of the plan, if a favorable letter of determination has not been obtained or maintained.
7. Identification of individual investments that represent 5% or more of the net assets available for benefits.
8. Significant real estate or other transactions between plan and the sponsor, employers, or employee organizations.
9. Unusual or infrequent events or transactions occurring subsequent to the latest benefit information date but before issuance of the financial statements, such as a plan amendment occurring after the latest benefit information date that significantly increases future benefits that are attributable to employee service rendered before that date.

(i) DECISION TO PREPARE PLAN FINANCIAL STATEMENTS.   The number of accounting decisions required to prepare the plan's financial statements is not large.

For many plans the first and most important decision will be whether to issue a statement at all. Plans subject to ERISA requirements must issue a statement, but public employee plans and ERISA plans with fewer than 100 participants are not required by ERISA to issue statements. The usual reason for not publishing plan financial statements, particularly for smaller employers, will be to avoid the additional expenses of preparing, auditing and distributing the statement. The usual reasons for publishing statements when not required by ERISA will include the following:

1. The employer wishes to present a strong, positive image to employees (or the public) about the administration and financial strength of the plan.
2. The number of participants may not be indicative of the financial values involved. Plan assets could be very significant in relation to the company's net worth.
3. The employer wants to protect the plan's fiduciaries against legal liability.
4. Publication is required by state or local law.

Other reasons for decisions are practical, largely affecting the ease and expense with which financial statements can be prepared. One subtle decision occurs when there have been multiple changes during the year, such as plan amendments and changes in assumptions. The order in which these items are presented can affect the reader's perception of what actually happened during the year. The FASB in SFAS No. 35 commented:

> The Board recognized that the determined effects of factors comprising the net change in the benefit information will vary depending on the order in which the effects are calculated. . . . Thus, the Board concluded that at this time it would not prescribe an order.

This can be cleared up through footnote disclosures as desired. Some of the practical decisions involved include:

1. Whether to use a **benefit information date** other than year-end. Many plans (if not most) will find it more convenient to use a beginning of the year date. However, that approach does require more information to be furnished regarding both net assets available and changes in such assets during the preceding year. Another approach when the regular actuarial valuation (to determine funding) is performed at the beginning of the year is to value the accumulated benefits at that point, and project to year-end, using "reasonable approximation." The FASB makes permissive reference to that type of an approach, provided that the results are substantially the same as those contemplated by SFAS No. 35. For many plans this approach will produce very acceptable results. An employer that discloses the funded status of its pension plan under SFAS No. 87 in its year-end financial statements may find it convenient to satisfy the SFAS No. 35 disclosure requirements by using the accumulated and vested benefit obligations disclosed under SFAS No. 87.
2. Whether to make a more complete **disclosure** of the plan's circumstances. In the interest of doing so, some plan sponsors may wish to present the benefit value information in more than the three minimum categories specified by SFAS No. 35. For example, the other vested benefit category could be expanded to include the value of vested benefits for employees eligible for normal or early retirement.

(j) DEFINED CONTRIBUTION PLANS.   Although SFAS No. 35 does not cover defined contribution plans, many of the concepts and principles included are applicable to defined contribution plans. Defined contribution plans require the maintenance of **individual accounts** for each participant, to record each one's share of the total net assets of the plan. Typically, a defined contribution plan will require a certain contribution from the employer without specifying the amount of benefits to be provided to the participants. The types and amounts of benefits, as well as the eligibility requirements, are frequently determined by the plan's trustees, who can be totally "unrelated" to the employer; in other cases the employer reserves those rights. Employer contributions are based on a formula that may be a certain rate per hour of work or per unit of production, a function of the employee's contribution, a percentage of the employer's annual profitability, or some other specified method. The employer's obligation here differs from that under a defined contribution plan. With a defined contribution plan, the employer is not obligated to make up any shortfalls in actual versus assumed experience. This can be particularly significant, of course, in the case of the investment experience.

(i) Separate Accounts.   Employer contributions, changes in the value of the plan's net assets, and forfeitures, if any, are allocated to individual participant accounts maintained for each participant. In addition, employee contributions, if any, are credited to the account.

(ii) Types of Plans.   Defined contribution plans include:

1. Profit-sharing plans, which provide for an employer contribution based on current or accumulated profits.
2. Money purchase plans, which provide for an employer contribution based on employee compensation, units of production, hours worked, or some criterion other than profits.
3. Stock bonus and employee stock ownership plans which are qualified profit-sharing plans that invest substantially all the plan's assets in the stock of the employer company.
4. Thrift or savings plans, which provide for periodic employee contributions with matching, in whole or in part, by the employer—usually from current or accumulated profits.

(iii) Financial Statements.   Financial statements for a defined contribution plan should include a statement of net assets available for benefits and a statement of changes in net assets available for benefits. The disclosures would be similar to those required for a defined benefit pension plan, except for the references to actuarial information.

32.6 ACCOUNTING FOR POSTRETIREMENT BENEFITS OTHER THAN PENSIONS

(a) BACKGROUND.   On December 21, 1990, the FASB issued SFAS No. 106, "Employers Accounting for Postretirement Benefits Other Than Pensions." Retiree medical benefits are SFAS No. 106's primary focus, but life insurance and other welfare benefits provided to employees after retirement also are included. The specific approach and methodology of SFAS No. 106 closely parallel the pension accounting rules addressed in SFAS Nos. 87 and 88.

Prior to SFAS No. 106, most employers had recognized the cost of postretirement benefits other than pensions on the **"pay-as-you-go"** or cash basis. Under the accounting requirements of SFAS No. 106, postretirement benefits are viewed as a form of deferred compensation that should be recognized on an accrual basis during the periods that the employees render the service needed to qualify for benefits.

Many midsize and larger employers provide health care benefits for their retirees. Although some employers provide benefits only until retirees reach age 65 and become eligible for Medicare, many programs provide lifetime benefits. Typically, benefits for retirees are similar to those for active employees. Programs for retirees age 65 and over usually are coordinated with Medicare benefits. Although benefit plans for retirees age 65 and over may appear similar to plans for retirees under age 65, some of the specific details of post-age-65 benefit programs may have significant cost implications.

The practice of providing postretirement health care benefits took root after the Medicare program was established in 1965. Employers found that, for relatively few dollars, **Medicare supplements,** as they were called, bought much employee goodwill. The effect of inflation on medical costs, the trend toward earlier retirement, and longer life expectancies have made these benefits increasingly expensive. During recent decades the cost of medical care has risen at an average rate of more than 40%, which is twice the average inflation rate for the same period. Total medical costs, which were approximately 6% of the gross national product in the mid-1960s, reached 12% in 1990 and continue to rise.

(b) SFAS NO. 106.   Employers that provide medical or other affected benefits are now required to follow a prescribed method in determining the annual expense charge for such benefits and to provide extensive disclosures in their financial statements. Generally, as of the financial statement date (measurement date), the discounted value of all future benefits that are expected to be paid is calculated (expected postretirement benefit obligation). For a newly hired employee, this liability is accrued ratably over the period from date of hire, or a date after which service is credited under the plan, until such employee is first eligible to retire with full benefits (service cost), unless the plan has a benefit formula which attributes a disproportionate share of the benefit obligation to the employee's early years of service. Transition rules, like their pension counterparts, prescribe how the liability for prior service for existing retirees and their dependents and the active work force is amortized (transition obligation). Unlike the pension rules under SFAS No. 87, SFAS No. 106 does not require a minimum balance sheet liability.

(c) QUANTIFICATION OF MEDICAL BENEFITS TO RETIREES.   The basic building block for the expense and liability determinations is the **discounted value of future benefits.**

Unlike the pension model where the monthly benefit is fixed at retirement, future medical benefits depend on the likelihood and cost of future claims. Besides variations due to plan provisions that define the level or richness of benefits provided, claims experience varies significantly by age, sex, occupation, and geographical location. For a given employee population, future retiree medical costs will increase because:

- Medical inflation will continue to outpace overall price increases, but will likely decelerate in the future.
- More active employees will retire.
- Per capita costs will rise as the retiree group ages.
- Advances in medical technology will introduce better and more costly treatment methods.

For example, for the projection year 19X2 assume that an employer expects to have 18 retirees as shown below and cash flow of $20,000:

	Number of Retirees		Per Capita Cost		
Age	Males	Females	Males	Females	Cash Flow
60	4	—	$2,100	—	$ 8,400
65	—	8	—	$700	5,600
70	6	—	1,000	—	6,000
				Total	$20,000

This process is repeated for 1993 and each subsequent year to arrive at a stream of expected cash flow. The total value in 1992 of the employer's future liabilities is calculated by discounting this stream of cash flow to 1992 to reflect the time value of money.

The number of retirees or other beneficiaries for each year is projected by applying actuarial assumptions to the current employee and retiree group. Rates of mortality, disability, retirement, and termination of employment are used to estimate how the current beneficiary group will change from one year to the next.

The **per capita costs** are projected in a similar fashion. Expected future costs are calculated by using actual base year figures and medical trend factors. These factors reflect the expected effects of future price inflation, technological changes, and an individual's propensity to use medical goods and services. Cost reductions after an individual has qualified for medicare or other governmental programs are taken into consideration.

The **expected postretirement benefit obligation** (EPBO) represents the actuarial present value of the future postretirement benefits expected to be paid to or for an employee, including benefits for the employee's beneficiaries and dependents. This differs from the projected benefit obligation in pension accounting in that the EPBO represents the value of all future postretirement benefits, not just those that have been attributed to employees' service as of the reporting date. The service cost is the portion of EPBO attributed to the current period.

The **accumulated postretirement benefit obligation** (APBO) represents the portion of the EPBO that has been attributed to employees' service rendered to date. If all employees have reached their full eligibility date, the APBO would be the same as the EPBO.

SFAS No. 106 specifies that a **transition obligation**, at the date that the new standard is adopted, would be measured as the unfunded APBO less any accrued postretirement benefit cost already recognized on the employer's balance sheet. This transaction obligation may be recognized immediately on the balance sheet (except for any amount attributable to plan initiation or benefit improvements adopted after December 21, 1990) through the cumulative effect of an accounting change (included as a charge against income in the year SFAS No. 106 is adopted), or may be recognized prospectively as a component of **net periodic postretirement benefit cost** through **straight-line amortization** over:

- The average remaining service period of active participants, or 20 years if longer.
- The average remaining life expectancy of the participants if almost all participants are retirees.

Note that a single method of transition must be used for all of an employer's plans.

Additional amortization of the transition obligation would be required if the cumulative cost computed under SFAS No. 106 is less than cumulative benefit payments less any plan assets or any recognized accrued cost at transition. This provision may require additional amortization for a few mature plans with very high pay-as-you-go costs.

(d) ILLUSTRATION—POSTRETIREMENT BENEFITS OTHER THAN PENSIONS. The FASB's proposed accrual method for postretirement benefits other than pensions is illustrated by Exhibit 32.14.

32.7 EMPLOYERS' ACCOUNTING FOR POSTEMPLOYMENT BENEFITS

(a) BACKGROUND. SFAS No. 112, "Employers' Accounting for Postemployment Benefits," was issued by the FASB in November 1992, established accounting standards for the estimated cost of benefits provided by an employer to former or inactive employees in the window of time after employment but before retirement (hereafter referred to as postemployment benefits). Postemployment benefits include such items as salary continuation, supplemental unemployment benefits, disability-related benefits (including workers' compensation), job training, and the continuation of health care benefits and life insurance coverage.

Prior to the issuance of SFAS No. 112, the accounting for the cost of postemployment benefits varied from employer to employer. Although some employers accounted for these benefits under a form of accrual accounting (e.g., cliff accounting—where the cost of the benefit is accrued at the time the event giving rise to the payment of benefits occurs), most still used a cash basis to recognize the costs associated with such benefits.

(b) SFAS NO. 112. SFAS No. 112 requires employers to recognize the obligation to provide postemployment benefits under an accrual method of accounting. Specifically, postemployment benefits that meet the following conditions should be accounted for in accordance with SFAS No. 43, "Accounting for Compensated Absences":

1. The employer's obligation relating to employee's rights to receive compensation for future absences is attributable to employees services already rendered;
2. The obligation relates to rights that vest or accumulate;

Expected postretirement benefit obligation (January 1, 19X3)	$20,000,000
Accumulated postretirement benefits obligation (January 1, 19X3)	12,000,000
Recognized accrued postretirement benefit cost (January 1, 19X3)	0
Transition obligation	12,000,000[1]
Service cost	750,000[2]
Net periodic postretirement benefit cost for 19X3:	
Service cost	$ 750,000
Interest cost on APBO	960,000
Return on assets	0[3]
Amortization of transition obligation over 20 years	600,000
Net periodic postretirement benefit cost	$ 2,310,000
Pay-as-you-go cost charged to expense under current practice	$ 700,000

[1] The transition obligation is equal to the APBO because the plan is unfunded and there is no recognized accrued postretirement benefit cost for this employer.
[2] Service cost represents the portion of the EPBO that is attributed to employees' service during the current period.
[3] This employer continues to operate the plan on a pay-as-you-go basis rather than prefunding it.

Exhibit 32.14. Postretirement benefits other than pensions.

3. Payment of compensation is probable; and
4. The amount can be reasonably estimated.

Postemployment benefits that do not meet the four conditions specified about should be accounted for in accordance with SFAS No. 5, "Accounting for Contingencies."

32.8 SOURCES AND SUGGESTED REFERENCES

American Academy of Actuaries, "An Actuary's Guide to Compliance with Statement of Financial Accounting Standards No. 87," AAA, Washington, DC, 1986.

———, "Actuarial Compliance Guideline for Statement of Financial Accounting Standards No. 88," Actuarial Standards Board, Washington, DC, 1989.

Accounting Principles Board, "Accounting for the Cost of Pension Plans," APB Opinion No. 8, AICPA, New York, 1966.

———, "Accounting Changes," APB Opinion No. 20, AICPA, New York, 1971.

———, "Reporting the Results of Operation—Reporting the Effects of Disposal of a Segment of a Business, and Extraordinary, Unusual and Infrequently Occurring Events and Transactions," APB Opinion No. 30, AICPA, New York, 1973.

Financial Accounting Standards Board, "A Guide to Implementation of Statement 87 on Employers' Accounting for Pensions: Questions and Answers," FASB, Stamford, CT, 1986.

———, "A Guide to Implementation of Statement 88: Questions and Answers," FASB, Norwalk, CT, 1988.

———, "Accounting and Reporting by Defined Benefit Pension Plans," Statement of Financial Accounting Standards No. 35, FASB, Stamford, CT, 1980.

———, "Employers' Accounting for Pensions," Statement of Financial Accounting Standards No. 87, FASB, Stamford, CT, 1985.

———, "Employers' Accounting for Settlements and Curtailments of Deferred Benefit Pension Plans and for Termination Benefits," Statement of Financial Accounting Standards No. 88, FASB, Stamford, CT, 1985.

———, "Employers' Accounting for Postretirement Benefits Other than Pension," Statement of Financial Accounting Standards No. 106, FASB, Norwalk, CT, 1990.

————, "Accounting for Income Taxes," Statement of Financial Accounting Standards No. 109, FASB, Norwalk, CT, 1992.

————, "Reporting by Defined Benefit Pension Plans of Investment Contracts," Statement of Financial Accounting Standards No. 110, FASB, Norwalk, CT, 1992.

————, "Employers' Accounting for Postemployment Benefits," Statement of Financial Accounting Standard No. 112, FASB, Norwalk, CT, 1992.

Munnell, Alicia H., *Economics of Private Pensions,* The Brookings Institution, Washington, DC, 1982.

CHAPTER 33

STOCK-BASED COMPENSATION

Peter T. Chingos, CPA

KPMG Peat Marwick LLP

Scott L. Decker, CPA, CMA

KPMG Peat Marwick LLP

John R. Deming, CPA

KPMG Peat Marwick LLP

CONTENTS

33.1 HISTORY OF ACCOUNTING FOR STOCK-BASED COMPENSATION

The nature and types of stock-based compensation plans and awards have constantly changed over the years. However, the most significant problems in determining the appropriate accounting for such awards have remained the same:

   1. Measurement of compensation cost (i.e., the determination of total compensation cost to be allocated to expense for financial reporting purposes).

2. Allocation of compensation cost (i.e., the determination of the period(s) over which total compensation cost should be allocated to expense and the method of allocation).

The authoritative accounting literature addresses the accounting in two pronouncements which are as follows:

1. APB Opinion No. 25, "Accounting for Stock Issued to Employees" (AICPA, 1972). Also see Interpretation of APB Opinion No. 25, "Accounting for Stock Issued to Employees" (AICPA, 1973).
2. Statement of Financial Accounting Standard No. 123, "Accounting for Stock-Based Compensation," (FASB, 1995).

APB Opinion No. 25 is applicable "to all stock option, purchase, award and bonus rights granted by an employer corporation to an individual employee. . . ." The Opinion contains substantial guidance in the application of its provisions to such plans.

Subsequent to the issuance of APB Opinion No. 25, the trend toward the adoption by enterprises of more complex plans and awards continued. Of particular significance was the increase in the number of combination plans—plans that provide for the granting of two or more types of awards to individual employees. In many combination plans, the employee, or the enterprise, must make an election from alternative awards as to the award to be exercised, thereby canceling the other awards granted under the plan.

Following the issuance of APB Opinion No. 25, there was also a significant increase in the number of plans that provided for the granting of variable awards to employees. A variable award is one that at the date the grant is awarded, either (1) the number of shares of stock (or the amount of cash) an employee is entitled to receive, (2) the amount an employee is required to pay to exercise his rights with respect to the award, or (3) both the number of shares an employee is entitled to receive and the amount an employee is required to pay, are unknown. One of the most popular variable awards is the stock appreciation right (SAR). SARs are rights granted that entitle an employee to receive, at a specified future date(s), the excess of the market value of a specified number of shares of the granting employer's capital stock over a stated price. The form of payment for amounts earned under an award of SARs may be specified by the award (i.e., stock, cash, or a combination thereof), or the award may permit the employee or employer to elect the form of payment.

Notwithstanding the guidance provided in APB Opinion No. 25, considerable disagreement continued to exist as to the appropriate method of accounting for variable awards. As a result, significant differences arose in the methods used by employers to account for variable awards, which led to numerous requests of the FASB for clarification. In December 1978 the FASB provided this clarification through the issuance of FASB Interpretation No. 28, "Accounting for Stock Appreciation Rights and Other Variable Stock Option or Award Plans," an interpretation of APB Opinion Nos. 15 and 25. In paragraph No. 2 of the Interpretation, the FASB specifies that:

APB Opinion No. 25 applies to plans for which the employer's stock is issued as compensation or the amount of cash paid as compensation is determined by reference to the market price of the stock or to changes in its market price. Plans involving stock appreciation rights and other variable plan awards are included in those plans dealt with by [APB] Opinion No. 25.

The Interpretation provides specific guidance in the application of APB Opinion No. 25 to variable awards, particularly in those more troublesome areas where the greatest divergence in accounting existed prior to its issuance.

However, APB Opinion No. 25, as interpreted, failed to incorporate criteria that can be consistently applied to all types of plans. As a result, as new types of plans have evolved and changes in the tax laws have occurred, new interpretations and guidance have been required, resulting in a steady stream of pronouncements by the FASB and the EITF since 1978, as shown in Exhibit 33.1.

The nature and the frequency of these additional pronouncements underscore the difficulties in applying the primary pronouncements to the myriad of stock-based compensation awards that have arisen since their issuance.

To address this problem, the FASB undertook a major project in 1984 to reconsider the accounting for stock-based compensation, whether issued to employees or issued to vendors, suppliers, or other nonemployees. On October 10, 1995, the FASB issued FASB Statement No. 123, "Accounting for Stock-Based Compensation." The FASB Statement No. 123 allows companies to retain the current approach set forth in APB Opinion No. 25, as amended, interpreted and clarified; however, companies are encouraged to adopt a new accounting method based on the estimated fair value of employee stock options. Companies that do not follow the new fair value based method are required to provide expanded disclosures in the footnotes. Thus, the FASB settled on a compromise solution to a complex issue that had become extremely politicized. The authors anticipate that the majority of entities will not elect the fair-value based method of accounting for stock options. Therefore, the financial statements of

FASB AND EITF PRONOUNCEMENTS SINCE 1978

Year	Issued By	Title
1980	FASB	FASB Interpretation No. 31: "Treatment of Stock Compensation Plans in EPS Computations," an interpretation of APB Opinion No. 15 and a modification of FASB Interpretation No. 28
1982	FASB	FASB Technical Bulletin No. 82-2: "Accounting for the Conversion of Stock Options into Incentive Stock Options as a Result of the Economic Recovery Tax Act of 1981"
1984	FASB	FASB Interpretation No. 38: "Determining the Measurement Date for Stock Option, Purchase, and Award Plans Involving Junior Stock," an interpretation of APB Opinion No. 25
1984	EITF	EITF Issue No. 84-13: "Purchase of Stock Options and Stock Appreciation Rights in a Leveraged Buyout"
1984	EITF	EITF Issue No. 84-18: "Stock Option Pyramiding"
1984	EITF	EITF Issue No. 84-34: "Permanent Discount Restricted Stock Purchase Plans"
1985	EITF	EITF Issue No. 85-45: "Business Combinations: Settlement of Stock Options and Awards"
1987	EITF	EITF Issue No. 87-6: "Adjustments Relating to Stock Compensation Plans"
1987	EITF	EITF Issue No. 87-23: "Book Value Stock Purchase Plans"
1987	EITF	EITF Issue No. 87-33: "Stock Compensation Issues Related to Market Decline"
1988	EITF	EITF Issue No. 88-6: "Book Value Stock Plans in an Initial Public Offering"
1990	EITF	EITF Issue No. 90-7: "Accounting for a Reload Stock Option"
1990	EITF	EITF Issue No. 90-9: "Changes to Fixed Employee Stock Option Plans as a Result of Equity Restructuring"
1994	EITF	EITF Issue No. 94-6: "Accounting for the Buyout of Compensatory Stock Options"
1995	EITF	EITF Issue No. 95-16: "Accounting for Stock Compensation Arrangements with Employer Loan Features under APB Opinion No. 25"

Exhibit 33.1.   Accounting pronouncements related to stock compensation plans and awards since 1978.

most companies will now include two presentations of a company's results of operations rather than the normal presentation of a single net income.

Given the belief that the majority of companies will continue to use the intrinsic value approach prescribed by APB Opinion No. 25, the authors have separated the chapter into two distinct parts. The first part will cover the application of APB Opinion No. 25, and its related interpretations and EITF issues. The remainder of the chapter will address the application of FASB Statement No. 123.

33.2 APPLICATION OF APB OPINION NO. 25

(a) NONCOMPENSATORY AND COMPENSATORY PLANS. APB Opinion No. 25 provides that a plan must have the following characteristics in order to be considered as noncompensatory:

1. Substantially all full-time employees meeting limited employment qualifications may participate (employees owning a specified percentage of the outstanding stock and executives may be excluded).
2. Stock is offered to eligible employees equally on the basis of a uniform percentage of salary or wages (the plan may limit the number of shares of stock that an employee may purchase through the plan).
3. The time permitted for exercise of an option or purchase right is limited to a reasonable period.
4. The discount from the market price of the stock is no greater than would be reasonable in an offer of stock to stockholders or others.

A compensatory plan is any plan that does not have all four characteristics of a noncompensatory plan. It should be recognized, however, that awards granted under compensatory plans do not necessarily result in recognition of compensation expense by the employer. An employer recognizes compensation expense with respect to awards granted pursuant to a compensatory plan only if the application of the measurement principle results in the determination of compensation cost.

(b) MEASUREMENT OF COMPENSATION: GENERAL PRINCIPLE. Paragraph 10 of APB Opinion No. 25 sets forth the following "measurement principle" for the measurement of compensation cost related to stock option, purchase, and award plans:

> *Measurement Principle*—Compensation for services that a corporation receives as consideration for stock issued through employee stock option, purchase, and award plans should be measured by the quoted market price of the stock at the measurement date less the amount, if any, that the employee is required to pay. . . . If a quoted market price is unavailable, the best estimate of the market value of the stock should be used to measure compensation. . . . The measurement date for determining compensation cost in stock option, purchase, and award plans is the first date on which are known both (1) the number of shares that an individual employee is entitled to receive, and (2) the option or purchase price, if any.

When both of the factors specified in paragraph 10 of APB Opinion No. 25 are known at the grant or award date (i.e., a fixed award), total compensation cost for an award is measured at the grant date. However, when either or both of these factors are not known at the grant or award date (i.e., a variable award), an employer should estimate total compensation cost each period from the date of grant or award to the measurement date based on the quoted market price of the employer's capital stock at the end of each period. This latter point is clarified in FASB Interpretation No. 28, which defines the compensation related to variable plan awards as:

The amount by which the quoted market value of the shares of the employer's stock covered by the grant exceeds the option price or value specified, by reference to a market price or otherwise, subject to any appreciation limitations under the plan. Changes, either increases or decreases, in the quoted market value of those shares between the date of grant and the measurement date [as defined in APB Opinion No. 25] result in a change in the measure of compensation for the right or award.

(c) APPLICATION OF THE MEASUREMENT PRINCIPLE.   A proper understanding of the measurement principle of APB Opinion No. 25 (including the clarification set forth in FASB Interpretation No. 28) is essential to determining the appropriate accounting, including the amount of compensation expense to be recognized. Paragraphs 11(a) through 11(h) of APB Opinion No. 25, as well as subsequent FASB and EITF pronouncements, contain guidance on the application of the measurement principle, as discussed in the following paragraphs.

(i) Measurement of Compensation Cost Based on Cost of Treasury Stock.   Paragraph 11(a) states:

> Measuring compensation by the cost to an employer corporation of reacquired (treasury) stock that is distributed through a stock option, purchase, or award plan is not acceptable practice. The only exception is that compensation cost under a plan with all the provisions described in paragraph 11(c) may be measured by the cost of stock that the corporation (1) reacquires during the fiscal period for which the stock is to be awarded and (2) awards shortly thereafter to employees for services during that period.

Thus compensation cost of an award of stock for current services may be measured by the cost of reacquired treasury stock only if the above conditions and those specified in paragraph 11(c) (see below) of the Opinion are met. Otherwise, compensation cost should be measured as of the measurement date otherwise determined in accordance with the criterion set forth in paragraph 10 of the Opinion.

(ii) Vesting Contingent on Continued Employment.   Paragraph 11(b) states:

> The measurement date is not changed from the grant or award date to a later date solely by provisions that termination of employment reduces the number of shares of stock that may be issued to an employee.

This paragraph makes it clear that a requirement that an employee remain employed by the granting enterprise for a specified period of time in order for his rights to become vested under a stock-based compensation award does not preclude a determination, as of the grant or award date, of the total compensation cost to be recognized as an expense by the granting employer.

(iii) Designation of Measurement Date.   Paragraph 11(c) states:

> The measurement date of an award of stock for current service may be the end of the fiscal period, which is normally the effective date of the award, instead of the date that the award to an employee is determined if (1) the award is provided for by the terms of an established formal plan, (2) the plan designates the factors that determine the total dollar amount of awards to employees for the period (for example, a percent of income), although the total amount or the individual awards may not be known at the end of the period, and (3) the award pertains to current service of the employee for the period.

The effect of this paragraph is to allow the designation of the end of a fiscal period as the measurement date when all of the conditions specified in paragraph 11(c) are met, even though the actual awards to individual employees may not be determined until after the close of the fiscal period.

(iv) Impact of Renewals, Extensions, and Other Modifications of Stock Options and Purchase Rights. Paragraph 11(d) states:

> Renewing a stock option or purchase right or extending its period establishes a new measurement date as if the right were newly granted.

This paragraph reflects a very important concept. Its application could result in measurement of compensation cost with respect to outstanding stock option or purchase rights upon their renewal or extension, even though no compensation cost was ascribable to the original award under the measurement principle of APB Opinion No. 25. For example, any excess of the quoted market price of an employer's capital stock over the exercise price of a stock option at the date of renewal or extension is compensation cost; this may require recognition of compensation cost in addition to any compensation cost associated with the original award.

Paragraph 11(d) addresses "renewals" and "extensions" of stock purchase rights. There are modifications other than renewals and extensions that could also have an impact on the accounting for previously granted awards.

EITF Issue No. 87-33, "Stock Compensation Issues Related to Market Decline," addresses a series of issues related to modifications to stock option and award plans as a result of market decline. The EITF's consensus on these issues generally precludes reversals of previously recognized compensation expense when outstanding awards are modified because of market value declines and, in many instances, require measurement and recognition of compensation cost for both the original and the modified award.

(v) Transfer of Stock or Assets to a Trustee, Agent, or Other Third Party. Paragraph 11(e) states:

> Transferring stock or assets to a trustee, agent, or other third party for distribution of stock to employees under the terms of an option, purchase, or award plan does not change the measurement date from a later date to the date of transfer unless the terms of the transfer provide that the stock (1) will not revert to the corporation, (2) will not be granted or awarded later to the same employee on terms different from or for services other than those specified in the original grant or award, and (3) will not be granted or awarded later to another employee.

This paragraph reinforces the principle that the measurement date is the first date on which are known both (1) the number of shares that an individual employee is entitled to receive, and (2) the option or purchase price, if any. The authors are not aware of any awards that have been structured in a manner that has resulted in an acceleration of the otherwise determined measurement date as a result of the application of paragraph 11(e).

(vi) Awards of Convertible Stock or Rights. Paragraph 11(f) states:

> The measurement date for a grant or award of convertible stock (or stock that is otherwise exchangeable for other securities of the corporation) is the date in which the ratio of conversion (or exchange) is known unless other terms are variable at that date (paragraph 10b). The higher of the quoted market price at the measurement date of (1) the convertible stock granted or awarded or (2) the securities into which the original grant or award is convertible should be used to measure compensation.

Awards to employees of convertible stock or rights to purchase convertible stock are not common. Nevertheless, this paragraph provides guidance in measuring the compensation cost of such awards. Further guidance can be found in FASB Interpretation No. 38, "Determining the Measurement Date for Stock Option, Purchase, and Award Plans Involving Junior Stock," an interpretation of APB Opinion No. 25.

(vii) Settlement of Awards.   Paragraph 11(g) states:

> Cash paid to an employee to settle an earlier award of stock or to settle a grant of option to the employee should measure compensation cost. If the cash payment differs from the earlier measure of the award of stock or grant of option, compensation cost should be adjusted (para. 15). The amount that a corporation pays to an employee through a compensation plan is "cash paid to an employee to settle an earlier award of stock or to settle a grant of option" if stock is reacquired shortly after issuance. Cash proceeds that a corporation receives from sale of awarded stock or stock issued on exercise of an option and remits to the taxing authorities to cover required withholding of income taxes on an award is not "cash paid to an employee to settle an earlier award of stock or to settle a grant of option" in measuring compensation cost.

The intent of this paragraph seems quite clear. If an earlier award of stock or stock options is ultimately settled by cash payment to the employee, the amount actually paid is the final measure of compensation cost to be recognized by the employer, regardless of the amount of compensation cost previously determined. However, in practice, application of this paragraph has often proved difficult and, as a result, a number of EITF Issues have dealt with cash settlements of awards, as discussed in the following paragraph.

EITF Issue No. 84-13, "Purchase of Stock Options and Stock Appreciation Rights in a Leveraged Buyout." This pronouncement sets forth the EITF's consensus that the "target company" in a leveraged buyout should recognize compensation expense in the amount of cash paid by the target company to acquire outstanding stock options and stock appreciation rights.

EITF Issue No. 85-45, "Business Combinations: Settlement of Stock Options and Awards." Similar to the consensus in EITF Issue No. 84-13, this consensus indicates that when a target company settles outstanding stock options or awards "voluntarily, at the direction of the acquiring company, or as part of the plan of acquisition, APB Opinion No. 25 requires that the settlement be accounted for as compensation expense in the separate financial statements of the target company."

EITF Issue No. 87-6, "Adjustments Relating to Stock Compensation Plans." This consensus addresses stock option plans that contain a cash bonus feature that provides for a reimbursement to employees of the taxes payable as a result of the exercise of a nonqualified stock option (a "tax-offset bonus"). The consensus indicates that awards under such plans are variable awards. Thus, the existence of a tax-offset bonus related to a stock option award requires that the entire award (the stock option *plus* the cash bonus feature) be accounted for as a variable award, as the option and the tax-offset bonus are viewed as a single variable award. This consensus is consistent with footnote 1 to FASB Interpretation No. 28, "Accounting for Stock Appreciation Rights and Other Variable Stock Option or Award Plans" which states, in part, "Plans under which an employee may receive cash in lieu of stock or additional cash upon the exercise of a stock option are variable plans for purposes of the Interpretation as the amount is contingent upon the occurrence of future events." The significant point here is that two different awards, one being a fixed award and the other a variable award, should be accounted for as a single, variable award.

EITF Issue No. 87-23, "Book Value Stock Purchase Plans." This consensus provides much-needed guidance in accounting for formula-based plans, under which employees purchase shares, or are granted options to acquire shares, of the employer's common stock at a formula price. The formula price is usually based on book value, a multiple of book value, or earnings. Additionally, the employee must sell the acquired shares back to the employer upon retirement or other termination of employment, at a selling price determined in the same manner as the original purchase price.

Privately held companies only:

No compensation expense should be recognized for changes in the formula price during the employment period "if the employee makes a substantive investment that will be at risk for a reasonable period of time." This consensus applies to plans where the employee is allowed to resell all or a portion of the acquired shares to the company at fixed or determinable dates, as well as plans where the shares are resold to the company only upon retirement or other termination of employment.

Privately held and publicly held companies:

If **options** are granted to employees to purchase shares at the formula price and the employees can resell the options, or the shares acquired upon exercise of the options, to the company upon retirement or other termination of employment, or at fixed or determinable dates, the consensus of the EITF is the same for both privately held and publicly held companies. The consensus indicates that compensation expense should be recognized for increases in the formula price from the grant date to the exercise date (i.e., the award should be accounted for as a variable award). The consensus further indicates that the expense previously recognized should not be reversed upon exercise of the option, and that "additional expense would be recognized if the shares are sold back to the company shortly after exercise, as required by paragraph 11(g) of APB Opinion No. 25."

The SEC Observer at the EITF provided the following clarification of the SEC staff's views of book value plans for publicly held companies:

The SEC Observer indicated that the SEC staff views a book value plan for a publicly held company as a performance plan and noted that it should be accounted for like an SAR.

As previously noted, a difference exists between accounting for book value purchase (and other formula-based) awards by privately held and publicly held companies. This difference, of course, raised questions as to the accounting to be applied to these types of awards when a privately held company becomes publicly held. This issue was subsequently addressed EITF in EITF Issue No. 88-6, "Book Value Stock Plans in an Initial Public Offering."

EITF Issue No. 87-33, "Stock Compensation Issues Related to Market Decline."   This consensus addresses a number of issues related to the October 1987 stock market decline, including "How to account for the repurchase of an outstanding option and the issuance of a 'new' option." The Task Force consensus on this issue was that "paragraph 11(g) of APB Opinion No. 25 does not apply if an existing option is repurchased in contemplation of the issuance of a new option that contains terms identical to the remaining terms of the original option except that the exercise price is reduced. . . ." The consensus also indicates that "the cash paid to repurchase the original option represents additional compensation that should be charged to expense in the current period."

The effect of this consensus is to preclude an employer from decreasing compensation cost associated with a stock option award, by "settling" the award through a cash payment that is less than the amount of compensation cost previously determined, and then granting a "new" option to the same employee that contains terms identical to the remaining terms of the original option except that the exercise price is reduced. In the event such an arrangement were entered into, application of the consensus would (1) require the employer to charge the amount of the cash payment to expense in the current period, (2) prohibit the reversal of previously recognized expense associated with the original option, (3) require continued amortization of any compensation measured at the original measurement date that had not been amortized and, additionally, could result in the measurement of additional compensation expense associated with the "new" award.

The consensus also requires similar accounting when an option is "repriced," as opposed to the situation described above where an option is canceled and reissued.

EITF Issue No. 88-6, "Book Value Stock Plans in an Initial Public Offering." As previously noted, EITF Issue No. 87-23 addresses certain issues related to the accounting for stock purchase awards to employees, where the purchase price is a formula price based on book value or earnings, and where the shares must ultimately be sold back to the company by the employee at a price determined in the same manner as the original purchase price. The consensus set forth in EITF Issue No. 87-23 makes certain distinctions between privately and publicly held companies with respect to the accounting for these types of awards.

In EITF Issue No. 88-6, the Task Force reached a consensus that a book value stock purchase plan of a publicly held company should be viewed as a performance plan, and should be accounted for like an SAR (this is consistent with the SEC Observer's comment noted under the discussion of EITF Issue No. 87-23 above). Thus, for a publicly held company, compensation expense should be recognized for increases in book value (or other formula price based on earnings) on awards outstanding under such a plan. For a privately held company, however, under the consensus reached in EITF Issue No. 87-23, no compensation expense would be recognized for such increases in the book value or other formula price, regardless of when the awards were granted.

The Task Force also reached consensuses in EITF Issue No. 88-6 related to the recognition and measurement of compensation expense by a privately held company for such awards in the event of a subsequent IPO (i.e., when a privately held company becomes a publicly held company). These consensuses are set forth in Exhibit 33.2.

EITF Issue No. 88-6 also contains certain guidance regarding pro forma disclosures for these types of plans in the event of an IPO, as well as an exhibit that contains "Examples of the Application of APB Opinion No. 25 and the EITF Consensus from Issue Nos. 87-23 and 88-6 in an IPO."

EITF Issue No. 94-6, "Accounting for the Buyout of Compensatory Stock Options." EITF Issue No. 87-33 addressed the settling of options and the issuance of new options. In this issue, the Task Force was asked to address the buyout, or settling, of options without an issuance of new options. In the consensus, the Task Force imposes a rebuttable presumption that options granted within six months of the buyout of the outstanding options would be considered replacement options. In such a case, the issuer would have to consider the implications of EITF Issue No. 87-33.

The Task Force reached a consensus that the total amount of compensation cost to be recognized is the sum of (1) the compensation cost amortized to the buyout date; (2) the options' intrinsic value, if any, at the buyout date in excess of the compensation cost recognized as expense to the buyout date; and (3) the amount, if any, paid for the options in excess of their intrinsic value at the buyout date. In addition, any remaining unamortized compensation cost related to the original options would not be included in income for any period. Exhibit 94-6A of the EITF Issue No. 94-6 provides examples.

(viii) Combination Plans and Awards. Paragraph 11(h) states:

> Some plans are a combination of two or more types of plans. An employer corporation may need to measure compensation for the separate parts. Compensation cost for a combination plan permitting an employee to elect one part should be measured according to the terms that an employee is most likely to elect based on the facts available each period.

If more than one type of award is granted to an employee under a plan, the measurement principle must be applied to each award for purposes of measuring compensation cost to an

**ACCOUNTING FOR BOOK VALUE OPTIONS AND SHARES
OF A PRIVATELY HELD COMPANY AT TIME OF IPO**

Type of Award Outstanding	Status at Time of IPO	Accounting
Book value option	Converts to an option to purchase unrestricted (market value) stock	In addition to compensation expense previously recognized for changes in book value, compensation expense should be recognized on successful completion of the IPO for the difference between market value and book value at the date of the IPO, because conversion of the book value option to a market value option results in a new measurement date. Subsequent to the IPO, no further compensation expense would be recognized, assuming the plan otherwise remains a fixed plan under APB Opinion No. 25.
	Remains a book value option	Any change in book value resulting from successful completion of the IPO should be recognized as compensation expense at the time of the IPO in accordance with variable plan (SAR) accounting. Subsequent to the IPO, the plan should continue to be accounted for like an SAR based on the consensus reached in conjunction with EITF Issue No. 87-23.
Book value shares	Converts to unrestricted (market value) stock	No compensation expense should be recognized at the time of the IPO; however, shares issued under the purchase plan within one year of the IPO are presumed to have been issued in contemplation of the IPO and would result in compensation expense for the difference between the book value of those shares and their estimated fair value at date of issuance. Subsequent to the IPO, no further compensation expense would be recognized, assuming the plan remains a fixed plan under APB Opinion No. 25.
	Remains book value stock	No compensation expense should be recognized upon successful completion of the IPO for any impact that the IPO may have on book value; however, shares issued under the purchase plan within one year of the IPO are presumed to have been issued in contemplation of the IPO, and would result in variable award (SAR) accounting for actual changes in book value of the shares since the date of their issuance. Subsequent to the IPO, compensation expense would be recognized for increases in book value after the IPO (variable award accounting).

Exhibit 33.2.   Accounting for book value options and book value shares at time of an IPO.

employer. Furthermore, if a combination plan permits an employee to elect one award from a number of alternative awards, compensation cost should be measured in terms of the award the employee is considered most likely to elect in view of the facts available each period. In many combination plans involving alternative awards, an employer retains the right to approve or reject an employee's election under certain circumstances, giving the employer significant control over the determination of the award under which compensation cost will be measured.

FASB Interpretation No. 28 provides additional guidance with respect to combination plans. In that Interpretation, the FASB specifies that in combination plans involving both an SAR or other variable award and a fixed award (e.g., a stock option), compensation cost should normally be measured and allocated to expense under the presumption that the variable award will be elected by the employee. However, this presumption may be overcome if experience or other factors, such as ceilings on the appreciation available to the employee under the variable feature, provide evidence that the employee will elect to exercise the fixed award.

(ix) Stock Option Pyramiding.   Stock option pyramiding is a stock option exercise approach that developed subsequent to the issuance of APB Opinion No. 25. This approach involves the payment by the employee of the option exercise price by transferring to the employer previously owned shares with a current fair value equal to the exercise price. In EITF Issue No. 84-18, "Stock Option Pyramiding," the Task Force reached a consensus that "some holding period" for the exchanged shares is necessary to "avoid the conclusion that the award of the option is, in substance, a variable plan (or a stock appreciation right), thereby requiring compensation charges." A majority of the Task Force members indicated that a 6-month period would satisfy the holding period requirement.

In a subsequent consensus set forth in EITF Issue No. 87-6, "Adjustments Relating to Stock Compensation Plans," the Task Force addressed a "phantom" stock-for-stock exercise arrangement, under which an employee holds "mature" shares meeting the holding period requirement discussed in EITF Issue No. 84-18. In this consensus, the Task Force indicated that if the exercise is accomplished by the enterprise issuing a certificate for the "net" shares (i.e., the shares issuable upon exercise of the option less the number of shares required to be relinquished to pay the exercise price), as opposed to the enterprise accepting the mature shares in payment of the exercise price and then issuing a new certificate for the total number of shares covered by the exercised option, the plan remains a fixed plan.

Thus, even though the "net" number of shares to be issued under either of the arrangements described above is not known at the date of grant, the use of qualifying mature shares to pay the option exercise price does not, under these two consensuses, change a plan that otherwise qualifies as a fixed plan to a variable plan. As a result, the enterprise is not required to recognize compensation expense for appreciation in shares under option subsequent to the date of grant solely because the award allows for payment of the exercise price of an option by surrendering mature shares owned by the employee or through a phantom stock-for-stock exercise involving mature shares owned by the employee.

(x) Use of Stock Option Shares to Cover Required Tax Withholding.   EITF Issue No. 87-6, "Adjustments Relating to Stock Compensation Plans," addresses an issue that is similar to the stock option pyramiding issue discussed under (ix) above. The Task Force reached a consensus that "an option that allows the use of option shares to meet tax withholding requirements may be considered a fixed plan if it meets all the other requirements of APB Opinion No. 25. No compensation needs to be recorded for the shares used to meet the tax withholding requirements. The Task Force noted that this treatment would be limited to the number of shares with a fair value equal to the dollar amount of only the *required* tax withholding." Therefore, even though the net number of shares to be issued would not be known at the date of grant under these circumstances (since the shares to be withheld to cover the required tax withholding will not be known until the exercise date), plans with tax withholding features may be accounted for as fixed plans as long as they meet the other requirements for a fixed plan under APB Opinion No. 25.

(d) ALLOCATION OF COMPENSATION COST: DETERMINING THE SERVICE PERIOD.
APB Opinion No. 25 requires that compensation cost related to "stock option, purchase and award plans should be recognized as an expense of one or more periods in which an employee performs services. . . . The grant or award may specify the period or periods during which the employee performs services or the periods may be inferred from the terms or from the past pattern of grants or awards."

FASB Interpretation No. 28 also indicates that compensation cost with respect to variable awards should be allocated to expense over the period(s) in which the employee performs the related services. However, the FASB went a step further in this interpretation by specifying that the service period is presumed to be the vesting period. The vesting period is normally the period from the date of the grant of the rights or awards to the date(s) they become exercisable. These criteria for determining the service period are considerably more definitive than the guidance provided in APB Opinion No. 25 and, in the authors' view, should be used for determining the service period for awards made pursuant to all stock-based compensation awards (i.e., both fixed and variable awards).

(i) Allocation of Compensation Cost Related to Fixed Awards.   Compensation cost related to fixed awards should normally be allocated to expense over the service period on a straight-line basis. On rare occasions, however, circumstances may arise that would justify allocation on another basis. In any event, the method used should be systematic, reasonable, and consistently applied.

(ii) Allocation of Compensation Cost Related to Variable Awards.   Allocating compensation cost related to variable awards to expense is more complex, because the measurement date and, thus, the final determination of compensation cost, occur subsequent to the date of grant. Total compensation cost with respect to a variable award must be estimated from the date of grant to the measurement date, based on the quoted market price of the employer's stock at the end of each interim period. Compensation cost so determined should be allocated to expense in the following manner:

1. If a variable award is granted for current and/or future services, estimated total compensation cost determined at the end of each period **prior to the expiration of the service period** should be allocated to expense over the service period. Changes in the estimated total compensation cost attributable to increases or decreases in the quoted market price of the employer's capital stock **subsequent to the expiration of the service period** (but prior to the measurement date) should be charged or credited to expense each period as the changes occur.

2. If a variable award is granted for past services, estimated total compensation cost determined at the date of grant is charged to expense of the period in which the award is granted. Changes in the estimated total compensation cost attributable to increases or decreases in the quoted market price of the employer's capital stock subsequent to the date of grant (but prior to the measurement date) should be charged or credited to expense each period as the changes occur.

(e) CANCELED OR FORFEITED RIGHTS.   APB Opinion No. 25 states in paragraph 15: "If a stock option is not exercised (or awarded stock is returned to the corporation) because an employee fails to fulfill an obligation, the estimate of compensation expense recorded in previous periods should be adjusted by decreasing compensation expense in the period of forfeiture." Application of this paragraph to a situation where an award is canceled or forfeited because employment is terminated prior to vesting of the award is straightforward; the previously accrued compensation should be eliminated by decreasing compensation expense in the period of cancellation or forfeiture.

However, prior to the issuance of FASB Interpretation No. 28, the application of this paragraph to combination plans was unclear. In a combination plan that permits an employee to elect either a fixed award (e.g., a stock option) or a variable award (e.g., an SAR), FASB Interpretation No. 28 specifies that compensation cost should be accrued based on the presumption that the employee will elect the variable award, unless there is evidence to the contrary. In cases involving combination plans where the employer has accrued compensation based on the presumption that the employee will elect to exercise the variable award and, due to a change in circumstances, it becomes more likely that settlement will be based on the fixed award (e.g., when appreciation in the quoted market price of the employer's capital stock exceeds the maximum appreciation an employee is entitled to receive upon exercise of an SAR), FASB Interpretation No. 28 specifies that the compensation accrued with respect to the variable award should not be adjusted by decreasing compensation expense, but should be recognized as consideration for the stock issued upon settlement of the fixed award. However, FASB Interpretation No. 28 further specifies that, if both the fixed award and the variable award are forfeited or canceled, accrued compensation should be eliminated by decreasing compensation expense during the period of forfeiture or cancellation.

EITF Issue No. 87-33, "Stock Compensation Issues Related to Market Decline," provides further clarification of APB Opinion No. 25, paragraph 15. In this pronouncement, "Task Force members agreed that the reversal of previously measured compensation would be appropriate only if the forfeiture or cancellation of an option or award results from the employee's termination or nonperformance."

(f) ACCOUNTING FOR INCOME TAXES UNDER APB OPINION NO. 25.   Compensation expense associated with stock-based compensation awards is often deductible by the employer for income tax purposes in a different period than such expense is recognized for financial reporting purposes. Such differences are temporary differences and should be accounted for as specified in FASB Statement No. 109, "Accounting for Income Taxes."

In many instances, however, there is a permanent difference between the amount of compensation expense recognized for financial reporting purposes and compensation expense deductible for income tax purposes. These differences generally arise because an employer is normally entitled to an income tax deduction for such awards equal to the amount of compensation reportable as income by the employee, and this amount is often different from the amount of compensation expense recognized by an employer for financial reporting purposes. In addressing this situation, APB Opinion No. 25 specifies that the reduction in income tax expense recorded by an employer with respect to a stock option, purchase, or award plan should not exceed the proportion of the tax reduction related to the compensation expense recognized by the employer for financial reporting purposes. Any additional tax reduction should not be accounted for as a reduction of income tax expense but, rather, should be credited directly to paid-in capital in the period that the additional tax benefit is realized through a reduction of current income taxes payable.

Occasionally, the amount of compensation expense for financial reporting purposes exceeds the amount of compensation deductible for income tax purposes. In these situations, an employer may, in the period of the tax reduction, deduct from paid-in capital and credit to income tax expense or previously recognized deferred taxes the amount of the additional tax reduction that would have resulted had the compensation expense recognized for financial reporting purposes been deductible for income tax purposes. However, this reduction is limited to the amount of tax reductions attributable to awards made under the same or similar plans that have been previously credited to paid-in capital.

(g) OTHER APB OPINION NO. 25 ISSUES

(i) Time Accelerated Restricted Stock Award Plan (TARSAP).   One type of plan that possesses certain aspects of a variable award while providing for fixed award accounting is the "Time Accelerated Restricted Stock Award Plan" (TARSAP). Under a TARSAP, restricted stock is awarded to the participant. The plans generally provide for a lifting of the restrictions based on the passage of time (for example, 20% per year for 5 years, 10% per year for 10 years). The restrictions may be lifted quicker based on certain performance criteria; however, they can never be lifted later than the original schedule. The lifting of the restrictions only affects the timing of the recognition of the compensation expense, not the amount of the compensation expense. The earnings per share and balance sheet classification of a TARSAP follow the same rules as any restricted stock plan.

Another form of a TARSAP involves stock options. For example, a company grants stock options, at the market price, with cliff vesting after 7 years. The plan provides for accelerated vesting if certain performance criteria are met.

It is important for companies to establish realistic vesting schedules in order to follow fixed plan accounting. If the employee cannot realistically expect to vest in the award, absent the achievement of the performance criteria, then fixed plan accounting would not be appropriate. An example of such a situation would be a stock option that, absent the achievement of performance criteria, do not vest until after the retirement date of the employee or after the expiration of an employment contract.

(ii) Applying APB Opinion No. 25 to Nonemployees. Generally accepted accounting principles require that the issuance of stock-based awards issued to nonemployees be recorded at fair value. Given this, one might wonder how a company should account for stock-based awards issued to directors or consultants. While directors are not legally employees, they perform services very similar to employees and, accordingly, practice has extended the application of APB Opinion No. 25 to directors' stock based plans. The accounting for awards granted to consultants is not so clear. If the consultant is working essentially as an employee (that is, on a full-time basis) then APB Opinion No. 25 should be applied. However, if the consultant is truly consulting on a temporary basis, then the award should be recorded at its fair value.

(iii) Cheap Stock. If a company issues stock within a year of an initial public offering, the SEC will presume that fair value at the date of issuance for APB Opinion No. 25 purposes is the initial public offering price. This is rebuttable by the company if objective evidence exists to validate the fair value to be something different than the initial public offering price. One other point of interest is that these shares must be considered outstanding for earnings per share calculations for all periods presented, based on a treasury stock method, even if antidilutive in a loss year.

33.3 EARNINGS PER SHARE UNDER APB OPINION NO. 25

Computation of the impact of capital accumulation awards on earnings per share is addressed in two authoritative pronouncements:

1. APB Opinion No. 15, "Earnings per Share."
2. FASB Interpretation No. 31, "Treatment of Stock Compensation Plans in EPS Computations."

Stock-based compensation awards influence earnings per share to the extent of compensation expense or credits to compensation expense, net of income tax effects, recognized by the employer for financial reporting purposes. For awards that will be settled by payment of cash to the employee, there is no additional impact on earnings per share, since settlement of the award will not result in the issuance of shares of an employer's common stock. However, when awards will be settled through issuance of shares of common stock, additional dilution in earnings per share may result because of the incremental number of shares of the employer's common stock deemed to be outstanding. In a combination plan involving alternative awards that will be settled by either the issuance of common stock or payment of cash, depending on the election made, additional dilution in earnings per share will result only if compensation is being recognized by the employer based on the presumption that the award will be settled through issuance of common stock.

APB Opinion No. 15 states that "options, warrants and similar arrangements usually have no cash yield and derive their value from their right to obtain common stock at specified prices for an extended period. Therefore, these securities should be considered as common stock equivalents at all times." Accordingly, shares of an employer's common stock that are potentially issuable to settle a stock-based compensation award are common stock equivalents. The dilutive impact of common stock equivalents on earnings per share is computed under the treasury stock method, as prescribed by APB Opinion No. 15.

(a) PRIMARY EARNINGS PER SHARE CALCULATION.   In applying the treasury stock method, the incremental number of shares estimated to be outstanding each period for purposes of computing primary earnings per share is determined as if the shares issuable pursuant to the award were issued at the beginning of the period (or at the date the award was granted, if later), and as if the assumed exercise proceeds were used by the employer to acquire shares of common stock at the average market price during the period. Paragraph 3 of FASB Interpretation No. 31 defines exercise proceeds as follows:

> In applying the treasury stock method of paragraph 36 of APB Opinion No. 15 to stock options, including stock appreciation rights and other variable plan awards, the exercise proceeds of the options are the sum of the amount the employee must pay, the amount of measurable compensation ascribed to future services and not yet charged to expense (whether or not accrued), and the amount of any "windfall" tax benefit to be credited to capital. Exercise proceeds shall not include compensation ascribed to past services.

The difference between the shares issuable and the shares deemed to be acquired from the assumed exercise proceeds is the incremental number of shares deemed to be outstanding for purposes of computing primary earnings per share. The number of shares so determined is not included, however, in the computation of primary earnings per share if the effect of inclusion is antidilutive, that is, if the effect of inclusion is to increase the earnings per share or to decrease the loss per share.

(b) FULLY DILUTED EARNINGS PER SHARE.   The impact of a compensation award on fully diluted earnings per share is computed in the same manner as the impact on primary earnings per share, with one exception. In order to reflect the maximum potential dilution, the market price of the employer's common stock at the end of each period, if higher than the average market price during the period, is used to compute the number of common shares deemed to be acquired by the employer with the assumed exercise proceeds. As in the case of primary earnings per share, the incremental number of shares deemed to be outstanding is not included in the computation of fully diluted earnings per share if the effect is antidilutive.

(c) EARNINGS PER SHARE COMPUTATIONS FOR FIXED AWARDS.   Computations of the impact of fixed awards on earnings per share are relatively straightforward. At the date an award is granted, both the number of shares that an individual employee is entitled to receive (i.e., the shares issuable pursuant to the award) and the option or purchase price, if any, are known. Thus the number of shares issuable pursuant to the award remains constant until the award is settled by issuance of shares. However, the reduction in the number of incremental shares for common shares deemed to be acquired by an employer with the assumed exercise proceeds might vary each period, because of changes in (a) the quoted market price of the employer's common stock, and (b) the amount of measurable compensation ascribed to future services and not yet charged.

(d) EARNINGS PER SHARE COMPUTATIONS FOR VARIABLE AWARDS. Computations of the impact of variable awards on earnings per share are considerably more complex than computations involving fixed awards. In the case of variable awards, either (1) the number of shares issuable pursuant to the award, (2) the option or purchase price, if any, or (3) both the number of shares issuable and the option or purchase price are not known at the date the award is granted. For example, in the case of SARs to be settled by issuance of shares of an employer's common stock, there is no option or purchase price. However, the estimated number of shares issuable will vary each period in which an award is outstanding, based on changes in the quoted market price of the employer's common stock. Furthermore, the number of shares deemed to be acquired by the employer from the assumed exercise proceeds will also vary each period in which an award is outstanding, due to changes in (a) the quoted market price of the employer's common stock, and (b) the amount of measurable compensation ascribed to future services and not yet charged to expense.

(e) EARNINGS PER SHARE COMPUTATIONS INVOLVING RESTRICTED SHARES. When restricted shares of an employer's common stock are issued to an employee, the ultimate benefit to be realized by the employee with respect to such shares is dependent on the employee's performance of future services. After the required services have been performed (e.g., continued employment for a specified period), the employee has the unrestricted right to the issued shares. Thus, upon performance of the required services, the issued shares entitle the holder to the same rights and privileges as those held by other common shareholders.

Accountants hold differing views as to the appropriate method of calculating the dilution in earnings per share resulting from outstanding restricted shares. Some argue that all outstanding restricted shares should be included in the computation of earnings per share. Others argue that the number of restricted shares included in the calculation should be determined by application of the treasury stock method. In their view, the number of shares included in computations of earnings per share should equal the total number of restricted shares outstanding, reduced by the number of shares deemed to be acquired by the employer from the assumed exercise proceeds (i.e., the amount of measurable compensation ascribed to future services and not yet charged to expense and the amount of any "windfall" tax benefit to be credited to capital). Additionally, if the shares are deemed to be repurchased under the treasury stock method, some consider the dividends related to this number of shares to be after-tax compensation expense which should reduce the numerator.

Since the existing authoritative literature does not specifically address the treatment of restricted stock plans in earnings per share computations, companies should apply consistently the method chosen.

(f) EARNINGS PER SHARE COMPUTATION INCLUDING SHARES SUBJECT TO REACQUISITION BY THE ISSUER. When book value shares or other shares subject to reacquisition by the issuer at a formula price (e.g., shares subject to reacquisition at book value, at a multiple of book value, or at a formula price based on earnings) are issued to an employee, the ultimate benefit to be realized by the employee with respect to such shares is dependent on the employee's performance of future services. However, after the specified services have been performed (e.g., continued employment for a specified period), the employee's rights become vested. Further, the employee is normally permitted, or in some instances required, to sell the shares back to the employer, either upon retirement, termination of employment, or at other fixed or determinable dates.

The appropriate method of calculating the dilution in earnings per share as a result of outstanding book value shares is not clear. Some believe the preferable method is to consider the awarded shares as outstanding shares from the date of their issuance for purposes of computing both primary and fully diluted earnings per share, assuming the shares entitle the holders to the same voting and dividend rights that other common shareholders possess. If this method is used, no reduction in the number of shares outstanding is made for any shares that would be deemed to be acquired by the employer through application of the treasury stock method. Others argue that the number of outstanding shares included in the earnings per share computation should be reduced through application of the treasury stock method. These differing views are similar to the differing views on earnings per share computations involving restricted stock, as previously discussed.

However, for book value and other shares subject to reacquisition by the employer at a formula price, there is also a third view. It suggests that any such shares that will ultimately be sold or "put" back to the employer should be excluded from computations of earnings per share. The rationale for this approach is that such shares are, in effect, mandatorily redeemable securities. This last view finds some support, at least for publicly held companies, in EITF Issue No. 88-6, which includes the following statement:

> For publicly held companies with existing book value stock plans and for privately held companies with book value stock plans that will remain in existence after an IPO, the SEC Observer noted that the SEC staff will require that the redemption amount of the book value stock be classified in the balance sheet outside stockholders' equity, consistent with the requirements of ASR 268, if the plan includes any conditions under which the company must redeem the stock with the payment of cash.

Consistent with this position expressed by the SEC Observer, it would appear to be appropriate for publicly held companies to exclude book value and other shares subject to repurchase by the company at a formula price from stockholders' equity "if the plan includes any conditions under which the company **must** redeem the stock with the payment of cash" (emphasis added). When this presentation is followed, the authors believe it would also be appropriate to exclude such shares from the calculation of earnings per share. However, the other requirements set forth in ASR No. 268 (incorporated into FRR § 211), should be followed, including a requirement to reduce net income by dividends on such shares in computing earnings available for common stock to be used in the earnings per share computation.

33.4 ILLUSTRATIONS OF ACCOUNTING UNDER APB OPINION NO. 25

This section includes (a) definitions of certain stock-based compensation awards; (b) a summary of the accounting consequences of the awards, including the impact on compensation expense and federal income tax expense to be recognized for financial reporting purposes, and the impact on earnings per share; (c) a summary of the federal income tax consequences of the awards to both the employer and the employee; and (d) exhibits illustrating the accounting and federal income tax consequences of hypothetical awards.

The discussion and exhibits demonstrate the application of the principles and concepts discussed in this chapter. Stock-based compensation plans and awards, however, tend to be unique; accordingly, the income tax and accounting consequences of any stock-based compensation award should be determined based on the specific terms of the award and the authoritative accounting literature and the tax laws and rulings in effect at the time of the award. State and local income tax consequences of stock-based compensation awards are not addressed in this section; such consequences should be determined pursuant to the tax laws of the applicable state and local governments. Finally, the exhibits ignore any employer withholding tax requirements; however, an employer should institute measures to ensure compliance with any requirements to withhold income taxes from recipients of awards. Failure to comply with applicable withholding requirements could jeopardize the employer's right to a tax deduction with respect to an award.

The discussion and exhibits address the accounting and income tax consequences of a fixed award, a variable award, and a formula award, as follows:

Fixed Award. Nonstatutory stock option (nondiscounted).

Variable Award. Stock appreciation right.

Formula Award. Book value share.

(a) FIXED AWARD

(i) Definition.   A nonstatutory stock option is an employee stock option that does not qualify for the special tax treatment afforded incentive stock options under IRC § 422A, or the special tax treatment afforded stock option issued under employee stock purchase plans under IRC § 423.

A nonstatutory stock option (nondiscounted) entitles an employee to purchase shares of the employer's capital stock for an amount equal to the fair market value of the shares as of the grant date. The employee's right is nontransferable and normally vests over a specified period (e.g., 3–5 years) although, in some instances, the right is vested at the date of grant. The right to exercise the option expires after a specified period of time (e.g., 10 years).

(ii) Accounting by Employer for Compensation Expense.   A nonstatutory stock option (nondiscounted) is a fixed award (i.e., both the number of shares the employee is entitled to receive and the option price are known at the date of grant). However, for financial reporting purposes, there is no compensation expense associated with such an award, since the option exercise price is equal to the fair market value of the employer's capital stock at the date of grant.

(iii) Accounting by Employer for Federal Income Taxes.   Upon exercise by an employee of a nonstatutory stock option, the employer is entitled to an income tax deduction for compensation expense, based on the difference between the option exercise price and the fair market value of the shares acquired through exercise, determined as of the exercise date. (Note: If the employee qualifies as an "insider" pursuant to the Securities Exchange Act of 1934, the computation of the tax deduction may differ.)

Thus, a difference usually arises between the amount of compensation expense recognized for financial reporting purposes and the amount of compensation expense that is deductible for income tax purposes. Any reduction of income taxes payable resulting from an excess of compensation expense deducted for income tax purposes over compensation expense recognized for financial reporting purposes should be credited to paid-in capital in the period of the reduction.

(iv) Accounting by Employer for Earnings per Share.   A reduction of earnings per share occurs as a result of the incremental number of common shares of the employer's stock deemed to be outstanding as a result of such awards if the award is dilutive. The incremental number of outstanding shares, if any, is computed using the treasury stock method in accordance with APB Opinion No. 15.

(v) Illustration of a Fixed Award.   Exhibit 33.3 demonstrates the accounting and earnings per share consequences of a hypothetical nonstatutory stock option award (nondiscounted).

(b) VARIABLE AWARD

(i) Definition.   An SAR is a right granted by an employer to an employee that entitles the employee to receive the excess of the quoted market price of a specified number of shares of the employer's capital stock over a specified value (usually the market price of the specified number of shares of the employer's capital stock at the date the right is granted). An SAR sometimes contains a limitation on the amount an employee may receive upon exercise. Further, an SAR may be the only compensation feature of an award; however, an SAR is often granted as part of a combination award in tandem with a nonstatutory stock option, whereby an employee or the employer must make an election to settle the award pursuant to either (but not both) the SAR or the nonstatutory stock option. The form of payment for amounts earned pursuant to an SAR may be specified by the award (i.e., stock, cash, or a combination thereof),

FIXED AWARD
Assumptions

Event	Date	Market Price of Employer's Common Stock
Grant of options to acquire common shares	January 1, 1994	$20
Vesting date (i.e., the date options become exercisable)	January 1, 1997	27
Exercise of options	December 31, 1998	42
Options granted	100	
Exercise price (options are nondiscounted, so exercise price equals fair market value at date of grant)	$20	
Par value of employer's common stock	$ 5	
Employer's effective tax rate	40%	

The year-end and average market prices of the employer's common stock between the date of grant and the exercise date (required for purposes of determining the impact of the award on earnings per share) are as follows:

Year Ended December 31	Market Price of Employer's Common Stock	
	End of Year	Average During the Year
1994	$25	$24
1995	29	27
1996	27	28
1997	34	30
1998	42	36

ACCOUNTING ENTRIES

Date	Description	Debit	Credit
December 31, 1998	Cash	$2,000	
	Common stock		$ 500
	Paid-in capital		1,500
	To record proceeds from exercise of stock option ($20 × 100)		
December 31, 1998	Income taxes payable	880	
	Paid-in capital		880
	To record the federal income tax benefit resulting from the deduction of compensation expense [40% (($42 − $20) × 100)]		

Exhibit 33.3.   Accounting for a fixed award.

EARNINGS PER SHARE

	Incremental Number of Shares Primary Earnings per Share Year Ended December 31,				
	1994	1995	1996	1997	1998
Average market price of employer's common stock	$24	$27	$28	$30	$36
Less exercise price	20	20	20	20	20
Difference	4	7	8	10	16
Multiplied by shares issuable	100	100	100	100	100
Tax deductible compensation expense	400	700	800	1,000	1,600
Effective tax rate	40%	40%	40%	40%	40%
Tax benefit to be credited to additional paid-in capital	160	280	320	400	640
Proceeds from employee upon exercise ($20 × 100)	2,000	2,000	2,000	2,000	2,000
Total assumed proceeds	2,160	2,280	2,320	2,400	2,640
Divided by average market price of employer's common stock	24	27	28	30	36
Shares deemed acquired with assumed proceeds	(90)	(84)	(83)	(80)	(73)
Shares issuable upon exercise	100	100	100	100	100
Incremental shares to be added to the denominator of the primary earnings per share calculation	10	16	17	20	27

	Incremental Number of Shares Fully Diluted Earnings per Share Year Ended December 31,				
	1994	1995	1996	1997	1998
Greater of year end or average market price of employer common stock	$25	$29	$28	$34	$42
Less exercise price	20	20	20	20	20
Difference	5	9	8	14	22
Multiplied by shares issuable	100	100	100	100	100
Tax deductible compensation expense	500	900	800	1,400	2,200
Effective tax rate	40%	40%	40%	40%	40%
Tax benefit to be credited to additional paid-in capital	200	360	320	560	880
Proceeds from employee upon exercise ($20 × 100)	2,000	2,000	2,000	2,000	2,000
Total assumed proceeds	2,200	2,360	2,320	2,560	2,880
Divided by greater of year end or average market price of employer common stock	25	29	28	34	42
Shares deemed acquired with assumed proceeds	(88)	(81)	(83)	(75)	(69)
Shares issuable upon exercise	100	100	100	100	100
Incremental shares to be added to the denominator of the fully diluted earnings per share calculation	12	19	17	25	31

Exhibit 33.3. *Continued.*

or the award may allow the employee or employer to elect the form of payment. If the award is settled in stock, the number of shares issued to the employee is determined by dividing the amount earned by the fair market value of this stock, determined as of the exercise date. The employee's right to exercise an SAR normally vests after a specified period (e.g., 5 years) and the right to exercise expires after a specified period (e.g., 10 years). In the case of an SAR granted in tandem with a nonstatutory award (or other alternate award), the vesting and expiration dates for both awards are usually identical.

(ii) Accounting by Employer for Compensation Expense. An SAR is a variable award, that is, the number of shares, or the amount of cash, an individual is entitled to receive is not known at the date the award is granted. The measurement date and, thus, the determination of total compensation cost associated with an SAR, occur at the exercise date. Total compensation, determined at the exercise date, is equal to the number of rights multiplied by the difference between the quoted market price of the employer's capital stock at the exercise date and the value specified in the award (normally the quoted market price of the employer's capital stock at the grant date).

For purposes of allocating compensation cost to expense of interim periods between the date of grant and the exercise date, compensation cost is estimated as of the end of each interim period by multiplying the number of shares specified in the award times the difference between the quoted market price of the employer's capital stock as of the end of the period and the value specified in the award. During the service period, the amount of compensation cost so determined is allocated to interim periods by recording an expense (or a decrease in expense) in an amount required to adjust accrued compensation at the end of each period to an amount equal to the percentage of the total service period that has elapsed times the estimated compensation cost. For interim periods ending after the service period and up to the exercise date, compensation expense is recorded in an amount sufficient to adjust accrued compensation at the end of each period to the estimated total compensation cost.

In some cases, an SAR awarded to an employee vests over various periods (e.g., 25% per year for 4 years). In these situations, each portion of the SAR that vests on a different vesting date is accounted for as a separate award. Thus, compensation cost attributable to each group should be separately determined and allocated to expense of interim periods from the date of grant to the measurement date in the manner set forth in the preceding paragraph. The accounting for an SAR that vests in this manner is illustrated in Appendix B to FASB Interpretation No. 28.

(iii) Accounting by Employer for Federal Income Taxes. When the amount earned by an employee under an SAR is settled by payment of cash, the employer is entitled to a tax deduction for compensation expense, in the year of payment, equal to the amount of cash paid. Accordingly, the entire amount of the tax benefit is credited to previously recorded deferred taxes and/or income tax expense.

When the amount earned by an employee under an SAR is settled by issuance of shares of the employer's capital stock, the employer is entitled to a tax deduction for compensation expense in the year in which the shares to be issued are delivered to the transfer agent. The amount of the deduction is equal to the fair market value of the shares, determined as of the date of delivery to the transfer agent. Thus, the deduction for compensation expense for tax purposes may differ from the amount of compensation expense recognized for financial reporting purposes if shares are delivered to the transfer agent after the measurement date (i.e., the exercise date). The treatment of this difference is discussed in subsection 33.2(f), "Accounting for Income Taxes Under APB Opinion No. 25."

(iv) Accounting by Employer for Earnings per Share. Earnings per share are affected each period from the date of the award of an SAR to the measurement (exercise) date as a result of compensation expense (net of related income taxes) recognized for financial reporting purposes. If the award is expected to be settled in cash, there would be no impact on earnings per share other than the impact due to compensation expense charged against earnings. However, if the award is expected to be settled by issuance of shares of the employer's common stock, additional dilution may occur as a result of the incremental number of shares of the employer's common stock deemed to be outstanding. It should be noted that for SARs that "are payable in stock or cash at the election of the enterprise or the employee, the decision of whether such rights or awards are common stock equivalents shall be made according to the terms most likely to be elected based on the facts available each period. It shall be presumed that such rights or awards will be paid in stock, but that presumption may be overcome if past experience or a stated policy provides a reasonable basis to believe that the rights or awards will be paid partially or wholly in cash." The incremental number of shares, if any, deemed to be outstanding is computed under the treasury stock method in accordance with APB Opinion No. 15 and FASB Interpretation No. 31. Appendix B of FASB Interpretation No. 31, "Treatment of Stock Compensation Plans in EPS Computations," includes illustrations of the computation of earnings per share for variable plan awards.

(v) Illustration of a Variable Award.   Exhibit 33.4 shows the consequences of a hypothetical SAR award.

(c) FORMULA AWARD

(i) Definition.   Book value shares must be sold back to the company upon retirement or earlier termination of employment, and the arrangement may also permit the employee to sell some or all of his shares back to the company at other fixed or determinable dates. The initial purchase price (or, in the case of a full value award where the employee is not required to pay for the shares, the initial measurement of compensation cost) is equal to the book value of the shares. When the shares are subsequently sold back to the company, the selling price is determined in the same manner as the initial valuation (i.e., book value). An employee-holder of book value shares is entitled to the same voting and dividend rights as other holders of the same class of stock. Shares for which the valuations are based on a multiple of book value, or on another formula based on earnings, are similar to book value shares, and the guidance in this illustration is generally applicable to such shares.

(ii) Accounting by Employer for Compensation Expense.   As previously discussed, and as addressed in EITF Issue Nos. 87-23 and 88-6, there is a distinction, for accounting purposes, between book value shares of publicly held and privately held companies. Subsection 33.2(c)(vii) provides a detailed discussion of the accounting for these plans.

(iii) Accounting by Employer for Federal Income Taxes.   The federal income tax treatment of book value plans differ based on specific provisions and elections made by the employee. Accordingly, the authors strongly urge companies to consult with their tax advisors. Suffice it to say, the tax deduction can differ from the expense recognized in the financial statements. The treatment of this difference is discussed in subsection 33.2(f), "Accounting for Income Taxes Under APB Opinion No. 25."

(iv) Accounting by Employer for Earnings per Share.   For publicly held companies, (as well as privately held companies if the conditions specified in EITF Issue No. 87-23 are not met), earnings per share are affected each period from the date of the award to the date the book value shares are sold back to the employer by the amount of compensation expense, net of income taxes, recognized for financial reporting purposes as described above. For privately held companies that elect to present earnings per share information in their financial statements, the authors believe that additional dilution results from the inclusion of the book value shares in the earnings per share computation. For publicly held companies, book value shares

HYPOTHETICAL AWARD OF A VARIABLE AWARD

Event	Date	Market Price of Employer's Common Stock
Grant of SAR	January 1, 1994	$20
Vesting of SAR (i.e., the date SAR becomes exercisable)	December 31, 1997	$23
Expiration date of SAR	December 31, 1998	No significance
Exercise of SAR and delivery of shares to the transfer agent	December 31, 1998	$29
Fair market value of employer's common stock:	January 1, 1994	$20
	December 31, 1994	21
	December 31, 1995	22
	December 31, 1996	26
	December 31, 1997	23
	December 31, 1998	29
Number of shares/rights covered by award	1,000	
"Base price" of SAR	$20	
Par value of employer's common stock	$ 5	
Employer's effective tax rate	40%	

ACCOUNTING BY EMPLOYER
(Entries required)

Date	Description	Debit	Credit
December 31, 1994	Compensation expense	$ 250	
	Accrued compensation		$ 250
	Deferred income taxes	100	
	Income tax expense		100
December 31, 1995	Compensation expense	750	
	Accrued compensation		750
	Deferred income taxes	300	
	Income tax expense		300
December 31, 1996	Compensation expense	3,500	
	Accrued compensation		3,500
	Deferred income taxes	1,400	
	Income tax expense		1,400
December 31, 1997	Accrued compensation	1,500	
	Compensation expense		1,500
	Income tax expense	600	
	Deferred income taxes		600
December 31, 1998	Compensation expense	6,000	
	Accrued compensation		6,000
	Deferred income taxes	2,400	
	Income tax expense		2,400
	To record compensation expense and the related federal income tax effect for each of the years in the 5-year period ended December 31, 1998 (see computation)		

Exhibit 33.4.   Accounting for a variable award.

December 31, 1998	Accrued compensation	9,000	
	Income taxes payable	3,600	
	Common stock		1,550
	Paid-in capital		7,450
	Deferred income taxes		3,600

To record issuance of 310 earned shares
($9,000 ÷ $29) and the related adjustments
to accrued compensation and deferred
income taxes

Computation of compensation expense and the related federal income tax effect:

	Year Ended December 31				
	1994	1995	1996	1997	1998
Increase in fair market value of employer's capital stock over base price	$ 1	$ 2	$ 6	$ 3	$ 9
Shares covered by SAR	× 1,000	× 1,000	× 1,000	× 1,000	× 1,000
Estimated total compensation cost	$1,000	$2,000	$6,000	$3,000	$9,000
Service period elapsed (%)	× 25%	× 50%	× 75%	× 100%	× 100%
Cumulative compensation expense	$ 250	$1,000	$4,500	$ 3,000	$9,000
Accrued compensation— beginning of period	—	− 250	− 1,000	− 4,500	− 3,000
Compensation expense— current period	$ 250	$ 750	$3,500	$(1,500)	$6,000
Effective tax rate	× 40%	× 40%	× 40%	× 40%	× 40%
Tax effect	$ 100	$ 300	$1,400	$ (600)	$2,400

EARNINGS PER SHARE

Dilution occurs as a result of the incremental number of shares deemed to be outstanding, computed under the treasury stock method, as set forth below.

Computation of incremental number of shares for purposes of computing primary earnings per share[a]:

	Year Ended December 31				
	1994	1995	1996	1997	1998
Accrued compensation—end of period	$250	$1,000	$4,500	$3,000	$9,000
Market price of employer's common stock—end of period	÷ 21	÷ 22	÷ 26	÷ 23	÷ 29
Incremental number of shares—end of period	12	45	173	130	310
Incremental number of shares— beginning of period	—	+ 12	+ 45	+ 173	+ 130
Combined incremental number of shares—beginning and end of period	12	57	218	303	440
	÷ 2	÷ 2	÷ 2	÷ 2	÷ 2
Incremental number of shares (average)[b]	6	29	109	152	220

(continued)

Exhibit 33.4.   Continued.

[a] The incremental number of shares determined under this computation is added to the number of shares otherwise included in the computation of primary earnings per share if the effect is dilutive. If the effect is antidilutive, the number of shares issuable upon exercise of the SAR is ignored in the computation of primary earnings per share.

[b] The examples in Appendix B to FASB Interpretation No. 31 illustrate a slightly different method of computing the incremental number of shares; however, a note to Exhibit 1 indicates, "These computations could also be done using other methods of averaging."

Computation of incremental number of shares for purposes of computing fully diluted earnings per share:

	Year Ended December 31				
	1994	1995	1996	1997[c]	1998
Accrued compensation—end of period	$250	$1,000	$4,500	$3,000	$9,000
Market price of employer's common stock—end of period	÷ 21	÷ 22	÷ 26	÷ 23	÷ 29
Incremental number of shares	12	45	173	130	310

[c] The more dilutive of the incremental number of shares included in the computation of primary earnings per share and the incremental number of shares determined under this computation is used in the computation of fully diluted earnings per share. In 1997, the primary calculation yields a more dilutive result, and, accordingly, the incremental number of shares used would be 152. If the effect is antidilutive, the number of shares issuable upon exercise of the SAR is ignored in the computation of fully diluted earnings per share.

Exhibit 33.4.   *Continued.*

that are viewed as a form of mandatorily redeemable equity security (see ASR No. 268) should be classified outside of stockholders' equity. As a result, such shares do not increase the number of shares used in the computation of earnings per share for publicly held companies.

(v) Illustration of a Formula Award.   Exhibit 33.5 illustrates the consequences of a hypothetical book value purchase award made by a privately held company.

33.5 APPLICATION OF FASB STATEMENT NO. 123

FASB Statement No. 123 provides elective accounting for stock-based employee compensation arrangements using a fair value model. Companies currently accounting for such arrangements under APB Opinion No. 25, "Accounting for Stock Issued to Employees," may continue to do so; however, FASB Statement No. 123 supersedes the disclosure requirements of APB Opinion No. 25 and is applicable to all companies with stock-based compensation arrangements. Companies not electing the fair value accounting method must disclose the pro forma net income and, for public companies, earnings per share as if this method had been elected. The guidance provided by FASB Statement No. 123 applies equally to companies adopting the fair value accounting as well as to companies determining the pro forma amounts that must be disclosed if a company continues to apply APB Opinion No. 25.

(a) SCOPE OF FASB STATEMENT NO. 123.   FASB Statement No. 123 applies to all transactions in which an employer grants shares of its common stock, stock options, or other equity instruments to employees, except for employee stock ownership plans (ESOPs). Accounting for ESOPs is specified in AICPA Statement of Position No. 93-6, "Employers' Accounting for Employee Stock Ownership Plans." FASB Statement No. 123 also applies to transactions in which

HYPOTHETICAL FORMULA AWARD
(Privately Held Company)

Assumptions

General: Common shares are acquired by an employee at their net book value. Acquired shares (book-value shares) can be sold back to the employer by the employee at their net book value 3 years from the date of purchase, or at any time thereafter, but must be resold upon termination of employment. If employment is terminated prior to 3 years from the date of purchase, the shares must be resold to the employer at a price equal to the lower of their net book value at date of termination or the amount originally paid for the shares.

Date of award and acquisition of shares by employee	January 1, 1994	
Vesting date (i.e., the first date on which shares may be sold back to the employer at net book value)	January 1, 1997	
Number of shares acquired	1,000	
Book value per share of employer's common stock	January 1, 1994	$10
	December 31, 1994	11
	December 31, 1995	13
	December 31, 1996	14
	January 1, 1997	14
	September 30, 1997	17
Effective date as of which employee elects to sell shares back to the employer	September 30, 1997	
Date employer acquires shares from employee (based on book value per share as of September 30, 1997)	November 15, 1997	
Par value of employer's common stock	$5	
Employer's effective tax rate	40%	
Dividends		
Paid between the date shares are acquired by the employee and the vesting date	June 30, 1996	$0.50 per share
Paid between the vesting date and the date shares are sold back to the employer	June 30, 1997	0.50 per share

ACCOUNTING ENTRIES

Date	Description	Debit	Credit
January 1, 1994	Cash	$10,000	
	Common stock		$5,000
	Paid-in capital		5,000
	To record issuance of 1,000 book-value shares ($10 × 1,000)		
June 30, 1996	Retained earnings	500	
	Cash		500
	Income taxes payable	200	
	Paid-in capital		200
	To record dividends paid on book-value shares ($0.50 × 1,000) and the related tax benefit (40% (500))		
			(continued)

Exhibit 33.5.   Illustration of a formula award.

January 1, 1997	Income tax payable	1,600	
	Paid-in capital		1,600
	To record reduction of taxes payable due to vesting of book value shares ($4,000 × 40%)		
June 30, 1997	Retained earnings	500	
	Cash		500
	To record dividends paid on book-value shares ($0.50 × 1,000)		
November 15, 1997	Treasury shares	17,000	
	Cash		17,000
	To record acquisition of book-value shares		

EARNINGS PER SHARE

Earnings per share are diluted as a result of the inclusion of the book value shares (1,000) in the earnings per share computation. There is no additional dilution, since no compensation expense is recognized for financial reporting purposes.

Exhibit 33.5. *Continued.*

an employer incurs a liability to employees that will be settled in cash based on the market price of the employer's stock or other equity instruments (e.g., cash-based stock appreciation rights). A company may not elect accounting on a plan-by-plan basis (for example, elect FASB Statement No. 123 for variable plans and retain accounting under APB Opinion No. 25 for fixed plans).

Shares of stock, stock options, or other equity instruments transferred directly to employees or other provider of goods or services by a principal shareholder (generally a shareholder who owns 10% or more of a company's common stock) are subject to the provisions of FASB Statement No. 123, unless the transfer was for a purpose other than compensation. In substance, these arrangements are considered to be capital contributions by a principal shareholder to the entity, with a subsequent award of equity instruments by the entity to its employees or other provider of goods or services.

(b) MEASUREMENT OF AWARDS. FASB Statement No. 123 requires compensation cost for all stock-based compensation awards, including most plans currently considered noncompensatory under APB Opinion No. 25 (i.e., broad-based plans), to be measured by a new fair value based method of accounting. For those companies adopting the recognition provisions of FASB Statement No. 123, the current accounting distinction between fixed options and performance options will be substantially eliminated.

As discussed earlier in the chapter, compensation cost for fixed and variable stock-based awards under APB Opinion No. 25 is measured by the excess, if any, of the market price of the underlying stock over the amount the individual is required to pay (the intrinsic value). Compensation cost for fixed awards is measured at the grant date, while compensation cost for variable awards is estimated until both the number of shares an individual is entitled to receive and the exercise or purchase price are known (measurement date). Compensation cost under variable awards is ultimately based on the intrinsic value on the vesting or settlement date.

FASB Statement No. 123 calls for different accounting and recognition of compensation cost for stock-based compensation plans, depending on whether an award qualifies as a liability or an equity instrument at the grant date. Inherent in the distinction between a liability and an equity instrument is an expectation as to the manner in which the award will ultimately be settled. A stock-based plan expected to be settled by issuance of equity securities would be considered an equity instrument when it is granted. Accordingly, compensation cost would be based on the stock price at the date of grant and would not be adjusted for subsequent changes in the stock price. In contrast, a stock-based plan that requires settlement in cash, or that allows an employee to require settlement in cash, indicates that the employer has incurred a liability. The amount of the liability for such an award would be measured each period based on the end-of-period stock price, similar to variable plan accounting under APB Opinion No. 25.

FASB Statement No. 123 specifies that measurement of an equity instrument award should be based on its estimated fair value at grant date, with the resulting compensation cost recognized over the employee service period (typically the vesting period). Changes in the stock price subsequent to the grant date will have no impact on determining the value of an award at grant date.

The fair value of a stock option award will be estimated using an option-pricing model that considers certain variables and assumptions. Restricted stock awards (called nonvested stock in FASB Statement No. 123) will be measured using the market price of an unrestricted share (or vested share) of the same stock if the stock is publicly traded, or the estimated market price if it is not publicly traded. In other words, shares subject to vesting provisions will not be afforded a discount in measuring compensation cost.

Exhibit 33.6 provides a comparison of compensation cost measured under FASB Statement No. 123 and APB Opinion No. 25 for a fixed stock option and a performance stock award.

(c) MEASUREMENT DATE. FASB Statement No. 123 indicates that the measurement date for stock options or other equity instruments granted to employees as compensation should be the date at which the stock price that enters into measurement of the fair value of an award is fixed. Measurement of compensation cost should be based on the underlying stock price at the date the terms of a stock-based award are agreed to by the employer and the employee (in most cases, the grant date). Awards made under a plan that is subject to shareholder approval are not deemed to be granted until that approval is obtained unless approval is essentially a formality.

The estimated fair value at the grant date should be subsequently adjusted, if necessary, to reflect the outcome of both performance conditions and service-related factors. No compensation cost will be recognized for options that do not vest due to either forfeitures upon termination of service or failure to meet specified performance targets or conditions. Companies may base their accruals of compensation cost on the best estimate of the number of options or other equity instruments expected to vest and revise that estimate, it necessary, to reflect actual forfeitures. Alternatively, for awards subject only to a service requirement, a company may begin accruing compensation cost as if all instruments were expected to vest and recognize the effect of actual forfeitures when they occur. However, vested options that expire unexercised at the end of their contractual terms do not avoid recognition of compensation cost. Only options forfeited because of failure to meet vesting requirements are excluded from determination of compensation cost.

In certain circumstances, due to the terms of a stock option or other equity instrument, it may not be feasible to reasonably estimate the fair value of a stock-based award at the grant date. For example, the fair value of a stock option whose exercise price adjusts by a specified amount with each change in the underlying price of the stock cannot be reasonably estimated using an option pricing model. If the fair value cannot be estimated at the grant date, fair value at the first date at which it is possible to reasonably estimate that value should be used as the final measure of compensation cost. For interim periods during which it is not possible to determine fair value, companies should estimate compensation cost based on the current intrinsic value of the award.

(d) OPTION PRICING MODELS. In addressing the issue of estimating fair value of equity instruments, the FASB noted that it was not aware of any quoted market prices that would be appropriate for employee stock options. Accordingly, FASB Statement No. 123 requires that the fair value of a stock option (or its equivalent) be estimated using an option-pricing model,

---

COMPARISON OF COMPENSATION COST RECOGNIZED UNDER
FASB STATEMENT NO. 123 AND APB OPINION NO. 25

Assume the following for stock compensation awards made by Company A, a public company:

Stock price at date of grant (January 1, 2000)	$40
Expected life of options	6 years
Risk-free interest rate	7.0%
Expected volatility in stock price	30%
Expected dividend yield	1.5%
Vesting schedule for options	100% at end of third year
Options expected to vest	
(5,000 forfeited each year)	285,000
Estimated fair value of each option*	$15
Stock price at December 31, 2002	$60
*Fair value calculated using an acceptable pricing model.	

Fixed Stock Option Award

On January 1, 2000, Company A grants 300,000 stock options to officers and other employees with a maximum term of ten years and an exercise price equal to the market price of the stock at date of grant.

	APB Opinion 25	FASB Statement No. 123
Compensation cost recognized:		
Year 2000	$ 0	$1,425,000
Year 2001	0	1,425,000
Year 2002	0	1,425,000
Total	$ 0	$4,275,000

Performance Stock Award

On January 1, 2000, Company A also grants 30,000 restricted shares to certain employees. The restrictions lapse at the end of three years if certain annual earnings per share targets are met during the three-year period. For purposes of this example, assume the earnings per share targets were met during the three-year period and the restrictions lapsed on December 31, 2002.

	APB Opinion 25	FASB Statement No. 123
Compensation cost recognized	$1,800,000	$1,200,000

Exhibit 33.6. Comparison of compensation cost recognized under FASB Statement No. 123 and APB Opinion No. 25.

such as the Black-Scholes or a binomial pricing model, that considers the following assumptions or variables:

- Exercise price of the option.
- Expected life of the option—Considers the outcome of service-related conditions (i.e., vesting requirements and forfeitures) and performance-related conditions. Expected life is typically less than the contractual term.
- Current price of the underlying stock—Stock price at date of grant.
- Expected volatility of the underlying stock—An estimate of the future price fluctuation of the underlying stock for a term commensurate with the expected life of the option. Volatility is not required for nonpublic companies.

- Expected dividend yield on the underlying stock—Should reflect a reasonable expectation of dividend yield commensurate with the expected life of the option.

- Risk-free interest rate during the expected term of the option—The rate currently available for zero-coupon U. S. government issues with a remaining term equal to the expected life of the options.

FASB Statement No. 123 requires that the option pricing model utilized consider management's expectations relative to the life of the option, future dividends, and stock price volatility. Both the volatility and dividend yield components should reflect reasonable expectations commensurate with the expected life of the option. As there is likely to be a range of reasonable expectations about factors such as expected volatility, dividend yield, and lives of options, a company may use the low end of the range for expected volatility and expected option lives and the high end of the range for dividend yield (assuming that one point within the ranges is no better estimate than another). These estimates introduce significant judgments in determining the value of stock-based compensation awards.

During the FASB's discussions prior to issuance of FASB Statement No. 123, those favoring retention of the basic requirements of APB Opinion No. 25 emphasized the imprecision of measuring fair value through option pricing models, particularly in light of the fact that most stock options issued to employees are not transferable and are forfeitable. The Board believes that it has addressed these issues by valuing at zero options that are expected to be forfeited, and by valuing options that vest based on the length of time they are expected to remain outstanding rather than on the stated term of the options.

During the last 20 years, a number of mathematical models for estimating the fair value of traded options have been developed. The most commonly used methodologies for valuing options include the Black-Scholes model, binomial pricing models, and the minimum value method. The minimum value of a stock option can be determined by a simple present value calculation which ignores the effect of expected volatility. (See Exhibit 33.8 for an illustration of the minimum value method.) The fair value of an option exceeds the minimum value because of the volatility component of an option's value, which represents the benefit of the option holder's right to participate in stock price increases without having to bear the risk of stock price decreases.

The Black-Scholes and binomial pricing models were originally developed for valuing traded options with relatively short lives and are based on complex mathematical formulas. Option values derived under these models are sensitive to both the expected stock volatility and the expected dividend yield. Exhibit 33.7 illustrates the relative effect of changes in expected volatility and dividend rates using a generalized Black-Scholes option-pricing model. Software packages that include option pricing models are readily available from numerous software vendors.

As demonstrated in Exhibit 33.7, option values increase as expected volatility increases, and option values decrease as expected dividend yield increases. It is interesting to note that in instances where higher expected volatility is coupled with higher dividend yields, the binomial model generally produces higher option values than the Black-Scholes model due primarily to increased sensitivity to compounded dividend yields in the binomial model. Nevertheless, FASB Statement No. 123 permits the use of either model.

(i) Expected Volatility.   Volatility is the measure of the amount that a stock's price has fluctuated (historical volatility) or is expected to fluctuate (expected volatility) during a specified period. Volatility is expressed as a percentage; a stock with a volatility of 25% would be expected to have its annual rate of return fall within a range of plus or minus 25 percentage points of its expected rate about two-thirds of the time. For example, if a stock currently trades at $100 with a volatility of 25% and an expected rate of return of 12%, after one year the stock price should fall within the range of $87 to $137 approximately two-thirds of the time (using simple interest for illustration). Stocks with high volatility provide option holders with greater

---

ESTIMATED OPTION VALUES

Assumptions:

Exercise price—$40 (equals current price of underlying stock)
Expected dividends—0%, 2%, and 4%
Expected risk-free rate of return—7%
Expected volatility—0%, 20%, 30%, and 40%
Expected term—six years

Fair values calculated using a Black-Scholes option pricing model

Dividend Rate	Volatility			
	0%	20%	30%	40%
0%	$13.35	$15.14	$17.56	$20.16
2%	8.87	11.42	13.98	16.57
4%	4.96	8.45	11.05	13.58

Exhibit 33.7.   Estimated option values.

economic "up-side" potential and, accordingly, result in higher option values under the Black-Scholes and binomial option pricing models.

FASB Statement No. 123 suggests that estimating expected future volatility should begin with calculating historical volatility over the most recent period equal to the expected life of the options. Thus, if the weighted-average expected life of the options is six years, historical volatility should be calculated for the six years immediately preceding the option grant. FASB Statement No. 123 provides an illustrative example for calculating historical volatility. Companies should modify historical stock volatility to the extent that recent experience indicates that the future is reasonably expected to differ from the past. Although historical averages may be the best available indicator of expected future volatility for some mature companies, there are legitimate exceptions including: (1) a company whose common stock has only recently become publicly traded with little, if any, historical data on its stock price volatility, (2) a company with only a few years of public trading history where recent experience indicates that the stock has generally become less volatile, and (3) a company that sells off a line of business with significantly different volatility than the remaining line of business. In such cases, it is appropriate for companies to adjust historical volatility for current circumstances or use the average volatilities of similar companies until a longer series of historical data is available.

FASB Statement No. 123 does not allow for a company with publicly traded stock to ignore volatility simply because its stock has little or no trading history. A company with only publicly traded debt is not considered a public company under FASB Statement No. 123. Subsidiaries of public companies are considered public companies for purposes of applying FASB Statement No. 123's provisions.

(ii) Expected Dividends. The assumption about expected dividends should be based on publicly available information. While standard option pricing models generally call for expected dividend yield, the model may be modified to use an expected dividend amount rather than a yield. If a company uses expected payments, any history of regular increases in dividends should be considered. For example, if a company's policy has been to increase dividends by approximately 3% per year, its estimated option value should not assume a fixed dividend amount throughout the expected life of the option.

Some companies with no history of paying dividends might reasonably expect to begin paying small dividends during the expected lives of their employee stock options. These companies may use an average of their past dividend yield (zero) and the mean dividend yield of an appropriately comparable peer group.

(iii) Expected Option Lives.   The expected life of an employee stock option award should be estimated based on reasonable facts and assumptions on the grant date. The following factors should be considered: (1) the vesting period of the grant, (2) the average length of time similar grants have remained outstanding, and (3) historical and expected volatility of the underlying stock. The expected life must at least include the vesting period and, in most circumstances, will be less than the contractual life of the option.

Option value increases at a higher rate during the earlier part of an option term. For example, a two-year option is worth less than twice as much as a one-year option if all other assumptions are equal. As a result, calculating estimated option values based on a single weighted-average life that includes widely differing individual lives may overstate the value of the entire award. Companies are encouraged to group option recipients into relatively homogeneous groups and calculate the related option values based on appropriate weighted-average expectations for each group. For example, if top level executives tend to hold their options longer than middle management, and nonmanagement employees tend to exercise their options sooner than any other groups, it would be appropriate to stratify the employees into these three groups in calculating the weighted-average estimated life of the options.

(iv) Minimum Value Method.   FASB Statement No. 123 indicates that a nonpublic company may estimate the value of its options without consideration of the expected volatility of its stock. This method of estimating an option's value is commonly referred to as the minimum value method. The underlying concept of the minimum value method is that an individual would be willing to pay at least an amount that represents the benefit of the right to defer payment of the exercise price until a future date (time value benefit). For a dividend-paying stock, that amount is reduced by the present value of dividends foregone due to deferring exercise of the option.

Minimum value can be determined by a present value calculation of the difference between the current stock price and the present value of the exercise price, less the present value of expected dividends, if any. Minimum value also can be computed using an option-pricing model and an expected volatility of effectively zero. Although the amounts computed using present value techniques may produce slightly different results than option-pricing models for dividend-paying stocks, the Board decided to permit either method of computing minimum value.

Exhibit 33.8 illustrates a minimum value computation for an option, assuming an expected five-year life with an exercise price equal to the current stock price of $40, an expected annual dividend yield of 1.25%, and a risk-free interest rate available for five-year investments of 6%.

MINIMUM VALUE METHOD	
Current stock price	$40.00
Less:	
Present value of exercise price	(29.89)
Present value of expected dividends	(2.11)
Minimum value of option[1]	$ 8.00

[1] The $8.00 minimum value was determined by a present value calculation. By way of contrast, application of a Black Scholes option-pricing model results in a minimum value of $7.70.

Exhibit 33.8.   Minimum value computation.

FASB Statement No. 123 does not allow public companies to account for employee stock options based on the minimum value method because that approach was considered inconsistent with the overall fair value concept. However, the FASB acknowledged that estimating expected volatility for the stock of nonpublic companies is not feasible. Accordingly, FASB Statement No. 123 permits nonpublic companies to ignore expected volatility in estimating the value of options granted. As a result, nonpublic entities are allowed to use the minimum value method.

(e) RECOGNITION OF COMPENSATION COST.   As previously discussed, FASB Statement No. 123 requires either recognition of compensation cost in an employer's financial statements for those companies adopting the new standard or disclosure of pro forma net income and earnings per share for companies remaining under APB Opinion No. 25 for all awards of stock options and other stock-based instruments. FASB Statement No. 123 applies the same basic accounting principles to all stock-based plans, including those currently considered noncompensatory under APB Opinion No. 25. At the date of grant, compensation cost is measured as the fair value of the total number of awards expected to vest. Adjustments to the amount of compensation cost recognized should be made for actual experience in performance and service-related factors (i.e., forfeitures, attainment of performance goals, etc.). Changes in the price of the underlying stock or its volatility, the life of the option, dividends on the stock, or the risk-free interest rate subsequent to the grant date do not adjust the fair value of options or the related compensation cost.

A stock option for which vesting or exercisability is conditioned upon achievement of a targeted stock price or specified amount of intrinsic value does not constitute a performance award for which compensation expense would be subsequently adjusted. For awards that incorporate such features, compensation cost is recognized for employees who remain in service over the service period regardless of whether the target stock price or amount of intrinsic value is reached. FASB Statement No. 123 does indicate, however, that a target stock price condition generally affects the value of such options. Previously recognized compensation cost should not be reversed if a vested employee stock option expires unexercised.

Awards for past services would be recognized as a cost in the period the award is granted. Compensation expense related to awards for future services would be recognized over the period the related services are rendered by a charge to compensation cost and a corresponding credit to equity (paid-in capital). Unless otherwise defined, the service period would be considered equivalent to the vesting period. Vesting occurs when the employee's right to receive the award is not contingent upon performance of additional services or achievement of a specified target.

Compensation cost for an award with a graded vesting schedule should be recognized in accordance with the method described in FASB Interpretation 28, "Accounting for Stock Appreciation Rights and Other Variable Stock Option or Award Plans," if the fair value of the award is determined based on different expected lives for the options that vest each year, as it would be if the award is viewed as several separate awards, each with a different vesting date. However, if the value of the award is determined based on a composite expected life, or if the award vests at the end of a period (i.e., cliff vesting), the related compensation cost may be recognized on a straight-line basis over the service period, presumed to be the vesting period. FASB Statement No. 123 does require that the amount of compensation cost recognized at any date must at least equal the value of the vested portion of the award at that date.

FASB Statement No. 123 requires that dividends or dividend equivalents paid to employees on the portion of restricted stock or other equity award that is not expected to vest be recognized as additional compensation cost during the vesting period. Also, certain awards provide for reductions in the exercise or purchase price for dividends paid on the underlying stock. In these circumstances, FASB Statement No. 123 requires use of a dividend yield of zero in estimating the fair value of the related award. This provision would have the effect of increasing the fair value of a stock option on a dividend-paying stock.

(f) ADJUSTMENTS OF INITIAL ESTIMATES.   Measurement of the value of stock options at grant date requires estimates relative to the outcome of service- and performance-related conditions. FASB Statement No. 123 adopts a grant date approach for stock-based awards with service requirements or performance conditions and specifies that resulting compensation cost should be adjusted for subsequent changes in the expected or actual outcome of these factors. Subsequent adjustments would not be made to the original volatility, dividend yield, expected life, and interest rate assumptions or for changes in the price of the underlying stock. Exhibit 33.9 illustrates the impact on compensation cost when actual forfeitures resulting from terminations deviate from the rate anticipated at grant date.

A performance requirement adds another condition that must be met in order for employees to vest in certain awards, in addition to rendering services over a period of years. Compensation cost for these awards should be recognized each period based on an assessment of the probability that the performance-related conditions will be met. Those estimates should be subsequently adjusted to reflect differences between expectations and actual outcomes. The cumulative effect of such changes in estimates on current and prior periods should be recognized in the period of change.

(g) MODIFICATIONS TO GRANTS.   FASB Statement No. 123 requires that a modification to the terms of an award that increases the award's fair value at the modification date be treated, in substance, as the repurchase of the original award in exchange for a new award of greater value. Additional compensation cost arising from a modification of a vested award should be recognized for the difference between the fair value of the new award at the modification date and the fair value of the original award immediately before its terms are modified, determined based on the shorter of (a) its remaining expected life or (b) the expected life of the modified option. For modifications of nonvested options, compensation cost related to the original award not yet recognized must be added to the incremental compensation cost of the new award and recognized over the remainder of the employee's service period.

As an example of a modification of a vested option, assume that, on January 1, 2000, Company A granted its employees 300,000 stock options with an exercise price of $50 per share and a contractual term of 10 years. The options vested at the end of three years and 15,000 of the original 300,000 options were forfeited prior to vesting. On January 1, 2004, the market price of Company A stock has declined to $40 per share and Company A decides to reduce the exercise price of the options. Under FASB Statement No. 123, Company A has effectively

---

ADJUSTMENT OF FORFEITURE RATE UNDER FASB STATEMENT NO. 123

Assumptions:

Options granted	10,000
Vesting schedule	100% at end of third year (cliff vesting)
Estimated forfeiture rate	6% per year (upon termination)
Actual forfeiture rate	6% in years 1 and 2; 3% in year 3
Option value at grant date	$10

Estimated fair value of award at grant date: $(10,000 \times .94 \times .94 \times .94) \times \$10 = \underline{\$83,100}$

Compensation cost recognized in years 1 and 2: $\$83,100 \div 3 = \underline{\$27,700}$

Compensation cost recognized in year 3 (3% forfeiture rate):

Total compensation cost to be recognized: $(10,000 \times .94 \times .94 \times .97) \times \$10 = \$85,700$

Cost recognized in year 1	(27,700)
Cost recognized in year 2	(27,700)
Cost recognized in year 3	$30,300

Exhibit 33.9.   Adjustment of forfeiture rate under FASB Statement No. 123.

issued new options and would recognize additional compensation cost as a result of the reduction in exercise price. The estimated fair value of the original award at the modification date would be determined using the assumptions for dividend yield, volatility, and risk-free interest rate at the modification date. Exhibit 33.10 illustrates the measurement of additional compensation cost upon modification of the terms of this award.

In certain cases, modifications may be made to options that were granted before FASB Statement No. 123 was effective. Under APB Opinion No. 25, compensation cost would not have been recognized upon initial issuance of an option if the exercise price was equal to the market price on the grant date. Because no compensation cost was recognized for the original options, the modified options are treated as a new grant. For modifications of vested options, compensation cost is recognized immediately for the fair value of the new option on the modification date. However, if the options had intrinsic value on the modification date (i.e., the options were in the money), the intrinsic value would be excluded from the amount of compensation cost recognized because an employee could have exercised the options immediately before the modification and received the intrinsic value without affecting the amount of compensation cost recognized by the company. For modifications to nonvested options, previously unrecognized compensation cost, if any, is added to incremental compensation cost from the new award and recognized over the employee's service period.

Exchanges of options or changes in their terms in conjunction with business combinations, spin-offs, or other equity restructurings are considered modifications under FASB Statement No. 123, with the exception of those changes made to reflect the terms of the exchange of shares in a business combination accounted for as a pooling-of-interests. This represents a change in practice, as such modifications do not typically result in a new measurement date under APB Opinion No. 25, and therefore, additional compensation expense is not recorded.

MODIFICATIONS TO GRANTS UNDER STATEMENT FASB NO. 123

Assume the following for stock options granted and subsequently modified by Company A, a public company:

	Fair Value of Original Award January 1, 2000	Fair Value of New Award January 1, 2004	Fair Value of Original Award January 1, 2004
Exercise price	$50	$40	$50
Stock price	$50	$40	$40
Expected volatility	30%	35%	35%
Expected dividend yield	1.5%	2.0%	2.0%
Expected option life	6 years	5 years	2 years[1]
Risk-free interest rate	6.5%	5.75%	5.75%
Estimated fair value of each option[2]	$18	$13	$ 5

[1] Lesser of remaining expected life of original award or expected life of new award.

[2] Fair value calculated using an acceptable pricing model.

The computation of additional compensation cost resulting from this modification would be as follows:

Estimated fair value of new award ($13/option × 285,000)	$ 3,705,000
Estimated fair value of original award at modification date ($5/option × 285,000)	(1,425,000)
Incremental compensation cost of new award	$ 2,280,000

Because the award is fully vested at the modification date, the additional compensation cost of $2,280,000 would be expensed in the period of modification.

Exhibit 33.10.   Modifications to grants under FASB Statement No. 123.

However, changing the terms of an award in accordance with antidilution provisions that are designed, for example, to equalize an option's value before and after a stock split or a stock dividend is not considered a modification.

(h) OPTIONS WITH RELOAD FEATURES.   Reload stock options are granted to employees upon exercise of previously granted options whose original terms provide for the use of "mature" shares of stock that the employee has owned for a specified period of time (generally six months) rather than cash to satisfy the exercise price. When an employee exercises the original options using mature shares (a stock for stock exercise), the employee is automatically granted a reload option for the same number of shares used to exercise the original option. The exercise price of the reload option is the market price of the stock at the date the reload option is granted, and the term is equal to the remainder of the term of the original option. Compensation cost related to options with reload features should be calculated separately for the initial option grant and each subsequent grant of a reload option.

In the Basis for Conclusions (Appendix A to FASB Statement No. 123), the FASB states its belief that, ideally, the value of an option with a reload feature should be estimated at the grant date, taking into account all of its features. However, the Board concluded that it is not feasible to do so because no reasonable method currently exists to estimate the value added by a reload feature. Accordingly, the Board decided that compensation cost for an option with a reload feature should be calculated separately for the initial option grant and for each subsequent grant of a reload option as if it were a new grant.

(i) SETTLEMENT OF AWARDS.   Employers occasionally repurchase vested equity instruments issued to employees for cash or other assets. Under FASB Statement No. 123, amounts paid up to the fair value of the instrument at the date of repurchase should be charged to equity, and amounts paid in excess of fair value should be recognized as additional compensation cost. For example, a company that repurchases a vested share of stock for its market price does not incur additional compensation cost. A company that settles a nonvested award for cash has, in effect, vested the award, and the amount of compensation cost measured at the grant date and not yet recognized should be recognized at the repurchase date.

A repurchase of vested stock options would be treated in a manner similar to a modification of an option grant. Incremental compensation cost, if any, to be recognized upon cash settlement should be determined as the excess of cash paid over the fair value of the option on the date the employee accepts the repurchase offer, determined based on the remainder of its original expected life at that date. Additionally, if unvested stock options are repurchased, the amount of previously unrecognized compensation cost should be recognized at the repurchase date because the repurchase of the option effectively vests the award. Exhibit 33.11 illustrates the accounting for the repurchase of an award by the employer.

In certain circumstances, awards granted prior to adoption of FASB Statement No. 123 may be settled in cash subsequent to adoption of FASB Statement No. 123. Compensation cost would not have been recognized for the original award under APB Opinion No. 25 if the exercise price equaled the market price on the grant date. Because no cost was previously recognized for the original award, the cash settlement of the vested options is treated as a new grant and recognized as compensation cost on the repurchase date. However, if the original options had been in-the-money and thus had intrinsic value immediately before the settlement, the intrinsic value is excluded from compensation cost, similar to the accounting for a grant modification.

(j) TANDEM PLANS AND COMBINATION PLANS.   Employers may have compensation plans that offer employees a choice of receiving either cash or shares of stock in settlement of their stock-based awards. Such plans are considered tandem plans. For example, an employee may be given an award consisting of a cash stock appreciation right (SAR) and an SAR with the same terms except that it calls for settlement in shares of stock with an equivalent value. The employee may demand settlement in either cash or in shares of stock and the election of

---

REPURCHASE OF AWARD UNDER FASB STATEMENT NO. 123

On January 1, 2000, Company A grants a total of 10,000 "at-the-money" options to employees. The options vest after three years and are exercisable through December 31, 2009. The market price of Company A stock is $50 at grant date. It is expected that a total of 8,500 options will vest, based on projected forfeitures. The fair value of an option at grant date is $18, using an acceptable option pricing model. At grant date, Company A would compute compensation cost of $153,000 (8,500 × $18 per option) to be recognized ratably over the service period.

On January 1, 2005, Company A repurchases 2,000 of the vested options for $30 per option. On that date, the market price of Company A's stock is $60 and the option's fair value is $24. Additional compensation cost would be recognized for the difference between the cash paid and the fair value of the option at the date of repurchase.

Calculations:

Repurchase price of options	$30	
Fair value of options at repurchase date	24	
Additional compensation cost	$ 6	× 2,000 options = $12,000

Journal entry:

Compensation expense	$12,000	
Additional paid in capital[1]	48,000	
Cash		$60,000

[1] Fair value of options repurchased (2,000 × $24)

Exhibit 33.11.   Repurchase of award under FASB Statement No. 123.

one component of the plan (cash or stock) cancels the other. Because the employee has the choice of receiving cash, this plan results in the company incurring a liability. The amount of the liability will be adjusted each period to reflect the current stock price. If employees subsequently choose to receive shares of stock rather than receive cash, the liability is settled by issuing stock.

If the terms of a stock-based compensation plan provide that settlement of awards to employees will be made in a combination of stock and cash, the plan is considered a combination plan. In a combination plan, each part of the award is treated as a separate grant and accounted for separately. The portion to be settled in stock is accounted for as an equity instrument and the cash portion is accrued as a liability and adjusted each period based on fluctuations in the underlying stock price.

Exhibit 33.12 illustrates the accounting for an award expected to be settled in a combination of cash and stock.

(k) EMPLOYEE STOCK PURCHASE PLANS.   Some companies offer employees the opportunity to purchase company stock, typically at a discount from market price. If certain conditions are met, the plan may qualify under Section 423 of the Internal Revenue Code which allows employees to defer taxation on the difference between the market price and the discounted purchase price. APB Opinion No. 25 treats employee stock purchase plans that qualify under Section 423 as noncompensatory.

Under FASB Statement No. 123, broad-based employee stock purchase plans are compensatory unless the discount from market price is relatively small. Plans that provide a discount of no more than 5% would be considered noncompensatory; discounts in excess of this amount would be considered compensatory under FASB Statement No. 123 unless the company could justify a higher discount. A company may justify a discount in excess of 5% if the discount from market price does not exceed the greater of (a) the per-share discount that would be reasonable in a recurring offer of stock to stockholders or (b) the per-share amount of stock issuance costs avoided by not having to raise a significant amount of capital by a public offering.

COMBINATION PLAN UNDER FASB STATEMENT NO. 123

Company A has a performance-based plan which provides for a maximum of 900,000 performance awards to be earned by participants if certain financial goals are met over a three-year period. Each performance award is equivalent to one share of Company A stock. The terms of the plan call for the awards to be settled two-thirds in stock and one-third in cash at the date the performance goals are attained (the settlement date). This plan may be viewed as a combination plan consisting of 600,000 shares of restricted stock and 300,000 cash SARs.

The market price of Company A stock is $30 at grant date. The Company estimates that 750,000 performance awards will ultimately be earned based on the Company's expectations of meeting benchmark goals and estimated forfeitures. Company A intends to settle the award by issuing 500,000 shares of stock and settling the remaining 250,000 units in cash based on the market price of Company A stock at the settlement date.

The stock portion of the award is accounted for as a grant of an equity instrument. Company A would recognize compensation cost of $15 million (500,000 × $30 per unit) over the three-year service period for the portion of the award expected to be settled in stock.

The cash portion of the award would result in initial compensation cost of $7.5 million (250,000 × $30) to be accrued as a liability over the participants' service period. The amount of the liability will be adjusted each period based on fluctuations in the market price of the stock. If the market price of Company A stock is $36 at the end of the service period, additional compensation cost of $1.5 million would be recognized (250,000 × $6).

Exhibit 33.12.   Combination plan under FASB Statement No. 123.

If a company cannot provide adequate support for a discount in excess of 5%, the entire amount of the discount should be treated as compensation cost.

For example, if an employee stock purchase plan provides that employees can purchase the employer's common stock at a price equal to 85% of its market price as of the date of purchase, compensation cost would be based on the entire discount of 15% unless the discount in excess of 5% can be justified.

If an employee stock purchase plan meets all of the following criteria, the discount from market price is not considered stock-based compensation:

1. The plan incorporates no option features other than the following, which may be incorporated: (a) employees are permitted a short period of time (not exceeding 31 days) after the purchase price has been fixed in which to enroll in the plan, and (b) the purchase price is based solely on the stock's market price at the date of purchase and employees are permitted to cancel participation before the purchase date.

2. The discount from the market price is 5% or less (or the company is able to justify a higher discount).

3. Substantially all full-time employees meeting limited employment qualifications may participate on an equitable basis.

(I) LOOK-BACK OPTIONS.   Some companies offer options to employees under Section 423 of the Internal Revenue Code, which allows employees to defer taxation on the difference between the market price of the stock and a discounted purchase price if certain requirements are met. One requirement is that the option price may not be less than the smaller of (a) 85% of the market price when the option is granted or (b) 85% of the market price at exercise date. Options that provide for the more favorable of several exercise prices are referred to as "look-back" options. Under APB Opinion No. 25, Section 423 look-back plans generally are considered noncompensatory.

Under the FASB Statement No. 123, the effect of a look-back feature would be recorded at fair value at the grant date similar to other stock-based compensation. Accordingly, the fair value of a look-back option should be estimated based on the stock price and terms of the option at the grant date by breaking it into its components and valuing the option as a combination position.

For example, on January 1, 2004, a company offers its employees the opportunity to sign up for payroll deductions to purchase its stock at either 85% of the stock's current $50 price or 85% of the stock price at the end of the year when the options expire, whichever is lower. Assume that the dividend yield is zero, expected volatility is 35% and the risk-free interest rate available for the next 12 months is 7 percent.

The look-back option consists of 15% of a share of nonvested stock and 85% of a one-year call option. The underlying logic is that the holder of the look-back option will always receive 15% of a share of stock upon exercise, regardless of the stock price at that date. For example, if the stock price fell to $40, the exercise price will be $34 ($40 × .85), and the holder will benefit by $6 ($40 − $34), or 15% of the exercise price. If the stock price exceeds the $50 exercise price, the holder of the look-back option receives a benefit that is more than equivalent to 15% of a share of stock. A standard option-pricing model can be used to value the one-year call option on 85% of a share of stock represented by the second component.

Total compensation cost at the grant date is computed in Exhibit 33.13.

(m) AWARDS REQUIRING SETTLEMENT IN CASH.   In most cases, an employer settles stock options by issuing stock rather than paying cash. However, under certain stock-based plans, an employer may elect or may be required to settle the award in cash. For example, a cash stock appreciation right derives its value from increases in the price of the employer's stock but is ultimately settled in cash. Such plans include phantom stock plans, cash stock appreciation rights, and cash performance unit awards. In other instances, an employee may have the option of requesting settlement in cash or stock.

Under APB Opinion No. 25, cash paid to settle a stock-based award is the final measure of compensation cost. The repurchase of stock shortly after exercise of an option is also considered cash paid to settle an earlier award and ultimately determines compensation cost. FASB Statement No. 123 indicates that awards calling for settlement in stock are considered equity instruments when issued, and their subsequent repurchase for cash would not necessarily require an adjustment to compensation cost if the amount paid does not exceed the fair value of the instruments repurchased. Awards calling for settlement in cash (or other assets of the employer) are considered liabilities when issued, and their settlement would require an adjustment to previously recognized compensation cost if the settlement amount differs from the carrying amount of the liability. Also, if the choice of settlement (cash or stock) is the employee's, FASB Statement No. 123 specifies that the employer would be settling a liability rather than issuing an equity security; accordingly, compensation cost should be adjusted if the settlement amount differs from the carrying amount of the liability.

FASB Statement No. 123 indicates that the accounting for stock compensation plans as equity or liability instruments should reflect the terms as understood by the employer and the employee. While the written plan generally provides the best evidence of its terms, an

---

COMPUTATION OF COMPENSATION COSTS OF A
LOOK-BACK OPTION UNDER FASB STATEMENT NO. 123

.15 of a share of nonvested stock ($50 × .15)	$ 7.50
Call option on .85 of a share of stock, exercise price of $50 ($8.48* × .85)	$ 7.21
Total compensation cost at grant date	$14.71

*Fair value calculated using an acceptable pricing model.

Exhibit 33.13.   Computation of compensation costs of a look-back option under FASB Statement No. 123.

employer's past practices may indicate substantive terms that differ from written terms. For example, an employer that is not legally obligated to settle an award in cash but that generally does so upon exercise of stock options whenever an employee asks for cash settlement is probably settling a substantive liability rather than repurchasing an equity instrument. In that instance, the Statement requires accounting for the substantive terms of the plan.

FASB Statement No. 123 does not change current accounting practice for nonpublic companies with stock repurchase agreements, provided that the repurchase price is the fair value of the stock at the date of repurchase. Alternatively, many nonpublic companies sponsor stock purchase plans that provide for employees to acquire shares in the company at book value or a formula price based on book value or earnings. In addition, these arrangements frequently require the company to repurchase the shares when the employee terminates at a price determined in the same manner as the purchase price.

Under current practice, a nonpublic company is not required to recognize compensation cost for share repurchases under book value or formula plans if the employee has made a substantive investment that will be at risk for a reasonable period of time. FASB Statement No. 123, however, requires fair value as the basic method of measuring compensation cost for all stock-based plans, including those of private companies. FASB Statement No. 123 indicates that each plan will need to be assessed on a case-by-case basis to determine whether the book value or formula price is a reasonable estimate of fair value and whether the plan is subject to additional compensation cost.

(n) TRANSACTIONS WITH NONEMPLOYEES. Except for stock-based awards to employees that are currently within the scope of APB Opinion No. 25, FASB Statement No. 123 provides that all transactions in which goods or services are the consideration received for the issuance of equity instruments should be accounted for based on the fair value of the consideration received or the fair value of the equity instruments issued, whichever is more reliably measurable. In some cases, the fair value of goods or services received from suppliers, consultants, attorneys, or other nonemployees is more reliably measurable and indicates the fair value of the equity instrument issued.

If the fair value of the goods or services received is not reliably measurable, the measure of the cost of goods or services acquired in a transaction with nonemployees should be based on the fair value of the equity instruments issued. However, FASB Statement No. 123 does not specify the measurement date for determining the fair value of equity instruments issued to other than employees, such as when contingent stock purchase warrants are issued in conjunction with sales agreements with major customers or purchase business combinations.

(o) ACCOUNTING FOR INCOME TAXES UNDER FASB STATEMENT NO. 123. The cumulative amount of compensation cost recognized that ordinarily results in a future tax deduction under existing tax law is a deductible temporary difference under FASB Statement No. 109, "Accounting for Income Taxes." Under current tax law, incentive stock options do not result in tax deductions for an employer (provided employees comply with requisite holding periods) and, accordingly, do not create a future deductible temporary difference. Tax benefits arising because employees do not comply with requisite holding periods (i.e., disqualifying dispositions) are recognized in the financial statements only when such events occur.

Nonqualified stock options and grants of restricted stock do generate tax deductions for employers. In general, the tax deduction equals the intrinsic value of the award at the date of exercise. Under FASB Statement No. 123, the cumulative amount of compensation cost recognized in a company's income statement is considered to be a deductible temporary difference under FASB Statement No. 109. Deferred tax assets recognized for deductible temporary differences should be reduced by a valuation allowance if, based on available evidence, such an allowance is deemed necessary. The deferred tax benefit or expense resulting from increases or decreases in that temporary difference (for example, as additional compensation cost is recognized over the vesting period) is recognized in the income statement because those tax effects relate to continuing operations. Similar to the provisions of APB Opinion No. 25 on accounting for the income tax effects of stock compensation awards, the amount of tax benefits recognized in the income statement is limited to the effects of deductions based on reported compensation cost. If the deduction for income tax purposes exceeds the amount of compensation cost recognized for financial reporting purposes, the benefit of the excess tax deduction is credited to additional paid-in capital.

(p) EFFECTIVE DATES AND TRANSITIONS.   The recognition provisions of FASB Statement No. 123 may be adopted immediately by companies wishing to do so and will apply to all awards granted after the beginning of the fiscal year in which the recognition provisions are first applied. Awards granted prior to the fiscal year in which initial application is adopted should not be adjusted except to the extent that prior awards are modified or settled in cash. The disclosure provisions of FASB Statement No. 123 , as discussed below, are effective for fiscal years beginning after December 15, 1995. However, disclosure of the pro forma net income and earnings per share, as if the fair value based accounting method had been used to account for stock-based compensation cost, is required for all awards granted in fiscal years beginning after December 15, 1994. Accordingly, for calendar year companies, 1996 financial statements will include the pro forma net income and earnings per share for both 1995 and 1996, as well as the other required disclosures for 1995 awards.

During the initial phase-in period, the effects of applying FASB Statement No. 123 for either recognizing compensation cost or providing pro forma disclosures may not be representative of the effects on reported net income for future years. Financial statements should include a supplemental disclosure to this effect if applicable.

33.6 EARNINGS PER SHARE UNDER FASB STATEMENT NO. 123

Under APB Opinion No. 15, "Earnings Per Share," stock options, stock appreciation rights, and other awards expected to be settled in stock are common stock equivalents for purposes of computing earnings per share. All dilutive common stock equivalents, regardless of whether they are exercisable, are treated as if they have been exercised for earnings per share purposes.

Under FASB Statement No. 123, the number of common stock equivalents used in computing primary earnings per share is the same as the number expected to vest in measuring compensation cost. This represents a change from current earnings per share rules that require all dilutive common stock equivalents, regardless of whether they are expected to vest, to be treated as if they had been exercised. Fully diluted earnings per share calculations are based on the actual number of common stock equivalents outstanding, as in current practice.

In applying the treasury stock method of APB Opinion No. 15, the assumed proceeds are the sum of (1) the amount the employee must pay (exercise price), (2) the amount of compensation cost attributed to future services and not yet recognized, and (3) the amount of any expected tax benefit that would be credited to equity (paid-in capital) upon exercise.

Under APB Opinion No. 25, common stock equivalents typically are dilutive when the market price of the underlying stock exceeds the related exercise price. However, in applying the treasury stock method under FASB Statement No. 123, common stock equivalents may be anti-dilutive even when the market price of the underlying stock exceeds the related exercise price. This result is possible because compensation cost attributed to future services and not yet recognized is included as a component of assumed proceeds upon exercise in applying the treasury stock method. Since this component represents an amount over and above the intrinsic value of the award at grant date, it is possible that common stock equivalents with a positive intrinsic value would be considered anti-dilutive and thereby excluded from earnings per share calculations under APB Opinion No. 15.

Exhibit 33.14 illustrates a primary earnings per share calculation under APB Opinion No. 25 and under FASB Statement No. 123.

EARNINGS PER SHARE UNDER FASB STATEMENT NO. 123 AND APB OPINION NO. 25

For purposes of this example, assume that 2006 is the first year that pro forma net income and earnings per share must be disclosed in the financial statements.

On January 1, 2006, Company A granted 100,000 options with an exercise price equal to the market price of the stock at that date ($30). The fair value of each option granted was $9, and the options vest at the end of three years. Company A expects that 85,000 options granted in 2006 will vest and be exercised. Assume a 40 percent tax rate.

On January 1, 2006, Company A computed compensation cost of $765,000 (85,000 × $9) to be recognized ratably at $255,000 per year. During 2006, 5,000 options were forfeited.

The market price of Company A stock at December 31, 2006 is $42, and the average stock price during 2006 was $36. Net income for 2006 (before recognition of compensation expense related to the option grant) was $2,700,000. Weighted average common shares outstanding are 1,500,000 at December 31, 2006.

Calculation of primary earnings per share for the year ended December 31, 2006:

	FASB STATEMENT No. 123	APB OPINION No. 25
Assumed proceeds from exercise of options	$2,550,000	$2,850,000
Average unrecognized compensation cost related to future services	637,500 [1]	0
Tax benefits credited to equity on assumed exercise based on average market price less weighted average exercise price[2]	0	228,000
Total assumed proceeds	$3,187,500	$3,078,000
Shares assumed issued upon exercise of options	85,000	95,000
Shares repurchased at average market price	88,542	85,500
Incremental shares	(3,542)*	9,500
Net income before stock-based compensation expense	$2,700,000	$2,700,000
Stock-based compensation expense, net of income taxes	(153,000)[3]	0
Net income	$2,547,000	$2,700,000
Weighted average shares outstanding	1,500,000	1,500,000
Incremental shares	0 *	9,500
Total weighted average shares outstanding	1,500,000	1,509,500
Primary earnings per share	$ 1.70	$ 1.79

*Impact on earnings per share is anti-dilutive; therefore, options are excluded from weighted average shares outstanding.

Calculations:

[1] ($765,000 + $510,000) ÷ 2 = $637,500.

[2] Under FASB Statement No. 123, the tax deduction based upon average market price ($6 per option) is less than the cost recognized for financial statement purposes ($9 per option); therefore, there is no tax benefit upon exercise that would be credited to paid-in capital. Under current practice (APB Opinion No. 25) the tax deduction of $6 for each of the 95,000 remaining options at a tax rate of 40% would result in a tax benefit of $228,000.

[3] ($765,000 ÷ 3) × .60 = $153,000.

Exhibit 33.14.   Earnings per share under FASB Statement No. 123 and APB Opinion No. 25.

33.7 DISCLOSURES FOR YEARS BEGINNING AFTER DECEMBER 15, 1995

(a) DISCLOSURE REQUIREMENTS FOR ALL COMPANIES.   FASB Statement No. 123 supersedes the disclosure requirements under APB Opinion No. 25 and requires disclosure of the following information by employers with one or more stock-based compensation plans regardless of whether a company has elected the recognition provisions or retained accounting under APB Opinion No. 25:

1. A description of the method used to account for all stock-based employee compensation arrangements should be included in the company's summary of significant accounting policies.

2. A description of the plans, including the general terms of the awards under the plans such as vesting requirements, the maximum term of options granted, and the number of shares authorized for grants of options or other equity instruments.

3. The following information should be disclosed for each year for which an income statement is presented:

   a. The number and weighted-average exercise prices of options for each of the following groups of options: (1) those outstanding at the beginning and end of the year, (2) those exercisable at the end of the year, and (3) the number of options granted, exercised, forfeited, or expired during the year.

   b. The weighted-average grant-date fair values of options granted during the year. If the exercise prices of some options differ from the market price of the stock on the grant date, weighted-average exercise prices and fair values of options would be disclosed separately for options whose exercise price (1) equals, (2) exceeds, or (3) is less than the market price of the stock on the date of grant.

   c. The number and weighted-average grant-date fair value of equity instruments other than options (e.g., shares of nonvested stock) granted during the year.

   d. A description of the method and significant assumptions used to estimate the fair values of options, including the weighted-average (1) risk-free interest rate, (2) expected life, (3) expected volatility, and (4) expected dividend yield.

   e. Total compensation cost recognized in income for stock-based compensation awards.

   f. The terms of significant modifications to outstanding awards.

   A company that has both fixed and indexed or performance-based plans should provide certain of the foregoing information separately for different types of plans. For example, the weighted-average exercise price at the end of the year would be shown separately for plans with a fixed exercise price and those with an indexed exercise price.

4. For options outstanding at the date of the latest balance sheet presented, disclosure of the range of exercise prices, the weighted-average exercise price and the weighted-average remaining contractual life. If the range of exercise prices is wide (for example, the highest exercise price exceeds 150% of the lowest exercise price), the exercise prices should be segregated into meaningful ranges. The following information should be disclosed for each range:

   a. The number, weighted-average exercise price, and weighted-average remaining contractual life of options outstanding, and

   b. The number and weighted-average exercise price of options currently exercisable.

FASB Statement No. 123 provides an extensive example disclosure.

(b) DISCLOSURES BY COMPANIES THAT CONTINUE TO APPLY THE PROVISIONS OF APB OPINION NO. 25.   In addition to the disclosures described above, companies who continue to apply the provisions of APB Opinion No. 25, must disclose the following for each year an income statement is presented:

- The pro forma net income and, for public entities, the pro forma earnings per share, as if the fair value based accounting method prescribed by FASB Statement No. 123 had been used to account for stock-based compensation cost.

- Those pro forma amounts should reflect the difference between compensation cost, if any, included in net income in accordance with APB Opinion No. 25 and the related cost measured by the fair value based method, as well as additional tax effects, if any, that would have been recognized in the income statement if the fair value based method had been used.

- The required pro forma amounts should reflect no other adjustments to reported net income or earnings per share.

FASB Statement No. 123 provides an extensive example disclosure.

33.8 SOURCES AND SUGGESTED REFERENCES

Accounting Principles Board, "Earnings per Share," APB Opinion No. 15, AICPA, New York, 1969.

————, "Accounting for Stock Issued to Employees," APB Opinion No. 25, AICPA, New York, 1972.

————, "Stock Plans Established by a Principle Stockholder," Accounting for Stock Issued to Employees: Interpretation of APB Opinion No. 25, AICPA, New York, 1973.

Financial Accounting Standards Board, "Purchase of Stock Options and Stock Appreciation Rights in a Leveraged Buyout," EITF Issue No. 84-13, FASB, Stamford, CT, 1984.

————, "Stock Option Pyramiding," EITF Issue No. 84-18, FASB, Stamford, CT, 1984.

————, "Permanent Discount Restricted Stock Purchase Plans," EITF Issue No. 84-34, FASB, Stamford, CT, 1984.

————, "Business Combinations: Settlement of Stock Options and Awards," EITF Issue No. 85-45, FASB, Stamford, CT, 1985.

————, "Adjustments Relating to Stock Compensation Plans," EITF Issue No. 87-6, FASB, Stamford, CT, 1987.

————, "Book Value Stock Purchase Plans," EITF Issue No. 87-23, FASB, Stamford, CT, 1987.

————, "Stock Compensation Issues Related to Market Decline," EITF Issue No. 87-33, FASB, Stamford, CT, 1987.

————, "Book Value Stock Plans in an Initial Public Offering," EITF Issue No. 88-6, FASB, Norwalk, CT, 1988.

————, "Accounting for a Reload Stock Option," EITF Issue No. 90-7, FASB, Norwalk, CT, 1990.

————, "Changes to Fixed Employee Stock Option Plans as a Result of Equity Restructuring," EITF Issue No. 90-9, FASB, Norwalk, CT, 1990.

————, "Accounting for the Buyout of Compensatory Stock Options," EITF Issue No. 94-6, FASB, Norwalk, CT, 1994.

————, "Accounting for Stock Compensation Arrangements with Employer Loan Features under APB Opinion No. 25," EITF Issue No. 95-16, FASB, Norwalk, CT, 1995.

————, "Accounting for Stock Appreciation Rights and Other Variable Stock Option or Award Plans," FASB Interpretation No. 28, FASB, Stamford, CT, 1978.

————, "Treatment of Stock Compensation Plans in EPS Computations," FASB Interpretation No. 31, FASB, Stamford, CT, 1980.

————, "Determining the Measurement Date for Stock Option, Purchase, and Award Plans Involving Junior Stock," FASB Interpretation No. 38, FASB, Stamford, CT, 1984.

————, "Accounting for the Conversion of Stock Options into Incentive Stock Options as a Result of the Economic Recovery Tax Act of 1981," FASB Technical Bulletin No. 82-2, FASB, Stamford, CT, 1982.

————, "Suspension of the Reporting of Earnings per Share and Segment Information by Nonpublic Enterprises," Statement of Financial Accounting Standards No. 21, FASB, Stamford, CT, 1978.

————, "Accounting for Income Taxes," Statement of Financial Accounting Standards No. 109, FASB, Norwalk, CT, 1992.

————, "Accounting for Stock-Based Compensation," Statement of Financial Accounting Standards No. 123, FASB, Norwalk, CT, 1995.

Securities and Exchange Commission, "Codification of Financial Reporting Policies," Financial Reporting Release No. 1, § 211 (ASR No. 268), SEC, Washington, DC, 1982.

CHAPTER 34

PROSPECTIVE FINANCIAL STATEMENTS

Don M. Pallais, CPA

CONTENTS

34.1 TYPES OF PROSPECTIVE FINANCIAL STATEMENTS

(a) DEFINITIONS. **Prospective financial information** is future-oriented; that is, financial information about the future. **Prospective financial statements** are future-oriented presentations that present, at a minimum, certain specific financial information.

The AICPA *Guide for Prospective Financial Information* (1993) defines prospective financial statements as presentations of an entity's financial position, results of operations, and cash flows for the future. In addition to the AICPA Guide, there is also a Statement on Standards for Attestation Engagements, "Financial Forecasts and Projections" (AT 200), which establishes standards for accountants' services. Since all the guidance in that statement is duplicated in the AICPA Guide, this chapter refers only to the Guide.

Entity means an individual, organization, enterprise, or other unit for which financial statements could be prepared in conformity with GAAP. It is not necessary for the entity to have been formed at the time the prospective financial statements are prepared—prospective financial statements may be prepared for entities that may be formed in the future. In fact, before committing capital to proposed entities, prospective investors or lenders often insist on seeing prospective financial statements covering the early years of proposed operations.

Although the AICPA Guide defines prospective financial statements as presentations of future financial position, results of operations, and cash flows, three full financial statements are not always required. Prospective financial statements may be presented in summarized or condensed form. A presentation of future financial data would be considered to be a prospective financial statement if it disclosed at least the following items, to the extent they apply to the entity and would be presented in the entity's historical financial statements for the period covered:

1. Sales or gross revenue.
2. Gross profit or cost of sales.
3. Unusual or infrequently occurring items.
4. Provision for income taxes.
5. Discontinued operations or extraordinary items.
6. Income from continuing operations.

7. Net income.

8. Primary and fully diluted earnings per share (required only when disclosure is also required for the entity's historical financial statements).

9. Significant changes in financial position (that is, significant balance sheet changes not otherwise disclosed in the presentation).

The definition of prospective financial statements does not specify the **length** of the future period. For a presentation to be prospective, however, **some** of the period covered must be in the future even though a part of the period may have expired. Thus, a calendar 19X1 presentation done on December 30, 19X1, would still, in theory, be a prospective presentation since there would still be an unexpired day in the period. Determining the period to be covered by prospective financial statements is discussed in more detail in subsection 34.3(c)(ii).

There are two kinds of prospective financial statements: financial forecasts and financial projections. In practice, though, prospective financial statements are often given other names, such as "budgets," "business plans," and "studies."

Although the terms **forecast** and **projections** are sometimes used interchangeably in popular usage, in the technical accounting literature, forecasts and projections differ in what they purport to represent. Forecasts represent expectations, whereas projections are hypothetical analyses.

(i) Financial Forecasts. Financial forecasts are defined as prospective financial statements that present, to the best of management's knowledge and belief, an entity's expected financial position, results of operations, and cash flows based on management's assumptions reflecting conditions it expects to exist and the course of action it expects to take. In some cases forecasts can be prepared by persons other than current management, such as a potential acquirer of the entity, but usually the person (or persons) who takes responsibility for the assumptions is someone who expects to be in a position to influence the entity's operations during the forecast period. The AICPA Guide refers to the person who takes responsibility for the assumptions as the **responsible party.**

Despite the inherent uncertainty of future events and the softness of prospective data, a forecast cannot be prepared without a **reasonably objective basis.** That is, sufficiently objective assumptions must be capable of being developed to present a forecast. Without a reasonably objective basis, management has no grounds for any expectations; all it would have is guesses.

The determination of whether a reasonably objective basis for a forecast exists is primarily an exercise in judgment. The key question is whether assumptions, based on the entity's plans, made by persons who are informed about the industry in which the entity operates would generally fall within a relatively narrow range. If so, there may be a reasonably objective basis for the forecast. On the other hand, if there is so much uncertainty regarding significant assumptions that consensus would be unlikely to be reached, there may not be a reasonably objective basis, precluding preparation of a forecast (although a projection could be developed). For example, there would be no reasonably objective basis to forecast the winnings of a thoroughbred being reared to race.

If prospective financial data are necessary, but no reasonably objective basis exists to present a forecast, management might hypothesize the assumption that is not subject to reasonable estimation and call the presentation a **projection** or quantify only those assumptions that have a reasonably objective basis and prepare a **partial presentation.** However, both of these alternatives are limited in their usefulness (see subsections 34.2(a)–(d) for a further discussion).

Exhibit 34.1 presents factors to consider in determining whether there is a reasonably objective basis to present a forecast.

Occasionally, an entity may need to present a forecast but cannot do so because of an uncertainty about the **actions** the **users** of the forecast may take. For example, an assumption may relate to passage of a referendum when the forecast is to be used by voters deciding on the

SUFFICIENTLY OBJECTIVE ASSUMPTIONS—MATTERS TO CONSIDER

Basis	Less Objective	More Objective
Economy	Subject to uncertainty	Relatively stable
Industry	Emerging or unstable—high rate of business failure	Mature or relatively stable
Entity		
• Operating history	Little or no operating history	Seasoned company; relatively stable operating history
• Customer base	Diverse, changing customer group	Relatively stable customer group
• Financial condition	Weak financial position; Poor operating results	Strong financial position; Good operating results
Management's Experience With:		
• Industry	Inexperienced management	Experienced management
• The business and its products	Inexperienced management; high turnover of key personnel	Experienced management
Products or Services		
• Market	New or uncertain market	Existing or relatively stable market
• Technology	Rapidly changing technology	Relatively stable technology
• Experience	New products or expanding product line	Relatively stable products
Competing Assumptions	Wide range of possible outcomes	Relatively narrow range of possible outcomes
Dependency of Assumptions on the Outcome of Forecasted Results	More dependency	Less dependency

Exhibit 34.1.   Determining a reasonably objective basis. *Source: Guide for Prospective Financial Information,* (§ 7.05).

referendum. In those cases, despite the high level of uncertainty, management may select one of the alternatives as its assumption and then call the presentation a forecast if:

1. The assumption is subject to only two possible outcomes (an either/or situation).
2. The outcome of that assumption is dependent on the actions of the users of the presentation.
3. The alternative selected is not unreasonable on its face.
4. The presentation discloses that the forecast represents management's expectations only if the prospective action of users takes place.

Regardless of the need for a reasonably objective basis and management's efforts to present its expectations, a forecast is not a **prediction.** A forecast is not judged on whether, in hindsight, it came true. A forecast is a presentation intended to provide financial information regarding management's plans and expectations for the future. It augments information in historical financial statements and other sources of data to help prospective investors, lenders, or others make better financial decisions.

(ii) Financial Projections. Financial projections present, to the best of management's knowledge and belief, an entity's future financial position, results of operations, and cash flows given the occurrence of one or more **hypothetical assumptions.** Financial projections are sometimes prepared to analyze alternative courses of action, as in response to a question such as "What would happen if . . . ?"

The hypothetical assumptions in a projection are those that are not necessarily expected to occur but are consistent with the reason the projection was prepared. There is no explicit limit on the number of hypothetical assumptions used in a projection. However, since a projection is a presentation of expectations based on the occurrence of the hypothetical assumptions; a presentation in which all significant assumptions have been hypothesized would not be a projection because it depicts no dependent expectations. Thus, at some point the number of hypothetical assumptions may grow so large that the presentation is not a projection.

Hypothetical assumptions need not be reasonable or plausible; in fact, they may even be improbable if their use is consistent with the reason the projection is prepared. For example, it is generally improbable that a hotel would experience 100% occupancy. But use of that occupancy rate as a hypothetical assumption would be appropriate if the projection were prepared to demonstrate the maximum return on investment of a hotel. However, there are special disclosure rules when hypothetical assumptions are improbable (see subsection 34.4(c)(ii)).

All the nonhypothetical assumptions in a projection are expected to occur **if the hypothetical assumption occurred,** which may be different from expecting the nonhypothetical assumption actually to occur. For example, a company may hypothesize adding a new product line and intend to use the resulting projection in deciding whether to do so. As a result of the assumption about a new product line, the projection might include assumptions about hiring new sales personnel. Management may not actually expect to hire new sales personnel, but it would hire them if it started a new product line; thus the assumption is not actually expected, but it is expected given the occurrence of the hypothetical assumption.

(b) OTHER PRESENTATIONS THAT LOOK LIKE PROSPECTIVE FINANCIAL STATEMENTS. A number of presentations look like prospective financial statements but are not, including **presentations for wholly expired periods, partial presentations, pro forma financial statements,** and **financial analyses.**

(i) Presentations for Wholly Expired Periods. Prospective financial statements are presentations for a future period. If the period covered by a presentation is wholly expired, such as a prior-year budget, it is not a prospective financial statement.

(ii) Partial Presentations. Partial presentations are presentations of prospective financial information that omit one or more minimum items required of prospective financial statements (see subsection 34.1(a)). They are not subject to the same rules as prospective financial statements.

(iii) Pro Formas. Pro forma financial statements are historical financial statements adjusted for a prospective transaction. Although one transaction has not occurred at the time of presentation, the statements are essentially historical ones. In essence, such statements answer the question "What would have happened if . . . ?" Guidance for accountants' reports on pro forma presentations can be found in the SSAE "Reporting on Pro Forma Financial Information" (AT 300).

(iv) Financial Analyses. Financial analyses are defined in the AICPA Guide as presentations in which the independent accountant rather than management develops and takes responsibility for the assumptions. Such presentations are normally a by-product of a consulting engagement in which management asks the accountant to analyze a condition and make recommendations about possible or prudent courses of action.

These analyses are not prospective financial statements because the party who takes responsibility for the assumptions (the accountant) is not, and does not expect to be, in a position to influence the entity's operations in the future period. If, however, management adopts the assumptions used, it may present the statements as a forecast or projection.

34.2 LIMITATIONS ON THE USE OF PROSPECTIVE FINANCIAL STATEMENTS

(a) HOW PROSPECTIVE FINANCIAL STATEMENTS ARE USED.   The use of prospective financial statements is neither required nor recommended by AICPA literature. Nonetheless, they are used for many purposes in practice. For example, they are used by management in internal planning, by potential suppliers of capital in making investment decisions, and by government agencies for monitoring or approving an entity's operations.

The AICPA Guide (Chapter 4) categorizes all the potential uses of prospective financial statements into two broad classes: **general use,** which refers to passive users, and **limited use,** which refers to use by management only or use by persons who are negotiating directly with management.

The AICPA Guide states that forecasts are appropriate for either general or limited use; projections are generally appropriate only for limited use.

Unlike SEC registration rules, the type of use is not dependent on the **number** of users of the prospective financial statements. A user is considered a limited user if it is negotiating directly with the entity; if it is not, it is a general user. Thus, even one passive user would constitute general use; whereas an entity may negotiate directly with numerous users, each of whom can change the terms of the transaction, and each would be considered a limited user.

(b) GENERAL USE.   General use means use of the prospective financial statements by persons who are **not** negotiating directly with management. General users are passive users; that is, they can review the prospective financial statements to determine their own course of action, but they cannot affect the company's actions or the terms of their investment. For example, after reviewing an entity's prospective financial statements, a potential investor in a limited partnership can decide whether to invest in it and if so, how much to invest, but he cannot change the terms of the investment; thus he would be considered a general user. If he can change the terms of the investment, he would be considered a limited user.

Because general users cannot negotiate the terms of their involvement with the entity, their information needs are much like those of shareholders in a public company. To make informed decisions, general users would ordinarily be served best by a presentation of management's estimate of future financial results—a forecast.

A presentation of results based on a hypothetical assumption that does not reflect management's expectations (that is, a projection) would not serve general users because such a presentation would only tell them what is **not** necessarily expected to happen, not what is. This would be analogous to providing shareholders with pro forma financial statements including transactions that did not occur instead of with historical financial statements.

Accordingly, financial projections are not ordinarily issued to general users unless the projections supplement a forecast **for the period covered by the forecast.** Thus, general users may benefit from an analysis of a hypothetical course of action when it supplements a presentation of management's expectations for that period, but not when it stands alone as the only presentation of prospective results for a period.

That forecasts are appropriate for general use, of course, does not suggest that they will meet all the users' information needs. Potential investors or lenders often need to consider other information as well before making economic decisions, just as they do when presented with historical financial statements.

(c) LIMITED USE.   Limited use of prospective financial statements means use by the entity itself or use by persons with whom the entity is negotiating directly. **Negotiating** is an active concept. It includes more than the user's ability to ask questions of the entity; it refers to the user's ability to affect the terms of its business with the entity beyond merely deciding whether to participate and the amount of its participation.

There is no limit on the potential number of limited users in a particular circumstance except for the limit of the number of parties that management can practically negotiate with at any one time. It is also unnecessary to specifically identify the limited users at the time the prospective financial statements are prepared.

Because limited users can negotiate the terms of their involvement and challenge or propose changes to the hypothetical assumptions, they can use presentations that don't present management's best estimates. Accordingly, projections are often useful for limited users.

Similarly, because limited users can demand additional information as a condition of their participation (or, when there is a lack of needed information, increase the cost of capital in response to a perceived increase in risk), it may also be appropriate for limited users to use **partial presentations** or **financial analyses.**

Of course, financial forecasts are appropriate for limited users as well as general users.

(d) INTERNAL USE.   Internal use means use of the prospective financial statements only by the entity itself. It is a type of limited use. Limitation of the prospective financial statements to internal use does not affect the type of statements that are appropriate in the circumstances, but it affects the type of services that an independent accountant can perform on them. This is discussed in more detail in subsection 34.9(a).

34.3 DEVELOPING PROSPECTIVE FINANCIAL STATEMENTS

(a) GENERAL GUIDELINES.   Chapter 6 of the AICPA Guide presents 11 guidelines for **preparation of prospective financial statements.** Although forecasts and projections can be developed without adhering to those guidelines, using them often results in more reliable prospective data.

The AICPA guidelines are listed in Exhibit 34.2. They apply to projections as well as forecasts, though in many cases they do not apply to the **hypothetical assumptions** in projections.

A general approach to developing prospective financial statements involves three steps:

1. Identifying key factors.

2. Developing assumptions for each key factor.

3. Assembling the prospective financial statements.

(b) IDENTIFYING KEY FACTORS.   The AICPA Guide (§ 6.28) states: "Key factors are those significant matters upon which an entity's future results are expected to depend. Those factors are basic to the entity's operations and serve as a foundation for the prospective financial statements."

Key factors vary by entity and industry. They are general matters such as manufacturing labor, sales, or capital asset needs. A knowledge of the entity's industry and proposed operations is necessary to identify all the key factors that will form the basis for the prospective financial statements.

(c) DEVELOPING ASSUMPTIONS.   Assumptions are developed for each key factor. In a **forecast,** the assumptions represent management's best estimate of future conditions and

Financial forecasts should be prepared in good faith.

Financial forecasts should be prepared with appropriate care by qualified personnel.

Financial forecasts should be prepared using appropriate accounting principles.

The process used to develop financial forecasts should provide for seeking out the best information that is reasonably available at the time.

The information used in preparing financial forecasts should be consistent with the plans of the entity.

Key factors should be identified as a basis for assumptions.

Assumptions used in preparing financial forecasts should be appropriate.

The process used to develop financial forecasts should provide the means to determine the relative effect of variations in the major underlying assumptions.

The process used to develop financial forecasts should provide adequate documentation of both the financial forecasts and the process used to develop them.

The process used to develop financial forecasts should include, where appropriate, the regular comparison of the financial forecasts with attained results.

The process used to prepare financial forecasts should include adequate review and approval by the responsible party at the appropriate levels of authority.

Exhibit 34.2.   Guidelines for preparation of prospective financial statements. *Source:* **AICPA,** *Guide for Prospective Financial Information* (§ 6.08).

courses of action. In a **projection,** the hypothetical assumptions are consistent with the purpose of the projection, and all the other assumptions represent management's best estimate of future conditions and courses of action **given the occurrence of the hypothetical assumptions.**

Approaches to developing assumptions range from highly sophisticated mathematical models to estimates based on personal opinion. Regardless of the approach taken to quantify the assumptions, to determine whether the assumptions are appropriate, management considers whether:

1. There appears to be a rational relationship between the assumptions and the underlying facts and circumstances.
2. Assumptions have been developed for each key factor.
3. Assumptions have been developed without undue optimism or pessimism.
4. Assumptions are consistent with the entity's plans and expectations.
5. Assumptions are consistent with each other.
6. Individual assumptions make sense in the context of the prospective financial statements taken as a whole.

It is not always necessary to obtain support for each significant assumption, but developing support often results in more reliable prospective financial information. In any case, the significant considerations in developing a forecast are (1) whether management has a reasonably objective basis (see subsection 34.1(a)(i)) to base its expectations on and (2) whether the assumptions are consistent with its expectations.

(i) Mathematical Models.   Forecasts may be based on sophisticated mathematical techniques such as regression analysis. However, merely extrapolating historical results into the future does not result in a forecast. To forecast, management satisfies itself that it has identified the conditions and course of action it intends to take in the future period. If, based on consideration of key factors, management believes that historical conditions are indicative of future results, it then might use an estimation technique based on historical results.

(ii) Length of the Prospective Period.   The AICPA Guide states that length of time to be covered by prospective financial statements, should be based on the needs of the user and management's ability to estimate future financial results.

In establishing a **minimum length** the AICPA Guide (§ 8.33) states that to be meaningful to users, a forecast or projection should include at least one full year of normal operations. For example, an entity forecasting a major acquisition would present at least the first full year following the acquisition; a newly formed entity would show at least the first full year of normal operations in addition to its start-up period.

When the entity has a long operating cycle or when long-term results are necessary to evaluate the investment consequences involved, it may be necessary to forecast farther into the future to meet the needs of users.

Uncertainty increases as to periods farther in the future. At some point, the underlying assumptions become so subjective that no reasonably objective basis exists to present a forecast.

The AICPA Guide (§ 8.33) limits the **maximum length** of the forecast period to three to five years. It states that ordinarily it would be difficult to establish that a reasonably objective basis for a forecast exists for a longer period. However, the Guide recognizes that, in some cases, forecasts can be presented for longer periods, such as when long-term contracts exist that specify the timing and the amount of revenue and costs can be controlled within reasonable limits (as in the case of real estate projects with long-term leases). It also recognizes that in some cases it may be hard to justify even a 3-year forecast, such as for certain start-up or high technology companies.

The **SEC rules** are generally more restrictive than the AICPA's. For prospective financial statements included in SEC filings, the SEC has stated that "[F]or certain companies in certain industries a [forecast] covering a two or three year period may be entirely reasonable. Other companies may not have a reasonable basis for [forecasts] beyond the current year" (Reg. 229.10(b)(2)).

In determining how far into the future it can forecast, management considers the key factors and resulting assumptions for each future period presented. Considering them in detail for, say, 1 year and merely extrapolating the results for an additional 2 years beyond that does not result in a 3-year forecast, but in a 1-year forecast and a 2-year projection.

(d) ASSEMBLING THE PROSPECTIVE FINANCIAL STATEMENTS.   Assembling the prospective financial statements involves converting the assumptions into prospective amounts and presenting the amounts and assumptions in conformity with AICPA presentation guidelines. Those guidelines are discussed in more detail in the following sections.

34.4 PRESENTATION AND DISCLOSURE OF PROSPECTIVE FINANCIAL STATEMENTS

(a) AUTHORITATIVE GUIDANCE.   The primary source of guidance for presentation and disclosure of financial forecasts and projections is Chapter 8 of the AICPA Guide. In the absence of FASB pronouncements, the Guide establishes the equivalent of GAAP for prospective financial statements.

Although the Guide establishes guidelines for presentation and disclosure, it does not require or recommend the presentation of prospective financial statements in any circumstance. The decision to present prospective financial statements is generally management's, based on its need and desires and those of potential financial statement users.

Other bodies have also established rules concerning presentation and disclosure of forecasts and projections. For example, the SEC, the North American Security Administrators Association, and individual state securities commissions have established rules that are applicable in certain situations. Issuers of prospective financial statements used in offering statements should be aware of those rules as well, but it is beyond the scope of this chapter to discuss all of them.

Occasionally, potential users of prospective financial statements also require a specific form or content for the statements. For example, users may specify the level of detail presented or the period covered, or they may require the completion of prescribed forms. Issuers of prospective financial statements should consider how those requirements compare with those in the AICPA Guide and whether compliance with the user's requirements may cause difficulties in obtaining an independent accountant's services on the statements.

(b) FORM OF PROSPECTIVE FINANCIAL STATEMENTS. Unlike historical financial statements, the **form** of prospective financial statements is flexible. Flexibility is permitted to present the most useful information in the circumstances.

Presenting prospective financial statements in the same form as the historical financial statements expected to be issued at the end of the prospective period facilitates later comparison. Accordingly, if later comparison is expected, an entity may issue a prospective balance sheet, income statement, and statement of cash flows.

If no later comparison is intended, or if more aggregated data are desired, the prospective financial statements may be presented in a summarized or condensed format. The amount of condensation or summarization is flexible as long as the following minimum items, to the extent they are applicable and would be presented in the historical financial statements, are either presented or otherwise derivable from the presentation:

1. Sales or gross revenue.
2. Gross profit or cost of sales.
3. Unusual or infrequently occurring items.
4. Provision for income taxes.
5. Discontinued operations or extraordinary items.
6. Income from continuing operations.
7. Net income.
8. Primary and fully diluted earnings per share.
9. Significant changes in financial position.

A summarized presentation should disclose significant cash flows and other significant changes in balance sheet accounts for the prospective period. The specific items to be presented depend on the circumstances, but often include cash flows from operations.

Exhibit 34.3 illustrates a condensed format for a financial forecast.

(i) Amounts Presented.   The prospective financial statements may be presented in terms of single-point estimates or ranges.

Ranges are sometimes presented when management wants to present a forecast but cannot refine its estimate of expected results sharply enough to present a single point as its best estimate. If the prospective financial statements are presented in terms of ranges, the range is not selected in a biased manner. That is, one end of the range is not significantly more likely than the other. In addition, the range is not characterized as representing the best and worst cases, since actual results might fall outside of the range.

Any of the following formats for a forecast might be acceptable.

Single-point estimate:

Sales	$XXX
Cost of sales	XXX

Range (from X to Z) showing an intermediate point (Y):

	X	Y	Z
Sales	$XXX	$YYY	$ZZZ
Cost of sales	XXX	YYY	ZZZ

Range showing a one line item only; example assumes the range is based on a forecasted range of sales prices and demand is inelastic:

Sales	$XXX—$YYY
Cost of sales	$XXX

(ii) Titles. The **titles** of financial forecasts should include the word "forecast" or "forecasted." Financial projections' titles should refer to the hypothetical assumptions. Titles such as "budget" are avoided since they offer no indication whether the presentation is a forecast or a projection.

XYZ COMPANY, INC.

Summarized Financial Forecast
Year Ending December 31, 19X3
(in thousands except per-share amounts)

		Comparative Historical Information*	
	Forecasted 19X3	**19X2**	**19X1**
Sales	$101,200	$91,449	$79,871
Gross profit	23,700	21,309	19,408
Income tax expense	3,400	3,267	2,929
Net income	4,500	3,949	3,214
Earnings per share	4.73	4.14	3.37
Significant anticipated changes in financial position:			
Cash provided by operations	4,100	3,103	4,426
Net increase (decrease) in long-term borrowings	3,400	300	(300)
Dividend			
(per share 19X3: $1.50; 19X2: $1.35; 19X1: $1.00)	1,400	1,288	954
Additions to plant and equipment	4,400	2,907	2,114
Increase (decrease) in cash	1,400	(334)	1,017

See accompanying Summary of Significant Forecast Assumptions and Accounting Policies [not illustrated in exhibit].

*Comparative historical information is not part of the minimum presentation.

Exhibit 34.3. Illustration of condensed format for prospective financial statements. *Source:*

(c) DISCLOSURES.   In addition to the items listed at the beginning of subsection 34.4(b), the AICPA Guide requires that the following matters be **disclosed** in prospective financial statements:

1. Description of what the presentation intends to depict.
2. Summary of significant assumptions.
3. Summary of significant accounting policies.

Each page of the prospective financial statements should direct the readers' attention to the summaries of significant assumptions and accounting policies. A legend such as "The accompanying summaries of significant assumptions and accounting policies are an integral part of the financial forecast" or "See accompanying summaries of significant assumptions and accounting policies" is generally used.

(i) Description of the Presentation.   The prospective financial statements should include a description of what management intends the statements to present, a statement that the assumptions are based on management's judgment at the time the prospective information was prepared, and a caveat that the prospective results may not be achieved.

The description is usually presented as the introduction to the summary of significant assumptions.

The **introduction** to the assumptions for a financial forecast would disclose the necessary information as follows:

> This financial forecast presents, to the best of management's knowledge and belief, the Company's expected financial position, results of operations, and cash flows* for the forecast period. Accordingly, the forecast reflects its judgment, as of [date], the date of this forecast, of the expected conditions and its expected course of action. The assumptions disclosed herein are those that management believes are significant to the forecast. There will usually be differences between the forecasted and actual results, because events and circumstances frequently do not occur as expected, and those differences may be material.

---

* If the presentation is summarized or condensed, this might read ". . . summary of the Company's expected results of operations and changes in financial position . . . ."

The introduction to the summary of significant assumptions for a financial projection would be similar to that for a forecast except that it would clearly explain the **special purpose** and **limitations** on the usefulness of the presentation. Such an introduction might read as follows:

> This financial projection is based on sales volume at maximum productive capacity and presents, to the best of management's knowledge and belief, the Company's expected financial position, results of operations, and cash flows* for the projection period if such volume were attained. Accordingly, the projection reflects its judgment, as of [date], the date of this projection, of the expected conditions and its expected course of action if such sales volume were experienced. The presentation is designed to provide information to the Company's board of directors concerning the maximum profitability that might be achieved if current production were expanded through the addition of a third production shift and should not be considered to be a presentation of expected future results. Accordingly, this projection may not be useful for other purposes. The assumptions disclosed herein are those that management believes are significant to the projection. Management considers it highly unlikely that the stated sales volume will be experienced during the projection period. Further, even if the stated sales volume were attained, there will usually be differences between the projected

and actual results, because events and circumstances frequently do not occur as expected, and those differences may be material.

---

* If the presentation is summarized or condensed, this might read ". . . summary of the Company's expected results of operations and changes in financial position . . . ."

If the presentation is shown as a range, the introduction also makes it clear that presentation is shown as a range, that the range represents managements' expectations, and that there is no assurance that actual results will fall within the range. A sample introduction follows:

> This financial forecast presents, to the best of management's knowledge and belief, the Company's expected financial position, results of operations, and cash flows for the forecast period at occupancy rates of 75% and 95% of available apartments. Accordingly, the forecast reflects its judgment, as of [date], the date of this forecast, of the expected conditions and its expected course of action at each occupancy rate. The assumptions disclosed herein are those that management believes are significant to the forecast. Management reasonably expects, to the best of its knowledge and belief, that the actual occupancy rates achieved will be within the range shown; however, there can be no assurance that it will. Further, even if the actual occupancy rate is within the range shown, there will usually be differences between the forecasted and actual results, because events and circumstances frequently do not occur as expected, and those differences may be material, and the actual results may be outside the range presented by the forecast.

(ii) Significant Assumptions.   The assumptions form the basis for the prospective financial statements; for the statements to be meaningful to users, the assumptions should be disclosed.

Numerous assumptions are made in developing prospective financial statements. Only **significant assumptions** are required to be disclosed. Significance is generally considered to be measured in terms of the magnitude of an assumption's effect on the prospective financial statements.

Assumptions, however, may be considered significant even though they may not have a direct and large dollar effect on the statements. Those assumptions, which need to be disclosed as well, include:

1. Sensitive assumptions, that is, assumptions about which there is a reasonable possibility of the occurrence of a variation that may significantly affect the prospective results.
2. Significantly changed conditions, that is, assumptions about anticipated conditions that are expected to be significantly different from current conditions.
3. Hypothetical assumptions used in a projection.
4. Other matters deemed important to the statements or their interpretation.

The form and placement of assumptions is flexible and can be based on management's judgment in the circumstances. The guiding principle is that the disclosure is understandable by the persons expected to use the statements.

Disclosure of the basis or rationale underlying the assumptions assists users in understanding and making decisions based on prospective financial statements. Such disclosure is recommended, but not required, by the AICPA Guide.

The following examples show the form of disclosure of significant assumptions that might be appropriate in various circumstances.

As a footnote in a formal presentation:

2. *Sales.* Sales of the Company's product in 19X2 are expected to increase 20% over those experienced in 19X1 ($1,000,000).

As a footnote in a formal presentation, including basis and rationale:

2. *Sales.* Based on commitments received and its current expansion into the Midwest market, management expects unit sales to increase by 15% over the number of units sold in 19X1. In addition, the Company expects to increase sales prices by an average of 5% over the year to cover expected increases in raw material costs. Increasing sales prices is not expected to adversely affect units sold since raw material cost increases will affect the entire industry and management anticipates industry-wide price increases. (Disclosure might also include discussion of other product lines, marketing plans, and other related information.)

Informal, shown on the face of the statements:

Sales (units up 15% over 19X1, price up 5%) $1,200,000

Informal, shown as output of factors used in a computer spreadsheet:

Sales = 1.2* 19X1Sal

The appropriateness of each approach would depend on the expected use of the prospective financial statements. The formal presentation that includes the basis and rationale would be most useful for general users; the informal printout of factors from a spreadsheet might be appropriate, and least costly to prepare, for internal use.

The disclosure of significant assumptions should also indicate which assumptions are **hypothetical** and which are **particularly sensitive.**

The **hypothetical** assumptions used in a projection should be specifically identified. In addition, if any of the hypothetical assumptions are considered **improbable,** the disclosure should indicate that.

Particularly sensitive assumptions are those for which there is a relatively high probability of variation that would significantly affect the prospective financial statements. The presentation should indicate which assumptions appeared to be particularly sensitive at the time of preparation of the statements (even though hindsight might indicate that others actually were particularly sensitive).

The disclosure of sensitivity is flexible. Below are examples of disclosures that might be appropriate in the circumstances.

With sensitivity quantified:

9. *Interest Expense.* The forecast assumes that the debt to be placed will carry an interest rate of 10%; however, the rate will not be determined until closing. For each $\frac{1}{4}$ of 1% that the actual interest rate differs from the rate assumed, forecasted income before income taxes would be raised or lowered by $25,000 and after-tax cash flow would change by approximately $16,000. If the rate exceeds $11\frac{1}{4}$%, the forecast would not indicate sufficient cash flow from the new project to service the debt.

Without sensitivity quantification:

9. *Interest Expense.* The forecast assumes the debt to be placed will carry an interest rate of 10%. The actual rate will not be determined until closing and may be higher or lower. To the extent that the actual rate exceeds 10%, forecasted income would be adversely affected.

Informal, printout of factors in computer spreadsheet:

Int exp = 0.1*debt! part. sensitive

(iii) Significant Accounting Principles. The prospective financial statements should include disclosure of the **significant accounting principles** used in the statements. The basis of accounting and the accounting principles used in the prospective statements are generally those that are expected to be used during the prospective period. Thus, if the prospective statements accompany historical financial statements, this disclosure may be accomplished by referring the reader to the appropriate note in the historical statements.

If the basis of accounting used in the prospective statements is a **comprehensive basis of accounting other than GAAP,** the basis used should be disclosed as well as that it is different from GAAP.

If the basis of accounting used is different from that expected to be used in the historical financial statements for the prospective period (such as presenting cash-flow forecast for an entity that uses GAAP for its historical financial statements), the use of a different basis of accounting in the prospective statements should be disclosed. The differences in prospective results that are caused by the use of the different basis would usually be reconciled in the statements unless the reconciliation would not be useful.

If the accounting principles used differ from those expected to be used (such as in a projection that analyzes the effect of a possible change in accounting principles), the use of a different principle in the projection should be disclosed. The results in the projection may also be reconciled to those that would result from using the principle used in the historical financial statements.

If management expects to change an accounting principle during the prospective period, the change in principle should be reflected in the prospective financial statements the same way it would be in the historical financial statements covering the prospective period. Other specific disclosures required for historical financial statements, such as those regarding pensions and income taxes, are not required for prospective financial statements.

(iv) Other Matters. The **date** of preparation of the prospective financial statements should be disclosed. This disclosure provides information to users about how current the information underlying the statements is likely to be. The date is generally disclosed in the introduction to the summary of significant assumptions.

Occasionally, management recognizes that users need information for periods beyond its ability to forecast. For example, management may plan a refinancing of debt or the introduction of new products after the end of the forecast period. Or, management may expect expiration of a significant contract or future adverse tax consequences to investors.

If users are considered limited users, management may present projections or partial presentations for the more distant periods.

If, however, the users are general users, presentation of a projection outside of the forecast period would be considered inappropriate. The AICPA Guide (§ 8.40) provides guidance for disclosure of significant post-forecast period matters.

Such a disclosure should:

1. Include a title indicating that it presents information about periods beyond the financial forecast period.
2. Include an introduction indicating that the information presented does not constitute a financial forecast and indicating its purpose.
3. Disclose significant assumptions and identify those that are hypothetical, as well as the specific plans, events, or circumstances that are expected to have a material effect on results beyond the forecast period.
4. State that (a) the information is presented for analysis purposes only, (b) that there is no assurance that the events and circumstances described will occur, and, if applicable, (c) that the information is less reliable than the forecast.

The disclosures are part of the forecast presentation; they're generally in the summary of significant assumptions. The Guide prohibits presenting them comparative to the forecasted results on the face of the forecast, in related summaries of benefits (such as in a summary of investor benefits), or as a financial projection.

34.5 TYPES OF ACCOUNTANTS' SERVICES

(a) OBJECTIVES OF ACCOUNTANTS' SERVICES.   Companies generally retain independent accountants to provide services on prospective financial statements for either of two reasons: to add credibility to prospective statements expected to be used by third parties or to provide consultation or assistance in developing statements expected to be used primarily by the client. The AICPA performance and reporting standards recognize that the type of service that is appropriate in the circumstances may vary depending on the expected use.

The AICPA Guide provides three standard accountants' services for prospective financial statements expected to be used by third parties: **compilation, examination,** and application of **agreed-upon procedures.** (No review, or moderate-level assurance, service is permitted.) When third-party use is not reasonably expected, the accountant may provide the three standard services or other types of services and reports that more closely reflect the purpose of the engagement.

(b) STANDARD ACCOUNTANTS' SERVICES.   The accountant is required to either compile, examine, or apply agreed-upon procedures whenever:

1. The presentation includes prospective financial statements.
2. The statements are, or reasonably might be, expected to be used by a third party.
3. The accountant either (a) submits to his client or others statements that he has assembled or assisted in assembling or (b) reports on the statements.

There are three exceptions to this rule:

1. The accountant need not report on **drafts** of prospective financial statements submitted if they are clearly marked as such.
2. The accountant need not provide one of the standard services when the prospective financial statements are used solely in connection with engagements involving potential or pending litigation before a trier of fact in connection with the resolution of a dispute between two or more parties (often called **litigation support services**). In such circumstances the accountant's work is ordinarily subjected to detailed analysis and challenge by each party to the dispute. However, the exception does not apply when the prospective financial statements are used by third parties who do not have the opportunity for such analysis and challenge. For example, creditors may not have that opportunity when a financial forecast is submitted to them to secure their agreement to a plan of reorganization.
3. The accountant who submits interim historical financial statements in a document that also contains prospective financial statements need not provide one of the standard services on the prospective statements if the prospective statements are labeled "budget," they do not extend beyond the end of the current fiscal year, the accountant's report states that he did not apply any of the standard services to them, and the accountant's report disclaims an opinion or any other form of assurance on the statements.

(i) Prospective Financial Statements.   If the presentation doesn't meet the minimum disclosure requirement of prospective financial statements, (see subsection 34.1(a)), it is a

partial presentation rather than prospective financial statements. In that case, the accountant is not required to provide a standard service on the prospective data. Chapter 23 of the AICPA Guide contains guidelines for compilations, examinations, and application of agreed-upon procedures to partial presentations. It does not **require** those services on partial presentations, but provides guidance for the accountant who is engaged to provide them.

(ii) Third-Party Use.   Third parties generally are any persons outside the entity presenting the prospective financial statements. Sometimes, however, such persons may not need to be considered third parties for the purpose of determining whether the guidance on accountants' services applies.

The AICPA Guide (§ 10.02) provides the following guidelines for determining whether outsiders are considered third parties:

> In deciding whether a party that is or reasonably might be expected to use an accountant's report is considered to be a third party, the accountant should consider the degree of consistency of interest between [management] and the user regarding the forecast. If their interests are substantially consistent (for example both the [preparer] and the user are employees of the entity about which the forecast is made), the user would not be deemed to be a third party. On the other hand, where the interests of the [preparer] and user are potentially inconsistent (for example, the [preparer] is a nonowner manager and the user is an absentee owner), the user would be deemed a third party. In some cases, this determination will require the exercise of considerable professional judgment.

In considering whether the statements will be restricted to internal use, the accountant may generally rely on management's oral or written representations, unless something leads him to believe that, despite management's representations, the statements are likely to be distributed to a third party.

(iii) Assemble and Submit.   **Assembly** means the "manual or computer processing of mathematical or other clerical functions related to the presentation of the prospective financial statements." (AICPA Guide, § 3.16). This refers to converting the assumptions into prospective amounts or putting the amounts into the form of statements. Assembly does not mean merely copying or collating statements prepared by someone else.

(c) INTERNAL USE.   The accountant may provide compilation, examination, or agreed-upon procedures engagements for internal use if engaged to do so. However, for internal use, the accountant has more flexibility to accommodate the varying circumstances of the engagement. Normally, these engagements involve consulting or planning (such as in management-consulting or tax-planning services) rather than third-party reliance. Common reporting options for internal use include **assembly reports** and **plain paper** prospective financial statements. Internal-use services are discussed in more detail in subsection 34.9(a).

(d) PROHIBITED ENGAGEMENTS.   The AICPA Guide prohibits the accountant from submitting or reporting on prospective financial statements intended for third-party use if those statements omit the disclosure of significant assumptions. Similarly, the accountant is prohibited from submitting or reporting on a projection for third-party use if it does not identify the hypothetical assumption or describe the limitations on the usefulness of the presentation.

The accountant also may not submit or report on a financial projection that is intended for general use (unless it supplements a forecast for the same period) because such use is considered inappropriate (see subsection 34.2(b)). This prohibition means that the accountant could not assemble and submit such a presentation even if management agreed not to present the accountant's report or refer to him in the document containing the projection that would be presented to general users.

(e) MATERIALITY. Accountants consider **materiality** in conducting engagements on prospective financial statements much as they do for historical financial statements. The AICPA Guide (§ 10.31) states, however, "Materiality is a concept that is judged in light of the expected range of reasonableness of the information; therefore, users should not expect prospective information (information about events that have not yet occurred) to be as precise as historical information."

It follows, then, that materiality criteria would be higher for prospective statements than for the same company's historical statements. That is, an amount that would be material to the historical statements might not be material to the prospectives. There is no consensus in practice, however, as to just how much higher materiality should be for prospective financial statements.

(f) SEC PERSPECTIVE. Relevant SEC rules regarding accountants' services on prospective financial statements in filings subject to the SEC's authority include the Safe Harbor Rule for Projections and the Guides for Disclosure of Projections. These rules, however, add relatively little to the requirements for accountants' procedures and reports established by the AICPA Guide. The more significant SEC policies in this area are less formal ones. Two particularly significant positions taken by the SEC involve **compilation services** and **independence rules.**

(i) Compilations in SEC Filings. Although not stated in formal SEC rules, the Commission's staff has been reluctant to accept compilations of prospective financial statements. Thus, although that service is allowed under the AICPA literature for both public and nonpublic entities (unlike compilations of historical statements, which are only appropriate for nonpublic companies), they generally are not an option for filings subject to SEC authority.

(ii) Independence. SEC independence rules differ from those established by the AICPA. As a general rule, AICPA literature considers independence impaired when the accountant either has a direct financial interest in the client or when he is acting in the capacity of management or an employee. Thus, providing a service on prospective financial statements would not, in and of itself, affect the auditor's independence for the audit of its historical financial statements or any other service.

The SEC rules, however, are based on a different concept, which the SEC refers to as "mutuality of interest." The SEC considers that the accountant's assistance in preparing prospective financial statements creates a mutuality of interest in the prospective results. Thus, it has stated that, generally if the accountant actively participates in the preparation of the prospective data, he has lost the independence necessary to examine and report on that prospective data (see SEC Guides, 33-5992 and 34-15305).

In a letter to an accountant, the SEC staff pursued this reasoning even further, stating that active assistance in the preparation of a company's prospective financial statements would also affect the accountant's independence in regard to its **historical financial statements** for the length of the prospective period. This independence impairment would occur regardless of whether the prospective statements were forecasts or projections or whether they were issued to the public or restricted to internal use (see Letter from Chief Accountant to Amper, Politzner, and Mattia, April 14, 1987; CCH, 1990, ¶7986).

(g) IRS PERSPECTIVE. IRS Circular 230 applies to prospective financial statements included in tax shelter offerings. It states that an accountant who reports on prospective financial statements in such offerings must either provide a **tax shelter opinion** or rely on one issued by another professional, such as another accountant or a lawyer.

A tax shelter opinion under Circular 230 states whether, in the professional's opinion, it is more likely than not that an investor will prevail on the merits of each material tax issue that involves a reasonable possibility of challenge by the IRS and an overall evaluation of the extent to which the material tax benefits are likely to be realized in the aggregate.

34.6 COMPILATION SERVICES

(a) SCOPE OF THE COMPILATION SERVICE.   A **compilation** of prospective financial statements is similar to a compilation of historical financial statements performed subject to SSARS No. 1, "Compilation and Review of Financial Statements" (1978). It relies primarily on an informed reading of the statements with an eye for obvious problems, but it doesn't provide any assurance on the statements.

The AICPA Guide states that a compilation of prospective financial statements involves:

1. Assembling, to the extent necessary, the prospective financial statements based on management's assumptions.

2. Performing the required compilation procedures, including reading the prospective financial statements with their summaries of significant assumptions and accounting policies and considering whether they appear to be (a) presented in conformity with AICPA presentation guidelines and (b) not obviously inappropriate.

3. Issuing a compilation report.

(b) ASSEMBLY.   Assembly, which is defined in subsection 34.5(b)(iii), refers to performing the necessary mathematics to turn assumptions into prospective financial data and drafting prospective financial statements in the appropriate form. In some cases, such as when the client has a sophisticated financial reporting function and prepares its own statements, assembly may not be required in a compilation. Often, however, assembly assistance is one of the primary benefits the client receives from the accountant.

Assembly does not include identifying key factors or developing assumptions, although accountants often help clients in these areas in a compilation.

(c) COMPILATION PROCEDURES.   The compilation procedures required by AICPA standards are listed in Exhibit 34.4.

In performing a compilation of prospective financial statements the accountant should, where applicable—

a. Establish an understanding with the client, preferably in writing, regarding the services to be performed.

b. Inquire about the accounting principles used in the preparation of the prospective financial statements.
   - For existing entities, compare the accounting principles used to those used in the preparation of previous historical financial statements and inquire whether such principles are the same as those expected to be used in the historical financial statements covering the prospective period.
   - For entities to be formed or entities formed that have not commenced operations, compare specialized industry accounting principles used, if any, to those typically used in the industry. Inquire about whether the accounting principles used for the prospective financial statements are those that are expected to be used when, or if, the entity commences operations.

c. Ask how the responsible party identifies the key factors and develops its assumptions.

d. List, or obtain a list of, the responsible party's significant assumptions providing the basis for the prospective financial statements and consider whether there are any obvious omissions in light of the key factors upon which the prospective results of the entity appear to depend.

e. Consider whether there appear to be any obvious internal inconsistencies in the assumptions.

(continued)

Exhibit 34.4.   Standard compilation procedures. *Source:* **AICPA, Statement on Standards for Attestation Engagements (AT 200).**

f. Perform, or test the mathematical accuracy of, the computations that translate the assumptions into prospective financial statements.

g. Read the prospective financial statements, including the summary of significant assumptions, and consider whether—

- The statements, including the disclosures of assumptions and accounting policies, appear to be not presented in conformity with the AICPA presentation guidelines for prospective financial statements.[1]
- The statements, including the summary of significant assumptions, appear to be not obviously inappropriate in relation to the accountant's knowledge of the entity and its industry and, for
  a— *Financial forecast,* the expected conditions and course of action in the prospective period.
  Financial projection, the purpose of the presentation.

h. If a significant part of the prospective period has expired, inquire about the results of operations or significant portions of the operations (such as sales volume), and significant changes in financial position, and consider their effect in relation to the prospective financial statements. If historical financial statements have been prepared for the expired portion of the period, the accountant should read such statements and consider those results in relation to the prospective financial statements.

i. Confirm his understanding of the statements (including assumptions) by obtaining written representations from the responsible party. Because the amounts reflected in the statements are not supported by historical books and records but rather by assumptions, the accountant should obtain representations in which the responsible party indicates its responsibility for the assumptions. The representations should be signed by the responsible party at the highest level of authority who the accountant believes is responsible for and knowledgeable, directly or through others, about matters covered by the representations.

- *For a financial forecast,* the representations should include a statement that the financial forecast presents, to the best of the responsible party's knowledge and belief, the expected financial position, results of operations, and cash flows for the forecast period and that the forecast reflects the responsible party's judgment, based on present circumstances, of the expected conditions and its expected course of action. If the forecast contains a range, the representation should also include a statement that, to the best of the responsible party's knowledge and belief, the item or items subject to the assumption are expected to actually fall within the range and that the range was not selected in a biased or misleading manner.
- *For a financial projection,* the representations should include a statement that the financial projection presents, to the best of the responsible party's knowledge and belief, the expected financial position, results of operations, and cash flows for the projection period given the hypothetical assumptions, and that the projection reflects its judgment, based on present circumstances, of expected conditions and its expected course of action given the occurrence of the hypothetical events. The representations should also (i) identify the hypothetical assumptions and describe the limitations on the usefulness of the presentation, (ii) state that the assumptions are appropriate, (iii) indicate if the hypothetical assumptions are improbable, and (iv) if the projection contains a range, include a statement that, to the best of the responsible party's knowledge and belief, given the hypothetical assumptions, the item or items subject to the assumption are expected to actually fall within the range and that the range was not selected in a biased or misleading manner.

j. Consider, after applying the above procedures, whether he has received representations or other information that appears to be obviously inappropriate, incomplete, or otherwise misleading and, if so, attempt to obtain additional or revised information. If he does not receive such information, the accountant should ordinarily withdraw from the compilation engagement.[2] (Note that the omission of disclosures, other than those relating to significant assumptions, would not require the accountant to withdraw).

---

[1] Presentation guidelines for entities that issue prospective financial statements are set forth and illustrated in the AICPA *Guide for Prospective Financial Information.*

[2] The accountant need not withdraw from the engagement if the effect of such information on the prospective financial statements does not appear to be material.

Exhibit 34.4. *Continued.*

There are two principal differences between the procedures done in a compilation of prospective statements and a compilation of historical statements: the requirement to consider the **actual results** for any expired portion of the prospective period and the requirement to obtain **signed representations** from the client.

Another difference between prospective and historical compilations is that **working papers** are required in a compilation of prospective financial statements. The working papers should be sufficient to show that the compilation was adequately planned and supervised and that the required procedures were performed. Signing off a checklist of procedures similar to Exhibit 34.4 may be considered evidence of both in some cases and may serve as sufficient documentation of the engagement.

(d) REPORTING ON A COMPILATION. The **standard report** on a compilation of prospective financial statements includes:

1. An identification of the prospective financial statements.
2. A statement that the accountant compiled the statements in accordance with standards established by the AICPA.
3. A statement that a compilation is limited in scope and does not enable the accountant to express an opinion or any other form of assurance on the statements or assumptions.
4. A caveat that the prospective results may not be achieved.
5. A statement that the accountant assumes no responsibility to update the report for events and circumstances occurring after the date of the report (the date of the report is the date of the completion of the compilation procedures).
6. For a projection, a paragraph that describes the limitations on the usefulness of the presentation.

The standard form of compilation report for a financial forecast is as follows:

We have compiled the accompanying forecasted balance sheet, statements of income, retained earnings, and cash flows of XYZ Company as of December 31, 19XX* and for the year then ending in accordance with standards established by the American Institute of Certified Public Accountants.

A compilation is limited to presenting in the form of a forecast information that is the representation of management and does not include evaluation of the support for the assumptions underlying the forecast. We have not examined the forecast, and, accordingly, do not express an opinion or any other form of assurance on the accompanying statements or assumptions. Furthermore, there will usually be differences between the actual and forecasted results, because events and circumstances frequently do not occur as expected, and those differences may be material. We have no responsibility to update this report for events and circumstances occurring after the date of this report.

---

* If the presentation is summarized, the opening sentence of the report would begin, "We have compiled the accompanying summarized projection of XYZ Company as of December 31, 19XX . . . ."

The standard form of compilation report for a financial projection is as follows:

We have compiled the accompanying projected balance sheet, statements of income, retained earnings, and cash flows of XYZ Company as of December 31, 19XX* and for the year then ending in accordance with standards established by the American Institute of Certified Public Accountants.

The accompanying projection and this report were prepared for [description of the special purpose, e.g., "the DEF National Bank for the purpose of negotiating a loan to expand XYZ Company's plant"] and should not be used for any other purpose.

A compilation is limited to presenting in the form of a projection information that is the representation of management and does not include evaluation of the support for the assumptions underlying the projection. We have not examined the projection, and, accordingly, do not express an opinion or any other form of assurance on the accompanying statements or assumptions. Furthermore, even if [description of the hypothetical assumption, e.g., "the loan is granted and the plant is expanded"], there will usually be differences between the actual and projected results, because events and circumstances frequently do not occur as expected, and those differences may be material. We have no responsibility to update this report for events and circumstances occurring after the date of this report.

---

* If the presentation is summarized, the opening sentence of the report would begin, "We have compiled the accompanying summarized projection of XYZ Company as of December 31, 19XX . . . ."

If the presentation is shown as a range, the accountant's report also includes a paragraph that states that management has shown the results of one or more assumptions as a range. The following is an example of such a paragraph:

As described in the summary of significant assumptions, management of XYZ Company has elected to portray forecasted [description of the financial statement element or elements for which the expected results of one or more assumptions fall within a range, and identification of the assumptions expected to fall within a range, e.g., "revenue at the amounts of \$XX and \$YY, which is predicated upon occupancy rates of XX% and YY% of available apartments"] rather than as a single-point estimate. Accordingly, the accompanying forecast presents forecasted financial position, results of operations, and cash flows [description of the assumptions expected to fall within a range, e.g., "at such occupancy rates"]. However, there can be no assurance that the actual results will fall within the range of [description of the assumptions expected to fall within a range, e.g., "occupancy rates"] presented.

(e) PROBLEM SITUATIONS. Potential problems in a compilation engagement include **scope limitations, deficiencies in the prospective financial statements,** and lack of **independence.**

(i) Scope Limitations. Scope limitations might include a client's inadequate responses to the limited inquiries required in a compilation or its refusal to supply signed representations. The AICPA Guide does not allow a scope-limitation compilation report. If the accountant cannot apply all the necessary procedures, he cannot complete the engagement and ordinarily should withdraw.

(ii) Presentation Deficiencies. Possible deficiencies in the prospective financial statements might affect either the assumptions or the other required disclosures. If the deficiency affects disclosures **other than assumptions,** the accountant may mention it in his compilation report. For example, if management chose to omit the disclosure of significant accounting policies, the accountant might add the following paragraph to his compilation report:

Management has elected to omit the summary of significant accounting policies required by the guidelines for presentation of a financial forecast established by the American Institute of Certified Public Accountants. If the omitted disclosures were included in the forecast, they might influence the user's conclusions about the Company's financial position, results of operations, and cash flows for the forecast period. Accordingly, this report is not intended for those who are not informed about such matters.

If the deficiency affects the disclosure of **assumptions** and the accountant is unable to have it corrected, he is not permitted merely to mention it in his report. In that case, he ordinarily would withdraw from the engagement.

(iii) Independence. Since a compilation provides no assurance, an accountant may compile prospective financial statements when he is not independent. In that case his report would indicate his lack of independence, but not the reason for it. The following sentence would be added to the compilation report to indicate the lack of independence:

We are not independent with respect to XYZ Company.

34.7 EXAMINATION SERVICES

(a) SCOPE OF AN EXAMINATION. An examination of prospective financial statements is similar to an audit of historical financial statements. It is based on evidence-gathering procedures and results in positive assurance about the statements. The main difference between the two services involves the evidence-gathering procedures. Because completed transactions do not generally constitute the bulk of the data underlying prospective financial statements, the accountant's procedures generally consist primarily of inquiry and analysis rather than of document inspection and confirmation.

An examination of prospective financial statements involves:

1. Evaluating the preparation of the statements.
2. Evaluating the support underlying the statements.
3. Evaluating the presentation of the statements for conformity with AICPA presentation guidelines.
4. Issuing a report as to whether, in the accountant's opinion,
   a. The prospective financial statements are presented in conformity with AICPA presentation guidelines and
   b. The assumptions provide a reasonable basis for the forecast or, for a projection, whether the assumptions provide a reasonable basis given the hypothetical assumptions.

(i) Evaluating Preparation. The accountant considers the process that management uses to develop its prospective financial statements to determine how much support he will need to accumulate. This consideration is similar to the consideration an auditor gives to a company's internal control in planning and performing an audit of historical financial statements. The better controlled the process of developing the financial statements, the less work the accountant generally needs to do in obtaining support for them.

In judging the process the entity uses in developing its prospective financial statements, the accountant generally compares the process to the guidelines discussed in subsection 34.3(a).

(ii) Evaluating Assumptions. The accountant performs procedures to determine whether the assumptions provide a reasonable basis for the prospective financial statements. He can decide that they do if he can conclude that:

1. Management has identified all key factors expected to affect the entity during the prospective period.
2. Management has developed assumptions for each key factor.
3. The assumptions are suitably supported.

To determine whether management has identified all **key factors** and developed assumptions for each one, the accountant needs to possess, or obtain during the engagement, an appropriate knowledge of the industry in which the entity will operate and the accounting principles and practices of that industry.

The accountant can conclude that the assumptions are **suitably supported** if the preponderance of information supports each significant assumption. Preponderance, here, does not imply a statistical majority of information. A preponderance exists if the weight of available information tends to support the assumption. The AICPA Guide states, however, "Because of the judgments involved in developing assumptions, different people may arrive at somewhat different but equally reasonable assumptions based on the same information."

The accountant need not obtain support for the **hypothetical** assumptions in a projection, since they are not necessarily expected to occur. For a projection, the accountant considers whether the hypothetical assumptions are consistent with the purpose of the projection and whether the other assumptions are suitably supported given the hypothetical assumption.

In evaluating the support for the assumptions, the accountant considers:

1. Whether sufficient pertinent sources of information, both internal and external to the entity, have been considered.
2. Whether the assumptions are consistent with the sources from which they are derived.
3. Whether the assumptions are consistent with each other.
4. Whether the historical financial information and other data used in developing the assumptions are sufficiently reliable for that purpose.
5. Whether the historical information and other data used in developing the assumptions are comparable over the periods specified or whether the effects of any lack of comparability were considered in developing the assumptions.
6. Whether the logical arguments or theory, considered with the data supporting the assumptions, are reasonable.

Support for assumptions may include market surveys, engineering studies, general economic indicators, industry statistics, trends and patterns developed from an entity's operating history, and internal data and analysis, accompanied by their supporting logical argument or theory.

The accountant determines whether the assumptions provide a reasonable basis for the statements, but he cannot conclude that any outcome is expected because (1) realization of prospective results may depend on management's intentions, which cannot be examined; (2) there is substantial uncertainty in the assumptions; (3) some of the information accumulated about an assumption may appear contradictory; and (4) different but similarly reasonable assumptions concerning a particular matter might be derived from common information.

(iii) Evaluating Presentation.   The accountant compares the presentation of the prospective financial statements to the AICPA presentation guidelines (see subsections 34.4(b) and (c)).

(b) STANDARD EXAMINATION REPORT.   The accountant's **standard report** on an examination of prospective financial statements includes:

1. An identification of the statements presented.
2. A statement that the examination of the statements was made in accordance with AICPA standards and a brief description of the nature of such an examination.
3. The accountant's opinion that the statements are presented in conformity with AICPA presentation guidelines and, for a forecast, that the underlying assumptions provide a reasonable basis for the forecast or, for a projection, that the underlying assumptions provide a reasonable basis for the projection given the hypothetical assumptions.
4. A caveat that the prospective results may not be achieved.

5. A statement that the accountant assumes no responsibility to update the report for events and circumstances occurring after the date of the report, which is the date of the completion of the examination procedures.

6. For a projection, a separate paragraph describing the limitations on the usefulness of the presentation.

The standard report on the examination of a financial forecast is as follows:

We have examined the accompanying forecasted balance sheet, statements of income, retained earnings, and cash flows of XYZ Company as of December 31, 19XX,* and for the year then ending. Our examination was made in accordance with standards for the examination of a forecast established by the American Institute of Certified Public Accountants and, accordingly, included such procedures as we considered necessary to evaluate both the assumptions used by management and the preparation and presentation of the forecast.

In our opinion, the accompanying forecast is presented in conformity with guidelines for presentation of a forecast established by the American Institute of Certified Public Accountants and the underlying assumptions provide a reasonable basis for management's forecast. However, there will usually be differences between the forecasted and actual results, because events and circumstances frequently do not occur as expected, and those differences may be material. We have no responsibility to update this report for events and circumstances occurring after the date of this report.

---

* If the presentation is summarized as discussed in subsection 34.4(b), the first sentence would read, in part, "We have examined the accompanying summarized forecast of XYZ Company as of . . . ."

The standard report on the examination of a financial projection is as follows:

We have examined the accompanying projected balance sheet, statements of income, retained earnings, and cash flows of XYZ Company as of December 31, 19XX,* and for the year then ending. Our examination was made in accordance with standards for the examination of a projection established by the American Institute of Certified Public Accountants and, accordingly, included such procedures as we considered necessary to evaluate both the assumptions used by management and the preparation and presentation of the projection.

The accompanying projection and this report were prepared for [description of the special purpose, e.g., "the DEF National Bank for the purpose of negotiating a loan to expand XYZ Company's plant"] and should not be used for any other purpose.

In our opinion, the accompanying projection is presented in conformity with guidelines for presentation of a projection established by the American Institute of Certified Public Accountants, and the underlying assumptions provide a reasonable basis for management's projection [description of the hypothetical assumption, e.g., "assuming the granting of the requested loan for the purpose of expanding XYZ Company's plant as described in the summary of significant assumptions"]. However, even if [description of the hypothetical assumption, e.g., "the loan is granted and the plant is expanded"], there will usually be differences between the projected and actual results, because events and circumstances frequently do not occur as expected, and those differences may be material. We have no responsibility to update this report for events and circumstances occurring after the date of this report.

---

* If the presentation is summarized as discussed in subsection 34.4(b), the first sentence would read, in part, "We have examined the accompanying summarized projection of XYZ Company as of . . . ."

When the prospective financial statements are presented as a range, the report also includes a separate paragraph describing the range (see subsection 34.6(d) for an example).

(c) MODIFIED EXAMINATION REPORTS.   There are four types of modified examination reports:

1. A **qualified** report, used when the statements depart from the AICPA presentation guidelines but the deficiency does not affect the assumptions (although if the matter is highly material, the accountant may issue an adverse report).
2. An **adverse** report, used when the statements fail to disclose significant assumptions or when the assumptions do not provide a reasonable basis for the presentation.
3. A **disclaimer** used when the accountant is precluded from applying procedures he considers necessary in the circumstances.
4. A **reference** to another accountant, used when another accountant examines the prospective financial statements of a significant portion of the entity, such as a major subsidiary.

(i) Qualified Opinion.   The accountant issues a qualified opinion if there is a material presentation deficiency that does not affect the assumptions. The following is an examination report qualified because of a presentation deficiency:

We have examined the accompanying forecasted balance sheet, statements of income, retained earnings, and cash flows of XYZ Company as of December 31, 19XX, and for the year then ending. Our examination was made in accordance with standards for the examination of a forecast established by the American Institute of Certified Public Accountants and, accordingly, included such procedures as we considered necessary to evaluate both the assumptions used by management and the preparation and presentation of the forecast.

The forecast does not [description of the presentation deficiency, such as "disclose the significant accounting principles underlying the presentation, which we believe is required by the guidelines for presentation of a forecast established by the American Institute of Certified Public Accountants"].

In our opinion, except for [description of the presentation deficiency, e.g., "the omission of the disclosure of significant accounting policies"] as discussed in the preceding paragraph, the accompanying forecast is presented in conformity with guidelines for presentation of a forecast established by the American Institute of Certified Public Accountants and the underlying assumptions provide a reasonable basis for management's forecast. However, there will usually be differences between the actual and forecasted results, because events and circumstances frequently do not occur as expected, and those differences may be material. We have no responsibility to update this report for events and circumstances occurring after the date of this report.

(ii) Adverse Report.   If the accountant believes a significant assumption to be unsupported or not disclosed, he issues an adverse opinion. He may also issue one if he believes that a departure from the presentation guidelines not involving the assumptions is serious enough to warrant it. The following is an example of an adverse report issued by the accountant because he believed an assumption was unreasonable:

We have examined the accompanying forecasted balance sheet, statements of income, retained earnings, and cash flows of XYZ Company as of December 31, 19XX, and for the year then ending. Our examination was made in accordance with standards for the examination of a forecast established by the American Institute of Certified Public Accountants and, accordingly, included such procedures as we considered necessary to evaluate both the assumptions used by management and the preparation and presentation of the forecast.

[Description of the problem assumption, e.g., "As discussed under the caption "sales" in the summary of significant assumptions, the forecasted sales include, among other things, revenue from the Company's federal defense contracts continuing at the current level. The

Company's present federal defense contracts will expire in March 19XX. No new contracts have been signed, and no negotiations are under way for new federal defense contracts. Furthermore, the federal government has entered into contracts with another company to supply the items being manufactured under the Company's present contracts."]

In our opinion, the accompanying forecast is not presented in conformity with guidelines for presentation of a forecast established by the American Institute of Certified Public Accountants because management's assumptions, as discussed in the preceding paragraph, do not provide a reasonable basis for management's forecast. We have no responsibility to update this report for events and circumstances occurring after the date of this report.

There is no caveat about actual results differing from those forecasted since the accountant believes the forecast assumptions to be unreasonable.

(iii) Disclaimer.   If the accountant cannot apply all the procedures he believes necessary to support an opinion on the statements, he issues a disclaimer. An example of a disclaimer follows:

We have examined the accompanying forecasted balance sheet, statements of income, retained earnings, and cash flows of XYZ Company as of December 31, 19XX, and for the year then ending. Except as explained in the following paragraph, our examination was made in accordance with standards for the examination of a forecast established by the American Institute of Certified Public Accountants and, accordingly, included such procedures as we considered necessary to evaluate both the assumptions used by management and the preparation and presentation of the forecast.

[Description of the scope limitation, e.g., "As discussed under the caption 'income from investee' in the summary of significant assumptions, the forecast includes income from an equity investee constituting 23% of forecasted net income, which is management's estimate of the Company's share of the investee's income to be accrued for the year ending December 31, 19XX. The investee has not prepared a forecast for the year ending December 31, 19XX, and we were therefore unable to obtain suitable support for this assumption."]

Because, [description of the scope limitation, e.g., "as described in the preceding paragraph, we were unable to evaluate management's assumption regarding income from an equity investee and other assumptions that depend thereon"], we express no opinion with respect to the presentation of or the assumptions underlying the accompanying forecast. We have no responsibility to update this report for events and circumstances occurring after the date of this report.

In a disclaimer there is no caveat about differences between actual and forecasted assumptions since the accountant cannot satisfy himself about the reasonableness of the assumptions.

Notwithstanding his scope limitation, if the accountant is aware of material deficiencies in the forecast, those deficiencies should be discussed in the disclaimer.

(iv) Divided Responsibility.   When another accountant is involved in the examination, the principal accountant may refer to the work of the other accountant as a basis, in part, for his own report. The reference is done in essentially the same way divided-responsibility reports are done for audits of historical financial statements.

(d) INDEPENDENCE.   The accountant who examines prospective financial statements is required to be independent. If he is not, the accountant generally issues a compilation report rather than disclaim an opinion after his examination.

34.8 AGREED-UPON PROCEDURES

(a) SCOPE OF SERVICE.   An engagement to apply agreed-upon procedures to prospective financial statements involves applying the procedures specified by the users of the statements and reporting the results of their application. The level of service is flexible; the accountant's report may only be distributed to the users who specified the procedures. Thus, it is a limited-distribution service.

Standards for agreed-upon procedures engagements discussed in the AICPA Guide were amended by SSAE No. 4, "Agreed-Upon Procedures Engagements" (1995).

(b) PROCEDURES. The procedures applied in an engagement may be limited or extensive, depending on the users' needs. For example, the service may consist of procedures below the level done in a compilation (such as mere assembly) or may be similar to those done in an examination. Alternatively, the service may consist of different levels of procedures applied to different amounts in the statements, such as a high level of work done on forecasted sales and very limited procedures on forecasted expenses.

Any level of procedures is appropriate in an agreed-upon procedures engagement as long as (1) the user takes responsibility for the adequacy of the procedures for his purposes, (2) the procedures are expected to result in reasonably consistent findings using the criteria, and (3) the procedures are more extensive than a mere reading of the prospective financial statements.

(c) REPORTS. The accountant's report on the results of applying agreed-upon procedures should contain the following elements:

1. A title that includes the word **independent.**
2. Reference to the prospective financial statements covered by the accountant's report and the character of the engagement.
3. Identification of the specified users.
4. A statement that the procedures performed were those agreed to by the specified users identified in the report.
5. Reference to standards established by the American Institute of Certified Public Accountants.
6. A statement that the sufficiency of the procedures is solely the responsibility of the specified users and a disclaimer of responsibility for the sufficiency of those procedures.
7. A list of the procedures performed (or reference thereto) and related findings.
8. Where applicable, a description of any agreed-upon materiality limits.
9. A statement that the accountant was not engaged to, and did not, perform an examination of prospective financial statements, a disclaimer of opinion on whether the presentation of the prospective financial statements is in conformity with AICPA presentation guidelines and on whether the underlying assumptions provide a reasonable basis for the forecast, or reasonable basis for the projection given the hypothetical assumptions; and a statement that if the practitioner had performed additional procedures, other matters might have come to his attention that would have been reported.
10. A statement of restrictions on the use of the report because it is intended to be used solely by the specified users. (However, if the report is a matter of public record, the accountant should include the following sentence: "However, this report is a matter of public record and its distribution is not limited.")
11. Where applicable, reservations or restrictions concerning procedures or findings.
12. A caveat that the prospective results may not be achieved.
13. A statement that the accountant assumes no responsibility to update the report for events and circumstances occurring after the date of the report.
14. Where applicable, a description of the nature of the assistance provided by a specialist.

The report should not provide negative assurance about the statements. That is, it should not state that nothing came to the accountant's attention to indicate that amounts or disclosures are inappropriate.

The accountant is not required to perform procedures beyond those requested by the specified users. However, if matters that contradict the assertions in the prospective financial statements come to the accountant's attention by means other than the procedures requested, he should include these matters in the report.

The following is an example of a report on the application of agreed-upon procedures:

Board of Directors—XYZ Corporation

Board of Directors—ABC Company

At your request, we have performed certain agreed-upon procedures, as enumerated below, with respect to the forecasted balance sheet and the related statements of income, retained earnings, and cash flows of DEF Company, a subsidiary of ABC Company, as of December 31, 19XX and for the year then ending. These procedures, which were specified by the Boards of Directors of XYZ Corporation and ABC Company, were performed solely to assist you in evaluating the forecast in connection with the proposed sale of DEF Company to XYZ Corporation. This agreed-upon procedures engagement was performed in accordance with standards established by the American Institute of Certified Public Accountants. The sufficiency of these procedures is solely the responsibility of the specified users of the report. Consequently, we make no representation regarding the sufficiency of the procedures described below either for the purpose for which this report has been requested or for any other purpose.

a. With respect to forecasted rental income, we compared the assumptions about expected demand for rental of the housing units to demand for similar housing units at similar rental prices in the city area in which DEF Company's housing units are located. We found that the forecasted occupancy rates were within the range of those comparable units.

b. We tested the forecast for mathematical accuracy. We noted no exceptions.

We were not engaged to, and did not, perform an examination, the objective of which would be expression of an opinion on the accompanying prospective financial statements. Accordingly, we do not express an opinion on whether the prospective financial statements are presented in conformity with AICPA presentation guidelines or on whether the underlying assumptions provide a reasonable basis for the presentation. Had we performed additional procedures, other matters might have come to our attention that would have been reported to you. Furthermore, there will usually be differences between the forecasted and actual results, because events and circumstances frequently do not occur as expected, and those differences may be material. We have no responsibility to update this report for events and circumstances occurring after the date of this report.

This report is intended solely for the use of the boards of directors of ABC Company and XYZ Corporation and should not be used by those who have not agreed to the procedures and taken responsibility for the sufficiency of the procedures for their purposes.

34.9 INTERNAL USE SERVICES

(a) SCOPE OF SERVICES. When the accountant assembles and submits or reports on prospective financial statements for **third-party use,** he must compile, examine, or apply agreed-upon procedures to them. However, for **internal use** the accountant's services and reports can be more flexible.

Internal use services generally are provided in the form of consulting, tax planning, or so-called controllership services. In these types of service the objective of the service is not to lend credibility to the statements and there is no third-party reliance on them, so AICPA guidelines allow the accountant to structure the engagement and report to fit the circumstances.

The accountant **may** provide compilation, examination, or agreed-upon procedures for internal use prospective financial statements, but he is not required to do so.

(b) DETERMINING WHETHER USE IS INTERNAL. The accountant may provide internal use services if he believes that third party use is not reasonably expected. In arriving at his belief, the accountant may rely on the oral or written representation of management, unless something comes to his attention to contradict management's representation.

The AICPA Guide (§ 10.02) provides the following guidelines for determining whether outsiders are considered third parties:

> In deciding whether a party that is or reasonably might be expected to use an accountant's report is considered to be a third party, the accountant should consider the degree of consistency of interest between [management] and the user regarding the forecast. If their interests are substantially consistent (for example both the [preparer] and the user are employees of the entity about which the forecast is made), the user would not be deemed to be a third party. On the other hand, where the interests of the [preparer] and user are potentially inconsistent (for example, the [preparer] is a nonowner manager and the user is an absentee owner), the user would be deemed a third party. In some cases, this determination will require the exercise of considerable professional judgment.

(c) PROCEDURES. The procedures applied in an internal use engagement are usually based on the nature of the engagement. They may focus on developing prospective data, or they may focus on improving operations or financial planning with prospective data being only a by-product of the engagement.

(d) REPORTS. The accountant's report for internal use services is flexible. Such reports sometimes speak solely to the prospective financial statements, but often they focus on alternative or recommended courses of action.

The standard compilation, examination, or agreed-upon procedures reports may be utilized for internal use, but often they are not used.

Reports on prospective financial statements for internal use generally take three broad forms: **plain paper, legend,** and **formal.** Where there is a report on the statements, it may stand alone or may be incorporated into another report, such as a consultant's report.

(i) Plain Paper. Plain paper means that the accountant provides neither a report on the statements nor any other written communication that accompanies them. In a plain-paper situation there would be nothing apparent to the reader to associate the accountant with the statements.

(ii) Legend. When an accountant's written communication (such as a transmittal letter) accompanies the prospective financial statements, the AICPA Guide (§ 22.09) requires that the accountant include (1) a caveat that prospective results may not be achieved and (2) a statement that the prospective financial statements are for internal use only. Many accountants choose to present this as a **legend** on the statement itself.

(iii) Formal Report. If the accountant decides to issue a report on a service, he may do so. However, the accountant is not permitted to report on a forecast or projection, even for internal use, if it does not disclose the significant assumptions.

According to the AICPA Guide (§ 22.06), a report for internal use preferably:

1. Is addressed to management.
2. Identifies the statements being reported on.

3. Describes the character of work performed and the degree of responsibility taken with respect to the statements.

4. Includes a caveat that the prospective results may not be achieved.

5. Indicates the restrictions as to the distribution of the statements and report.

6. Is dated as of the date of the completion of the accountant's procedures.

7. For a projection, describes the limitations on the usefulness of the presentation.

The following is an example of a report on an internal use service consisting of assembly of a forecast:

To Mr. John Doe, President
XYZ Company

We have assembled from information provided by management, the accompanying forecasted balance sheet, and the related forecasted statements of income, retained earnings, and cash flows of XYZ Company as of December 31, 19XX,* and for the year then ending. We have not compiled or examined the financial forecast and express no assurance of any kind on it. Further, there will usually be differences between the forecasted and actual results, because events and circumstances frequently do not occur as expected, and those differences may be material. In accordance with the terms of our engagement, this report and the accompanying forecast are restricted to internal use and may not be shown to any third party for any purpose.

---

* If the presentation is summarized as discussed in subsection 34.4(b), the first sentence would read, in part, "We have assembled . . . the accompanying summarized forecast of XYZ Company . . . ."

An example of a report on the assembly of a projection is as follows:

To Mr. John Doe, President
XYZ Company

We have assembled from information provided by management, the accompanying projected balance sheet, and the related projected statements of income, retained earnings, and cash flows, and summaries of significant assumptions and accounting policies of XYZ Company as of December 31, 19XX,* and for the year then ending. The accompanying projection and this report were prepared for [description of the special purpose, e.g., "presentation to the Board of Directors of XYZ Company for its consideration as to whether to add a third operating shift"]. We have not compiled or examined the financial projection and express no assurance of any kind on it. Further, even if [description of the hypothetical assumption, e.g., "the third operating shift is added"], there will usually be differences between the projected and actual results, because events and circumstances frequently do not occur as expected, and those differences may be material. In accordance with the terms of our engagement, this report and the accompanying projection are restricted to internal use and may not be shown to any third party for any purpose.

If the presentation is summarized as discussed in subsection 34.4(b), the first sentence would read, in part, "We have assembled . . . the accompanying summarized projection of XYZ Company . . . ."

In addition to the above, the accountant's report on prospective financial statements for internal use would:

1. Indicate if he is not independent with respect to the client (the report would not express any assurance on the statements if there is a lack of independence) and

2. Note any disclosures required under the presentation guidelines (see subsection 34.4(a)) whose omission comes to the accountant's attention (other than omitted assumptions).

The report might either describe the omitted disclosures or merely note the omission of disclosures in a manner such as:

> This financial forecast was prepared to help you develop your personal financial plan. Accordingly, it does not include all disclosures required by the guidelines established by the American Institute of Certified Public Accountants for presentation of a financial forecast.

34.10 SOURCES AND SUGGESTED REFERENCES

American Institute of Certified Public Accountants, Accounting and Review Services Committee, "Compilation and Review of Financial Statements," Statement on Standards for Accounting and Review Services No. 1, AICPA, New York, 1978.

————, Auditing Standards Board, "Financial Forecasts and Projections," Statement on Standards for Accountant's Services on Prospective Financial Information, AICPA, New York, 1985.

————, "Reporting on Pro Forma Financial Information," Statement on Standards for Attestation Engagements, AICPA, New York, 1988.

————, "Agreed-Upon Procedures Engagements," Statement on Standards for Attestation Engagements No. 4, AICPA, New York, 1995.

————, *Guide for Prospective Financial Information,* AICPA, New York, 1993.

Commerce Clearing House, *SEC Accounting Rules,* CCH, Chicago, 1990.

Financial Accounting Standards Board, "Statement of Cash Flows," Statement of Financial Accounting Standards No. 95, FASB, Stamford, CT, 1987.

Pallais, Don, and Holton, Stephen D., *Guide to Forecasts and Projections,* 10th ed., Practitioners Publishing, Fort Worth, TX, 1995.

CHAPTER 35

PERSONAL FINANCIAL STATEMENTS

Thomas D. Hubbard, PhD, CPA, CFE
University of Nebraska, Lincoln
Dennis S. Neier, CPA
Goldstein Golub Kessler, P.C.

CONTENTS

35.1 GUIDANCE

The authoritative guide in the preparation of personal financial statements is AICPA SOP No. 82-1, "Accounting and Financial Reporting for Personal Financial Statements." This SOP establishes the use of estimated current value rather than historical cost as the basis for measuring assets and liabilities in personal financial statements. It also provides guidance on how to determine estimated current value for several kinds of assets and liabilities.

Accountants are often engaged to compile, review, or audit personal financial statements. The specific guide for such engagements is the AICPA "Personal Financial Statements Guide," which includes SOP No. 82-1.

The general guidance provided by the AICPA in SSARS No. 1, "Compilation and Review of Financial Statements," applies to compilations and reviews of all financial statements, including personal financial statements.

A subsequent AICPA release, SSARS No. 6, "Reporting on Personal Financial Statements Included in Written Personal Financial Plans," allows accountants to prepare personal financial statements that omit disclosures required by GAAP so long as the statement will be used solely in the development of the client's personal financial plan and not to obtain credit or to meet other disclosure requirements. If an accountant prepares a personal financial statement under this exemption, he or she should issue a written report stating the restricted purpose of the statement and noting that it has not been audited, reviewed, or compiled.

35.2 GENERAL DESCRIPTION AND REQUIREMENTS

(a) DEFINITION. A personal financial statement presents the personal assets and liabilities of an individual, a husband and wife, or a family. It is not a financial statement on a business owned by the person; in fact, it differs from a business financial statement in several important ways (see Exhibit 35.1).

The essential purpose of a personal financial statement is to measure wealth at a specified date—to take a snapshot of the person's financial position. It does this by presenting:

- Estimated current values of assets.
- Estimated current amounts of liabilities.
- A provision for income taxes based on the taxes that would be owed if all the assets were liquidated and all the liabilities paid on the date of the statement.
- Net worth.

	Personal	Business
Objective	Measurement of wealth	Reporting of earnings, evaluation of performance
Uses	Facilitation of financial planning; procural of credit; provision of disclosures to the public or the court	Procural of credit, information for shareholders, regulatory requirements
Valuation	Current value	Historical cost
Method of accounting	Accrual	Accrual
Classification	None: assets presented in order of liquidity, liabilities in order of maturity	Assets and liabilities classified current or long-term
Excess of assets over liabilities	Net worth	Equity earnings

Exhibit 35.1.   Personal and business financial statements compared.

The basic personal financial statement containing this information is called a **statement of financial condition,** not a balance sheet. Values and amounts for one or more prior periods may be included for comparison with the current values and amounts, but this is optional. The **statement of changes in net worth** is also optional. It presents the major sources of increase or decrease in net worth (see Exhibit 35.2).

(b) OWNERSHIP.   A personal financial statement covering a whole family usually presents the assets and liabilities of the family members in combination, as a single economic unit. However, the members may have different ownership interests in these assets or liabilities. For example, the wife may have a remainder interest in a testamentary trust, whereas the husband

JAMES AND JANE PERSON
Statements of Financial Condition
December 31, 19X3 and 19X2

	December 31	
	19X3	19X2
Assets		
Cash	$ 3,700	$ 15,600
Bonus receivable	20,000	10,000
Investments		
Marketable securities (Note 2)	160,500	140,700
Stock options (Note 3)	28,000	24,000
Kenbruce Associates (Note 4)	48,000	42,000
Davekar Company, Inc. (Note 5)	550,000	475,000
Vested interest in deferred profit-sharing plan	111,400	98,900
Remainder interest in testamentary trust (Note 6)	171,900	128,800
Cash value of life insurance ($43,600 and $42,900), less loans payable to insurance companies ($38,100 and $37,700) (Note 7)	5,500	5,200
Residence (Note 8)	190,000	180,000
Personal effects (excluding jewelry) (Note 9)	55,000	50,000
Jewelry (Note 9)	40,000	36,500
	$1,384,000	$1,206,700
Liabilities		
Income taxes—current year balance	$ 8,800	$ 400
Demand 10.5% note payable to bank	25,000	26,000
Mortgage payable (Note 10)	98,200	99,000
Contingent liabilities (Note 11)		
	132,000	125,400
Estimated income taxes on the differences between the estimated current values of assets and the estimated current amounts of liabilities and their tax bases (Note 12)	239,000	160,000
Net worth	1,013,000	921,300
	$1,384,000	$1,206,700

The notes are an integral part of these statements.

(continued)

Exhibit 35.2.   Illustrative financial statements. *Source:* Reproduced with permission from AICPA, Personal Financial Statements Guide, Appendix E: Statement of Position No. 82-1, "Accounting and Financial Reporting for Personal Financial Statements," 1992, pp. 53–58.

JAMES AND JANE PERSON
Statements of Changes in Net Worth
For the Years Ended December 31, 19X3 and 19X2

	Year ended December 31	
	19X3	19X2
Realized increases in net worth		
Salary and bonus	$ 95,000	$ 85,000
Dividends and interest income	2,300	1,800
Distribution from limited partnership	5,000	4,000
Gains on sales of marketable securities	1,000	500
	103,300	91,300
Realized decreases in net worth		
Income taxes	26,000	22,000
Interest expense	13,000	14,000
Real estate taxes	4,000	3,000
Personal expenditures	36,700	32,500
	79,700	71,500
Net realized increase in net worth	23,600	19,800
Unrealized increases in net worth		
Marketable securities (net of realized gains on securities sold)	3,000	500
Stock options	4,000	500
Davekar Company, Inc.	75,000	25,000
Kenbruce Associates	6,000	
Deferred profit-sharing plan	12,500	9,500
Remainder interest in testamentary trust	43,100	25,000
Jewelry	3,500	
	147,100	60,500
Unrealized decrease in net worth		
Estimated income taxes on the differences between the estimated current values of assets and the estimated current amounts of liabilities and their tax bases	79,000	22,000
Net unrealized increase in net worth	68,100	38,500
Net increase in net worth	91,700	58,300
Net worth at the beginning of year	921,300	863,000
Net worth at the end of year	$1,013,000	$921,300

The notes are an integral part of these statements.

Exhibit 35.2.   Illustrative financial statements. *Source:* Reproduced with permission from AICPA, Personal Financial Statements Guide, Appendix E: Statement of Position No. 82-1, "Accounting and Financial Reporting for Personal Financial Statements," 1992, pp. 53–58.

JAMES AND JANE PERSON
Notes to Financial Statements

Note 1. The accompanying financial statements include the assets and liabilities of James and Jane Person. Assets are stated at their estimated current values, and liabilities at their estimated current amounts.

Note 2. The estimated current values of marketable securities are either (a) their quoted closing prices or (b) for securities not traded on the financial statement date, amounts that fall within the range of quoted bid and asked prices.

Marketable securities consist of the following:

	December 31, 19X3		December 31, 19X2	
	Number of Shares or Bonds	Estimated Current Values	Number of Shares or Bonds	Estimated Current Values
Stocks				
Jaiven Jewels, Inc.	1,500	$ 98,813		
McRae Motors, Ltd.	800	11,000	600	$ 4,750
Parker Sisters, Inc.	400	13,875	200	5,200
Rosenfield Rug Co.			1,200	96,000
Rubin Paint Company	300	9,750	100	2,875
Weiss Potato Chips, Inc.	200	20,337	300	25,075
		153,775		133,900
Bonds				
Jackson Van Lines, Ltd. (12% due 7/1/X9)	5	5,225	5	5,100
United Garvey, Inc. (7% due 11/15/X6)	2	1,500	2	1,700
		6,725		6,800
		$160,500		$140,700

Note 3. Jane Person owns options to acquire 4,000 shares of stock of Winner Corp. at an option price of $5 per share. The option expires on June 30, 19X5. The estimated current value is its published selling price.

Note 4. The investment in Kenbruce Associates is an 8% interest in a real estate limited partnership. The estimated current value is determined by the projected annual cash receipts and payments capitalized at a 12% rate.

Note 5. James Person owns 50% of the common stock of Davekar Company, Inc., a retail mail order business. The estimated current value of the investment is determined by the provisions of a shareholders' agreement, which restricts the sale of the stock and, under certain conditions, requires the company to repurchase the stock based on a price equal to the book value of the net assets plus an agreed amount for goodwill. At December 31, 19X3, the agreed amount for goodwill was $112,500, and at December 31, 19X2, it was $100,000.

A condensed balance sheet of Davekar Company, Inc., prepared in conformity with generally accepted accounting principles, is summarized below:

(continued)

Exhibit 35.2.   *Continued.*

	December 31	
	19X3	**19X2**
Current assets	$3,147,000	$2,975,000
Plant, property, and equipment—net	165,000	145,000
Other assets	120,000	110,000
Total assets	3,432,000	3,230,000
Current liabilities	2,157,000	2,030,000
Long-term liabilities	400,000	450,000
Total liabilities	2,557,000	2,480,000
Equity	$ 875,000	$ 750,000

The sales and net income for 19X3 were $10,500,000 and $125,000 and for 19X2 were $9,700,000 and $80,000.

Note 6. Jane Person is the beneficiary of a remainder interest in a testamentary trust under the will of the late Joseph Jones. The amount included in the accompanying statements is her remainder interest in the estimated current value of the trust assets, discounted at 10%.

Note 7. At December 31, 19X3 and 19X2, James Person owned a $300,000 whole life insurance policy.

Note 8. The estimated current value of the residence is its purchase price plus the cost of improvements. The residence was purchased in December 19X1, and improvements were made in 19X2 and 19X3.

Note 9. The estimated current values of personal effects and jewelry are the appraised values of those assets, determined by an independent appraiser for insurance purposes.

Note 10. The mortgage (collateralized by the residence) is payable in monthly installments of $815 a month, including interest at 10% a year through 20Y8.

Note 11. James Person has guaranteed the payment of loans of Davekar Company, Inc., under a $500,000 line of credit. The loan balance was $300,000 at December 31, 19X3, and $400,000 at December 31, 19X2.

Note 12. The estimated current amounts of liabilities at December 31, 19X3, and December 31, 19X2, equaled their tax bases. Estimated income taxes have been provided on the excess of the estimated current values of assets over their tax bases as if the estimated current values of the assets had been realized on the statement date, using applicable tax laws and regulations. The provision will probably differ from the amounts of income taxes that eventually might be paid because those amounts are determined by the timing and the method of disposal or realization and the tax laws and regulations in effect at the time of disposal or realization.

The estimated current values of assets exceeded their tax bases by $850,000 at December 31, 19X3, and by $770,300 at December 31, 19X2. The excess of estimated current values of major assets over their tax bases are—

	December 31	
	19X3	**19X2**
Investment in Davekar Company, Inc.	$430,500	$355,500
Vested interest in deferred profit-sharing plan	111,400	98,900
Investment in marketable securities	104,100	100,000
Remainder interest in testamentary trust	97,000	53,900

Exhibit 35.2.   Continued.

may own life insurance with a net cash surrender value. It may be useful, especially when the statement is to be used in a divorce case, to disclose each individual's interests separately. This may be done in separate columns within the statement, in the notes to the statement, or in additional statements for each individual.

Often an individual covered by the statement is one of a group of joint owners of assets, as with community property or property held in joint tenancy. In this case, the statement should include only the individual's interest as a beneficial owner under the laws of the state. If the parties' shares in the assets are not clear, the advice of an attorney may be needed to determine whether the person should regard any interest in the assets as his or her own, and if so, how much. The statement should make full disclosure of the joint ownership of the assets and the grounds for the allocation of shares.

(c) USES. Many individuals or families use personal financial statements for investment, tax, retirement, gift and estate planning, and for obtaining credit. A personal financial statement may also be required for disclosure to the court in a divorce case, or to the public when the individual is a candidate or an incumbent of public office.

(d) ACCOUNTING BASIS. SOP No. 82-1 establishes the use of estimated current values and amounts and the accrual basis of accounting as GAAP for personal financial statements. The AICPA "Personal Financial Statements Guide" allows accountants to prepare, compile, review, or audit personal financial statements on other comprehensive bases of accounting, such as historical cost, tax, or cash.

(e) ORDER OF PRESENTATION. Assets are presented in order of liquidity, and liabilities in order of maturity. No distinction is made between current and long-term assets and liabilities because there is no operating cycle in a person's financial affairs.

Assets and liabilities of a closely held business that is conducted as a separate entity are not combined with similar personal items in a personal financial statement. Instead, the estimated current net value of the person's investment in the entity is shown as one amount. But if the person owns a business activity that is not conducted as a separate entity, such as a real estate investment with a related mortgage, the assets and liabilities of the activity are shown as separate amounts.

35.3 ASSETS

(a) ESTIMATED CURRENT VALUE. Assets are presented at their estimated current value. This is defined by SOP No. 82-1 (AICPA, par. 12) as "the amount at which the item could be exchanged between a buyer and a seller, each of whom is well informed and willing, and neither of whom is compelled to buy or sell." Sales commissions and other costs of disposal should be considered if they are expected to be material.

SOP No. 82-1 recognizes that determining the estimated current value of some assets may be difficult, and if the costs of doing so would appear to exceed the benefits, recommends that the person use his or her judgment.

In general, the best way to determine estimated current value is by reference to recent market prices of similar assets in similar circumstances. If recent market prices are not available, other methods may be used, including the use of appraisals, the adjustment of historical cost by reference to a specific price index, the capitalization of past or prospective earnings, the use of liquidation values, or the use of discounted amounts of projected cash receipts.

Whatever method is used, it should be consistently applied from period to period for the same asset.

(b) RECEIVABLES. Receivables are presented at the discounted amounts of cash expected to be collected, using the prevailing interest rate at the date of the statement.

(c) MARKETABLE SECURITIES. Marketable securities are stocks, bonds, unfulfilled futures contracts, options on traded securities, CDs, and money market accounts for which market quotations are publicly available. The estimated current value of a marketable security is its closing price on the date of the statement, less the expected sales commission. IRAs and Keogh accounts should be presented net of the penalty charge for early withdrawal.

If the security was not traded on that date, but published bid and asked prices are available, SOP No. 82-1 states that the estimated current value should be within the range of those prices. Some accountants (Kinsman and Samuelson, 1987, p. 139), however, believe that only the bid price should be used, because "people can ask all they want for an asset, but what matters is what others will pay for it."

If bid and asked prices are not available for the date of the statement, the estimated current value is the closing price on the last day that the security was traded, unless the trade occurred so far back in the past as to be meaningless by the date of the statement.

On over-the-counter securities, unfortunately, the market does not speak with a single voice. Different quotations may be given by the financial press, quotation publications, financial reporting services, and various brokers. In such a case, the mean of the bid prices, of the bid and asked prices, or of the prices quoted by a representative sample of brokers may be used as the estimated current value.

Large blocks of stock may also pose a problem. If a large block of stock were dumped on the market, the price might not hold up. On the other hand, a controlling interest might be worth more, share for share, than a minority interest. Market prices may need to be adjusted for these factors to determine estimated current value. Preparers should consult a qualified stockbroker for an opinion on this problem.

Restrictions on the transfer of a stock are yet another factor that might call for an adjustment of market prices to determine estimated current value.

(d) LIMITED PARTNERSHIP INTERESTS.   If interests in a limited partnership are actively traded, the estimated current value of such an interest should be based on the prices of recent trades. If interests in the partnership are not actively traded, the current value of the partnership's underlying assets may be used to measure the value of the interest (see subsections 35.3(a) and (h)). When this method is used, the person should consider discounting the value of the interest for lack of marketability and lack of control over the general partner.

If it is not feasible to estimate the current value of the partnership's underlying assets (and the interests are not actively traded), the estimated current value of the interest may be shown at the amount of cash that the person has invested. If the underlying assets of the partnership are considered to be virtually worthless, however, the interest should be valued at zero.

The person's share of the partnership's negative tax basis, if any, should be included in the computation of the provision for income taxes (see section 35.5).

The statement should disclose the person's share of any recourse debts of the partnership, and any commitments for future funding. If the person's interest in the partnership represents a substantial proportion of ownership, it may be useful to disclose summarized financial information about the partnership as an investment in a closely held business (see subsection 35.3(h)).

(e) PRECIOUS METALS.   The estimated current value of precious metals, like that of marketable securities, is their closing price on the date of the statement, less the expected sales commission.

(f) OPTIONS ON ASSETS OTHER THAN MARKETABLE SECURITIES.   Options to buy assets other than marketable securities should first be valued at the difference between the exercise price and the asset's current value. Then this difference should be discounted at the person's borrowing rate over the option period, if this is material. The borrowing rate should reflect the cost of a loan secured by the asset.

(g) LIFE INSURANCE.   The estimated current value of a life insurance policy is its cash surrender value, less any loans against it. This information may be obtained from the insurance company.

Disclosure of the face value of the policy is required by SOP No. 82-1. It may also be useful to disclose the death benefits that would accrue to family members covered by the statement.

(h) CLOSELY HELD BUSINESSES.   If the person has a material investment in a closely held business that is conducted as a separate entity, the statement should disclose the name of the company, the person's percentage of ownership, and the nature of the business. It should also disclose summarized financial information on the company's assets, liabilities, and results of operations, based on the company's financial statements for the most recent year. The basis of presentation of these statements, such as GAAP, tax, or cash, should also be disclosed, and so should any significant loss contingencies.

Determining the estimated current value of an investment in a closely held business, whether a proprietorship, partnership, joint venture, or corporation, is notoriously difficult. The objective is to approximate the amount at which the investment could be exchanged, on the date of the statement, between a well-informed and willing buyer and seller, neither of whom is compelled to buy or sell. This value is presented as a single item in the statement of financial condition, and a condensed balance sheet of the company should be presented in the notes.

SOP No. 82-1 recognizes several methods, or combinations of methods, for determining the estimated current value of a closely held business: appraisals, multiple of earnings, liquidation value, reproduction value, discounted amounts of projected cash receipts, adjustments of book value, and cost of the person's share of the equity of the business. If a buy-out agreement exists specifying the amount that the person will receive when he or she withdraws, retires, or sells out, SOP No. 82-1 says that it should be considered but that it does not necessarily determine estimated current value.

A prior question that SOP No. 82-1 does not address is whether an accountant preparing a personal financial statement should try to value a closely held business at all. Competence in valuing businesses requires a considerable degree of concentration on the subject, and some accountants' litigation liability coverage excludes valuations. Qualified appraisers, such as members of the American Society of Appraisers or the Institute of Business Appraisers, are readily available to value the business. Thus, some accountants (Siegel and Lederfich, 1988, p. 67) believe that "the accountant should refrain from valuing the business interest himself."

(i) REAL ESTATE.   The estimated current value of an investment in real estate or a leasehold may be based on sales of similar properties in similar circumstances; on assessed value for property taxes, considering the basis of the assessment and its relationship to market values in the area; on the discounted amounts of projected cash flows from the property; or on an appraisal from a qualified real estate appraiser.

The estimated current value of a property should be presented net of expected sales commissions and closing costs.

(j) PERSONAL PROPERTY.   Personal property includes but is not limited to cars, jewelry, antiques, and art. These items should be valued at appraisal values derived from a specialist's opinion or at the values given in published guides such as the *Blue Book* for cars. If the costs of an appraisal seem to outweigh the benefits, historical cost should be used.

(k) INTANGIBLE ASSETS.   Patents, copyrights, and other intangible assets should be presented at the net proceeds of a current sale of the asset or the discounted amount of cash flow arising from its future use. If the amounts and timing of receipts from the asset cannot be reasonably estimated, the asset should be presented at its purchased cost.

(l) FUTURE INTERESTS.   The following future interests should be shown in a personal financial statement: guaranteed minimum portions of pensions, vested interests in pension or profit-sharing plans, deferred compensation contracts, beneficial interests in trusts, remainder interests in property subject to life estates, fixed amounts of alimony for a definite future period, and annuities. Any other future interests should also be shown, so long as they are nonforfeitable rights for fixed or determinable amounts; are not contingent on the holder's life expectancy or the occurrence of a particular event, such as disability or death; and do not require future performance of service by the holder.

Such future interests should be presented at their discounted amounts. Suppose, for example, that Sally Smith has an $80,000 interest in her employer's profit-sharing plan, 75% of it vested. She would receive her benefits in a lump sum one year after leaving the company. Assume the current interest rates on similar investments are 10%, the present value of $1 to be received in one year is $0.9091. Thus, Smith's interest in the profit-sharing plan would be calculated as $80,000 × 0.75 × 0.9091, and would be shown at $54,546.

35.4 LIABILITIES

(a) ESTIMATED CURRENT AMOUNT.   Payables and other liabilities are presented at their estimated current amount. This is the amount of cash to be paid, discounted by the rate implicit in the transaction in which the debt was incurred. APB Opinion No. 21, "Interest on Receivables and Payables," explains how to determine this rate.

Although certain kinds of liabilities are not discounted in business financial statements, all liabilities should be presented at their discounted amounts in personal financial statements. No distinction is made between current and long-term liabilities.

With some home mortgages and other debts, the person may be able to pay off the debt currently at an amount less than the present value of future payments. If this alternative exists, the debt should be presented at the lower amount.

Personal liabilities such as home mortgages are shown separately from investment liabilities such as margin accounts. Obligations related to limited partnership investments should be shown if the person is personally liable for them. Debt that was included in the valuation of an investment in a closely held business, however, should not be shown again here.

(b) NONCANCELABLE COMMITMENTS.   Child support, alimony, pledges to charities, and other noncancelable commitments to pay future sums should be presented as liabilities at their discounted amounts if they have all of the following characteristics:

- The commitment is for a fixed or determinable amount.
- The commitment is not contingent on someone else's life expectancy or the occurrence of a particular event, such as death or disability.
- The commitment does not require future performance by others, as an operating lease does.

(c) CONTINGENT LIABILITIES.   Among the contingent liabilities that should be considered for disclosure are personal guarantees on others' loans, liabilities for limited partnership obligations, lawsuits against the person, inadequate medical insurance coverage, and noncoverage for personal liability. SFAS No. 5, "Accounting for Contingencies," as amended, provides guidance on whether a contingent liability should be recorded, disclosed in a footnote, or omitted. This pronouncement says, in short, that a liability should be recorded if its related contingent loss or range of loss can be estimated and its occurrence is probable. If the amount of loss cannot be estimated but its occurrence is either probable or possible, the related liability should be recognized in a footnote. If its occurrence is remote, neither recording nor footnote recognition is required.

(d) INCOME TAXES PAYABLE.   Income taxes currently payable include any unpaid income taxes for past tax years, deferred income taxes arising from timing differences, and the estimated amount of income taxes accrued for the elapsed portion of the current tax year to the date of the statement. If the statement date coincides with the tax year-end, there is obviously no difficulty in estimating the amount for the current year. If the dates do not coincide, the estimate should be based on taxable income to date and the tax rate applicable to estimated taxable income for the whole year. The taxes for the current year should be shown net of amounts withheld from pay or paid with estimated tax returns.

35.5 PROVISION FOR INCOME TAXES

(a) DEFINITION. The personal financial statement presents a provision for the income taxes that would be owed if all of the person's assets were sold, and all of his or her liabilities paid, on the date of the statement. This provision should be shown under its full title as given in SOP No. 82-1 (par. 30): "Estimated income taxes on the differences between the estimated current values of assets and the estimated current amounts of liabilities and their tax bases." It is presented in the statement as one amount and is shown between liabilities and net worth. A note discloses the methods and assumptions used to compute it (see Exhibit 35.2).

(b) COMPUTING THE PROVISION FOR INCOME TAXES. Currently applicable income tax laws and regulations, state and local as well as federal, should be used in computing the provision for income taxes. Negative tax bases of tax shelters, recapture of depreciation, available carryovers, the one-time exclusion for sale of a residence, the deductibility of state income taxes against federal income taxes, and alternative minimum taxes should all be considered.

Because most of these considerations apply to one or two assets or liabilities but not to others, the provision for income taxes should be computed separately for each asset and each liability. It is not necessary, however, to disclose all these computations in the note. For example, note 12 in Exhibit 35.2, which is reproduced from SOP No. 82-1, shows only the excess of estimated current values over the tax bases of major assets.

(c) TAX BASIS. It is often difficult to determine the tax basis of an asset or liability acquired long ago, or by inheritance or trade. In such a case the preparer may use a conservative estimate of the tax basis in computing the provision for income taxes, with a note disclosing how the estimate was determined.

(d) DISCLAIMER. SOP No. 82-1 (par. 31) requires a statement that "the provision will probably differ from the amounts of income taxes that might eventually be paid because those amounts are determined by the timing and the method of disposal, realization, or liquidation and the tax laws and regulations in effect at the time of disposal, realization, or liquidation." This statement should be made in the note (see Exhibit 35.2, note 12).

35.6 STATEMENT OF CHANGES IN NET WORTH

(a) DEFINITION. A statement of changes in net worth is an optional supplement to the statement of financial condition. It presents the major sources of change in the person's net worth.

Whereas the statement of financial condition may or may not show amounts for prior periods and thus may not show change in net worth at all, the statement of changes in net worth should present:

- Increases in net worth produced by income, by increases in the estimated current values of assets, by decreases in the estimated current amounts of liabilities, and by decreases in the provision for income taxes.
- Decreases in net worth produced by expenses, by decreases in the estimated current values of assets, by increases in the estimated current amounts of liabilities, and by increases in the provision for income taxes.

The statement of changes in net worth does not attempt to measure net income. It combines income and other changes because the financial affairs of an individual or family are a mixture of business and personal activities.

(b) USES. Accountants have often found that lenders do not require a statement of changes in net worth from persons seeking credit; and that credit-seekers, for their part, are not eager to reveal so much information about their standard of living. But a statement of changes in net worth can be very useful in financial planning. As one accountant (Bull, 1984, p. 42) observes, knowing the amounts and sources of increase or decrease in wealth enables the person to estimate how much he or she will have to increase earnings or decrease consumption to achieve a desired level of wealth—or on the other hand, how much he or she may decrease earnings or increase consumption and still achieve the same goal.

(c) FORMAT. The sample statement of changes in net worth shown in Exhibit 35.2, which is reproduced from SOP No. 82-1, distinguishes realized from unrealized sources of increase or decrease in net worth, thus dividing the sources into four categories: Realized increases, realized decreases, unrealized increases, and unrealized decreases.

35.7 DISCLOSURES

A personal financial statement should include sufficient disclosures to make it adequately informative. These disclosures may be made either in the body of the statement or in the notes. The following list, although not exhaustive, indicates the nature and type of information that should ordinarily be disclosed:

- The names of the individuals covered by the statement.
- The fact that assets are presented at their estimated current values and liabilities at their estimated current amounts.
- The methods used to determine current values and amounts, and any change in these methods from one period to the next.
- If any assets shown in the statement are jointly held, the nature of the joint ownership.
- If the person's investments in securities are material in relation to his or her other assets, and if they are concentrated in one or a few companies or industries, the names of those companies or industries and the estimated current value of each security.
- Information on material investments in closely held businesses, including the name of the company; the person's percentage of ownership; the nature of the business; summarized financial information on the company's assets, liabilities, and results of operations, based on the company's financial statements for the most recent year; the basis of presentation of these statements, such as GAAP, tax, or cash; and any significant loss contingencies.
- Description of intangible assets and their estimated useful lives.
- The face amount of life insurance.
- Nonforfeitable rights, such as pensions based on life expectancy, that were omitted from the statement because they do not have all the characteristics required for inclusion (see subsection 35.3(1)).
- The following tax information:
    The methods and assumptions used in computing the provision for estimated income taxes on the differences between the estimated current values of assets and the estimated current amounts of liabilities and their tax bases.

A statement that this provision will probably differ from the amounts of income taxes that might eventually be paid, because these amounts will be determined by the actual timing and method of disposal, realization, or liquidation, and by the tax laws and regulations in effect at the time of disposal, realization, or liquidation.

Unused operating-loss and capital-loss carryforwards.

Other unused deductions and credits, with their expiration periods, if applicable.

The differences between the estimated current values of major assets and the estimated current amounts of major liabilities, or categories of assets and liabilities, and their tax bases.

- Maturities, interest rates, collateral, and other pertinent details on receivables and debt.
- Related-party transactions such as notes receivable or notes payable to other family members.
- Contingencies such as pending lawsuits and loan guarantees.
- Noncancelable commitments, such as operating leases, that do not have all the characteristics required for inclusion (see subsection 35.4(b)).
- Subsequent events, such as a decline in value of an asset after the statement date.

35.8 COMPILATION AND REVIEW

An accountant can compile or review personal financial statements based on an individual's representation of the estimated current values of assets and the estimated current amounts of liabilities. The accountant, however, should obtain an understanding of the methods the individual used to reach the conclusions regarding estimated values of assets and amounts of liabilities and determine that those methods were appropriate in the circumstances. In many engagements, the accountant will be involved with the client in determining the estimated values.

The standards applicable to compilations of financial statements in SSARS No. 1, "Compilation and Review of Financial Statements," are applicable to personal financial statements.

The SSARS No. 1 performance standards require an accountant, in both a compilation and a review, to reach an understanding with the client as to the services to be performed—compilation, review, or audit. The understanding may be oral or written. However, the use of a well-written engagement letter spelling out all services to be performed and establishing the fee structure is advised to avoid subsequent disputes and fee disagreements. The AICPA *Personal Financial Statement Guide* (Guide) includes sample engagement letters for compilations, reviews, and audits in Appendix A.

The accountant should also have a general understanding of the nature of the individual's financial transactions, form of available records, qualifications of accounting personnel, if any, the accounting basis on which the statements are to be presented, and the form and content of the statements. For example, the statements may be on a GAAP, cash, or tax basis.

In compilation, an understanding of the individual's business and personal records is necessary to compile personal financial statements in appropriate format. Similarly an understanding is necessary in a review engagement to determine the appropriate inquiry and analytical procedures necessary to support the review assurance on the individual's financial statements.

Knowledge required is generally gained through experience with the client's records and statements and through inquiries. The accountant must consider other services that may be necessary to compile an individual's financial statements, such as assembling records, determining values for assets, establishing current amounts of liabilities, income tax services, and so forth.

Ordinarily an accountant can compile personal statements based on the individual's representation of the estimated current values of assets and the estimated current amounts of liabilities, although, as indicated, assistance in determining these amounts is often required of the accountant. At a minimum, the accountant should have a clear understanding of the methods used to determine the estimated current values of significant assets and the estimated current amounts of significant liabilities and be satisfied that those methods are appropriate considering the circumstances of the engagement.

Although it will be necessary, in most engagements, for the accountant to assist the client in gathering the current values and amounts for the statements, it must be recognized that the accountant is not an appraiser of assets or an expert in determining present values for items such as pension plans and other assets and liabilities that may appear in personal financial statements. Therefore, it is appropriate for the accountant to rely on the services of an expert, such as a real estate appraiser or an actuary in gathering and evaluating client information.

In a compilation, the accountant is not required to make inquiries or perform other procedures to verify, corroborate, or review information supplied by the individual. However, if the accountant has reason to believe that the information supplied by the client is not correct, is incomplete, or is otherwise unsatisfactory to support the compilation of personal financial statements, he or she should attempt to obtain additional or revised information. If the client refuses to provide additional or revised information, or the accountant cannot otherwise obtain the needed information, he or she should withdraw from the engagement.

Before issuing his or her report, the accountant should read the compiled personal statements and consider whether they appear to be appropriate in form and free from obvious material errors.

The term "errors" refers to mistakes in compiling financial statements, including arithmetical or clerical mistakes, and mistakes in applying accounting standards, which includes inadequate disclosure. Examples of errors that might occur in personal financial statements prepared in conformity with GAAP (SOP No. 82-1) include failure to record estimated income taxes on the differences between the estimated current values of assets and the estimated current amounts of liabilities and their tax bases; not disclosing the way estimated current values and amounts were determined; and presenting asset or liability amounts at an obviously inappropriate value or amount.

Performance standards for reviews of personal financial statements are identical to those established in SSARS No. 1 for compilation engagements. In addition, however, in review engagements, the accountant must perform inquiry and analytical procedures sufficient to provide a reasonable basis for expressing limited assurance that there are no material modifications that should be made to the client's personal financial statements for them to be in conformity with GAAP or other comprehensive basis of accounting.

A review is not an audit and does not include a study and evaluation of internal accounting control, tests of accounting records, and other evidential procedures normally performed during an audit. Thus, a review does not provide assurance that the accountant will become aware of all significant matters that would be disclosed in an audit. However, if the accountant becomes aware of information that appears incorrect, incomplete, or otherwise unsatisfactory, he or she should perform the additional procedures considered necessary to achieve limited assurance that there are no material modifications that should be made to the financial statements for them to be in conformity with the basis of reporting.

SSARS No. 1, as amended, requires a written representation letter in all review engagements. Auditing standards require such a representation letter in audit engagements. Also, the Guide encourages use of the representation letter in personal financial statement compilation engagements. An example representation letter appropriate for a compilation, review, or audit engagement is reproduced in Appendix C of the Guide.

35.9 AUDITS

Generally accepted auditing standards (GAAS) apply to audits of personal financial statements, as they do to other audit engagements. As with any financial statement, the audit objective in personal financial statement engagements is to attest to the fairness of the assertions in the statements. Special attention must be given to the establishment of estimated current values and amounts in accordance with SOP No. 82-1.

GAAS requires a study and evaluation of internal accounting control, tests of accounting records and of responses to inquiries, and other evidence procedures considered necessary in the circumstances of the engagement. Because internal control is not usually a consideration, most of the independent auditors's effort in forming an opinion of personal financial statements consists of gathering evidential matter to support the assertions of existence and valuation of assets and the rights and obligations associated with those assets.

Often, as a result of the inadequacy of personal financial records, significant restrictions are imposed on the auditor's efforts to obtain needed evidential matter to support an opinion on personal financial statements. Accordingly, expressing an unqualified opinion is not possible. For this reason, most personal statement engagements are compilations, with some reviews.

35.10 REPORTS

The Guide discusses specific reporting standards for compilation, review, and audit engagements that incorporate the basic reporting standards in the SSARSs and the SASs.

Because a statement of financial condition is the only personal financial statement required by SOP No. 82-1, the accountant is frequently engaged to report on that statement only. Occasionally, an individual will need or want the accountant to report on both the statement of financial condition and a statement of changes in net worth. Usually the accountant is asked to report on current period statements only, although sometimes comparative statements are required.

Reporting standards in the SSARSs apply to compilations and reviews of personal financial statements. In a compilation or review engagement, an accountant is required to issue a report whenever the compilation or review is complete; and this requirement is applicable to the personal financial statements of an individual, as specified by SSARS No. 1, paragraph 4.

Personal financial statements compiled by an accountant should be accompanied by a report stating that:

A compilation has been performed in accordance with Statements on Standards for Accounting and Review Services issued by the American Institute of Certified Public Accountants (modified by SSARS No. 7)

A compilation is limited to presenting in the form of a personal financial statement(s) information that is the representation of the individual.

The financial statement(s) have not been audited or reviewed and, accordingly, the accountant does not express an opinion or any other form of assurance on them.

(SSARS No. 1, paragraph 14, modified for personal financial statements)

Any other procedures the accountant performs in connection with the engagement should not be mentioned in the report.

The compilation report is addressed to the individual whose financial statement(s) are compiled and the date of the report is the date of the completion of the compilation. Also, each page of the statement of financial condition (and the statement of changes in net worth, if presented) should include a reference "See Accountant's Compilation Report."

The standard compilation report, covering both the statement of financial condition and the statement of changes in net worth, follows (from Chapter 5, paragraph 3 of the Guide, modified appropriately by SSARS No. 7):

I [we] have compiled the accompanying statement of financial condition of [James and Jane Person] as of [date], and the related statement of changes in net worth for the [period] then ended, in accordance with Statements on Standards for Accounting and Review Services issued by the American Institute of Certified Public Accountants.

A compilation is limited to presenting in the form of financial statements information that is the representation of the individuals whose financial statements are presented. I [we] have not audited or reviewed the accompanying financial statements and, accordingly, do not express an opinion or any other form of assurance on them.

An accountant may be asked to compile personal financial statements that omit substantially all disclosures required by GAAP (SOP No. 82-1), including disclosures that might appear in the body of the statements. Such reporting is appropriate provided the omission of the disclosures is clearly indicated in the accountant's compilation report and the accountant is not aware that the disclosures are being omitted for the purpose of misleading the intended users of the statements. For example, it would not be appropriate to omit from personal financial statements intended for use in obtaining a home mortgage informative disclosures that would be important to the financial institution in making the loan decision. If disclosures are omitted, and certain selected information is presented in the footnotes, for example, information important in obtaining a mortgage loan, such information should be labeled "Selected Information—Substantially All Disclosures Required by Generally Accepted Accounting Principles Are Not Included." (SSARS No. 1, paragraph 19)

If substantially all disclosures are omitted from the personal financial statements and the statements do not disclose that the assets are presented at their estimated current values and that the liabilities are presented at their estimated current amounts, the accountant should include this disclosure in his or her compilation report. If the statements have been presented on a comprehensive basis of accounting other than GAAP, that basis of accounting, if not disclosed in the statements, must be included in the accountant's report.

The standard compilation report for personal financial statements, omitting substantially all disclosures, covering both the statement of financial condition and the statement of changes in net worth, is presented below from the Guide, Chapter 5, paragraph 4, modified appropriately by SSARS No. 7:

> I [we] have compiled the accompanying statement of financial condition of [James and Jane Person] as of [date], and the related statement of changes in net worth for the [period] then ended, in accordance with Statements on Standards for Accounting and Review Services issued by the American Institute of Certified Public Accountants.
>
> A compilation is limited to presenting in the form of financial statements information that is the representation of the individuals whose financial statements are presented. I [we] have not audited or reviewed the accompanying financial statements and, accordingly, do not express an opinion or any other form of assurance on them.
>
> [James and Jane Person] have elected to omit substantially all of the disclosures required by generally accepted accounting principles. If the omitted disclosures were included in the financial statements, they might influence the user's conclusions about the financial condition of [James and Jane Person] and changes in their net worth. Accordingly, these financial statements are not designed for those who are not informed about such matters.

As previously stated, if the statements do not disclose the basis of valuing assets and the basis of presentation of liabilities, this information must be included in the above report. The following sentence should be included at the end of the first paragraph of the above report:

> The financial statements are intended to present the assets of [James and Jane Person] at estimated current values and their liabilities at estimated current amounts.

Also, if the statements are presented on a comprehensive basis of accounting other than GAAP and that basis is not disclosed in the statements, the following sentence (which assumes the individual is reporting on the tax basis) would be appropriate as the last sentence of the first paragraph of the compilation report (SSARS No. 1, Interpretation No. 12, "Reporting on a Comprehensive Basis of Accounting Other Than Generally Accepted Accounting Principles):

> The financial statements have been prepared on the accounting basis used by the individual for federal income tax purposes, which is a comprehensive basis of accounting other than generally accepted accounting principles.

An accountant may issue a compilation report on the personal financial statements of an individual even though he or she is not independent with respect to that individual. In such cases, the "not independent" accountant must modify the compilation report to clearly state the non-independent status. The specific reason or reasons for the lack of independence should not be discussed. The accountant should simply add a bland additional paragraph to the compilation report stating:

> I am [we are] not independent with respect to [name of individual].

Sometimes an accountant is requested by an individual to assist in assembling data for the completion of a standard preprinted loan form and sign the form, or to sign such a form the client has compiled. SSARS No. 3, "Compilation Reports on Financial Statements Included in Certain Prescribed Forms," provides an alternative form of standard compilation report when a prescribed form or related instructions call for departure from GAAP by specifying a measurement principle not in conformity with GAAP or by failing to request the disclosures required by GAAP.

SSARS No. 3 reporting standards are appropriate for prescribed forms that request information from personal financial statements that have been compiled or reviewed by an accountant.

As stated in SSARS No. 3, paragraph 2, a **prescribed form** is any standard preprinted form designed or adopted by the body to which it is to be submitted, for example, forms used by credit agencies. There is a **presumption** in SSARS No. 3 that the information required by a prescribed form is sufficient to meet the needs of the body that designed or adopted the form and there is no need for that body to be advised of departures from GAAP (SOP No. 82-1 for personal financial statements on prescribed forms) required by the prescribed form or related instructions.

If engaged to report on information included in a prescribed form meeting the definitions in SSARS No. 3 regarding personal financial statements, an accountant should follow the standard form for such compilation reports prescribed by the Guide, Chapter 5, paragraph 8, as modified by SSARS No. 7. It is important to remember to use the following form of accountant's report for personal financial statements included in prescribed forms that call for departures from GAAP. Such statements call for departures from GAAP by not requesting footnotes or by requesting information in the body of the statements that is not in conformity with SOP No. 82-1, i.e., GAAP:

> I [we] have compiled the [identification of financial statements, including period covered and name of individual(s)] included in the accompanying prescribed form, in accordance with Statements on Standards for Accounting and Review Services issued by the American Institute of Certified Public Accountants.
>
> My [our] compilation was limited to presenting in the form prescribed by [name of body] information that is the representation of the individuals whose financial statements are presented. I [we] have not audited or reviewed the financial statements referred to above and, accordingly, do not express an opinion or any other form of assurance on them.
>
> These financial statements (including related disclosures) are presented in accordance with the requirements of [name of body], which differ from generally accepted accounting

principles. Accordingly, these financial statements are not designed for those who are not informed about such differences.

If the information presented in the prescribed form does not disclose that the personal statements present assets at their estimated current values and liabilities at their estimated current amounts, the accountant's compilation report should include the following as the final paragraph of the above report:

> Except as prescribed by the requirements of [name of body], the financial statements are intended to present the assets of [James and Jane Person] at estimated current values and their liabilities at estimated current amounts.

If there are departures from the requirements of the form, other than GAAP, and the accountant is aware of these departures, he or she must modify the compilation report by adding an additional paragraph or paragraphs, if necessary, to alert the reader to the deficiencies. For example, the final paragraph of a compilation report with departures from the requirements of the form might read:

> However, I did become aware of a departure from generally accepted accounting principles that is not called for by the prescribed form or related instructions [describe the departure and its effect on the statements, if known, or state that the effect has not been determined].

An accountant should not sign a preprinted accountant's report that does not conform with the guidance in SSARS No. 1 regarding the standard compilation report. If the preprinted report form cannot be appropriately revised, the accountant should attach his or her own report following the guidance provided in SSARS No. 3 or SSARS No. 1, as appropriate.

An accountant compiling or reviewing personal financial statements may become aware of a departure from GAAP—SOP No. 82-1 involving either measurement principles or disclosure principles, or both. If the accountant decides that attempting to explain the GAAP deficiencies in the personal financial statements in his or her report will not adequately communicate the problems to potential statement users, the accountant should withdraw from the engagement and issue no report.

If the accountant believes he or she can appropriately communicate the departure in the compilation or review report, the problem should be described in a separate paragraph of the report. The separate paragraph(s) should explain what GAAP requires, what the client has done, and the effects of the departure on the statements, if such effects have been determined. If the effects have not been determined, this fact should also be disclosed in the separate paragraph(s).

For example, if the client has reported an investment at cost, rather than fair value as required by GAAP for personal financial statements, and the accountant cannot persuade the individual to change the amount, the following might be added to a standard compilation on a "statement of financial condition"—note that the last sentence of the second paragraph of the report has been modified to reference the GAAP departure explained in the third paragraph:

> I have compiled the accompanying statement of financial condition of [Tom Shipp] as of [date], in accordance with Statements on Standards for Accounting and Review Services issued by the American Institute of Certified Public Accountants.
>
> A compilation is limited to presenting in the form of financial statements information that is the representation of the individual whose financial statements are presented. I have not audited or reviewed the accompanying financial statement and, accordingly, do not express an opinion or any other form of assurance on it. However, I did become aware of a departure from generally accepted accounting principles that is described in the following paragraph.

As disclosed in Note x to the financial statements, generally accepted accounting principles require that assets be presented at their estimated current values and that liabilities be presented at their estimated current amounts. [Tom Shipp] has informed me that his investment in Brooks, Inc., is stated in the accompanying financial statements at cost and that the effects of this departure from generally accepted accounting principles on his financial condition have not been determined.

If the above GAAP departure existed in a review engagement, an identical description paragraph would be added to the review report explaining the use of the cost basis in place of estimated current amounts. In the case of a review, the third paragraph of the review report would read:

Based on my review, with the exception of the matter described in the following paragraph, I am not aware of any material modifications that should be made to the accompanying financial statement in order for it to be in conformity with generally accepted accounting principles.

The final paragraph would be as presented above in the compilation report for Tom Shipp. (Modified from the Guide, Chapter 5, paragraph 12, to conform to current standards.)

The standard review report should express limited assurance that, based on the performance of inquiry and analytical procedures, the accountant is not aware of any material modifications that should be made to the personal financial statements for them to be in conformity with GAAP or other comprehensive basis of accounting.

The standard review report, from the Guide, Chapter 5, paragraph 10, modified by SSARS No. 7, follows:

I [We] have reviewed the accompanying statement of financial condition of [James and Jane Person] as of [date], and the related statement of changes in net worth for the [period] then ended, in accordance with Statement on Standards for Accounting and Review Services issued by the American Institute of Certified Public Accountants. All information included in these financial statements is the representation of [James and Jane Person].

A review of personal financial statements consists principally of inquiries of the individuals whose financial statements are presented and analytical procedures applied to financial data. It is substantially less in scope than an audit in accordance with generally accepted auditing standards, the objective of which is the expression of an opinion regarding the financial statements taken as a whole. Accordingly, I [we] do not express such an opinion.

Based on my [our] review, I am [we are] not aware of any material modifications that should be made to the accompanying financial statements in order for them to be in conformity with generally accepted accounting principles.

Reviews of personal financial statements are not nearly as frequent as compilations. Reviews are more involved, requiring inquiry and analytical procedures, and carry considerably more professional responsibility on the part of the accountant than does a compilation engagement. Also, they are more expensive. Generally, reviews are viewed by the public and the legal system as something just below an audit in professional responsibility, when in fact a review does not include any of the evidence gathering procedures found in audit engagements. Reviews are generally considered by the profession to be just a step or two above a compilation and far below the responsibility associated with an audit engagement.

Audits of personal financial statements are the rarest of the three types of engagements primarily because of the general lack of adequate accounting records supporting personal assets, liabilities and equities, and the transactions data affecting those balances. Also, the standards requiring presentation of a statement of financial condition with assets at estimated fair values and liabilities at estimated current amounts create audit problems. The auditor frequently is unable to obtain sufficient competent evidential matter to support an opinion on personal financial statements. Many such engagements involve a "disclaimer of opinion" because of scope restrictions on the auditor's ability to obtain necessary evidence.

The auditor will attempt to obtain evidence as to the individual's assertions regarding the existence of assets and the proper determination of their fair values and the amount of liabilities and the appropriateness of the underlying estimates.

Following is the auditor's standard report appropriate for personal financial statements (Guide, Chapter 5, paragraph 13):

INDEPENDENT AUDITOR'S REPORT

I [We] have audited the accompanying statement of financial condition of [James and Jane Person] as of [date], and the related statement of changes in net worth for the [period] then ended. These financial statements are the responsibility of [James and Jane Person]. My [Our] responsibility is to express an opinion on these financial statements based on my [our] audit.

I [We] conducted my [our] audit in accordance with generally accepted auditing standards. Those standards require that I [we] plan and perform the audit to obtain reasonable assurance about whether the financial statements are free of material misstatement. An audit includes examining, on a test basis, evidence supporting the amounts and disclosures in the financial statements. An audit also includes assessing the accounting principles used and significant estimates made by [James and Jane Person], as well as evaluating the overall financial statement presentation. I [We] believe that my [our] audit provides a reasonable basis for my [our] opinion.

In my [our] opinion, the financial statements referred to above present fairly, in all material respects, the financial condition of [James and Jane Person] as of [date], and the changes in their net worth for the [period] then ended in conformity with generally accepted accounting principles.

The Guide presents examples of auditor's reports on personal financial statements modified because of scope restrictions (qualified opinions and disclaimer of opinions) and reports modified because of departures from GAAP (qualified opinions and adverse opinions). These reports are very unusual because the individual will usually request a compilation or, at most a review of personal statements. Only individuals in political office or those in positions where their financial status is being challenged will need an audit of their personal wealth.

Statement on Auditing Standards No. 62, "Special Reports," paragraphs 9 and 10 probably apply to disclosure in personal financial statements presented on the cash or tax basis of accounting (OCBOA). The disclosure standards in OCBOA statements are essentially the same as for GAAP statements, especially for those items appearing in the tax basis or modified cash basis statements that are the same as or similar to items that appear in GAAP basis statements. For those items, such as depreciation, long-term debt and owners' equity, the disclosures should be comparable to those in GAAP statements.

Presented below, from paragraph 19 of the Guide, modified by SSARS No. 7, is an illustrative compilation report on the income tax basis of accounting. Note the wording used in the first paragraph to describe the financial statements and how that wording varies from the GAAP format:

I [We] have complied the accompanying statement of assets and liabilities—income tax basis of [James and Jane Person] as of [date], and the related statement of changes in net assets—income tax basis for the [period] then ended, in accordance with Statements on Standards for Accounting and Review Services issued by the American Institute of Certified Public Accountants.

A compilation is limited to presenting in the form of financial statements information that is the representation of the individuals whose financial statements are presented. I [we] have not audited or reviewed the accompanying financial statements and, accordingly, do not express an opinion or any other form of assurance on them.

SSARS No. 6 provides an exception for the performance and reporting standards in SSARS No. 1 for personal statements included in written personal financial plans. Such statements included in written personal financial plans frequently exclude disclosures required by GAAP and contain other GAAP departures. These exceptions exist because the statements are prepared to facilitate the financial plan and not for credit purposes.

An accountant, according to SSARS No. 6, may submit a written personal financial plan containing unaudited personal financial statements to a client without complying with the compilation and review performance and reporting standards when all the following conditions are met:

An understanding is reached with the client, preferably in writing, that the financial statements,

Will be used solely to assist the client's advisers to develop the client's personal financial goals and objectives.

Will not be used to obtain credit or for any purposes other than developing the personal financial plan.

Nothing comes to the accountant's attention during the engagement to cause him or her to believe that the statements will be used to obtain credit or for any purposes other than the personal financial plan or its implementation by an insurance agent, broker, attorney, or like agent.

If the above objectives are met, the following report, from paragraph 25, Chapter 5, of the Guide, may be used in place of the standard compilation report for personal financial statements included in personal financial plans:

The accompanying statement of financial condition of [James and Jane Person], as of [date], was prepared solely to help you develop your personal financial plan. Accordingly, it may be incomplete or contain other departures from generally accepted accounting principles and should not be used to obtain credit or for any purposes other than developing your financial plan. We have not audited, reviewed, or compiled the statement.

Each of the personal financial statements should include a reference to the accountant's report.

35.11 SOURCES AND SUGGESTED REFERENCES

Accounting Principles Board, APB Opinion No. 21, "Interest on Receivables and Payables," AICPA, New York, 1971.

American Institute of Certified Public Accountants, Accounting and Review Services Committee, "Compilation and Review of Financial Statements," Statement on Standards for Accounting and Review Services No. 1, AICPA, New York, 1979.

————, "Reporting on Personal Financial Statements Included in Written Personal Financial Plans," Statement on Standards for Accounting and Review Services No. 6, AICPA, New York, 1986.

————, "Accounting and Financial Reporting for Personal Financial Statements," Accounting Standards Division, Statement of Position No. 82-1, AICPA, New York, 1982.

————, Personal Financial Statements Task Force, Personal Financial Statements Guide, AICPA, New York, 1983.

Bull, I. O., "Personal Financial Statements—Suggestions for Improvement," *CPA Journal,* December 1984, p. 42.

Financial Accounting Standards Board, "Accounting for Contingencies," Statement of Financial Accounting Standards No. 5, FASB, Stamford, CT, 1975.

Kinsman, M. D., and Samuelson, B., "Personal Financial Statements: Valuation Challenges and Solutions," *Journal of Accountancy,* September 1987, p. 139.

Siegel, J. G., and Lederfich, L., "Accounting and Disclosures for Personal Financial Statements," CPA Journal, February 1988, p. 67.

CHAPTER 36

PARTNERSHIPS AND JOINT VENTURES

Gerard L. Yarnall, CPA

American Institute of Certified Public Accountants

Ronald J. Patten, PhD, CPA

College of Commerce
DePaul University

CONTENTS

36.1 NATURE AND ORGANIZATION OF PARTNERSHIP ENTITY

(a) DEFINITION OF PARTNERSHIP.   The Uniform Partnership Act (UPA), which has been adopted by most of the states, defines a partnership as an association of two or more persons who contribute money, property, or services to carry on as co-owners a business for profit.

A partnership may be **general** or **limited.** In the general partnership each partner may be held personally responsible for all the firm's debts, whereas in the limited partnership the liability of certain partners is limited to their respective contributions to the capital of the firm. The limited partnership is composed of a general partner and limited partners with the latter playing no role in the management of the business. Limited partnerships are discussed in section 36.6.

While partnerships remain popular as a form of business organization, they are not as commonly used as they once were. The Tax Reform Act of 1986 has served to dampen the attractiveness of limited partnerships as tax shelters. Similarly, new accounting standards that are more prone to require consolidation of investees have made the use of partnerships and joint venture for purposes such as research and development less advantageous. At the same time, many law firms and public accounting firms that were organized as general partnerships are tending to organize themselves as professional corporations as a result of the favorable tax status that can flow from that structure, as well as the easing of state laws forbidding professional firms to incorporate.

(b) ADVANTAGES AND DISADVANTAGES OF PARTNERSHIP.   Bogen (1968, Section 12, p. 5) states:

> The partnership form of organization is superior to the proprietorship because it permits several persons to combine their resources and abilities to conduct a business. It is easier to form than a corporation, and retains a personal character making it more suitable in professional fields.

A distinct advantage of a partnership over a corporation is the close relationship between ownership and management. This provides more flexible administration, as well as more management talent with a personal interest in the problems and success of the business.

Historically, the three outstanding disadvantages of the partnership form of organization, as compared with corporate form, were recognized as (1) **unlimited liability of the partners for business debts,** (2) **mutual agency power of each partner as it pertains to business actions,** and (3) **limited life of the partnerships.** However, the existence of a number of large partnerships, particularly in the fields of law, accountancy, and investment banking, indicates that to a great degree many of these disadvantages may be more apparent than real. In addition, partnerships have devised a number of ways to overcome some of the drawbacks. For example, since the partnership is subject to dissolution upon the death, bankruptcy, insanity, or retirement of a partner—which events do not affect the continuity of a corporation—long-term commitments for the business unit are difficult to obtain. Many partnerships agreements overcome this drawback by providing for automatic continuation by the remaining partners subject to liquidation of the former partner's interest. In a sense, these partnerships have an unlimited life.

Still, the unlimited liability condition, which creates the possibility of loss of personal assets on the part of each partner, is a retardant to many. This is especially important when one considers that each party is assumed to be an agent for all partnership activities, with the power to bind other partners as a result of his or her actions. Again, however, some partnerships have managed to overcome these difficulties, at least partially, by adopting variations of the partnership form of organizations. Such variants include the following:

Limited Liability Companies. Limited liability companies (LLC) are a relatively new form of business entity in the United States and have characteristics of both corporations and partnerships. LLCs shield their owners (or members) from personal liability for certain of the entity's debts and obligations, in much the same manner as a corporation. At the same time, a properly organized LLC can be treated as a partnership for federal income tax purposes, enabling it to enjoy the tax item pass-through and other benefits of the standard partnership form.

Registered Limited Liability Partnerships. Registered limited liability partnerships (LLPs), a distant relative of the limited liability company (LLC) are a type of general partnership that protect the partners' *personal* assets if another of their partners is sued for malpractice. However, the assets of the partnership itself remain at risk, as do the personal assets of the accused partner, and all partners still retain the standard joint-and-several liabilities of the partnership (e.g., lease obligations and bank loans).

Limited Partnerships. The limited partnership form has proliferated in recent years as a vehicle for raising capital for a particular project or undertaking. Limited partnerships are particularly common in the leasing and oil and gas industries. Prior to the Tax Reform Act of 1986, the limited partnership form also served as the organizational structure for a number of tax shelters. Limited partners risk losing their limited liability the more they participate in the management or control of the partnership's activities, thus reducing the attractiveness of the limited partnership structure for some potential partners. See section 36.6 for further discussion of limited partnerships.

Joint Ventures. Partnerships are often encountered in the formation and operation of joint ventures. In a typical corporate joint venture, two or more entities form a partnership to undertake a specific business project, often for a specific, agreed-upon period. Each party's contributions to the venture may vary widely from case to case. For example, one corporation may provide technology, personnel, or facilities while the other contributes only the cash or other operating capital required for the undertaking. Alternatively, the venturers may jointly provide some or all of these elements. In any event, the entities form an enterprise that will function as a partnership, even if that partnership has the legal status of a corporation. See section 36.7 for further discussion of joint ventures.

(c) TAX CONSIDERATIONS. Even though a partnership is not considered a separate taxable entity for purposes of paying and determining federal income taxes, it is treated as such for purposes of making various elections and for selecting its accounting methods, taxable year, and method of depreciation.

Under Section 761 (a) of Subchapter K of the Internal Revenue Code of 1954, certain unincorporated organizations may be excluded, completely or partially, from treatment as partnerships for federal income tax purposes. This exclusion applies only to those organizations used (1) for investment purposes rather than as the active conduct of a business, or (2) for the joint extraction, production, or use of property, but not for the purpose of selling the products or services extracted or produced.

The use of limited partnerships because of favorable tax considerations has been significantly reduced as a result of the Tax Reform Act of 1986. Prior to passage of that Act, limited partnerships as a form of tax-sheltered investment, had been used in real estate, motion picture production, oil drilling, cable TV, cattle feeding, and research and development. The limited partnership gave investors the tax advantages of the partnership such as the pass-through of losses, while at the same time limiting their liability to the original investment. The Tax Reform Act of 1986 changed the situation considerably, however.

I.R.C. § 465 generally limits a partner's loss to the amount that the partner has "at risk" and could actually lose from an activity. These rules, which apply to individuals and certain closely held corporations, are designed to prevent taxpayers from offsetting trade, business, or professional income with losses from investments in activities that are, for the most part, financed by nonrecourse loans for which they are not personally liable. If it is determined that the loss is deductible under these "at-risk" rules, the taxpayer is subjected to "passive activity" loss rules. Generally, losses from passive trade or business activities, such as in a partnership where the partner is not active, may not be deducted from other types of income such as wages, interest, or dividends according to I.R.C. § 469.

Some substantial tax benefits can still be enjoyed by investing in a triple net lease limited partnership. These partnerships buy buildings that are used by fast-food, auto parts, and other chains and franchises that do not want mortgage debt on their balance sheet. The partnerships collect rent and pass it along to the partners net of three costs—insurance, upkeep, and property taxes—paid by the tenants.

(d) IMPORTANCE OF PARTNERSHIP. In the United States, the single proprietorship is the most common form of business organization in terms of number of establishments, and the corporate form does by far the greatest volume of business. Nevertheless, the partnership form of organization holds an important place in both respects and fills a significant need. It is widely employed among the **smaller business units** and in **professional fields** such as medicine, law, dentistry, and accountancy, activities in which the partners are closely identified with the operation of the business or profession. Partnerships are also found in financial lines, such as investment banks. Occasionally a substantial trading or other business is conducted as a partnership.

(e) FORMATION OF PARTNERSHIP. The agreement among the copartners that brings the partnership into existence may be oral or written. The latter is much to be preferred. Note the following from Bedford, Perry, and Wyatt (1979):

> Since a partnership is based on a contract between two or more persons, it is important, although not necessarily a legal requirement, that special attention be given to the drawing up of the partnership agreement. This agreement is generally referred to as the "Articles of

Copartnership." In order to avoid unnecessary and perhaps costly litigation at some later date, the Articles should contain all of the terms of the agreement relating to the formation, operation, and dissolution of the partnership.

Each partner should sign the Articles and retain a copy of the agreement. It is desirable that a copy of the agreement be filed with the recorder, clerk, or other official designated to receive such documents in the county in which the partnership has its principal place of business. In the case of a limited partnership such filing is imperative. There may also be a requirement that the agreement be published in newspapers.

According to Bogen (1968), the following matters should be covered by the articles:

1. Names of partners and the firm name.
2. Kind of business to be conducted.
3. Capital contribution of each partner.
4. Duration of the partnership contract.
5. The time to be devoted to the business by each, and any limitation upon outside business interests.
6. Method of dividing profits and losses.
7. Restrictions upon the agency powers of the partners.
8. Salaries to be paid partners, or limitations upon the withdrawal of profits.
9. Method of admitting new partners.
10. Provision for insurance on lives of partners for benefit of firm.
11. Procedure to be followed in voluntary dissolution.
12. Procedure upon death or withdrawal of partner, including method of valuation of tangible assets and goodwill, and provision for continuation of the business by the remaining partners.

In the event that contributions of assets other than cash are being made to the new firm, the articles should also cover the matter of **income tax treatment** upon the subsequent disposal of such assets. In general, such assets retain the tax basis of the previous owner so that the taxable gain or loss when ultimately disposed of may be greater or less than the gain or loss to the partnership.

Many partnerships have been plagued, if not entirely destroyed, through disagreements that could have been avoided, or greatly minimized, by the exercising of more care and skill in the drafting of the original agreement.

(f) INITIAL BALANCE SHEET.   Section 8 of the UPA states that:

1. All property originally brought into the partnership or subsequently acquired by purchase or otherwise, on account of the partnership is partnership property.
2. Unless the contrary intention appears, property acquired with partnership funds is partnership property.

It follows that the initial balance sheet should explicitly identify the assets contributed by partners as belonging to the partnership and assign values to these assets that are agreeable to all partners. Debts assumed by the partnership will receive comparable treatment. The initial balance sheet should also show the total initial proprietorship and the partners' shares therein. According to Moonitz and Jordan (1963):

The most direct manner of accomplishing this result is to include the initial balance sheet in the partnership agreement itself. If it is not expedient to include it as an integral part of the agreement, reference to the initial balance sheet should be made in the agreement, and the balance sheet, as a separate document, should be signed by each partner.

Unambiguous **identification** of assets and obligations at the inception of the partnership is important for at least two reasons. (1) Partnership creditors have no claim against the assets of individual partners until the partnership assets have been exhausted (special cases are discussed in Parts III and VI of the UPA). (2) Unless specifically provided for in the partnership agreement, partnership assets may be used only for partnership purposes; partners' personal assets are, of course, subject to no such limitations.

36.2 ACCOUNTING FOR PARTNERSHIP OPERATIONS

(a) PECULIARITIES OF PARTNERSHIP ACCOUNTING.   In many respects, the accounting problems of the partnership are the same as those of other forms of business organization. The underlying pattern of the accounting for the various assets and current goods and service costs, including departmental classification and assignment, is not modified by the type of ownership and method of raising capital employed. The same is true of the recording of revenues and the treatment of liabilities. The **special features** of partnership accounting relate primarily to the recording and tracing of capital, the treatment of personal services furnished by the partners, the division of profits, and the adjustments of equities required upon the occasion of reorganization or liquidation of the firm.

(b) METHODS OF DIVIDING PROFITS AND LOSSES.   As stated in § 18 of the UPA, partnership income is shared equally unless otherwise provided for in the partnership agreement. In some cases the agreement may specify division of profits in an arbitrary ratio (which of course includes the equal ratio already mentioned), referred to elsewhere in this discussion as the **income ratio.** Such a specified ratio (e.g., 60 − 40, $\frac{2}{3}$ − $\frac{1}{3}$) may or may not be related to the original capital contributions of the respective partners. It is reiterated that the essential point is agreement among the partners as to how they wish profits to be divided.

Another example of profit division by a single set of relationships is afforded by division in **proportion to capital balances.** Since this phrase is ambiguous, the agreement should specify which of the following bases are intended: (1) original capital, (2) capital at the beginning of the year, (3) capital at the end of the year, or (4) average capital. If the last is specified, the method of computation should be outlined.

(c) EXAMPLE USING AVERAGE CAPITAL RATIO.   The following example shows the division of profits and losses on the basis of average capital ratios.

The Articles of Copartnership of Bracey and Maloney provide for the division of profits on the basis of the average capital balances as shown for the year by the books of the partnership. Effect is to be given to all contributions and withdrawals during the year. The capital accounts for the year appear as follows:

	Bracey		*Maloney*	
	Debit	*Credit*	*Debit*	*Credit*
January 1		$60,000		$48,000
March 1	$6,000			
April 1			$3,000	
June 1		12,000		
July 1			6,000	
September 1		3,000		21,000
October 1	9,000		9,000	
December 1				6,000

Computation of average capital is as follows:

			Bracey		
	Debits	Credits	Balance	Time Maintained	Dollar-Months
January 1		$60,000	$60,000	2 mos.	$120,000
March 1	$ 6,000		54,000	3	162,000
June 1		12,000	66,000	3	198,000
September 1		3,000	69,000	1	69,000
October 1	9,000		60,000	3	180,000
	$15,000	$75,000	$60,000	12 mos.	$729,000
Average capital ($729,000 ÷ 12)					$ 60,750

			Maloney		
	Debits	Credits	Balance	Time Maintained	Dollar-Months
January 1		$48,000	$48,000	3 mos.	$144,000
April 1	$ 3,000		45,000	3	135,000
July 1	6,000		39,000	2	78,000
September 1		21,000	60,000	1	60,000
October 1	9,000		51,000	2	102,000
December 1		6,000	57,000	1	57,000
	$18,000	$75,000	$57,000	12 mos.	$576,000
Average capital ($576,000 ÷ 12)					$ 48,000

If net profit for the year is $36,000, it is distributed as follows:

Bracey	$ 60,750	6,075 ÷ 10,875 × $36,000 = $20,110.35
Maloney	48,000	4,800 ÷ 10,875 × 36,000 = $15,889.65
	$108,750	$36,000.00

The method above assumes each month to be of equal significance. If the contributions and withdrawals are dated irregularly, it might be desirable to use days rather than months as the time unit.

(d) TREATMENT OF TRANSACTIONS BETWEEN PARTNER AND FIRM. It has often been pointed out that no single profit-sharing ratio can yield equitable results under all circumstances in view of the various contributions of the partners to the firm activities. Accordingly, the articles may well include provisions regarding allowances for (1) interest on invested capital, (2) salaries for services rendered, and (3) bonuses. The ratio for dividing the profit or loss remaining after applying such provisions must, of course, also be specified.

(i) Interest on Invested Capital. The partnership agreement should cover at least four points in the matter of allowing interest on invested capital:

1. Specific rate or directions for determining the rate.
2. Procedure to be followed if the net income before interest is less than the interest requirement.
3. Procedure to be followed if the partnership experiences a loss.

4. Capital balance (beginning, closing, or average) on which interest is to be allowed (and, if an average balance, method by which the average is to be determined).

The **rate of interest** may be stated specifically or it may be determined by reference to the call money market, the yield of certain governmental obligations, the charge made by local banks for commercial loans, or some other available measure.

If the articles provide for a regular interest allowance, there should be included a statement of how to deal with the cases in which the firm operates at a loss or has a net profit of less than the interest. Following are two ways of dealing with these contingencies: (1) the interest allowance may be dropped or reduced (when there is some profit) for the period in question; (2) the full interest may be allowed and the resulting net debit in the income account apportioned in the income (profit-sharing) ratio. The second procedure is customary for cases in which the articles do not cover the point precisely.

(ii) Partners' Salaries.   Each working partner should be entitled to a stated salary as compensation for his services just as each investing partner should receive interest on his capital investment. (The general rule, from a legal standpoint, is that a partner is not entitled to compensation for services in carrying on the business, other than his share in the profits, unless such compensation is specifically authorized in the partnership agreement.) It is always desirable that the articles of partnership specify the amounts of salaries or wages to be paid to partners, or indicate clearly how the amounts are to be determined. The agreement regarding salaries should also cover the contingencies of inadequate income and net losses in particular periods.

Charges for salaries designed to represent reasonable allowances for personal services rendered by the partners are often viewed as **operating expenses,** and this interpretation may be included in the agreement. Under this interpretation, there would seem to be good reason for concluding that regular salaries should be allowed, whether or not the business is operated at a profit. As is the case with interest allowances on capital investments, there is strong presumption that if salaries are authorized in the agreement, they must be allowed, regardless of the level of earnings, in all cases in which a contrary treatment is not prescribed.

Treatment of salary allowances as business expenses is convenient from the standpoint of accounting procedure, particularly in that this treatment facilitates appropriate departmentalization of such charges. On the other hand, it must not be forgotten that partners' salaries, like interest allowances, are essentially devices intended to provide equitable treatment of partners who are supplying unlike amounts of capital and services to the firm; the purpose, in other words, is to secure an equitable apportionment of earnings.

According to Bedford (1962), a distinct rule, "derived from custom and from law," that applies in accounting for partnership owners' equities, is that "the income of a partnership is the income before deducting partners' salaries; partners' salaries are treated as a means of dividing partnership income."

Dixon, Hepworth, and Paton (1966), on the other hand, indicate that the interpretation of partners' salaries should vary with the circumstances:

> Where there are a substantial number of partners, and salaries are allowed to only one or two members who are active in administration, there is practical justification for treating such salaries as operating charges closely akin to the cost of services furnished by outsiders. This is especially defensible where the salaries are subject to negotiation from period to period and are in no way dependent upon the presence of net earnings. Where there are only two partners, and both capital investments and contributions of services are substantially equal, there is less need for salary adjustments; if "salaries" are allowed in such a situation it would seem to be reasonable to interpret them as preliminary distributions of net income—an income derived from a coordination of capital and personal efforts in a business venture. Between these two extremes there lies a range of less clear-cut cases . . . .

(iii) Bonuses. Where a particular partner furnishes especially important services, the device of a bonus—usually expressed as a percentage of net income—may be employed as a means of providing additional compensation. The principal question that arises in such cases is the interpretation of the bonus in relation to the final net amount to be distributed according to the regular income ratio, as illustrated in the following example.

Stark and Bruch share profits equally. Per the partnership agreement, Bruch is to receive a bonus of 20% of the net income of the firm, before allowing the bonus, for special services to the firm. If in a particular year the credit balance of the expense and revenue account is $27,000 before allowing the bonus, profits are divided as follows:

	Stark	Bruch	Total
Bonus, 20% of $27,000		$ 5,400	$ 5,400
Balance equally	$10,800	10,800	21,600
	$10,800	$16,200	$27,000

If the bonus is to be treated as an expense item in the computation of the final net income, the $27,000 credit balance of the expense and revenue account represents both the bonus and the final net income. Hence the $27,000 is 120% of the net income, and the net income is 100% or $22,500. Under this method the profits are divided as follows:

	Stark	Bruch	Total
Bonus, 20% of $22,500		$ 4,500	$ 4,500
Balance equally	$11,250	11,250	22,500
	$11,250	$15,750	$27,000

(iv) Debtor–Creditor Relationship. At times, when a partnership is formed, a partner may not be interested in investing more than a certain amount of assets on a permanent basis. He, therefore, may make an advance to the partnership that is viewed as a loan rather than an increase in his capital account. The firm may thus obtain the initial financing it needs without having to negotiate with an outside source on less favorable terms. The loan may be interest bearing and may be repayable in installments. As noted by Meigs, Johnson, and Keller (1966), **interest charges** on such loans should be treated as an expense of the partnership, and the loan itself should be disclosed clearly as a liability of the firm.

Occasionally, a partner may withdraw a sum from the partnership. This type of transaction should be treated in the manner dictated by the circumstances. If the loan is material relative to the partner's net personal assets, if no repayment terms are stipulated, and if the loan has been long outstanding, the loan is, in effect, a **withdrawal** and should be viewed as a contraction of the firm's capital. If, on the other hand, the partner has every intention of repaying the sum, the loan may be regarded as a valid receivable.

(v) Landlord–Tenant Relationship. In some cases, a partner may rent property from or to the partnership. Transactions of this type should be handled exactly as rental agreements with others are handled. The only possible difference in recording this type of event would find the rent receivable from a partner being debited to his drawing or capital account instead of to a "rent receivable" account. If the rent was owed to the partner, the payable could be recorded as a credit to either the partner's drawing or capital account. To minimize the possibility of confusion, it is preferable to record rental transactions with partners in the same manner as other rental agreements.

(vi) Statement Presentation. Receivables and payables arising out of transactions between a partner and the firm of which he is a partner should be classified in the balance sheet in the same manner as are receivables and payables arising out of transactions with nonpartners. However, any such receivables and payables included in the balance sheet should be set forth separately; they should not be combined with other receivables and payables. SFAS No. 57 (FASB, 1982) indicates that receivables or payables involving partners stem from a related party transaction and, as such, if material, should be disclosed in such a way as to include:

1. The nature of the relationship(s) involved.
2. A description of the transactions including transactions to which no amounts or nominal amounts were ascribed, for each of the periods for which income statements are presented, and such other information deemed necessary to an understanding of the effects of the transaction on the financial statements.
3. The dollar amounts of transactions for each of the periods for which income statements are presented and the effects of any change in the method of establishing the terms from that used in the preceding period.
4. Amounts due from or to related parties as of the date of each balance sheet presented and, if not otherwise apparent, the terms and manner of settlement.

(e) CLOSING OPERATING ACCOUNTS.   The operating accounts are closed to the expense and revenue account in the usual manner. That account is then closed by crediting each partner's capital account with his share of the net income or debiting it with his share of the net loss. The drawing account of each partner is then closed to the respective capital account.

(i) Division of Profits Illustrated.   The articles of copartnership of (the fictitious firm of) Ahern and Ciecka include the following provisions as to distribution of profits:

Partners' loans. Loans made by partners to the firm shall draw interest at the rate of 6% per annum. Such interest shall be computed only on December 31 of each year regardless of the period in which the loan was in effect.

Partners' salaries. On December 31 of each year, salaries shall be allowed by a charge to the expense and revenue account and credits to the respective drawing accounts of the partners at the following amounts per annum: Ahern $14,400; Ciecka, $12,000. Partners' salaries are to be allowed whether or not earned.

Interest on partners' invested capital. Each partner is to receive interest at the rate of 6% per annum on the balance of his capital account at the beginning of the year. Such interest is to be allowed whether or not earned.

Remainder of profit or loss. The balance of net income after provision for salaries, interest on loans, and interest on invested capital is to be divided equally. Any loss resulting after provision for the above items is to be divided equally.

On December 31, the books of the partnership show the following balances before recognition of interest and salary adjustments.

Sundry assets	$309,000	
Sundry liabilities		$ 66,000
Ahern, capital		120,000
Ahern, drawings	15,000	
Ciecka, capital		60,000
Ciecka, drawings	9,000	
Ciecka, loan		30,000
Expense and revenue		57,000
	$333,000	$333,000

AHERN AND CIECKA, PARTNERSHIP
Schedule of Division of Net Income
For the year ended December 31, 19XX

	Total	Ahern	Ciecka
Interest on loan	$ 1,350		$ 1,350
Interest on capital	9,180	$6,300	2,880
Salaries allowed	26,400	14,400	12,000
Remainder—equally	20,070	10,035	10,035
Profit earned	$57,000	$30,735	$26,265

Exhibit 36.1.   Division of profits.

Balances of the capital accounts on January 1 were: Ahern $105,000; Ciecka $48,000. The loan from Ciecka was made on April 1. Division of profits is as shown in Exhibit 36.1.

(ii) Statement of Partners' Capitals Illustrated.   Formal presentation of the activity of the partners' capital accounts is often made through the **statement of partners' capitals** (Exhibit 36.2).

(f) INCOME TAXES.   According to Hoffman (1978, p. 359):

Unlike corporations, estates, and trusts, partnerships are not considered separate taxable entities. Instead, each member of a partnership is subject to income tax on their distributive share of the partnership's income, even if an actual distribution is not made. (Section 701 of Subchapter K of the 1954 Code contains the statutory rule that the partners are liable for income tax in their separate or individual capacities. The partnership itself cannot be subject to the income tax on its earnings.) Thus, the tax return (Form 1065) required of a partnership serves only to provide information necessary in determining the character and amount of each partner's distributive share of the partnership's income and expense.

Some states, however, impose an unincorporated business tax on a partnership that for all practical purposes is an income tax.

AHERN AND CIECKA, PARTNERSHIP
Statement of Partners' Capitals
For the year ended December 31, 19XX

	Total	Ahern	Ciecka
Balances: January 1	$153,000	$105,000	$48,000
Add: additional investments	27,000	15,000	12,000
net income for year—per schedule	57,000	30,735	26,265
Total	$237,000	$150,735	$86,265
Less: withdrawals	24,000	15,000	9,000
Investment, December 31	$213,000	$135,735	$77,265

Exhibit 36.2.   Sample statement of partners' capitals.

36.3 ACCOUNTING FOR CHANGES IN FIRM MEMBERSHIP

(a) EFFECT OF CHANGE IN PARTNERS.   From a legal point of view, the withdrawal of one or more partners or the admission of one or more new members has the effect of dissolving the original partnership and bringing into being a **new firm.** This means that the terms of the original agreement as such are not binding on the successor partnership. As far as the continuity of the business enterprise is concerned, on the other hand, a change in firm membership may be of only nominal importance; with respect to character of the business, operating policies, relations with customers, etc., there may be no substantial difference between the new firm and its predecessor.

To determine the value of the equity of a retiring partner, or the amount to be paid for a specified share by an incoming partner, a complete **inventory and valuation of firm resources** may be required. Estimation of **interim profits** and unrealized profits on long-term contracts may be involved. In any event, there should be a careful adjustment of partners' equities in accordance with the new relationships established.

A withdrawing partner may continue to be liable for the firm obligations incurred prior to his withdrawal unless the settlement includes specific release therefrom by the continuing partners and by the creditors.

A person admitted as a partner into an existing partnership is liable for all the obligations of the partnership arising before his admission as though he had been a partner when such obligations were incurred, except that this liability shall be satisfied only out of partnership property.

(b) NEW PARTNER PURCHASING AN INTEREST.   It is possible for a party to acquire the interest of a partner without becoming a partner. A member of a partnership may sell or assign his interest, but unless this has received the **unanimous approval** of the other partners, the purchaser does not become a partner; one partner cannot force his copartners into partnership with an outsider. Under the Uniform Partnership Act, the buyer in such a case acquires only the seller's interest in the profits and losses of the firm and, upon dissolution, the interest to which the original partner would have been entitled. He has no voice in management, nor may he obtain an accounting except in case of dissolution of the business; ordinarily he can make no withdrawal of capital without the consent of the partners.

To illustrate some of the possibilities in connection with purchase of an interest, assume that the firm of Hirt, Thompson, and Pitts negotiates with Davis for the purchase of a capital interest. Data are as follows:

	Capital Accounts	Income Ratio
Hirt	$20,000	50%
Thompson	12,000	40
Pitts	8,000	10
	$40,000	100%

(i) Purchase at Book Value.   If Davis purchases a one-fourth interest for $10,000, it is clear that he is paying exactly book value, and the entry would be:

Hirt, capital	$5,000	
Thompson, capital	3,000	
Pitts, capital	2,000	
Davis, capital		$10,000

The cash payment would be divided in the same manner (i.e., Hirt $5,000, Thompson $3,000, and Pitts $2,000), and would pass directly from Davis to them without going through the firm's cash account.

(ii) Purchase at More than Book Value.   Assume now that Davis agrees to pay $12,000 for a one-fourth interest; this is more than book value. In general, two solutions are possible.

Bonus Method.   Under this method, the extra $2,000 paid by Davis is considered to be a bonus to Hirt, Thompson, and Pitts and is shared by them in the income ratio. The entry is:

Hirt, capital	$5,000	
Thompson, capital	3,000	
Pitts, capital	2,000	
Davis, capital		$10,000

The cash payment of $12,000 is divided as follows:

	Hirt	Thompson	Pitts	Total
Capital transferred	$5,000	$3,000	$2,000	$10,000
Premium—in income ratio	1,000	800	200	2,000
Cash received	$6,000	$3,800	$2,200	$12,000

Goodwill Method.   That Davis is willing to pay $12,000 for a one-fourth interest indicates that the business is worth $48,000. Existing assets are therefore undervalued by $8,000. Under the goodwill or revaluation of assets method, if specific assets can be revalued, this should be done. If not, or if the agreed revaluation is less than $8,000, the difference may be assumed to be goodwill. Dividing the gain in the income ratio results in this entry:

Sundry assets and/or goodwill	$8,000	
Hirt, capital		$4,000
Thompson, capital		3,200
Pitts, capital		800

The entry to record Davis' admission would then be:

Hirt, capital	$6,000	
Thompson, capital	3,800	
Pitts, capital	2,200	
Davis, capital		$12,000

The cash payment will be received in amounts equal to the transfer from the capital accounts.

(iii) Purchase at Less than Book Value.   Assume next that Davis agrees to pay only $9,000 for a one-fourth interest—that is, less than book value. Again two solutions are possible.

Bonus Method.   Under this method, the same transfers are made from the three partners to Davis' capital account as if he had paid book value, but the difference of $1,000 is apportioned to determine the cash settlement, as follows:

	Hirt	Thompson	Pitts	Total
Capital transferred	$5,000	$3,000	$2,000	$10,000
Loss—in income ratio	500	400	100	1,000
Cash received	$4,500	$2,600	$1,900	$ 9,000

Revaluation of Assets Method.   This approach reasons that a price of $9,000 for a one-fourth interest indicates that the business is worth $36,000 and that assets should be revalued downward by $4,000. Where a portion of the write-down can be identified with specific tangible assets, the appropriate accounts should be adjusted. Otherwise, existing goodwill should be included in the write-down.

	(1)	
Hirt, capital	$2,000	
Thompson, capital	1,600	
Pitts, capital	400	
Sundry, assets and/or goodwill		$4,000

	(2)	
Hirt, capital	$4,500	
Thompson, capital	2,600	
Pitts, capital	1,900	
Davis, capital		$9,000

(c) NEW PARTNER'S INVESTMENT TO ACQUIRE AN INTEREST.   The admission of a new partner when he makes an investment in the firm to acquire a capital interest is illustrated by the following cases.

Assume that the capital account balances of the partnership of Andrews and Bell prior to the admission of Cohen are:

	Capital Accounts	*Income Ratio*
Andrews	$18,000	60%
Bell	12,000	40
	$30,000	100%

(i) Investment at Book Value.   If Cohen invests $10,000 in the firm for a one-fourth interest, the entry is:

Cash (or other assets)	$10,000	
Cohen, capital		$10,000

(ii) Investment at More than Book Value.   If Cohen is willing to invest $14,000 for a one-fourth interest, the total capital will be $44,000.

Bonus Method.   Under this method, Cohen's share is one-fourth or $11,000, and the $3,000 premium is treated as a bonus to the old partners by the entry:

Cash (or other assets)	$14,000	
Andrews, capital		$ 1,800
Bell, capital		1,200
Cohen, capital		11,000

Goodwill Method.   If Cohen invests $14,000 for a one-fourth interest, it would seem that the total worth of the firm should be $56,000. Since total capital is $44,000, under the **goodwill or revaluation of assets method,** there is justification in assuming that existing assets are undervalued to the extent of $12,000. Circumstances may indicate that the $12,000 under-valuation is in the form of goodwill. If it is to be recognized, the entries are as follows:

	(1)	
Goodwill	$12,000	
Andrews, capital		$ 7,200
Bell, capital		4,800

	(2)	
Cash	$14,000	
Cohen, capital		$14,000

If the understatement of the capital of the old partners was attributable to excessive depreciation allowances, land appreciation, an increase in inventory value, or to some combination of such factors, an appropriate adjustment of the asset or assets involved would be substituted for the charge to "goodwill."

(iii) Investment at Less than Book Value

Bonus Method.   If Cohen invests $8,000 for a one-fourth interest, it may indicate the willingness of the old partners to give Cohen a bonus to enter the firm.
    Since the total capital is now $38,000, a one-fourth interest is $9,500 and the entry is:

Cash	$8,000	
Andrews, capital	900	
Bell, capital	600	
Cohen, capital		$9,500

Revaluation of Assets Method.   Under this method, the investment by Cohen of only $8,000 for a one-fourth interest may be taken to mean that the existing net assets are worth only $24,000. The overvaluation of $6,000 could be corrected by crediting the overvalued assets and charging Andrews and Bell in the income ratio.

	(1)	
Andrews, capital	$3,600	
Bell, capital	2,400	
Sundry assets		$6,000

	(2)	
Cash	$8,000	
Cohen, capital		$8,000

Goodwill Method.   A third method sometimes offered to handle this situation is the goodwill method, which assumes that the new partner contributes goodwill (of $2,000 in this case) in addition to the cash, and is credited for the amount of his interest at book value ($10,000 in this case). This seems illogical, however, since it contradicts the original fact that Cohen's investment was to be $8,000.

(d) SETTLING WITH WITHDRAWING PARTNER THROUGH OUTSIDE FUNDS.   The withdrawal of a partner where settlement is effected by payments made from personal funds of the remaining partners directly to the retiring partner is illustrated by the firm of Adams, Bates, & Caldwell:

	Capital Balances	Income Ratio
Adams	$30,000	50%
Bates	24,000	30
Caldwell	16,000	20
	$70,000	100%

(i) Sale at Book Value. If Caldwell retires, selling his interest at book value to the other partners in their income ratio and receiving payment from outside funds of Adams and Bates, the entry is:

Caldwell, capital	$16,000	
Adams, capital		$10,000
Bates, capital		6,000

The total payment to Caldwell is $16,000, and payments by Adams and Bates are $10,000 and $6,000, respectively.

(ii) Sale at More than Book Value. If payment to Caldwell exceeds book value, either the bonus or the goodwill method may be used.

Bonus Method. If total payment to Caldwell is $18,000, the premium of $2,000 may be treated as a bonus to Caldwell. The entry to record the withdrawal of Caldwell is the same as above, and payment would be as follows:

	Adams	Bates	Total
Capital per books	$10,000	$6,000	$16,000
Premium paid	1,250	750	2,000
Cash required	$11,250	$6,750	$18,000

Goodwill Method. In the following situation, Adams and Bates are willing to pay a total of $2,000 more than book value for Caldwell's interest. Since the latter receives 20% of the profits, this implies that assets are undervalued by $10,000. Under the **goodwill or revaluation of assets method,** all or part of this amount may be goodwill. The entries to record this situation are:

	(1)	
Goodwill or sundry assets	$10,000	
Adams, capital		$ 5,000
Bates, capital		3,000
Caldwell, capital		2,000

	(2)	
Caldwell, capital	$18,000	
Adams, capital		$11,250
Bates, capital		6,750

(iii) Sale at Less than Book Value. If Caldwell should agree to accept $15,000 for his interest, this is $1,000 less than book value.

Bonus Method. The $1,000 may be considered to be a **bonus** to Adams and Bates. The entry would be the same as in the first example, but the cash payments would be calculated as follows:

	Adams	Bates	Total
Capital, per books	$10,000	$6,000	$16,000
Less discount allowed	625	375	1,000
Cash required	$ 9,375	$5,625	$15,000

Revaluation of Assets Method.   In this example, it can be argued under the revaluation of assets approach that the discount of $1,000 for a 20% share in firm profits implies an overstatement of book values of assets by $5,000. If this correction is to be made, the entries to adjust the books and record the subsequent withdrawal of Caldwell are:

	(1)	
Adams, capital	$ 2,500	
Bates, capital	1,500	
Caldwell, capital	1,000	
Sundry assets		$5,000

	(2)	
Caldwell, capital	$15,000	
Adams, capital		$9,375
Bates, capital		5,625

In preceding examples, the so-called bonus method and revaluation of assets method have been presented as alternatives. Although each method results in different capital account balances in the new firm that comes into being, it should be observed that the partners in the new firm are treated relatively the same under either method. This is subject to the basic qualification that the old partners who remain in the new firm must continue to share profits and losses as between themselves in the same ratio as before.

(e) SETTLEMENT THROUGH FIRM FUNDS.   The withdrawal of a partner where settlement is to be made from funds of the business is illustrated by the firm of Arnold, Brown & Cline.

	Capital Balances	*Income Ratio*
Arnold	$ 40,000	30%
Brown	50,000	30
Cline	60,000	40
	$150,000	100%

(i) Premium Paid to Retiring Partner.   Payment is to be made to Cline from the assets of the partnership. Payment is $64,000, to be made one-half in cash and the balance in notes payable. Under one treatment, the premium of $4,000 is viewed as chargeable to the remaining partners in their income ratio. The entry is:

	$ 2,000	
Arnold, capital	$ 2,000	
Brown, capital	2,000	
Cline, capital	60,000	
Cash		$32,000
Notes payable		32,000

A second method treats the $4,000 premium as payment for Cline's share of the unrecognized goodwill of the firm. The following entry would be made:

	$ 4,000	
Goodwill	$ 4,000	
Cline, capital	60,000	
Cash		$32,000
Notes payable		32,000

A third possibility for recording the retirement of Cline is to recognize a total goodwill or asset revaluation implied by the premium paid for the retiring partner's share. Since a $4,000 premium was paid for a 40% share, total implied goodwill or asset revaluation is $10,000 and the entries are:

	(1)	
Goodwill or sundry assets	$10,000	
Arnold, capital		$ 3,000
Brown, capital		3,000
Cline, capital		4,000

	(2)	
Cline, capital	$64,000	
Cash		$32,000
Notes payable		32,000

Many accountants are inclined to approve of the first treatment on the ground that it is "conservative." Meigs, Johnson, and Keller (1966) state that it is "consistent with the current trend toward viewing a partnership as a continuing business entity, with asset valuations and accounting policies remaining undisturbed by the retirement of a partner." The second treatment is supported by reference to the rule that it is proper to set up goodwill only when it has been purchased. The third interpretation relies on the idea that it is inconsistent to recognize the existence of an intangible asset and then to record it at only a fraction of the proper amount.

The accountant may distinguish between a payment for goodwill and one that represents a partner's share of the increase in value of one or more of the firm's assets. In the latter case, it is generally not reasonable to record only the increase attaching to the retiring partner's equity. Suppose, for example, that an inventory of merchandise has a **market value** on the date of settlement substantially above book value. Clearly, the most appropriate treatment here is that under which the inventory is adjusted to market value—the value at which it is in effect acquired by the new firm; to add to book value only the withdrawing partner's share of the increase would result in figures unsatisfactory from the standpoint both of financial accounting and operating procedure.

(ii) Discount Given by Retiring Partner.   Assuming that Cline receives $57,000 for his interest in the firm and payment is made by equal amounts of cash and notes payable, two possible accounting treatments are available.

First, the discount of $3,000 may be credited to the remaining partners in their income ratio:

Cline, capital	$60,000	
Cash		$28,500
Notes payable		28,500
Arnold, capital		1,500
Brown, capital		1,500

In the second method the implied overvaluation of assets is recognized. Since Cline's share (40%) was purchased at a discount of $3,000, the total overvaluation of firm assets may be considered as $7,500. The following entries are made:

	(1)	
Arnold, capital	$ 2,250	
Brown, capital	2,250	
Cline, capital	3,000	
Sundry assets		$ 7,500

	(2)	
Cline, capital	$57,000	
Cash		$28,500
Notes payable		28,500

(f) ADJUSTMENT OF CAPITAL RATIOS. Circumstances may arise in partnership affairs when it becomes desirable to adjust partners' capital account balances to certain ratios—most often the income ratio. This may happen in connection with the admission of a new partner, the withdrawal of a partner, or at some time when no change in personnel has occurred. Only a simple case involving a continuing firm is illustrated here.

Assume the following data for the firm of Emmett, Frye, and Gable:

	Capital Balances	*Income Ratio*
Emmett	$50,000	50%
Frye	25,000	30
Gable	15,000	20
	$90,000	100%

If the partners wish to adjust their capital balances to the income ratio without changing total capital, it is obvious that Frye should pay $2,000 and Gable $3,000 directly to Emmett, and that the entry should be:

Emmet, capital	$5,000	
Frye, capital		$2,000
Gable, capital		3,000

Adjustment of the capital balances to the income ratio by the minimum **additional investment into the firm** (as distinguished from the preceding personal settlement) could, of course, be effected by the additional investment of $5,000 each by Frye and Gable.

36.4 INCORPORATION OF A PARTNERSHIP

According to Meigs, Johnson, and Keller (1966):

> Most successful partnerships give consideration at times to the possible advantages to be gained by incorporating. Among the advantages are limited liability, ease of attracting outside capital without loss of control, and possible tax savings.
>
> A new corporation formed to take over the assets and liabilities of a partnership will usually sell stock to outsiders for cash either at the time of incorporation or at a later date. To assure that the former partners receive an equitable portion of the total capital stock, the assets of the partnership will need to be adjusted to fair market value before being transferred to the corporation. Any goodwill developed by the partnership should be recognized as part of the assets transferred.
>
> The accounting records of a partnership may be modified and continued in use when the firm changes to the corporate form. As an alternative, the partnership books may be closed and a new set of accounting records established for the corporation. . . .

36.5 PARTNERSHIP REALIZATION AND LIQUIDATION

(a) BASIC CONSIDERATIONS. A partnership may be disposed of either by selling the business as a unit or by the sale (realization) of the specific assets followed by the liquidation of the liabilities and final distribution of the remaining assets (usually cash) to the partners. A basic principle to be observed carefully in all such cases is that losses (or gains) in realization or sale must first be apportioned among the partners in the income ratio, following which, if outside creditors have been paid in full or cash reserved for that purpose, payments may be made according to the remaining capital balances of the partners.

Discussions of partnership liquidations usually point out that the proper **order of cash distribution** is: (1) payment of creditors in full, (2) payment of partners' loan accounts, and (3) payment of partners' capital accounts. Actually the stated priority of the **partners' loans** appears to be a legal fiction. An established legal doctrine called the **right of offset** requires that any credit balance standing in a partner's name be set off against an actual or potential debit balance in his capital account. Application of this right of offset always produces the same final result as if the loan or undrawn salary account were a part of the capital balance at the beginning of the process. For this reason, no separate examples are given that include loan accounts. If they are encountered, they may be added to the capital account balance at the top of the liquidation statement. (The existence of partners' loan accounts might have an effect on profit sharing, however, in the sense that interest on partners' loans is usually provided for and profits might be shared in the average capital ratio: loans would presumably be excluded from the computation.)

Realization of all assets and liquidation of liabilities may be completed before any cash is distributed to partners. Or, if the realization process stretches over a considerable period of time, so-called **installment liquidation** may be employed.

(b) LIQUIDATION BY SINGLE CASH DISTRIBUTION.   The illustration below demonstrates the realization of assets, payment of creditors, and final single cash distribution to the partners. Losses are first allocated to the partners in the income ratio, followed by cash payment to creditors and then to partners.

Rogers, Stevens, and Troy are partners with capital balances of $20,000, $15,000 and $10,000, respectively. Profits and losses are shared equally. On a particular date they find that the firm has assets of $80,000, liabilities of $47,000, and undistributed losses of $12,000. At this point the assets are sold for $59,000 cash. The proper distribution of the cash is as follows:

		Total	Rogers	Stevens	Troy
Capital balances		$45,000	$20,000	$15,000	$10,000
Less undistributed losses		12,000	4,000	4,000	4,000
Adjusted balances		$33,000	$16,000	$11,000	$ 6,000
Less loss on sale of					
assets		21,000	7,000	7,000	7,000
Adjusted balances		$12,000	$ 9,000	$ 4,000	$(1,000)
Payment by Troy for					
deficiency		1,000			1,000
Balances before					
distribution		$13,000	$ 9,000	$ 4,000	-0-
Cash available	$60,000				
Paid to creditors	47,000				
Cash paid to partners		$13,000	$ 9,000	$ 4,000	-0-

In this example it was assumed that Troy was financially able to make up the $1,000 deficiency that appeared in his capital account. Only by making this payment does he bear his agreed share of the losses. If Troy had been personally insolvent and therefore unable to make the $1,000 payment, the statement from that point on would have taken the following form:

	Total	Rogers	Stevens	Troy
Adjusted balances	$12,000	$ 9,000	$ 4,000	$(1,000)
Apportion deficiency in income ratio		(500)	(500)	1,000
Balances before distribution	$12,000	$ 8,500	$ 3,500	-0-
Cash available	$59,000			
Paid to creditors	47,000			
Cash paid to partners	$12,000	$ 8,500	$ 3,500	-0-

Troy is now personally indebted to Rogers and Stevens in the amount of $500 each. Just how this debt would rank in the settlement of Troy's personal affairs depends on the state having jurisdiction. Under the UPA his personal creditors (not including Rogers and Stevens) have prior claim to his personal assets; because he was said to have been personally insolvent, the presumption is that Rogers and Stevens would collect nothing. In a common-law state, a deficiency of this sort is considered to be a personal debt and would generally rank along with the other personal creditors. In this event Rogers and Stevens would presumably make a partial recovery of the $500 due each of them.

(c) LIQUIDATION BY INSTALLMENTS. It is sometimes necessary to liquidate on an installment basis. Two of the many possible cases are illustrated—in the first there is no capital deficiency to any partner when the first cash distribution is made; in the second there is a possible deficiency of one partner at the time of the first cash distribution. The situation involving a final deficiency of a partner is discussed above in the partnership of Rogers, Stevens, and Troy. If this situation should appear in the winding up of an installment liquidation, its treatment would be the same as described there.

The role of the liquidator is especially important in the case of installment liquidation. In addition to his obvious responsibility to see that outside creditors are paid and to convert the various assets into cash with a maximum gain or a minimum loss, he must protect the interests of the partners in their relationship to each other. Other than for reimbursement of liquidation expenses, no cash payment can be made to a partner, even on loan accounts or undrawn profits, except as the total standing to his credit exceeds his share of total possible losses on assets not yet realized. Improper payment by the liquidator might result in personal liability therefore, recovery could not be made from the partner who was overpaid.

(d) CAPITAL CREDITS ONLY—NO CAPITAL DEFICIENCY. Below is the balance sheet of Burns & Mantle as of April 30, when installment liquidation of the firm began. The partners share profits and losses equally.

Assets		Liabilities and Capital	
Cash	$ 6,200	Liabilities	$ 56,000
Other assets	350,000	Burns, capital	220,200
		Mantle, capital	80,000
	$356,200		$356,200

During May assets having a book value of $220,000 are sold for cash of $198,000, and $39,000 is paid to creditors. During June the remaining assets are sold for $90,000, the balance due creditors is paid, and liquidation expenses of $8,000 are paid. Distribution of cash to the partners should be made as follows:

	Total	Burns	Mantle
Capital, per balance sheet	$300,200	$220,200	$80,000
Less realization loss in May	22,000	11,000	11,000
Balance after loss	$278,200	$209,200	$69,000
Cash available to partners	148,200		
Possible loss divided	$130,000	65,000	65,000
Balances paid in cash		$144,200	$ 4,000
Balances, June 1		$ 65,000	$65,000
Less realization loss in June	40,000	20,000	20,000
Balances after loss	$ 90,000	$ 45,000	$45,000
Less liquidation expense	8,000	4,000	4,000
Final cash payment	$ 82,000	$ 41,000	$41,000

Cash available to partners at May 31 is calculated as follows:

Cash, per balance sheet	$ 6,200	
Received from sale of assets—May	198,000	$204,200
Paid to creditors—May	$ 39,000	
Reserved for creditors	17,000	56,000
Available for distribution to partners		$148,200

In this example the first payment of $148,200 reduces the capital claims to the profit and loss ratios, and all subsequent charges or credits to the partners' capital accounts are made accordingly.

(i) Capital Credits Only—Capital Deficiency of One Partner. This situation is illustrated in Exhibit 36.3 using the previous balance sheet but assuming the following liquidation data:

	Assets Sold	Cash Received	Creditors Paid	Expenses Paid
May	$ 80,000	$ 50,000	$39,000	
June	100,000	60,000	17,000	
July	170,000	145,000		$8,000

In Exhibit 36.3 each partner received in total the balance of his capital account per the balance sheet minus his share (50%) of realization losses and expenses, the same as if one final cash payment had been made on July 31. Note that if Mantle had had a loan account of, say, $20,000 and a capital balance of $60,000, the first cash distribution of $60,200 would still have gone entirely to Burns. At this point, after exercising the right of offset, Mantle would still have had a future possible deficiency of $40,000.

(ii) Installment Distribution Plan. A somewhat different approach to the problem of installment liquidation is illustrated below.

Fox, Green, and Harris are partners sharing profits equally. Following is the partnership balance sheet as of December 31, at which time it is decided to liquidate the firm by installments.

Assets		Liabilities and Capital	
Cash	$ 3,000	Liabilities	$ 24,000
Other assets	186,000	Fox, capital	79,000
		Green, capital	52,000
		Harris, capital	34,000
	$189,000		$189,000

BURNS & MANTLE
Statement of Liquidation
May 1 to July 31

	Total	Burns	Mantle
Capital balances, May 1	$300,200	$220,200	$ 80,000
Less realization loss in May	30,000	15,000	15,000
Balances after loss, May 31[a]	$270,200	$205,200	$ 65,000
Less realization loss in June	40,000	20,000	20,000
Balances after loss, June 30	$230,200	$185,200	$ 45,000
Cash available to partners[b]	60,200		
Possible loss apportioned	$170,000	85,000	85,000
Balances after apportionment		$100,200	$(40,000)
Further possible loss to Burns		(40,000)	40,000
Cash payment to Burns		$ 60,200	
Balances, July 1		$125,000	$ 45,000
Less realization loss in July	25,000	12,500	12,500
Balances after loss, July 31	$145,000	$112,500	$ 32,500
Less liquidation expense	8,000	4,000	4,000
Final cash payment	$137,000	$108,500	$ 28,500

[a] No cash was distributed to partners at May 31 because only $200 was available at that time. The calculation:

Cash, per balance sheet	$ 6,200	
Received from sale of assets—May	50,000	$ 56,200
Paid to creditors—May	$ 39,000	
Reserved for creditors	17,000	$ 56,000
Available to partners—not distributed, May 31		$ 200

[b] This amount is the $200 not distributed at May 31 plus the $60,000 received in June from sale of assets.

Exhibit 36.3.   Sample statement of liquidation.

Using the balance sheet above, computation of correct cash distribution is as follows:

	Total	Fox	Green	Harris
Partners' capital balances	$165,000	$79,000	$52,000	$34,000
Loss that would eliminate Harris, who is least able to absorb	102,000	34,000	34,000	34,000
Balances	$ 63,000	$45,000	$18,000	
Loss that would eliminate Green	36,000	18,000	18,000	
Balances	$ 27,000	$27,000		

The amount of the loss that will extinguish each partner's capital account is determined by dividing his capital account by his percentage of income and loss sharing. Hence, for Harris this amount is $34,000 ÷ 33⅓%, or $102,000.

From the computations, it is possible to prepare a schedule for the distribution of cash as follows:

	Cash	Liabilities	Fox	Green	Harris
First	$21,000	$21,000			
Next	27,000		All		
Next	36,000		$\frac{1}{2}$	$\frac{1}{2}$	
All in excess of	84,000		$\frac{1}{3}$	$\frac{1}{3}$	$\frac{1}{3}$

It is assumed that the $3,000 cash on hand on December 31 is used in payment of liabilities. The following liquidation data are given:

	Assets Sold	Cash Received	Creditors Paid
January	$ 64,000	$ 41,000	$24,000
February	60,000	37,000	
March	62,000	54,000	
Totals	$186,000	$132,000	$24,000

Based on these data, the application of the computations already made results in the following payments to creditors and partners:

	Amount	Liabilities	Fox	Green	Harris
January	$ 41,000	$21,000	$20,000		
February	37,000		7,000		
			15,000	$15,000	
March	54,000		3,000	3,000	
			16,000	16,000	$16,000
Totals	$132,000	$21,000	$61,000	$34,000	$16,000

36.6 LIMITED PARTNERSHIPS

(a) DEFINITION OF LIMITED PARTNERSHIPS.   Limited partnerships are business partnership structures that permit partners to invest capital with the proviso that there will be limited control over business operations and, accordingly, assumption of liability limited to the extent of capital contributions.

In general partnerships, the potential liability that can accrue to individual partners is unlimited. That unlimited liability has always been a major drawback of the partnership structure. Limited partnerships evolved to a great extent in order to overcome that disadvantage.

The legal provisions governing limited partnerships are provided by the Uniform Limited Partnership Act and the Revised Uniform Limited Partnership Act, which have been adopted in some form by each state government.

(b) DIFFERENCES BETWEEN LIMITED PARTNERSHIPS AND GENERAL PARTNERSHIPS. In addition to limitations on the liability of partners, limited partnerships differ from general partnerships in the following ways:

- Limited partners have no participation in the management of the limited partnership.
- Limited partners may invest only cash or other assets in a limited partnership; they may not provide services as their investment.
- The surname of a limited partner may not appear in the name of the partnership.

(c) FORMATION OF LIMITED PARTNERSHIPS. The formation of limited partnerships is generally evidenced by a **certificate** filed with the county recorder of the principal place of business of the limited partnership rather than a partnership agreement such as that described in subsection 36.1(e). Such certificates include many of the items present in the typical partnership contract of a general partnership. In addition, certificates must include the name and residence of each general partner and limited partner; the amount of cash and other assets invested by each limited partner; provision for return of a limited partner's investment; any priority of one or more limited partners over other limited partners; and any right of limited partners to vote for election or removal of general partners, termination of the partnership, amendment of the certificate, or disposal of all partnership assets.

Interests in limited partnerships are offered to prospective limited partners in **units** subject to the Securities Act of 1933. Thus, unless provisions of that Act exempt a limited partnership, it must file a registration statement for the offered units with the Securities and Exchange Commission (SEC) and undertake to file periodic reports with the SEC. Large limited partnerships that engage in ventures such as oil and gas exploration and real estate development and issue units registered with the SEC are called **master limited partnerships.** The SEC has provided guidance for such registration and reporting in *Industry Guide 5: Preparation of Registration Statements Relating to Interests in Real Estate Limited Partnerships.*

(d) ACCOUNTING AND FINANCIAL REPORTING CONSIDERATIONS. As a general rule, the accounting records of limited partnerships are kept on a cash basis. However, the SEC requires that limited partnerships registrants prepare and file basic financial statements in conformity with generally accepted accounting principles (GAAP). For example, SEC Staff Accounting Bulletin Topic 4F requires the equity section of the limited partnership's balance sheet to distinguish between general partner and limited partner equity, with a separate statement of changes in partnership equity for each type of participation provided for each period for which a limited partnership income statement is presented.

The SEC also believes it is appropriate for a limited partnership registrant to include financial data on a tax basis of accounting, with an appropriate reconciliation of differences in major disclosure areas between tax and financial accounting. Whether GAAP-basis financial statements (along with the data necessary for income tax return preparation) should be distributed to the participants of SEC-reporting limited partnerships is a matter covered by the proxy rules.

36.7 JOINT VENTURES

(a) DEFINITION OF JOINT VENTURE. Joint ventures are partnerships formed when two or more parties pool resources for the purpose of undertaking a specific project such as the development or marketing of a product. Joint ventures are owned, operated, and jointly controlled by a small group of owners or investors as separate business projects operated for the mutual benefit of the ownership group. Joint ventures may take the legal form of partnerships or they may be separately incorporated entities.

The owners or investors (venturers) in a joint venture may or may not have equal ownership interests in the venture. A venturer's share may range from as low as 5% or 10% to over 50%, but no less. All venturers usually participate in the overall management of the venture. Significant decisions generally require the consent of all venturers regardless of the percentage of ownership so that no individual venturer has unilateral control.

(b) ACCOUNTING BY JOINT VENTURES. Regardless of their legal form of organization, joint ventures must maintain accounting records and prepare financial statements just like any other enterprise. The primary users of the joint ventures financial statements are the venturers, who need to record their share of the profit or loss of the venture and to value their investment in it. Most of the accounting principles and procedures used by joint ventures are the same as those used by other business enterprises.

The most significant accounting issue for most joint ventures is the recording of initial capital contributions, particularly noncash cash contributions. Such contributions should be recorded on the books of the venture at the fair value of the assets contributed on the date of contribution, unless the fair value of the assets is not readily or reliably determinable or the recoverability of that value is in doubt. This general rule does not apply, however, to assets contributed by a venturer who controls a venture. In those circumstances, the assets should be recorded on the books of the venture at the same amount at which they were carried on the venturer's books because there has been no effective change in control over the assets.

(c) ACCOUNTING FOR INVESTMENTS IN JOINT VENTURES.   Since joint venturers have rights and obligations that may differ from their ownership percentages assuring them of significant influence even at ownership percentages of less than 20%, the application of customary equity or consolidation accounting is not always appropriate. Interests in incorporated joint ventures are accounted for in accordance with APB Opinion No. 18, which mandates use of the equity method. Accounting for interests in joint ventures that are organized as partnerships or undivided interests is discussed in an AICPA staff interpretation of APB Opinion No. 18 that states that many of the provisions of that Opinion are appropriate in accounting for such investments.

In 1979, the AICPA's Accounting Standards Executive Committee issued an Issues Paper entitled *Joint Venture Accounting.* The Issues Paper contains the following advisory conclusions:

- The portion of APB Opinion No. 18 dealing with investments in joint ventures should be re-examined.
- The one-line equity method described in APB Opinion No. 18 should be required for investments in joint ventures (whether incorporated or unincorporated) that are subject to joint control, except that the cost method should be permitted for investments that are not material to the investor.
- If an entity that otherwise meets the definition of a joint venture is, in fact, controlled by majority voting interest or otherwise, the entity should be required to be accounted for as a subsidiary of the controlling investor and to be fully consolidated by that investor.
- If an entity that otherwise meets the definition of a joint venture is not subject to joint control, by reason of its liabilities being several rather than joint as in some undivided interests, investments in the entity should be required to be accounted for by the proportionate consolidation method.
- The use of the same method in the balance sheet and income statement should be required.
- Disclosure of supplementary information as to the assets, liabilities, and results of operations should be mandatory if the investments in the aggregate are material.

(i) Financial Statement Presentation.   There are a number of different methods that venturers use to display their interest in joint ventures in their financial statements. The AICPA Issues Paper mentioned previously describes seven different methods, only four of which are considered acceptable. The methods described in the AcSEC advisory conclusions are not interchangeable; that is, each should be applied when specified circumstances exist. The four methods are briefly described in the following paragraphs.

One-Line Equity Method.   This method involves the application of the "traditional" equity method of accounting described in APB Opinion No. 18. The Issues Paper expresses the position that this method should remain the prevalent method of accounting for joint venture investments. Since most joint ventures give each investor significant influence over the venture, the equity method is generally more appropriate than the historical cost method used when an investor has only minor influence. The equity method of accounting is described in Chapter 8 of this handbook.

Many venturers prefer to use the equity method because it reflects the venturer's exposure to only the net liabilities of the venture by presenting the investment as a net position. The equity method also reflects the investor's share of the net income of the venture in the income statement for the period in which the net income is earned by the joint venture. Critics point out that it tends to obscure the nature and volume of the business of investors that conduct significant operation through joint ventures. It also excludes certain assets and liabilities that may be essential to an investor's business from the investor's balance sheet and elements of revenue and expense that arise from the venture's operations from the investor's income statement.

Proportionate Consolidation Method.   Under this method, the investor's proportionate share of the assets, liabilities, revenues and expenses is combined with similar items in the investor's financial statements. This method is often used in the real estate and oil and gas industries. The Issues Paper on joint venture accounting recommends that the proportionate consolidation method be used only in situations in which venturer's liabilities are several rather than joint. The Securities and Exchange Commission, however, generally has not favored proportionate consolidation and use of the method in other industries has thus been constrained. AICPA SOP No. 78-9, "Accounting for Investments in Real Estate Ventures" states that the usual full consolidation or equity methods should be applied to *corporate* joint ventures in the real estate industry.

While the proportionate consolidation method provides information in an entity's financial statements that may be useful to present and potential investors on past and prospective changes in the economic resources and obligations of the entity, its critics point out that it is based on the concept of control over pieces of the joint venture even though such control does not actually exist. Similarly, the method combines net assets in the balance sheet and operations in the income statement that the investor owns and controls directly with those over which the investor may have little or no control.

Full Consolidation.   The Issues Paper recommends that when a venturer has control of a joint venture, the full or traditional consolidation method of accounting be used as described in FASB Statement No. 94, "Consolidation of All Majority-Owned Subsidiaries." That method involves the combination of the assets, liabilities, revenues and expenses of the joint venture with those of the venturer in the venturer's financial statements. The portion of the venture's net assets owned by the other venturers is shown as a liability on the venturer's balance sheet and is usually described as a *minority interest.*

Cost Method.   Presenting an investment in a joint venture at cost is permissible only for immaterial investments.

(ii) Combination of Methods.   Some investors believe that a combination of these methods is the most appropriate way to present an investment in a joint venture in their financial statements. Those investors might use one method for the balance sheet and another for the income statement. When a combination of methods is used, it generally involves use of the one-line equity method in the balance sheet and the proportionate consolidation method in the income statement. The AICPA Issues Paper recommends against using a combination of methods.

(iii) Income Tax Issues.   Differences may arise between an investor's accounting treatment of an investment in a joint venture for purposes of financial reporting and for income tax purposes. In such circumstances, deferred taxes are required to be recognized. For joint ventures organized as partnerships, investors generally use the equity method for both tax and financial reporting purposes and therefore deferred taxes do not arise. No less, there may be differences between the book and tax carrying amount of the investment. Such differences are *temporary* *differences* as defined by FASB Statement No. 109, "Accounting for Income Taxes," and therefore do require recognition of deferred taxes. The length of time over which such differences may reverse depends on the specific differences in the carrying method used.

(d) CURRENT DEVELOPMENTS.   The FASB currently has on its agenda a project dealing with consolidation and related matters. One phase of that project covers unconsolidated entities and is intended to address presentation in an investor's financial statements of investments in noncontrolled corporations and partnerships, including joint ventures and undivided interests. The presentation methods currently being considered include the equity method, proportionate consolidation, and an expanded equity method.

In October 1995, the Board issued an exposure draft of a proposed statement that would establish standards that specify when entities should be included in consolidated financial statements and how consolidated financial statements should be prepared. It would apply to business enterprises that control other entities regardless of the legal form of the controlling and controlled entities.

The proposed Statement would require a controlling entity to consolidate all entities that it controls unless control is temporary at the time the entity becomes a subsidiary. For purposes of this requirement, control of an entity would be defined as the power to use or direct the use of the individual assets of another entity in essentially the same ways as the controlling entity can use its own assets.

The proposed Statement would supersede Accounting Research Bulletin No. 51, "Consolidated Financial Statements," and FASB Statement No. 94, "Consolidation of All Majority-Owned Subsidiaries."

This proposed Statement would be effective for financial statements for fiscal years beginning after December 15, 1996. Earlier application would be encouraged. The proposed Statement would be applied by restatement of comparative financial statements for earlier periods except certain consolidation procedures could be applied prospectively if retroactive application is not practicable.

The FASB's Emerging Issues Task Force has also discussed several matters that may affect the appropriate accounting for investments in joint ventures. Those matters include—

- Issue No. 95-6, "Accounting by Real Estate Investment Trust for an Investment in a Service Corporation," which sets forth criteria for determining whether significant influence exists. While the criteria were developed specifically for real estate investment trusts and service corporations, they may be useful in making that determination for other entities as well.

- Issue No. 94-1, "Accounting for Tax Benefits Resulting from Investments in Affordable Housing Projects," which describes the Task Force's consensus position about how an entity that invests in a qualified affordable housing project through a limited partnership should account for its investment.

- Appendix D-46, "Accounting for Limited Partnership Investments," which describes discussion of the SEC staff's position that investments in all limited partnerships should be accounted for pursuant to paragraph 8 of AICPA SOP No. 78-9, "Accounting for Investments in Real Estate Ventures." That guidance requires the use of the equity method unless the investor's interest "is so minor that the limited partner may have virtually no influence over partnership operating and financial policies."

36.8 SOURCES AND SUGGESTED REFERENCES

American Institute of Certified Public Accountants, "Related Party Transactions," Statement of Auditing Standards No. 6, AICPA, New York, 1975.

Anderson, R. J., *External Audit,* Pitman Publishing Co., Toronto, Ontario, Canada, 1977.

Bedford, Norton M., *Introduction to Modern Accounting,* Ronald Press, New York, 1962.

————, Perry, Kenneth W., and Wyatt, Arthur H., *Advanced Accounting—An Organization Approach,* Wiley, New York, 1979.

Bogen, Jules I., "Advantages and Disadvantages of Partnership," in *Financial Handbook,* 4th ed., Ronald Press, New York, 1968.

Defliese, Philip L., Johnson, Kenneth P., and Macleod, Roderick K., *Montgomery's Auditing,* 9th ed., Ronald Press, New York, 1975.

Dixon, Robert L., Hepworth, Samuel R., and Paton, William A., Jr., *Essentials of Accounting,* Macmillan, New York, 1966.

Financial Accounting Standards Board, "Related Party Disclosures," Statement of Financial Accounting Standards No. 57, FASB, Stamford, CT, 1982.

Hoffman, William H., Jr., (Ed). *West's Federal Taxation: Corporations, Partnerships, Estates and Trusts,* West, St. Paul, MN, 1978.

Internal Revenue Service & Internal Revenue Code of 1954, Section 761, Subchapter K.

Meigs, Walter B., Johnson, Charles E., and Keller, Thomas F., *Advanced Accounting,* McGraw-Hill, New York, 1966.

Moonitz, Maurice, and Jordan, Louis H., *Accounting—An Analysis of Its Problems,* 2 vols., rev. ed., Holt, Rinehart and Winston, New York, 1963.

CHAPTER 37

ESTATES AND TRUSTS

Philip M. Herr, JD, CPA

Guardian Life Insurance Company of America
Estate, Business & Financial Planning Department

CONTENTS

37.1 ESTATES—LEGAL BACKGROUND

(a) EXECUTING A WILL.   A **will** is a revocable instrument whereby a person makes a disposition of his property to take effect at death. A prudent person should secure legal advice upon reaching the age of majority (age 18 in many states). If the attorney deems it advisable, such person should execute a will. In the will, the testator (maker) should spell out in detail who is to inherit his property upon his death. The testator may also name a person to administer the estate and select a **guardian** (a protector of the body and property of his children, if any). A will can be very simple or very complex depending on the extent of the testator's property and desires. To be valid, the will must be properly executed according to state law. Such state laws normally require the maker to declare that the document is his last will and testament and to sign it in the presence of at least two witnesses, who also sign. Such witnesses, called **subscribing witnesses,** may later be called upon to testify about the maker's appearance of mental competence at the time of the execution of the will.

(b) WILL PROVISIONS.   Every will provision must be adhered to by the executor and the courts unless it is contrary to law or against public policy.

A typical will provides for:

1. A statement revoking all prior wills and codicils.
2. An instruction to pay all just debts, expenses of administration, funeral expenses, and sometimes final burial instructions. (However, these instructions are better left in a letter of instruction left with a close family member or friend in case the will should be found after the funeral.)
3. General bequests or legacies of money or property to named individuals payable out of the general assets of the estate.
4. Devises of real property to specified individuals.
5. Specific bequests or legacies of specific property. They fail if the property does not exist at the testator's death.
6. Demonstrative bequests or legacies. These are gifts of money or property payable out of a particular fund; if the fund is insufficient, the balance becomes a general legacy.
7. Provisions concerning disposal of the residuary estate. The residuary estate is all property not otherwise provided for in the will.
8. The duties and powers of the executor (described later in this section).
9. The naming of fiduciaries (executors, trustees, guardians, committees for incompetents) and their successors; and often, the exemption of having to post a fidelity bond.
10. Definitions of terms used in the will.
11. Provisions apportioning federal and state death taxes among the various classes of beneficiaries (marital vs. nonmarital, specific vs. residuary, charitable vs. noncharitable).
12. Simultaneous death provision that provides who shall be presumed to have survived whom as between the testator and other beneficiaries taking under the will.
13. The terms of any testamentary trusts that might be established under the will (i.e., for a minor beneficiary).
14. Signature of testator and subscribing witnesses, which may also be notorized in an attempt to "self-prove" the will.

(c) RULES UNDER INTESTACY.   "Intestacy" is defined as the state or condition of dying without having made a valid will, or without having disposed by will of a part of the deceased's property. Thus it arises not only when the deceased died without having made a will, but also if the will is invalid, or if it contains ineffective or no provisions concerning the disposal of the residuary estate.

When an intestacy is present, state law provides who is to receive the property. In effect, state statutes make a will for the deceased. The plan of distribution of the property, sometimes called **intestate succession** or **laws of descent and distribution,** is strictly defined by state statute and is based on degree of relationship to the deceased. New York State, for example, provides that if a decedent dies without a will and leaves a wife and two children, the wife receives $50,000 and one-half of the residuary estate and the children share the other one-half. Under the same circumstances, Oregon allows the spouse one-half of the estate and the children share the other one-half. Distribution plans under state laws vary even more if a spouse or children do not survive the decedent. It could result, for example, in a surviving parent, who may have made lifetime gifts to the decedent for the parent's own estate planning purposes, receiving those assets back. Distribution plans under intestacy do not take into account financial needs or close bonds of a decedent to certain relatives. It may result in relatives with whom a decedent has had no contact for many years inheriting a portion of the property. Absence of a will can result in fights over the appointment of administrators and in custody battles over the guardianship of minor children and their property. The failure to make a will should be a conscious decision of an informed individual to allow state law to make it for him and not a result of ignorance or procrastination.

(d) DOMICILE.   Generally most states take the position that the property of a person domiciled in a state at the time of death is subject to court jurisdiction (and the estate and inheritance tax) of that state. **Domicile** is defined as the place where a person has a true, fixed, and permanent home to which, whenever absent, the person has the intention of returning.

In addition, states generally also claim court jurisdiction over (and estate and inheritance tax on) real and tangible personal property located within their boundaries for persons domiciled outside the state at the time of their death.

These two concepts often force an executor or administrator to bring court proceedings in more than one state. Proceedings brought outside the state of domicile are called **ancillary proceedings.** The distribution by the executor or administrator of ancillary property is governed by the state law of the property's location.

Sometimes more than one state claims that a decedent was domiciled in that state at the time of death. Such a situation can lead to expensive litigation and excessive estate or inheritance tax. A person with dual residences should clearly establish which state he considers to be his domicile. This can be done by consistency in such evidence of domicile as voter registration, automobile registration, state income tax returns, declaration in will, and positions taken in documents executed during life.

Separate issues arise if the decedent is not a U.S. citizen. If the decedent was a resident alien with a U.S. citizen spouse, his estate will be administered and taxed as if a U.S. citizen. The executor or administrator, however, should determine whether the United States has an estate tax treaty with the decedent's country of citizenship, especially if the decedent owned assets in that country, and review the laws of that country to determine if any death taxes are owed to that country. If the surviving spouse is not a U.S. citizen, the executor or administrator must carefully review the estate tax rules relating to this situation. For example, the regular marital deduction rules do not apply. A marital deduction is permitted only if the will provides for a qualified domestic trust, or if the spouse elects to become a U.S. citizen.

If the decedent is not a U.S. citizen and not a resident alien, the estate taxation and administration of the estate take on a whole new complexion. The issue of domicile becomes extremely important and could have a major impact on the U.S. taxation of the estate, as well as the number of ancillary international proceedings that may have to be conducted. A situation like this behooves an executor or administrator to seek expert advice and counsel.

(e) PROBATE PROCEDURES: WILL.   The courts having jurisdiction over decedents' estates have different names. Some states call such a court a "probate court"; others, a "surrogate court." Often the same court governs both decedents leaving wills and those dying without wills.

Most wills are drafted by an attorney; however, a **holographic will** is written entirely in the decedent's handwriting. Most state statutes recognize these wills and impose only minimal requirements to establish their validity. Two universal requirements are that the will be executed with testamentary intent, and be signed by the testator. A holographic will need *not* be witnessed to be valid in certain states. A court's determination of whether a holographic will is valid becomes part of the probate process.

A **codicil** to a will, or will codicil, is an amendment to or modification of an otherwise valid will. Testators will often use a codicil to make minor or modest changes instead of going through the whole process of redrafting the entire will. In certain cases this may be a misconception on their part since a codicil must meet certain statutory requirements of its own and must be executed in the same manner as a will (i.e., signed by the testator and two or more witnesses). In any event, a codicil becomes part of the last will and testament document.

After a decedent's will has been located, it should be presented to the court for **probating,** that is, proving it valid. The named executor (executrix if a female), if qualified and willing to act, is issued **letters testamentary,** that is, a document authorizing him to act on behalf of the estate. In some states temporary letters are issued with formal letters issued at a later date.

(f) PROBATE PROCEDURES: FAILURE OF EXECUTOR.   If the executor named in the will is unqualified because of such factors as age, competency, or residency, any named successor if qualified is allowed to take the executor's place. Should all successors fail to qualify or refuse the appointment, any beneficiary of the estate may petition the court for appointment. State laws generally provide an order of priority, the appointment going first to a qualified surviving spouse, then to qualified children (sometimes in age order), then to qualified grandchildren, and so on.

The person who qualifies and accepts the appointment is called an **administrator** (or **administratrix**) **CTA** (*cum testamento annexo,* that is, "with the will annexed"). The administrator CTA has the same duties and powers as an executor and looks to the will for authority to act.

(g) PROBATE PROCEDURES: INTESTACY.   The death of a person without a will necessitates the appointment of an administrator. As mentioned above, appointments are made by interested parties petitioning the court and the court appointing the first person who can qualify in the order of priority outlined under state law. Letters of administration are issued after compliance with the governing statutes. The administrator must distribute the estate in accordance with the laws of intestacy of the state in which he is appointed.

(h) SETTLEMENT OF SMALL ESTATES.   Most state statutes provide special rules for the settlement of small estates with either no court administrative involvement or some form of an abbreviated procedure. The definition of "small" depends on the gross value of the estate. These values can be as low as $5,000 to $15,000, or as high as $50,000 to $60,000. Utilization of these special rules results in greatly reduced administration costs and a quicker settlement of the estate.

(i) FIDUCIARY RESPONSIBILITIES

(i) Executor versus Administrator.   Although the executor's powers and duties come primarily from the will and secondarily from state law if the will is silent, the administrator of a person dying intestate must look solely to state law for authority to act.

The term **personal representative** or simply **representative** as used in this section encompasses both executors and administrators. The term **fiduciary** includes executors, administrators, guardians, and trustees.

(ii) General Duties of Representatives.   Duties of a representative, stated generally, are to collect the decedent's assets, pay creditors, account for all income and expenses, and distribute the assets remaining according to the provisions of the will or in accordance with state law in the absence of will provisions.

In the performance of these duties, the personal representative must use the **"reasonable man" rule,** that is, duties must be exercised with the prudence a reasonable person would exercise with his own property. The representative does not guarantee estate assets against loss. However, he is responsible for acting reasonably and can be asked to make good estate losses should he fail to act reasonably. Since the representative is not required to possess the expertise of an accountant, attorney, or investment counselor (although a decedent may often name such a professional in the will), a representative acting in a "reasonable" manner should determine whether the will or state law authorizes the retention of such advisors whenever necessary.

(iii) Preliminary Administration.   Often a death is sudden and unexpected. Determining whether the decedent left a will is sometimes a problem. Finding it and determining whether it is the last will executed may be even bigger problems. A careful search must be made of the decedent's personal papers. If the decedent had an attorney, accountant, banker, or insurance broker, the person may be helpful in ascertaining the existence of a will and locating it. The importance of the will lies not only in carrying out the decedent's plan for distribution of his assets, but also in determining the persons named as executors, trustees, and guardians of minors or others incapable of caring for themselves. Administration of the estate must begin, however, at the moment of death. There are too many important acts, such as carrying out the decedent's instructions for bodily organ donations, arranging for the funeral, and safeguarding valuable or perishable assets, to await the location of the will or formal appointment of a representative. Someone must take responsibility at once. Should it later turn out that another person was named executor or appointed administrator, an orderly transition of authority can be made.

(iv) Specific Duties of Representatives.   Other specific duties of the personal representative are to:

1. Arrange to have all estate assets inventoried and title transferred to the name of the executor or administrator.
2. Obtain possession of the decedent's important papers and personal property and arrange for safekeeping.
3. Arrange for adequate insurance coverage for estate assets.
4. Collect all debts owed to the decedent and litigate if necessary.
5. Arrange for an appraisal of all estate assets by qualified appraisers before distributing any assets.
6. Keep clear and accurate records of all estate receipts and disbursements. This is necessary for tax returns and for accountings to courts and beneficiaries.
7. Determine whether assets coming under the control of representatives are sufficient to meet both claims against the estate and legacies allowed by will and/or state law.
8. Review cash requirements to pay legacies, taxes, debts, and administration expenses, and determine whether assets are sufficiently liquid to pay such claims as they become due.
9. Arrange for the preparation of any payment of tax due on the decedent's final income tax returns, federal estate return, state or foreign estate or inheritance tax returns, and estate income tax returns.
10. Advertise for creditors (publish notification of decedent's death, allowing statutory period for claim presentation) and pay all valid claims against the estate.
11. Pay legacies at times specified under state law and distribute the remainder of the estate after payment of all debts and administration expenses to persons directed by will or by state law in the absence of will direction.
12. Prepare interim and/or final accountings for beneficiaries and courts as required by state law.

A graphic outline of the administration of a decedent's estate is presented in Exhibit 37.1.

(v) Possession of Assets.   After the appointment of the administrator or executor, the next step is to assemble the property belonging to the estate. The representative is required to

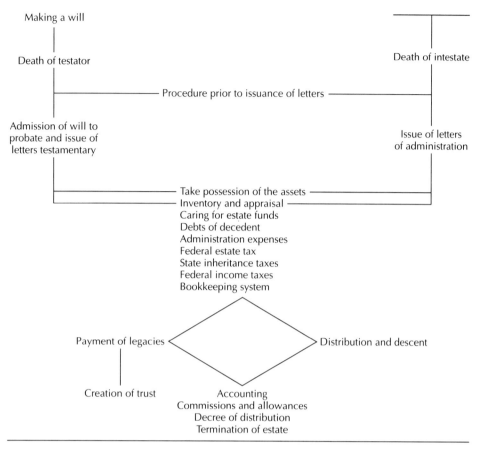

Exhibit 37.1.   Graphic outline of the administration of decedent's estate.

exercise due diligence in the discovery of assets and must take all proper legal steps to obtain possession of them.

(vi) Probate versus Nonprobate Assets.   Probate assets are those assets whose disposition is controlled by the decedent's will. Nonprobate assets pass to the designated beneficiary by either operation of law (i.e., joint tenancy with right to survivorship, tenants by the entirety), or by operation of contract (i.e., designated beneficiary of an insurance policy, qualified retirement plan, or other form of deferred compensation). Although the value of nonprobate assets is includable in the decedent's gross estate for tax purposes, the administrator or executor is not responsible for the collection of these assets. However, the estate representative's cooperation in assisting a beneficiary obtain possession of these assets is a usual occurrence.

(vii) Personal Property Exemptions.   Personal property of the deceased passes directly to the personal representative of the decedent. However, certain items of personal property must be exempted by statute for the benefit of the family of the decedent.

(viii) Real Property.   Title to real property passes directly to the heirs, or devisees, and such property does not ordinarily come under the control of the representative unless left to the estate by will, sold by order of the court to pay valid obligations of the estate, or administered by the representative as a requirement of state law. If real estate does come under the control of the representative, it is handled in the same manner as personal property. In some states, the representative may manage the real estate and collect rents during the period of administration. The balance due on a **land contract** receivable is personal property of the estate, although the title to the land passes to the heirs and is retained by them until the contract is paid.

(ix) Inventory of Assets.   A detailed inventory of all assets taken over, which will form the basis of the accounting of the representative, should be prepared and filed with the court. Schedules should be prepared of all cash on hand and on deposit; all furniture, fixtures, and articles of personal use; all claims against others **(choses in action)**; all contract rights that do not involve personal services; all unpaid fees, commissions, and salaries; all life insurance policies payable to the estate; all interest in partnerships; all unpaid dividends of record as of the date of death, or other accrued income; all leases; and all other personal property owned by the decedent. The inventory does not include goods or money held by the decedent for others. Claims canceled by will are included in the inventory, as are articles exempted for the decedent's family and articles of no apparent value. No liabilities are mentioned in the inventory, and assets pledged to secure a loan are listed without deduction for the amount of the loan. Accruals are to be computed up to midnight following the death of the decedent.

(x) Valuation of Assets.   The asset values are usually set by appraisers appointed by the court and will presumably be the market values at the time of death. The executor should keep a copy of the inventory and incorporate its details into the bookkeeping system.

(xi) Management of Estate Funds.   Generally, the function of the administrator or executor of an estate is to **liquidate,** whereas the role of the trustee or guardian is to manage. Nonetheless, the administrator or executor may have important managerial functions to perform. Perishable goods, speculative investments, and burdensome property should be disposed of promptly. Unless forgiven in the will, every effort should be made to collect all claims due the estate. Articles of a personal nature are usually distributed among legatees or next of kin at their inventory value but may be sold if such a distribution is not feasible.

All **estate funds** should be kept in a separate bank account in the name of the representative, with an indication of the fiduciary relationship, and should not be mingled with those of the representatives (except in the case of a trust company). All **disbursements** should be made by check. Interest should be secured on bank balances if possible. Stock certificates in the name of the decedent should be transferred to the name of the representative in his fiduciary capacity. Adequate insurance should be carried against fire, theft, public liability, and other risks. In general, the representative, to avoid personal liability for loss of funds and property, must care for the assets as diligently as if they were his own, assuming the representative to be a reasonably prudent businessman.

An executor or administrator may not be under legal compulsion to invest the funds of the estate, but it is certainly good business practice to make interim investments in guaranteed obligations, such as short-term U.S. securities or bank savings certificates or savings accounts if significant amounts of cash are accumulated for taxes, expenses, or future distribution. If investments are made, the representative must be guided by the procedure required of trustees (see later discussion).

The representative is not justified in continuing to operate a business owned by the decedent unless authorized to do so by the will. In the case of a closely held business, either a corporation or partnership, the representative will be guided by the provisions, if any, in the partnership or shareholder agreement. The terms of a buy–sell agreement may obligate and bind the representative to sell the decedent's business interest to either the surviving shareholders or partners, or to the corporation or partnership itself. In the absence of any such agreements or provisions, the business should be liquidated by the surviving partners.

(xii) Payments of Debts.   The administrator or executor has a duty to satisfy himself as to the validity of the claims made against the estate and should interpose objections to any doubtful claims. A judgment cannot be rejected. A doubtful claim may be settled by a reasonable compromise in good faith. A partial payment of a debt barred by the statute of limitations does not revive the debt.

The representative is not required to pay any debt or make any distribution of assets until the expiration of a statutory period of time. If any payment or distribution is made during the period, the representative may be held responsible for the remaining assets not being sufficient to meet the remaining liabilities.

(xiii) Advertising for Creditors.   The representative is permitted to advertise for creditors and should do so for personal protection. Notices are inserted in one or more newspapers published in the county requesting persons who have claims to present them with supporting affidavits and vouchers within a specified time, usually 6 months. Claims not yet due should be presented for proof so that funds will be set aside for their payment.

(xiv) Order of Debt Payment.   When the list of debts is completed and presented to the court, the solvency or insolvency of the estate can be determined. If the estate is solvent, the order of payment is immaterial, but if the liabilities are in apparent excess of the value of the assets, a statutory order must be followed. The following order of payment is, according to Stephenson (Estate and Trusts), representative:

1. Debts that by law have a special lien on property to an amount not exceeding the value of the property.
2. Funeral expenses.
3. Taxes.
4. Debts due to the United States and to the state.
5. Judgments of any court of competent jurisdiction, within the state, docketed and in force, to the extent to which they are a lien on the property of the deceased person at death.
6. Wages due to any domestic servant or mechanical or agricultural laborer for a period of not more than one year immediately preceding the death.
7. Claim for medical services within 12 months preceding death.
8. All other debts and demands.

(xv) Source of Funds for Debt Payment.   Unless the will directs otherwise, the assets of the estate are used in the following order in the payment of debts:

1. Personal property not bequeathed.
2. Personal property bequeathed generally.
3. Personal property bequeathed specifically.
4. Realty not devised.
5. Realty devised generally.
6. Realty devised specifically.

The sale, lease, or mortgaging of real estate to provide funds for the payment of debts must, in the absence of a provision to the contrary in the will, follow a petition to the court for permission so to use the realty, and the court must approve of the disposition made by the representative. Property descended to heirs is usually used before that distributed by will. Land sold by an heir or devisee before the estate is settled is subject to a possible claim for unpaid debts of the estate. All **dower or curtsey rights** (statutory rights for surviving wife or husband) and estates for life or years are adjusted, and heirs or devisees must be reimbursed if any assets are subsequently discovered from which the debts could have been paid.

In many instances, if the decedent was an owner of a closely held business, he may have entered into some form of a **buy sell agreement** with his co-owners. The agreement usually provides that the executor shall sell the decedent's interest in the business to one or more co-owners, or to the business entity itself, at the price set forth therein in exchange for cash. Depending upon the arrangement, the buy sell agreement will be referred to as either a cross purchase or entity redemption (or corporate stock redemption) agreement. The decedent's agreement to be bound by the terms of the agreement contractually binds the executor to sell the decedent's interest in the business pursuant to the terms of the agreement. This sales price also works to establish the estate tax value of the business interest in the gross estate.

The decedent, anticipating his need to provide liquidity for the estate, may have established and funded an irrevocable life insurance trust. In this arrangement, the trust applies for a life insurance policy on the decedent's life. The trustee is both the owner and beneficiary of the policy. Upon the decedent's death, the trustee collects the insurance proceeds. While neither the trustee nor the executor are contractually bound to do so, the trustee usually purchases assets from the estate, hence providing the needed liquidity. This technique also eliminates the need for the executor to sell assets in a rush at liquidation, or "estate sale," prices.

The executor should be sure to review the decedent's personal papers thoroughly, and interview the surviving spouse and business associates or partners, to determine the existence of a buy sell agreement or irrevocable life insurance trust.

(xvi) Administration Expenses.   Reasonable and necessary outlays made by the representative in collecting and distributing assets will be allowed by the court. The representative is personally liable for amounts disallowed. The compensation of the representative, court costs, and an allowance for preparing the accounting are allowed specifically when an accounting is made. Attorney's fees, accountant's fees, fire insurance premiums, necessary repairs to property, collection costs, and other ordinary expenses will be allowed. The character and amount of the estate and the complications of the particular situation will govern the decisions of the courts as to the reasonableness or necessity of a particular expenditure.

Most states statutorily regulate attorney's fees by prescribing a set fee schedule based on the size of the probate estate. Should an attorney's fee exceed the statutory maximum, he or she will need to seek the court's approval. In many instances, the estate's attorney may also be one of the executors, or the sole executor. This may entitle the attorney/executor to both a fee and a commission; however, the attorney/executor will have to keep detailed records of time spent and duties performed in order to sustain dual compensation.

(xvii) Distribution of Estate Assets.   After making appropriate provisions for the payment of all claims against the estate, the personal representative proceeds to distribute the remaining assets according to the instructions in the will or in compliance with the laws of descent and distribution.

(xviii) Payment of Legacies.   Legacies are usually payable one year after the death of the testator. General legacies ordinarily draw interest after that date and should be charged with interest for payments prior to the due date. General legacies to the testator's dependent children usually bear interest from the date of death. If the estate appears to be solvent, the executor may pay or deliver legacies at any time but should, for his own protection, take a bond from the legatee providing for a refund to the estate in case the assets prove to be inadequate to meet the prior claims. Otherwise a suit in equity may be necessary to recover the improper payments.

(xix) Abatement of Legacies.   If there are insufficient assets to meet the debts and other prior claims, the legacies are reduced or abated. A complete revocation is referred to as an **ademption.** The rules governing priority in the abatement of legacies are as follows:

1. A specific legacy takes priority over a general legacy. If the testator bequeaths specific shares of stock to A and $5,000 in cash to B, B's legacy will be diminished or, if necessary, entirely wiped out before the stock left to A is resorted to.

2. A legacy for the support of the testator's widow or children, who are not otherwise adequately provided for, takes priority over legacies to strangers or more distant relatives.

3. In most states, the personal assets of the estate will be used for the payment of debts before resorting to the real estate. As a result, the bequests of money or personal property may be diminished or wiped out, although the devisees of the real property are not affected.

4. Subject to the foregoing rules, all legacies are reduced pro rata in case of a deficiency.

If the will directs that real estate be sold to pay debts, the sale will take place before any legacies are abated.

(xx) Deductions from Legacies. There may be certain required deductions from legacies, the most common one being state inheritance taxes. A debt due by a legatee to the testator should be deducted, but a debtor who becomes a legatee is not entitled to retain funds applicable to the payment of all charges and legacies.

(xxi) Lapsed Legacies. A legacy is said to have "lapsed" if the legatee dies before the testator, and the assets involved revert to the undistributed or residuary portion of the estate. An exception is sometimes made when the deceased legatee is a child or other near relative who has left surviving children; the children then receive the legacy.

The children would receive the legacy on either a **per stirpes** or **per capita** basis. **Per stirpes** means that the children of a deceased parent receive an equal share of the deceased parents' share. **Per capita** means that the children of a deceased parent receive their own share. For example: A's will leaves everything to spouse or A's children should spouse predecease. A's spouse and one adult child predecease A. A is survived by a second adult child (B) and the predeceased child's two children (C and D). A **per stirpes** distribution would leave 50% to B and 25% to each of C and D. A **per capita** distribution would leave 33⅓% to B, C, and D.

(xxii) Advancement and Hotchpot. An advancement is a transfer of property by a parent to a child in anticipation of the share of the estate the child would receive if the parent died intestate. If a person indicates in his will that the advances are to be part of the child's legacy, these advances are considered as part of the corpus of the estate and must be taken into account in making the final distribution. An **allowance to a widow** for the support of the family is not an advance, nor is it a direct charge against items devised or bequeathed to her.

If there is no will and the advancement exceeds the child's distributable shares of the estate, the legatee is entitled to no further distribution but is not required to return the excess; if the advancement is less than the child's share, he is entitled to the difference. **Hotchpot** or **collation** is the bringing together of all the estate of an intestate with the advancements made to the children in order that it may be divided in accordance with the statutes of distribution.

(xxiii) Surviving Spouse's Right of Election against the Will. Should a decedent's will completely disinherit a surviving spouse or provide less than a certain percentage of the estate to her, the spouse may petition the court to elect to receive a specified percentage of the estate, normally ranging between 30% to 50%, "against the will" (e.g., in lieu of the existing dispositive will provisions). The right to make this election will vary among the states depending on whether the probated will was executed before the marriage or during the marriage between the decedent and surviving spouse.

(xxiv) Disclaimers. It is often recommended that an intended legatee or beneficiary forfeit, give up, or disclaim, an estate distribution. In other words, the legatee or beneficiary waives his or her right to receive all or part of their interest in an estate asset or distribution of assets. The effect of a proper disclaimer is that the intended legatee or beneficiary is presumed to have predeceased the decedent, and the asset is distributed to the contingent legatee or beneficiary. Disclaimers are governed both by state statute and the IRC in §§ 2046 and 2518. The requirements of both must be carefully observed in order to obtain the desired result. In general, the following steps must be observed:

1. The disclaimer must be made in writing.
2. It must be received by the executor and filed with the surrogate or probate court that has jurisdiction of the estate within 9 months of the date of death.
3. The intended legatee or beneficiary must renounce all right, title, and interest in the item(s) and must not have received, or be deemed to have received, any economic benefit of the assets being disclaimed.
4. The disclaimed interest must pass to someone other than the disclaiming legatee or beneficiary, and he may not direct to whom the asset will pass in lieu of himself.

(xxv) Decree of Distribution and Postdecree Procedure. The principal distribution of estate properties is made after the issuance by the court of a decree of distribution. Upon the filing of an acceptable final accounting (see below) and the expiration of the time for objections by interested parties, the court approves the accounting, allows the expenses of preparing the accounting and the representative's commission, and issues a decree that disposes of the balance of the estate according to the will or according to the statutes of descent and distribution in that jurisdiction.

The representative distributes the estate assets according to the decree, pays his commission, settles any other expenses allowed in the decree, closes his books, presents his vouchers to the court, and asks for a discharge from his responsibilities and for the cancellation of his bond.

(xxvi) Funding of Trusts. It is not uncommon for part of the estate to be distributed to a testamentary trust or to a preexisting intervivos trust. The distribution to the trust may make up part of a marital, residuary, or charitable bequest. A testamentary trust may also be funded to hold assets for a minor beneficiary. The appointment and approval of the trustee(s), and the distribution of the estate assets to the trust would be included in the courts' decree described above.

(j) POWERS OF ESTATE REPRESENTATIVE

(i) Executor versus Administrator. The personal representative's powers, as distinguished from duties, are those acts that he is authorized, rather than required, to perform. As previously mentioned, the powers of an executor or administrator CTA are outlined in the will and are often broader than those allowed to an administrator of an intestate, who must look solely to statutory authority.

The most common statutory and will clause powers of the personal representative are to invest and reinvest estate assets, to collect income and manage the estate property, to sell estate property as he sees fit, to mortgage property (in some states), and to deliver and execute agreements, contracts, deeds, and other instruments necessary to administer the estate. Most properly drawn wills reproduce the statutory powers and add additional desired powers not granted by statute.

(ii) Will Powers Not Conferred by Statute.   Using New York State law as outlined by Harris (1984) as an example, the powers listed below, when included in a will of a New York decedent, would grant additional powers not conferred by statute. These powers would not be available to an executor unless enumerated in the will (and never available to an administrator of an intestate):

1. To distribute the estate immediately after death. Many states require the executor to delay any distribution for as much as one year after letters testamentary are issued.
2. To hold property without regard to the limitations imposed by law on the proper investment of estate assets.
3. To make "extraordinary repairs" to estate assets. New York allows the representative to make only "ordinary repairs"; he has to secure the permission of all beneficiaries and possibly of the court to make "extraordinary repairs" such as replacing a heating system on real estate administered by the estate.
4. To charge the cost of agents such as attorneys, accountants, and investment advisors as estate expenses.
5. To continue a business of decedent.
6. To keep funds uninvested or invested in nonincome-producing assets.
7. To abandon, alter, or demolish real estate.
8. To borrow on behalf of the estate and give notes or bonds for the sums borrowed, and to pledge or mortgage any property as security for the borrowing.
9. To pay all necessary or proper expenses and charges from income or principal, or partly from each as the fiduciary deems advisable. (This important power will be expanded on in the discussion of income and principal of trusts.)
10. To do all acts not specifically mentioned as if the fiduciary were the absolute owner of the property.

(iii) Will Powers versus Statutory Powers.   It is important to remember that state law is looked to only where the will is silent. Any will provision will be adhered to, even if it is broader or more restrictive than statutory powers, unless such provision is contrary to law or public policy.

(k) COMMISSIONS OF REPRESENTATIVES.   Many states make executors' and administrators' commissions statutory. However, with an executor, the first step is to look to the will. Testators may specifically provide the amount of commission or prohibit commissions for fiduciaries. These will provisions will be adhered to, although several states allow an executor to renounce the will provisions and receive statutory commissions. Other states force the executor to renounce the appointment and petition to be appointed administrator, thereby becoming eligible for the statutory commissions of an administrator. Some states do not have statutory commission rates, leaving the awarding of commissions to the court's discretion.

It is important to bear in mind that commissions are allowed only on the **probate assets,** that is, assets that come under the administration of the personal representative. As previously mentioned, real property does not generally come under the control of the representative and thus is not usually a probate asset. When real property is a probate asset, the representative is entitled to commissions. In several states, specific bequests and the income thereon are treated as nonprobate and thus noncommissionable assets. In addition, if an asset is secured by a liability, only the net equity should enter into the commission base.

Sometimes a will provides for more than one executor. State law must then be examined to determine whether each is entitled to statutory commission or whether one such commission must be shared.

(I) TAXATION OF ESTATES

(i) Final Individual Income Taxes.   One of the responsibilities of the personal representative is to file any unfiled federal and state income tax returns, as well as final income tax returns for the short taxable year that ends on the date of death of the decedent. If the deceased left a surviving spouse, the personal representative can elect to file a joint federal tax return for the year of death. A joint return will normally be prepared on the cash basis for the calendar year, including the decedent's income only through the date of death, and the income of the surviving spouse for the full calendar year. An election in the final return to accrue medical expenses unpaid at death that are paid within one year of death may be made. Accrued interest on U.S. Government Series E Bonds owned by the decedent may be included as income in the final federal income tax return. Expert tax advice should be secured by the representative before making these or various other available elections.

Unused capital loss carryforwards and unused charitable contribution carryforwards of decedent are no longer deductible after the final year. Unused passive activity losses are allowed on the final return to the extent they exceed the estate tax value over the decedent's adjusted basis.

If a joint return is being filed, the tax shown on the return must be allocated between the decedent and the surviving spouse. The allocation will take into account the decedent's withholding tax and his actual payments of estimated tax, leaving the estate of the decedent with either an asset (representing overpayment of taxes) or a liability (representing underpayment of taxes). If the surviving spouse had income or paid some portion of the tax, she would owe the estate or be entitled to reimbursement from it, depending on the relationship of her tax payments to the separate tax liability on her income.

(ii) Federal Estate Tax.   Decedents with gross estates valued at over $600,000 are required to file a Federal Estate Tax Return, Form 706, regardless of the fact that there may be no federal estate tax liability. The federal estate tax is a tax on the value of the decedent's gross estate less certain deductions. Generally, the tax is paid from the estate property and reduces the amount otherwise available to the beneficiaries. Therefore, in the absence of specific directions in a will or trust, taxes are generally apportioned to the property that causes a tax. If property passes without tax because of a marital or charitable deduction, no taxes are chargeable to the property.

The gross estate for tax purposes includes all of the decedent's property as defined in the IRC, not merely probate property. The following are examples of property that is part of the gross estate for estate tax purposes, though not part of the probate estate and thus not accounted for in the representative's accounting:

1. Specifically devised real property.
2. Jointly owned property passing to the survivor by operation of law.
3. Life insurance not payable to the estate when the decedent possessed "incidents of ownership" such as the right to borrow or change the beneficiary of the policy, and policies transferred within 3 years of death.
4. Lump-sum distributions from retirement plans paid to someone as a result of surviving the decedent.
5. Gift taxes paid by the decedent within 3 years of death.
6. Fair market value of the principal of any revocable "living" trust of which the decedent was the grantor or settlor.
7. Fair market value of the principal of any irrevocable trust in which the decedent, as grantor or settlor, had retained any rights to income, or over the beneficiaries' rights to the use, enjoyment, or possession of the trust principal.

In putting a value on the gross estate for estate tax purposes, the representative has an election to value the estate as of the date of death or an alternative date. The alternative date is either 6 months after the date of death or at disposition of an asset if sooner. If the election to use the alternative date is not made, all property must be valued as of the date of death; if the alternative date is elected, all property must be valued at the alternative valuation date or dates. Alternate valuation is available only if there is a reduction in estate taxes.

Deductions from the gross estate to arrive at the taxable estate include administration expenses (if an election has not been made to deduct them on estate income tax returns), funeral expenses, debts of the decedent, bequests to charitable organizations, and a marital deduction for property passing to a surviving spouse.

The 1976 Tax Reform Act unified estate and gift tax rates by provisions for a unified table to be applied both to taxable gifts made after 1976 and to taxable estates for persons dying after 1976. In computing estate taxes on the taxable estate, gifts made after 1976 are added to the taxable estate and the unified tax is recomputed with credit given for the gift tax previously paid on such gifts. This computation has the effect of treating gift taxes paid as only payments on account of future estate and gift tax brackets. A marital deduction is now available for 100% of property passing to the surviving spouse. The property may be left in trust with income to the spouse for life, together with either a general power of appointment, or limited power of appointment. The latter may qualify for the marital deduction if the representative makes a Qualified Terminable Interest Property (QTIP) election with the return. Eventually, the property would be taxable in the surviving spouse's estate and the tax thereon would be payable from the property.

Estates are also allowed an unlimited charitable deduction for bequests left directly to charities. A prorated charitable deduction is allowed for a split-interest bequest to charity either in the form of a remainder interest or an income interest.

A **unified credit** is allowed against the computed estate tax. The unified credit is subtracted from the taxpayer's estate or gift tax liability. However, the amount of the credit available at death will be reduced to the extent that any portion of the credit is used to offset gift taxes on lifetime transfers. The amount of the credit is equivalent to a taxable estate of $600,000. Therefore, a decedent can have a taxable estate of up to $600,000 before any estate tax is due.

Several other credits may be allowed against the computed estate tax. Most common is a credit for state estate and inheritance taxes (described next). Depending upon the nature, situs, and other aspects of certain assets included in the gross estate, the following other credits may be allowed against the computed estate tax: prior transfers, foreign death taxes, death taxes on remainders, and recovery of taxes claimed as credits.

Filing of the Form 706 is due nine months after the decedents' date of death. The executor or administrator may request a six-month extension of time to file the return. If any tax is due with the return, an estimated payment of said tax is due six months from the date of death, with any balance due with the filing of the return.

While payment of the estate tax cannot normally be extended, IRC Section 6166 provides relief for certain estates. Should the estate assets include an interest in a closely held business, that exceeds 35% of the adjusted gross estate, an election by the executor or administrator would permit the deferral and payment of the estate tax, that is attributable to the inclusion of the closely held business interest in the estate, in installments over several years. The requirements of this code section are strict; therefore, the executor or administrator should carefully consider all available options, advantages, and consequences of making this election.

One of these options, available to closely held corporations, is an IRC Section 303 stock redemption. If funds are available, the corporation may redeem stock held by the executor or administrator equal to an amount that may not exceed the sum of the estate taxes, outstanding debts and administration expenses. While this option does not serve to defer the payment of estate taxes, it is an option that may be used in conjunction with or in lieu of the deferred payments under Section 6166 described above.

(iii) State Estate and Inheritance Taxes.   The estate tax in some states, such as New York, take the form of a tax on the right to transmit wealth that is similar to the federal estate tax. In other states, like New Jersey, an inheritance tax is applied to one's right to receive a portion of a decedent's estate. The state inheritance taxes are paid from estate funds by the representative, who will therefore withhold an appropriate amount from each legacy or establish a claim against those beneficiaries responsible for the tax by the terms of the will or by state law. Kinship of the beneficiary to the decedent is usually the controlling factor in determining exemptions and tax rates with close relatives being favored.

Other states such as Florida assess an estate tax based upon the amount of credit for state death taxes claimed on the federal estate tax return.

Almost all states provide for the tax to be at least equal to the federal credit for state death taxes if total inheritance taxes are less.

The timing of the state's estate or inheritance tax return and payment of any taxes may differ from the federal rules. An executor or administrator should be acquainted with these rules to avoid penalty and interest assessments. A state return may be required to be filed even though no federal return is required if the gross estate is less than $600,000, and even if no state tax is due.

(iv) Generation Skipping Transfer Tax.   The Tax Reform Act of 1986 revised and imposes a new generation skipping transfer tax on most transfers made to individuals two generations (i.e., grandchildren) down from the donor or decedent. Most transfers prior to 1987 are exempt. Direct transfers or distributions from trusts to individuals two generations down will be subject to the tax if the transfer exceeds the allowable exemption.

A donor/decedent has a lifetime exemption of $1,000,000. Transfers in excess of this amount to grandchildren are subject to a flat tax in addition to the estate and gift tax. This flat tax is imposed at the highest marginal estate and gift tax rate, which is currently 55%. Consequently, it is conceivable that transferring $100 could cost $110 in estate/gift and generation skipping taxes. The law is relatively new and complex. Therefore, knowledge of the law and planning are important in order to minimize the impact of the tax.

(v) Estate Income Taxes.   The representative may be responsible for filing annual federal income tax returns for the estate for the period beginning the day after the date of death and ending when the estate assets are fully distributed. The returns are generally prepared on a cash basis and can be prepared on a fiscal year, rather than a calendar year, basis. Such an election is made with the filing of the initial return and is often done to cut off taxable income in the first year of the estate. Maintenance of books on a fiscal year basis and filing the request for an extension of time to file the return will also establish the fiscal year. If returns are not timely filed, the estate will then be required to file on a calendar year basis.

A federal income tax return is due if the estate earns gross income of $600 or more per year. A $600 exemption is allowed in computing the income subject to federal income taxes. Administration expenses such as executor's commission and legal and accounting fees may be deducted if the representative does not elect to take these expenses on the federal estate tax return. If the estate distributes net income (gross income less expenses), such **distributable net income** is taxed to the recipient and the estate is allowed a corresponding deduction in computing its taxable income. Any remaining taxable income after deductions for exemption, expenses, and distributions is taxed at a rate specified in a table to be used exclusively for estates and trusts.

The income tax basis of estate assets are stepped up to their estate tax value. Therefore, should the executor or administrator sell any assets to raise cash, the assets' estate tax value is used to determine whether any gain or loss is realized upon the sale. There are, however, certain assets includable in the estate whose income tax basis carries over from the decedent. These assets are called **income in respect of a decedent,** or **IRD,** and are described in IRC Section 691. The following are examples of IRD: proceeds of U.S. savings bonds in excess of decedent's purchase price, IRAs, tax sheltered annuities and regular annuities, deferred compensation, and final paychecks and other remittances of compensation. Certain IRD give rise to income taxation upon receipt, while others do not cause taxation until they are redeemed or otherwise liquidated. Should an item of IRD be paid directly to an estate beneficiary, or be distributed to the beneficiary from the estate, the same rules regarding income tax basis apply. An offsetting deduction is available to the executor or beneficiary who must recognize IRD in their gross income. The deduction is equal to that items attributable share of the estate tax its inclusion in the estate has caused.

Estates must now make quarterly estimated tax payments in the same manner as individuals, except that an estate is exempt from making such payments during its first 2 taxable years. Accordingly, the penalties for underpayment of income tax are applicable to fiduciaries.

Some states also tax the income of estates, and the representative must see to it that such state statutes are complied with.

37.2 ACCOUNTING FOR ESTATES

(a) GOVERNING CONCEPTS. The general concepts governing the accounting for decedent's estates are for the most part similar to those applicable to trusts, but there are some differences. The underlying equation expressing the accounting relationship is assets = accountability. However, the representative is concerned, *not* with the long-term management of property for beneficiaries, but rather with the payment of debts and the orderly realization and distribution of the estate properties. The collection and the distribution of income are incidental to the main function of the estate's fiduciary.

Whenever an estate accounting is prepared, a reconciliation of the gross estate as finally determined for estate tax purposes should be made with the schedule of principal received at the date by the representative. Every difference should be explainable.

(i) Accounting Period. The accounting period of the estate is determined by the dates set by the fiduciary or by the court for intermediate and final accountings; nevertheless, the books must be closed at least once a year for income tax purposes.

(ii) Principal and Income. Unless otherwise provided for, the rules outlined below for the trustee should generally be followed by the representative in the allocation of receipts and disbursements to principal and income. Such distinctions, although not called for under the will, are frequently mandated by requirements of estate, inheritance, and income tax laws and regulations.

(iii) Treatment of Liabilities. The representative picks up only the inventory of assets of the decedent at the inception of the estate. Claims against the estate, after presentation and review, are paid by the representative and are recorded as "debts paid." The payment of such debts reduces in proportion the accountability of the representative.

(b) RECORD-KEEPING SYSTEM. No special type of bookkeeping system is prescribed by law, but a complete record of all transactions must be kept with sufficient detail to meet the requirements of the courts, and of the estate, inheritance, and income tax returns. Much of the information may be in memorandum form outside of the formal accounting system.

The federal estate tax law requires information regarding assets beyond those ordinarily under the control of the representative (e.g., real estate). Such information must be assembled in appropriate form by the representative, who has responsibility for the estate tax return.

(i) Journals. A single multicolumn journal is usually sufficient. It should incorporate cash receipts, cash disbursements and asset inventory adjustments. Further, it is important to note and keep track of the distinction between principal and income.

(ii) Operation of a Going Business.   If the decedent was the **individual proprietor** of a going business and if the court or the will instructs the administrator or executor to continue the operation of the business, the bookkeeping procedure becomes somewhat complicated. The books of the business may be continued as distinct from the general estate books, or the transactions of the business may be combined with other estate transactions in one set of records. The best procedure, if the business is of at least moderate size, is to keep the operations of the business in a separate set of books and to set up a controlling accounting in the general books of the executor or administrator.

As soon as the representative takes charge of the business, the assets should be inventoried and the books closed, normally as of the date of death. The liabilities should be transferred to the list of debts to be paid by the representative, leaving the assets, the operating expenses and income, and the subsequently incurred liabilities to be recorded in the books of the company. An account should be opened in the books of the business for the representative that will show the same amount as the controlling account for the business in the books of the representative.

(iii) Final Accounting.   The "final" accounting is the report to the court of the handling of the estate affairs by the representative, if required. It presents, among other things, a plan for the distribution of the remainder of the assets of the estate and a computation of the commission due the representative for his services. If the court approves the report, it issues a decree putting the proposals into effect.

(c) REPORTS OF EXECUTOR OR ADMINISTRATOR.   The form of the reports of the fiduciary will vary according to the requirements of the court and to the character of the estate. In general, however, the representative "charges" himself with all of the property received and subsequently discovered plus gains on realizations, and "credits" (or discharges) himself with all disbursements for debts paid, expenses paid, legacies distributed, and realization losses. Each major item in the charge and discharge statement should be supported by a schedule showing detailed information. At any time during the administration of the estate, the excess of "charges" over "credits" should be represented by property in the custody of the fiduciary. It may be necessary to show the market value of property delivered to a legatee or trustee at the date of delivery, in which case the investment schedule will show the increase or decrease on distribution of assets, as well as from sales. The **income schedule,** when needed, should be organized to show the total income from each investment, the expenses chargeable against income, and the distribution of the remainder.

Exhibit 37.2 is typical of the **charge-and-discharge statement,** each item being supported by a schedule.

37.3 TRUSTS AND TRUSTEES—LEGAL BACKGROUND

(a) NATURE AND TYPES OF TRUSTS.   The trust relationship exists whenever one person holds property for the benefit of another. The **trustee** holds legal title to the property for the benefit of the **beneficiary,** or *"cestui que trust."* The person from whom trust property is received is known as the grantor, donor, settler, creator, or trustor.

An **express trust** is one in which the trustee, beneficiary, subject matter, and method of administration have been explicitly indicated. An **implied** trust may be created whether language of an instrument indicates the desirability of a trust but does not specify the details, or when the trust relationship is assumed in order to prevent the results of fraud, breach of trust, or undue influence. The terms "constructive," "resulting," and "involuntary" trust are sometimes applied to such situations.

A **testamentary trust** is one created by a will. A **living trust,** or *"trust inter vivos,"* is created to take effect during the grantor's lifetime. Trusts are sometimes created by court order, as in the case of a guardianship.

ESTATE OF JOHN SMITH
Charge and Discharge Statement
A. L. White, Executor
From April 7, 19XX, to December 15, 19XX

First, as to Principal:

The Executor charges himself as follows:

With amount of inventory at the date of death, April 7, Schedule A	$xxx	
With amount of assets discovered subsequent to date of death, Schedule B	xxx	
With gain on realization of assets, Schedule C	xxx	
		$xxx

The Executor credits himself as follows:

With loss on realization of assets, Schedule C	$xxx	
With amount paid for funeral and administrative expenses, Schedule D	xxx	
With amount paid on debts of the estate, Schedule F	xxx	
With distributions to legatees, Schedule G	xxx	
		xxx
Leaving a balance of principal, Schedule C, of		$xxx

Second, as to Income:

The Executor charges himself as follows:

With amount of income received, Schedule H		$xxx	

The Executor credits himself as follows:

With amount of administrative expenses chargeable to income, Schedule D	$xxx		
With distribution of income to legatees, Schedule I	xxx	xxx	
Leaving a balance of income, Schedule J			xxx
Leaving a balance of principal and income of			$xxx

Balance of principal and income to be distributed to those entitled thereto, subject to the deduction of the Executor's commissions, legal fees, and the expenses of this accounting, Schedule K.

Exhibit 37.2. Sample charge and discharge statement.

A **private trust** is created for the benefit of particular individuals, while a **public** or **charitable trust** is for the benefit of an indefinite class of persons. Charitable trusts are discussed in Chapter 29.

A **simple trust** directs the trustee to distribute the entire net income of the trust to the named beneficiary. A **complex trust** gives the trustee the discretionary authority to distribute or accumulate the trust net income to or on behalf of the named beneficiary. In some instances, the trust may start off as complex and then convert to a simple trust upon the happening of a specified event, that is, the beneficiary's attainment of age 21 or 25.

A **grantor trust** exists when both the grantor and beneficiary are the same individual. A grantor trust may be implied if the grantor retains sufficient rights or controls over disposition of trust income and/or principal.

A trust may include a **spendthrift clause** that prohibits the beneficiary from assigning his interest before receiving it or prevents creditors from enforcing their claims against the income or principal of a trust fund, or both.

Trusts are often used for business purposes, as when property is transferred by a deed of trust instead of a mortgage, when trustees are appointed to hold title and perform other functions under a bond issue, or when assets are assigned to a trustee for the benefit of creditors. Bankruptcy and insolvency are discussed in Chapter 39.

(i) Limitations on Private Trusts. A public trust may be established for an indefinite period, but a trust may not suspend indefinitely the power of anyone to transfer the trust property. The common law rule, otherwise known as the **Rule against Perpetuities,** limits the duration of a private trust to 21 years after the death of some person who is living when the trust is created. Another common limitation in certain states is "two lives in being" at the origin of the trust.

Accumulation of the income of a trust is also restricted by state law. A common provision, for example, is that in the case of a trust created for the benefit of a minor, the income can be accumulated only during the minority of the beneficiary. Even the income of a charitable trust cannot be accumulated for an "unreasonable" period.

(ii) Revocation of Trusts. A completed trust cannot be revoked without the consent of all the beneficiaries unless the right to revoke has been expressly reserved by the grantor. Trusts are therefore sometimes classified as "revocable" or "irrevocable."

(b) APPOINTMENT AND REMOVAL OF TRUSTEES. In general, anyone competent to make a will or a contract is competent to create a trust. The trustee must be one who is capable of taking and holding property and who has the legal capacity and natural ability to execute the trust.

(i) Choice of Trustee. The decedent's will usually names the trustee for a testamentary trust. A grantor who is establishing an inter vivos trust will usually appoint one or more of the following to act as trustee: a relative; his professional advisor, that is, attorney, accountant, broker; a business associate; or an institutional entity, such as a bank or trust company. Each type of trustee has its pros and cons; however, the most important concern is not to choose a trustee that will cause adverse income tax consequences.

(ii) Methods of Appointment. Some of the means by which trustees are appointed are:

1. By deed or declaring of trust. The creator of the trust names the trustees in the instrument.
2. By will. The same person may be both executor and trustee under a will, but this dual capacity should be clearly indicated.
3. By agreement.
4. By the court. The court will appoint a trustee when a trust may fail for lack of a trustee, when a trustee refuses to serve or has died, or when a vacancy from any cause exists and no other means have been provided for filing the vacancy.
5. By implication of law.
6. By self-perpetuating boards. When vacancies occur, they are filed by the remaining members of the board.
7. By the exercise of a power of appointment. The instrument creating the trust may give the remaining trustees, beneficiaries, or any other person the power to appoint a trustee to fill a vacancy. Specific instructions should be included in the instrument as to the situation establishing a vacancy, the persons who may be appointed, and the manner of making the appointment.

(iii) Acceptance or Disclaimer. Acceptance of an appointment as trustee may be made by positive statement, by qualifying as executor if the appointment is by will, by the acceptance of property of the trust, or by other acts from which acceptance may be presumed. An individual may refuse to accept an appointment as a trustee and should execute and deliver a disclaimer expressing rejection of the appointment.

(iv) Resignation of Trustee. According to the Restatement of the Law of Trusts 2d (1 Trusts A.L.I. 234):

> A trustee who has accepted the trust cannot resign except (a) with the permission of a proper court; or (b) in accordance with the terms of the trust; or (c) with the consent of all the beneficiaries, if they have capacity to give such consent.

(v) Removal of Trustee. The court has power to remove a trustee and appoint a successor under certain circumstances. Scott (1987) cites, among others, the following grounds upon which trustees have been removed:

1. Failure to exercise discretion.
2. Self-dealing.
3. Failure to keep proper accounts, and mingling with trustee's own funds.
4. Incompetency and neglect of duty.
5. Conversion of trust property.
6. Refusal to obey orders of the court.

(c) POWERS AND DUTIES OF TRUSTEES. The powers of trustees are obtained both from the provisions and implications of the instrument creating the trust and from the general laws pertaining to the trust relationship. The instrument may either expand or restrict the general powers, except that it may not relieve the trustee from liability for gross negligence, bad faith, or dishonesty. The powers of a trustee may be either (1) imperative or mandatory, or (2) permissive or discretionary. In other words, they must either be exercised definitely and positively within a given length of time or upon the occurrence of some contingency, or they may be exercised at the discretion of the trustee.

(i) General Powers. The general powers of a trustee, which include all necessary incidental powers, are:

1. To take and retain possession of the trust property.
2. To invest trust funds so as to yield a fair income.
3. To sell and reinvest when necessary.
4. To sell and convey real estate when necessary to carry out the provisions of the trust.
5. To release real estate so that it may earn income.
6. To pay for repairs, taxes, and other such expenses in connection with trust property.
7. To sue or defend suits when necessary.
8. To make contracts that are necessary to carry out the purposes of the trust.
9. To pay over and distribute the trust property to those entitled to it.

The trustee secures possession of the trust property and holds title in his own name. All debtors should be notified of the change in ownership of claims against them in order to hold them directly liable to the trustee. All debts due the trust estate should be collected promptly. Trust property must be kept separate from the property of anyone else. The trustee will be liable for any loss occurring as a result of their mingling of funds or other property. An exception is usually made when a trust company is acting as trustee; it may deposit cash in trust funds with itself or may mingle various trust funds and deposit same with designated depositories.

(ii) Duties.   The duties of the trustee are outlined by Scott (1987) as follows:

1. To administer the trust as long as he continues as trustee.
2. To administer the trust solely in the interest of the beneficiary (the duty of loyalty as a fiduciary).
3. Not to delegate to others the performance of acts which the trustee sought personally to perform.
4. To keep clear and accurate accounts.
5. To give to beneficiaries upon their request complete and accurate information as to the administration of the trust.
6. To exercise such care and skill as a man of ordinary prudence would exercise in dealing with his own property; and if the trustee possesses greater skill than that of an ordinary prudent man, he must exercise the skill he has.
7. To take reasonable steps to secure control of trust property and to keep control of it.
8. To use care and skill to preserve the trust property. The standard of care and skill is that of a man of ordinary prudence.
9. To take reasonable steps to realize on claims which he holds in trust and to defend claims of third persons against the trust estate.
10. To keep the trust property separate from his own property and separate from property held upon other trusts; and to designate trust property as property of the trust.
11. To refrain in ordinary circumstances from lending trust money without security.
12. To invest trust funds so that they will be productive of income.
13. To pay the net income of the trust to the beneficiary at reasonable intervals; and if there are two or more beneficiaries he must deal with them impartially.
14. Where there are several trustees, it is the duty of each of them, unless otherwise provided by the trust instrument, to participate in the administration of the trust, and each trustee must use reasonable care to prevent the others from committing a breach of trust.

(d) PROPER TRUST INVESTMENTS.   The trustee is under a duty to invest funds in such a way as to receive an income without improperly risking the loss of the principal. The only general rule as to investment is that the trustee is under a duty to make such investments as a prudent man (the **"prudent man" rule** or "Massachusetts" rule) would make of his own property, having primarily in view the preservation of the estate and the amount and regularity of the income to be derived. In some states ("legal-list" states), the legislatures tell trustees in what they must or may invest funds unless the terms of the trust otherwise provide.

Kinds of investments that are almost universally condemned are summarized by Scott (1987) as follows:

1. Purchase of securities on margin.
2. Purchase of speculative shares of stock.
3. Purchase of bonds selling at large discount because of uncertainty of repayment at maturity.
4. Purchase of securities in new and untried enterprises.
5. Use of trust property in the carrying on of a trade or business, even though it is not an untried enterprise.
6. Purchase of land or other things for the purpose of resale, unless authorized by the terms of the trust.
7. Purchase of second and other junior mortgages.
8. Making unsecured loans to individuals or firms or corporations.

Types of investments that are almost universally permitted include:

1. Bonds of the United States or of the state or of a municipality thereof.
2. First mortgages on land.
3. Corporate bonds of a high investment grade.

In 1990, the American Law Institute published the Restatement 3d of Trusts, which incorporates a new Prudent Investor Rule. Since then, California, Delaware, Georgia, Illinois, Minnesota, New York, Tennessee, and Washington have adopted provisions similar to, or somewhat comparable to, the scope of these new rules. The Restatement embodies three main themes:

1. Although it is thought that a trustee may not delegate any of his duties, other than certain ministerial duties, this position is relaxed in that a trustee should, or even must, delegate investment authority to skilled professionals should they lack the required expertise or experience to properly manage the assets within the trust.
2. The costs incurred by the trustee in performing his duties must be reasonable.
3. A trustee is now charged with the responsibility for maintaining the trust portfolio in such a manner as to keep pace with inflation. This is much broader than merely preserving capital, but rather a need to manage for both growth in principal and in income.

(e) TRUSTEE'S PERSONAL LIABILITIES AND LIABILITY FOR ACTS OF CO-TRUSTEE.
A trustee is liable to the beneficiary for failure to fulfill his duties under the statutes, general rules of equity, or the provisions of the trust indenture.

A trustee must be particularly circumspect in all matters affecting his own property or benefit. He is personally liable for torts committed by himself or his agents and, unless his agreement states otherwise, is personally liable on all contracts made on behalf of the trust.

A trustee is not responsible for **loss** by theft, embezzlement, or accident if he has taken all the precautions that a careful businessman takes in guarding his own property, and if he is strictly following his line of duty as a trustee. If a trustee is not insolvent and mixes trust property with his own, the beneficiary may take the whole, leaving the trustee to prove his own part. If the trustee is insolvent, the beneficiary shares with the other creditors unless definite property can be identified as belonging to the trust. Interest will be charged against a trustee who has mingled trust funds with his own. If bank deposits are made in the individual name of the trustee, he will be treated as a guarantor of the solvency of the bank, even though he uses care in his choice of the bank and has not in any way misused the funds.

In general, a trustee is not liable for losses caused by the default or negligence of a co-trustee unless he has cooperated with the trustee who is at fault, or has known of the trustee's misconduct and has not taken any steps to prevent it. If, however, each trustee should have interested himself in the matter in question, such as the proper investment of funds, each would be responsible even though he took no part in or knew nothing of the misconduct. All trustees should act together in handling the trust property and should apply to the court for instructions in case they cannot agree. Unanimity is usually required for all important decisions in the case of private trusts, but a majority of a board of trustees may act for a charitable trust.

In certain circumstances, a trustee may become personally liable for the unpaid estate taxes of a decedent under the theory of **transferee liability.** Ordinarily, the beneficiary of an estate or trust is ultimately liable for any unpaid estate or gift taxes due on the transfer. The liability is equal to the value of the property received by the recipient as of the date of transfer. A review of IRC Sections 6324 and 6901, primarily, is in order. For example, the trustee of an inter vivos trust that is included in the gross estate for estate tax purposes could result in the trustee being personally liable, as opposed to the beneficiaries, for payment of any attributable estate taxes. Certain trust distributions trigger the GSTT, discussed in § 37.1(1), requiring the trustee to pay this tax. As a result of this possibility, a trustee should consider maintaining a reserve until he is satisfied that all such taxes are satisfied. Upon making distributions, the trustee should also consider requesting that the beneficiaries indemnify him for any taxes that may be assessed against him.

(f) GUARDIANS.   If a person is incompetent to manage his own property because of a disability such as infancy or mental incompetency, a guardian will be appointed by the probate or other appropriate court. The court must approve the appointment of a guardian by will. A guardian is a trustee in the strictest sense of the term. He is directly under the supervision of the court. If possible, only the income from the property should be used for the maintenance and education of the beneficiary; permission must be granted by the court before the principal can be used for this purpose. Any **sale of real estate** must be authorized by the court. A guardian should have the authorization of the court or the direction of a will before paying money to a minor or to anyone for the minor; otherwise he may be compelled to pay the amount again when the minor becomes of age.

(g) TESTAMENTARY TRUSTEE.   The work of the trustee appointed by a will begins when the executor sets aside the trust fund out of the **estate assets.** One person may serve as both executor and trustee under a will.

The testamentary trustee has slightly more freedom in handling the funds than does the executor, and his responsibility may be made less rigorous by provisions of the will. He holds, invests, and cares for the property, and disposes of it or its income as directed by the will. A trustee should have specific authority of a will or the court, or the consent of everyone interested, before carrying on a business. If there are several executors, one can act alone, but trustees must act jointly.

(h) COMPENSATION OF TRUSTEES.   Trustees are usually allowed compensation for their work, either by provision of the trust instrument or by statute. The **statutory provision** is usually a graduated percentage of the funds handled.

A trustee is entitled to be repaid expenditures reasonably and properly incurred in the care of trust property. The compensation is usually allocated to principal and income in accordance with the specific provision of the indenture or as provided by statute or rules of law.

(i) RIGHTS OF BENEFICIARY.   The beneficiary has an equitable title to the trust property, that is, he can bring suit in a court of equity to enforce his rights and to prevent misuse of the property by the trustee. Unless the instrument by which the trust is created provides otherwise, the beneficiary, if of age, can sell or otherwise dispose of his equitable estate in the property.

The beneficiary has the **right to inspect** and take copies of all papers, records, and data bearing on the administration of the trust property and income that are in the hands of the trustee. The beneficiary may have an accounting ordered whenever there is any reason for suspicion, or any failure to allow inspection or to make satisfactory reports and statements. Whenever it seems advisable, a court of equity will order an accounting.

The beneficiary may have an injunction issued to restrain the trustee from proceeding with any unauthorized action, if such action will result in irremediable damage. The beneficiary may present a petition to the court for the removal of a trustee but must be able to prove bad faith, negligence, lack of ability, or other such cause for the removal. The trustee is entitled to a formal trial.

The beneficiary can, if it is possible to do so, follow the trust property and have it subjected to the trust, even if a substitution has been made for the original property, unless it comes into hands of an innocent holder for value. If the trust property cannot be traced or is in the hands of an innocent holder for value, the beneficiary may bring action against the trustee in a court of equity for breach of trust.

If the beneficiary is of age and mentally competent, he may approve or ratify acts of the trustee that would otherwise be a violation of the trustee's duties or responsibilities.

(j) DISTINCTION BETWEEN PRINCIPAL AND INCOME.   Probably the most difficult problem of the trustee is to differentiate between principal (corpus) and income. The intention of the creator of the trust is binding if it can be ascertained, but in the absence of instructions to the contrary the general legal rules must be followed.

The **life tenant** (the present beneficiary) is entitled to the net income and the **remainderman** (the future beneficiary) to the principal, as legally determined. The principal is the property itself that constitutes the trust fund, and the income is the accumulation of funds and other property arising from the investment or other use of the trust principal. Increases or decreases in the value of the assets that constitute the trust fund affect only the principal. The income determined under these rules is not always the same as taxable income or income as determined by GAAP. The life tenant is entitled to receive only the net income from all sources for the entire term of his tenancy. He is not allowed to select the income from only those investments that are lucrative.

(i) Receipts of Principal.   The following receipts of cash or other property have been held to be part of the **corpus** of the trust and therefore to belong to the remainderman or persons entitled to the corpus:

1. Interest accrued to the beginning of the trust. Bond coupons are not apportioned in the absence of a statute providing for such a division.
2. Rent accrued to the beginning of the trust. Under the common law, rent was not apportioned according to the time expired.
3. Excess of selling price of trust assets over their value in the original inventory or over its purchase price. Appreciation, in general, belongs to the trust corpus.
4. The value of assets existing at the time of the original inventory was taken but not included in the inventory.
5. Dividends (see discussion below).
6. Proceeds of the sale of stock rights.
7. Profit from the completion of executory contracts of a decedent.
8. Profits earned prior to the beginning of the trust on the operations of a partnership or sole proprietorship.
9. Insurance money received for a fire that occurred prior to the date of the beginning of the trust, or after that date if the property is in the hands of the trustee for the benefit of the trust in general.
10. If trust property is mortgaged, the proceeds may be said to be principal assets, although there is no increase in the equity of the remainderman.

(ii) Disbursements of Principal.   The following payments, distribution, and exhaustion of assets have been held to be chargeable to the corpus:

1. Excess of the inventory value or purchase price of an asset over the amount realized from its sale.
2. Payment of debts owed, including accruals, at the date of the beginning of the trust.
3. Real estate taxes assessed on or before the date of the beginning of the trust. In the case of special assessments made during the administration of the trust, the remainderman may pay the assessment and the life tenant may be charged interest thereon annually during the life of the trust, or else some other equitable adjustment will be made between them.
4. Any expenditures that result in improvements of the property, except those made voluntarily by a life tenant for his own benefit, and all expenditures on newly acquired property that are necessary to put it into condition to rent or use.

5. Wood on the property that the life tenant uses for fuel, fences, and other similar purposes. The life tenant may operate mines, wells, quarries, and so on, that have been
opened and operated on the property.

6. Losses due to casualty and theft of general trust assets.

7. Expenses of administration except those directly pertaining to the administration of
income. For example, legal expenses incurred in defending the trust estate are chargeable to principal; however, the expenses of litigation in an action to protest only the income are payable out of income.

8. Trustee's commissions in respect to the receipts or disbursements out of principal.
Commissions computed on income are ordinarily payable out of income.

9. Brokerage fees and other expenses for changing investments should generally be
chargeable to principal, since they are a part of the cost of purchase or sale.

10. Income taxes on gains made from disposition of principal assets.

11. Carrying charges on unproductive real estate, unless the terms of the trust direct the
trustee to retain the property even though it is unproductive.

12. Cost of improvements to property held as part of the principal.

(iii) Receipts of Income.   The following receipts have been held to be income and to belong
to the life tenants or persons entitled to the income.

1. Interest, rent, and so on, accruing after the date of the beginning of the trust. The proceeds of a foreclosed mortgage may be apportionable between principal and income. Interest includes the increment in securities issued at a discount.

2. Increase in value of investments made by the trustee from accumulated undistributed
income.

3. Dividends (see discussion below).

4. Crops harvested during the trust.

5. Royalties or other income from operation of mines, quarries, or wells that were made
productive prior to the beginning of the trust, or were developed or leased in cooperating
with the remainderman.

6. Net profit from the operation of a business.

(iv) Disbursements of or Charges to Income.   The following items have been held to be
chargeable against the income of the trust:

1. Interest payable, accruing during the life of the trust.

2. Any expenses incurred in earning or collecting income, caring for trust property, or
preserving its value, and an appropriate share of administration fees and expenses.

3. Income tax except those levied on gains from sale of principal assets.

4. Premiums on trustee's bond.

5. Provision for amortization of wasting property, including leasehold interests, royalties,
oil and gas wells, machinery, and farm implements (see discussion of depreciation
below).

6. Provision for amortization of improvements to trust property when such improvements
will not outlive the duration of the trust.

7. Losses of property due to the negligence of the life tenant.

8. Losses due to casualty and theft of income assets.

(k) PRINCIPAL AND INCOME—SPECIAL PROBLEMS.   The distinction between principal
and income also involves a consideration of such problems as unproductive property, accruals,
dividends, bond premium and discount, and depreciation and depletion.

(i) Unproductive Property.   When the trustee is required to sell unproductive property and the sale is delayed, the net proceeds of the sale should be apportioned between principal and income. The net proceeds are allocated by determining the sum that, with interest thereon at the current rate of return on trust investments, would equal the net proceeds, and the sum so determined is treated as principal and the balance as income (Restatement of Trusts 2d, § 241). Apportionment between principal and income is generally applicable to real estate, but it has been applied in the case of personal property also. It does not matter whether the property is sold at a gain or a loss.

(ii) Accruals.   There are two dates at which the matter of accruals becomes significant. The first is the date at which the trust begins. Income and expenses accrued at that date belong to the corpus of the estate. The second date is the one when the life interest terminates. Income and expenses accrued at that date belong to the life tenant or his estate.

Larsen and Mosich (1994) provide a summarization of the general rule of accrual as applied to certain items, from which the following is taken:

1. *Interest.* Interest accrued on receivables and investments at the date the trust is established is considered part of the trust corpus. Exceptions are interest on (a) savings accounts when the interest is paid only if the deposit remains until the end of the interest period, and (b) coupon bonds when the payment is contingent upon the owner presenting the coupon, in which case the date of receipt is controlling. Similar rules apply to the accrual of interest expense.

2. *Rent.* The accrual of rent prior to the beginning of the trust is considered by many states as a portion of a trust corpus. Any rent accruing between the date of the establishment of the trust and the termination of the tenancy belongs to the income beneficiary. Rent expense is handled similarly.

3. *Dividends.* Ordinary cash dividends are not divisible. If the dividend is declared and the date of record has passed before the trust is created, the dividend is a part of the corpus. Otherwise it is considered income to the trust. A stock dividend is treated in the same manner in many states. . . . [For a discussion of special treatment of cash and stock dividends under the Massachusetts and Pennsylvania rules, see below.]

4. *Property taxes.* Taxes which have been levied on trust property prior to the beginning of the trust are charges against the principal. Any taxes assessed on the basis of trust property held for the benefit of the income beneficiary are chargeable against income. Special assessments made during the administration of the trust are usually paid by the remainderman, although in some cases where the assessment is for improvements which benefit the life tenant, a part or all of the assessment may be charged against income. When the assessment is paid from the corpus, interest on the funds advance may be charged against income.

5. *Profits.* Income earned by a partnership or proprietorship does not accrue. The income which is earned prior to the creation of the trust is considered a part of the principal of the trust. In many cases a partnership is dissolved upon the death of a partner, and there may be no income earned after the trust is established. In the event that the business continues by specific direction of the grantor or provision of the partnership agreement, any income earned after the trust is created is income of the trust.

6. *Executory contracts.* Any profits earned on the completion of an executory contract by the trustee is an addition to the principal of the trust.

7. *Livestock and crops.* Any livestock born during the tenancy under the trust is considered income, except to the extent that the herd must be maintained as directed by the grantor, in which case the increase must be divided between principal and income in a manner which honors this intention. If the principal includes land, any crops harvested during this tenancy are considered income of the trust.

8. *Premium returns.* Any return of premium or dividend on insurance policies which was paid prior to the creation of the trust is a part of the principal. This is considered realization of assets.

9. *Royalties.* Royalties or other income from the operation of mines or other natural resource deposits which were made operative before the trust was created or which were developed in cooperation with the remainderman are income to the trust.

(iii) Dividends.   The determination of whether a dividend is principal or income involves a consideration of applicable state laws. Ordinary cash dividends declared during the period of the trust belong to the income beneficiary. An ordinary stock dividend is usually regarded as income except in states that follow the **Massachusetts rule.** This rule holds that all cash dividends are treated as income and that stock dividends are entirely principal.

Some states follow the **Pennsylvania rule,** which holds that, in regard to extraordinary dividends, it is not the form of the dividend but its source that determines whether and to what extent it is income or principal. Generally, under this rule extraordinary dividends are income if declared out of earnings accruing to the corporation during the period of the trust, but they are principal if declared out of earnings accruing prior to the creation of the trust. Thus, if such dividends cause the book value of the corporation's stock to be reduced below the book value that existed at the creation of the trust, that portion of the dividend equivalent to the impairment of book value is principal and only the remainder is income. The present Pennsylvania law provides that stock dividends of 6% or less "shall be deemed income" unless the instrument provides to the contrary.

Although there is still wide diversity among the courts and state statutes in the apportionment of corporate distributions, Scott (1987) points out that the recent trend has been in favor of the Massachusetts rule. The Uniform Principal and Income Act (Uniform Laws Annotated, Vol. 7B, § 5) follows the essence of the Massachusetts rule in treating cash and other property dividends as income and stock dividends as principal.

(iv) Premium and Discount on Bonds.   The necessity of accumulating bond discount or amortizing bond premium in order to determine the **correct interest income** still gives rise to a great deal of confusion in trust and estate administration. In general, it appears that most courts support the amortization of premium on bonds purchased by the trustee, but there has been little or no support of the accumulation of discount. Any difference between the inventory value and the face value of the bonds taken over by the trustee is usually treated as an adjustment of principal.

In the event of **redemption before maturity,** it has been held that the proper procedure is to amortize the premium to the date of redemption; the unamortized balance is a loss borne by principal. If a bonus is received, it should be credited to principal.

Scott (1987) suggests:

> It might well be held that the whole matter [of amortizing premium and discount] should be left to the discretion of the trustee, and if he is not guilty of an abuse of discretion in unduly favoring some of the beneficiaries at the expense of the others, the court should not interpose its authority. This, of course, is the result reached where such discretion is expressly conferred upon the trustee by the terms of the trust.

(v) Depreciation and Depletion.   In determining whether provision must be made for depreciation and depletion, it is essential to consider carefully the intentions and wishes of the trustor. If the trustor intended to give the full, undiminished income to the life tenant even though the principal would thereby be partially or completely exhausted, no deduction from income for depletion or depreciation is allowed. If, however, there is an expressed or implied intention to preserve the principal intact, the trustee is required to withhold from income an amount sufficient to maintain the original property of the trust.

When the trustor's intentions regarding the receipts from wasting property cannot be determined from the trust instrument, then, according to Scott (1987), the inference is that the trustor did not intend that the life beneficiary should receive the whole income at the expense of the principal. Thus, when the trustee holds wasting property, including royalties, patents, mines, timberlands, machinery, and equipment, he is under a duty to make a provision for amortization of such property. The general rule has been applied to new buildings erected and improvements made by the trustee; however, the courts have generally held that buildings that were part of the trust estate at the beginning of the trust need not be depreciated. The courts have, in effect, refused to treat the buildings as wasting property.

The trend appears to be in the direction of adopting principles of depreciation followed in accounting practice. For example, the position taken in § 13 of the Revised Uniform Principal and Income Act is that, with respect to charges against income and principal, there shall be:

> . . . a reasonable allowance for depreciation under generally accepted accounting principles, but no allowance shall be made for depreciation of that portion of any real property used by a beneficiary as a residence or for depreciation of any property held by the trustee on the effective date of this Act for which the trustee is not then making an allowance for depreciation.

(l) TAX STATUS OF TRUST.   Unless the trust qualifies as an exempt organization (charitable, educational, etc.), or unless the income of the trust is taxable to the grantor (revocable, or grantor retains substantial dominion and control), the income of the trust is subject to the federal income tax in a manner similar to the case of an individual. In general, the trust is treated as a conduit for tax purposes and is allowed a deduction for its income that is distributed or distributable currently to the beneficiaries. The trust may also be subject to state income taxes, personal property taxes, and so on. A tax service should be consulted for the latest provisions and rulings as to deductions, credits, rates, and filing requirements.

It is important to note that although trusts and estates are taxed similarly, there are two major differences. Trusts must be operated on a calendar year basis, whereas estates may operate on a fiscal year, usually tied to the decedent's date of death. Secondly, trusts must pay estimated taxes in the same fashion as individuals. Estates, on the other hand, are exempt from this requirement; but only for their first 2 tax years.

The impact of RRA '93 (the Revenue Reconciliation Act of 1993) substantially compressed the income tax rates applicable to trust and estates. Indexed from its original level effective for tax years beginning in 1993, trusts reach the top 36% bracket at $7,650 of income in 1995. Trusts are also subject to the 10% surtax resulting in an effective top rate of 39.6%. Compare this to married individuals filing jointly, for example, where the 39.6% top bracket is not reached until taxable income exceeds $256,500 in 1995. That is quite a disparity. Trustees of existing trusts need to consider their responsibility to take this disparity into consideration when reviewing the mix of assets in the current trust portfolio, and when exercising their discretion to make discretionary distributions of income. In certain cases, where older trusts were established with a different rate structure in mind, and where state law permits, a trustee may want to consider bringing a court proceeding to reform the terms of the trust accordingly. If the settlor is still alive, all of the beneficiaries are adults, and trust is irrevocable, it may be possible under state law, as it is in New York, to revoke the trust and create a new one if the gift tax cost is not excessive.

(m) TERMINATION OF TRUST.   A trust may be terminated by the fulfillment of its purpose or by the expiration of the period for which the trust was created. A trust may also be terminated under a power reserved by the grantor, or by the consent of all beneficiaries unless continuance of the trust is necessary to carry out a material purpose for which it was created.

When the trust is terminated, the trustee is discharged when he has transferred the property to those entitled to it according to the terms of the trust instrument. The trustee, to protect himself, may secure a formal release of all claims from all who receive any of the property and are competent to consent, may require a bond of indemnity from the beneficiaries, or may refuse to act without a decree of court.

37.4 ACCOUNTING FOR TRUSTS

(a) GENERAL FEATURES.   Generally, accounting for a trust is the same as accounting for an estate. The emphasis for a trust, however, is that principal or corpus versus income should be properly distinguished. Two interests, that is, current or life versus future or remainder, usually serve different parties. One party may have a current or income interest whereas another party holds a future or remainder interest. Therefore, allocation between principal and income is important.

(i) Accounting Period.   The accounting period for a trust depends somewhat on the nature of the trust and the provisions of the trust instrument. Reports may be required by the court or may be submitted to other interested parties at various intervals during the life of the trust.

(ii) Recording Principal and Income.   A careful distinction must be made between principal (corpus) and income in recording the transactions. The **legal theory** seems to be that the principal of a trust is not a certain amount of monetary value but is a certain group of assets that must be capable of isolation from the assets that compose the undistributed income. Actual **separation of cash and investments** is difficult because of such factors as accrued interest and amortization of bond premium and discount. Ordinarily it is sufficient to keep one account for cash and one for each type of investment, and to indicate the claims of the principal and income in the total.
   Accounts should be kept with the beneficiaries to show the amounts due and paid to each.
   The trustee should keep records that will meet both the requirements of the income tax law and regulations and the law relating to principal and income. There are apt to be conflicts at various points in the determination of taxable income and of income belonging to the life tenant. The only solution is to keep sufficiently detailed records so that all of the information is available for both purposes. In some cases, it may be necessary to prepare **reconciliation schedules** in order to keep a record of the differences between the income tax calculation of net income and the application of trust accounting principles of accounting income.

(iii) Accounting for Multiple Trusts.   Several trusts may be created by a single instrument, such as trusts originating through the provisions of a will, and a single trustee may have to keep his accounts so as to be able to prepare a report of the administration of the estate as a whole and also a separate report of each trust.

(iv) Treatment of Liabilities.   In some cases, trust property will be encumbered with an unpaid mortgage or other obligation of which the trustee must keep a record. It is also possible that in handling the business of the trust some liabilities will be incurred. These are usually current in character and the entry made at the time of payment, charging the amount to an asset or expense account, is usually sufficient.

(b) RECORD-KEEPING SYSTEM.   The bookkeeping system requirements for the trust, like those for any other enterprise, vary with the complexity of the situation. The trustee should keep a complete record of all transactions relating to the trust in order to protect himself, to make reports to the court, to prepare income tax returns, and to give the beneficiaries of the trust an adequate accounting. No special type of bookkeeping system is prescribed by law, but a complete record of all transactions must be kept in such a way that the reports required by the courts can be prepared. All records should be kept in permanent form and should be carefully preserved and filed for possible future reference.

(i) Journals.   In a comparatively simple situation, one multicolumn journal may be satisfactory, but in most cases a set of various journals should be kept.

(ii) Principal and Income Accounts.   It is necessary to distinguish carefully between principal and income in the administration of trusts. The Trust Principal account and the Undistributed Trust Income account record the net worth or capital of the trust. It will usually be necessary to analyze those accounts for income tax purposes, just as equity is analyzed in corporation accounts to obtain all of the information required for the income tax return. There may be some conflicts between income as defined by the law relating to the administration of trusts and taxable income as defined by the income tax law and regulations.

(iii) Opening Books of Account.   If an inventory has been filed with the court, such as an executor's or guardian's inventory, the trustee must record the same values in his accounts. If no such inventory was filed, the trustee should have one prepared that will serve as the basis of his property accounting. Whenever possible, the inventory should contain the same values as those required for income tax purposes in determining the gain or loss from the sale of property. In any case a record of such values must be available.

(iv) Amortization of Bond Premium or Discount.   When bonds are taken over in the inventory at more or less than their face value, the difference between the inventory value and the amount received at maturity is ordinarily treated as a loss or gain on realization; but when bonds are purchased at a premium or discount, the difference between the amount paid and the amount to be received at maturity should be treated as an adjustment of the interest earned and should be written off during the remaining life of the bond. If the amount is not large, the "straight-line" method may be used, that is, the total premium or discount is divided by the number of remaining interest payments to obtain the amount to be written off at each interest date. If the amount is large, amortization tables may be used in which the **effective rate** of interest is applied to the present value of the bond to obtain the income due to the life tenant.

(v) Depreciation.   Except for buildings forming part of the inventory at the date of origin of the trust, or in trusts where contrary provisions were intended by the grantor, wasting assets, including buildings and equipment, should be preserved by reflecting depreciation as a charge to income, if allowed by the trust instrument or state law. Many states have no provision for depreciation.

   If all of the trust income is distributed to beneficiaries without regard for depreciation, the entire periodic deduction for depreciation is taken for income tax purposes by the beneficiaries, and the trustee has no occasion to record depreciation in his records. In all instances the trustee should be guided by the provisions of the trust instrument or state law in his handling of depreciation.

(vi) Payments of Expenses.   A distinction must be made between expenses chargeable to principal and income. In the absence of direction in the instrument the fiduciary should rely upon state law as to allocation of trust expenses. Generally if an expense is recurring each year it is usually charged to income. It could also be allocable one-half to principal and one-half to income. If an expense is attributable to corpus, it should be charged to principal. If the expense was to maintain and collect income, then it should be charged to income. For example, capital gains are allocated to principal, and the income tax paid by the trustee on capital gains should also be charged to principal; however, when a bank assesses an annual fee for a custody account, the custody fee could be charged to income or split 50/50 between income and principal.

(c) TRUSTEE'S REPORTS.   Trustee's reports vary in form and in frequency according to the nature and provisions of the trust, and whether it is being administered under the jurisdiction of a court. Moreover, the form of the report varies among jurisdictions. Before preparing the report, the accountant should ascertain from the court whether a particular form is required. The valuations to be used must always be the same as those appearing on the inventory unless specific permission has been granted to change them. If assets have been written off as worthless, they must nevertheless appear in the new inventory without value.

If income and principal cash accounts have been properly maintained, the balance of the undistributed income would be represented by an equal amount of cash in the bank. If specific investments have been made with the intention that the funds used were still to be considered as undistributed income, the assets acquired should be shown as assets belonging to the trust income account.

The reports consist primarily of an analysis of the principal and income accounts. In addition, a statement showing the changes in the investments, an inventory of the property at the date of the report, and supporting schedules of various items will be required. A reconciliation of cash receipts and disbursements is also often prepared.

37.5 SOURCES AND SUGGESTED REFERENCES

Denhardt, J.G., Jr. and Denhardt, J.W., *Complete Guide to Trust Accounting and Trust Income Taxation,* Prentice-Hall, Englewood, NJ, 1977.

Denhardt, J.G., Jr. and Grider, John D., *Complete Guide to Estate Accounting and Taxes,* 4th ed., Prentice-Hall, Englewood, NJ, 1988.

Denhardt, J.G., Jr. and Grider, John D., *Complete Guide to Fiduciary Accounting,* Prentice-Hall, Englewood, NJ, 1981.

Executors and Administrators, 31 Am Jur 2d (rev.), Lawyer's Cooperative Publishing, Rochester, NY, 1989, April 1995 Cum. Suppl.

Federal Taxes Weekly Alert, *Effect of Death on an Individual's Income Tax Attributes,* November 16, 1995 Practice Alert, Research Institute of America.

Ferguson, M. Carr, Freeland, James J. and Ascher, Mark L., *Federal Income Taxation of Estates, Trusts and Beneficiaries,* 2nd ed., Little Brown, Boston, 1993.

Gillett, Mark R., and Stafford, Joel D., *Steps to Prepare and File Estate Tax Returns Effectively,* Estate Planning May/June 1995, Warren Gorham & Lomant.

Harris, Ann C., *Proper Disposition if IRD Items Can Produce Tax Savings,* Estate Planning September/October 1994, Warren Gorham & Lomant.

Harris, Homer I., *Estates Practice Guide,* 4th ed. Lawyer's Co-Operative Publishing, Rochester, NY, 1984, Nov. 1994 Suppl.

Harrison Louis S., *Coordinating Buy-Outs and Installment Payment of Estate Tax,* Estate Planning May/June 1995, Warren Gorham & Lomant.

Herr, Philip M., and Etkind, Steven M., *When and How an Interest in a Tax Shelter Should Be Disposed of Before Death,* Estate Planning September/October 1990, Warren Gorham & Lomant.

Larsen, E.J. and Mosich, A.N., *Modern Advanced Accounting,* 6th ed., Shephards McGraw-Hill, New York, 1994.

Nossman, Walter L., Wyatt, Joseph L., Jr. and McDaniel, James R., *Trust Administration and Taxation,* rev. 2nd ed., Matthew Bender, New York, 1988, Aug. 1995 Cum. Suppl.

Peschel, John L. and Spurgeon, Edward D., *Federal Taxation of Trusts, Grantors and Beneficiaries,* 2nd ed., Warren, Gorham & Lamont, New York, 1989, 1995 Cum. Suppl.

Restatement 3rd Trusts (Prudent Investor Rule) §§ 227-229, American Law Institute, 1990.

Restatement, Second, Trusts, American Law Institute, 1959.

Sages, Ronald A., *The Prudent Investor Rule and The Duty Not To Delegate,* Trust & Estates May 1995.

Schlesinger, Sanford J., and Weingast, Fran Tolins, *Income Taxation of Estates and Trust: New Planning Ideas,* Estate Planning May/June 1995, Warren Gorham & Lomant.

Scott, Austin Wakeman, *The Law of Trusts,* 4th ed., Little Brown, 1987, 1995 Suppl.

Share, Leslie A., *Domicile Is Key in Determining Transfer Tax of Non-Citizens,* Estate Planning January/February 1995, Warren Gorham & Lomant.

Stephens, Richard B., Maxfield, Guy B., Lind, Stephen A. and Calfee, Dennis A., *Federal Estate and Gift Taxation,* 6th ed., Warren, Gorham & Lamont, New York, 1991, 1995 Cum. Suppl. No. 3.

Stephenson, G.T. and Wiggins, Norman, *Estates and Trusts,* 5th ed., Appleton-Century-Crofts, New York, 1973.

Tractenberg, Beth D., *Transferee Liability Can Reach Trustee as Well as a Beneficiary,* Estate Planning, September/October 1994, Warren Gorham & Lomant.

Trusts & Estates Staff, *Uniform Laws Provide A Road Map For Estate Planners,* Trust & Estates May 1994.

Trusts, 76 Am Jur 2d (rev.), Lawyer's Cooperative Publishing, Rochester, NY, 1992, April 1995 Cum. Suppl.

Turner, George M., *Trust Administration and Fiduciary Responsibility,* Shephards McGraw-Hill, 1994.

Uniform Principal and Income Act, American Laws Annotated, Vol. 7.

Uniform Probate Code, American Laws Annotated, Vol. 8, 8A and 8B

Waggoner, Lawrence W., *The Revised Uniform Probate Code,* Trust & Estates May 1994.

VALUATI
NONPU

Allyn A. J

Allyn A. Joy

Jacob P.

Deloitte & To

R. MILES, CPA, CFE

MOSS-ADAMS LLP

Certified Public Accountants

212 North Naches Avenue
P.O. Box 22650
Yakima, WA 98907-2650

Phone 509.248.7750
FAX 509.457.5204
ericm@mossadams.com
www.mossadams.com

A member of
Moores Rowland International
an association of independent
accounting firms throughout the world.

CONTENTS

38.1 DEFINITION OF VALUE

(a) DEFINITION OF NONPUBLIC. A **public company** is one whose common stock has widespread ownership and investment interest and such active trading that market quotations ordinarily represent fair market value. In contrast, the common stock of a **nonpublic company** generally has concentrated ownership and such few trades that the transactions do not provide reliable indications of fair market value.

(b) PURPOSES FOR VALUATIONS. The need for valuing the common stock of a nonpublic or closely held company arises on many occasions. Among the more important situations requiring the valuation of nonpublic stock are filing estate and gift tax returns, estate planning, financial planning, employee stock ownership plan transactions and reports, granting stock options, drawing stock purchase agreements, marital dissolutions, structuring recapitalizations, sales, mergers, and divestitures.

(c) FAIR MARKET VALUE. Briefly stated, **fair market value** is that value at which a willing buyer and a willing seller, both well informed and neither under any compulsion to act, would arrive in an arm's-length sale of the asset in question. Such value is always determined as of a specific date and is based on all pertinent facts and conditions that are known or reasonably might be anticipated on that date. The existence of a willing buyer and a willing seller is assumed in the very definition of fair market value.

38.2 GENERAL PROCEDURE FOR VALUATION

(a) COMPILE BACKGROUND INFORMATION ABOUT THE COMPANY. In valuing the common stock of a nonpublic company it is necessary to become as informed as the well-informed buyer and seller assumed in the definition of value.

The appraiser should review the **history** of the corporation including date and state of incorporation, the products originally made, evolutionary developments to the present, and changes in control over the years. A list of stockholders and a listing of officers' names, salaries, ages, and experience should be obtained.

The appraiser must understand the nature of the company's products, raw materials used, and the methods of manufacture. A facilities tour is helpful. He or she should inquire as to how technologically advanced (or backward) the company is and review anticipated capital expenditures.

Information on the size of the labor force, the existence of collective bargaining agents, and background information on employee relations, as well as the corporation's strike experience should be obtained. The risk of customer loss during a strike must be evaluated.

The analyst should carefully analyze the structure of the industry, including the identity of existing competitors, barriers to entry and exit, and the bargaining position of customers and suppliers.

Obtain information on the sales force, including its size, structure, methods of compensation and radius of distribution. Information on markets, including principal industries served and principal customers served, is also important. Any material dependence on a single industry (25% or more of sales) or on a single customer (10% or more of sales) should be carefully reviewed and the risk of a sudden loss evaluated. The nature of the markets served (e.g., replacement vs. original equipment market or job shop vs. proprietary) should be examined. The economic forces that give rise to demand for the company's products or services should be understood. Market share data, when available, can be helpful. Price, quality, and service as competitive factors should be assessed. The role of **patents** and proprietary or secret technology in the competitive structure of the industry should be examined, and if these are important, the possible effects of patent expirations should be reviewed. **Research and development** projects underway should be reviewed with management.

Changes in the industry, particularly those of a technological or marketing nature, must be analyzed in terms of the company's outlook. The analyst should obtain a "feel" for the industry. Background information can usually be obtained from trade sources. He should compile and analyze long-term sales data on the industry (preferably in terms of both dollars and units), to examine the growth and cyclical characteristics of the industry. He should compare the performance of the company relative to its industry, and he should understand the reasons for any pronounced differences in trends between the company and its industry.

(b) COMPILE FINANCIAL INFORMATION REGARDING THE COMPANY. The appraiser should obtain **audit reports** for the past 5 years. If audit reports are not available, he will have to use unaudited statements. Some situations may require a complete audit of the books or even the services of an investigation accountant. In any event, the appraiser must clearly state the source of the financial information upon which he has relied.

The appraiser should prepare a 5-year spreadsheet of the income accounts and should review such areas as officers' compensation, the company's relationship with affiliated entities, and travel and entertainment.

It is helpful to restate the income account in ratios, at least down as far as operating income. This frequently discloses trends in cost-price relationships that should be discussed with management. Margins by product lines should be reviewed for a multiline company. The appraiser should obtain the **latest interim statement** and interview management with regard to the company's outlook for the current fiscal year. It is useful to get the interim statement for the same period of the previous year.

It is helpful to prepare and review a 5-year comparison of the **balance sheets.** Analyze changes that may be occurring in financial position. If the company is growing, evaluate its capacity to finance future growth. The latest balance sheet should be most carefully scrutinized for **nonoperating assets,** which, if substantial, should be segregated and valued separately. Hidden assets or hidden liabilities not adequately disclosed in the statements or notes must be ferreted out in interviews with management. The capital structure must be carefully reviewed, as well as the terms of any stock purchase agreements or stock options.

The appraiser should get sales, income, and dividend data back for a longer period of years, generally 10 to 20 years, if readily available, to review both the **growth and cyclical characteristics** of the company, as well as its long-term dividend policy. It is particularly important to review the long-term outlook with management. Most managements will have given it a great deal of thought and will be very insightful. Some, however, may be quite reticent on the subject, requiring a number of probing questions on the part of the appraiser. It is helpful to get insights from production, finance, and sales and marketing people, as well as the CEO.

(c) SELECT GUIDELINE COMPANIES. Having reviewed the quantitative and qualitative factors discussed above, the appraiser must translate this complex array of facts into value. This requires an analysis of the most relevant facts from the actual marketplace. This is ordinarily done through the selection and analysis of guideline companies that can be used to formulate objective guidelines for the evaluation of the subject company. Guideline companies are publicly held companies that come as close as possible to the investment characteristics of the company being valued. Ideally, they are in the same industry. Frequently, however, there are no public companies in the same industry, so it is necessary to select companies with an underlying similarity of investment characteristics based on markets, products, growth, cyclical variability, and other factors.

Such companies were traditionally called "comparative companies," a term that seems to connote companies "just like" the company being valued. It is seldom, if ever, possible to find publicly held companies "just like" the company under consideration. Appraisers have come to generally use the term "guideline companies" as a more appropriate term than "comparative companies."

The importance of a thorough, objective selection of guideline companies cannot be overestimated. The credibility of any valuation analysis is dependent on the demonstrated objectivity of the selection of guideline companies.

In searching for guideline companies, the best available **sources** are usually *Moody's Industrial Manual* and Standard & Poor's *Standard Corporation Records*. Both manuals are updated annually. The **Directory of Companies Required to File Annual Reports with the SEC** can also be helpful. These sources classify companies by industry, and the appropriate industry groupings can be reviewed for possible guideline companies. If no appropriate industry classification can be found, it is sometimes necessary to review all the companies listed in either Standard & Poor's or Moody's. In recent years many appraisers have switched from printed sources of information on possible guideline companies to computerized databases. It must be recognized that the breadth and depth of coverage and the accuracy of the information contained in such services will affect the results. Although they are far more efficient than the traditional printed sources, if such databases are not comprehensive in the number of companies they cover or in the way they classify businesses, some actively traded companies that meet the criteria established for the selection of guideline companies may be missed.

The appraiser must clearly state the criteria used in selecting guideline companies and prepare a list of all reasonable potential guideline companies. The list should state the reasons for rejecting or retaining the potential companies. A description of each guideline company finally selected should be part of the report.

(i) Compile Data on Guideline Companies. It is necessary to compile financial and operating data on the guideline companies. Annual reports should be obtained on the guideline companies, and 10-K reports often are helpful. As much information as possible must be gleaned from official reports, trade sources, prospectuses, and so on, regarding products, markets, and customer dependence, for each of the guideline companies. Five-year **balance sheet** and **income account** comparisons are recommended. Where possible, **adjustments** should be made to the income and balance sheets of the guideline companies and/or the subject company to minimize differences in accounting when such differences are material.

Generally, public companies compute **depreciation** on the straight-line basis for financial reporting purposes. If the company being valued uses accelerated depreciation, its income and net worth should be adjusted to a straight-line basis when the difference is substantial (10% or more of average income over the past 5 years).

Adjustments should be considered when there is a difference in **inventory accounting** method between the subject company and the guideline companies. The most common difference is that most or all the guideline companies are on LIFO and the subject company is on FIFO. Most appraisers tend to ignore this difference unless the impact exceeds 10% of income or net worth. Pratt advocates adjusting both the balance sheet and income account of LIFO comparatives to value a FIFO company. This is the most common approach to the problem, but a surprising number of appraisers simply ignore the issue altogether.

When the subject company and all the guideline companies are on LIFO, most appraisers make no adjustments. However, even here, some adjustment of the balance sheet should be considered. If the subject company has been on LIFO for an appreciably longer or shorter time than the guideline companies, there may be a substantial difference in the understatement of inventories on the LIFO method. This is readily handled by simply adjusting all balance sheets to a FIFO basis which, in any event, provides a more current measure of the value of inventories. This procedure can be followed even though earnings comparisons are left on a LIFO basis. However, when LIFO inventory liquidations occur, resulting profits should be adjusted out as nonrecurring.

The income accounts of the subject company should be carefully reviewed and the management interviewed with regard to **extraordinary factors** affecting income, such as inventory write-downs, uninsured losses, plant moving expenses, or anything of a substantial and nonrecurring nature. Adjustments should be made to eliminate the effects of these extraordinary, nonrecurring items.

(ii) Calculate Market Value Ratios.   Next, the appraiser should calculate the **market values** of the guideline companies by multiplying the number of shares outstanding by the price per share on the valuation date. If the company has preferred stock outstanding, include it in this computation.

It is necessary to compute the **price-earnings ratio.** Generally, but by no means always, a weighted average of earnings over the past 5 years is used. (The weighted average places a weight of five on the earnings of the most recent year, a weight of four to income of the year before that, etc.) When earnings are variable, an unweighted average may be appropriate. The period selected must be the one that best measures the earning power of the subject company relative to the earning power of the guideline group. Generally, median ratios are used to avoid the distorting effect of extremes on the arithmetic average.

Compute the **average cash flow** (net income plus noncash charges) for each of the guideline companies using the same period. Compute the median price-cash flow ratio of the guideline group.

Compute the **price-dividend ratio** of each of the guideline companies. Generally, the dividend of the latest year is suitable for this purpose. However, if there has been an abrupt change in the dividend rate in a recent quarter, the new rate may be more indicative of dividend expectations. Compute the median price-dividend ratio of the guideline group.

Compute market-value-to-book-value ratios and the median of these ratios.

(d) ESTIMATE DIVIDEND-PAYING CAPACITY.   The use of the price-dividend ratio raises the question of the significance of the actual dividend payments of a nonpublic corporation. In many cases, even though the company has the capacity to pay dividends, it pays small ones, or none at all. This inevitably raises the question of whether actual dividend payments or dividend-paying capacity should be capitalized. That dividend-paying capacity must be considered is quite clearly the position of the IRS (Rev. Rul. 59-60, ¶ 3e), but the courts have not always been as clear.

In estimating dividend-paying capacity, the guideline companies are useful. Compute the payout ratio (dividends as a percentage of net income) of the guideline companies and derive the median payout ratio of the group. Then examine the financial position of the company being valued relative to that of the guideline companies. Consider also that the company being valued, as a closely held company, does not have the same **access to capital markets** for equity capital as the guideline companies and must, therefore, rely on the retention of earnings to a greater extent than publicly held companies. As a reasonable rule of thumb, when the company being valued has a financial position roughly similar to that of the guideline companies, construct dividends at a **payout ratio** equal to two-thirds that of the guideline companies. That is, if the guideline companies are paying out 60% of their earnings, a privately held company of similar financial position could be expected to pay out about 40% of earnings. This lesser payout ratio (40% as opposed to 60%) recognizes the nonpublic company's greater reliance on the retention of earnings to finance its business. When the financial position of the company being valued is weaker than that of the guideline companies, the dividend-paying capacity is correspondingly less. If the financial position of the company being valued is significantly stronger than that of the guideline companies, it may have a dividend-paying capacity equal to or greater than that of the guideline companies, despite its inferior access to capital markets.

A second part to this question is, if dividend-paying capacity should be capitalized, how? Does a dollar of dividend that could be paid, but is not paid, have a value to the minority interest investor equal to a dollar of dividend that is actually paid? One reasonable procedure is to capitalize actual dividend payments at the same rate as the guideline companies and capitalize unpaid dividend-paying capacity (the excess of the capacity to pay dividends over the actual dividends paid) at half the multiplier derived from the guideline companies. This procedure recognizes that the minority interest investor does benefit from that unpaid dividend-paying capacity because the company builds its equity base faster than it would if such dividends were paid. However, it also recognizes that the benefit is not as direct nor as immediate as the actual payment of dividends.

(e) JUDGMENTAL MODIFICATION OF THE VALUATION RATIOS.   These market value ratios provide useful valuation guidelines. However, they are nothing more than guidelines and must inevitably be combined with the appraiser's judgment in arriving at a sound valuation conclusion. The appraiser must, after careful consideration of all relevant factors, come to one of three possible conclusions:

1. Investors would find the subject company to be more attractive than the group of guideline companies. (In this case a premium must be added to the median valuation ratios.)
2. Investors would find the subject company to be less attractive than the guideline companies. (In this case a discount from the median valuation ratios is required.)
3. Investors would regard the subject as being neither more nor less attractive than the group of guideline companies. (In this case the use of the median ratios would be appropriate.)

This decision requires a careful comparative analysis of the subject company and the guideline companies in terms of both qualitative and quantitative differences.

In addition to the basic nature of the product, qualitative considerations may include such factors as **market position, geographic, product, and market diversification, patent protection, depth of management, research and development capabilities,** and many others. Often, but by no means always, public companies are larger and more diversified, and have more professional management. When they are used as guideline companies for the valuation of a smaller, weaker, less diversified company, a judgmental adjustment to the valuation ratios may be necessary. However, in making these judgmental adjustments, care must be taken to avoid "counting the same trick twice." For instance, in valuing a company with low earnings, one should not take a discount for poor management, if it is the poor management that causes the low earnings. That would obviously be "doubling up."

In terms of quantitative differences, one should first look to **long-term trends of sales and income.** Place the sales and income of each of the guideline companies on an index basis, selecting a base period that is not affected by abnormal factors. Determine the median sales index of the group of guideline companies and compare it to the company being valued. Charts of these comparisons are particularly helpful.

Differences in **trends** may be properly reflected in the valuation procedure through the use of a weighted average. However, a pronounced long-term inferiority of sales trend, and particularly of income trend, may require a further discount to the valuation ratios derived from the guideline companies. Conversely, a decided long-term superiority of trends may require an upward adjustment to those valuation ratios.

One should also look to the factor of **variability.** A company with a highly variable earnings is less attractive to investors than a company with a stable earnings trend. However, be careful in comparing the trend of earnings of a single company to that of the group average or median. The averaging process tends to have a stabilizing influence, and it may therefore be desirable to make a comparison on an individual company basis.

A comparison of financial ratios is also recommended. This should include the current ratio (current assets divided by current liabilities), liquidity ratio (current assets as a percentage of total assets), and leverage ratios (total liabilities as a percentage of total assets and net worth as a percentage of total assets). Differences in financial position can be appropriately reflected in the estimation of dividend-paying capacity. In most cases, the use of dividend-paying capacity as a valuation factor makes a reasonable allowance for differences in financial position. When there are extreme differences, some further adjustment may be necessary. The financial position of the company being valued may be so weak that the nonpayment of dividends does not adequately reflect its poor financial position. In this case, an appraiser must make a judgmental negative adjustment to the valuation ratios. On the other hand, a strong financial position is normally adequately reflected through either liberal dividend payments or a strong dividend-paying capacity. A company with an extremely strong financial position relative to the guideline companies represents an unusual situation, which is covered in subsection 38.3(h).

Operating ratios, including sales times net worth, net income as a percentage of sales and income as a percentage of net worth, should be computed and charted. These ratios should be reviewed with particular attention to the profit margin. A profit margin that is well below average may indicate a high-cost operation and, when accompanied by highly variable earnings, may require some discount to the valuation ratios. However, frequently a low profit margin is accompanied by a high ratio of sales to net worth, and together these characteristics are symptomatic of integration lesser than that of the guideline companies.

Finally, examine the fundamental assumption in the valuation procedure that the **earnings outlook** of the subject company is roughly similar to that of the guideline companies. If there are strong indications that such an assumption is not reasonable, make an appropriate adjustment to the valuation ratios.

(f) APPLICATION OF THE MARKET VALUE RATIOS. At this point, the appraiser has derived four valuation ratios that have been derived from the guideline companies: price-net worth ratio, price-earnings ratio, price-cash flow ratio, and price-dividend ratio. The application of the four ratios provides four indicators of value, and there may be considerable variation among them. This inevitably raises the question of their relative importance. There is close to universal acceptance of the notion that, except under unusual circumstances, earnings are the most important valuation factor.

Some appraisers and some courts completely ignore the concept of **cash flow.** The use of cash flow in valuation analysis is most appropriate when the company has large assets that do not necessarily decline in value with time and are not "used up" in production. An obvious example is a real estate holding company. The use of cash flow in the valuation of companies with very little investment in depreciable assets (service companies, for instance) is somewhat redundant, in that cash flow may be almost identical to earnings, and its use is simply a repetition of the price-earnings ratio analysis.

If the subject company is significantly more or less capital intensive than the guideline companies, the cash flow approach should be modified or eliminated.

Some appraisers completely ignore dividends and dividend-paying capacity. Some give no weight to the book value factor.

The necessity of translating these indicators into a value presents a dilemma to the appraiser. If he uses specific weights, he must defend these as reasonable and not constituting a formula. On the other hand, deriving a value from only one of these factors also constitutes a weighting procedure because it assigns a weight of 100% to that one factor and zero to the others. Some appraisers cope with this problem by simply stating that "all things considered, I think the value is X," but they must face the obvious question: What factors did you consider and how much weight did you give to them?"

The following tabulation gives a cross section of the weightings commonly used by business appraisers in valuing industrial corporations.

Valuation Basis	Weights							
Price—Book Value	20	25	20	10	33⅓	0	10	0
Price—Earnings	30	25	40	60	33⅓	60	90	100
Price—Cash Flow	20	25	0	0	0	20	0	0
Price—Dividends	30	25	40	30	33⅓	20	0	0

For the most part, courts do not specify the weight they accord to these various valuation factors. In the few cases where the courts have been specific, they have tended to ascribe **primary importance to earnings and dividends,** and they have demonstrated a tendency to give more weight to earnings than to dividends. The factor of book value has generally received relatively little weight in court decisions involving industrial companies. However, it is not totally ignored.

Whatever weights are used, the appraiser must thoughtfully analyze the resulting value for **reasonableness.** If this stock were publicly traded at this price, would it be more attractive than the shares of the guideline companies? Would it be significantly less attractive than shares of the guideline companies? If the appraiser can answer both of these questions in the negative, he has probably arrived at a reasonable result.

(i) Discount for Lack of Marketability.   The value derived from the guideline analysis is the freely traded price, that is, the price at which the common stock of the subject company would trade if it had an active public market.

Clearly, lack of ready marketability makes a stock considerably less attractive than it would be if it were readily marketable. This was recognized by the IRS in its Rev. Rul. 77-287 when, in discussing the value of unregistered shares of public companies, it stated: "The discount from the market price provides the main incentive for a potential buyer to acquire restricted securities."

In recent years appraisers have generally used transactions in the restricted shares of public companies as the best guideline for determining the appropriate discount for lack of marketability. A number of studies have been made of this market, and they indicate a rather wide dispersion of discounts but most indicate a median discount of about 35%. The two seminal studies, those of Maher (1976) and Moroney (1973) indicated median discounts of 34.73% and 33% respectively. More recent studies have been made by Williamette Management Associates (median 31.2%) and Standard Research Consultants (45%).

Willamette Associates has also analyzed the relationship of original public offering prices to arm's-length trades during the 3 years preceding the public offering, which suggests discounts in the 40% to 60% range.

(ii) Discount for Minority Interest.   The discount for lack of marketability should not be confused with a discount for minority interest. This chapter has explained the use of publicly held guideline companies in making a judgment as to the value of stock in a nonpublic company. The prices at which the common stocks of those guideline companies sell reflect minority interest values; therefore the comparative analysis enables the appraiser to express an opinion about the price at which the stock of the subject closely held company would trade if it had an active public market (the freely traded value). It is therefore a minority interest value to begin with, and a minority interest discount is inappropriate. However, the stock of a closely held company is lacking in marketability, and a discount for lack of marketability is appropriate.

(g) DISCOUNTED FUTURE BENEFITS APPROACHES.   A discounted future benefits valuation involves two fundamental, difficult, and very imprecise steps:

1. The long-term projection of the benefit, and
2. The determination of an appropriate discount rate, by which the future benefits may be reduced to present value.

It is essential that the discount rate and the benefit be matched. That is, a dividend or net-free cash flow discount rate must be applied to projected dividends or net-free cash flow. An earnings discount rate must be applied to projected earnings. The use of a net cash flow discount rate to discount earnings, for instance, is erroneous.

Data on past rates of return on publicly traded common stocks are readily available and can be used as a reference point in estimating the appropriate rate of return (dividend or net-free cash flow discount rate) of a subject company. However, there is no commonly accepted database for establishing an earnings discount rate or total cash flow discount rate. As a result, discounted future benefits valuations are almost always done on the basis of dividends. (The term **net cash flow** is often used, usually in the context of an enterprise valuation. Because net cash flow is the total cash flow of the business minus its capital (fixed assets and working capital) needs, it is essentially the same as dividends or dividend paying capacity. Moreover, some appraisers use the term **cash flow** meaning cash flow to the stockholder, which is dividends.

The projection of net-free cash flow or dividends is a three-step procedure:

1. Project total cash flow (total revenues less cash expenses).
2. Project the capital needs of the business.
   a. Project required capital expenditures.
   b. Project required net working capital changes.
3. Compute dividend paying capacity (total cash flow minus total capital needs).

The general theory used in estimating the expected rate of return is that investors' return expectations are based on past returns. In establishing the required rate of return for a nonpublic company, practitioners almost invariably use long-term stock return data compiled by Ibbotson Associates, whose Annual Yearbook includes two series of stock return data, one for large companies (those in the Standard & Poor's Composite Index) and one for smaller companies (companies in a size category defined by the smallest quintile of New York Stock Exchange companies). Generally, it is the second of these series that is used, because nonpublic companies are almost always closer in size to the group of smaller companies.

In deriving the required rate of return for a subject company, it is first necessary to estimate the rate of return investors expect on the small companies themselves on the valuation date. Then, if the appraiser believes that an investment in the subject company is riskier than in the small companies, he or she must add an increment to their rate of return to reflect that greater risk. Conversely, if the appraiser believes the risk is less, the rate of return must be reduced. Such additions and deductions are made essentially on a judgmental basis.

The actual (geometric average) long-term (1926–1994) rate of return on Ibbotson's group of small companies was 12.2%. However, the arithmetic mean of the 69 rates of return was 17.4% and there is considerable difference of opinion as to which of these two numbers should be used as a base point in expected rate of return formulation. The decision on which rate to use can have a major impact on value (commonly ± 50% or more). Despite its overriding importance, the Business Valuation Committee of the American Society of Appraisers, the entity charged with fostering high standards in the business appraisal profession, has never taken a stand on this very important issue. Most business appraisers seem to use the arithmetic mean, but most investment bankers seem to use the geometric mean of the returns, which is the actual return. The best justification for the use of the arithmetic mean can be found in *Ibbotson's 1995 Yearbook* pages 149–151 and the best justification for the use of the actual rate or return (the geometric mean) can be found on pages 62 through 68 of the June 1995 issue of *Business Valuation Review.*

The expected return on stocks, on any given date, is affected by the rate of return available on risk free investments. For instance, when risk free interest rates are 10%, common stock investors expect a higher return than when such interest rates are 5%. Therefore, it is necessary to adjust the historic rate of return of the small companies for the difference between historic and current risk free interest rates. When using actual returns, this is done geometrically.

The 1926–1994 return on small company common stocks was 12.2% and on long term governments was 4.8%. The geometric differential is 1.071 (1.122 ÷ 1.048). Assuming a valuation date rate of return on long term governments of 6.0%, the expected rate of return on the small companies' stocks is 13.5% (1.071 × 1.06 gives a return relative of 1.135).

The use of the arithmetic mean requires arithmetic differencing. The 1926–1994 arithmetic mean rate of return on the common stocks of small companies was 17.4% and that on long-term governments was 5.2%, giving an arithmetic difference of 12.2 (17.4 − 5.2) which, added to the 6.0% return available on the long-term governments on the valuation date gives an expected rate of return for small companies of 18.2%.

Two aspects of these procedures should be readily apparent. The first is that the *expected* rate of return on the small companies (13.5% derived from actual long term returns and 18.2% derived from the arithmetic means of long-term returns) is fundamentally an assumption as to the rate of return expected by investors based on a long-term measurement of long term returns. The Ibbotson data are used as empirical evidence of the past returns. The second is that the use of the arithmetic mean of the returns, as opposed to actual returns, makes a huge difference. (It does so because its use assumes that investors expect dramatically higher returns in the future than they have received in the past.)

In the above example, long-term governments have been used in measuring the available risk free rate of return. However, there is not unanimity of opinion among business appraisers as to the appropriate risk-free rate of return that should be used. Some use government securities with maturities that parallel the horizon of the assumed buyer of the stock being valued, a 90-day Treasury bill if the buyer is assumed to have a 90-day horizon, a long term government if the investor is assumed to have a long horizon. Others always use long-term governments on the grounds that, for valuation purposes, horizon is an attribute of the investment, not the investor, and common stocks, except under unusual circumstances, have a horizon of infinity, a horizon that is best reflected by the use of long term governments to measure the available risk-free return.

The value of stock is the present value of future returns in perpetuity. This axiom requires, at least theoretically, that future dividends or net-free cash flows be projected, and their present value determined, in perpetuity, or, as a practical matter, so far into the future that present value increments become insignificant. There are three ways of doing this:

1. The arithmetic method,
2. The algebraic method, or
3. The semi-algebraic method.

Under the arithmetic method, each year's dividend is projected and its present value determined using the expected rate of return. This is done for all future years until the annual present value increments become insignificant. Then the present values are totaled to give value.

In the algebraic method, the appraiser used the Gordon Model, which is:

$$\text{Value} = \frac{D}{ROR - g}$$

where D = dividends for the first year after the valuation date, ROR = the expected rate of return, and g = expected rate of growth in perpetuity.

The algebraic method produces the same value as the arithmetic method. It is simply a computational shortcut. It can be used only if the assumed growth rate of dividends is constant.

In the semi-algebraic method, dividends or net-free cash flows are projected for a few years, usually five, and then present value is determined. Then the Gordon Model is used to determine the value at the end of the projection period, and the present value of that "terminal value" is added to the present value of the cash flows during the projection period.

Appraisers rarely use the arithmetic method because it tends to highlight the fact that their valuation depends on a projection of dividends decades into the future. Also, appraisers do not commonly use the algebraic method, possibly because it seems embarrassingly simple. By far the most common method used is the semi-algebraic, probably because it give the appearance of suitable complexity and tends to obscure the inherently infinite nature of the projection.

However, unlike the algebraic method, it can accommodate changes in the growth rates and capital needs during the projection period.

The discounted future net-free cash flow or dividends approach, as a valuation model, is eminently sound. However, the problems inherent in its application to a specific fact situation, primarily the inexactitude of the two major inputs, return and benefits, render the results obtained only as good as the assumption incorporated in its application. Moreover, its total divorce from valuation date actual stock prices of any sort, impairs its credibility and highlights the totally abstract nature of the method.

In recent years, as discounted future benefits approaches have been subjected to increasingly critical review, exclusive reliance on the technique seems to have waned considerably. Few appraisers now rely entirely on these approaches in valuing established companies. These approaches are generally used in valuing startups and as an adjunct to the guideline company approach in valuing established companies.

If the guideline company approach and the discounted future benefits approach produce substantially different values, the appraiser should carefully analyze the reasons for the difference. Such differences usually indicate that the investing public is using a different discount rate and/or growth rate from those used by the appraiser in his discounted benefits approach.

(h) USE OF FORMULAS.   Rev. Rul. 59-60, the courts, and the ESOP Association have discredited the use of valuation formulas. The ESOP Association made the point very clearly: "Formula appraisals are totally unacceptable, because they will virtually always result in an unfair, if not absurd, appraisal at some time in the future."

Valuation formulas can be as simple as "Value = net book value," "Value = net asset value," or "Value = 10 × earnings." On the other hand, they can be so complex as to defy comprehension. Doctors and engineers seem particularly enamored of complex valuation formulas.

The most widely employed type of formula still in use by some business appraisers, is the "excess earnings formula." The original formula of this type was ARM-34, which was used for many years by IRS in the valuation of closely held companies.

ARM-34 was as follows:

$$\text{Value} = \text{book value} + \text{capitalized excess earnings}$$

Generally, excess earnings were defined as earnings in excess of 10% of net worth, and a 20% capitalization rate was generally used in capitalizing excess earnings so that, in practice, the formula was:

$$\text{Value} = \text{book value} + 5 \left(\text{earnings} - \frac{\text{book value}}{10} \right)$$

The formula has long since been discredited and abandoned by the IRS as well as the courts because it is arbitrary and not market oriented and can therefore produce very unrealistic values.

However, a variation of ARM-34 is still in use by some appraisers. The basic formula is the same:

$$\text{Value} = \text{book value} + \text{capitalized excess earnings}$$

Excess earnings are defined as the earnings in excess of the industry's average rate of earnings on stockholders' equity. Typically, these excess earnings are capitalized at 20% (or multiplied by 5). The shortcomings of this approach are fundamentally the same as ARM-34. The underlying assumption that a company is worth its book value if it has an average rate of earnings on net worth for its industry is arbitrary, unsupported, and often absurd. In fact, companies in industries marked by low rates of earnings on book value, will tend, on average, to be worth less than book value, whereas companies in industries with high rates of earnings on equity tend, on average, to have values in excess of book value, sometimes by a factor of 4 or 5.

(i) NET ASSET VALUE APPROACH.   Net asset value is simply computed by adjusting all assets to a market value basis and deducting all liabilities. Fundamentally, this is yet another formula approach, the formula being "Value = net asset value." There is ample evidence in the marketplace that the common stocks of industrial companies can sell appreciably above or below net asset value. This is not surprising because the normal expectation of investors is that the benefits of ownership will be received by them by way of dividends and a rising market price. However, if the liquidation of a company is pending, net asset value is of paramount importance.

Net asset value has greater relevance to the appraisal of holding companies, notably investment companies and real estate holding companies. Even here, however, the evidence of the marketplace is that the stocks of such companies almost always trade below net asset value.

38.3 SPECIAL SITUATIONS

(a) WHOLESALE AND RETAIL COMPANIES.   The valuation of wholesale and retail companies is essentially similar to that of an industrial company as described above. Attention should be given to costs of store openings, as well as to credit and inventory management. Particular attention should be paid to the factor of **geographic diversification** in valuing distribution companies. For example, a supermarket chain whose stores are concentrated in a single city involves greater investment risk than a regional supermarket company operating in a number of cities, and special allowance should be made for such differences.

(b) VALUATION OF SERVICE COMPANIES.   The U.S. economy is increasingly dominated by companies engaged in the performance of services for their customers as opposed to manufacturing. Service companies range in the size and scope of activities from small businesses having a considerable dependence on one or a few specialized employees to large businesses such as the major payroll/computer service businesses. The size and scope of activities will determine the valuation method employed. For larger, institutionalized businesses, the guideline company approach will ordinarily be employed. Since the value of a business engaged in the provision of services typically attaches to human resources as opposed to capital assets, the factor of size of capital generally is accorded less weight than size of the financial benefits of ownership in the valuation of an industrial or manufacturing company. Moreover, the factor of cash flow may in many instances simply be duplicative of earnings in service businesses having modest capital needs.

Smaller businesses having a particular dependence on relatively few employees and a special market niche may not lend themselves to the publicly traded guideline company approach. Services providing limited information on small company transactions exist and can be helpful in delineating valuation parameters provided the business in question is reasonably similar to the businesses reported on in these services. The appraiser ordinarily will employ a capitalization of earnings approach employing an appropriate risk adjusted capitalization factor giving consideration to the special risks associated with their small size. Such capitalization factors inevitably involve a considerable injection of professional judgment on the part of the appraiser.

(c) COMPANIES WITH LOW EARNINGS. The valuation of a company with a very low rate of earnings on stockholders' equity can present a particular problem. The extreme form of this is a company that over a period of years has had no earnings and no capacity to pay dividends. The use of the valuation procedure described earlier can be misleading in this instance, since primary weight is given to evidence of earning power. Obviously, the company with no earnings has no value based solely on the factor of earning power. These cases must be carefully judged on their own merits. If liquidation is certain, or even probable, **liquidating value** is governing. If not, a going-concern valuation is called for, recognizing that companies that are "worth more dead than alive" because of chronically low earnings may go on for years without liquidating, and the minority interest investor cannot force a liquidation.

In estimating going-concern value, it is helpful to examine the range of the ratios of market value to book value of the guideline companies. Frequently there are, among the guideline companies, two or three companies with low rates of earnings on stockholders' equity (5% or less) and these tend to have low price-book value ratios. In a group where the median price-book value ratios might be 80% or 90%, there may very well be two or three companies earning less than 5% on capital, which may have price-book value ratios of 40% or 50%. Under such circumstances, these data would lead to the conclusion that the company with no earnings at all should be valued below that 40% or 50%.

The influence of judgment in this situation can be reduced through the use of a **statistical regression technique.** Examine the relationship between the market value-book value ratio and the rate of earnings on book value of the guideline companies. Generally there is a definite relationship that can be described precisely through the use of a simple linear correlation. This technique makes it quite clear that the companies with high rates of earnings on stockholders' equity tend to have high price-book value ratios, and the companies with low rates of earnings on stockholders' equity tend to have low market price-book value ratios. The statistical definition of this relationship can constitute a satisfactory basis for the valuation of a company with little or no earnings.

(d) HOLDING COMPANIES. The guideline company technique is also used in valuing holding companies, that is, companies whose assets consist largely of securities. Guideline companies must be selected that parallel, to the extent possible, the nature of the assets of the company being valued. If the holding company being valued has a **diversified portfolio of common stocks,** it is desirable to select closed-end diversified investment companies. The analyst can then examine the relationship between the market value of the stocks of such companies and **underlying net asset values.** The relationships of market value to earnings and of market value to dividends should also be reviewed. However, the ratio of market value to net asset value is generally conceded to be the primary determinant of value and, as a practical matter, this ratio generally shows far greater consistency than the price-earnings or price-dividends ratios of closed-end investment companies. In determining the net asset value of the holding company, the **capital gains tax** on unrealized capital gains may be deducted as a way to reflect the tax disadvantage of the holding company vis-a-vis regulated investment companies. However, some simply modify the median price to net asset value derived from comparatives on the theory that the subject company, unlike the guideline companies, may be "locked in" to some investments by virtue of the capital gains tax.

The procedure involving a **nondiversified investment company** is essentially similar to that just described for diversified companies, except that nondiversified investment companies are selected for comparison. The other difference is that some of the nondiversified investment companies may be taxed as ordinary corporations; therefore the holding company may not be at a tax disadvantage relative to such guideline companies.

If the portfolio of the subject company is concentrated in just a few investments, it may be difficult to find public companies so lacking in diversification. Under these circumstances it will be necessary to apply a discount to the ratios derived from the guideline companies.

If the investment portfolio is largely **debt securities** of good quality, one should examine the relationship between market value and underlying net asset value of closed-end bond funds. As a general rule, the market value-net asset value ratio among these companies is quite close to net asset value.

(e) REAL ESTATE COMPANIES.   The valuation of a minority interest in a real estate holding company requires an **appraisal of the underlying assets** by a qualified real estate appraiser.

The **net asset value** of the real estate holding company can then be computed by adjusting stockholders' equity for the difference between the appraisal value of the real estate and net book value.

The appraiser should select publicly held real estate companies owning similar types of real estate, which disclose the estimated appraised value of their assets. This can be used in calculating net asset value. This, in turn, can be used to calculate the price-net asset value relationship. It is also recommended that the relationship between market value and earnings, cash flow, and dividends be examined.

In applying such ratios to the company being valued, primary weight should be given to the market price-net asset value ratio. However, the factors of earnings, cash flow, and dividends certainly should not be ignored.

In applying these ratios, judgment must be brought to bear on qualitative differences between the guideline companies and the subject company. Diversification by property and neighborhood must be considered. A comparison of financial position and the operating record is also important.

(f) COMPANIES WITH NONOPERATING ASSETS.   Industrial companies with large nonoperating assets present a particular valuation problem. The company whose **cash** clearly exceeds its operating needs by a substantial margin is a case in point. Another is a company owning a large portfolio of **securities.** Another example is a company owning valuable **real estate** unrelated to its basic business. In these instances it is best to remove such assets from the balance sheet and deduct the related earnings, with an appropriate tax adjustment, from reported earnings. Dividends must also be adjusted. Value the company as though it did not own the nonoperating assets. It is then necessary to determine the appropriate increment to the value of the stock determined on an operating basis. If the nonoperating assets are securities, the best procedure is that recommended for an investment company (see subsection 38.3(d)). Similarly, if such assets are real estate, the procedure used in valuing a minority interest in a real estate company is appropriate.

(g) LIFE INSURANCE PROCEEDS.   In valuing common stock for estate tax purposes it is necessary to reflect any windfall to the company arising from any life insurance on the deceased. This may be done by considering the company's improved financial position and its higher earning power related to the proceeds. If the proceeds result in a level of cash beyond the needs of the business, then the excess should be treated as a nonoperating asset, as reviewed above.

If the deceased was a key man it may be necessary to apply a special discount to reflect the higher risk related to his loss.

(h) COMPANIES WITH AN EXTREMELY STRONG FINANCIAL POSITION.   A company with an extremely strong financial position can present a particular valuation problem. An example is a real estate company with no long-term debt. The publicly held companies that might be used for comparative purposes, without exception, have large amounts of long-term debt outstanding. Thus any price-earnings ratio or price-net asset value ratio that can be derived from them reflects the way in which the investing public values a real estate company with significant leverage.

One might approach this problem in the usual way and then adjust the valuation ratios derived from publicly held real estate companies to reflect the superior financial position of the subject company. However, the influence of the appraiser's judgment can be minimized by changing to the **"total invested capital technique,"** to quantify better the effect of extreme superiority in financial position.

In employing the total invested capital technique, the total market value of all preferred and common stock is combined with the total market value of all the outstanding long-term debt of each of the guideline companies. That represents the total market value of the total invested capital. That amount is then related to the book value of that total invested capital (net worth plus long-term debt), adjusted for underlying asset values in the case of real estate companies.

Similarly, the total market value of the total invested capital is related to the earnings available for that total invested capital (net income plus interest on long-term debt), to the cash flow available for that invested capital (net income plus noncash charges, plus interest on long-term debt), and finally it is related to the earnings paid out on that total invested capital (dividends plus interest on long-term debt). The application of these ratios to a company with a decidedly stronger financial position is recommended when the company being valued is stronger than the guideline companies by a very wide margin, a circumstance that tends to occur in the valuation of real estate companies but may be encountered in the valuation of an industrial company.

One important drawback of this technique should be noted. It is necessary to ascertain the market value of the long-term debt of the guideline companies and, when the debt is not publicly traded, it is necessary to estimate its market value. This introduces an element of judgment that the basic procedure does not entail.

(i) PREFERRED STOCK.   A standard preferred stock is a security which has the following features:

1. The right to receive a stated cumulative cash dividend before any cash dividends are paid to the company's common stock.
2. The right to receive a stated amount upon liquidation of the company before any proceeds are distributed to the company's common stock.
3. No voting rights in normal circumstances.
4. No participation rights in dividends or liquidation proceeds beyond its stated preferences.
5. No conversion rights.
6. No redemption rights at the option of the holder; may be callable by the company.
7. No sinking fund or other feature that provides a definite maturity.

There are two key elements in the valuation of a standard preferred stock.

1. The probability that the company will meet the obligations of the preferred stock. This entails consideration of:
   a. The earnings coverage for the dividend preference.
   b. The asset coverage for the liquidation preference.
   c. The characteristics of the corporation, which could affect these coverages, particularly its prospective growth, financial position, and stability.
2. The yields available from comparable fixed income investments.

The valuation of preferred stock requires the selection and analysis of publicly traded preferred stocks that can be used to formulate the best possible valuation guidelines. There are surprisingly few actively traded standard preferred stocks of industrial companies, and it is not possible to confine comparatives to a single industry. It is necessary to compute the earnings coverage of each of these securities. Earnings coverage is computed as follows:

$$\frac{\text{Earnings before interest and taxes}}{\text{Interest} + \left(\dfrac{\text{preferred dividend requirement}}{1 - \text{tax rate}} \right)}$$

Asset coverage is measured relative to both current assets and total assets and is computed as follows:

$$\text{Current assets coverage:} = \frac{\text{Current assets}}{\text{Total liabilities} + \text{par value of preferred}}$$

$$\text{Total assets coverage:} = \frac{\text{Total assets}}{\text{Total liabilities} + \text{par value of preferred}}$$

Compute the yield (**dividend divided by market price**) on each of these securities, looking for a relationship between the yield and the earnings and asset coverages of the comparative preferreds. Qualitative factors should also be considered. Precise relationships are seldom ascertainable. However, a careful review of the data should provide a good base for the exercise of informed judgment in determining the freely traded value.

A discount to the freely traded value is required. General practice among appraisers is to apply a discount of 15% to 20% for lack of marketability of standard preferred stocks.

It is sometimes necessary to appraise a preferred stock that deviates in significant ways from a standard preferred stock. An exhaustive list of such preferred stocks is not practical. However, a few of the more common variations are as follows:

1. *Noncumulative Preferred Stock.* Some increase in the yield is warranted for the risk that the dividend may be skipped and "gone forever."

2. *Preferred Stock with Share Convertibility.* This is preferred stock that is convertible into a specified number of shares of common stock. It is necessary to determine the fair market value of the common stock into which the preferred is convertible. If the conversion value (the value of the common stock into which the preferred is convertible) is substantially less than the value as a standard preferred, the premium for convertibility is small or even nonexistent. On the other hand, if the conversion value exceeds the value as a standard preferred stock, the market value is equal to the conversion value plus a small premium.

3. *Preferred Stock with Dollar Convertibility.* This type of preferred is typically convertible into an amount of common stock having a specified dollar value, usually $100, on the conversion date. Even though its dividend may not warrant a value of $100, the conversion feature may give it a value close to or at the conversion price, depending on the assurance that the owner of the preferred can convert and receive $100 worth of common stock at any time.

4. *Preferred Stock with Participation Rights.* This type of preferred is entitled to the standard fixed dividend and liquidation preferences **plus** a share of the residual dividends or asset values, or both, which would otherwise pass to the common stock. Such rights give the preferred some of the attributes of a common stock and these attributes should be valued in a similar manner.

5. *Preferred Stock with an Adjustable Dividend Rate.* The dividend rate on such preferreds is typically adjusted quarterly to reflect prevailing market yields. This adjustment feature, depending on its specific structure, generally maintains the value of these preferreds at or

near par. Many public companies have issued adjustable rate preferred stocks, but they are uncommon among nonpublic companies.

(j) EMPLOYEE STOCK OWNERSHIP PLANS.   Over the past 15 years there has been an enormous growth in the number of companies with employee stock ownership plans. The trust established under an ESOP requires a determination of fair market value for a variety of reasons, including:

1. Contributions of stock by the company or sales by its stockholders to the ESOP.
2. Sales of stock by the ESOP to third parties.
3. Transfer of shares from the ESOP to a beneficiary.
4. Repurchase of shares from a beneficiary exercising his or her put.
5. Reports required by ERISA.

The appraiser of ESOP shares should be familiar with the Department of Labor proposed regulations regarding ESOP appraisals. These regulations stress the requirement that the appraiser be independent of all parties to the transaction other than the plan. They also stress the requirement of a fully documented appraisal. The proposed regulation affirms Rev. Rul. 59-60 as a reasonable statement of general valuation principles, but the DOL seems to go out of its way to mandate the use of guideline companies.

The valuation of ESOP shares is fundamentally the same as valuation for other purposes except that the put obligation, providing it is enforceable, constitutes a kind of marketability that may reduce or even eliminate the lack of marketability discount that would otherwise be required. The appraiser, in deriving the freely traded value of the shares, will have used publicly held guideline companies as valuation guidelines. If the appraiser concludes that the put gives the beneficiary about the same assurance of marketability that he would enjoy if the trust held stock of the guideline companies, then no discount is appropriate. However, if the business risks of the subject company are such that the assurance of marketability is less, then some discount for lack of marketability is required. The size of such discount depends on the appraiser's assessment of the probability that the company will be financially able to honor its put obligations. This requires an analysis of the company's growth, stability, financial position, and cash flow—all factors that the appraiser will have considered in the basic appraisal process. Consideration should also be given to the timing and size of stock distributions to terminating employees since these factors could affect the company's ability to honor its put obligations.

Some appraisers believe that an additional discount is required for the lack of marketability of the stock in the hands of the trust, because the put does not affect the marketability of shares until they are distributed out of the trust. Others, viewing the trust as a device by which stock is held for ultimate distribution to terminating employees, conclude that the degree of marketability to the trust need not be reflected in valuing the stock.

There has been considerable discussion within the appraisal profession as to the effect that the stock repurchase liability may have on the fair market value of the stock. ("Stock repurchase liability" is not a liability in the normal sense of the word because it is an obligation to purchase an asset at its market value.) To date, no consensus has developed, and most appraisers seem to ignore the issue or list it as "a factor that has been considered."

Leveraged ESOPs present additional problems to the appraiser beyond the scope of this book.

(k) VALUATIONS FOR MARITAL DISSOLUTIONS.   The classic definition of fair market value is not always appropriate for a business valuation to be used in a divorce proceeding. This is particularly true in the case of professional practices that cannot be sold. The standard of value may not be clear from the statutes or the case law. It is imperative that the appraiser get guidance from the attorney with regard to the standard of value and the ways in which that standard can be applied to the case at hand.

The date as of which the marital estate is to be valued frequently is not clear from the statutes or case law and can, in some states, be set at the discretion of the trier of fact.

(l) RESTRICTIVE AGREEMENTS.   The existence of certain restrictive agreements can be determinative of value for estate tax purposes. If such an agreement restricts the sale of the stock during the stockholder's lifetime and obligates the estate to sell after death, and if the price is readily ascertainable from the agreement (and was reasonable at the time the agreement was signed), then the agreement is normally determinative of the value for estate tax purposes. However, where the parties to the agreement are family members, there is the possibility that "IRC Chapter 14—Special Valuation Rules" will apply and require a different valuation standard. This question should be resolved by the attorney for the estate.

(m) S CORPORATIONS.   There is no consensus among appraisers as to the impact of the Subchapter S election on value. Some appraisers simply adjust the earnings of the S corporation to a C corporation basis. (This methodology may be found on Page 7–14 in the IRS Valuation Guide for Income, Estate and Gift Taxes—Valuation for Appeals Officer.) Others develop price earnings ratios from the pretax earnings of guideline companies. These methods assume that the S election has no effect on value. Other appraisers have concluded that the premium can be as much as 100% or more, depending upon the payout ratio (Schackelford, 1988). The premium, if any, attributable to a minority interest in an S Corporation is derived from the tax benefit associated with the avoidance of the corporate level income tax.

Any such calculation of the tax advantage associated with the avoidance of corporate tax must inherently assume that the S advantage will remain unchanged in perpetuity. In fact it can be lost by changes within the legal structure of the company or its ownership or by changes in the tax code. Moreover, because it reduces the type and number of possible purchasers of the stock, an increment to the discount for lack of marketability seems warranted.

(n) START-UP COMPANIES.   Start-up companies are all future, no past; therefore the guideline company approach will be of limited use in appraising a start-up company. Some form of discounted future benefit approach must be used. The projections will be of the utmost importance and, in the case of a high-technology company, the appraiser will need significant input from an expert familiar with the technology and its market potential. The present value discount rate associated with the valuation of start-up companies will reflect the high inherent risks associated with an unproven business. Venture capitalists typically employ expected rates of return ranging upwards of 25% to 40% in determining the value of a start up business, depending on the nature of the contemplated enterprise and the perceived degree of risk.

(o) NONVOTING STOCK.   Many corporations have a voting and a nonvoting common stock, which presents a valuation problem. One SEC study indicates a value differential of about 8% between high vote and low vote common shares where voting power is the only difference in the rights of each class.

Courts have been rather erratic on this question. In one case the court held that the voting stock, which constituted 1% of the equity, had 40% of the value. However, in other cases the courts were more moderate, and a number of cases have used relatively modest discounts for nonvoting stock, generally about 5%. A 5% to 10% differential seems reasonable in considering minority interest blocks.

(p) VALUATION OF A CONTROLLING INTEREST.   The ultimate controlling interest is the **100% interest.** The value of such an interest is the greater of the liquidating value of the corporation or the price it would fetch as a going concern in a sale or merger. If the company has relatively low earnings, the liquidating value should be estimated. **Liquidating value**

may differ substantially from book value. Receivables may be difficult to collect by a company in liquidation, particularly if the company has granted credit to a large number of small accounts. The value of inventories tends to vary with the complexity of the inventory. An inventory of raw material, steel or copper, for example, has a fairly ascertainable value. On the other hand, a complex inventory of plumbing supplies, for example, can generally be sold only at a deep discount.

An appraisal should be obtained for real estate, as well as machinery and equipment. Standard machinery, a machine tool for instance, has an established market, and an experienced machinery and equipment appraiser can readily ascertain its value. Special machinery may have no more than scrap value. Consideration must be given to operating costs during the wind-up period and to severance pay and **pension obligations** under the Employee Retirement Income Security Act (ERISA). If liquidating value exceeds going-concern value, then the value of the 100% interest is the present value of the estimated proceeds of liquidation.

Most companies are worth more as **going concerns** than they are in liquidation and, under those circumstances, it is necessary to estimate the value of the company as a going concern. This presents essentially the same problem as a minority valuation in the sense that the appraiser must make a judgment as to the proper capitalization of earnings. It is desirable to examine the objective evidence of the marketplace. The preferred approach is to analyze available data on similar companies that have been involved in a sale or merger. There are two good sources of information to be used in obtaining information on such transactions. The first of these is *F&S Index of Corporate Change,* a quarterly published by Predicasts, Inc., which tabulates corporate sales and mergers by SIC number. The second is *Mergers & Acquisitions—The Journal of Corporate Venture,* a quarterly published by Information for Industry, Inc., which summarizes recent merger activity.

These sources should reveal a number of companies of a similar nature that have been sold or merged near the valuation date. Often it is not possible to obtain extensive details on such transactions. However, when the analyst can obtain a minimum of information, such as the sale price of the company, combined with a recent balance sheet and at least one year's income account, the transaction can serve as a useful guideline in the valuation of a 100% interest. When the acquiring company reports to the SEC, 10-K and S-4 reports may contain useful information.

Frequently this "direct approach" to the valuation of a 100% interest is not feasible because there have been no transactions involving similar companies or because information cannot be obtained on the transactions that have occurred. In that case, standard practice is to determine a minority interest value, following essentially the procedure outlined previously. Having determined this minority interest value, it is necessary to apply an appropriate **premium** to derive the value of a 100% interest. A useful guideline in this respect can be developed from the premiums that have been paid for publicly held industrial companies generally in recent months. This premium can be derived by examining the relationship between the sale price of the stock of each company and its stock price before the pending merger was influencing its market value. If this is done on a sufficient number of companies, a useful guideline to an appropriate merger premium for the company being valued can be obtained. However, there tends to be considerable variation among merger premiums, and the appropriate merger premium for the subject company is essentially a matter of judgment. The merger premium analysis is a very rough guideline, but it is a very useful one.

Lesser percentages of ownership can constitute absolute control. In some states 50% plus one share can force the sale, merger, or liquidation of a company. In other states it is two-thirds plus one share. Blocks of stock having legal absolute control are worth a substantial premium over minority interest values. However, some large companies have a policy of avoiding less than 100% acquisitions because they may prevent consolidation for income tax purposes or involve possible minority interest or dissenting stockholder problems. Therefore, a block of stock, substantially less than 100%, but legally constituting absolute control, has a per share value greater than that of a minority interest but somewhat less than that of a 100% interest.

In some states (Illinois, Ohio, Minnesota, and others) a two-thirds majority is required for sale, merger, or liquidation. In these states it is possible to own more than 50% of the voting securities and still not have absolute control. In these states the owner of, for example, 55% of the voting securities has **working control,** but not absolute control. He can control the dividend-paying policy of the company, its operating policies, and its employment policies. The owner of that 55% block is certainly in a better position than the owner of a minority interest. However, because he cannot force the sale or liquidation of the company, the 55% interest is not proportionately as valuable as an interest that can force the sale or merger of the company.

The premium that should be attached to a minority interest value to reflect this kind of working control tends to vary from company to company, and considerable judgment must be used by the appraiser in reflecting this factor. The premium should be 10% or more, but it should be significantly less than the premium for absolute control.

(q) FIFTY PERCENT INTEREST.   Sometimes it is necessary to value a block of stock that represents exactly 50% of the voting power. Obviously, this block of stock is not a controlling interest. However, 50% of the vote does have "veto power." Although it cannot force any number of basic moves that may be deemed desirable, it can prevent the remaining half from undertaking action it deems to be undesirable. A holder of a 50% interest is in a better position than an owner of a minority interest; therefore a 50% block should have some premium in value over a minority interest value. This premium should be small, certainly no more than 10%.

38.4 COURT DECISIONS ON VALUATION ISSUES

The U.S. Tax Court probably hears more business valuation cases than any other court. However, looking to Tax Court opinions for guidance with regard to "factors considered," discounts, premiums, and so on can be a rather frustrating exercise because the opinions are not always clear. The best summary of court decisions related to business valuations is the *Federal Tax Valuation Digest.*

An analysis of cases is beyond the scope of this book. However, two developments in court decisions should be mentioned.

For many years the U.S. Tax Court seemed to reflect a "split it down the middle" attitude, which fostered extreme valuations by the government as well as by taxpayers. This was explicitly changed by a series of decisions in the early 1980s. The most important of these was *Buffalo Tool & Die v. Commissioner* (74 TC 441, 1980), in which the court indicated that it would lean heavily toward the party that presents the better appraisal. Subsequent cases that made the same point include *Donald Strutz v. Commissioner* (40 TCM 757, 1980), *Sirloin Stockade, Inc. v. Commissioner* (40 TCM 928, 1980), and *Hooker Industries v. Commissioner* (44 TCM 258, 1982). The cumulative effect of these cases, together with the imposition of tax penalties for overappraisal or underappraisal (see IRC ¶¶ 6659 and 6660) has been to increase drastically the risk of relying on a poorly documented or poorly reasoned appraisal.

The second development concerns the definition of what constitutes a minority interest, as opposed to a controlling interest, in a family-owned corporation. In the early 1980s the IRS took the position in Rev. Rul. 81-253 that individual minority interest blocks of stock owned by family members in a family-controlled corporation should be valued as parts of a control block. This theory has not been accepted by any court so far (see, e.g., *Estate of Bright v. U.S.,* 658 F. 2d 999 (5th Cir. 1981); *Estate of Andrews,* 79 TC 938 (1982); *Victor J. Minahan v. Commissioner,* 88 TC 492 (1987)).

The Service has finally acknowledged the existence of minority interests in family corporations with the issuance of Rev. Rul 93-12.

Valuations in matrimonial cases vary greatly among jurisdictions and may involve a standard of value different from the classic definition of fair market value.

38.5 SAMPLE CONDENSED VALUATION ANALYSIS

(a) COMPANY BACKGROUND. The following abbreviated valuation of a company is presented for illustrative purposes. Many of the facts and most of the tables and charts used in a full valuation analysis have been omitted here for the sake of brevity. The subject company and the guideline companies are fictional.

The purpose of the appraisal is to determine the fair market value of a 20% interest in ABC Snack Foods Inc., as of March 31, 1989.

ABC Snack Foods, Inc. (hereinafter referred to as ABC), is a producer of potato chips, tortilla and corn chips, and popcorn. The company has two plants, one of 205,000 sq. ft. in Houston, Texas, and a second of 100,000 sq. ft. in Amarillo, Texas, which was opened in 1988.

Products are distributed through 350 routes, of which 225 are company owned and 125 are independent distributors. In each of its major markets ABC is either the first or second brand. Advertising, which averages 1.75% of sales, is done primarily by TV and radio and, to a lesser extent, by billboards. Promotions normally account for 2.5% of sales. No single customer accounts for more than 5% of sales.

The analysis indicated that ABC was growing somewhat faster than both the potato chip and the popcorn industries. Both the potato chip and popcorn businesses are marked by fairly intense competition in terms of price, promotions, distribution, and advertising. The company competes with several companies that are substantially larger than ABC, as well as with a large number of small local firms, some of which are industry leaders in their locality.

Financial and income data with appropriate adjustments are shown for ABC Snack Foods in Exhibit 38.1.

(b) SELECTION OF GUIDELINE COMPANIES. In selecting guideline companies certain criteria were established:

1. The common stock must be publicly held and actively traded.
2. The stock must trade above $2.00 per share. This criterion was established to eliminate very cheap stocks whose prices frequently do not have realistic relationships to basic determinants of value.
3. Guideline companies must be primarily engaged in the production and sale of dessert and snack foods.

In searching for companies that would meet these criteria, we reviewed all companies classified as food companies in *Standard Corporation Records* and in *Moody's Industrial Manual* and *Moody's OTC Industrial Manual*. These sources published financial data concerning virtually all securities in which there is sufficient public interest to warrant such publication. All the companies in the industry classifications listed were reviewed and eight were selected as being the best possible companies that could be used as a valuation guideline. The reasons for the exclusion of the others were given. A very brief description of each of these companies follows:

Alabaster Ice Cream, Inc., manufactures premium ice cream for distribution throughout the West and in several major cities in the Midwest.

Hi-Grade Enterprises, Inc., manufactures and distributes potato chips, fried pork skins, peanut butter crackers, and popcorn. Products are sold throughout the South.

Hudson Foods Corp., produces meat sticks and beef jerky under the names Slim Jim and Pemmican. Distribution is national.

Interlaken Foods Corp. is primarily a producer of chocolate and confectionary products distributed nationally.

ABC SNACK FOODS, INC.
Condensed Balance Sheets and Computations of Total Net Worth
Net Income, Cash Flow and Dividends
(Figures in Thousands of Dollars)

Fiscal Years Ending March 31,	1984	1985	1986	1987	1988	1989
Condensed Balance Sheets						
Assets:						
Current assets						
Cash and equivalent	$ 3,827	$ 4,818	$ 4,578	$ 3,130	$ 4,259	$ 4,157
Accounts receivable	3,599	5,433	7,627	7,289	7,203	9,552
Inventories	1,385	2,402	2,408	2,236	2,576	3,861
Other current assets	909	419	434	843	914	1,322
Total current assets	9,720	13,072	15,047	13,498	14,360	18,892
Net fixed assets	7,615	8,665	9,254	13,949	17,464	16,875
Net fixed assets	7,615	8,665	9,254	13,949	17,464	16,875
Other assets	131	178	176	1,075	454	426
Other assets	131	178	176	1,075	454	426
Total assets	$17,467	$21,915	$24,477	$28,522	$32,278	$36,193
Capital and liabilities:						
Current liabilities	$ 3,501	$ 4,613	$ 4,008	$ 4,382	$ 4,313	$ 5,070
Current liabilities	3,501	4,613	4,008	4,382	4,313	5,070
Other credits	—	—	—	—	—	—
Other liabilities	784	989	1,103	1,593	2,004	2,524
Total net worth	13,180	16,314	19,369	22,545	25,963	28,599
Total capital and liabilities	$17,465	$21,916	$24,480	$28,520	$32,280	$36,193
Computation of Total Net Worth						
Preferred stock	$ —	$ —	$ —	$ —	$ —	$ —
Common stock	2,045	2,045	2,045	2,045	2,045	2,045
Additional paid-in capital	3,554	3,554	3,554	3,554	3,554	3,554
Retained earnings	7,581	10,716	13,771	16,946	20,365	23,001
Treasury stock	—	—	—	—	—	—
Adjustments:						
Total net worth	$13,180	$16,314	$19,369	$22,545	$25,963	$28,599
Additional Information						
Total liabilities	$ 4,285	$ 5,602	$ 5,111	$ 5,975	$ 6,317	$ 7,594
Net working capital	6,219	8,459	11,040	9,116	10,047	13,822
Net sales	51,581	58,880	62,376	66,037	70,671	76,499
Computation of Adjusted Net Income and Cash Flow						
Reported net income		$ 3,481	$ 3,431	$ 3,679	$ 3,924	$ 4,386
Adjustments:						
Flood loss (net)		—	—	—	—	843
Adjusted net income		3,481	3,431	3,679	3,924	5,229
Depreciation & amortization		1,140	1,479	1,825	2,023	2,197
Cash flow		$ 4,620	$ 4,911	$ 5,504	$ 5,947	$ 7,426
Computation of Total Dividends						
Preferred stock dividends		$ —	$ —	$ —	$ —	$ —
Common stock dividends		342	376	505	505	1,686
Total dividends		$ 342	$ 376	$ 505	$ 505	$ 1,686

Exhibit 38.1.   Adjusted financial and income data.

King Foods Inc. produces and markets soft pretzels, baked cookies and muffins, and semifrozen carbonated beverages and frozen juice treats and desserts. Distribution is national.

Munchies, Inc., produces and distributes snack items including peanut butter or cheese-filled cracker sandwiches, cookie sandwiches, potato chips, popcorn, and fried pork skins. Sales are primarily through the company's own sales organization to service stations and drug stores in 35 states, primarily east of the Mississippi River.

Sweetgoods Corp. produces sweet goods, including single portion cakes, frozen cakes and pies, doughnuts, and cookies. Distribution is primarily in 23 eastern and southeastern states.

Tri-State Snacks Corp. is a producer of candy and other snack items, primarily under its own brand names. Products are marketed nationally.

The market value of each of the guideline companies has been computed by simply multiplying the closing price on March 31, 1989, by the number of shares outstanding. That market value appears on Column I of Exhibit 38.2.

Column II shows the weighted average earnings of each company during the 5 years preceding the valuation date. (The weighting procedure places a weight of one on 1984, two on 1985, up to five on the earnings of 1988.) Column III shows the price-earnings ratios. The median price earnings ratio is 16.8. The next column shows the 5-year weighted average cash flow over the same period and shows that the median market price to cash flow ratio is 10.7 times. Column VI shows the dividends of each company in the year preceding the valuation date and this is followed by the price dividend ratio. The median is 41.0. Column VIII shows the payout ratio of each company, indicating that the median payout ratio is 42.5%. Finally we show the total net worth of each company, and that is followed by the market value to net worth percentage.

These market value ratios provide useful guidelines for the valuation of ABC. However, they are nothing more than guidelines and must inevitably be combined with the appraiser's judgment in arriving at a sound valuation conclusion. The appraiser must, after careful consideration of all relevant facts, come to one of three possible conclusions:

1. Investors would find ABC to be more attractive than the group of guideline companies. (In this case a premium must be added to the median valuation ratios.)
2. Investors would find ABC to be less attractive than the guideline companies. (In this case a discount from the median valuation ratios is required.)
3. Investors would regard ABC as being neither more nor less attractive than the group of guideline companies. (In this case the use of the median ratios would be appropriate.)

(c) QUALITATIVE CONSIDERATIONS.   ABC has an excellent trade name in its marketing territory as evidenced by the fact that it is the number one or number two brand in all its major markets. We think that the ABC trade name, in its markets, is as good as some of the guideline companies and inferior to several of them. On balance we think that this is a small negative consideration for ABC.

In terms of size, ABC is at the low end of the range of the guideline companies and it has less geographic diversification than the group of guideline companies. This is a small negative consideration for ABC.

ABC's new plant in Amarillo positions it to expand geographically and results to date exceed expectations. We think that this is a positive factor.

ABC uses two commodities, potatoes and corn, and both of these commodities are subject to rather considerable price variability. However, some of the guideline companies' businesses are as vulnerable as ABC to price changes of a limited number of commodities.

Mr. A. B. Caldwell, the founder of the company, is 64 and in ill health. Mr. John Grundy, the company's executive vice president has been groomed to succeed Mr. Caldwell. However,

	MARKET VALUE RATIOS			
	I	II	III	IV
Company	3/31/89 Total Market Value	Latest 5-Year Weighted Average Earnings	Market Value Times Latest 5-Year Weighted Average Earnings	Latest 5-Year Weighted Average Cash Flow
	($000)(a)	($000)		($000)
Alabaster Ice Cream, Inc.	$ 112,258	$ 5,076	22.1	$ 10,252
Hi-Grade Enterprises, Inc.	121,617	6,957	17.5	14,143
Hudson Foods Corp.	63,129	4,153	15.2	6,091
Interlaken Foods Corp.	2,389,938	116,487	20.5	161,127
King Foods Inc.	75,842	4,784	15.9	8,191
Munchies, Inc.	561,257	38,060	14.7	53,736
Sweetgoods Corp.	137,542	7,291	18.9	12,372
Tri-State Snacks Corp.	235,345	14,518	16.2	17,144
Guideline company median			16.8	

NOTE: (a) On a minority interest basis.

Exhibit 38.2.   Market value data for the guideline companies.

there is no one other than Mr. Grundy with the depth of experience needed to run the company. We conclude that ABC has somewhat less depth of management than the guideline companies and that this is a negative consideration.

(d) QUANTITATIVE CONSIDERATIONS.   A comparison of sales and income growth appears in Exhibit 38.3. The sales of each company were placed on a index basis with the years 1985–1986 equal to 100, and the group median was determined. The upper portion of that chart shows that the sales growth of ABC has been similar to that of the guideline companies.

The lower portion of that chart shows that the long-term trend of ABC's net income has been close to the group of guideline companies.

A comparison of certain operating ratios is shown in Exhibit 38.4. The top section shows that in 1984 and 1985 ABC was generating more sales per dollar of equity capital than the group of guideline companies. However, during the last 3 years ABC has been almost identical to the group median.

The middle portion of the chart shows that ABC's net profit margin has remained fairly constant at about 6%, whereas the guideline companies have declined from 7.7% in 1984 to 5.2% in 1988.

The lower portion of that chart shows that ABC's rate of earnings on stockholders' equity was above the group median in 1984 but has been slightly inferior to the group median since then. Since 1984 the trends have been parallel.

ABC's current ratio of 3.7 times is considerably better than the group median of 2.2 times. Both ABC and the guideline companies have about 50% of their assets in the form of current assets and about 50% in fixed assets. In terms of leverage, ABC is significantly better than the group median. ABC's ratio of total liabilities to total assets is 21%, compared to the group median of 43%. We conclude that the overall financial position of ABC is better than the group of guideline companies.

V Market Value Times Latest 5-Year Weighted Average Cash Flow	VI Latest Year Dividends	VII Market Value Times Latest Year Dividends	VIII Latest Year Dividends as a % of Latest 5-Year Weighted Average Earnings	IX Total Net Worth	X Market Value as a % of Net Worth
	($000)			($000)	
10.9	$ 1,421	79.0	28.0	$ 29,888	375.6
8.6	4,097	29.7	58.9	58,914	206.4
10.4	1,537	41.1	37.0	24,935	253.2
14.8	58,530	40.8	50.2	679,284	351.8
9.3	2,037	37.2	42.6	33,113	229.0
10.4	20,999	26.7	55.2	201,593	278.4
11.1	3,096	44.4	42.5	50,651	271.5
13.7	4,077	57.7	28.1	42,693	551.2
10.7		41.0	42.5		275.0

The quantitative analysis revealed no important differences between ABC and the group of guideline companies that would require modification of the median ratios. Its growth rates were not significantly different. The comparison of operating ratios did not reveal any significant differences that would require adjustment. The analysis did reveal that ABC has significantly less leverage than the guideline companies. However, that low leverage has enabled ABC to pay out about the same percentages of its earnings as the guideline companies (40% vs. 42.5%) despite its inferior access to capital markets. We think that the better financial position is reasonably reflected through the capitalization of dividends.

We summarize as follows:

NEGATIVE DIFFERENCES

1. Slight inferiority in trade name.
2. Inferior depth of management.
3. Less geographic diversification.

POSITIVE DIFFERENCES

1. ABC's promising geographic expansion.

We think that, on balance, these differences make ABC somewhat less attractive than the guideline companies and are appropriately reflected by a 10% reduction in the median valuation ratios.

(e) APPLICATION OF THE VALUATION RATIOS.   The valuation ratios are applied to ABC's own figures on Exhibit 38.5. Primary weight (60%) is applied to the value derived from

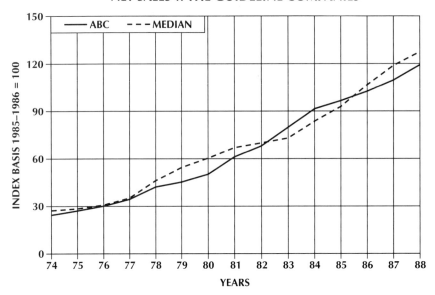

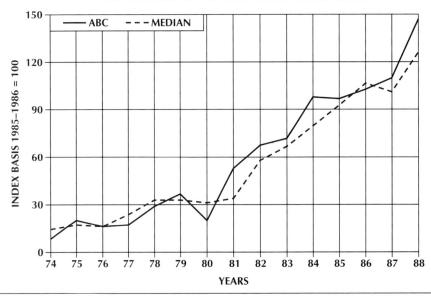

Exhibit 38.3.   A comparison of sales and income growth.

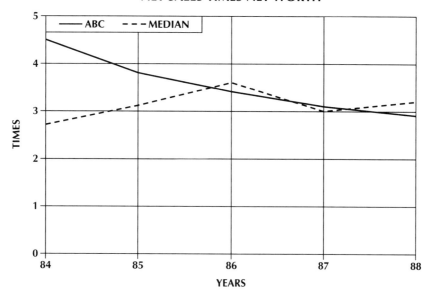

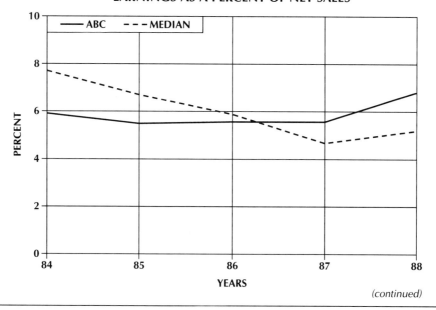

(continued)

Exhibit 38.4.   A comparison of certain operating ratios.

ABC SNACK FOODS, INC.

EARNINGS AS A PERCENT OF NET WORTH

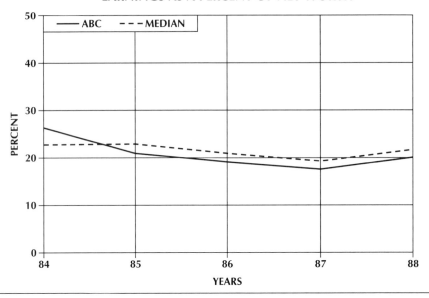

Exhibit 38.4.   *Continued.*

VALUATION OF THE COMMON STOCK OF ABC SNACK FOODS, INC.
Modified Valuation Ratios Derived on Exhibit 38.2

	Median Ratios	Modified Valuation Ratios	
Market value × 1984–1988 weighted average earnings	16.8	15.1	
Market value × 1984–1988 weighted average cash flow	10.7	9.6	
Market value × 1988 dividends	41.0	36.9	
Application of valuation ratios to ABC's earnings, cash flow, and dividends			
15.1 × ABC's 1984–1988 weighted average earnings of $4,214,000 = $63,631,000 × a weight of 60%			$38,179,000
9.6 × ABC's 1984–1988 weighted average cash flow of $6,125,000 = $58,800,000 × a weight of 20%			11,760,000
36.9 × ABC's 1988 dividends of $1,686,000 = $62,213,000 × a weight of 20%			12,443,000
			$62,382,000
Freely traded value per share (based on 100,000 shares issued and outstanding)			$624
Less: Discount for lack of marketability (30%)			187
Fair market value per share			$437

Exhibit 38.5.   Valuation of the common stock of ABC Snack Foods, Inc., as of March 31, 1989.

earnings and 20% each to the values derived from cash flow and dividends. This weighting procedure results in a value of $62,382,000.

It should be noted that the value of $62,382,000 is 218% of ABC's book value of $28,599,000. This is well within the range of the guideline companies and is reasonable. No separate weight has been given to the guideline companies' ratio of market value to book value because we believe that investors give little, if any, weight to book value in appraising the securities of companies with the high rates of earnings on capital that are characteristic of this industry.

It should also be noted that we have not used a discounted future benefits approach because ABC's prospective growth rates are roughly comparable to those of the guideline companies. The adjusted valuation ratios are, therefore, a reflection of both the growth rate and the capitalization rate appropriate to ABC Snack Foods, Inc., on the valuation date.

Dividing the preliminary value of $62,382,000 by the 100,000 shares outstanding results in a freely traded value (the price at which the stock would trade in an active market) of $624 per share.

The fact that the ABC stock lacks ready marketability must be reflected by a discount for lack of marketability. We think that a discount of 30% is appropriate. This results in a value for the common stock of $437 per share.

It is our conclusion that a block of 20,000 shares had a fair market value of $437 per share, as of March 31, 1989, or $8,740,000 for the entire block.

38.6 SOURCES AND SUGGESTED REFERENCES

Blackman, L., The Valuation of Privately-Held Businesses, Probus Publishing, Chicago, 1986.

Brown, Ronald L., *Valuing Professional Practices and Licenses: A Guide for the Matrimonial Practitioner,* Prentice-Hall, 1987.

Burke, Frank M., Jr., *Valuation and Valuation Planning for Closely-Held Businesses,* Prentice-Hall, 1981.

Ibbotson, Roger A., *Stocks, Bonds, Bills and Inflation,* Ibbotson Associates, Chicago, 1989.

Internal Revenue Service, *IRS Valuation Guide for Income, Estate & Gift Taxes,* Commerce Clearing House, Chicago, 1985.

———, Revenue Ruling No. 59-60, U.S. Treasury Dept., Washington, DC.

Maher, J. Michael, "Discounts for Lack of Marketability for Closely-Held Business Interests," *Taxes— The Tax Magazine,* September 1976, pp. 562–71.

Moroney, Robert E., "Most Courts Overvalue Closely Held Stocks," *Taxes—The Tax Magazine,* March 1973, pp. 144–154.

Pratt, Shannon P., Ed., *Readings in Business Valuation,* American Society of Appraisers Educational Foundation, 1986.

———, *Valuing a Business,* 2nd ed., Dow Jones-Irwin, Homewood, IL, 1989.

———, *Valuing Small Businesses and Professional Practices,* Dow Jones-Irwin, Homewood, IL, 1986.

Schackelford, Aaron L., "Valuation of S Corporations," Business Valuation Review, December 1988, pp. 159–162.

Schnepper, J. A., *The Professional Handbook of Business Valuation,* Addison-Wesley, Reading, MA, 1982.

Smith, Gordon V., *Corporate Valuation,* Wiley, New York, 1988.

Standard & Poor's Corporation, *Standard Corporation Records,* Standard & Poor's, New York, annual update.

CHAPTER 39

BANKRUPTCY

Grant W. Newton, PhD, CPA, CMA
Pepperdine University

CONTENTS

39.1 OVERVIEW

This chapter contains a brief description of the Bankruptcy Code, a discussion of the services that can be rendered by the accountant, and an introduction to the problems faced by accountants working in the bankruptcy area.

39.2 ALTERNATIVES AVAILABLE TO TROUBLED COMPANIES

The debtor's first alternatives are to locate new financing, to merge with another company, or to find some other basic solution to its situation that avoids the necessity of discussing its problems with representatives of creditors. If none of these alternatives is possible, the debtor may be required to seek a remedy from creditors, either informally (out of court) or with the help of judicial proceedings.

(a) OUT-OF-COURT SETTLEMENTS. The informal settlement is an out-of-court agreement that usually consists of an extension of time (stretch-out), a pro rata cash payment for full settlement of claims (composition), an issue of stock for debt, or some combination. The debtor, through counsel or credit association, calls an informal meeting of the creditors for the purpose of discussing its financial problems. In many cases, the credit association makes a significant contribution to the out-of-court settlement by arranging a meeting of creditors, providing advice, and serving as secretary for the creditors' committee.

A **credit association** is composed of credit managers of various businesses in a given region. Its functions are to provide credit and other business information to member companies concerning their debtors, to help make commercial credit collections, to support legislation favorable to business creditors, and to provide courses in credit management for members of the credit community.

At the **creditors' meeting** the debtor describes the causes of failure, discusses the value of assets (especially those unpledged) and unsecured liabilities, and answers any questions the creditors may ask. The main objective of this meeting is to convince the creditors that they would receive more if the business were allowed to operate than if it were forced to liquidate, and that all parties would benefit from working out a settlement.

(i) Appointment of Creditors' Committee.   To make it easier for the debtor to work with the creditors, a committee of creditors is normally appointed during the initial meeting of the debtor and its creditors, providing, of course, the case is judged to warrant some cooperation by the creditors. It should be realized that the creditors are often as interested in working out a settlement as is the debtor. The **creditors' committee** serves as the bargaining agent for the creditors, supervises the operation of the debtor during the development of a plan, and solicits acceptance of a plan once the committee has approved it. Generally, the creditors' committee meets immediately after appointment for the purpose of selecting a presiding officer and counsel.

(ii) Plan of Settlement.   Provided there is enough time, it is often advisable that the accountant and the attorney assist the debtor in preparing a suggested **plan of settlement** for presentation and discussion at the first meeting with creditors. Typically only the largest creditors and a few representatives of the smaller creditors are invited so that the group is a manageable size for accomplishing its goals.

There is no set pattern for the form that a plan of settlement proposed by the debtor must take. It may call for 100% payment over an extended period of time, payments on a pro rata basis in cash for full settlement of creditors' claims, satisfaction of debt obligations with stock, or some combination. A carefully developed forecast of projected operations, based on realistic assumptions developed by the debtor with the aid of its accountant, can help creditors determine whether the debtor can perform under the terms of the plan and operate successfully in the future.

(b) ASSIGNMENT FOR BENEFIT OF CREDITORS.   A remedy available under state law to a corporation in serious financial difficulties is an **assignment for the benefit of creditors.** In this instance the debtor voluntarily transfers title to its assets to an assignee, who then liquidates them and distributes the proceeds among the creditors. Assignment for the benefit of creditors is an extreme remedy because it results in the cessation of the business. This informal liquidation device (although court-supervised in many states) is like the out-of-court settlement devised to rehabilitate the debtor, in that it requires the consent of all creditors or at least their agreement to refrain from taking action. The appointment of a custodian over the assets of the debtor gives creditors the right to file an involuntary bankruptcy court petition.

Proceedings brought in the federal courts are governed by the Bankruptcy Code. Normally it is necessary to resort to such formality when suits have been filed against the debtor and its property is under garnishment or attachment or is threatened by foreclosure or eviction.

(c) BANKRUPTCY COURT PROCEEDINGS.   Bankruptcy court proceedings are generally the last resort for the debtor whose financial condition has deteriorated to the point where it is impossible to acquire additional funds. When the debtor finally agrees that bankruptcy court proceedings are necessary, the liquidation value of the assets often represents only a small fraction of the debtor's total liabilities. If the business is liquidated, the creditors get only a small percentage of their claims. The debtor is discharged of its debts and is free to start over; however, the business is lost and so are all the assets. Normally, liquidation proceedings result in large losses to the debtor, the creditors, and the business community in general. Chapter 7 of the Bankruptcy Code covers the proceedings related to liquidation. Another alternative under the Bankruptcy Code is to seek some type of relief so that the debtor, with the help of the bankruptcy court, can work out agreements with creditors and be able to continue operations. Chapters 11, 12, and 13 of the Bankruptcy Code provide for this type of operation.

(i) Title 11—Bankruptcy Code.   Title 11 U.S. Code contains the bankruptcy law. The code is divided into eight chapters:

- Chapter 1   General Provisions
- Chapter 3   Case Administration
- Chapter 5   Creditors, the Debtor, and the Estate
- Chapter 7   Liquidation
- Chapter 9   Adjustment of Debts of a Municipality
- Chapter 11   Reorganization
- Chapter 12   Adjustment of Debts of a Family Farmer with Regular Income
- Chapter 13   Adjustment of Debts of an Individual with Regular Income

Chapters 1, 3, and 5 apply to all proceedings under the code except chapter 9, where only specified sections of chapters 1, 3, and 5 apply. A case commenced under the Bankruptcy Code—chapter 7, 9, 11, 12, or 13—is referred to as a **Title 11 case.** Chapter 13, which covers the adjustment of debts of individuals with regular income, is beyond the scope of this presentation because it can be used only by individuals with unsecured claims of less than $250,000 and secured claims of less than $750,000. Provisions relating to chapter 11 are discussed in detail in a separate section.

(ii) Chapter 7—Liquidation.   Chapter 7 is used only when the corporation sees no hope of being able to operate successfully or to obtain the necessary creditor agreement. Under this alternative, the corporation is liquidated and the remaining assets are distributed to creditors after administrative expenses have been paid. An individual debtor may be discharged from liabilities and entitled to a fresh start. A corporation's debt is not discharged.

The decision as to whether rehabilitation or liquidation is best also depends on the amount that can be realized from each alternative. The method resulting in the greatest return to the creditors and stockholders should be chosen. The amount received from liquidation depends on the resale value of the firm's assets minus the costs of dismantling and legal expenses. The value of the firm after rehabilitation must be determined (net of the costs of achieving the remedy). The alternative leading to the highest value should be followed.

Financially troubled debtors often attempt an informal settlement or liquidation out of court; if it is unsuccessful, they will then initiate proceedings under the Bankruptcy Code. Other debtors, especially those with a large number of creditors, may file a **petition for relief** in the bankruptcy court as soon as they recognize that continuation of the business under existing conditions is impossible.

As soon as the **order for relief** has been entered, the U.S. trustee appoints a disinterested party from a panel of private trustees to serve as the **interim trustee.** The functions and powers of the interim trustee are the same as those of an **elected trustee.** Once an interim trustee has been appointed, the creditors meet to elect a trustee that will be responsible for liquidating the business. If a trustee is not elected by the creditors, the interim trustee may continue to serve in the capacity of the trustee and carry through with an orderly liquidation of the business.

The objective of the trustee is to liquidate the assets of the estate in an orderly manner. Once the property of the estate has been reduced to money and the security claims have been satisfied to the extent allowed, then the property of the estate is distributed to the holders of the claims in the order specified by the Bankruptcy Code. The first order, of course, is priority claims; when they have been established, the balance goes to unsecured creditors. After all the funds have been distributed, the remaining debts of an individual are discharged. As mentioned earlier, if the debtor is a corporation, the debts are not discharged. Thus it is necessary for the corporation to cease existence. Any funds subsequently coming into the corporate shell would be subject to attachment.

(iii) Chapter 12—Adjustment of Debt of a Family Farmer with Regular Annual Income.
To help farmers resolve some of their financial problems Congress passed chapter 12 of the Bankruptcy Code. It became effective November 26, 1986, and lasts until October 1, 1998. Because chapter 12 is new and relates to a specific class of debtors, Congress will evaluate whether the chapter is serving its purpose and whether there is a need to continue this special chapter for the family farmer. After Congress makes this evaluation it will be able to determine whether to make this chapter permanent. If Congress does not act to either extend the date or make chapter 12 permanent, chapter 12 will terminate on October 1, 1998.

Under current law, a family farmer in need of financial rehabilitation may file either a chapter 11 or 13 petition. Most family farmers, because they have too much debt to qualify, cannot file under chapter 13 and are limited to chapter 11. Many farmers have found chapter 11 needlessly complicated, unduly time-consuming, inordinately expensive, and, in too many cases, unworkable. Chapter 12 is designed to give family farmers an opportunity to reorganize their debts and keep their land. According to legislative history, chapter 12 gives debtors the protection from creditors that bankruptcy provides while, at the same time, it prevents abuse of the system and ensures that farm lenders receive a fair repayment.

In order to file a petition, an individual or an individual and spouse engaged in farming operations must have total debt that does not exceed $1,500,000, and at least 80% of noncontingent, liquidated debts (excluding debt from principal residence unless debt arose out of family operations) on the date the petition is filed must have arisen out of farming. Additionally more than 50% of the petitioner's gross income for the taxable year prior to the filing of the petition must be from farming operations.

A corporation or partnership may file if more than 50% of the outstanding stock or equity is owned by a family and:

1. More than 80% of the value of its assets consist of assets related to farming operations.
2. The total debts do not exceed $1,500,000 and at least 80% of its noncontingent, liquidated debts on the date the case is filed arose out of farming operations.
3. The stock of a corporation is not publicly traded.

Only the debtor can file a plan in a chapter 12 case. The requirements for a plan in chapter 12 are more flexible and lenient than those in chapter 11. In fact, only three requirements are set forth in § 1205 of the Bankruptcy Code. First, the debtor must submit to the supervision and control of the trustee all or such part of the debtor's future income as is necessary for the execution of the plan. Second, the plan must provide for full payment, in deferred cash payments, of all priority claims unless the creditors agree to a different treatment. Third, where creditors are divided into classes, the same treatment must apply to all claims in a particular class. The plan can alter the rights of secured creditors with an interest in real or personal property, but there are a few restrictions. To alter the right of the secured claim holder, the debtor must satisfy one of the following three requirements:

1. Obtain acceptance of the plan.
2. Provide in the plan that the holder of such claim retain the lien and as of the effective date of the plan provide that the payment to be made or property to be transferred is not less than the amount of the claim.
3. Surrender the property securing such claim.

If a holder of an allowed unsecured claim does not accept the plan, then the court may not approve the plan unless:

1. The value of the property to be distributed is equal to at least the amount of the claim.
2. The plan provides that all of the debtor's projected disposable income to be received within 3 years, or longer if directed by the court, after the first payment is made will be a part of the payments under the plan.

To facilitate the operation of the business and the development of a plan, § 1206 of the Bankruptcy Code allows family farmers to sell assets not needed for the reorganization prior to confirmation without the consent of the secured creditor, provided the court approves such a sale.

(iv) Prepackaged Chapter 11 Plans.   Before filing a chapter 11 plan, some debtors develop a plan and obtain approval of the plan by all impaired claims and interests. The court may accept the voting that was done prepetition provided that the solicitation of the acceptance (or rejection) was in compliance with applicable nonbankruptcy laws governing the adequacy of disclosure in connection with the solicitation. If no nonbankruptcy law is applicable, then the solicitation must have occurred after or at the time the holder received adequate information as required under section 1125 of the Bankruptcy Code.

It is often necessary for a chapter 11 plan to be filed for several reasons including the following:

1. Income from debt discharge is taxed in and out of court workout to the extent that the debtor is or becomes solvent. While some tax attributes may be reduced in a bankruptcy case, the gain from debt discharged is not taxed.
2. A larger percent of the net operating loss may be preserved if a chapter 11 petition is filed. For example, the provisions of section 382(1)(5) and 382(1)(6) of the I.R.C. dealing with net operating losses only apply to bankruptcy cases.
3. A smaller percentage of creditor approval is needed in chapter 11. Only two-thirds of the dollar amount of debt represented by those creditors voting and a majority in number in each class are necessary in chapter 11. However, for any out of court workout to succeed, the percentage accepting the plan must be much greater. For example, some bond indenture agreements provide that amendments cannot be made unless all holders of debt approve the modifications. Since it is difficult, if not impossible, to obtain 100% approval, it is necessary to file a bankruptcy plan to reduce interest or modify the principal of the bonds.

Since the professional fees and other costs, including the cost of disrupting the business, of a prepackaged plan are generally much less than costs of a regular chapter 11, a prepackaged bankruptcy may be the best alternative.

(d) THE ACCOUNTANT'S SERVICES IN PROCEEDINGS.   One of the first decisions that must be made at an early meeting of the debtor with bankruptcy counsel and accountants is whether it is best to liquidate (under provisions of state law or Bankruptcy Code), to attempt an out-of-court settlement, to seek an outside buyer, or to file a chapter 11 petition. To decide which course of action to take, it is also important to ascertain what caused the debtor's current problems, whether the company will be able to overcome its difficulties, and, if so, what measures will be necessary. Accountants may be asked to explain how the losses occurred and what can be done to avoid them in the future. To help with this determination, it may be necessary to project the operations after a 30-day period over at least the next 3 to 6 months, and to indicate the areas where steps will be necessary in order to earn a profit.

For existing clients, the information needed to make a decision about the course of action to make may be obtained with limited additional work; however, for a new client, it is necessary to perform a review of the client's operations to determine the condition of the business. Once the review has been completed, the client must normally decide to liquidate the business, attempt an informal settlement with creditors, or file a chapter 11 petition, unless additional funds can be obtained or a buyer for the business is located. For example, where the product is inferior, the demand for the product is declining, the distribution channels are inadequate, or other similar problems exist that cannot be corrected, either because of the economic environment or management's lack of ability, it is normally best to liquidate the company immediately.

The decision whether a business should immediately file a chapter 11 petition or attempt an out-of-court settlement depends on several factors. Among them are the following:

1. Size of company.
   a. Public.
   b. Private.
2. Number of creditors.
   a. Secured.
   b. Unsecured.
   c. Public.
   d. Private.
3. Complexity of matter.
   a. Nature of debt.
   b. Prior relationships with creditors.
4. Pending lawsuits.
5. Executory contracts, especially leases.
6. The impact of alternatives selected.
7. Nature of management.
   a. Mismanagement.
   b. Irregularities.

39.3 GENERAL PROVISIONS OF BANKRUPTCY CODE

(a) **FILING OF PETITION.** A **voluntary case** is commanded by the debtor's filing of a bankruptcy petition under the appropriate chapter.

An **involuntary petition** can be filed by 3 or more creditors (if 11 or fewer creditors, only one creditor is necessary) with unsecured claims of at least $10,000 and can be initiated only under chapter 7 or 11. An indenture trustee may be one of the petitioning creditors. The Court allows a case to proceed only if (1) the debtor generally fails to pay its debts as they become due, provided such debts are not the subject of a bona fide dispute; or (2) within 120 days prior to the petition a custodian was appointed or took possession. The latter excludes the taking of possession of less than substantially all property to enforce a lien.

(b) TIMING OF PETITION—TAX CONSIDERATIONS.   The timing for filing the petition is important. For example, if the debtor delays filing the petition until the creditors are about to force the debtor into bankruptcy, the debtor may not be in a position to effectively control its destiny. On the other hand, if the petition is filed when the problems first develop and while the creditors are reasonably cooperative, the debtor is in a much better position to control the proceeding. If possible, it is best to file the petition near the end of the month, or even better, near the end of the quarter, to avoid a separate closing of the books.

Tax factors should also be considered in deciding when to file the petition. For example, if a debtor corporation that has attempted an unsuccessful out-of-court settlement decides to file a petition, the tax impact of the out-of-court action should be considered. If, in the out-of-court agreement, the debtor transferred property that resulted in a gain and a substantial tax liability, it would be best for the debtor to file the petition after the end of the current taxable year. By taking this action the tax claim is a **prepetition tax claim** and not an administrative expense. If the tax claim is a prepetition claim, interest and penalties stop accruing on the day the petition is filed and the debtor may provide in the plan for the deferral of the tax liability up to 6 years. If the tax claim is an administrative expense, penalties and interest on any unpaid balance will continue to accrue and the provision for deferred payment of up to 6 years does not apply.

(c) ACCOUNTING SERVICES—ACCOUNTING DATA REQUIRED IN THE PETITION.
The accountant must supply the attorney with certain information necessary for filing a Chapter 11 petition. This would normally include the following:

List of Largest Creditors. A list containing the names and addresses of the 20 largest unsecured creditors, excluding insiders, must be filed with the petition in a voluntary case. In an involuntary situation, the list is to be filed with the petition in a voluntary case. In an involuntary petition the list is to be filed within two days after entry of the order for relief. See Bankruptcy Rule 1007 and Bankruptcy Form 4.

List of Creditors. The debtor must file with the court a list of the debtor's creditors of each class, showing the amounts and character of any claims and securities and, so far as is known, the name and address or place of business of each creditor and a notation whether the claim is disputed, contingent, or unliquidated as to amount, when each claim was incurred and the consideration received, and related data.

List of Equity Security Holders. It is necessary to provide a list of the debtor's security holders of each class showing the number and kind of interests registered in the name of each holder and the last known address or place of business of each holder.

Schedules of Assets and Liabilities. The schedules that must accompany the petition (or filed within 15 days after the petition is filed—unless the court extends the time period) are sworn statements of the debtor's assets and liabilities as of the date the petition is filed under chapter 11. These schedules consist primarily of the debtor's balance sheet broken down into detail, and the accountant is required to supply the information generated in the preparation of the normal balance sheet and its supporting schedules. The required information is supplied on Schedules A through C, which include a complete statement of assets, and Schedules D through F, which are a complete statement of liabilities. Schedule G requires the debtor to list all executory contracts and unexpired leases. It is crucial that this information be accurate and complete because the omission or incorrect listing of a creditor might result in a failure to receive notice of the proceedings, and consequently the creditor's claim could be exempted from a discharge when the plan is later confirmed. Also omission of material facts may be construed as a false statement or concealment.

Statement of Financial Affairs. The **statement of affairs,** not to be confused with an accountant's usual use of the term, is a series of detailed questions about the debtor's property and conduct. The general purpose of the statement of affairs is to give both the creditors and the court an overall view of the debtor' operations. It offers many avenues to begin investigations into the debtor's conduct. The statement (Official Form No. 7) consists of 21 questions to be answered under oath concerning the following areas:

1. Income from employment or operation of business.
2. Income other than from employment or operation of business.
3. Payments to creditors.
4. Suits, executions, garnishments, and attachments.
5. Repossessions, foreclosures, and returns.
6. Assignments and receiverships.
7. Gifts.
8. Losses.
9. Payments related to debt counseling or bankruptcy.
10. Other transfers.
11. Closed financial accounts.
12. Safe deposit boxes.
13. Setoffs.
14. Property held for another person.
15. Prior address of debtor.
16. Nature, location, and name of business.
17. Books, records, and financial statements.
18. Inventories.
19. Current partners, officers, directors, and shareholders.
20. Former partners, officers, directors, and shareholders.
21. Withdrawals from a partnership or distributions by a corporation.

Exhibit "A" to the Petition. This is a thumbnail sketch of the financial condition of the business listing total assets, total liabilities, secured claims, unsecured claims, information relating to public trading of the debtor's securities, and the identity of all insiders.

The debtor must also file any additional reports or documents that may be required by local rules or by the U.S. trustee.

(d) ADEQUATE PROTECTION AND AUTOMATIC STAY. A petition filed under the Bankruptcy Code results in an automatic stay of the actions of creditors. The **automatic stay** is one of the fundamental protections provided the debtor by the Bankruptcy Code. In a chapter 7 case it provides for an orderly liquidation that treats all creditors equitably. For business reorganizations under chapter 11, 12, or 13, it provides time for the debtor to examine the problems that forced it into bankruptcy court and to develop a plan for reorganization. As a result of the stay, no party, with minor exceptions, having a security or adverse interest in the debtor's property can take an action that will interfere with the debtor or his property, regardless of where the property is located, until the stay is modified or removed. Section 362(a) provides a list of eight kinds of acts and conduct subject to the automatic stay.

Under section 362 of the Bankruptcy Code, a tax audit, a demand for a tax return, or the issuance of a notice and demand for payment for such assessment are not considered a violation of the automatic stay.

The stay of an act against the property of the estate continues, unless modified, until the property is no longer the property of the estate. The stay of any other act continues until the case is closed or dismissed, or the debtor is either granted or denied a discharged. The earliest occurrence of one of these events terminates the stay.

(i) Relief from the Stay.   The court may grant relief after notice and hearing, by terminating, annulling, modifying, or conditioning the stay. The court may grant relief for cause, including the lack of adequate protection of the interest of the secured creditor. With respect to an act against property, relief may be granted under chapter 11 if the debtor does not have an equity in the property and the property is not necessary for an effective reorganization.

Section 361 identifies acceptable ways of providing adequate protection. First, the trustee or debtor may be required to make periodic cash payments to the entity entitled to relief as compensation for the decrease in value of the entity's interest in the property resulting from the stay. Second, the entity may be provided with an additional or replacement lien to the extent that the value of the interest declined as a result of the stay. Finally, the entity may receive the indubitable equivalent of its interest in the property.

The granting of relief when the debtor does not have any equity in the property solves the problem of real property mortgage foreclosures where the bankruptcy court petition is filed just before the foreclosure takes place. It was not intended to apply if the debtor is managing or leasing real property, such as a hotel operation, even though the debtor has no equity, because the property is necessary for an effective reorganization of the debtor.

The automatic stay prohibits a secured creditor from enforcing its rights in property owned by the debtor until the stay is removed. Without this right a creditor could foreclose on the debtor's property, collect the proceeds, invest them, and earn income from the investment, even though a bankruptcy petition has been filed. Since the Bankruptcy Code does not allow this action to be taken, the creditor loses the opportunity to earn income on the proceeds that could have been received on the foreclosure. The courts refer to this as **creditor's opportunity costs.** Four circuit courts have looked at this concept of opportunity cost. Two circuits (ninth and fourth) have ruled that the debtor is entitled to opportunity cost, the eighth circuit ruled that under certain conditions opportunity costs may be paid, and the fifth circuit ruled that opportunity cost need not be paid. In January 1988 the Supreme Court held in *In re Timbers of Inwood Forest Associates* (484 U.S. 365 (1988)) that creditors having collateral with a value less than the amount of the debt are not entitled to interest during the period that their property is tied up in the bankruptcy proceeding. Because of the extended time period during which the creditors' interest in the property is tied up in bankruptcy proceedings, this decision will most likely encourage creditors to properly collateralize their claim and may in limited ways restrict the granting of credit.

If **relief from the stay** is granted, a creditor may foreclose on property on which a lien exists, may continue a state court suit, or may enforce any judgment that might have been obtained before the bankruptcy case.

(ii) Accounting Services—Determining Equity in Property.   The accountant may assist either the debtor or the creditor in determining the value of the collateral to help determine if there is any equity in the property. As a result of the *Timbers* decision the court is more closely considering the prospects for successful reorganization. In cases where there is considerable question about the ability of the debtor to reorganize, courts are now allowing the stay to be removed, providing there is no equity in the property. The debtor, creditors' committee, or secured creditor(s) may ask accountants to provide evidences as to the ability of the debtor to reorganize.

(e) EXECUTORY CONTRACTS AND LEASES.   Section 365(a) provides that the debtor or trustee, subject to court approval, may assume, assign, or reject any executory contract or unexpired lease of the debtor. **Executory contracts** are contracts that are "so far unperformed that the failure of either [the bankrupt or nonbankrupt] to complete performance would constitute a material breach excusing the performance of the other" (see Countryman, 1973). Countryman's definition seems to have been adopted by Congress in the statement that "executory contracts include contracts under which performance remains due to some extent on both sides" (see S. Rep. No. 95-989, 95th Cong., 2nd Sess. (1977)]. However, before a contract can be assumed, § 361 indicates that the debtor or trustee must:

1. Cure the past defaults or provide assurance they will be promptly cured.
2. Compensate the other party for actual pecuniary loss to such property or provide assurance that compensation will be made promptly.
3. Provide adequate assurance of future performance under the contract or lease.

(i) Limitations on Executory Contracts.   To be rejected, the contract must still be an executory contract. For example, the delivery of goods to a carrier before the petition is filed, under terms that provide that the seller's performance is completed upon the delivery of the goods to the carrier, would not be an executory contract in chapter 11. Furthermore, the seller's claim would not be an administrative claim. On the other hand if the terms provide that the goods are received on delivery to the buyer, the seller under U.C.C. § 2-705 would have the right to stop the goods in transit and the automatic stay would not preclude such action. If the goods are delivered, payment for such goods would be an administrative expense.

The damages allowable to the landlord of a debtor from termination of a lease of real property are limited to the greater of 1 year or 15% of the remaining portion of the lease's rent due not to exceed 3 years after the date of filing or surrender whichever is earlier. This formula compensates the landlord while not allowing the claim to be so large as to hurt other creditors of the estate. The damages resulting from the breach of an employment contract are limited to 1 year following the date of the petition or the termination of employment, whichever is earlier.

(ii) Accounting Services—Rejection of Executory Contracts.   The accountant may render several services relating to the rejection of executory contracts, including the following:

1. Estimating the amount of the damages that resulted from the lease rejection for either the debtor or landlord.
2. Evaluating for the landlord the extent to which the debtor has the ability to make the payments required under the lease.
3. Assisting the debtor in determining (or evaluating for the creditor's committee) the leases that should be rejected. To the extent possible, this assessment should be made at the beginning of the case to help reduce the expenses of administration during the chapter 11 case. Amounts paid for rent for period after filing petition to the date of rejection are considered administrative expenses. Each lease needs to be analyzed to determine if there is equity in the lease or if the debtor needs it to successfully reorganize.

(f) AVOIDING POWER.   The Bankruptcy Code grants to the trustee or debtor in possession the right to avoid certain transfers and obligations incurred. For example § 544 allows the trustee to avoid unperfected security interest and other interests in the debtor's property. Thus if the creditor fails to perfect a real estate mortgage, the trustee may be able to avoid that security interest and force the claim to be classified as unsecured rather than secured.

The trustee needs these powers and rights to ensure that actions by the debtor or by creditors in the prepetition period do not interfere with the objective of the bankruptcy laws, to provide for a fair and equal distribution of the debtor's assets through liquidation—or rehabilitation, if this would be better for other creditors involved.

In addition the trustee has the power to avoid preferences, fraudulent transfers, and postpetition transfers.

(g) PREFERENCES.   A **preferential payment** as defined in § 547 of the Bankruptcy Code is a transfer of any of the property of a debtor to or for the benefit of a creditor, for or on account of an antecedent debt made or suffered by the debtor while insolvent and within 90 days before the filing of a petition initiating bankruptcy proceedings, when such transfer enables the creditor to receive a greater percentage of payment than it would receive if the debtor were liquidated under chapter 7. Insolvency is presumed during the 90-day period. A transfer of property to an insider between 90 days and 1 year before the filing of the petition is also considered a preferential payment. Preferences include the payment of money, a transfer of property, assignment of receivables, or the giving of a mortgage on real or personal property.

A preferential payment is not a fraud but rather a legitimate and proper payment of a valid antecedent debt. The voidability of preferences is created by law to effect equality of distribution among all the creditors. The 90-day period (1 year for transactions with insiders) prior to filing the bankruptcy petition has been arbitrarily selected by Congress as the time period during which distributions to the debtor's creditors may be redistributed to all the creditors ratably. During this period, a creditor who accepts a payment is said to have been preferred and may be required to return the amount received and later participate in the enlarged estate to the pro rata extent of its unreduced claim.

(i) Exceptions to Preferential Transfers. Section 547(c) contains eight exceptions to the power the trustee has to avoid preferential transfers. Five of the assumptions are discussed below.

1. *Contemporaneous Exchange.* A transfer intended by the debtor and creditor to have a contemporaneous exchange for new value given to the debtor and that is in fact a substantially contemporaneous exchange is exempted. The purchase of goods or services with a check would not be a preferential payment, provided the check is presented for payment in the normal course of business.

2. *Ordinary Course of Business.* The second exemption protects payments of debts that were incurred in the ordinary course of business or financial affairs of both the debtor and the transferee when the payment is made in the ordinary course of business according to ordinary business terms.

3. *Purchase Money Security Interest.* The third exception exempts security interests granted in exchange for enabling loans when the proceeds are used to finance the purchase of specific personal property. For example, a debtor borrowed $75,000 from a bank to finance a computer system and subsequently purchased the system. The "transfer" of this system as collateral to the bank would not be a preference provided the proceeds were given after the signing of the security agreement, the proceeds were used to purchase the system, and the security interest was perfected within 20 days after the debtor received possession of the property.

4. *New Value.* This exception provides that the creditor is allowed to insulate from preference attack a transfer received to the extent that the creditor replenishes the estate with new value. For example, if a creditor receives $10,000 in preferential payments and subsequently sells to the debtor, on unsecured credit, goods with a value of $6,000, the preference would be only $4,000. The new credit extended must be unsecured and can be netted only against a previous preferential payment, not a subsequent payment.

5. *Inventory and Receivables.* This exception allows a creditor to have a continuing security interest in inventory and receivables (or proceeds) unless the position of the creditor is improved during the 90 days before the petition. If the creditor is an insider, the time period is extended to 1 year. An improvement in position occurs when a transfer causes a reduction in the amount by which the debt secured by the security interest exceeds the value of all security interest for such debt.

   A two-point test is to be used to determine if an improvement in position occurred: The position 90 days (1 year for insiders) prior to the filing of the petition is compared with the position as of the date of the petition. If the security interest is less than 90 days old, then the date on which new value was first given is compared to the position as of the date of the petition. The extent of any improvement caused by transfers to the prejudice of unsecured creditors is considered a preference.

To illustrate this rule, assume that on March 1, the bank made a loan of $700,000 to the debtor secured by a so-called floating lien on inventory. The inventory value was $800,000 at that date. On June 30, the date the debtor filed a bankruptcy petition, the balance of the loan was $600,000 and the debtor had inventory valued at $500,000. It was determined that 90 days prior to June 30 (date petition was filed) the inventory totaled $450,000 and the loan balance was $625,000. In this case there has been an improvement in position of $75,000, ($600,000 − $500,000) − ($625,000 − $450,000) and any transfer of a security interest in inventory or proceeds could be revoked to that extent.

(ii) Accounting Services—Search for Preferential Payments.   The trustee or debtor-in-possession will attempt to recover preferential payments. Section 547(f) provides that the debtor is presumed to be insolvent during the 90-day period prior to bankruptcy. This presumption does not apply to transfers to insiders between 91 days and 1 year prior to bankruptcy. This presumption requires the adverse party to come forth with some evidence to prove the presumption. The burden of proof, however, remains with the party in whose favor the presumption exists. Once this presumption is rebutted, insolvency at the time of payment is necessary and only someone with the training of an accountant is in a position to prove insolvency. The accountant often assists the debtor or trustee in presenting evidence showing whether the debtor was solvent or insolvent at the time payment was made. In cases where new management is in charge of the business or where a trustee has been appointed, the emphasis is often on trying to show that the debtor was insolvent in order to recover the previous payments and increase the size of the estate. The creditors' committee likewise wants to show that the debtor was insolvent at the time of payment to provide a larger basis for payment to unsecured creditors. Of course, the specific creditor recovering the payment looks for evidence to indicate that the debtor was solvent at the time payment was made.

Any payments made within the 90 days preceding the bankruptcy court filing and that are not in the ordinary course of business should be very carefully reviewed to see if the payments were preferences. Suspicious transactions would include anticipations of debt obligations, repayment of officers' loans, repayment of loans that have been personally guaranteed by officers, repayment of loans made to personal friends and relatives, collateral given to lenders, and sales of merchandise made on a countraaccount basis.

In seeking to find voidable preferences, the accountant has two crucial tasks: to determine the earliest date on which insolvency can be established within the 90-day period (1 year for insiders), and to report to the trustee' attorney questionable payments, transfers, or encumbrances that have been made by the debtor after that date. It is then the attorney's responsibility to determine the voidable payments. However, the accountant's role should not be minimized, for it is the accountant who initially determines the suspect payments. See Newton (1994) for a discussion of the procedures to follow in a search for preferences.

(h) FRAUDULENT TRANSFERS.   Fraudulent transfers and **obligations** are defined in § 548 and include transfers that are presumed fraudulent regardless of whether the debtor's actual intent was to defraud creditors. A transfer may be avoided as fraudulent when made within 1 year prior to the filing of the bankruptcy petition, if the debtor made such transfer or incurred such obligation with actual intent to hinder, delay, or defraud existing or real or imagined future creditors. Also avoidable are constructively fraudulent transfers where the debtor received less than a reasonably equivalent value in exchange for such transfer or obligation and (1) was insolvent on the date that such transfer was made or such obligation was incurred, or became insolvent as a result of such transfer or obligation; (2) was engaged in business, or was about to engage in business or a transaction, for which any property remaining with the debtor was an unreasonably small capital; or (3) intended to incur, or believed that the debtor would incur, debts that would burden the debtor's ability to pay as such debts matured.

Under § 544 of the Bankruptcy Code, fraudulent transfers may also be recovered under state law for payments made between 1 and 6 years. Section 546 provides that any action to recover a preference or a fraudulent transfer under § 548 through the Bankruptcy Code or under § 544 through state law must commence the action within two years after the order for relief or if a trustee is appointed during the second year after the petition is filed within one year after the trustee is appointed.

In the determination of fraudulent transfers, insolvency is defined by § 101(32) as occurring when the present fair salable value of the debtor's property is less than the amount required to pay its debts. The fair value of the debtor's property is also reduced by any fraudulently transferred property, and for an individual, by the exempt property under § 522.

(i) LBO as a Fraudulent Transfer.   A fraudulent transfer may occur in a LBO. For example, in a LBO transaction where the assets of the debtor were used to finance the purchase of the debtor's stock and the debtor became insolvent, operated with an unreasonably small capital, or incurred debt beyond the ability to repay, a fraudulent transfer may have occurred. Note that the transfer may have been made without adequate consideration because the debtor corporation received no benefit from the proceeds from the loan that were used to retire former stockholder's stock.

(ii) Accounting Services—Search for Fraudulent Transfers.   It is important for the accountant to ascertain when a fraudulent transfer has in fact occurred because it represents a possible recovery that could increase the value of the estate. It can, under certain conditions, prevent the debtor from obtaining a discharge. To be barred from a discharge as the result of a fraudulent transfer, the debtor must be an individual and the proceedings must be under chapter 7 liquidation or the trustee must be liquidating the estate under a chapter 11 proceeding.

In ascertaining if the debtor has made any fraudulent transfers or incurred fraudulent obligations, the independent accountant would carefully examine transactions with related parties within the year prior to the petition or other required period, look for the sale of large amounts of fixed assets, review liens granted to creditors, and examine all other transactions that appear to have arisen outside the ordinary course of the business.

(i) POSTPETITION TRANSFERS.   Section 549 allows the trustee to avoid certain transfers made after the petition is filed. To be avoidable, transfers must not be authorized either by the court or by an explicit provision of the Bankruptcy Code.

(i) Adequate Value Received.   The trustee can avoid transfers made under § 303(f) and 542(c) of the Bankruptcy Code even though authorized. Section 303(f) authorizes a debtor to continue operating the business before the order for relief in an involuntary case. Section 549 does, however, provide that a transfer made prior to the order for relief is valid to the extent of value received. Thus, the provision of § 549 cautions all persons dealing with a debtor before an order for relief has been granted to evaluate the transfers carefully. Section 542(c) explicitly authorizes certain postpetition transfers of real property of the estate made in good faith by an entity without actual knowledge or notice of the commencement of the case.

(ii) Accounting Services—Preventing Unauthorized Transfers.   To prevent unauthorized transfers, the procedures that the accountant should see are operative include the following:

1. Establishing procedures to ensure that prepetition debt payments are made only with proper authorization.
2. Designating an individual to handle all requests for prepetition debt payments.

3. Acquainting accounting personnel with techniques that might be used to obtain unauthorized prepetition debt payments.

(j) SETOFFS. Setoff is that right existing between two parties to net their respective debts where each party, as a result of unrelated transactions, owes the other an ascertained amount. The right to setoff is an accepted practice in the business community today. When one of the two parties is insolvent and files a bankruptcy court petition, the right to setoff has special meaning. Once the petition is filed, the debtor may compel the creditor to pay the debt owed and the creditor may in turn receive only a small percentage of the claim—unless the Bankruptcy Code permits the setoff.

The Bankruptcy Code gives the creditor the right to offset a mutual debt, providing both the debt and the credit arose before the commencement of the case. Major restriction on the use of setoff prevents the creditor from unilaterally making the setoff after a petition is filed. The right to setoff is subject to the automatic stay provisions of § 362 and the use of property under § 363. Thus, a debtor must obtain relief from the automatic stay before proceeding with the setoff. This automatic stay and the right to use the amount subject to setoff is possible only when the trustee or debtor in possession provides the creditor with adequate protection. If adequate protection—normally in the form of periodic cash payments, additional or replacement collateral, or other methods that will provide the creditor with the indubitable equivalent of its interest—is not provided, then the creditor may proceed with the offset as provided in § 553.

(i) Early Setoff Penalty. Section 553(b) contains a penalty for those creditors who, when they see the financial problems of the debtor and threat of the automatic stay, elect to offset their claim prior to the petition. The Code precludes the setoff of any amount that is a betterment of the creditor's position during the 90 days prior to the filing of the petition. Any improvement in position may be recovered by the debtor in possession or trustee. The amount to be recovered is the amount by which the insufficiency on the date of offset is less than the insufficiency 90 days before the filing of the petition. If no insufficiency exists 90 days before the filing of the petition, then the first date within the 90-day period where there is an insufficiency should be used. **Insufficiency** is defined as the amount by which a claim against the debtor exceeds a mutual debt owing to the debtor by the holder of such claim. The amount recovered is considered an unsecured claim.

(ii) Accounting Services—Setoffs. In addition to developing a schedule that helps determine the amount of the penalty, the accountant may assist in determining the amount of debt outstanding.

(k) RECLAMATION. One area where the avoiding power of the trustee is limited is in a request for reclamation. Section 546(c) provides that under certain conditions the creditor has the right to reclaim goods if the debtor received the goods while insolvent. To **reclaim** these goods, the seller must demand in writing, within 10 days after their receipt by the debtor, that the goods be returned. The court can deny reclamation, assuming the right is established, only if the claim is considered an administrative expense or if the claim is secured by a lien. A creditor faces some problems in attempting to reclaim goods. One is that the request must be made within 10 days. If the 10-day period expires after the commencement of the case, the seller may reclaim the goods within 20 days after the receipt of the goods by the buyer. Requests made after this time period are denied.

Another problem is that the right of reclamation under UCC § 2-702 is basically a right to obtain the physical return of particular goods in the hands of the debtor. If the goods have been sold or used, the ability to obtain the goods may be limited. For example, it is doubtful that the seller could reclaim goods that were sold by the debtor to a purchaser in good faith that had no knowledge of the debtor's financial problems. Also, the reclamation rights of the seller are subject to any superior right of other creditors, which most likely would include the good faith purchaser or buyer in the ordinary course of business.

The court may deny reclamation to a seller that has the right to the reclamation only if the court either grants an administrative expense for the amount of the claim or secures such claim with a lien.

(l) U.S. TRUSTEE.   Chapter 30 of Title 28, U.S. Code, provides for the establishment of the U.S. trustee program. The Attorney General is responsible for appointing one U.S. trustee in each of the 21 regions, and one or more assistant U.S. trustees perform the supervisory and appointing functions formerly handled by bankruptcy judges. They are the principal administrative officers of the bankruptcy system. The judicial districts of Alabama and North Carolina were not to be a part of the expansion of the U.S. Trustee program until 1992. The Judicial Improvements Act of 1990 (P.L. 101-650) extended the time period in which the six districts must be a part of the system to October 1, 2002. In these districts, some of the functions performed by the U.S. trustee in other districts are assigned to an administrator in the bankruptcy court.

The U.S. trustee establishes, maintains, and supervises a panel of private trustees that are eligible and available to serve as trustee in cases under chapter 7 or 11. Also, the U.S. trustee supervises the administration of the estate and the trustees in cases under chapter 7, 11, 12 or 13. The intent is not for the U.S. trustee system to replace private trustees in chapters 7 and 11. Rather, the system should relieve the bankruptcy judges of certain administrative and supervisory tasks and thus help to eliminate any institutional bias or the appearance of any such bias that may have existed in the prior bankruptcy system.

The U.S. trustees are responsible for the administration of cases. They appoint the committees of creditors with unsecured claims and also appoint any other committees of creditors or stockholders authorized by the court. If the court deems it necessary to appoint a trustee or examiner, a U.S. trustee makes this appointment (subject to court approval) and also petitions the court to authorize such an appointment.

U.S. trustees monitor applications for compensation and reimbursement for officers and accountants and other professionals retained in the case, raising objections when deemed appropriate. Other responsibilities include monitoring plans and disclosure statements, creditors' committees, and the progress of the case.

39.4 HANDLING OF CLAIMS UNDER CHAPTER 11

A claim antedating the filing of the petition that is not a priority claim or that is not secured by the pledge of property is classified as an **unsecured claim.** Claims where the value of the security interest is less than the amount of the claims are divided into a secured and unsecured part.

(a) PROOF OF CLAIMS.   A proof of claim or interest is deemed filed in a chapter 11 case provided the claim or interest is listed in the schedules filed by the debtor, unless the claim or interest is listed as disputed, contingent, or unliquidated. A creditor is thus not required to file a proof of claim if it agrees with the debt listed in the schedules. It is, however, advisable for creditors to file a proof of claim in most situations. Creditors who for any reason disagree with the amount admitted on the debtor's schedules, such as allowable prepetition interest on their claims, or creditors desiring to give a power of attorney to a trade association or lawyer, should always prepare and file a complete proof of claim. Special attention must also be devoted to secured claims that are undersecured.

(b) UNDERSECURED CLAIMS.   Section 506 provides that if a creditor is undersecured, the claim will be divided into two parts. The first part is secured to the extent of the value of the collateral or to the extent of the amount of funds subject to setoff. The balance of the claim is considered unsecured. The value to be used to determine the amount of the secured claim is, according to § 506(a), to "be determined in light of the purpose of the valuation and of the proposed disposition or use of such property, and in conjunction with any hearing on such disposition or use or on a plan affecting such creditors' interest." Bankruptcy Rule 3012 provides that any party in interest may petition the court to determine the value of a secured claim.

Thus, the approach used to value property subject to a lien for a chapter 7 may be different from that for a chapter 11 proceeding. Even within a chapter 11 case, property may be valued differently. For example, fixed assets that are going to be sold because of the discontinuance of operations may be assigned liquidation values, whereas assets that will continue to be used by the debtor may be assigned going concern values. Although courts have to determine value on a case-by-case basis, it is clear that the **value** is to be determined in light of the purpose of the valuation and the proposed disposition or use of the property.

Section 1111(b) allows a secured claim to be treated as a claim with recourse against the debtor in chapter 11 proceedings (that is, where the debtor is liable for any deficiency between the value of the collateral and the balance due on the debt) whether the claim is nonrecourse by agreement or by applicable law. This preferred status terminates if the property securing the loan is sold under § 363 or is to be sold under the terms of the plan, or if the class of which the secured claim is a part elects application of § 1111(b)(2).

Another available section under § 1111(b) is that a class of undersecured creditors can elect to have its entire claim considered secured. A class of creditors will normally be only one creditor. For example, in chapter 11 cases where most of the assets are pledged, very little may be available for unsecured creditors after paying administrative expenses. Thus, the creditor might find it advisable to make the § 1111(b)(2) election. On the other hand, if there will be a payment to unsecured creditors of approximately 75 cents per dollar of debt, the creditor may not want to make this election.

The purpose of the election is to provide adequate protection to holders of secured claims where the holder is of the opinion that the collateral is undervalued. Also, if the treatment of the part of the debt that is accorded unsecured status is so unattractive, the holder may be willing to waive his unsecured deficiency claims. The class of creditors making this election has the right to receive full payment for its claims over time. If the members of the class do not approve the plan, the court may confirm the plan as long as the plan provides that each member of the class receives deferred cash payments totaling at least the allowed amount of the claim. However, the present value of these payments as of the effective date of the plan must be at least equal to the value of the creditors' interest in the collateral. Thus, a creditor who makes the election under § 1111(b)(2) has the right to receive full payment over time, but the value of that payment is only required to equal the value of the creditor's interest in the collateral.

(c) ADMINISTRATIVE EXPENSES.   The actual, necessary costs of preserving the estate, including wages, salaries, and commissions for services rendered after the commencement of the case, are considered administrative expense. Any tax including fines or penalties is allowed unless it relates to a tax-granted preference under § 507(a)(8). Compensation awarded a professional person, including accountants, for postpetition services is an expense of administration. Expenses incurred in an involuntary case subsequent to the filing of the petition but prior to the appointment of a trustee or the order for relief are not considered administrative expenses. They are, however, granted second priority under § 507. Administrative expenses of a chapter 11 case that is converted to chapter 7 are paid only after payment of chapter 7 administrative expenses.

(d) PRIORITIES.   Section 507 provides for the following priorities:

1. Administrative expenses.
2. Unsecured claims in an involuntary case arising after commencement of the proceedings but before an order of relief is granted.

3. Wages earned within 90 days prior to filing the petition (or the cessation of the business) to the extent of $4,000 per individual.

4. Unsecured claims to employee benefit plans arising within 180 days prior to filing petition limited to $4,000 times the number of employees covered by the plan less the amount paid in (3) above and the amount previously paid on behalf of such employees.

5. Unsecured claims of grain producers against a grain storage facility or of fishermen against a fish storage or processing facility to the extent of $4,000.

6. Unsecured claims of individuals to the extent of $1,800 from deposits of money for purchase, lease, or rental of property or purchase of services not delivered or provided.

7. Claims for debts to a spouse or former spouse or child for alimony, maintenance or support payments.

8. Unsecured tax claims of governmental units:

    a. Income or gross receipts tax, provided tax return was due (including extension) within 3 years prior to filing petition, tax is assessable after commencement of the case; or tax was assessed within 240 days before petition was filed.

    b. Property tax last payable without penalty within 1 year prior to filing petition.

    c. Withholding taxes.

    d. Employment tax on wages, and so forth, due within 3 years prior to the filing of the petition.

    e. Excise tax due within 3 years prior to the filing of the petition.

    f. Customs duty on merchandise imported within 1 year prior to the filing of the petition.

    g. Penalties related to a type of claim above in compensation for actual pecuniary loss.

9. Allowed unsecured claims based on any commitment by the debtor to the Federal depository institutions regulatory agency (or predecessors to such agency), to maintain the capital of an insured depository institution.

Priority claims in a Chapter 11 case must be provided for in the plan.

(e) PROCESSING OF CLAIMS.   Several accounting firms and other businesses have developed models to handle the processing of claims of both small and large debtors. Some of their features include:

1. Capture of all the various formats of claims needed by the bankruptcy court.

2. Information needed for management to review and evaluate each claim.

3. Mailing lists and labels.

4. Creditor statements.

5. On-line update and inquiry capability.

6. Modeling and decision analysis capability that enables management to evaluate settlement alternatives efficiently.

One system uses a multifield data base to help debtors deal with the complexities of a bankruptcy. Creditors' files can be sorted in terms of classes of creditors, priorities of claims, and so on, and then alphabetically within these categories. Notices sent to creditors include all the necessary information, such as the amount of a claim and its current status. Ongoing information that changes over time is constantly updated. This could include the extent to which proofs of claim differ from the recorded debt, the assessment of market values of collateral pledged as security, other assets that are not pledged as security, distributions made during the course of a chapter 11 case, and changes to or withdrawals of claims. Automatically prepared and mailed notices keep creditors current on the proceedings of a case. The system, through automatic mailings, answers telephone inquiries as they are entered.

39.5 OPERATING UNDER CHAPTER 11

No order is necessary under the Bankruptcy Code for the debtor to operate the business in chapter 11. Sections 1107(a) and 1108 grant the debtor all the rights, powers, and duties of a trustee, except the right to compensation under § 330, and provide that the trustee may operate the business unless the court directs otherwise. Thus, the debtor will continue to operate the business unless a party in interest requests that the court appoint a trustee. Until action is taken by management to correct the problems that caused the adverse financial condition, the business will most likely continue to operate at a loss. If the creditors believe new management is necessary to correct the problem, they will press for a change in management or the appointment of a trustee. In most large bankruptcies as well as in many smaller cases, the management is replaced, often by **turnaround specialists,** who have particular expertise in taking over troubled companies. They often eliminate the unprofitable aspects of the company's operations, reduce overhead, and find additional financing as part of the turnaround process. Once the plan has been confirmed, turnaround specialists frequently move on to other troubled companies. In small cases where management is also the stockholders, creditors are apt to be uncomfortable with existing management, which may have created the problems.

(a) USE OF PROPERTY.   The debtor or trustee must be able to use a secured party's collateral, or in most situations there would be no alternative but to liquidate the business. Section 363(c) gives the trustee or debtor the right to use, sell, or lease property of the estate in the ordinary course of business without a notice and a hearing. As a result of this provision the debtor may continue to sell inventory and receivables and use raw materials in production without notice to secured creditors and without court approval. The use, sale, or lease of the estate's property other than in the ordinary course of business is allowed only after notice and an opportunity for a hearing.

(i) Cash Collateral.   One restriction on the use of the property of the bankruptcy estate is placed on the trustee or debtor where cash collateral is involved. **Cash collateral** is cash, negotiable instruments, documents of title, securities, deposit accounts, or other cash equivalents where the estate and someone else have an interest in the property. Also included would be the proceeds of noncash collateral, such as inventory and accounts receivable and proceeds, products, offspring, and rents, profits, or property subject to a security interest, if converted to proceeds of the type defined as cash collateral, provided the proceeds are subject to the prepetition security interest.

To use cash collateral, the creditor with the interest must consent to its use, or the court, after notice and hearing, must authorize its use. The court may authorize the use, sale, or lease of cash collateral at a preliminary hearing if there is a reasonable likelihood that the debtor in possession will prevail at the final hearing. The Bankruptcy Code also provides that the court is to act promptly for a request to use cash collateral.

(ii) Accounting Services—Assisting Debtor in Providing Information to Secured Lender.
In many cases, a company cannot operate unless it can obtain use of its cash collateral. For example, cash in bank accounts subject to setoff or collections from pledged receivables and inventory prior to the filing of the petition are not available for use until the company obtains the consent of the appropriate secured creditor or of the court.

Thus, an immediate concern of many companies that need to file a chapter 11 petition is how to procure enough cash to operate for the first week or so after filing the petition. Often the best way to obtain the use of the cash is to get approval from the secured creditor prior to the filing of the petition. Accountants can work with the debtor in putting together information for the secured lender that may result in the pledge of additional property or an extension of a receivable or inventory financing agreement for the release of cash to allow operation of the business once the petition is filed.

(b) OBTAINING CREDIT.   In most chapter 11 proceedings the debtor must obtain additional financing in order to continue the business. Although the debtor was allowed to obtain credit under prior law, the power granted to the debtor under the Bankruptcy Code is broader. Section 364(a) allows the debtor to obtain unsecured debt and to incur unsecured obligations in the ordinary course while operating the business. This right is automatic unless the court orders otherwise. Also the holder of these claims is entitled to first priority as administrative expenses.

If the debtor is unable to obtain the necessary unsecured debt under § 364(a), the court may authorize the obtaining of credit and the incurring of debt by granting special priority for claims. These priorities may include the following:

1. Giving priority over any or all administrative expenses.
2. Securing the debt with a lien on unencumbered property.
3. Securing the debt with a junior lien on encumbered property.

Debtor-in-possession (DIP) financing may be obtained from the existing lender or from a new lender. Most all major banks are involved in DIP financing as well as several other financial entities, including funds that are established to make loans to companies in chapter 11 and on emergence from chapter 11. At times existing creditors will lend to the chapter 11 debtor in order to prevent other lenders from obtaining a position that may be superior to that of the existing lender. The bankruptcy court may allow the debtor to prime* the position of the existing lender. However, for the court to authorize the obtaining of credit with a lien on encumbered property that is senior or equal to the existing lien, the debtor must not be able to obtain credit by other means and the existing lien holder must be adequately protected.

Credit obtained other than in the ordinary course of business must be authorized by the court after notice and a hearing. Where there is some question whether the credit is related to the ordinary course of business, the lender should require court approval.

(c) APPOINTMENT OF TRUSTEES.   The Bankruptcy Code provides that a trustee can be appointed in certain situations based on facts in the case and not related to the size of the company or the amount of unsecured debt outstanding. The trustee is appointed only at the request of a party in interest after a notice and hearing. A party in interest includes the debtor, the trustee (in other contexts), creditors' or stockholders' committees, creditors, stockholders, or indenture trustees. Also, a U.S. trustee, while not a party in interest, may petition the court for an appointment of a trustee.

Section 1104(a) states that a trustee be appointed:

1. for cause, including fraud, dishonesty, incompetence, or gross mismanagement of the affairs of the debtor by current management, either before or after the commencement of the case, or similar cause, but not including the number of holders of securities of the debtor or the amount of assets or liabilities of the debtor; or
2. if such appointment is in the interest of creditors, any equity security holders, and other interests of the estate, without regard to the number of holders of securities of the debtor or the amount of assets or liabilities of the debtor.

---

*Priming allows a new lender to obtain a lien in all or some of the property of the debtor that is above that of the existing lender for the new funds lent to the debtor.

The U.S. trustee is responsible for the appointment of the trustee from a panel of qualified trustees, once the appointment has been authorized by the court. It also appears that the U.S. trustee would have the right to replace trustees who fail to perform their functions properly.

The Bankruptcy Code, as originally enacted, provided that in a chapter 7 case, the interim trustee appointed by the U.S. trustee would serve as the trustee unless a trustee is elected by a majority of at least 20% of the unsecured creditors voting in an election at a meeting of creditors under section 341 of the Bankruptcy Code. In most chapter 7 cases the interim trustee serves as the trustee. The Bankruptcy Reform Act of 1994 modified section 1104 of the Bankruptcy Code to provide that on request of a party in interest (made within 30 days after the court authorized the appointment of a trustee), the U.S. trustee must call a meeting of unsecured creditors for the purpose of electing a chapter 11 trustee. This change might encourage more creditors to petition the court for the appointment of a trustee in a chapter 11 case because the creditors now have some impact as to who is appointed.

(d) APPOINTMENT OF EXAMINER.   Under the Bankruptcy Code, the trustee's major functions are to (1) operate the business, and (2) conduct an investigation of the debtor's affairs. Under certain conditions it may be best to leave the current management in charge of the business, without resolving the need for the investigation of the debtor. The Code provides for the appointment of an examiner to perform this function. Section 1104(b) states that if a trustee is not appointed:

> . . . [O]n request of a party in interest, and after notice and hearing, the court shall order the appointment of an examiner to conduct such an investigation of the debtor as is appropriate, including an investigation of any allegations of fraud, dishonesty, incompetence, misconduct, mismanagement, or irregularity in the management of the affairs of the debtor of or by current or former management of the debtor, if
>
> 1. Such appointment is in the interest of creditors, any equity security holders, and other interests of the estates; or
> 2. The debtor's fixed, liquidated, unsecured debts, other than debts for goods, services, or taxes, or owing to an insider, exceed $5 million.

(i) Functions of Examiner.   The function of the examiner is to conduct an investigation into the actions of the debtor, including fraud, dishonesty, mismanagement of the financial condition of the debtor and the operation of the business, and the desirability of the continuation of such business. The report is to be filed with the court and given to any creditors' committee, stockholders' committees, or other entities designated by the court. In addition to these two provisions, § 1106(b) also states that an examiner may perform other functions as directed by the court. In some cases the court has expanded the role of the examiner. For example, the bankruptcy judges may prefer to see additional controls exercised over the management of the debtor, but may not see the need to incur the costs of the appointment of a trustee. These functions are assigned to the examiner.

(ii) Accountants as Examiners.   Accountants may serve as examiners, and in some regions U.S. trustees have expressed a preference for appointing accountants in certain situations. Where a financial investigation is needed, an accountant may be the most qualified person to perform as an examiner. In many cases where the role of the examiner has been expanded, accountants were serving as examiners.

(e) OPERATING STATEMENTS.   Several different types of reports are required while the debtor is operating the business in a chapter 11 reorganization proceeding. The nature of the reports and the time period in which they are issued depend to some extent on local rules and on the type of internal controls of the debtor and the extent to which large losses are anticipated.

Districts establish local bankruptcy rules that generally apply to all cases filed in that particular district. These rules cover some of the procedural matters that relate to the handling of a bankruptcy case, including appearance before the court, forms of papers filed with court, assignment of case, administration of case, employment of professionals, and operating statements. The rules for the filing of operating statements have become primarily the responsibility of the U.S. trustee and, as a result, the specific procedures for these statements are those of the U.S. trustee.

One statement required by all regions is an operating statement—profit and loss statement. This statement may include, in addition to the revenue and expense accounts needed to determine net income on the accrual basis, an aging of accounts payable (excluding prepetition debts) and accounts receivable, status of payments to secured creditors, analysis of tax payments, analysis of insurance payments and coverage, and summary of bankruptcy fees that have been paid or are due.

The U.S. trustee also requires cash receipts and disbursement statements. In some cases it may be necessary to prepare this statement for each bank account of the debtor. For example the U.S. trustee for the central district of California requires that the debtor, in addition to the regular account, establish separate accounts for payroll and taxes. Separate cash receipts and disbursements statements are also required for each account.

An independent accountant may assist the debtor in the preparation of these monthly operating reports. See section 39.7(c) of this chapter.

(f) REPORTING IN CHAPTER 11. In November of 1990, the AICPA issued Statement of Position (SOP) No. 90–7, *Financial Reporting by Entities in Reorganization Under the Bankruptcy Code,* which represents the first major pronouncement to be issued on financial reporting by companies in bankruptcy. The SOP applies to any company that files a chapter 11 petition after December 31, 1990. In addition, the provisions regarding fresh start reporting apply to any entity that has its plan confirmed after June 30, 1991, even though the chapter 11 petition was filed before January 1, 1991. Earlier use of the provisions of the SOP is encouraged for companies still in chapter 11.

The SOP was designed to eliminate some of the significant divergences in accounting for bankruptcies and to increase the relevance of financial information provided to debtors, creditors, stockholders, and other interested parties who make decisions regarding the reorganization, especially the reorganization plan, of the debtor. The SOP applies to financial reporting by companies that have filed chapter 11 petitions and expect to reorganize as going concerns, and to companies that emerge from chapter 11 under confirmed plans. It does not apply to companies that are restructuring their debt outside of chapter 11 or to those that adopt chapter 11 plans of liquidation. It deals with how to report the activities of the chapter 11 company during the reorganization proceeding and how to report the emergence of the company from chapter 11.

A major objective of financial statements issued by the debtor in chapter 11 should be to reflect the financial evolution of the debtor during the proceeding. Thus, for financial statements issued in the year the petition is filed and in subsequent years, a distinction should be made between transactions and events directly associated with the reorganization, as opposed to those related to the ongoing operations of the business. This principle is reflected in several significant areas of the financial statements.

(i) Balance Sheet. Paragraphs 23–26 of the SOP provide specific guidance for the preparation of the balance sheet during the reorganization.

Liabilities subject to compromise should be separated from those that are not and from postpetition liabilities. Liabilities that are subject to compromise include unsecured claims, undersecured claims and fully secured claims that may be impaired under a plan. Paragraph 23 indicates that if there is some uncertainty as to whether a secured claim is undersecured or will be impaired under the plan, the entire amount should be included with prepetition claims subject to compromise.

In view of this, it is expected that most prebankruptcy claims will be reported initially as liabilities subject to compromise. There are a number of reasons for this. For example, at the time the balance sheet is prepared the collateral may not have been appraised. Also, it might be determined as the case progresses that estimated cash flows from property are less than anticipated. All security interests may not have been fully perfected. Due to these and other factors, it is not unusual for claims which appeared fully secured at the onset of a case to be found to be compromised during the proceedings.

Paragraph 26 also indicates that circumstances arising during the reorganization may require a change in the classification of liabilities between those subject to compromise and those not subject to compromise.

The principal categories (such as priority claims, trade debt, debentures, institutional claims, etc.) of the claims subject to compromise should be disclosed in the notes to the financial statements. Note that the focus of the reporting requirement is on providing information about the nature of the claims rather than whether the claims are current or noncurrent.

Liabilities that are not subject to compromise consist of postpetition liabilities and liabilities not expected to be impaired under the plan. They are reported in the normal manner and thus should be segregated into current and noncurrent categories if a classified balance sheet is presented.

Liabilities that may be affected by the plan should be reported at the amount expected to be allowed even though they may be settled for a lesser amount. For example, once the allowed amount of an existing claim is determined or can be estimated, the carrying value of the debt should be adjusted to reflect that amount. Paragraph 25 provides that debt discounts or premiums as well as debt issue costs should be viewed as valuations of the related debt. When the allowed claim differs from the net carrying amount of the debt, the discount or premium and deferred issue costs should be adjusted to the extent necessary to report the debt at the allowed amount of the claim. If these adjustments are not enough, then the carrying value of the debt will be adjusted. The gain or loss resulting from the entries to record these adjustments is to be reported as a reorganization item as described below.

Prepetition claims that become known after the petition is filed, such as a claim arising from the rejection of a lease, should also be reported on the basis of the expected amount of the allowed claim and not at an estimate of the settlement amount. Paragraph 48 of the SOP suggests that these claims should be reported at the amount allowed by the court because that is the amount of the liability until it is settled and the use of the allowed amount is consistent with the amounts at which other prepetition liabilities are stated.

FASB Statement No. 5, *Accounting for Contingencies,* applies to the process of determining the expected amount of an allowed claim. Claims that are not subject to reasonable estimation should be disclosed in the notes to the financial statements based on the provisions of FASB Statement No. 5. Once the accrual provisions of FASB Statement No. 5 are satisfied, the claims should be recorded.

(ii) Statement of Operations.   The objective of reporting during the chapter 11 case is to present the results of operations of the reporting entity and to clearly separate those activities related to the normal operations of the business from those related to the reorganization. Thus, revenues, expenses (including professional fees), realized gains and losses, and provisions for losses resulting from the chapter 11 reorganization and restructuring of the business should be separately reported. According to paragraph 27 of SOP No. 90-7, items related to the reorganization (except for the reporting of discontinued operations which are already reported separately) should be reported in a separate category within the income (loss) from operations section of the statement of operations. Appendix A in the SOP 90-7 contains an example of the form to use for operating statements issued during a chapter 11 case. The part of the operating statement that relates to the reporting of reorganization items is as follows:

Earnings before reorganization items and income tax benefits	47
Reorganization items:	
Loss on disposal of facility	(60)
Professional fees	(50)
Provision for rejected executory contracts	(10)
Interest earned on accumulated cash resulting from chapter 11 proceeding	1
	(119)
Loss before income tax benefit and discontinued operations	(72)

Note that the reader of the statement of operations is able to determine the amount of income generated from continuing operations without the impact of the reorganization being reflected in these totals. While it will involve some judgment on the part of management to determine the part of income that relates to ongoing operations, a reasonable estimate of the segregation will be much more beneficial to the reader than including all items in the same category as is current practice.

A summary of the provisions relating to the operating statements follows:

1. Gains or losses as a result of restructuring or disposal of assets directly related to the reorganization are reported as a reorganization item (unless the disposal meets the requirement for discontinued operations). The gains or losses include the gain or loss on disposal of the assets, related employee costs and other charges related to the disposal of assets or restructuring of operations. Note that the reporting of a reduction in business activity does not result in reclassification of revenues or expenses identified with the assets sold or abandoned, unless the transaction is classified as a disposal of a business segment under APB Opinion No. 30.

2. Professional fees are expensed as incurred and reported as a reorganization item.

3. Interest income that was earned in chapter 11 that would not have been earned but for the proceeding is reported as a reorganization item.

4. Interest expense should be reported only to the extent that it will be paid during the proceeding or to the extent that it may be allowed as a priority, secured or unsecured claim. The extent to which the reported interest expense differs from the contractual rate should be reflected in the notes to the operating statement or shown parenthetically on the face of the operating statement (the SEC prefers the latter). Under current practice, some debtors have accrued interest even though this procedure has been somewhat questionable. This practice should cease under the new SOP.

5. Income from debt discharge in a chapter 11 case where fresh start reporting is required should be shown as an extraordinary item. Paragraph 41 of the SOP indicates that this should also be the case for debtors not qualified for fresh start reporting. Although most debtors have already been reporting the income from debt discharge as an extraordinary item, it is now clear that this is the acceptable practice.

(iii) Statement of Cash Flows.   Paragraph 31 of the SOP indicates that reorganization items should be disclosed separately within the operating, investing and financing categories of the statement of cash flows. The SOP also indicates that reorganization items related to operating cash flows are better reflected if the direct method is used to prepare the statement of cash flows. An example of the statement of cash flows issued during a chapter 11 case using the direct approach is found in Appendix A of the SOP.

The SOP indicates that if the indirect method is used, the details of the operating cash receipts and payments resulting from the reorganization should be disclosed in a supplementary schedule or in the notes to the financial statement. The footnote or supplementary schedule should include the information from the reorganization section of the statement of cash flows that is presented above.

It would also be acceptable to reflect this information in the cash flow statement as shown next:

Net loss	$(118)
Adjustment to determine net cash provided by operating items before reorganization items:	
Depreciation	20
Loss on disposal of facility	60
Provision for rejection of executory contracts	10
Loss on discontinued operations	56
Increase in postpetition liabilities and other liabilities	250
Increase in accounts receivable	(180)
Reorganization items	49
Net cash provided by operating activities before reorganization items	147
Reorganization items:	
Interest received on cash accumulated because of the chapter 11 proceeding	1
Professional fees paid for services rendered in connection with the chapter 11 proceeding	(50)
Net cash provided by reorganization items	(49)
Net cash provided by operating activities	98

Any reorganization items included in financing and investing activities should also be disclosed separately.

39.6 CHAPTER 11 PLAN

The accountant advises and gives suggestions to the debtor and attorney in drawing up a plan. Section 1121 of the Bankruptcy Code provides that only the debtor may file a plan of reorganization during the first 120 days of the case (unless a trustee has been appointed). This breathing period permits the debtor to hold lawsuits and foreclosures in status quo and to determine economic causes of its financial predicament while developing a plan. Using the schedules of assets and liabilities, statement of affairs, and past and projected financial statements, the debtor and its accountant examine the liabilities of the debtor and the value of the business and explore sources of funding for the plan such as enhanced profitability, partial liquidation, issuing debt securities, or outside capitalization. They outline the classes of debt that cannot be deferred or reduced and negotiate with the rest.

(a) CLASSIFICATION OF CLAIMS.   Section 1122 provides that claims or interests can be divided into classes provided each claim or interest is substantially similar to the others of such class. In addition, a separate class of unsecured claims may be established consisting of claims that are below or reduced to an amount the court approves as reasonable and necessary for administrative convenience. For example, claims of less than $1,000, or those creditors who will accept $1,000 as payment in full of their claim, may be placed in one class and the claimants will receive the lesser of $1,000 or the amount of their claim. All creditors or equity holders in the same class are treated the same, but separate classes may be treated differently.

Generally, all unsecured claims, including claims arising from rejection of executory contracts or unexpired leases, are placed in the same class except for administrative expenses. They may, however, be divided into different classes if separate classification is justified. The Bankruptcy Code does not require placing all claims that are substantially the same in the same class.

Courts have stated that § 1122(a) "does not require that similar claims must be grouped together, but merely that any group created must be homogeneous."

(b) DEVELOPMENT OF PLAN. The items that may be included in the plan are listed in § 1123. Certain items are listed as mandatory and others are discretionary. The mandatory provisions are:

1. Designate classes of claims and interests.
2. Specify any class of claims or interest that is not impaired under the plan.
3. Specify the treatment of any class of claims or interest that is impaired under the plan.
4. Provide the same treatment for each claim or interest in a particular class unless the holders agree to less favorable treatment.
5. Provide adequate means for the plans' implementation, such as:
   - Retention by the debtor of all or any part of the property of the estate.
   - Transfer of all or any part of the property of the estate to one or more entities.
   - Merger or consolidation of the debtor with one or more persons.
   - Sale of all or any part of the property of the estate, either subject to or free of any lien, or the distribution of all or any part of the property of the estate among those having an interest in such property of the estate.
   - Satisfaction or modification of any lien.
   - Cancellation or modification of any indenture or similar instrument.
   - Curing or waiving any default.
   - Extension of a maturity date or a change in an interest rate or other term of outstanding securities.
   - Amendment of the debtor's charter.
   - Issuance of securities of the debtor, or of any entity involved in a merger or transfer of the debtor's business for cash, for property, for existing securities, or in exchange for claims or interests, or for any other appropriate purpose.
6. Provide for the inclusion in the charter of the debtor, if the debtor is a corporation, or of any corporation referred to in (5) above, of a provision prohibiting the issuance of nonvoting equity securities, and providing, as to the several classes of securities possessing voting power, an appropriate distribution of such power among such classes, including, in the case of any class of equity securities having a preference over another class of equity securities with respect to dividends, adequate provisions for the election of directors representing such preferred class in the event of default in the payment of such dividends.
7. Contain only provisions that are consistent with the interests of creditors and stockholders and with public policy with respect to the selection of officers, directors, or trustee under the plan.

In addition to these requirements, the plan may also:

1. Impair or leave unimpaired any class of unsecured or secured claims or interests.
2. Provide for the assumption, rejection, or assignment of executory contracts or leases.
3. Provide for settlement or adjustment of any claim or interest of the debtor or provide for the retention and enforcement by the debtor of any claim or interest.
4. Provide for the sale of all of the property of the debtor and the distribution of the proceeds to the creditors and stockholders.
5. Include any other provision not inconsistent with the provisions of the Bankruptcy Code.

In determining the classes of creditors' claims or stockholders' interests that must approve the plan, it is first necessary to determine if the class is **impaired.** Section 1124 states that a class of claims or interest is impaired under the plan, unless the plan leaves unaltered the legal, equitable, and contractual rights of a class, cures defaults that led to acceleration of debts, or pays in cash the full amount of their claims.

(c) DISCLOSURE STATEMENT.   A party cannot solicit the acceptance or rejection of a plan from creditors and stockholders affected by the plan unless they receive a written disclosure statement containing adequate information as approved by the court. Section 1125(b) requires that the court must approve this disclosure statement, after notice and a hearing, as containing adequate information.

(i) Definition of Adequate Information.   Section 1125(a) states that adequate information means information of a kind, and in sufficient detail, as far as is reasonably practicable in light of the records, that would enable a hypothetical reasonable investor typical of holders of claims or interests of the relevant class to make an informed judgment about the plan. This definition contains two parts. First it defines adequate information and then it sets a standard against which the information is measured. It must be the kind of information that a typical investor of the relevant class, not one that has special information, would need to make an informed judgment about the plan. Section 1125(a)(1) provides that adequate information need not include information about other possible proposed plans.

(ii) Content.   As noted above, the information disclosed in the statement should be adequate to allow the creditor or stockholder to make an informed judgment about the plan. The following paragraphs describe the types of information that might be included.

1. *Introduction.* The statement should provide information about voting on the plan, as well as background information about the debtor and the nature of the debtor's operations.
2. *Management.* It is important to identify the management that will operate the debtor on emergence from bankruptcy and to provide a summary of their background.
3. *Summary of the Plan of Reorganization.* Typical investors want to receive a description of the terms of the plan and the reasons the plan's proponents believe a favorable vote is advisable.
4. *Reorganization Value.* Included in the disclosure statement should be the reorganization value of the entity that will emerge from bankruptcy. One of the first, as well as one of the most difficult, steps in reaching agreement on the terms of a plan is determining the value of the reorganized entity. Once the parties—debtor, unsecured creditors' committee, secured creditors, and shareholders—agree on the reorganization value, this value is then allocated among the creditors and equity holders. Thus, before determining the amount that unsecured creditors, secured creditors, or equity holders will receive, it is necessary to determine the reorganization value. An unsecured creditors' committee or another representative of creditors or equity holders is generally unable, and often unwilling, to agree to the terms of a plan without any knowledge of the emerging entity's reorganization value. It also appears that if this value is needed by the parties that must agree on the terms of a plan, it is also needed by each unsecured creditor to determine how to vote on the plan.

   Paragraph 37 of SOP 90-7 states that while the court determines the adequacy of information in the disclosure statement, entities that expect to adopt fresh start reporting should report information about the reorganization value in the disclosure statement. The reporting of this value should help creditors and shareholders make an informed judgment about the plan.

   The SOP suggests that the most logical place to report the reorganization value is in the pro forma balance sheet that shows the financial position of the entity as though the proposed plan was confirmed.

5. *Financial Information.* Among several types of information that may benefit creditors and stockholders considerably in assessing the potential of the debtors' business are the following: audited reports of the financial position as of the date the petition was filed or as of the end of a recent fiscal year, and the results of operations for the past year; a detailed analysis by the debtor of its properties, including a description of the properties, the current values, and other relevant information; and a description of the obligations outstanding with identification of the material claims in dispute. If the nature of the company's operations is going to change significantly as a result of the reorganization, historical financial statements for the past 2 to 5 years are of limited value.

In addition to the historical financial statements, it may be useful to present a **pro forma balance sheet** showing the impact that the proposed plan, if accepted, will have on the financial condition of the company. Included should be the source of new capital and how the proceeds will be used, the postpetition interest obligation, lease commitments, financing arrangements, and so forth.

To provide the information needed by creditors and stockholders for effective evaluation of the plan, the pro forma statement should show the reorganization value of the entity. Thus the assets would be presented at their current values and, if there is any excess of the reorganization value (going concern value) over individual assets, this value would be shown. Liabilities and stockholder's equity should be presented at their discounted values based on the assumption that the plan will be confirmed. If appraisals of the individual assets have not been made, it appears appropriate to reflect the differences between the book value and reorganization value as an adjustment to the asset side of the pro forma balance sheet.

If the plan calls for future cash payments, the inclusion of projections of future operations will help the affected creditors make a decision as to whether they believe the debtor can make the required payments. Even if the plan calls for no future cash payments, it may still be advisable to include the financial information in the disclosure statement that will allow creditors and stockholders to see the business's potential for operating profitably in the future. These projections must, of course, be based on reasonable assumptions, and the assumptions must be clearly set forth in the projections accompanying the disclosure statement.

6. *Liquidation Values.* Included in the disclosure statement should be an analysis of the amount that creditors and equity holders would receive if the debtor was liquidated under chapter 7. In order to effectively evaluate the reorganization alternative, the creditors and equity holders must know what they would receive through liquidation. Also, the court, in order to confirm the plan, must ascertain, according to § 1129 (a)(7), that each holder of a claim or interest who does not vote in favor of the plan must receive at least an amount that is equal to the amount that would be received in a chapter 7 liquidation.

Generally, it is not acceptable to state that the amount provided for in the plan exceeds the liquidation amount. The presentation must include data to support this type of statement.

7. *Special Risk Factors.* In any securities that are issued pursuant to a plan in a chapter 11 proceeding, certain substantial risk factors are inherent. It may be advisable to include a description of some of the factors in the disclosure statement.

(d) CONFIRMATION OF PLAN. Prior to the confirmation hearing on the proposed plan, the proponents of the plan will seek its acceptance. Once the results of the vote are known, the debtor or other proponent of the plan will request confirmation of the plan.

The holder of a claim or interest, as defined under § 502, is permitted to vote on the proposed plan. Voting is based on the classification of claims and interests. A major change from prior law is that the acceptance requirements are based on those actually voting and not on the total value or number of claims or interests allowed in a particular class. The Secretary of the

Treasury is authorized to vote on behalf of the United States when the United States is a creditor or equity security holder.

A class of claim holders has accepted a plan if at least two-thirds in amount and more than one-half in number of the allowed claims for that class that are voted are cast in favor of the plan. For equity interests it is only necessary that votes totaling at least two-thirds in amount of the outstanding securities in a particular class that voted are cast for the plan. The majority in number requirement is not applicable to equity interests.

(e) CONFIRMATION REQUIREMENTS. Section 1129(a), which contains the requirements that must be satisfied before a plan can be confirmed, is one of the most important sections of the Bankruptcy Code. The provisions follow:

1. *The Plan Complies with the Applicable Provisions of Title 11.* Section 1122 concerning classification of claims and § 1123 on the content of the plan are significant sections.

2. *The Proponents of the Plan Comply with the Applicable Provisions of Title 11.* Section 1125 on disclosure is an example of a section that is referred to by this requirement.

3. *The Plan Has Been Proposed in Good Faith and Is Not by Any Means Forbidden by Law.*

4. *Payments Are Disclosed.* Any payment made or to be made for services, costs, and expenses in connection with the case or plan has been approved by, or is subject to the approval of, the court as reasonable.

5. *There Is Disclosure of Officers.* The proponent of the plan must disclose the persons who are proposed to serve after confirmation as director, officer, or voting trustee of the reorganized debtor. Such employment must be consistent with the interests of creditors and equity security holders and with public policy. Also, names of insiders to be employed and the nature of their compensation must also be disclosed.

6. *Regulatory Rate Has Been Approved.* Any governmental regulatory commission that will have jurisdiction over the debtor after confirmation of the plan must approve any rate changes provided for in the plan.

7. *The Plan Satisfies the Best-Interest-of-Creditors Test.* It is necessary for the creditors or stockholders who do not vote for the plan to receive as much as they would if the business were liquidated under chapter 7.

8. *The Plan Has Been Accepted by Each Class.* Each class of creditors or stockholders impaired under the plan must accept the plan. Section 1129(b), however, provides an exception to this requirement—the **"Cram Down."**

   This section allows the court under certain conditions to confirm a plan even though an impaired class has not accepted it. The plan must not discriminate unfairly, and it must be fair and equitable, with respect to each impaired class of claims or interest that has not accepted the plan. The Code states conditions for secured claims, unsecured claims, and stockholder interests that would be included in the "fair and equitable" requirement. It should be noted that because the word "includes" is used, the meaning of fair and equitable is not restricted to these conditions. A discussion of the "cram down" provision is found in § 5.33 of Newton's *Bankruptcy and Insolvency Accounting: Practice and Procedure* (1994).

9. *Priority Claims Have Been Satisfied.* This requirement provides that priority claims must be satisfied with cash payment as of the effective date of the plan unless the holders agree to a different treatment. An exception to this general rule is allowed for taxes. Taxes must be paid over a period of 6 years from date of assessment with a present value equal to the amount of the claim.

10. *At Least One Class Accepts the Plan.* If a class of claims is impaired under the plan, at least one class that is impaired, other than a class of claims held by insiders, must accept the plan.

11. *Plan Is Feasible.* Confirmation of the plan is not likely to be followed by liquidation or by the need for further financial reorganization unless the plan provides for such liquidation or reorganization.

12. *Payment of Fees.* The filing fees and quarterly fees must be paid or provided in the plan that they will be paid as of the effective date of the plan.

13. *Retiree Benefit Continuation.* The plan must provide, as of the effective date, for the continuation of all retiree benefits as defined under section 1114 and at the level established under section 1114.

(f) ACCOUNTING SERVICES—ASSISTANCE TO DEBTOR.   Accountants can provide considerable services to their client relating to the formulation of the plan, some of which are described in the following subsections.

(i) Liquidation Value of Assets.   Section 1129(a)(7) provides that each holder of a claim must either accept that plan or receive or retain interest in property of a value that is at least equal to the amount that would have been received or retained if the debtor were liquidated under chapter 7. Accountants can help the debtor establish these values.

(ii) Projections of Future Operations.   Section 1129(a)(11) contains the feasibility standard of chapter 11 requiring that confirmation of the plan of reorganization is not likely to be followed by liquidation or further reorganization (unless contemplated). The accountant may assist the debtor or trustee to formulate an acceptable plan by projecting the ability of the debtor to carry out and perform the terms of the plan. To establish feasibility, the debtor must project the profitability potential of the business. Where the plan calls for installment payments, the accountant may be requested to prepare or review projected budgets, cash flow statements, and statements of financial position. The creditors must be assured by the projected income statement and cash flow statement that the debtor will be in a position to make the payments as they become due. The forecast of the results of operations and financial position should be prepared on the assumption that the proposed plan will be accepted, and the liability and asset accounts should reflect the balance that would be shown after all adjustments are made relative to the debt forgiveness. Thus, interest expense is based on the liabilities that will exist after the discharge occurs.

(iii) Reorganization Value.   Not only are cash projections needed for the feasibility test as mentioned in the previous paragraph, but they are an important part of the negotiation process. The creditors want to receive the maximum amount possible in any chapter 11 plan and often want the payment in cash as of the effective date of the plan. The creditors realize, however, that if their demands are beyond the ability of the debtor to make payments, the plan will not work and they will not receive the payments provided for in the plan. Cash flow projections assist both parties in developing reasonable conclusions regarding the value of the entity emerging from chapter 11. In some reorganizations, there is considerable debate over cash flow projections and the discount rate to be used in determining the value of the debtor's continuing operations, to which must be added the amount to be realized on the sale of nonoperating assets plus excess working capital. Once the debtor and its creditors' committee can agree on the basic value of the entity, it is easier to negotiate the terms of the plan.

During the formulation of the plan the accountant can assist the debtor considerably by helping to determine the reorganized value of the debtor or by helping the debtor to assess the valuation of an investment banker or other specialists. If the accountant develops the cash projections supporting the valuation, the accountant will be precluded from being independent for SEC purposes. Once the debtor has determined an estimate of the value of the entity that will emerge from bankruptcy, the accountant can provide assistance to the debtor in negotiating the terms of the plan with the creditor.

(iv) Pro Forma Balance Sheet.   Also of considerable help in evaluating a plan is a pro forma balance sheet showing how the balance sheet will look if the plan is accepted and all provisions of the plan are carried out. By using reorganization models or simulation models, the pro forma balance sheet may be prepared based on several possible courses of action that the debtor could take. The pro forma balance sheet illustrates the type of debt equity position that would exist under different alternatives.

This pro forma balance sheet should reflect the debts at discounted values. Assets are generally presented at their historical cost values unless the debtor has made a decision to apply the concept of quasi reorganization. A pro forma balance sheet that reflects the reorganized values of the entity is of considerable benefit to the debtor in developing the terms for a plan.

Once the terms of the proposed plan have been finalized, the pro forma balance sheet based on historical values reflecting these terms is generally included in the disclosure statement that must be submitted prior to or at the time votes are solicited on the plan. The pro forma balance sheet reflecting reorganized values, however, provides information for the creditors and stockholders that is much more relevant in making an informed judgment about how to vote on the plan.

(v) Reorganization Model.   Accountants can develop a model to help the debtor in developing a plan. The outcome of a reorganization plan depends on a variety of assumptions, including the creditors' willingness to accept different mixes of cash and securities, economic trends, possible sources for financing continuing operations or acquisitions, and many other factors. Using a model, these assumptions can be altered one at a time with all else held constant, and the possible courses of action can be analyzed according to the needs of management. Using this technique, creditors or the debtor can identify potential problem areas and request clarifications. Once these have been received and entered into the system, a new set of comparisons is made and the process is repeated until both sides are satisfied that the most favorable course is being pursued. Breakdowns of reorganization plans by computer models allow debtors and creditors to focus on the financial data most relevant to the case at hand.

(g) ACCOUNTING SERVICES—ASSISTANCE TO CREDITORS' COMMITTEE.   The following subsections describe several of the services that the accountant can render for the creditors' committee or for a committee of equity holders.

(i) Assistance in the Bargaining Process.   One of the basic functions performed by the creditors' committee is to negotiate a settlement and then make its recommendation to the other creditors. The accountant should be familiar with the bargaining process that goes on between the debtor and the creditors' committee in trying to reach a settlement. Bargaining can be both vigorous and delicate. The debtor bargains, perhaps, for a settlement that consists of a small percentage of the debt, demanding only a small immediate cash outlay, with payments to be made in the future. The debtor may want the debts outstanding to be subordinated to new credit or may ask that the agreement call for partial payment in preferred stock. The creditors want a settlement that represents a high percentage of the debt and consists of a larger cash down payment with the balance to be paid as soon as possible. In cases where there is very little cash available for debt repayment on confirmation, unsecured creditors may be interested in obtaining most of the outstanding stock of the company. In the past 10 years, the creditors of public companies have received an increasing interest in the ownership of the debtor. It is not unusual for the creditors to own between 80% and 95% of the outstanding stock of the emerging entity. For example, Wickes' creditors received 84% ownership, and the existing equity of Emmons Industries retained only 3% interest whereas creditors received the balance. The shareholders of failed leveraged-buyouts often receive no equity interest in the reorganized entity.

The services that the accountant may render for the creditors' committee in the negotiations with the debtor vary significantly depending on several factors, including the size of the debtor, the experience of the members of the creditors' committee, the nature of the debtor's operations, and the creditors' committee confidence in the debtor and in the professionals—especially attorneys and accountants—who are helping the debtor. The committee in most cases, to varying degrees, depends on the accountant to help evaluate the debtor's operations, the information provided about those operations, and the terms of a proposed plan. Often accountants may be engaged to investigate selected aspects of the debtor's operations and to obtain an overall understanding of the debtor's problems and possible solutions.

(ii) Evaluation of Debtor's Projections.   Of primary significance to a creditors' committee is determining whether the projections and forecasts submitted by the debtor are realistic. The representatives of the largest unsecured creditors on the committee typically are not accountants and thus may need assistance in evaluating the financial data prepared by the debtor. The accountant for the creditors' committee may be in a strong position to evaluate the debtor's projections and to make recommendations. The intention is not to perform an audit of such data but rather to review the information to determine whether the projections can be supported to some extent by hard evidence. The level of involvement by the accountant for the creditors' committee will vary, depending on the sophistication of the company or of the financial people who prepared the data. The review in some cases could be limited to a discussion of the data with those who prepared the projections, to determine whether the forecasts seem to make sense. In other situations, however, the accountant may find that the preparation of this information has been somewhat loose or vague. In these circumstances, the accountant for the committee may need to get involved in the preparation or to perform a review of the appropriate accounting records to see whether the basic underlying data have some foundation in fact.

(iii) Reorganization Value.   In some cases accountants for the creditors' committee develop their own models of the debtor's operations. Cash flow projections can then be prepared for determining the reorganized entity's value. Operational changes made by the debtor are entered in the model as are proposed sales or other major actions, providing a basis for the committee's response to the debtor's proposals. Evaluation by the creditors' committee focuses on the impact these actions will have on the value of the reorganized entity and on the amount of potential settlement.

(iv) Review of Plan and Disclosure Statement.   As was noted earlier, the accountant for the debtor provides advice and assistance in the formulation of a plan of reorganization in a chapter 11 proceeding and a plan of settlement in an agreement out of court. An important function of an accountant employed by the creditors is to help evaluate the proposed plan of action. In a chapter 11 case where the debtor has not proposed a plan within 120 days, a proposed plan has not been accepted within 180 days after the petition was filed, or where the trustee has been appointed, the accountant may assist the creditors in developing a plan to submit to the court. The accountant is able to provide valuable assistance to the committee because of familiarity with the financial background, nature of operations, and management of the company gained during the audit. In committee meetings a great deal of discussion goes on between the committee members and the accountant concerning the best settlement they can expect and how it compares with the amount they would receive if the business were liquidated.

The creditors are interested in receiving as much as possible under any reorganization plan. The accountant may work with the creditors' committee to see that the amount proposed under the plan is reasonable and fair based on the nature of the debtor's business. First, it must be determined that the plan provides for at least as much as would be received in a chapter 7 liquidation. Second, the creditors must leave for the debtor enough assets to operate the business after reorganization. If a reasonable basis does not exist for future operations, the judge may not confirm the plan because it is not feasible.

If an audit has not been performed, the accountant for the creditors' committee must rely on the information contained in the disclosure statement and in other reports that have been issued. Thus, the content of the disclosure statement may be most important. Also, since the disclosure statement serves as the basic report used by the creditors to evaluate the plan, it is critical that it be properly prepared and contain the type of information that allows the creditors to effectively evaluate the proposed plan.

The accountant for the creditors' committee may be asked to evaluate the disclosure statement. If, in the accountant's opinion, it does not contain adequate information, the deficiencies may be conveyed to the debtor informally (normally through creditors' committee counsel) prior to submission of the plan to the court, or an objection to the content of the statement may be raised at the disclosure hearing.

In evaluating the information in the disclosure statement, the accountant for the creditors' committee may be asked to review the financial statements contained in the disclosure statement or others that were issued by the debtor. Special consideration must be made in reviewing pro forma and liquidation statements of financial condition. The pro forma statement provides the creditors with an indication of the debtor's likely financial condition if the plan is accepted. This statement should show that the creditors will receive more if they accept the plan than they would receive if the debtor were liquidated. The pro forma statement also should demonstrate that the plan is feasible in that, after satisfying the provisions of the plan, the debtor retains an asset base with which to operate. In reviewing the pro forma statement prepared by the debtor, special consideration must be given to the analysis of the assumptions used to prepare it and to the evaluation of the value of the assets (which may differ from book values). If the pro forma statements are based on historical costs, the accountant for the creditors' committee may want to restate them to reflect the reorganized values of the entity. The creditors' committee will be able to evaluate the terms of the plan more effectively if it can compare the terms to pro forma statements containing the reorganized value of the entity rather than historical values.

Liquidation statements show what the unsecured creditors would receive if the business were liquidated. The assumptions used in the adjustments to book values must be evaluated carefully. The accountant for the creditors' committee may be asked to review statements of this nature and to provide advice as to the reasonableness of the analysis. There may be a tendency for the debtor to understate liquidation values in order to make the terms of the plan more appealing to the unsecured creditors.

(h) ACCOUNTING FOR THE REORGANIZATION. SOP 90-7 explains how the debtor emerging from chapter 11 should account for the reorganization both when fresh start reporting should be adopted and when it is not allowed. Fresh start reporting requires the debtor to use current values (going concern or reorganization values) in its balance sheet for both assets and liabilities and to eliminate all prior earnings or deficits.

(i) Requirements for Fresh Start Reporting. The two conditions that must be satisfied before fresh start reporting can be used are:

1. The reorganized value of the emerging entity immediately before the confirmation of the plan is less than the total of all postpetition liabilities and allowed claims.
2. Holders of existing voting shares immediately before confirmation retain less than 50% of the voting share of the emerging entity.

Paragraph 36 of the SOP indicates that the loss of control contemplated by the plan must be substantive and not temporary. Thus, the new controlling interest must not revert to the shareholders existing immediately before the plan was confirmed. For example, a plan that provides for shareholders existing prior to the confirmation to reacquire control of the company at a subsequent date may prevent the debtor from adopting fresh start reporting.

Debtors that meet both of the above conditions will report the assets and liabilities at their going concern (reorganization) values. Reorganization value is defined as the "fair value of the entity before considering liabilities and approximates the amount that a willing buyer would pay for the assets of the entity immediately after the restructuring." The focus in determining the reorganization value is on the value of the assets, normally determined by discounted future cash flows. The reorganization value of the entity may be determined by several approaches depending on the circumstances. [For a discussion of reorganization values see Chapter 10 of Newton's Bankruptcy and Insolvency Accounting: Practice and Procedure, Fifth Edition, Wiley, 1994. In most cases, it is not the responsibility of the accountant to determine the reorganization value of the debtor, but to report in the financial statements the value that is determined through the negotiations by the debtor, creditors' and stockholders' committees and other interested parties.

Professionals involved in bankruptcy cases have been aware of the limited usefulness of book values for some time. For example, market values are required in the schedules that are filed with the bankruptcy court, and fair market value of assets are determined under section 506 of the bankruptcy code for assets pledged.

Reorganization values will be used only when both conditions for a fresh start are satisfied. For example, fresh start reporting will not be used by most nonpublic companies because in most cases there is no change of ownership. Thus, the provisions of the SOP will primarily apply to public companies.

(ii) Allocation of Reorganization Value.   For entities meeting the criteria discussed above (reorganization value less than liabilities and old shareholders own less than 50% of voting stock of the emerging entity), fresh start reporting will be implemented in the following manner:

1. The reorganization value is to be allocated to the debtor's assets based on the market value of the individual assets. The allocation of value to the individual assets is to be made in accordance with the provisions of APB Opinion No. 16, *Business Combinations,* for transactions reported on the basis of the purchase method. Any part of the reorganization value not attributable to specific tangible assets or identifiable intangible assets should be reported as an intangible asset (reorganization value in excess of amounts allocable to identifiable assets) and amortized over a period not to exceed forty years in accordance with the provisions of APB Opinion No. 17, *Intangible Assets.* The SOP indicates that the allocation period will generally be substantially less than forty years. It suggests that there are usually overriding pertinent factors that will result in a life of less than 40 years for the reorganization value in excess of amounts allocable to identifiable assets. The SOP states that at a minimum, "the same considerations used in determining the reorganization value should be applied in determining the period of amortization."

2. Liabilities that survive the reorganization should be shown at present value of amounts to be paid determined at appropriate current interest rates. Thus, all liabilities will be shown at their discounted values (the practice of discounting debt has not always been followed in the past).

3. Deferred taxes are to be reported in conformity with generally accepted accounting principles. Benefits realized from preconfirmation net operating loss carryforwards should be used to first reduce reorganization value in excess of amounts allocable to identifiable assets and other intangibles. Once the balance of the intangible assets are exhausted, the balance is reported as a direct addition to the additional paid-in capital.

(iii) Disclosure Requirements.   Paragraph 39 of the SOP indicates that when fresh start reporting is adopted, the notes to the initial financial statement should disclose the following:

1. Adjustments to the historical amounts of individual assets and liabilities.
2. The amount of debt forgiven.

3. The amount of prior retained earnings or deficit eliminated.

4. Significant matters relating to the determination of reorganization value.

The SOP indicates that the following are some of the other significant matters that should be disclosed:

1. The method or methods used to determine reorganization value and factors such as discount rates, tax rates, the number of years for which cash flows are projected, and the method of determining terminal value.

2. Sensitive assumptions (those assumptions about which exists a reasonable possibility of the occurrence of a variation that would significantly affect measurement of reorganization value).

3. Assumptions about anticipated conditions that are expected to be different from current conditions, unless otherwise apparent.

(iv) Reporting by Debtors Not Qualifying for Fresh Start.   Debtors that do not meet both of the conditions for adopting fresh start reporting should state any debt issued or liabilities compromised by confirmed plans at the present values of amounts to be paid. Thus, the debtor will no longer have the option to elect to discount or not to discount debt issued in a chapter 11 case.

These provisions apply only to chapter 11 cases. However, in out-of-court workouts where liabilities are generally restated, it will be difficult to justify accounting for issuance of new debt in a manner different from the discounting procedure described in the SOP.

39.7 REPORTING REQUIREMENTS IN BANKRUPTCY CASES

Accountants often issue various types of reports and schedules as part of services rendered in the bankruptcy and insolvency area. These services include the preparation of operating reports, evaluation or development of a business plan, valuation of the business and search for preferences. Many of the reports or schedules produced would generally be classified as financial statements. Because financial statements are issued, the accountant must determine if a compilation, review or audit report must be issued, or if the service that generated the statements is exempted from professional standards related to compilation of financial statements from the records and the attestation standards. This issue has involved considerable controversy among accountants that practice in the bankruptcy and insolvency area.

(a) LITIGATION SERVICES.   When the accountant begins an engagement involving bankruptcy or insolvency issues, a decision needs to be made as to application of the attestation standards. Section 9100.48 of *Attestation Engagements Interpretation,* "Applicability of Attestation Standards to Litigation Services," excludes litigation services that "involve pending or potential formal legal or regulatory proceedings before a trier of fact in connection with the resolution of a dispute between two or more parties. . . ." Guidance in this area is provided by the AICPA's Management Consulting Division, in *Consulting Services Special Report 93-1,* "Application of AICPA Professional Standards in the Performance of Litigation Services" (CSSR 93-1). This report concludes in paragraph 71/105.03 that "[b]ankruptcy, forensic accounting, reorganization, or insolvency services, as practiced by CPA's, generally are acceptable as forms of litigation services."

CSSR 93-1 notes that the role of the accountant in a litigation engagement is different from the role in an attestation services engagement. When involved in an attestation engagement, the CPA firm expresses "a conclusion about the reliability of a written assertion of another party." In the performance of litigation services, the accountant helps to "gather and interpret facts and must support or defend the conclusions reached against challenges in cross-examination or regulatory examination and in the work product of others."

Appendix 71/B of CSSR 93-1 describes the delivery of reorganization services to include items such as the following:

- Preparing or reviewing valuations of the debtor's business.
- Analyzing the profitability of the debtor's business.
- Preparing or reviewing the monthly operating reports required by the bankruptcy court.
- Reviewing disbursements and other transactions for possible preference payments and fraudulent conveyances.
- Preparing or reviewing the financial projections of the debtor.
- Performing financial advisory services associated with mergers, divestitures, capital adequacy, debt capacity, and so forth.
- Consulting on strategic alternatives and developing business plans.
- Providing assistance in developing or reviewing plans of reorganization or disclosure statements.*

CSSR 93-1 then concludes that bankruptcy services similar to those listed above that are provided by CPA's generally are accepted as a form of litigation services. Appendix 71/B of CSSR 93-1 provides that:

> This acceptance is due to many fundamental and practical similarities between bankruptcy services and the consulting services associated with other forms of litigation. Bankruptcy law, as promulgated by the Bankruptcy Code and case law, is applied by bankruptcy judges and lawyers to resolve disputes between a debtor and its creditors (for example, distribution of the debtor's assets). Bankruptcy cases frequently include actions related to claims for preferential payments and fraudulent conveyances; negligence of officers, directors, or professionals engaged by the debtors; or other allegations common to commercial litigation. The bankruptcy court has the power and authority to value legal claims and resolve such common litigation as product liability, patent infringement, and breach of contract. The decisions of bankruptcy judges can be appealed as can the decisions of other courts.

The above guidelines according to CSSR 93-1 should also apply to services rendered in an out of court workout as described in the following paragraph from Appendix 71/B:

> Out-of-court restructuring holds the potential for litigation. Therefore, the settlement process is generally conducted with the same scrutiny, due diligence, and intense challenge as that of a formal court-administered process. Furthermore, bankruptcy services provided by CPAs are typically not three-party attest services (the three parties in attest services are the asserter, the attester, and the third party). Instead, affected parties have the opportunity to question, challenge, and provide input to the bankruptcy findings and process.

For services to be exempted, they must be rendered in connection with the litigation and the parties to the proceeding must have an opportunity to analyze and challenge the work of the accountant. For example, when the CPA expresses a written conclusion about the reliability of a written assertion by another party, and the conclusions and assertions are for the use of others who will not have the opportunity to analyze and challenge the work, the professional standards would apply. Also, when the CPA is specifically engaged to perform a service in accordance with the attestation standards or accounting services standards (SAARS), professional standards are applicable.

---

*CSSR 93-1 notes that the words *review* and *reviewing* are not intended to have the same meaning as they do in the AICPA SSARSs.

(b) DISCLOSURE REQUIREMENTS. If it is determined that the analysis or report that will be issued comes under the guidelines as a form of litigation services, it is advisable to explain both the association and the responsibility, if any, through a transmittal letter or a statement affixed to documents distributed to third parties. Appendix 71/B of CSSR 93-1 suggests the following format for a statement that would explain the association of the CPAs and their responsibility, if any:

> The accompanying schedules (projected financial information; debt capacity analysis; liquidation analysis) were assembled for your analysis of the proposed restructuring and recapitalization of ABC Company. The aforementioned schedules were not examined or reviewed by independent accountants in accordance with standards promulgated by the AICPA. This information is limited to the sole use of the parties involved (management; creditors' committee; bank syndicate) and is not to be provided to other parties.

If it is determined that the service does not qualify as litigation service, any financial statements that might be issued from the services rendered should be accompanied with an accountant's report based on the compilation of the financial statements. Prior to the issuance of a compilation report the format and nature of the report must be cleared with the Firm Administrator.

(c) OPERATING REPORTS. Another area where there is considerable uncertainty is in the issuance of operating reports. All regions of the U.S. trustee require monthly operating reports be submitted to the court as well as annual operating reports. Among those items that were listed in CSSR 93-1 that might fall under litigation services was the preparation or review the monthly operating reports required by the bankruptcy court. These reports, especially for larger public companies, are often prepared in accordance with generally accepted accounting principles, including SOP 90-7. For example, in the region of New York, Connecticut and Vermont, the U.S. trustee has issued guidelines that require the statements to confirm to SOP 90-7. Other U.S. trustees have on request by the accountant allowed the statements to be prepared in the format that conforms to the manner in which the accountant normally prepares monthly financial statements. Additionally, the accountant is asked to prepare supplemental data not generally presented in monthly financial statements such as an aging schedule of postpetition payables and a schedule of postpetition taxes paid and accrued.

As noted above in CSSR 93-1, the professional standards would apply under two conditions:

1. When the CPA expresses a written conclusion about the reliability of a written assertion by another party, and the conclusions and assertions are for the use of others who will not have the opportunity to analyze and challenge the work.
2. When the CPA is specifically engaged to perform a service in accordance with the attestation standards or accounting services standards (SAARS).

In most situations the second requirement—specifically engaged to perform attestation or compilation services—is not satisfied. Thus, based on this condition the professional standards would not apply. CPAs are generally engaged to prepare the operating reports that the U.S. trustee and the bankruptcy court require and not specifically to perform an audit or review of the financial records or even compile the financial statements in accordance with the professional standards.

It is the first requirement—expressing a written conclusion about the reliability of a written assertion by another party who will not have the opportunity to analyze and challenge the work—that needs further consideration by the profession. While, no specific hearing is scheduled to review the reports, creditors or other parties in interest might raise objections to the content of the reports. Objections to the operating reports have been raised, but rarely. The preparation or the review of monthly operating reports that are required by the court is one of the items listed in the services that are rendered by accountants in the performance of reorganization services. CSSR 93-1 notes that "[b]ankruptcy services provided by CPAs generally are accepted as a form of litigation services."

Since operating reports are considered a form of litigation services, a compilation report should not be issued on the reports. Rather, the following statement should be included in a transmittal letter or affixed to the operating reports.

> The accompanying operating reports for the month of _____ were assembled for your analysis of the proposed restructuring of the ABC Company under chapter 11 of the Bankruptcy Code. The aforementioned operating reports were not examined or reviewed by independent accountants in accordance with the standards promulgated by the AICPA. This information is limited to the sole use of the parties in interest in this chapter 11 case and is not to be provided to other parties.

If, on the other hand, it is determined in a particular engagement that professional standards are applicable and the CPA is associated with the financial statements, then a compilation report should be issued based upon the prescribed form as set forth in SAARS No. 3. As noted above, prior to the issuance of a compilation report the format and nature of the report must be reviewed for conformity to applicable standards.

(d) INVESTIGATIVE SERVICES.   Preference analysis or other special investigative services performed in a bankruptcy proceeding, receivership or out of court settlement, are considered a litigation service. As a result the accountant is not required to issue an agreed-upon procedures report. This would not preclude the professional from issuing a report that described the procedures performed and the results ascertained from the performance of the stated procedures. For example, using the above format, a report issued to a trustee based upon an analysis of preferences, might be worded:

> The accompanying analysis of preferential payments was assembled (or prepared) for your analysis (or consideration) in conjunction with the proposed reorganization of _____ under chapter 11 of the Bankruptcy Code. The aforementioned analysis of preferential payments was not examined or reviewed by independent accountants in accordance with standards promulgated by the AICPA. This information is limited to the sole use of the trustee in this chapter 11 case and is not to be provided to other parties.

(e) FINANCIAL PROJECTIONS.   Section 200.03 of the AICPA, "Statements on Standards for Attestation Engagements" states that the standards for prospective financial statements does not apply for engagements involving prospective financial statements used solely in connection with litigation support services. CSSR 93-1 clearly indicates that prospective financial information qualifies as a litigation service. CSSR 93-1 states that parties-in-interest can challenge prospective financial information during negotiations or during bankruptcy court hearings often dealing with the plan's feasibility and adequacy of disclosure. Projections that are included in a disclosure statement would not be subject to the attestation standards since there is a hearing on the disclosure statement and the court must approve the disclosure statement before votes for the plan can be solicited. Parties-in-interest have an opportunity to challenge the prospective information included. Any projections provided for the debtor or for the creditors committee that is used in the negotiations of the plan would also not fall under the attestation standards.

CSSR 93-1 does, however, indicate that in situations where the users of the prospective financial information cannot challenge the CPA's work, the attestation standards apply. CSSR 93-1 suggests that the attestation standard might apply in situations where exchange offers are made to creditors and stockholders with whom the company has not negotiated or who are not members of a creditor group represented by a committee. Section 200.03 of the AICPA, "Statements on Standards for Attestation Engagements" indicates that if the prospective financial statements are used by third parties that do not have the opportunity to analyze and challenge the statements, the litigation exception does not apply.

Section 200.02 of the AICPA, "Statements on Standards for Attestation Engagements" indicates that when an accountant submits, to his client or others, prospective financial statements that he has assembled (or assisted in assembling) or reports on prospective financial statements that might be expected to be used by third parties, a compilation, examination, or agreed-upon procedures engagement should be performed. Thus for prospective financial statements that do not qualify for the litigation exception, the engagement must be in the form of a compilation, examination or agreed-upon procedures if the accountant is associated with the financial statements.

The determination of the reorganization or liquidation values to be included in the disclosure statement or to be used by the debtor or creditors' committee in the negotiations of the terms of a plan, as well as other service that involve financial projections, would fall under the litigation exception. If it is determined that the report regarding the issuance of financial projections would not fall under litigation services the format and nature of the report must be reviewed for conformity to applicable standards.

The following wording might be in the transmittal letter or in a statement affixed to the documents:

> The accompanying projected financial statements (or information) were assembled for your analysis of the proposed restructuring and reorganization of _____ under chapter 11 of the Bankruptcy Code. The aforementioned statements were not examined or reviewed by independent accountants in accordance with standards promulgated by the AICPA. This information is limited to the sole use of _____ and is not to be provided to other parties.

39.8 SOURCES AND SUGGESTED REFERENCES

Accounting Principles Board, "Business Combinations," Accounting Principles Board Opinion No. 16, AICPA, New York, 1970.

———, "Interest on Receivables and Payables," Accounting Principles Board Opinion No. 21, AICPA, New York, 1971.

———, Accounting Standards Executive Committee, *Statement of Position (SOP) No. 90-7, Financial Reporting by Entities in Reorganization Under the Bankruptcy Code,* AICPA, New York, 1990.

Behrenfield, William H., and Biebl, Andrew R., "Bankruptcy/Insolvency," *The Accountant's Business Manual,* AICPA, New York, 1989.

Countryman, "Executory Contracts in Bankruptcy," *Minnesota Law Review,* Vol. 57, (1973), pp. 439, 460.

Financial Accounting Standards Board, "Reporting Gains and Losses from Extinguishment of Debt," Statement of Financial Accounting Standards No. 4, FASB, Stamford, CT, 1975.

———, "Accounting for Contingencies," Statement of Financial Accounting Standards No. 5, FASB, Stamford, CT, 1975.

———, "Accounting by Debtors and Creditors for Troubled Debt Restructurings," Statement of Financial Accounting Standards No. 15, FASB, Stamford, CT, 1977.

King, Lawrence P., ed., *Collier Bankruptcy Manual,* Matthew Bender, New York, 1994.

Newton, Grant W., *Bankruptcy and Insolvency Accounting,* 5th ed., Wiley, New York, 1994.

Patterson, George F., Jr., & Newton, Grant, "Accounting for Bankruptcies: Implementation SOP 90-97," *Journal of Accountancy,* 46, (April 1993).

Securities and Exchange Commission, "Push down" Basis of Accounting for Parent Company Debt Related to Subsidiary Acquisitions," Staff Accounting Bulletin No. 73, SEC, Washington DC, 1987.

———, "Views Regarding Certain Matters Relating to Quasi-Reorganizations, Including Deficit Eliminations," Staff Accounting Bulletin No. 78, SEC, Washington DC, 1988.

Summers, Mark Stevens, *Bankruptcy Explained: A Guide for Businesses,* Wiley, New York, 1989.

CHAPTER 40

FORENSIC ACCOUNTING AND LITIGATION CONSULTING SERVICES

Jeffrey H. Kinrich, CPA

Price Waterhouse LLP

M. Freddie Reiss, CPA

Price Waterhouse LLP

Elo R. Kabe, MBA, CPA

Price Waterhouse LLP

CONTENTS

The authors would like to thank the following Price Waterhouse staff members for their valuable research and editorial assistance: John Bednarski, Gloria Gowan, Jess Hines, Albert Lilienfeld, Linda Morris, Neil Murdoch, Raymond Sims, Leslie Spiller, and Daniel Wray.

40.1 INTRODUCTION

Forensic accounting can be broadly defined as the application of accounting principles, theories, and discipline to facts and hypotheses at issue in a legal context. This legal context is generally litigation, but any dispute resolution proceeding (e.g., arbitration or mediation) is a candidate for the application of forensic accounting. Similarly, forensic accounting applies equally to both civil and criminal litigation. The principal focus of this chapter will be civil litigation because it is by far the most frequent dispute resolution proceeding in which the professional accountant will be involved.

The terms "forensic accounting," "litigation support," or "litigation consulting" are sometimes used as synonyms. Attorneys, however, sometimes use "litigation support" to mean automated document management. For purposes of this chapter, forensic accounting includes all financial and accounting analysis performed by a professional accountant to assist counsel in connection with its investigation, assessment, and proof of issues in a dispute resolution proceeding.

This chapter provides a brief description of the litigation process and a discussion of the accountant's role in, and contribution to, that process. It includes a description of the types of cases in which professional accountants typically get involved and a discussion of analytical techniques and approaches that the accountant can apply to these cases. The last section of this chapter, "Testimony" provides suggestions as to how to prepare and deliver deposition and trial testimony.

40.2 THE LEGAL CONTEXT

(a) THE ADVERSARIAL PROCESS.   In civil disputes it is generally up to the parties (the plaintiff and defendant), not the court, to initiate and prosecute litigation, to investigate the pertinent facts, and to present proof and legal argument to the adjudicative body. The court's function, in general, is limited to adjudicating the issues that the parties submit to it, based on the proofs presented by them. The adversarial system is based on the belief that the truth is more likely to emerge from bilateral investigation and presentation, motivated by the strong pull of self-interest, rather than from judicial investigation motivated only by official duty.

(b) STAGES IN A CIVIL SUIT.   There are three basic phases or stages in a civil suit, barring appeal. These stages are the same for virtually all adversarial proceedings, whether in a federal, state, or administrative court.

(i) Pleadings.   A lawsuit is started by a **complaint** that is filed with the clerk of the trial court and served on the defendants. The complaint lays out the facts and causes of action alleged by the plaintiff. The defendants may file a **motion** to dismiss (arguing that the defendant is not legally liable even if the alleged facts are true) or an **answer** to the complaint. The answer may contain a denial of the allegations or an affirmative defense (e.g., statute of limitations has expired). The defendant also may file a **counterclaim** which presents a claim by the defendant (counterplaintiff) against the plaintiff (counterdefendant).

(ii) Pretrial Discovery.   The purpose of pretrial discovery is to narrow the issues that need to be decided at trial and to obtain evidence to support legal and factual arguments. It is essentially an information-gathering process. Evidence is obtained in advance to facilitate presentation of an organized, concise case, as well as to prevent any surprises at trial. This sharing of information often will result in the settlement of the case before trial.

The first step in discovery typically involves the use of **interrogatories** and **document requests.** Interrogatories are sets of formal written questions directed by one party in the lawsuit to the other. They are usually broad in nature and are used to fill in and amplify the fact situation set out in the pleadings. Interrogatories are also used to identify individuals who may possess unique knowledge or information about the issues in the case.

Requests for production of documents identify specific documents and records that the requesting party believes are relevant to its case and that are in the possession of and controlled by the opposing party. The opposing party is only required to produce the specific documents requested. Accordingly, when drafting these requests, care must be taken to be as broad as possible so as to include all relevant documents but narrow enough to be descriptive. It is not unusual for more than one set of interrogatories and document requests to be issued during the course of a lawsuit. The accountant is often involved in developing interrogatories and document requests on financial and business issues.

Depositions are the second step in the discovery process. They are the sworn testimony of a witness recorded by a court reporter. During the deposition, the witness may be asked questions by the attorneys for each party to the suit. The questions and answers are transcribed, sworn to, and signed. The testimony will allow the party taking the deposition to better understand the facts of the case and may be used as evidence in the trial. The accountant expert witness may be heavily involved at this stage, both in being deposed and in developing questions for opposing witnesses.

(iii) Trial.   The third stage of the litigation/adversarial process is the trial. It is the judicial examination and determination of issues between the parties to the action. The trial begins with the attorneys for each party making opening statements concerning the facts they expect to prove during the trial. Then the plaintiff puts forth its case, calling all of the witnesses it believes are required to prove its case. Each witness will be subject to direct examination and then cross-examination by the opposing party's attorney. After the plaintiff has called all of its witnesses and presented all of its evidence, the defendant will then present its case in the same manner. The plaintiff then has an opportunity to present additional evidence to refute the defendant's case in a rebuttal. The defendant can respond in a surrebuttal. Finally, each party has the opportunity to make a closing statement before the court.

The U.S. Constitution and most state constitutions provide for the right of trial by jury in most cases. This right does not have to be exercised and many cases are tried without a jury. In most states and in federal courts, one of the parties must request a jury or the right is presumed to be waived.

(c) REQUIRED PROOFS.   In order for a plaintiff to succeed in a claim for damages, it must satisfy three different but related proofs: liability, causation, and amount of damages. If the burden of proof is not met on any one of these, the claim will fail.

(i) Liability.   The plaintiff must prove that one of its legal rights has been transgressed by the defendant. It will present evidence attempting to prove that the actions of the defendant were in violation of the plaintiff's legal rights. Similarly, the defendant will present evidence in an effort to prove that the plaintiff's rights were not violated, or at least, were not violated by the defendant.

(ii) Causation.   If the plaintiff proves that the defendant has violated one of its legal rights, it must be shown that this violation resulted in some harm to the plaintiff. Here, attorneys for the plaintiff and defendant will try to prove or disprove the nexus between the defendant's actions and some harm to the plaintiff.

(iii) Damages.   After presenting the evidence relating to the liability and causation issues, the parties' next step in most cases is to prove damages.

Damages are one of a number of remedies that may be available to a prevailing plaintiff. Other types of remedies include specific performance (performance of the act that was promised), injunctions (an order by the court forbidding or restraining a party from doing an act), and restitution (the return of goods, property, or money previously conveyed). Damages are the only type of remedy discussed in this chapter.

The general principle in awarding damages is to put the plaintiff in the same position it would have been if its legal rights had not been transgressed. There are three main categories of damages: compensatory, consequential, and punitive. Compensatory damages compensate the injured party only for injuries or losses actually sustained and proved to have arisen directly from the violation of the plaintiff's rights. Consequential damages are foreseeable damages that are caused by special circumstances beyond the action itself. They flow only from the consequences or results of an action. Punitive damages are intended to penalize the guilty party and to make an example of the party to deter similar conduct in the future. They are awarded only in certain types of cases (e.g. fraud).

The quantification of damages is primarily a question of fact. The burden of proving the damage amount normally falls on the plaintiff. It is in this area that accountants are most frequently utilized. Many different methods can be used to quantify the economic loss. They are discussed in subsection 40.6(b).

40.3 THE ACCOUNTANT'S ROLE IN THE LITIGATION PROCESS

Typically the accountant is hired by attorneys representing either the plaintiff or the defendant. In some cases, however, an accountant may be engaged directly by one of the parties to the action, often by an audit client. No matter who engages the accountant, a number of possible services might be provided. The accountant can work as either testifying expert or as consultant. The basic difference between the two is discoverability of the accountant's work product.

(a) THE TESTIFYING EXPERT.   Frequently, the accountant's purpose in the case will be to develop and render an opinion regarding financial or accounting issues. Ordinarily, only facts and firsthand knowledge can be presented by witnesses at trial. The only exception to this rule is the testimony of experts, which can include an expression of the expert's **opinions.**

According to the courts and the law, experts are those who are qualified to testify authoritatively because of their education, special training, and experience. Clearly, a professional accountant can qualify as an expert in issues relating to accounting and financial data.

As discussed in subsections 40.5(a–e) and 40.6(a–d), the accountant as expert may be asked to develop and present evidence in support of any or all of the required proofs. For example, the accountant can review and offer an opinion as to the adequacy of the work performed by another accountant in a professional liability suit (proof of liability). Or, the accountant might review the financial records and the business environment of a company to determine whether a bank's withdrawal of credit caused the company to go out of business (proof of causation). Most commonly, the accountant will be asked to provide an opinion regarding the economic loss suffered by the plaintiff in the case (proof of damages).

(b) NONTESTIFYING CONSULTANT.   In certain situations, the accountant will be asked to be a consultant rather than a testifying expert. The accountant will take on more of an advisory role and will not provide testimony. The work the accountant performs for the attorney as a consultant is generally protected by the attorney's work product privilege and as such is not discoverable by the opposing party. For this reason, accountants are often engaged initially as consultants. This enables the attorney to explore avenues and conduct analyses from which he might want to shield his testifying expert. However, once the accountant has been designated as an expert, **all** work products may be subject to discovery.

(c) CASE ANALYSIS AND PLANNING.   Whether in the role as testifying expert or nontestifying consultant, the professional accountant can provide valuable assistance throughout the litigation process.

In many circumstances, the accountant can be of use to the attorney before the complaint is even filed. The accountant can help the attorney understand the accounting, financial, and economic issues involved in the case, and can also assess the potential value of the claim by providing an estimate of the amount of damages. In certain cases, especially those involving accountant's liability, the accountant may actually help to identify causes of action to be included in the complaint.

Once a case has been filed, the accountant can help the attorney understand and evaluate critical accounting, financial, and economic issues and assist with the formulation of an appropriate strategy. Strategy formulation is a continual process; as new information is received and additional issues uncovered, the overall strategy is revised. During the planning phase, the accountant will evaluate alternative approaches and determine the most reasonable approach to take based on all available information. At the same time, the accountant will assess the strengths and weaknesses of the opponent's case. The accountant's involvement in this phase will help the attorney to focus on those issues that have the greatest impact on proving the case.

(d) DISCOVERY.   Discovery is the information-gathering stage of the litigation process. During discovery each party attempts to identify and obtain all the information and documents necessary to prove its case. The accountant's initial assistance may be in formulating specific accounting and financially oriented questions to be included in interrogatories. The accountant will also assist in drafting document requests by identifying in a very specific manner the types of documents (particularly accounting records and reports) that would be of interest and that the opposing party is likely to have retained. The more specific the requests are, the more likely the response will be useful. The accountant will also be able to assist the attorney with the preparation of **responses** to the opposing party's interrogatories and document requests.

Depositions provide each side with an opportunity to elicit relevant facts and to identify weaknesses in an opponent's argument. The accountant can be helpful in this area by assisting the attorney in identifying subjects to be explored and in developing specific deposition questions, especially when financial executives or experts are being deposed. Frequently, an attorney will request the accounting expert to be present at these key depositions. Here the accountant can help the attorney understand and interpret the deponent's responses and formulate follow-on questions to probe more deeply into the subject area. Having the accountant present at the deposition will enable the attorney to completely understand and consider the financial issues. The accountant who will be a testifying expert may be subject to deposition by the opposing attorney. The opposition will attempt to gain a thorough understanding of the accountant's analysis and conclusions and, when possible, identify weaknesses and lay the groundwork for attack at trial. The importance of giving effective deposition testimony is obvious. The last section of this chapter, "Testimony," presents a description of the deposition process and some pointers for giving deposition testimony.

(e) SETTLEMENT ANALYSIS.   Settlement negotiations can occur at any point during the litigation process. They can be greatly facilitated by the use of an accounting expert. The accountant can be instrumental in evaluating existing alternatives and terms as well as in proposing other strategic approaches. The accountant's evaluation may involve (1) the determination of economic value and feasibility of various strategies, or (2) an analysis of the strengths and weaknesses of the two sides' positions.

When determining value and evaluating feasibility, the accountant can estimate damages under various scenarios and help to assess the probability of occurrence for each, thereby giving the attorney a better understanding of the risks involved. Just as importantly, the accountant can evaluate the true economic value of various settlement alternatives (e.g., structured settlements and noncash settlements) and determine possible tax effects of each. This will enable the attorney and client to make a more informed decision regarding settlement options and perhaps offer alternatives that benefit both parties.

The accountant also can provide an evaluation of the relative strengths and weaknesses of both the plaintiff's and the defendant's positions, thereby helping the attorney strengthen his bargaining position and anticipate potential problems.

(f) TRIAL.   If the case does not settle, the final role of the accountant will be to assist during the trial itself. The accountant's testimony in court is a key part of this role. In testimony, the accountant presents the opinions developed as a result of his information gathering, review, and analysis. This role is clearly the most important one the accountant will play in the process. It is imperative that the accountant present opinions in a straightforward, cogent, and concise manner. The last section of this chapter describes the course of direct testimony and suggests ways to enhance the effectiveness of the testimony.

Although opinion testimony is of paramount importance at the trial stage, the accountant can play other valuable roles. For example, the accountant can be of tremendous value to attorneys during the cross-examination of opposing experts and financial witnesses. The accountant can work with the attorney to prepare cross-examination questions in an effort to undermine the testimony or the credibility of the witness. The accountant will be important in this phase because of his ability to formulate accounting and financially oriented questions that will be difficult for the witness to evade or deflect. More importantly, the accountant will be able to assess the responses and provide follow-on questions to "close the loop" on important issues.

(g) PROFESSIONAL STANDARDS RELEVANT TO LITIGATION CONSULTING.   Throughout the litigation process, the accountant will be asked to provide input, conduct analyses, and offer advice or opinions regarding facts at issue in the case. Clearly, the attorney-client will expect that appropriate standards of care are followed by the accountant during the course of the engagement. However, although the litigation process itself is a formal, structured process with many rules and procedures that must be followed, the nature of the accountant's work is typically very unstructured and loosely defined. For this reason, the AICPA has established certain exemptions for CPAs engaged as expert witnesses as discussed below. Despite the lack of specifically defined standards, the general standards established by the AICPA form a framework for a responsible practitioner in the role as a forensic accountant. These standards serve as reasonable guidelines to ensure that the accountant does not jeopardize the interests of the attorney or the attorney's client.

The AICPA has published nonauthoritative educational guidance for practitioners, including Consulting Services Special Report 93-1, "Application of AICPA Professional Standards in the Performance of Litigation Services," Report 93-2, "Conflicts of Interest in Litigation Services Engagements," Report 93-3, "Comparing Attest and Consulting Services: A Guide for the Practitioner," Report 93-4, "Providing Litigation Services," and Consulting Services Practice Aid 95-2, "Communicating Understandings in Litigation Services: Engagement Letters."

No rules or standards are substitutes for professional judgment. The following discussion of selected AICPA standards is by no means all inclusive. The standards and guidelines that follow define a base on which a responsible professional can comfortably rely while conducting litigation services engagements.

Regardless of the service or engagement the accountant is called upon to provide, key elements of the AICPA's Code of Professional Conduct will apply. Notably, Article IV—Objectivity and Independence (AICPA, 1988, pp. 7–8) advises the accountant to be "impartial, intellectually honest and free of conflicts of interest." The attorney and client should not expect less.

(i) Litigation Support Exemptions. Litigation support services are specifically exempted from the reporting requirements concerning financial forecasts and projections in the Statement on Standards for Accountants' Services on Prospective Financial Information (AICPA, 1985). The basis for this exemption is that prospective financial information in a litigation context is open to challenge, that is, cross-examination. Absent this opportunity for scrutiny and challenge, the professional standard applies.

Section 9100.48 of *Attestation Engagements Interpretations,* "Applicability of Attestation Standards to Litigation Services," excludes litigation services that "involve pending or potential formal legal or regulatory proceedings before a trier of fact in connection with the resolution of a dispute between two or more parties . . . ."

Litigation services are recognized as a management consulting service in Statement on Standards for Consulting Services issued by the AICPA, and are defined in Consulting Services Practice Aid No. 93-4, "Providing Litigation Services" (AICPA, 1993) as "any professional assistance nonlawyers provide to lawyers in the litigation process." Bankruptcy, forensic accounting, reorganization, or insolvency services, as provided by CPAs, generally are accepted as forms of litigation services. Also, guidance on providing litigation services is available in the AICPA Management Advisory Services Technical Consulting Practice Aid No. 7, "Litigation Services," (Wagner and Frank, 1986). This practice aid provides insights into types of engagements, relationships with attorneys and clients, approach to the work, and other unique aspects of this practice.

(ii) Conflicts of Interest. Conflicts of interest warrant special attention and concern by the accountant in a litigation engagement. Not only is the practitioner exposed to conflicts with his general practice clients, but the discovery of a conflict during the litigation engagement could jeopardize the ability of the attorney to serve the client, not to mention cause embarrassment to the accountant and high likelihood that fees will not be collected. The AICPA's Consulting Services Special Report 93-2, "Conflicts of Interest in Litigation Services Engagements," provides definitions and guidance on identifying and handling conflicts of interest.

A conflict of interest exists in a litigation engagement when the ability of the accountant to be objective and independent may be affected by prior or current business relationships. The accountant should avoid engagements that involve conflicts of interest. Conflicts may arise from the accountant's ethical obligation to preserve existing client confidences, or from other relationships that may affect the accountant's ability to present adequately an issue for the client. An accountant may decline an engagement on the basis of perceived conflicts or business considerations. Accepting a litigation engagement on behalf of an audit client would not be a conflict; accepting an engagement against an audit client may be a professional conflict and would likely be a business conflict. Often, potential conflicts can be resolved through agreements between the parties, establishment of "fire walls" (procedural barriers between teams within the firm), or other methods.

Before the accountant accepts a litigation engagement, all current and prior relationships, if any, with all known parties in a litigation must be evaluated for possible conflicts of interest. Known parties include potential clients, opposing parties, and each of their respective counsels. Also, throughout the engagement, potential conflicts of interest could surface, and these situations should be evaluated as if they occurred before the engagement began.

(iii) Legal Liability.   Historically, CPA services to the litigation process had not been the subject of litigation themselves. However, two recent cases (*Mattco Forge v. Arthur Young* and *Shadow Traffic v. Superior Court*) have changed the risk profile to the litigation consultant.

Until *Mattco Forge,* many believed that litigation support services were subject to the "litigation privilege," thereby immunizing the accountant-witness from liability for courtroom testimony or related preparation. However, *Mattco Forge* held that litigation services are subject to the traditional contract and tort standards. Accordingly, the accountant-witness is advised to be sure his or her services comply with the standards of the profession as well as any contractual commitments made. *Crain, et al.* (1994) provides a more thorough discussion of this case.

In *Shadow Traffic,* the accountant-witness had been contacted by one party to the litigation and had had what were deemed confidential discussions regarding the case. The accountant was not retained by that party, but shortly thereafter, the accountant was retained by the opposing party. The court found this to be a conflict of interest; as a result, the client's law firm was disqualified. (The accountant had already withdrawn, or he would have been disqualified as well.) This case demonstrates not only the risk but also the embarrassment that can result from improper or incomplete conflicts clearance procedures.

40.4 TYPES OF CASES

(a) GENERAL ROLE OF ACCOUNTANT-EXPERT.   An accountant may be called as an expert in almost any case where there are numbers or dollars in dispute. Since most civil lawsuits are about money, this means that an accountant may be involved in almost any type of litigation.

Accountants are also used as experts in cases that require a knowledge of business records and transactions. However, there are certain types of cases in which the accountant is more likely to be involved.

A lawsuit typically requires proof of liability, causation, and damages. An accountant may be involved in any or all of these areas. Cases requiring an accountant's testimony on liability typically revolve around professional liability (e.g., was the audit performed properly?) or investigatory accounting (e.g., can the accountant determine what really happened?). Damages cases usually involve the computation of lost economic value, including lost profits, lost royalties, or loss of asset value.

(b) BUSINESS-ORIENTED CASES.   The accountant's work often involves business disputes. This section presents a summary of common types of cases and the accountant's role.

(i) Breach of Contract.   Typically, the plaintiff has a contract with the defendant that the defendant is accused of breaching. For example, the contract may call for the defendant to buy a certain quantity of product for a certain price. The defendant, however, fails to make the required purchases. Or, the defendant may be accused of breaching a warranty on its goods or services. The accountant may be asked to quantify the damages suffered by the plaintiff as a result of the breach. Usually, the damages are measured by lost profits, that is, the additional profits the plaintiff would have earned but for the defendant's breach. Among the issues the accountant may address are lost revenues, avoided costs, available capacity, and possible mitigating actions, including sale of the product to others.

(ii) Business Interruption. A business interruption claim may arise from an accident, fire, flood, strike, or other unexpected event. It may even arise from a contract or warranty claim where the defendant's breach has caused the plaintiff to suspend operations. Typically, these claims are filed by a business against its insurance carrier, though a claim against the entity causing the event is possible. In a business interruption case, the plaintiff claims the event caused the business to suffer losses.

Often, the accountant is asked to quantify the loss. Elements to be considered may include lost profits, loss of tangible assets, loss of intangible assets (including goodwill), loss of an entire business or business line, cost to repair or reestablish the business, cost of downtime, or cost of wasted effort (time spent fixing the problem instead of generating operating profits).

(iii) Intellectual Property. Intellectual property disputes involve the rights to use patents, copyrights, and trademarks. The plaintiff claims that the defendant infringed on the plaintiff's intellectual property by illegally using the patent, copyright, or trademark. For patents, damages are defined by law to be plaintiff's lost profits (if reasonably provable), but not less than a reasonable royalty. Damages in a copyright case are the market value of the infringed work, the profits that the owner lost or will lose as a result of the infringement, or the defendant's profit. In a trademark case, where the mark has been registered with the Patent and Trademark Office, the owner may recover actual damages and also the infringer's profits.

Often computations are made separately for lost profits and for reasonable royalties. Sometimes the accountant can perform both analyses. Other times the accountant's opinion on reasonable royalty may be supplemented by another expert with experience in negotiating royalties in the particular industry.

(iv) Antitrust. The plaintiff in antitrust litigation may be either the government or a private party. The government usually brings suit to oppose a merger or to break up a monopolist. Government suits are usually not for monetary damages. Experts in these suits, particularly in liability issues involving monopolistic practices, relevant market share, and the like, are often economists, not accountants.

In a private suit, the plaintiff accuses the defendant of violating antitrust laws, resulting in injury to competition, including (or especially) injury to the plaintiff. The accountant's role again may be the computation of lost profits.

A company may be accused of violating antitrust laws by selling the same goods at different prices to different parties in the same channel of distribution. This ostensibly discriminatory pricing may be refuted if the defendant can show that the price differences are justified by differences in cost of production, service, freight, and so on. An accountant may conduct these cost justification studies.

Accusations of predatory pricing also fall under the antitrust laws. The defendant in a predatory pricing case is accused of pricing so low that competitors lose money and are driven out of business. Once the competition is eliminated, the defendant presumably raises prices and enjoys monopoly profits. One legal standard for predatory pricing is pricing below cost of production. Depending on the law, the standard may be either incremental costs or fully allocated costs. An accountant may help establish or refute this claim by studying product pricing and production costs, and measuring the resulting profit margins.

(v) White Collar Crime and Fraud.   Lawsuits in this area usually relate to actions that resulted in the failure of a venture. Accountants are typically engaged to determine whether the venture was structured, organized, or managed as a conduit to abscond with investor money. Some of the more egregious examples typically are "boiler room" solicitations that appeal to investors because of the promised high return on investment.

Other examples of white collar crime and fraud activities include schemes involving the "penny stock" market and high-yielding investment certificates that may actually be nothing more than "Ponzi" transactions. In a typical Ponzi arrangement, real profits do not exist. Instead, money from new investors is used to pay investment returns to existing investors, giving the impression of profits.

Other types of fraud cases include various schemes by executives, employees, and customers to siphon funds from financial institutions for their personal use, check kiting, lapping, computer fraud, embezzlement, defense procurement fraud, costing fraud, schemes involving kickbacks, insider trading cases, and fraudulent bankruptcy actions.

The accountant's role in white collar crime and fraud cases is usually twofold. First, the accountant may assist counsel in the investigation of the venture to document what happened and establish liability. Second, the accountant may be involved in calculating damages that result from the fraud.

(vi) Securities Act Violations.   Lawsuits in this area usually involve alleged violations of the federal acts, specifically §§ 11 and 12(2) of the Securities Act of 1933 and § 10(b) of the Securities and Exchange Act of 1934. These sections concern making false or misleading public statements about a company or omitting a material fact (either in a prospectus or in public statements, including financial statements), resulting in an alleged overvaluing of the company's stock. Typically, when the correct information becomes public, the value of the stock drops. Plaintiffs claim that, but for the misleading statements, they would not have bought the stock or they would have bought at a lower price. These lawsuits are often brought against officers, directors, investment bankers, lawyers, accountants, and others who may have been party to misstatements. Accountants may be involved in the liability, causation, and damages portions of securities cases. Involvement with liability issues is most common when an auditor has been accused of violating § 10(b)5 by failing to perform a GAAS audit and/or by giving a clean opinion to non-GAAP financial statements. The accountant will review the auditor's work papers and other relevant materials to reach a conclusion as to the adequacy of the audit of the financial statements. For more on this topic, see subsection 40.4(b)(ix) below.

The causation and damages phases of securities cases are closely linked. They consist of determining whether the information had any impact on the stock price and quantifying the losses suffered by the plaintiff investors as a result. Typically, this involves determining what the stock price **would have been** if the proper information had been released at the proper time. The methods for doing this are beyond the scope of this chapter; see de Silva, et al (1995) for a treatment of this subject.

(vii) Bankruptcy.   Bankruptcy matters may require an accountant's services for many different tasks. The role of the accountant and scope of services to be performed is influenced by the size of the company and by whether the accountant is working for the trustee, debtor in possession, secured creditors, or the creditors' committee(s).

Accountants for the debtor in possession may be asked to prepare analyses supporting the solvency or insolvency of the debtor, which may affect creditors' claims, recoveries, or security interests. Such accountants also may be involved in preparing prospective financial information filed with the U.S. Trustee's Office or used in negotiating plans of reorganization with the parties of interest. Another important role may require making analyses to support a debtor's use of cash collateral and analyses showing that adequate protection is available to the secured creditor.

An accountant for the creditors' committee, in addition to reviewing any analyses prepared for the debtor, will have additional responsibilities. The accountant may initially be asked to determine the cause for the business failure and may need to determine quickly whether the debtor's operation may be further depleting the assets available for creditors. The creditors' accountants also may need to investigate the conduct of the debtor. The scope and depth may vary significantly based on the relationship and confidence the creditors have with existing management. At a minimum, a review to determine possible preferential payments, fraudulent conveyances, and insider transactions is usually performed. The roles, definitions, and exceptions to preferences and fraudulent conveyances are detailed in the Bankruptcy Code as well as in Newton (1994).

(viii) Lender Liability. Common law verdicts in numerous states have established a duty requiring banks to act in good faith and to provide a reasonable time period for a customer to arrange alternative financing should the bank no longer wish to continue the relationship. Other cases involve inaccurate or incomplete responses from banks to inquiries by third parties or failure to honor financing commitments. In some situations the bank's activity, either as a member of the business's Board of Directors, or in selecting those members, or the bank's insistence on designating workout consultants, places them in a position of being too close to operating the business; and they may find themselves accountable for its losses or ultimate bankruptcy.

The accountant's role is to assist with liability, causation, and damage issues. With respect to liability issues, the accountant may develop financial data to determine whether the borrower was in compliance with various loan covenants at various intervals during the banking relationship, including at its commencement. A review of debt and equity items in the financial statements could identify differences in definitions or inconsistencies between GAAP and the bank loan document terminology.

Accounting consultants working with defendants to lender liability actions may provide useful information to show the bank was acting prudently in calling a loan or in refusing to extend it based on the results of a financial analysis of the debtor. On the causation issue, the accountant can determine whether the bank's actions caused the business failure, or whether other circumstances were involved.

The accountant's role in damages is important for both the plaintiff and defendant. Damage theories may include both the actual cost of the termination of the credit relationship and more complex damages, including punitive and RICO claims where business failure occurs.

(ix) Employment Litigation. Employment litigation typically involves claims of employment discrimination (including discrimination on the basis of age, race, or gender) or wrongful discharge. Claims may involve discrimination in hiring, promotion, or wages.

The accountant may be involved in both liability and damages phases of employment claims. For liability, the accountant may compile hiring rates, promotion rates, salary levels, or similar historical information to prove or refute a claim of differential treatment. This liability work often may be performed in conjunction with a statistician.

On damages, the accountant may determine what the plaintiff's income would have been had the alleged discrimination not occurred. The accountant will consider the proper level of earnings, the likely duration of the earnings, and any offset from amounts actually earned. The issues are very similar to loss of earnings claims in personal injury cases. Although specific approaches are not discussed in this chapter, the methods are logically similar to lost profits claims.

(x) Accountant's Liability. Most litigated claims against accountants have arisen from audit work. Recently, significant litigation has come from compilation, review, and prospective financial statement engagements.

Litigation over audited financial statements generally involves allegations that GAAP was not applied, or that the audit was not conducted in accordance with GAAS, or both. In class action securities litigation, noncompliance with SEC Regulations S-X and S-K as well as Financial Reporting Releases may also be alleged.

The accountant will review and analyze the company's financial records and auditor's work papers to determine if information can be discovered to prove or disprove compliance with GAAP or GAAS.

(c) NONBUSINESS CASES. Important nonbusiness issues include marital dissolution, partnership dissolution, and personal injury matters.

(i) Marital Dissolution. In many states the financial aspects of a marital dissolution are governed by family law statutes that establish rules for sharing of income and the division of property. The tax laws have also greatly influenced the allocation of income and assets during and after a marital dissolution. Most states divide assets "equitably"; a few states are governed by community property rules. Awareness of the local rules and practices is of critical importance to accountants in their financial analyses.

In community property states the impact of community versus separate property is important. Simply stated, in community property states both spouses share equally in all income earned and property acquired during the marriage using community property funds. Separate property owned prior to marriage or acquired during marriage using separate property assets may retain its distinction. However, where funds and assets are commingled, the ultimate sharing of such items is complicated. The accountant's role is often to trace receipts and disbursements to determine which assets are community property.

Accountants often are asked to determine the value of the assets owned by the litigants as well as the income sources from which spousal and child support can be calculated. The valuation of assets often includes business valuation and, in the case of professionals, the value of their shareholdings or partnership interest. Issues such as professional goodwill or celebrity goodwill are important and contested often in marital dissolution litigation.

(ii) Partnership Dissolution. Partnerships sometimes break up in a manner similar to a divorce. The accountant's work is also similar, focusing on tracing, valuation, and fair apportionment of assets and liabilities.

(iii) Personal Injury. Personal injury cases stem from automobile accidents, slip-and-falls, and the like. Typically, damage components include medical expenses, pain and suffering, and lost earnings. The accountant is usually involved in the last item only. For identification of the issues involved, see 40.4(b)(ix).

40.5 THE ACCOUNTANT'S ROLE IN THE LIABILITY ISSUE

Accountants can play a critical role in assisting counsel in issues related to liability. Because attorneys are usually not knowledgeable about accounting or auditing issues, the accounting expert may provide critical insights into the nature of the liability aspects of a case. Although the issues vary by the type of case, the role that an accountant performs frequently focuses on the following areas.

(a) VIOLATIONS OF GAAP. An accountant is often called on to assess whether there have been violations of GAAP. At one time, GAAP was simply common practice, that is, those principles that were generally used by professionals. GAAP has become more codified with pronouncements from the FASB, the EITF, government bodies (e.g., SEC) and industry organizations. The accounting expert must be cognizant of the literature and must be able to bring knowledge of the ever-increasing corpus of pronouncements and standards that constitute GAAP to the issues of the case.

During the discovery process, the accountant has the opportunity to explore the underlying documents and associate the facts with the accounting pronouncements. The accountant will refer to a company's general accounting records and documents as well as to the work papers of the independent auditor. The ability to review an independent auditor's work papers is essential. Such a review process requires the expert either to be an auditor or to have some auditing background. Issues related to the auditing firm's consideration of GAAP, their consultation with parties in their firm who provide technical expertise, and the extent to which they have researched a specific area of accounting should be documented in the auditor's work papers.

GAAP issues often arise in **securities cases.** In securities class action suits, the company's auditor may be named as a defendant along with the officers and directors of the company. The plaintiff's complaint usually enumerates a number of GAAP violations, centering around the timing and nature of revenues and expenses. That is, the complaint often alleges that the earnings of the defendant company were due to the overrecognition of revenues and the under-recognition of expenses.

For example, a recent securities case involved, in part, the recognition by the company of revenues related to sales of territorial rights for franchisees. The complaint alleged that the defendant recognized the revenue before the earning process was complete and therefore committed a fraud on the market through reporting higher revenues to the public. Another case involved the recognition of production expense related to a film company's extensive inventory of products for the theatrical and ancillary markets. In this instance, the company was alleged to have used accounting methods that were not in conformity with SFAS No. 53. As a result, one of the major allegations in the lawsuit was that the company did not write-down film costs to their net realizable value when supposedly it became known that the company would not realize revenues to cover their unamortized costs.

GAAP is also an issue in disputes over the **contractual purchase** of a company. With such purchases, the audited financial statements are used as the basis for the purchase or condition of the sale. The expert in these cases is called on by the seller to review the working papers of the independent auditor of the financial statements. From these working papers and the notes to the financial statements, the expert can determine what accounting methods were employed and whether they are in conformity with GAAP and common industry practice.

In contractual purchases litigation, the issues center on the valuation of assets or the quantification and disclosure of liabilities. Asset values in dispute may include such issues as proper use of LIFO or FIFO, inventory write-downs, unrecorded liabilities, accounting for impaired assets, amortization of goodwill, replacement cost versus book value, and realizable value of accounts receivable.

Liabilities are of critical importance since the buyer needs to be alerted to all potential and contingent debts and encumbrances. The accountant would determine whether there was adequate disclosure of the liabilities in the financial statements that were either issued or relied on by the buyer. The accountant may also need to evaluate whether subsequent events were reasonably foreseeable.

(b) VIOLATIONS OF GAAS OR OTHER PROFESSIONAL STANDARDS.   The accountant may review and assess potential violations of GAAS or other applicable professional standards. Such violations may range from the failure of the defendant auditing firm to adequately observe the physical inventory, to not confirming sufficient accounts receivable, to not performing an adequate subsequent events review. GAAS violations are usually alleged in conjunction with GAAP violations. Liability issues related to a failure to perform an audit in accordance with GAAS are usually not unearthed until a review of the auditing firm's work papers has taken place.

Bankruptcy cases often focus on the liability of the auditor of the failed company's financial statements. For example, in the savings and loan industry, independent auditors of some failed institutions have been charged with violations of the ethical rule on independence, with failure to adequately circularize loans, and with inadequately documenting audit findings. In these cases, attorneys for both the plaintiff and defendant have turned to accounting experts to assist them, particularly in determining whether any GAAS violations have occurred.

With the increasing number of authoritative pronouncements being issued by the AICPA in areas related to compilations and reviews, forecasts and projections, the detection of fraud, and the need for auditors to communicate significant deficiencies in internal control structure, the accounting expert may be frequently called on by attorneys to address the issue of compliance with professional standards.

(c) TRANSACTIONAL ANALYSES. The accountant provides expertise in several types of transactional disputes.

In **white collar crime** cases where "Ponzi" schemes are suspected, the accountant will want to document how the enterprise was structured and to develop organizational charts and flow charts. Tracing transactions from the receipt of investor funds to its ultimate investment or disposition will be required. Analyses that illustrate the lack of any positive cash flow other than by raising additional investor funds will be useful to the attorney in showing liability. The flow of all cash transactions, identification of all bank accounts, location of any safe deposit boxes, investment accounts, or custodial arrangements are all within the accountant's scope.

The accountant should also analyze cash disbursements to see whether any patterns indicating self-dealing emerge, or to identify possible related entities or personal use or benefit of company assets. Unusual expenses should be vouched and particular attention should be devoted to traditionally sensitive areas such as travel and entertainment expenses. Some suspicious transactions are easily detected. Many illegal activities involve disguised transactions, but it is just as likely that the paid bills and supporting evidence will be fairly explanatory.

In the case of **penny stock fraud** schemes, the accountant may shift greater attention to the financial results and reports to shareholders, press releases and the like, to determine if evidence exists that such data were incorrect or inaccurate. Income recognition abuses or improper capitalization of expenses are typical categories of abuses used by penny stock promoters to misstate the operating results and mislead investors. In addition, the accountant should analyze key contracts, employment agreements, and other consulting arrangements. A time line analysis that reflects all key "publicized events" should be developed and used to determine if such events did occur. From the time line it can be determined whether, in the same time frame, all acquisitions or dispositions of assets and other financial transactions were accounted for properly.

Marital dissolution is another transactional area where the accountant can assist the attorney. Actual "liability" is usually not an issue in marital dissolutions. Most states have no-fault statutes that allow either party to seek a dissolution. The "liability" role of the accountant is to identify all assets and liabilities of the parties so that a fair and equitable distribution of assets results. Most family law courts are equity oriented, so the substance of transactions should carefully be considered when analyzing financial data. The forensic accountant has to examine financial data with concern for diversion of assets, improper cash transactions, and padded payroll and other fringe benefits and perks that may deprive the nonworking spouse of a fair share of the business's net worth as well as a share of spousal support.

If financial statements do not exist for closely held companies, such financial statements may need to be prepared. The accountant must be familiar with the local state family law. The accountant must also be familiar with tax implications of various asset transfers or split-ups so that neither spouse later finds unexpected tax consequences. The accountant should be aware of the proper handling of pension plan assets, individual retirement accounts, 401(k) plans, and the like, so that each party receives a fair share of assets, and so that income tax or excise taxes are not triggered unnecessarily.

In community property states, the existence of separate property and the impact of prenuptial agreements may also require analysis. Significant tracing of funds may become necessary if a total segregation of separate property assets has not been maintained. The marital community may have rights to a contribution for increased value of separate property that arises from services provided by the community after marriage. Lastly, the community may have some interest in separate property if joint tax returns have been filed and no separate tax cost was allocated to each category of assets.

(d) BANKRUPTCY AND BANKRUPTCY FRAUDS.   The work required to establish liability in bankruptcy cases is similar to that discussed in subsection 40.5(c) on transactional work, particularly in relation to white collar crime. One difference is that liability issues in bankruptcy have the benefit of explicit rules in the Bankruptcy Code (Title 11 USC, more specifically, §§ 543–549). These sections of the Bankruptcy Code detail the powers of a trustee to avoid transfers that defraud, hinder, or delay creditors, give preferential treatment to certain creditors, or do not give the bankrupt person or entity fair value for the transfer. Since these code sections define the scope of the trustee's power, an accountant engaged by the trustee should first read and understand the relevant provisions before planning the work. In addition, an accountant must obtain an understanding of certain sections of the Uniform Commercial Code and in particular the Uniform Fraudulent Transfer Act of the state where the business is situated. The location of the business may influence the scope of the work since the time period under the bankruptcy statute only allows for recovery one year prior to the bankruptcy, whereas state laws vary from 3 to 10 years.

Once the appropriate time period and scope have been determined, the accountant needs to review all material transactions to gain an understanding as to the economic benefit of the exchange to the bankrupt, including all monetary and nonmonetary exchanges. In addition, the accountant needs to determine the timing and explanation for any liens or other security interest granted or recorded during the time period. This review should include any asset sales, purchases, foreclosures, and tax assessments. Transactions between related entities or commonly controlled entities or their affiliates must be reviewed. Unlike the typical audit where discovery of fraud is not an objective unless it would materially misstate the financial statements, in a bankruptcy case the accountant is trying to develop **any** evidence that might show fraud or fraudulent intent.

A **preferential payment** analysis covers a review of transactions within 90 days (one year for insiders) prior to bankruptcy wherein a creditor is paid for an antecedent debt at a time the debtor is insolvent and such payment is not in the ordinary course of business. The definition of insolvency for this purpose is the fair value of assets compared with the fair value of liabilities—a balance sheet approach. "Ordinary course of business" is not defined except by reference to case precedents. For example, if creditors are routinely paid in 90 days but certain creditors get paid just before bankruptcy within 30 days, such payments are probably **not** in the ordinary course of business.

Certain **leveraged buyouts** (LBOs) have encountered financial difficulty shortly after consummation, and some creditors have used various security law and bankruptcy law theories to unwind these transactions and seek recoveries from selling shareholders, secured creditors, and others.

The accountant's work in establishing or defending liability is critical. Analyses that show the cash flow of the entity before and after the LBO help establish whether sufficient capital or working capital was available to the company. Changes in a company's borrowing, especially where a significant amount of assets have been recently pledged, also illustrate the potential damage to unsecured creditors. The accountant's ability to distinguish operating losses caused by the form and structure of the buyout from losses due to the economy or other competing companies will also assist counsel in determining whether the LBO can be attacked as a fraudulent transfer.

(e) ECONOMIC FORECASTS AND PROJECTIONS.   Accountants are sometimes retained by attorneys to address liability issues in the areas of economic forecasts, projections, and market definitions. The accountant sometimes works with and assists other experts whose testimony has direct bearing on the financial issues of the case.

In antitrust cases, the accountant's insights into pricing and costs complement the economic expert's development of liability issues surrounding predatory pricing, price discrimination, and monopolistic behavior. Attorneys may use the accountant to assist an economist rather than to testify to these issues. Because of their familiarity with the underlying financial and accounting documents of the company, accounting experts are often used to assist marketing experts in liability issues related to market definition in antitrust cases and product substitution in patent and intellectual property cases.

40.6 CAUSATION AND DAMAGES

(a) PROVING THE CAUSE OF DAMAGES.   The issues of causation and damages arise after the proof of liability. In discussing damages, we rely on the concept of the "but-for" world. The but-for world is the economic and physical environment that would have existed "but for" the actions of the defendant. In other words, it is the "undamaged" world, in contrast to the "actual," damaged world that did occur, and in which the defendant performed the alleged illegal acts.

In proving liability, the plaintiff must prove that the complained-of actions occurred and were illegal. In moving logically from liability toward damages, the plaintiff must demonstrate that the actions caused injury—that the but-for world arises logically out of the liability claims. Only then can the amount of damage be assessed.

This step is often omitted or glossed over. Often, the nexus between liability and damages is clear, and the act of calculating damages is enough to show the relationship. For example, if the lawsuit is over the loss of a specific contract, it may be obvious that damages should be the lost profit on that contract. However, there are situations where, if this step is overlooked, the plaintiff (and its expert accountant acting as damage witness) may not succeed in demonstrating its case.

As an example, consider the following situation. Company P's growth was at 20% during Year 1, and it has grown at that rate for many years. A conspiracy by two competitors, D1 and D2, to injure P is alleged to have started on January 1, Year 2. This conspiracy consists of sharing internal information between D1 and D2, but does **not** affect market prices, customer perceptions, or any other external matters. Nevertheless, Company P's growth has fallen to 12% during Year 2, and it sues.

Assume that the conspiracy was illegal. It would be inappropriate for a damage expert to measure damages based on the 8% shortfall in expected growth. Growth is determined in the marketplace, and the liability acts do not have a clear relationship to actions by customers. Absent such a showing, whether through logic or quantitative analysis, a damage study based on the 8% shortfall would be flawed.

Often, in proving causation, the accountant must eliminate or take into account possible causes other than the complained-of liability acts. In the example above, the parties may have cut prices (legally), a new competitor may have entered the market, or a specific contract may have been lost (legally). In a securities case, where the allegation is that stock prices fell after bad news was released, it is possible that the entire market or industry declined at the same time. The accountant must analyze the specific facts and discriminate between legal and illegal causes and effects. Only after the link between the correct cause (liability) and effect (damages) is established can the accountant proceed to calculate damages.

(b) PROVING THE AMOUNT OF DAMAGES

(i) Measures of Damages.   Depending on the case, there are many different standards by which damages are measured:

1. Lost profits (past profits, prospective profits, or both, including increased costs).
2. Lost asset value (the appraised value of identified assets, including goodwill, or other intangibles).
3. Lost personal earnings (wages, salary, etc.).
4. Lost royalties or licensing fees (amounts due for use of the plaintiff's assets or rights).

In most cases, these approaches are all attempts to compute the difference between the but-for world and the actual world. That is, an attempt to measure the difference between what **should have** happened and what **actually did** happen.

Lost profits are the most common standard for business cases. Valuations are used in both business disputes and marital dissolution proceedings. Personal earnings is the damages standard for the economic component of personal injury suits. (Other components are medical costs and pain and suffering.) Reasonable royalty is used in intellectual property disputes, especially patent cases.

The basics of a lost profits computation are discussed below, but valuation methods are beyond the scope of this chapter. Loss of personal earnings was mentioned briefly above; many of the principles of lost profits computation can be applied. Reasonable royalty computations depend to some extent on a lost profits analysis, but the specific requirements of a reasonable royalty analysis are also beyond the scope of this chapter. For more on reasonable royalty, see Frank and Wagner (1987).

(ii) Mitigation.   A plaintiff has the obligation to mitigate damages. This means that the plaintiff must take reasonable steps to minimize the damages suffered. More specifically, the courts (and damages experts) will compute damages as if the plaintiff mitigated, whether the mitigation really occurred or not. Consider the following examples of mitigation:

1. Plaintiff company lost a production contract. Plaintiff should lay off staff, sell the product to someone else, cancel subcontractors or purchase orders, and so on. Damages would be lost revenues less unavoidable costs.
2. Plaintiff individual was injured and unable to work at his old job, which involved physical labor. However, his injuries allow him to perform office work. Plaintiff is obligated to look for an appropriate job, commensurate with his abilities and skills, which he is able to perform. Damages would be lost wages less alternative wages which were or should have been earned (plus, of course, damages for medical costs and pain and suffering).
3. Plaintiff had a binding contract with defendant for sale of plaintiff's business. Defendant breached. Plaintiff must make a good faith effort to find a new buyer. Damages would be computed as difference between the contract value and the market value that would be paid by a new buyer, plus any increased costs or time-value-of-money costs caused by the breach.

In many cases, reasonable mitigation will have occurred, and the expert may look at the difference between what should have occurred and what did occur as the measure of damages. After all, the plaintiff's recovery through litigation is uncertain, and plaintiff has every incentive to reduce damages to itself. However, if reasonable mitigation did not occur, the accountant should make the necessary adjustments.

(c) QUANTIFYING LOSSES UNDER THE LOST PROFITS APPROACH.   Basically, the procedure to follow in quantifying losses is to determine lost sales volume and the related incremental revenue, consider the plaintiff's capacity to produce, and compute the costs associated with generating the projected revenue.

Lost profits may be computed using either the **incremental** or **overall** methods. Under the incremental method, all incremental (additional) revenues and costs are computed; the difference between incremental revenues and incremental costs is the lost profit. Under the overall method, the company's overall revenues and costs (historical plus incremental) are computed; lost profits are the difference between historical and but-for profits. For more on the basics of lost profits, see Sims and Haller (1988).

If done carefully, the incremental and overall methods are identical. In practice, errors may occur in applying the incremental method because incremental costs are overlooked. In particular, this may happen when, in the but-for world, the cost of an **historical** activity changes. For example, assume 200 units of raw material were purchased historically for $10 per unit. In the but-for world, 300 units would be required. Due to volume discounts, the material can be purchased at $9 per unit. A pure incremental analysis would compute incremental costs as 100 units times $9 per unit, or $900. This is wrong, for it fails to take into account the cost savings on the 200 historical units. Either an overall analysis or a proper incremental analysis would show the incremental cost to be $(300 \times \$9) - (200 \times \$10) = \$700$.

Quantifying lost profits is essentially a three-step procedure:

Determine Lost Sales Volume and the Related Incremental Revenues. Lost sales volume should be estimated based on the liability theory of the but-for world. Often, certain benchmarks are used to establish lost sales. Some common methods are:

The Direct Approach. In many cases, the facts support a direct computation of lost sales. For example, in a breach of contract matter, the contract may call for a certain quantity of product to be produced.

The Before-and-After Approach. Compare sales or sales growth before the liability act to the comparable figures afterward.

The Yardstick (or Benchmark) Approach. Compare the subject company to other companies or to industry averages. This requires the accountant to conclude that, but for the liability acts, the subject company would have performed as well as the comparable company or the industry average. If the defendant has gained the sales lost by the plaintiff, a comparison to the plaintiff may be appropriate. A variation of this method incorporates the before-and-after approach: Compare the subject company to a standard or the industry average before the liability act; use that relationship to project the but-for world.

The Market Forecast Approach. Project the market or the company's market share directly based on other evidence in the case. Sometimes, prior market forecasts are available. In other circumstances, the accountant may make the forecast or rely on another expert or witness in the case to provide the forecast.

A sales forecast may be made in units or dollars. If units are used, the forecast must be converted into dollars by using an assumed price. The accountant should consider whether the but-for economic environment would result in different prices than the actual environment. If the plaintiff was illegally constraining prices (for example, through predatory pricing or producing goods in violation of a patent), the but-for price may be higher than the historical price. If the plaintiff illegally constrained competition (for example, through antitrust violations), the historical price may be too high.

The combination of the sales forecast and but-for prices yields a but-for revenue projection.

Consider the Plaintiff's Capacity to Produce. The plaintiff must be able to produce the projected sales for them to be recoverable as damages. If the plaintiff is selling all it can produce, the incremental sales forecast may not be achievable.

Capacity can always be expanded, but at a cost. Within some production range, there are no significant production constraints. If projected sales are within this range, the analysis may be straightforward. Beyond this range, the plaintiff may only be able to expand production by adding overtime, moving to a second or third shift, or by building additional production facilities. If the plaintiff's claim requires an expansion of production capacity, the accountant must evaluate the increased capacity for three factors: reasonableness, timing, and cost.

Reasonableness may be judged by a company's responses to similar situations. When capacity constraints arose in the past, did the company expand, or did it simply operate with constraints? Were additional shifts or mandatory overtime instituted to expand capacity, or were capital expenditures made? If additional shifts or hours were run, was this a long-term solution, or was it only until additional capacity could be constructed? Is the increased demand permanent, or it is better to lose sales now to avoid excess capacity later? How does increased demand relate to production of the company's other products?

Once reasonableness is established, **timing** must be considered. Can capacity be expanded quickly? What lead time is required? What evidence of increased demand does company management require before committing to an expansion? Are there supply constraints on getting the required capital goods?

Finally, consider **cost.** How much will the expanded capacity cost? If required production is within the usual production range, a special cost analysis may not be needed. If overtime, shift differentials, or capital expenditures are required, their costs should be estimated.

Compute the Costs Associated with Generating the Projected Revenue.   The accountant must be careful to identify all costs associated with projected revenue. As with revenues, either a total cost or incremental cost approach may be appropriate. Costs include both capacity expansion costs (see above) and ordinary production, selling, and administrative costs.

Costs may be estimated using a variety of techniques. Among the most common are:

Direct Assignment. Costs are specifically identified and associated with the incremental sales. This is often used for direct costs, such as materials and direct labor.

Cost Allocations. Accounting or engineering judgments are used to allocate costs to units. The techniques used are similar to those of cost accounting. In allocating costs, it is important to have a thorough understanding of the magnitude of the incremental volume, and of the related fixed and variable costs. Costs which are considered fixed for a small change in volume may be variable for a larger change.

Statistical Methods. Statistical methods, especially regression analysis, may be used to find the relationship between historical costs and volumes. Once such a relationship is established, it may be used to estimate costs for the but-for volume. These methods are powerful, but require significant training to apply correctly.

For more on cost estimation methods, see Kinrich (1995).

(d) OTHER ISSUES.   Besides the basic procedures for determining lost profits, there are other issues to take into consideration.

(i) Cash Flow.   When accountants speak of lost profits, they often mean net income according to GAAP. However, in computing damages, it may be appropriate to measure lost cash flow. The computation of net income includes numerous accounting conventions and techniques (depreciation, LIFO, etc.) that may not reflect actual out-of-pocket losses. Depending on the legal standard, lost cash flow may be more appropriate. Even if net income is the proper standard, cash flow is clearly relevant if interest is to be earned on past damages.

(ii) Interest on Damage Awards.   Some or all of most damage awards are to compensate for past losses. In order to be made whole in economic terms, it might be supposed that the plaintiff should earn interest on past losses from the date of loss to the date of payment. However, the law does not always allow interest, and when it does, the interest rate is not always the rate applicable to the economic circumstances.

In general, the treatment of interest is governed by the applicable law. The courts distinguish between prejudgment interest (accrued between the date of loss and the date of trial or final judgment) and postjudgment interest (accrued from the date of judgment to the date of payment, which can be years if the judgment is appealed). In some jurisdictions, the rate of interest is set by law, often at a rate between 6% and 10%. Depending on the case, some jurisdictions do not allow prejudgment interest; most allow postjudgment interest.

Some interest awards are within the province of the court. Some judges may allow calculations of interest to go to the jury as part of the damage claim; others may reserve the right to separately compute interest (either at the statutory rate or at a rate depending on proof) after the jury awards damages. If the court allows economic testimony as to the amount of interest, what is the proper approach? The accountant should determine interest by recreating what would have happened to the plaintiff had the money been received at the times the damage claim asserts. The issues to be analyzed include:

The Amount of Cash That Would Have Been Received. This is not necessarily the amount of net income. Adjustments should be made for changes in working capital, capital expenditures, depreciation, repayment of principal, and so on.

The Income Taxes That Would Be Paid on the Income. Interest should be calculated on after-tax cash available for investment, as that is the amount that would be available in the but-for world. Only if net income approximates cash flow would a calculation based on net income be acceptable.

The Interest Rate That Would Make the Plaintiff Whole. The courts reject any "speculative" damage claim, including a speculative interest rate. This means that it is normally inappropriate to treat interest as equivalent to a lost investment opportunity (since the results of that investment may be speculative), thereby computing interest as a return on equity. Appropriate interest rates may include a risk-free (short-term or long-term government rates such as T-bills or bonds), money market rates, the plaintiff's or defendant's borrowing rate (if the plaintiff or defendant has debt outstanding), or the prime rate. The choice of rate depends on circumstances.

Taxes to Be Paid on Interest Earned. Interest earned is subject to taxes. If a before-tax interest rate is used, taxes must be subtracted before compounding the interest in future periods. Alternatively, an after-tax interest rate may be used. For more on the treatment of taxes, see below.

(iii) Present Value and Inflation. Time is a factor in most damage claims. A violation typically occurs sometime prior to the loss suffered by the plaintiff; the loss can continue into the future (e.g., lost earnings in a personal injury case); the trial can occur either after the entire loss has been suffered or prior to the full recovery from the impact of the violation; and the award may not be paid until sometime after the trial. Thus, a damage award must compensate the plaintiff for both past and future losses, but it must be made in full at the present time. This requires that the accountant accumulate both past and future lost profits to the present. This accumulation is accomplished by discounting the projected lost profits to the date of violation using a rate of interest and compounding the resulting amount to the present at some prejudgment interest rate. The choice of discount rate depends on circumstances. A nominal discount rate (such as the T-bill rate, the prime rate, or any other market rate) includes both a real rate of interest and an inflation premium. If the damages into the future are computed in constant (uninflated) dollars, then discounting at a real rate (net of inflation) may be appropriate. If inflation has been built into the projected damage figures, a nominal interest rate is correct. In either case, the appropriate discount rate should include an adjustment for risk.

For more on determining the present value of a damage award, see Kabe (1996).

(iv) Income Taxes. Under the law, some damage awards are taxable to the recipient, whereas others are tax-free. In computing damages, the goal is to properly account for taxes so the plaintiff is in the same position as it would have been if the liability act had never occurred.

If the award is taxable, then the damages should be computed on a before-tax basis. The plaintiff then receives the damage award, pays taxes, and is in the proper after-tax position. If the amount is tax-free, only the after-tax amount should be assessed as damages.

Complications arise in the two areas: (1) if prejudgment interest is due, and (2) if tax rates have changed from the damage date to the payment date. As discussed above, prejudgment interest is computed on the after-tax amount, since that is the amount the plaintiff would have had to invest. However, if the award is taxable, the damages must be expressed in pretax dollars. The solution is simple. Compute the entire award, including damages and interest, in after-tax dollars. Then, gross up the award by the tax rate in the year of payment. When the plaintiff receives this amount and pays tax on it, plaintiff will be in the proper after-tax position. This approach, although accurate, has been relatively untested in court.

A similar situation arises if tax rates have changed. If pretax damages are used, the change in tax rates will result in an incorrect after-tax award. The solution is again to compute the after-tax amounts, then gross up the award for the current tax rate.

40.7 SUPPORT FOR OPINIONS

(a) SOURCES OF INFORMATION. The accountant must be aware of the many facts and statistics that relate to the subject and issues of the case and must have adequate data to authoritatively support opinions or conclusions. The data should be of high reliability since the accountant is subject to cross-examination.

There are two basic sources for data: the litigating parties (either the client or the opposition), and external sources, such as industry publications, economic statistics, and so on. The former is obtained through the discovery phase discussed previously. The latter is discussed here.

Many reference books list sources of business information. Also, computer databases are widely available and eliminate the need for data entry as the information can be downloaded into a computer file.

Often, an accountant may need to call on other experts or persons knowledgeable in the particular industry. A few state CPA societies have formed litigation services committees that the accountant may contact. Also, a research library may have an index of experts who can be contacted.

(b) RELIANCE ON OTHERS. The accountant as an expert witness may rely on the work of employees as well as personal research or sources in forming his opinion. Federal Rule of Evidence No. 703 describes permissible bases on which expert testimony may be founded: (1) information acquired through firsthand observation, (2) facts observed by, or presented to, the expert witness at the trial or at the hearing, (3) data considered by the expert witness outside of court. Rule 703 permits an expert to rely on facts that are not normally admissible in evidence if they are of a type reasonably relied on by experts in the field. "Reasonably" means trustworthy. "Type relied on" is left to the discretion of the trial judge. In turn, the judge may question the accountant-witness as to the appropriate degree of reliance.

(c) DOCUMENTATION. All materials prepared, accumulated, or referred to by the accountant acting as an expert witness in a case may be made available to the opposing side. At the outset the attorney and accountant should develop a clear understanding of exactly what the accountant will be preparing and retaining for the engagement. Then the accountant should carefully control the content of work papers and correct or avoid collecting materials that are irrelevant to forming an opinion. This should be an ongoing process, as the accountant may not be able to remove anything after receiving a subpoena. All work products of an expert may be discoverable and could be thoroughly scrutinized by the opposing party. Errors, inconsistencies, and irrelevant materials may form the basis for an effective challenge to the testimon of the accountant.

(d) ENGAGEMENT LETTERS.   The accountant may feel that it is appropriate to issue an engagement letter specifying the engagement's purpose, the tasks that need to be performed, and the terms of compensation. If the accountant is identified as an expert witness, the opposing party can discover the engagement letter. If, due to subsequent events, tasks enumerated in the engagement letter are not completed or are completed with adverse consequences to the accountant's client, opposing counsel may use this information to imply that the accountant's opinion is defective, or that the accountant did not perform all the analyses required to substantiate the conclusions presented. Accordingly, under many circumstances the engagement letter should describe the tasks in general terms only.

The AICPA provides guidance regarding the use and content of engagement letters in Consulting Services Practice Aid 95-2, "Communicating Understanding in Litigation Services: Engagement Letters."

40.8 TESTIMONY

Testimony is the ultimate result of expert witness work. This section provides advice on giving testimony and suggestions for the expert.

(a) GIVING DEPOSITION TESTIMONY.   A deposition of an expert witness is part of the discovery process in which counsel seeks to fulfill several major objectives. The most obvious objective is to find out what opinions the expert is going to offer at trial, and why. A deposition is also an opportunity to commit the expert to sworn testimony that can later be used for impeachment purposes, should the expert try to change his opinion. Additionally, counsel will use the deposition to assess the expert's effectiveness as a witness and the strength of the case for purposes of settlement negotiation and development of trial strategy. Consequently, expert depositions may be more important than the trial testimony and should be regarded with due respect.

Adequate preparation is crucial to giving an effective deposition. Naturally, a thorough review of one's opinions and underlying support is in order. The expert should also review any prior writings and testimony for previous positions that may be construed as contradictory. Being caught unaware in an apparent contradiction can have a debilitating effect on the credibility of a deponent's testimony. Know the information and sources relied on, the various analyses performed, the opinions reached, and the strengths as well as the weaknesses of the case. Above all, tell the truth.

Finally, insist on a detailed predeposition briefing with counsel. This briefing should include a conclusion regarding disclosure strategy. If the objective is to cause a settlement to occur, a complete disclosure of all the strengths of the case should be made. If the case is likely to proceed to trial, then a restrictive approach may be called for, in which the expert should answer only the question asked and should not volunteer related issues to opposing counsel.

There are some general rules an expert should follow when giving a deposition:

- *Bring No Documentation unless Required or Advised by Counsel.* To do so will only make opposing counsel more effective in conducting discovery and provide additional avenues of questions. Of course if the deposition is in response to a subpoena, all documents identified in that subpoena must be provided.

- *Think before Answering and Do Not Answer unless You Are Sure You Understand the Question.* Word crafting is an attorney's stock in trade. If a question is not totally understood, at best the answer will be unresponsive. At worst, the *accountant* may fall into a trap. Or, the attorney may not even understand his own question, and the response will only serve to lead the attorney to more effective questioning.

- *Answer Questions Directly—Then Stop.* Do not fill dead air, ramble, or volunteer information. The "pregnant pause" is a favorite gambit to elicit additional information when opposing counsel is not quite sure what to ask next and wants the expert's help.

- *Stop Talking and Listen When Your Counsel Objects.* The question may be improper, or the accountant's counsel may have noticed the infamous "trick" question. Common trick questions include the use of compound questions, double negatives, absolute terms, and prefacing a question with a misstatement of prior testimony.

  Absolute terms are typified by questions such as, "Were those **all** the documents you reviewed?" or, "Are those **all** your opinions regarding this case?" An affirmative answer may preclude a temporarily forgotten item that is important to the case from later being cited at trial. Consequently, if appropriate, qualify with responses such as, "Those are the items that I recall at the present time."

  A misstatement of prior testimony typically starts with, "Earlier you testified . . . ," and ends with a question which is often not directly related to the mischaracterized testimony. By answering the question while failing to correct the mischaracterization, an argument can be made that the witness agrees with the misstatement.

- *Refuse to Engage in Speculation.* Either the expert knows the answer or does not know. Opposing counsel may have the fact in hand and is hoping to trap the expert in a conflict. Being asked to interpret an unfamiliar document can be particularly treacherous. Likewise, an incorrect guess on a forgotten minor detail can be as damaging as an error on a major one. Do not be afraid to respond "I don't know" or "I don't recall." No one knows everything and very few, if any, people have perfect recall.

- *Resist Being Provoked into Anger or Arguing with Counsel.* Chances are the provocation is calculated, and there is no upside potential. Anger will cloud reasoned logic and possibly blind the expert to a trap that is just about to open.

- *Review the Court Reporter's Transcript, Correct All Errors and Typographical Errors, and Sign.* Once the deposition has been completed and the court reporter has prepared a transcript, read your testimony carefully. If you said something you did not mean, now is the only time you will have to change it.

(b) GIVING TRIAL TESTIMONY

(i) Direct Testimony. The objective of direct testimony is to present an opinion in a manner such that it will be understood and believed by the judge and jury. The testimony will begin by reviewing the witness's qualifications, which provide the prerequisite skill and training enabling the witness to provide the court with expert testimony.

The expert's opinions then will be solicited. It is imperative that the expert not appear to be an advocate for the plaintiff or defendant, but rather fair and unbiased. The job of advocacy should be reserved for the attorney. Violation of this precept will tend to undermine the expert's credibility.

Finally, the basis for the expert's opinion will be presented. The engagement scope is reviewed, including who retained the expert and why, documents reviewed, interviews conducted, the engagement team, manner of supervision and time spent, compensation, and any engagement scope limitations imposed. Next the methodology employed is explained, which leads to the conclusions and opinions reached. Typically any weaknesses are acknowledged and explained in a preemptive fashion to reduce potential damage on cross-examination.

The key to persuasive and effective testimony is communication. The expert's position may be a technical marvel, but it is worthless if the jury is not convinced. Therefore, the expert should speak English and eliminate accounting and financial jargon. Concepts should be explained by way of common, everyday occurrences. Condescending or patronizing speech is inappropriate. There is an old saying: "If you can't say it in simple English, you don't understand it." You can be sure that if you do not express it in simple terms, the judge or jury will not understand it.

The expert's job is to educate the jury and the court in an interesting fashion. This job can be facilitated by the use of and reference to trial exhibits. It is difficult to devote too much attention to trial exhibits. Trial exhibits are used to lead the jury, court, and oneself through the basis of the opinion, as well as to keep everyone's attention focused. Like the language used in testimony, the exhibits should be kept clear and simple so the point is unmistakable and memorable. In many jurisdictions, the jury cannot take notes, and visual exhibits are the most effective method to ensure a point or conclusion is remembered.

(ii) Cross-Examination.   The purpose of cross-examination is to cast doubt on or, if possible, undermine the expert witness's credibility and testimony. One of the simpler ways to accomplish this objective is through impeachment. Consequently, a thorough review of prior testimony, writings, and the deposition transcript is required. Make sure you are not on record as holding a view that is or appears to be contrary to the one you are now presenting, or be able to provide an explanation.

Be calm and polite, even if opposing counsel is manipulating responses. The expert is in the attorney's ballpark, and any anger will be turned against the witness. Cross-examining attorneys will frequently use "yes/no" questions to manipulate an opposing expert. The expert should generally resist the tendency to provide lengthy qualifications to such questions, as a skilled attorney may succeed in having the expert admonished by the court to answer only the question asked. An admonishment will taint the expert in the jury's mind, as well as leave the expert with less maneuvering room during the remainder of cross-examination. However, this is not to suggest the expert should timidly follow the yes/no trail. Make explanations when necessary.

Another favored approach is the hypothetical question. Care must be taken not to appear too defensive or restrictive when answering a hypothetical question. Select the appropriate moment to cleanly sever the link between the hypothetical and the reality of the case at hand. Finally, remember that redirect examination can rehabilitate mischaracterizations by opposing counsel. So even if you must admit something that appears damaging, you will have a chance to explain why the admission is irrelevant in the current context.

If opposing counsel has discovered an error, the expert should acknowledge the error, but not necessarily the implications or conclusions drawn by counsel. Again, redirect examination can salvage errors, especially immaterial errors.

It is important to know the opposing expert's opinion and basis, and the key differences between both experts' work. The ultimate objective of cross-examination is to get the expert to agree with the opposing expert's opinion and basis. Nearly as damaging is an acknowledgment that the opposing expert is a leading expert in the field. Failing this, an admission that reasonable minds can differ is a likely parting shot.

The expert must also be prepared for questions concerning fees and any scope limitations, especially if opposing counsel has not engaged an expert witness. A comfortable, matter-of-fact response is called for. The expert is a professional who has been asked to conduct certain analyses and offer an opinion. This is not unlike any other engagement an accountant conducts, and you should not feel guilty about being compensated for your time and effort.

Finally, the expert must stay within his field of expertise. By straying, the expert will end up in unnecessary difficulties.

(iii) Redirect Examination.   The purpose of redirect examination is to rehabilitate points made by the opponent and clarify responses and mischaracterizations. It is generally counterproductive to a witness's credibility to argue with opposing counsel or to resist answering questions which, to the jury, appear reasonable and straightforward. An evasive witness generally is a less credible witness. The expert is back in friendly hands during redirect, and this is the time to mitigate real or perceived damage.

During the redirect examination the attorney will typically select two or three areas where additional explanation is necessary to counter the points made on cross-examination. This is the witness's opportunity to clearly explain **why** the points made during cross-examination are irrelevant and have no bearing on the expert's opinion.

40.9 SOURCES AND SUGGESTED REFERENCES

American Institute of Certified Public Accountants, Code of Professional Conduct, AICPA, New York, 1988.

————, *Statement on Standards for Consulting Services (SSCS) No. 1,* "Consulting Services: Definitions and Standards," AICPA, New York, 1986.

————, Auditing Standards Board, *Statement on Standards for Accountants' Services on Prospective Financial Information,* "Financial Forecasts and Projections," AICPA, New York, 1985.

————, *Application of AICPA Professional Standards in the Performance of Litigation Services,* AICPA Special Report 93-1, n.d.

————, *Conflicts of Interest in Litigation Services Engagements,* AICPA Consulting Services Special Report 93-2, n.d.

————, *Comparing Attest and Consulting Services: A Guide for the Practitioner,* AICPA Consulting Services Special Report 93-3, n.d.

————, *Providing Litigation Services,* AICPA Consulting Services Practice Aid 93-4, n.d.

————, *Communicating Understandings in Litigation Services,* AICPA Consulting Services Practice Aid 95-2, n.d.

————, *Statement on Standards for Attestation Engagements,* AICPA, 1986.

Black, Henry C., *Black's Law Dictionary,* 5th ed., West Publishing, St. Paul, MN, 1979.

Crain, Michael A., Goldwasser, Dan L., and Harry, Everett P., "Liability: Expert Witness—In Jeopardy?," *Journal of Accountancy,* AICPA, December 1994, Vol. 42.

de Silva, Harindra, Lo, Nancy N., and Nells, Tara N., "Securities Act Violations: Estimation of Damages," *Litigation Services Handbook: The Role of the Accountant as Expert* by Weil, Roman L., Wagner, Michael J., and Frank, Peter B., eds., Wiley, New York, 1995.

Dunn, Robert L., *Recovery of Damages for Lost Profits,* 4th ed., Lawpress, Tiburon, CA, 1992.

Dykeman, Francis C., *Forensic Accounting: The Accountant as Expert Witness,* Wiley, New York, 1982.

Federal Rules of Evidence: 703.

Federal Rules of Civil Procedure: 26, 30, 33, 34, 36, 45.

Frank, Peter B., and Wagner, Michael J., "Computing Lost Profits and Reasonable Royalties," *AIPLA Quarterly Journal,* Vol. 15, No. 4, AIPLA, Arlington, VA 1987, pp. 391–425.

Kabe, Elo R., and Blonder, Brian L., "Discounting Concepts and Damages," *Litigation Services Handbook: The Role of the Accountant as Expert,* 1996 Supplement by Weil, Roman L., Wagner, Michael J., and Frank, Peter B., eds., Wiley, New York, 1996.

Kinrich, Jeffrey H., "Cost Estimation," *Litigation Services Handbook: The Role of the Accountant as Expert* by Weil, Roman L., Wagner, Michael J., and Frank, Peter B., eds., Wiley, New York, 1995.

Knapp, Charles L., *Commercial Damages,* Matthew Bender, New York, 1986.

Kraft, Melvin D., *Using Experts in Civil Cases,* Practicing Law Institute, New York, 1977.

Newton, Grant W., *Bankruptcy and Insolvency Accounting,* 5th ed., Wiley, New York, 1994.

Sims, Raymond S., and Haller, Mark W., "Lost Profits: Covering All the Bases in the 'But For' World," *Inside Litigation,* Vol. 2, No. 4, Prentice-Hall Law & Business, New York, February 1988.

Wagner, Michael J., and Frank, Peter B., *Litigation Services: Management Advisory Services Technical Consulting Practice Aid No. 7,* AICPA, New York, 1986.

Weil, Roman L., Wagner, Michael J., and Frank, Peter B., eds., *Litigation Services Handbook: The Role of the Accountant as Expert,* 2nd ed., Wiley, New York, 1995.

INDEX

1